PERSIAN LITERATURE

A BIO-BIBLIOGRAPHICAL SURVEY

BY

C. A. STOREY

VOLUME I

QUR'ĀNIC LITERATURE; HISTORY AND BIOGRAPHY

PART 2

BIOGRAPHY

ADDITIONS AND CORRECTIONS

INDEXES

SUBSIDISED BY THE TRUSTEES OF THE "E. J. W. GIBB MEMORIAL"

LUZAC & COMPANY, LTD.

46 GREAT RUSSELL STREET, LONDON.

1972.

First Published . . . 1953
Reprinted 1972

SBN 7189 0144 4

Printed in England by
Stephen Austin and Sons, Ltd., Hertford, Herts.

PREFACE

THE present instalment of my survey of Persian literature completes the first volume. In view of the inconveniently large size to which it has grown I have felt myself compelled, for purposes of binding, to regard the previous four fasciculi as Part 1 and the present instalment as Part 2.

Among those who since the date of my last acknowledgment have been so kind as to send me additions and corrections I remember particularly Professor A. J. Arberry, Mr. J. D. Pearson, Mr. G. M. Wickens and, above all, Professor V. Minorsky. To the Trustees of the " E. J. W. Gibb Memorial ", who generously agreed to bear the cost of printing this second part of Volume I, I am greatly indebted.

C. A. STOREY.

April, 1953.

LIST OF
AUTHORITIES AND ABBREVIATIONS

[Supplementary to the lists printed on pp. ix–xxiii, xxix–xxxv (prefixed to p. 61), [xliv] facing p. 237, and [xlviii] facing p. 433]

Breslau Richter = *Verzeichnis der orientalischen Handschriften der Staats- und Universitätsbibliothek Breslau von G. Richter.* Leipzig, 1933.

Bull. E.O.I.F. de Damas = *Bulletin d'études orientales de l'Institut Français de Damas.*

Dharī'ah = *al-Dharī'ah ilā taṣānīf al-Shī'ah*, [an Arabic work] by M. Muḥsin known as Sh. Āghā Buzurg Ṭihrānī. Al-Najaf (vols. i–iii) 1355–7/1936–8 and Ṭihrān (vol. iv onwards) 1360/1941– , *in progress.* [I regret that I have been unable to make full use of this work, which, though ordered by me from a bookseller in 1943, did not come into my hands until 1951, when most of the present volume was already printed.]

Edinburgh New Coll. = *A handlist of the Arabic, Persian and Hindustani MSS. of New College, Edinburgh. By R. B. Serjeant.* London, 1942.

Ellis Coll. = [The MSS. belonging to the collection of the late A. G. Ellis described, mainly by A. J. Arberry, in] Luzac's *Bibliotheca Orientalis* xlv (1945) pp. 3–35 [where they bear numbers from M1 to M446].

Karatay = *Istanbul Üniversitesi Kütüphanesi farsça basmalar kataloğu*, by Fehmi Edhem Karatay. Istanbul, 1949.

Madrās I, II = *A descriptive catalogue of the Islamic manuscripts in the Government Oriental Manuscripts Library, Madras.* [Vol. i by P. P. Subrahmanya Sāstrī (, Mīr Mushtāq Aḥmad and S. 'Abd al-Wahhāb Bukhārī), vol. ii by T. Chandrasēk'haran.] Madrās, 1939, 1950.

Majlis II = *Fihrist i Kitāb-khānah i Majlis i Shūrā-yi Millī (Kutub i khaṭṭī: Fārsī) ta'līf i . . . Ibn i Yūsuf i Shīrāzī. Jild i siwwum az nashrīyāt i Kitāb-khānah.* **Tihrān** A.H.S. 1318–21/1939–42.

Mashhad IV, V = *Fihrist i Kitāb-khānah i Āstānah i quds i Riḍawī. Jild i chahārum (panjum).* Mashhad A.H.S. 1325 (A.H. 1366/1947), 1329 (A.H. 1370/1951. This volume arrived too late to be used for more than a few addenda of special interest). [Future cataloguers of Arabic and Persian printed books will do well to follow the example of this catalogue (and of the Āṣafīyah catalogue) in regarding the date of composition, when easily ascertainable from the author's preface or conclusion, as a necessary part of the description of a work. Descriptions of biographical works, moreover, will often be unsatisfactory, if they do not indicate when the subject of the biography lived and what he was.]

OCM. = *Oriental College Magazine* [in Urdu, edited successively by Prof. M. Shafīʻ and Prof. M. Iqbāl], vols. i–xxii (Lahore, 1925–46). [References have been given to most of the relevant articles in the volumes issued from 1925 to 1939, but from 1940 onwards few of the issues reached me.]

OLZ. = *Orientalistische Literaturzeitung.*

PL. = *Persian literature*, i.e., the present work.

Princeton [nos. 1–206] = *Descriptive catalog of the Garrett Collection of Persian, Turkish and Indic manuscripts . . . in the Princeton University Library. By Mahomed E. Moghadam [and] Yahya Armajani under the supervision of Philip K. Hitti.* Princeton, 1939. [The numbers sufficiently distinguish these MSS. from those described and numbered 393–469 in Martinovitch's catalogue (cf. *PL.* p. xxxiii).]

Rossi = *Elenco dei manoscritti persiani della Biblioteca Vaticana.* [By] *Ettore Rossi.* Città del Vaticano 1948 (Studi e testi, 136).

Sipahsālār = *Fihrist i Kitāb-khānah i Madrasah i ʻĀlī i Sipahsālār ta'līf i . . . Ibn i Yūsuf i Shīrāzī.* Tihrān A.H.S. 1315/1936 (vol. i), 1318/1940 (vol. ii), *in progress* (?).

Tashkent Univ. = *A descriptive catalogue of the Persian, Arabic and Turkish manuscripts preserved in the Library of Middle Asiatic State University* [in Russian], by A. A. Semenov. Tashkent, 1935.

FURTHER ADDITIONS AND CORRECTIONS (UNINDEXED)

P. 22, l. 19 (cf. p. 1201, l. 25) [Walī Allāh Dihlawī]. Also *Shah Wali-Ullah Dehlavi and Indian politics in the 18th century*, by Khalīq Aḥmad Niẓāmī (in *Islamic culture*, xxv/1 (Jan.–Oct. 1951) pp. 133–45); *Shah Wali Allah as a mystic*, by Faḍl i Maḥmūd Asīrī (in *Islamic culture*, xxvi/2 (April 1952) pp. 1–15).

P. 24, l. 7. [M. Riḍā Hamadānī.] See p. 1426*a*, l. 12.

P. 25, l. 9 (cf. p. 1203, l. 19) [Rafī' al-Dīn Dihlawī]. Also *Ency. Isl.* under Rafī' al-Dīn (M. Shafī'); Brockelmann *Sptbd.* ii p. 850.

P. 30 (15). S. Abū 'l-Qāsim Riḍawī Qummī Lāhaurī died on 14 Muḥ. 1324 [14 March 1906] according to Mashhad iv p. 315.

P. 32 (48) and p. 33 (57). For an Arabic work completed by 'Ubaid Allāh Khān Tarkhān at Delhi in 1140/1728 at the age of twenty-one see Mingana's Rylands Library catalogue no. 415, Brockelmann *Sptbd.* i p. 841[12].

P. 38, l. 6. [*Lughāt al-Qur'ān.*] Also **Delhi** 1270/1853–4 (see 'Alīgaṛh Subḥ. ptd. bks. p. 39).

P. 43, l. 8, and pp. 1220–1. [*Naẓm al-la'ālī.*] Edition: **Lucknow** 1264/1848 (Sprenger p. 532).

P. 48 (5). See *Dharī'ah* iii p. 373 no. 1358.

P. 48 (6). Edition: 1319/1901–2 (*Dharī'ah* i p. 367 no. 1331).

P. 55, l. 5. [*Tuḥfat al-gharā'ib.*] Edition: Persia 1268/1851–2 (*Dharī'ah* iii p. 457[6]).

P. 56, l. 21. [Kaṛawī.] For Kaṛā, on the Ganges opposite to Mānikpūr, see Raḥmān 'Alī p. 167[13].

P. 77, l. 9. [*Jāmi' al-tawārīkh*. Translations.] *Insert*:

(**1a**) *Sbornik lyetopisei* [cf. *PL.* p. 76[3]], i/2 [History of Chingiz Khān and his ancestors [including the passages omitted by Berezin] translated into Russian by O. I. Smirnóva [mainly from the Tashkent and Rawān Kö͟shkü (1518) MSS.] with notes by B. Pankratov and O. Smirnóva under the editorship of A. A. Semenov]. **USSR,** Academy of Sciences 1952 (315 pp.). [Information from V. Minorsky.]

P. 156, l. 24. *Read* Yūsuf b. 'Abd al-Laṭīf's work.

P. 169 (16) is probably the same work as p. 170 (34).

P. 182, l. 20. [*Rāḥat al-arwāḥ.*] Also **Ma͟shhad** v p. 90 no. 533 (A.H. 1105/1694).

P. 182, l. 26. [*Bahjat al-mabāhij.*] Also **Ma͟shhad** v p. 36 no. 408.

P. 197, l. 20. [*Ḥayāt al-qulūb.*] For other editions see Ma͟shhad v pp. 263–4.

P. 198, l. 10. [*Jalā' al-'uyūn.*] For other editions see Ma͟shhad v pp. 256–7.

P. 203. ['Alī Akbar " Bismil ".] See p. 1396 n.

P. 215, l. 7. [*Manāqib i Murtaḍawī.*] Editions : **Bombay** 1269/1852–3 (Ma͟shhad v p. 332) ; **Ṭihrān** 1273/1856 (*ibid.* p. 333).

Pp. 221–2. [M. Ḥasan b. Ma'ṣūm Qazwīnī.] See p. 1423 n.

P. 229 (14). [*Durr Baḥr al-manāqib.*] Edition : **Tabrīz** 1313/1895–6 (*D͟harī'ah* viii p. 62).

P. 234 (68). The *Tuḥfat al-d͟hākirīn* was completed in 1278/1861–2 by M. " Bīdil " Kirmāns͟hāhānī b. 'Alī M. C͟hulābī Māzandarānī (see Ma͟shhad v p. 244 no. 382, *D͟harī'ah* iii p. 433 no. 1568, p. 186 no. 668, *Majma' al-fuṣaḥā'* ii p. 75).

P. 234 (69). The *Tuḥfat al-Riḍawīyah* was completed in 1270 (see Ma͟shhad v p. 40 no. 413, where a MS. is described). Another edition : **Ṭihrān** 1288/1871–2 (Ma͟shhad v p. 245, *D͟harī'ah* iii p. 436). Naurūz 'Alī died in 1309/1891–2.

P. 357, l. 16 (cf. p. 1297[22]). [*Badā'i' al-azmān.*] Supplement : *Al-muḍāf ilā Badā'i' al-azmān* [= Vatican Arab. (but the text is in Persian) 523 foll.151*a*–171*b*] . . . *ba-taṣḥīḥ u ihtimām i 'Abbās Iqbāl.* **Ṭihrān** A.H.S. 1331/1952 (60 pp.). [Information from V. Minorsky.]

P. 429, l. 26. *Read* M. Raḍī Tabrīzī (cf. pp. 147, 1245).

P. 433, l. 14. [*Futūḥ al-salāṯīn*. Editions.] Also **Madrās** 1948 (Madras Univ. Islamic Series, 9). [Information from Kh. A. Niẓāmī.]

P. 591, l. 8 from foot. [*Sharḥ i Aḥadīyah*.] See p. 1389 n.2.

P. 790, n. 8. Cf. *Emir Nizameddin Nevâî, Muhâkemet ül-Lugateyn, farsçaya terceme eden Turhan Genceî* (see *Oriens* iv/1 (1951) p. 126).

P. 793, l. 5. The words "and dedicated to Sulṭān Salīm" should be deleted. Sulṭān Salīm (reigned 918–26/1512–20) is mentioned in the preface, but the work was begun after his death.

P. 862 (7). Cf. *Dīwān i Āzād*, Ḥaidarābād, n.d. (2 vols., 60; 61 pp. Karatay p. 82).

P. 873. [Amr Allāh Ilāhābādī.] See also Rieu i 25*a*.

P. 908, n. 4. The correct spelling seems to be Īrawānī (see *Farhang i Niẓām* i p. 513).

P. 914, l. 30. ['Alī Ḥasan Khān.] See p. 1436*a*, n.1.

P. 973 penult. The references to p. 177 *supra* and *Laṭā'if-nāmah* p. 17 should be deleted. The Kamāl al-Dīn Ḥusain Khwārazmī mentioned on those pages died in 839/1435–6 and is different from the saint of the same name who died in 956/1549 (see *Safīnat al-auliyā'* p. 191, *Khazīnat al-aṣfiyā'* ii p. 331) and who is doubtless the person to whom the *Miftāḥ al-ṭālibīn* is devoted. The index and p. 1253^{11-13} should be corrected accordingly.

P. 983. ['Ālim Shaikh 'Azīzān.] See p. 1397 n.

Pp. 992–9. [Dārā-Shukōh.] Also *Three little-known works of Dara Shukuh* [*Risālah i Ḥaq-numā*, *Ṭarīqat al-ḥaqīqat*, *Ḥasanāt al-'ārifīn*], by Bikrama Jīt Ḥasrat (in *Islamic culture*, xxv/1 (Jan.–Oct. 1951) pp. 52–72, where bibliographical information about some other works will be found).

P. 994 n.3. For a different version of the *Su'āl u jawāb* (Delhi 1885°) see Edwards col. 461 (cf. *Islamic culture*, xxv/1 p. 72).

P. 1047, l. 32. ['Alī Anwar Qalandar.] Also M. Idrīs p. 59.

P. 1058 (40). For S. Wāriṯẖ 'Alī Sẖāh (b. 1232/1816 at Dēwah, near Bārah Bankī, d. 30 Muḥ. 1323/7 March 1905) see Niẓāmī Badāyūnī *Qāmūs al-masẖāhīr* (in Urdu) ii p. 274.

P. 1059 (57). For "Wāṣil" Kẖāliṣpūrī (b. 1263/1847 at Lucknow) see M. Idrīs p. 29, where he is called Sikandar 'Alī Kẖān.

P. 1074, l. 2. Sẖaraf al-Dīn Ḥusain: so C. C. Edwards (*BSOS*. x/1 p. 200, l. 10 from foot), but Ḥusain is here perhaps a corruption of Ḥusainī, since "Suhailī" Kẖwānsārī (*Ḏẖail i Tārīkẖ i 'Ālam-ārāy i 'Abbāsī* [cf. *PL.* i p. 1281], *muqaddamah*, p. 2, n. 1) gives the Mīr Munsẖī's name as Muḥammad.

P. 1074, l. 28. [*Taḏẖkirah i kẖwusẖ-nawīsān* . . .]. The title is *Gulistān i hunar* according to "Suhailī" Kẖwānsārī (see the preceding addendum).

P. 1079, l. 8. *For* waiting on *read* writing about.

P. 1080, l. 21. *Read* Burhān Kẖān.

P. 1104, l. 3. For Aḥmad 'Alī "Rasā" see *Sẖam' i anjuman* p. 178.

P. 1115, n. 1. Cf. *Ansāb i Sẖuyūkẖ i Farsẖūrī* [*Farsẖaurī?*] *i Badāyūn*, by M. Raḍī al-Dīn Badāyūnī, Sẖāhābād 1899 (see Blumhardt's Supplementary cat. of Hindustani books in the BM., col. 345).

P. 1117, l. 5. *Insert*:
1521*a*. Prince **Nāṣir al-Dīn Tūrā** b. Amīr Muẓaffar.
Tuḥfat al-zā'irīn, on the cemeteries and saints' graves in Bukẖārā with biographical information, composed in 1324/1906: **Bukẖārā** 1328/1910 (see Semenov *Kurzer Abriss* p. 9).

P. 1123. [*Sẖadd al-izār.*] Edition of the Arabic text: **Tihrān** A.H.S. 1328/1950 (ed. M. Qazwīnī and 'Abbās Iqbāl. See *Oriens* v/1 p. 188).

P. 1128 antepenult. *Read* p. 1136[23] *infra*.

P. 1141, l. 19. [Nāṣir b. Kẖusrau.] Also *Nasir-i Khusraw and Ismailism*, by W. Ivanow, Bombay 1948 (70 pp. The Ismaili Society's Series, Series B, no. 5). [This work, mentioned in the Ismaili Society's lists of its publications, may not have reached this country, since it does not seem to be traceable in Luzac's and Probsthain's catalogues or in the lists of books received by the RAS. and SOAS.]

P. 1150, l. 8. [*Risālah i S.M.*] See p. 1420 n.

P. 1162, l. 6. *Insert*:

(24*a*) *Tuḥaf i ahl i Bukhārā*, adventures in foreign lands by Mīrzā Sirāj al-Dīn, a Bukhārā merchant: **Bukhārā** 1330/1912 (see Semenov *Kurzer Abriss* p. 10).

P. 1181, n. 3. Mīrzā Muḥammad is described in the *Dharī'ah* (viii p. 278 no. 1186 and elsewhere) as *al-Būshahrī al-muḥāmī fī 'l-Baṣrah*.

P. 1183 (32). For Col. M. Taqī Khān see *Rijāl i Ādharbayjān* p. 43.

P. 1191, l. 12. [*Kashf al-asrār* . . .] *Insert*:

Edition: *K. al-a. wa-'u. al-a.* (*ma'rūf bi-Tafsīr i Khwājah 'Abd Allāh i Anṣārī*) *ta'līf i Abū 'l-Faḍl Rashīd al-Dīn al-Maibudī*, **Tihrān** A.H.S. 1331/1952–3 (Vol. i (Sūrahs I–II), ed. 'Alī Aṣghar Ḥikmat, 805 pp.). [Information from V. Minorsky.]

P. 1203, l. 23. For M. Bāqir Nawwāb see *Rauḍāt al-jannāt* p. 651.

P. 1209, l. 7. Read *Ḥaqā'iq*.

P. 1215, l. 8. Warnūsfādarān [vocalization ?] is one of the quarters (*maḥāll*) of Sidih, near (*min tawābi'*) Iṣfahān (*Dharī'ah* iv p. 320 n.).

P. 1225, l. 4 from foot. Kāshī is perhaps a corruption of Kāsī, that being, according to the *Ency. Isl.* (i p. 152*b*, under Afghānistān), the name of the ancestor of the Shinwārī tribe.

P. 1253, ll. 11–13. See the correction to p. 973 penult.

P. 1259, l. 12. The word Khān should not be in thick type.

P. 1264, l. 29. [*Majālis al-muttaqīn*.] Also [**Persia**] 1275/1858–9 (Mashhad v p. 314); **Ṭihrān** 1284/1867–8 (*ibid*., p. 315).

P. 1265, l. 5. [*Mātam-kadah*.] Also **Ṭihrān** 1284/1868 (Mashhad v p. 311).

P. 1266, l. 4 from foot. [M. Mahdī Tunakābunī.] See p. 1425 n.1.

P. 1308, l. 25. *For* a verse *read* in verse.

P. 1310, l. 10. This appears to be the *Chahār gulshan* of Chaturman [*PL.* p. 472], not the work of Daulat Rāy [*PL.* p. 481].

P. 1345, l. 5. For a similar name, S. Irtaḍā Ḥusain Amrōhawī, see *Dharī'ah* iii p. 418 (1505).

P. 1346, l. 5. Shahrawānī is probably a corruption of Nahrawālī (see p. 1023[6]).

P. 1348, l. 22. MT'LWY seems to be the name of a place, since M. Idrīs in speaking of a certain Ḥājī La'l Muḥammad (p. 70[7]) says that he was born at MT'LWY [vocalisation ?] commonly called (*'urf*) Maṭārī in the District of Ḥaidarābād, Sind'h. Maṭārī is 16 miles N. of Ḥaidarābād.

P. 1352, l. 4. *Read* p. 51.

N. BIOGRAPHY : (*a*) POETS

A list of 51 sources of information concerning Persian poets (all *tadhkirahs* except one or two histories containing biographical sections) was prefixed by H. Ethé to his account of Persian poetical literature in the *Grundriss der iranischen Philologie*. An Urdu translation of this list was published in the *Oriental College Magazine*, vol. iii/2 (Lahore, Feb. 1927), pp. 21–37, by Dr. 'Abd al-Sattār Ṣiddīqī. In a *takmilah* to Dr. 'Abd al-Sattār's article (pp. 40–56) Prof. M. Shafī' enumerated 41 additional *tadhkirahs* (and other works) known to be extant as well as eleven which seem to be lost. In the next two issues of the *OCM*. (vol. iii/3 (May 1927) pp. 48–52 and vol. iii/4 (Aug. 1927) p. 31) he added four more and raised the total to 107. This total was successively increased to 135 and 142 [1] by Ḥakīm S. Shams Allāh Qādirī (*OCM*. v/1 (Nov. 1928) pp. 1–7, v/4 (Aug. 1929) pp. 112–13) and to 143 by M. Shajā'at-'Alī Khān, who described the *Ma'āthir al-Bāqirīyah* in *OCM*. vi/2 (Feb. 1930) pp. 111–13. Subsequently Prof. M. Iqbāl described two more (nos. 144 and 145), both belonging to Prof. Maḥmūd Shērānī, namely the *Zubdat al-mu'āṣirīn* written in 1240/1824–5 by Mīr Ḥusain al-Ḥusainī, a resident of Shīrāz (*OCM*. x/1 (Nov. 1933) pp. 32–42 and x/2 (Feb. 1934) pp. 129–37, where extracts relating to Persian poetesses are published) and the *Laṭā'if al-khayāl* written in 1076/1665 by a Persian who had visited India (*OCM*. xi/1 (Nov. 1934) pp. 58–73, where some extracts are given).

1088. Sadīd al-Dīn [2] M. b. M. b. Imām Sharaf al-Dīn Abī Ṭāhir Yaḥyā b. Ṭāhir b. 'Uthmān **al-'Aufī** al-Bukhārī, who claimed descent from 'Abd al-Raḥmān b. 'Auf,[3] was probably born at Bukhārā and was certainly educated there. In 597/1200–1 he

[1] One of these, however, the *Mu'nis al-aḥrār*, is an anthology without biographical information. A considerable proportion are histories containing biographical sections.

[2] See Niẓām al-Dīn *Introduction* pp. 3–5. The authorities who give his *laqab* as Nūr al-Dīn are apparently in error.

[3] A prominent *Ṣaḥābī*, for whom see *Ency. Isl.* and Caetani *Chronographia Islamica* pp. 341–2. He was one of *al-'Asharat al-Mubashsharah* and a member of the committee of six which elected 'Uthmān to the Caliphate. He died in 32/652–3.

went to Samarqand, where his maternal uncle, the physician Majd al-Dīn M. b. 'Adnān Surkhakaṭī (see p. 431 *supra*), was in the service of the Īlak Khān, Qilich Ṭamghāch Khān Ibrāhīm. The *Walī-'ahd*, 'Uthman b. Ibrāhīm, appointed 'Aufī his secretary, but before long he had started on travels which took him to Khwārazm, Shahr i Nau, Nasā (in 600/1203–4), Khūjān = Khabūshān (in 603/1206–7), Isfarāyin, Nīshāpūr, Harāt, Isfizār (after 607) and other places. By 617/1220,[1] if not before, he was in Sind, ruled at that time by Nāṣir al-Dīn Qabājah, for whom, as mentioned below, two of his works were written. In a note discovered by A. H. M. Niẓām al-Dīn at the end of an India Office MS.[2] a contemporary who prefixes to 'Aufī's name, among other titles, those of *Qāḍī* and *Wā'iẓ al-mulūk wa-'l-salāṭīn*, speaks of meeting him at Cambay, where he had been living for some time (*rūzī chand ān-jā sukūnat sākhtah būd*). It may be surmised that he was *Qāḍī* of that place, which was included in Nāṣir al-Dīn Qabājah's dominions. In 625/1228 he was in Bhakkar when Qabājah was besieged there by the troops of Īltutmish, the Sulṭān of Delhi. After Qabājah's capitulation and suicide 'Aufī became a subject of Īltutmish and the *Jawami' al-ḥikāyāt* is dedicated to that monarch's *Wazīr*, Qiwām al-Dīn al-Junaidī. He was still alive in 628/1230–1, the date of an event which is referred to in the *Jawāmi' al-ḥikāyāt* (see A. H. M. Niẓām al-Dīn *Introduction* p. 20).

In addition to the *Lubāb al-albāb* he wrote

(1) *Tarjamah i kitāb al-Faraj ba'd al-shiddah*, a translation of al-Tanūkhī's work (for which see Brockelmann i 155, 519 (*ad* 155), *Suppltbd.* i p. 253) written about 620/1223 for Malik Nāṣir al-Dīn Qabājah (see Niẓām al-Dīn *Introduction to the Jawámi'u 'l-ḥikáyát* pp. 14–19, where it is shown that the I.O. MSS. Ethé 737 and 738 contain the second half of this translation),

(2) *Jawāmi' al-ḥikāyāt wa-lawāmi' al-riwāyāt*, a collection of more than two thousand anecdotes planned at the request of

[1] In a *khuṭbah* composed in this year and quoted in the *Lubāb al-albāb* (i pp. 115–16) 'Aufī referred to the conquests made on behalf of Nāṣir al-Dīn Qabājah by Malik Bahā' al-Dīn 'Alī al-Jāmajī.

[2] Ethé 737. See Niẓām al-Dīn *Introduction* pp. 16–17, where the Persian text is given.

Malik Nāṣir al-Dīn Qabājah, not yet finished at his death in 625, resuscitated at the suggestion of Sulṭān Īltutmish's *Wazīr* Niẓām al-Mulk Qiwām al-Dīn M. b. Abī Sa'īd al-Junaidī, to whom it was eventually dedicated not earlier than 628/1230–1 (see Niẓām al-Dīn *Introduction to the Jawámi'u 'l-ḥikáyát*, G.M.S., N.S. viii, London 1929),

(3) *Madā'iḥ al-Sulṭān*, mentioned in the *Jawāmi' al-ḥikāyāt* but now apparently lost (see Niẓām al-Dīn *op. cit.* p. 14 n. 1).

***Lubāb al-albāb*,**[1] notices of nearly 300 poets written probably in 618/1221–2 and dedicated to Malik Nāṣir al-Dīn Qabājah's *Wazīr*, 'Ain al-Mulk Fakhr al-Dīn al-Ḥusain b. Abī Bakr al-Ash'arī : Sprenger no. 1 = **Berlin** 637 (defective. 15th cent. ?), **Lindesiana** p. 124 no. 308 (16th or 17th cent.).

The *Bazm-ārāy* (Rieu Suppt. 106. Early 17th cent.), completed in 1000/1591–2 by S. 'Alī b. Maḥmūd al-Ḥusainī and dedicated to the Khān i Khānān 'Abd al-Raḥīm b. Bairam Khān (for whom see p. 533 *supra*) is largely plagiarized from the *Lubāb al-albāb* and may be regarded as virtually an additional manuscript (see M. Khān Qazwīnī's *muqaddimah* pp. h–w).

Edition : *Part II of the Lubábu 'l-albáb of Muḥammad 'Awfí edited . . . by E. G. Browne*, **London and Leyden** 1903°* (Persian historical texts, vol. ii), *Part I of the Lubábu 'l-albāb . . . edited . . . by E. G. Browne and Mírzá Muḥammad ibn 'Abdu 'l-Wahháb-i-Qazwíní*, **London and Leyden** 1906°* (Persian historical texts, vol. iv).

Corrections : *Taṣḥīḥ i Lubāb al-albāb*, by " Waḥīd " Dastgirdī (in *Armaghān XI*, pp. 335–6, 652–4, 747–52, XII, pp. 843–4).

List of the poets (not quite complete) : Sprenger, pp. 3–6.

Descriptions : (1) *On the earliest Persian Biography of Poets, by Muhammad Aúfi, and on some other works of the class called Tazkirat ul Shuârá. By N. Bland* (in the *JRAS*. 1848, pp. 111–76), (2) *An early Persian anthology* (in R. A. Nicholson's *Studies in Islamic poetry*, Cambridge 1921, pp. 1–42. With many verse translations).

[1] A still earlier *tadhkirah*, the *Manāqib al-shu'arā'* by Abū Ṭāhir al-Khātūnī, who flourished at the end of the 11th century, was known to Daulat-Shāh and is mentioned by Ḥājjī Khalīfah, who, however, seems to have known it only by name, since he does not give the opening words.

[Autobiographical statements in the *Lubāb al-albāb* and the *Jawāmi' al-ḥikāyāt* (for these see the *muqaddimah* of M. Khān Qazwīnī and the preface of E. G. Browne to Part I of the *Lubāb al-albāb* and Niẓām al-Dīn's *Introduction to the Jawámi'u 'l-ḥikáyát*); Rieu ii 749–50; Browne, *Lit. Hist.* ii pp. 477–9; *Ency. Isl.* under 'Awfī (short and unsigned).]

1089. For the *Tārīkh i Guzīdah*, which was written in 730/1329–30 by **Ḥamd Allāh Mustaufī** Qazwīnī and of which the fifth and penultimate *bāb* (pp. 755–829 in the G.M.S. facsimile) is devoted to very brief notices of *imāms* and *mujtahids* (*Faṣl* 1 = pp. 755–9), ten *qurrā'* (*Faṣl* 2 = pp. 759–60), seven traditionists (*Faṣl* 3 = p. 760), *mashāyikh* (*Faṣl* 4 = pp. 760–97), *'ulamā'* (*Faṣl* 5 = pp. 797–812), and poets (*Faṣl* 6 = pp. 812–29), see pp. 82–4 *supra*. A translation of *Faṣl* 6 by E. G. Browne is mentioned on p. 84.

1090. For the *Firdaus al-tawārīkh*, which was written in 808/1405–6 by **Khusrau Abarqūhī** and which contains at the end a biographical dictionary of Arabic and Persian poets, see p. 86 *supra*.

1091. For the *Mujmal* of **Faṣīḥ** al-Dīn Aḥmad b. M. **Khwāfī,** a compendium of Islāmic history and biography to 845/1441–2, see pp. 90–1 *supra*.

1092. The *Bahāristān*, a collection of anecdotes written in 892/1487 by the poet 'Abd al-Raḥmān b. Aḥmad "**Jāmī**", does not belong to this section, but it deserves a passing mention, since the seventh of its eight *rauḍahs* is devoted to short biographies of twenty-eight poets.

1093. **Daulat-Shāh** b. 'Alā' al-Daulah Bakhtī-Shāh al-Ghāzī al-**Samarqandī,** as he calls himself (*T. al-sh.* pp. 11^6, 541^1), or Amīr [1] Daulat-Shāh, as he is called in the *Laṭā'if-nāmah*, was the son of Amīr 'Alā' al-Daulah Isfarāyinī (*Laṭā'if-nāmah* p. 180^7), an intimate friend of Sulṭān Shāh-Rukh (*T. al-sh.* p. 337^{19-20}). He was present [2] at the battle of Chakman [3] Sarāy [4], near

[1] This title was hereditary in families belonging to the aristocracy of high officialdom (see Barthold in *Mir-Ali-Shir* p. 113).

[2] *dar ān muṣāff dar rikāb i ẓafar-ma'āb būdam* (*T. al-sh.* p. 533^2).

[3] Vocalization not verified.

[4] According to the *Ḥabīb al-siyar*, iii, pt. 3, p. 202^{19}, this battle took place at the end of 875/1471.

Andkhūd, in which his sovereign, Abū 'l-Ghāzī Sulṭān Ḥusain defeated Sultān Maḥmūd Mīrzā, the third son of Sulṭān Abū Sa'īd,[1] but he did not rise to the dignities and influence of his ancestors, being apparently content to live a simple life as a landed proprietor (*az imārat u 'aẓamat kih āyīn i ajdād i ū būd gudhasht* [2] *u sar-rishtah i faqr u qanā'at u dahqanat ba-dast āward*, *Laṭā'if-nāmah* p. 180[10]). Mīr 'Alī-Shīr says in the *Majālis al nafā'is*, which was begun in 896/1490–1, that news of his death had recently been received. According to the *Mir'āt al-ṣafā'*, cited by Rieu, he died in 900/1494–5. He was about fifty years old when he began to write the *Tadhkirat al-shu'arā'*.[3]

Tadhkirat al-shu'arā', notices of ancient and modern poets completed in 892/1487, dedicated to Mīr 'Alī-Shīr (for whom see pp. 789–95 *infra*) and divided into a *muqaddimah* (on the art of poetry) seven *ṭabaqāt* (" each containing accounts of some twenty more or less contemporary poets and the princes under whose patronage they flourished ") and a *khātimah* on seven poets contemporary with the author and the merits of Sulṭān Ḥusain: Ḥ. Kh. ii p. 262 no. 2819, Sprenger no. 3, **Cairo** p. 502 (A.H. 892, autograph [4]), p. 501 (A.H. 980/1572), p. 502 (n.d.), **British Museum** (A.H. 895/1489–90),[5] **Rieu** iii 977*b* (A.H. 973/1565), ii 809*b* (16th cent.), i 364*a*–365*b* (8 copies, one of the 16th cent. and three of the 17th), **Bodleian** 348 (A.H. 942/1536), 349 (A.H. 975/1567–8), 350 (A.H. 978/1571), 351–8, **Oxford** Ind. Inst. MS. Pers. A. ii. 21 (A.H. 994/1586), **Edinburgh** New Coll. p. 6 (A.H. 952/1545), **Ethé** 656 (A.H. 960/1553), 657–63, **I.O.** 3777 (18th cent.), **I.O.** D.P. 620, **Blochet** ii 1129 (A.H. 967/1560), 1130 (A.H. 974), 1131–41, iii 2452 (late 16th cent.), **Rosen** Inst. 31 (A.H. 971/1563–4), **Berlin** 638 (A.H. 974/1567), 639–42. **Dorn** 320 (A.H. 975/1567–8), **Flügel** ii 1199 (A.H. 979/1571), 1200

[1] For whom see *Ency. Isl.* under Abū Sa'īd.

[2] Cf. his own words *Az jāh u marātib i ābā' u ajdād bī bahrah māndah* (*T. al-sh.* p. 11[19]).

[3] *Chūn az rūy i muḥāsabat u murāqabat ba-rūz-nāmah i ḥayāt naẓar numūdam dīdam kih kārawān i 'umr i girān-māyah dar tīh i gum-rāhī panjāh marḥalah qaṭ' numūdah būd* (*T. al-sh.* p. 11[10]. Cf. p. 12[5, 8]).

[4] The cataloguer may perhaps have been misled by the author's colophon, which is reproduced in some of the manuscripts (as in the G.M.S. edition).

[5] For information concerning this recently acquired MS. I am indebted to the kindness of Prof. A. J. Arberry.

(A.H. 985/1577), **Browne** Pers. Cat. 113 (A.H. 979/1572), 112 (A.H. 984/1576–7), 114, Suppt. 292–5 (the last = King's 106), **Browne** Coll. J. 8 = Houtum-Schindler 36 (A.H. 908/1502–3 or 980/1572–3), **Būhār** 90 (A.H. 980/1572), **Krafft** p. 125 no. 312 (A.H. 982/1574), **Ivanow** 218 (A.H. 984/1576–7), Curzon 49, 50, **Kapurthala** (A.H. 999/1590–1. See *Oriental College Magazine* vol. iii/4 (Lahore, Aug. 1927) p. 11), **Tashkent** Univ. 69 (16th cent.), **Sipahsālār** ii pp. 475–7 (4 copies, one of 16th cent.), **Lindesiana** p. 132 no. 838 (not later than A.D. 1600), no. 54, no. 310, no. 309, **Rehatsek** p. 130 no. 15 (A.H. 1033/1623–4. LIST OF POETS), p. 95 no. 45, p. 103, no. 59 (apparently, though the title is given as *Maḥbūb al-qulūb*), **Bānkīpūr** viii 680 (A.H. 1051/1641), 681, **'Alīgaṛh** Subḥ. MSS. p. 61 no. 32, **Āṣafīyah** i p. 318 no. 36, iii p. 162 no. 119, **Aumer** 1 (" ziemlich alt "), **Bombay** Univ. p. 274 (old), **Bukhārā** Semenov 48, **Chanykov** 105, **Lahore** Panjab Univ. Lib. (2 copies. See *Oriental College Magazine* vol. iii, no 1 (Nov. 1926) p. 74), **Leningrad** Pub. Lib. (see *Mélanges asiatiques* iii (St. Petersburg 1859) p. 728), Mus. Asiat. (at least 3 copies. See *Mélanges asiatiques* vi (1873) p. 126, vii (1876) p. 402), **Madras** 440, **Majlis** 327, **Peshawar** 1451, **R.A.S.** P. 163, **Salemann-Rosen** p. 13 nos. 61*, 147*. A copy described as written by Sulṭān-'Alī Mashhadī (a celebrated calligraphist [1] contemporary with Daulat-Shāh) and adorned with six full-page miniatures occurred in Sotheby's sale catalogue for 22–23 May 1930.

Editions: (**1**) **Bombay** 1887°, (**2**) *The Tadhkiratu 'sh-Shu'ará . . . of Dawlatsháh . . . edited . . . by E. G. Browne* . . ., **London and Leyden** 1901°* (Persian historical texts, vol. i), (**3**) **Allahabad** 1921* (*Ṭabaqahs* i–v only. Ed. S. M. Ḍāmin 'Alī).

Extracts: (**1**) [Life of "ANWARĪ"] *Vitae poetarum persicorum ex Dauletschahi Historia Poetarum . . . excerptae . . . persice edidit latine vertit . . . J. A. Vullers. Fasc. II. Anvarii vitam tenens*, **Giessen** 1868°. (**2**) [Life of " ANWARĪ "] *Ali Aukhadeddin Enveri. Materialy dlya ego biographii i kharakteristiki* [by V. A. Zhukovsky], **St. Petersburg** 1883°. (**3**) [Life of " 'AṬṬĀR "] *Pend-namèh, ou Le Livre des Conseils de Férid-eddin Attar, traduit et publié*

[1] Cf. *Laṭā'if-nāmah* p. 170, *Tuḥfah i Sāmī* p. 69, *Ḥabīb al-siyar* iii pt 3, p. **344** antepenult., etc.

par M. le Bon Silvestre de Sacy, **Paris** 1819°*, *Pand-nāmah i . . . Farīd al-Dīn ʻAṯṯār* [reprinted from the Paris edition of 1819] [**Ṭihrān**] 1873°. (**4**) [Life of " Ḥāfiẓ "] *Vitae poetarum persicorum ex Dauletschahi Historia Poetarum . . . excerptae . . . persice edidit latine vertit . . . J. A. Vullers. Fasc. I. Hâfizi Schirâzensis vitam tenens*, **Giessen** 1839°* (cf. no. 1 *supra*). (**5**) [Life of " Jāmī "] *Tuhfat ul Ahrār, the Gift of the Noble: being one of the Seven Poems, or Haft Aurang, of Mullā Jāmī . . . edited . . . by F. Falconer* [with biographies of " Jāmī " from Daulat-Shāh's *tadhkirah*, the *Ātash-kadah* and the *Haft iqlīm*], **London** 1848°* (Society for the Publication of Oriental Texts). (**6**) [Life of " Niẓāmī "] *De expeditione Russorum Berdaam versus auctore inprimis Nisamio disseruit F. Erdmann* [with Daulat-Shāh's notice of " Niẓāmī "], **Kazan** 1826–32°. (**7**) [Life of " Niẓāmī "] *Behram-Gur und die russische Fuerstentochter. Muhammed Niszamiu-d-din, dem Gendscher, nachgebildet und durch . . . Anmerkungen erlaeutert von F. von Erdmann* [with Daulat-Shāh's notice of " Niẓāmī "] *2te Auflage*, **Kazan** 1844°*. (**8**) [Life of " Saʻdī "] *The Persian and Arabick works of Sâdee* [edited by J. H. Harington and M. Rāshid. With Daulat-Shāh's notice of " Saʻdī " in Persian text and English translation], vol. i, **Calcutta** 1791°*.

Turkish translation (abridged) : *Safīnat al-shuʻarā'*, written in 1233 by Fahīm Sulaimān Efendī (for whom see *Ency. Isl.* under Fehīm) : **Flügel** ii 1258. Edition : **Istānbūl** 1259/1843 (cf. Babinger *Geschichtsschreiber der Osmanen* p. 351, n. 1).

English translation of *Ṭabaqahs* i–iii : *Translation with notes—critical and explanatory of Tadhkiratush-shu'ara . . . (the portion prescribed for the B.A. Examination) of Dawlatshah-e-Samarqandi. By P. B. Vachha.* **Bombay** [1909*].

J. von Hammer-Purgstall's *Geschichte der schönen Redekünste Persiens, mit einer Blüthenlese aus zweyhundert persischen Dichtern* (Vienna 1818) is for the most part an abridged paraphrase of the *Tadhkirat al-shuʻarā*, supplemented with selected notices from the *Tuḥfah i Sāmī* and a few from other sources.

Translations of extracts : (**1**) [Life of " Anwarī " (Latin)] see Extracts (1) above, (**2**) [Life of " Anwarī " (Russian)] see Extracts (2) above, (**3**) [Life of " ʻAṭṭār " (French)] see

Extracts (3) above, (**4**) [Life of Firdausī (French)] *Tezkirat alschoara, Histoire des poëtes. Par Douletschah . . . Par M. Silvestre de Sacy*, pp. 230–8 (in *Notices et extraits*, Tome iv (**Paris**, An 7 [= 1798°*]). (**5**) [Life of Firdausī (German) *Fragmente ueber die Religion des Zoroaster. Aus dem Persischen uebersetzt und mit einem ausfuehrlichen Commentar versehen nebst dem Leben des Ferdusi aus Dauletscha'h's Biographieen der Dichter. Von Dr. J. A. Vullers* . . ., **Bonn** 1831°. (**6**) [Life of Ḥāfiẓ (French)] *Tezkirat alschoara. Histoire des poëtes. Par Douletschah . . . Par M. Silvestre de Sacy*, pp. 238–45 (in *Notices et extraits*, Tome IV (**Paris,** An 7 [= 1798°*]). (**7**) [Life of "Ḥāfiẓ" (Latin)] see Extracts (4) above. (**8**) [Life of " Sa'dī " (English)] see Extracts (8) above. (**9**) [Account of the Sarbadār dynasty = Browne's ed. pp. 277–88[1] (French)] *Tezkirat alschoara. Histoire des poëtes. Par Douletschah . . . Par M. Silvestre de Sacy*, pp. 251–62 (in *Notices et extraits*, tome iv (**Paris,** An 7 [= 1798°*). (**10**) [Account of Sulṭān Ḥusain's conquests (abridged) = Browne's ed. pp. 522–39 [2] (French)] *Tezkirat alschoara. Histoire des poëtes. Par Douletschah . . . Par M. Silvestre de Sacy*, pp. 262–9 (in *Notices et extraits*, tome iv (**Paris,** An 7 [= 1798°*]).

Descriptions : (**1**) *Tezkirat alschoara.*[3] *Histoire des poëtes. Par Douletschah ben-Alaëddoulet algazi alsamarcandi . . . Par M. Silvestre de Sacy* (in *Notices et extraits des manuscrits de la Bibliothèque nationale,* tome iv (**Paris,** An 7 [= 1798°*]), pp. 220–72 (with List of Poets), (**2**) Sprenger 3.

Lists of the poets : (1) See under Descriptions (1) above, (2) Rehatsek pp. 130–1.

Sources : *The sources of Dawlatshāh . . . By E. G. Browne* (in *JRAS.* 1899, pp. 37–45).

Metrical abridgment (about 250 verses) : *Āsmān i sukhun*, a remodelling by Luṭf Allāh M. Muhandis b. Aḥmad, who lived in Aurangzēb's time, of a versification made in Akbar's time by " Fā'iḍī " Kirmānī : Sprenger no. 15 (Top-khānah).

[Autobiographical statements (for which see Browne's English

[1] In the notice of Ibn i Yamīn, the seventh biography in *Ṭabaqah* v.
[2] In the final section of the *Khātimah.*
[3] In the Arabic character, but transliterated in a footnote.

preface p. 15); *Majālis al-nafā'is; Laṭā'if-nāmah* p. 180; Rieu i p. 364; *Ency. Isl.* under Dawlat-Shāh (Huart); Browne *Lit. Hist.* iii pp. 436–7.]

1094. Amīr, or Mīr,[1] Niẓām al-Dīn **'Alī-Shīr " Nawā'ī "** and " Fānī "[2] b. Amīr Ghiyāth al-Dīn Kichkīnah[3] was born at Harāt on 17 Ramaḍān 844[4]/9 Feb. 1441. He is said to have been a schoolfellow of Sulṭān Ḥusain b. Manṣūr, who, on becoming ruler of Harāt in 873/1469, appointed him Keeper of the Great Seal (*Muhr-dār*).[5] Before long, however, he resigned that appointment, being by nature averse from holding office. He continued nevertheless to occupy a position of great influence and intimacy at court, and in 876/1472 he was formally given the rank of *amīr* (*manṣab i 'ālī-marātib i imārat i dīwān i a'lā*).[6] On occasions when Sulṭān Ḥusain was absent from Harāt Mīr 'Alī-Shīr acted as Governor (*ḥākim*) of the town. In 892/1487 he reluctantly accepted the Governorship of Astarābād, but after little more than a year he returned to Harāt. On 12 Jumādā II A.H. 906/3 Jan. 1501 he died.

Barthold states (in the *Ency. Isl.* under Turks. III. Čaghatāi literature (English edition, Vol. IV p. 916)) that, although in European works Mīr 'Alī-Shīr is frequently described as a

[1] 'Alī-Shīr was an *amīr* (in Turkish *bēg*) by birth, this title being hereditary in families belonging to the aristocracy of high officialdom (Barthold in *Mir-Ali-Shir* p. 113. Cf. *Laṭā'if-nāmah* p. 218^{12}: *Mīr masnad i imārat rā maurūthī dāsht*). In Turkish works he is called 'Alī-Shīr Bēg.

[2] It is usually said that " Nawā'ī " was his *takhalluṣ* in Turkish poetry and " Fānī " in Persian (*Dar fārisī Fānī takhalluṣ kardah* (*Tārīkh i Rashīdī*): *Dar shi'r i turkī muṭlaqan takhalluṣ i īshān Nawā'ī ast u dar dīwān i fārisī takhalluṣ-ash Fanā'ī* (*sic. Tuḥfah i Sāmī* p. 180^{21})). This doubtless corresponds roughly to the facts, but it is shown by Berthels (*Mir-Ali-Shir* pp. 34–6: cf. *Der Islam* xix pp. 43–4, where, however, the sense is not quite correctly rendered) that " Fānī " is the *takhalluṣ* used in the *Lisān al-ṭair*, which is a Turkish work, and that according to Mīr 'Alī-Shīr's own statement at the end he used that *takhalluṣ* to emphasise the Ṣūfī character of the work.

[3] *Ḥabīb al-siyar* iii, pt. 3, p. 179^{6}. Kijīkīnah (Kījīkīnah, KJKNH) Bakhshī according to the *Tārīkh i Rashīdī*.

[4] The authority for this date is Khwānd-Amīr's *Makārim al-akhlāq* (see Rieu i p. 366).

[5] *Ḥabīb al-siyar* iii pt. 3, p. 230^{21} (*muḥāfaẓat i muhr i buzurg i humāyūn rā dar 'uhdah i ān-janāb kard*).

[6] *Ḥabīb al-siyar* iii pt. 3, p. 231 $^{24 seqq.}$. The same rank was conferred immediately afterwards on Amīr S. Ḥasan [b.] Ardashīr (*Ḥabīb al-siyar* iii pt. 3, p. 232^{5}: *u ham-dar-ān rūz kih Amīr Niẓām al-Dīn 'Alī-Shīr bar masnad i imārat i dīwān nishast Amīr Saiyid Ḥasan i Ardashīr nīz ba-d-ān manṣab sarfarāz gasht.*). Cf. Belin p. 15.

minister or vizier, he never in fact held any such official position.[1] "His influence on affairs of state and his activity as a patron of arts and sciences were the result of his friendship (not always unclouded) with his prince Sulṭān Ḥusain (1469–1506)."

Mīr 'Alī-Shīr was the author of a Persian *dīwān*,[2] but his reputation as a Persian poet was not high.[3] In the history of Eastern-Turkish literature, on the other hand, he is an important figure. "Mīr 'Ali Shīr," says Rieu, "has done more than any other to raise Turki to the rank of a literary language, and is universally considered as the most elegant, as he certainly is the most prolific, of Chaghatāi writers." His Turkī works (at least 29 in number [4]) include (1) four *dīwāns*,[5] (2) a *khamsah*,[6] (3) *Lisān al-ṭair* (A.H. 904/1498–9), modelled on 'Aṭṭār's *Manṭiq al-ṭair*, (4) *Khamsat al-mutaḥaiyirīn*, a memoir of his friend Jāmī,[7] (5) *Nasā'im al-maḥabbah* (A.H. 901/1495–6), a translation of Jāmī's *Nafaḥāt al-uns*, (6) *Muḥākamat al-lughatain* (A.H. 905/1499–1500), on the superiority of Turkish to Persian,[8] (7) *Maḥbūb al-qulūb* (A.H. 906/1500–1) on morals and manners.[9] According

[1] His contemporary Khwānd-Amīr mentions him several times incidentally in the *Dastūr al-wuzarā'*, but does not include him in the series of *wazīrs*.

[2] *Dīwān i Fānī*. MSS.: Blochet iii 1765, 1766, Āyā Ṣōfyah 3882, Ghorlulu 'Alī Pāshā 295, Fātiḥ 3886–7 ("*Dīwān i Nawā'ī*", but both described as Persian), Nūr i 'Uthmānīyah 3850, Yildiz 2781/30 (cf. Edhem and Stchoukine p. 43) etc.

[3] Cf. the opinion expressed by Bābur (*Bābur-nāmah* tr. 'Abd al-Raḥīm p. 109[1]: *ba'ḍī abyāt i ū bad nīst wa-lī akthar sust u firūd and*).

[4] For lists see Belin pp. 59–62, *ZDMG.* ii pp. 249–51 (Berezin), Rieu Turkish Cat. p. 265*b*, *Islâm Ansiklopedisi*, 5. cüz, pp. 353–6.

[5] *Gharā'ib al-ṣighar* (Edition: Khīwah 1881 (*Isl. Ansikl.*). *Muntakhabāt* printed several times at Tashkent, Bukhārā, Tabrīz and Istānbūl acc. to *Isl. Ansikl.*), *Nawādir al-shabāb*, *Badā'i' al-wasaṭ*, *Fawā'id al-kibar*. For MSS. (some of them containing collections antedating the division into four *dīwāns* or selected from them) see Rieu Turkish Cat. pp. 294–7, Dorn 561–4, Jackson-Yohannan 21 (beg. *Zihī ẓuhūr*. No title. A.H. 905/1499–1500), 22 (*Nawādir al-shabāb*. A.H. 988/1580), Philadelphia Lewis 95 (beg. *Ai ṣafḥah*), Princeton 150–1, Tashkent 130, etc.

[6] *Ḥairat al-abrār*, *Farhād wa Shīrīn*, *Majnūn wa Lailā*, *Sab'ah i saiyārah*, *Sadd i Iskandarī*. Editions: Khīwah 1880 and Tashkent 1904 (according to *Isl. Ansikl.*), Tashkent 1893 and 1901 (acc. to Tashkent Cat. no. 128). Cf. Rieu Turkish Cat. pp. 292–4, Dorn 560 (A.H. 898/1492–3), Tashkent 128 etc.

[7] French translations of selected portions in Belin, *Notice*, pp. 101–58.

[8] Editions: Paris 1841 (in Quatremère's *Chrestomathie turke-orientale* pp. 1–39), Istānbūl 1899, Khōqand 1918 (see *Isl. Ansikl.*).

[9] Editions: Istānbūl 1889 (so *Isl. Ansikl.*, but perhaps 1289/1872–3 should

to the *Islâm Ansiklopedisi* the oldest and finest manuscripts of his *Kullīyāt* are (1) Istānbūl, Rawān Köshkü no. 808 (A.H. 901/1496), (2) Istānbūl, Fātiḥ no. 4059, (3) Paris, Suppl. turc. 316–17 (A.H. 933/1526) and (4) Leningrad Pub. Lib. [Dorn 558. Cf. *ZDMG*. ii pp. 248–56.]

Mīr 'Alī-Shīr is famous also as a patron of writers and artists. Mīr Khwānd, Khwānd-Amīr, Ḥusain Kāshifī and Bihzād are among those who were indebted to his encouragement.

Majālis al-nafā'is, short notices of contemporary Persian and Turkī poets, begun in 896/1490–1,[1] written in Eastern Turkish and divided into eight *majālis* ((1) deceased poets personally unknown to the author, (2) poets deceased before 896 whom the author had met, (3) living poets known to the author, (4) men of letters who occasionally wrote poetry, (5) noblemen of Khurāsān who occasionally wrote poetry (6) non-Khurāsānī poets, (7) kings and princes of Tīmūr's house, (8) Sulṭān Ḥusain): Ḥ. Kh. v p. 381 no. 11388 (cf. ii p. 263 no. 2822), **Flügel** ii 1209 (A.H. 903/1497–8?), **Blochet** iii 1765 (early 16th cent.), **Browne** Coll. J. 7 (A.H. 937/1530–1), **Rieu** Turkish Cat. p. 273*a* (A.H. 987/1579), p. 274*b* (A.H. 1232/1817), **Lindesiana** p. 244 no. 149 (A.H. 1031/1621–2), **Bukhārā** Semenov 28, 98, **Ethé** 664, **Leningrad** Asiat. Mus. (see Dorn p. 504), Institut (A.H. 1224/1809. See Smirnow p. 189 no. 96), Pub. Lib. nos. 558 (9) (in the *Kullīyāt i Nawā'ī*) and 553 (the latter only a fragment. See Smirnow p. 190[1], Dorn pp. 510, 503),

be read, since an edition of that date is mentioned by Browne, *L.H.* iii p. 453), Bukhārā 1907 and Tashkent (so *Isl. Ansikl.*). Described at length by Belin in *Journal asiatique*, 6e série, tom. vii pp. 523–52, tom. viii pp. 126–54. For MSS., extracts and translations of extracts see Rieu Turkish Cat. pp. 275–6. The Persian translation made in 1204/1789–90 by "Āẓfarī" (see pp. 642–3 *supra*) was described by S. M. 'Abd Allāh from a MS. at Lahore (Panjāb Univ. Lib.) in *OCM*. xi/4 (Aug. 1935) pp. 41–8.

[1] On this date see Barthold's remarks in *Mir-Ali-Shir*, p. 124, Hinz's trans. p. 35: Leider lässt sich die Schrift keiner bestimmten Zeit im Leben des Verfassers zuweisen, obschon sie ein Datum (896/1490–1491) enthält; denn dieses entspricht anderen Stellen der *Mağālis* nicht. So wird beispielsweise als Zeitgenosse des Verfassers von diesem als Beherrscher Samarqands der Sohn Sulṭān Maḥmūds genannt, Sulṭān 'Alī Mīrzā; dieser herrschte in Samarqand zuerst kurze Zeit während des Jahres 1496, etwas länger sodann von 1498–1500 . . .

Univ. no. 618 (see Salemann-Rosen p. 24), **Mas͟hhad** iii p. 103, **Munich** Turkish Cat. p. 41 no. 148 (modern), **Velyaminov-Zernov** p. 861 no. 12, and probably also in the Istānbūl and Paris MSS. of the *Kullīyāt* mentioned above (p. 791).[1]

Editions: **Tashkent** 1326/1908 (together with the *tad͟hkirah* entitled *Bāg͟h i Iram* and Afḍal Mak͟hdūm i Pīrmastī's *Afḍal al-tad͟hkār fī d͟hikr al-s͟hu'arā' wa-'l-as͟h'ār*, composed in 1322. See Semenov's Tashkent Cat., *vvedenie*, p. [3]), 1330/1912 (see Semenov's *Kurzer Abriss* p. 3, n. 1).

Extracts: (1) [The preface] Belin *Notice biographique et littéraire sur Mir Ali-Chir-Névâii* (tirage à part) pp. 65–8, (2) [parts of *Majlis* iii] Berezin *Chrestomathie turque* pp. 146–61, (3) [*Majlis* vii] Belin *op. cit.* pp. 73–82.

Translations of extracts: (1) [The preface (French)] Belin *op. cit.* pp. 68–72, (2) [*Majlis* vii (French)] Belin *op. cit.* pp. 83–100.

Description: Browne *Lit. Hist.* iii pp. 437–9.

Persian translations: (1) *Laṭā'if-nāmah*, a translation made by Sulṭān-Muḥammad "Fak͟hrī" b. "Amīrī" Harawī (see pp. 795–7 *infra*), who added a ninth *majlis* (on living poets not mentioned in the original) and dedicated his work to the *Wazīr* Ḥabīb Allāh [Sāwajī] at the time of Sām Mīrzā's appointment to the [titular] Governorship of K͟hurāsān with Durmis͟h K͟hān as his vice-gerent [i.e. in 927/1521 according to *Ḥabīb al-siyar* iii, *juz'* 4, p. 100]: **Lindesiana** p. 122 no. 55 [2] (A.H. 939/1532–3), **Rieu** i 365*b* (A.H. 965/1558).

Editions: (1) *Laṭā'if-nāmah i Fak͟hrī* [with preface, notes and indexes by S. M. 'Abd Allāh] (in the *Oriental College Magazine*, vol. vii no. 4 (**Lahore** Aug. 1931), vol. viii no. 1 (Nov. 1931), no. 2 (Feb. 1932), no. 3 (May 1932), no. 4 (Aug. 1932), vol. ix no. 1 (Nov. 1932) and no. 2 (Feb. 1933), (2) *The Majalis-un-Nafa'is* [sic] " *Galaxy of poets* " *of Mir 'Ali Shir Nava'i* [sic]. *Two*

---

[1] This list of Eastern-Turkish MSS. makes no claim to completeness.

[2] Probably the *Laṭā'if-nāmah*, though this is not expressly stated in the catalogue. An inquiry addressed to the John Rylands Library failed to elicit the desired information, since the manuscript, owing to war-time precautions, was not available.

16th. century Persian translations edited with an introduction and annotations, etc., by Ali Asghar Hekmat, **Tihrān** A.H.S. 1323/1945 pp. 1–178.

(2) (*Tarjamah i Majālis al-nafā'is*), begun at Istānbūl in 927/1521, completed in 929/1522–3 and dedicated to Sulṭān Salīm by Ḥakīm [Shāh] M. b. Mubārak al-Qazwīnī (cf. *al-Shaqā'iq al-Nu'mānīyah* I pp. 371–2, Rescher's trans. p. 216), who compressed the matter of the original (with some additions) into seven *bihishts* and appended an eighth in two *rauḍahs* ((1) ancient and modern poets, mostly extracts from Jāmī's *Bahāristān*, (2) Salīm and the poets of his court): **As'ad** 3877, **Tihrān** Sa'īd Nafīsī's private library.

Edition: *The Majalis-un-Nafa'is* [*sic*] . . . *Two 16th century Persian translations edited* . . . *by Ali Asghar Hekmat*, **Tihrān** A.H.S. 1323/1945 pp. 179–409.

(3) *Majālis al-nafā'is*, a translation made by Shāh 'Alī b. 'Abd al-'Alī in the time of Sulṭān Dīn Muḥammad [b. Jānī Bēg, who ruled over part of Khurāsān during the reigns of 'Abd Allāh Khān Uzbak [A.H. 991/1583–1006/1598) and 'Abd al-Mu'min Khān and after the latter's death in 1006/1598 was proclaimed Khān in Harāt, but was defeated soon afterwards by Shāh 'Abbās and died during his flight]: **Rieu** Suppt. 104 (breaks off in the middle of the account of Ulugh Bēg, the sixth in *Majlis* vii. 17th cent.).

(4) *Majālis al-nafā'is*, a translation made by 'Abd al-Bāqī Sharīf Riḍawī at the instance of Ghulām-Ghauth Khān, Nawwāb of the Carnatic: **Madras** 445 (A.H. 1242/1827, probably autograph).

[Daulat-Shāh 494–509; Jāmī *Bahāristān* (the last notice in *Rauḍah* vii); *Makārim al-akhlāq*, a panegyric by Khwānd-Amīr (for whom see pp. 101–9 *supra*) written in the rough before 'Alī Shīr's death but finished afterwards and dedicated to Sulṭān Ḥusain (MS.: Rieu i p. 367*a*): *Majālis al-'ushshāq* (the fourth biography from the end); *The Babur-nama in English* (see p. 532 *supra*) i p. 271 (summarised in Browne's *Lit. Hist.* iii pp. 456–7); *Bābur-nāmah* tr. 'Abd al-Raḥīm pp. 108^{18}–109^{9}; *Laṭā'if-nāmah* pp. 218–23 (the first *qism* in *Majlis* ix); *Ḥabīb* *al-siyar* iii, *juz'* 3, pp. 217 etc. ; *Tārīkh i Rashīdī* (the passage, omitted in Ross's translation, is quoted in *Mélanges asiatiques* ix (St. Petersburg, 1888) pp. 358–60 and in *Oriental College Magazine*, vol. x no. 3 (Lahore, May 1934) pp. 155–7 ; *Tuḥfah i Sāmī*, Ṭihrān A.H.S. 1314, pp. 179–81 (the first biography in *Ṣaḥīfah* vi. French translation by Silvestre de Sacy in *Notices et extraits*, tome iv (Paris, An 7 = 1798°*) pp. 290–3) : *Mir'āt al-adwār* (Ethé 109, fol. 411*b* seq.) ; Taqī Kāshī *Khulāṣat al-ashʻār* (cf. Sprenger p. 20) : Ḥasan Rūmlū *Aḥsan al-tawārīkh* xii pp. 55[9]–57[10], Seddon's trans. pp. 24–5 ; *Mir'āt al-khayāl* (Bodl. 374) no. 57 ; *Safīnah i Khwushgū* (Bodl. 376 no. 8) ; *Ātash-kadah* no. 60 (Bombay 1277 p. 19[1]) ; *Khulāṣat al-afkār* no. 197 ; Elliot *Bibliographical index* pp. 114–16 ; M. Nikitski *Emir-Nizam-ed-Din-Ali-Shir, v gosudarstvennom i literaturnom ego znachenii*, St. Petersburg 1856 (diss. For a criticism see Barthold in *Mir-Ali-Shir*, Leningrad 1928, p. 101, Hinz's trans. p. 3) ; *Notice biographique et littéraire sur Mir Ali-Chir Névâïi, suivie d'extraits tirés des œuvres du même auteur par M.* [F.A.] *Belin* (in the *Journal asiatique*, 5e série, tome xvii (1861) pp. 175–256, 281–357, published also as an offprint. For a criticism see Barthold, *op. cit.* pp. 101–2, Hinz's trans. pp. 3–4) ; Elliot and Dowson *History of India* iv pp. 527–8 ; Browne *Lit. Hist.* iii pp. 505–6 and elsewhere ; *Mir-Ali-Shir : sbornik k pyatisotletiyu so dnya rozhdeniya*, Leningrad (Akademiya Nauk SSSR) 1928 (containing articles in Russian ((1) Contribution to the history of the literary language of Central Asia by A. Samoylovich pp. 1–23, (2) Nevāyi and 'Attār by E. Berthels, pp. 24–82, (3) A new Chaghatāy-Persian dictionary by A. Romaskevich, pp. 83–99, (4) Mīr 'Alī-Shīr and political life by W. Barthold pp. 100–64) as well as reviews of some books, mostly in Turkish, on Mīr 'Alī-Shīr. See a summary by H. Ritter in *Der Islam* xix (1930–1) pp. 42–9 and W. Barthold *Herat unter Ḥusein Baiqara, dem Timuriden. Deutsche Bearbeitung* [of B.'s article in *Mir-Ali-Shir* pp. 100–64] *von W. Hinz* (D.M.G. Abhandlungen für die Kunde des Morgenlandes, xxii, 8 (Leipzig 1937)) ; *Oriental College Magazine* vol. x no. 2 (Lahore, Feb. 1934) pp. 3–34, vol. xi no. 2 (Feb. 1935) pp. 3–25 (articles in Urdu by S. M. 'Abd Allāh) ; *Ency. Isl.* in the section ČAGHATĀI LITERATURE (Barthold), which forms part of the article Turks (there is no separate article on Mīr 'Alī-Shīr); *Islâm Ansiklopedisi* under Ali Şîr (an article of 18 columns by A. Zeki Velidi Togan), where some further works are mentioned, including *Ali Şîr Beg, hayatı ve eserleri* by A. Zeki Velidi Togan (a forthcoming publication of the University of Istanbul) and a Russian bibliography of 'Alī-Shīr and his works by A. A. Semenov (Tashkent 1940); 'Alī Aṣghar Ḥikmat's introduction to his edition of two Persian translations of the *Majālis al-nafā'is* pp. Z–KH; Portraits in the *Burlington Magazine*, Jan. 1931, plate IV B, and in Binyon, Wilkinson, and Gray's *Persian miniature painting*, London, 1933, pl. lxxvi.]

1095. For the (*Tārīkh i Ṣadr i Jahān*), which was written, partly at least, in 907/1501–2 by Ṣadr i Jahān Faiḍ Allāh Banbānī and which concludes with a biographical chapter, see p. 110 *supra*.

1096. For the *Ḥabīb al-siyar* of **Khwānd-Amīr** which extends to 930/1524 and which contains biographies of celebrities at the end of reigns, see pp. 104–8 *supra*. In addition to this and other works he wrote

Makārim al-akhlāq, a pompous panegyric on Mīr 'Alī-Shīr, who died in 906/1501 (see p. 789 *supra*) before its completion: **Rieu** i 367*a* (A.H. 965/1558).

1097. At the end of his narrative of the year 911/1505–6 Bābur has inserted in the *Bābur-nāmah* (see pp. 530–5 *supra*) short accounts of some poets, scholars, musicians and other celebrities contemporary with Sulṭān Ḥusain at Harāt. In the Bombay edition of 'Abd al-Raḥīm's translation these will be found on pp. 112 antepenult.—116^{10}. A corrected text of the passage was published by M. Shafī' in *OCM*. x/3 (May 1934) pp. 140–9.

1098. For the *Tārīkh i Rashīdī*, which was completed by Mīrzā Ḥaidar Dūghlāt in 952/1546 and which contains biographies of poets and other celebrities, see pp. 274–5 *supra*.

1099. Sulṭān-Muḥammad "**Fakhrī**" b. M. "Amīrī" al-Harawī was, according to "Ilāhī", a panegyrist of Shāh Ṭahmāsp (reigned 930/1524–984/1576). His *Laṭā'if-nāmah* (for which see p. 792 *supra*) was written at the time when Shāh Ismā'īl's son,

Sām Mīrzā (b. 923/1517) was appointed titular Governor of Khurāsān,[1] Durmish Khān, his tutor, being the real Governor and Ḥabīb Allāh Sāwajī the *Wazīr*. It was to the latter that "Fakhrī" dedicated both the *Laṭā'if-nāmah* and the *Tuḥfat al-ḥabīb*, an anthology of ghazals.[2]

In the *Jawāhir al-'ajā'ib*, according to Sprenger, "The author informs us that with the intention to perform the pilgrimage to Makkah, he came during the reign of Sháh Tahmásb Ḥosayny (reigned from 930 to 984) to Sind, the ruler of that country was then[3] Moḥammad 'ysá Tarkhán (died in 974), and it would appear that he wrote this book at his Court." M. 'Īsā Tarkhān reigned from 961/1554 or 962/1555 to 974/1564 or 975/1565, but apparently "Fakhrī's" connexion with Sind began at an earlier date. In the *Tārīkh i Ma'ṣūmī* (for which see p. 652 *supra*) "Maulānā Fakhrī Harawī"[4] is mentioned in a list of celebrities contemporary with Mīrzā Shāh Ḥasan [Arghūn], M. 'Īsā Tarkhān's predecessor, who reigned from 930/1524 to 961/1554 and who is presumably identical with Abū 'l-Fatḥ Shāh Ḥasan Ghāzī,[5] the dedicatee of the *Rauḍat al-salāṭīn*.[6] To Shāh Ḥasan Arghūn he dedicated[7] also his *Ṣanā'i' al-ḥusn* [perhaps *Ṣanā'i'*

[1] i.e. in 927/1521, from which date he held the appointment, residing at Herāt, until his father's death in 930/1524.

[2] For which see Sprenger no. 6, Rieu Suppt. 375, Bānkīpūr xi 1101, Bānkīpūr Suppt. i 1993, Lindesiana p. 137 no. 864, Āṣafīyah i p. 716 no. 303, Peshawar 1892, and probably also Blochet iii 1978.

[3] This word probably misrepresents the sense of the original.

[4] *Maulānā Fakhrī Harawī mardī khwush-ṭab' u akābir būḍah u shi'r nīz mī-guftah. Ba'ḍī taṣnīfāt dārad dar ṣanā'i' u badā'i' u 'arūḍ u qāfiyah* (p. 206).

[5] Blochet on the other hand says (tome iii p. 450) probably quite arbitrarily that the *Rauḍat al-salāṭīn* is dedicated "au sultan du Bengale, Aboul-Fath Shah Hoseïn Ghazi (†925 de l'hégire = 1519)." The Sulṭān of Bengal was called Ḥusain Shāh, not Shāh Ḥusain.

[6] Curiously enough on the same page on which the *Tārīkh i Ma'ṣūmī* speaks of Fakhrī Harawī it ascribes (according to the printed text) a work entitled *Rauḍat al-salāṭīn* to another author, who is described as follows: *Shāh Ḥusain TKDRY* [corrected in the index to NKDRY]: *dar silk i umarā-yi Mīrzā Shāh Ḥasan intiẓām dāsht. bah ḥiddat i ṭab' u jaudat i dhihn u makārim i akhlāq u maḥāsin i ādāb sar-āmad i fuḍalā-yi zamān i khwud būdah. u dar fann i shi'r u tārīkh mahāratī kāmil dāsht. u Rauḍat al-salāṭīn az jumlah i muṣannafāt i ūst.*

[7] According to 'Abd al-Muqtadir the dedicatee's name is introduced into the following line of a *qiṭ'ah* at the beginning of the work: *Rashk i Jam u Farīdūn naqd i Shujā' i Dhū 'l-Nūn* * *Chashm u chirāgh i Arghūn Shāh i Ḥasan-khaṣā'il.* Amīr Dhū 'l-Nūn was the father of Shāh-Bēg Arghūn, the founder of the Arghūn dynasty in Sind. Shujā' Bēg Arghūn, another son of Dhu 'l-Nūn, was the father of Shāh Ḥasan.

al-Ḥasan, as 'Abd al-Muqtadir transliterates], a work on poetical figures (MSS. : Bodleian 1371–2, Bānkīpūr ix 848 i).

(1) ***Rauḍat al-salāṭīn***, notices of royal poets in seven *bābs*, written at the request of Abū 'l-Fatḥ Shāh Ḥasan [1] Ghāzī : **Blochet** ii 1142 (early 17th cent.), 1143 (late 17th cent.), **Berlin** 644.

(2) ***Jawāhir al-'ajā'ib***, notices of 20 poetesses, written probably at the court of M. 'Īsā Tarkhān [2] : Sprenger 5 (Tōpkhānah. 143 pp.), **Bodleian** 362 (apparently an abridgment (9 foll. only). A.H. 1185/1771), **Bānkīpūr** xi 1098 xxxii (abridgment (4 foll. only). 18th cent.), **Būhār** 482 (1) (abridgment (16 foll. only). 19th cent.)

Edition : **Lucknow** 1873°* (23 pp.).

List of the poetesses : Sprenger p. 11.

[*Tārīkh i Ma'ṣūmī* p. 206 ; *Khazīnah i ganj i Ilāhī* (see Sprenger p. 83) ; *Makhzan al-gharā'ib*, no. 1901 (?) ; Sprenger p. 9 ; Rieu i p. 366.]

1100. Abū 'l-Naṣr **Sām Mīrzā,** son of Shāh Ismā'īl I, was born at Marāghah on 21 Sha'bān 923/19 Sept. 1517 (*Ḥabīb al-siyar* iii, pt. 4, p. 83^{17}). Durmish Khān b. 'Abdī Bēg [Shāmlū], a close friend of the Shāh, was appointed his tutor (*lalah, ibid.* p. 83^{22}). In 927/1521 the four-year-old prince was made titular Governor of Khurāsān with Durmish Khān as the real Governor (*Ḥ. al-s.* p. 100 ult.—101^{6}). Durmish Khān [3] reached Harāt in Dhū 'l-Ḥijjah (*Ḥ. al-s.* p. 101^{12-13}), but it was not until the following year that Sām Mīrzā was actually sent to Khurāsān. He reached Harāt in Ramaḍān 928 (*Ḥ. al-s.* p. 104^{21}). In 939/1532–3 his brother Shāh Ṭahmāsp, who had acceded to the throne in 930/1524, appointed him for the second time Governor at Harāt [4] with Āghziwār [5] Khān as his guardian. They rebelled

[1] The Berlin MS. has Ḥusain according to Pertsch, and Blochet also writes Ḥusain.

[2] In the verse which Sprenger supposed to be a chronogram the word *tārīkh* is a corruption of *fārigh*.

[3] After his death in 931 his brother Ḥusain Khān was appointed Governor of Harāt by Shāh Ṭahmāsp (*Aḥsan al-tawārīkh*, tr. Seddon, p. 94).

[4] *Aḥsan al-tawārīkh* i p. 246 penult.

[5] Vocalization unconfirmed.

in 941/1534–5 [1] and laid siege to Qandahār, at that time governed by Khwājah Kalān Bēg [2] on behalf of Mīrzā Kāmrān.[3] After a siege of eight months Āghziwār Khān was killed in battle outside Qandahār, and Sām Mīrzā sought and received his brother's forgiveness. In 951/1544 he and his brother Bahrām Mīrzā were sent by Shāh Ṭahmāsp to welcome Humāyūn,[4] the Mogul Emperor, who had gone to Persia as a refugee to seek the Shāh's help. Having rebelled again in 969/1561–2,[5] he was punished by confinement in the fortress of Qahqahah,[6] and there he died in 974/1566–7,[7] when an earthquake destroyed the building in which he was seated.

Tuḥfah i Sāmī, notices of poets [8] who flourished from the later years of the 9th/15th century to the middle of the

[1] *A. al-t.* i p. 260.

[2] Formerly one of Bābur's chief amīrs. For an account of him see *Ma'āthir al-umarā'* iii pp. 179–81 (in the biography of his son Muṣāḥib Bēg).

[3] Brother of the Mogul Emperor Humāyūn and Governor of Kābul, Qandahār and the Panjāb. For a summary of his career see Bānkīpūr Cat. ii pp. 217–22. Cf. *Ency. Isl.* under Kāmrān (H. Beveridge).

[4] *A. al-t.* i p. 309[8]. This seems to be the last mention of Sām in the *A. al-t.*

[5] This is stated by Rieu and M. 'Alī Tarbiyat apparently on the authority of the *Riyāḍ al-shu'arā'* and the *Takmilat al-akhbār* (what is this work ?) respectively.

[6] Iskandar Munshī in speaking of Qahqahah at a later date (p. 579[11]) mentions Sām Mīrzā, Ismā'īl Mīrzā and Alqās Mīrzā as persons who had been confined there. He describes it as a fortress or castle (*qal'ah*) on a mountain peak in the region (*ulkā*) of Yāft [doubtless = "Yāft (Māft, or Bāft)," *Nuzhat al-qulūb* tr. le Strange p. 86] in the administrative division (*az a'māl*) of Qarājah-Dāgh [a mountainous tract rich in iron and other minerals stretching east of Marand in Northern Ādharbāyjān and including Ahar, the chief town. For a map of the region (on which, however, neither Yāft nor Qahqahah is marked) see S. M. 'Alī Jamāl-Zādah's *Ganj i shāygān*, Berlin 1335, p. 102]. Cf. Seddon's note in *Aḥsan al-t.* ii (trans.) p. 293, and also Minorsky in *BSOS.* vii (1933–5) pp. 991–2, where it is stated that Yāft is "on the Qara-su". That Qahqahah was not in the immediate neighbourhood of Yāft is shown by the fact that Ismā'īl ii, having left Qahqahah on Tuesday, 22 Safar 984, did not camp at Yāft until the following Thursday (*A. al-t.* trans. p. 205[11]).

[7] According to M. 'Alī Tarbiyat, who quotes (again apparently from the *Takmilat al-akhbar* : see n. 5 on this page) a chronogram (*Daulat i Ṭahmāsb shud bāqī*) by 'Abdī Shīrāzī. Rieu on the other hand says (presumably on the authority of the *Riyāḍ al-shu'arā'*) that "having rebelled in A.H. 969 against his brother Shāh Ṭahmāsp, he was thrown into prison, and afterwards put to death with other princes of the royal house, on the accession of Shāh Ismā'īl II, A.H. 984." Iskandar Munshī mentions the names of some princes put to death by Ismā'īl II, but Sām Mīrzā is not among them.

[8] 664 according to Sprenger, 663 in Berlin 643, but there are only 399 names in Silvestre de Sacy's list.

10th/16th, composed, at least partly, in or about 957/1550,[1] and divided into seven *ṣaḥīfahs* ((1) S̲h̲āh Ismāʻīl and contemporary princes, p. 6 in the Ṭihrān edition, (2) Saiyids and *ʻulamā'*, p. 21, (3) *wazīrs* and other officials, p. 55, (4) persons of distinction who occasionally wrote poetry, p. 63, (5) poets best known by their pen-names (*s̲h̲āʻirānī kih bi-tak̲h̲alluṣ mas̲h̲hūr-and*), p. 85, (6) poets of Turkish race, p. 179, (7) jesters and poets of the lower classes, p. 188): Ḥ. K̲h̲. ii p. 263 no. 2823 (*Tad̲h̲kirat al-s̲h̲uʻarā' fārisī li-Sām Mīrzā*), Sprenger p. 12 no. 7, **Bānkīpūr** viii 682 (A.H. 968/1561), 683 (A.H. 971/1564), **Rieu** i 368*a* (very defective. A.H. 969/1561–2), 367*b* (late 16th cent.), Suppt. 103 (A.H. 976/1569), **Flügel** ii 1201 (A.H. 972/1564–5), **Krafft** p. 126 no. 313 (A.H. 972/1565), **Lindesiana** p. 215 no. 317 (A.H. 977/1569–70), **Sipahsālār** ii p. 462 (probably *circ.* A.H. 983/1575), **Cairo** p. 501 (A.H. 997/1588–9), **Blochet** ii 1144 (A.H. 1001/1593), 1145 (late 16th cent.), 1146 (17th cent.), 1147 (early 18th cent.), **Bombay** Univ. p. 41 no. 25 (bears seal dated 1007/1598–9), **Aumer** 2, **Berlin** 643, 643*a*, **Browne** Suppt. 272, **Buk̲h̲ārā** Semenov 41, **Ethé** 665 (about 579 biographies), 666 (only 474 biographies), **Leningrad** Asiat. Mus. (defective. See *Mélanges asiatiques* vii (St. Petersburg 1876) p. 402), **Leyden** iii p. 19 no. 933, **Madras** 305. Some other MSS. are mentioned in the Bombay University catalogue p. 42, including one dated 972 at Kābul (library unspecified). There are several at Istānbūl (e.g. Fātiḥ 4241–2, Ḥakīm-og̲h̲lū ʻAlī Pās̲h̲ā 718).

Edition: **Ṭihrān** A.H.S. 1314/1936 (ed. Waḥīd Dastgirdī. Supplement to the periodical *Armag̲h̲ān*, Year 16).

Edition of *Ṣaḥīfah* v: *The Tuhfa i Sami* (*Section V*) *of Sam Mirza Safawi edited . . . by Mawlawi Iqbal Husain*, **Patna** (Allahabad printed) 1934* (Patna University).

Extracts: *Iqtibāsāt i Tuḥfah i Sāmī rājiʻ bah hunarwarān* [edited with notes by M. S̲h̲afīʻ in *Oriental College Magazine*, vol. x no. 2 (**Lahore,** Feb. 1934) pp. 73–128].

[1] This date occurs in the notice of Humāyūn towards the end of *Ṣaḥīfah* i, where it is mentioned as the current year (*Notices et extraits* iv p. 281). In the Ṭihrān edition the passage (p. 17[4]) is corrupt (*tā aknūn kih sanah i k̲h̲ams wa-tisʻmi'ah i Hijrīst*). In the Bombay University MS. the date is given as 956 (*tā ḥāl kih 956 ast*).

Abridgment: *Intikhāb i Tuḥfah i Sāmī*, by Ānand Rām "Mukhliṣ" (for whom see pp. 612–14 *supra*): **I.O.** D.P. 718.

Descriptions: (**1**) . . . *Le présent sublime, ou Histoire des poëtes de Sam-mirza . . . Par A. I. Silvestre de Sacy* (in *Notices et extraits des manuscrits de la Bibliothèque nationale*, Tome IV (**Paris**, An 7 = 1798°*) pp. 273–308. With List of 399[1] poets). (**2**) *Ueber die morgenländischen Handschriften der königlichen Hof- und Central-Bibliothek in München. Bemerkungen von Othmar Frank*, **Munich** 1814°*, pp. 34–69 and Anhang pp. xv–xlix (List of 518[2] poets).

[*Ḥabīb al-siyar* iii pt. 4, pp. 83, 100, 104; Ḥasan Rūmlū *Aḥsan al-tawārīkh*, Seddon's trans., pp. 90^{16}, 118–19; *Khazīnah i ganj i Ilāhī* (Sprenger p. 77); *Safīnah i Khwushgū* (Bodl. 376 no. 58); *Muntakhab al-ash'ār* (Bodl. 379) no. 285; *Riyāḍ al-shu'arā*; *Ātash-kadah*, Bodl. 384 no. 35, Bombay 1277 p. 14; *Makhzan al-gharā'ib* no. 1000; *Majma' al-fuṣaḥā'* i 31 (where Sām is inadvertently described as a son of Shāh Ṭahmāsp); *Sham' i anjuman* p. 199; *Ency. Isl.* under Sām (Huart); M. 'Alī Tarbiyat *Dānishmandān i Ādharbāyjān*, Ṭihrān A.H.S. 1314, pp. 173–4.]

1101. Mīr **'Alā' al-Daulah "Kāmī"** b. Yaḥyā Saifī Ḥusainī[3] **Qazwīnī** was the second son of the author of the *Lubb al-tawārīkh* (see pp. 111–13 *supra*), the younger brother and foster-son[4] of Mīr 'Abd al-Laṭīf Qazwīnī, Akbar's teacher[5] and friend,[6] and the uncle of Naqīb Khān (for whom see p. 118 *supra*). When Shāh Ṭahmāsp sent orders from Ādharbāyjān in 960/1552–3 for the arrest of Mīr Yaḥyā and his family (cf. p. 111 *supra*) on the charge of excessive Sunnism, Mīr 'Alā' al-Daulah, who was

[1] The fifth *ṣaḥīfah* in the MS. described (Ancien fonds 247 = Blochet ii 1144) contains only 104 biographies, whereas there are 296 in the corresponding part of the Munich MS.

[2] The Munich MS. is defective.

[3] Ḥasanī according to the printed text of Badā'ūnī.

[4] *Ham birādar i khurd i 'Abd al-Laṭīf u ham tarbiyat-kardah i ū būd u ū-rā ḥaḍrat i āqā mī-guft* (Badā'ūnī iii 97^{16}).

[5] *Pādshāh pīsh i īshān sabaqī chand az dīwān i Khwājah Ḥāfiẓ u ghair i ān khwāndah and* (Badā'ūnī iii 98^{18}); *Dar sāl i duwwum ba-mu'allimī i 'Arsh-āshyānī iftikhār andūkht* (*Ma'āthir al-umarā'* iii 814^{3}).

[6] For 'Abd al-Laṭīf see Badā'ūnī iii pp. 97–8; *Ā'īn i Akbarī* tr. Blochmann pp. 447–8; *Memoirs of Jahāngīr* tr. Rogers and Beveridge i pp. 28 n. 2, 264; *Ma'āthir al-umarā'* iii pp. 813–15; Raḥmān 'Alī p. 132, etc.

then in Ādharbāyjān (Badā'ūnī p. 98[10]), warned his father. The latter was arrested and died later in prison, but Mīr 'Abd al-Laṭīf fled to the mountains of Gīlān. Invited to India by Humāyūn, Mīr 'Abd al-Laṭīf arrived there shortly after Humāyūn's death and was received by Akbar in 963/1556, the first year of his reign (*Akbar-nāmah*, tr. Beveridge, ii, p. 35; Badā'ūnī i p. 30[15]). Naqīb Khān had accompanied him (*A.-n.*, *ibid.*), but whether "Kāmī" reached India at this time or another is not recorded. A son of his, Mīr Yaḥyā Ḥusainī Saifī, is one of the poets included in the *Nafā'is al-ma'āthir* (Sprenger p. 55).

Nafā'is al-ma'āthir (a chronogram = 973/1565–6, the date of inception [1]), a *tadhkirah* dedicated to Akbar and containing (in the Munich MS.) a *maṭla'* (subdivided into two *miṣra's*, (1) *dar kaifīyat i ṣudūr i shi'r*, (2) *dar ta'rīf u taqsīm i shi'r*), notices of about 350 poets, mainly of the 10th/16th century, arranged alphabetically in 28 *baits* (one for each letter), a fragment relating to the history of Gujrāt in the years 980–5,[2] and a *maqṭa'* dealing in three *maṭlabs* with the history of Bābur, Humāyūn and Akbar: Sprenger 10 (Mōtī Maḥall. LIST OF POETS), **Aumer** 3 (old), **Rieu** iii 1022*a* (only extracts, viz. the preface, table of contents, history of Bābur, Humāyūn and Akbar to Jumādā II 982/1574, and a few detached lives of poets. Circ. A.D. 1850), **Ross-Browne** 247 (2) (circ. A.D. 1864. Cf. **Rehatsek** p. 169 no. 147, of which R.-B. 247 is probably a transcript).

Extracts (poets of Akbar's time in India only): *Muntakhab al-tawārīkh*, by 'Abd al-Qādir Badā'ūnī (cf. pp. 439–40 *supra*), iii pp. 170–390 [3] (166 poets).

[1] Sprenger points out that considerably later dates occur in the MS. seen by him. The latest of those mentioned in his catalogue seems to be 996, the year of "Hādī's" death. He says further that "according to a Postscript" the work was completed in 979, and Aumer quotes, doubtless from the same "postscript", the chronogram *Tammat 'alā yadaihi* (= 979).

[2] Is this by any chance a portion of the history of Akbar misplaced?

[3] This section is headed *Dhikr i shu'arā-yi 'aṣr i Akbar-Shāhī kih dar Nafā'is al-ma'āthir madhkūr-and kih ma'khadh i īn 'ujālah ast u mashhūr bah Tadhkirah i Mīr 'Alā' al-Daulah ast.* Similarly in his notice of "Kāmī" (p. 316) Badā'ūnī says that Mīr 'Alā' al-Daulah's *tadhkirah* is *ma'khadh i īn 'ujālah.* Among the poets noticed by Badā'ūnī are an appreciable number who do not appear in Sprenger's account of the *Nafā'is al-ma'āthir*. Badā'ūnī may of course have used a later edition of the *N. al-m.* than that represented by the Lucknow MS. which Sprenger examined.

List of the poets: Sprenger pp. 47–55.

[*Muntakhab al-tawārīkh* iii pp. 97–8 (in the notice of Mīr 'Abd al-Laṭīf); *Ā'īn i Akbarī* tr. Blochmann p. 447 37 and n. 2; *Mir'āt i jahān-numā* (fol. 389 in a B.M. MS. cited by Rieu, iii p. 1022*b*); *Ma'āthir al-umarā'* iii p. 813 (in the life of Naqīb Khān).]

1102. S. Bahā' al-Dīn Ḥasan "**Nithārī**" **Bukhārī**,[1] or, as on the title-page[2] of Berlin 645, S. Ḥasan Khwājah[3] Naqīb al-Ashrāf[4] Bukhārī.

Mudhakkir i aḥbāb (a chronogram = 974/1566–7), notices of 275 poets who lived in Bukhārā or its dependencies after the time of Mīr 'Alī-Shīr (for whom see pp. 789–95 *supra*), divided into a *maqālah* ((*a*) Chingīz-Khānī Sulṭāns, i.e. Shaibānī Khān etc., (*b*) Chaghatāy Sulṭāns, i.e. Bābur etc.), four *bābs* ((1) deceased poets not personally known to the author, (2) deceased poets known to the author, (3) living poets known to the author, (4) living poets unknown to the author) and a *khātimah* (the author's family): Ḥ. Kh. v p. 478, **British Museum** (A.H. 987/1579. See *British Museum Quarterly* iv/4 (1930) p. 112), **Berlin** 645, **Ivanow** 219 (bad and defective. 17th cent.), **Leningrad** Institut Oriental de l'Académie (see an article by A. Boldyrev in *Musée de l'Ermitage, Travaux du Département oriental*, iii (1940) pp. 291–300).

Extracts relating to seven calligraphists: *OCM.* xi/2 (Feb. 1935) pp. 39–45 (ed. Nawwāb Ṣadr Yār Jang, from a MS. in his private library).

[1] "Nitháry Bokháry, Bahâ aldyn Ḥasan" according to the *Nafā'is al-ma'āthir*.

[2] That the author does not mention his name in the preface seems probable from the fact that in the *British Museum Quarterly* the *Mudhakkir i aḥbāb* is described as anonymous. On the title-page (fol. 1*a*) of Berlin 645 his name is given in an ornate gold-lettered inscription quoted by Pertsch (*Tadhkirat al-shu'arā afḍal al-muta'akhkhirīn Maulānā Saiyid Ḥasan Khwājah Naqīb al-Ashrāf Bukhārī sallama-hu 'llāh ta'ālā . . .*). The dedicatee was Abū 'l-Ghāzī Iskandar Bahādur Khān [the Shaibānid, 968/1561–991/1583: see *Ency. Isl.* under Iskandar Khān] according to Pertsch, Amīr M. Badī' al-Ḥusainī according to the *BMQ.* Nawwāb Ṣadr Yār Jang and the *BMQ.* (but not Pertsch) describe the work as written in the time of 'Abd Allāh Bahādur Khān, which suggests that he is mentioned in the preface.

[3] This title is appended to the names of several of the author's relations in the *khātimah* (e.g. Bābā Khān Khwājah, 'Abd al-Salām Khwājah b. Pādshāh Khwājah, Walī Allāh Khwājah b. Mīram Khwājah).

[4] For this office see *Ency. Isl.* s.v. Sharīf.

List of the poets : Berlin pp. 605–9.

[*Nafā'is al-ma'āthir* (Sprenger p. 54).]

1103. For the *Mir'āt al-adwār*, a general history to 974/1566–7 by Muṣliḥ al-Dīn Lārī, which contains in the latter part biographies of writers and other celebrities inserted after the most important reigns, see p. 117 *supra*.

1104. For the *Aḥsan al-tawārīkh* of Ḥasan Rūmlū (A.H. 985/1577), which concludes the record of each year with obituary notices, mostly very short, see pp. 307–8 *supra*.

1105. Taqī al-Dīn M. "Dhikrī" b. Sharaf al-Dīn 'Alī Ḥusainī Kāshānī, usually called **Taqī Kāshī,** was born circ. 943/1536–7 [1] and was still alive in 1016/1607–8. He was a pupil of Muḥtasham Kāshī, who during the illness from which he died in 996/1588 sent for him and asked him to collect and arrange his poetical works. This he did and wrote a preface, which is prefixed to the British Museum MS. of Muḥtasham's *dīwān* (Rieu ii, p. 665).

Khulāṣat al-ash'ār wa-zubdat al-afkār, a remarkable *tadhkirah* containing "the fullest biographical details, the most copious and best chosen extracts (seldom less than a thousand verses [2] and in all 350,000 couplets), the soundest critical and most exact and complete bibliographical remarks on the Persian poets" [3] (Sprenger), divided into a *muqaddimah* (reasons for writing the work, four *faṣls* on *'ishq*, selections from 'Alī's *dīwān* with Persian paraphrase, and a *lāḥiqah* on poetry and the beginnings of Persian poetry), four *rukns* completed in 985/1577–8 [4] ((1) (= *Mujallads* i and ii) 54 ancient poets, mainly

[1] "He was born at Káshán about A.H. 946" according to Sprenger, who does not say how he obtained this information. If it is correct that when he wrote the *dhail* to the *khātimah* of the *Khulāṣat al-ash'ār* he had "now arrived at the fiftieth year of his age" (Bland p. 131) and if the date was then 993, as indicated by the chronogram quoted by Bland (who misinterpreted it) and Sprenger, he must have been born about 943.

[2] Thus according to 'Abd al-Muqtadir the selections from Ḥāfiẓ amount to almost the whole *dīwān*.

[3] "The only fault is that he dwells at too great a length on the love adventures of the subjects of his biography which are generally most disgusting."

[4] Rieu Suppt. 105, Berlin 647, Ethé 667 and Lindesiana 312 (Bland's MS.) contain at the beginning a eulogy on Shāh Ṭahmāsp, which must have been written before 984. Rieu Suppt. 105 contains also a later dedication to Shāh 'Abbās, at the end of which the author says that the work was completed early in 996. In the Bland MS. *Rukn* ii opens with a dedication to Shāh 'Abbās, but at the beginning of the work this MS. seems to contain no mention of

qaṣīdah-writers from Subuktigīn's time to the 8th century, (2) (= *Mujallad* iii) 42 *ghazal*-writers and later *qaṣīdah*-writers of the 8th and early 9th centuries, (3) (= *Mujallad* iv) 49 modern poets of the 9th and a few of the 10th century, (4) (= *Mujallad* v) 101 poets from Sulṭān Ḥusain Mīrzā's time to that of the author), a *khātimah* added in 993/1585 [1] (contemporary poets in 12 *aṣls* devoted to particular places [2], (1) Kāshān, (2) Iṣfahān, (3) Qumm, etc.), and a short *dhail* [3], the whole existing also in a revised and enlarged edition completed in 1016/1607–8, which ends with a [second] *khātimah* (poems, without biographies, of 60 poets, most of whom sent their *dīwāns* to the author after the completion of his work [4]) and an expanded *dhail* (the author's reflections on his work : see Bland pp. 131–2),[5] and of which there is an abridgment containing the biographies without the poetical quotations : Sprenger 8 (Mōtī Maḥall), 9 (Mōtī Maḥall. The abridged 2nd ed. LIST OF POETS [6]), **Blochet** iii 1242 (Notices of 'Am'aq, Sūzanī, Rashīd i Waṭwāṭ, Falakī, 'Imādī [from *Rukn* i]. " Ce volume est l'un des tomes du manuscrit original du grand tezkéré de Taki ed-Din . . . el Kashani." Late 16th cent.), **Bānkīpūr** viii 684 (*Mujallad* iv = *Rukn* iii only.[7] Revised and annotated by the author. Late 16th or early 17th cent.), **Ethé** 667 (abridged 2nd ed. (without the poems), lacking *Rukn* IV), 668 (*Khātimah* only. 1st ed. (with the poems). A.H. 993/1585), **Dorn** 321 (*Rukn* iii only. A.H. 933/1526 ! ! LIST OF 41 POETS), **Rieu** Suppt. 105 (introductory chapters and *Mujallad* i only, defective at end. 16th cent. LIST OF 22 POETS.), **Majlis** 334

Shāh 'Abbās but (in its place ?) a dedication (dated 1006) to Ibrāhīm 'Ādil-Shāh [II, of Bījāpūr, A.H. 987/1579–1035/1626]. In his *dhail* the author, writing in 1016, says that the work had occupied him during thirty years and that so much had been inserted in it, since its completion in its original form, that a sixth *mujallad* had become necessary.

[1] After 14 years had been spent on the work (Sprenger p. 13).

[2] The places of the poets' origins, their birthplaces.

[3] Ethé 668, a MS. of 993, ends with a short *dhail*.

[4] For the author's statements concerning this second *khātimah* see *JRAS*. ix (1848) p. 131.

[5] It seems from Bland's description that the *dhail* in his MS. consists of the *dhail* of 993 (with its chronogram) supplemented by the author's final remarks and the chronogram for 1016.

[6] For emendations of this list see Ethé 667.

[7] On foll. 270–395 of this MS. there is a *tadhnīb* added after the completion of the work and containing quotations from about 250 poets concerning whom the author had been unable to obtain any biographical information.

(only *Khātimah, aṣls* 1–7. A.H. 1013/1604–5), **Lindesiana** p. 223 no. 312 (unabridged 2nd ed., lacking *Rukn* iv. A.H. 1038–9/1628–30. Bland's MS.), **Berlin** 647 (abridged 2nd ed. 19th cent.), 647*a* (only *Khātimah*, second *Khātimah* and *Dhail*. 19th cent. LIST OF POETS IN 2ND KHĀTIMAH), **Ivanow** 2nd Suppt. 932 (fragment of vol. iv = *Rukn* iii, viz. poets numbered 109–16 in Sprenger's list. Circ. A.D. 1873).

Description: *On the earliest Persian Biography of Poets, by Muhammad Aúfi, and on some other Works of the class called Tazkirat ul Shuârá. By N. Bland* (in *JRAS.* ix (1848), pp. 126–34).

[*Ṣuḥuf i Ibrāhīm* (Berlin Cat. p. 640); Bland in *JRAS.* ix (1848) pp. 131–2.]

1106. S. **'Alī b. Maḥmūd al-Ḥusainī** completed in 1000/1591–2 and dedicated to his patron, the *Khān i Khānān* 'Abd al-Raḥīm [1] b. Bairam Khān, his

Bazm-ārāy, an anthology of ancient and modern poets with rhetorical and uninformative biographies largely plagiarized from the *Lubāb al-albāb* (see p. 783 *supra*): **Rieu** Suppt. 106 (early 17th cent.).

1107. For the *Ṭabaqāt i Akbarī*, written in 1001–2/1592–4 by Niẓām al-Dīn Aḥmad Harawī, which contains brief notices of 81 poets of Akbar's time (Calcutta ed. vol. ii pp. 484–520) see pp. 433–5 *supra*.

1108. The *Haft iqlīm*, completed in 1002/1594 by Amīn b. Aḥmad Rāzī, which contains geographically arranged notices of celebrities including many poets, will be described in the sub-section of this work devoted to general biography.

1109. For the *Muntakhab al-tawārīkh* of 'Abd al-Qādir Badā'ūnī, which was written in 1004/1595–6 and which contains notices of 166 poets of Akbar's time, see pp. 439 and 801[26] *supra*.

1110. For the *Ā'īn i Akbarī*, which contains brief notices of poets of Akbar's time (Calcutta ed. pp. 235–62, Blochmann's trans. pp. 548–611) see pp. 549–51 *supra*.

[1] For whom see p. 533 n. 4 *supra*.

1111. The *Majālis al-mu'minīn*, which was completed in 1010/1602 by Nūr Allāh Shūshtarī, and of which the 12th and last *majlis* deals with Persian poets, will be described in the subsection of this work devoted to general biography.

1112. Mullā **Muḥammad** "Muḥammad" [1] **Ṣūfī** [2] **Māzandarānī**,[3] poet, mystic, traveller and in his time a celebrated personage,[4] was born at Āmul (*Mai-khānah* p. 345[5]), but early in life he migrated to Shīrāz and lived there for a prolonged period (*ibid.*). According to Taqī Kashī (Sprenger p. 33) he travelled much in Persia. In Akbar's reign (963/1556–1014/1605) he went to India [5] and settled at Aḥmadābād. It was there that he became the teacher and friend (*Ma'āthir al-umarā'* iii p. 450[17]) of Mīr S. Jalāl Bukhārī,[6] member of a saintly Gujrātī family, who was later (1052/1642) to become *Ṣadr* of Hindūstān. There too, until an estrangement supervened, he enjoyed the companionship of the poet "Naẓīrī" Nīshāpūrī (Bānkīpūr iii p. 61), and there he was visited repeatedly by Taqī Auḥadī (*ibid.*, doubtless on the authority of the *Khulāṣat al-ash'ār*). From time to time he travelled to other parts of India, and it was during a visit to Ajmēr that the author of the *Mai-khānah* had the felicity of meeting the devout, unworldly and evidently impressive *ṣūfī*, who informed him that he had lived for 15 years in Mecca (*Mai-khānah* p. 346[1]) and that there were few parts of the world

[1] According to Sprenger and 'Abd al-Muqtadir "Muḥammad" is the *takhalluṣ* used in the copies of the *dīwān* seen by them, though some of the *tadhkirahs* put him under "Ṣūfī". Bland says on the authority of the *Ṣuḥuf i Ibrāhīm*, but perhaps erroneously, that he used both pen-names.

[2] *Chūn ṣūfī-ṭabī'at u ṣāfī-ṭawīyat wāqi' shudah binā-bar-ān bi-Maulānā M. i Ṣūfī ishtihār yāftah* (*Mai-khānah*, p. 345).

[3] 'Abd al-Muqtadir says that the *tadhkirahs* mention several poets called Ṣūfī or M. Ṣūfī with various *nisbahs* (Māzandarānī, Shīrāzī, Kirmānī, Ardistānī, Hamadānī, Āmulī, Iṣfahānī, Kashmīrī), but that some of these are merely repetitions of M. Ṣūfī Māzandarānī, since verses ascribed to them are to be found in the Bānkīpūr *dīwān*.

[4] Taqī Kāshī describes him as "a mystical poet who enjoyed great celebrity during his life time" (Sprenger p. 33). In the *Ma'āthir al-umarā'* (iii p. 450) he is called *Mullā M. i Ṣūfī i Māzandarānī i mashhūr*.

[5] With Abū Ḥaiyān i Ṭabīb and Mullā Ḥasan 'Alī Yazdī according to the *Majma' al-fuṣaḥā'*. Ṭāhir Naṣrābādī mentions in his account of Ḥusain [so in the printed text] 'Alī Yazdī (*Tadhkirah* pp. 157–8) that he became a close friend of M. Ṣūfī (*Ba'd az ān ba-Hindūstān raftah bā Mullā M. i Ṣūfī marbūṭ shudah muddatī chūn shīr u shakar u āb u guhar ba-ham āmīzish dāshtand ba-ḥasb i taqdīrāt az yak-dīgar judā shudah and*). Cf. *Safīnah i Khwushgū* no. 626.

[6] b. 1003/1595, d. 1057/1647.

he had not seen(!). It is said that he was summoned to Court by Jahāngīr and died on the way thither [1] at Sirhind [2] in 1032/1623 [3] or 1035/1625–6.[4]

According to Taqī Kāshī "he was accused of being a free-thinker by men learned in law" (Sprenger p. 33). He is one of the ten poets enumerated in the list of names at the end of the *Iqbāl-nāmah i Jahāngīrī* and in the *Haft iqlīm* his poetry is highly praised (*shi'r dar ghāyat i jaudat u hamwārī dārad*). His *dīwān* is preserved at Bānkīpūr (iii no. 301), Hamburg (191 iv) and Munich (Aumer 18 (6)). A MS. in a private library was described by Sprenger (no. 382). His *sāqī-nāmah*, written in 1000/1591–2, is preserved at Bānkīpūr (two copies—iii p. 62 and xi p. 139), Berlin (18 ii 10 (*a*)), Hamburg (191 (4)) and Munich (Aumer 18 (3)). A Lucknow MS. was described by Sprenger (no. 187). His *But-khānah* was compiled in collaboration with Ḥasan Bēg Khākī, who was sent as *Bakhshī* to Gujrāt in 1007/1598–9 (see p. 123 *supra*).

But-khānah, a large selection from the *dīwāns* of 126 poets, mostly early, compiled in 1010/1601–2, but amplified in 1021/1612–13 by 'Abd al-Laṭīf b. 'Abd Allāh 'Abbāsī Gujrātī,[5] who

[1] From Gujrāt (*Ma'āthir al-umarā'* iii p. 451), from Aḥmadābād (to Lahore, *Safīnah i Khwushgū*), from Kashmīr (*Ṣuḥuf i Ibrāhīm*). According to the *Muntakhab al-ash'ār* (no. 629) he died in Kashmīr.

[2] So *Ṣuḥuf i Ibrāhīm*.

[3] So Khwushgū.

[4] So *Riyāḍ al-shu'arā'* (according to Bānkīpūr i p. 61 antepenult.) and other works. According to the passage translated from the *Ṣuḥuf i Ibrāhīm* by Bland (*JRAS*. 1848 pp. 165–6) he was a resident of Aḥmadābād in Gujrāt in 1038 and afterwards, for some time, of Kashmīr, but the date is evidently corrupt, since the passage goes on to say that "by desire of the Emperor Jehangir [who died in 1037 !] he came from Kashmir, but arriving at Serhind, died there".

[5] 'Abd al-Laṭīf 'Abbāsī after a period in the service of Lashkar Khān Mashhadī (*Dīwān* and afterwards *Ṣūbah-dār* of Kābul) became *Dīwān i Tan* with the title of 'Aqīdat Khān in Shāh-Jahān's fifth year. For some time he was Court Chronicler. He died in the twelfth year of the reign, 1048–9/1638–9. He was the author of (1) *Nuskhah i nāsikhah i Mathnawīyāt i saqīmah*, a revised and annotated edition of Jalāl al-Dīn Rūmī's *Mathnawī* completed in 1032/1622–3 (MSS.: Blochet iii 1340, Ethé 1088–90, 2993, Bodleian 663–5, Rieu ii 589*a*, 590*a*, Browne Pers. Cat. 227, etc.), (2) *Laṭā'if al-ma'nawī min ḥaqā'iq al-Mathnawī*, a commentary on the same work (Editions: Lucknow 1282/1866 (see Berlin p. 795[7]), Cawnpore 1876°. MSS.: Bombay Univ. p. 240, Ethé 1101, Rieu ii 590*a*, Bānkīpūr i 74, Ivanow 507, etc.), (3) *Mir'āt al-Mathnawī*, another commentary on the same work (MS.: Ethé 1102), (4) *Laṭā'if al-lughāt*, a glossary to the same work (Editions: Lucknow 1294/1877°*, Cawnpore 1905°*. MSS.: Bodleian 1748–51, Ethé 1091–7, Rieu ii 590*b*,

prefixed a preface and brief biographies of the poets entitled *Khulāṣah i aḥwāl al-shu'arā'* : **Bodleian** 366 (slightly defective. LIST OF POETS).

Edition of the selections from "Muṭahhar's" *dīwān* : *OCM.* xi/3 (May 1935) pp. 152–60, xi/4 (Aug. 1935) *ḍamīmah*, pp. 161–216 (ed. M. Shafī').

[*Haft iqlīm* no. 1191 (a quotation from this in *Mai-khānah, ḥawāshī* p. 67) ; *Ā'īn i Akbarī* p. 254, Blochmann's trans. p. 590 ; Taqī Kāshī (Sprenger p. 33) ; Taqī Auḥadī ; 'Abd al-Nabī *Mai-khānah* pp. 345–60 and *ḥawāshī* pp. 67–9 ; *Safīnah i Khwushgū* no. 583 ; *Yad i baiḍā'* ; *Muntakhab al-ash'ār* no. 629 (Bodl. col. 252. Passage quoted in *Mai-khānah, ḥawāshī* p. 67) ; *Riyāḍ al-shu'arā'* ; *Majma' al-nafā'is* ; *Ātash-kadah* no. 402 (under Iṣfahān. M. Zamān in the Bodl. Cat. is a corruption) ; *Ma'āthir al-umarā'* iii pp. 450–1 ; *Ṣuḥuf i Ibrāhīm* (summarised in *JRAS.* 1848 pp. 165–6) ; *Makhzan al-gharā'ib* no. 2434 ; *Nishtar i 'ishq* ; *Majma' al-fuṣaḥā'* ii p. 38 ; Bānkīpūr iii pp. 60–1.]

1113. **Taqī Auḥadī,**[1] or, as he calls himself, Taqī b. Mu'īn al-Dīn M.[2] b. Sa'd al-Dīn M. al-Ḥusainī al-Auḥadī[3] al-Daqqāqī[4]

591*a*, 810*a*, iii 1000*a*, Bānkīpūr i 75, Eton 106, Glasgow, etc.), (5) *Laṭā'if al-ḥadā'iq min nafā'is al-daqā'iq*, a revised text of Sanā'ī's *Ḥadīqah* with a commentary begun in 1040/1630–1 and completed in 1042/1632–3 with help from Mīr 'Imād al-Dīn Maḥmūd "Ilāhī" (for whom see pp. 815–16 *infra*). (Edition : Lucknow 1887 (see Bānkīpūr i p. 29 1 and 15). MSS. : Edinburgh 273, Lahore Panjāb Univ., Bānkīpūr i 21, Būhār 283–4, 'Alīgaṛh Subḥ. MSS. p. 49 no. 12), (6) *Sharḥ i Ḥadīqah*, the same revised text with an abridgment of the same commentary completed by the commentator himself in 1044/1634 (MSS. : Ethé 923–4, Ivanow 445, Ivanow Curzon 192).

['*Amal i Ṣāliḥ* iii pp. 437–8 ; Rieu ii p. 589 ; Bānkīpūr i pp. 25–8.]

[1] According to 'Abd al-Muqtadir he "adopted the *takhalluṣ* Auḥadī", but this seems to be incorrect. Ivanow in describing a MS. of his *dīwān* calls it the *Dīwān i Taqī* and Sprenger, who had the same MS. before him, treats Taqī as the *takhalluṣ*. Similarly he is placed under the letter T in the *Makhzan al-gharā'ib* and elsewhere.

[2] For his father, Sh. Mu'īn al-D. M. Auḥadī, see *Makhzan al-gharā'ib* no. 2297, where it is said that his *majlis* at Qazwīn was frequented by Shāh Ṭahmāsp, that from Qazwīn he went to Shīrāz and afterwards to India and that he died in the Deccan in 979.

[3] Taqī was "descended by seven steps" (Bland p. 134) from Shaikh Auḥad al-Dīn 'Abd Allāh Balyānī [b. Mas'ūd b. M. b. 'Alī b. Aḥmad b. 'Umar b. Ismā'īl b. Abī 'Alī al-Daqqāq, d. 686/1287 : see Sprenger p. 95, *Nafaḥāt al-uns* p. 291, *Safīnat al-auliyā'* p. 180 (no. 338)].

[4] For Abū 'Alī al-Daqqāq, who died in 405/1015 or 406/1016, see *Tadhkirat al-auliyā'* i pp. 187–201, *Nafaḥāt al-uns* pp. 328–31, *Safīnat al-auliyā'* p. 159 (no. 283).

al-Balyānī [1] al-Iṣfahānī, was born at Iṣfahān in Muḥarram 973/1565. He was presented to S̲h̲āh 'Abbās I (A.H. 985/1587–1038/1629) soon after his accession and enjoyed his favour for some years. In 1003/1594–5 he went on a pilgrimage to Najaf and other holy places, returning home in 1009/1600–1. In Rajab 1015/Nov. 1606 he left for India via S̲h̲īrāz, Kirmān and Qandahār. After staying for 18 months in Lahore and more than a year in Āgrah he went to Gujrāt (Gujarat) and lived there for three years, returning to Āgrah in 1020/1611–12. It was in that year, apparently while still in Gujrāt, that he compiled an anthology entitled *Firdaus i k̲h̲ayāl i Auḥadī* (a chronogram = 1020 [2]), containing " all the specimens of poetry he had collected in the six years between Shiraz and Guzarat " (Bland p. 135). Later on at Āgrah one of the nobles of Jahāngīr's court " induced him to remodel the work, and to accompany the extracts with memoirs of the several authors quoted ". Thus it became the *'Arafāt al-'ās̲h̲iqīn* completed at Āgrah in 1024. That he returned to Gujrāt is shown by the fact that his abridgment, the *Ka'bah i 'irfān* was written at Aḥmadābād [3] in 1036. The date of his death does not seem to be recorded, but the A.S.B. MS. of his *Tad̲h̲kirat al-'ās̲h̲iqīn* (Ivanow 733) contains poems dated 1038 and 1039.[4]

His own list of his works, quoted from the *Ka'bah i 'irfān* in the *Guldastah* and thence in the Bānkīpūr catalogue, viii pp. 77–8, includes several *mat̲h̲nawīs* [5] and several

---

[1] Balyān " bi-fatḥ i awwal bar wazn i G̲H̲LYĀN " is the name of a village in the *wilāyat* of Kāzarūn (*Burhān i qāṭi'*). Cf. *S̲h̲īrāz-nāmah* p. 140 : *BLYĀN qarya'ī az qurā i Kāzarūn ast.*

[2] " In later life," says Bland " he indulged his poetic inclination by compiling an anthology, which he named Firdúsi Khayáli Auhadi, of which the value of the letters contains also the date." Unfortunately Bland explains in a footnote that *Firdaus i k̲h̲ayāl* = 991, which is true but irrelevant, since at that date Taqī Auḥadī was eighteen years old.

[3] This is stated in Taqī Auḥadī's own list of his works quoted from the *Ka'bah i 'irfān* by the author of the *Guldastah* and thence by 'Abd al-Muqtadir in the Bānkīpūr catalogue viii p. 77 ult. (*In nusk̲h̲ah kih Ka'bah i 'irfān-ast az 'Arafāt dar Aḥmadābād i Gujrāt sanah i 1036 muntak̲h̲ab s̲h̲ud.*)

[4] If these dates are correct, the poems in question must be later additions to the *Tad̲h̲kirat al-'ās̲h̲iqīn*, which is already mentioned in Taqī's list of his own works in the *Ka'bah i 'irfān* written in 1036.

[5] *Dar mat̲h̲nawīyāt-as̲h̲ as̲h̲'ār i s̲h̲utur-gurbah ba-naẓar rasīd* (*Riyāḍ al-s̲h̲u'arā*', quoted in Bānkīpūr viii p. 78 ult.).

dīwāns.[1] Little of this large output seems to have survived. Of the *Tadhkirat al-'āshiqīn*, a *dīwān* of *ghazals*, the first half (*alif* to *dāl*) is preserved at Calcutta (Ivanow 733), and there is another *dīwān* (beginning *Īn charkh i gard-gard i kawākib-nigār chīst*) at Madras (no. 7). The *Surmah i Sulaimānī*, a dictionary of non-Arabic words utilised later (1062/1652) in the compilation of the *Burhān i qāṭi'*, is preserved at Leningrad (Salemann-Rosen p. 16 no. 174). The Lucknow (Tōp-khānah) MS. of the *Kullīyāt* (*sic*) described by Sprenger (p. 576) seems to have been only a comparatively small collection of his shorter poems.

(1) ***'Arafāt*** [?] ***al-'ārifīn*** [or ***al-'āshiqīn***] ***wa-'araṣāt al-'āshiqīn*** [or ***al-'ārifīn***],[2] begun at Āgrah in 1022/1613 and completed there in 1024/1615, an alphabetically arranged dictionary of about 3000 poets divided into 28 *'arṣahs* (one for every letter of the alphabet) each subdivided into three *'arafahs* devoted respectively to ancient, mediaeval and modern poets[3]: **Bānkīpūr** viii 685–6 (apparently complete

[1] *Shi'r i bisyār guftah ammā hamwār-ast* (Ṭāhir i Naṣrābādī p. 303).

[2] In Taqī's own list of his works as quoted from the *Ka'bah i 'irfān* in the *Guldastah* the title of his *tadhkirah* is mentioned in two abbreviated forms, viz. *'.rafāt* and *'.rafāt al-'ārifīn wa-'araṣāt al-'ashiqīn* (Bānkīpūr viii p. 77 penult. and p. 78[10]). Similarly the author of the *Guldastah* in his preface calls it *'.rafāt al-'ārifīn* (Bānkīpūr viii p. 117 antepenult.). In the Āṣafīyah catalogue it is called *Gh.rafāt al-'ārifīn*. The full title as given in the preface to the *tadhkirah* itself is, according to Bland, " Urfát u ghurfáti ââshikín wa ârsát u ârzáti âârifīn ", which comes to the same thing as 'Abd al-Muqtadir's " 'Urafât wa Gurafât-i 'Âshiqîn wa 'Araṣât wa 'Araḍât-i 'Ârifîn ". Neither the vocalisation nor the meaning can be regarded as obvious. That Bland did not understand the words is shown by his description of them as " one of those titles, in which, as in those of many Arabic books, the translatable sense is sacrificed to a sort of rhythm, if not rhyme." Since his time the *tadhkirah* has been generally known to European orientalists as the *'Urafāt al-'āshiqīn*, but no European seems to have ventured to translate these words. It seems probable that the first word should be read *'Arafāt* (the name of the hill and adjoining plain 12 miles from Mecca, where the pilgrims assemble on the 9th day of the pilgrimage) and that the first element of the title means " The 'Arafāt of gnostics ", the word 'Arafāt having been selected as suggesting a place of assembly. This interpretation receives perhaps a little support from the fact that the abridgment, *Ka'bah i 'irfān*, is named after another place of assembly for pilgrims. The word *'araṣāt* may have been used in allusion to yet another place of assembly, the court of the last judgment. The transposition of *al-'āshiqīn* and *al-'ārifīn* may have been an afterthought of the author's.

[3] " Wālih " (quoted in Bānkīpūr viii p. 78) says that this *tadhkirah* contains many idle tales (*muzakhrafāt i bisyār*). In the Bānkīpūr catalogue (iii p. 61) the *Majma' al-nafā'is* is credited with the strange statement that Taqī Auḥadī's *tadhkirah* [which contains some 3000 biographies] consists of selections from M. Ṣūfī's *But-khānah* [which, at least as represented by the Bodleian MS., deals with 126 poets].

except for the omission of the 2nd and 3rd *'arafahs*, i.e. 138 poets, under *ḥā'*. A.H. 1050/1640–1), **I.O.** 3654 (= Lindesiana p. 223 no. 313. Circ. A.D. 1760), **Lindesiana** p. 223 no. 635 (verses only without biographies. Circ. A.D. 1780), **Āṣafīyah** iii p. 164 no. 209.

Description : *On the earliest Persian Biography of Poets . . . By N. Bland* (in *JRAS*. 1848) pp. 134–6.

(2) ***Ka'bah i 'irfān,*** an abridgment of the preceding made at Aḥmadābād [1] in 1036/1626 : **Lindesiana** p. 223 no. 314 (A.H. 1036/1626).

(3) ***Intikhāb i Ka'bah i 'irfān,*** an abridgment of the preceding made at Jahāngīr's request and divided into three *rukns* devoted respectively to ancient, mediaeval and modern poets : no MSS. recorded.

Selections from the *Intikhāb* : ***Guldastah*** compiled in 1155/1742 by 'Abd al-Wahhāb 'Ālamgīrī b. S. Manṣūr Khān, a grandson of S. Dilāwar Khān on his father's side and of Ghiyāth al-Dīn Khān b. Jumlat al-Mulk Islām Khān Riḍawī Mashhadī on his mother's side : **Bānkīpūr** viii 692 (18th cent.).

[*'Arafāt al-'āshiqīn*, preface (summarised in *JRAS*. ix (1848) pp. 134–5 and Bānkīpūr catalogue viii pp. 76–7) ; *Tadhkirah i Ṭāhir i Naṣrābādī* p. 303 ; *Safīnah i Khwushgū* ii no. 364 (Bodleian col. 223) ; *Riyāḍ al-shu'arā'* ; *Majma' al-nafā'is* (I.O. D.P. 739 fol. 194*b*) ; *Khulāṣat al-afkār* no. 56 ; *Ātash-kadah* no. 685 ; *Ṣuḥuf i Ibrāhīm* (summarised in Bland's article pp. 135–6) ; *Makhzan al-gharā'ib* no. 424 ; *JRAS*. ix (1848) pp. 134–6 ; Sprenger p. 95 note.]

1114. For 'Abd al-Bāqī Nihāwandī's *Ma'āthir i Raḥīmī*, which was completed in 1025/1616 and of which the *khātimah* (vol. iii, 1699 pp., in the Calcutta ed.) is devoted to contemporary celebrities, especially poets (pp. 66–1576), see p. 553 *supra*.

1115. **'Abd al-Nabī** "Nabī" b. Khalaf **Fakhr al-Zamānī** [2] **Qazwīnī** was born at Qazwīn about 998/1590.[3] In his youth he

[1] See p. 809[19].

[2] Fakhr al-Zamān, the maternal grandfather of 'Abd al-Nabī, was *Qāḍī* of Qazwīn (*M.-kh.* p. 499[11]).

[3] This is an inference from his statements that he was 19 years old when he went to Mashhad and that he reached Āgrah in 1018, apparently not many months later.

had some poetical talent as well as a remarkable memory which enabled him to learn by heart without difficulty such tales as the *Qiṣṣah i Amīr Ḥamzah*. At the age of 19 he visited Mas̲h̲had and there met merchants and travellers who spoke to him of India and inspired him with a desire to see that country. Travelling via Qandahār and Lahore he reached Āgrah in 1018/1609–10. His relative Mīrzā Niẓāmī Qazwīnī, who was *Wāqi'ah-nawīs*, gave him employment, apparently as his *qiṣṣah-k̲h̲wān*. In 1022/1613 at Ajmēr Mīrzā Amān Allāh b. Mahābat K̲h̲ān [1] appointed him his librarian (*kitāb-dār*). Subsequently he was in Kas̲h̲mīr for nearly two years and then in Bihār for a time, when his patron Mīrzā Niẓāmī was successively *Dīwān* of those two provinces. In the former period he completed his *Dastūr al-fuṣaḥā'*, a work now apparently lost, on the art of reciting the *Qiṣṣah i Ḥamzah*. In 1028/1619 at Patnah he came into contact with Nawwāb Sardār K̲h̲ān [2] and experienced so much kindness at his hands that he dedicated to him the *Mai-k̲h̲ānah*, which was completed in that year. In 1041/1631–2 he

[1] Amān Allāh "Amānī" Ḥusainī, who received the title of K̲h̲ānah-zād K̲h̲ān from Jahāngīr and that of K̲h̲ān i Zamān from S̲h̲āh-Jahān, died in 1046/1637. In Jahāngīr's 17th year, A.H. 1031–2/1622–3, he was appointed to govern Kābul as deputy for his father, and he subsequently held other governorships. For his career, etc., see *Ma'āt̲h̲ir al-umarā'* i pp. 740–8, Beveridge's trans. pp. 212–19, *Memoirs of Jahāngīr* tr. Rogers and Beveridge i p. 252, ii pp. 44, 94, 99, 231, 239, 257, 275, *Tad̲h̲kirah i Ṭāhir i Naṣrābādī* pp. 59–60, etc. Among his works were (1) a *dīwān* (see Sprenger 97, Bodleian 1095), (2) *Ruqa'āt i Amān Allāh i Ḥusainī*, a collection of 99 short letters on Ṣūfī matters addressed to numerous *s̲h̲aik̲h̲s*, beg. *Ḥamd i wāfir*. MSS.: Āṣafīyah i pp. 114, 124, Bānkīpūr xi 1098 xviii, Berlin 62 (14), Brelvi-Dhabhar p. 59, Browne Suppt., 699 (King's 202), Būhār 270 ii, Ethé 1763 (7), 1893, 2934, Ethé ii 3046, Ross-Browne 191, Gotha Arabic Cat. p. 489, Ivanow 1st Suppt. 787 (3), 2nd Suppt. 951, Lahore (*OCM*. vii/3 (May 1931) p. 59). Editions: Calcutta, date ? (see Berlin p. 129), Lucknow 1269 (*v. ibid.*), 1871†, 1873°, Cawnpore 1271*, 1874†, 1881†, 1883†, 1885†, 1888†, 1899†. (3) *Ins̲h̲ā i K̲h̲ānah-zād K̲h̲ān*, a collection of political, social and other letters and prose compositions in four *faṣls*, beg. *Sar-nawis̲h̲t i k̲h̲āmah*. MSS.: Ethé 2077, Rieu ii 877*a*, Brelvi-Dh bbar p. 59. (4) *Umm al-'ilāj* a treatise on purgatives written in 1036 and dedicated to Jahāngīr. MSS.: Rieu ii 794*a*, Ivanow 1554, Blochet ii 887 (6). Editions: Cawnpore 1873°*, 1880°. (5) *C̲h̲ahār 'unṣur i dānis̲h̲*, an Arabic-Persian dictionary (MS. Rieu 509*a*). (6) *Ganj i bād-āward*, on agriculture (?). MS.: Āṣafīyah ii p. 968. Cf. Rieu ii 489*b*.

[2] K̲h̲wājah Yādgār, brother of 'Abd Allāh K̲h̲ān Fīrōz-Jang, received from Jahāngīr the title of Sardār K̲h̲ān in 1022 (*Memoirs of Jahāngīr*, tr. Rogers and Beveridge, i p. 237) and the *jāgīr* of Monghyr in 1028 (*op. cit.* ii p. 89). For his career see *Ma'āt̲h̲ir al-umarā'* ii pp. 411–12.

wrote the preface to his collection of anecdotes, *Nawādir al-ḥikāyāt wa-gharā'ib al-riwāyāt,* which is preserved in MSS. at the British Museum (Rieu iii 1004*b*. Only the 1st of the 5 *Ṣaḥīfahs*) and in Manchester (Lindesiana p. 118 no. 194. What part or parts ?). In the *Mai-khānah* (p. 510) he tells us that in addition to his *sāqī-nāmah* he had written 1500 lines of poetry.

Mai-khānah, a collection of *sāqī-nāmahs* with biographies of their authors,[1] mostly contemporaries of the compiler, who began the work at Ajmēr in 1022/1613 or 1023/1614 and completed it at Patnah in 1028/1619 [2] : **Rāmpūr** (A.H. 1039/1629–30. Cf. Nadhīr Aḥmad 96), **Lahore** Prof. M. Shafī''s private library, **Nūr i 'Uthmānīyah** 4328.

Edition : **Lahore** 1926* (ed. M. Shafī').

Description : *Tadhkirah i Mai-khānah aur us-kā mu'allif*, by M. Shafī' (in *OCM*. iii/1 (Nov. 1926) pp. 3–22, iii/2 (Feb. 1927) pp. 3–10). This differs little from the first 16 pages of the introduction to the Lahore edition.

Textual emendations : *Taṣḥīḥ i Mai-khānah*, by M. Shafī' (in *OCM*. iii/4 (Aug. 1927) pp. 79–90, iv/1 (Nov. 1927) pp. 55–62, iv/2 (Feb. 1928) pp. 43–55).

[*Mai-khānah* pp. 498–523 and the editor's Urdu introduction pp. *bā'-qāf* ; *OCM*., *loc. cit.* ; *Nawādir al-ḥikāyāt*, preface and fol. 35*a* (see Rieu iii 1004*b*) ; *Tarīkh i Muḥammad-Shāhī* (Berlin Cat. p. 479 no. 179).]

1116. A certain "**Qāṭi'ī**" [3] dedicated to Jahāngīr (reigned 1014/1605–1037/1628) his

Majma' al-shu'arā' i Jahāngīr-Shāhī, notices of 151 poets who wrote in praise of Jahāngīr, being the third *daftar* of a larger work : **Bodleian** 371 (autograph).

1117. Shāh **Ḥusain b.** Malik **Ghiyāth al-Dīn Maḥmūd** has

[1] In all 71 poets arranged in three *martabahs* ((1) 26 deceased authors of *sāqī-nāmahs* from Niẓāmī Ganjawī to Faghfūr Gīlānī (d. 1029), (2) 20 living authors of *sāqī-nāmahs*, (3) 25 living poets who had not yet written *sāqī-nāmahs*.

[2] So according to the chronogram at the end, but later additions were made.

[3] The *tadhkirah* of Mullā "Qāṭi'ī" is one of the sources of "Āzād's" *Khizānah i 'āmirah*. Sprenger says (p. 144) that he could find no account of the book or of its author.

already been mentioned (pp. 364–5 *supra*) as the author of a history of Sīstān, the *Iḥyā' al-mulūk*, completed in 1028/1619.

Khair al-bayān, begun in 1017/1608–9, completed in 1019/1610, revised and enlarged in 1035/1625–6, further enlarged in 1036/1626–7, and dedicated to Shāh 'Abbās, notices of ancient and modern poets in a *muqaddimah* (history of Muḥammad, the Twelve Imāms, and the Ṣafawī dynasty to 1033/1623–4), two *faṣls* ((1) ancient poets (2) modern poets), a *khātimah* (royal and noble poets), and a *khatm i khātimah* (scholars): **Rieu** Suppt. 108 (A.H. 1041/1631), 109 (defective. 18th cent.).

1118. **"Muṭribī" al-Aṣamm al-Samarqandī** was born in 966/1559 and was still alive in 1037/1628, when he went to Balkh.

Tārīkh i Jahāngīrī (beg. *Ai nām i Tu iftitāḥ i har dīwānī . . . Ba'd az tadhkirah i ḥamd i Ilāhī ta'ālā wa-ta'aẓẓam*), a *tadhkirah* begun in Rajab 1034/April–May 1625, dedicated to Jahāngīr [who died in 1037/1628] and divided into two *silsilahs* ((1) poets [of Transoxiana according to Ethé], who flourished at the courts of the Chaghatāy sulṭans [Akbar and Jahāngīr], (2) poets of Transoxiana under the Ūzbaks) and a *khātimah* (begun in Jumādā II A.H. 1036/Feb. 1627 and containing "a memoir of the author's own attachment to and personal attendance on the emperor Jahângîr . . . together with an additional number of Transoxanian poets . . ."): **Ethé** ii 3023 (A.H. 1075/1665).

1119. For Iskandar Munshī's *Tārīkh i 'ālam-ārāy i 'Abbāsī* (*Ṣaḥīfah* ii, *Maqṣad* 1 completed in 1025/1616 and *Maqṣad* 2 in 1038/1628–9) which concludes the record of Shāh Ṭahmāsp's reign with biographies of princes, high officials and other celebrities (pp. 95–136; poets on pp. 129–35) and which in the subsequent part contains obituary notices at the end of particular years, see pp. 310–12 *supra*.

1120. **Ḥasan b. Luṭf Allāh Ṭihrānī Rāzī** was only a boy in 968/1560–1 when his father, Khwājah Luṭf Allāh, was appointed *Wazīr* of Khurāsān by Shāh Ṭahmāsp and went to Harāt. After his father's death in 981/1573–4 he succeeded him as *Wazīr*.

Mai-khānah, or *Kharābāt* (see Rieu Suppt. p. 76b[14]), notices

of poets written for Ḥasan Bēg [Shāmlū, Bēglarbēgī of Khurāsān 1027/1618–1050/1640–1] and completed in 1040/1630–1 : **Rieu** Suppt. 107 (very defective. A.H. 1227/1812).
List of the poets : Rieu Suppt. 107.

1121. Mīr **" Ilāhī " Hamadānī,** or, as he calls himself,[1] 'Imād al-Dīn Maḥmūd Ilāhī Ḥusainī, was the son of Ḥujjat al-Dīn [2] and was one of the Saiyids of Asadābād,[3] near Hamadān. In 1010/1601–2, he tells us,[4] he went to prosecute his studies at Shīrāz [5] and stayed there for 3½ years. After leaving Persia he spent some time at Kābul, where Ẓafar Khān " Aḥsan ", a poet [6] and a patron of poets, was Governor [7] from 1033/1624, Jahāngīr's 19th regnal year, until 1037/1628,[8] the first year of Shāh-Jahān's reign. A poem addressed to him by Mīr " Ilāhī " in 1033 is mentioned by Rieu (ii 687*b*). It was at Kābul that he went to see the arrogant and irascible Ḥakīm Ḥādhiq [9] on the latter's return [in 1040/1630–1 : see *Pādshāh-nāmah* i, pt. 1, p. 318 [12]] from his mission to Imām-Qulī Khān, of Bukhārā.

" After some years spent at Court, under Jahāngīr and Shāh-jahān," says Rieu,[10] " he accompanied Ẓafar Khan to Kashmīr, A.H. 1041–2,[11] and resided there till his death, the date of which,

[1] In his notice of " Ādharī ", where also the title of his *tadhkirah* is mentioned (Sprenger p. 66).
[2] Sprenger p. 435. Ḥujjat Allāh according to *Muntakhab al-ash'ār* no. 46.
[3] See le Strange *L.E.C.* p. 196.
[4] *Khazīnah* fol. 61*b*.
[5] So Pertsch, correcting Sprenger, who said Iṣfahān.
[6] For an autograph MS. of his *Kullīyāt* written in 1053 see Bānkīpūr ii no 329. For his *dīwāns* and other poems see Ethé 1601, Bānkīpūr iii 330, Ivanow 780, Sprenger 90, Madras 3, 3(*a*) and 3(*b*), Nadhīr Aḥmad 199 (Rāmpūr), Blochet iii 1900, *OCM.* VII/1 (Nov. 1930) p. 141. For his life see *Ma'āthir al-umarā'* ii pp. 756–62, Bānkīpūr Cat. iii pp. 117–18. In one of the prefaces contained in his *Kullīyāt* he mentions Mīr " Ilāhī " and four other poets with whom he associated at Kābul (Bānkīpūr Cat. iii p. 118[1]).
[7] Technically Deputy Governor for his father, Khwājah Abū 'l-Ḥasan Turbatī, who was the absentee titular Governor.
[8] When he was succeeded by Lashkar Khān Mashhadī (*Pādshāh-nāmah* i, pt. 1, p. 120[10]).
[9] For whom see *Ma'āthir i Raḥīmī* iii pp. 845–55, *Ma'āthir al-umarā'* i pp. 587–90, Bānkīpūr iii p. 109, Sprenger no. 238, Rieu Suppt. 325, etc.
[10] Rieu's authority for all the statements, correct or incorrect, made in this sentence is doubtless the *Wāqi'āt i Kashmīr*.
[11] It was early in 1042 that Ẓafar Khān was sent to Kashmīr as deputy for his father, the absentee Governor. He was made Governor on his father's death in Ramaḍān 1042/1633 (*P.-n.* i pt. 1, p. 474[7]), was removed in 1048 (*P.-n.* ii p. 125 ult.) and was reappointed in 1051/1642 (*P.-n.* ii p. 283[2]).

A.H. 1063,[1] is expressed in some verses engraved on his tomb, and quoted in the Vāḳiʻāt i Kashmīr, fol. 122*a*, by the chronogram *Būd sukhun-āfrīn.*"

For a MS. of his *dīwān* transcribed in 1042/1632 see Rieu ii 687*b*, and for another, which contained (but seems no longer to contain) a chronogram for 1052/1642-3, see Sprenger 277 = Berlin 939.

Khazīnah i ganj i Ilāhī, alphabetically arranged notices of about 400 poets, chiefly of the 9th/15th and 10th/16th centuries: Sprenger 11 = **Berlin** 646 (unfinished autograph).

List of the poets (with some biographical details): Sprenger pp. 67–87.

[Mubtalā *Muntakhab al-ashʻār* no. 46; *ʻAmal i Ṣāliḥ* iii pp. 415–16 (not very informative); Ṭāhir Naṣrābādī pp. 255–6; *Kalimāt al-shuʻarā'* (Sprenger p. 109); *Mir'āt al-khayāl* no. 74 (p. 119 in the 1324 edition); *Hamīshah bahār* (Sprenger p. 117); *Wāqiʻāt i Kashmīr* p. 153; *Riyāḍ al-shuʻarā'*; *Dīwān i muntakhab* (Sprenger p. 150[3]); *Ātash-kadah* no. 598; *Khulāṣat al-afkār* no. 36; *Makhzan al-gharā'ib* no. 113; *Riyāḍ al-afkār* (Bānkīpūr Suppt. i p. 50); *Haft āsmān* pp. 146–7; Rieu ii 687*b*, iii 1091*b*.]

1122. For the *Ṭabaqāt i Shāh-Jahānī* of M. Ṣādiq, in which 1046/1636–7 is spoken of as the current year and which contains 871 biographies of (1) Saiyids and saints, (2) scholars, physicians and men of letters (*ʻulamā'*, *ḥukamā'* and *fuḍalā'*), (3) poets, who lived under the House of Tīmūr, see the subsection of this work relating to General Biography.

1123. For the *Ṣubḥ i ṣādiq*, which was begun in 1041/1631-2 and finished in 1048/1638–9 by M. Ṣādiq Iṣfahānī and of which the 3rd *mujallad* is devoted to celebrated men of the first eleven centuries, see p. 126 *supra*.

1124. For the *Pādshāh-nāmah* of M. Amīn Qazwīnī, which contains a *khātimah* devoted to the *shaikhs*, scholars, physicians and poets of Shāh-Jahān's time, see p. 567 *supra*.

[1] Sprenger says (p. 436) that according to a chronogram by Ghanī he died in 1052, but that [Abū] Ṭālib places his death in 1060 and Sirāj in 1064. According to Rieu (iii p. 1091*b*) the date 1057 is given in the *Mir'āt i jahān-numā*.

1125. For the *Muntakhab al-tawārīkh*, which was completed in 1056/1646–7 by M. Yūsuf Aṭakī Kan'ānī and of which the fifth *qism* is devoted to biographies of Imāms, saints, scholars and poets, see p. 127 *supra*.

1126. For the *Pādshāh-nāmah* of 'Abd al-Ḥamīd Lāhaurī, which contains at the end of vol. i notices of 13 *mashāyikh* (pp. 328–39), 13 *fuḍalā'* (pp. 339–46), 8 physicians (pp. 346–51) and four poets (pp. 351–9), and at the end of vol. ii notices of 4 *mashāyikh* (pp. 753–4), six *'ulamā'* (pp. 754–6), one physician (pp. 756–7), and two poets (pp. 757–9), see pp. 575–6 *supra*.

1127. For the *'Amal i Ṣāliḥ* of M. Ṣāliḥ Kanbō Lāhaurī, which was completed in 1070/1659–60 and which contains at the end of vol. iii notices of 16 *Saiyids* and *shaikhs* (pp. 357–82), 13 scholars (pp. 382–93), 8 physicians (pp. 393–7), 18 poets (pp. 397–435), 14 prose-writers (pp. 435–43), and 7 calligraphists (pp. 443–6), see pp. 580–1 *supra*.

1128. The *tadhkirah* entitled *Laṭā'if al-khayāl*[1] was written by a Persian, probably a native of Fārs, who was at Daulatābād in 1062/1652 and who also visited Aḥmadābād and Sūrat. In 1067/1656–7 he returned to Persia and met Ruknā "Masīḥ" Kāshī at Shīrāz and "Ṣā'ib", who showed him much kindness, at Iṣfahān. He went again to India at some date unspecified, and it was there that he wrote (part of ?) the *Laṭā'if al-khayāl* in 1076/1665–6. Prof. M. Iqbāl in an article on the work (see below) demonstrated that the author was almost certainly **M. b. M. al-Dārābī,** who wrote the *Laṭīfah i ghaibī*,[2] a defence of Ḥāfiẓ against certain criticisms. From the *Laṭīfah i ghaibī* Rieu ascertained that M. b. M. al-Dārābī left his birthplace, Dārābjird, for Shīrāz, where he spent most of his life, and that in 1062/1652 he was at Aḥmadābād. From a passage absent from the B.M. MS. but occurring on p. 122 of the lithographed edition it appears that the *Laṭīfah i ghaibī* was written at Shīrāz

[1] To be distinguished from the *Laṭā'if al-khayāl* of Mīr M. Ṣāliḥ Nawwāb Riḍawī b. Mīrzā Muḥsin Nawwāb, which is an anthology without biographical information (see Bodleian 1143, Ethé 1739, Sipahsālār ii p. 479, *JRAS*. 1848 p. 168).

[2] MSS.: Rieu Suppt. 417 (1), Ivanow 983. Edition: Ṭihrān 1304/1887. Cf. Browne *Lit. Hist.* iii pp. 300–1.

in 1087/1676. Rieu adds that the author left also a Ṣūfī work, *Maqāmāt al-ʿārifīn*, and a treatise on the lawfulness of singing entitled *Shauq al-ʿārifīn wa-dhauq al-ʿāshiqīn*. Rieu says nothing about a *tadhkirah*, but Ṭāhir Naṣrābādī in a brief notice of him says that he had recently (*dar īn sāl* [1]) returned from India and was writing a *tadhkirah* of poets.[2]

Laṭāʾif al-khayāl, notices of 454 poets, mainly contemporary, arranged in 28 *ṭabaqahs* each devoted to a particular town, district or country ((1) Fārs and Shabānkārah, (2) tawābiʿ i Fārs, (3) Iṣfahān, and so on) and written (at least partly) in 1076/1665–6 [3] : MS. (less than half of the work) in Prof. Maḥmūd Shērānī's private library at Lahore.

Description and extracts : *OCM*. xi/1 (Nov. 1934) pp. 58–73 (article by M. Iqbāl).

[Autobiographical statements in *Laṭāʾif al-khayāl* (see *OCM*. xi/1 pp. 61–5) and *Laṭīfah i ghaibī* (see Rieu Suppt. 417 (1)) ; *Tadhkirah i Ṭāhir i Naṣrābādī* p. 186.]

1129. For the *Mirʾāt al-ʿālam*, which was written in 1078/1667 by Sh. M. Baqā Sahāranpūrī (nominally by Bakhtāwar Khān), and of which the *khātimah* contains alphabetically arranged notices of poets, see pp. 132–3 *supra*.

1130. M. **Ṭāhir Naṣrābādī** was born at Naṣrābād,[4] near Iṣfahān, probably in 1027/1618, since he tells us (*Tadhkirah* p. 458[12]) that in 1044/1634–5, when his father [5] died, he was

[1] Unfortunately *dar īn sāl* does not always refer to the same year. Thus on p. 173 it is explained as 1077, but on p. 170 as 1083.

[2] *Mullā Shāh Muḥammad—az wilāyat i Dārāb-ast ṭālib-ʿilm i munaqqaḥīst muddatī dar Hind būd dar īn sāl tashrīf āwardand tadhkirah i shuʿarā mī-nawīsad umīd kih muwaffaq bāshad. . . .*

[3] According to Iqbāl this year is several times mentioned as the current year, but Ṭāhir Naṣrābādī, writing later than 1076 presumably, speaks of M. Dārābī's *tadhkirah* in terms which imply that it was not yet completed.

[4] For information concerning Naṣrābād, a village now of five or six thousand inhabitants in the *dihistān* of Mārbīn half a parasang west of Iṣfahān, see the editor's introduction to the Ṭihrān edition of Ṭāhir's *tadhkirah*. Descendants of the author are still living in the village.

[5] Ṭāhir does not mention his father's name. Rieu's statement that he was Mīrzā Ḥasan ʿAlī is due apparently to hasty reading of a sentence (*Tadhkirah* p. 451, l. 5 *ab infra*), in which the author says that his father was a son of Mīrzā Ḥasan ʿAlī's sister. It seems highly probable, however, that Ṭāhir's father was Mīrzā M. Taqī, since Mīrzā Ṣādiq, Ṭāhir's paternal uncle (see p. 125

seventeen years old. His great-grandfather, K͟hwājah Ṣadr al-Dīn ʿAlī, was a wealthy landowner (*Tad͟hkirah* p. 457⁶) and the founder of three *madrasahs*,[1] but the family had become impoverished, and more than one of its members had gone to seek his fortune in India.[2] After a frivolous youth he went to live in a coffee-house frequented by scholars and poets and there he seems to have spent most of his life, since it was to it that he returned after his pilgrimage to Mas͟hhad, Najaf, and Mecca some years before he wrote his *tad͟hkirah*. Enjoying the society and esteem of the learned, talented, and pious (such as Mīr ʿAbd al-ʿĀl "Najāt"), winning by his compositions in prose and verse the approbation of men like Āqā Ḥusain K͟hwānsārī (for whom see p. 20, n. 2 *supra*, and *Tad͟hkirah* p. 152), and receiving from S͟hāh Sulaimān (1077/1666–1105/1694) on his visits to Naṣrābād marks of gracious favour, though not the material benefits he would have preferred, he lived no doubt happily enough, until the death of several friends, especially that of Āk͟hund Darwīs͟h Naṣīrā Qazwīnī in 1079[3] (*Tad͟hkirah* pp. 463⁹ and 531¹), robbed the coffee-house of its charm. He retired to a life of pious devotion in the mosque of Lunbān,[4] and had been there for seven years when he wrote his account of his own life. He had an only[5] son, Badīʿ al-Zamān (*Tad͟hkirah* p. 455), or Mīrzā Badīʿ Iṣfahānī, who became Malik al-s͟huʿarāʾ under S͟hāh Sulṭān-Ḥusain (according to "Ḥazīn": see Sprenger p. 138, *Kullīyāt i Ḥazīn* p. 993). His specimens of his own poetry, which in style resembles that of "Ṣāʾib"

supra and *Tad͟hkirah* pp. 64 and 452¹⁸), mentions in the *Ṣubḥ i ṣādiq* (see Bānkīpūr vi p. 47, l. 12 *ab infra*) that his father, M. Ṣāliḥ, "died on the 18th S͟hawwâl, A.H. 1043 = A.D. 1638, leaving besides the author [i.e. M. Ṣādiq] three sons, viz. Muḥammad Taqî, who was then in Persia, Muḥammad Saʿîd and Muḥammad Jaʿfar, who were then living in Bengal."

[1] One of these was at Naṣrābād, where the doorway is still standing (photograph in the Ṭihrān edition of the *Tad͟hkirah* p. *bā*).

[2] E.g. Mīrzā Ṣāliḥ (*Tad͟hkirah* p. 452¹⁷) and Mīrzā Ismāʿīl (p. 454¹³). In spite of Bland's statement (*JRAS*. 1848 p. 139¹⁰) there seems to be no evidence that Ṭāhir himself was ever in India.

[3] In 1089 according to the Bānkīpūr MS. If 1079 is correct and if Ṭāhir had subsequently spent seven years in the mosque at Lunbān, his account of his own life must have been written (or at any rate completed) later than 1083.

[4] A village near Iṣfahān.

[5] *munḥaṣir dar fard*. These words are the foundation for Bland's statement that Ṭāhir's son "was, at the time he wrote, still in Merv".

and "Kalīm" no longer admired in Persia (see the editor's introduction, p. *jīm*), include a *qaṣīdah* in praise of Shāh Sulaimān, lines from a *mathnawī* modelled on one by "Ahlī" Shīrāzī, and chronograms for the building of the Hasht Bihisht palace in 1080 (*Tadhkirah* p. 487). For his *Gulshan i khayālāt* (or *khayāl*), a short tract in ornate prose, see Rieu Suppt. 376, Bodleian 1636(6) and 1906 : for his *Intikhāb i dīwān i Ṣā'ib* see Ethé 1623, Būhār 432 (1).

Tadhkirah i Ṭāhir i Naṣrābādī, short notices of more than 1,000[1] contemporary poets, begun in 1083/1672–3,[2] dedicated to Shāh Sulaimān and divided into a *muqaddimah* (kings and princes), five *ṣaffs* subdivided into *firqahs* ((1) (*a*) *amīrs* and *khāns* of Persia, p. 15, (*b*) *amīrs* of India, p. 53, (*c*) *wazīrs, mustaufīs*, and *kuttāb*, p. 69, (2) Saiyids and *nujabā'*, p. 95, (3) (*a*) scholars, p. 149, (*b*) calligraphists, p. 206, (*c*) *faqīrs*, p. 209, (4) professional poets of (*a*) 'Irāq and Khurāsān, p. 212, (*b*) Transoxiana, p. 432, (*c*) India, p. 444, (5) the author and his relations, p. 451) and a *khātimah* (a collection of old and new chronograms, riddles, etc., p. 468) : Sprenger p. 88, **Blochet** ii 1148 (ostensibly an autograph dated 1083/1672–3, although the date 1089[3] occurs in the biography of Mīr Luṭf Allāh), **Rieu** Suppt. 110 (A.H. 1097/1686. Lacunæ), i 368 b (18th cent.), **Bānkīpūr** viii 687 (A.H. 1105[4]/1694), **Lindesiana** p. 196 no. 315 (circ. A.D. 1700), **Berlin** 648 (A.H. 1114/1702), 649,

[1] In the Berlin MS. 649 there are 838 notices according to a marginal numeration.

[2] This date is mentioned in the preface (p. 5 ult.) and also, as the current year, at least once elsewhere (p. 170). Expressions like *dar-īn sāl* occur repeatedly in the work, but only very rarely (three times ?) are they further defined, and then (at any rate in the printed text) not always as the same year. Thus on pp. 170 and 173 *dar-īn sāl* is explained as meaning 1083 and 1077 respectively, while on p. 450 *al-ḥāl* is said to be 1081. "Current years" anterior to 1083 are probably corrupt, and so doubtless are some of the later dates that occur (always, it seems, in figures not words). The year 1089 found by Rieu on fol. 331 of a B.M. MS., apparently corresponds to 1081 in the printed edition (p. 450), Similarly the date of Darwīsh Naṣīrā's death is given as 1089 in the Bānkīpūr MS. (Cat. vol. viii p. 80[20]), but as 1079 in the printed text. According to Sprenger eight or nine biographies were added in 1092. This date does not seem to occur in the printed edition, where the latest dates appear to be 1085 (p. 326), 1086 (p. 342), 1112 (p. 20), and 1115 (p. 174).

[3] 1081 in the printed edition (p. 450).

[4] The chronogram *Shud ākhir* = 1105, not 1150. Presumably therefore *panjāh* in the colophon is a *lapsus calami* for *panj*.

Edinburgh 88 (A.H. 1118/1706. Lacunæ), **Bodleian** 373 (A.H. 1132/1720), **I.O.** D.P. 587 (A.H. 1244/1829), **Ethé** 669, **Ivanow** 220 (A.D. 1870).

Edition : *Tadhkirah i Naṣrābādī*, **Ṭihrān** A.H.S. 1316–17/1937–8 (supplements to the periodical *Armaghān*).

Edition of *Ṣaff* iii, *firqah* 2 (calligraphists) : *OCM.* xii/4 (Aug. 1935) pp. 154–9 (ed. M. Shafī').

Description : *On the earliest Persian Biography of Poets . . . By N. Bland* (in *JRAS.* ix (1848)) pp. 137–140.

List and epitome of the biographies in *Ṣaff* iii, *firqahs* 2–3, and *Ṣaff* iv : Sprenger pp. 88–108.

[*Tadhkirah i Naṣrābādī*, *Ṣaff* v, at end (pp. 457–68 in the printed edition. Summarised by Bland, Sprenger, Rieu, 'Abd al-Muqtadir, etc.) ; *Safīnah i Khwushgū* (summarised in Bānkīpūr viii p. 85) ; *Ṣuḥuf i Ibrāhīm* (passage translated by Bland, pp. 139–40) ; Bland's article in *JRAS.* 1848 pp. 139–40 (see above) ; Rieu i 368b ; Blochet ii 1148 ; Bānkīpūr viii 687 ; editor's introduction to the Ṭihrān edition.]

1131. For the *Jāmi' i Mufīdī*, a history of Yazd, which was completed in 1090/1679 and of which the 9th *faṣl* of the 2nd *maqālah* of the 3rd volume is devoted to the poets of Yazd, see p. 352 *supra*.

1132. Mīrzā M. Afḍal " **Sarkhwush** " [1] was, according to his pupil " Khwushgū ", the second son of M. Zāhid [2] and was born in Kashmīr in 1050/1640-1 (Bānkīpūr viii pp. 92–3). M. Zāhid, says " Khwushgū ", was in the service of 'Abd Allāh Khān Zakhmī,[3] after whose death all Zāhid's five sons entered the Emperor's service. Naṣrābādī's statement that " Sarkhwush " was a Lāhaurī and was living in Lahore [in, or about, 1083] is described by " Khwushgū " as incorrect (Bkp. viii p. 93^{1-3}). " Sarkhwush " himself tells us (cf. Sprenger p. 108, Rieu i p. 369)

[1] He " was generally called Chélá " according to Sprenger. This is a Hindī word meaning " servant, slave, disciple ".

[2] According to Shēr Khān (cited by Rieu) his grandfather was Mīr La'l Bēg, of Badakhshān. This fact is not mentioned in the 1324 edition of the *Mir'āt al-khayāl*.

[3] In the *Mir'āt al-khayāl* (Bombay 1324 p. 290) " Sarkhwush " is described as " *az Mughūlān i 'Abd-Allāh-Khānī* ". For 'Abd Allāh Khān see *Ma'āthir al-umarā'* iii p. 92^{6}.

that he was a hereditary servant of 'Ālamgīr, that in his youth he had been anxious to acquire rank and wealth, but that when he wrote he was living in retirement at Delhi. According to " Khwushgū ", his pupil, he died in Muḥarram 1126/1714 [1] at the age of seventy-six.

" Khwushgū " says that his *Kullīyāt* consisted of about 45,000 verses (Bkp. viii p. 93[6]. Cf. *JRAS*. 1848 p. 169, where the number is given as nearly 40,000). They included six *mathnawīs*, (1) *Nūr 'alā nūr*, modelled on Rūmī's *Mathnawī*, (2) *Ḥusn u 'ishq*, (3) *Sāqī-nāmah*, (4) *Qaḍā u qadar*, (5) *dar bayān i ba'ḍī khuṣūṣīyāt i Hindūstān*, (6) *Jang-nāmah i M. A'ẓam Shāh*, and, according to the *Gul i ra'nā* (cited Bkp. viii p. 82), two *dīwāns*, which (like his other poetical works ?) were lost through his son's carelessness. No MSS. of these works are recorded.

Kalimāt al-shu'arā' (a chronogram = 1093/1682, but dates as late as 1108/1696–7 occur), very short notices of about 200 poets who flourished (nearly all in India) during the reigns of Jahāngīr, Shāh-Jahān, and Aurangzēb : Sprenger 13, **Ivanow** Curzon 51 (A.H. 1111/1700), 52 (defective at end. 18th cent.), 53 (19th cent.), 54 (defective at end. 19th cent.), **Ivanow** 221 (small portion only), 222 (portion only), **Rāmpūr** (A.H. 1129/1716. Pictures. See Nadhīr Aḥmad 88), **Madras** 441 (A.H. 1154/1741), 442–3, **Ethé** 670 (A.H. 1154/1742), 671 (n.d.), 672 (fragment), ii 3024 (A.H. 1270/1853–4), **I.O.** D.P. 709(e) (A.H. 1164/1750), **I.O.** 4046 (defective. A.H. 1237/1822), **Rieu** i 369*a* (A.H. 1156/1743), **Oxford** Ind. Inst. (A.H. 1157/1745) **Lindesiana** p. 216 no. 322 (circ. A.D. 1760), **Blochet** ii 1149 (18th cent.), 1150 (A.H. 1179/1765–6), **Berlin** 650 (1) (A.H. 1242/1826), 651 (A.D. 1784), **Āṣafīyah** i p. 318 no. 14 (A.H. 1222/1807–8), p. 322 no. 51 (circ. A.D. 1912), no. 54 (circ. 1912), no. 97 (circ. 1912), **Bānkīpūr** viii 688 (19th cent.), Suppt. ii 2175 (19th cent.), **Būhār** 91 (19th cent.), **Browne** Suppt. 296 (King's 92), **Peshawar** 1413.

List of the poets (with some biographical details) : Sprenger pp. 109–115.

[*Tadhkirah i Naṣrābādī* p. 450 ; *Kalimāt al-shu'arā'* (see Sprenger p. 108, Rieu i p. 369) ; *Mir'āt al-khayāl* no. 106 (Bombay

[1] So also *Tārīkh i Muḥammadī* (cited by Rieu iii 1086*a*), etc. : in 1125 according to Sirāj, in 1127/1715 according to the *Ṣuḥuf i Ibrāhīm*.

1324 p. 290, but Rieu quotes from the work some information absent from this edition); *Hamīshah bahār* (Sprenger p. 123); *Safīnah i Khwushgū* (summarised in Bānkīpūr viii pp. 92–3); *Muntakhab al-ash'ār* no. 317; Sirāj *Dīwān i muntakhab* (Sprenger p. 150); *Khizānah i 'āmirah* no. 60, pp. 263–4; *Gul i ra'nā* (cited Bānkīpūr viii p. 82); *Farḥat al-nāẓirīn* (*OCM. IV*/4 (Aug., 1928) p. 95); *Ṣuḥuf i Ibrāhīm* (passage translated by Bland, *JRAS.* 1848 p. 169); *Khulāṣat al-afkār* no. 135; *Makhzan al-gharā'ib* no. 1034; *Nishtar i 'ishq*; Sprenger p. 108; Rieu i p. 369, iii p. 1086*a*; Bānkīpūr viii p. 82.]

1133. For the *Lubb al-lubāb*, which was composed in 1097/1685–6 by Ḥājjī Muḥammad-Qulī Qājār and of which the twenty-third *faṣl* contains short notices of 220 Persian poets, see p. 134 *supra*.

1134. For the *Mir'āt i jahān-numā*, an enlarged edition of the *Mir'āt al-'ālam* existing in two posthumous recensions completed in 1095/1684 and 1111/1699 respectively, which, like the original edition, contain towards the end alphabetically arranged notices of Persian poets, see p. 133 *supra*.

1135. **Shēr Khān** b. 'Alī Amjad Khān **Lōdī**[1] spent at least part of his boyhood in Bengal, whither his father had gone in the service of Sulṭān M. Shāh-Shujā', Shāh-Jahān's second son.[2] He received some instruction there from Mullā Farrukh Ḥusain "Nāẓim",[3] who after completing his studies had left his home,

[1] The author's name and the title of the work occur shortly before the notice of Rūdakī (p. 20^{10-11} in the 1324 edition). Lōdī is an Afghān clan-name (see *Ency. Isl.* under Afghānistān).

[2] b. 1025/1616, Governor of Bengal 1048/1638, defeated by Aurangzēb at K'hajwah in 1069/1659, d. 1071/1660.

[3] In spite of the *Ency. Isl.* (and the *Makhzan al-gharā'ib*, no. 2854) it is impossible to identify Farrukh Ḥusain "Nāẓim", who left Harāt evidently in early manhood, settled in Bengal and died there in 1068, with Mullā Nāẓim Harawī, who spent his whole life as court poet to the Bēglarbēgīs of Harāt (Rieu ii p. 692), never visited India (according to "Sarkhwush": see Sprenger p. 114), was upwards of 60 years old [in 1076], when the *Qiṣaṣ al-Khāqānī* was written (Rieu *loc. cit.*), died in 1081 (according to Sirāj: see Sprenger p. 151) and is best known as the author of a *Yūsuf u Zalīkhā*, begun in 1058 and completed in 1072, which is popular especially in Central Asia (Edition: Lucknow 1286/1870°*. MSS.: Ethé 1593–6, Ivanow 779, Bānkīpūr iii 336, Blochet iii 1901–4, iv 2195, Rieu ii 692*b*, Browne Suppt. 1381, Bodleian 1130, etc.).

Harāt,[1] and had settled in Jahāngīrnagar (D'hākah, i.e. Dacca in Eastern Bengal). He was, however, too young to profit fully from the Mullā's teaching, as his brothers had done, and he had read only some elementary Persian and Arabic text-books (*mukhtaṣarāt i fārisī u 'arabī*), when "Nāẓim" died on the day of 'Āshūrā' 1068/1657. His regular education then ceased, but he learned much from the conversation of his father and his father's erudite friends. In 1084/1673–4 his father died, in 1087/1676 his brother, 'Abd Allāh Khān, was killed (*sharbat i shahādat chashīd*) in the mountains of Kābul, and in 1090/1679 he sought employment under S. Shukr Allāh Khān [Khwāfī], who had been a friend of his father's in his Bengal days and who is described in the 1324 edition of the *Mir'āt al-khayāl* as *Faujdār* of the *chaklah* of Sirhind [2] and in Rosen's transcription of the same passage from a Leningrad MS. as *Faujdār* of the town of [Shāh-]Jahānābād.[3]

Mir'āt al-khayāl, completed in 1102/1690–1, chronologically arranged notices of about 136 [4] poets, viz. (1) 60 [5] ancient poets from "Rūdakī" to "Āṣafī", p. 21, (2) 8 modern poets from Jalāl i "Asīr" to "Saḥābī", p. 75, (3) 28 poets of Shāh-Jahān's reign from "Qudsī" to "Fiṭrat", p. 85, (4) 11 living poets from 'Āqil Khān "Rāzī" to Aḥmad "'Ibrat", p. 238, (5) 9 living Indian poets whose fame had spread to Īrān and Tūrān from Nāṣir 'Alī Sirhindī to Sh. 'Abd al-Qādir (or to "Waḥshat", as in the Bombay edition, where there are some differences of

[1] *Aṣl-ash az Harāt ast ba'd az takmīl i khwīsh az waṭan bar-āmadah ba-ḥasb i qismat ba-mulk i Bangālah uftād. . . .*

[2] *kih ba-taqrīb i faujdārī dar chaklah i Sirhind kāmrawā'ī u kāmyābī dārad* (p. 120 ult.).

[3] *kih ba-taqrīb i faujdārī dar shahr i Jahānābād u nawāḥī i ān kāmrānī u kāmyābī dārad* (Rosen Inst. p. 163[3]). Rieu cites the *Ma'āthir i 'Ālamgīrī*, p. 214, for the statement that Shukr Allāh Khān, a son-in-law of 'Āqil Khān Rāzī [for whom see pp. 584–5 *supra*], was appointed *Faujdār* of Delhi in 1092. He wrote a commentary on Rūmī's *Mathnawī* (MSS.: Ivanow Curzon 211 and, probably, 'Alīgaṛh p. 49), and died in 1108 (Sprenger p. 151, from "Sirāj") or 1112 ("Khwushgū"). See also *Mir'āt al-khayāl* pp. 240–50, *Hamīshah bahār* (Sprenger p. 121), *Safīnah i Khwushgū* (Bānkīpūr viii p. 87), *OCM.* ix/i p. 66.

[4] So in the Bodleian MS. Sprenger says that some of the numerous MSS. are abridgments. According to Bland the MS. described by him contained notices of seventy poets and fifteen poetesses.

[5] So in the Bodleian MS.: Rosen says 61. The numbers for the succeeding classes are in accordance with Rieu's list.

arrangement) p. 291, (6) 15 poetesses from "Mihrī" to "Hamdamī", p. 334, the whole interspersed with short treatises on prosody, music, ethics, the interpretation of dreams and other subjects: Sprenger 14, **Bodleian** 374 (A.H. 1133/1721), 375 (A.H. 1213/1798–9), **Blochet** ii 1152 (early 18th cent.), 1151 (mid 18th cent.), **Bānkīpūr** Suppt. i 1785 (A.H. 1141/1728), **Ivanow** 223 (A.H. 1141/1729), 224 (late 18th cent.), **Ethé** 673 (A.H. 1147/1734), 674 (lacks the *tadhkirah* of poetesses at the end. N.d.), **Rieu** i 369*b* (18th cent.), 371*a* (A.H. 1183/1769), 371*a* (defective at end. 18th cent.), **Āṣafīyah** i p. 324 no. 25 (A.H. 1211/1796–7), no. 62 (n.d.), p. 170 no. 243, **Lindesiana** p. 222 no. 316 (circ. A.D. 1800), **Aumer** 4 (A.H. 1220/1805), **Berlin** 650 (2) (little more than the 1st quarter of the work. A.H. 1242/1826), **Lahore** Panjab Univ. Lib. (defective at both ends. See *Oriental College Magazine*, vol. iii, no. 1 (Lahore, Nov. 1926), p. 74), **Rosen** Institut 32, **Bukhārā** Semenov 104, **Peshawar** 1471.

Editions: [**Calcutta**] 1246/1831*, **Barēlī** 1264/1848* (cf. Sprenger 14), **Bombay** 1324/1906°.[1]

Descriptions: (**1**) *On the earliest Persian Biography of Poets . . . By N. Bland* (in *JRAS*. 1848) pp. 140–2, (**2**) Rosen Institut pp. 161–8.

List of the poets (with some biographical details): Bodleian coll. 207–11.

Lists of the "modern" and contemporary poets: (**1**) Rieu i p. 370, (**2**) Rosen Institut pp. 161–8 (with epitomes of some biographies).

[*Mir'āt al-khayāl*, under Farrukh Ḥusain "Nāẓim" = Bombay 1324 pp. 120–1 (Persian text quoted by Rosen, Inst. pp. 162–3), and in *khātimah* = Bombay 1324 pp. 339—42 (summarised by Bland, pp. 141–2, and Sprenger p. 115); Rieu i 370 (where both passages are summarised).]

1136. Qāḍī **M. Badī' b. M. Sharīf Samarqandī** wrote in the reign of Subḥān-Qulī Khān, the Ashtarkhānī Sulṭān of Bukhārā (A.H. 1091/1680–1114/1702).

Tadhkirat al-shu'arā' i Subḥān-Qulī-Khānī, notices of

[1] Perhaps an abridgment. The date of printing (1324) will be found on p. 343.

poets and scholars of Subḥān-Qulī Khān's time: **Bukhārā** Semenov 50 (cf. Semenov *Kurzer Abriss* p. 6).

1137. **Kishan Chand "Ikhlāṣ,"** son of Achal Dās and a pupil of 'Abd al-Ghanī Bēg "Qabūl", was a K'hatrī (i.e. a Kshatriya) of Shāhjahānābād, who died in the reign of Aḥmad Shāh (1161/1748–1167/1754).

Hamīshah bahār, alphabetically arranged notices of about 200 poets who flourished (mainly in India) from the time of Jahāngīr (1014/1605–1037/1628) to the accession of Muḥammad Shāh (1131/1719) with a few of Akbar's time (963/1556–1014/1605), written in 1136/1723–4: Sprenger 16 (Tōpkhānah), **I.O.** 4401 (A.H. 1138/1726), **Ethé** 675 (A.H. 1139/1727), **Lindesiana** p. 156 no. 323 (circ. A.D. 1830), **Bānkīpūr** viii 689 (19th cent.), **Āṣafīyah** i p. 318 no. 13.

List and epitome of the biographies: Sprenger pp. 117–30.

[*Hamīshah bahār* (Sprenger p. 119); *Gul i na'nā* (Bānkīpūr viii p. 129); *Ṣuḥuf i Ibrāhīm* (passage translated by Bland, *JRAS.* 1848 pp. 169–70); *Makhzan al-gharā'ib* no. 260; Sprenger p. 117; Beale *Oriental biographical dictionary.*]

1138. For the *Mir'āt i wāridāt,* of which the fourth *ṭabaqah* completed in 1142/1730 contains *inter alia* biographies of Indian poets and authors, see p. 611 *supra.*

1139. **Bindrāban Dās "Khwushgū"** a Hindu "of the Bais tribe" (i.e. presumably of the Vaishya caste), was a native of Mat'hurā [1] (i.e. "Muttra", 30 miles N.N.W. of Āgrah). At the age of 14 he became a pupil of M. Afḍal "Sarkhwush", who suggested his *takhalluṣ* "Khwushgū" [2] and who died in 1126/1714 (see p. 822 *supra*). Having spent the ten years 1137–47/1724–35 in compiling his *Safīnah,* he was prevented from making a fair copy and publishing the work by Nādir Shāh's invasion [1151/1739], in consequence of which he had

[1] So 'Abd al-Muqtadir (Bkp. viii p. 83). According to the *Gul i ra'nā* as summarized in Bkp. viii p. 130 he was "a Hindû of the Bais tribe of Mathrâ", which perhaps does not necessarily imply that he was born there. "Ḥairat" describes him (incorrectly ?) as "a Banya of Benares and a pupil of By-dil" (Sprenger p. 155).

[2] This is stated by "Khwushgū" himself in his notice of "Sarkhwush" (see Rieu Suppt. p. 79 and Bānkīpūr viii p. 93).

to go with the army to Kōt Kāngrah (Sprenger p. 130). He remained seven or eight years [1] in the Panjāb, but in 1155/1742 he returned to Delhi and gave his *Safīnah* to "his master" Sirāj al-Dīn ʿAlī Khān "Ārzū", who wrote some notes and added a preface (*ibid.*). "Ārzū" himself says in his *Majmaʿ al-nafāʾis* (for which see p. 839 *infra*) that "Khwushgū" was his constant companion for 25 years (Bānkīpūr viii p. 84[1]). Among other distinguished friends of his were ʿAbd al-Qādir Bē-dil (for whom see Rieu ii 706*b*, Bānkīpūr iii pp. 194–5, viii p. 96, etc.), Saʿd Allāh "Gulshan" (for whom see Bānkīpūr viii p. 98) and ʿUmdat al-Mulk Amīr Khān "Anjām" (for whom cf. p. 843[7] *infra*, Sprenger pp. 153, 203). The last of these was, according to "Ārzū", the dedicatee of the *Safīnah* (Bkp. viii p. 84[2]). Towards the end of his life he renounced the world and lived piously at Allahabad. According to the *Gul i raʿnā* (quoted in Bānkīpūr viii p. 84) he died at ʿAẕīmābād (i.e. Patna) between 1161/1748 and 1170/1756–7.[2] For his uncle Sadānand "Bē-takalluf" see Bānkīpūr vii p. 94.

Safīnah i Khwushgū (a chronogram = 1137/1724–5, the date of inception), or *Safīnah i Khwushgūʾī* (a chronogram = 1147/1734–5, the date of completion), more or less chronologically arranged notices of poets in three *daftars* ((1) 362 ancient poets from "Rūdakī" to "Kāfī", (2) 811 [3] "mediæval" poets from "Jāmī" to "Shugūnī" (d. some years after 1060), (3) modern and contemporary poets : Sprenger pp. 130–2 = **Berlin** 652–3 (*Daftars* I–II, defective), **Bānkīpūr** viii pp. 83–115 (*Daftar* III, apparently defective. A.H. 1182/1768–9), Suppt. i 1786 (*Daftar* II, defective, extending from "Jāmī" to "Surūrī" (no. 636 in Bodleian MS.). 19th cent.), **Majlis** 403 (*Daftar* II (?) A.H. 1268/1851–2), **Bodleian** 376 (*Daftar* II), **I.O.** 4023 (*Daftar* I), **Lahore** Panjāb Univ. (*Daftar* II, defective, 775 poets from Jāmī to Mīrzā Raḍī (no. 775 in Bodleian MS.). See *OCM. III*/1 (Nov. 1926) p. 75).

[1] Apparently an overestimate, if it was in 1155 that he returned to Delhi.

[2] *dar ʿasharah i sābiʿ baʿd i miʾah wa-alf dar ʿAẕīmābād Paṭnah paikar i ʿunṣurī wā-gudhāsht.* ʿAbd al-Muqtadir understands this as meaning 1170 (Bkp. viii p. 84[2]).

[3] So in the Bodleian MS. In the Berlin MS. there are 545, extending from Jāmī to Mīrzā Aḥmad Bēg (no. 554 in the Bodleian MS.).

List and epitome of the biographies: [*Daftar* II] Bodleian coll. 212–39 [*Daftar* III] Bānkīpūr viii pp. 84–115 (excellent epitome).

Alphabetical rearrangement ("991 notices")[1] made at Shūshtar by "Durrī" Shūshtarī and completed in 1241/1825: **Sipahsālār** ii p. 474 (770 poets. Some marginal notes in "Durrī's" hand), **Rieu** Suppt. 111 (A.H. 1252/1836).

[Autobiographical information in *Safīnah*, preface (?) (see Sprenger p. 130) and elsewhere (cf. Bānkīpūr viii pp. 87^{14}, 92^{14}, 93^{3}, 94^{26}, 95 ult., 98^{18}, 103^{17}, 108^{9}, 110^{3}, 112^{18}, 113^{37}, 114^{17}, ^{25} and many passages where "Khwushgū" says that particular poets were friends of his, etc.); "Ḥairat" *Maqālāt al-shu'arā'* (Sprenger p. 155); *Gul i ra'nā* (passage summarised in Bānkīpūr viii pp. 130–1); *Majma' al-nafā'is*; *Makhzan al-gharā'ib* no. 736; Sprenger pp. 130–1.]

1140. For the *Burhān al-futūḥ*, which was composed in 1148/1735–6 by M. 'Alī b. M. Ṣādiq Nīshāpūrī and of which the 16th *bāb* is devoted to poets, see p. 137 *supra*.

1141. **'Aṭā' Allāh "Nudrat"**, entitled Dānishwar Khān, is the author of a Persian dictionary, *'Ain i 'Aṭā* (MS.: Ethé 2515), which he completed after twenty years' work in 1162/1749. The India Office MS. Ethé 1699 (*Kullīyāt i Nudrat*) is probably his *dīwān*.

Tadhkirah i Nudrat, notices of ancient and modern poets in two *chamans* ((1) the 3rd century, (2) the 4th century), seven *gulshans* (the 5th to the 11th century) and one *ḥadīqah* or *khātimah* (contemporary poets of the 12th century), completed in Muḥammad Shāh's 19th regnal year, 1149–50/1737: **Ethé** 676 (breaks off in *Gulshan* III).

1142. For the *Tārīkh i Hindī*, which was completed in 1154/1741–2 by Rustam 'Alī Shāhābādī and of which the *khātimah* is devoted to contemporary or nearly contemporary *shaikhs*, *'ulamā'* and poets, see p. 471 *supra*.

[1] Although described (correctly, it seems) by Rieu as "taken from all three volumes of the original work", "Durrī's" recension is said in the Sipahsālāh catalogue to be a rearrangement of the second of the four [*sic* ?] *qisms*. The beginning (misplaced ?) of a third *qism* (= *daftar* apparently) is noted in Bānkīpūr viii p. 86^{13}.

1143. For the *Tārīkh i Muḥammad-Shāhī*, or *Nādir-al-zamānī*, a history, mainly of India, to 1159/1746, by Khwush-ḥāl Chand, which contains at the end of *Maqālah* ii short notices of 258 poets (list in Berlin cat. pp. 477–80), see pp. 136–7 *supra*.

1144. For the *Wāqi'āt i Kashmīr*, which was completed in 1160/1747 by Khwājah M. A'ẓam and which is devoted largely to the saints, poets, and scholars of Kashmīr, see p. 683 *supra*.

1145. **Mardān 'Alī Khān** [1] **"Mubtalā"** b. M. 'Alī Khān Mashhadī composed in 1161/1748 his

Muntakhab al-ash'ār, a poetical anthology with short biographical notices: **Lahore** Prof. Maḥmūd Shērānī's private library (A.H. 1166/1753. See 'Abd al-Nabī *Mai-khānah*, editor's preface p. BK), **Nadhīr Aḥmad** 94 (A.H. 1166/1753. 'Abd al-Ḥusain, Lucknow. Perhaps the same MS. as the preceding), **Bodleian** 379.

List of the 755 poets (with some biographical details): Bodleian coll. 239–55.

[*Muntakhab al-ash'ār* no. 662.]

1146. **'Abd al-Ḥakīm "Ḥākim" Lāhaurī** b. Shādmān Khān Uzbak received a *manṣab* and the title of Ḥakīm Bēg Khān from Muḥammad Shāh at the beginning of his reign (1131/1719–1161/1748), but he subsequently left the royal service and became a wandering *faqīr*. "Āzād" Bilgrāmī made his acquaintance at Aurangābād. He was the author of a *dīwān* and of a *tadhkirah*, the title of which he changed at "Āzād's" suggestion from *Tuḥfat al-majālis* to *Mardum i dīdah* (see *Khizānah i 'āmirah* p. 200[18]). When "Muṣḥafī" wrote his *'Iqd i Thuraiyā* (in 1199/1784–5) he was still alive. According to the *Naghmah i 'andalīb* he died in Kashmīr.

Muntakhab i Ḥākim (a chronogram = 1161/1748), or [?] *Nuskhah i pasandīdah dar dhikr i ba'ḍī shu'arā* [?], a small *tadhkirah* of poets including "Āfrīn", "Āzād", "Ummēd",

[1] In the Bodleian catalogue the author's name is given (wrongly, it seems) as Muḥammad 'Alîkhân bin Muḥammad.

and " Ārzū ",[1] with a *takmilah* relating to Mīr 'Abd al-Ḥaiy [2] and Sh. Nūr-Muḥammad: **Rehatsek** p. 133 no. 21 (A.H. 1175/1761–2 (?),[3] partly autograph), **Rieu** iii 1037*b* iv (extracts only (1 fol.), from a MS. in Munīr al-Mulk's library).

It is not clear whether this work is identical with

Mardum i dīdah,[4] a small *tadhkirah* of poets whom the author had seen, composed, according to " Āzād " (*Khizānah i 'āmirah* p. 200[18]), during a visit paid by " Ḥākim " to Aurangābād (evidently, to judge from the context, the second of the three visits mentioned by " Āzād ", i.e. 15 Jumādā 'l-ūlā–19 Shawwāl 1175/1761–2): no MSS. recorded.

[*Safīnah i Khwushgū* (Bānkīpūr viii p. 107); " Ḥairat " *Maqālāt al-shu'arā'* (Sprenger p. 155); *Khizānah i 'āmirah* pp. 200–4 (no. 37); *'Iqd i Thuraiyā* (Rieu i 377*b*) fol. 42; *Makhzan al-gharā'ib* no. 642; *Naghmah i 'andalīb* (Rieu iii 978*b*) fol. 70; Rieu iii 1086*b*.]

1147. Nawwāb Khān-i-Zamān Bahādur [5] Ẓafar-Jang [6] **'Alī-Qulī Khān " Wālih "** b. M. 'Alī Khān Shamkhālī Lakzī Dāghistānī,[7] a descendant of the Shamkhāls, or rulers, of the Lesgians [8] of Dāghistān, was born at Iṣfahān in Ṣafar 1124/1712. His father, appointed in 1126/1714 Bēglarbēgī of Erivan, died

[1] The *Muntakhab i Ḥākim* is described by Rieu as compiled from the *Majma' al-nafā'is* of " Ārzū ", with additional lives. If this is correct, " Ḥākim " must have used " Ārzū's " work before its completion in 1164.

[2] Doubtless the editor of the *Ma'āthir al-umarā'*.

[3] According to Rehatsek " this copy bears towards the end the date 1175 ". Presumably Rehatsek means that 1175 was the date of transcription, not that the year 1175 is mentioned in the text towards the end. It will be observed that apparently 1175 is the date assigned by " Āzād " to the *Mardum i dīdah*.

[4] With the double meaning " pupil of the eye " and " men seen ".

[5] Kh.-i-Z. B., a title conferred by Aḥmad Shāh (*Khizānah i 'āmirah* p. 448[14]).

[6] Title conferred by Muḥammad Shāh (*Khizānah i 'āmirah* p. 448[13]).

[7] Usually known as 'A.-Q.Kh. Dāghistānī, he is called 'A.-Q.Kh. Lakzī in the *Ātash-kadah* (no. 15) and 'A.-Q.Kh. Shamkhālī in the *Makhzan al-gharā'ib* (no. 3018). He appears to be the same person as " Nawāb 'Alī Qulī Khān, commonly called Chhangā or Shash Angushtī (from having six fingers on each hand), a mansabdār of 5000 horse " (Beale), the father of Gannā Begam, Urdu poetess and wit, who became the wife of 'Imād al-Mulk Ghāzī al-Dīn Khān (see p. 623 *supra* and Beale *Oriental Biographical Dictionary* under Ghazi-uddin Khan III) and who died in 1189/1775 (see Beale under " Gunna or Ganna Begam ", Sprenger p. 227, Garcin de Tassy i pp. 488–90). P.S. This identification is confirmed by *Nujūm al-samā'* p. 47 penult.: *'Alī Qulī-Khān Wālih i Dāghistānī i Shash-angushtī dar Riyāḍ al-shu'arā āwardah kih . . .*

[8] For the Lesgians and their Shāmkhāls or Shamkhāls see *Ency. Isl.* under Dāghistān, *Ḥudūd al-'ālam* tr. Minorsky p. 455, etc.

in 1128/1716 or 1129/1717.[1] When still a schoolboy "Wālih" fell in love with his cousin, Khadījah Sulṭān, and was betrothed to her, but her forced marriage to Karīm-dād, the slave of Maḥmūd Khān,[2] and after his death to a succession of other persons saddened the rest of his life.[3] His father's uncle, Fatḥ-'Alī Khān, was Prime Minister to Shāh Sulṭān-Ḥusain (reigned 1105/1694–1135/1722) and other relatives of his held high office, but in 1133/1720 they were all dismissed.[4] This calamity was followed by the Afghān invasion (1721–2), the seven years of Afghān rule and in 1144/1731 by the death of Shāh Ṭahmāsp II, to whom he had attached himself. "Wālih" left for India,[5] reached Delhi in 1147/1734–5,[6] and received in course of time from Muḥammad Shāh (reigned 1131/1719–1161/1748) a *manṣab* of 4000, the title of Ẓafar-Jang and the appointment of Second Mīr-Tūzuk. In Aḥmad Shāh's reign (1161/1748–1167/1754) he was promoted to a *manṣab* of 6000 and the title of Khān-i-Zamān Bahādur. In the reign of 'Ālamgīr II (1167/1754–1173/1759) his *manṣab* was increased to 7000 and on 1 Rajab 1169/1 April 1756[7] he died at Delhi. For his *dīwān*, completed in 1157/1744–5,

[1] See Bānkīpūr viii p. 119[11–12].

[2] Mīr Maḥmūd b. Mīr Wais, ruler of Qandahār, led an Afghān invasion of Persia in 1134/1721, defeated the Persians and sealed the fate of the Ṣafawī dynasty at the decisive battle of Gulnābād (some 3 leagues E. of Iṣfahān) in March 1722/Jum. II 1134, took Iṣfahān after a siege in October 1722 and forced Shāh Sulṭān-Ḥusain to abdicate (see Browne *Lit. Hist.* iv pp. 125–9, *Ency. Isl.* under Ḥusain b. Sulaiman, etc.).

[3] The romantic story of this 18th-century Majnūn and Lailā is the subject of a *mathnawī*, *Wālih u Sulṭān*, written in 1160/1747 at "Walih's" request by Mīr Shams al-Dīn "Faqīr" Dihlawī (MSS.: Rieu Suppt. 343, Eton 144, Ivanow 866, Ivanow Curzon 297, Ethé 1711, I.O. D.P. 1262, Bānkīpūr iii 413. English translation: *The story of Valeh and Hadijeh. Translated . . . by Mirza Mahomed and C. Spring Rice*, London 1903°*).

[4] For his dismissal see Malcolm *History of Persia* i p. 416 n. His successor, Muḥammad-Qulī Khān, was the maternal uncle of Luṭf-'Alī Bēg "Ādhar".

[5] According to "Āzād" (*Khizānah* p. 194[1]) "Wālih" and "Ḥazīn" travelled together from Kirmān to Bandar i 'Abbāsī, but "Wālih", leaving by an earlier boat, reached Tattah ten days before "Ḥazīn". "Azād" says (*Khizānah* p. 194[10]) that when Nādir Shāh was at Delhi "Ḥazīn" lay concealed in "Wālih's" house. "Ḥazīn" himself seems to make no mention of "Wālih", who according to "Khwushgū" (Bkp. viii p. 110) was his disciple and pupil.

[6] "Āzād," when returning in this year from Sīwistān, met "Wālih" at Lahore and accompanied him to Delhi (*Khizānah* p. 448[3]).

[7] In support of this date Rieu (iii p. 1086*a*) cites the *Ṣūrat i ḥāl*, an autobiographic *mathnawī* by "Gulshan" Jaunpūrī, who was employed by "Wālih" till his death (see Rieu ii 715*b*). The date 1170/1756–7 is given in the *Khizānah i 'āmirah*.

see Bodleian 1182, Ethé 1708, Edinburgh New Coll. p. 9, Āṣafīyah i p. 736 no. 345. A theological or Ṣūfī *mathnawī* composed in 1149/1736–7 and entitled *Najm al-hudā* (MSS.: Bānkīpūr Suppt. i 1921, Ivanow 855) is ascribed to "Wālih" Dāghistānī by Sprenger and Ivanow, but a verse quoted by 'Abd al-Muqtadir shows that the author is a different "Wālih", namely S. M. Mūsawī, who was born in Khurāsān, migrated to Ḥaidarābād and then to Arcot and died in 1184/1770 (see Madras no. 61, *Gulzār i A'ẓam* pp. 365–8, *Guldastah i Karnāṭak* (Ivanow 1st Suppt. 776 no. 68)). Another *mathnawī*, *Mīrzā-nāmah*, on the love adventures of Mīrzā Shīr-afgan (MS.: Ivanow 856), is likewise ascribed to "Wālih" Dāghistānī by Sprenger and Ivanow, but probably this too is by S. M. Mūsawī.

Riyāḍ al-shu'arā', "alphabetically" arranged notices of "2500"[1] poets (very few of the author's contemporaries, especially of the contemporary poets of India, whom he held in small estimation) written mainly in 1160/1747 (a year often referred to, according to Ivanow) and completed in 1161/1748 (according to a chronogram quoted and explained by Bland, quoted without explanation by 'Abd al-Muqtadir) or 1162/1749 (a year explicitly mentioned, according to Ivanow, as that in which the last portion was written)[2]: Sprenger no. 18, **Berlin** 657 (an abstract containing only the biographies and one line by each poet. Autograph ?), 656 (2497 articles ? A.H. 1224/1809), **Ivanow** 230 (A.H. 1171/1757–8), **Ivanow** Curzon 57 (defective. A.D. 1794 ?), **Lindesiana**[3] p. 121 no. 311 (circ. A.D. 1770), no. 57 (A.H. 1210/1795–6), no. 58 (defective at end. Modern), **Būhār** 92 (A.H. 1191/1777–8), **Rieu** i 371*a* (A.H. 1203/1788) Suppt. 112 (A.H. 1216/1801), 113 (breaks off in *kāf*. 19th cent.), **Āṣafīyah** iii p. 164 no. 120 (A.H. 1258/1842), **Bānkīpūr** viii 693 (19th cent.), **Bodleian** 377 (n.d.), 378 (short fragment only), **I.O.** 3653,

[1] "The notices," according to Rieu, "are stated to amount to 2500 in number."

[2] The author, according to Rieu, claims as special excellences of his *tadhkirah* that he has confined his quotations to verses of undoubted merit and that he has inserted observations relating to prosody and poetical figures, historical information and critical judgments on poetical quality. "In India," says Sprenger, "this Tadzkirah is more esteemed than any other."

[3] One of the three MSS. described in the Lindesiana catalogue is identical with the I.O. MS. mentioned below.

Lahore Panjab Univ. Lib. (extracts, 94 poets. See *Oriental College Magazine*, vol. iii, no. 1 (Lahore, Nov. 1926), p. 75).

Epitome (with some additions) : ***Lubb i lubāb***, written by Qamar al-Dīn ʻAlī b. Sanā Allāh Ḥusainī Nāṣirī for Richard Johnson : **Ethé** 695 (A.H. 1194/1780, autograph).

Description : *On the oldest Persian Biography of Poets . . . By N. Bland* (in *JRAS*. 1848) pp. 143–7.

List of the 2594 biographies in Ivanow 230 and Ivanow Curzon 57 : **Ivanow** Curzon pp. 28–63.

[Autobiography in *Riyāḍ al-s̲h̲uʻarā'*, *k̲h̲ātimah* (summarised by Rieu and ʻAbd al-Muqtadir) ; " Mubtalā " *Muntak̲h̲ab al-as̲h̲ʻār* no. 725 ; *Safīnah i K̲h̲wus̲h̲gū* (summarised in Bānkīpūr viii p. 110) ; " Guls̲h̲an " Jaunpūrī *Ṣūrat i ḥāl* (Rieu ii p. 715*b*) ; " Ḥairat " *Maqālāt al-s̲h̲uʻarā'* (Sprenger p. 160) ; *K̲h̲izānah i ʻāmirah* pp. 446–50 (Bodleian 381 no. 129) ; *Ātas̲h̲-kadah* no. 841 ; *Ṣuḥuf i Ibrāhīm* (passage translated or summarised by Bland, pp. 145–6) ; *K̲h̲ulāṣat al-afkār* no. 301 (cf. Bland p. 147) ; *Mak̲h̲zan al-g̲h̲arā'ib* no. 3018 ; *Riyāḍ al-ʻārifīn* pp. 263–4 ; *Majmaʻ al-fuṣaḥā* ii p. 558 ; *S̲h̲amʻ i anjuman* p. 491.]

1148. Mīr **Ḥusain-Dōst** " Ḥusainī " b. S. Abī Ṭālib **Sanbhalī** left Sanbhal (i.e. " Sambhal ", 22 miles S.W. of Murādābād) at the age of 19 for Delhi, where he spent his time in the company of poets. In 1173/1759–60, having left Delhi for Bareilly (Barēlī), he wrote a Persian grammar, *Tas̲h̲rīḥ i nādir* (MSS. : Calcutta Madrasah p. 104, Rāmpūr (see Nad̲h̲īr Aḥmad 302)). In 1203/1789 he made a prose abstract of " Hātifī's " *Tīmūr-nāmah* (see p. 290 *supra*).

Tad̲h̲kirah i Ḥusainī, completed in 1163/1749–50, short alphabetically arranged notices of about 200 ancient and modern poets (as well as some saints and princes) : Sprenger no. 20 (Mōtī Maḥall), **Rieu** i 372*a* (18th cent.), 372*b* (18th cent.), **Bānkīpūr** viii 694 (different beginning. 19th cent.), **Berlin** 654 (breaks off in *sīn*), **Lahore** Panjāb Univ. (defective. See *OCM*. III/1 (Nov. 1926) p. 75).

Edition : **Lucknow** 1875°*.

Abridgment : **I.O.** 3847 (A.H. 1187/1773), **Ivanow** 2nd Suppt. 933 (A.H. 1250/1834).

1149. **Sirāj al-Dīn 'Alī Khān "Ārzū"** Akbarābādī, entitled Isti'dād Khān,[1] b. Sh. Ḥusām al-Dīn "Ḥusām"[2] was born at Gwalior[3] or Akbarābād in 1099/1687–8 or 1101/1689–90.[4] According to "Āzād"[5] he was descended on his father's side from Sh. Kamāl al-Dīn, the son of a sister of the great saint Naṣīr al-Dīn Maḥmūd called Chirāgh i Dihlī,[6] and on his mother's side from another celebrated saint M. Ghauth Guwāliyārī.[7] In 1132/1719–20 he went from Gwalior to Delhi and found a patron in Anand Rām "Mukhliṣ" (d. 1164/1751: see p. 612 *supra*), who obtained for him a *manṣab* and a *jāgīr*. Influential support came to him also from Muḥammad Shāh's *Khān-sāmān*, Mu'taman al-Daulah Isḥāq Khān "Isḥāq" Shūstarī[8] and after

[1] See Bānkīpūr viii p. 112.

[2] According to "Khwushgū" (Bānkīpūr viii p. 87) "Shaykh Ḥusâm-ud-Dîn, father of the writer's master, Sirâj-ud-Dîn 'Alî Khân Ârzû; was a Manṣabdâr under 'Âlamgîr, and died A.H. 1115 (A.D. 1703)".

[3] "Ḥairat" (Sprenger p. 153) says that he was born at Gwalior, studied first at Āgrah, proceeded thence to Delhi, and subsequently, with the sons of Nawwāb Isḥāq Khān, to Lucknow. In the *Ṣuḥuf i Ibrāhīm* also it is stated that he was born at Gwalior (see Berlin cat. p. 765[5]). Neither "Āzād", who had obtained a written autobiography from "Ārzū" (see the next note), nor "Khwushgū" specifies the place of his birth. On the other hand both Rieu and 'Abd al-Muqtadir say (on what authority ?) that he was born at Akbarābād (i.e. Āgrah). If this is an inference from the *nisbah* Akbarābādī appended to his name (e.g. in the *Khizānah i 'āmirah*), it is not of course necessarily correct. According to Sprenger (p. 133[1]) "he was born in 1101 either at Agra or Gwályár, but brought up in the former city".

[4] According to "Khwushgū" (Bānkīpūr viii p. 112) the date 1099 has the authority of "Ārzū" himself and the support of a chronogram (*Nuzl i ghaib*) composed by "Ārzū's" father. The date 1101/1689–90 is given by "Āzād", who had never met "Ārzū" but had written to him from the Deccan, when compiling his *Sarw i āzād*, and had obtained from him a written autobiography (*Khizānah i 'āmirah* p. 119). Possibly therefore both dates are derived from "Ārzū" himself.

[5] Doubtless on "Ārzū's" own authority (cf. the previous note).

[6] d. 757/1356. See *Safīnat al-auliyā'* p. 100 (Ethé 647 no. 116); Beale *Oriental biographical dictionary* under Nasir-uddin Mahmud; *Ency. Isl.* under Čirāgh Dihlī; etc.

[7] d. 970/1562–3, author of the Arabic Ṣūfī work *al-Jawāhir al-khamsah* (see Brockelmann ii p. 418, *Supptbd.* ii p. 616, and, for the Persian translation, Ethé 1875–6, Bombay Univ. p. 227, etc.). Cf. *Ency. Isl.* under Muḥammad Ghawth Gawāliyārī. For his tomb at Gwalior see V. A. Smith *Akbar* p. 435 (and the references given there), *Annual Report of the Director General of Archæology in India* 1920–1 p. 14, 1921–2 pp. 37–8.

[8] See *Ma'āthir al-umarā'* iii pp. 774–6, Bānkīpūr viii p. 103, Beale *Oriental biographical dictionary* under Is-haq Khan. His daughter became the wife of Shujā' al-Daulah, who succeeded Ṣafdar-Jang as Nawwāb-Wazīr of Oudh in 1754.

his death in 1152/1739–40 from his eldest son Najm al-Daulah,[1] who paid "Ārzū" a monthly stipend of 150 rupees. In 1163/1750 Najm al-Daulah was killed, but his younger brother Sālār-Jang maintained the friendly relations of the family towards "Ārzū", and in 1168/1754–5, when Sālār-Jang went to Oudh, "Ārzū" accompanied him. Thus he reached the town of Awad'h (Ajōd'hyā, now part of Fyzabad), the home of his remote ancestor, the aforementioned Sh. Kamāl al-Dīn. Soon afterwards he was presented by Sālār-Jang to Shujā' al-Daulah, the Nawwāb-Wazīr of Oudh. He did not, however, enjoy for long the monthly stipend of 300 rupees granted to him by the Nawwāb-Wazīr, since he died at Lucknow on 23 Rabī' II 1169/26 Jan. 1756. He was buried at Delhi.

An incomplete list of "Ārzū's" works given in the preface to his '*Aṭiyah i kubrā* was reproduced by Blochmann in *JASB*. 37, pt. 1 (1868) pp. 70–1. They are (**1**) *Khiyābān*, a commentary on the *Gulistān* (MSS.: Sprenger 481, Bodleian 725, Berlin 49(2). Edition: Cawnpore 1293/1876–7°*), (2) *Shigūfah-zār*,[2] a commentary on the first part of the *Sikandar-nāmah* (MSS.: Sprenger 426, Rieu Suppt. 232, I.O. D.P. 1243A, 1243B, Lahore (Panjāb Univ.), 'Alīgaṛh p. 49, Āṣafīyah ii p. 1482, Berlin 736). This commentary "given in extenso, with a few additions, in the margins of the Iskandar Nāmah lithographed at Bombay A.H. 1277 [°*] . . . forms the basis of the glosses in the Calcutta and Lucknow editions, as stated by Sprenger, Oude Catalogue, no. 426" (Rieu), (**3**) *Sharḥ i qaṣā'id i 'Urfī* (MSS.: I.O. D.P. 1286A, 1286C, 1286D, (**4**) *Sirāj i wahhāj, muḥākamah i shu'arā'*,[3] (**5**) *Sirāj i munīr, ajwibah i i'tirāḍāt i Mullā Munīr bar ash'ār i ba'ḍ i muta'akhkhirīn* [namely "Qudsī" (for whom see pp. 568–9, *supra*) according to Bkp. iii p. 218], (**6**) *Risālah i adab i 'ishq, dar taḥqīq i adab i 'ishq*, (**7**) *Mi'yār al-afkār, dar qawā'id i ṣarfīyah*

[1] See *Ma'āthir al-umarā'* iii pp. 775–6.

[2] This title apparently does not occur in the MSS. of the work, which is usually called *Sharḥ i abyāt i Iskandar-nāmah*.

[3] This seems to be a conflation of two different works, since the list of "Ārzū's" works quoted in the Berlin catalogue, p. 765, from the *Ṣuḥuf i Ibrāhīm* describes the *Sirāj i wahhāj* as *dar ḥall i abyāt i Khwājah i Shīrāzī* and the *Dād i sukhun* (no. 19 below) as *dar muḥākamah i ash'ār i qaṣīdah i Qudsī u Shaidāb* [*sic*, apparently for *Shaidā-yi*] *Hindī*.

u naḥwīyah i fārisī, (**8**) *Mat͟hnawī i Jūs͟h u k͟hurūs͟h, ba-muqābalah i Sūz u gudāz i Mullā Nau'ī*, (**9**) *Mat͟hnawī i Sūz u sāz* [*sic*, apparently = *S͟hūr i 'is͟hq*, Sprenger p. 337] *dar barābar i Maḥmūd u Ayāz i Mullā Zulālī*, (**10**) *'Ālam i āb, dar jawāb i Sāqī-nāmah i Mullā Ẓuhūrī*, (**11**) *Mat͟hnawī i 'Ibrat-fasānah, dar tatabbu' i Qaḍā u qadar i Mullā M.-Qulī Salīm*, (**12**) *Dīwān i g͟hazal, mus͟htamil bar panj hazār bait*,[1] (**13**) *Nat͟hr i Payām i s͟hauq dar jawāb i murāsalāt i a'izzah*, (**14**) *Gulzār i k͟hayāl, dar ta'rīf i faṣl i Hōlī i Hindūstān*, (**15**) *Ābrūy i suk͟hun, dar waṣf i ḥauḍ u fawākih u tāk*, (**16**) *qaṣā'id u rubā'īyāt u k͟huṭab*.

The *'Aṭīyah i kubrā*, like most of " Ārzū's " works, seems to be undated, but the foregoing list is doubtless earlier than 1147/1734–5, since it does not include the *Sirāj al-lug͟hah*, which was written in that year. To that list can be added

(**17**) *'Aṭīyah i kubrā*, on simile, metaphor and metonymy [2] (MSS.: Ivanow 394, Ivanow Curzon 177, Ivanow 2nd Suppt. 969 (4), Bānkīpūr ix 854 (2), Madras 482. Editions: [Calcutta] 1832* (followed by the *Mauhibat i 'uẓmā*), Cawnpore 1897°), (**18**) *Mauhibat i 'uẓmā*, on rhetoric [3] (MSS.: Bānkīpūr ix 854 (1), Ivanow 2nd Suppt. 969 (5), 970. Edition: [Calcutta] 1832* (preceded by the *'Aṭīyah i kubrā*), (**19**) *Dād i suk͟hun, dar muḥākamah i as͟h'ār i qaṣīdah i Qudsī u S͟haidā-yi* [*sic lege*] *Hindī* [4]

[1] " Ārzū " wrote *dīwāns* in which he imitated those of " Salīm ", " At͟har " and " Fig͟hānī ", composing a counterpart to each poem in the same metre and rhyme (cf. Sprenger p. 337, Berlin Cat. p. 765). A MS. of the *dīwān* modelled on that of " At͟har " is described by Sprenger, who says that " Ârzú informs us in his Tadzkirah, *voce* Athar, that these poems formed first a separate Dywán as they do in this copy, but subsequently he incorporated them in his large Dywán ". Ivanow Curzon 295 and 296 (both beginning *C͟hih parwarī*) seem to be copies of this same *dīwān*. Bānkīpūr iii 399 (*Dīwān i Ārzū: g͟hazals* beginning *Ai basmalah*, followed by *rubā'īs* beginning *'Ālam bāg͟hīst*) opens with the same poem as Sprenger 107, which is described as *Intik͟hāb az dīwān i Ārzū*.

[2] On *bayān* only (*fa-qaṭ dar bayān*, Berlin cat. p. 765).

[3] *dar fann i ma'ānī wa-bayān* (Berlin cat. p. 765).

[4] " A short treatise on various questions of style, versification, etc. . . . The author states that he undertook an analysis of a *qaṣīda* by Abū'l-Barakāt Munīr (d. 1054/1644), and tried to be as impartial as possible. He refers also to Muḥammad Jān Qudsī (d. 1056/1646), and others." (Ivanow.) Presumably this work is concerned with " S͟haidā's " *qaṣīdah*, " in which he enumerates at length the defects and the shortcomings of each and every couplet of a *kaṣīda* by his contemporary Ḳudsī . . ." (*Ency. Isl.*, supplement, under S͟haidā). For " Ārzū's " reply to " Munīr's " criticisms of " Qudsī " see no. 5 *supra* (*Sirāj i munīr*).

(Berlin cat. p. 765). (MSS.: Ivanow 393, Lahore (Panjāb Univ. See *OCM*. V/4 (Aug. 1929) p. 17).) (**20**) *Zā'id al-fawā'id*, a dictionary of Persian verbs and the abstract nouns derived from them (MS.: Ivanow 2nd Suppt. 969 (11)), presumably related in some way to the *Zawā'id al-fawā'id*, a work on the same subject by 'Abd al-Wāsi' Hānsawī (MS.: Lahore, Panjāb Univ. See *OCM*. VIII/2 (Feb. 1932) p. 73). (**21**) *Sirāj al-lughah*, completed in 1147/1734–5, a dictionary of non-Arabic words used by the old poets (*mutaqaddimīn*) with many criticisms of the *Burhān i qāṭi'*, whose mistakes and to a much smaller extent those of the *Farhang i Rashīdī* it was the author's primary purpose to correct [1] (MSS.: Ethé 2513, Lindesiana p. 216 no. 766, Ivanow 1434). For a description of this work and the *Chirāgh i hidāyat* see Blochmann in *JASB*. 37, pt. 1 (1868) pp. 25–7. (**22**) *Chirāgh i hidāyat*, a dictionary of words used by modern poets (*muta'akhkhirīn*), forming the second *daftar* of the *Sirāj al-lughah* (MSS.: Rieu ii 501*b*, iii 997*a*, 1070*b*, Ivanow 1435–6, Ivanow Curzon 526, Bānkīpūr ix 807–9, Berlin 120 (1), Browne Pers. Cat. 147 I, Browne Suppt. 375 (King's 125), Ethé 2514, Lahore (Panjāb Univ. 2 copies). Editions (on the margin of Ghiyāth al-Dīn M. Rāmpūrī's *Ghiyāth al-lughāt*): Cawnpore 1868*, 1870*, 1874°, 1878°, 1307/1890*, Lucknow 1296/1879°, Bombay 1880–1°.) (**23**) [*Taṣḥīḥ i* [2]] *Gharā'ib al-lughāt* [3], a corrected edition of 'Abd al-Wāsi' Hānsawī's *Gharā'ib al-lughāt*, which is a glossary of Urdū words with their equivalents in Persian, Arabic, and Turkish (MSS.: Rieu iii 1030*a*, Bānkīpūr ix 838, Ivanow 2nd Suppt. 969 (7), 'Alīgaṛh p. 56 nos. 16, 21, Lahore (Panjāb Univ. 2 copies).) (**24**) *Tanbīh al-ghāfilīn*, a criticism

[1] "The Siráj is rather voluminous, as it contains the words of the Burhán with lengthy remarks attached to each" (Blochmann p. 27). "The critical remarks on the Burhán are so numerous, that the Burhán should never have been printed without the notes of the Siráj" (Blochmann p. 25).

[2] So in the 'Alīgaṛh catalogue. The other cataloguers call "Ārzū's" revised edition by the same title as the original, *Gharā'ib al-lughāt*.

[3] In the list of "Ārzū's" works quoted from the *Ṣuḥuf i Ibrāhīm* in the Berlin catalogue, p. 765, there is mentioned *Nawādir al-alfāẓ dar bayān i lughāt i Hindīyah kih Fārisī u 'Arabī i ān shuhrat na-dārad*. According to Rieu "Ārzū's" revision of the *Gharā'ib al-lughāt* "is confined to those Hindī words the Arabic or Persian equivalents of which are not commonly known in India". Possibly, therefore, the *Nawādir al-alfāẓ* and the revised edition of the *Gharā'ib al-lughāt* are the same work.

of the poems of "Ḥazīn"[1] (MSS.: I.O. D.P. 423 (*c*), Lahore (Panjāb Univ. See *OCM*. V/4 (Aug. 1929) p. 16).) Blochmann described this work briefly in *JASB*. 37, pt. 1 (1868) p. 27. A rejoinder, *Qual i faiṣal*, written in 1267/1850–1[2] by Maulawī Imām-Bakhsh "Ṣahbā'ī", was published at Cawnpore in 1862 (Blochmann *loc. cit.*) and in vol. iii of "Ṣahbā'ī's" *Kullīyāt*, Cawnpore and Lucknow [1878–80°*]. According to Blochmann another rejoinder was written by a nephew of "Ārzū's", Mīr Muḥsin 'Ālī, "and Ték Chand, Mirzá Qatíl and Wárastah take frequently occasion to justify Ḥazín." (**25**) *Iḥqāq al-ḥaqq*, another tract relating to "Ḥazīn". No MSS. seem to be recorded, but a rejoinder, *I'lā' al-ḥaqq*, was published in vol. i of "Ṣahbā'ī's" *Kullīyāt*, Cawnpore and Lucknow [1878–80°]. (**26**) *Mihr u Māh*, a *mathnawī* (MSS.: Lindesiana p. 216 no. 620, Lahore (Panjāb Univ. See *OCM*. VII/1 (Nov. 1930) p. 144)), (**27**) *Muthmir*, on the principles of the Persian language (*dar 'ilm i uṣūl i lughat*), a counterpart to al-Suyūṭī's *Muzhir*, (MS.: Ivanow Curzon 550).

Some others, of which no MSS. have yet been recorded, are mentioned by Sprenger and 'Abd al-Muqtadir.

"Ārzū's" reputation as a scholar was, and still is, high in India, if not in Persia.[3] According to Blochmann (*Contributions to Persian lexicography* p. 25) "He is the best commentator whom India has produced. His commentaries to Nizámí's Sikandarnámah, the Qaçídahs of Kháqání and 'Urfí, and his *sharh* to the Gulistán, entitled Khiyábáni Gulistán, are of great

[1] "Being proud of his affluence and ability, Ḥazîn, remark some of his biographers, began to look down on the Amîrs and nobles, and commenced, says his friend Wâlih, as the poet's nature was, to write satires against the citizens, and did not even spare the king and his nobles. In spite of his friend Wâlih's advice, Ḥazîn continued his satirical writings, till, says Wâlih, the poet lost all esteem in the eyes of the public. Wâlih . . . had at last, to his deep regret, to give up his friendship with Ḥazîn, and cut off all communication with the poet. . . . Ḥazîn then began to criticise the eminent poets of the imperial court, and wrote satires against many of them, such as Sirâj-ud-Dîn 'Alî Khân Ârzû, . . . Mîr Muḥammad Afḍal Ṣâbit, and others. In revenge Ârzû wrote the . . . Tanbîh-ul-Ġâfilîn . . ., in which he collected a large number of frail verses from Ḥazîn's dîwân, and criticisingly pointed out mistakes therein" (Bānkīpūr cat. iii p. 225).

[2] So Āṣafīyah ii p. 908.

[3] Cf. *Majmū'ah i naghz* i p. 24[11]: *Agar-chih zabān-dānān i Īrān az mamarr i ḥasad bā nafs al-amr az-ū ḥisābī na-mī-girand ammā ḥaqq ān-ast kih wujūd i īn chunīn kas dar khāk i pāk i Hindūstān ḥukm i iksīr i a'ẓam dārad.*

value." Blochmann's opinion that the *Burhān i qāṯiʿ* should never have been printed without the notes of the *Sirāj al-lughah* has already been quoted. Another work commended by Blochmann is the *Tanbīh al-ghāfilīn* (*Contributions* p. 27[10]: "Of his other works which compilers ought to read, I may mention the *Tanbíh ul gháfilín*. . . . As most remarks refer to Persian style and idiom, compilers [of dictionaries] and grammarians will do well to procure copies").

Several distinguished Urdū poets received instruction from "Ārzū" in the *ars poetica*, and thus he has a place in the history of Urdū poetry, though he himself rarely composed poetry in Urdū. His Persian poetry—if we may judge from the paucity of manuscripts—seems not to have retained such popularity as it may have enjoyed in his own day.

Majmaʿ al-nafāʾis, completed in 1164/1750–1, meagre alphabetically arranged notices [1] of 1419 [2] or 1735 [3] ancient and modern poets with extracts from their works: Sprenger 19, **Ethé** 680 (vol. ii only, beginning with *ḍād* (Ḍiyāʾ al-Dīn Fārisī) and ending with *yāʾ*. A.H. 1166/1753, transcribed from an autograph), **I.O.** D.P. 739 (omits preface, breaks off in *ṣād* (Amīr Rūzbihān "Ṣabrī") and lacks the latter half of *thāʾ*, the whole of *jīm*, *ḥāʾ*, *khāʾ* and *dāl* and the first part of *dhāl*), **Bānkīpūr** viii 695–6 (A.H. 1179/1765–6), **Bodleian** 380 (n.d.), **Ivanow** 231 (*alif* to *jīm* only. 19th cent.).

Abridgments: (1) ***Muntakhab i Majmaʿ al-nafāʾis***: **Ethé** 681 (A.H. 1243/1827), (2) **I.O.** 4015 (possibly identical with the preceding).

Selection of notices containing critical or other comments by "Ārzū" on the verses quoted: ***Jāmiʿ al-fawāʾid***, compiled by K'harakpat Rāy Kāyat [i.e. Kāyat'h = Kāyast'ha] in 1195/1781 or 1196/1782, or both: **I.O.** 4081 (A.H. 1196/1782).

[Autobiography in *Majmaʿ al-nafāʾis*; *Hamīshah bahār* (Sprenger p. 118[6]); *Safīnah i Khwushgū* (passage summarised in Bānkīpūr viii p. 112); "Mubtalā" *Muntakhab al-ashʿār*

[1] The biographies were added as an afterthought, the author's original intention having been to compile an anthology (*safīnah*), and he paid much less attention to the biographies than to the extracts.

[2] So Sprenger.

[3] So ʿAbd al-Muqtadir.

no. 84 ; *Riyāḍ al-shu'arā'* ; *Sarw i Āzād* ; Sirāj *Dīwān i muntakhab* (Sprenger p. 150[2]) ; "Ḥairat" *Maqālāt al-shu'arā'* (Sprenger p. 153) ; *Khizānah i 'āmirah* pp. 116–21 (Bodleian 381 no. 11) ; *Dhikr i Mīr* pp. 63–4 ; *Khulāṣat al-kalām* no. 8 (passage summarised in Bānkīpūr viii p. 140) ; *Ṣuḥuf i Ibrāhīm* no. 393 ; *Khulāṣat al-afkār* no. 40 ; *Makhzan al-gharā'ib* no. 229 ; *Majmū'ah i naghz* i pp. 24–6 ; Sprenger pp. 132–3 ; Blochmann *Contributions to Persian lexicography* (in *JASB*. 37, Pt. 1 (1868)) pp. 25–8, 70–1 ; Garcin de Tassy i pp. 226–8 ; Beale *Oriental biographical dictionary* under Siraj-uddin 'Ali Khan ; M. Ḥusain "Āzād" *Āb i ḥayāt* (in Urdu) pp. 123–5 ; Rieu ii 501–2 ; Raḥmān 'Alī p. 71 ; Bānkīpūr iii pp. 217–18, viii p. 112 ; Rām Bābū Saksēna *History of Urdu literature* pp. 47–8 ; S. Shams Allāh Qādirī *Qāmūs al-a'lām* (in Urdu), pt. 1 (Ḥaidarābād 1935), coll. 26–9, where several further references will be found.]

1150. Sh. Jamāl al-Dīn Abū 'l-Ma'ālī[1] **M. 'Alī**[2] "**Ḥazīn**" b. Abī Ṭālib Zāhidī[3] Lāhijī **Jīlānī** was born on 27 Rabī' II 1103/17 Jan. 1692 at Iṣfahān, to which his father had migrated from Lāhijān.[4] Educated at his birthplace by his father and others[5] and subsequently at Shīrāz, he developed into a scholar, who both taught[6] and wrote on the subjects of his study. Even as a child he had composed poetry in spite of some early discouragement from his father (Autobiography pp. 19–20, 22,

[1] So in the subscription to the *Ṣafīr i dil*, Bodleian 1185. There is no such subscription in the lithographed *Kullīyāt*.

[2] *Muḥammad al-mad'ū* (or *al-mushtahir*) *bi-'Alī*, etc.

[3] He was sixteenth (according to Balfour's text) in descent from a great saint, Sh. Zāhid Gīlānī, the spiritual director of Sh. Ṣafī al-Dīn Ardabīlī, the ancestor of the Ṣafawī kings (see Browne *Lit. Hist.* iv pp. 38–44).

[4] At the age of ten (*Tadhkirat al-mu'āṣirīn* p. 951[15], Sprenger p. 136) "Ḥazīn" was taken by his father on a visit to Lāhijān and stayed there for nearly a year during which time he read the *Khulāṣat al-ḥiṣāb* with his uncle Sh. Ibrāhīm Zāhidī Jīlānī (d. 1119/1707–8).

[5] The names of his teachers and the books which he studied under them are faithfully recorded in the autobiography. That M. Bāqir Majlisī (for whom see pp. 196–8 *supra*) was not one of them (as alleged by "some of his biographers": see Bānkīpūr iii p. 223) seems clear from "Ḥazīn's" statement that he had seen him three or four times (Autobiography p. 32, trans. p. 32). He died when "Ḥazīn" was seven or eight years old.

[6] Cf. Autobiography p. 59[9] (*u dar ḍimn i īn mashāghil kutub i mutadāwalah rā dars mī-guftam*), trans. p. 64, and other passages. His abandonment of the practice of teaching (apparently in 1143/1730–1) is recorded on p. 178, trans. p. 195. The last works taught by him were the *Uṣūl i Kāfī*, the *Man lā yaḥḍuruhu l-faqīh*, the *Ilāhīyāt i Shifā'* and the *Sharḥ i Tajrīd*.

trans. pp. 18, 21). More remarkable than all this, however, is that in his desire for knowledge he associated at Iṣfahān with Christian priests like "the Caliph Avanus" [1] (Autobiog. p. 57, trans. pp. 62–3) and, secretly, with a Jew named Shu'aib (*op. cit.* p. 58, trans. p. 63), read many Christian books and had a translation of the *Taurāt* written down for his use. Similarly at a later date [2] he obtained information concerning Zoroastrianism from a *dastūr* at Baiḍā (*op. cit.* p. 83, trans. p. 93).

Even before his father's death [in 1127/1715] "Ḥazīn" had visited many towns in Fārs [3] and some elsewhere, but until then and for a few years afterwards his main place of residence was Iṣfahān, and he was there when the Afghān invasion and the siege of 1134–5/1721–2 [cf. p. 831 n. 2 *supra*] brought misery to the inhabitants and compelled him to sell most of his possessions including two thousand volumes from his library, the rest of which was subsequently looted by the Afghāns. Before the end of the siege, however, "Ḥazīn" escaped in disguise, and the next eleven years were spent in wandering from place to place,[4] meeting scholars, composing poetry, writing philosophical and other treatises and occasionally teaching. More than once he came in contact with Shāh Ṭahmāsp (reigned 1135/1722–1144/1731): at Mashhad the king visited him (Autobiog. p. 161, trans. p. 174) and subsequently [early in 1142/1729] invited him to accompany the royal army on the march against Ashraf the Afghān (Autobiog. p. 175, trans. p. 192), later at Iṣfahān "Ḥazīn" gave the king advice and outlined measures calculated

[1] Khalīfah Āwānūs, as he is called in Belfour's text, or Awānūs Khalīfah, as he calls himself at the beginning of his Persian work on Christian evidences completed in 1690 (MSS.: Rieu i p. 5, Browne Suppt. 1388), is judged by Rieu to have been a Roman Catholic, probably of French origin. Lady Sheil in her *Glimpses of life and manners in Persia* (London 1856, p. 349 [14]) speaks of being called on by "a Nestorian khaleefa, or bishop". According to Morier's *Adventures of Hajji Baba* (ch. 40) the Armenian patriarch of Echmiadzin was known in Persia as the Khalīfah.

[2] Before his father's death in 1127/1715 (Autobiog. p. 100, trans. p. 110): it is not clear how long before.

[3] In one journey alone "Ḥazīn" says that he saw most of Fārs (Autobiog. p. 91 penult. (*u dar ān safar kamtar nāḥiyah az mamlakat i Fārs māndah bāshad kih na-dīdah bāsham*), trans. p. 100).

[4] An incomplete list of the towns visited in the course of these wanderings, which included pilgrimages to the holy places of al-Ḥijāz and al-'Irāq (nearly 3 years at Najaf), is given by Browne iv p. 279.

to preserve his dynasty (Autobiog. p. 190, trans. p. 206). These were years of revolution and disorder in Persia, and much space in "Ḥazīn's" autobiography is devoted to accounts of Afghān and Turkish invasions, local insurrections, the rise of Nādir Shāh and other historical events. Eventually the prevailing misery became so painful to him that he decided to leave the country.[1] Sailing from Bandar i 'Abbāsī on 10 Ramaḍān 1146/14 Feb. 1734, "Ḥazīn" reached Tattah, in Sind, early in Shawwāl.[1] After a stay of more than two months [2] he continued his journey and halted successively at Khudā-ābād (7 months ill), Bhakkar [3] (nearly 1 month), a village near Multān (nearly 2 years), Lahore (3 months), Delhi (more than 12 months), Lahore again (where he heard that Nādir Shāh was besieging Qandahār [4] and where he remained through the period of the protracted siege and afterwards until Nādir Shāh entered the district of Kābul), Sulṭānpūr, Sirhind, and again Delhi, where he was during the period of Nādir Shāh's invasion [5] and where he had been living for more than three years at the time when he wrote his *Tadhkirat al-aḥwāl* late in 1154/1742 at the age of 53 [*sic*]. He had then spent eight unhappy years in India, constantly regretting his advent to a country which he found extremely uncongenial. His first return to Lahore was in fact intended to be only a stage on his way from India via Kābul and Qandahār to Khurāsān, where he hoped to settle, but this

[1] According to the account given by 'Abd al-Muqtadir (Bānkīpūr iii p. 224), presumably on the authority of "Ḥazīn's" acquaintance "Wālih" (for whom see pp. 830–3 *supra*), the immediate cause of "Ḥazīn's" departure was that he had incurred suspicion of complicity in the assassination of Walī-M. Khān Shāmlū, who had been sent to Lār as Governor by Nādir Shāh, and that he was consequently unsafe in Persia.

[1] According to "Āzād" (*Khizānah i 'āmirah* p. 194[3]) "Wālih" had reached Tattah ten days before.

[2] The periods of residence up to the second arrival in Lahore make too large a total.

[3] Here "Āzād", who was returning from Sīwistān to Delhi, met "Ḥazīn" and received from him an autograph copy of some verses as a memento (*Khizānah i 'āmirah* p. 194[4]).

[4] Nādir Shāh reached Qandahār before Naurūz 1149/March 1737 and the town capitulated on 2 Dhū 'l-Qa'dah 1150/23 March 1738.

[5] Nādir Shāh won the battle of Karnāl on 15 Dhū 'l-Qa'dah 1151/24 Feb. 1739, entered Delhi on 9 Dhū 'l-Ḥijjah/20 March and left the city on 7 Ṣafar 1152/16 May 1739. "Āzād" says that while Nādir was in Delhi "Ḥazīn" lay concealed in "Wālih's" house (*Khizānah i 'āmirah* p. 194[10]).

design was frustrated by Nādir Shāh's approach. After Nādir Shāh's departure "Ḥazīn" went back for the second time to Lahore, but here he incurred the enmity of the Governor, Zakarīyā Khān, and was in a position of some danger until "Wālih" (see pp. 830–3 *supra*) arranged for his return to Delhi (*Khizānah i 'āmirah* p. 194$^{10-13}$, Bānkīpūr iii p. 225$^{3-9}$). 'Umdat al-Mulk Amīr Khān "Anjām"[1] obtained for him a *suyūrghāl* from Muḥammad Shāh[2] (*Khizānah i 'āmirah* p. 194^{14}, Bānkīpūr iii p. 225), and his financial position was thus rendered secure, but his tactlessness and his disparagement of India and Indians aroused animosity against him at Delhi,[3] and it was not long before he moved first to Āgrah (*Khizānah i 'āmirah* p. 194^{18}) and then to Benares, which became his permanent place of residence. Apparently he continued for some time to cherish hopes of returning to Persia, since we are told by Ghulām-Ḥusain Khān that several times he went to Paṭnah and had made up his mind to leave India, when obstacles intervened (*Siyar al-muta'akhkhirīn*, Cawnpore, 1866, p. 615^{17} : *chand bār ān 'ālī-miqdār tā ba-'Aẓīmābād rasīdah 'āzim i ba-dar raftan az khāk i siyāh i Hind būd : taqdīr musā'adat nah numūd*). At Benares he was repeatedly visited by Ghulām-Ḥusain Khān (for whom see pp. 625–40 *supra*) and more than once in 1177/1764 by the Emperor [Shāh-'Ālam], the *Wazīr* [Shujā' al-Daulah of Oudh] and Mīr Qāsim [the *Nāẓim* of Bengal], who were advised by him not to make war against the British (*Siyar al-muta'akhkhirīn*, ii 746$^{22-24}$). When he finally became resigned to the prospect of spending the rest of his days in India, he built a tomb for himself at Benares, and in it he was buried when he died on the 10th, 11th, 13th, or 18th of Jumādā I 1180/November 1766. According to 'Abd al-Muqtadir the tomb and the two

[1] For whom cf. p. 827^{11} *supra*.

[2] According to Ghulām-Ḥusain Khān "Ḥazīn" more than once declined invitations from Muḥammad Shāh to undertake the office of *Wazīr* (*Siyar al-muta'akhkhirīn*, Cawnpore 1866, ii p. 615^{11} : *Muḥammad Shāh ba-wasāṭat i 'Umdat al-Mulk u dīgar muqarrabān i daulat-khwāh mukarrar paighām dādah mas'alat numūd kih muta'ahhid i imḍā-yi umūr i wizārat gashtah raunaq-afzā-yi salṭanat i ū shawad ammā chūn sar firū āwardan ba-dunyā nang u 'ār i ān nuqāwah i akhyār būd rāḍī na-shud*).

[3] One outcome of this animosity, "Ārzū's" *Tanbīh al-ghāfilīn*, has been mentioned above (p. 837).

lines of poetry[1] inscribed thereon by his own hand can still be seen in the part of Benares known as Fāṭimān.

Ghulām-Ḥusain Khān, who knew Ḥazīn well in his later years, was impressed by the depth of his learning and his omniscience (*Siyar al-muta'akhkhirīn* ii 615[6]: *makhfī na-mānad kih faqīr u kasānī-kih ba-hamah wujūh bihtar az-īn ḥaqīr būdah and i'tirāf dārand kih dar-īn juzw i zamān chūn ū kasī dīdah na-shudah bal-kih mutaraddidīn i 'Arab u 'Ajam nīz ba-jāmi'īyat i ān janāb dar jamī' i 'ulūm i ẓāhir u bāṭin aḥadī rā dar aṭrāf u aknāf i 'ālam nishān na-dādah and āyatī būd az āyāt i Ilāhī* . . .). Raymond (Ḥājjī Muṣṭafā), the translator of the *Siyar al-muta'akhkhirīn*, who visited him in 1764 and 1765, found him " a man of sense and also of knowledge ". He was also a pious and devout man, but it is not clear whether his reputation as a saint was so great in his lifetime as it seems to have become after his death. According to the *Ārāyish i maḥfil* written in 1219–20/1804–5 (see p. 456 *supra*) he received revelations, performed miracles and was credited with some power over the sun. For the ill-nature which he seems to have shown in India a sufficient explanation can perhaps be found in the ill-health to which he so often refers in his autobiography.

In the course of the *Tadhkirat al-aḥwāl* (pp. 64, 97, 101, 163, trans. pp. 71, 106, 111, 176) " Ḥazīn " records the completion of four *dīwāns*, the third of which was collected at Shīrāz [evidently in, or soon after, 1127] and the fourth at Mashhad [evidently between 1139 and 1142]. The first three of these *dīwāns* do not seem to be extant, but the fourth may be more or less identical with an extant *dīwān* of 1155, which the author describes as his fourth, and which may be a re-issue or a later recension of that collected at Mashhad. The *dīwān* of 1155 (preserved in a B.M. MS., Rieu ii p. 715*a*, of about that date, as well as in other MSS.) opens with a prose preface (beginning *Iftitāḥ i nāmah*), which contains the statement that, having previously published three *dīwāns*, the author, then resident in India and over fifty years old, had collected in a fourth, A.H. 1155, the

[1] *Zabān-dān i maḥabbat būdah am dīgar na-mī-dānam * Hamīn dānam kih gūsh az Dūst paighāmī shunīd īn-jā. Ḥazīn az pāy i rah-paimā basī sar-gashtagī dīdam * Sar i shūrīdah bar bālīn i āsāyish rasīd īn-jā.*

remainder of his detached pieces, and that the four *dīwāns* together amounted to about 30,000 lines. This 1155 *dīwān* contains *qaṣīdahs*, *ghazals*, fragments of *ghazals* (*mutafarriqāt i ghazalīyāt*, mostly pieces of two or three lines), *rubāʿīs*, *muqaṭṭaʿāt* and parts of the four *mathnawīs*,[1] *Chaman u anjuman*, *Kharābāt*[2] (*mukhtaṣar*), *Maṭmaḥ al-anẓār* (prologue), and *Tadhkirat al-ʿāshiqīn*[3] (prologue and epilogue).

The 1155 *dīwān* seems to be the basis of the poetical portion of the Lucknow and Cawnpore *Kullīyāt*[4] (see p. 847[3] *infra*), in which, however, are included two other short *mathnawīs*, namely, the *Ṣafīr i dil*, composed in 1173, and the *Farhang-nāmah*. A seventh *mathnawī*, the *Wadīʿat al-badīʿah*, written on the model of "Sanāʾī's" *Ḥadīqah*, when the author was about 70 years old (and therefore circ. 1173), is preserved in several MSS.[5] Apparently "Ḥazīn" did not collect any fifth *dīwān*, but he seems to have made additions to the fourth, since a *dīwān* preserved in the British Museum and containing *qaṣīdahs* and *ghazals* (the latter defective at the end) is described by Rieu (ii p. 717*a*) as being "richer than the corresponding sections in the preceding copies".

Twenty prose works, several of them *ḥawāshī* on standard text-books, are mentioned by title in "Ḥazīn's" autobiography (pp. 59, 82, 84, 96–7, 150, 162, 201, 237; trans. pp. 64, 92, 93,

[1] In a prose preface prefixed to these four *mathnawīs* in a B.M. MS. (Rieu ii p. 716*b*) the author says "that the original drafts had been scattered in various countries, and that he had now written what he describes as a sample of each, in order to comply with the desire of a noble friend in India".

[2] Cf. Autobiography pp. 164–73, trans. pp. 176–90, where it is stated that of the *Kharābāt*, a *mathnawī* modelled on Saʿdī's *Būstān*, 1200 verses had been written [apparently at Mashhad between 1139 and 1142], but that it had never been completed. Some extracts are quoted in the autobiography, and the same extracts with others occur in the Lucknow and Cawnpore editions of the *Kullīyāt*.

[3] Cf. Autobiography pp. 97–99, trans. pp. 106–9, from which it appears that this *mathnawī* was begun at Iṣfahān [evidently before 1127] and that it consisted of about 4000 verses.

[4] And indeed of all the later MSS. of his poems. It is noteworthy that among the *muqaṭṭaʿāt* in the lithographed *Kullīyāt* (p. 920) are the lines on his father's death, which are quoted in the autobiography (pp. 16–17, trans. pp. 15–16) and which were written long before the collection of any fourth *dīwān*.

[5] E.g. Bodleian 1185 (2), 1184 (5), Bānkīpūr iii 407, Blochet iii 1940, Browne Suppt. 1139 (1), Ivanow 862 (1).

105, 163, 175, 219, 256). Of these the *Risālah i tajarrud i nafs* written at Kirmānshāh (Autobiog. p. 150, trans. p. 163) must be similar to, if not identical with, the *Risālah dar tajarrud i nafs*. or *Risālah dar ḥaqīqat i nafs u tajarrud*, preserved in several MSS. (Ethé 1903, Bānkīpūr iii p. 231, Ivanow-Curzon 502 (2), Ivanow 2nd Suppt. 1043 (5)). The extant *Faras-nāmah* (Bānkīpūr iii pp. 232, 234, Lindesiana p. 152, Rieu ii p. 483) was written in India as a substitute for an unprocurable work on farriery composed by the author at Iṣfahān in his youth [about 1127: see Autobiog. p. 97, trans. p. 106], and is "a mere sample" of that earlier work. None of the other prose works mentioned in the autobiography seem to be recorded in library catalogues, but several prose works by him, mostly short tracts, are extant. These include (1) *al-Lam'ah* [*min* ?] *mir'āt Allāh fī sharḥ Āyat Shahida 'llāh*, an Arabic commentary on Sūrah iii 16 composed at Ardabīl in 1139 (MSS.: Ethé 1904, Ivanow-Curzon 752 (4), I.O. Cat. of Arabic MSS. ii 1165 (2)), (2) *Shajarat al-Ṭūr fī sharḥ Āyat al-Nūr*, an Arabic commentary on Sūrah xxiv 35 composed in 1140 at Mashhad (MSS.: Ethé 1904, Ivanow-Curzon 752 (3), I.O. Cat. of Arabic MSS. ii 1165 (1)), (3) *Taḥqīq i ma'ād i rūḥānī* (Bānkīpūr iii p. 233, Ivanow-Curzon 752 (1), Ivanow 2nd Suppt. 1043 (3)), (4) *Risālah i auzān i shar'ī*, or *Risālah dar auzān i mithqāl u dirham u dīnār wa-ghairah* (Bānkīpūr iii p. 232, Rieu ii p. 483, Ivanow-Curzon 502 (7)), (5) *Mas'alah i ḥudūth u qidam* (Bānkīpūr iii p. 232, Ivanow-Curzon 502 (3), Ivanow 2nd Suppt. 1043 (4)), (6) *Jawāb i ruqa'āt i Shaikh Ḥasan i marḥūm* (Bānkīpūr iii p. 232), (7) *Sharḥ i Qaṣīdah i Lāmīyah*, a commentary on a *qaṣīdah* of his own in praise of 'Alī (Bānkīpūr iii pp. 232, 235), (8) *Risālah i ṣaidīyah*, or *Risālah dar khawāṣṣ i ḥayawān* ('Alīgarh Subḥ. MSS. p. 8, Bānkīpūr iii p. 232, Rieu ii p. 483), (9) a short note on the Persian invasions of India completed at Ḥusainābād in 1180 (see p. 615 *supra*), (10) *Dastūr al-'uqalā'*, on administrative ethics, etc., composed at Delhi in 1153/1740 (MSS.: I.O. D.P. 1207, Ivanow-Curzon 502 (1)), (11) *Mawā'id al-asḥār*, on Shī'ite theology (Browne Suppt. 1280), (12) *Mudhākarāt fī 'l-muḥāḍarāt* (I.O. D.P. 1207), (13) *Maṣābīḥ al-ẓalām fī ārā' al-kalām* (Āṣafīyah i p. 170, under Balāghat). A long, but confessedly incomplete, list of his own works evidently compiled late in "Ḥazīn's" life is quoted in the *Nujūm al-samā'* (pp. 287–93).

The *Kullīyāt i Ḥazīn* published by Nawal Kishōr at [Lucknow] in 1293/1876°* and at Cawnpore in 1893 (cf. Browne *Lit. Hist.* iv p. 281 n. 5) contains (1) *Tārīkh i aḥwāl bi-tadhkirah i ḥāl i Maulānā-yi Shaikh Muḥammad 'Alī Ḥazīn kih khwud nawishtah ast*, pp. 2–144, (2) [Preface to the 1155 *dīwān*, beginning] *Iftitāḥ i nāmah*, etc., pp. 145–50, (3) *Qaṣā'id*, pp. 150–255, (4) *Dīwān* [i.e. *ghazals*], pp. 257–689, (5) *Mutafarriqāt*, pp. 691–748, (6) *Rubā'īyāt*, pp. 749–89, (7) *Mathnawīyāt* [viz. *Ṣafīr i dil*, pp. 791–822, *Chaman u anjuman*,[1] pp. 823–38, *Mukhtaṣarī az kitāb i mathnawī i musammā bi-Kharābāt*, pp. 839–61, *Dībāchah i Maṭmaḥ al-anẓār*, pp. 863–9, *Farhang-nāmah*, pp. 871–87, *Fātiḥah u khātimah i mathnawī i mausūm bi-Tadhkirat al-'āshiqīn*, pp. 889–902], (8) *Muqaṭṭa'āt*, pp. 903–29, (9) *Tadhkirah* [*al-mu'āṣirīn*], pp. 931–1031.

(1) (***Tadhkirat al-aḥwāl***),[2] an autobiography containing a considerable amount of historical information written at the end of 1154/1742 in Delhi: Sprenger 22, **Bānkīpūr** vii 624 (A.H. 1162/1749), 625 (A.H. 1281/1865), **Ivanow** 225 (circ. A.H. 1180/1766–7), 226 (18th cent.), 227 (19th cent.), **Ivanow-Curzon** 55 (18th cent.), 56 (18th cent.), **Lindesiana** p. 151 no. 446 (circ. A.D. 1780–90), no. 447 (circ. A.D. 1800), no. 559 (A.H. 1218/1803–4), **Bodleian** 383 (A.H. 1197/1783), **Browne** Suppt. 300 (before A.D. 1788. King's 74), **Rieu** ii 823*a* (late 18th cent.), i 381*a* (A.H. 1216/1801), ii 843*b* (A.H. 1244/1829), **Rehatsek** p. 218 no. 11 (apparently. A.H. 1214/1799), **I.O.** D.P. 674*a* (A.H. 1223/1808), **Ethé** 677 (A.H. 1227/1812), **I.O.** 3952 (A.H. 1259/1843), 3967(*c*), **Ross and Browne** 240 (2) (A.H. 1280/1864), **Vollers** 987 (2).

Editions: **London** 1831°* (*The Life of Sheikh Mohammed Ali Hazin . . . edited . . . by F. C. Belfour*. Persian title: *Tārīkh i aḥwāl bi-tadhkirah i ḥāl i Maulānā-yi Shaikh Muḥammad 'Alī Ḥazīn kih khwud nawishtah ast*. Oriental Translation Fund),

[1] Doubtless only the "sample" referred to above (p. 845 n. 1).

[2] The author having given his work no formal title, various quasi-titles are found on the title-pages of MSS. and editions, e.g. *Tārīkh i aḥwāl i Ḥazīn*, *Ḥālāt i Shaikh 'Alī Ḥazīn*, etc.

Benares 1851* (title ?), [**Lucknow**] 1293/1876°* (*Kullīyāt i Ḥazīn* pp. 2–144), **Cawnpore** 1893 (*Kullīyāt i Ḥazīn* pp. 2–144. Cf. Browne *Lit. Hist.* iv p. 281 n. 5), **Delhi** 1319/1902°* (*Sawāniḥ i 'umrī i . . . 'Alī Ḥazīn*).

Translations : (**1**) *The Life of Sheikh Mohammed Ali Hazin . . . translated . . . by F. C. Belfour*, **London** 1830°* (Oriental Translation Fund), **Bombay** [1901*. " Part 2 " only ?], **Bombay** [1910*. 2 pts.], (**2**) *The translation of the Tarikh-i-ahwal of Mowlana Muhammad Shaykh Ali Hazin. With an introduction and appendix. By M. C. Master.* **Bombay** 1911°*.

(2) (*Tadhkirat al-mu'āṣirīn*), notices of about 100 contemporary poets of Persia written in nine days towards the end of 1165/1752 and divided into two *firqahs* ((1) *'ulamā'* who wrote poetry, (2) professional poets) : Sprenger 21, **Bānkīpūr** iii 407 (A.H. 1178/1764), 408 (19th cent.), Suppt. ii 2350, **Rieu** ii 873*b* (before A.H. 1182/1768), i 372*b* (A.H. 1193/1779), ii 843*b* (A.H. 1244/1829), **Ivanow** 228 (18th cent.), 229 (19th cent.), **Ethé** 678 (A.D. 1806), 679 (probably A.H. 1227/1812), **I.O.** D.P. 493 (*p*) (early 19th cent.), **I.O.** 586 (*a*) (A.H. 1249/1833), I.O. 3967 (*a*) (early 19th cent.). **'Alīgaṛh** Subḥ. MSS. p. 60 no. 11 (A.H. 1245/1829–30), **Berlin** 655 (breaks off in the notice of " Shaghaf " Qummī).

Editions : *Kullīyāt i Ḥazīn* [**Lucknow**] 1293/1876°*, pp. 931–1025, **Cawnpore** 1893 (cf. Browne *Lit. Hist.* iv p. 281 n. 5), pp. 931–1025.

List and epitome of the biographies : Sprenger pp. 135–41.

Description : *JRAS.* ix (1848) pp. 147–9 (by N. Bland).

[*Tadhkirat al-aḥwāl; Tadhkirat al-mu'āṣirīn* (contains no autobiography, but autobiographical statements occur here and there : see Sprenger pp. 135–41) ; *Safīnah i Khwushgū* (summarised in Bānkīpūr viii p. 110) ; " Mubtalā " *Muntakhab al-ash'ār* (Bodleian 379 no. 187) ; " Wālih " *Riyāḍ al-shu'arā'* (the main source of 'Abd al-Muqtadir's account of " Ḥazīn " in Bānkīpūr iii pp. 223–7) ; *Majma' al-nafā'is; Khizānah i 'āmirah* pp. 193–200 (no. 36) ; *Tārīkh i Muḥammadī; Ātash-kadah* no. 783 ; *Siyar al-muta'akhkhirīn*, Lucknow 1866, vol. ii pp. **615**[2–26], 632[17], 672[4], 743[23], 744[3 22], 746[22–3], 776[18], trans. Calcutta 1926, vol. ii pp. 176–8, 433–4, 525 and footnote ;

Khulāṣat al-kalām no. 19 ; *'Iqd i Thuraiyā ; Khulāṣat al-afkār* no. 86 ; Short anonymous account of " Ḥazīn " (MS. : I.O. 4036) ; *Makhzan al-gharā'ib* no. 652 ; *Mir'āt i āftāb-numā ; Ārāyish i maḥfil* (see p. 456 *supra*. The passage relating to " Ḥazīn " is translated in Garcin de Tassy's *Mémoire sur les particularités de la religion musulmane dans l'Inde*, Paris 1869, pp. 104–6) ; *Nishtar i 'ishq ; Naghmah i 'andalīb ; Majma' al-fuṣaḥā'* ii p. 94 (3 lines !) ; *Haft āsmān* pp. 161–4 ; *Sham' i anjuman* p. 130 ; *Nujūm al-samā'* pp. 283–93 (on pp. 287–93 a long list by " Ḥazīn " of his own works) ; Rieu i p. 372, ii pp. 715–16 ; Bānkīpūr iii pp. 223–7 (an account of some length based mainly on the *Riyāḍ al-shu'arā'*) ; Browne *Lit. Hist.* iv pp. 115–18, 277–81 ; *Ency. Isl.* under Ḥazīn (Hidayet Hosain) ; *Shaikh Muhammad 'Ali Hazin, his life, times and works. By Sarfaraz Khan Khatak*, Lahore 1944 (see *Luzac's Oriental list*, Jan.–March 1946, p. 6. Not utilised above) ; etc.]

1151. **Afḍal Bēg Khān Qāqshāl** [1] **Aurangābādī.**

Tuḥfat al-shu'arā', written in 1165/1751–2 and dealing with poets of the Deccan who flourished under Niẓām al-Mulk I : **Āṣafīyah** i p. 316 no. 10 (A.H. 1185/1771–2. Cf. Nadhīr Aḥmad 77), iii p. 162 no. 122, **Madrās** 439 (defective at end).

1152. Mīr **M. Taqī " Mīr "** b. Mīr M. 'Alī [2] was born at Āgrah about 1137/1724–5.[3] His grandfather had been *Faujdār* of the

[1] A Turkish clan-name. Two members of this clan were *amīrs* in Akbar's reign, Majnūn Khān Qāqshāl (see *Ā'īn i Akbarī* tr. Blochmann pp. 369–70, *Ma'āthir al-umarā'* iii 207–11) and Bābā Khān Qāqshāl (see *Ā'īn i Akbarī* tr. Blochmann p. 369 n. 3, *Ma'āthir al-umarā* i pp. 391–3, Beveridge's trans. pp. 335–7).

[2] *Dhikr i Mīr* p. 62[11] (*chūn marā dīd pursīd kih īn pisar az kīst guft az Mīr Muḥammad 'Alī ast*). Elsewhere in the *Dhikr i Mīr* (e.g. pp. 5[13], 16[4], 25[13]) he calls his father 'Alī Muttaqī (not *Mīr* 'Alī Muttaqī) and on p. 5[4] he describes this appellation as a *khiṭāb* (*Jawān i ṣāliḥī 'āshiq-pīshah būd dil i garmī* (or *dil-garmī* ?) *dāsht ba-khiṭāb i 'Alī Muttaqī imtiyāz yāft*). These passages seem to show that his real name was Mīr M. 'Alī and that on account of his piety he was nicknamed or surnamed 'Alī Muttaqī. Apparently those authorities who give his name as Mīr 'Abd Allāh are wrong.

[3] " Mīr " says in the *Dhikr i Mīr* (p. 152[12]) that he had reached the age of sixty (*aknūn kih pīrī rasīd ya'nī 'umr i 'azīz ba-shaṣt-sālagī kashīd*). The date of the *Dhikr i Mīr* appears to be 1197/1783 (according to a chronogram quoted in 'Abd al-Ḥaqq's introduction but absent from the printed text of the work itself, presumably because it occurs in the *khātimah*, a collection of " facetiæ "

environs of Āgrah (*Dhikr i Mīr* p. 4[3]: *bah faujdārī i gird i Akbarābād sar-afrāz gasht*): his father was a pious *darwīsh*. At the age of ten or eleven he lost his father, sought employment without success at Āgrah, went to Delhi, was presented to the Amīr al-Umarā' Ṣamṣām al-Daulah [Khān i Daurān],[1] a friend of his father's, and was granted by him a pension of one rupee a day (*op. cit.* p. 62). This pension (*rūzīnah*) came to an end when the Amīr al-Umarā' died [in 1151/1739] of a wound received in Nādir Shāh's invasion (p. 63[6]). "Mīr" went again to Delhi, lived for a time with his elder brother's maternal uncle [2] Sirāj al-Dīn 'Alī Khān "Ārzū" (for whom see pp. 834–40 *supra*), and studied under some of his Delhi friends (p. 63[17]: *u kitābī chand az yārān i shahr khwāndam*). He complains bitterly of the unfriendly treatment that he received from "Ārzū" (pp. 63[18]–64[7]). After leaving "Ārzū's" house he was for some time the protégé, or perhaps the employee, of Ri'āyat Khān (p. 67 ult.: *bā khwud rafīq-am kard tamattu'ī az-ū bastam u az qaid i tang-dastī rastam*); subsequently he was in the service of the Nawwāb Bahādur [3] (p. 71[6]: *talāsh i rūzgār ba-khānah i Nawwāb Bahādur kardam u naukar shudam*), until his murder [in 1165/1752] deprived him of employment (p. 72[7]). In the long period of his residence at Delhi he found either employers or patrons in a number of prominent Muslims and Hindus, but his autobiography contains several references to straitened circumstances. In

omitted by 'Abd al-Ḥaqq). It is true that on the page immediately preceding that on which "Mīr" gives his age as sixty he refers to the blinding of Shāh-'Ālam by Ghulām-Qādir, an event of 1202/1788, but this may well be a later insertion. In any case it cannot be supposed that his birth took place sixty years before 1202, i.e. in 1142, since in that case he would have been only nine years old in 1151/1738–9, whereas we know that he was at least ten when his father died (p. 54[16]: *al-Ḥamdu li-llāh kih dah-sāla'ī*, in his father's words), and that for some time after that event he had been in receipt of a pension from the Amīr al-Umarā' Ṣamṣām al-Daulah [Khān i Daurān], which terminated on the latter's death [in 1151/1739] from a wound received at the Battle of Karnāl.

[1] Khwājah 'Āṣim, for whom see *Ma'āthir al-umarā'* i pp. 819–22.

[2] *khālū-yi birādar i kalān* (p. 63[16]), that is to say, the mother of "Mīr's" half-brother was "Ārzū's" sister. Elsewhere (pp. 73[8], 75[1]) Mīr calls "Ārzū" *khālū* or *khālū-yi man*.

[3] Jāwīd Khān, a eunuch who became a great favourite of Aḥmad Shāh and was murdered by Ṣafdar-Jang (see Beale *Oriental biographical dictionary* under Jawid Khan).

1197/1783 [1] he migrated to Lucknow at the invitation of Āṣaf al-Daulah (p. 138 ult.), and there he lived in receipt of a stipend [2] from Āṣaf al-Daulah (d. 1212/1797) and his successor, Saʻādat-ʻAlī Khān (1798–1814), until his death in 1225/1810.

" Mīr " is regarded as one of the greatest Urdu poets. According to ʻAbd al-Ḥaqq (*Ency. Isl.* under Urdu) " his ghazals and mathnawīs are by far the best to be found in Urdū literature ". His *Kullīyāt* were published at Calcutta in 1811 and at Lucknow in 1867 and 1874. Several of his works have been published separately. His Urdu writings do not concern us here, but the two following are in Persian.

(1) ***Nikāt al-shuʻarā'***, about 100 short notices of Rēkhtah (i.e. Urdu) poets written nearly one year after the death of " Mukhliṣ ",[3] which occurred in 1164/1751 (see p. 612 *supra*): Sprenger no. 42, **Bodleian** 392 (A.H. 1211/1796), **Berlin** 668 (A.D. 1852), **Rāmpūr** (see *OCM*. VI/2 (Feb. 1930) p. 114).

Edition: **Aurangābād** (Badāyūn printed) [1920*] (Anjuman i Taraqqī i Urdu. With Urdu introduction by Ḥabīb al-Raḥmān Khān Shirwānī).

(2) ***Dhikr i Mīr***, an autobiography containing a good deal of historical information written (mainly ?) at the age of sixty [4]: Sprenger p. 627, **Etawah** K. B. Maulawī Bashīr al-Dīn Aḥmad's private library (A.H. 1222/1807), **Lahore** K. B. Maulawī M. Shafī''s private library.

Edition: **Aurangābād** 1928* (Anjuman i Taraqqī i Urdū. With Urdu introduction by ʻAbd al-Ḥaqq).

[*Dhikr i Mīr* and the editor's Urdu introduction; *Makhzan al-gharā'ib* no. 2684; *Majmūʻah i naghz* ii pp. 229–54; *Gulshan i bī-khār*; various Urdu *tadhkirahs* and other works; Sprenger pp. 175, 627; Garcin de Tassy ii pp. 305–21; Blumhardt's Catalogue of Hindustani MSS. in the I.O. Library, p. 85 and

[1] This date, not mentioned by " Mīr ", who seems to have had little interest in dates, is given in the Urdu *tadhkirahs Gulshan i Hind* and *Gulzār i Ibrāhīm* (cited by ʻAbd al-Ḥaqq, *Dhikr i Mīr*, introduction p. *ṣād*).

[2] *Majmūʻah i naghz* ii p. 229 penult.: *ba-ṣīghah i shāʻirī ba-mawājib i mablagh i dū ṣad rūpiyah mulāzim i sarkār i daulat-madār i Nawwāb i ghufrān-ma'āb Wazīr al-Mamālik Āṣaf al-Daulah Yaḥyā Khān Bahādur gashtah.*

[3] *Qarīb i yak-sāl ast kih dar gudhasht* (p. 10 in the Berlin MS.).

[4] See n. 3 on p. 849 *supra*.

elsewhere; Saksena *History of Urdu literature* pp. 70–80; *Ency. Isl.* under Mīr (Hidāyat Ḥusain) and under Urdū ('Abd al-Ḥaqq); T. Grahame Bailey *History of Urdu literature* pp. 47–50.]

1153. **Fatḥ-'Alī,** commonly called (*al-mad'ū bi-*) 'Alī, **Ḥusainī Gardēzī** or, as he is called in the *Majmū'ah i naghz*, S. (Mīr) Fatḥ-'Alī Khān Ḥusainī, was, according to that work (ii p. 20[14]), the elder brother of S. Ghālib 'Alī Khān "'Iyān", one of the Saiyids of Gardēz.[1] His father, therefore, was S. 'Iwaḍ Khān, who in the reign of Aḥmad Shāh was Deputy-Governor of the province of Lahore. S. Fatḥ-'Alī adopted the life of a *ṣūfī* and became an influential shaikh. In the *Majmū'ah i naghz*, which was completed in 1221/1806–7, his name is mentioned incidentally several times (vol. ii pp. 20, 184, 355, 369) and is followed by formulæ (*sallamahu Rabbuhu* and the like) showing that he was still alive at the time of writing (possibly long before 1221).

Tadhkirah i 'Alī i Ḥusainī i Gardēzī, an alphabetically arranged *tadhkirah* of about 100 Urdu poets written at Delhi six years after the death of "Anjām" (and therefore in 1165/1751–2,[2] if the authorities cited by Sprenger, p. 203, are correct in saying that "Anjām" died in 1159): Sprenger no. 43, **Ethé** 698 (A.H. 1180/1766–7), 699 (A.H. 1216/1802), 700 (B.S. 1213/1805), **Ivanow** 233 (defective. Late 18th cent.), 1st Suppt. 767 (late 18th cent.), **Madras** 437 (*l*) (A.H. 1230/1815), **Bānkīpūr** Suppt. i 1787 (19th cent.), **Rieu** iii 1071*a* (19th cent.).

Edition: *Tadhkirah i Rēkhtah-gōyān*, **Aurangābād** date? (Anjuman i Taraqqī i Urdu. With introduction by 'Abd al-Ḥaqq. See a review in *OCM*. x/3 (May 1934) p. 134).

[*'Iyār al-shu'arā'* under Yūsuf (cf. Sprenger p. 178); *Majmū'ah i naghz* ii p. 20[14]; Garcin de Tassy i pp. 523–4; 'Abd al-Ḥaqq's introduction to his edition (not utilised above).]

1154. Sh. M. Qiyām al-Dīn "**Qā'im**" **Chāndpūrī** belonged to

[1] According to Khwājah 'Abd al-Majīd's Urdu dictionary *Jāmi' al-lughāt*, s.v. Gardēzī, the Gardēzī Saiyids are a clan (*qabīlah*) of Saiyids settled at Muẓaffargaṛh (in the Panjāb). Gardēz, from which doubtless their ancestor, or ancestors, migrated, is in Afghānistān, some fifty miles from Ghaznī.

[2] The date 1172 is mentioned in the *Oriental College Magazine* x/3, p. 134, and this, if based on Prof. 'Abd al-Ḥaqq's researches, is doubtless more correct.

Chāndpūr (presumably the place of that name 19 miles S. of Bijnaur), but he went early in life to Delhi and obtained employment under the Emperor. According to Saksena he was *Dārōghah* of the Royal Armoury. When he wrote his *Makhzan i nikāt* (in 1168/1754–5), he had left Delhi owing to the decay of the empire. The date of his death is variously given (1202/1787–8, 1207/1792–3, 1208/1793–4, 1210/1795–6). He was himself an Urdu poet and the author of a *dīwān* (for which see Blumhardt's I.O. catalogue of Hindustani MSS., no. 143, and Sprenger p. 631). According to T. Grahame Bailey his poems were published in 1927.

Makhzan i nikāt (a chronogram = 1168/1754–5), a *tadhkirah* of Rēkhtah (i.e. Urdu) poets : Sprenger no. 44 (Mōtī Maḥall, autograph), **Ethé** 701.

Edition : **Aurangābād** 1929 (ed. 'Abd al-Ḥaqq. See *BSOS*. v/4 (1930) p. 928).

[Autobiography at end of *Makhzan i nikāt* (summarised in Sprenger p. 179) ; Sprenger p. 179 ; Garcin de Tassy i pp. 360–71 ; Blumhardt *Catalogue of the Hindustani manuscripts in the Library of the India Office* pp. 74–5 ; Saksēna *A history of Urdu literature* p. 97 ; 'Abd al-Ḥaqq's introduction to his edition of the *Makhzan i nikat* (not utilised above) : T. Grahame Bailey *A history of Urdu literature* p. 50.]

1155. Sirāj al-Dīn "**Sirāj**" Ḥusainī **Aurangābādī,** a Ṣūfī poet in Persian and Urdu, died in 1177/1763–4.

Majmū'ah i shu'arā' or *Dīwān i muntakhab*, an anthology completed in 1169/1755–6 from the works of about 680 poets without biographical details apart from dates of death : Sprenger no. 29 (F. Hall) = **Ethé** 691 (A.H. 1191/1777).

List of the poets : Sprenger pp. 149–51.

[*Majmū'ah i naghz* I p. 293 ; Sprenger pp. 148–9, 292 ; Garcin de Tassy III pp. 145–7 ; *Ṣubḥ i gulshan* p. 200 ; etc.]

1156. Nawwāb Ṣamṣām al-Daulah **Shah-nawāz Khān** Mīr 'Abd al-Razzāq b. Ḥasan 'Alī Ḥusainī Khwāfī **Aurangābādī** was born at Lahore on 28 Ramaḍān 1111/20 March 1700 and murdered at Aurangābād on 3 Ramaḍān 1171/11 May 1758. An account of his life will be given later in this fasciculus, when the time comes to deal with the *Ma'āthir al-umarā'*, his best-known work. At this point it will be sufficient to note that Ghulām-'Alī "Āzād" describes him as *shi'r-fahm i bī-naẓīr* (*Khizānah i 'āmirah* p. 56³. Cf. *Ma'āthir al-umarā'* i p. 35¹²: *u dar shi'r-fahmī dam i yaktā'ī mī-zad*).

Bahāristān i sukhun, a *tadhkirah* of ancient and modern poets left incomplete at the author's death in 1171/1758 and completed in 1194/1780 by his son, Mīr 'Abd al-Ḥaiy (according to the *Sawāniḥ i Dakan* cited by Rieu iii p. 1025*a*): **Āṣafīyah** i p. 316 no. 17, iii p. 162 no. 121 (A.H. 1194/1780), no. 193 (A.H. 1204/1789–90), **Madras** p. 542 no. 528 (A.H. 1259/1843).

1157. S. **'Abd al-Wahhāb** "Iftikhār" Bukhārī **Daulatābādī**, a descendant of S. Jalāl Bukhārī called Makhdūm i Jahāniyān,[1] was born at Aḥmadnagar but settled at Daulatābād on his marriage to the daughter of S. Murtaḍā Khān, commandant of the fort.[2] His instructor in the art of poetry was Mīr Ghulām-'Alī "Āzād" Bilgrāmī (for whom see pp. 855–66 *infra*). M. Mīranjān, who did not know the precise date of his death, says that he died towards the end of the eighth decade of the twelfth century (*tā awākhir i 'asharah i thāminah i mi'ah i ithnā-'ashar*).

Bī-naẓīr (a chronogram = 1172/1758–9), notices of 136 poets of the 12th/18th century.

Edition: *Tazkira-e-Benazir*, Allahabad 1940 (ed. S. Manẓūr 'Alī. Allahabad Univ. Arabic-Persian Series, 1. See *JRAS*. 1941 p. 198).

[*Sarw i āzād*; *Khāzin al-shu'arā'* fol. 38*a*]

1158. Mīr **'Alī Shēr "Qāni'" Tattawī,** born in 1140/1727–8, was still alive in 1202/1787–8 (see pp. 138, 656 *supra*).

Maqālāt al-shu'arā' (a chronogram = 1174/1760–1, the date of completion), alphabetically arranged notices of the poets of Sind: **Rieu** ii 848*a* (A.H. 1246/1830), **I.O.** 4397 (A.H. 1271/1855).

1159. Sh. Qiyām al-Dīn "**Ḥairat**" b. Sh. Amān Allāh **Akbarābādī.**

[1] For whom see *Ency. Isl.* under Djalāl and the index to the present work.
[2] For whom see *Ma'āthir al-umarā'* III pp. 644–5.

Maqālāt al-shuʿarāʾ (a chronogram = 1174/1760–1), short notices of 150 poets who flourished from the time of Aurangzēb to that of ʿĀlamgīr II (d. 1173/1759): Sprenger no. 31 (Mōtī Maḥall), **Rāmpūr** (A.H. 1228/1813. See *OCM*. VI/2 (Feb. 1930) pp. 114–16).

List and epitome of the biographies: Sprenger pp. 153–60.

1160. **Naqsh ʿAlī** wrote in India.

Bagh i maʿānī (probably a chronogram = 1174/1760–1, but there are later additions), an extensive but concise dictionary of Persian poets: Sprenger p. 152 (*Chamans* iii (Kings), iv (Wazīrs and Amīrs) and v (322 poets from time of Hārūn al-Rashīd to A.H. 800/1397–8). Mōtī Maḥall), **Bānkīpūr** viii 698 (*Chamans* vi and vii (?). Poets, mainly Indian or connected with India, from the 9th/15th century to the author's time, defective, ending with "Ẓarīf". Probably autograph), **Rieu** iii 1022*b* (extracts from *Chamans* iii and iv. Circ. A.D. 1850).

1161. **Durgā Dās.**

Safīnah i ʿishrat (a chronogram = 1175/1761–2), alphabetically arranged notices of ancient and modern poets: **Bānkīpūr** viii 699 (breaks off in *sīn*. 19th cent.).

1162. Ḥassān al-Hind[1] Mīr **Ghulām-ʿAlī "Āzād"** b. S. M. Nūḥ Ḥusainī Wāsiṭī[2] **Bilgrāmī** Ḥanafī Chishtī[3] was born at Bilgrām[4] on 25 Ṣafar 1116/29 June 1704. It was there that he received instruction in the *kutub i darsīyah* from Mīr Ṭufail Muḥammad Utraulawī Bilgrāmī (for whom see *Subḥat al-marjān* pp. 90–4, Raḥmān ʿAlī p. 98, etc.). In 1134/1721–2 he went to Delhi and remained there for two years studying Arabic lexicology

[1] Like Ḥassān b. Thābit (for whom see *Ency. Isl.*, etc.) "Āzād" composed Arabic *qaṣīdahs* in praise of the Prophet (quotations from some of these *qaṣāʾid i Nabawīyah* are made in the *Subḥat al-marjān*, e.g. twenty or so on pp. 218–20). The title dates back to "Āzād's" lifetime, since it occurs in the puff by his pupil, Qāḍī ʿAbd al-Qādir "Mihrbān" Aurangābādī, appended to the *Subḥat al-marjān* (p. 297[19]).

[2] For the Wāsiṭī Saiyids, who claim descent from a Saiyid said to have migrated from Wāsiṭ to India in the reign of Sulṭān Maḥmūd Ghaznawī (or at some other time), see *Āʾīn i Akbarī* tr. Blochmann i pp. 390–5, Blumhardt *Cat. of the Hindustani MSS. in the I.O. Library* pp. 21–22, etc.

[3] *wa-'l-Ḥanafī madhhaban wa-'l-Chishtī ṭarīqatan* (*Subḥat al-marjān* p. 118[16]).

[4] 15 miles South of Hardoi in Oudh. See *Ency. Isl. s.v.*

(*lughat*), the Traditions and the life of the Prophet and belles lettres (*ḥadīth u siyar i Nabawī u funūn i adab*) with his maternal grandfather, Mīr 'Abd al-Jalīl Bilgrāmī (for whom see p. 712 *supra*, footnote, and *Islamic culture* ii/1 (Jan. 1928) p. 133). Possibly it was in these same two years that his maternal uncle, Mīr M. b. 'Abd al-Jalīl Bilgrāmī (for whom see pp. 712–13 *supra*) taught him prosody and certain branches of *adab*. At the end of 1142/1730 he left Bilgrām for Sīwistān (i.e. Sehwan, in Sind) at the request of his uncle,[1] the aforesaid Mīr M. b. 'Abd al-Jalīl Bilgrāmī, who was *Mīr Bakhshī* and *Waqā'i'-nigār* at that town. Having appointed him, or caused him to be appointed,[2] his *nā'ib*, Mīr Muḥammad went back to Bilgrām for four years. It was in 1147/1734 that "Āzād" on his return-journey from Sīwistān met "Ḥazīn" at Bhakkar, as has already been mentioned (p. 842 n. 3 *supra*). In Rajab 1150/Nov. 1737 he left Bilgrām on a pilgrimage to the Ḥijāz, sailed from Sūrat on 24 Dhū'l-Qa'dah, reached Jiddah on 18 Muḥarram 1151/8 May 1738, Mecca on 23 Muḥarram and al-Madīnah on 25 Ṣafar. Here he studied the *Ṣaḥīḥ* of al-Bukhārī under M. Ḥayāt Sindī Madanī (for whom see *Subḥat al-marjān* pp. 95–7, Raḥmān 'Alī pp. 186–7, Brockelmann Supptbd. ii p. 522). At the end of this year he performed the *ḥajj* and on 3 Jumādā I 1152/8 Aug. 1739 he sailed from Jiddah, reaching "Swally" on the 29th of that month and Sūrat on the 2nd of Jumādā II. After a stay of five months at Sūrat he settled at Aurangābād, where he spent the next seven years in seclusion at the *takyah* of Shāh Musāfir Ghujduwānī. Towards the end of 1159/1746 he became the friend and constant companion of Nawwāb Niẓām al-Daulah Nāṣir-Jang, Āṣaf-Jāh's second son,[3] who in 1161/1748 succeeded

[1] *Wa-fī sanati thalāth wa-arba'īn wa-mi'ah wa-alf ṭalabanī 'l-khāl . . . ilā baldati Sīwistān* (*Subḥat al-marjān* p. 88[5]). In the *Khizānah i 'āmirah* (p. 124[11]) Dhū 'l-Ḥijjah 1142 is given as the date of his leaving Bilgrām for Sīwistān.

[2] *Wa-ja'alanī nā'iban fī dhālika 'l-makān* (*Subḥat al-marjān* p. 88[6]): *u ān-janāb faqīr rā niyābat i har dū khidmat muqarrar kardah* (*Khizānah* p. 124[15]).

[3] *wa-fī awākhiri sanati tis'ah* [*sic*] *wa-khamsīn wa-mi'ah wa-alf ḥaṣalat al-muwāfaqah bainī wa-bain al-Nawwāb Niẓām al-Daulah Nāṣir-Jang khalaf al-Nawwāb Niẓām al-Mulk Āṣaf-Jāh fa-aḥabbanī ḥubban 'ajaz al-qalam 'an bayānihi wa-rafa'anī makānan mā ḥāma aḥadun ḥauma arkānihi wa-kāna lā yada'unī fī 'l-ẓa'n wa-'l-iqāmah wa-lā yamallu min ṣuḥbatī ḥīnan min azminat al-istidāmah* (*Subḥat al-marjān* p. 122[5]).

his father as *Ṣūbah-dār* of the Deccan (i.e. as Niẓām of Ḥaidarābād), and who was murdered in Muḥarram 1164/December 1750. According to Shams Allāh Qādirī " Āzād " received a stipend from Nāṣir-Jang, and this is not unlikely, but he resisted suggestions that he should seek office [1] and doubtless maintained this attitude to the end of his life. At any rate he describes himself in the *Khizānah i 'āmirah* (p. 125[12]) as living at Aurangābād in retirement at the age of sixty-one (*chand bār ba-tamāshā-yi aṭrāf i mulk i Dakan bar-khāstam aknūn dar dār al-amn i Aurangābād gūshah-gīr-am* . . .). Shortly before this, in 1170/1757, when his great friend, the Prime Minister Ṣamṣām al-Daulah Shāh-nawāz Khān, was dismissed from office, " Āzād "—one of the few who remained faithful to the fallen minister—exerted himself on his behalf and took a prominent part in the negotiations which ended in his restoration to favour (*Ma'āthir al-umarā'* i pp. 28–9, Beveridge's trans. p. 22). In the following year, when Shāh-nawāz Khān's house was looted after his murder (3 Ramaḍān 1171/11 May 1758) and the unfinished manuscript of his great work, the *Ma'āthir al-umarā'*, disappeared, " Āzād " instituted a search, recovered eventually [most of] the dispersed fragments (see vol. i pp. 3, 11–12, trans. pp. 3, 10), wrote a preface (*khuṭbah u tamhīd* = vol. i pp. 10–13) and a biography of Shāh-nawāz Khān (pp. 14–41) and inserted a few additional biographies.[2]

One of the last of the contemporary accounts of " Āzād " must be that published by William Chambers in the *Asiatick Miscellany*, vol. i, Calcutta 1785, pp. 496–7. It runs as follows :

> " The author . . . [of the extracts mentioned on p. 865 *infra*] is at this day alive at Aurungabad, in the Decan, where, after a series of years spent in literary pursuits and extensive travels, he resides, in great repute, and with some splendour, at the age of eighty-five. The present Nizam has visited him

[1] *wa-lammā . . . tawallā 'l-Nawwāb Niẓām al-Daulah Nāṣir-Jang ri'āsat al-Dakan . . . bālagha 'l-aktharūna an akhtāra manṣiban min manāṣib al-imārah . . . fa-nafaḍtu dhailī min al-habā' al-manthūr wa-mā miltu 'an jāddat al-istiqāmah ilā sharak al-ghurūr* . . . (*Subḥat al-marjān* p. 122[16]).

[2] " Āzād's " edition, containing 260–290 biographies exists in several manuscripts. A much enlarged edition containing about 730 biographies, was completed in 1194/1780 by the author's son, Mīr 'Abd al-Ḥaiy (Ṣamṣām al-Mulk) and was published at Calcutta in 1887–91 (Bibliotheca Indica. 3 vols.).

twice in person at that city; and the Translator [i.e. W. Chambers] is in possession of the copy of a letter addressed to him, in the year 1775, by the celebrated Gâzy ud Dîn Khân, wherein he pays him the highest compliments. The work in question [i.e. the *Khizānah i ʻāmirah*] was published by him there in the sixty-first year of his age; and he is the author of several others in verse and prose: among which, he tells Gâzy ud Dîn Khân, in his answer to the above-mentioned letter, that his Arabick poems amounted to 4000 couplets, and his Persian to 8000; confessing, at the same time, that he was constantly adding something to each, though he had then passed the age of seventy. But his historical writings [e.g. the biographies of Āṣaf-Jāh and his sons, the account of the Marāṭ'hās, etc., in the *Khizānah i ʻāmirah*] are, to European readers, the most curious and valuable of his productions; and they have this particular recommendation, that he was the eye-witness of most of the facts which he relates, and has himself travelled over the countries which are the scene of his narrations:—circumstances that deserve to be more especially remarked, in regard to the ensuing Extracts, which have been the more readily selected, as they have a tendency to throw light on transactions, in which both the English and the French have been concerned, and, in their accounts of which, they have in some points differed from each other."

According to Wajīh al-Dīn Ashraf (*Baḥr i zakhkhār* (Rieu iii p. 976*b*) fol. 315) he died on 21 Dhū 'l-Qaʻdah 1200/15 September 1786 [1] (see Rieu i p. 373*b*). He is buried at Rauḍah ("Rauza", "Roza", "Raoza") or Khuldābād,[2] about seven miles from Daulatābād, and, according to T. W. Haig (*Historic landmarks of the Deccan*, Allahabad 1907, p. 58), "the fame of the poet's learning is such that parents take their children to his shrine

[1] The date 1200 is given also in the *Khulāṣat al-afkār* and elsewhere. Rieu says that in the *Tārīkh i dil-afrūz* (cf. p. 754 *supra*) Ghulām-Ḥusain Khān "Jauhar", who saw "Āzād" at Aurangābād in 1198/1783–4, gives 1199/1784–5 as the date of his death.

[2] For the vast cemetery of Rauḍah or Khuldābād, which contains the tombs of Aurangzēb, Abū 'l-Ḥasan Quṭb-Shāh, Āṣaf-Jāh, some kings of Aḥmadnagar and several well-known saints, see Haig, *Historic Landmarks the Deccan* pp. 56–8.

in order that they may, by picking up with their lips a piece of sugar from the tomb, obtain both a taste for knowledge and the ability to acquire it."

Lists of " Āzād's " works are given in S. Shams Allāh Qādirī's Urdu *Qāmūs al-a'lām* i coll. 33–5, the Bombay Univ. Cat. pp. 201–2 (based on the preceding), S. Wajāhat-Husain's article in the *JRASB.* 1936, Letters, pp. 123–30, and Brockelmann Supptbd. ii p. 600 (Arabic works only). The following list omits an Urdu work mentioned by S. Wajāhat-Ḥusain.

ARABIC WORKS

(**1**) *Ḍau' al-darārī*, a commentary on al-Bukhārī's *Ṣaḥīḥ* to the end of the *kitāb al-zakāh* (*Subḥat al-marjān* p. 122 antepenult. No MSS. recorded ?), (**2**) *Subḥat al-marjān fī āthār Hindustān*, written in 1177/1763–4 and divided into four *fuṣūl*, viz. :

(I, p. 4) on references to India in Qur'ānic commentaries and in the Traditions of the Prophet, originally an independent work completed at Arcot in Sha'bān 1163/1750 and entitled *Shammāmat al-'anbar fī-mā warada fī 'l-Hind min Saiyid al-Bashar*,[1] (II, p. 24) biographies of Indian scholars, originally a part of the author's work *Tasliyat al-fu'ād*,[2] which also supplied material for *Faṣl* iii, (III, p. 123) *fī muḥassināt al-kalām*, on certain rhetorical figures, viz., (*a*) 23 figures of Indian (i.e. Sanskrit) rhetoric, which the author exemplifies from Arabic poetry, especially his own (*maqālah* 1, p. 123), (*b*) 37 figures discovered or invented or first recognised as such by the author himself (*maqālah* 2, p. 162 : *fī 'l-muḥassināt allatī 'stakhraja-hā 'l-mu'allif*. The first is *al-tafā'ul*, i.e. euphemism), (*c*) one figure invented by Amīr Khusrau, namely *bū-qalamūn* (*maqālah* 3, p. 204), (*d*) two figures peculiar to

[1] For MSS. of the *Shammāmat al-'anbar* see Āṣafīyah iii p. 258 nos. 853, 857, 859.

[2] Cf. *Subḥat al-marjān* p. 122 antepenult. (*wa-Tasliyat al-fu'ād dhakartu fīhā ba'ḍ qaṣā'idī wa-fawā'idī* [*sic* : read *fawā'id* ?] *ukhar wa-qad naqaltu 'anhā tarājim al-'ulamā' wa-maṭālib ukhrā fī hādhā 'l-kitāb*), p. 123[10] (*al-maqālat al-ūlā fī 'l-muḥassināt allatī naqaltuhā 'an al-Hindīyah ilā 'l-'Arabīyah wa-'l-muḥassināt ḥilyah li-l-kalām muṭlaq*[an] *lākinna lahā jilwat*[an] *ukhrā fī 'l-kalām al-mauzūn fa-'alaiya an adhkura hāhunā madḥ al-manẓūm min al-kalām wa-'l-ḥamā'il al-manūṭah bi-'awātiq* [*sic lege*] *al-aqlām wa-qad ḥarrartu lahu faṣl*[an] *fī kitābī Tasliyat al-fu'ād fa-aj'aluhu juz'*[an] [*sic lege*] *min hādhā 'l-sawād*).

the Arabs, viz. *ḥusn al-takhallus* and *istikhdām al-muḍmar* (*maqālah* 4, p. 218), together with a *qaṣīdah badī'īyah*, in which the foregoing figures are exemplified (*maqālah* 5, p. 220), (IV, p. 234) *fī bayān al-ma'shūqāt wa-'l-'ushshāq*, on the types of lovers depicted by the poets, in five *maqālahs*, (*a*) *fī bayān al-ghizlān*, introductory matter followed by an enumeration of the types of female lovers recognized by the Hindūs (*al-ṣāliḥah, al-mu'linah, al-sūqīyah*, etc. p. 234), (*b*) types labelled by the author (*fī aqsām al-ghizlān allatī hiya min mustakhrajāt al-mu'allif*, p. 255. The first is *al-zā'irah fī 'l-ru'yā*, the second *al-nāfirah 'an al-shaib*, and so on), (*c*) *al-qaṣīdat al-ghizlānīyah*, a *qaṣīdah* describing each of the foregoing types, p. 260, (*d*) *fī aqsām al-'ushshāq*, on the types of male lovers, p. 263, (*e*) *al-qaṣīdat al-hayamānīyah*, a *qaṣīdah* on the types of male lovers, p. 295.

An edition of this curious work was published at [Bombay] in 1303/1886°*, and MSS. of it are preserved at Manchester (Cat. Arab. MSS. 292), the Calcutta Madrasah (p. 47 no. 88), and (extracts only) the British Museum (Rieu iii pp. 1022*b*, 1055*b*). A Persian translation of the third and fourth *faṣl* was made by the author himself and entitled *Ghizlān al-Hind* (a chronogram = 1178/1764–5). For MSS. see no. (12) below. A Persian translation of the first and second *faṣl* was made by S. Shams al-Dīn b. Shāh Wārith 'Alī Ḥasanī Ḥusainī Banārasī at the request of the Rājah of Benares, Mahārāj Īsarī Parshād, in whose service the translator was in 1286/1869 (MS.: Bānkīpūr viii 653).

(**3**) *Dīwāns*. In the list of his own works given on pp. 122–3 of the *Subḥat al-marjān*, which was written in 1177/1763–4, "Āzād" mentions two Arabic *dīwāns* consisting of 3000 verses [1] (p. 122 penult.: *wa-'l-dīwānān . . . wa-jumlatu ash'ārī fī 'l-dīwānain thalāthatu ālāf wa-arsaltuhumā ilā ba'ḍ al-fuḍalā' bi-'l-Madīnat al-Munawwarah*). Shams Allāh Qādirī in speaking

[1] In the *Khizānah i 'āmirah* written in 1176 only one Arabic *dīwān* is mentioned and this is said to consist of 3000 verses (p. 125^{17}: *Dīwān i fārisī u 'arabī i faqīr murattab ast. Dīwān i 'arabī sih hazār bait bāshad*).

of "Āzād's" Arabic *dīwān* [so—in the singular] says that it contains more than 3000 verses and that it was published in four volumes at Ḥaidarābād in 1300. The Āṣafīyah catalogue (i p. 696) records two MSS. and a printed (i.e. doubtless lithographed) edition, speaks of *har sih ḥiṣṣah*, but says nothing about place or date of publication. Sarkis (*Dictionnaire encyclopédique de bibliographie arabe*, col. 1) records editions of (1) *al-dīwān al-awwal* completed in 1187 [1] and lithographed at the Kanz al-'ulūm Press, Ḥaidarābād, (2) *al-dīwān al-thānī* (pp. 59) printed (or lithographed) at the Lauḥ i maḥfūẓ Press, Ḥaidarābād,[2] and (3) *al-dīwān al-thālith* printed (or lithographed) at the Kanz al-'ulūm Press without date. Seven *dīwāns* entitled *al-Sab'at al-saiyārah* (beginning *Lamaḥat ilaiya bi-'ainihā 'l-kaḥlā'u*) were begun in 1179 and completed in 1194 (Autograph MS.: Nawwāb Nūr al-Ḥasan's library, Lucknow. See Nadhīr Aḥmad in *JASB*. 1917 p. cxxxix, no. 152. According to S. Maqbūl Aḥmad Ṣamdanī, *Ḥayāt i Jalīl* ii p. 175 note 139, a selection from these seven *dīwāns* was published under the title *Mukhtār dīwān Āzād* at the Āsī Press, Lucknow, in 1328). A *dīwān i tāsi'* and a *dīwān i 'āshir* are preserved at 'Alīgaṛh (Subḥ. MSS. p. 126). For MSS. described simply as *Dīwān i Āzād* (*i Bilgrāmī*) see the 'Alīgaṛh catalogue (Subḥ. MSS. p. 126), the Āṣafīyah catalogue (i p. 696) and the Rāmpūr Arabic catalogue (i p. 586). (**4**) *Maẓhar al-barakāt*, a Ṣūfī *muzdawijah*, or *mathnawī*, in seven *daftars*, of which the first was completed in 1194/1780 and the second, third and fourth in 1195/1781, the rest being undated (MSS.: Āṣafīyah (autograph. See *Qāmūs al-a'lām* col. 34), Manchester Arab. Cat. 481 (*a*), Princeton Arab. Cat. (1938) no. 136). (**5**) *Shifā' al-'alīl fī iṣlāḥ* [3] *kalām Abī 'l-Ṭaiyib al-Mutanabbī* (MS.: S. 'Alī Ḥusain Bilgrāmī's library, Ḥaidarābād.

[1] *Atamma ta'līfahu sanata* 1187 according to Sarkis. If this *dīwān* is correctly described as *al-dīwān al-awwal*, 1187 cannot be the date of collection. If 1187 is an error for 1287, that may be the date of printing (see the next note).

[2] A copy of this second *dīwān* is mentioned in the 'Alīgaṛh catalogue (Subḥān Allāh Printed Books p. 25), and there 1287 is given as the date of printing.

[3] Wajāhat-Ḥusain writes *iṣṭilāhāt* (as in the *Ḥadā'iq al-Ḥanafīyah*), but the correctness of *iṣlāḥ* is shown by the words quoted by Nadhīr Aḥmad from the preface (*wa-lā yakhfā 'alā 'l-ṭabīb al-'ārif bi-mu'ālajat al-amrāḍ anna manṣib al-islāḥ a'lā wa-arfa' min manṣib al-i'tirāḍ fa-waqa'a fī khāṭirī an uṣliḥa mā fī kalāmihi min al-fasād*).

See Nadhīr Aḥmad in *JASB.* 1917 p. cxxiii). (**6**) *Kashkūl*[1] (MSS.: Āṣafīyah iii p. 642 nos. 242 (mainly autograph), 261).

PERSIAN WORKS

(**7**) *Dīwān*, beginning *Bar-ār az madd i bi-smi'llāhi tīgh i khwash-maqālī rā* (*Subḥat al-marjān* p. 123[8]. MSS.: Sprenger 146, Bānkīpūr iii 423, Ethé 1722, Ivanow-Curzon 304–6, Madras 75 (*c*) (*muntakhab*), and doubtless also Āṣafīyah iii p. 288 no. 830), (**8**) *Mathnawī ba-jawāb i Mathnawī i Mīr 'Abd al-Jalīl i Bilgrāmī*[2] (MS.: Āṣafīyah iii p. 632), (**9**) *Mathnawī i sarāpā-yi ma'shūq* (MS.: 'Alīgaṛh Subḥ. MSS. p. 43 no. 90). It seems at least possible that this may be identical with the *Mir'āt al-jamāl*, which is placed among the Persian MSS. in the catalogue of the Bibliotheca Lindesiana (p. 144 no. 592), though S. Wajāhat-Ḥusain, who gives references to *Itḥāf al-nubalā'* p. 331 and *Ḥadā'iq al-Ḥanafīyah* p. 455, describes that work as " an Arabic poem containing 105 verses and describing the beauties of a beloved from head to foot ". The language is not specified in the *Ḥadā'iq al-Ḥanafīyah*: the *Itḥāf al-nubalā'* is not at the moment accessible. (**10**) *Sanad al-sa'ādāt fī ḥusn khātimat al-Sādāt* (*Subḥat al-marjān* p. 123[7]. MSS.: Āṣafīyah ii p. 1346 no. 372, iii p. 662 no. 101, Ethé 2670. According to Shams Allāh Qādirī an edition was published at Bombay in 1282/1865–6). (**11**) *Ghizlān al-Hind* (a chronogram = 1178/1764–5), a translation of the third and fourth *faṣl* of the *Subḥat al-marjān* (no. 2 above) made at the request of the author's two friends, 'Abd al-Qādir " Mihrbān " Aurangābādī (cf. p. 855 n. 1 *supra*) and Lachhmī Narāyan " Shafīq " Aurangābādī (cf. pp. 476–8 *supra* and p. 867 *infra*) (MSS.: Āṣafīyah i p. 168 no. 164, Berlin 1051, Ethé 2135, Nadhīr Aḥmad 310). (**12**) *Shajarah i ṭaiyibah*, on the pedigrees and lives of the *shaikhs* of Bilgrām (*Qāmūs*

[1] Classed among the *Muḥāḍarāt i 'Arabī* in the Āṣafīyah catalogue. Shams Allāh Qādirī places it among " Āzād's " Persian works. It may of course contain extracts in both languages. Wajāhat-Ḥusain does not mention it.

[2] Mīr 'Abd al-Jalīl, " Āzād's " maternal grandfather, has already been mentioned (p. 856 *supra*). The *mathnawī* in question is doubtless that on the marriage of the Emperor Farrukh-siyar (Edition: Lucknow 1299/1882°*. MSS.: Nadhīr Aḥmad 210, Panjāb Univ. Lib., Āṣafīyah iii p. 632 (?). Cf. S. Maqbūl Aḥmad Ṣamdanī *Ḥayāt i Jalīl* ii pp. 62–72).

al-a'lām i col. 35. MSS. : Āṣafīyah i p. 322 no. 35, ii p. 1778 no. 114). (**13**) *Rauḍat al-auliyā'*, written in 1161/1748, lives of ten saints buried at Rauḍah or Khuldābād, near Daulatābād, the first being al-Gharīb al-Hānsawī and the last " Āzād " himself (Edition : Aurangābād 1310/1892–3*. MSS. : Āṣafīyah i p. 320, iii p. 164, Ethé 655). (**14**) *Ma'āthir al-kirām tārīkh i Bilgrām*, completed in 1166/1752–3 and divided into two *faṣls*, viz. (1) lives of about 80 *fuqarā'*, i.e. saints and mystics, connected, in some cases rather remotely, with Bilgrām and its neighbourhood, (2) lives of about 70 similar *fuḍalā'*, i.e. men of learning (Edition : Ḥaidarābād 1910 (with introduction by 'Abd al-Ḥaqq. See *OCM*. III/2 (Feb. 1927) p. 33 footnote). MSS. : Āṣafīyah i p. 348 no. 105, Ethé 682 (sent by the author to Richard Johnson in 1785), Rieu iii 971*a*, Bānkīpūr viii 723, Berlin 603 (*Faṣl* 2 only. For a list of the biographies in this *faṣl* see Berlin pp. 567–8)).

The second volume of this work is the *Sarw i āzād* (no. (16) below). The *Sharā'if i 'Uthmānī* of Ghulām-Ḥasan Ṣiddīqī Bilgrāmī (MSS. : Ivanow 277, I.O. 3913, Āṣafīyah iii p. 164) was written expressly for the purpose of correcting numerous alleged inaccuracies in the *Ma'āthir al-kirām* and the *Sarw i āzād*. Another attack on the two volumes, more especially on " Āzād's " style and his poetry, is the *Taḥqīq al-sadād fī madhallat al-Āzād* written soon after 1167/1754 by M. Ṣiddīq " Sukhunwar " 'Uthmānī Bilgrāmī (MS. : Ivanow 397). A reply to the second attack is the *Ta'dīb al-zindīq fī takdhīb al-Ṣiddīq* of 'Abd al-Qādir Samarqandī Dihlawī (MS. : Ivanow 398).

(15) **Yad i baiḍā'**,[1] alphabetically arranged lives of 532 ancient and modern poets, compiled originally at Sīwistān in 1145/1732–3 and thereupon published, later revised and enlarged at Allahabad in 1148/1735–6, and still further enlarged after the author's return from Mecca by additional matter sent to some friends for insertion : Sprenger no. 23, **Bānkīpūr** viii 691 (partly autograph), **I.O.** 3966 (*b*) (A.H. 1178/1764), **Āṣafīyah** iii p. 162 no. 186 (*Tadhkirah i Yad i baiḍā mausūm bah Tadhkirah*

[1] An alternative title, *Ṣubḥ i khandān*, is attributed to this work in the Āṣafīyah catalogue.

i Ṣubḥ i khandān. A.H. 1297/1880), no. 155 (*Tadhkirah i Ṣubḥ i khandān ya'nī Yad i baiḍā*).

(16) *Sarw i āzād*, completed in 1166/1752–3 as the second volume of the work whose first volume is entitled *Ma'āthir al-kirām* (no. (14) above) and consisting likewise of two *faṣls*, viz. (1) notices of 143 poets who were born in India, or visited the country, after 1000/1591–2, including some learned men and poets of Bilgrām, (2) notices of 8 Rēkhtah (i.e. Urdū) poets: Sprenger no. 24, **Nadhīr Aḥmad** 86 (Ḥakīm 'Abd al-Ḥaiy, Lucknow. Autograph), **Āṣafīyah** i p. 320 no. 16 (A.H. 1194/1780), **Ivanow** 1st Suppt. 765 (A.H. 1223/1808), **Ivanow** Curzon 58 (19th cent.), **Lindesiana** p. 144 no. 330*g* (A.H. 1237/1821–2), **Ethé** 683 (n.d.), 684 (lacking *Faṣl* 2. A.H. 1265/1849), **Bānkīpūr** viii 697 (19th cent.), **Bombay** Univ. 122 (fragment only, 39 poets).

Edition: **Lahore** 1913* (published by the Āṣafīyah Book Depot, Ḥaidarābād. Cf. *OCM*. III/2 (Feb. 1927) p. 33 n. 2).

Lists of the poets: Ivanow-Curzon pp. 64–6 (132 Persian poets), Ivanow 1st Suppt. p. 7 (8 Urdu poets).

Criticisms: see under *Ma'āthir al-kirām* (no. (14) above).

(17) *Khizānah i 'āmirah*, written in 1176/1762–3,[1] alphabetically arranged notices of about 135 [2] ancient and modern poets, together with valuable biographies of Āṣaf-Jāh, his sons and some other contemporary nobles as well as historical accounts of the Marāṭ'hās and of Aḥmad Shāh Durrānī: Sprenger no. 25, **Lindesiana** p. 144 no. 319 (A.H. 1176/1762–3), no. 925 (A.H. 1196/1782), no. 320 (extracts. Circ. A.D. 1780), **Ethé** 685 (A.H. 1182/1768, transcribed from an autograph), 686 (A.H. 1193/1779), 687–90 (four undated copies), 490 (historical extracts only), **I.O.** D.P. 644, **I.O.** 3991 (only the account of Āṣaf-Jāh, etc.), 4078, **Rieu** i 798*a* (first portion only, ending with the account of Aḥmad Shāh Durrānī. A.H. 1197/1783), 373*a* (fragment, breaking off in the notice of "Āzād". Late 18th cent.), 374*b* (extract, Āṣaf-Jāh to "Āzād". Early 19th cent.), 374*b* (extract, Āṣaf-Jāh, his children, etc. A.H. 1232/1817), **Bodleian** 381

[1] The death of Dargāh-Qulī Khān in 1180/1766 is recorded on p. 224 of the printed text.

[2] In the Bodleian MS. the poets are 135, counting Āṣaf-Jāh, but not the other *amīrs*. Sprenger gives the number as 106.

(A.H. 1199/1785), **Blochet** ii 1157 (18th cent.), 1158 (extracts. Late 18th cent.), **Āṣafīyah** i p. 318 no. 26 (A.H. 1221/1806–7), **Bānkīpūr** viii 700 (19th cent.), 658 (extract, Āṣaf-Jāh, etc. A.H. 1203/1789), Suppt. i 1788 (19th cent.), **'Alīgaṛh** Subḥ. MSS. p. 60 no. 20 (A.H. 1266/1849–50), **Ivanow** 232 (19th cent.), Curzon 59 (A.H. 1282/1865), **Browne** Pers. Cat. 115, **Browne** Coll. H. 23 (4) (only the account of Āṣaf-Jāh, etc.), **R.A.S.** P. 116 (possibly also P. 164 and P. 165).

Editions: **Cawnpore** 1871*, 1900°.

Extracts: (**1**) *A short history of the origin and progress of the Marratta State.*—[Persian text] *Extracted from the Khazanah e Aamerah* [Cawnpore editions pp. 39–47[13]], *and translated by William Chambers* (in *The Asiatick Miscellany*, vol. ii (**Calcutta** 1786*) pp. 86–122), (**2**) *Extracts from the Khazanah e Aamerah* [viz. *A short account of Naser Jung* (= Cawnpore editions pp. 54–56) and *A short account of Muzaffer Jung* (= Cawnpore editions pp. 59–60)].—*Translated by W. Chambers* [with the Persian text] (in *The Asiatick Miscellany*, vol. i (**Calcutta** 1785*) pp. 494–511).

Translations of extracts: (**1**) see Extracts (1) above, (**2**) see Extracts (2) above, (**3**) *History of Asof Jah, shewing by what means he acquired the Territory in the Dekhan, which is now in the Possession of his Son Nizaum-ul-Moolk; extracted from a Biographical Work, written in the Persian language* [= Cawnpore editions pp. 35[8]–38[2]], *and translated by Henry Vansittart* [without the Persian text] (in *The Asiatick Miscellany*, vol. i (**Calcutta** 1785*) pp. 327–31), (**4**) *The History of Ahmed Shah, King of the Abdallies, who are also called Duranees, from a Custom of wearing a Pearl in one of their Ears; extracted from the same Persian Book which furnished the History of Asof Jah* [= Cawnpore editions pp. 97–116 with omissions], *and translated by Henry Vansittart* [without the Persian text] (in *The Asiatick Miscellany*, vol. i (**Calcutta** 1785*) pp. 332–42).

List and epitome of the biographies: Bodleian coll. 255–60.

Descriptions: (**1**) *On the earliest Persian Biography of Poets ... By N. Bland* (in the *JRAS.* ix (1848)) pp. 152–3, (**2**) Sprenger pp. 143–5.

Sources: (**1**) Sprenger pp. 144–5, (**2**) Rieu i pp. 373–4, (**3**) Blochet ii pp. 328–9.

[Autobiographies in *Yad i baiḍā'* (A.H. 1148. Cf. Bānkīpūr viii pp. 115–16), *Rauḍat al-auliyā'* (A.H. 1161), *Ma'āthir al-kirām* (A.H. 1166), *Sarw i āzād* (A.H. 1166. Passage summarised in Bombay Univ. Cat. pp. 200–1), *Khizānah i 'āmirah* (A.H. 1176) no 13, pp. 123–45 (passage summarised by Bland, *JRAS.* ix (1848) pp. 150–2, Blochet, ii pp. 326–8, and much more briefly by Rieu, i p. 373, and 'Abd al-Muqtadir, Bānkīpūr iii pp. 252–3) and *Subḥat al-marjān* (A.H. 1177) pp. 118–23 ; *Safīnah i Khwushgū* (passage summarised in Bānkīpūr viii p. 108[1-4]) ; *Riyāḍ al-shu'arā' ; Gul i ra'nā* (a long biography by his pupil " Shafīq ". Cf. Rieu iii p. 978*a*) ; *Asiatick Miscellany* i (Calcutta 1785) pp. 496–7 (passage quoted pp. 857–8 *supra* and in Bodleian Cat. col. 260) ; *Ṣuḥuf i Ibrāhīm* no. 199 (cf. Bland in *JRAS.* ix (1848) p. 152) ; *Khulāṣat al-afkār* no. 41 (summarised by Bland in *JRAS.* ix (1848) pp. 152–3) ; *Ārāyish i maḥfil* (for which see p. 456 *supra.* The passage is translated in Garcin de Tassy i p. 259) ; *Natā'ij al-afkār* ; Bland in *JRAS.* ix (1848) pp. 150–3 ; Garcin de Tassy i pp. 259–60 ; *Ḥadā'iq al-Ḥanafīyah* (in Urdu) pp. 454–6 ; Raḥmān 'Alī pp. 154–5 ; Bānkīpūr iii pp. 252–3 ; *Ency. Isl.* under Ghulām 'Alī (unsigned) ; *Ḥayāt i Jalīl* (in Urdu), by S. Maqbūl Aḥmad Ṣamdanī, Allahabad 1929, vol. ii pp. 163–77 ; *Qāmūs al-a'lām* (in Urdu) by S. Shams Allāh Qādirī, pt. 1 (Ḥaidarābād 1935) coll. 32–5 ; Bombay Univ. Cat. pp. 200–3 ; *Āzād Bilgrāmī. By Sayyid Wajahat Husain* (in *JRASB.*, 3rd series, Letters, vol. ii (1936) pp. 119–30) ; Brockelmann Supptbd. ii pp. 600–1.]

1163. As yet unidentified is—

A very large *tadhkirah* written probably between 1170/1757 and 1180/1766 and containing alphabetically arranged notices of 2200 poets, each letter forming a *ḥadīqah* subdivided into three *gulshans* ((1) ancient, (2) " mediæval," (3) modern poets), the last of which comprises two *chamans* ((1) Īrān and Tūrān, (2) India) : **Ethé** 692 (apparently a rough draft. No preface or colophon).

Here may be mentioned also—

Safīnat al-shu'arā', a large and apparently unfinished anthology of ancient and modern poets with useful biographies, written, at least partly, in 1170/1756–7 (mentioned on fol. 264*b* as the current year) by an unidentified author, who was an associate of Anand Rām "Mukhliṣ" (see pp. 612–14 *supra*): **Ivanow** Curzon 326 (some 700 poets, about one-third of the work, very defective and much disarranged. Foll. 503. Late 18th cent. LIST OF POETS).

1164. For the *Tuḥfat al-kirām*, which was begun in 1180/1766–7 and completed in 1181/1767–8 by Mīr ʻAlī Shēr "Qāniʻ" Tattawī and which contains much biographical information concerning the celebrities of Sind and other places, see p. 656 *supra*.

1165. **Lachhmī Narāyan "Shafīq" Aurangābādī** has already been mentioned as the author of the *Ḥaqīqat-hā-yi Hindustān* (p. 477 *supra*), the *Bisāṭ al-ghanāʼim* (p. 762), the *Tanmīq i shigarf* (p. 738), the *Maʼāthir i Āṣafī* (p. 750) and other works. For his life and other particulars see pp. 476–8 *supra*.

(1) ***Chamanistān i shuʻarāʼ***, notices of Rēkhtah (i.e. Urdu) poets, written in 1761 and "taken largely from Mīr's *Nikāt ush Shuʻarā*, 1752, and *Tazkira e Fatḥ ʻAlī*, together with considerable additions of his own from earlier *tazkiras*" (T. Grahame Bailey in *BSOS*. v/4 (1930) p. 927).

Edition: **Aurangābād** 1928 (ed. ʻAbd al-Ḥaqq. See *BSOS*. *loc. cit.*).

(2) ***Gul i raʻnā***, begun in 1181/1767–8 and completed in 1182/1768–9, alphabetically arranged notices ("extremely rich in biographical detail") of Indian poets in two *faṣls*, (1) Muslims, (2) Hindus: **Bānkīpūr** viii 701 (1204 *Faṣlī*), **I.O.** 3692–3, **Rieu** iii 977*b* (extracts from *Faṣl* 1. 19th cent.), **Āṣafīyah** iii p. 162 no. 183 (ending with *fāʼ*), **Rehatsek** p. 161 nos. 121 (complete), 122 (defective, ending in *ẓāʼ*).

List and epitome of the biographies in *Faṣl* 2: Bānkīpūr viii pp. 129–34.

(3) ***Shām i gharībān***, written in 1182/1768–9, a *tadhkirah* of poets of Persian birth who visited India (see Rieu iii 1085*b*): no MSS. yet recorded in any published catalogue?

1166. It has already been mentioned (p. 140 *supra*) that **Yūsuf ʻAlī Khān** b. Ghulām-ʻAlī Khān appended to his *Ḥadīqat* *al-ṣafā'* a *khātimah* which is sometimes called the *Tadhkirah i Yūsuf 'Alī Khān.*

(*Tadhkirah i Yūsuf 'Alī Khān*), completed at Murshidābād in 1184/1770–1, short alphabetically arranged notices of about 300 ancient and modern poets with an appendix relating to 20 contemporary poets not included in "Ārzū's" *tadhkirah* (for which see p. 839 *supra*): Sprenger no. 62, **Bodleian** 118 (autograph), **Berlin** 661 (A.H. 1213/1799), **Bānkipūr** vi 480 (appendix only. 19th cent.), **Ivanow** 45.

List and epitome of the 20 biographies in the appendix: Sprenger pp. 193–4.

1167. For M. Aslam's *Farḥat al-nāẓirīn*, which was completed in 1184/1770–1 and of which the *khātimah* contains notices of *shaikhs*, *'ulamā'* and poets contemporary with Aurangzēb (published by M. Shafī' in *OCM.*), see pp. 140–1 *supra*.

1168. Mīr **Ghulām-Ḥasan** b. Mīr Ghulām-Ḥusain b. Mīr 'Azīz Allāh Rātmanā'ī [?].

Tadhkirah i sukhun-āfrīnān i Hindī-zabān, meagre notices of a large number of Urdu poets written apparently in 1191/1777: **Ivanow** Curzon 62 (A.D. 1861).

1169. S. **Ghulām-Ḥusain "Shōrish"**, familiarly called Mīr Bhainā, was a native of Patna. When he compiled his *tadhkirah* he had already written a Persian *dīwān* of about 4000 verses. According to Sprenger, who does not specify his authority, he died in 1195/1781.

Tadhkirah i Shōrish, short notices of 314 Urdu poets compiled probably in 1193/1779, "for the latest date that occurs in it is 1192, and men who died in 1194 are mentioned as being alive" (Sprenger): Sprenger no. 46 = **Bodleian** 387.

[Sprenger p. 182; Garcin de Tassy iii pp. 134–5.]

1170. Ḥājjī **Luṭf-'Alī Bēg "Ādhar"** b. Āqā Khān Bēgdilī[1] Shāmlū Iṣfahānī was born at Iṣfahān on 20 Rabī' II 1134/

[1] This Turcoman clan-name is explained by Luṭf-'Alī Bēg early in the historical introduction with which the second *Mijmarah* of the *Ātash-kadah* opens. Bēgdil Khān, according to him, was the third of the four sons of Ildigiz Khān, who was the third of the six sons of Oghūz Khān. [For this eponymous ancestor of the Oghuz Turks see the articles Ghuzz, Toghuzghuz and Turks in the *Ency. Isl.*] In the time of Maḥmūd Ghaznawī, or in that of Chingiz Khān, the Bēgdilīs

7 Feb. 1722,[1] the year of Maḥmūd Khān's Afghān invasion,[2] on account of which his family fled from Iṣfahān to Qum, his home for the next fourteen years. At the beginning of Nādir Shāh's reign [A.H. 1147/1736–1160/1747] his father[3] was appointed Governor (*ḥākim*) of Lār and the coast of Fārs (*sawāḥil i Fārs*), and Luṭf-'Alī Bēg moved from Qum to Shīrāz. Two years later his father died near Bandar i 'Abbāsī, and he went with his paternal uncle, Ḥājjī M. Bēg, on a pilgrimage to Mecca and al-Madīnah and then to the sanctuaries of al-'Irāq. Having spent a year in Fārs, he set out on a pilgrimage to Mashhad and he was there when Nādir Shāh reached the town [in Shawwāl 1153/Dec. 1740] on his return from his campaigns in India and Turkistān. When Nādir Shāh left Mashhad for the Lesghian mountains [*Jibāl i Lakzīyah*, to punish the Lesghians[4] of Dāghistān for the murder of his brother, Ibrāhīm Khān], Luṭf-'Alī Bēg went with the army through Māzandarān to Ādharbāyjān. From there he returned to his birthplace, Iṣfahān. After Nādir

with other Turkish tribes migrated to Persia and, while some remained there, others went on and settled in Syria. In Tīmūr's reign Amīr Jahāngīr, when campaigning in Syria, recognized the Syrian Bēgdilīs as his countrymen and led them back to Persia with the intention of restoring them to Turkistān. On reaching Ardabīl, however, the Bēgdilī leaders had the honour of meeting Sulṭān 'Alī Siyāh-pūsh Ṣafawī [Sulṭān Khwājah 'Alī, as he is called in the *Silsilat al-nasab i Ṣafawīyah* p. 45 (= *JRAS*. 1921 p. 407)] and, having solicited his intercession, they obtained permission to leave the Tīmūrid camp (*urdū-yi Tīmūrī*] and stay at Ardabīl as *murīds* of that saintly personage. In the 250 years since Shāh Ismā'īl's accession they had given faithful service to the Ṣafawī family and many of them had held high positions. The descendants of those Bēgdilīs who had returned from Syria were known as Bēgdilī Shāmlū, while the descendants of those who had never gone to Syria were called simply Bēgdilī [see *JRAS*. 1843 pp. 380–1, where a less corrupt text than that of the 1277 edition is summarised. Cf. the articles Ḳizil-bāsh and Shāh-sewan in the *Ency. Isl.*].

[1] The incorrect date 1123/1711 given by Browne comes from the corrupt 1277 edition of the *Ātash-kadah*. Its incorrectness is shown by the words which immediately follow: *u muqārin i īn ḥāl fitnah i Maḥmūd i Gh.lījān* [*sic*, for *Ghiljāy*] *i Afghān rūy dādah*.

[2] Cf. p. 831 n. 2 *supra*.

[3] Several of Luṭf-'Alī Bēg's relations held prominent positions. His maternal uncle Muḥammad-Qulī Khān succeeded Fatḥ-'Alī Khān, "Wālih's" great-uncle (cf. p. 831 *supra*), as Prime Minister to Shāh Sulṭān-Ḥusain. His paternal uncles, Walī-Muḥammad Khān and Muṣṭafā Khān Bēgdilī, and another maternal uncle, Riḍā-Qulī Khān Bēgdilī, were sent on missions to the Ottoman Sulṭān.

[4] For the Lesghians, who have already been mentioned (p. 830 *supra*) in connexion with 'Alī-Qulī Khān "Wālih" Dāghistānī, see the *Ency. Isl.* under Dāghistān.

S͟hāh's death he was in the service of 'Alī S͟hāh,[1] Ibrāhīm S͟hāh,[2] S͟hāh Ismā'īl[3] and S͟hāh Sulaimān[4] (*ba'd az qatl i Nādir S͟hāh c͟handī dar silk i mulāzimān i rikāb i 'Alī S͟hāh u Ibrāhīm S͟hāh u S͟hāh Sulaimān būdah*, to quote his own words). At the time when Ibrāhīm Mīrzā [afterwards Ibrāhīm S͟hāh] arrived in 'Irāq, to the Governorship of which he had been appointed by his brother, 'Alī S͟hāh, Luṭf-'Alī Bēg was *Dārūg͟hah i Daftar i Dīwān i A'lā*. After these troubled years Luṭf-'Alī Bēg adopted the life of a *ṣūfī* and cultivated the society of scholars, mystics, poets and wits. Mīr S. 'Alī "Mus͟htāq" instructed him in the art of poetry and became his intimate friend. According to the *Anjuman i K͟hāqān* and the *Majma' al-fuṣaḥā'* he died in 1195/1781 (see Rieu Suppt. p. 81a^{5-7}). It is true that in the *'Iqd i T͟huraiyā* "Muṣḥafī", writing in 1199/1785, said that Luṭf-'Alī Bēg "was then still alive in Iṣpahān, and was considered the greatest poet of the period" (Rieu[5] p. 375*a*), but "Muṣḥafī" lived in Delhi, and his information from Iṣfahān may not have been up to date.

MSS. of "Ād͟har's" *dīwān* are preserved at Bānkīpūr (Cat. iii no. 400), Rāmpūr (*g͟hazals* only? See Nad͟hīr Aḥmad 106) and Lahore (*g͟hazals* only. See *OCM*. VI/4 (Aug. 1930) p. 67). Extensive extracts from his *Yūsuf u Zalīk͟hā*, which is dated 1176/1762–3, are given in the *Ātas͟h-kadah*.

His son, Ḥusain (or Ḥasan) 'Alī Bēg "S͟harar", is one of the poets noticed in the *Zīnat al-madā'iḥ* (Rieu Suppt. 118) and the *Majma' al-fuṣaḥā'* II p. 262.

[1] 'Alī S͟hāh = 'Ādil S͟hāh = 'Alī-Qulī K͟hān, who succeeded his uncle, Nādir S͟hāh, in 1160/1747 but was deposed in S͟hawwāl 1161/Sept. 1748 by his brother Ibrāhīm (see Malcolm *History of Persia* ii pp. 53–5, Watson *History of Persia* pp. 40–1, Sykes *History of Persia* ii pp. 272, 275–6, Zambaur *Manuel de généalogie* p. 261).

[2] 'Alī S͟hāh's younger brother, deposed in Muḥarram 1163/Dec. 1749–Jan. 1750 (see Malcolm ii pp. 54–5, Watson p. 41, Sykes p. 276, Zambaur p. 261).

[3] S͟hāh Ismā'īl III [Ṣafawī], a boy of eight or nine, was proclaimed king at Iṣfahān in 1163 by 'Alī Mardān K͟hān Bak͟htyārī (see Malcolm ii p. 59, Watson p. 44, Zambaur p. 261).

[4] S͟hāh Sulaimān II [Ṣafawī] was proclaimed king at Mas͟hhad in Muḥarram or Ṣafar 1163 (cf. p. 320 *supra*) and after reigning for 40 days was deposed and blinded (see Malcolm ii pp. 55–6, Watson p. 41, Zambaur p. 261).

[5] According to 'Abd al-Muqtadir "Muṣḥafî, who composed his tad͟kirah in A.H. 1199, speaks of Âd͟ur in the present tense, and says that the poet was then of about sixty years of age".

Ātash-kadah,[1] notices of about 845 ancient and modern poets begun by the author at the age of forty [2] [and therefore about 1174/1760–1], continued or added to over a number of years (e.g. 1179, mentioned under Delhi as the current year, 1180,[3] described as the current year under " Anwarī ", 1185, 1190, 1191 and 1193, dates given, with chronograms, for the deaths of " 'Udhrī ", " Ṭūfān ", " Ṣahbā " and " Firībī " [4]), arranged for the most part geographically under towns or provinces and divided into two *mijmarahs* (*Mijmarah* I, ancient poets, subdivided into a *shu'lah* (kings, princes and *amīrs* of all countries), three *akhgars* ((1) poets of Īrān, (2) poets of Tūrān, (3) poets of Hindūstān) and a *furūgh* (poetesses) ; *Mijmarah* II, about seventy contemporary poets alphabetically arranged, with a subdivision into two *partaus* ((1) contemporaries, preceded by a historical introduction mainly on the Afghān invasion and subsequent events, (2) autobiography) : Sprenger no. 32, **Blochet** iv 2453 (Iṣfahān, A.H. 1180/1767, transcribed by Asad Allāh b. 'Abd al-Raḥīm al-Shirwānī), ii 1153 (A.H. 1213/1799), 1154 (A.H. 1217/1802), 1155 (A.H. 1231/1816), 1156 (A.H. 1234/1819, collated with an autograph (?)), **Ethé** 693 (A.H. 1196/1782), 694 (A.H. 1215/1800, transcribed possibly by the author's son[5]), **Lindesiana** p. 182 no. 918 (A.H. 1202/1787–8), no. 56 (A.H. 1215/1800–1), **Sipahsālār** ii pp. 452–6 (four copies, one of 1207/1792–3), **Rieu** i 375*b* (defective. A.H. 1214/1800), Suppt. 114 (A.H. 1234/1818), i 375*a* (A.H. 1238/1823), **Oxford** Ind. Inst. MS. Whinfield 6 (A.H. 1219/1805), **Bodleian** MS. Pers. d. 80 (A.H. 1222/1807), Bodleian 384 (A.H. 1227/1812), 385 (A.H. 1228/1813), 386,

[1] According to Blochet (ii p. 325) the *Ātash-kadah* " est un ouvrage très peu considéré en Perse. . . . Les lettrés persans prétendent que le choix des vers cités a été très mal fait. . . ."

[2] *Chūn shumār i sinīn i 'umr az thalāthīn ba-arba'īn rasīd* (fol. 3b[9] in the 1277 edition).

[3] It will be noticed that a MS. dated 1180/1767 exists at Paris. According to Blochet the date is certain.

[4] According to 'Abd al-Muqtadir the Bānkīpūr MS. contains no mention of " Firībī " and no date later than 1187. The biography of " Firībī " is in the Bombay edition of 1277, as well as in Bodleian 384 and the MS. or MSS. described by Bland.

[5] Ibn al-marḥūm Luṭf-'Alī 'Alī Muḥammad al-Shīrāzī maskinan al-Burūjirdī mauṭinan, described by Ethé as the author's son, but, if these words are the sole evidence, it is not decisive.

Berlin 658 (A.H. 1223/1808), 659 (A.H. 1235/1820), 660, **Rehatsek** p. 68 no. 3 (A.H. 1224/1809–10), **Brelvi-Dhabhar** p. xiii (A.H. 1226/1811), **Majlis** 322 (A.H. 1225/1810), 321, **Bānkīpūr** viii 702 (A.D. 1823), **Browne** Suppt. 1 (A.H. 1273/1856–7), **As'ad** 2507–9, **Āṣafīyah** i p. 316 no. 4, **Leningrad** Pub. Lib. (2 copies. See *Mélanges asiatiques* iii (St. Petersburg 1859) p. 728), Institut (Rosen 33. A.H. 1230/1814–15), Mus. Asiat. (see *Mélanges asiatiques* vi (1873) p. 127), Univ. 1027*, 1183* (Romaskewicz p. 3), 1230 (A.H. 1241/1825–6. Romaskewicz p. 19), **Mashhad** iii p. 157 (defective at end).

Editions: **Calcutta** 1249/1833*, **Bombay** 1277/1860° (a bad edition), 1299/1882°.

Extract (the *Shu'lah* only, i.e. the kings, princes and *amīrs*): *The Atesh Kedah, or Fire-temple, by Hajji Lutf Ali Beg, of Isfahan, now first edited . . . by N. Bland*, **London** 1844°* (40 pp.).

Descriptions: (**1**) *Account of the Atesh Kedah, a biographical work on the Persian Poets, by Hajji Lutf Ali Beg, of Ispahan, by N. Bland* (in *JRAS*. vii (1843) pp. 345–92), (**2**) Browne *Lit. Hist.* iv pp. 282–4.

List and epitome of the biographies: Bodleian coll. 262–93.

Turkish translation: **Istānbūl** 1259/1843 (see *Ency. Isl.*).

Abridgment (the poems rearranged under four headings, (1) *qaṣā'id*, (2) *muqaṭṭa'āt*, (3) *ghazalīyāt*, (4) *rubā'īyāt*, in the alphabetical order of the rhymes, with omission of the biographies): *Tadhkirah i Isḥāq*, by Isḥāq Bēg "'Udhrī" Bēgdilī Shāmlū, a younger brother of Luṭf-'Alī Bēg, who died at an early age in 1185/1771–2[1]: **Sipahsālār** ii pp. 469–72.

[Autobiography in *Ātash-kadah, Mijmarah* II, *Partau* 2 (passage translated by Bland, *JRAS*. 1843, pp. 381–3, and briefly summarised in Sprenger p. 161, Browne *Lit. Hist.* iv pp. 283–4 and Bodleian coll. 292–3), statements concerning his tribe, his ancestors and himself in the historical narrative (some 18 pp. in the 1277 edition) with which *Mijmarah* II begins (passage relating to the Bēgdilīs translated by Bland, *JRAS*. 1843, pp. 380–1); *Riyāḍ al-shu'arā'* (passage summarised by Bland, *JRAS*. 1848 p. 161 n. 2); *Tadhkirah i Muṣḥafī* (for a translated

[1] See *Ātash-kadah, Mijmarah* ii, *Partau* i (Bodleian 384 no. 813; *JRAS*. 1843 p. 384); *Anjuman i Khāqān*; *Majma' al-fuṣaḥā'* ii p. 345.

extract see Bānkīpūr iii pp. 219–20); *Ṣuḥuf i Ibrāhīm* (passage summarised in *JRAS.* 1848 p. 161); *Makhzan al-gharā'ib* no. 235; *Tadhkirah i Akhtar* (Berlin 664); *Tajribat al-aḥrār* (Rieu Suppt. 132); *Anjuman i Khāqān; Majma' al-fuṣaḥā'* ii pp. 73–5; *Sham' i anjuman* p. 65; Rieu i p. 375*a*; Bānkīpūr iii pp. 219–20, viii p. 135; Browne *Lit. Hist.* iv pp. 283–4; *Ency. Isl.* under Luṭf 'Alī Beg (Kramers).]

1171. Abu 'l-Ḥasan Amīr al-Dīn Aḥmad, known as (*al-mushtahir bi-*) **Amr Allāh Ilāhābādī,** travelled to 'Aẓīmābād (i.e. Patna) in Ṣafar 1192/1778 and there decided to write a *tadhkirah.* He composed it during his journey to Calcutta and finished it on 3 Jumādā II 1193/18 June 1779. On his return, as he tells us in his conclusion, he reached Lucknow in 1194/1780 and there he obtained much information about other poets but did not incorporate it in his work, since he felt obliged to confine himself to the poets of whom he had given a list in his introduction. The list referred to is dated 1197/1783. "Accordingly we have to suppose, that the preface and the work itself were composed A.H. 1193, but that the conclusion was added at the same time with the index of the poets, viz. A.H. 1197."

Tadhkirah i masarrat-afzā, alphabetically arranged notices of 247 Rēkhtah (i.e. Urdu) poets completed in 1193/1779 [1]: **Bodleian** 388 (possibly autograph).

1172. Maulawī Gulshan 'Alī **"Gulshan" Jaunpūrī,** the younger brother of the grammarian and mathematician Raushan 'Alī "Naẓmī" Anṣārī Jaunpurī, was born at Jaunpūr, went as a young man to Delhi, where he witnessed Nādir Shāh's sack of the city (A.H. 1151/1739) and met the poets "Ḥazīn" and "Wālih", to the latter of whom he attached himself. After "Wālih's" death in 1169/1756 he returned home, but soon went in search of employment to Shamsābād (in the Farrukhābād District of the United Provinces), where Saiyid Basālat Jahān

[1] "The careful biographical information, along with the many and extensive extracts from Dîwâns, renders the work very valuable indeed. There occur many poets whom Garcin de Tassy (in his Histoire de la Littérature Hindouie et Hindoustanie) does not even mention, and the very useful list of Rêkhta poets given by A. Sprenger (in his Catalogue, p. 195 sq.) might be considerably enriched from this source with valuable biographical information."

(d. 1176/1762–3) became his patron. He was already over sixty years of age when he wrote his autobiography. According to the *Tajallī i nūr* he died in 1200/1786 and was the author of a Persian *dīwān* and other works including treatises on *raml*, *jafr*, prosody and *mu'ammā*.

Ṣūrat i ḥāl, an autobiography in *mathnawī* verse: **Rieu** ii 715*a* (18th cent.).

[*Makhzan al-gharā'ib* no. 2196; *Tajallī i nūr* II pp. 20–21.]

1173. For the *Ḥadīqat al-aqālīm*, which was written mainly in 1192/1778–1196/1782 by Murtaḍā Ḥusain Bilgrāmī and which contains biographies of poets and other celebrities, see pp. 142–3 *supra*.

1174. **Mōhan La'l "Anīs"** Kāyat'h [1] was the son of Rāy Tūlā (?) Rām, *Qānūngō* of the *parganah* of Gōpāmau in Oudh. In the art of poetry he was a pupil of Mirzā M. Fākhir "Makīn" Dihlawī.[2] He had been resident at Lucknow for more than fifty years when he wrote the first edition of his *Anīs al-aḥibbā'* [in 1197/1783], and for more than ninety years when he completed the second edition [in 1235/1819–20]. The work was undertaken at the request of Mahārājah Tikēt Rāy,[3] who had been delighted with the *Tadhkirah* of "Ḥazīn" (for which see p. 848 *supra*) and had asked "Anīs" to write a counterpart to it on Indian poets. For his *dīwān* (MS. at Rāmpūr) see *OCM*. VI/4 (Aug. 1930) p. 75.

Anīs al-aḥibbā', notices of "Makīn" and the poets of his school completed in 1197/1783 and divided into an *Iftitāḥ* (on "Makīn's" teacher, Mirzā 'Aẓīmā-yi "Iksīr" i Iṣfahānī),[4] a *Fatḥ al-bāb* (on "Makīn"), a *Faṣl* (on 31 Muslim pupils of

[1] I.e. Kāyast'h, the name of the Hindū caste of clerks and accountants.

[2] Born at Delhi, migrated to Lucknow in 1173/1759–60, lived for some time at Faiḍābād and at Ilāhābād, where the Emperor Shāh-'Ālam became his pupil in the art of poetry, died at Lucknow in 1221/1806–7. See Rieu i 376*a*, Bānkīpūr iii pp. 258–9, Sprenger p. 481, *Ṣuḥuf i Ibrāhīm* (penultimate biography under *Mīm*), *Khulāṣat al-afkār* no. 475, *Makhzan al-gharā'ib* no. 2699, *Tadhkirah i dil-gushā* (Berlin p. 672 no. 112).

[3] *Dīwān* to Sarfarāz al-Daulah Mirzā Ḥasan Riḍā Khān, who was *Nā'ib* of Āṣaf al-Daulah, the Nawwāb-Wazīr of Oudh. Tikēt Rāy died in 1215/1800–1.

[4] Went to Delhi [presumably from Persia] in Muḥammad Shāh's reign, and was afterwards invited by Nawwāb Mahābat-Jang (for whom see p. 717 *supra*) to Murshidābād, where he died in the time of Sirāj al-Daulah (A.H. 1169–70).

" Makīn "), a *Fāṣilah* (on six Hindū pupils), an *Ikhtitām* (on five Muslim pupils of " Makīn's " pupils) and a *Ḥusn i khātimah* (on six Hindū pupils of his pupils) : Sprenger no. 33, **Rieu** i 376*a* (18th cent., apparently written or revised by the author), 377*a* (an enlarged recension begun in 1209/1794–5, completed in 1235/1819–20 and containing 50 notices in the *Faṣl*, 12 in the *Fāṣilah*, 11 in the *Ikhtitām* and 18 in the *Ḥusn i khātimah*. A.H. 1237/1822), **Berlin** 662 (A.H. 1218/1803–4), **Bānkīpūr** viii 703 (19th cent.).

List of the poets in the 1st edition : Sprenger pp. 162–3.

[Autobiography in *Anīs al-aḥibbā'* at end of *Fāṣilah*.]

1175. **Ghulām-Hamadānī " Muṣḥafī "** b. Walī-Muḥammad belonged to a family connected with Amrōhah (20 miles N. of Moradabad), but, if not born at Lucknow,[1] he lived there in early, or comparatively early, life. In, or about, 1190/1776 he went to Delhi where he spent twelve years cultivating Rēkhtah (i.e. Urdu) poetry, which he found to be in vogue there, though his early predilection had been for Persian poetry. Eminent poets of the time used to forgather at his house. On returning to Lucknow he found a patron in Prince Sulaimān-Shukōh,[2] the second son of Shāh-'Ālam II and brother of Akbar-Shāh. He died in, or about, 1240/1824-5 at an advanced age. He was a facile writer of verse, and composed several *dīwāns*. In the *Tadhkirah i Hindī* he mentions three [3] in Persian and, apparently, four in Urdu. According to Sprenger, who cites the *Gulshan i bī-khār*, he subsequently wrote three more in Urdu. A volume of selections from four of his Urdu *dīwāns* was published

[1] According to Rieu " he was born in Lucknow ". Garcin de Tassy, citing the *Tadhkirah i Hindī* and paraphrasing doubtless the same words as Rieu, says " Mashafi habita d'abord Lakhnau ". According to Saksena he was born at Akbarpūr. There is one place of that name near Fyzabad and another near Cawnpore. Shēftah (cited by Garcin ii p. 286) says that he was born at Delhi : Grahame Bailey that he " belonged to Amrohā, but went as a young man to Delhi, which he considered his native place ".

[2] See Garcin de Tassy iii pp. 171–3, Beale *Oriental biographical dictionary* p. 390.

[3] Four according to Sprenger, who speaks of " a rough copy of a Persian Dywán in the style of Jalál Asyr, and one in the style of Nácir 'alyy ", whereas 'Abd al-Muqtadir regards these two as a single *dīwān* " in the style of Jalâl Asîr and Nâṣir 'Alî ".

at [Lucknow] in 1296/1879°. He enjoyed a considerable reputation in his time and he had many pupils.

(1) *'Iqd i Thuraiyā*, a *tadhkirah* written at Delhi in 1199/1784–5 at the suggestion of Mīrzā "Qatīl" and devoted to 133 Persian poets who flourished, chiefly in India, from the time of Muḥammad Shāh (A.H. 1131–61/1719–48) to that of Shāh-'Ālam (A.H. 1173/1759–1221/1806): **Rieu** i 377*b* (late 18th cent.), **Bānkīpūr** viii 709 (A.H. 1244/1829).

Edition: **Aurangābād** date ? (ed. 'Abd al-Ḥaqq. Anjuman i Taraqqī i Urdū. See a review in *OCM*. XI/4 (Aug. 1935) pp. 119–20).

(2) *Tadhkirah i Hindī*, notices of about 350 Rēkhtah (i.e. Urdu) poets, from the time of Muḥammad Shāh to that of the author, written at the request of Mīr Mustaḥsan "Khalīq" and completed in 1209/1794–5: Sprenger no. 47 = **Ivanow** 1st Suppt. 769 (A.H. 1219/1804), **Rieu** i 378*a* (late 18th cent.), **Bānkīpūr** viii 710 (A.H. 1238/1822).

Edition: **Aurangābād** date ? (ed. 'Abd al-Ḥaqq. Anjuman i Taraqqī i Urdū. See a review in *OCM*. XI/4 (Aug. 1935) pp. 131–4).

(3) *Tadhkirah i Fārisī*, written in 1236/1820–1, notices of modern Urdu and Persian poets of India, with extracts, nearly all Urdū, from their works: **Bānkīpūr** viii 711 (A.H. 1237/1821–2).

(4) *Riyāḍ al-fuṣaḥā'*, brief notices of about 325 contemporary Urdu poets.

Edition: **Aurangābād** date ? (ed. 'Abd al-Ḥaqq. Pp. 378. Anjuman i Taraqqī i Urdū, no. 77. See a review in *OCM*. XI/4 (Aug. 1935) pp. 134–5).

[Autobiography in the *Tadhkirah i Hindī* (summarised by Rieu, i p. 377*b*, Sprenger, pp. 182–3, and Garcin de Tassy, ii pp. 284–5); *Tadhkirah i 'Ishqī; Majmū'ah i naghz* ii pp. 188–95; *Gulshan i bī-khār; Natā'ij al-afkār* p. 420; Sprenger pp. 182–3, 625; Garcin de Tassy ii pp. 283–8 (under Mashafi); Rieu i p. 377*b*; M. Ḥusain "Āzād" *Āb i ḥayāt* (in Urdu), several editions; Beale *Oriental biographical dictionary* p. 246 (under Mas-hafi): Bānkīpūr viii pp. 149–50; Blumhardt *Catalogue of Hindustani manuscripts in the . . . India Office* p. 125; *Ency. Isl.*

under Maṣḥafī ; Saksēna *History of Urdu literature* pp. 90–3 : T. Grahame Bailey *History of Urdu literature* p. 53.]

1176. Nawwāb **'Alī Ibrāhīm Khān** " Khalīl " died in 1208/ 1793–4 (see pp. 700–2 *supra*).

(1) *Gulzār i Ibrāhīm*, notices of about 300 Rēkhtah (i.e. Urdū) poets completed in 1198/1784 : Sprenger 45, **Rieu** i 375*b* (18th cent.), iii 1069*a* (19th cent.), **Bānkīpūr** viii 707 (A.H. 1220/1806), **Ivanow** 1st Suppt. 768 (19th cent.), **Bodleian** 389.

Urdu translation made at the request of J. B. Gilchrist : **Browne** Suppt. 1084 (Corpus 159[1]).

(2) *Khulāṣat al-kalām*, notices of 78 writers of *mathnawīs* completed in 1198/1784 : **Lindesiana** p. 177 no. 318 (circ. A.D. 1790), **Bodleian** 390 (A.H. 1246/1831), **Bānkīpūr** viii 704–5 (lacks *dāl-ḍād*. 19th cent.), 706 (lacks the poetical extracts. 19th cent.).

Lists and epitomes of the biographies : (**1**) Bodleian coll. 295–302, (**2**) Bānkīpūr viii pp. 138–46 (lacking *dāl-ḍād*).

Description : *On the earliest Persian Biography of Poets . . . By N. Bland* (in *JRAS*. ix (1848)) pp. 158–9, 161–3.

(3) *Ṣuḥuf i Ibrāhīm*, notices of about 3278 [1] ancient and modern poets completed at Benares in 1205/1790 : **Berlin** 663, **Bānkīpūr** viii 708 (defective, ending with " 'Urfī ". 19th cent.).

Description : *On the earliest Persian Biography of Poets . . . By N. Bland* (in *JRAS*. ix (1848)) pp. 158–61, 163–4.

List of the biographies : Berlin pp. 628–67.

1177. Maulawī M. **Qudrat Allāh " Shauq "** b. Sh. Qabūl Muḥammad has already been mentioned (p. 143 *supra*) as the author of the general history *Jām i jahān-numā* begun in 1191/1777 and completed in 1199/1785.

(1) *Ṭabaqāt al-shu'arā'*, : **Āṣafiyah** i p. 322 no. 40 (A.H. 1210/1795–6).

(2) *Takmilat al-shu'arā' Jām i Jamshīd*, an alphabetically arranged *tadhkirah* of ancient and modern poets written

[1] Apparently the largest number of biographies in any *tadhkirah* yet described. The *Makhzan al-gharā'ib* (for which see p. 881 *infra*) contains **3148**.

after the *Jām i jahān-numā*: **Rāmpūr** (A.H. 1218/1803–4. See *OCM*. VII/1 (Nov. 1930) pp. 68–9 and Nadhīr Aḥmad 83).

1178. Mirzā **Abū Ṭālib Khān** Tabrīzī **Iṣfahānī**, the author of the *Lubb al-siyar u jahān-numā* (see p. 145 *supra*) and the *Tafḍīḥ al-ghāfilīn* (p. 705 *supra*), died at Lucknow in 1220/1805-6 or 1221/1806-7.

(1) *Khulāṣat al-afkār*, notices of about 494 ancient and modern poets written in 1206–7/1791–3 on the basis of material collected during 25 years, divided into a *muqaddimah* (on Persian poetry and the rules to be observed in compiling *tadhkirahs*), 28 *ḥadīqahs* (one for each letter, under which the poets are arranged chronologically),[1] a *dhail* (160 supplementary notices) and a *khātimah* (on the author himself and 23 poets personally known to him) and followed in most manuscripts by five treatises, viz. (1) *Risālah dar 'ilm i akhlāq*, (2) *Muṣṭalaḥāt i mūsīqī*, (3) *dar 'ilm i 'arūḍ u qāfiyah*, (4) *Mukhtaṣar dar funūn i khamsah i ṭibb*, (5) *Lubb al-siyar u jahān-numā* (see p. 145 *supra*)[2]: Sprenger no. 34 (where parts of the preface are quoted), **Ethé** 696 (transcribed by G. Swinton[3] from an autograph and corrected by the author in 1804), 697 (lacks the first four of the appended treatises), **Bodleian** 391 (A.H. 1210/1796), **Rieu** i 378*b* (very imperfect. Early 19th cent.), iii 1003*b* (poetical extracts only. Circ. A.D. 1850), Suppt. 116 (early 19th cent.), **Bānkīpūr** viii 712 (lacks the last three of the appended treatises. 19th cent.).

Description: *On the earliest Persian Biography of Poets . . . By N. Bland* (in *JRAS*. ix (1848)) pp. 153–8, where the *muqaddimah* is summarised.

List and epitome of the biographies: Bodleian coll. 302–15.

(2) *Masīr i Ṭālibī fī bilād i Afranjī*, a narrative completed in 1219/1804–5 from rough notes of a journey to Europe from 1 Ramaḍān 1213/6 Feb. 1799, when he left Calcutta, to 15 Rabī' I 1218/5 July 1803, when he reached Calcutta on his

[1] In his selections the compiler devotes special attention to *mathnawīs*, "from which he gives extracts of considerable extent" (Rieu i p. 379*b*).

[2] The third *bāb* of the *Lubb al-siyar* contains biographies of celebrities including poets.

[3] G. Swinton studied Persian under Abū Ṭālib Khān in London previously to his appointment to the Bengal Civil Service (see Ethé col. 357 ult.).

return : **Rieu** i 384*a* (A.H. 1221/1806),[1] 384*b* (vol. iii. Early 19th cent.), **Bodleian** 1855 (A.H. 1222/1807–8), **Blochet** i 647 (A.H. 1228/1813), **'Alīgaṛh** Subḥ. MSS. p. 57 no. 1, **Āṣafiyah** ii p. 836 no. 29, **Bānkīpūr** vii 627, **Browne** Pers. Cat. 116 (less than half the work), **Edinburgh** 90, **Ethé** 2727, **Madras** 449, **R.A.S.** P. 177.

Edition : *Masīrī* [*sic*] *Ṭālibī. Travels in Europe and Asia, by Mírza Abu Taleb Khán. Published and edited by his son Mírza Hasein* [*sic*] *Âli and Mír Kudrut Âli.* **Calcutta** 1812°* (pp. 865).

English translation : *The Travels of Mirza Abu Taleb Khan, in Asia, Africa, and Europe, during the years* 1799, 1800, 1801, 1802, *and* 1803. *Written by himself, in the Persian language. Translated by C. Stewart.* **London** (Broxbourne printed) 1810° (2 vols.) ; *Second edition, with additions,* **London** (Broxbourne printed) 1814°* (3 vols.).

French translations (from the English) (1) *Voyages de Mirza Abu Taleb Khan . . . Suivis d'une réfutation des idées qu'on a en Europe sur la liberté des femmes d'Asie ; par le même auteur. Le tout traduit du persan en anglais, par C. Stewart . . . et traduit de l'anglais en français par M. J. C. J.* [2] **Paris** 1811°. (2) *Voyages de Mirza Abou Taleb Khan . . . trad. de l'anglais en français par Ch. Malo.* **Paris** 1819 (see Zenker i no. 1025).

German translation (from the French of J. C. J.) : *Reise des Mirza Abu Taleb Khan durch Asien, Afrika, und Europa, in den Jahren* 1799, 1800, 1801, 1802 *und* 1803. *Nebst einer Widerlegung der Begriffe, welche man in Europa von der Freyheit der asiatischen Weiber hat. Aus dem Französischen.* **Vienna** 1813°.

Urdu translation by Mīrzā 'Alī Riḍā " Maḥzūn " Murādābādī : *Masīr i Ṭālibī,* **Murādābād** 1904* (Pt. 1 only ?).

Abridgment by David Macfarlane (beg. *Ba'd i ḥamd i mutakāthir*) : **Berlin** 358.

Editions of the abridgment : *The Travels of Mirza Aboo Talib Khan. In the Persian language. Abridged by David Macfarlane* (*Masīr i Ṭālibī*). **Calcutta** 1827°* (pp. 157), 1836* (pp. 132).

[1] This MS., from which Major C. Stewart made his translation, is described by him in a note on a fly-leaf as " very superior to the printed edition ".

[2] I.e. Hendrik Jansen according to Edwards, col. 312.

1179. Sh. M. Wajīh [al-Dīn][1] **"'Ishqi"** b. Ghulām-Ḥusain "Mujrim" 'Aẓīmābādī was for ten years *Taḥṣīldār* at Kharwar[2] and subsequently went to Dacca. In 1224/1809–10 he was still alive, but his sight was much impaired. For his *dīwān* see Sprenger 286.

Tadhkirah i 'Ishqī, short alphabetically arranged notices of 439 Rēkhtah (i.e. Urdū) poets, written probably in, or soon after, 1215/1800–1: Sprenger 48 = **Bodleian** 393 (n.d.).

[*Tadhkirah i 'Ishqī* no. 272, *Nishtar i 'ishq*; Garcin de Tassy ii p. 47; Sprenger pp. 183 and 441; *Nigāristān i sukhan* p. 65.]

1180. **Rafī' al-Dīn Qandahārī** died in 1241/1825–6.

Naubahār, notices of 57 ancient and modern poets written in 1216/1801–2: MS. in the possession of Ḥakīm S. Shams Allāh Qādirī (see *OCM*. V/4 (Aug. 1929) p. 113).

1181. Sh. **Aḥmad 'Alī Khān**[3] Hāshimī **Sandīlawī** (or Sandīlī)[4] b. Sh. Ghulām-Muḥammad b. Maulawī M. Ḥājjī must have been born about 1163/1750, since according to his own statement in the preface he was in his fifty-fifth year when he compiled the *Makhzan al-gharā'ib*, a work in which 1217/1802–3 is mentioned[5] as the current year and which was completed in 1218/1803–4. Having been recommended to Nawwāb Dhū 'l-Faqār al-Daulah Mirzā Najaf Khān Bahādur Ghālib-Jang[6] by Nawwāb 'Izzat al-Daulah Mirzā Ḥasan Suhrāb-Jang,[7] he was enrolled through the former's influence in the *risālah* of Shāh-'Ālam (reigned 1173/1759–1221/1806). After Nawwāb

[1] The proper name of "Mujrim's" son is given as Miyān Raḥmat Allāh by Garcin (and, presumably on Garcin's authority, by Ethé in the Bodleian catalogue), but Miyān Raḥmat Allāh "'Ishqī" (Sprenger p. 241, *Majmū'ah i naghz* II p. 396[2]) seems to be a different person.

[2] Presumably K'harwar, described in the *Jāmi' al-lughāt* (an Urdu dictionary) as a village in the Midnāpūr District [of Bengal].

[3] So in the contemporary colophon quoted in Bānkīpūr viii p. 155.

[4] Evidently a different person from Sh. Aḥmad 'Alī "Khādim" Sand'hīlawī [so], author of an anthology entitled *Anīs al-'ushshāq*, if Sprenger is right in saying (p. 147) that the latter "flourished in India in 1165" [P.S. Cf. *Mai-khānah* ed. M. Shafī' p. 347 n. 3]. Sandīlah is a town 32 miles N.W. of Lucknow.

[5] In the notice of Ghulām-Fakhr al-Dīn Khān "Ḥairat" (see Bānkīpūr viii p. 154[1]).

[6] For Nawwāb Najaf Khān see p. 474 *supra*, Beale *Oriental biographical dictionary* under Najaf Khān, etc.

[7] Son of Mirzā M. Muḥsin, the elder brother of Nawwāb Ṣafdar-Jang. The latter was *Nawwāb-Wazīr* of Awad'h ("Oudh") and died in 1167/1754.

Najaf Khān's death [in 1196/1782], "which was followed by anarchy and a massacre of the inhabitants of Dihlî" (Bānkīpūr viii p. 154), Aḥmad 'Alī began to cultivate the society of Persians from Khurāsān, 'Irāq and Fārs and to collect Persian poems. Encouraged by his master, Mirzā M. Ḥasan "Qatīl", he decided to compile a *tadhkirah*.

Makhzan al-gharā'ib, alphabetically arranged notices of 3148[1] ancient and modern poets completed in 1218/1803–4 at Delhi: Sprenger no. 27 (Faraḥ-bakhsh), **Bodleian** 395 (A.H. 1224/1809), **Bānkīpūr** viii 713–14 (A.H. 1224/1809), **Rieu** Suppt. 117 (1st half of 19th cent.), iii 1015*b* (34 notices only. A.D. 1850–1), **Lahore** Prof. Maḥmūd Shērānī's private library (see 'Abd al-Nabī *Mai-khānah*, editor's introduction, penultimate page), **A'ẓamgaṛh** Dār al-Muṣannifīn (see *OCM*. III/2 (Feb. 1927) p. 36 n.).

List of the biographies (with epitomes of some): Bodleian coll. 317–96.

[*Makhzan al-gharā'ib*, preface.]

1182. For the *Mir'āt i āftāb-numā* of Nawwāb Shāh-nawāz Khān Dihlawī, which was written in 1218 and which contains biographies of Ṣūfīs, '*ulamā*', poets and calligraphists, see p. 146 *supra*.

1183. **Bhagwān Dās "Hindī"**[2] (originally "Bismil") was the son of Dalpat Dās b. Harbans Rāy, a Kāyast'h[3] who held high offices at Lucknow. He was born in 1164/1750–1 and received his early education from Maulawī S. Yūsuf Sahāranpūrī. In the art of poetry his instructor was Mirzā M. Fākhir "Makīn" Dihlawī, who, as has already been mentioned (p. 874 n. 2 *supra*), migrated to Lucknow in 1173/1759–60 and died there in 1221/1806–7. "In his youth, he held the post of Mîr Baḥr" (Bānkīpūr viii p. 156[28]), and subsequently, in the time of Āṣaf al-Daulah [1189–1212/1775–97], became *Dīwān* to Rājah Nid'hī [?] Sing'h Bahādur. After the Rājah's death he entered the service of

[1] Of the *tadhkirahs* hitherto described only the *Suḥuf i Ibrāhīm* (for which see p. 877 *supra*) contains a larger number of biographies.

[2] In the *Anīs al-aḥibbā'* (A.H. 1197/1783) he is called Bhagwān Dās "Bismil". In the Bānkīpūr Catalogue Hindī is not expressly said to be a *takhalluṣ*, but that is doubtless implied by the statement that "he at first adopted the *takhalluṣ* Bismil". Moreover, his autobiography, to judge from its position (fol. 93*b* in a volume of 102 foll.), must be under "Hindī".

[3] For this word see p. 874 n. 1 *supra*.

Rājah Paṭar [?] Chand Bahādur and later that of Mahārājah Tikēt Rāy [who died in 1215/1800–1. See p. 874 n. 3 *supra*]. He was the author of (1) *Silsilat al-maḥabbat*, a *mathnawī* modelled on "Jāmī's" *Silsilat al-dhahab*, (2) *Maẓhar al-anwār*, a *mathnawī* modelled on "Niẓāmī's" *Makhzan al-asrār*, (3) *Mihr i ḍiyā*, a *mathnawī* modelled on "Jāmī's" *Yūsuf u Zalīkhā*, (4) *Shauqīyah*, a *dīwān*, (5) *Dhauqīyah*, another *dīwān*, (6) *Tadhkirah i Ḥadīqah i Hindī*, on ancient and modern Indian poets to the year 1200/1786, (7) *Sawāniḥ al-nubuwwah*, an account of the Prophet and the Twelve Imāms written at the request of S. Khairāt 'Alī, and

(8) *Safīnah i Hindī*, alphabetically arranged notices of Persian poets who flourished in India from the accession of Shāh-'Ālam in 1173/1759 to 1219/1804–5, the date of completion: **Bānkīpūr** viii 715 (A.H. 1220/1805).

[Autobiography in *Safīnah i Hindī*; *Anīs al-aḥibbā'*.]

1184. For the *Zīnat al-tawārīkh*, a general history to 1221/1806–7 by M. Raḍī [not Riḍā apparently] Tabrīzī and 'Abd al-Karīm Ishtihārdī, which contains notices of poets and other celebrities at the end of *Pīrāyah* i, see p. 147 *supra*.

1185. S. Abū 'l-Qāsim, commonly called (*'urf*) Mīr **Qudrat Allāh** Qādirī (*Majmū'ah i naghz* ii p. 92 ult.), who used the *takhalluṣ* "**Qāsim**", studied medicine under Ḥakīm M. Sharīf Khān and poetics under Hidāyat Allāh Khān "Hidāyat" [of Delhi. See Sprenger p. 238]. In his brief account of himself he says that he had written [doubtless in Urdū] a *dīwān* of about 7000 verses and two *mathnawīs*, the first of 3500 verses on the story of the *Mi'rāj* in the metre of Jalāl al-Dīn Rūmī's *Mathnawī*, and the second of about 5200 verses on the miracles of 'Abd al-Qādir al-Jīlānī in the metre of the *Būstān*.

Majmū'ah i naghz[1] (a chronogram = 1221/1806–7, the date of completion), or (*Tadhkirah i Qāsim*), alphabetically arranged notices of about 800 Urdū poets: Sprenger no. 52, **Lahore** Panjāb Univ. Lib. (probably autograph. See *OCM.* III/1 (Nov. 1926) pp. 77–8 and the editor's introduction to the

[1] This is only the first of several chronograms given in the preface and is not stated to be the title, but it may now be accepted as such.

Lahore edition), **Bānkīpūr** Suppt. i 1789 (A.D. 1822), **Berlin** 669, **Ethé** 2849.

Edition: *Majmu'a-i-Naghz, or Biographical notices of Urdu poets by Hakim Abu'l Qasim Mir Qudratullah Qasim. Edited by Hafiz Mahmud Shairani*, **Lahore** 1933 (Panjāb University Oriental Publications).

[Autobiography in *Majmū'ah i naghz* ii pp. 92–3 (summarised in Sprenger p. 186 and Bānkīpūr Suppt. i p. 65); Garcin de Tassy i pp. 353–6 (under Cacim); *Mīr Qudrat Allāh Khān "Qāsim" aur un kī tālīf Majmū'ah i naghz*, by Ḥāfiẓ Maḥmūd Shērānī (in *OCM*. IX/1 (Nov. 1932) pp. 28–51); the editor's Urdu introduction to the Lahore edition.]

1186. Nawwāb A'ẓam al-Daulah Mīr **M. Khān "Sarwar"** b. Nawwāb Abū 'l-Qāsim Muẓaffar-Jang was the author of a large Urdu *dīwān*. He died in 1250/1834–5.

Tadhkirah i Sarwar, notices of about 1200 Urdu poets completed, according to a statement at the end (see Ethé 2850), on 9 Muḥarram 1222/19 March 1807, though other dates are indicated by various chronograms, including *'Umdah i muntakhabah* (1216), which Sprenger supposed to be the title: Sprenger no. 51, **Blochet** ii 1159 (A.D. 1829), **Ethé** 2850.

[*Gulshan i bī-khār*; Sprenger pp. 185, 285; Garcin de Tassy iii pp. 64–5.]

1187. Sh. **Ghulām-Muḥyī 'l-Dīn "'Ishq"** (originally "Mubtalā") Qurashī Mēraṭ'hī was the son of Sh. Ni'mat Allāh "Ni'amī", whose bulky Persian *dīwān* he helped to arrange at the age of twelve. Having thus acquired a taste for poetry, he wrote a *dīwān* in which he used the *takhalluṣ* "Mubtalā". Subsequently he devoted much of his time to archery, without however neglecting his studies. "When Sháh 'álam came from Patna [or rather, from Ilāhābād ?] to Dilly [in 1185/1771] he gained the friendship of one of his courtiers, whose title was Nawáb Najaf Khán, and his name Ibráhym Bég, and his takhalluç, Alam, he was induced by him to write another Dywán in which he used the takhalluç of 'ishq" [1] (Sprenger p. 187), and a Persian

[1] A [Persian] *Dīwān i 'Ishq* by Khalīfah Ghulām-Muḥyī 'l-Dīn 'Ishq is preserved at Ḥaidarābād (Āṣafīyah i p. 728 no. 483).

mathnawī, *Fusūn i 'ishq*, telling the story of Shāh-Rukh and Māh-Rukh. He wrote also an *inshā'* entitled *Chahār daftar i sharq*,[1] as well as *Nuskhah i sarā'ir*, on chronograms, *Bihār al-tashrīh*, composed in 1220/1805–6, and *Ashi''āt* [*sic ?*] *al-'ishq*, on Ṣūfism, composed in the same year.

(1) ***Bāgh i gulhā-yi ḥusn*** (a chronogram = 1187/1773), or ***Majmū'ah i 'ishq***, or ***Chār chaman***, "a Persian Tadzkirah," which "fills about 1280 pages" (Sprenger): **'Alīgaṛh** Subḥ. MSS. p. 53 no. 8 (A.H. 1187, autograph).

(2) ***Ṭabaqāt i sukhun*** (a chronogram = 1222), biographies, which "have the advantage of being original" (Sprenger), divided into two *ṭabaqahs* ((1) Rēkhtah, i.e. Urdū, poets, 196 in number, (2) Persian poets of the same period): Sprenger no. 53 = **Berlin** 670 (lacking *Ṭabaqah* ii).

List of the poets in *Ṭabaqah* i: Berlin pp. 675–6.

[Autobiographical information in the *Ṭabaqāt i sukhun* under "'Ishq" and "Mubtalā" (summarised in Sprenger p. 187); *Majmū'ah i naghz* ii p. 401.]

1188. **M. Ṣādiq "Humā"** Marwazī has already been mentioned (pp. 335–6 *supra*) as the author of the *Tārīkh i jahān-ārā*.

Zīnat al-madā'iḥ, a collection of poems composed in praise of Fatḥ-'Alī Shāh from the first to the seventh year of his reign (A.H. 1218/1803–4) with a sequel (vol. ii) compiled in 1223/1808, together with notices of their authors: **Rieu** Suppt. 118, 119 (vol. ii), **Majlis** 397, 398 (A.H. 1223/1808–9).

Lists of the poets: Rieu Suppt. 118–19.

1189. Mīrzā **M. 'Alī Kātib i Ṣafawī** was first employed by Shah-zādah Abū 'l-Naṣr Mīrzā M. Sulaimān-Shukōh, Shāh-'Ālam's son,[2] to copy Persian and Urdū *dīwāns* and subsequently became *Muṣāḥib* and *Kātib*[3] to Sulṭān Abū 'l-Fatḥ Muḥammad "Ṭulū'ī" Ṣafawī [the last (nominal) king of the Ṣafawī dynasty, who was proclaimed at Ṭihrān in 1200/1785 by Āqā Muḥammad,

[1] Or *shauq* ? This title is erroneously said by Sprenger to be a chronogram for 1199.

[2] Cf. p. 875[20] *supra*.

[3] *Īn dharrah i khāksār . . . dar sarkār i . . . Sulṭān M. i Ṣafawī al-mutakhalliṣ Ṭulū'ī . . . dar muṣāḥabat u shughl i sharīf i kitābat būd* (quoted by Nadhīr Aḥmad from the preface to the *Tadhkirah i Kātib*).

fled to Sind in 1205/1790–1 and settled at Lucknow in 1210/1795–6 (cf. pp. 319–20 *supra*)].

Ta<u>dh</u>kirah i Kātib, alphabetically arranged notices of poets selected from the *Ma<u>kh</u>zan al-<u>gh</u>arā'ib* (cf. p. 881 *supra*) and completed in 1225/1810 : **Rampūr** (see Na<u>dh</u>īr Aḥmad no. 81 and a more detailed description by M. <u>Sh</u>ajā'at 'Alī <u>Kh</u>ān in *OCM*. VI/2 (Feb. 1930) pp. 108–11).

1190. **Aḥmad Bēg "A<u>kh</u>tar"** Gurjī is one of the poets of Fatḥ-'Alī <u>Sh</u>āh's time included in Bahman Mīrzā's *Ta<u>dh</u>kirah i Muḥammad-<u>Sh</u>āhī* (Rieu Suppt. 124 fol. 182*b*) and 'Alī Akbar <u>Sh</u>īrāzī's *Ta<u>dh</u>kirah i dil-gu<u>sh</u>ā* (Berlin p. 671 no. 45).

Ta<u>dh</u>kirah i A<u>kh</u>tar, alphabetically arranged notices of contemporary poets written in 1227/1812–13 : **Berlin** 664 (not later than 1264/1847).

List of the poets : Berlin pp. 665–7.

1191. Mun<u>sh</u>ī **<u>Dh</u>ū 'l-Faqār 'Alī <u>Kh</u>ān "Mast"** wrote in addition to the *Riyāḍ al-wifāq* several other works, of which the titles and subjects are mentioned by Sprenger.

Riyāḍ al-wifāq (a chronogram = 1229/1814), notices of 144 poets, mainly contemporaries of the author connected with Calcutta and Benares (at the latter of which places the work seems to have been compiled) : Sprenger no. 36 = **Berlin** 665.

List and epitome of the biographies : Sprenger pp. 165–72.

1192. For the *Zubdat al-<u>gh</u>arā'ib*, which was written in 1231/1816 by M. Riḍā "Najm" Ṭabāṭabā and of which the fifth volume contains biographies of philosophers, saints and poets, see p. 148 *supra*.

1193. Āqā **Ḥusain-Qulī <u>Kh</u>ān "'Ā<u>sh</u>iqī"**[1] **'Aẓīmābādī** b. Āqā 'Alī <u>Kh</u>ān <u>Sh</u>āhjahānābādī was born at Patnah in 1194/1780. In the course of several visits to Akbarābād and <u>Sh</u>āhjahānābād he met many learned men, from whom he collected numerous poems. In 1223/1808 he was shown a copy of "Wālih's" *ta<u>dh</u>kirah* (for which see p. 832 *supra*) by Mīr M. Ja'far "Masīḥ" Barēlawī, the *Taḥṣīl-dār* of Atraulī [in the 'Alīgaṛh District]

[1] The statement that his *ta<u>kh</u>alluṣ* was "'I<u>sh</u>q" (Sprenger p. 644, Bānkīpūr VIII p. 157) seems to be erroneous.

and, finding the selections contained in it uninteresting,[1] he decided to write a *tadhkirah* himself [2] and spent eight years in collecting material. According to Sprenger's summary of his biography in the *Gulshan i bī-khār* (under " 'Āshiqī " if Sprenger is correct) " it is said that he now, 1252, resides at Lucnow, he is the author of the نشتر عشق in Persian, but as he does not know Arabic he fell into many errors " (Sprenger p. 205).

Nishtar i 'ishq, alphabetically arranged notices of 1470 ancient and modern poets with copious extracts, mainly *ghazals* and *rubā'īs*, begun in 1224/1809–10 and completed in Rajab 1233/1818 [3]: Sprenger no. 732, **Rāmpūr** (A.H. 1236/1820–1. See Nadhīr Aḥmad no. 97), **Bānkīpūr** viii 716–17 (late 19th cent.), **Lahore** Panjāb Univ. Lib. (slightly defective. See *OCM*. III/1 (Nov. 1926) p. 76 and *Mai-khānah* ed. M. Shafī' p. *bā lām*).

[*Gulshan i bī-khār* (see Sprenger p. 205); Garcin de Tassy I p. 235 (under 'Aschiqui); *Nigāristān i sukhun* p. 59 (under " 'Āshiqī "); *Ṣubḥ i gulshan* p. 271 (under " 'Āshiqī ").]

1194. **M. Fāḍil Khān** [4] **" Rāwī "** Bāyandurī **Garrūsī** was born in the district of Garrūs in Dhū 'l-Ḥijjah 1198/Oct.–Nov. 1784. After his father's death in 1214/1799–1800 he left his birthplace and pursued his studies in 'Irāq and elsewhere, eventually reaching Ṭihrān, where he studied the art of poetry under the Malik al-Shu'arā', Fatḥ-'Alī Khān " Ṣabā " Kāshānī (for whom see pp. 333–4 *supra*). Impressed by his abilities, which included a keen intelligence and a retentive memory, " Ṣabā " presented him to Fatḥ-'Alī Shāh, who appointed him Reciter of Panegyrics [5] at court. Subsequently he became Chief Herald [6]

[1] Abū Ṭālib Khān Tabrīzī Iṣfahānī, on the other hand, regarded " Wālih's " *tadhkirah* as " abounding in beautiful poetry " and was greatly charmed with it (see *JRAS*. 1848 p. 155, where the preface to his *Khulāṣat al-afkār* is summarized).

[2] According to Sprenger " he undertook it at the request of Mr. Elliot " and completed it in 1230. Perhaps Sprenger's copy was an early edition with a preface specially written for Mr. Elliot.

[3] See the previous note.

[4] So *Majma' al-fuṣaḥā'*.

[5] *Rāwī i madāyiḥ i Khāqānī shud* (*Majma' al-fuṣaḥā'*).

[6] *Bar jārchiyān i darbār buzurg u sālār shud dar safar u ḥaḍar az multazimīn i rikāb i a'lā būd* (*ibid.*): *manṣab i Jārchī-Bāshī yāft* (*Rauḍat al-ṣafā-yi Nāṣirī* vol. ix).

in constant attendance upon the Shāh. He committed " Ṣabā's " poems to memory and acted as his rhapsodist.[1] When the Shāh issued instructions that a collection of poems by the court poets should be compiled and two successive compilers, Aḥmad Bēg " Akhtar " (see p. 885 *supra*) and M. Bāqir Bēg " Nashāṭī " Gurjī, had died before completing the task, Fāḍil Khān was ordered to undertake it and he accordingly compiled the *Anjuman i Khāqān*. After Fatḥ-'Alī Shāh's death [in 1250/1834] Fāḍil Khān retired and lived in receipt of a pension from Muḥammad Shāh Qājār. He died in 1252/1836–7.[2]

Anjuman i Khāqān, notices of the poets of Fatḥ-'Alī Shāh's reign in four *anjumans* and a *khātimah*, undertaken at the Shāh's request in 1234/1818–19 and completed in five months: **Rieu** Suppt. 120 (A.H. 1234/1819), **Sipahsālār** ii p. 461 (A.H. 1236/1820–1), **As'ad** 2075, **Lahore** Panjāb Univ. Lib. (See *OCM.* III/1 (Nov. 1926) p. 77), **Majlis** 324.

List of the poets: Rieu Suppt. p. 86.

[*Anjuman i Khāqān, khātimah; Tadhkirah i dil-gushā* (Berlin p. 672 no. 134); *Nigāristān i Dārā* fol. 92*b*; *Tadhkirah i Muḥammad-Shāhī* fol. 187*b*; *Majma' al-fuṣaḥā'* ii p. 142; *Rauḍat al-ṣafā-yi Nāṣirī* vol. ix, 6th page from end.]

1195. **Maḥmūd Mīrzā** b. Fatḥ-'Alī Shāh **Qājār** has already been mentioned (p. 336 *supra*) as the author of the *Tārīkh i Ṣāḥib-qirānī*, completed in 1248/1832.[3] He died at Tabrīz in 1852 or 1853. His *Bayān al-Maḥmūd*, an anthology of initial lines of *ghazals* by contemporary poets (see Rieu Suppt. 377, Bānkīpūr Suppt. i 1997), was compiled in 1240/1824–5. For other works of his, mentioned in the preface to the *Safīnat al-Maḥmūd*, see Rieu Suppt. p. 87.

(1) *Gulshan i Maḥmūd*, notices of forty-eight sons of Fatḥ-'Alī Shāh with specimens of their poetry, compiled by order of the Shāh in 1236/1820–1: **Rieu** Suppt. 121 (A.H. 1239/1823), **As'ad** 2876.

[1] *Ash'ār i janāb i Malik* [*sc. al-Shu'arā'*] *rā ḥāfiẓ u ḥāwī u nāqil u rāwī āmad* (*Majma' al-fuṣaḥā'*).

[2] So apparently *Majma' al-fuṣaḥā'* and certainly *Rauḍat al-ṣafā-yi Nāṣirī* vol. ix.

[3] Another MS.: Leningrad Univ. 1142 (Romaskewicz p. 4).

List of the poets: Rieu Suppt. p. 87.

(2) ***Safīnat al-Maḥmūd,*** notices of the poets of Fatḥ-'Alī Shāh's reign preceded in the B.M. MS. by two prefaces, the first of which gives *Majma' i Maḥmūd* as the title and 1235/1819–20 as the date of compilation,[1] while the second says that in 1240/1824–5 the author was commanded by the Shāh to write an account of contemporary poets and that the title *Safīnat al-Maḥmūd* was given to it by the latter: **D.M.G.** 18 (lacks the earlier preface. A.H. 1256/1840), **Rieu** Suppt. 122 (mid 19th cent.), **As'ad** 3874.

(3) ***Nuql i majlis,*** notices of ancient and modern poetesses, composed in 1241/1825–6 at Nihāwand: MS. formerly in Vambéry's possession.

Extracts (biographies translated or summarised in German, verses in Persian and German): *Aus dem Geistesleben persischer Frauen. Von H. Vambéry* (in *ZDMG.* 45 (1891) pp. 403–28).

1196. **'Alī Akbar "Bismil" Shīrāzī,** who has already been mentioned (p. 203 *supra*) as the author of the *Baḥr al-la'ālī*, died a few years before 1283/1866–7.

Tadhkirah i dil-gushā, on the poets of Fatḥ-'Alī Shāh's reign, begun in 1237/1821–2 by order of Ḥusain 'Alī Mīrzā and divided into a *gulzār* (subdivided in the Browne MS. into 3, in the Berlin MS. into 7, *gulbuns*, on Shīrāz, its history, buildings, gardens and celebrities, especially Sa'dī, Ḥāfiẓ and Waṣṣāf), two *būstāns* ((1) on Fatḥ-'Alī Shāh and 15 members of his family, (2) on 157 other poets arranged alphabetically under the *final* letter of the *takhalluṣ*, the first being "Bī-nawā", the second "Shaidā" and the last "Yārī"), and a *khātimah* (autobiography, ending (at least in the Browne MS.) with an account of the earthquake of 4 Shawwāl 1239/2 June 1824): **Browne** Coll. J. 18 = Houtum-Schindler 37 (apparently written by or for the author), **Berlin** 667 (A.H. 1252/1836).

[1] According to Vambéry, however, the *Majma' i Maḥmūd*, of which he possessed a MS. (see *ZDMG.* 45 (1891) pp. 403–5), is a collection of works by Maḥmūd Qājār, eleven in his MS., namely, (1) *Safīnat al-Maḥmūd*, (2) *Muntakhab al-Maḥmūd*, (3) *Gulshan i Maḥmūd*, (4) *Makhzan al-Maḥmūd*, (5) *Nuql i majlis*, (6) *Sunbulistān*, (7) *Parwardah i khayāl*, (8) *Maqṣūd i jahān*, (9) *Maḥmūd-nāmah*, (10) *Naṣā'iḥ al-Maḥmūd* or *Durar al-Maḥmūd* (Rieu, Suppt. p. 87, gives these as two different works), (11) *Bayān al-Maḥmūd*.

List of the poets : Berlin pp. 669–73.

[See p. 203 *supra*, also *Riyāḍ al-ʿārifīn* (Ṭihrān A.H.S. 1316) pp. 422–4.]

1197. S. **ʿAbd al-Raḥīm " Munṣif "** al-Mūsawī b. Mīr M. Bāqir ʿAlī-ābādī was born at Sārī in 1197/1783.

Badīʿ al-afkār, an anthology of ancient and modern poems with biographical notices, begun at Sārī in 1237/1821–2 for M. Kāẓim Mīrzā b. Muḥammad-Qulī Mīrzā b. Fatḥ-ʿAlī S͟hāh, completed in 1239/1824 and divided into six *qisms* ((1) *qaṣīdahs*, (2) *g͟hazals*, (3) *mat͟hnawīs*, (4) *muqaṭṭaʿāt*, (5) *rubāʿīs*, (6) *tarjīʿ-bands*), in which the poets are arranged alphabetically except the royal princes, who come first : **Rieu** Suppt. 378.

[Autobiography at end of *Badīʿ al-afkār*.]

1198. Mīr **Ḥusain al-Ḥusainī**, having travelled from S͟hīrāz to ʿUmān and thence to Sind, was admitted to the court of Mīr Karam ʿAlī K͟hān and Mīr Murād ʿAlī K͟hān Tālpur, the latter of whom has already been mentioned (p. 658 *supra*). On his return home (presumably to S͟hīrāz) Mīr Ḥusain compiled a *tad͟hkirah* as an *armag͟hān* for the two Sindī princes.

Zubdat al-muʿāṣirīn, a *tad͟hkirah* of contemporary poets compiled in 1240/1824–5 : MS. in the possession of Prof. Maḥmūd S͟hērānī at Lahore.

Description with some extracts (verses by poetesses) : *Fārisī kī baʿḍ s͟hāʿir ʿauratēṅ aur un kā kalām* by M. Iqbāl (in *OCM*. X/1 (Nov. 1933) pp. 31–42).

1199. **ʿAbd al-Razzāq Bēg " Maftūn " b. Najaf-Qulī K͟hān Dunbulī** died in 1243/1827–8 (see pp. 344–5 *supra*).

(1) *Tajribat al-aḥrār wa-tasliyat al-abrār*, personal memoirs with notices of his contemporaries written in 1228/1813 : **Rieu** Suppt. 132, **Majlis** 534.

(2) *Nigāristān i Dārā*, notices of poets contemporary with Fatḥ-ʿAlī S͟hāh written in 1241/1825–6 and divided into five *nigār-k͟hānahs* or *aiwāns* ((1) Fatḥ-ʿAlī S͟hāh, (2) 21 royal princes and noble amīrs, i.e. sons, grandsons and nephews of Fatḥ-ʿAlī S͟hāh, (3) 55 " favourites of the Shāh and of the princes, men of letters, Vazirs and other officials ", beginning with " Ṣabā " and ending with " Humā ", (4) about 120 other poets

beginning with " Āzād " (M. 'Alī Kashmīrī) and ending with " Yaghmā ", (5) the author) and an appendix (on " 'Andalīb ") : **Rieu** Suppt. 123.

List of the poets in *Nigār-khānahs* i–iii : Rieu Suppt. pp. 88–9.

1200. Ḥakīm **'Alī-Riḍā** (in full, Ghulām-'Alī-Mūsā-Riḍā) **" Rā'iq "**, usually known as **Bāqir Ḥusain Khān Nā'iṭī**, was the son of Rukn al-Dīn Ḥusain Khān. He died in 1248/1832–3.

Guldastah i Karnāṭak (a chronogram = 1210/1795–6, the date of inception), alphabetically arranged notices of seventy poets who lived in the Carnatic towards the close of the eighteenth century and in the early years of the nineteenth, completed some time between 1244/1828–9 and 1248/1832–3, the date of the author's death : **Ivanow** 1st Suppt. 766 (early 20th cent.).

List of the poets : Ivanow 1st Suppt. pp. 8–10.

[Autobiography in *Guldastah i Karnāṭak; Natā'ij al-afkār* p. 189 ; *Ṣubḥ i waṭan* pp. 81–8 ; *Gulzār i A'ẓam* p. 202 ; *Ishārāt i Bīnish* (Ivanow-Curzon p. 69 no. 49) ; M. Mahdī " Wāṣif " Madrāsī *Ḥadīqat al-marām* (in Arabic), Madras 1279/1862, pp. 23–4.]

1201. Rājah **Ratan Sing'h " Zakhmī "**, who was born at Lucknow on 23 Muḥarram 1197/29 Dec. 1782 and died in 1851, has already been mentioned (p. 709 *supra*) as the author of the *Sulṭān al-tawārīkh*.

Anīs al-'āshiqīn, an alphabetically arranged *tadhkirah* of ancient and modern poets written at Lucknow in 1245/1829–30 [1] and divided into a *muqaddimah* (in praise of Naṣīr al-Dīn Ḥaidar) [2] and 31 *ḥarfs*, in which are given brief biographies and selections, almost exclusively from the poets' *ghazals* and *rubā'īs* : **Lahore** Panjāb Univ. Lib. (vol. i only, ending with " Ḍiyā'ī ". See M. Shafī' in *OCM*. III/3 (May 1927) pp. 48–51), **Nadhīr Aḥmad** 73 (vol. ii only, beginning with " Ṭālib " Jājarmī and containing about 1176 notices. Gaurī Parshād, Lucknow. A.H. 1239/1820).[3]

[Autobiography in *Anīs al-'āshiqīn* under " Zakhmī " (summarised by M. Shafī' in *OCM*. III/3 (May 1927) pp. 49–50).]

[1] It will be observed that the MS. described by Nadhīr Aḥmad is dated 1239. If this date is correct the MS. must represent an edition earlier than the *muqaddimah* in praise of Naṣīr al-Dīn Ḥaidar.

[2] King of Awad'h (" Oudh ") 1243/1827–1253/1837.

[3] See n. (1) on this page.

1202. S. **M. 'Alī** b. S. M. Ṭabāṭabā'ī **Zawārī** was born on 29 Ṣafar 1195/24 Feb. 1781 at Iṣfahān, to which his father had been forced by stress of circumstances to migrate from Zawārah,[1] the home of his family. At the age of nineteen S. M. 'Alī went to Zawārah and pursued his studies there for two years, but misfortunes compelled him to leave the town and to wander for a period from place to place. In Fatḥ-'Alī Shāh's reign (1211/1797–1250/1834) he returned and obtained an appointment as clerk (*kātib*) in the Madrasah of Mīrzā 'Abd al-'Aẓīm at Ardistān. In the time of Saif al-Daulah Sulṭān-Muḥammad Mīrzā [2] an accusation having been laid against him and a summons issued, he fled from Ardistān, but some time afterwards successful intercession was made on his behalf, his offence was pardoned, and he was commanded to write a history of the Kākh i 'Asharah [?].

Ma'āthir al-Bāqirīyah, notices of 52 panegyrists of S. M. Bāqir al-Mūsawī al-Ḥusainī, written in 1245/1829–30 : **Rāmpūr** (A.H. 1247/1832. See a description by M. Shajā'at 'Alī Khān in *OCM*. VI/2 (Feb. 1930) pp. 111–13. Cf. Nadhīr Aḥmad no. 89).

[Autobiography in *khātimah* to *Ma'āthir al-Bāqirīyah* (summarised by Shajā'at 'Alī Khān).]

1203. **Khūb Chand "Dhakā'"** b. Bhawānī Chand Kāyat'h **Dihlawī,** a pupil of Mīr Naṣīr al-Dīn "Naṣīr",[3] lived at Sikandarābād and died in 1846. He was the author of a *dīwān* [in Urdū], of some Persian poetry, and of some compositions in ornate prose.

'Iyār al-shu'arā', an inaccurate and uncritical alphabetically arranged dictionary of nearly 1500 Rēkhtah (i.e. Urdū) poets, begun in 1208/1793–4 or 1213/1798–9 [4] at the suggestion of "Naṣīr", but containing a date as late as 1247/1831–2 : Sprenger no. 50 = (?) **Ethé** 702 (n.d.).

[Autobiography in *'Iyār al-shu'arā'* ; Sprenger pp. 184–5 ; Garcin de Tassy iii pp. 350–1.]

[1] For Zawārah, near Ardistān, see p. 14 *supra*.
[2] Who was appointed Governor of 'Irāq in 1240/1824–5 (see p. 892 *infra*).
[3] d. at Ḥaidarābād in, or about, 1840 (see Sprenger p. 269, Garcin de Tassy ii pp. 418–20, Beale *Oriental biographical dictionary*, Saksēna *History of Urdu literature* pp. 146–7, T. Grahame Bailey *History of Urdu literature* p. 59, etc.).
[4] "According to a rather ambiguous chronogram on fol. 2*b*, l. 8" (Ethé).

1204. Saif al-Daulah **Sulṭān-Muḥammad** "Sulṭān" b. Fatḥ-'Alī Sh̲āh **Qājār** was born on 26 Jumādā I 1228/27 May 1813.[1] In 1240/1824–5 he was appointed Governor of 'Irāq and spent the next ten years at Iṣfahān, where learned and pious men frequented his court. After the death of Fatḥ-'Alī Sh̲āh [in 1250/1834][2] he returned to Ṭihrān and in Muḥammad Sh̲āh's campaigns against Gurgān and Harāt he had the rank of *mīr-panjah* (*Majma' al-fuṣaḥā'* I p. 32[4] : *az Iṣfahān ba-Ṭihrān āmadah dar safar i Gurgān u Harāt dar kamāl i 'izzat ba-manṣab i mīr-panjagī manṣūb u mak̲h̲ṣūṣ gardīd*). Some time later he visited Najaf and Karbalā'. In 1279/1862–3 he travelled via Gīlān and Sh̲īrwān to Istānbūl, Alexandria, Cairo, Mecca, Damascus, Ḥimṣ, Aleppo, Diyārbakr, al-Mauṣil and Bag̲h̲dād. After a year in Ṭihrān he made a pilgrimage to Mash̲had. Apparently he was still alive when the *Majma' al-fuṣaḥā'*, completed in 1288/1871, was written. Of his works Riḍā-Qulī K̲h̲ān mentions (1) a *dīwān* of nearly twenty thousand verses, (2) *Mulūk al-kalām*, an anthology of passages in Arabic and Persian prose and verse on various subjects, (3) *Tuḥfat al-Ḥaramain wa-saif al-rasā'il*, a *math̲nawī*.

Tadhkirat al-salāṭīn (as it is called in the preface of the Sipahsālār MS.), or *Bazm i K̲h̲āqān* (as it is called in the preface of the Majlis MS.), written at Iṣfahān in 1245/1829–30, recast perhaps in 1250/1834–5,[3] and divided into a *muqaddimah* (consisting of the *Anīs al-'ushshāq* of Sh̲araf al-Dīn "Rāmī" appropriated without acknowledgment) and three *bābs* ((1) kings and princes with verses by them, (2) a brief account of Fatḥ-'Alī Sh̲āh and specimens of his poetry, (3) on the author's life and poems), or, as in the Majlis MS., into a *muqaddimah* (= the *Anīs al-'ushshāq*) and five *anjumans* ((1) *dar ba'ḍī az ash̲'ār u ḥālāt i salāṭīn u pādsh̲āh-zādagān i pīsh̲īn*, (2) *dar manāqib i pādsh̲āh i 'aṣr* [Fatḥ-'Alī Sh̲āh] *u ash̲'ārī az ū*, (3) *dar ash̲'ār u ḥālāt i sh̲āh-zādagān*, (4) *dar ash̲'ār u aḥwāl i mīr-zādagān*, (5) *dar dhikr i ash̲'ār u ḥālāt i mu'allif*) : **Sipahsālār** ii p. 477 (breaking

---
[1] So *Nāsik̲h̲ al-tawārīk̲h̲* (*Tārīk̲h̲ i Qājārīyah* vol. i, at end. Quoted in Sipahsālār ii p. 477). The date 1227 is given in the *Majma' al-fuṣaḥā'*.
[2] Riḍā-Qulī K̲h̲ān says 1249.
[3] 1245 is the date given in the preface of the Majlis MS. The Sipahsālār MS. seems to give the two dates 1250 and 1245 in a rather obscure way.

off before the end of *Bāb* II), **Majlis** (containing in *Anjuman* v the author's biography only, not his poems. For some account of this MS., not described in the Majlis catalogue, see Sipahsālār ii p. 478, footnotes).

[*Majma' al-fuṣaḥā'* i pp. 31–4 (summarised in Sipahsālār ii pp. 477–8).]

1205. **Bahman Mīrzā** b. Nā'ib al-Salṭanah 'Abbās Mīrzā [1] comes fourth in the list of 'Abbās Mīrzā's twenty-six surviving sons given in the *Rauḍat al-ṣafā-yi Nāṣirī* (vol. ix, fol. 166*a* (the 30th page from the end), l. 9). His eldest brother, Muḥammad Mīrzā, who acceded to the throne in 1250/1834 and died in 1264/1848, was born on 6 D̲h̲ū 'l-Qa'dah 1222/5 Jan. 1808. Probably therefore Bahman Mīrzā was born about 1225/1810. In the preface to the *Tad̲h̲kirah i Muḥammad-S̲h̲āhī* he " says that he was residing in Ardabīl, to the government of which he had been appointed by his father, when he was invited by his elder brother, Muḥammad Shāh, to join him, and, at his request, compiled the present work " (Rieu). The date of composition, 1247/1831–2, is indicated by a chronogram and at the end of the work 1249/1833–4 is given as the date of completion. He evidently returned to Ardabīl, since according to the *Rauḍat al-ṣafā-yi Nāṣirī* (x, fol. 2*a*, l. 11) he was there in Rajab 1250/Nov. 1834, when Muḥammad S̲h̲āh came to the throne. In that year he was appointed Governor of Burūjird (*op. cit.* x fol. 6*b*, l. 25, fol. 7*a*, l. 6 *ab infra*). In 1257/1841 (apparently) he was made Governor of Ād̲h̲arbāyjān (*op. cit.* x fol. 26*a*, l. 6 *ab infra*), but in 1263/1847 he was superseded in favour of Nāṣir al-Dīn Mīrzā (*op. cit.* x fol. 42*a*, l. 18). He was then under suspicion of desiring to secure for himself the succession to the throne, and it was with some trepidation that he set out for Ṭihrān. Muḥammad S̲h̲āh gave him a friendly reception, but, when an inquiry into the finances of Ād̲h̲arbāyjān revealed a large deficit, Bahman Mīrzā thought it prudent to take refuge in the Russian Embassy (*op. cit.* x fol. 42*b*, l. 21). Permission to live in Russian territory was granted to him, and there the remainder of his life was spent, though his recall was suggested

[1] For 'Abbās Mīrzā, Fatḥ-'Alī S̲h̲āh's eldest (surviving) son, see p. 338 *supra*.

early in Nāṣir al-Dīn S͟hāh's reign.¹ He seems to have gone to Georgia ² and to have died there in 1883.³

Tad͟hkirah i Muḥammad-S͟hāhī, notices of poets completed in 1249/1833-4 and divided into three *ris͟htahs* ((1) about 150 ancient and modern poets to the end of the 12th century of the Hijrah, (2) Fatḥ-'Alī S͟hāh and twelve Qājār princes, (3) 57 contemporary poets in alphabetical order) : **Rieu** Suppt. 124 (A.H. 1257/1841).

List of the poets in *Ris͟htahs* 2 and 3 : Rieu Suppt. pp. 90-1.

1206. Darwīs͟h Ḥusain "**Nawā**" ⁴ **Kās͟hānī** is described in the *Majma' al-fuṣaḥā'* as a contemporary who after a period spent in travel (*muddatī siyāḥat kardah*) had settled in Tabrīz, where his *takyah* and its beautiful garden used to be visited by the children of the *Walī-'ahd* and others. After his death [which must have occurred before 1288/1871] his *tad͟hkirah*, without

---

¹ Cf. R. G. Watson *History of Persia* p. 380 : There were at this time absent from the kingdom, in banishment, two men who had been the most powerful, as well as perhaps the ablest, statesmen of Persia. One of the two was the Shah's uncle, Bahman Meerza, who had been implicated in the proceedings of the Asef-ed-Dowleh at Meshed. It was believed that the latter had offered to him the crown of Persia, and the discovery of this conspiracy had led to Prince Bahman being deprived of his government of Azerbaeejan, and to his being forced to retire to Georgia, where he remained under Russian protection. The other exiled Persian statesman was the Asef-ed-Dowleh, the uncle of the late Mahomed Shah. The Ameer-i-Nizam was urged to recall both of these illustrious exiles ; but with regard to the case of Bahman Meerza, he observed that, should the prince be permitted to return to his country, his wealth, influence and popularity would quickly secure for him his former government of Azerbaeejan, which he would be likely to constitute an independent province.

² See the preceding footnote.

³ " Mr. Churchill states in a letter that Bahman Mirza subsequently fled to the Caucasus and died there a few years ago " (Rieu Suppt. p. 90. From Rieu's preface it appears that the Churchill MSS. were acquired from 1884 to 1894). Cf. Browne Coll. p. 119, where it is said that a certain MS. " was originally transcribed in 1277/1860 for Prince Bahman Mírzá *Bahá'u'd-Dawla*, who according to a note in Schindler's writing attached to the volume, died in the Caucasus in A.D. 1883." [Bahman Mīrzā Bahā' al-Daulah, however, was not the same person as the Bahman Mīrzā who died in the Caucasus. The former was a son of Fatḥ-'Alī S͟hāh (47th in the list given in the *Rauḍat al-ṣafā-yi Nāṣirī* ix fol. 172*b*) and was Governor of Kās͟hān (*op. cit.* x fol. 22*a*, l. 21), Yazd (*op. cit.* x fol. 23*b*, l. 5), Simnān (*op. cit.* ix fol. 172*b* (17th page from end), l. 4) and doubtless of other places. He is presumably the Bahman Mīrzā who " died at Ṭihrán in Rabí' II, 1277 = Oct.–Nov. 1860 " (Browne Coll. p. 90).]

⁴ " Bí-Nawá " according to the catalogue of the Browne Collection, but this is not supported by the *Tad͟hkirah i Muḥammad-S͟hāhī*, the *Majma' al-fuṣaḥa*', or the " endorsement " on " Sipihr's " MS. seen by S. Churchill (cf. the next note).

preface or conclusion, had been seen by Riḍā-Qulī Khān, who mentions it in his *muqaddimah* (vol. i p. [8^8]) as well as in his notice of Darwīsh "Nawā". Riḍā-Qulī Khān did not regard him as a good judge of poetry (*quwwah i tashkhīṣ i shi'r nadāshtah*).

Tadhkirah i Darwīsh Nawā, short biographical notices of ancient and modern poets with extensive extracts from their works: **Rieu** Suppt. 115 (*Silsilah* i, *Ṭabaqah* 1 only, containing 50 ancient poets (specified by Rieu) in alphabetical order from Abū 'l-Faraj Rūnī to Niẓāmī Ganjawī.[1] Before A.H. 1253/1837, probably written by, or for, the author), **Browne** Coll. V. 68 (contains not only the poets given in the preceding MS. but also in "*Ṭabaqa* i, *Silsila* 2" an enormous number of minor poets, some ancient, others "at least as modern as the Ṣafawí period", and in a third section (untitled and apparently incomplete, since it breaks off in the letter *Ṣād*) further poets, mostly quite modern).

[*Tadhkirah i Muḥammad-Shāhī* (Rieu Suppt. 124) fol. 221*a*; *Majma' al-fuṣaḥā'* ii p. 527.]

1207. Nawwāb 'Aẓīm al-Daulah Sarfarāz al-Mulk M. **Muṣṭafā Khān "Shēftah"** [2] Dihlawī Muẓaffar-Jang was a son of Nawwāb 'Aẓīm al-Daulah Sarfarāz al-Mulk Murtaḍā Khān, a Bangash Afghān, who in 1813 purchased the estate of Jahāngīrābād in the Bulandshahr District. He was born at Delhi in 1806 [3] and educated by local scholars and *ṣūfīs*. In the art of poetry he received instruction from "Mūmin" and "Ghālib" (for the latter of whom see pp. 525–7 *supra*). In Dhū 'l-Ḥijjah 1254/Feb. 1839 he started on a pilgrimage to Mecca and al-Madīnah and did not return to Delhi until Dhū 'l-Ḥijjah 1256/Feb. 1841. Of this journey he published (where ? when ?) an account entitled

[1] The MS. described by Rieu was acquired through Sidney Churchill, who "states that a MS. belonging to Sipihr, of Teheran [for whom see pp. 152–4 *supra*], and containing, besides the above Ṭabaḳah, two Silsilahs, treating of later and contemporary poets, is endorsed "Taẓkirah i Darvīsh Navā".

[2] This *takhalluṣ* used by him in his Urdu poetry is better known than "Ḥasratī", which he used in his Persian poetry.

[3] This is the date given by Niẓāmī Badāyūnī in the *Qāmūs al-mashāhīr*. If the catalogues are right in saying that he was 26 when he *completed* the *Gulshan i bī-khār* in 1250, he must have been born in 1223 or 1224, i.e. in 1808 or 1809.

Targhīb al-sālik ilā aḥsan al-masālik, or *Rah-āward*, of which an Urdu translation, *Sirāj i munīr*, by S. Zain al-'Ābidīn, was published (where ?) in 1910. After the Mutiny of 1857 he was imprisoned for a time on a charge of seditious correspondence with the King of Delhi, but was subsequently pardoned. Thenceforward he lived mainly at Jahāngīrābād. He died in 1869 and was buried at Delhi.

He is the author of (1) the *safar-nāmah* mentioned above, (2) *Dīwān i Shēftah*, an Urdu *dīwān* published at Meerut, probably two or three years before 1857, and republished in the *Kullīyāt i Shēftah u Ḥasratī* (Badāyūṅ 1916), (3) *Dīwān i Ḥasratī*, a Persian *dīwān* published in the *Kullīyāt*, (4) a number of Persian *ruqa'āt* published in the *Kullīyāt*, and

(5) **Gulshan i bī-khār,** very short notices of about 600 Rēkhtah (i.e. Urdū) poets, "more correct than most other Tadzkirahs" (Sprenger), begun in 1248/1832–3 and completed in 1250/1834–5; **Rieu** iii 1069*a* (A.H. 1252/1837), **Bānkīpūr** viii 718 (A.H. 1255/1840).

Editions: **Delhi** 1253/1837–8 (see Sprenger p. 189 and *Kullīyāt i Shēftah u Ḥasratī*, introductory biography p. 43), 1843°*, **Lucknow** 1874°*.

For the *Gulistān i bī-khazān*, an Urdū *tadhkirah* written in 1265/1859 by Ḥakīm S. Ghulām-Quṭb al-Dīn "Bāṭin", of Āgrah, as an improved version of the *Gulshan i bī-khār*, which according to "Bāṭin" contains much satirical and unjust criticism, see Sprenger no. 57 and Blumhardt's *Catalogue of the Hindustani manuscripts in . . . the India Office* no. 61, as well as Blumhardt's catalogues of Hindustani printed books in the B.M. and I.O., where a lithographed edition (Lucknow 1875°*) is described. According to Sprenger it may be considered a translation of the *Gulshan i bī-khār* "into unintelligible Hindústány, with some idiotical remarks".

[Garcin de Tassy iii pp. 123–4; *Sham' i anjuman* 134–6; *Kullīyāt i Shēftah u Ḥasratī*, Badāyūṅ 1916 (published for his son, Nawwāb Ḥājjī M. Isḥāq Khān), introductory biography by Niẓāmī Badāyūnī; Niẓāmī Badāyūnī *Qāmūs al-mashāhīr* (in Urdū) ii p. 33; Rām Bābū Saksēna *A history of Urdu literature*, Allahabad 1927, pp. 150–1.]

1208. **Aḥmad,** known as (*al-shahīr bi-*) **Hulāgū** (or Halākū, which according to Blochet is the modern pronunciation), "**Kharāb**" **Qājār** set out on a pilgrimage to Mecca and, being unaccompanied by friends who could speak his language, he sought to occupy his time by writing down such ancient and modern poetry as he could remember. Having visited Mecca and Medina, he went to Istānbūl (on an embassy, according to Blochet: *ba-jihat i muhimm i umūrāt i ẓāhirī i khwud wārid i marz i Qusṭanṭīn u idrāk i sharaf-yābī i āstānah i A'lā Ḥaḍrat muyassar shud,* as "Kharāb" himself says). The business of his embassy having kept him fully occupied during the year that he spent at Istānbūl, it was only after this delay that he could re-examine his manuscript. Finding the contemporary poetry most agreeable to his taste, he rejected the rest and confined his *Maṣṭabah i Kharāb* to the poets of Fatḥ-'Alī Shāh's time. The Turkish poetry at the end of the work was collected by him during his visit to the Ottoman dominions.

Maṣṭabah i Kharāb, brief notices of Fatḥ-'Alī Shāh's Persian, Indian and Turkish contemporaries who wrote Persian and Turkish poetry, compiled in 1253/1837–8: **Blochet** ii 1160 (A.H. 1271/1855).

[Autobiographical statements in the preface (summarised by Blochet, who quotes some of the original Persian).]

1209. H. H. Nawwāb Wālā-Jāh Amīr al-Hind A'ẓẓam al-Umarā' [afterwards 'Umdat al-Umarā' ?][1] Mukhtār al-Mulk Sirāj al-Daulah **M. Ghauth Khān** [afterwards Ghulām-M. Ghauth Khān ?][2] "A'ẓẓam" Bahādur-Jang [afterwards Shahāmat-Jang ?][3] was the last titular[4] Nawwāb of the Carnatic. He

[1] 'Umdat al-Umarā' in the *Madras almanac* for 1854.

[2] In the *Ṣubḥ i waṭan* "he" calls himself M. Ghauth Khān and says that his original name was M. Ghauth (cf. *Madras almanac* for 1842). In the *Madras almanac* for 1854 and in the official announcement of his death he is called Ghulām-M. Ghauth Khān.

[3] Shahāmat-Jang in the *Ishārat i Bīnish* (Ivanow-Curzon p. 69 no. 10).

[4] His grandfather 'Aẓīm al-Daulah in 1801 ceded his rights and authority in the Carnatic to the East India Company. Since the death of M. Ghauth Khān the successive heads of this family have borne the title Prince of Arcot (*Amīr i Arkāṭ*). For the present Prince of Arcot see *Who's Who* under Arcot, Prince of. This house, to quote *The Times* of 3.12.1855, "was a century ago one of the most prominent in Southern India. His [i.e. M. Ghauth Khān's]

was born on 29 Dhū 'l-Ḥijjah 1239/25 August 1824 [1] and succeeded his father, Nawwāb A'ẓam-Jāh, in 1825. During his minority his uncle, H.H. Prince 'Aẓīm-Jāh Bahādur Nā'ib i Mukhtār, acted as Regent. On 25 August 1842 he was installed as *Nawwāb Ṣūbah-dār* of the Carnatic at Chepauk Palace. After a life "spent in rioting and profligacy" (*The Times*) he died without issue on 7 October 1855 at the age of thirty-one years and was buried to the north of the Great Mosque at Triplicane. He "is said to have possessed considerable natural intelligence, but he never evinced any predilection for European society, and he had long forgotten the little knowledge of English he had once acquired. He was by nature of a lavish disposition, and the only value he seems to have set on money was to have it to give to his attendants" (*The* [*Madras*] *Athenaeum*). For his *dīwān*, the *Dīwān i A'ẓam*, see Ivanow 1st Suppt. no. 814. A published edition of a work of his entitled *Bahāristān i A'ẓam* (probably an anthology) is mentioned without date or place of publication under the heading *Dawāwīn* in the Āṣafīyah catalogue (i p. 714). M. Mahdī "Wāṣif" in his *Ḥadīqat al-marām* (p. 7) denies that he wrote any books and says that the poet "Rāqim" [2] wrote a work on prosody and a *tadhkirah* of poets which he ascribed to the Nawwāb.

(1) ***Ṣubḥ i waṭan***, notices of about 90 poets of the Carnatic with eleven *ghazals* by each, completed in 1257/1841 and intended to correct and supplement the *Guldastah i Karnāṭak* of "Rā'iq" (see p. 890 *supra*).

Edition: **Madras** 1258/1842* (cf. Sprenger p. 172).

ancestor it was who was supported as Nawab by the English, in opposition to a relative and rival, whose cause was espoused by the French. The struggle between the two European nations lasted long, but in the end, spite of the genius and devotion of men like Labourdonnais, Dupleix and Lally, the English triumphed and with them their ally the Nawab. But the power of his race was soon at an end. In 1801 Lord Wellesley, as Governor-General, entered into a treaty with the reigning Nawab by which that Prince ceded his rights and authority in the Carnatic to the British, one-fifth of the yearly revenues being guaranteed to him for the maintenance of himself and his retainers." For the Persian histories of the Carnatic see pp. 777–80 *supra*.

[1] 1 Dhū 'l-Ḥijjah 1239 according to the *Ishārāt i Bīnish* (Ivanow-Curzon p. 69 no. 10).

[2] Presumably M. Ḥusain "Rāqim" Qādirī, of whom there is a notice in the *Ishārāt i Bīnish* (Ivanow-Curzon p. 69 no. 50).

List of the poets common to the *Guldastah i Karnāṭak* and the *Ṣubḥ i waṭan*: Ivanow 1st Suppt. pp. 8–10.

(2) *Gulzār i Aʿẓam* (a chronogram = 1269/1852–3): **Āṣafīyah** i p. 322 no. 38 (A.H. 1302/1884–5).

Edition: [**Madrās** ?] 1272/1855–6 (see Ḥaidarābād Coll. p. 23 and Ivanow 1st Suppt. p. 40. The former gives Ḥaidarābād as the place of publication, the latter says " [Madras ?] ").

[*Ṣubḥ i waṭan* pp. 3–8; *Madras almanac* 1842 pp. 282, 284: 1854 p. 109: and other dates; *Ishārāt i Bīnish* (Ivanow-Curzon p. 69 no. 10); *The Athenaeum* [a Madras newspaper] 9.10.1855 p. 482, 11.10.1855 p. 486; *The Times* [London newspaper] 3.12.1955 p. 8 col. 3; M. Mahdī "Wāṣif" Madrāsī *Ḥadīqat al-marām* (in Arabic), Madras 1279/1862, p. 7; Buckland *Dictionary of Indian biography* p. 73. Unfortunately some of the above works have not been available for the verification of certain details in the revision of this article.]

1210. **Wazīr ʿAlī "ʿIbratī" ʿAẓīmābādī** was born at ʿAẓīmābād (i.e. Paṭnah) and was a pupil of Rājah Piyārē Laʿl "Ulfatī" Dihlawī (d. 1254/1838).[1] After a period in the service of Nawwāb Raushan al-Mulk Mubārak al-Daulah M. Mahdī-Qulī Khān Bahādur Shaukat-Jang he was appointed *Munshī* to Nawwāb Mubāriz al-Mulk Ḍiyāʾ al-Daulah S. M. Ḥasan Khān Bahādur Tahawwur-Jang. Later he became the constant companion of Rājah Bhūp Sing'h.

He is the author of several works preserved at Calcutta, viz. *Iʿjāz al-maḥabbat*, written in 1247/1831–2, a prose version of "Faiḍī's" *Nal Daman* (Ivanow Curzon no. 259), *Miṣbāḥ al-akhlāq*, written in 1250/1834–5, a collection of 76 short bombastic letters (Ivanow Curzon no. 507), *Miʿrāj al-ʿushshāq*, written in 1251/1835–6, a prose version of "Hātifī's" *Lailā u Majnūn* (Ivanow Curzon no. 246) and *Sirāj al-maḥabbat*, written in 1252/1836, a prose version of "Minnat's" *mathnawī* on the story of Hīr and Rānjhā (Ivanow Curzon no. 314).

(1) *Miʿrāj al-khayāl*, an alphabetically arranged dictionary

[1] For accounts of his life see *Miʿrāj al-khayāl* and *Riyāḍ al-afkār* (the latter summarised in Bānkīpūr Suppt. i p. 50).

of poets, chiefly Indians of the 18th and 19th centuries, completed in 1257/1841 (but later dates occur): **Ivanow** Curzon 60 (A.H. 1282/1865).

List of 23 contemporary poets: Ivanow-Curzon pp. 67–8.

(2) *Riyāḍ al-afkār*, alphabetically arranged biographies of elegant prose-writers (many of them also poets), mostly of the 17th, 18th and 19th centuries and mostly Indians or Persians who settled in India, completed in 1268/1852 and divided into 28 *khiyābāns*: **Būhār** 93 (A.H. 1282/1866), **Bānkīpūr** Suppt. i no. 1784 (1272 *Faṣlī*).

List and epitome of the biographies: Bānkīpūr Suppt. i pp. 49–61.

[Autobiographies in *Mi'rāj al-khayāl* and *Riyāḍ al-afkār* (the latter summarised in Bānkīpūr Suppt. i p. 48).]

1211. M. **Qudrat Allāh Khān "Qudrat"** b. M. Kāmil Gōpāmawī "left his native place" (i.e. Gōpāmau[1] presumably) for the Carnatic in 1227/1812 and subsequently entered the service of the Nawwāb. In 1239/1823–4 the title of Khān was conferred upon him and he was appointed custodian of the late Nawwāb's tomb. He was the author of two *dīwāns*.

Natā'ij al-afkār, about 525 short notices of ancient and modern poets completed in 1258/1842 and dedicated to Nawwāb M. Ghauth Khān (for whom see pp. 897–9 *supra*): Sprenger no. 730, **Rieu** iii 1024*b* (extracts only. Circ. A.D. 1850), **I.O.** 4027 (A.D. 1895).

Edition: **Madras** 1843 (see Sprenger p. 644).

[*Natā'ij al-afkār*, preface (summarised by Rieu); *Guldastah i Karnāṭak* (Ivanow 1st Suppt. p. 9 no. 51); *Ṣubḥ i waṭan* pp. 148–53; *Ishārāt i Bīnish* (Ivanow-Curzon p. 69 no. 48); M. Mahdī "Waṣif" Madrāsī *Ḥadīqat al-marām* (in Arabic), Madras 1279/1862, pp. 47–8; *Sham' i anjuman* p. 392.]

1212. S. **Murtaḍā "Bīnish"** b. Ṣādiq 'Alī Riḍawī Ḥusainī Madrāsī, whose family came from Gulbargah, was born in 1226/1811 at Madras.

Ishārāt i Bīnish (a chronogram = 1265/1848–9, the date of

[1] 14 miles East of Hardoi in Oudh.

completion), notices of 69 (66 ?) contemporary poets of the Carnatic, dedicated to Nawwāb M. Ghauth Khān Shahāmat-Jang (for whom see pp. 897–9 *supra*): **Ivanow** Curzon 61 (many additions and emendations, possibly by the author).

Edition: *Tadhkirah i Bīnish*, [**Madras**] 1268/1851–2*.

List of the poets: Ivanow-Curzon pp. 68–70.

[Autobiography in *Ishārāt i Bīnish*; *Ṣubḥ i waṭan* pp. 38–42; *Ṣubḥ i gulshan* p. 75.]

1212. **M. Riḍā " Najm "** b. Abī 'l-Qāsim **Ṭabāṭabā** has already been mentioned as the author of the general histories *Zubdat al-gharā'ib* (begun in 1231/1816. See p. 148 *supra*) and *Majma' al-mulūk* (begun about 1260/1844. See p. 148), and of the Indian histories *Akhbārāt i Hind* (completed in 1264/1848. See p. 488 *supra*), and *Mafātīḥ al-ri'āsat* (extending to 1251/1835–6. See p. 523 *supra*).

Naghmah i 'andalīb (a chronogram = 1261/1845), or *Chahār bāgh* (?)[1], a *tadhkirah* of 226 foll. dedicated to Wājid 'Alī Shāh, King of Oudh, and divided into two *rauḍahs*, of which the first is subdivided into five *bahārs* ((1) on Persian grammar, fol. 7*b*, (2) forms of Persian poetry, fol. 11*a*, (3) poetical figures, fol. 13*a*, (4) metre and rhyme, fol. 15*b*, (5) short alphabetically arranged notices of ancient and modern poets, not usually very informative biographically except in the case of Indian poets, especially the more recent, foll. 19*a*–200*b*), and the second into two *ḥadīqahs* ((1) on Greek music, fol. 201*a*, (2) on Indian music, fol. 203*b*), **Rieu** iii p. 978*b* (circ. A.D. 1850. Received by H. M. Elliot from the author), 1014*b* (extracts only), 1018*b* (extracts only).

1213. Mīrzā **Amīr Bēg " Amīr " Banārasī** was in the service of the rulers of Oudh from the time of Sa'ādat-'Alī Khān [1212–29/1797–1814] to that of M. Amjad 'Alī Shāh [1258–63/1842–7].

Ḥadā'iq al-shu'arā', begun in 1211/1796–7 at the request of Ẓafar al-Daulah Fatḥ-'Alī Khān Kaptān, completed on 7 Sha'bān 1262/31 July, 1846, and containing alphabetically arranged and biographically not very informative

[1] This second title, written on the fly-leaf of Elliot's MS., does not appear in the text.

notices of 2609 poets (the first " Ābrū ", the last M. Yūnus Khān " Yūnus " Abharī) in 31 *ḥadīqahs* (foll. 8–166*b*), followed by 30 *shajarahs* on the correct forms of the titles of kings and poets (foll. 166*b*–183), 31 *dauḥahs* on the correct forms of geographical names (foll. 183–217), two *thamarahs* on the names, dates of accession and length of reign of kings in Pre-Islamic Persia and the Muḥammadan world (foll. 217–29), seven *nakhlahs* on the seven dialects of Persian (Harawī, Sagzī, etc., foll. 229*b*–230), and 30 *natījahs* forming a large anthology of poetical quotations arrayed alphabetically according to the rhymes (foll. 230–853): **Ivanow** Curzon 702 (probably autograph), **Būhār** Arabic cat. pp. 529–30 (*ḥadīqahs* and *shajarahs* only).

1214. **M. 'Alī " Bahār "** b. Āqā Abū Ṭālib mudhahhib **Iṣfahānī** was, like his father, an illuminator by trade. According to *al-Ma'āthir wa-'l-āthār* he lived for a time in Ṭihrān, but returned to Iṣfahān and died there. He is the author of the facetious tales entitled *Yakhchālīyah* (Editions: [Persia] 1290/1873°, 1298/1881°).

Madā'iḥ al-Mu'tamadīyah, poems in praise of Mu'tamad al-Daulah Minūchihr Khān,[1] a memoir of whom by " the late " Āqā 'Alī Rashtī is prefixed to the work, with rhetorical and mostly uninformative notices of their authors: **Rieu** Suppt. 127 (A.H. 1259/1843, apparently the copy presented to Minūchihr Khān, " whose portrait is found inside the original painted cover "), 128 (A.H. 1263/1847, an enlarged edition, in which the opening memoir is brought down from 1259/1843 to Minūchihr Khān's death on 5 Rabī' i 1263/21 Feb., 1847, and notices of 19 additional poets are given).

List of the poets (87 + 19): Rieu Suppt. pp. 93–5.

[*al-Ma'āthir wa-'l-āthār* p. 213.]

1215. S. **'Alī Kabīr,** commonly called (*al-mad'ū* or *'urf*)

[1] Minūchihr Khān Gurjī Tiflīsī, a Georgian eunuch taken captive in Fatḥ-'Alī Shāh's Georgian Campaign of 1219/1804, became Īch-Āqā-sī in charge of the royal Ḥaram and was given the title of Mu'tamad al-Daulah after the death of the previous holder of the title, 'Abd al-Wahhāb " Nashāṭ ", on 5 Dhū 'l-Ḥijjah 1244/8 June 1829 (cf. *Rauḍat al-ṣafā-yi Nāṣirī* **ix** fol. 146*b*, l. 20). Early in 1258/1842 he was appointed Governor of Iṣfahān, Luristān and 'Arabistān (*op. cit.* **x** fol. 24*a* antepenult). Cf. Browne, *A year amongst the Persians* pp. 60, 201.

M. Mīranjān, " Saiyid," originally " Ajmalī ", b. S. 'Alī Ja'far Ḥusainī **Muḥammadī** Ḥanafī Naqshbandī **Ilāhābādī** has already been mentioned (p. 223 *supra*) as the author of a translation of 'Abd al-'Azīz Dihlawī's *Sirr al-shahādatain*, completed at Ghāzīpūr in 1251/1835 and entitled *Iẓhār al-sa'ādah fī tarjamat Asrār al-shahādah.* He was born on 28 Muḥarram 1212/1797, both his father and his mother being descendants of a well-known scholar and mystic, Shāh Khūb Allāh (properly M. Yaḥyā) Ilāhābādī.[1] In addition to a number of theological and other works in prose [2] he wrote a *dīwān* and several *mathnawīs.*[3]

Khāzin al-shu'arā' (a chronogram = 1260/1844, the date of inception), or *Wāqi'āt al-nādirāt* (= 1265/1848–9, the date of completion), notices of 190 modern [4] poets, nearly all Indians and most of them disciples, pupils, friends, or relatives of Shāh Khūb Allāh, his uncle M. Afḍal " Muḥaqqar " Ilāhābādī, or of someone connected with them : **I.O.** 3899 (A.D. 1908).

[*Khāzin al-shu'arā'*, *khātimah* (foll. 180–96).]

1216. Mīrzā **'Abd Allāh "Raunaq"** b. M. Āqā Kurdistānī was born at Sinandij,[5] to which an ancestor of his had migrated from Hamadān. He was appointed *Munshī Bāshī*, or Chief Secretary, by Amān Allāh Khān II, who was made Governor (*Wālī*) of Kurdistān by M. Shāh Qājār in 1262/1846, was deposed after a year's tenure, and was reinstated by Nāṣir al-Dīn Shāh in 1265/1848–9.

Ḥadīqah i Amān-Allāhī, notices of the poets of Sinandij, completed in 1265/1848–9, and dedicated to Amān Allāh Khān II, the Governor : **Rieu** Suppt. 129 (A.H. 1266/1850).

[Autobiography in the *khātimah* to the *Ḥadīqah i Amān-Allāhī* (summarised by Rieu) ; *Majma' al-fuṣaḥā'* ii pp. 150–1.]

1217. S. **Murtaḍā " Bīnish "** b. Ṣādiq 'Alī Riḍawī Ḥusainī Madrāsī, whose family came from Gulbargah, was born in 1226/1811 at Madrās.

[1] d. 1144/1731. See *Khāzin al-shu'arā* fol. 173*a* (under " Yaḥyā "), Raḥmān 'Alī pp. 58–9.
[2] Titles in *Kh. al-sh.* fol. 185*b*.
[3] Titles in *Kh. al-sh.* fol. 186*a*.
[4] Nāṣir 'Alī Sirhindī (d. 1108/1697) seems to be among the earliest.
[5] The capital of Persian Kurdistān : see *Ency. Isl.* under Senna.

Ishārāt i Bīnish (a chronogram = 1265/1848–9, the date of completion), notices of 69 (66 ?) contemporary poets of the Carnatic, dedicated to Nawwāb M. Ghauth Khān Shahāmat-Jang (for whom see pp. 897–9 *supra*): **Ivanow** Curzon 61 (many additions and emendations, possibly by the author).

Edition: *Tadhkirah i Bīnish*, [**Madras**] 1268/1851–2*.

List of the poets: Ivanow-Curzon pp. 68–70.

[Autobiography in *Ishārāt i Bīnish*; *Ṣubḥ i waṭan* pp. 38–42; *Ṣubḥ i gulshan* p. 75.]

1218. Qāḍī **Nūr al-Dīn "Fā'iq"**[1] b. Qāḍī S. Aḥmad Ḥusain Riḍawī.

Makhzan i shu'arā', (a chronogram = 1268/1851–2), a *tadhkirah* of the Rēkhtah (i.e. Urdu), poets of Gujrāt: **Bombay** Univ. (see *JBBRAS*, n.s. iv (1928), p. 142).

Edition: **Aurangābād** (Delhi printed) date ? (Anjuman i Taraqqī i Urdū. With introduction by 'Abd al-Ḥaqq. See review in *Oriental College Magazine* x/3 (May 1934), p. 135).

1219. 'Abd al-'Alīm **Naṣr Allāh Khān** "Qamar" Aḥmadī Khwēshgī[2] Khūrjawī, who died in 1299/1881, has already been mentioned (pp. 756–7) as the author of a *Tārīkh i Dakan*.

Gulshan i hamīshah-bahār, brief and almost dateless notices of 414 Indian, mostly Urdū, poets, written by the author at the age of thirty[3] after reading "Shēftah's" *Gulshan i bī-khār* (cf. p. 896 *supra*) at Bijnaur and finding it unsatisfactory: Fatḥ al-akhbār Press, **Kōl** [i.e. 'Alīgaṛh], A.H. 1270/1854* (p. 173 in Arberry).

[Autobiography in *G. i h.-b.* pp. 92–4; see also p. 757 *supra*.]

1220. Mīrzā **Ṭāhir "Shi'rī" Iṣfahānī,** surnamed (*mulaqqab bah*) Dībājah-nigār, one of the Iṣfahānī shaikhs descended, like "Ḥazīn" (see p. 840 *supra*), from Sh. Zāhid Jīlānī, was born at Iṣfahān in 1224/1809. Educated at his birthplace and at Ṭihrān, he entered the service of Nawwāb I'tiḍād al-Salṭanah (for whom

[1] Qāḍī Nūr al-Dīn Ḥusain Khān Riḍawī Fā'iq according to the *Oriental College Magazine*.

[2] For this Afghān clan-name see *An Afghan colony at Qasur*, by M. Shafī' (in *Islamic culture* iii/3 (July 1929) pp. 452–73).

[3] Naṣr Allāh Khān does not mention the date of his birth.

see p. 238 *supra*). His death must have occurred between 1272/1856, the date of the *Ganj i shāygān*, and 1288/1871, the date of the completion of the *Majma' al-fuṣaḥā'*, in which, apparently through a misprint, he is said to have died in 1270. The same date is given in *al-Ma'āthir wa-'l-āthār*.

Ganj i shāygān, notices of 41 or 42 panegyrists of the Ṣadr i A'ẓam, Mīrzā Āqā Khān, written in 1272/1856 [1] and divided into a *durj i nukhustīn* (*dar dhikr i āthār u aṭwār i shāh-zādagān*), a *durj i duwum* (*dar sharḥ i ḥasab u nasab i Ṣadr i A'ẓam u marātib i faḍl u adab i shu'arā-yi buzurgwār*) and a *silk* (*dar tarjamah i aḥwāl u shamma'ī az aqwāl i mu'allif i kitāb*) : **Majlis** 428.

Edition : [**Ṭihrān**] 1272/1856°.

Description with a list of the poets : *Mélanges asiatiques* iv (St. Petersburg 1863), pp. 57–60.

[*Ganj i shāygān, silk* ; *Majma' al-fuṣaḥā'* ii, pp. 246–7 ; *al-Ma'āthir wa-'l-āthār* p. 204.]

1221. For the *Rauḍat al-ṣafā-yi Nāṣirī*, which was completed in 1274/1857 by Riḍā-Qulī Khān and which contains biographies of celebrities including poets (e.g. vol. ix, foll. 173*a*–179*a*), see p. 910[32] *infra*.

1222. For the *Khwurshīd i jahān-numā*, which was begun in 1270/1853–4 and completed in 1280/1863–4 by S. Ilāhī Bakhsh Angrēzābādī and of which the ninth *burj* contains biographies of saints, poets, etc., see p. 152 *supra*.

1223. S. **'Abd al-Laṭīf "Alṭaf"** Ḥusainī is the author of an Urdu verse translation of Jāmī's *I'tiqād-nāmah* published with the Persian text at Madras in 1272/1855–6*.

Sham' i maḥfil i sukhan, notices of Persian and Indian poets : **Madrās** 1279/1862*.

1224. Maulawī Āghā **Aḥmad 'Alī** "Aḥmad" b. Āghā Shajā'at-'Alī was born at D'hākā (Dacca) in Eastern Bengal on 10 Shawwāl

[1] The chronogram quoted in the Majlis catalogue (*Āgandah shud ba-durj i guhar Ganj i shāygān*) really indicates 1273, but is apparently intended to indicate 1272.

1255/17 Dec. 1839. In 1862 he founded at Calcutta the Madrasah i Aḥmadīyah, over which he presided until his death. In 1864 he was appointed a Persian teacher in the Calcutta Madrasah, and on 6 Rabīʿ ii A.H. 1290/6 June 1873 he died of fever at Dacca. He was the author of (1) *Mu'aiyid i Burhān*, a defence of the *Burhān i qāṭiʿ* against the criticisms of " G͟hālib " [1] (475 pp. Maẓhar al-ʿajā'ib Press, Calcutta 1865),[2] (2) *S͟hams͟hīr i tīz-tar*, a reply to " G͟hālib's " rejoinder, the *S͟hams͟hīr i tīz* (106 pp. Calcutta 1868),[2] (3) *Risālah i tarānah* (*A treatise on the Rubá'í entitled Risálah i Taránah by Ágha Ahmad 'Alí . . . with an introduction and explanatory notes by H. Blochmann*, Calcutta 1867°*, pp. 11, 17), (4) *Risālah i is͟htiqāq*, an elementary Persian grammar (1872). He was editor, or co-editor, of the Bibliotheca Indica editions of the *Akbar-nāmah* (see p. 547 *supra*), the *Iqbāl-nāmah i Jahāngīrī* (see p. 562 *supra*), the *Ma'āt͟hir i 'Ālamgīrī* (see p. 593 *supra*), the *Muntak͟hab al-tawārīk͟h* (see p. 439 *supra*), the *Sikandar-nāmah i baḥrī*, and the *Wīs u Rāmīn*.

Haft āsmān, an account of Persian *mat͟hnawīs* and their writers, begun in 1869 and intended to consist of an *auj* (on the nature of *mat͟hnawī* verse, the earliest writers of *mat͟hnawīs* and " Niẓāmī ", the " imām " of *mat͟hnawī-gūyān*), seven *āsmāns* (each devoted to *mat͟hnawīs* in one of the seven metres used in that kind of verse) and an *ufuq*, but never continued beyond the *auj* and the first *āsmān* (on *mat͟hnawīs* in the *sarīʿ* metre).

Edition: *The Haft ásmán or History of the Masnawí of the Persians. By the late Maulawí Ágha Ahmad 'Alí . . . with a biographical notice of the author, by H. Blochmann.* **Calcutta** 1873°* (Bibliotheca Indica).

[Blochmann's biographical notice.]

1225. Amīr al-S͟huʿarā' **Riḍā-Qulī K͟hān " Hidāyat "** b. M. Hādī Ṭabaristānī [3] was born at Ṭihrān on 15 Muḥarram

[1] For whom see pp. 525–7 *supra*.

[2] Neither the British Museum nor the India Office seems to have the *Mu'aiyid i Burhān* or the *S͟hams͟hīr i tīz-tar*.

[3] The autobiographies in the *Majmaʿ al-fuṣaḥā'* and the *Rauḍat al-ṣafā-yi Nāṣirī* are headed Hidāyat i Ṭabaristānī and Hidāyat i Māzandarānī respectively.

1215/8 June 1800. His father, who died in 1218/1803–4 at Shīrāz, had been Treasurer [1] to Āqā Muḥammad Shāh Qājār (reigned 1193/1779–1211/1797) and after serving Fatḥ-'Alī Shāh for a short time in the same capacity had been appointed Treasurer of the province of Fārs [2] under the Governor, Ḥusain 'Alī Mīrzā. Having lost his father in early childhood, Riḍā-Qulī lived for some years with relatives of his mother at Bārfurūsh,[3] and later, having returned to Fārs, he was cared for by another relative, M. Mahdī Khan "Shiḥnah" Māzandarānī,[4] who held high office in the province. On the completion of his education he entered the service of the Governor, Ḥusain 'Alī Mīrzā,[5] and held various appointments in attendance upon him and his sons.[6] In 1245/1829–30, when Fatḥ-'Alī Shāh visited Shīrāz (3 Rajab/29 Dec. to 11 Sha'bān/5 Feb.), Riḍā-Qulī was presented and was given the titles of Khān and Amīr al-Shu'arā.[7] After Muḥammad Shāh's accession [in 1250/1834] and the defeat and

[1] *Dar ḥaḍrat i . . . M. Shāh Qājār . . . ba-manṣab i khazīnah-dārī maḥsūd i aqrān būdah* (*Riyāḍ al-'ārifīn* p. 627^{11}) : *Āqā M. Shāh wai rā rīsh-safīd i 'amalah i khalwat u ṣandūq-dār i jinsī i khwud kardah* (*Majma' al-fuṣaḥā'* ii p. 581^{21}).

[2] *Pas az intiqāl i ān daulat ba-ḥaḍrat i . . . Fatḥ-'Alī Shāh . . . dar ān darbār . . . ba-manṣab i madhkūr* [i.e. *manṣab i khazīnah-dārī*] *muftakhir u ḥasb al-amr ma'mūr ba-khidmatgudhārī i Farmān-farmā-yi mamlakat i Fārs shudah ba-Shīrāz āmadah* (*Riyāḍ al-'ārifīn* p. 627^{12}) : *Ba'd az sālī dū ba-Taḥwīl-dārī u Ṣāḥib-jam'ī i kull i mutawajjihāt i dīwānī i Fārs ma'mūr u ba-khidmat i . . . Ḥusain 'Alī Mīrzā-yi Farmān-farmā-yi Fārs mashghūl būd* (*Majma' al-fuṣaḥā'* ii p. 581^{23}).

[3] *Majma' al-fuṣaḥā'* ii p. 581^{25}. It appears from *Rauḍat al-ṣafā-yi Nāṣirī* ix fol. 95, l. 12, that he was there in 1224/1809 at the age of nine.

[4] For accounts of him see *Anjuman i Khāqān*, *Nigāristān i Dārā*, *Tadhkirah i Muḥammad-Shāhī*, *Rauḍat al-ṣafā-yi Nāṣirī* ix fol. 177*b* penult. (7th page from end), *Majma' al-fuṣaḥā'* ix pp. 252–3. He died in 1247/1831–2.

[5] Son of Fatḥ-'Alī Shāh and for thirty years Governor of Fārs, he became a pretender to the throne on his father's death but was defeated and he died on his way to the fortress prison of Ardabīl.

[6] *Chūn zamān i khurd-sālī dar-gudhasht ba-mulāzamat i Shāh-zādah i Farmān-farmā u farzandānash ba-sar mī-raft u mu'azzaz u mukarram mī-zīst u manāṣib i munāsib dāsht* (*Majma' al-fuṣaḥā'* ii p. 581) ; *rūzgārī chand nīz ba-ḥukm i wirāthat mulāzamat numūd 'āqibat ba-khwud sitīzān u az khidmat gurīzān dar kunj i 'uzlat pā ba-dāman kashīd hamginān-rā kārash shigift āmadah* etc. (*Riyāḍ al-'ārifīn* p. 628^{2}). In speaking of Riḍā-Qulī Mīrzā, Ḥusain 'Alī Mīrzā's eldest son, Riḍā-Qulī Khān says *Bandah i mu'allif sāl-hā dar khidmatash ḥarīf i ḥujrah u garmābah u gulistān būdah am* (*Rauḍat al-ṣafā-yi Nāṣirī* x fol. 5*a*, l. 19).

[7] *Rauḍat al-ṣafā-yi Nāṣirī* ix fol. 148*b*, l. 10 *ab infra*, *Majma' al-fuṣaḥā'* ii p. 581 penult.

arrest of Ḥusain ʻAlī Mīrzā the province of Fārs came under the authority of Fīrūz Mīrzā[1] and Muʻtamad al-Daulah Minūchihr Khān (for whom see p. 902 n. 1 *supra*). Riḍā-Qulī Khān was appointed Companion[2] to the former and held this position for a year or two, but when Fīrūz Mīrzā was transferred to the Governorship of Kirmān, he remained in Shīrāz at the court of the new Governor, Farīdūn Mīrzā.[3] In 1254/1838 he was sent to Ṭihrān by Farīdūn Mīrzā with presents for Muḥammad Shāh,[4] who had just returned from his unsuccessful expedition against Harāt.[5] Muḥammad Shāh instructed him to remain at court and in 1257/1841 appointed him guardian to his son ʻAbbās Mīrzā.[6] He became the constant companion of the king, with whom he used to discuss history and poetry.[7] At the end of 1263/1847 he was appointed Governor of the district of Fīrūzkūh and in accordance with a recognized custom sent his eldest son, ʻAlī-Qulī, to administer

[1] The Shāh's brother, twelfth in the list of the sons of ʻAbbās Mīrzā b. Fatḥ-ʻAlī Shāh given in the *Rauḍat al-ṣafā-yi Nāṣirī* ix fol. 166*a*.

[2] *Faqīr-rā ba-munādamat i Nawwāb Fīrūz Mīrzā manṣūb dāshtand* (*Majmaʻ al-fuṣaḥā'* ii p. 582^{4}); *chūn man i bandah . . . dar ān zamān ba-ṣawāb-dīd i Muʻtamad al-Daulah ba-munādamat u muṣāḥabat i amīr-zādah i madhkūr muftakhir u ma'mūr būdam u jamʻī az mutaʻalliqīn u ʻiyāl dar mauṭin i ma'lūf yaʻnī Shīrāz dāshtam li-hādhā Nawwāb i ashraf Farmān-farmā-yi jadīd i Fārs Farīdūn Mīrzā marā az ḥarakat manʻ u ba-sukūn amr farmūd u ba-khilʻat u inʻām u raḥmat u ikrām dar ḥaḍrat i khwud muʻazzaz u mashʻūf hamī-dāsht chunān-kih dar tahniyat i wurūdash midḥatī kih ziyādah az hashtād bait būd mauzūn u maʻrūḍ dāshtam ba-ʻadad i abyāt ashrafī i tūmānī jā'izah jā'iz shumurd u adā farmūd* (*Rauḍat al-ṣafā-yi Nāṣirī* x fol. 10*b*, l. 1).

[3] Another of Muḥammad Shāh's brothers, fifth in the list referred to in the last footnote but one.

[4] *u dar īn aiyām Nawwāb . . . Farīdūn Mīrzā . . . bandah i mu'allif u ʻAlī-Qulī Khān Sartīb i Afshār rā bā baʻḍī tuḥaf u hadāyā rawānah i Dār al-khilāfah numūd u pas az sharaf-yābī i ḥuḍūr i ḥaḍrat i sulṭānī u maʻrūfīyat dar khidmat i janāb i Ḥājjī* [Mīrzā Āqāsī] *i Airawānī ba-tawaqquf i rikāb ma'mūr shudīm* (*Rauḍat al-ṣafā-yi Nāṣirī* x fol. 22*a*, l. 22). Riḍā-Qulī Khān reached Ṭihrān on 15 Ramaḍān and stayed at the house of Ḥājjī Mīrzā Āqāsī, the Prime Minister (*Majmaʻ al-fuṣaḥā'* ii p. 582^{7}).

[5] For this expedition see R. G. Watson, *History of Persia* pp. 297–319.

[6] *Ham dar īn sāl Shāh-zādah ʻAbbās Mīrzā pas az faut i birādar i akbar i khwud dar shab i iḥyā-yi Ramaḍān mutawallid gardīd u samī i birādar i raftah shud u ḥaḍrat i Shāhanshāhī bandah i mu'allif rā ba-tarbiyat u khidmat i ū ma'mūr farmūd* (*Rauḍat al-ṣafā-yi Nāṣirī* x fol. 25*a*, l. 19).

[7] *Majmaʻ al-fuṣaḥā'* ii 582^{9-11}. Cf. *op. cit.* i fol. 5*a*, l. 13: *ba-khidmat i tarbiyat i yakī az shāh-zādagānam ma'mūr u ba-manṣab i tarkhānī i ḥuḍūr i bāhir al-nūr dar safar u ḥaḍar u khalwat u jalwat masrūr dāsht.* For the word *tarkhānī* cf. *op. cit.* ii p. 515^{1}: *dar zamān i jawānī dar khidmat i . . . Fatḥ-ʻAlī Shāh simat i munādamat dāshtah dar khalawāt ba-kitāb-khwānī u dar jalawāt ba-tarkhānī makhṣūṣ būdah kamāl i maḥramīyat dar ān-ḥaḍrat yāftah.*

the district as his deputy.[1] After the accession of Nāṣir al-Dīn Shāh in 1264/1848 he retired from official life for a time,[2] but on 5 Jumādā II 1267/7 April 1851 he left for Khīvah on the embassy which he has described in his *Sifārat-nāmah i Khwārazm*. On his return after an absence of eight months [3] he was appointed Principal of the newly founded Dār al-Funūn College, or École polytechnique, at Ṭihrān.[4] About the same time he was instructed to bring the *Rauḍat al-ṣafā'* up to date.[5] For nearly fifteen years he remained at the College and then he was appointed *Lālah-bāshī*, or Tutor, to the Crown Prince, Muẓaffar al-Dīn Mīrzā, who had just been nominated Governor of Ādharbāyjān and with whom he spent some years at Tabrīz. He died at Ṭihrān on 10 Rabī' II 1288/30 June 1871. Gobineau says of him : "J'ai vu dans un diner Ryza-Kouly-Khan, ancien gouverneur du frère du roi, ambassadeur à Bokhara, historiographe, grammairien, et poëte excellent en persan littéraire et en dialecte. C'est un des hommes les plus spirituels et les plus aimables que j'aie rencontrés dans aucune partie du monde." [6]

Riḍā-Qulī Khān's works [7] include (1) *ghazalīyāt* and *qaṣā'id*. In the *Riyāḍ al-'ārifīn*, completed in 1260/1844,[8] his *Dīwān*

[1] *Rauḍat al-ṣafā-yi Nāṣirī* x fol. 41*b* penult. : *u ḥukūmat i wilāyat i Fīrūzkūh nīz ba-īn-ghulām mufawwaḍ gardīd u 'Alī-Qulī pisar i akbar i khwud rā bah niyābat rawānah kardam.*

[2] *Majma' al-fuṣaḥā'* ii p. 582[14] : *ba-rikāb-būsī sharaf-yāb gashtah ba-khidmat i muqarrarah ma'mūr āmadam ba-sababī chand az ān khidmat isti'fā numūdam u ba-kunj i 'uzlat uftādam.*

[3] *az safar i dūr i Khwārazm kih hasht-māh imtidād yāftah būd* (*Rauḍat al-ṣafā-yi Nāṣirī* x fol. 106, l. 8).

[4] *pas ba-riyāsat u nāẓimīyat i Madrasah i Dār al-Funūn . . . muftakhir gashtam u dar-īn ḍimn ḥasb al-amr ba-itmām i tārīkh i Rauḍat al-ṣafā ḥukmī raft . . .* (*Majma' al-fuṣaḥā'* ii p. 582[17]). The Dār al-Funūn was opened on 5 Rabī' II 1268/28 January 1852 (*al-Ma'āthir wa-'l-āthār* p. 111).

[5] See p. 910[32] *infra*.

[6] *Trois ans en Asie*, Paris 1859, tome ii pp. 454–5 (chapitre v : les caractères).

[7] Of the twenty works enumerated below all but the *Jāmi' al-asrār* (no. 14), the *Nizhād-nāmah* (no. 17) and the *Farhang* (no. 18) are mentioned in the *Majma' al-fuṣaḥā'* (ii p. 582). The *Jāmi' al-asrār* is mentioned without information concerning its subject in the author's list of his own works in the *Riyāḍ al-'ārifīn* (pp. 628–9). That list, although it immediately follows a statement that 1260 was the current year and that the author's age was then forty-five, contains (at least in the printed edition of A.H.S. 1316) several works written after 1260, since it includes all the twenty enumerated below except the *Sifārat-nāmah* (no. 15), the *Nizhād-nāmah* (no. 17) and the *Farhang* (no. 18).

[8] That it contains later additions (at least in its printed form) is clear from the preceding note.

i ghazalīyāt is described as consisting of 8,000 verses and his *qaṣā'id* as amounting to more than 10,000 verses. In the *Majma' al-fuṣaḥā'*, completed in 1288/1871,[1] his *qaṣā'id* and *ghazalīyāt* together are said to comprise more than 30,000 verses. A MS. *dīwān* transcribed in 1283/1866 and consisting mainly of *ghazals* is preserved in the British Museum (Rieu Suppt. 365). **(2)–(8)** seven *mathnawīs*,[2] namely (2) *Anwār al-wilāyah* in the metre of the *Makhzan al-asrār*, (3) *Gulistān i Iram* or *Baktāsh-nāmah*, on the love-story of Baktāsh and Rābi'ah (Edition: [Ṭihrān [3]] 1270/1854°), (4) *Baḥr al-ḥaqā'iq* in the metre of "Sanā'ī's" *Ḥadīqah*, (5) *Anīs al-'āshiqīn*, "a religious and mystic poem, with anecdotes of saints and Sufis" (M.S.: Rieu Suppt. 364 ii, dated 1253/1837), (6) *Khurram bihisht* (metre *mutaqārib*) completed in 1277/1860–1 (MS.: Majlis 433), (7) *Hidāyat-nāmah* (metre *ramal*), "a poem containing moral and religious precepts illustrated by apologues and anecdotes in the style of the Masnavi of Jalāl ud-Dīn Rūmi and in the same metre" (MS.: Rieu Suppt. 364 i, dated 1253/1837), (8) *Manhaj al-hidāyah*,

(9) *Madārij al-balāghah*, "(lith. 1331) . . . a glossary of rhetorical and poetical terms with many examples taken from different poets" (*Ency. Isl.*), **(10)** *Maẓāhir al-anwār* (see p. 224 *supra*), **(11)** *Miftāḥ al-kunūz*, a commentary on the *dīwān* of Khāqānī (MS.: Rieu Suppt. 221 ii, dated 1259/1843), **(12)** *Laṭā'if al-ma'ārif*,[4] **(13)** *Fihris al-tawārīkh*, a concise chronology presented to Nāṣir al-Dīn Shāh just before the author's departure on his embassy to Khīwah (*Rauḍat al-ṣafā-yi Nāṣirī* x, fol. 70*a*, l. 5 *ab infra*), which "appears to have been lost save that portion which was lithographed at Tabríz in A.H. 1280, but which has never been distributed" (S. Churchill in *JRAS*. 1887 p. 318), **(14)** *Jāmi' al-asrār* (see footnote 7 on p. 909 *supra*), **(15)** *Sifārat-nāmah i Khwārazm* (see p. 342 *supra*), **(16)** *Rauḍat al-ṣafā-yi Nāṣirī*, an edition of the seven volumes of the *Rauḍat al-ṣafā'*

[1] For the date see p. 911 *infra*.
[2] The first six have the title *Sittah i ḍarūrīyah*.
[3] Tabrīz according to *Ency. Isl.* (Massé).
[4] Probably the work referred to in S. Churchill's statement that "The Lataáif ul-'Árifín is a Súfí tract in prose mixed with verse" (*JRAS*. 1887 p. 318).

(see p. 92 *supra*), followed by a continuation in three [1] volumes extending to 1274 [2]/1857 (Edition: Ṭihrān 1270–4/1853–7°), (**17**) *Nizhād-nāmah i pādshāhān i Īrānī-nizhād* (see p. 239 *supra*), (**18**) *Farhang i anjuman-ārāy i Nāṣirī*, a dictionary of which the introductory remarks were written in 1286/1869–70 and which is devoted mainly to words used by the poets (Edition: Ṭihrān 1288/1871°*. For a description see *JRAS*. 1886 pp. 200–3),

(19) ***Riyāḍ al-ʿārifīn***, notices of saints who were also poets with selections from their poems, completed in 1260/1844, dedicated to Muḥammad Shāh and divided into a *ḥadīqah* (on Ṣūfism, the life of the Ṣūfīs and their conventional terms), two *rauḍahs* ((1) *dar dhikr i ʿurafā u mashāyikh ba-tartīb i tahajjī*, notices of about 170 saints and mystics who composed poetry, (2) *dar dhikr i fuḍalā u muḥaqqiqīn i ḥukamā*, alphabetically arranged notices of about 100 poets and philosophers (the first Avicenna, the last Yaḥyā Lāhijī), who at times wrote mystical poetry), a *firdaus* (*dar sharḥ i ḥāl i muta'akhkhirīn u muʿāṣirīn*, alphabetically arranged notices of about 70 modern and contemporary Ṣūfī poets) and a *khuld* (autobiography): **Rieu** Suppt. 126 (19th cent.).

Editions: **Ṭihrān** 1305/1888°, A.H.S. 1316/1937‡.

(20) ***Majmaʿ al-fuṣaḥā'***, notices of 862 ancient [3] and modern poets completed in 1288/1871 [4] and divided into four chapters [5]

[1] The *R. al-ṣ. i N.* is in ten volumes, each with its own title-page. In the B.M. description " 2 vols." should properly be " 10 vols. in 2 ".

[2] Not 1270, as stated in the *Ency. Isl.*

[3] Riḍā-Qulī Khān criticises his predecessors for including in their so-called *tadhkirahs* only inferior specimens of ancient poetry.

[4] 1288 is given as the date of completion on p. 678¹ of vol. ii. In the preface (vol. i, fol. 6*a*, l. 7) and in the heading to *Bāb* ii (vol. i p. 64) 1284 and 1285 respectively are mentioned as the current year, but earlier years are elsewhere described as current, e.g. 1274 (vol. ii p. 548¹⁵) and 1275 (vol. ii p. 81¹³). The work, based in part on material collected over a period of thirty years (see vol. i, fol. 4*b* ult.), would doubtless have remained unfinished, if the author had not been instructed first by Muḥammad Shāh (vol. i, fol. 5*a*, l. 14) and later by Nāṣir al-Dīn Shāh (fol. 6*a*, l. 4) to finish it.

[5] The word *bāb* is applied to these divisions at the end of the preface (vol. i, fol. 6*a*, l. 14), at the beginning of the biography of Nāṣir al-Dīn Shāh (fol. 10*b*, ll. 1 and 5) and in the heading to *Bāb* ii (vol. i p. 64. *Bābs* iii and iv are without headings). On the other hand the word *rukn* is used, but doubtless only by way of comparison, a few lines before the divisions are called *abwāb* (vol. i, fol. 6*a*, l. 10: *u ān-rā murattab u mubawwab sākhtam u bunyān i ān-rā mānand i ʿālam i jusmānī bar chār rukn nihādam*). On p. 657 of vol. i the words *qismat* and *ṭabaqah* are used.

((1) 115 kings and princes who wrote poetry, the first being Nāṣir al-Dīn Shāh, the last Yūsuf ʻĀdil-Shāh (vol. i, fol. 10*b*–p. 63), (2) 323 ancient poets from A.H. 173/789–90 to 800/1397–8,[1] the first Abū Ḥafṣ Sughdī, the last Yūsuf Ghaznawī (vol. i pp. 64–657), (3) 66 " mediaeval " poets (*shuʻarā-yi mutawassiṭīn*), the first " Āhī " Turshīzī, the last Yaḥyā Gīlānī (vol. ii pp. 2–57), (4) 358 modern and contemporary poets, the first " Adīb " Marāgha'ī, the last two " Yaghmā " and " Hidāyat " (vol. ii pp. 58–678) : **Rieu** Suppt. 125 (an early recension dedicated to Muḥammad Shāh. The MS. breaks off in the notice of Niẓāmī, vol. i p. 639 in the Ṭihrān edition. Circ. A.H. 1250/1835, said to be partly autograph).

Edition : **Ṭihrān** 1295/1878°* (2 vols.).

Descriptions : 1) *Relation de l'ambassade au Kharezm* (see p. 342 *supra*), introduction, pp. xx–xxi ; (2) *JRAS.* 1886 pp. 203–4 (by S. Churchill. With list of *tadhkirahs* mentioned in the preface).

In addition Riḍā-Qulī Khān was editor of (1) the *Dīwān i Minūchihrī* (Ṭihrān, date ? See *JRAS.* 1886 p. 200. The Ṭihrān edition of 1297/1880° was based on his edition), (2) the *Qābūs-nāmah* and the *Tuzuk i Tīmūrī* (Ṭihrān 1285/1868°), (3) the *Nafthat al-maṣdūr* (Ṭihrān A.H.S. 1307–8/1928–30 [2]).

[Autobiographies in *Riyāḍ al-ʻārifīn*, last chapter (Ṭihrān 1316 pp. 627–52), *Rauḍat al-ṣafā-yi Nāṣirī* ix foll. 178*b* (5th page from end), *Majmaʻ al-fuṣaḥā'* ii pp. 581–677 ; biography by Mānakjī (cf. p. 239 *supra*) prefixed to the *Farhang i anjuman-ārāy i Nāṣirī* (Ṭihrān 1288/1871°*) ; *Relation de l'ambassade au*

[1] These dates are given in the heading to the table of contents on fol. 7*b* in vol. i, but there is some confusion in the arrangement of the poets, since, although *Bāb* ii includes some poets of the eighth century (e.g. Ṣafī al-Dīn Ardabīlī, d. 735, vol. i p. 313, and ʻAlī Hamadānī, d. 786, p. 340), there are far more in *Bāb* iii (e.g. Ibn i Yamīn, d. 763, vol. ii p. 2, Ḥāfiẓ, d. 791, p. 11, Khwājū, d. 734, p. 15, Salmān i Sāwajī, d. 769, p. 19). The *mutawassiṭīn* in *Bāb* iii seem to be poets who died between 701 and 1151 (A.H. 1150 being given on p. 56 (cf. *Ṭarā'iq al-ḥaqā'iq* iii p. 42[33]) as the date of the death of " Hāshimī " Dihlawī b. M. Mu'min " ʻArshī ", who is erroneously described as the author of the *Maẓhar al-āthār* (cf. Rieu ii 802, Ethé 1765), a *mathnawī* really written in 940). Here again, however, there is some overlapping, since *Bāb* iv contains Fatḥ Allāh " Janāb " Iṣfahānī, who died in 1146 (vol. ii p. 92).

[2] 1307 *Shamsī* on title-page, 1308 on cover, but 1341 [*Qamarī* = 1922–3] in the lithographer's colophon.

Kharezm de Riza Qouly Khan traduite et annotée par C. Schefer (see p. 342 *supra*), introduction, pp. xv–xxiv ; *A modern contributor to Persian literature, Rizá Ḳulí Khán and his works. By Sidney Churchill* (in *JRAS*. 1886 pp. 196–206. Cf. *JRAS*. 1887 pp. 163 and 318) ; *al-Ma'āt͟hir wa-'l-āt͟hār*, p. 189 ; Berthels *Ocherk istorii persidskoi literatury*, Leningrad 1928 pp. 110–13 ; *Ency. Isl.* under Riḍā Ḳulī K͟hān (Massé).

Portraits : *Farhang i anjuman-ārāy i Nāṣirī*, plate ; *Naft͟hat al-maṣdūr*, frontispiece ; *Riyāḍ al-'ārifīn* A.H.S. 1316, frontispiece ; Browne *Lit. Hist.* iv p. 344.]

1226. Nawwāb M. **Ṣiddīq Ḥasan K͟hān** " Nawwāb " died in 1890 (see p. 27 *supra*).

S͟ham' i anjuman, notices of 989 ancient and modern poets, completed in 1292/1875.

Edition : [**Bhōpāl**,] 1292–3/1876°*.

[See p. 27 *supra* as well as *S͟ham' i anjuman* pp. 474–86 and Brockelmann *Supptbd.* ii pp. 859–61.]

1227. [Nawwāb] Raḍī al-Daulah Niẓām al-Mulk [1] S. Abū'l-K͟hair **Nūr al-Ḥasan K͟hān** " Ṭaiyib ",[2] originally " Nūr ", b. M. Ṣiddīq Ḥasan K͟hān, elder son of the author of the *S͟ham' i anjuman* (see § 1226 *supra*) by his first wife, a daughter of the Prime Minister of Bhōpāl, M. Jamāl al-Dīn K͟hān Dihlawī, was born at Bhōpāl on 21 Rajab 1278/22 January 1862. Among his teachers was Maulawī Ilāhī Bak͟hs͟h Faiḍābādī, Head Teacher of the Madrasah i Sulaimānī at Bhōpāl. His publications include (1) *'Arf al-jādī min jinān hudā 'l-hādī* (Edition : Bhōpāl 1296/1879. See Āṣafīyah iii p. 444, from which it would seem to be a Persian work on Ḥanafī Law, though Sarkis (*Dictionnaire encyclopédique*, col. 1873) treats it as an Arabic work), (2) *al-Nahj al-maqbūl min s͟harā'i' al-Rasūl* (Edition : place ? 1296/1879. See Āṣafīyah iii p. 446, where it is placed among the Persian works on Ḥanafī Law), (3) *al-Jawā'iz wa-'l-ṣilāt min jam' al-asāmī wa-'l-ṣifāt* (an Arabic work " on Muḥammadan names,

[1] These two titles, conferred doubtless by the State of Bhōpāl, are mentioned in *Ma'āt͟hir i Ṣiddīqī* (cf. p. 28[26] *supra*) iv p. 216.

[2] *Ma'āt͟hir i Ṣiddīqī* iv p. 216.

titles, and epithets." Edition: Delhi[1] 1297/1880°), (4) *al-Raḥmat al-muhdāh ilā man yurīd ziyādat al-'ilm 'alā aḥādīth al-Mishkāh*, in Arabic (Edition: place ? 1301/1883–4. See Sarkis, col. 1873, and Āṣafīyah i p. 628, from the latter of which it appears that Nūr al-Ḥasan was the editor rather than the author of this *Takmilah i Mishkāt*), (5) *Sulṭān al-adhkār min aḥādīth Saiyid al-abrār*, an abridgment of the *'Amal al-yaum wa-'l-lailah* of Ibn al-Sunnī[2] (Edition: Ḥaidarābād 1318/1900–1. See Sarkis, col. 1873).

In the Āṣafīyah catalogue, vol. i, published in 1332/1914, he is described as *maujūd* (i.e. still alive), but on p. 49 of the *Ma'āthir i Ṣiddīqī*, vol. ii, published in 1342/1924, his name is followed by the word *marḥūm*.

(1) ***Nigāristān i sukhan***, a supplement to the *Sham' i anjuman*, devoted primarily to poets of Bengal and elsewhere whose verses sent for inclusion in that work arrived too late but containing also many other ancient and modern poets, 651 in all. Edition: [**Bhōpāl**], 1293/1876*°.

(2) ***Tadhkirah i Ṭūr i Kalīm***. Edition: place ? 1299/1881–2 (see Āṣafīyah i p. 318).

[*Sham' i anjuman* pp. 486–7; *Nigāristān i sukhan* pp. 130–3; Ellis ii col. 446; Edwards col. 599; Sarkis *Dictionnaire encyclopédique de bibliographie arabe*, col. 1873; *Ma'āthir i Ṣiddīqī* (cf. p. 28 *supra*), iv p. 216; Brockelmann *Supptbd.* ii p. 861. Very full information would doubtless be obtainable from the fifth volume of the *Ma'āthir i Ṣiddīqī*, if ever published, since that volume was to deal with Ṣiddīq Ḥasan Khān's descendants. Only vols. i–iv have been accessible to me.]

1228. Nawwāb Ṣafī al-Daulah Ḥusām al-Mulk[3] S. Abū Naṣr M. **'Alī Ḥasan Khān** "Ṭāhir", originally "'Āshiqī", b. M. Ṣiddīq Ḥasan Khān was the younger son of the author of the *Sham' i anjuman* (see p. 913 *supra*) by his first wife, a daughter of the Prime Minister of Bhōpāl, M. Jamāl al-Dīn Khān Dihlawī.

[1] So Ellis. Sarkis says Bhōpāl.
[2] See Brockelmann i p. 165.
[3] For these titles see *Ma'āthir i Ṣiddīqī* vi p. 216 and the description of the author's work *Ta'līm u tarbiyat* on the back covers of the *Ma'āthir i Ṣiddīqī*.

He was at one time Honorary Director of the Department of Education in the State of Bhōpāl. Among his works were *al-Bunyān al-marṣūṣ min bayān ījāz al-fiqh al-manṣūṣ*, a Persian work on Ḥanafī Law (Edition: place ? 1299/1881–2. See Āṣafīyah iii p. 444), *Khirman i gul*, a Persian *dīwān*, *Nālah i dil*, an Urdu *dīwān*, *Ma'āthir i Ṣiddīqī*, a detailed Urdu biography of his father (Edition: Lucknow 1342/1924–1343/1925), and several other Urdu works (e.g. *Fiṭrat al-Islām*, *Sīrat al-Islām*, *al-Madanīyah fī'l-Islām*, *Intiẓām i khānah-dārī*), of which descriptions (without dates and places of publication) are given on the back covers of the *Ma'āthir i Ṣiddīqī*.

(1) ***Ṣubḥ i gulshan***, a supplement to the *Sham' i anjuman* (see p. 913 *supra*) and the *Nigāristān i sukhan* (see p. 914 *supra*), begun in 1294/1877 and completed in 1295/1878.

Edition: **Bhōpāl** 1295/1878° (cf. *OCM*. iii/2 (Feb. 1927) p. 51).)

(2) ***Bazm i sukhan***, biographies of Urdu poets, written in 1297/1880.

Edition: place ? date ? (see Āṣafīyah iii p. 162 no. 133 and Peshawar 1482 (1)).

[*Ma'āthir i Ṣiddīqī* iv p. 216. Very full information would doubtless be obtainable from the fifth volume of the *M.i.Ṣ.*, if ever published, since that volume was to deal with Ṣiddīq Ḥasan Khān's descendants. Only vols. i-iv have been accessible to me.]

1229. M. **Muẓaffar Ḥusain "Ṣabā"** Gōpāmawī.[1]

Rūz i raushan, written in 1297/1880 as a supplement to the *Sham' i anjuman* (see p. 913 *supra*), the *Nigāristān i sukhan* (see p. 914 *supra*), and the *Ṣubḥ i gulshan* (see p. 915[12] *supra*).

Edition: **Bhōpāl** 1297/1880° (cf. *OCM*. iii/2 (Feb. 1927) p. 51).)

1230. Qārī **Raḥmat Allāh "Wāḍiḥ"** b. 'Ashūr Muḥammad

[1] Gōpāmau is 14 miles East of Hardoi in Oudh.

Bukhārī [1] was a contemporary of the Manghit Amīr Muẓaffar al-Dīn (reigned 1277/1860–1303/1885).

Tuḥfat al-aḥbāb fī tadhkirat al-aṣḥāb, usually called *Tadhkirah i Qārī Raḥmat Allāh*, notices of Central Asian poets of the nineteenth century: **Bukhārā** Semenov 38.

Edition: *Tuḥfat al-aḥbāb . . . ma' Tārīkh i kathīrah u Majmū'ah i Salīmī*, **Tashkent** 1332/1913–14 (with additions by Mīrzā Salīm Bēk. Cf. p. 378 *supra* and Semenov *Kurzer Abriss* pp. 9–10).

1231. **Abū 'l-Qāsim Muḥtasham** was the son of M. 'Abbās "Rif'at" Shirwānī (for whom see pp. 226, 421 *supra*) and the grandson of Aḥmad b. Muḥammad al-Yamanī al-Shirwānī (for whom see p. 226 n. *supra*, Brockelmann *Sptbd* ii pp. 850–1, *Dānishmandān i Ādharbāyjān* p. 31 and Sarkis *Dictionnaire encyclopédique de bibliographie arabe* coll. 1120–1).

Akhtar i tābān, or *Tadhkirat al-nisā'*, brief notices of 82 poetesses.

Edition: **Bhōpāl** 1299/1881–2 (see M. Shafī''s description in *OCM*. iii/3 (May 1927) p. 52).

1232. Mīrzā **Muḥammad b. M. Rafī'**, entitled Malik al-kuttāb, **Shīrāzī** has already been mentioned as the author of the *Zīnat al-zamān* or *Tāj al-tawārīkh* (p. 492 *supra*, where some biographical information will be found), the *Iksīr al-tawārīkh* (p. 210 *supra*), the *Tārīkh i Ingilistān* and the *Tārīkh i qadīm i Yūnān* (p. 429 *supra*) and the *Mir'āt al-zamān* (p. 432 *supra*).

Tadhkirat al-khawātīn, alphabetically arranged notices of Arabian, Persian, Indian, and Turkish poetesses.

Edition: [**Bombay**] 1306/1889°.

1233. Kunwar [2] **Durgā-Parshād** "Mihr" **Sandīlī** has already been mentioned as the author of the *Gulistān i Hind* (p. 491 *supra*, where some biographical information will be found) and the *Būstān i Awad'h* (p. 712 *supra*).

[1] Ibn-i-Aschur-Muhammad-Rahmatullah-i-Bukhari according to Semenov's *Kurzer Abriss* p. 9. This might conceivably represent M. Raḥmat Allāh b. 'Ashūr Bukhārī. According to Semenov's Bukhārā catalogue the name appears as Ibn-e 'Ashur-Rehmetolla-ol-Bokhari in the lithographed edition.

[2] A Hindī word meaning "prince (son of a Rājah)".

Ḥadīqah i ʿishrat, notices of poetesses[1] written in 1893.
Edition : **Sandīlah** 1894°*.

1234. "**Afḍal**" **Makhdūm i Pīrmastī** is described by Semenov (Bukhārā Catalogue p. 5) as a contemporary Bokharan poet and prose-writer.

Afḍal al-tadhkār fī dhikr al-shuʿarāʾ wa-ʾl-ashʿār, notices of Central Asian poets of the nineteenth century written in 1322/1904 : **Bukhārā** Semenov 4.

Edition : Tashkent 1326/1908 (see Semenov *Kurzer Abriss* p. 10).

[Mīrza Salīm Bēk's additions to the *Tuḥfat al-aḥbāb* (see p. 916[3] *supra*), Tashkent 1332/1913–14, pp. 2, 6, 310–11.]

1235. **Dīnshāh** Jījībhā'ī **Īrānī,** a Bombay solicitor (B.A. 1902, from St. Xavier's College, Judge Spencer Prizeman 1904, Muncherji Nowroji Banaji Scholar 1904, LL.B. 1905 from the Government Law School), was President of the Iranian Zoroastrian Anjuman in 1928. Among his publications are (1) *The Resurrection of the ancient sovereigns of Iran in the ruins of Madayen. A Persian operetta by Syed Mirzadeh Eshqi* [i.e. "ʿIshqī's" *Rastākhīz*]. *Translated* [and edited] *by Dinshaw J. Irani*, Bombay 1924*. (2) *The divine songs of Zarathustra*, London 1927. (3) *Paik i Mazdayasnān* [essays on Zoroastrianism, originally written in English or Gujarati, translated into Persian by Pūr-Dāwud. Pts. 1–8], Bombay 1927–9*. (4) *Pouran-dokht-nâmeh* [*Pūrān-dukht-nāmah*]. *The poems of Poure-Davoud.* [Edited] *with their English translation by D. J. Irani*, Bombay 1928*. (5) *Akhlāq i Īrān i bāstān*, Bombay [1930*], Ṭihrān 1932. (6) *Falsafah i Īrān i bāstān*, Bombay 1933, as well as English translations of a number of Persian texts prescribed for Bombay University examinations.

Poets of the Pahlavi regime [selections from the works of contemporary poets with English translations and short biographies (in Persian with English epitomes)], **Bombay** 1933 (vol. i, 98 poets).

[Bombay University Calendar ; list of publications facing

[1] So Edwards. Arberry says "famous women".

title-page of *Poets of the Pahlavi regime*; portrait in group with R. Tagore and members of the Literary Society, Ṭihrān, reproduced as frontispiece to the same work.]

1236. **Sa'īd Nafīsī,** the son of Dr. Mīrzā 'Alī Akbar Khān Nafīsī Nāẓim al-aṭibbā, was born at Ṭihrān in A.H.S. 1274/1895. After completing his education in Europe[1] he returned to Persia in A.H.S. 1297/1918–19 and received an appointment in the Ministry of Public Works. In A.H.S. 1306/1927–8 (so Īrānī) or 1308/1929–30 (so Ishaque) he entered the service of the Ministry of Education and was nominated to lectureships in Literature and History in the Faculties of Law and Literature [presumably at the University of Ṭihrān]. His works, of which seventeen are mentioned in a list accompanying his edition of the *Rubā'īyāt* of Bābā Afḍal Kāshānī (Ṭihrān A.H.S. 1311/1933, with bio-bibliographical introduction), include novels, a French-Persian dictionary, a life of Sh. Zāhid Gīlānī (Rasht A.H.S. 1307/1928–9. Cf. p. 840, n. 3, *supra*), and editions of classical Persian texts (e.g. 'Umar Khaiyām's *Rubā'īyāt*, Ṭihrān A.H.S. 1306/1927–8, 2nd ed. A.H.S. 1309/1930–1, the *Qābūs-nāmah*, Ṭihrān A.H.S. 1312/1933, Sanā'ī's *Sair al-'ibād ilā 'l-ma'ād*, Ṭihrān A.H.S. 1316/1937, Khwānd-Amīr's *Dastūr al-wuzarā'*, Ṭihrān A.H.S. 1317/1938, Ḥusain Kāshifī's *Lubb i lubāb i Ma'nawī*, Ṭihrān (see *Luzac's Oriental List* 1940, p. 108), " 'Aṭṭār's " *Dīwān i qaṣā'id u-ghazalīyāt*, Ṭihrān A.H.S. 1319/1940–1, and the *Tārīkh i Baihaqī*, vol. i, Ṭihrān A.H.S. 1319/1940).

(1) *Aḥwāl u muntakhab i ash'ār i Khwājū-yi Kirmānī*: **Ṭihrān** A.H.S. 1307/1928.

(2) *Aḥwāl u ash'ār i . . . Rūdakī i Samarqandī*: vol. i. **Ṭihrān** A.H.S. 1309–10/1930–2; vol. ii. **Ṭihrān** A.H.S. 1310/1931–2.

(3) *Majd al-Dīn i Hamgar i Shīrāzī*: **Ṭihrān** A.H.S. 1314/1935–6.

(4) *Aḥwāl u ash'ār i fārisī i Sh. Bahā'ī*: **Ṭihrān** 1316/1937–8.

[1] Neither Īrānī nor Yāsimī specifies the part or parts of Europe to which he went.

[Īrānī *Poets of the Pahlavi regime* pp. 344 i-344 xviii (portrait); Rashīd Yāsimī *Adabīyāt i mu'āṣir* pp. 57–9 (portrait), 110, 114, 116.]

1237. Ghulām-Riḍā Khān **Rashīd Yāsimī** is the son of M. Walī Khān, Mīr Panj, Īl i Gūrān, Qal'ah i Zanjī, and was born in 1314/1896–7 at Kirmānshāh. In 1333/1914–15 he went to Ṭihrān and after completing his education served for a time in the Ministry of Education and subsequently in the Ministry of Finance. At the time when Ishaque and Īrānī wrote [circ. 1932] he held an appointment at the Imperial court. On the title-page of his *Adabīyāt i mu'āṣir* [1937–8] he is described as a Professor in the University of Ṭihrān. A list of his published works printed on the cover of his translation of E. G. Browne's *Literary History of Persia*, vol. iv, comprises twenty titles and includes seven translations. The *Dīwān i Mas'ūd i Sa'd i Salmān* published at Ṭihrān in A.H.S. 1318/1939 was edited by him.

(1) *Aḥwāl i Ibn i Yamīn*: **Ṭihrān** A.H.S. 1303/1924.

(2) *Tatabbu' u intiqād i aḥwāl u āthār i Salmān i Sāwajī*: **Ṭihrān** [circ. 1928 ?].

(3) *Adabīyāt i mu'āṣir*, mainly notices of contemporary poets[1] followed by brief sketches of other branches of literature: **Ṭihrān** A.H.S. 1316/1937–8 (printed as an appendix to the *Tārīkh i adabīyāt i Īrān*, i.e. Rashīd Yāsimī's translation of the fourth volume of E. G. Browne's *Literary History of Persia*).

[Ishaque *Sukhanvarān-i-Īrān* i pp. 92–105 (portrait); Īrānī *Poets of the Pahlavi regime* pp. 284–307 (portrait).]

1238. Dr. **Qāsim Ghanī**, a medical graduate of the American University at Bairūt, is a physician practising in Ṭihrān. In

[1] As sources of biographical information concerning contemporary poets Rashīd Yāsimī mentions (in addition to the works of Ishaque and Īrānī) the *Bihtarīn ash'ār* of " Pizhmān " Bakhtyārī [Ṭihrān 1313/1934*], the *Muntakhabāt i āthār* of M. Ḍiyā' Hashtrūdī [A.H. 1342/1923–4], the *Gulhā-yi adab* of Sa'ādat Nūrī [Iṣfahān A.H.S. 1312/1933–4], and the *Asrār i khilqat* of Muṭī'ī [cf. Ishaque *Modern Persian poetry* p. 195, from which it appears that this work is the *A. i kh.* of Sarhang Aḥmad Akhgar, ed. Ḥusain Muṭī'ī, Ṭihrān A.H.S. 1314/1935–6].

1924–5, five or six years after graduating at Bairūt, he spent eighteen months in Paris, and he was there for a second visit in 1928. Two of Anatole France's novels, *Thaïs* and *La révolte des anges*, have been translated by him into Persian. He and M. b. 'Abd al-Wahhāb Qazwīnī were joint editors of the *Dīwān i Ḥāfiẓ* published at Ṭihrān in A.H.S. 1320/1941.

Baḥth dar āthār u afkār u aḥwāl i Ḥāfiẓ. Vol. i: *Tārīkh i 'aṣr i Ḥāfiẓ*, **Ṭihrān** A.H.S. 1321/A.H. 1361/1942 (with preface by Prof. M. Qazwīnī); vol. ii pt. 1: *Tārīkh i taṣawwuf dar Islām*, **Ṭihrān** A.H.S. 1322/A.H. 1362/1943.

[M. Qazwīnī's preface.]

1239. **Badī' al-Zamān Furūzān-far** b. Āqā Sh. 'Alī Bushrūya'ī Khurāsānī was born at, or near, Bushrūyah in A.H.S. 1318/1900–1. Educated first at local schools and later at Mashhad under the well-known poet "Adīb" Nīshāpūrī (d. 1344/1926), he went to Ṭihrān early in A.H.S. 1303/1924 and studied philosophy and other subjects. In 1308/1929 he was appointed Lecturer in Persian Literature (as well as Arabic Literature and Logic, according to Īrānī) at the Teachers' Training College (*Dār al-Mu'allimīn*, now called *Dānish-sarāy i 'Ālī*). When the Madrasah i Sipahsālār was reconstituted as the Faculty of Theology and Philosophy (A.H.S. 1313/1934–5), he was made Assistant Director(?) (*mu'āwin i ān dānish-kadah gardīd*). In 1316/1937–8 he became Director of the newly-founded Institute for the Training of Preachers. On the title-page of his life of Rūmī [1315/1937] he is described as a Professor in the University of Ṭihrān (*ustād i Dānish-gāh i Tihrān*), a title doubtless held concurrently with more than one of the aforementioned appointments.

(1) *Sukhan u sukhanwarān*, a poetical anthology with a biographical and critical introduction to the selections from each poet: vol. i (44 poets of Khurāsān and Transoxiana from the third to the sixth century), **Ṭihrān** A.H.S. 1308–9/1930; vol. ii, pt. 1 (11 poets of 'Irāq and Ādharbāyjān in the fifth and sixth centuries), **Ṭihrān** [A.H.S. 1312/1933]; *in progress*? (Vols. i and ii, pt. 1, reviewed by R. A. Nicholson in *JRAS*. 1936 pp. 122–3).

(2) *Risālah dar taḥqīq i aḥwāl u zindagānī i Maulānā Jalāl al-Dīn i Rūmī*: **Ṭihrān** 1315/1937‡ (vol. i).

[Autobiographical statements in the *muqaddimah* to no. (2); Ishaque *Sukhanvarān-i-Īrān* i pp. 32–7 (portrait); Īrānī *Poets of the Pahlavi regime* pp. 178E–194 (portrait); Yāsimī *Adabīyāt i mu'āṣir* pp. 27–9 (portrait)].

1240. **M. Isḥāq** (M. Ishaque), M.A., B.Sc., Ph.D., Lecturer in Arabic and Persian in the Post-Graduate Department of the University of Calcutta and formerly Assistant Lecturer in the Department of Arabic and Islamic Studies at the University of Dacca, was born at Calcutta in 1900 and educated at Calcutta University. He visited Persia in 1930 and 1934 and in the eight months that he spent in the country he made the acquaintance of many prominent writers and collected the literary and biographical material which formed the basis for his *Sukhanwarān i Īrān dar 'aṣr i ḥāḍir*. Subsequently he obtained the degree of Ph.D. at the University of London for a thesis substantially identical with his work *Modern Persian Poetry* (Calcutta 1943).

Sukhanvarān-i-Īrān dar 'aṣr-i-ḥāẓir. Poets and poetry of Modern Persia, vol. i [notices of 33 poets] *with thirty-two portraits and two Musical Notes* . . . **Calcutta** (Delhi printed), 1933‡, *vol. ii* [notices of 51 poets] *with fifty-one portraits and one Musical Note* . . . **Calcutta** (Delhi printed), 1937‡ [vol. iii, devoted to prose-writers, is to follow].

[*Armaghān* xi/7 (Sept.-Oct. 1930), pp. 559–60 (with portrait).]

1241. **Ḥabīb Yaghmā'ī** b. Mīrzā Asad Allāh is a grandson of the poet "Yaghmā" and was born in 1320/1902–3 at the village of Khūr in the district (*bulūk*) of Jandaq and Biyābānak. Educated at the Teachers' Training College (*Dār al-Mu'allimīn*) in Ṭihrān, he was for two years Director of Education and Charitable Bequests at Simnān (*ba-riyāsat i ma'ārif u auqāf i Simnān manṣūb gasht*) before being appointed Lecturer in Persian Literature at the Dar al-Funūn in Ṭihrān and a member of the staff of the Press Department (*u ba'd^an ba-mu'allimī i adabīyāt i Fārisī dar Dār al-Funūn u 'uḍwīyat i Idārah i Kull i Inṭibā'āt bar qarār gardīd*). His poems have been published mainly in newspapers and periodicals. An edition of Asadī's *Karshāsp-nāmah* was published by him at Ṭihrān in A.H.S. 1317/1938. Several unpublished works of his are mentioned by Ishaque.

Sharḥ i ḥāl i Yaghmā, an account of the poet "Yaghmā",[1] who died on 16 Rabīʿ II 1276/13 Nov. 1859, preceded by a description of the district of Jandaq and Biyābānak: **Ṭihrān** [circ. 1927 ?‡].

[Ishaque *Sukhanvarān-i-Īrān* i pp. 64–9 (portrait); Yāsimī *Adabīyāt i muʿāṣir* pp. 96–7 (portrait).]

1242. For ʿAbd al-Ḥusain "Āyatī's" *Tārīkh i Yazd*, which was completed in A.H.S. 1317/1938–9, and of which pp. 268–351 are devoted to the poets of Yazd, see the Additions and Corrections to this work.

1243. Appendix

(1) *Bazm i wiṣāl*, a metrical account by "Ṣabūrī" of his journey from Persia to India and his doings there: **Lucknow** 1873°*.

(2) *Ḥiṣār i Nāy: sharḥ i ḥāl i Masʿūd i Saʿd i Salmān*, completed in A.H.S. 1317/1938 by Suhailī Khwānsārī: Islāmīyah Press [**Ṭihrān** ? 1938 ? ‡].

(3) *Life and Times of Hafiz of Shiraz*, by M. Ḥamīd Allāh: [**Allahabad** 1892*].

(4) *Madhāq i sukhan*, "a biographical dictionary of famous Persian poets,"[2] by Shāh Ḥaidar Ḥasan b. Shāh M. Ḥasan Ilāhābādī: [**India**] 1300/1883*.

(5) *Sharḥ i aḥwāl i Nāṣir i Khusrau*, drawn up for Charles Schefer by the Persian Minister of Public Instruction and Jaʿfar-Qulī Khān b. Riḍā-Qulī Khān: **Blochet** i 637.

(6) *Tadhkirah i mukhtaṣar dar ḥāl i Rēkhtah-gōyān i Hind*, by M. Ṣadr al-Dīn: **Browne** Suppt. 304 (Corpus 159²).

(7) *Tadhkirah i mutaʾakhkhirīn i shuʿarāʾ i Fārs*,

[1] Cf. Browne, *List. Hist.* iv pp. 337–44.

[2] So Arberry. According to the Quarterly Catalogue it contains lives of the poets of Allahabad.

short notice of modern poets, mainly of Fārs, with copious extracts from their works: **Browne** Coll. J. 19 (apparently only about half of the work).

(8) ***Tadhkirah i shuʿārāʾ***, by Maulawī ʿAbd al-Ghanī "Ghanī" Farrukhābādī. Edition: place ? 1916 (Āṣafīyah iii p. 162 no. 198).

(9) ***Tadhkirah i shuʿarāʾ i Qāʾināt***, notices of thirty poets of Qāʾināt or Bīrjand, by Ḍiyāʾ al-Dīn Qāʾinātī (contemporary): **Nadhīr Aḥmad** 80 (W. Ivanow's collection. A.H. 1330/1912, transcribed from an autograph).

(10) ***Tadhkirah u tabṣirah***, notices of popular Persian poets, by Mahdī Ḥusain Nāṣirī: **Allahabad** [1915*].

(11) ***Tadhkirat al-nisāʾ***, on the poetesses of India, without author's name: **Nadhīr Aḥmad** 82 (Ḥājjī Ḥabib Allāh's library, Nellore. A.H. 1182/1768).

(12) ***Tadhkirat al-shuʿarāʾ***, by Bahāʾ al-Dīn Ḥasan Khān "ʿUrūj", probably the author of the *Payām i ulfat* (Ivanow 402, 1st Suppt. 793): **Āṣafīyah** i p. 318 nos. 12, 99.

(13) ***Tadhkirat al-shuʿarāʾ***, by Ṣiddīq Khān b. Amīr Muẓaffar: **Bukhārā** Semenov 49.

(14) ***Yaghmā-yi Biyābānak***, a life of "Yaghmā" (cf. p. 922[5] *supra*) by ʿAlī Muqaddam: **Ṭihrān** A.H.S. 1313/1934*.

N. BIOGRAPHY: (*b*) SAINTS, MYSTICS, ETC.

[The series of works enumerated in the preceding subsection includes not only the *tadhkirahs* primarily concerned with poets but also a number of histories containing biographies of poets in appendices or special sections or otherwise. Most of these histories treat similarly of saints and other celebrities, but except in special cases they are not mentioned below. For information concerning them the preceding subsection should be consulted. Works concerned primarily with the utterances of saints are not included in the following subsection, unless they contain an appreciable amount of biography.]

1244. The *Kashf al-maḥjūb* written probably about 450/1058 by ʻAlī b. ʻUthmān al-Jullābī al-Hujwīrī is a general work on Ṣūfism and does not belong to this subsection,[1] but of the 420 pages to which it extends in Nicholson's translation pp. 70–175 are biographical and deserve mention here.

1245. Shaikh al-Islām Abū Ismāʻīl **ʻAbd Allāh** b. M. b. ʻAlī **al-Anṣārī** al-Harawī al-Ḥanbalī, who in his poems calls himself "Anṣārī", "Pīr i Harī", or "Pīr i Harāt", and who in Ṣūfī works is often called simply Shaikh al-Islām, was born at Quhunduz [2] on 2 Shaʻbān 396/4 May 1006. He was a disciple of Abū 'l-Ḥasan al-Kharaqānī (for whom see p. 927, n. 1, *infra*) and is one of the most famous Ṣūfīs. He was a learned man, especially in Arabic linguistics, the Traditions, history, genealogy, and Qur'ānic exegesis, but his uncompromising Ḥanbalism and his polemics against non-Ḥanbalīs made him the victim of more than one heresy-hunt.[3] He died in Dhū 'l-Ḥijjah [4] 481/Feb.–March 1089 and is buried near Harāt.[5]

ʻAbd Allāh Anṣārī's extant works, and more especially the MSS. of them preserved at Istānbūl, are the subject of H. Ritter's *Philologika* viii/1 (in *Der Islam* 22/2 (1934) pp. 89–100). The Arabic works are enumerated by Brockelmann. They include the *Manāzil al-sā'irīn*, the *Dhamm al-kalām*, and *al-Arbaʻīn fī 'l-ṣifāt*, an anthropomorphic tract (MS.: Baghdād Köshkü 510. See *Der Islam* 17/3–4 (1928) p. 255 (*Philologika* ii), where the

[1] It may nevertheless be permissible to record two articles dealing with Hujwīrī's work, namely (1) *Persian Sufiism, being a translation* [by Sidney Jerrold] *of* [the literary portions of] *Professor Zhukovsky's introduction to his edition of the Kashf al-Maḥjūb* (in *BSOS*. v/3 (1929) pp. 475–88), and (2) *The Kashfu-l-Maḥjūb of Abū-l-Ḥasan ʻAlī al-Jullābī. By L. S. Dugin* (in *JRASB*., Letters, viii/2 (1942) pp. 315–79).

[2] *Man ba-Quhunduz zādah am* (*Nafaḥāt* p. 377[1]): *maulūdash . . . dar Quhunduz min maḥallāt i Ṭūs* (*Riyāḍ al-ʻārifīn* p. 50[21]): *dar Quhunduz i Ṭūs mutawallid shudah* (*Majmaʻ al-fuṣaḥā'* p. 65). It seems probable that the Quhunduz referred to was at Harāt rather than Ṭūs.

[3] *Wa-kāna saifan maslūlan ʻalā 'l-mukhālifīn wa-jidhʻan fī aʻyun al-mutakallimīn wa-'mtuḥina ghaira marrah* (*Ṭabaqāt al-Ḥanābilah* p. 401).

[4] So *Ṭabaqāt al-ḥuffāẓ*. The *Safīnat al-auliyā'* says 9 Rabīʻ II.

[5] For a description of his shrine see Yate, *Northern Afghanistan* pp. 33–7, and for some views see Niedermayer and Diez *Afganistan*, Leipzig 1924, p. 61.

work is briefly described by Ritter). The surviving Persian works are mostly brief Ṣūfī tracts in rhymed prose.[1] According to Ḥ. Kh̲ (iii p. 293) Anṣārī was the author of three Persian *dīwāns*. No copies of these are recorded, but twenty *g̲h̲azals* occurring in the Persian tract or collection of tracts which passes in Central Asia under the incorrect title of *Manāzil al-sā'irīn* (see Berthels in *Islamica* iii/1 (1927) p. 10) and which Zhukovski called the Pseudo-*Manāzil al-sā'irīn* [2] were published by him in an article entitled *Pesni Kheratskago Startsa*, which he contributed to the *Vostochnyya Zametki* (St. Petersburg 1895), pp. 79–113, and of which an English translation, *The songs of the Elder of Herat*, was published by L. Bogdanov in the *JRASB.*, Letters, vol. v, 1939, pp. 205–55. A small collection of *rubā'iyāt* ascribed to Anṣārī has been published several times in the East.

Anṣārī finds a place in the *ṭabaqāt al-mufassirīn*,[3] and a *tafsīr* by him " *ba-zabān i darwīs̲h̲ān* " is mentioned in the *Majālis al-'us̲h̲s̲h̲āq* (p. 56. Cf. *Islamica* iii/1 (1927) p. 15). Of this Ṣūfī *tafsīr* no copies seem to have survived. A MS. at Mas̲h̲had

[1] The best known is the *Munājāt*, of which there are several editions. The *Naṣīḥat-nāmah i wazīr* or *Naṣīḥah i Niẓām al-Mulk* was published by Berthels in the *Izvestiya Akademii Nauk*, series vi, vol. 20 (Leningrad 1926) pp. 1139–50.

[2] Three MSS. of this work were known to Zhukovski, one in the Leningrad Public Library (III.2.8., called *Manāzil al-sā'irīn* in the copyist's colophon) and two in his own possession (one of which has the title *Manāzil al-sā'irīn* written in a later hand on the first leaf). This tract, or collection of tracts, begins with the words *Ḥamd i bī-ḥadd Ilāhī rā u durūd i bī-'adad* (*t̲h̲anā-yi bī-'add*) *pādshāhī rā kih bardās̲h̲t az dīdah i dilhā ramad* (*Vostoch. Zam.* p. 82), which, as Ritter has pointed out, are the opening words of the tract or collection of tracts usually called *Kanz al-sālikīn* (Āṣafīyah i p. 466 no. 303, Bānkīpūr Suppt. i 1995 xxii, Bombay Univ. p. 139 no. 65, Browne Coll. D.7, Būhār 165, Cairo p. 422, Dresden 172 (1), Ethé 1919 (5), Ivanow 1158–9, Lahore (see *OCM.* VIII/3 (May 1932) p. 133), Leipzig Fleischer 110 (5), Rieu ii 738*a*, S̲h̲ahīd 'Alī Pās̲h̲ā 1383 (see *Der Islam* 22/2 pp. 97–8, where other Istānbūl MSS. are mentioned)). Some of these MSS. (e.g. the Asiatic Museum MS. Nov. 3, of which the sections are enumerated by Berthels (*Islamica* III/1 (1927) p. 11), and Ivanow 1158) contain far more matter than others and appear to be extensively interpolated.

[3] A precise statement concerning his activities in this field occurs in the biographical note written in 746/1345–6 by M. b. M. sibṭ al- . . . al-Mālikī on the first leaf of the B.M. MS. of the *Ḏh̲amm al-kalām* and quoted in Cureton-Rieu p. 711. It runs as follows : . . . *'ālim bi-'l-ḥadīt̲h̲ ṣaḥīḥihi wa-saqīmihi wa-bi-āt̲h̲ār al-salaf wa-lug̲h̲āt al-'Arab wa-'k̲h̲tilāfihā wa-bi-tafsīr al-Kitāb al-'Azīz wa-ma'ānīhi wa-aqwāl al-mufassirīn iftataḥa 'l-Qur'ān al-'Azīz fa-fassarahu ilā qaulihi Yuḥibbūnahum ka-ḥubbi 'llāhi* [II 160] *fa-fiataḥa majālis fī 'l-ḥaḍrah . . . fī hād̲h̲ihi 'l-āyah muddah ṭawīlah min 'umrihi wa-kad̲h̲ā fī qaulihi 'azza wa-jalla Inna 'lladh̲īna sabaqat lahum minnā 'l-ḥusnā* [XXI 101] *fa-fassara fīhā t̲h̲alāt̲h̲-mi'ah wa-sittīn majlis*ᵃⁿ*. Wa-qad jama'a 'Abd al-Qādir*

containing a Persian commentary on *Sūrahs* xxi 6–xxv is indeed described in the catalogue (vol. i, fṣl. 3, MSS., p. 11 no. 30) as the *Tafsīr i Khwājah 'Abd Allāh i Anṣārī*, but this Mashhad *tafsīr*, which deals separately with translation, explanation and *ta'wīl* in three *naubats*, is apparently the same as that of which *Sūrahs* vi–ix are preserved in the Sipahsālār Library (Catalogue, vol. i p. 148) and which, though it often quotes Anṣārī in the third *naubat*, cannot be the work of Anṣārī himself (see the cataloguer's remarks on p. 149). [P.S. See the Additions and Corrections.]

Ṭabaqāt al-Ṣūfīyah,[1] notices of 120 saints based on the Arabic *Ṭabaqāt al-Ṣūfīyīn* of M. b. al-Ḥusain al-Sulamī (d. 412/1021, see Brockelmann i 200, *Sptbd.* i pp. 361–2), apparently taken down from 'Abd Allāh Anṣārī's oral discourses and arranged after his death by an anonymous disciple: **Nāfidh Pāshā** 426 (A.H. 771/1370. See *Der Islam* 22/2 (1934) p. 93), **Nūr i 'Uthmānīyah** 2500 (A.H. 839/1436. See *Der Islam* 22/2 p. 93), **Ivanow** 234 (collated A.H. 1015/1606–7).

Extracts: (1) L. Massignon *La passion d'al-Hallaj*, Paris 1922, i pp. 368–9 (with French translation). (2) L. Massignon *Essai sur les origines du lexique technique de la mystique musulmane* 1922, pp. 99–100.

List of the saints: Ivanow pp. 80–82.

Description of the work and discussion of the language: *Tabaqat of Ansari in the Old Language of Herat. By W. Ivanow* (in *JRAS*. 1923 pp. 1–34 and 337–82).

[*Ṭabaqāt al-Ḥanābilah ta'līf al-Qāḍī Abī 'l-Ḥusain M. b. Abī Ya'lā M. . . . ikhtiṣār Shams al-Dīn Abī 'Abd Allāh M. b. 'Abd al-Qādir . . . al-Nābulusī* (cf. Brockelmann *Sptbd.* i pp. 308, 557), Damascus 1350/1931, pp. 400–1; *Kharīdat al-qaṣr* (see Leyden cat., 2nd ed., ii/1 p. 217); al-Dhahabī *Ta'rīkh al-Islām*, apparently under A.H. 481 (B.M. Or. 50 (Cureton-Rieu p. 739) fol. 176. See Cureton-Rieu p. 710*b* n. , where this

al-Ruhāwī kitāban sammāhu 'l-Mādiḥ wa-'l-mamdūḥ . . . mu'ẓam al-kitāb fī tarjamatihi fa-man ṭāla'a dhālika 'arafa manzilatahu wa-jalālatahu fī 'l-ummah. . . .

[1] This work is one of the main sources of Jāmī's *Nafaḥāt al-uns* (see W. Ivanow *The sources of Jami's Nafahat* (in *JASB*. 1922, pp. 385–91)).

biography is described as *notitia uberrima*); Idem *Tadhkirat al-ḥuffāẓ* iii pp. 354–60; *Tārīkh i Guzīdah* pp. 785–6; biographical note written in 746/1345–6 by M. b. M. sibṭ al- . . . al-Mālikī on the first leaf of the B.M. MS. of the *Dhamm al-kalām* and quoted in Cureton-Rieu p.711 (cf. p. 925, n. 3, *supra*, where a part of it is quoted); al-Yāfi'ī *Mir'āt al-janān* under A.H. 481 (vol. iii p. 133); al-Subkī *Ṭabaqāt al-Shāfi'īyat al-kubrā* iii p. 117; al-Ṣafadī *al-Wāfī bi-'l-Wafayāt* (cf. Gabrieli *Indice* p. 105); *Mujmal i Faṣīḥī* under A.H. 481; al-Suyūṭī *Ṭabaqāt al-mufassirīn* p. 15, *Ṭabaqāt al-ḥuffāẓ* iii p. 24; *Nafaḥāt al-uns* pp. 576–80; *Majālis al-'ushshāq* no. 8; *Haft iqlīm* no. 619; *Safīnat al-auliyā'* pp. 165–6 (no. 300); *Shadharāt al-dhahab* iii pp. 365–6; *Riyāḍ al-shu'arā'*; *Ātash-kadah* no. 287; *Khulāṣat al-afkār* no. 2; *Makhzan al-gharā'ib* no. 4; *Rauḍāt al-jannāt* p. 450; *Khazīnat al-aṣfiyā'* ii pp. 235–6; *Riyāḍ al-'ārifīn* pp. 50–1; *Majma' al-fuṣaḥā'* i p. 65; Rieu i p. 35; V. A. Zhukovsky *Pesni Kheratskago Startsa* (in *Vostochnyya Zametki*, St. Petersburg 1895, pp. 79–113) and L. Bogdanov's English translation, *The songs of the Elder of Herat* (in *JRASB.*, Letters, vol. v, 1939, pp. 205–55); *Ṭarā'iq al-ḥaqā'iq* ii pp. 162–3; *GIP.* ii p. 282; Ethé col. 974; Browne *Lit. Hist.* ii pp. 269–70; *Ency. Isl.* under Anṣārī (unsigned) and Herewī (M. Ben Cheneb); Ivanow pp. 78–9; Berthels *Grundlinien der Entwicklungsgeschichte des ṣūfischen Lehrgedichts in Persien* (in *Islamica* iii/1 (Leipzig 1927), pp. 1–31) pp. 7–15; Brockelmann i p. 433, *Sptbd.* i pp. 773–5.]

1246. For *al-Qand fī ma'rifat 'ulamā' Samarqand*, an Arabic work on the holy places, graves of holy men, etc., at Samarqand by 'Umar b. M. al-Nasafī (d. 537/1142), which seems not to have survived in its original form but only in the Persian translation of an Arabic abridgment, see p. 371 *supra*.

1247. Of unknown date but certainly earlier than 698/1299, the date of the British Museum MS., is an account of Abū'l-Ḥasan al-Kharaqānī,[1] the teacher of Abū Sa'īd b. Abī 'l-Khair

[1] d. 425/1033, aged 73. See *Kashf al-maḥjūb* tr. Nicholson p. 163; Sam'ānī *Ansāb* fol. 194b⁹; *Tadhkirat al-auliyā'* ii pp. 201–55; *Nafaḥāt al-uns* pp. 336–8; *Majālis al-'ushshāq* no. 6; *Haft iqlīm* no. 837; *Safīnat al-auliyā'* p. 74 (no. 67); *Majma' al-gharā'ib* no. 5; *Riyāḍ al-'ārifīn* pp. 47–8; *Khazīnat al-aṣfiyā'* i pp. 522–7; Nicholson *Mystics of Islam* pp. 133–8, *Studies in Islamic mysticism* pp. 42–4. Kharaqān, four leagues from Bisṭām on the road to Astarābād,

(see p. 928, n. 2, *infra*), abridged from a work entitled *Nūr al-ʿulūm.*

Nūr al-ʿulūm *min kalām al-Shaikh Abī 'l-Ḥasan al-Kharaqānī* : no MSS. recorded.

Abridgment : *al-muntakhab min kitāb Nūr al-ʿulūm min kalām al-Shaikh Abī 'l-Ḥasan al-Kharaqānī*,[1] an account of the utterances and mode of life of Abū 'l-Ḥasan al-Kharaqānī in ten *bābs* : **Rieu** i p. 342*a* (lacks much of *Babs* iii and vi. A.H. 698/1299).

Edition with Russian translation by E. Berthels : *Nūr al-ʿulūm. Zhizneopisanie sheykha Abū-l-Ḥasana Kharakānī* (in *Iran* iii (**Leningrad** 1929) pp. 155–224).

1248. In the preface to the *Asrār al-tauḥīd* (see § 1249 *infra*) M. b. al-Munawwar says that a cousin (*pisar i ʿamm*) of his [who must, like himself, have been a great-great-grandson of Abū Saʿīd b. Abī 'l-Khair] had written a work in five chapters entitled *Ḥālāt u sukhanān i shaikh i mā.* M. b. al-Munawwar does not mention his name, but Zhukovsky, who identified an untitled British Museum manuscript as the *Ḥālāt u sukhanān*, came to the conclusion that his name was Muḥammad and that he was probably the son of Abū Rauḥ Luṭf Allāh b. Abī Saʿīd [b. Abī Ṭāhir b. Abī Saʿīd b. Abī'l-Khair]. Most of this work (nearly five-sixths apparently) is incorporated in the *Asrār al-tauḥīd.*

Ḥālāt u sukhanān i Shaikh Abū Saʿīd Faḍl Allāh b. Abī 'l-Khair al-Maihanī[2], written probably about 540/1145–6 : **Rieu** i 342*b* ii (A.H. 699/1299).

is spelt *bi-fatḥ al-khā' wa-'l-rā' wa-'l-qāf al-maftūḥāt* according to Samʿānī (*Ansāb* fol. 194*b*[7]), and he had visited the place (according to a quotation, not from the *Ansāb* apparently, in Yāqūt's *Muʿjam albuldān* s.v.). In the *Qāmūs*, on the other hand, it is said to be pronounced " like Saḥbān " (*wa-taḥrīkuhu laḥn*), and al-Suyūṭī (*Lubb al-lubāb* p. 91) spells it *bi-'l-ḍamm wa-'l-qāf* (cf. le Strange *L.E.C.* p. 366).

[1] These are the words of a heading in the MS., whereas in the subscription the tract is called *Nūr al-ʿulūm.*

[2] b. 357/967 at Maihanah (between Abīward and Sarakhs, not the place of this name south of Turbat i Ḥaidarī), d. there 440/1049. See Nicholson's *Studies in Islamic Mysticism* pp. 1–76 and his article in the *Ency. Isl.*; Browne *Lit. Hist.* ii pp. 261–9 ; *Kashf al-maḥjūb* tr. Nicholson, pp. 164–6 ; *Tadhkirat al-auliyā'* ii pp. 322–37 ; Subkī iv p. 10 ; *Nafaḥāt al-uns* pp. 339–47 ; *Haft iqlīm* no. 525 ; *Safīnat al-auliyā'* pp. 162–3 (no. 294) ; *Makhzan al-gharā'ib* no. 1 ; *Khazīnat al-aṣfiyā'* ii pp. 228–9 ; etc.

Edition : *Zhizn' i ryechi startsa Abu-Sa'ida Meykheneyskago* (*Ḥālāt u sukhunān etc.*). **St. Petersburg** 1899°* (ed. V. A. Zhukovsky. Publications of the Faculty of Oriental Languages in the University of St. Petersburg, no. 2).

Many passages of this work are translated in R. A. Nicholson's essay *Abú Sa'íd ibn Abi 'l-Khayr* (*Studies in Islamic mysticism*, Cambridge 1921, pp. 1–76).

Descriptions : (**1**) Browne *Lit. Hist.* ii 263 ; (2) Nicholson *op. cit.* p. 1.

1249. **M. b. al-Munawwar** b. Abī Sa'īd b. Abī Ṭāhir b. Abī Sa'īd b. Abī 'l-Khair Maihanī was, like the author of the *Ḥālāt u sukhanān*, a great-great-grandson of Abū Sa'īd.

Asrār al-tauḥīd fī maqāmāt al-Shaikh Abī Sa'īd, an account of the saint much larger than the *Ḥālāt u sukhanān*, most of which it incorporates, written probably in 574/1178–9,[1] or at any rate not earlier than 552/1157, the date of Sanjar's death, and not later than 599/1202, since Ghiyāth al-Dīn M. b. Sām, King of Ghōr, to whom it is dedicated, died in that year : **Mehren** 16 (lacks foll. 1–13. A.H. 711/1311), **Leningrad** Pub. Lib. (defective. 8th/14th cent.), **Cairo** p. 412.

Editions : **St. Petersburg** 1899°* (*Tainy edineniya s Bogom v podvigakh startsa Abu-Sa'ida. Tolkovanie na chetverostishie Abu-Sa'ida* [Persian text edited by V. A. Zhukovsky and followed (pp. 487–93) by the *Risālah i Ḥaurā'īyah*, an explanation of one of Abū Sa'īd's quatrains by 'Ubaid Allāh b. Maḥmūd Shāshī. Publications of the Faculty of Oriental Languages in the University of St. Petersburg, no. 1]) ; **Ṭihrān** A.H.S. 1313/1934–5 (ed. Aḥmad Bahmanyār. Based on Zhukovsky's edition and containing the *Risālah i Ḥaurā'īyah* as well as a Persian translation of Zhukovsky's preface but modernised in spelling and shorn of textual notes).

Many passages of this work are translated in R. A. Nicholson's

[1] Bahmanyār draws attention to statements of the author implying that his work was written 100 + 34 years (*sī u chahār sāl* according to the Copenhagen MS.) or 100 + 30 or 40 years (*sī sāl u chihil sāl* [*sic*] according to the Leningrad MS., Ṭihrān ed. p. 287²) after Abū Sa'īd's death [in 440], i.e. in 574, if the former reading is correct, in 570 or 580, if the latter reading be accepted.

essay *Abú Sa'íd ibn Abi 'l-Khayr* (*Studies in Islamic mysticism*, Cambridge 1921, pp. 1–76).

Descriptions: (**1**) Browne *Lit. Hist.* ii pp. 262–3, (**2**) Nicholson *Studies in Islamic mysticism* pp. 1–3.

1250. The celebrated mystic and poet **Farīd al-Dīn** M. b. Ibrāhīm al-**'Aṭṭār** was born at Kadkan or Shādyākh, villages near Nīshāpūr. He spent thirteen years of his youth at Mashhad and after many wanderings settled finally in Nīshāpūr. Like his father he was a druggist by profession. According to Daulat-Shāh he died in 627/1230, possibly the correct date, but various other dates are given.

Tadhkirat al-auliyā', notices (practically confined to sayings and anecdotes) of about 70 saints mainly of the first three Islāmic centuries, to which is added in some MSS. an appendix (called sometimes vol. ii) containing 20–25 notices of later saints: Ḥ.Kh ii p. 258 no. 2797, **Blochet** iv 2306 (slightly defective at both ends. Early 13th cent.), i 403 (late 13th or early 14th cent.), 404 (late 13th or early 14th cent.), 405 (A.H. 888/1483), 406 (16th cent.), 407 (A.H. 1049/1639), 153 (1) (defective. 18th cent.), **Berlin** 580 (A.H. 687/1288 or 689/1290), 578 (old), 579 (A.H. 999/1591), 581 (with appendix (20 saints)), 582 (with appendix. A.H. 1099/1688), 583 (defective), 584 (fragments), **Bānkīpūr** viii 659 (A.H. 724/1324. LIST OF THE 77 NOTICES), 660 (A.H. 830/1426–7), 661 (A.H. 939/1532–3), **Upsala** Zetterstéen 408 (defective. A.H. 791/1388–9), **Peshawar** 1053B (14th cent.), **Rieu** i 344*a* (14th cent.), 344*b* (17th cent.), **Ivanow** 235 (defective, late 15th or early 16th cent.), 236 (A.H. 1094/1683(?)) 237 (A.H. 1171/1757–8), 238 (late 18th cent.), Curzon 63 (slightly defective. 17th–18th cent.), 1st Suppt. 770 (part only. 19th cent.), 771 (part only. A.H. 1112/1700), **I.O.** D.P. 584A (A.H. 920/1514–15 ?), 584B (slightly defective. 17th cent.), **Ethé** 1051 (with appendix. A.H. 1091/1680), 1052 ("very old"), 1053 (n.d.), 1054 (fragment), **Leyden** iii p. 17 no. 930 (A.H. 941/1534–5), no. 929 (old), **Āṣafīyah** i p. 316 nos. 3 (A.H. 978/1570–1), 11 (A.H. 1082/1671–2), 15, 31, 34, **Rehatsek** p. 190 no. 29 (?) (author not stated. A.H. 984/1576–7), no. 28 (?) (author not stated. Defective at both ends), **Būhār** (with appendix. 16th cent.), **Leningrad**

Mus. Asiat. (A.H. 1003/1594–5. See *Mélanges asiatiques* vii (St. Petersburg 1876) pp. 505–11), Pub. Lib. (Chanykov 104), Univ. nos. 579*, 580* (Salemann-Rosen p. 13), **Bodleian** 622 i-ii (with appendix (23 saints). Seals dated 1020/1611–12), 623 i (A.H. 1026–7/1617–18), 624 i-ii (with appendix. A.H. 1078/1668), 625 ix-x (with appendix. n.d.), **'Alīgaṛh** Subḥ. MSS. p. 61 no. 22 ("old"), **Browne** Suppt. 291 (King's 75), **Browne** Coll. J. 4 (9) (only 40 notices. A.H. 1269/1852–3), J. 3 (7) (selections. A.H. 1297/1880), V.7 (14 (1) ("of no great antiquity"), **Cairo** p. 501 (four copies, one dated 1267/1850–1, the rest undated).

Editions: Fakhr al-maṭābi' [**Delhi** ? circ. 1852 ?*], Mujtabā'ī Press, **Delhi** (date ? see Ḥaidarābād Coll. p. 27), **Lahore** 1306/1889*, 1308/1891*, **Lucknow** 1891°, **London and Leyden** 1905–7°* (ed. R. A. Nicholson. 2 vols. Persian Historical Texts, iii, v).

Translated extracts: (**1**) [Life of Ḥallāj], F. A. D. Tholuck *Blüthensammlung aus der morgenländischen Mystik*, **Berlin** 1825, pp. 310–27. (**2**) [Shaqīq Balkhī, Ḥātim Aṣamm, Aḥmad Khiḍrūyah Abū Ḥafṣ Ḥaddād] *Vier turkestanische Heilige. Ein Beitrag zum Verständnis der islamischen Mystik. Von P. Klappstein*, **Berlin** 1919 (Türkische Bibliothek, 20. A Kiel dissertation). (**3**) J. Hallauer *Die Vita des Ibrahim b. Edhem in der Tedhkiret el-Ewlija des Ferid ed-din Attar, eine islamische Heiligenlegende*, **Leipzig** 1925 (Türkische Bibliothek, 24. A Zürich dissertation. Cf. H. H. Schaeder's review in *Islamica* iii/2 (1927) pp. 282–94).

Lists of the saints: (**1**) Leyden iii pp. 17–19, (**2**) *Mélanges asiatiques* vii (St. Petersburg 1876), pp. 505–11, (**3**) Ethé coll. 622–5 (includes appendix), (**4**) Bānkīpūr viii pp. 17–18.

Abridgments: (**1**) by 'Abd al-Wāḥid Bilgrāmī, i.e. probably Sh. 'Abd al-Wāḥid "Shāhidī" Bilgrāmī, who died in 1017/1608–9 (see *Ā'īn i Akbarī* tr. Blochmann p. 547, Badā'ūnī *Muntakhab al-tawārīkh* iii pp. 65–6, Raḥmān 'Alī p. 136), **Berlin** 585. (**2**) **Mehren** 15 (45 saints. 41st regnal year [of Aurangzēb ?]).

Swedish translation: *Ur Tazkiratú 'l-Awliyá skrifven af Shaikh Farídu 'd-Dín 'Attár öfversatt af Baron Erik Hermelin efter Professor Reynold A. Nicholson's text.* **Stockholm** 1931–2* (2 vols.).

Persian metrical version: *Walī-nāmah*, composed by Ḥāfiẓ 'Allāf for Ibrāhīm Sulṭān, Shāh-Rukh's son, and completed at Mecca in 821/1418: **Rosen** Institut 79 (A.H. 887/1482).

Turkish translations [1]: (**1**) [Eastern Turkish] **Paris** Bib. Nat. 100 (Uighur script), **Fātiḥ** 2848 (Arabic script. See *Islâm Ansiklopedisi* ii p. 10*a*). Edition: *Tezkereh-i evliâ. Manuscrit ouïgour de la Bibliothèque Nationale reproduit par l'héliogravure typographique*, **Paris** 1890. French translation: *Tezkereh-i evliâ. Le Mémorial des saints traduit sur le manuscrit ouïgour de la Bibliothèque Nationale par A. Pavet de Courteille*, **Paris** 1889. (**2**) [Eastern Turkish] by Khwājah Shāh b. S. Aḥmad b. S. Asad Allāh . . . al-Khuwārazmī: **Leningrad** Mus. Asiat. (A.H. 1234/1828–9). See *Mélanges asiatiques* vii (1876) pp. 511–12). (**3**) [Eastern Turkish. Unidentified] **Bukhārā** Semenov 44, **Schefer** 989 (14 saints only? 19th cent.), **Upsala** Zetterstéen 636. (**4**) [Old Anatolian Turkish] a translation dedidated to Āydīn-oghlū Meḥmed Bey (A.H. 707–34. See *Islâm Ansiklopedisi* ii p. 10, which is the authority for the date just given), **Bāyazīd** 1643. (**5**) [Ottoman Turkish] by Sinān al-Dīn Yūsuf b. Khiḍr, called Khwājah Pāshā (d. 891/1486. See *Ency. Isl.* under Sinān Pasha I), Ḥ.Kh ii p. 258 no. 2798, **Nūr i 'Uthmāniyah** 2299 (presumably the autograph referred to in *Ency. Isl.*). (**6**) [Ottoman Turkish] by 'Alī Riḍā Qarāḥiṣārī (see *Islâm Ansiklopedisi* ii p. 10*b*[3]). (**7**) [Miscellaneous, including unidentified or inadequately described MSS.] **Browne** Handlist 232 (first 20 notices only. A.H. 931/1524), **Dresden** 18 (a translation or adaptation by M. b. Ghāzī), 99, 141 (different from 99. A.H. 1018/1609–10), 174 (A.H. 1039/1629–30 and 1093/1682), **Leyden** iii p. 19 no. 931 (A.H. 952/1545), **Upsala** 306 (*Maqālāt al-auliyā'*, written by order of Sulṭān Abū 'l-Fatḥ Malik Isfandiyār [if Tornberg's Effendijar is to be so read] Bahādur Khān), and the Istānbūl MSS. mentioned in *Islâm Ansiklopedisi* ii p. 10*b*.

Urdu translation by Mīrzā Jān: *Anwār al-adhkiyā'*, **Cawnpore** 1914*.

[*Lubāb al-albāb* ii pp. 337–9; Daulatshāh pp. 187–92; *Majālis al-mu'minīn*, *majlis* 6 (pp. 296–300); *Rauḍāt al-jannāt*

[1] This list makes no claim to completeness. No attempt has been made to search the catalogues of Turkish MSS.

iv pp. 196–7; Rieu i 344*a*; *Grundriss der iranischen Philologie* ii 284–5; M. Qazwīnī's *muqaddimah i intiqādī dar sharḥ i aḥwāl i Sh. 'Aṭṭār* prefixed to vol. ii of R. A. Nicholson's edition of the *Tadhkirat al-auliyā'*; Browne *Lit. Hist.* ii 506–15; *Ency. Isl.* under 'Aṭṭār (less than one column, unsigned); Bombay Univ. Cat. pp. 60–4; *Philologika. Von Hellmut Ritter. X. Farīdaddīn 'Aṭṭār* (in *Der Islam* 25/2 (1938) pp. 134–73); *Islâm Ansiklopedisi* under Attâr (12 columns by H. Ritter); etc., etc.]

1251. Nūr al-Dīn 'Alī b. Yūsuf **al-Shaṭṭanūfī** [1] al-Lakhmī al-Shāfi'ī was born at Cairo in Shawwāl 647/Jan.–Feb. 1250 and died there on 19 Dhū 'l-Ḥijjah 713/6 April 1314 (see *al-Durar al-kāminah* iii p. 141, *Bughyat al-wu'āt* pp. 358–9, Brockelmann ii 118, *Sptbd* ii p. 147).

Bahjat al-asrār wa-ma'din al-anwār, an Arabic biography of 'Abd al-Qādir al-Jīlānī [2]: Ḥ.Kh. ii p. 71 (inaccurate), **Ahlwardt** ix nos. 10,072–6, **Cureton-Rieu** p. 737, etc., etc. (see Brockelmann).

Editions: **Cairo** 1301/1883–4 (Sarkis col. 1127), 1304/1887 (Ellis i col. 262, Sarkis *loc. cit.*), **Tunis** 1302–4/1884–7 (Sarkis *ibid*).

Persian translations: (1) *Kashf al-āthār* (a chronogram = 1133/1720–1), written in the reign of Muḥammad Shāh (1131–61/1719–48) by M. Ḥabīb Allāh Akbarābādī (*maulid*^{an}) Dihlawī (*tawaṭṭun*^{an}), the author of the *Dhikr i jamī' i auliyā' i Dihlī* (see p. 1019 *infra*): **I.O.** D.P. 711 (A.H. 1140/1727, transcribed from an autograph), **Āṣafīyah** i p. 462 no. 431 (A.H. 1270/1853), iii p. 200 no. 1338. (2) *Zubdat al-āthār muntakhab i Bahjat*

[1] Shaṭṭanūf (*bi-'l-fatḥ wa-tashdīd al-ṭā'* according to Suyūṭī's *Lubb al-Lubāb*) or Shaṭanūf (*ka-ḥalazūn* according to the *Qāmūs*) is in Egypt, *min a'māl al-Manūfiyah* according to the *Tāj al-'arūs*. The spelling Shaṭṭanaufī comes from Veth's edition of the *Lubb al-Lubāb*, but this seems to be a mistranscription.

[2] For this celebrated saint (b. 470/1078 or 471/1079 in Gīlān, d. 561/1166 at Baghdād) see al-Dhahabī *Ta'rīkh al-Islām* (published in Margoliouth's article *Contributions to the biography of 'Abd al-Ḳādir of Jīlān*, *JRAS*. 1907 pp. 267–310); al-Yāfi'ī *Mir'āt al-janān* iii pp. 347–66; *Fawāt al-Wafayāt* ii pp. 2–3; *Nafaḥāt al-uns* pp. 586–90; *Akhbār al-akhyār* pp. 9–22; *Haft iqlīm* no. 1195, *Safīnat al-auliyā'* pp. 43–58 (no. 36); M. al-Dilā'ī *Natījat al-taḥqīq* (partially translated by T. H. Weir in *JRAS*. 1903 pp. 155–66); *Khazīnat al-aṣfiyā'* i pp. 94–5; *Ency. Isl.* under 'Abd al-Ḳādir (Margoliouth); Brockelmann i pp. 435–6, *Sptbd* i pp. 777–9, where numerous biographies are mentioned.

al-asrār, an abridged translation by 'Abd al-Ḥaqq Dihlawī (for whom see p. 194 *supra*) : **I.O.** D.P. 759*a* (defective. Early 19th cent.).

Edition : **Delhi** [1890°. With Urdu translation].

Another translation, *Maqāmāt i Ghauth al-thaqalain*, was made by Badr al-Dīn b. Ibrāhīm Sihrindī (see p. 1002[9] *infra*), but no copies seem to be recorded.

1252. **Ibrāhīm b.** Shaikh al-Islām Ṣadr al-Dīn **Rūzbihān** b. Fakhr al-Dīn Aḥmad b. Rūzbihān wrote the life of his great-grandfather[1] in response to a request made ninety-four years after his death, i.e. in or about 700/1300–1.

(***Sīrat-nāmah i Shaikh Rūzbihān***),[2] or (***Aḥwāl i Rūzbihān***), a life of Rūzbihān b. Abī Naṣr al-Baqlī divided into seven *bābs* ((1) on his birth and early life, (2) on the great *shaikhs* who were his contemporaries, (3) anecdotes concerning him and his miracles (*dar ḥikāyāt u karāmāt i shaikh*), (4) his observations relating to Qur'ānic exegesis, the Traditions, etc., (5) various observations of his to his associates (*dar fawā'id i mutafarriqah bar aṣḥāb*), (6) on his children and grandchildren and some merits (*shaṭrī az faḍā'il*) of the author's father Shaikh al-Islām Ṣadr al-Millah wa-'l-Dīn Rūzbihān al-Thānī al-Shaikh al-Thānī, (7) on his death) : MS. (two fragments of 36 and 9 leaves (early 13th cent.) containing portions of *Bābs* 1, 3, 4, and 7) acquired at Shīrāz by W. Ivanow.

Description : (**1**) [1st fragment] *A biography of Ruzbihan al-Baqli. By W. Ivanow* (in *JASB.* xxiv/4 (1928) pp. 353–61, (**2**) [2nd fragment] *More on biography of Ruzbihan al-Baqli* [with the

[1] Rūzbihān b. Abī Naṣr al-Baqlī, of whose works the best known is an Arabic Ṣūfī commentary on the *Qur'ān* entitled *'Arā'is al-bayān fī ḥaqā'iq al-Qur'ān*, died at Shīrāz in 606/1209. See *Shīrāz-nāmah* p. 116 ; *Shadd al-izār* (Rieu Arab. Suppt. p. 462) ; *Nafaḥāt al-uns* pp. 288–90 ; *Majālis al-'ushshāq* no. 17 ; *Haft iqlīm* no. 173 ; *But-khānah* (Bodleian 366) no. 119 ; *Safīnat al-auliyā'* p. 176 (no. 324) ; *Majma' al-gharā'ib* no. 812 ; *Riyāḍ al-'ārifīn* p. 128 ; *Khazīnat al-aṣfiyā'* ii pp. 253–4 ; *Majma' al-fuṣaḥā'* i pp. 235–6 ; *Ṭarā'iq al-ḥaqā'iq* ii pp. 286–7 ; Massignon *La passion d'al Ḥallâj* pp. 374–7, 45* (at end of book), *Recueil de textes inédits concernant l'histoire de la mystique* pp. 113–14 ; Brockelmann i p. 414, *Sptbd.* i pp. 734–5 ; etc.

[2] The place in the preface where the title should come has been left blank, but the author uses the expression *sīrat-nāmah* at least twice in referring to his work.

Persian text of the surviving portion of *Bāb* i]. *By W. Ivanow* (in *JBBRAS*. vii (1931) pp. 1–7).

1253. **Farīdūn** b. Aḥmad **Sipah-sālār**, a high military officer under the Saljūqids, says that he was Jalāl al-Dīn Rūmī's disciple for forty years.

(*Risālah i Sipah-sālār*) or (*Manāqib i Jalāl al-Dīn i Rūmī*), an account of Jalāl al-Dīn Rūmī and his successors, dependent largely upon the *Walad-nāmah* of Sulṭān Walad and including a supplement by the Sipah-sālār's son which brings it down to the period when Chelebī 'Ābid (d. 739/1338) was head of the order: **Heidelberg** P. 233 (A.H. 1006/1597. See *Zeitschrift für Semitistik* Bd. 6 (1928) p. 223), **Breslau** Richter 89 (?) (*Manāqib al-Ḥusain al-Khaṭībī al-Balkhī*, called at the end of the MS. *Risālah i Sipah-sālār*, but described by Richter as a biography of Bahā' al-Dīn Walad. A.H. 1292/1875).

Editions: place ? 1302/1884–5 (see Āṣafīyah i p. 428 no. 984), **Cawnpore** 1319/1901 (Maḥmūd al-Maṭābi'. See the bibliography to Nicholson's article on Tibrīzī in the *Ency. Isl.*); **Tihrān** (*Aḥwāl i Maulawī*. Date ? See *Luzac's Oriental list* 1947 p. 41).

Turkish translation: *Manāqib i ḥaḍrat i Khudāwandgār*, tr. Midḥat Bahārī Ḥusāmī, **Salonica** (so Kramers in *Ency. Isl.* under Sulṭān Walad) or **Constantinople** (so Nicholson in *Ency. Isl.* under Tibrīzī) 1331/1913.

[Nicholson in *Ency. Isl.* under Tibrīzī.]

1254. 'Afīf al-Dīn 'Abd Allāh b. As'ad **al-Yāfi'ī,** already mentioned (p. 53 *supra*) as the author, or epitomator, of *al-Durr al-naẓīm fī faḍā'il al-Qur'ān al-'aẓīm*, was born in the Yemen, settled at Mecca in 718/1318, and died there in 768/1367.

I. *Rauḍ al-rayāḥīn fī ḥikāyāt al-ṣāliḥīn*, five hundred anecdotes of saints, Ḥ.Kh. iii p. 488 (for MSS. and editions see Brockelmann ii 177, *Sptbd* ii p. 228).

Persian translations: (1) *Tuḥfat al-murshidīn min ḥikāyāt al-ṣāliḥīn*, by Jalāl [al-Dīn] M. b. 'Abbādī [or 'Ubādī or 'Ibādī] Kāzarūnī [1] [with a *dhail* on the life of the translator's *murshid*

[1] Jalāl al-Dīn M. b. al-'.bādī al-Kāzarūnī according to the Āyā Ṣōfyah catalogue.

S͟h. Bū Isḥāq Kāzarūnī [1]] : **Lahore** Panjāb Univ. (A.H. 818/1415. See *OCM.* viii/3 p. 140), **Āyā Ṣōfyah** 1702.

(2) *Tarjamah i Rauḍat* [*sic*] *al-rayāḥīn,* written in the reign of Sulṭān M. Quṭb-S͟hāh (A.H. 1020–35/1612–26) by Faḍl Allāh "Jahānī" b. Asad Allāh al-Ḥusainī al-A'rābī al-Simnānī : **Ethé** 642 (A.H. 1026/1617).

II. *K͟hulāṣat al-mafāk͟hir fī 'k͟htiṣār manāqib al-s͟haik͟h 'Abd al-Qādir wa-jamā'ah mimman 'azzamahu min al-s͟huyūk͟h al-akābir,*[2] about 200 anecdotes, mainly of 'Abd al-Qādir Jīlānī,[3] written as a supplement (*'alā sabīl al-takmilah*) to the *Rauḍ al-rayāḥīn* : **Ahlwardt** 8804, **Loth** 708 ii, **Būhār** 275, etc.

Persian translations: (1) (*Tarjamah i K͟hulāṣat al-mafāk͟hir*) or (*Tarjamat al-Takmilah*), written by an anonymous disciple [4] of S. Jalāl al-Dīn Buk͟hārī,[5] at whose suggestion the work was undertaken : **Bodleian** 332 (before A.H. 910/1504), 333 (M. S͟hāh's reign (A.D. 1719–48)), **Bānkīpūr** viii 670 (A.H. 991/1584), **Āṣafīyah** i p. 410 no. 720 (*Takmilah i Imām 'Abd Allāh i Yāfi'ī* by Mīrān Muḥyī 'l-Dīn. A.H. 999/1590–1), **I.O.** D.P. 640 (A.H. 1012/1604), D.P. 596 (A.H. 1031/1621), **Ethé** 643 (A.H. 1089/1678), **Cairo** p. 502 (A.H. 1020/1611), **Edinburgh** 242 (old), **Ivanow** 242 (A.H. 1177/1763–4), Curzon 75 (late 18th or early 19th cent.), 1st Suppt. 857 (slightly defective at both ends. Early 19th cent.), **Būhār** 185 (lacunæ. 19th cent.), **Berlin** 19 (1) (begins with 101st anecdote). (2) *Tarjamah i Takmilah,* a verse translation in 105 *ḥikāyats* made by

[1] Presumably different from the work published at Istānbūl in 1945 as Vol. 14 of the Bibliotheca Islamica (Maḥmūd b. 'Uṯmān, *Die Vita des Scheich Abū Isḥāq al-Kāzarūnī.* Hrsg. von F. Meier). For Abū Isḥāq Ibrāhīm b. S͟hahryār Kāzarūnī, who died in 426/1035, see *Kas͟hf al-maḥjūb,* tr. Nicholson, pp. 172, 173; *Tad͟hkirat al-auliyā'* ii pp. 291–304; Ibn Baṭṭūṭah (ii p. 89); *Haft iqlīm* p. 206 (no. 162); *Safīnat al-auliyā'* p. 161 (no. 292); *K͟hazīnat al-aṣfiyā'* ii pp. 225–7; *Der Islam* xix/1–2 (1930) pp.18–26; etc.

[2] This, according to al-Yāfi'ī's preface, is the *laqab* of the work, its *ism* being *Aṭrāf 'ajā'ib al-āyāt wa-'l-barāhīn wa-ardāf g͟harā'ib ḥikāyāt Rauḍ al-rayāḥīn* (see the passage quoted in Bānkīpūr viii p. 32 : . . . *wa-sammaituhu kitāb Aṭrāf . . . wa-laqqabtuhu bi-K͟hulāṣat al-mafāk͟hir . . .*).

[3] See p. 933, n. 2, *supra.*

[4] In the copyist's colophon of I.O. D.P. 640 the work is ascribed to Mīrān Saiyid Muḥyī 'l-Dīn and in the Āṣafīyah catalogue Mīrān Muḥyī 'l-Dīn is given as the name of the author.

[5] See pp. 944–6 *infra.*

"'Abdī", who completed it in 1051/1641–2 in S͟hāh-Jahān's reign: Sprenger 63 = **Ivanow** 742 (18th cent.).

[Subkī vi p. 103; *al-Durar al-kāminah* ii pp. 247–9; *Nafaḥāt al-uns* pp. 681–2; *Safīnat al-auliyā'* p. 68 (no. 62); *K͟hazīnat al-aṣfiyā'* i 114; *Rauḍāt al-jannāt* p. 457; *Ency. Isl.* under Yāfi'ī (Krenkow); Brockelmann ii pp. 176–7, *Sptbd.* ii pp. 227–8, where further references will be found.]

1255. For the *S͟hīrāz-nāmah*, which was completed in 744/1343–4 by Aḥmad b. Abī 'l-K͟hair S͟hīrāzī and which contains notices of holy persons connected with S͟hīrāz, see p. 351 *supra*.

1256. S͟hams al-Dīn Aḥmad **Aflākī** was a disciple of Jalāl al-Dīn Rūmī's grandson, Jalāl al-Dīn al-'Ārif, at whose request he wrote the *Manāqib al-'ārifīn.*

Manāqib al-'ārifīn, lives of Jalāl al-Dīn Rūmī, his father, successors and associates, begun in 718/1318–19,[1] completed in 754/1353–4 [2] and divided into ten *faṣls* ((1) Bahā' al-Dīn Walad, his father, d. 628/1231, (2) Burhān al-Dīn Tirmid͟hi, his spiritual guide, (3) Jalāl al-Dīn himself, b. 604/1207, d. 672/1273, (4) S͟hams al-Dīn M. b. 'Alī Tabrīzī, his friend and guide, (5) Ṣalāḥ al-Dīn Farīdūn Qūnawī known as Zarkūb, a friend and *k͟halīfah*, d. 657/1258, (6) Ḥusām al-Dīn Ḥasan b. Ak͟hī Turk, a *k͟halīfah*, d. 683/1284, (7) Bahā' al-Dīn Sulṭān Walad, Jalāl al-Dīn's son d. 712/1312,[3] (8) Jalāl al-Dīn Farīdūn, known as C͟helebī Amīr 'Ārif al-Balk͟hī, Sulṭān Walad's son, b. 670/1272, d. 719/1320, (9) C͟helebī S͟hams al-Dīn Amīr 'Ābid, another of Sulṭān Walad's sons, d. 739/1338 and succeeded by his brother Ḥusām al-Dīn Amīr Wājid, who died in 742/1342, (10) descendants of the foregoing *s͟haik͟hs*): Ḥ. K͟h. vi p. 154, **Blochet** i 409 (A.H. 964/1556), 410 (*Faṣls* i-iii only. 16th cent.), 411–14 (all 17th cent.), 415 (18th cent.), **Rieu** i 345*b* (slightly defective. A.H. 997/1589), 344*b* (17th cent.), **Ethé** 630 (A.H. 1027/1618), **I.O.** D.P. 734 (A.H. 1034/1624), 1120 (defective.

[1] Or 710/1310–11, according to some MSS. (e.g. Ethé 630).

[2] This date is given in a note which occurs at the end in some of the MSS., e.g. Ethé 630 (*Ta'rīk͟h taṣnīf al-muṣannif ... Maulānā S͟h. al-D. A.* [*al-*]*Aflākī al-'Ārifī raḥimahu 'llāh sanat arba' wa-k͟hamsīn wa-sab'-mi'ah*). In the B.M. MS. Add. 25,025 the word *taṣnīf* is absent from the note.

[3] As Rieu mentions, notices of the foregoing seven *s͟haik͟hs* are given in the same order in the *Nafaḥāt al-uns*, pp. 528–44.

19th cent.), **Flügel** ii 1206 (1041/1632); **Ivanow** 240 (slightly defective. A.H. 1177/1763–4), **Āṣafīyah** i p. 324 no. 23, **Berlin** 587 (defective), **Chanykov** 103, **Salemann-Rosen** p. 19 no. 589, **Upsala** Zetterstéen 409, as well as several of the Istānbūl catalogues (see Horn p. 292).

Edition: *Sawāniḥ i 'umrī i ḥaḍrat i Maulānā Rūmī musammā bah Manāqib al-'ārifīn*, **Āgrah** 1897°.

French translation: *Les saints des derviches tourneurs, récits traduits . . . et annotés par Cl. Huart*, **Paris** 1918*, 1922* (Bibliothèque de l'École des Hautes Études, sciences religieuses, vols. 32 and 36).

Abridged Turkish translation of *Faṣls* i-viii: *Hasht bihisht* (beginning *Ḥamd i nā-maḥdūd awwal Munshī' i kā'ināt*), by an unknown translator: **Flügel** ii 1207 (A.H. 1015/1606).

English translation of extracts: *The Mesnevī . . . . of . . . Jelālu-'d-Dīn . . . er-Rūmī. Book the first . . . translated . . . by J. W. Redhouse*, **London** 1881°* (Trübner's Oriental Series), pp. 1–135.

Abridgment (with excision of all passages savouring of unorthodoxy): *Khulāṣat al-Manāqib*, by Aḥmad b. M., apparently a disciple of Jalāl al-Dīn Bukhārī (d. 785/1383. See pp. 944–6 *infra*), **Ivanow** 241 (18th cent.).

Revised version: *Thawāqib al-manāqib i auliyā' Allāh* (a chronogram = 947/1540–1), by 'Abd al-Wahhāb b. Jalāl al-Dīn M. al-Hamadānī,[1] who "revised and corrected the original work, curtailed it in some places by omitting superfluous stories and traditions, increased it in others by adding much needed explanations, . . . paid particular attention to dates, genealogy, etc." and divided the new edition into a *muqaddimah*, nine *dhikrs* or biographies (the tenth of the original being omitted) and a *khātimah* (containing the *tārīkh* and a *munājāt*): Ḥ.Kh. p. 154, **Ross-Browne** 218 (16th cent.), **Ethé** 631 (17th cent.).

Turkish translation of the revised version: *Tarjamah i Manāqib i thawāqib* [?], written in 998/1590[2] by Darwīsh Maḥmūd

[1] So Ross-Browne and Ethé. Ḥ.Kh. calls him al-Sh. 'A. al-W. al-Ṣābūnī al-Hamadānī.

[2] Ḥ.Kh. is the authority for this date. The dedication to Murād is mentioned by Palmer, not by Ḥ.Kh.

al-Maulawī and dedicated to the Sulṭān Murād [iii]: **Browne** Suppt. 1251 (Trinity R. 13, 1, Palmer p. 7), probably also **Flügel** ii 1208 (defective, beginning in the third biography).

1257. **Tawakkulī** b. Ismā'īl b. Ḥājjī **al-Ardabīlī** known as (*al-mushtahir bi-*) **Ibn i Bazzāz** [1] mentions his uncle (*'amm i mu'allif*) Pīrah Aḥmad al-Ardabīlī [2] as one of the disciples of the celebrated saint Ṣafī al-Dīn Isḥāq al-Mūsawī,[3] the ancestor of the Ṣafawīs, and says that he himself and Shams al-Dīn Ardabīlī called on the saint to condole with him on the death of his eldest son, Khwājah Muḥyī 'l-Dīn.[4] In 726/1325 he was with the same Shams al-Dīn at Marāghah.[5]

Ṣafwat al-ṣafā', or *al-Mawāhib al-sanīyah fī 'l-manāqib al-Ṣafawīyah* [6] (beginning *al-Ḥ. l. 'lladhī tajallā li-auliyā'ihi*),[7] an account of the life, sayings and miracles of the aforementioned Sh. Ṣafī al-Dīn Isḥāq (d. 12 Muḥarram 735/ 12 Sept. 1334), written in the time of his son and successor Ṣadr al-Dīn Mūsā,[8] completed in, or not very long before, 759/

[1] Tawakkulī . . . Bazzāz: so in the Bombay edition p. 6¹ (four lines above the table of contents with which the author's preface ends). This passage has perhaps been removed by Abū 'l-Fatḥ from his revised edition, since Rieu does not refer to it but says that "the author's name appears incidentally in the text, fol. 553*a*, as Tavakkulī, توکلی". A person of this name, Tawakkulī 'Atīqān [= b. 'Atīq] Ardabīlī, figures in an anecdote on p. 261 of the Bombay edition (*Bāb* vii, *faṣl* 5, *ḥikāyat* [24]). Browne says (*Lit. Hist.* iv p. 34) that in a note in A. G. Ellis's MS. the name is written Tūklī.

[2] Bombay edition p. 354¹³. The author's brother, Pīrah Ya'qūb, who according to Rieu is mentioned among the saint's disciples, does not seem to be among those enumerated in *Bāb* xii of the Bombay edition.

[3] For whom see *Ḥabīb al-siyar* iii, 4 pp., 5–9. *Majālis al-mu'minīn* p. 273 (*majlis* 6); *Haft iqlīm* no. 1359; *Silsilat al-nasab i Ṣafawīyah* pp. 10–38 (cf. *JRAS*. 1921 pp. 397–404); Browne *Lit. Hist.* iv pp. 38–44; *Dānishmandān i Ādharbāyjān* pp. 231–4.

[4] Bombay edition p. 293¹⁷ (*Bāb* viii, *faṣl* 16).

[5] Bombay edition p. 262² (*Bāb* vii, *faṣl* 5).

[6] See the Bombay edition p. 6²⁻³, where, however, the text is corrupt.

[7] These are the opening words of Ethé 1842 and all the Istānbūl MSS. described by Tauer. On the other hand the Bānkīpūr MS. begins *Sitāyish u niyāyish mar Khāliqī rā* and the Bombay edition *al-Ḥ. l. 'l-Walī al-Ḥamīd wa-'l-ṣalāt wa-'l-salām . . . ammā ba'd īn miskīn i kam-biḍā'at.* The first words of the Leyden and Leningrad MSS. are not given in the catalogues.

[8] According to the *Silsilat al-nasab i Ṣafawīyah* (p. 39 = *JRAS*. 1921 p. 404) he was born in 704/1305 and died in 794/1392. According to Rieu (iii p. 1085*b*) the date of his death is given as 779/1377–8 in the *Qiṣaṣ al-Khāqānī*, fol. 5*a*.

1358 [1] and divided into a *muqaddimah*, twelve *bābs* and a *khātimah* [2]: Ḥ.Kh. iv p. 105, **Ethé** 1842 (A.H. 759/1358, said to be an autograph), **Leyden** v p. 231 no. 2639 (A.H. 890/1485), **Āyā Ṣōfyah** 3099 = Tauer 434 (A.H. 896/1491), 2123 = Tauer 435 (A.H. 914/1509), **Ḥakīmoghlū ʻAlī Pāshā** 775 = Tauer 436 (A.H. 947/1540), **Bānkīpūr** viii 662 (A.H. 1035/1625–6), **Adabīyāt Kutubkhānah-si** 4675 = Tauer 437 (A.H. 1049/1639), **Chanykov** 90 (cf. *Mélanges asiatiques* i (St. Petersburg 1852) p. 543), **Dorn** 300 (from Ardabīl). A MS. written at Ardabīl in 1030/1621, which belonged to the late A. G. Ellis (= Ellis Coll. M. 163), is mentioned by Browne (*Lit. Hist.* iv p. 35). Ellis Coll. M. 164 is dated 964/1557.

Edition: **Bombay** 1329/1911°* [3] (ed. Aḥmad b. Karīm Tabrīzī).

Extracts (containing references to the Shīrwān-Shāhs): *Mélanges asiatiques* i (St. Petersburg 1852) pp. 543–8 (with French translation by Chanykov, pp. 549–52).

Description: Browne *Lit. Hist.* iv pp. 34–5, 38–9.

Revised edition (beginning *Sharīftarīn dhikrī*) prepared at the command of Shāh Ṭahmāsp (reigned 930/1524–984/1576) by Abū 'l-Fatḥ al-Ḥusainī (cf. p. 13 *supra*), whose additions, according to Rieu, "appear to be confined to the preface and to the Khātimah, in which an account of the descendants of Ṣafī ud-Din is brought down to Shāh Ṭahmāsp": **Rieu** i 345*b* (16th cent.), **Browne** Suppt. 837 (King's 87), **Mashhad** iii *fṣl.* 14, MSS., no. 68.

Turkish translation written in 949/1542–3, in Shāh Ṭahmāsp's reign by M. Kātib "Nashāṭī" Shīrāzī (*M. al-Kātib yuʻraf bi-Nashāṭī*): **Rieu** Turkish Cat. p. 281 (16th cent.), **Chanykov** 91. [4]

[1] It will be noted that Ethé 1842, described as an autograph, is dated 759. According to Rieu the author "states that, in the very year in which he wrote, Malik Ashraf (who reigned A.H. 745–758) had dismissed his Vazīr ʻAbd ul-ʻAlī".

[2] The subjects of the chapters are given by Browne (*Lit. Hist.* iv pp. 38–9).

[3] This edition contains also (1) an account of Ardabīl, pp. 25–7 marg., (2) an account of Ādharbāyjān, pp. 28–65 marg., (3) *al-Ṭibb al-jadīd al-kīmiyāʼī*, an Arabic medical work, being Part IV of Ṣāliḥ b. Naṣr Allāh al-Ḥalabī's *Ghāyat al-itqān* (see Brockelmann ii p. 365, *Sptbd.* ii p. 666), pp. 66–158 marg., (4) an Arabic translation of the *Basilica chymica* of Crollius, pp. 158–239 marg., (5) extracts from the Arabic *tafsīr* entitled *ʻArāʼis al-bayān* (see Brockelmann i p. 414, *Sptbd.* i p. 735) by Rūzbihān al-Baqlī (cf. p. 934 *supra*), pp. 241–358 marg., 359–383, (6) the *Gulshan i rāz* of Maḥmūd Shabistarī, pp. 384–98, (7) an extract from "ʻAṭṭār's" *Manṭiq al-ṭair*, pp. 384–98 marg.

[4] No attempt has been made to trace other MSS. of this translation.

1258. To Shāh Shujā' [i.e., according to Ethé, the Muẓaffarid, who reigned from 760/1359–786/1384] was dedicated—

A life of 'Abd al-Qādir al-Jīlānī [1] (beginning *Sazāwār i ḥamd u thanā Pādshāhīst*) : **Ethé** 1800 (A.H. 1052/1642).

1259. S. **M. b. Mubārak** b. M. 'Alawī **Kirmānī,** called Amīr, or Mīr, i Khwurd,[2] was the grandson of S. M. b. Maḥmūd Kirmānī,[3] a merchant who in the course of his journeyings between Kirmān and Lahore used to meet Sh. Farīd al-Dīn Ganj i Shakar [4] at Ajōd'han and became his disciple. After Farīd al-Dīn's death [in 664/1265] he became the friend of Sh. Niẓām al-Dīn Auliyā.[5]

[1] For whom see p. 933 n. 2 *supra*.

[2] Cf. *Rashaḥāt* p. 47², where two persons called Amīr [i] Buzurg and Amīr [i] Khwurd are mentioned.

[3] For biographies (based probably on the *Siyar al-auliyā'*) see *Akhbār al-akhyār* p. 96 ; *Kalimāt al-ṣādiqīn* no. 38 ; *Khazīnat al-aṣfiyā'* i p. 320.

[4] Farīd al-Dīn Mas'ūd called Ganj i Shakar or Shakar-ganj, the *khalīfah* of Quṭb al-Dīn Bakhtyār, died on 5 Muḥarram 664/17 Oct. 1265 aged 95 and was buried at Ajōd'han or Pattan (now called Pāk Pattan on his account), about half-way between Lahore and Multān in the Montgomery District of the Panjāb. Some Ṣūfī tracts by him are extant and there are two collections of his utterances, (1) *Rāḥat al-qulūb*, collected by Niẓām al-Dīn Auliyā (Edition : place ? date ? (Āṣafīyah iii p. 198). MSS. : 'Alīgaṛh Subḥ. MSS. p. 18 no. 5, p. 19 no. 23, Āṣafīyah i p. 420, Bānkīpūr **xvi** 1357, **xvii** 1641, Būhār 170, Ivanow 1181, Lindesiana p. 204). (2) *Asrār al-auliyā'*, collected by Badr al-Dīn Isḥāq (Editions : Lucknow 1876°*, place ? 1301/1883–4 (Āṣafīyah i p. 398), Cawnpore 1890†. MSS. : 'Alīgaṛh Subḥ. MSS. p. 13, Āṣafīyah i p. 396, nos. 354, 650, Browne Suppt. 47 (King's 35), Rieu iii 973*b* (extracts)). See *Siyar al-'ārifīn* no. 5 ; *Akhbār al-akhyār* pp. 52–4 ; Firishtah ii pp. 383–91 ; *Gulzār i abrār* nos. 14 and 21 ; *Jawāhir i Farīdī* ; *Safīnat al-auliyā'* pp. 96–7 (no. 113) ; *Mir'āt al-asrār, ṭabaqah* 19 ; *Sawāṭi' al-anwār* (Ethé col. 329 no. 17) ; *Ātashkadah* no. 755 ; *Ṣuḥuf i Ibrāhīm* ; *A brief account of Masúd, known by the name of Faríd Shakarganj or Shakarbár. By Munshí Mahan* [*sic*] *Lal* (*in JASB. V* (1836) pp. 635–8) ; *JASB. VI* (1837) pp. 190–3 (an account of Pākpattan in an article (pp. 169–217) entitled *Journal of Captain C. M. Wade's voyage from Lodiana to Mithankot by the river Satlaj on his mission to Lahór and Baháwulpur in 1832–33. By Lieut. F. Mackeson*) ; *Khazīnat al-aṣfiyā'* i pp. 287–305 ; Garcin de Tassy, *Mémoire sur . . . la religion musulmane dans l'Inde*, 2nd ed., Paris 1869, pp. 94–5 ; Beale *Oriental biographical dictionary* under Farid ; *The shrine of Bābā Farīd Shakarganj at Pakpattan. By Miles Irving* (in *Journal of the Punjab Historical Society*, i (1911–12) pp. 70–6) ; *I'lān i siyādat i Farīdī* (in Urdu), by Rashīd Aḥmad, Amrōhah 1915 ; Bānkīpūr **xvii** pp. 112–14 ; *Babā Farīd Ganj i Shakar, Sh. Ibrāhīm aur Farīd i Thānī*, an Urdu article by Mōhan Sing'h " Dīwānah " in *OCM*. xiv/2 (Feb. 1938) pp. 75–81, xiv/3 (May 1938) pp. 25–37, xiv/4 (Aug. 1938) pp. 88–90, xv/1 (Nov. 1938) pp. 67–84, xv/2 (Feb. 1939) pp. 44–71 (and later issues ?) ; *Nasab-nāmah i ḥaḍrat i Bābā Farīd al-Dīn Ganj i Shakar*, an Urdu article by Baldēv Sing'h in *OCM*. xvii/2 (Feb. 1941) pp. 118–27.

[5] N. al-D. M. b. A. Badā'ūnī, the most celebrated of the saints of Delhi, was born in 636/1238–9 at Badā'ūṅ, to which his grandfather is said to have migrated from Bukhārā. After spending four years at Delhi he went to Ajōd'han

He died in 711/1311–12 and was buried at Delhi. His grandson, M. b. Mubārak, received his initiation into Ṣūfism in childhood from Sh. Niẓām al-Dīn. Subsequently he became the disciple of Naṣīr al-Dīn Maḥmūd Chirāgh i Dihlī.[1] It is stated in the *Khazīnat*

and in 655/1257 became a disciple of Farīd al-Dīn Ganj i Shakar. Returning to Delhi he settled in the neighbouring village of Ghiyāthpūr (now called Niẓām al-Dīn Auliyā kī bastī, i.e. N. al-D. A.'s village) and died there in 725/1325. Among his disciples were Chirāgh i Dihlī and the poets Khusrau (see pp. 495–505 *supra*) and Ḥasan Dihlawī. Discourses of his are extant in four collections, (1) *Afḍal al-fawā'id*, collected (in part ?) by Khusrau before the *Rāḥat al-muḥibbīn*, in which it is mentioned as an earlier work (see Bānkīpūr **xvii** p. 115. According to Waḥīd Mirzā the first of its four parts was presented to the saint in 719 [i.e. long after the time at which the discourses of the *Rāḥat al-muḥibbīn* were collected] and permission was then obtained to continue the work, but the second part [unlike the third and fourth ? According to Waḥīd Mirzā the work " is divided into four parts ".] remained incomplete). Edition: Delhi 1887°. Description: Waḥīd Mirzā *Life and works of Amir Khusrau* pp. 225–7. (2) *Rāḥat al-muḥibbīn*, " discourses relating to the accounts of prophets and saints " and apparently to other matters taken down by Khusrau from 20 Rajab 689 to 9 Muharram 691 (MSS.: Bānkīpūr **xvii** 1642, Rieu 973*b* (extracts)). (3) *Fawā'id al-fu'ād*, taken down by Ḥasan Dihlawī in 707–19 and 719–22 and containing according to Ivanow " much biographical material concerning early Chishtī saints " (Edition: Lucknow 1885°. MSS.: 'Alīgaṛh Subḥ. MSS. p. 18, Ivanow 239, Rieu iii 972, 973*b* (extracts), 1040*b* (extracts)). (4) *Durar i Niẓāmīyah*, taken down by 'Alī b. Maḥmūd Jāndār . . . (presumably = 'Alī-Shāh b. Maḥmūd Jāndār, *Gulzār i abrār* no. 85. MS.: Būhār 183). His collection of the utterances of his master Ganj i Shakar, the *Rāḥat al-qulūb*, is mentioned in the preceding note. See *Nafaḥāt al-uns* pp. 584–6; *Siyar al-'ārifīn* no. 7; *Akhbār al-akhyār* pp. 54–60; *Haft iqlīm* no. 385; Firishtah, [Lucknow] 1281, ii pp. 391–8; *Gulzār i abrār* no. 78; *Kalimāt al-ṣādiqīn* no. 25; *Safīnat al-auliyā'* pp. 97–8 (no. 114); *Mir'āt al-asrār, ṭabaqah* 20; *Maṭlūb al-ṭālibīn* (Ethé 653); *Sawāṭi' al-anwār* (Ethé col. 331 no. 21); " Mubtalā " *Muntakhab al-ash'ār* no. 665; *Tadhkirah i Ḥusainī* p. 330; *Makhzan al-gharā'ib* no. 2716; *Khazīnat al-aṣfiyā'* i pp. 328–9; Garcin de Tassy *Mémoire sur les particularités de la religion musulmane dans l'Inde*, 2nd ed., 1869, pp. 97–9; *Ḥadā'iq al-Ḥanafīyah* pp. 277–8; *Nuzhat al-khawāṭir* pp. 122–8; Beale *Oriental biographical dictionary* under Nizam-uddin Aulia; Raḥmān 'Alī p. 240; Bānkīpūr **xvi** p. 19; *Ency. Isl.* under Niẓām al-Dīn (Hidayet Hosain); Waḥīd Mirzā *Life and works of Amir Khusrau* pp. 112–19.

[1] Naṣīr al-Dīn Maḥmūd b. Yaḥyā Awad'hī called Chirāgh i Dihlī was born at Awad'h, i.e. Ajōd'hyā. At the age of forty he became a disciple of Niẓām al-Dīn Auliyā and in 724/1324 was nominated by him as his successor (*khalīfah*). He died at Delhi in 757/1356. Among his disciples were Gēsu-darāz (see p. 950 n. 1) and M. b. Ja'far Makkī (see pp. 183–4 *supra*). A collection of his utterances, *Khair al-majālis*, begun in 755/1354 and completed in 756/1355 or 760/1359 by his disciple Ḥamīd Shā'ir Qalandar (*Akhbār al-akhyār* p. 86[15]), or Ḥamīd Qalandar (*op. cit.* p. 86[18], *Khazīnat al-aṣfiyā'* i p. 365), or Ḥamīd al-Dīn b. Tāj al-Dīn al-Qalandar al-Dihlawī (*Nuzhat al-khawāṭir* p. 37), is described in the last-mentioned work (p. 38[1]) as well-known (*mutadāwal fī aidī 'l-nās*), but no copies seem yet to be recorded in any published catalogue. See *Siyar al-'ārifīn* no. 12; *Akhbār al-akhyār* pp. 80–6; *Haft iqlīm* no. 402; Firishtah ii pp. 398–400; *Gulzār i abrār* no. 131; *Kalimāt al-ṣādiqīn* no. 33; *Safīnat al-auliyā'* pp. 100–1 (no. 116); *Mu'nis al-arwāḥ*; *Mir'āt al-asrār, ṭabaqah* 20; *Sawāṭi' al-anwār* (Ethé col. 331 no. 22); *Khazīnat al-aṣfiyā'* i pp. 353–7;

al-aṣfiyā' on the authority of the *Shajarah i Chishtīyah* that he died in 770/1368–9.

Siyar al-auliyā' fī maḥabbat al-Ḥaqq jalla wa-'alā, lives of Chishtī [1] saints, written in the reign of Fīrōz-Shāh Tughluq (752–90/1351–88), when the author was fifty years old, and divided into ten *bābs* ((1) *shaikhs* of the order from the Prophet to Niẓām al-Dīn,[2] (2) *khalīfahs* of Mu'īn al-Dīn Sijzī,[3] Quṭb al-Dīn Bakhtyār,[4]

Beale *Oriental biographical dictionary* under Nasir-uddin Mahmud ; Raḥmān 'Alī p. 238 ; *Nuzhat al-khawāṭir* pp. 158–60 ; *Ency. Isl.* under Čirāgh Dihlī (Hidayet Hosain) ; *Shaikh Nasīruddīn Mahmūd Chirāgh-i-Dehlī as a great historical personality*, by M. Ḥabīb (in *Islamic Culture* xx/2 (April 1946)).

[1] Chisht, a village near Harāt (marked as Khwajah Chisht on some maps), was the burial-place of Abu Aḥmad Abdāl Chishtī, the real founder of the Chishtī order, who died in 355/966 (see *Nafaḥāt* pp. 366–7, *Haft iqlīm* no. 622 ; *Safīnat al-auliyā'* p. 89 (no. 102) ; *Sawāṭi' al-anwār* (Ethé col. 328 no. 9) ; *Khazīnat al-aṣfiyā'* i pp. 241–3).

[2] See p. 941 n. 5.

[3] Mu'īn al-Dīn M. b. Ghiyāth al-Dīn Ḥasan Sijzī Chishtī, the founder of the Indian branch of the Chishtī order and one of India's most famous saints, is said to have been born in Sijistān but to have grown up in Khurāsān. Having resided for long or short periods at various places in Persia and the neighbouring countries (twenty years, according to Dārā-Shukōh, at Hārūn (" *az nawāḥī i Nīshāpūr* ") with his *pīr*, Khwājah 'Uthmān Hārūnī), he eventually settled at Ajmēr and died there in 633/1236 at an advanced age. A collection of 28 discourses by him was made by Quṭb al-Dīn Ūshī and entitled *Dalīl al-'ārifīn* (Editions : Cawnpore 1889°, Lucknow 1890°. MSS. : Āṣafīyah i p. 418 nos. 417 and 964, iii p. 196 no. 1505, Bānkīpūr xvii 1639, Rieu iii 973*b* (extracts), Ivanow-Curzon 460, 'Alīgaṛh Subḥ. MSS. p. 18 no. 9, p. 19 no. 17). He himself made a collection of 'Uthmān Hārūnī's utterances under the title *Anīs al-arwāḥ* (Edition : Lucknow 1890°. MSS. : Āṣafīyah i p. 402 nos. 599, 801, p. 404 no. 963, ii p. 848, Bānkīpūr xvii 1638, Būhār 169, I.O. D.P. 1153(*a*), Ivanow-Curzon 460 (1)). A *dīwān* of Ṣūfī poems by a poet who uses the *takhalluṣ* " Mu'īn " is ascribed to him (Editions : [Lucknow] 1285/1868°*, Lucknow 1316/1898°, 1327/1909*, Cawnpore 1288/1871*, 1875*, 1910‡, Lahore 1886*, [1904*], [1934*]. MS. : Bānkīpūr i 53). See *Siyar al-'ārifīn* no. 1 ; *Akhbār al-akhyār* pp. 22–5 ; Firishtah II pp. 375–8 ; *Gulzār i abrār* no. 5 ; *Safīnat al-auliyā'* pp. 93–4 (no. 110) ; *Mu'nis al-arwāḥ* (p. 1000 *infra*) ; *Mir'āt al-asrār*, *ṭabaqah* 17 ; 'Abd al-Ḥamīd *Pādshāh-nāmah* i, 1, p. 81 ; *Sawāṭi' al-anwār* (Ethé col. 329 no. 15) ; " Mubtalā " *Muntakhab al-ash'ār* no. 609 ; *Ātash-kadah* no. 756 ; *Ṣuḥuf i Ibrāhīm* ; *Makhzan al-gharā'ib* no. 2280 ; *Riyāḍ al-'ārifīn* pp. 220–1 ; *Miftāḥ al-tawārīkh* p. 57 ; *Waqā'i' i Shāh Mu'īn al-Dīn Chishtī* (p. 1066 *infra*) ; *Khazīnat al-aṣfiyā'* i pp. 256–67 ; Garcin de Tassy *Mémoire sur . . . la religion musulmane dans l'Inde*, Paris 1869, pp. 59–63 ; *Majma' al-fuṣaḥā'* i p. 542 ; *Ḥadā'iq al-Ḥanafīyah* p. 250 ; Beale *Oriental biographical dictionary* under Mu'in-uddin Chishti ; *Mu'īn al-auliyā'* (p. 1051 *infra*) ; *Tārīkh i Khwājah i Ajmēr ma'rūf bah Aḥsan al-siyar* (in Urdu), by M. Akbar Jahān, Āgrah [1905*] ; Bānkīpūr i p. 77 ; *Ency. Isl.* under Čishtī (unsigned) ; *Sawāniḥ i Khwājah i gharīb-nawāz rāh-numā i Ajmēr i sharīf* (in Urdu), by 'Āshiq Ḥusain " Sīmāb " Akbarābādī, Āgrah 1921* ; *Maḥfil i Khwājah 'urf Tārīkh i Sarwar i Ajmērī* (in Urdu), by Ghulām-Aḥmad Khān " Sarwar " Ajmērī, Āgrah [1924*] ; *Tārīkh al-salaf* (in Urdu), by " Ma'nī " Ajmērī, Āgrah 1344/1925–6 ; etc.

[4] Q. al-D. B. Ūshī, known as (*al-ma'rūf bah*) Kākī (in allusion to the

and Farīd al-Dīn,[1] (3) descendants of Farīd al-Dīn, relatives of Niẓām al-Dīn and Saiyids of the author's family, (4) *khalīfahs* of Niẓām al-Dīn, (5) some friends [2] who had the honour of being *murīds* and intimates of Niẓām al-Dīn (*ba'ḍī yārān i a'lā kih bi-sharaf i irādat u qurbat i Sulṭān al-mashāyikh . . . makhṣūṣ u musharraf būdah and . . .*), (6) duties of *khalīfahs* and *murīds*, (7) forms of prayer used by Farīd al-Dīn and Niẓām al-Dīn, (8) mystic love and visions of God, (9) *samā'* (music, trances and dancing), (10) sayings and letters of Niẓām al-Dīn) : **Ivanow** 243 (defective. A.H. 1040/1630–1), **I.O.** D.P. 668 (A.H. 1093/1682), **Berlin** 586 (lacks end of *Bāb* v and most of *Bāb* vi), **Rieu** iii 976*a* (extracts only. Circ. A.D. 1850), **Āṣafīyah** i p. 444 no. 939 (*Bāb* ix only. A.H. 1277/1860–1).

Edition : **Delhi** 1302/1885°*.

Urdu translation : *Urdū tarjamah i kitāb i S. al-a.*, **Lahore** [1923*].

[Autobiographical statements in the *Siyar al-auliyā'* ; *Akhbār al-akhyār* p. 97 ; *Maṭlūb al-ṭālibīn, maṭlab* 16 (Ethé col. 325 no. 45) ; *Dhikr i jamī' i auliyā' i Dihlī* ; *Khazīnat al-aṣfiyā'* i p. 366 ; *Nuzhat al-khawāṭir* p. 142 ; Raḥmān 'Alī p. 82]

1260. S. **Jalāl al-Dīn** Ḥusain b. Aḥmad Ḥusainī **Bukhārī,** surnamed **Makhdūm i Jahāniyān,** one of the great saints of India and a grandson of that S. Jalāl Bukhārī, called S. Jalāl i

cakes of bread (*kāk*) which used to appear miraculously for his sustenance), was born at Ūsh or Ōsh (both spellings are used by Barthold) in Farghānah. He became a disciple of Mu'īn al-Dīn Chishtī and it is said that in the course of his travels he met Shihāb al-Dīn Suhrawardī at Baghdād. He died at Delhi in 633/1235, the same (Hijrī) year as his *pīr* Mu'īn al-Dīn. A collection of his discourses was made under the title *Fawā'id al-sālikīn* by Farīd al-Dīn Ganj i Shakar (MSS. : Bānkīpūr xvii 1640, Ivanow Curzon 413). A *dīwān*, in which " Quṭb ", or " Quṭb i Dīn ", is the *takhalluṣ* used, is ascribed to him (Editions : Lucknow 1879°, 1882†, Cawnpore 1904*. MSS. : Sprenger 453, Rieu Suppt. 238), and also a *mathnawī*, *Mathnawī i mai-rang* (Edition : Cawnpore 1890°). See *Siyar al-'ārifīn* no. 4 ; *Akhbār al-akhyār* pp. 25–6 ; *Haft iqlīm* no. 1520 ; Firishtah ii pp. 378–83 ; *Gulzār i abrār* no. 13 ; *Kalimāt al-ṣādiqīn* no. 1 ; *Safīnat al-auliyā'* pp. 94–6 (no. 112) ; *Mir'āt al-asrār, ṭabaqah* 18 ; *Rauḍah i aqṭāb* ; *Sawāṭi' al-anwār* (Ethé col. 329 no. 16) ; *Riyāḍ al-shu'arā'* ; *Makhzan al-gharā'ib* no. 2047 ; *Riyāḍ al-'ārifīn* p. 206 ; *Khazīnat al-aṣfiyā'* i pp. 267–76 ; Garcin de Tassy *Mémoire sur les particularités de la religion musulmane dans l'Inde*, 2nd ed., Paris, 1869, pp. 89–92 ; *Sham' i anjuman* p. 387 ; Beale *Oriental biographical dictionary* under Qutb-uddin Bakhtiar ; Bānkīpūr xvii pp. 110–11.

[1] See p. 941 n. 4.

[2] *Yārān i a'lā* seems to be a term applied to friends of Niẓām al-Dīn, not, as Rieu supposed, the friends of the author.

Surkh, who migrated from Bukhārā to India and died at Uchh,[1] was born at Uchh in 707/1308. He became a disciple of Sh. Rukn al-Dīn Abū 'l-Fatḥ (see p. 971 n. 4 *infra*), associated with al-Yāfiʻī (see pp. 935–7 *supra*) at Mecca, and received the Chishtī investiture from Sh. Naṣīr al-Dīn Chirāgh i Dihlī (see p. 942 n. 1). In consequence of his travels, which took him to Egypt, Syria, the two 'Irāqs, Khurāsān, Balkh and Bukhārā, he is called Jahān-gasht. He died on 10 Dhū 'l-Ḥijjah 785/3 Feb. 1384 and is buried at Uchh. Two or three Ṣūfī works by him are recorded in the catalogues (e.g. 'Alīgaṛh Subḥ. MSS. p. 18 nos. 14, 15, Princeton 99). Collections of his utterances and teachings are the *Khizānah i Jalālī* (by Abū 'l-Faḍl b. Ḍiyā' 'Abbāsī, if Ivanow 1st Suppt. 856 is indeed a part of that work), the *Khulāṣat al-alfāẓ Jāmiʻ al-ʻulūm*, by 'Alī b. Sa'd b. Ashraf (Ivanow 1209), the *Sirāj al-hidāyah* (I.O. D.P. 1038), and a work of unknown title written by a descendant of the *shaikh* and divided into *majlises*, of which Ivanow 1210 is a fragment. A work based on his teachings is the *Khizānat al-fawā'id al-Jalālīyah* composed in 752/1351 by Aḥmad Bahā b. Ya'qūb (Ethé 2561, I.O. D.P. 998).

(*Safar-nāmah i Makhdūm i Jahāniyān*), an account of travels (but perhaps not genuine, since the work seems not to be mentioned by the biographers and the MSS. are (all ?) late) : **I.O.** D.P. 1107 (A.H. 1130/1718), 1123 (18th cent.), **Āṣafīyah** i p. 442 nos. 775 (A.H. 1159/1746), 429, ii p. 836 no. 16 (A.H. 1188/1774), **Lindesiana** p. 159 no. 624 (A.H. 1240/1824–5), **Madrās** i 448.

Urdu translations : (1) *Safar-nāmah i ḥaḍrat i Makhdūm i Jahāniyān Jahān-gasht*, by M. 'Abbās, **Lucknow** 1908* (described as 4th edition), (2) *S.-n. i M. i J.*, **Lahore** 1909 (possibly the same translation).

[Shams i Sirāj *Tārīkh i Fīrōz-Shāhī* pp. 514–16 ; " Yūsufī " *Maḥbūbīyah* (see p. 954 *infra*) ; *Siyar al-ʻārifīn* no. 13 ; *Akhbār al-akhyār* pp. 141–3 ; Firishtah, Bombay 1831–2, vol. ii pp. 779–84, [Lucknow] 1281/1864–5 pp. 415–17 ; *Gulzār i abrār* no. 128 ; *Dabistān i madhāhib*, tr. Shea and Troyer, New York 1937,

[1] See *Akhbār al-akhyār* p. 61 ; Firishtah, Bombay 1831–2, ii pp. 774–5, [Lucknow] 1281 ii pp. 412–13 ; *Khazīnat al-aṣfiyā'* ii pp. 35–8 ; etc. Uchh is now in the State of Bahāwalpūr.

p. 280; *Safīnat al-auliyā'* p. 116 (no. 157); *Mir'āt al-asrār*, *ṭabaqah* xxi; *Sawāṭi' al-anwār* (Ethé col. 332[29]); 'Abd al-Rashīd *Tārīkh i Qādirīyah* fol. 47*b*; *Khazīnat al-aṣfiyā'* ii pp. 57–63; Beale *Oriental biographical dictionary* under Shaikh Jalal; *Nuzhat al-khawāṭir* (in Arabic) pp. 28–35; *Ency. Isl.* under Djalāl (unsigned)].

1261. **Ḥājjī Rūmī** was a *khalīfah* of Maulānā Taqī al-Dīn M. Naqawī [Taqawī ?].

Taḥrīr al-mu'taqid fī ḥālāt al-murshid, a life of Taqī al-Dīn M. Naqawī [1] and his father 'Alī Murtaḍā, surnamed Māh i Sha'bān i Biyābānī and Sha'bān al-Millah [2]: **Rieu** iii 1042*a* (circ. A.D. 1850).

1262. S. Nūr Allāh Shūshtarī in his *Majālis al-mu'minīn* (p. 311[23]) cites the *Khulāṣat al-manāqib* as the work of **Nūr al-Dīn Ja'far Badakhshī**,[3] a disciple of S. 'Alī Hamadānī (*Maulānā N. al-D. J. B. kih az afāḍil i talāmidhah i ūst dar kitāb i Kh. al-m. dhikr numūdah kih . . .*). The ascription of the work to " 'Alā'ī " (*OCM*. iii/1, p. 70: *muṣannif kā nām " 'Alā'ī " lik'hā hai*) may be an inference from a poetical quotation, since " 'Alā'ī " (in addition to " 'Alī ") was used by S. 'Alī Hamadānī as a *takhalluṣ* (see Rieu ii p. 825*a* iii). Ethé's reason for ascribing the work to S. 'Alī himself is not clear.

Khulāṣat al-manāqib, an account of the life and more especially the sayings of Amīr S. 'Alī b. Shihāb al-Dīn Hamadānī,[4]

[1] A Bhakkarī Saiyid and Suhrawardī *shaikh*, who was born at Jhūnsī [Jhūsī, near Allahabad] in 720/1320–1 and died on 7 Dhū 'l-Ḥijjah 785/31 Jan. 1384. Cf. *Nuzhat al-khawāṭir* p. 93, where the authority is the *Manba' al-ansāb* (by Taqī al-Dīn's great-grandson Mu'īn al-Ḥaqq. See p. 949 *infra*), but where there is a discrepancy, since T. al-D. is called (not M. but) 'Alī b. 'Alī b. M. al-Ḥusainī al-Bhakkarī al-Shaikh T. al-D. al-Jhūnsawī.

[2] Cf. *Nuzhat al-khawāṭir* p. 92, where it is said on the authority of the *Manba' al-ansāb* that 'Alī b. M. b. M. b. M. b. Shujā' b. Ibrāhīm al-Ḥusainī al-Bhakkarī thumma 'l-Jhūnsawī al-mashhūr bi-Sha'bān al-Millah was born at Bhakkar on 24 Sha'bān 630 [in 660/1261–2 according to the *Taḥrīr al-mu'taqid*. See Rieu iii p. 1042*a*], that he travelled at the age of thirty to Multān, whence he moved successively to Bihār, Shaikhpūrah, and finally to the neighbourhood of Allahabad, where large numbers were converted by him to Islām, and that he died on 3 or 13 Dhū 'l-Ḥijjah 760/26 Oct. or 5 Nov. 1359 [at Jhūnsī according to the *Taḥrīr al-mu'taqid*].

[3] One of the authorities cited in the commentary on the *Aurād i Fatḥīyah* described in Rieu Suppt. 20.

[4] S. 'A. H., the " Second 'Alī " (*'Alī al-Thānī*) travelled extensively before settling in Kashmīr, where his influence contributed greatly to the spread of

begun in 787/1385–6 in Khuttalān[1]: **Berlin** 6 (8), **Bodleian** 1264, **Lahore** Panjāb Univ. Lib. (see *OCM.* iii/1 (Nov. 1926) p. 70).

1263. **Ṣalāḥ b. Mubārak al-Bukhārī** became a disciple of

Islām in the country. His arrival is said (e.g. by Firishtah, ii p. 339 penult., and by Abū 'l-Faḍl, *Ā'īn* p. 583^{11}) to have occurred in the reign of Sulṭān Quṭb al-Dīn (A.H. 780/1378–796/1393–4 according to W. Haig's tentative determination in *JRAS.* 1918 p. 468), but different authorities give different dates, e.g. 741 (!) (see Ethé 1850), 773 or 780 (*Nuzhat al-khawāṭir* p. 88^{3}), 781 (Rieu p. 447, perhaps from the *Wāqi'āt i Kashmīr*). His migration from Khurāsān (cf. *Nuzhat al-khawāṭir* p. 88^{2}) or, more probably, from Transoxiana (cf. *Majālis al-mu'minīn* p. 313^{20}) was prompted by a desire to escape the wrath of Tīmūr. The statement that he was expelled by Tīmūr from Hamadān cannot be correct, since Tīmūr did not reach Hamadān until after S. 'Alī's death, which occurred on 6 Dhū 'l-Ḥijjah 786/19 January 1385 at the age of seventy-three. He was buried by his own desire in Khuttalān (which may perhaps be the place from which he migrated to Kashmīr). He "may be regarded as a sort of patron saint of the Musulmán section of the population" [of Kashmīr] and "the mosque of Sháh-i-Hamadán is perhaps the most reverenced in the town" [of Srīnagar. *Tārīkh i Rashīdī* tr. Ross, p. 432 n. 2]. His works, of which forty-three are enumerated in the *Nuzhat al-khawāṭir*' are mostly short Ṣūfī tracts, and some are in Arabic. Collections of ten or more are preserved in the MSS. Rieu ii 835*b*, Blochet i no. 156, iv no. 2249, and Cairo p. 529. The best known are the *Aurād i fatḥīyah*, an Arabic litany repeatedly lithographed in India, and the *Dhakhīrat al-mulūk*, a fairly large treatise on political ethics (Edition: [Lahore] 1323/1905–6°*. MSS.: Leyden iv p. 220 nos. 1958–60, Berlin 6 (5), 295–7, Blochet ii 760–6, Rosen Inst. 110, Mashhad 9, MSS., no. 22, Bānkīpūr ix 943, Flügel iii 1853, Rieu ii 447*b*, 448*a*, 835*b*, Būhār 213–14, Āṣafīyah ii p. 1220, Bodleian 1451–3, Browne Suppt. 640 (King's 189), Browne Coll. N. 6, Ethé 2176–9, Lindesiana p. 121, Ivanow Curzon 490, Ivanow 1380, 'Alīgaṛh Subḥ. MSS. p. 11, Dresden 5, Panjāb Univ. (*OCM.* ix/2 (Feb. 1933) p. 44), Leningrad Univ. 1174 (Romaskewicz p. 9), Madras 425–6, Princeton 67, Upsala 456). For poems by him see Bānkīpūr i 150 (a "*dīwān*" of 14 foll.), Blochet iv 2249 (some *ghazals*), Rieu ii 825*a* (some *ghazals*), Āṣafīyah i p. 464 (*Gulshan i asrār*), p. 716 (*Chihil asrār*, an edition (place ?) of 1303. Cf. Edwards col. 112, where a *takhmīs* by Mastān Shāh (Edition: Lahore 1313/1897° in M. Sh.'s *Ātash-kadah i waḥdat*) is mentioned). See "Ādharī" *Jawāhir al-asrār* (Rieu i p. 43) fol. 121; *Nafaḥāt al-uns* p. 515; Daulat-Shāh p. 325^{9}; *Majālis al-'ushshāq* no. 36; *Ḥabīb al-siyar* iii, 3, p. 87 (based on the *Nafaḥāt*); *Tārīkh i Rashīdī*, tr. Ross, p. 432; *Haft iqlīm* no. 1019; *Majālis al-mu'minīn* pp. 311–13; Firishtah, [Lucknow] 1281, vol. ii p. 339 penult.; *Safīnat al-auliyā'* pp. 107–8 (no. 135); *Wāqi'āt i Kashmīr* pp. 36–7; *Makhzan al-gharā'ib* no. 1582; *Riyāḍ al-'ārifīn* pp. 178–9; *Khazīnat al-aṣfiyā'* ii pp. 293–9; *Majma' al-fuṣaḥā'* i p. 340; Rieu II p. 447; Beale *Oriental biographical dictionary* under Sayyad 'Ali; Raḥmān 'Alī p. 148; T. W. Arnold *The preaching of Islam*, 2nd ed., p. 292; 'Abd al-Ḥaiy Lak'hnawī *Nuzhat al-khawāṭir* (in Arabic) pp. 87–90; Ethé no. 1850; Bānkīpūr Cat. i pp. 229–31; Brockelmann ii p. 221, *Sptbd* ii p. 311; etc.

[1] Khuttal or Khuttalān (pronounced also Khutlān or Khatlān) was the name of a district between the Panj and the Wakhsh (tributaries of the Oxus) west of Badakhshān. See le Strange *L.E.C.* p. 438, Barthold *Turkestan* p. 69, *Ency. Isl.* under Khuttal (Barthold).

Khwājah 'Alā' al-Dīn 'Aṭṭār [1] in 785/1393 and was by him introduced to Bahā' al-Dīn Naqshband, after whose death in 791/1389 he began to write his *Anīs al-ṭālibīn*.

Anīs al-ṭālibīn wa-'uddat al-sālikīn, or *Maqāmāt i Khwājah Naqshband*, an account of Bahā' al-Dīn Naqshband,[2] his teachings and miracles: Ḥ. Kh. i p. 487, **Bānkīpūr** xvi 1377 (an abridgment (foll. 55) beginning *Ammā ba'd chunānkih dar ẓuhūr aḥwāl u āthār i auliyā rā*. A.H. 856/1452, ostensibly transcribed by 'Abd al-Raḥmān Jāmī), 1376 (A.H. 994/1586), **Ivanow** 244 (beg. as Bānkīpūr xvi 1377. A.H. 952/1545–6), **Ivanow** Curzon 64 (A.H. 993/1585), **Ethé** 1851 (A.H. 1008/1599–1600), **I.O.** D.P. (Bilg. 428) (A.H. 1041/1631–2), D.P. 1185 (an abridgment), **Blochet** i 113 (11) (A.H. 1009/1600),[3] **Āṣafīyah** iii p. 362 no. 236, **Berlin** 4 (23), **Cairo** p. 423 (apparently), **Istānbūl** (several copies, e.g. Fātiḥ 2560. See Horn p. 290, Brockelmann *Sptbd.* ii p. 282), **Lahore** Panjab Univ. Lib. (defective at end. See *OCM.* iii/1 (Nov. 1926) p. 70), **Romaskewicz** p. 3 no. 966*a*, **Upsala** Zetterstéen 472 (13) (defective).

1264. S. **Mu'īn al-Ḥaqq** b. Shihāb al-Ḥaqq b. M. Abū Ja'far b. Shāh Taqī al-Dīn [4] b. Sha'bān al-Millah,[5] a Bhak'harī Saiyid by descent, was a native of Jhūnsī [Jhusi, near Allahabad], where his great-grandfather, Shāh Taqī al-Dīn died in 785/1384.[6] His father, Shihāb al-Ḥaqq, was born in 760/1359 and died in 800/1397, leaving him an orphan at an early age. Desiring to ascertain his pedigree, he went via Multān, where he stayed with Sh. Kabīr, to Bhak'har and was affectionately received by his relatives. He obtained from them a copy of an old *nasab-nāmah* alleged to have been brought to Bhak'har by their ancestor,

[1] d. 802/1400, a disciple of Bahā' al-Dīn Naqshband. See *Rauḍat al-sālikīn* no. 5, *Rashaḥat* pp. 79–90, *Haft iqlīm* no. 1490, *Safīnat al-auliyā'* p. 80 (no. 85), *Khazīnat al-aṣfiyā'* i pp. 551–4.

[2] See p. 7, n. 3, *supra*; *Rauḍat al-sālikīn* no. 4; *al-Shaqā'iq al-Nu'mānīyah*, tr. Rescher, pp. 165–6; *Haft iqlīm* no. 1489; *Safīnat al-auliyā'* pp. 78–9 (no. 82); *Ency. Isl.* under Nakshband (Margoliouth); Brockelmann *Sptbd.* ii p. 282 (where some further references will be found).

[3] Blochet gives the author's name as Mullā Ḥusām al-Dīn Khwājah Yūsuf.

[4] See p. 946 n. 1 *supra*. [5] See p. 946 n. 2 *supra*.

Ḥāfiẓī Bukhārī and describes the ascription to Ṣalāḥ b. Mubārak as incorrect.

[6] This is the date given in the *Taḥrīr al-mu'taqid* (see p. 946 *supra* and Rieu iii p. 1042*a*). For two apparently corrupt dates given in the Bānkīpūr MS. of the *Manba' al-ansāb* see the Bānkīpūr catalogue, Suppt. ii p. 59 n.

S. M. Makkī, who according to him was born in 540/1145–6 and died in 644/1246–7. On this *nasab-nāmah* he based the *Manba' al-ansāb*, which cannot have been completed earlier than 830/1426–7, the latest date mentioned in his genealogical account of his family.

Manba' al-ansāb, an account of the Saiyids of Bhak'har and of various matters relating mainly to Ṣūfism in eleven[1] *faṣls* ((1) genealogy of Muḥammad, (2) genealogy of the Prophets, (3) history of Muḥammad, the twelve Imāms and the fourteen Ma'ṣūms, (4) genealogical account of the Saiyids in Arabia and elsewhere, (5) account of the four *Pīrs*, of the fourteen *khānawādahs* and of some minor orders, (6) rules, observances and prayers of the Ṣūfīs, (7) doctrines of the philosophers and the Ṣūfīs concerning the soul, (8) differences of opinion on some *ḥadīths* relating to Ṣūfism, (9) the meaning of the words *Āmantu bi-'llāh*, (10) eulogies on the early Caliphs and the twelve Imāms, (11) the origin and destiny of man and the various classes of *faqīrs*), being Mu'īn al-Ḥaqq's work retouched and greatly enlarged by his lineal descendant in the sixth degree, S. 'Alī Ghaḍanfar, commonly called Jār Allāh,[2] who lived probably about the close of the 10th/16th century, and who "professes to have added genealogical accounts of Sayyids of various countries, extracted from some standard historical works; further, a sketch of the Ṣūfī orders, borrowed from the Aḥvāl ul-Aṣfiyā and the Laṭāif i Ashrafī and finally the last six chapters of the work" (Rieu): **Rieu** i 348*a* (A.H. 1175/1761), iii 1042*a* (extracts only. Circ. A.D. 1850), **Bānkīpūr** Suppt. ii 2069 (lacunæ. A.D. 1876), **Āṣafīyah** iii p. 718.

1265. **M. 'Alī Sāmānī.**

Siyar i Muḥammadī, a biography of the Chishtī saint S. M. b. Yūsuf Ḥusainī known as Gēsū-darāz and Bandah-

[1] So Rieu. A twelfth *faṣl* (on the genealogy of the Imāms and of Shāh Taqī al-Dīn) is mentioned in the preface of the Bānkīpūr copy but is absent from that MS.

[2] This editor, not mentioned by 'Abd al-Muqtadir, is doubtless responsible for the references to Jāmī and his *Nafaḥāt*, which led 'Abd al-Muqtadir to suppose that the author wrote the work at a very advanced age.

nawāz,[1] written in 831/1427–8: **Āṣafīyah** iii p. 198 no. 1374 (A.H. 1312/1894–5).

1266. **Abū 'l-Makārim b. 'Alā' al-Mulk Jāmī.**[2]

Khulāṣat al-maqāmāt, a biography of Sh. Aḥmad i Jām[3], written at least partly in 840/1436–7, which is mentioned as the

[1] S. M. b. Yūsuf Ḥusainī, born at Delhi in 721/1321, became a disciple of the Chishtī *shaikh* Naṣīr al-Dīn Maḥmūd Chirāgh i Dihlī (d. 757/1356: see p. 942 n. 1 *supra*), migrated after the latter's death to Gujrāt, remained there many years with Khwājah Rukn al-Dīn Kān i Shakar, and in 815/1412–13 settled at Gulbargah, where he died on 16 Dhū 'l-Qa'dah 825/1 Nov. 1422, " at the age of 105 lunar years, leaving numerous descendants in the enjoyment of great wealth and honours " (Rieu i p. 347*b*). He wrote several Ṣūfī works, including *Asmār al-asrār* (Edition: Ḥaidarābād 1350/1931–2. MSS.: Ivanow 1220, 1219 (3), Princeton 120 (?), Ethé 1861, Bombay Univ. p. 158, Āṣafīyah iii pp. 194, 198), *Khātimah* (MSS.: Ethé 1920 (12), 1856–8, 1869 vi, Ivanow 1222, Āṣafīyah i p. 416), *Ḥadā'iq al-uns* (MSS.: Ethé 1869 v, Ivanow 1228, Āṣafīyah i p. 418), *'Ishq-nāmah* (Ḥ. Kh. iv p. 212. MSS.: Ethé 1869 iii, Ivanow 1229, Āṣafīyah i p. 430. Turkish translation by Firishtah-Zādah: Flügel iii 1968 I. Edition of the Turkish translation: Istānbūl 1288/1871), *Wujūd al-'āshiqīn* (MSS.: Bānkīpūr xvi 1374, Ivanow 1223–7, Ethé 1858–60, Āṣafīyah i p. 496), *Istiqāmat al-sharī'ah bi-ṭarīq al-ḥaqīqah* (MSS.: Ivanow 1219 (2), Bodleian 1267 (1), Ethé 1861–2). A collection of discourses by him, *Jawāmi' al-kalim* or *Malfūẓāt i Bandah-nawāz*, was made by his disciple M. b. M. Akbar Ḥusainī (MSS.: Āṣafīyah iii p. 196, i pp. 412, 486 (?), ii p. 1722 (?), Ivanow 1231, Rieu i 347). See *Tārīkh ḥabībī* (p. 952 *infra*), *Khawāriqāt* (p. 976 *infra*), *Akhbār al-akhyār* pp. 131–6; Firishtah, Bombay 1831–2, vol. i p. 607, vol. ii p. 748, [Lucknow] 1281/1864–5, vol. i pp. 319–20, vol. ii p. 399, Briggs's trans. vol. ii pp. 388, 398; *Gulzār i abrār* no. 158 (Ivanow p. 100[16]); *Riyāḍ al-auliyā'*; *Sawāṭi' al-anwār* (Ethé col. 331 no. 22 (*a*)); *Khazīnat al-aṣfiyā'* i pp. 381–2; Rieu i pp. 347–8; Beale *Oriental biographical dictionary* under Muhammad Gesu Daraz; Raḥmān 'Alī p. 82; *Ḥālāt i dil-gudāz ma'rūf bah Sawāniḥ i Bandah-nawāz* (in Urdū), by Ḥakīm M. 'Umar Dihlawī, Delhi 1320/1902–3; two views of his shrine at Gulbargah in *Pictorial Hyderabad ... by K. Krishnaswamy Mudiraj*, vol. i, Ḥaidarābād 1929, [plates] pp. 98, 99.

[2] The author's name, absent from the three MSS. mentioned here, is given in the *Ṭarā'iq al-ḥaqā'iq* (see Ivanow p. 88) and in Khanikoff's *Mémoire sur la partie méridionale de l'Asie centrale*, Paris, 1861, p. 116 (see Ivanow 1st Suppt., p. 158).

[3] Shaikh al-Islām Abū Naṣr A. b. Abī 'l-Ḥasan Nāmaqī Jāmī, called Zhandah Pīl, is said to have been born in 441/1049–50 and to have died in 536/1142. His tomb at Jām, or Turbat i Shaikh Jām, about half-way between Harāt and Mashhad [cf. *Ency. Isl.* under Turbat-i Shaikh-i Djām] is described in C. E. Yate's *Khurasan and Sistan*, pp. 36–7. The works ascribed to him are some Ṣūfī tracts (e.g. *Miftāḥ al-najāt* begun in 522/1128, Flügel iii 1679, and *Uns al-tā'ibīn*, Ivanow 1169) and a *dīwān* (Editions: Cawnpore 1879°, 1881°, 1885†, 1898†. MSS.: Bānkīpūr i 23, Ethé 2863, 910, Brelvi-Dhabhar p. xxiv, Rieu ii 551*b*, Ivanow 436, Ivanow-Curzon 191, Bombay Univ. p. 224, Āṣafīyah i p. 716, Panjāb Univ. (*OCM.* iii/2 p. 75), Sprenger 88). See *Nafaḥāt* pp. 405–17; *Haft iqlīm* no. 667; *Majālis al-mu'minīn* pp. 271–2; *Safīnat al-auliyā'* pp. 168–9 (no. 308); *Makhzan al-gharā'ib* no. 3; *Riyāḍ al-'ārifīn* pp. 51–3; *Khazīnat al-aṣfiyā'* ii pp. 243–4; *Majma' al-fuṣaḥā'* I pp. 67–8; Bānkīpūr i pp. 30–1; *Ency. Isl.* under Aḥmed Jāmī (A. S. Beveridge); *JRAS.* 1917 pp. 300–6 (*q.v.* together with Ivanow 245 for further references).

current year in *Bāb* 3 (*JRAS*. 1917 p. 355[12]), and divided into ten *bābs* and a *faṣl*: **Ivanow** 245 (foll. 106. Lacunæ. Late 17th cent.), **I.O.** D.P. 641 (17th cent.), **Leningrad**. Asiat. Mus. V 21 (a fragment corresponding to foll. 4–46 of Ivanow 245 and breaking off early in *Bāb* 8. 16th cent. ?).

Edition based on the Leningrad fragment: *A biography of Shaykh Ahmad-i-Jam. By W. Ivanow* (in *JRAS*. 1917, pp. 291–365).

1269. **'Abd al-'Azīz b. S̲h̲ēr Malik**[1] b. M. **Wā'iẓī** wrote the two works mentioned below in the time of 'Alā' al-Dīn Aḥmad S̲h̲āh II, the Bahmanid ruler of the Deccan, who reigned from 838/1435 to 862/1457 and whose father, S̲h̲ihāb al-Dīn Aḥmad S̲h̲āh I (825/1422–838/1435), was not only a disciple and patron of the famous saint of Gulbargah, S. M. b. Yūsuf Ḥusainī surnamed Gēsū-darāz,[2] but also an admirer of the still more famous saint, S̲h̲āh Ni'mat Allāh Walī, of Māhān, to whom he sent two missions.[3]

[1] An *amīr* named S̲h̲ēr Malik was put to death by S̲h̲ihāb al-Dīn Aḥmad S̲h̲āh, who was his maternal uncle (see *Burhān i ma'āt̲h̲ir* p. 73[21], W. Haig *The religion of Aḥmad Shāh Bahmanī* (in *JRAS*. 1924) p. 78).

[2] See W. Haig *op. cit*, pp. 74–5: "He had always shown an inclination for the society of holy men. In A.D. 1399, in the reign of his brother and predecessor, Fīrūz, the saint Sayyid Muhammad Gīsū Darāz, whose shrine is still the best known in the Dakan, came from Dihlī and settled at Gulbarga. He was at first received with much honour, but the accomplished and cultured Fīrūz soon wearied of the rude and unlettered saint, and treated him with neglect. Aḥmad, simpler and more devout than his brother, built a hospice for Gīsū Darāz, and was unremitting in his devotion to him. The misfortunes of Fīrūz in the latter part of his reign were attributed by many to his neglect of the saint, and Aḥmad certainly enjoyed the active sympathy of Gīsū Darāz in his intrigues to supplant his brother. . . . Aḥmad S̲h̲āh, on his accession to the throne, distinguished Sayyid Muhammad Gīsū Darāz with an even greater measure of his favour, with the result that the cult of the saint became the fashion among all classes. The predecessors of Aḥmad on the throne of the Dakan had been disciples of the family of Muhammad Sirāj-al-dīn Junaidī, but Aḥmad forsook the representative of this family and became the professed disciple of Gīsū Darāz, on whom he bestowed large endowments which were long enjoyed by his descendants."

[3] The purpose of the first mission was to seek the saint's acceptance of the Sulṭān as a disciple: the second mission conveyed a request that the saint would send a son to India to act as the Sulṭān's spiritual guide (see Firis̲h̲tah i p. 433, W. Haig *op. cit.* pp. 76–7, and Rieu ii p. 832*b* xv, where a document entitled *Nasab i k̲h̲irqah i Aḥmad S̲h̲āh* is recorded). Three of the saint's grandsons went to the Deccan, and at least two of them seem to have settled there permanently (Haig, *op. cit.* pp. 77–8; H. K. Sherwani *Maḥmūd Gāwān*, Allahabad 1942, p. 26, and elsewhere).

(1) *Manāqib i ḥaḍrat i Shāh Ni'mat Allāh Walī*,[1] dedicated to 'Alā' al-Dīn Aḥmad Shāh : **Rieu** ii 833*a* (17th cent.).

(2) *Tārīkh ḥabībī wa-tadhkirat murshidī*, a biography of Gēsū-darāz,[2] completed in 849/1445–6 : **Ivanow** 246 (A.H. 1159/1746).

1270. **Mīm**,[3] who was a *khalīfah* of Shāh M. Ṣalāḥ Dūndē,[4] himself a *khalīfah* of Shāh 'Uthmān Akbar, wrote—

Ḥālāt i Shāh 'Uthmān Akbar, an account of Shāh 'Uthmān Akbar (b. at Jhūnsī in 737/1336–7, d. 821/1418–19), a son of Maulānā Taqī al-Dīn M. Naqawī (for whom see p. 946 n. 1 *supra*) : **Rieu** iii 1042*b* (extract only. *Circ.* A.D. 1850).

1271. **M. b. Abī 'l-Qāsim** was a disciple of Sh. Aḥmad i K'haṭṭū (کھتّو), who is called also Sh. Aḥmad i Maghribī.[5]

[1] For this saint and poet, who was a disciple of al-Yāfi'ī (see p. 935 *supra*) and who died at Māhān (near Kirmān) in 834/1431, see Daulat-Shāh pp. 333–40; *Ḥabīb al-siyar* iii, 3, p. 143 ; Taqī Kāshī no. 102 (Sprenger p. 19) ; *Majālis al-mu'minīn* pp. 275–6 (in *Majlis* 6) ; *Khazīnah i ganj i Ilāhī* (Sprenger p. 86) ; *Jāmi' i Mufīdī* ; *Mir'āt al-khayāl* p. 60 (no. 43) ; Mubtalā *Muntakhab al-ash'ār* no. 664 ; *Ātash-kadah* no. 250 ; *Khulāṣat al-afkār* no. 277 ; *Makhzan al-gharā'ib* no. 2710 ; *Riyāḍ al-'ārifīn* pp. 241–8 ; *Majma' al-fuṣaḥā'* ii pp. 42–8 ; Rieu ii pp. 634–5 ; Bānkīpūr ii pp. 10–11 ; Browne *Lit. Hist.* iii pp. 463–73; *Ency. Isl.* under Ni'mat Allāh Walī (Berthels) ; " Āyatī " *Tārīkh i Yazd* pp. 229–32 ; etc. Editions of his *dīwān* have been published at [Ṭihrān] in 1276/1860° and A.H.S. 1316/1938 (for MSS. see Sprenger 419, Rieu Suppt. 279, Rieu ii 634*b*, Bānkīpūr ii 168–9, Berlin 856–8, Ivanow Curzon 234, Browne Suppt. 625, R.A.S. P. 299, etc.). For prose works by him see Ivanow 1239–40, Rieu ii 831–833*a*, 635*b*, 828*b*, 829*a*, Āṣafīyah i p. 472, etc.

[2] For whom see p. 950 n. 1 *supra*.

[3] For this name cf. Bānkīpūr viii p. 107, where an eighteenth-century " Shāh Mīm, with the *takhalluṣ* Mīm " is mentioned.

[4] For this name cf. p. 646 n. 5.

[5] A saint much revered in Gujrāt, who was born at Delhi, became the disciple and eventually the *khalīfah* of Bābā Isḥāq Maghribī (d. 776/1375. See *Khazīnat al-aṣfiyā'* ii pp. 289–90, *Nuzhat al-khawāṭir* p. 13) at K'haṭṭū, a village near Nāgaur (for which see p. 5 n. 4 *supra*), settled in Gujrāt, where he died on 10 Shawwāl 849/9 Jan. 1446 and was buried at Sark'hēj, 6 miles S.W. of Aḥmadābād (cf. Murray's *Handbook to India, Burma and Ceylon*, 4th ed., p. 117 : " To the rt. is the Tomb of the Saint Shaik Ahmad Khattu Ganj Bakhsh, called also Maghrabi. Ganj Bakhsh lived at Anhalwada, and was the spiritual guide of Sultan Ahmad I., and a renowned Mohammedan saint ; he retired to Sarkhej, and died there in 1445 [*sic*] at the age of 111. This magnificent tomb and mosque were erected to his memory. The tomb is the largest of its kind in Guzerat, and has a great central dome and many smaller ones . . ."). See *Akhbār al-akhyār* pp. 156–61 ; *Ā'īn i Akbarī* tr. Blochmann p. 507 ; *Gulzār i abrār* no. 164 ; *Tūzuk i Jahāngīrī* ed. S. Aḥmad p. 212[11], Rogers and Beveridge's trans. i p. 428 ; *Mir'āt al-asrār, ṭabaqah* 22 ; *Riyāḍ al-auliyā'* ; *Mir'āt i Aḥmadī, khātimah* pp. 33–4, English trans. pp. 32–3 ; *Khazīnat al-aṣfiyā'* ii pp. 314–20 ; Beale's *Oriental biographical dictionary* under Ahmad Khattu ; etc.

Malfūẓāt i Aḥmad i Maghribī, an account of the life and sayings of Sh. Aḥmad i K'haṭṭū in sixteen *faṣls* (166 foll.): **Ivanow** 247 (18th cent.).

1272. Aḥmad b. M., called **Mu'īn al-fuqarā'**, flourished probably in the 9th/15th century.

(*Kitāb i Mullā-zādah*), or (*Risālah i Mullā-zādah*), a list with some biographical details of celebrities, especially saints, buried at Bukhārā[1]: **Leningrad** Mus. Asiat. (at least two copies, one of A.D. 1600 and another of 1289/1872. See *Mélanges asiatiques* vii (St. Petersburg 1876) p. 173), **Leningrad** Univ. 947*b* (Salemann-Rosen p. 49), 948*b* (*ibid.*), probably also 593*c* (*Tadhkirah i shuyūkh i Bukhārā*, by A. b. M. called M. al-f. See Salemann-Rosen p. 13), **Tashkent Univ.** Semenov 64 (A.H. 1230/1814–15), **R.A.S.** P. 159 (2) (" An Account of the Holy and Learned Men of Bukhārā from A.H. 54 to 814 ". Author not stated. A.H. 1246/1830–1), **Majlis** 225 (A.H. 1301/1883–4), **Bukhārā** Semenov 92.

Edition: **Bukhārā** 1904 (with the *Tārīkh i Bukhārā* of Narshakhī (cf. p. 370 *supra*). See the Tashkent Univ. catalogue no. 64).

Extracts: W. Barthold *Turkestan v epokhu Mongolskago nashestviya* i p. 166–72.

Description: Barthold *Turkestan*, London 1928, p. 58.

1273. " **Yūsufī**," the author of the *Maḥbūbīyah*, is probably to be identified with Najm al-Dīn Yūsuf ibn Rukn al-Dīn M. Ni'am Allāh Gardēzī, the author of the *Aurād i Yūsufī* (for which see Ivanow 1st Suppt. 859). He was a disciple of S. Ḥāmid Kabīr and S. Rukn al-Dīn Abū 'l-Fatḥ, who were respectively the grandson and the great-grandson of the celebrated saint S. Jalāl al-Dīn Bukhārī called Makhdūm i Jahāniyān (d. 10 Dhū 'l-Ḥijjah 785/3 Feb. 1384 at Uchh: see pp. 944–6 *supra*). Probably, therefore, he flourished in the latter half of the 9th/15th century. S. Rukn al-Dīn Abū 'l-Fatḥ was (no doubt considerably) his junior and received instruction from him in the *Qur'ān* and some other Arabic books (cf. *Maḥbūbīyah*, I.O. D.P. 1107

[1] Cf. *Manāqib i mazārāt i Bukhārā-yi-sharīf* (Leningrad Univ. no. 390. Salemann-Rosen p. 17) and *Risālah i mazārāt i Bukhārā sharīf* (Peshawar 999A).

foll. 2*a*, 97*b*), but this did not prevent Yūsufī from becoming his pupil in the *'ulūm i bāṯin*.

Maḥbūbīyah, anecdotes of S. Jalāl al-Dīn Bu<u>kh</u>ārī, called Ma<u>kh</u>dūm i Jahāniyān, of his son, S. Maḥmūd Nāṣir al-Dīn, his grandson, S. Ḥāmid Kabīr, and his great-grandson, S. Rukn al-Dīn Abū 'l-Fatḥ : **I.O.** D.P. 1107*a* (A.H. 1130/1718), D.P. 658 (A.H. 1268/1851).

1274. The well known poet, scholar and mystic Nūr al-Dīn 'Abd al-Raḥmān b. Aḥmad **Jāmī** was born at <u>Kh</u>arjird in the district of Jām [1] on 23 <u>Sh</u>a'bān 817/7 Nov. 1414 and died at Harāt on 18 Muḥarram 898/9 Nov. 1492.

Nafaḥāt al-uns min ḥaḍarāt al-quds, more or less chronologically arranged notices of about 567 saints from Abū Hā<u>sh</u>im al-Ṣūfī (2nd/8th cent.) to Qāsim al-Anwār (d. 837/1433–4), as well as of 13 Ṣūfī poets from "Sanā'ī" to "Ḥāfiẓ" and 34 female saints, begun in 881/1476–7 at the request of Mīr 'Alī <u>Sh</u>īr (for whom see pp. 789–95 *supra*), completed in 883/1478–9 and constituting an enlarged, extended and linguistically modernized recension of 'Abd Allāh Anṣārī's *Ṯabaqāt*, which, as already mentioned (p. 926 *supra*), is itself an enlarged Persian version of the *Ṯabaqāt al-Ṣūfīyah* of M. b. al-Ḥusain al-Sulamī : Ḥ. <u>Kh</u>. vi p. 367 no. 13922, **'Ā<u>sh</u>ir** p. 109 no. 177 (autograph according to Brockelmann *Sptbd.* ii p. 286), **Blochet** iv 2307 (A.H. 883/1478–9, transcribed from an autograph), iii 1676 (A.H. 895/1490, transcribed from an autograph), i 416 (A.H. 907/1501), 417 (A.H. 934/1527), iv 2300 (2) (A.H. 968/1561), i 418–20, **Dorn** 422 (2) (A.H. 883/1478 (?)), **Leyden** iii p. 19 no. 932 (A.H. 896/1491), **Browne** Coll. J. 6 (10) = Houtum-Schindler 35 (A.H. 902/1497), **Browne** Pers. Cat. 276 (16th–17th cent.), Suppt. 1321 (A.H. 1100/1688–9), 1322 (fairly old. King's 118), **Rieu** i 349*b* (A.H. 916/1510. Said to have been collated with an autograph), 349*a* (A.H. 961/1554), 350*a* (Āgrah, A.H. 1012/1603. Calligraphic with 17 fine pictures), 350*b* (16th

[1] *Wilādat i ī<u>sh</u>ān <u>Kh</u>arjird i Jām būdah ast* (*Ra<u>sh</u>aḥāt* p. 133[8]) : *Aṣl u maulid i bandagī i Maulānā wilāyat i Jām ast u masqaṯ i ra's i mubāraka<u>sh</u> qaryah i <u>Kh</u>arjird u man<u>sh</u>a'a<u>sh</u> dār al-salṯanah i Harāt* (Daulat-<u>Sh</u>āh p. 483[23]). For the town of Jām see p. 950 n. 3 *supra*. <u>Kh</u>arjird, some seventy-five miles from the town of Jām, is about twenty-five miles south of <u>Kh</u>wāf.

cent.), 350*b* (16th cent.), 350*b* (17th cent.), **Flügel** iii 1944 (A.H. 919/1513), **Dresden** no. 408 (A.H. 930/1524), **Bānkīpūr** Suppt. i 1780 (A.H. 932/1525–6), **Bānkīpūr** ii 181 (5) 204, 205, 206 (A.H. 1074/1663–4) 181 (5), **Madras** 446 (A.H. 939/1532–3), **Bodleian** 894 (3) (A.H. 941/1534), 895 (3) (A.H. 963/1556), 957 (old), 958 (n.d.), **Peshawar** 889 (A.H. 942/1535–6) **Būhār** 84 (A.H. 954/1547), **Upsala** 301 (A.H. 958/1551), **Princeton** 103 (A.H. 962/1554–5), **Berlin** 592 (A.H. 971/1563), 593 (A.H. 1021/1612), 594, 595, 596, 38 (2) (A.H. 1096/1684–5), **Bombay** Fyzee 4 (A.H. 972/1565), **Ethé** 1357 (8) (612 biographies. A.H. 980/1572), 1366 (549 biographies. A.H. 987/1579), 1362 (A.H. 990/1582), 1361 (611 biographies. A.H. 1023/1614), 1359 (620 biographies. n.d.), 1360 (612 biographies. n.d.), 1363–4, 1365 (597 biographies. A.H. 1065/1654–5), 1367, **I.O.** D.P. 774 (A.H. 1032/1622), 774B, **Cairo** p. 428 (A.H. 983/1575), p. 534 (A.H. 985/1577–8), pp. 427–8 (3 undated copies), **Turin** 94 (A.H. 995/1587), **Rehatsek** p. 104 no. 61 (A.H. 1002/1593–4), **Āṣafīyah** i p. 350 nos. 98 (A.H. 1007/1598–9), 32, 52, 53, 74, 113, **Leningrad** Asiat. Mus. (A.H. 1008/1599. See *Mélanges asiatiques* vii (1876) p. 401), Univ. 591–2 (Salemann-Rosen p. 20), 1184 (Romaskewicz p. 15), **Ivanow** Curzon 65 (with Lārī's glosses. A.H. 1014/1605–6), 66, **Ivanow** 612 (2) (old), 248 (A.H. 1133/1720–1), 249 (A.H. 1144/1731–2), 250, **Lindesiana** p. 165 no. 527 (*circ.* A.D. 1700), **'Alīgaṛh** Subḥ. MSS. p. 16 no. 88, **Bukhārā** Semenov 112, **Chanykov** 102, **Eton** 39, 40 (selections), **Lahore** Panjāb Univ. (3 copies. See *OCM*, iii/i (Nov. 1926) pp. 71–2), **Majlis** 564, **Tashkent Univ.** 75, etc.

Editions : **Calcutta** 1858–9°* (*The Nafahtáal-ons* [*sic*] *min hadharát al-qods, or the lives of the Soofis. . . . Edited by Mawlawis Gholám 'Iisa* [,] *'Abd al Hamíd and Kabír al-Dín Ahmad, with a biographical sketch of the author, by W. Nassau Lees. . . .* Lees' Persian Series) ; [**Bombay**] Ḥaidarī Press, 1289/1872* (followed by the *Silsilat al-dhahab*) ; **Cawnpore** 1885† (followed by the *Silsilat al-dhahab*), 1893† (followed by the *Silsilat al-dhahab*) ; **Lahore** 1897† (with Lārī's *Takmilah*) ; **Tashkent** 1915 (with Lārī's commentary. See Harrassowitz's *Bücher-Katalog* 405 (1926) no. 856 and Bukhārā Semenov pp. 14, 26).

Eastern-Turkish translation (abridged) : *Nasā'im al-maḥabbah min shamā'im al-futuwwah*, begun in 901/1495–6 by Mīr 'Alī-Shīr

"Nawā'ī" (see pp. 789-95 *supra*), who omitted many notices (e.g. all the female saints), added some new ones (e.g. 33 Indian saints from Shakar-ganj onwards) and concluded the work with an account of "Jāmī" himself: **Rieu** Turkish Cat. p. 274*b*.

Ottoman Turkish translation: *Futūḥ al-mujāhidīn li-tarwīḥ qulūb al-mushāhidīn*,[1] completed in 927/1521 by "Lāmi'ī"[2]: Ḥ. Kh. vi p. 367 ult., **Schefer** MSS. turcs 1052 (A.H. 986/1579), **Fleischer** p. 522 no. 279, **Vatican** (see *ZDMG*. 51 (1897) p. 40 no. 25).

Edition of the Ottoman Turkish translation: **Istānbūl** 1270/1854 (see Harrassowitz's *Bücher-Katalog* 405 (1926) no. 1096, Zenker ii p. 39).

Arabic translation by Tāj al-Dīn b. Zakarīyā' b. Sulṭān al-'Abshamī al-Umawī al-'Uthmānī al-Hindī al-Ḥanafī al-Naqshbandī[3]: **de Slane** 1370 (A.H. 1104/1693), **Cairo** Arab. Cat. ii p. 75, **Rāmpūr** Arab. Cat. i p. 370.

Urdu translation: *Tarjamah i Nafaḥāt al-uns*, by S. Aḥmad 'Alī Chishtī Niẓāmī. Edition: place? date? (Āṣafīyah iii p. 184 no. 249).

Commentaries: (1) *Ḥāshiyah i Nafaḥāt al-uns*, "very meagre and almost of no importance" (Ivanow), written[4] at the request of Jāmī's son, Ḍiyā' al-Dīn Yūsuf, by 'Abd al-Ghafūr Lārī,[5] who had heard the author explain difficult passages in the *Nafaḥāt* and who appended a *khātimah*,[6] or *takmilah*,[7]

[1] So Fleischer. Ḥ. Kh. writes *F. al-mushāhidīn li-t. q. al-mujāhidīn*.

[2] Maḥmūd b. 'Uthmān Bursawī, for whom see *Ency. Isl.* under Lāmi'ī.

[3] d. 1050/1640. See p. 965 n. 1 *infra*.

[4] In 896/1490–1 according to Ethé (Bodleian 960), but hardly any of the other cataloguers mention this date. The *Khātimah*, written immediately after the completion of the *Ḥāshiyah* proper, contains the date of Jāmī's death.

[5] Raḍī al-Dīn 'A. al-Gh. L., both a pupil (*shāgird*) and a disciple (*murīd*) of Jāmī's, wrote also Arabic annotations on *al-Fawā'id al-Ḍiyā'īyah*, Jāmī's incomplete Arabic commentary on Ibn al-Ḥājib's *Kāfiyah* (for which see Brockelmann i p. 304, *Sptbd.* i p. 533, Loth 928–9, Ellis coll. 30–1, Fulton-Ellis col. 34 etc.). He died on 5 Sha'bān 912/21 Dec. 1506. See *Rashaḥāt* pp. 163–73; *The Bābur-nāmah in English* i p. 284; *Bābur-nāmah* tr. 'Abd al-Raḥīm p. 113 (text edited by M. Shafī' in *OCM*. x/3 (May 1934) pp. 141–2); *Tārīkh i Rashīdī* (the passage, omitted by Ross, is quoted by M. Shafī' in *OCM*. x/3 (May 1934) p. 153); *Safīnat al-auliyā'* p. 84 (no. 91); *Khazīnat al-aṣfiyā'* i p. 598.

[6] So styled by the author himself in the preface to the *Ḥāshiyah* (cf. Berlin p. 560[22–3]).

[7] The title most frequently given to the work by copyists.

on Jāmī's life and utterances, often absent from MSS. of the *Ḥāshiyah* and often transcribed as an independent work: Ḥ. Kh. vi p. 367[9], **I.O.** D.P. 1152(*c*) (*Khātimah* only. A.H. 947/1540–1), **Ethé** 1362 marg. (selections only? A.H. 1042/1632–3), 1923 (37) (*Khātimah* only. N.d.), **Blochet** i 421 (without *Khātimah*. A.H. 963/1555), **Cairo** p. 428 (*Khātimah* only? A.H. 983/1575), **Ivanow** Curzon 65 (with *Khātimah*. A.H. 1014/1605–6), **Ivanow** 249 marg. (without *Khātimah*. A.H. 1144/1731–2), Curzon 67 (defective. Without *Khātimah*), 68 (without *Khātimah*), **Berlin** 593 marg. (without *Khātimah*. A.H. 1021/1612), 594 marg. (without *Khātimah*. Defective), 595 marg. (without *Khātimah*. Portion only), 596 (with *Khātimah*), 597 (without *Khātimah*. Defective), **Āṣafīyah** i p. 346 no. 112 (A.H. 1156/1743–4), p. 414 no. 201, **Rieu** i 350*b* (with *Khātimah*. 18th cent.), 351*b* (*Khātimah* only. A.H. 1133/1721), **'Alīgaṛh** Subḥ. MSS. p. 13 no. 27, **Bodleian** 960 (without *Khātimah*), 958 (*Khātimah*), **Būhār** 85, **Bukhārā** Semenov 52–3 (both without *Khātimah*), **Tashkent Univ.** 75 (*Khātimah* only), etc. (**2**) *Ḥāshiyah i Nafaḥāt al-uns*, meagre notes by Khwājah M. Dihdār "Fānī" Shīrāzī [1]:

[1] M. b. Maḥmūd *al-mulaqqab bi*-Dihdār, as he calls himself in the preface to the *Ḥāshiyah*, belonged to a family of Arab descent which had migrated from Ḥuwaizah, in Khūzistān, to Shīrāz. According to the *Mi'yār i sālikān i ṭarīqat* (as quoted in Rieu, iii p. 1094*b*) he "stayed many years at the court of Burhān Niẓām Shāh [ruler of Aḥmadnagar 914–61/1508–53], who made him Nāẓir of his kingdom. After the death of that prince's successor (A.H. 972) he retired to Sūrat, where he died A.H. 1016". If this is correct, he must have gone to India before Akbar's reign (963–1014/1556–1605), not in it, as Rieu says (ii p. 816*a*). He does not seem to be mentioned in the *Burhān i ma'āthir*, but some connexion with Aḥmadnagar is indicated by the title of a Ṣūfī tract of his, *Risālah i Niẓām-Shāh*, or *Risālah ba-jihat i Niẓām-Shāh* (Bodleian 1298 (2)). It was doubtless after his retirement (if that is the right word) to Sūrat, that he "became intimate" (Rieu ii p. 816*a*) with the Khān i khānān 'Abd al-Raḥīm (cf. p. 533 n. 4 *supra*), to whom are dedicated at least three of his works, the '*Asharah i kāmilah* (Bānkīpūr xvii 1517, etc.), the *Alif al-insānīyah* (Bkp. xvii 1525, etc.) and the *Sharḥ Khuṭbat al-bayān* (Bkp. xvii 1527, Ethé 1922 (27)). He is not, however, one of the adherents of the Khān i khānān to whose biographies the *khātimah* of the *Ma'āthir i Raḥīmī* (cf. p. 553 *supra*) is devoted. Although according to the *Mi'yār i sālikān i ṭarīqat* he died at Sūrat, Taqī Auḥadī (cited in Bānkīpūr xvii p. 34[12–13]) says that he died at his birthplace, Shīrāz. Seventeen of his works, mostly short Ṣūfī tracts, are described in the Bānkīpūr catalogue, xvii 1516–32. For smaller collections see Rieu ii 816*a* (eleven), Leningrad Univ. 997 (ten. Romaskewicz pp. 3, 6, 9, 11, 12, 15), Flügel iii 1964 (seven), Bodleian 1298 (7)–(13) (seven) and Āṣafīyah iii p. 202 no. 1447 (five). Bodleian 1281 is a *Ḥāshiyah i Faṣl al-khiṭāb*. *Ḥāshiyahs* on the *Rashaḥāt* and the *Gulshan i rāz* are mentioned by Sprenger and Rieu, but no copies seem to be recorded. Of his poetical works a *Maulūd-nāmah*,

I.O. D.P 682 (A.H. 1108/1696), 990 (18th cent.), **Bodleian** 961 (fragment only). (**3**) *Mukāshafāt i 'Alī Akbar Wahbī* (a chronogram = 1198/1784, the date of completion), explanations of the Ṣūfī terms by 'Alī Akbar b. Mīrzā Asad Allāh b. Sirāj al-Ḥaqq Amr Allāh al-Maudūdī: **Bānkīpūr** ii 208 (2 vols., ending with the notice of M. b. al-Faḍl al-Balkhī, the 119th in the Calcutta edition (pp. 130–1). 18th cent.).

Description: *Notices et extraits* xii pp. 287–436 (by Silvestre de Sacy, whose description relates to the MS. Blochet i 419).

Sources: *The sources of Jami's Nafahat*, by W. Ivanow (in *JASB*. N.S. 18 (1922) pp. 385–402); *More on the sources of Jami's Nafahat*, by W. Ivanow (in *JASB*. N.S. 19 (1923) pp. 299–303).

Abridgments: (**1**) *Khulāṣat al-Nafaḥāt*, an abridgment containing utterances and often explanations of them but scarcely any dates or other biographical information, written not later than 923/1517, the date of the Bānkīpūr MS., by Jalāl, i.e. probably, as 'Abd al-Muqtadir suggests, Sh. Jalāl Harawī [1]: **Bānkīpūr** ii 207 (A.H. 923/1517), **I.O.** D.P. 642 (A.H. 968/1560–1). (**2**) *Khulāṣat al-Nafaḥāt*, an abridgment made in 927/1521 by Maḥmūd b. Ḥasan b. Maḥmūd al-Ḥasanī al-Āmulī and containing 232 biographies, some of which relate to saints of Fārs and 'Irāq not mentioned by Jāmī: **Bodleian** 959 (n.d.).

[Some biographical sources are mentioned on p. 11 *supra*: a fuller list will be given in the section POETRY. Meanwhile the following may be added—'Abd al-Ghafūr Lārī's *Khātimah* to his *Ḥāshiyah* (see p. 956[24] *supra*); Mīr 'Alī-Shīr *Majālis al-nafā'is* (cf. p. 791 *supra*), first notice in *Majlis* iii (but this contains no biographical information), *Khamsat al-mutaḥaiyirīn*

on the birth of Muḥammad, is preserved at Princeton (no. 86). A *mathnawī* entitled *Haft dilbar* dedicated to Akbar and a *dīwān* containing *qaṣā'id* and *tarjī'-bands* were described by Sprenger from MSS. in the Mōtī Maḥall and the Tōp-khānah.

[1] Sh. J. Harawī, the son of a high official, Khwājah M. b. 'Abd al-Malik (*kih dar silk i a'āẓim i ahl i qalam intiẓām dāsht*), early devoted himself to Ṣūfism and became the disciple of Shams al-Dīn M. Rūjī (d. 904/1499. See *Rashaḥāt* pp. 187–98, *Safīnat al-auliyā'* pp. 189–90 (no. 361); *Khazīnat al-aṣfiyā'* i pp. 590–2). At the time when Khwānd-Amīr wrote his biography (i.e. probably in 929/1523) he was in the habit of preaching a weekly sermon in the *masjid i jāmi'* at Harāt. According to the *Ṣuḥuf i Ibrāhīm* (cited by 'Abd al-Muqtadir) he was a grandson of Jāmī's. See *Ḥabīb al-siyar* iii, 3, p. 348; *Ṣuḥuf i Ibrāhīm*; *Makhzan al-gharā'ib* no. 500.

(cf. p. 790 *supra*. Translated extracts in Belin's *Notice biographique* pp. 101–58), *Nasā'im al-maḥabbah* (see p. 790 *supra*), at end; *Laṭā'if-nāmah* pp. 96–7 (no biographical information); *Tārīkh i Rashīdī* (passages quoted in *Mélanges asiatiques* ix pp. 327, 355–8, and one of them in *OCM*. x/3 p. 153); *Tuḥfah i Sāmī* pp. 85–90; *Haft iqlīm* no. 264; *Khazīnat al-aṣfiyā'* i pp. 586–90; *Jāmī . . . ta'līf i 'Alī Aṣghar Ḥikmat*, Tihrān, A.H.S. 1320/1942.]

1275. **'Alī b. Maḥmūd al-Abīwardī al-Kūrānī.**[1]

Rauḍat al-sālikīn, a detailed life of the Naqshbandī shaikh 'Alā' al-Dīn M. b. M. b. Mu'min al-Ābizhī [or al-Ābīzī][2] al-Qūhistānī, who was a disciple of Sa'd al-Dīn al-Kāshgharī and who died in 892/1487,[3] preceded by short notices of ten other shaikhs (from 'Abd al-Khāliq Ghujduwānī to 'Ubaid Allāh Aḥrār), who occur in the Naqshbandī pedigree: **Būhār** 186 (A.H. 948/1541), **Ethé** 632 (defective at end).

List of the biographies: Ethé coll. 260–1.

1276. Abū 'l-Ghāzī Sulṭān **Ḥusain** b. Sulṭān Manṣūr b. Bāyqarā b. 'Umar Shaikh b. Tīmūr, virtually the last of the Tīmūrid kings of Khurāsān, was born at Harāt[4] in Muḥarram 842/June-July 1438. After Sulṭān Abū Sa'īd's death (25 Rajab 873/8 Feb. 1469) he seized Harāt and ascended the throne there in Ramaḍān 873/March 1469. Having reigned for thirty-eight years he died on 11 Dhū 'l-Ḥijjah 911/5 May 1506. His patronage and that of his celebrated friend Mīr 'Alī-Shīr "Nawā'ī" (see pp. 789–95 *supra*) made his court a brilliant centre of letters and art. "Jāmī," "Hātifī," "Hilālī," Ḥusain Kāshifī, 'Abd Allāh Marwārīd, Mīr Khwānd, Khwānd-Amīr, Daulat-Shāh, Bihzād and Sulṭān 'Alī Mashhadī were among the famous men who found encouragement there. Sulṭān Ḥusain himself wrote poetry. A MS. of his Turkī *dīwān* is preserved in the Bibliothèque nationale at Paris.

[1] Kūrān was a village near Isfarāyin (Sam'ānī 489*b*, *Lubb al-Lubāb* 226).

[2] Ābizh or Ābīz was a village in Qūhistān (*Rashaḥāt* p. 176[6], where it is spelt Āpīz).

[3] For notices of him see *Rashaḥāt* pp. 176–86, *Gulzār i abrār* no. 237; *Khazīnat al-aṣfiyā'* i pp. 578–80.

[4] *Ḥabīb al-siyar* iii, 3, p. 203[18].

The *Majālis al-'ushshāq*, which is ostensibly[1] the work of Sulṭān Ḥusain, is said by Khwānd-Amīr (*Ḥabīb al-siyar* iii, 3 p. 330[7]) and Bābur (*Bābur-nāmah* tr. 'Abd al-Raḥīm p.112[8]. Cf. Browne *Lit. Hist.* iii p. 457) to be the work of Mīr[2] **Kamāl al-Dīn Ḥusain** b. Maulānā Shihāb al-Dīn Ṭabasī **Kāzargāhī.**[3] Kamāl al-Dīn Ḥusain, who, according to Khwānd-Amīr, was well acquainted with the usual subjects of study and occasionally wrote poetry, laid claim to special knowledge of *jafr* and *taṣawwuf*. Leaving Ṭabas, he went to Ādharbāyjān and lived for a time under the patronage of Sulṭān Ya'qūb [Āq-quyūnlū, A.H. 884–96/1479–90]. He then migrated to Harāt, was appointed Warden of the shrine of Khwājah 'Abd Allāh Anṣārī,[4] and wrote a commentary on the *Manāzil al-sā'irīn*[5]. In 904/1498–9 Sulṭān Ḥusain appointed him to the office of Ṣadr.[6] The date of his

[1] Except in so far as verses by Kamāl al-Dīn Ḥusain occurring in the book are headed "by the author" (cf. Bābur's statement quoted by Browne, *Lit. Hist.* iii p. 458).

[2] His mother, a sister of Amīr [i.e. Mīr] Rafī' al-Dīn Ḥusain (*Laṭā'if-nāmah* p. 161[3]), belonged to a distinguished family of Nīshāpūrī Saiyids (*dar silk i banāt i sādāt i 'iẓām i Nīshāpūr intiẓām dāsht*, *Ḥabīb al-siyar* iii, 3, p. 330[2]).

[3] Or Gāzargāhī ? His claim to this *nisbah*, which is applied to him in the *Bābur-nāmah*, but not in the *Laṭā'if-nāmah* or the *Ḥabīb al-siyar*, is presumably based on his connexion with the shrine of 'Abd Allāh Anṣārī at Kāzargāh or Gāzargāh, some two miles to the north-east of Harāt. A description of the shrine is given in C. E. Yate's *Northern Afghanistan* pp. 33–7, where the name of the place is spelt Gazargah. Doubtless this represents the modern, if not the ancient, pronunciation, though Kāzargāh would be expected, since the place is said to have received its name (properly Kārzār-gāh, battlefield) from a battle fought there in 206/821–2. See Barthold *Herāt unter Ḥusein Baiqara*, tr. Hinz, p. 78 n. 1 ; *Istorico-geograficheskу obzor Irana* p. 40.

[4] *Ḥabīb al-siyar* iii, 3 p. 330[4] : *Khāqān i manṣūr amr i shaikhī i tauliyat i mauqūfāt i mazār i muqarrab i ḥaḍrat i Bārī Khwājah 'Abd Allāh i Anṣārī rā ba-ān-janāb mufawwaḍ gardānīd*. The Warden who was at the shrine when Yate visited it in 1885 is called by him "the Mutawali [read Mutawallī], or superintendent of the endowment of the shrine". For 'Abd Allāh Anṣārī see pp. 924–7 *supra*.

[5] For the *Manāzil al-sā'irīn*, an Arabic work on Ṣūfism by 'Abd Allāh Anṣārī, see Brockelmann i p. 433, *Sptbd.* i p. 774. No MS. of Kamāl al-Dīn's commentary seems to be recorded.

[6] *Ḥabīb al-siyar* iii, 3, p. 330[5] : *manṣab i ṣadārat u pursīdan i muhimm i dād-khwāhān rā nīz ba-rāy i ṣawāb-numāyash tafwīḍ farmūd*. For the functions of a *ṣadr* see *Tadhkirat al-mulūk*, tr. Minorsky, p. 111. The number of these officials was increased by Sulṭān Ḥusain (*Ḥabīb al-siyar* iii, 3, p. 327, l. 5 *ab infra* : *chūn dar zamān i khujastah-nishān i Khāqān i 'ālī-makān mauqūfāt i bilād i Khurāsān ba-martaba'ī rasīdah būd kih yak kas az 'uhdah i ḍabṭ i ān bīrūn na-mī tuwānist āmad paiwastah ān pādshāh i 'ālī-jāh dū sih kas az a'āẓim i sādāt u fuḍalā rā ba-ta'ahhud i manṣab i ṣadārat sarfarāz mī sākht binā bar-ān dar awān i salṭanat i ān-ḥaḍrat jam'ī kathīr az arbāb i 'amā'im ba-saranjām i mahāmm i ān manṣab mashghūlī numūdand.*)

death is not mentioned in the *Ḥabīb al-siyar*, but he seems to have been dead at the time of writing (930/1524 probably), since the past tense is used in speaking of him.

Majālis al-ʻushshāq, romantic and panegyrical accounts in ornate prose and verse of about seventy-six great mystics (beginning with Jaʻfar al-Ṣādiq), famous lovers (e.g. Majnūn), and kings, of whom the last is Sulṭān Ḥusain himself, begun in 908/1502–3 and completed in the following year[1]: Ḥ. Kh. v p. 380, **Leningrad** Univ. 1024 (A.H. 909/1503–4. See Romaskewicz p. 13), 1076 (A.H. 972/1564–5. See Romaskewicz p. 13), 915 (see Salemann-Rosen p. 18), **Bodleian** 1271 (A.H. 959/1552. PICTURES), 1272 (A.H. 1029/1619–20), 1273, **Ethé** 1870 (A.H. 973/1565), 1871 (defective and disordered. PICTURES), **Ḥakīm-oghlū ʻAlī Pāshā** 667 (A.H. 982/1574. See Duda *Ferhād und Schīrīn* p. 206), **Nūr i ʻUthmānīyah** 4211 (A.H. 987/1579. See Duda *Ferhād und Schīrīn* p. 205), **Blochet** i 423 (late 16th cent. PICTURES described in *Revue des Bibliothèques*, 1898, p. 392), 424 (16th cent.), 425 (late 16th cent. PICTURES described in *Revue des Bibliothèques* 1898, p. 391), 426 (late 16th cent. PICTURES described in *Revue des Bibliothèques* 1900 p. 195), 427 (A.H. 988/1580. PICTURES described in *Revue des Bibliothèques* 1899, p. 60), **Bānkipūr** viii 663 (16th cent. PICTURES), **Lālā Ismāʻīl** 578 (A.H. 1050/1640–1. See Duda *Ferhād und Schīrīn* p. 206), **Rieu** i 351*b* (A.H. 1215/1800), 353*a* (first 26 *majālis* only. Early 18th cent.), **Amīrī Efendī** Pers. 93 (see Duda *Ferhād und Schīrīn* p. 206), **Āṣafīyah** i p. 472 no. 861 (A.H. 1146/1733–4), **Āyā Ṣūfiyah** 4238 (see Duda *Ferhād und Schīrīn* p. 206), **Berlin** 598 (PICTURES), 599 (defective at beginning), **Browne** Suppt. 1140 (n.d.), Coll. D. 21(3), **Flügel** iii 1949, **Leyden** v p. 232 no. 2642, **Majlis** 671 (defective), **Rāmpūr** (Nadhīr Aḥmad 90. PICTURES).

Editions: **Lucknow** 1870*; 1293/1876*; **Cawnpore** 1312/1897°.

Lists of the biographies: (**1**) G. Ouseley *Biographical notices*

[1] The work is severely criticized by Bābur, who calls it "a miserable production, mostly lies, and insipid and impertinent lies to boot, some of which raise a suspicion of heresy. Thus he [i.e. Kamāl al-Dīn Ḥusain] attributes carnal loves to many prophets and saints, inventing for each of them a paramour" (see Browne *Lit. Hist.* iii pp. 457–8).

pp. 247–50, **(2)** Flügel iii pp. 427–8, **(3)** Rieu i pp. 352–3, **(4)** Ethé coll. 1036–9.

[For Sulṭān Ḥusain see Daulat-Sẖāh pp. 521–40 (abridged French translation by Silvestre de Sacy in *Notices et extraits* iv (An 7 [= 1798]) pp. 262–6); *Majālis al-nafā'is, majlis* 8; *Bābur-nāmah* in the year 911 (pp. 103 penult.–105[16] in the Bombay edition of 'Abd al-Raḥīm's translation); *Laṭā'if-nāmah* pp. 215–16 (*majlis* 8); *Rauḍat al-ṣafā*'; *Ḥabīb al-siyar* iii, 3, pp. 201 foll. (H. Ferté's *Vie de Sultan Hossein Baïkara traduit de Khondémir* (Paris 1898) contains the early part of this narrative and, according to Bouvat,[1] goes as far as p. 254 of Vol. iii [evidently in the Ṭihrān edition [2]], in which according to the same authority the life of Sulṭān Ḥusain occupies pp. 239–83); *Tuḥfah i Sāmī* pp. 11–12; *Maṭla' al-sa'dain*; *Ency. Isl.* under Ḥusain Mīrzā (H. Beveridge); Browne *Lit. Hist.* iii pp. 390–1; W. Barthold *Herat unter Ḥusein Baiqara, dem Timuriden. Deutsche Bearbeitung von W. Hinz*, Leipzig (D.M.G.) 1938 (a translation of Barthold's article *Mir-Ali-Shir i politicheskaya zhizn'* in *Mir-Ali-Shir. Sbornik k pyatisotletiyu so dnya rozhdeniya*, Leningrad 1928, pp. 100–64); etc.

For Kamāl al-Dīn Ḥusain see *Ḥabīb al-siyar* iii, 3, p. 330; *Bābur-nāmah* towards the end of the account of the year 911 (p. 112[6] in the Bombay edition of 'Abd al-Raḥīm's translation); *The Bābur-nāma in English* i p. 280; *Laṭā'if-nāmah* p. 161; *Haft iqlīm* pp. 192–3 (no. 154); Browne *Lit. Hist.* pp. 440, 457–8.]

1277. Fakẖr al-Dīn **'Alī b. al-Ḥusain** al-Wā'iẓ **al-Kāsẖifī** known as (*al-musẖtahir bi-*) al-Ṣafī[3] was the son of Ḥusain b. 'Alī

---

[1] *L'empire mongol* (*2me phase*), Paris 1927, p. 163.

[2] In the Bombay edition the account of Sulṭān Ḥusain begins on p. 201 of vol. iii, pt. 3, and ends with his burial on p. 327 (after which come notices of his children and the celebrities of his reign), but a good deal of the intervening space is devoted to Bābur.

[3] Fakẖr ... Ṣafī: so in the preface to the *Rasẖaḥāt*. The *tadẖkirahs* give some curious variations—Maulānā Ṣafī al-Dīn (*Laṭā'if-nāmah*), Fakẖrī called Mullā-Zādah (" his name is Fakhr aldyn b. Ḥosayn Wā'itz Káshify, sometimes he used the takhalluç of Çafyy ". *Nafā'is al-ma'āṯẖir*, Sprenger p. 52), Ṣafī al-Dīn Muḥammad(!) (*Kẖazīnah i ganj i Ilāhī*, first notice, Sprenger p. 80, but Fakẖr al-Dīn 'Alī Ṣafī in the second notice, Sprenger p. 83), Maulānā Fakẖrī Kāsẖifī (*Makẖzan al-gẖarā'ib* no. 1902). The *Tuḥfah i Sāmī*, which calls him correctly Fakẖr al-Dīn 'Alī, says nothing about his *takẖalluṣ*. In the verses quoted at the end of the *Rasẖaḥāt* (p. 363[12], p. 363 ult., p. 364[1]) he calls himself Ṣafī.

al-Wāʿiẓ al-Kāshifī (for whom see pp. 12–13, 212–13 *supra*). In order to visit Khwājah ʿUbaid Allāh he went twice from Harāt (*L.-n.* p. 166[9]) to Samarqand : towards the end of Dhū 'l-Qaʿdah 889/Dec. 1484 and again early in Rabīʿ ii 893/March 1488, as he himself tells us (*Rashaḥāt* p. 2[5]), he was admitted to the presence of the saint and after every conversation made a written record of what he had heard. After his father's death [in 910/1504–5] he succeeded him as preacher in the *masjid i jāmiʿ* at Harāt (*Ḥ. al-s.* iii, 3, p. 341). In 939/1532–3 after one year's confinement at Harāt he went to Gharjistān and there completed his collection of anecdotes, the *Laṭāʾif al-ṭawāʾif*,[1] for the amusement of the Sulṭān, Shāh Muḥammad, who had received him kindly. Rieu says that he died in 939/1532–3, probably on the authority of the *Tuḥfah i Sāmī*, though the printed text gives the incorrect date 909.

Of his works only the *Maḥmūd u Ayāz* is mentioned by name in the *Ḥabīb al-siyar* and the *Tuḥfah i Sāmī*. This *mathnawī*, which according to the former was written in the same metre as the *Lailā u Majnūn* [of Niẓāmī] and was well known (*dar miyān i mardum mashhūr ast*), seems now, if extant at all, to be extremely rare. Possibly the Berlin MS. 692 (2), which begins with the words *Ai nām i tu ganj-nāmah i rāz* and which contains the hemistich *Sulṭān i jahān Ḥusain i ghāzīst*, may be a copy of it,[2] since the Sulṭān Ḥusain referred to is more likely to be Sulṭān Ḥusain of Harāt than Shāh Sulṭān-Ḥusain the Ṣafawī, who is suggested in the Berlin catalogue. Neither the *Maḥmūd u Ayāz* nor the *Rashaḥāt* is mentioned in the *Rauḍāt al-jannāt*, which speaks only of the *Laṭāʾif al-ṭawāʾif*, the *Ḥirz al-amān min fitan al-zamān*,[3] a work entitled *Anīs al-ʿārifīn* (*fī 'l-mawāʿiẓ wa-'l-naṣāʾiḥ wa-tafsīr al-āyāt wa-'l-akhbār wa-'l-qiṣaṣ*

[1] MSS. : Berlin 1013–15, Oxford Ind. Inst. MS. Pers. A. iv. 12, Bodleian 454–6, Lindesiana p. 154 no. 617, Lahore, Rieu ii 757*b*, 758*a*, Blochet iv 2091, Ivanow 297, Ivanow 1st Spt. 775, Būhār 443–4, Ethé 778–9, Bānkīpūr viii 732–4, Rehatsek p. 230, Browne Coll. x. 5, Bombay Univ. p. 229, Edinburgh New Coll. p. 10, Eton 86–7, Leyden v p. 295, Majlis 622 (2).

[2] Bodleian 1084 may be a fragment of this poem.

[3] On the talismanic virtues of letters of the alphabet, Qurʾānic verses, etc. MSS. : Lindesiana p. 120 no. 676, Ivanow Curzon 656, Āṣafīyah i p. 56, Ḥakīm-oghlū 453.

wa-'l-ḥikāyāt al-gharībah) [1] and an abridgment of his father's *Asrār i Qāsimī*.[2]

Rashaḥāt i ʻain al-ḥayāt, or simply *Rashaḥāt* (a chronogram = 909/1503–4, the date of completion), a memoir of Nāṣir al-Dīn ʻUbaid Allāh b. Maḥmūd Shāshī called Khwājah Aḥrār,[3] with notices of some other Naqshbandī *shaikhs*, divided into a *maqālah* (chronologically arranged notices of Naqshbandīs, p. 4 ult.), three *maqṣads* ((1) on Aḥrār, his parentage, early life, wanderings, etc., p. 207, (2) his sayings, p. 242, (3) his miracles, with notices of the disciples by whom they were related, p. 287), and a *khātimah* (on his death, p. 360): Ḥ. Kh. iii p. 461 no. 6453, **Lahore** Panjāb Univ. Lib. (2 copies dated 978/1570–1 and 1006/1597–8. See *OCM*. iii/1 (Nov. 1926), p. 72), **Ethé** 633 (A.H. 984/1577), 634 (collated in 1041/1632), 635 (n.d.), **I.O.** D.P. 653 (A.H. 985/1577), **Ivanow** 252 (A.H. 995/1587), 253 (A.H. 1005/1596–7), 254 (A.H. 1141/1728–9), 255 (defective. 19th cent.), **Ivanow** Curzon 69 (A.H. 1013/1605), 703 (early

[1] A work of this title in 32 *bābs* appears on p. 429 of the Cairo Persian catalogue (Section: *ʻIlm al-mawāʻiẓ*), where the author is said to be Ḥusain b. al-Raṣadī al-mushtahir bi-'l-Wāʻiẓ.

[2] The *A. i Q.*, a work of doubtful authorship, ostensibly by Ḥusain Wāʻiẓ (d. 910) but dedicated to Qāsim al-anwār (d. 837), on the five occult sciences *Kīmiyā*, *Līmiyā*, *Hīmiyā*, *Sīmiyā* and *Rīmiyā*, has been lithographed at Lūd'hiyānah in 1289/1872* and at Bombay in 1302/1885° and (a different recension, *Kashf al-asrār i Qāsimī*) in 1312/1894°*. MSS.: Mehren 132 (A.H. 907/1501–2, said to have been transcribed from an autograph in the author's lifetime), Browne Coll. Q. 3, Bānkīpūr Suppt. ii 2055, Peshawar 1954, Āṣafīyah ii p. 1690 nos. 5, 203, 193, p. 1692 no. 198. No copy of the abridgment seems to be recorded.

[3] Head of the Naqshbandī order in his time and dedicatee of Jāmī's *Tuḥfat al-aḥrār*, born in 806/1404, doubtless at or near Shāsh, i.e. Tāshkand (both his father and his maternal grandfather were Shāshīs, and when he was one year old they were living at Bāghistān (*Rashaḥāt* p. 220[18]), which is near Tāshkand, *az kūh-pāyah-hā-yi Tāshkand*, *op. cit.* p. 208[11]), settled in Samarqand, where he acquired great wealth by farming and trade and where he died on 29 Rabīʻ i 895/20 (21?) Feb. 1490. See *Nafaḥāt al-uns* pp. 465–74; *al-Ḍauʼ al-lāmiʻ* (in Arabic) v p. 120 (three lines only); *Rauḍat al-sālikīn* no. 10; *Majālis al-ʻushshāq* no. 54; *Ḥabīb al-siyar* iii, 3, pp. 200–1; *al-Shaqāʼiq al-Nuʻmānīyah* (in Arabic), tr. Rescher, pp. 167–71; *Haft iqlīm* no. 1533; *Gulzār i abrār* no. 187; *Safīnat al-auliyā'* pp. 80–1 (no. 87); *Khazīnat al-aṣfiyā'* i pp. 582–6; *JRAS*. 1916 pp. 59–75 (the article cited below under Description). Several small Ṣūfī works by him are extant, e.g. (1) *Wālidīyah* (MSS.: Browne Suppt. 684 (Trinity), Ethé 1923 (13), Tashkent Univ. 19 (1) (?), 20 (1)); (2) *Fiqarāt* (Edition: Ḥaidarābād, date ? (Āṣafīyah iii p. 200). MSS.: Āṣafīyah i p. 458, Gotha 21, Lindesiana p. 119, Tashkent Univ. 19 (3), Ethé 1919 (3), Būhār 190 (1)).

19th cent.), **Āṣafīyah** i p. 320 no. 1 (A.H. 1000/1591–2), no. 5 (A.H. 1017/1608–9), p. 346 no. 61 (A.H. 1085/1674–5), p. 438 no. 128, **Velyaminov-Zernov** p. 865 no. 9 (A.H. 1023/1614), **Bānkīpūr** viii 664 (A.H. 1036/1627), Suppt. i 1781 (defective. 17th cent.), **Rieu** i 353*a* (A.H. 1074/1664), **Berlin** 600 (A.H. 1080/1669), **Princeton** 460 (A.H. 1092/1681), **Blochet** i 422 (17th cent.), **Edinburgh** 243 (17th cent.), **Tashkent Univ.** Semenov 72 (17th cent.), 71 (A.H. 1250/1834), **Peshawar** 978 (A.H. 1111/1699–1700), **Būhār** 86 (A.H. 1286/1869), **'Alīgaṛh** Subḥ. MSS. p. 60 no. 7, **Bodleian** 360 (n.d.), **Bukhārā** Semenov 73, **Chanykov** 101, **Dorn** 310, **Gotha** p. 121 no. 32*a* (contains the *Maqālah* only), **Salemann-Rosen** p. 16 no. 293.

Editions: **Lucknow** 1890°; **Cawnpore** 1911–12* (described as a seventh edition); **Tashkent** 1329/1911 (see *Ency. Isl.* under Ṣafī and Barthold's *Uluġ Beg*, tr. Hinz, p. 234).

Description: *The Rashahat-i-'ainal-hayat (Tricklings from the fountain of life). By H. Beveridge* (in *JRAS.* 1916, pp. 59–75).

List of the biographies in the *maqālah*: Gotha pp. 122–26.

Persian commentary: *Tauḍīḥ al-Rashaḥāt*, by M. Ḥusain b. M. Hādī al-'Aqīlī al-'Alawī al-Shīrāzī, who based it on the explanations of his spiritual guide Ḥabīb Allāh: **Bānkīpūr** viii 665 (A.H. 1186/1772).

Arabic translation: *Ta'rīb* (or *Tarjamat*) *Rashaḥāt 'ain al-ḥayāt* written in 1029/1620 by Tāj al-Dīn b. Zakarīyā' b. Sulṭān al-'Abshamī al-Umawī al-'Uthmānī al-Hindī al-Ḥanafī al-Naqshbandī[1]: **Cairo** Arab. Cat. ii p. 75, 2nd ed. i p. 202, **Paris** de Slane 2044.

Edition of an Arabic translation[2]: **Mecca** 1307/1889–90 (with a continuation (*dhail*), *Nafā'is al-sāniḥāt fī tadhyīl al-bāqiyāt al-ṣāliḥāt*,[3] by M. Murād b. 'Abd Allāh al-Qāzānī al-Manzilawī (*tawallud*^{an}) al-Makkī (*tawaṭṭun*^{an}), who was alive at

[1] An Indian who settled in Mecca and died there in 1050/1640. See *Khulāṣat al-athar* i p. 464–70, Raḥmān 'Alī p. 35, Bānkīpūr Arab. Cat. xiii pp. 154–5, Brockelmann ii p. 419, *Sptbd* ii p. 618. For his translation of the *Nafaḥāt al-uns* see p. 956 *supra*.

[2] Perhaps not Tāj al-Dīn's translation, since both Sarkis and Ghulām-Rasūl Sūratī describe M. Murād as the translator.

[3] Cf. Cairo Arab. Cat. 2nd ed. v p. 394.

the time of publication. See Sarkis *Dictionnaire encyclopédique de bibliographie arabe* col. 1481, Brockelmann *Sptbd.* ii p. 287, and the catalogue of the Bombay bookseller G͟hulām-Rasūl Sūratī for 1914–15 p. 177).

Turkish translations: (1) completed in 993/1585 by M. Ma'rūf b. M. S͟harīf al-'Abbāsī, Qāḍī of Smyrna: Ḥ. K͟h. iii p. 463, **Rieu** Turkish cat. p. 74 (less than the first half of the *Maqālah*). Editions of M. Ma'rūf's translation: **Istānbūl** 1236/1820–1; **Būlāq** 1256/1840–1. (2) by 'Ārif C͟helebī: **Bānkīpūr** (A.H. 1046/1636–7, autograph. See Bānkīpūr Pers. Cat. viii p. 26), **Berlin** Turkish Cat. p. 31 (small portion only).

It is not clear from the description whether **Velyaminov-Zernov** 5 (p. 859) is one of the above translations or another.

[*Laṭā'if-nāmah* p. 166; *Ḥabīb al-siyar* iii, 3, p. 341; *Tuḥfah i Sāmī* p. 68 (in *Ṣaḥīfah* iv); *Nafā'is al-ma'āt͟hir* under "Fak͟hrī" (Sprenger p. 52); *K͟hazīnah i ganj i Ilāhī* (Sprenger pp. 80 and 83); *Mak͟hzan al-g͟harā'ib* no. 1902; *Rauḍāt al-jannāt* p. 257[21] (quotes from the *Riyāḍ al-'ulamā'*); Bānkīpūr viii p. 24; *Ency. Isl.* under Ṣafī (V. F. Büchner); Brockelmann *Sptbd.* ii p. 286.]

1278. M. b. Burhān al-Dīn Samarqandī called Maulānā **M. Qāḍī**[1] became a disciple of the great Naqs͟hbandī saint, K͟hwājah 'Ubaid Allāh Aḥrār,[2] in 885/1480 (*Ras͟haḥāt* p. 344[13]) and waited upon him for nearly twelve years. After 'Ubaid Allāh's death he went to Tās͟hkand (*Tārīk͟h i Ras͟hīdī* tr. Ross p. 213) and remained there until the destruction of the town [by S͟haibānī K͟hān Uzbak in 908/1503]. Having migrated to Buk͟hārā, he was well received by Maḥmūd Sulṭān, S͟haibānī's brother, who became his disciple for one winter (*ibid.*). In 916/1510 after the crushing defeat of the Uzbaks at Marw by S͟hāh Ismā'īl's forces he left Buk͟hārā for Andujān and Ak͟hsī (*op. cit.* pp. 214 and 277, in the latter of which places he is said to have left Samarqand [*sic*] and gone to Andujān). While resident in Farg͟hānah he was often visited by Ḥaidar Mīrzā Dūg͟hlāt (*op. cit.*

[1] An explanation of this appellation is given in *Tārīk͟h i Ras͟hīdī*, tr. Ross, p. 212 (correctly translated ?).

[2] d. 895/1490 or 896/1491 at Samarqand. See p. 964 n. 3 *supra*.

p. 278. Ḥaidar Mīrzā, born in 905/1499–1500, was then a mere boy), and he gained many followers and devotees (*op. cit.* p. 342). He was between sixty and seventy years of age when he died in 921/1516 [1] at Tāshkand, where he had gone from Akhsī on a visit to Suyunjuk Khān (*ibid.*).

(1) *Silsilat al-'ārifīn*, an account of Khwājah 'Ubaid Allāh: Ḥ. Kh. iii p. 607 no. 7211, **'Alīgaṛh** Subḥ. MSS. p. 15 no. 71.

(2) *Tadhkirat al-auliyā'* (beg. *Bi-gū, ai murgh i zīrak, ḥamd i Maulā'ī kih hast ū-rā * Sipās* etc.), perhaps identical with the preceding work: **Chanykov** 100 (A.H. 1189/1775).

[*Bayān i aḥwāl i Maulānā M.Q.* (see p. 973 *infra*); *Rashaḥāt* pp. 344–7; *Tārīkh i Rashīdī*, tr. Ross, pp. 212–14, 277–9, 341–2, and elsewhere (see the index under Hazrat Mauláná Muhammad Kázi (but the Maulānā M. who escaped with Ḥaidar to Badakhshān was a different person), and under Muhammad Kazi); *Gulzār i abrār* no. 195; *Ṭabaqāt i Shāh-Jahānī*; *Sanawāt al-atqiyā'* fol. 271*b*; *Khazīnat al-aṣfiyā'* i pp. 597–8; Rieu ii 859*b*.]

1279. Quṭb al-'ālam [2] **'Abd al-Quddūs** b. Ismā'īl b. Ṣafī al-Dīn Ḥanafī [3] **Gangōhī** [4] was the disciple, brother-in-law and *khalīfah* of Sh. M. b. 'Ārif b. Aḥmad 'Abd al-Ḥaqq [Rudaulawī], "but got besides an investiture from almost all the Khânwâdas or Ṣûfic branches" (Ethé col. 336). He spent thirty-five years in Rudaulī,[5] migrated thence in 896/1491, early in the reign of Sulṭān Sikandar Lōdī [894–923/1489–1517], at the suggestion of his disciple 'Umar Khān Kāsī, one of the Sulṭān's *amīrs*, to Shāhābād, "near Delhi," [6] where he remained another thirty-five years. In 932/1525–6, when Bābur defeated and killed Sulṭān Ibrāhīm b. Sikandar Lōdī and sacked Shāhābād, 'Abd al-Quddūs

[1] The chronogram *Naqd i Khwājah 'Ubaid Allah* comes to 921, not 922.
[2] According to the *Sawāṭi' al-anwār*.
[3] He is said to have been a descendant of Abū Ḥanīfah (*Safīnat al-auliyā'* p. 101).
[4] Gangōh is 23 miles S.W. of Sahāranpūr in the United Provinces.
[5] 38 miles from Bārā Bankī in Oudh.
[6] Shāhābād, formerly in the *sarkār* of Sirhind (*Ṣūbah* of Delhi), is now in the Anbālah ("Ambala") District of the Panjāb. It is about 110 miles N. of Delhi.

moved to Gangōh, where after fourteen years he died in 944/1537 or 945/1537 at the age of eighty-four.

Ṣūfī works by him are (1) *Nūr al-hudā* (MS. : Ethé 1924 (14)), (2) *Qurrat al-a'yun* (MS. : Ethé 1924 (16)), (3) *Rushd-nāmah* or *Risālah i Rushdīyah* (Edition : Jhajjar 1312/1897°.[1] MSS. : 'Alīgaṛh Subḥ. MSS. p. 16 no. 75, Princeton 113). A collection of his letters on Ṣūfī subjects (*Maktūbāt i 'Abd al-Quddūs* or *Maktūbāt i Quddūsīyah*) was made by his disciple Bud'han Jaunpūrī (Edition : Delhi 1287/1870°*. MSS. : Bodleian 1275, Ethé 1873), and there exists a collection of Ṣūfī dicta, *Laṭā'if i Quddūsī*, compiled by Sh. Rukn al-Dīn (Edition : Delhi 1311/1894. MS. : I.O. D.P. 1099).

Anwār al-'uyūn fī asrār al-maknūn, anecdotes of Aḥmad 'Abd al-Ḥaqq Rudaulawī[2] : **Āṣafīyah** i p. 486 no. 575 (? *Malfūẓ i Sh. A. 'A. al-Ḥ.*).

Editions : **'Alīgaṛh** 1905* ; **Lucknow** [1909*. With an Urdū translation by Khalīl al-Raḥmān Chaud'hurī].

[*Akhbār al-akhyār* pp. 221–4 ; *Zubdat al-maqāmāt* pp. 96–101 ; *Safīnat al-auliyā'* p. 101 (no. 118) ; *Mir'āt al-asrār, ṭabaqah* 23 ; *Sawāṭi' al-anwār* no. 30 (Ethé col. 336) ; *Khazīnat al-aṣfiyā'* i pp. 416–18.]

1280. Ḥāmid b. Faḍl Allāh known as (*al-ma'rūf bi-*) Darwīsh Jamālī (*Siyar al-'ārifīn*, Ethé 637, fol. 2*b*[2]), i.e. Shaikh, or Mullā, "**Jamālī**" Kanbō[3] **Dihlawī,** used at first the *takhalluṣ* "Jalālī",[4] but changed it to "Jamālī" at the suggestion of his *pīr*, Samā'

[1] One of these dates (given in the B.M. catalogue) is presumably incorrect, since they do not correspond.

[2] A Chishtī saint, who died in 836/1433 or 837/1434. See *Akhbār al-akhyār* pp. 187–90 ; *Mir'āt al-asrār, ṭabaqah* 23 (summarized in Bānkīpūr viii p. 62) ; *Riyāḍ al-auliyā'* (cited by Rieu, iii p. 1086a) ; *Sawāṭi' al-anwār* no. 27 (Ethé col. 336) ; *Khazīnat al-aṣfiyā'* i pp. 384–7.

[3] Cf. *Ṭabaqāt i Akbarī* i p. 340[2], *Muntakhab al-tawārīkh* i p. 325[5]. Kanbō, spelt also Kanbōh, Kambō and Kambōh, is the name of a mainly agricultural caste in the Panjāb and western United Provinces. According to "Āzād" (*Khizānah* p. 177 ult.) the *qāḍīs* and *muftīs* of Delhi were usually members of this caste (*khidamāt i shar'īyah i Dār al-khilāfah i Dihlī mithl i qaḍā u iftā akthar bah qaum i Kanbō ta'alluq dāsht u dārad*).

[4] As "Jamālī" himself gives his name as Ḥāmid b. Faḍl Allāh, it is difficult to understand the statement that his original name was Jalāl Khān or Jalāl (*Akhbār al-akhyār* p. 227 ult. : *Nām i aṣl i ū Jalāl Khān ast*).

al-Dīn,[1] who died in 901/1496. He himself tells us that after visiting the two holy cities, the Maghrib, the Yemen, Palestine, Rūm, Syria, the two 'Irāqs, Ādharbāyjān, Gīlān, Māzandarān and Khurāsān [2] he returned to Delhi and to the presence of his revered master, Samā' al-Dīn. The names of some Ṣūfīs met in the course of these wanderings are mentioned in the *Siyar al-'ārifīn* [3] and these might provide clues to the chronology. "Jamālī's" visit to Harāt, for example, and his meetings with Jāmī cannot have taken place later than 898/1492, the year in which Jāmī died. It seems probable that at the time of his travels he was still quite young. According to 'Abd al-Ḥaqq [4] his career began in the reign of Sulṭān Sikandar Lōdī [894–923/1488–1517]. He was one of the Sulṭān's intimate friends.[5] An elegy (*marthiyah*) on this Sulṭān is one of the poems from which quotations are given by Nawwāb Ṣadr-Yār-Jang (*OCM.* x/1 p. 156). Odes were written by him also in praise of Bābur [932–7/1526–30] and Humāyūn [937–63/1530–56]. He accompanied the latter on his expedition to Gujrāt and died there on 10 Dhū 'l-Qa'dah 942/1 May 1536.[6] "His tomb, a very elegant little building of white marble, is a short distance S.E. of the Koṭob minár, eleven miles from Dilly" (Sprenger p. 446). He left two sons, of whom the elder, Sh. 'Abd al-Raḥmān [7] Gadā'ī Kanbō,[8] became *Ṣadr* in Akbar's reign.

Badā'ūnī, who describes "Jamālī" as a famous poet [9] (*shā'ir i mashhūr, M. al-t.* iii p. 76[8]), says that in addition to the *Siyar*

[1] See *Siyar al-'ārifīn* no. 14 (Ethé col. 264); *Akhbār al-akhyār* pp. 211–12; *Kalimāt al-ṣādiqīn* no. 77; *Khazīnat al-aṣfiyā'* ii pp. 74–6 (Sh. S. al-D. Suhrawardī); *Ḥadā'iq al-Ḥanafīyah* p. 355; Raḥmān 'Alī p. 80. Badā'ūnī calls him Sh. S. al-D. Kanbō-yi Dihlawī (*M. al-t.* i p. 326[1]).

[2] According to a passage quoted in *OCM.* ix/3 p. 38 he visited Ceylon.

[3] It is not clear what authority Sprenger had for his statement that "Jamālī" wrote an account of his travels (*safar-nāmah*).

[4] *A. al-a.* p. 227[7] : *Ibtidā-yi ū az zamān i Sulṭān Sikandar b. Buhlūl ast.*

[5] *az muṣāḥibān u ham-zabānān i ū būd* (*Ṭabaqāt i Akbarī* i p. 340[2]); *ibtidā az nudamā-yi Sulṭān Sikandar Lōdī būdah* (*Ma'āthir al-umarā'* ii p. 539[5]).

[6] *A. al-a.* p. 228[14–16].

[7] *OCM.* xi/1 p. 74 on the authority of the *Ā'īnah i Muḥammadī* of M. Ḥārithī Badakhshī.

[8] See Badā'ūnī iii pp. 76–7; *Ma'āthir al-umarā'* ii pp. 539–41, Beveridge's trans. pp. 568–70; etc.

[9] He is to be distinguished from "Jamālī" (Pīr Jamāl) Ardistānī, who died in 879/1474–5 (see p. 185 *supra*).

al-'ārifīn he wrote other works in prose and verse (*u ghair i ān naẓm u nathr i dīgar dārad, M. al-t.* i p. 326[1]), including a *dīwān* of 8,000 or 9,000 verses. Of his *dīwān* only two manuscripts are at present known to exist, one, probably complete or nearly so, at Rāmpūr (described briefly by Nadhīr Aḥmad (no. 179) and much more fully by Imtiyāz 'Alī " 'Arshī " (*OCM.* xi/1 pp. 76–8)), and another, defective at both ends and containing only *qaṣā'id*,[1] *tarkīb-bands* and *marāthī*, in the private library of Nawwāb Ḥabīb al-Raḥmān Khān Shirwānī (see *OCM.* x/1 pp. 147–59). The latter library possesses also a Ṣūfī *mathnawī*, *Mir'āt al-ma'ānī* (*OCM.* x/1 pp. 145–7), which according to Imtiyāz 'Alī is not rare [though no copies seem to be recorded in published catalogues]. Another *mathnawī*, *Mihr u māh* (*OCM.* xi/1 p. 75), seems not to be extant.

Siyar al-'ārifīn,[2] completed in Humāyūn's reign [i.e. not earlier than 937/1530, nor later than 942/1536, the year of the author's death] and devoted to the lives of fourteen [3] Chishtī [4] saints, namely (1) Mu'īn al-Dīn Ḥasan Sijzī Chishtī,[5] (2) Badr al-Dīn Maḥmūd Mūyīnah-dūz Khujandī,[6] (3) Bahā' al-Dīn Zakarīyā' [Multānī],[7] (4) Quṭb al-Dīn Bakhtyār Ūshī,[8] (5) Farīd

[1] According to 'Abd al-Ḥaqq Dihlawī his *qaṣā'id* are better than his *ghazals* and *mathnawīs*.

[2] According to Badā'ūnī (*Muntakhab al-tawārīkh* i p. 325 penult.) this work *khālī az suqmī u tanāquḍī nīst.*

[3] Thirteen according to Rieu, who omits no. 2.

[4] See p. 943 n. 1 *supra*.

[5] See p. 943 n. 3 *supra*.

[6] Presumably identical with Khwājah Maḥmūd Mūyīnah-dūz, who is described as a disciple of Qāḍī Ḥamīd al-Dīn Nāgaurī (d. 643/1246 (?). See pp. 5–6 *supra*) and an associate (*muṣāḥib*) of Khwājah Quṭb al-Dīn [Bakhtyār Ūshī, d. 633/1235]. See *Akhbār al-akhyār* p. 50 ; *Kalimāt al-ṣādiqīn* no. 16 ; *Khazīnat al-aṣfiyā'* pp. 284–5.

[7] One of the great saints of India, born in 566/1170–1 (*Safīnat al-auliyā'* p. 115[10]) or 578/1182–3 (Firishtah ii p. 404[20]), disciple and *khalīfah* of Shihāb al-Dīn 'Umar Suhrawardī (d. 632/1234), with whom he associated at Baghdād on his way back from a *ḥajj*, and *pīr* of the poet " 'Irāqī ", died in 666/1267 at Multān. See *Nafaḥāt al-uns* pp. 583–4 ; *Akhbār al-akhyār* pp. 26–8 ; Firishtah ii pp. 404–9 ; *Safīnat al-auliyā'* pp. 114–15 (no. 152) ; *Mir'āt al-asrār*, *ṭabaqah* 18 ; *Makhzan al-gharā'ib* no. 280 ; *Khazīnat al-aṣfiyā'* ii pp. 19–26 ; Garcin de Tassy *Mémoire sur les particularités de la religion musulmane dans l'Inde* 2nd ed., Paris 1869, pp. 92–3 ; Beale *Oriental biographical dictionary* under Baha-uddin Zikaria [*sic*] ; Raḥmān 'Alī p. 32 ; *Ency. Isl.* under Bahā' al-Dīn Zakarīyā' (Arnold).

[8] See p. 943 n. 4 *supra*.

al-Dīn Mas'ūd [Ganj i Shakar],[1] (6) Ṣadr al-Din 'Ārif,[2] (7) Niẓām al-Dīn M. [Auliyā'] Badā'ūnī,[3] (8) Rukn al-Dīn Abū 'l-Fatḥ,[4] (9) Sh. Ḥamīd al-Dīn [Siwālī] Nāgaurī,[5] (10) Najīb [al-Dīn] Mutawakkil,[6] (11) Jalāl al-Dīn Abū 'l-Qāsim Tabrīzī,[7] (12) Naṣīr al-Dīn Maḥmūd Awad'hī,[8] (13) S. Jalāl al-Dīn Makhdūm i Jahāniyān Bukhārī,[9] (14) Samā' al-Dīn : **Lindesiana** p. 162 no 115 (A.H. 964/1556–7), **Rieu i** 354*a* (omits no. 2. A.H. 1019/1610), 355*a* (A.H. 1131/1719), **Ethé** 637 (A.H. 1043/1634), 638 (lacks no. 2. N.d.), 639 (a shorter redaction. A.H. 1123/1711), **Berlin** 590 (lacks no. 14. A.H. 1085/1674), 591, **Ivanow** Curzon 71 (18th cent.), **Bānkīpūr** Suppt. I 1782 (late 18th cent.).

Edition : **Delhi** 1311/1893°.

1 See p. 941 n. 4 *supra*.

2 Son, disciple and successor of Bahā' al-Dīn Zakarīyā' Multānī (no. 3 above), died in 684/1286 and was buried at Multān near his father. See *Akhbār al-akhyār* pp. 61–3 ; Firishtah ii pp. 409–11 ; *Safīnat al-auliyā'* p. 116 (no. 155) ; *Khazīnat al-aṣfiyā'* ii pp. 28–31.

3 See p. 941 n. 5 *supra*.

4 Son and successor of Ṣadr al-Dīn 'Ārif (no. 6 above), died in 735/1335 and was buried at Multān near his father. See *Akhbār al-akhyār*, pp. 63–6; Firishtah ii pp. 411–12 ; *Safīnat al-auliyā'* p. 116 (no. 156) ; *Maṭlūb al-ṭālibīn, majlis* 10 ; *Khazīnat al-aṣfiyā'* ii pp. 47–51.

5 See p. 6 *supra*.

6 Brother and successor of Ganj i Shakar (no. 5 above), died at Delhi in 669/1271 (*Sawāṭi' al-anwār*) or 671/1272–3 (*Khazīnah*). See *Akhbār al-akhyār* pp. 60–1 ; *Kalimāt al-ṣādiqīn* no. 26 ; *Mir'āt al-asrār, ṭabaqah* 19 ; *Sawāṭi' al-anwār* (Ethé, col. 331 no. 18) ; *Khazīnat al-aṣfiyā'* i pp. 305–7.

7 Originally a disciple of Badr al-Dīn Abū Sa'īd al-Tabrīzī (who according to the *Safīnat al-auliyā'*, p. 93[15], was visited at Tabrīz by Mu'īn al-Dīn Chishtī), he went after Abū Sa'īd's death to Baghdād and for seven years consorted with Shihāb al-Dīn 'Umar Suhrawardī (d. 632/1234), accompanied Auḥad al-Dīn Kirmānī (d. 697/1297–8) on a journey to Mecca, travelled much in company with Bahā' al-Dīn Zakarīyā' Multānī (d. 666/1267), went to Delhi in the reign of Īltutmish (607–33/1210–36), associated with Quṭb al-Dīn Ūshī (d. 633/1235), migrated from Delhi to Badāyūṅ and from there to Bengal, where he died after making many converts to Islām. According to the *Khazīnat al-aṣfiyā'* he died in 642/1244–5, but this date must be incorrect, and some of the other particulars given above are scarcely credible if, as seems probable, he is the same person as the aged Sh. Jalāl al-Dīn Tabrīzī, whom Ibn Baṭṭūṭah visited [probably about 740/1339–40] in the mountains of Kāmarū (i.e. Kāmrūp, or Western Assam), and who died not long afterwards at the alleged age of 150 years (Ibn Baṭṭūṭah iv p. 217[1]). He himself told Ibn Baṭṭūṭah that he was in Baghdad when the Caliph al-Musta'ṣim was put to death (in 656/1258). See *Akhbār al-akhyār* pp. 44–6 ; *Khazīnat al-aṣfiyā'* ipp. 278–83 ; *Nuzhat al-khawāṭir* pp. 20–2 ; *Dānishmandān i Ādharbāyjan* p. 97 (based on the *Khazīnat al-aṣfiyā'*).

8 i.e. Chirāgh i Dihlī, for whom see p. 942 n. 1 *supra*.

9 See pp. 944–6 *supra*.

Description: *OCM.* ix/3 (May 1933) pp. 44–7 (by Yā-Sīn Khān Niyāzī).

[*Tārīkh i Shēr-Shāhī* (an Urdū translation of the passage is given in *OCM.* ix/3 p. 35); *Akhbār al-akhyār* pp. 227–9; *Ṭabaqāt i Akbarī* i p. 340; *Haft iqlīm* no. 393; Badā'ūnī *Muntakhab al-tawārīkh* i pp. 325–6; *Kalimāt al-ṣādiqīn* no. 91; *Ṭabaqāt i Shāh-Jahānī*; *Khazīnah i ganj i Ilāhī*; *Mir'āt al-'ālam*; *Riyāḍ al-auliyā'*; *Safīnah i Khwushgū* no. 43; *Muntakhab al-ash'ār* no. 137; *Riyāḍ al-shu'arā'*; *Khizānah i 'āmirah* pp. 177–9 (no. 27); *Ātash-kadah* no. 751; *Ṣuḥuf i Ibrāhīm*; *Khulāṣat al-afkār* no. 67; *Makhzan al-gharā'ib* no. 493; *Nishtar i 'ishq*; *Natā'ij al-afkār*; S. Aḥmad Khān *Āthār al-ṣanādīd* (in Urdu), Delhi 1270/1853, p. 47; *Khazīnat al-aṣfiyā'* ii p. 84; *Sham' i anjuman* p. 106; Carr Stephen *The archæology . . . of Delhi* pp. 171–3; Rieu i p. 354*a*; Raḥmān 'Alī p. 43; Bānkīpūr Suppt. i pp. 43–4; *Sikandar Lōdī aur us-kē ba'd fārisī muṣannifīn*, by Yā-Sīn Khān "Niyāzī" (in *OCM.* ix/3 (May 1933) pp. 37–48); *Taṣānīf i Shaikh "Jamālī" Dihlawī* (in Urdu) by Nawwāb Ḥabīb al-Raḥmān Khān Shirwānī (in *OCM.* x/1 (Nov. 1933) pp. 145–59); *Istidrākāt* (in Urdu) by Imtiyāz 'Alī "'Arshī" (in *OCM.* xi/1 (Nov. 1934) pp. 74–8).]

1281. M. b. Yaḥyā b. Yūsuf al-Raba'ī **al-Tādifī,** or al-Tādhifī, al-Ḥalabī al-Ḥanbalī was born in 899/1493–4 and died at Aleppo in Sha'bān 963/1556.

Qalā'id al-jawāhir fī manāqib al-Shaikh 'Abd al-Qādir, an Arabic account of 'Abd al-Qādir al-Jīlānī [1] and some of his disciples and contemporaries: Ḥ. Kh. iv, p. 565, no. 6557, **Bānkīpūr** xii 752, etc. (see Brockelmann *Sptbd.* i p. 777, ii p. 463).

Edition: **Cairo** 1303/1886° (see Ellis ii, col. 274).

Persian translation of selected parts written in 1012/1603–4 by Ḥusain b. Sh. Ṣābir Sindī: *Qalā'id al-jawāhir*, **I.O.** D.P. 704 (defective at the end and elsewhere. 18th cent.).

[M. Rāghib al-Ṭabbākh *I'lām al-nubalā' bi-ta'rīkh Ḥalab*

[1] See p. 933 n. 2 *supra*.

al-shahbā' pp. 25–6: Sarkis *Dictionnaire encyclopédique de bibliographie arabe*, col. 287; Brockelmann *Sptbd.* ii p. 463.]

1282. Abū 'l-Muḥsin **M. Bāqir b. M. 'Alī** wrote in 947/1540–1—

A history of the Naqshbandī order in a *muqaddimah*, four *maqṣads* ((1) *shaikhs* prior to Bahā' al-Dīn, (2) Bahā' al-Dīn, (3) *shaikhs* from the time of Bahā' al-Dīn to that of Aḥrār, (4) Aḥrār) and a *khātimah*: **Ethé** 636 (16th cent.).

1283. An unknown disciple of Makhdūm i A'ẓam Aḥmad b. Saiyid Jalāl al-Dīn Khwājagī Kāsānī[1] completed in 949/1542—

Maqāmāt i ḥaḍrat i Makhdūm i A'ẓam: **Tashkent Univ.** Semenov 74 (1).

1284. **Maḥmūd** b. Sh. 'Alī b. 'Imād al-Dīn **Ghujduwānī.**

Miftāḥ al-ṭālibīn, a large biography of Sh. Kamāl al-Dīn Khwārazmī,[2] at one time head of the Kubrawī order, written in 950/1543–4: **Samarqand** V. L. Vyatkin's private library (see Semenov *Kurzer Abriss* p. 4).

Extracts: *Zapiski Vostochn. Otd. Imp. Russ. Arkheol. Obshchestva* xv pp. 205–12 (ed. W. Barthold).

1285. An unknown author, who had received his information from disciples of Maulānā M. Qāḍī, wrote—

Bayān i aḥwāl i ḥaḍrat i Maulānā M. Qāḍī, an account of M. b. Burhān al-Dīn Samarqandī called Maulānā M. Qāḍī (for whom see p. 966 *supra*): **Rieu** ii 859*b* (19th cent.).

1286. **Shams al-Dīn al-Qādirī** or, more fully, Shams al-Dīn Abū 'l-Fatḥ Muḥammad b. Sh. Isḥāq Walī Allāh al-Qādirī b. Quṭb al-Anām Shaikh al-Islām Shams al-Dīn Muḥammad al-Qādirī al-Multānī, was fifty years old when he wrote his *Makhāzin al-Qādirīyah* in the second half of the 10th/16th

[1] For this saint, who was born at Kāsān in Farghānah, became the spiritual director of 'Ubaid Allāh Khān Shaibānī and who, according to Semenov, died probably in 1512 (misprint for 1542?) see Semenov *Kurzer Abriss* p. 3 and p. 981[9] *infra*.

[2] Cf. p. 177 *supra* and p. 974 *infra* as well as *Laṭā'if-nāmah* p. 17 and *Majālis al-mu'minīn* pp. 321–9.

century,[1] apparently at Bīdar [2] in the Deccan. He had previously written in Arabic an account of his grandfather's miracles.

Makhāzin al-Qādirīyah, a defence of 'Abd al-Qādir al-Jīlānī against the attacks of ignorant persons : **Rieu** ii 874 (A.H. 1130/1717), **Ivanow** 1326 (2) (lacking the first three of the eleven *makhzans*. A.H. 1142/1729–30), **Āṣafīyah** i p. 474 no. 919 (A.H. 1199/1785), **I.O.** D.P. 730 (defective at end. 18th cent.).

1287. In 972/1564–5 [3] was written—

Risālah dar aḥwāl i ḥaḍrat i Kamāl al-Dīn i Khwārazmī[4]***:*** **Āṣafīyah** iii p. 164 no. 168.

1288. Maulānā Kamāl al-Dīn Maḥmūd Andujānī, [=Maḥmūd Ghujduwānī ?], who was a friend and confidant of " the great and highly renowned " Sh. Quṭb al-Dīn [Kamāl al-Dīn ?] Ḥusain [Khwārazmī ?], wrote in 949/1542–3 a work entitled *Miftāḥ al-ṭālibīn* [cf. p. 973]. An abridgment of that work was made by a pupil of Sh. Quṭb al-Dīn Ḥusain and enlarged by the addition of " many new and valuable details ". In 973/1565–6 the same pupil, whose name has not been ascertained,[5] abridged his own abridgment under the title *Jāddat al-'āshiqīn*.

Jāddat al-'āshiqīn, on the mystical doctrine, especially on the life and miracles of Sh. Quṭb al-Dīn [Kamāl al-Dīn ?] Ḥusain : **Ethé** 1877 (A.H. 989/1581), **'Alīgaṛh** Subḥ. MSS. p. 18 no. 1.

1289. **Ḥusain** Ḥāfiẓ **Qazwīnī** (or **Tabrīzī**) [6] settled in Damascus and there met Sh. Bahā' al-Dīn al-'Āmilī.

[1] This follows from his statements that he was "at present" (*ḥālā*) fifty years old (I.O. D.P. 730, fol. 218, l. 4) and that his father died in Shawwāl 945/1539 at the age of fifty-two (fol. 220*a*, l. 9).

[2] He states that his father was buried *dar-īn shahr i Bīdar*. His grandfather, Shaikh Muḥammad al-Qādirī al-Multānī, who died in 935/1529 (fol. 218*b*, ll. 12–13), was also buried at Bīdar.

[3] The Āṣafīyah catalogue adds *Dar Samarqand nawishtah shud*, but it is not clear whether this refers to the composition of the work or to the transcription of this particular MS.

[4] Cf. p. 973[13].

[5] In the catalogue of the Subḥān-Allāh MSS. at 'Alīgaṛh the *Jāddat al-'āshiqīn*, described as the *malfūẓāt* of Sh. Khwārazmī, is said to be the work of Sh. Sharaf al-Dīn Ḥusain commonly called (*'urf*) M. Ma'ṣūm.

[6] *Qazwīnī yā Tabrīzī ba-tardīdī kih dar khātimah i Mustadrakāt al-wasā'il dar tarjamah i Shaikh Bahā'ī madhkūr ast* (Mashhad catalogue).

Rauḍāt al-jinān wa-jannāt al-janān,[1] completed in 975/1567–8: **Mashhad** 14, MSS., no. 35 ("*jild i thānī*", i.e. *Rauḍah* vii to the end of the work).

1290. **Nūr al-Dīn M. b. Ḥusain** b. ʻAbd Allāh b. Pīr Ḥusain b. Shams al-Dīn **al-Qazwīnī.**

Silsilah-nāmah i Khwājagān i Naqshband, a spiritual pedigree of Naqshbandī shaikhs with biographical information about some of them, composed in 978/1570–1: **Blochet** i 428 (A.H. 993/1585, copied from an autograph), **Lālah-lī** 1381, **Ḥamīdīyah** p. 110 no. 155.

1291. Bābā **Dāwud Khākī** Kashmīrī Suhrawardī, a devoted disciple of Sh. Ḥamzah Kashmīrī,[2] used often to visit the members of his order at Multān. He was hostile to the Chak dynasty, accompanied the army sent by Akbar to invade Kashmīr and died in 994/1586, soon after their arrival in the country. Of his works M. Aʻẓam mentions (1) *Wird al-murīdīn,* (2) *Dastūr al-sālikīn,* a commentary on the preceding, (3) *Qaṣīdah i Jalālīyah,* and (4) *Risālah i ghuslīyah.*

Wird al-murīdīn, a short metrical life of Sh. Ḥamzah Kashmīrī: **Lahore** 1894° (in a pamphlet of 31 pp. with the title *Ḍarūrī i kalān, Ḍarūrī i khwurd, Wird al-murīdīn,* containing five short works, of which the first and the third are by Dāwud Khākī).

[*Wāqiʻāt i Kashmīr* pp. 108–10; *Khazīnat al-aṣfiyā'* ii pp. 88–9.]

1292. Khwājah **Isḥāq Qārī,**[3] another disciple of Sh. Ḥamzah Kashmīrī, lived in seclusion at Shīwah [spelling ?] for twenty-two years and died at al-Madīnah after performing a pilgrimage.

Ḥilyat al-ʻārifīn, a biography of Sh. Ḥamzah Kashmīrī written in 980/1572–3: **Rieu** iii 972*b* (acephalous. A.H. 1139/1726).

[1] The precise subject of this work is not stated in the Mashhad catalogue, where it appears in the section *Tārīkh u afsānah.* That it is concerned with saints may be inferred from the chronogrammatic verse

*Chu pursīdam zi tārīkhash khirad guft * Ziyārāt i qubūr i auliyā shud.*

[2] Sh. Ḥamzah, one of the great saints of Kashmīr, died on 24 Ṣafar 984/23 May 1576. See *Wāqiʻāt i Kashmīr* pp. 104–6; *Khazīnat al-aṣfiyā'* ii pp. 86–7.

[3] *Az ʻilm i qirā'at ḥifẓ i wāfir dāsht.*

[*Wāqiʿāt i Kas̲h̲mīr* pp. 121–2.]

1293. **Mann Allāh** b. ʿAlī Allāh M. Ḥusainī.[1]

K̲h̲awāriqāt (so Ethé), or *Tabṣirat al-k̲h̲awāriqāt* (*al-k̲h̲awāriq*) *i Gēsū-darāz i Ḥusainī*, on the life and miracles of Gēsū-darāz,[2] his descendants and spiritual successors, composed in 981/1573–4[3]: **Ethé** 1869 vii, **Āṣafīyah** i p. 406 nos. 337, 817 (A.H. 1311/1893–4), iii p. 194 no. 1378 (A.H. 1311/1893–4).

1294. **Ḥusain b.** Mīr **Ḥusain** Ḥusainī **Sarak̲h̲sī.**

Saʿdīyah, biographies of the Jūybārī K̲h̲wājahs Muḥammad Islām, a contemporary of the S̲h̲aibānids ʿUbaid Allāh K̲h̲ān (A.H. 940–6) and ʿAbd Allāh K̲h̲ān (A.H. 946–7/1539–40), and K̲h̲wājah Saʿd, written in 984/1586: **Tashkent** A. A. Semenov's private library (A.H. 984/1586, autograph. See Semenov *Kurzer Abriss* p. 4), **Buk̲h̲ārā** private libraries (see Semenov *Ukazatel'* p. 26, where the work is called *Manāqib i S̲h̲. K̲h̲wājah M. Islām* and where a reference is given to Zimin *Materialy k istorii Turkestana v XVI v.* (*Izv. T. Otd. Russ. Geogr. Obshchestva*, Tashkent 1918) p. 30).

1295. S. **Murs̲h̲id,** a Yasawī dervish, says in the preface to his *Ḥujjat al-abrār* that in accordance with Ṣūfī tradition he had left his monastery and travelled to Transoxiana, Syria, Egypt, al-Madīnah, Persia and Asia Minor. His *Tasallā'* [*sic*] *al-qulūb*, a diffuse commentary on the first three verses of Jalāl al-Dīn Rūmī's *Mat̲h̲nawī* (Blochet iii 1377 (1)), is dedicated to the memory of Prince Mubāriz al-Dīn S̲h̲irwān Girāy, a son of the K̲h̲ān of the Crimea, Abū 'l-Muẓaffar M. Girāy K̲h̲ān b. Daulat Girāy K̲h̲ān, who reigned from 985/1577 to 992/1584.

Ḥujjat al-abrār, a *mat̲h̲nawī* completed in 996/1588, dedicated to Sulṭān Murād b. Salīm [982–1003/1574–95] and

[1] The Āṣafīyah Catalogue is the authority for the author's name, which is not mentioned by Ethé.
[2] d. 825/1422. See p. **950** n. 1 *supra*.
[3] So Ethé and Āṣafīyah iii p. 194, but A.H. 891 according to Āṣafīyah i p. 406.

dealing with the orders of dervishes at Istānbūl and their chiefs, especially Aḥmad Yasawī[1]: **Blochet** iii 1377 foll. 103*b*–173 (17th cent.).

1296. The *Riyāḍ al-auliyā'*,[2] as it is called in an inscription of doubtful authority on a fly-leaf, is there said to be the work of Mu'īn al-Dīn Minbarī (?). The author, whatever his name may have been, was a disciple of Muḥammad Balkhī (M. al-Zāhid al-Jāmī al-Balkhī b. Abī Bakr b. M. b. Abī Sa'īd b. Khalīl Allāh al-Jāmī). The latter, whose biography is the last in the biographical part of the work, was born in 899/1493–4, lived in Balkh and Badakhshān, and died on 10 Rabī' i 979/2 Aug. 1571. Probably therefore the *Riyāḍ al-auliyā'* was written towards the end of the 10th/16th cent.

Riyāḍ al-auliyā' (?), biographies of the ancient prophets (foll. 1*b*–45, beginning *al-Ḥ. l. . . . ammā ba'd 'ulamā-yi ḥadīth u khabar*, possibly not a part of the main work), Muḥammad (fol. 45*b*, beginning *Ḥamd i bī-ghāyat u shukr i bī-nihāyat mar ān pādshāhī rā*), the first Caliphs, early and later Ṣūfīs (the latest being a number connected with Khurāsān) followed by discussions of various Ṣūfī topics: **Ivanow** Curzon 704 (late 17th cent.).

List of the 15 principal biographies of later *shaikhs*: Ivanow Curzon pp. 467–8.

1297. **Abū 'l-Ma'ālī M. "Muslimī"** (*Tuḥfat al-Qādirīyah*, foll. 2*b*[9], 3*a*[2]) or Shāh S. Khair al-Dīn Abū 'l-Ma'ālī Qādirī Kirmānī Lāhaurī b. S. Raḥmat Allah b. S. Fatḥ Allāh (*Khazīnat al-aṣfiyā'* i p. 149[12]) was born in 960/1553 and became a disciple of Sh.

[1] For Aḥmad Yasawī, who died in 562/1166–7 and is buried at his birthplace, Yasī, the town now called Turkistān, or Ḥaḍrat i Turkistān, see *Rashaḥāt* pp. 8–9; *Safīnat al-auliyā'* p. 76 (no. 75); *Khazīnat al-aṣfiyā'* i pp. 531–2; *Legenda pro Khakim Atà* [an Eastern-Turkish biography of Ḥakīm Atā (for whom see *Ency. Isl.* under Ḥakīm Atā) with extracts from several Persian works relating to his teacher Aḥmad Yasawī and his spiritual successors]. *Soobshchil K. G. Zaleman* [i.e. C. Salemann]. *Ottisk iz Izvestiy Imperatorskoy Akademii Nauk*, T. ix, no. 2 (St. Petersburg 1898) pp. 105–50; *Ency. Isl.* under Aḥmed Yesewī (Melioransky); *Der Islam* xiii (1923) p. 106 (Babinger), xiv (1925) p. 112 (Barthold).

[2] This is the title of a work completed in 1090/1679–80 by M. Baqā (see p. 1012).

Dāwud C͟hūnī-wāl,[1] presumably at or near C͟hūnī.[2] Subsequently he settled in Lahore, where he died on 16 Rabīʿ i 1024/15 April 1615 and was buried outside the Mōtī Darwāzah in a tomb which the K͟hazīnat al-aṣfiyāʾ describes as visited by hundreds of people on the anniversary of his death. In addition to the Tuḥfat al-Qādirīyah a work entitled Ḥilyah i Saiyid i ʿālam and a dīwān (in the possession of his descendants) are mentioned in the K͟hazīnat al-aṣfiyāʾ.

Tuḥfat al-Qādirīyah, a life of ʿAbd al-Qādir Jīlānī [3] in 21 bābs: **Lahore** Panjāb Univ. (A.H. 1101/1689–90. See *OCM*. viii/4 (Aug. 1932) p. 41), **Ethé** 1803 (A.H. 1137/1725), **Ivanow** 266 (18th cent.), **Ivanow** Curzon 77 (18th cent.), **Āṣafīyah** i p. 408 no. 495, ii p. 848 nos. 31, 32, **Tashkent Univ.** 18 (4).

Edition: **Siyālkōṭ** 1317/1899° (in a collectaneous volume entitled *Ism i aʿẓam* containing several Ṣūfī works, three of them by Abū 'l-Maʿālī).

Urdu translations (1) *Sīrat al-G͟hauth*, by M. Bāqir, **Lahore** 1905*, (2) *Urdū tarjamah i kitāb T. al-Q.*, by M. ʿAbd al-Karīm, **Lahore** 1906†, (3) **Lahore** [1919*].

Abridgment by the author himself: *Muk͟htaṣar i Tuḥfah i Qādirīyah*, in two qisms ((1) on ʿAbd al-Qādir, (2) on his associates): **Ivanow** Curzon 267 (A.H. 1101/1689–90).

[*Safīnat al-auliyāʾ* pp. 195–6; *K͟hazīnat al-aṣfiyāʾ* i pp. 149–51.]

1298. **ʿAbd al-Ḥaqq** b. Saif al-Dīn al-Turk [4] al-**Dihlawī** al-Buk͟hārī, who died in 1052/1642–3, has already been mentioned as the author of the *Madārij al-nubuwwah* (p. 194 *supra*), the *S͟harḥ Sufar al-saʿādah* (p. 181 *supra*), the *D͟hikr al-mulūk* or *Tārīk͟h i Ḥaqqī* (p. 441 *supra*), the *Aḥwāl i Aʾimmah i It͟hnā-ʿas͟har* (p. 214 *supra*) and the *Jad͟hb al-qulūb ilā diyār al-maḥbūb* (p. 427 *supra*).

---

[1] For whom see Badāʾūnī *Muntak͟hab al-tawārīk͟h* iii pp. 28–39; *Safīnat al-auliyāʾ* p. 193 (no. 369), *K͟hazīnat al-aṣfiyāʾ* i pp. 128–31. His tomb is at S͟hērgaṛh (kih dīhī az muḍāfāt i qaṣabah i C͟hūnī ast, *K͟hazīnah* i p. 130^{14}). According to the *K͟h. al-a.* Abū 'l-Maʿālī was not only his murīd and k͟halīfah but also his birādar-zādah i ḥaqīqī.

[2] Qaṣabah i C͟hūnī kih ba-fāṣilah i c͟hihal kurūh az Lāhaur ba-janūb wāqiʿ ast (*K͟hazīnah* i p. 129^{19}).

[3] For whom see p. **933** n. 2 *supra*.

[4] Not al-Turkī. The incorrect form should be corrected on p. 194 *supra*.

(1) ***Akhbār al-akhyār fī asrār al-abrār***, lives of 255 Indian saints preceded by a notice of ‘Abd al-Qādir Jīlānī (for whom see p. 933 n. 2 *supra*) and followed by a *khātimah* or *takmilah* on the author's ancestors and his own life, compiled before 996/1588 but revised and completed in 999/1590–1: **Bodleian** 363 (A.H. 1095/1684), **I.O.** D.P. 572 (A.H. 1107/1695–6, said to have been transcribed from a MS. corrected by the author), **Ethé** 640 (n.d.), **Browne** Suppt. 21 (A.H. 1109/1697–8. King's 18), 22 (A.H. 1243/1827–8. Corpus 126), **Bānkīpūr** viii 666 (A.H. 1133/1720), 667 (A.H. 1278/1861–2), **Blochet** i 431 (18th cent.), **Rieu** i 355*a* (A.H. 1218/1803), **Ivanow** 258 (19th cent.), **Āṣafīyah** i p. 346 nos. 33 and 99, **Berlin** 588 (defective), 52 (11)–(12) (extracts), **Bukhārā** Semenov 1, **Lahore** Panjāb Univ. Lib. (see *OCM*. iii/1 (Nov. 1926) p. 72).

Editions: Aḥmadī Press [**Delhi** presumably [1]] 1270/1853–4 (see Bānkīpūr viii p. 28), Muḥammadī Press, **Delhi** 1282/1865–6 (see ‘Alīgaṛh Subḥān Allāh ii p. 57 no. 19), **Delhi** 1309/1891–2 (see Āṣafīyah iii p. 182 no. 215 and Waḥīd Mirzā *Life and works of Amir Khusrau* p. 241 (5)), Mujtabā'ī Press, **Delhi** 1332/1914‡.[2]

(2) ***Zād al-muttaqīn fī sulūk ṭarīq al-yaqīn***, written in 1003/1594–5 and devoted to the lives of two Indian saints resident at Mecca in the 10th/16th century, namely ‘Alī b. Ḥusām al-Dīn al-Muttaqī [3] and ‘Abd al-Wahhāb b. Walī

[1] One of the publications of the Aḥmadī Press at Delhi was the 1285 edition of the *Sirr al-shahādatain* mentioned on p. 223 *supra*.

[2] The last is the edition cited in this work. It contains also the *rasā'il* or *makātīb* entitled *Irsāl al-makātīb wa-'l-rasā'il ilā arbāb al-kamāl wa-'l-faḍā'il* (cf. *Ta'līf qalb al-alīf*, ed. Shams Allāh, pp. 39–43).

[3] ‘A. b. Ḥ. al-D. Muttaqī Qādirī Shādhilī Madyanī Chishtī, born at Burhānpūr in 885/1480 or 888/1483 (*al-N. al-s.* p. 317[3]), went after his father's death (*A. al-a.* p. 259[2]) to Multān, where he became a pupil of Sh. Ḥusām al-Dīn Muttaqī Multānī (for whom see *A. al-a.* p. 213), lived for a time at Aḥmadābād in the reign of Bahādur Shāh (932–43/1526–36), departed thence when Bahādur Shāh was defeated by Humāyūn [in 941/1535], migrated [immediately ?] to Mecca [in 953/1546 according to *S. al-m.*, but this date seems to be incorrect], associated with Abū 'l-Ḥasan al-Bakrī [who died in 952/1545 according to *Shadharāt al-dhahab* viii p. 293, if the same person is meant] and Ibn Ḥajar [al-Haitamī (d. 974/1567), not al-‘Asqalānī (d. 852/1449)], died on 2 Jumādā i 975/4 Nov. 1567 at the age of 87 or 90 and was buried at al-Ma‘lāh (*al-N. al-s.* p. 315[15]), the cemetery outside Mecca. Of his numerous works the best known at the present day is the collection of traditions entitled *Kanz al-‘ummāl*, which was printed at Ḥaidarābād in 1312–15/1894–7. See *Akhbār al-akhyār*

Allāh al-Muttaqī [1] as well as to short notices of some contemporary Meccan _shaikhs_ and *faqīrs* [2]: **Rieu** i 356*a* (A.H. 1260/1844), **Peshawar** 1462 (1).

(3) *Zubdat al-āthār muntakhab i Bahjat al-asrār*,[3] an abridgment of al-Shaṭṭanūfī's life of 'Abd al-Qādir al-Jīlānī (for which see p. 933 *supra*): **I.O.** D.P. 759*a* (defective. Early 19th cent.).

Edition: *Zubdat al-āthār . . . aur kitāb i Urdū Kuḥl al-abṣār tarjamah i Zubdat al-asrār* [*sic* [4]], **Delhi** [1890°. With an Urdū translation].

1299. **M. Ṣāliḥ b. Amīr 'Abd Allāh** b. Amīr 'Abd al-Raḥmān wrote in the time of 'Abd al-Mu'min Khān b. 'Abd Allāh Khān Ūzbak (A.H. 1006/1598).

pp. 257–69; *al-Nūr al-sāfir* (in Arabic) pp. 315–19; *Ẓafar al-wālih* (in Arabic) i pp. 315–17; *Safīnat al-auliyā'* p. 191 (no. 365); *Ma'āthir al-kirām*; *Mir'āt i Aḥmadī, khātimah* pp. 85–7, English trans. pp. 73–5; *Subḥat al-marjān* p. 43; *Khazīnat al-aṣfiyā'* i pp. 429–31; *Ḥadā'iq al-Ḥanafīyah* p. 382; Rieu i p. 356; Raḥmān 'Alī p. 146; Bānkīpūr Arabic Cat. v p. 142; *Ency. Isl.* under al-Muttaqī al-Hindī (Hidāyat Ḥusain); Brockelmann ii p. 384, *Sptbd.* ii pp. 518–19. Biographies entitled *Itḥāf al-naqī* and *al-Qaul al-naqī* were written (see Bānkīpūr Cat. v. p. 143) by his pupils 'Abd al-Wahhāb al-Muttaqī (for whom see the next note) and al-Fākihī (for whom see Brockelmann ii p. 388, *Sptbd* ii p. 529), but no copies seem to be recorded in published catalogues.

[1] 'A. al-W. M., born at Mandū [usually spelt Māndū], went to Mecca before the age of twenty [*A. al-a.* p. 269[13]], attached himself in 963/1556 [*A. al-a.* p. 270[8]], apparently the year of his arrival, to 'Alī al-Muttaqī, a friend of his father's, transcribed and collated many copies of his works, was recognized as his successor, taught Fiqh, Ḥadīth and other subjects for many years in the Ḥaram i Sharīf and died in 1001/1592–3. 'Abd al-Ḥaqq Dihlawī was his pupil for upwards of two years from 996/1588 and derived from him most of the information concerning 'Alī al-Muttaqī which is contained in the *Zād al-muttaqīn*. See *Akhbār al-akhyār* pp. 269–78; *Mir'āt i Aḥmadī, khātimah* p. 88, English trans. p. 75; *Khazīnat al-aṣfiyā'* i pp. 138–40; *Ḥadā'iq al-Ḥanafīyah* p. 392; Raḥmān 'Alī p. 139.

[2] For a list of these 26 persons see S. Shams Allāh Qādirī, *A treatise of Shaikh Abd-ul-Haq Dehlawi . . . (Tadhkirah i muṣannifīn i Dihlī)* pp. 12–13.

[3] Mentioned in 'Abd al-Ḥaqq's own list of his works *Ta'līf qalb al-alīf* (Shams Allāh Qādirī's edition p. 31) and also, according to Shams Allāh Qādirī, in the *Akhbār al-akhyār*.

[4] Described by Edwards as "Zubdat ul-āṣār. 'Abd ul-Ḥaḳḳ's own Persian abridgment of his Arabic work Zubdat ul-asrār, anecdotes and sayings of 'Abd ul-Ḳādir Gīlānī. With the omitted passages of the Z. ul-asrār, translated into Persian by Amānat Khān, and a Hindustani translation of the original Arabic by the latter". In 'Abd al-Ḥaqq's list of his own works there is no suggestion that the *Zubdat al-āthār* was abridged from a work entitled *Zubdat al-asrār*.

Tārīkh i mazārāt i Balkh : **Kābul** National Library (see *Journal asiatique*, Jan.–March 1924, p. 150).

Presumably this is different from the

Tārīkh i madfūnīn i Balkh (*u ḥālāt i Samarqand*) : **Āṣafīyah** i p. 346 no. 168 (author's name not stated in the catalogue).

1300. A disciple of Khwājah Isḥāq wrote—

Ḍiyā' al-qulūb, a biography of Khwājah Isḥāq (d. 1007/1598), the son of Makhdūm i A'ẓam (d. 949/1542) : see p. 973 n. 1 *supra*) : MS. in private possession (see Semenov *Ukazatel'* p. 20, where a reference is given to Validov *Vostochnye rukopisi v Ferganskoi oblasti* (in *Zapiski Vostochn. Otd. Imp. Russ. Arkheol. Obshchestva*, xxii) p. 304).

1301. A different work on the same subject was written by "**the son of Mullā Mīr Muḥammad 'Iwaḍ**"

Manāqib i Maulānā Isḥāq : MS. in private possession (see Semenov *Ukazatel'* p. 27, where references are given to Validov *op. cit.* p. 312, Zimin *Materialy k istorii Turkestana v* xvi *v.* (*Izv. T. Otd. Russ. Geogr. Obshchestva*, Tashkent 1918) pp. 29–30, and Barthold *Otchet o komandirovke v Turkestan* (*Zapiski Vostochn. Otd. Imp. Russ. Arkheol. Obshchestva* xv) pp. 61–3).

1302. **'Ubaid Allāh Naqshband Samarqandī,** a disciple of Sh. Luṭf Allāh Chūstī, wrote probably at the beginning of the seventeenth century.

Sirāj al-sālikīn wa-laṭā'if al-'ārifīn, a biography of Sh. Luṭf Allāh Chūstī, who died in 979/1571–2, with information concerning other Naqshbandīs : MS. in private possession (see Semenov *Ukazatel'* p. 19, where a reference is given to Barthold *Otchet o komandirovke v Turkestan* (*Zapiski Vostoch. Otd. Imp. Russ. Arkheol. Obshchestva*, xv) pp. 61–3. Cf. Semenov *Kurzer Abriss* p. 5, where the title (apparently of this same work) is given as *Manāqib i Maulānā-yi Luṭf Allāh i Chūstī* and a MS. in Semenov's possession transcribed in 1173/1759–60 from one dated 1022/1613–14 is mentioned, and Semenov

Ukazatel' p. 27, where references are given to Zimin *Materialy k istorii Turkestana* (*Izv. T. Otd. Russ. Geogr. Obshchestva*, Tashkent 1918) pp. 29–30 and Validov *Vostochnye rukopisi v Ferganskoi oblasti* (*Zapiski Vostochn. Otd. Imp. Russ. Arkheol. Obshchestva*, xxii) p. 312).

1303. M. Amīn [1] "**Ḥas͟hrī**" **Tabrīzī** Anṣārī lived for a time at 'Abbāsābād, near Iṣfahān, on friendly terms with [2] Nawwāb Mīrzā Ḥabīb Allāh, the *Ṣadr*, and in receipt of a stipend from the Office of Pious Foundations (*mablag͟hī az sarkār i mauqūfāt waẓīfah dās͟ht*, Naṣrābādī p. 280[8]). Subsequently he went to Tabrīz and died there. His poetical works (of which no copies seem to be recorded) included a *mat͟hnawī* on the campaigns of S͟hāh 'Abbās I (reigned 985–1038/1587–1629) written by royal command and another entitled *Rauḍah i abrār*, which was composed in 1011/1602–3 in the same metre as the *Mak͟hzan al-asrār* and which, like the *Rauḍah i at͟hār*, dealt with the saints, mystics and poets buried at Tabrīz. In the preface to the *Rauḍah i at͟hār* he mentions an earlier work of his on persons buried at S͟hīrāz.

Rauḍah i at͟hār, a prose work composed in 1011/1602–3 and devoted to a bare enumeration [3] of the saints, etc., buried in Tabrīz and its neighbourhood: **Flügel** ii 836 (A.H. 1021/1612–13), **Chanykov** 111–12.

Edition: **Tabrīz** 1303/1885–6 (see *D. i Ā.* p. 118[18]).

[*Tad͟hkirah i Naṣrābādī* p. 280; *K͟hizānah i 'āmirah* p. 193; *Dānis͟hmandān i Ād͟harbāyjān* pp. 117–18.]

1304. "**Ḥusainī**" an Afg͟hān of Peshawar and a disciple of the local Qādirī *pīr* Qāsim b. Qadam, was born in 977/1569–70.

Tuḥfah i Qāsimī, a *mat͟hnawī* on the miracles of Mīr Dād and other Afg͟hān saints, begun in 1009/1600–1 and completed in 1012/1603–4: **Ivanow** Curzon 261 (18th–19th cent.).

[1] So *Dānis͟hmandān i Ād͟harbāyjān* p. 118[9]. Naṣrābādī and "Azād" call him simply Ḥas͟hrī Tabrīzī without mentioning his name.
[2] *az muṣāḥibān i Nawwāb būd* (Naṣrābādī p. 280[10]).
[3] eine schlichte Aufzählung (Flügel).

1305. **'Abd al-Ṣamad b. Afḍal M.** b. Yūsuf Anṣārī, the son of a sister of Abū 'l-Faḍl (for whom see pp. 541–51 *supra*), completed in 1015/1606–7 the collection of his uncle's official letters entitled *Mukātabāt i 'Allāmī*, which has been mentioned on p. 542 *supra*.

Akhbār al-aṣfiyā', short notices of about 250 saints, mostly the same as in the *Akhbār al-akhyār* (see p. 979 *supra*), completed in 1014/1605–6, in the reign of Jahāngīr: **Peshawar** 1057 (A.H. 1089/1678–9), **Ethé** 641 (A.H. 1098–9/1687–8), **Bānkīpūr** viii 668 (lacunae. 18th cent.), 669 (transcribed from the preceding).

1306. **'Abd al-Qādir ibn Hāshim** ibn M. al-Ḥusainī.

Ḥadīqat al-auliyā', biographies of saints who lived in Sind, completed in 1016/1607–8: **I.O.** 4399 (19th cent.).

1307. Khwājah **Kamāl**.

Tuḥfat al-su'adā' (beg. *al-Ḥ. li-walīyihi wa-'l-ṣ. 'alā Nabīyihi . . . 'ārifān ḥājjī 'l-Ḥaramain bandagī i Shaikh Qiwām al-Dīn i 'Abbāsī i Lak'hnawī*), short lives of the Chishtī saints, Sh. Sa'd (d. 988/1580),[1] Qiwām al-Dīn (d. 840/1436–7),[2] and Shāh Mīnā (d. 870/1465–6),[3] composed in 1016/1607–8 at the request of the author's son, Shāh Ḥamīd Abū 'l-Faiḍ: **Rāmpūr** (A.H. 1175/1761. See Nadhīr Aḥmad 75).

1308. Sh. **'Alīm** (or 'Ālim ?) **'Azīzān** was born in 972/1564 and died in 1041/1632.

Lamaḥāt min nafaḥāt al-quds, biographies of *shaikhs* belonging to a branch of the Naqshbandī order. Edition: **Tashkent** 1327/1909 (see Semenov *Kurzer Abriss* p. 5).

[1] This date is given by Nadhīr Aḥmad doubtless on the authority of the *Tuḥfat al-su'adā'*. Neither the *Akhbār al-akhyār* nor the *Khazīnat al-aṣfiyā'* contains a biography of Sh. Sa'd.

[2] Cf. *Akhbār al-akhyār* p. 155; *Sawāṭi' al-anwār* (Ethé col. 332[45]); *Khazīnat al-aṣfiyā'* i pp. 388–9. Q. al-D. was a disciple of Chirāgh i Dihlī (for whom see p. 942 n. 1 *supra*) and of Makhdūm i Jahāniyān (see pp. 944–6 *supra*).

[3] Shāh Mīnā, the saint of Lucknow, was a disciple of Sh. Qiwām al-Dīn and of Sh. Sārang. See *Akhbār al-akhyār* p. 156; *Malfūẓāt i Shāh Mīnā* (***Tuḥfat al-Sa'dīyah ?*** p. 1066 *infra*); *Khazīnat al-aṣfiyā'* i pp. 398–9; *Lucknow District Gazetteer* p. 214.

1309. For the *Tārīkh i Khān-i-Jahānī u Makhzan i Afghānī*, which was completed in 1021/1613 by Ni'mat Allāh b. Ḥabīb Allāh Harawī and of which the *khātimah* contains notices of 68 Afghān saints, see p. 393 *supra*. The third *daftar* of the shorter recension, *Makhzan i Afghānī* (p. 394 *supra*), is likewise devoted to Afghān saints.

1310. **M. Ghauthī** b. Ḥasan b. Mūsā Shaṭṭārī,[1] as he calls himself, or M. b. al-Ḥasan al-Manduwī, as he is called in the *Nuzhat al-khawāṭir* (p. 61¹⁰),[2] or Mullā Ghauthī Māndū-wālē,[3] as he is called in (the heading of ?) the extract contained in Ivanow-Curzon 74, was the son of Ḥasan b. Mūsā Aḥmadābādī, whose biography is the last in the *Gulzār i abrār* (or at any rate in Ivanow 259). He had contemplated writing the *Gulzār i abrār* as early as 998/1590, but circumstances compelled the postponement of the work until after 1010/1602. " In fact, the greater part of his book was written between 1020/1611 (cf. f. 29v) and 1022/1613 (cf. ff. 172v, 182v, 184v, etc.). Only once he mentions 1008/1599 as current (f. 65) " (Ivanow).

Gulzār i abrār, bombastic, but valuable,[4] notices of 575 Indian saints, many of them Gujrātīs, dedicated to Jahāngīr and divided into five *chamans* ((1)–(3) seventh, eighth and ninth century respectively, (4) tenth and early eleventh century, (5) Shaṭṭārīs) : **Lindesiana** p. 143 no. 185 (A.H. 1078/1667–8), **Bukhārā** Semenov 94 (A.H. 1078/1667–8), **Ivanow** 259 (A.H. 1155/1742–3), **Ivanow** Curzon 74 foll. 67*b*–70 (Mu'īn al-Dīn Chishtī only), **Āṣafiyah** iii p. 162 no. 177, **Rieu** iii 1041*b* (extracts only. *Circ*. A.D. 1850).

[1] Possibly identical with Maulānā Ghauthī, who is mentioned under Aḥmadābād in the *Haft iqlīm* (p. 88, no. 31) as a person known to everyone and of whose poetry four verses are quoted. " Ghauthî, a poet of Gujarât," whose " name was Ḥasan ", occurs in the *Makhzan al-gharā'ib* (no. 1816), but, if his name is correctly given as Ḥasan, he cannot be identical with the author of the *Gulzār i abrār*. Cf. *Riyāḍ al-shu'arā'* 688 (Ivanow-Curzon p. 37), where there is another notice of Ḥasan Ghauthī. There seems to be no mention of M. Ghauthī or of Ḥasan Ghauthī in the *khātimah* to the *Mir'āt i Aḥmadī*.

[2] Merely in a citation of the *Gulzār i abrār*.

[3] Māndūwālī (*sic* ?) according to Ivanow.

[4] " because of its exactitude in dates, richness in details, and its abundant information about a great many persons otherwise unknown, but especially for its large number of references to the history of Gujrāt and India in general " (Ivanow).

List of the saints: Ivanow pp. 97–180

1311. **M. Ṣādiq Kashmīrī Hamadānī** is best known as the author of the *Ṭabaqāt i Shāh-Jahānī*, which he wrote, partly at any rate, in 1046/1636–7. Another work of his, the *Silsilat al-ṣādiqīn*, is referred to in the *Kalimāt al-ṣādiqīn*.

Kalimāt al-ṣādiqīn, biographies of 125 saints buried at Delhi, completed in 1023/1614: **Bānkīpūr** viii 671 (18th cent.).

List and epitome of the biographies: Bānkīpūr viii pp. 35–45.

1312. **Naṣīb i Kashmīr,**[1] as he calls himself, or Abū 'l-Fuqarā' Bābā Naṣīb, as M. A'ẓam calls him, or Bābā Naṣīb al-Dīn Suhrawardī Kashmīrī, as he is called in the *Khazīnat al-aṣfiyā'*, was a disciple of Bābā Dāwud Khākī, who has already been mentioned in this work (p. 975). One of the great saints of Kashmīr, he was renowned for his austerity and for his kindness to the poor and wretched.[2] He died on 13 Muḥarram 1047/7 May 1637.

(Rīshī-nāmah),[3] lives of Kashmīrī saints, especially of Bābā Nūr al-Dīn Walī Rīshī,[4] the subject of the first and by far the longest biography (foll. 169*b*–332 in Ivanow 260), Bābā Bām al-Dīn,[5] Bābā Zain al-Dīn,[6] Bābā Laṭīf al-Dīn,[7] Bābā Naṣr al-Dīn,[8] Bābā Rajab al-Dīn,[9] Bābā Shukr al-Dīn,[10] Bābā

[1] Rhyming with *faqīr i ḥaqīr*.

[2] *Masākīn dar khidmatush rujū' i tamām dāshtand dar waqt i khwud malja' u ma'āb i ghurabā u bī-chāragān būd* (*Wāqi'āt i Kashmīr* p. 142[11]).

[3] Cf. *Wāqi'āt i Kashmīr* p. 63[14]: *Rīshī kasī rā gūyand kih az zumrah i zāhidān u 'ābidān dar riyāḍat sakht u ṣulb-tar bāshad u khwud rā az aulād u izdiwāj fārigh dārad dast az jamī' i ārzūhā u hawā u hawas bar-dārad chih jāy i mulk u māl*; *Khazīnat al-aṣfiyā'* ii p. 334[15]: *Darwīshān i Rīshī firqah dar Kashmīr az khānadān i Kubrawīyah būdand darwīsh* [*sic*, but read *u Rīshī*] *ba-zabān i Kashmīrī mard i 'ābid u zāhid rā gūyand kih faiḍ i Uwaisī dāshtah bāshad.* It is the Sanskrit word *ṛishi*, meaning "saint" or "anchorite". See *Some Account of the Rishis or Hermits of Kashmir*, by Lieut.-Col. D. J. F. Newall (in *JASB.* xxxix, pt. 1 (1870) pp. 265–70).

[4] Who died in 842/1438–9. See *Wāqi'āt i Kashmīr* pp. 63–4; *Khazīnat al-aṣfiyā'* ii pp. 312–13; Lawrence, *The Valley of Kashmir* pp. 287–8.

[5] *Wāqi'āt i Kashmīr* p. 64.

[6] *W. i K.* p. 64.

[7] *W. i K.* p. 65.

[8] *W. i K.* p. 65.

[9] *W. i K.* p. 70.

[10] *W. i K.* p. 70.

Laṭīf al-Dīn's disciples, Bābā Naurōz Rīs͟hī [1] [Malik Saif al-Dīn, Mirzā Ḥaidar Kās͟hg͟harī],[2] S͟h. Ḥamzah [3] and several of his disciples, with a long preliminary discourse on the merits of the first four Caliphs, etc. : **Ivanow** 260 (defective at the beginning and elsewhere. Foll. 519. Early 17th cent.), **Edinburgh** 245 (foll. 428), **I.O.** D.P. 731 (18th cent.).

[*Wāqi'āt i Kas͟hmīr* p. 142 ; *K͟hazīnat al-aṣfiyā'* ii p. 95 ; Rieu iii 1085*a*.]

1313. **Bahā' al-Dīn** "**Bahā**", whose *Rīs͟hī-nāmah* seems to be based on that of Naṣīb, is placed here for convenience in the absence of information concerning his date (which will probably be revealed approximately as soon as a cataloguer particularizes the latest Qādirīs mentioned in his poem).

Rīs͟hī-nāmah, a metrical account of the saints of Kas͟hmīr in three *daftars* ((1) S͟h. Nūr al-Dīn, his followers and contemporaries, (2) S͟h. Ḥamzah and some other *Rīs͟hīs*, (3) 'Abd al-Qādir Gīlānī and the *s͟haik͟hs* of his *silsilah* in Kas͟hmīr) : **Bānkīpūr** Suppt. i 1894 (A.H. 1284–5/1867–9), **I.O.** 3684, **London S.O.A.S.**

1314. **'Alī Aṣg͟har** b. S͟h. Maudūd b. S͟h. M. **Chis͟htī** Hindālawī (?) [4] Fatḥpūrī wrote his *Jawāhir i Farīdī* primarily to elucidate the complex genealogical relations of the descendants of S͟h. Farīd al-Dīn Ganj i S͟hakar,[5] who were so numerous that he had been surnamed Ādam i T͟hānī and many impostors had been able to claim privileges to which they were not entitled.

Jawāhir i Farīdī, an elaborate work on the lives of some Chis͟htī saints, especially Farīd al-Dīn Ganj i S͟hakar and his descendants, completed in 1033/1623 under Jahāngīr (but evidently supplemented later) [6] and divided into five *bābs* ((1) the Prophet, his wives and children, the early Caliphs and

---

[1] *W. i K.* p. 73.
[2] See pp. 273–6 *supra* ; *JRAS*. 1918, p. 461, etc.
[3] See p. 975 n. 2 *supra*.
[4] Ivanow writes Handālawī, 'Abd al-Muqtadir Bîdâlawî.
[5] See p. 941 n. 4 *supra*.
[6] According to Ivanow the years 1036 and 1038 are referred to as current and at the end of the work an event of 1057 is mentioned.

some *Tābi'īn*, (2) Mu'īn al-Dīn Chishtī,[1] Quṭb al-Dīn Bakhtyār Ūshī,[2] Farīd al-Dīn Ganj i Shakar, Najīb al-Dīn Mutawakkil,[3] their wives, children and disciples, (3) Zain al-'Ābidīn Chishtī Hindālawī, a descendant of Ganj i Shakar in the fourth generation and a contemporary of Sikandar Lōdī (894–923/1488–1517), who settled at Hindālī (?), near Fatḥpūr, (4) a list of *a'rās*, i.e. days of the month on which the anniversaries of the death of different saints are celebrated, together with some information concerning the affiliations of the author's father, (5) on the descendants of Sh. Sa'd Ḥājjī (so Ivanow), or Sa'īd Ḥājjī (so Būhār), a relation of Ganj i Shakar, and those of Sh. 'Abd Allāh Ghaffārī, known as Shaikh al-Islām, etc.) : **Ivanow** Curzon 72 (late 19th cent.), **Būhār** 87 (A.H. 1314/1896).

Edition : **Lahore** 1301/1884 *(author's name given as Aṣghar 'Alī).

1315. **S. M. Qāsim "Riḍwān"** was the younger son of the Yasawī saint Jamāl al-Dīn Khwājah Dīwānah S. Atā'ī of Khwārazm and Khīwaq (i.e. Khīwah). The latter, a son of S. Pādshāh Khwājah Pardah-pūsh and a descendant of Sulṭān Khwājah Aḥmad Yasawī called Atā,[4] was born shortly before Shāh Ismā'īl's invasion, i.e. in 916/1510,[5] and died in 1016/1607–8.

Maqāmāt i Saiyid Atā'ī, an account of the life, miracles and teachings of the aforementioned saint, completed on 1 Muḥarram 1036/22 September 1626 on the basis of a work by Ākhund Maulānā Darwīsh Tāshkandī and the *Maqāmāt al-'ārifīn* of Qāḍī Jān M. b. Qāḍī Khān BJĀRĪ (read Bukhārī ?) and divided into a *muqaddimah*, four *maqāms* and a *khātimah* : **Ethé** 644 (slightly defective at end).

1316. **M. Hāshim** b. M. Qāsim al-Nu'mānī (?) **al-Badakhshānī,**[6]

[1] See p. 943 n. 3 *supra*.
[2] See p. 943 n. 4 *supra*.
[3] See p. 971 n. 6 *supra*.
[4] See p. 977 n. 1 *supra*.
[5] Ethé quotes the passages *Chūn ḥaḍrat i īshān chahār māyah* [*sic*, apparently for *chahārmāhah*] *shudand fitnah i Shāh Ismā'īl wāqi' gardīd* (fol. 14b ult.) and *Ḥaḍrat i īshān dar hangām i shīr-khwāragī būdand kih fatarāt i gharībah numūd u bi-sabab i hujūm i Qizil-bāsh u fitnah i Shāh Ismā'īl kār i akthar i ān-ḥudūd ba-qatl anjāmīd* (fol. 31a, l. 1).
[6] M. al-Hāshim [*sic*] b. M. al-Qāsim al-Nu'mānī al-Badakhshānī in I.O.D.P. 1034 fol 105b (no other MS. is at present accessible to me). The Cawnpore edition has al-NBGHĀNĪ instead of al-Nu'mānī, but otherwise agrees with the MS. Al-Nu'mānī, if correct, refers doubtless to his *pīr*, Mīr M. Nu'mān.

who mentions his name not in the preface [1] to the *Zubdat al-maqāmāt* but in the second *faṣl* of the second *maqṣad* (p. 130[14] in the Cawnpore edition), and whom a later author [2] calls **Hāshim Kishmī**,[3] tells us that, although his ancestors were Kubrawīs, he had even in his youth been attracted towards the Naqshbandī order. Having gone to India, he made the acquaintance of Mīr M. Nu'mān [4] at Burhānpūr and in 1031/1621–2 visited Aḥmad Sirhindī. For nearly two years he was in constant attendance upon the latter. He is evidently identical with the poet "Hāshim", i.e. Khwājah Hāshim b. M. Qāsim, who, as Sprenger ascertained from his *dīwān*, was at Burhānpūr in 1030/1621 and was apparently still alive in 1056/1646. For this *dīwān*, which contains at least two poems in praise of Aḥmad Fārūqī, see Ivanow 747 = Sprenger 250, Ethé 2898, Rehatsek p. 144 no. 67, Madras 64 (?), Āṣafīyah i p. 437 (?).

(1) ***Zubdat al-maqāmāt***, or ***Barakāt al-Aḥmadīyat al-bāqiyah***, an account of the life, miracles and teachings of Sh. Aḥmad Fārūqī Sirhindī,[5] his preceptor, Khwājah M.

[1] Not at any rate in the preface as given in the Cawnpore edition and the Bānkīpūr MS.

[2] M. Iḥsān, author of the *Rauḍat al-Qaiyūmīyah*, who in his list of authorities mentions Hāshim Kishmī's *Zubdat al-maqāmāt wa-barakāt al-Aḥmadīyah* (see Ivanow-Curzon p. 87[5]). In S. 'Alī Bilgrāmī's description of the I.O. MS. D.P. 994(b) (Bilg. 480) the author's name is given as Khwājah Muḥammad Hāshim, probably on the authority of a colophon or a note on the title-page.

[3] Evidently from Kishm in Badakhshān, like M. Ṣiddīq Kishmī, who is said to have come from Kishm in Badakhshān (*Zubdat al-maqāmāt* p. 372[10] : *wai az Kishm i Badakhshān-ast*). Kishm, once the chief town of Badakhshān, still exists (see *Ency. Isl.* under Badakhshān) and is marked even on fairly small maps.

[4] One of Aḥmad Sirhindī's *khalīfahs*. He was born at Samarqand *circ.* 977/1569–70 (*Zubdat al-maqāmāt* p. 328[5]), though his father, Shams al-Dīn Yaḥyā known as Mīr Buzurg, belonged to Kishm (*op. cit.* p. 327[1])

[5] Badr al-Dīn Aḥmad b. 'Abd al-Aḥad Fārūqī Kābulī Sirhindī Naqshbandī, called Imām i Rabbānī, Maḥbūb i Subḥānī and Mujaddid i Alf i Thānī (i.e. the Renovator of the Second Millennium, in allusion to the tradition *Inna 'llāha yab'athu li-hādhihi 'l-ummati 'alā ra'si kulli mi'ati sanatin man yujaddidu lahā dīnahā*, Abū Dāwud, *malāḥim*, 1), was born in, or about, 971/1563–4 at Sirhind (or Sihrind, as it is also spelt) of a family Kābulī in origin but resident in India for many generations. In 1028/1619 he was imprisoned at Gwalior by Jahāngīr, who took exception to the apparent arrogance of some sentences in his *Maktūbāt*, but in the following year he was pardoned and dismissed with a *khil'at* and a present of 1,000 rupees. In 1032/1623 he received from Jahāngīr a present of 2,000 rupees, and on 29 Ṣafar 1034/11 December 1624 he died at Sirhind. Among his works were (1) *Maktūbāt*, a large collection of letters in three *daftars* (Editions : Delhi 1288/1871*, 1290/1873*, Lucknow 1294/1877°*,

Bāqī,[1] and their children, *khalīfahs* and friends, written at the request of Aḥmad Sirhindī's children and completed in 1037/1627–8: **Bānkīpūr** viii 672 (18th cent. FULL ANALYSIS), **I.O.** D.P. 994*b*, 1034 (much damaged. A.H. 1150/1737–8).

Editions: **Lucknow** 1885†, **Cawnpore** 1890°.

Urdu translation: *Urdū tarjamah i kitāb i Zubdat al-maqāmāt* . . ., **Lahore** [1909*].

Evidently this author is the M. Hāshim b. Qāsim who wrote—

(2) *Nasamāt al-quds min ḥadā'iq al-uns*, a continuation of the *Rashaḥāt i 'ain al-ḥayāt* (see p. 964 *supra*) written in 1031/1622 for Aḥmad Fārūqī Sirhindī and containing biographies of Naqshbandīs from the beginning of the tenth/sixteenth century to the first quarter of the eleventh/seventeenth:

Amritsar 1339/1921* (incomplete ?), etc. MSS.: Bānkīpūr xvi 1392–3, Ethé 1891, Ivanow 1268, etc.), (2) *Mabda' u ma'ād* (Editions: Cawnpore 1309/1891°, Amritsar 1330/1912*. MSS.: Peshawar 1067(6), Nadhīr Aḥmad 37, Panjāb Univ. (*OCM*. viii/4 p. 41). Urdu trans.: Lahore [1923*]), (3) *Ma'ārif i ladunīyah* (Edition: [Lahore] 1351/1933*. MSS.: Peshawar 1916(5) (?), Panjāb Univ. (*OCM*. viii/4 p. 41). Urdu trans.: Lahore [1923*]), (4) *Sharḥ i rubā'īyāt i Sh. M. Bāqī* (MSS.: Peshawar 1067(8), Panjāb Univ. (*OCM*. viii/4 p. 41)). See *Gulzār i abrār* no. 537; *Kalimāt al-ṣādiqīn* no. 123; *Tūzuk i Jahāngīrī* pp. 272 penult., 308[7], 370[28], Rogers and Beveridge's trans. ii pp. 91–3, 161, 276; *Safīnat al-auliyā'* pp. 197–8 (no. 376); *Ḥaḍarāt al-quds*, *daftar* 2; *Manāqib al-ḥaḍarāt* (p. 991 *infra*); *Rauḍat al-qaiyūmīyah* (p. 1023 *infra*); *Subḥat al-marjān* pp. 47–52; *Khazīnat al-aṣfiyā'* i pp. 607–19; Beale *Oriental biographical dictionary* under Ahmad Sarhindi; Raḥmān 'Alī pp. 10–12; *Maqāmāt i Imām i Rabbānī Mujaddid i Alf i Thānī* (in Urdu), by M. Ḥasan, Lahore [1923*]; *Sīrat i Mujaddid* (in Urdu), by Wilāyat 'Alī Shāh, Lahore, 1928; Ivanow-Curzon p. 85; etc. Accounts of his teachings are *Anwār i Aḥmadīyah* and *Hadīyah i Mujaddidīyah*, by Maulawī Wakīl Aḥmad "'Ājiz" Sikandarpūrī published in one volume at Delhi in 1309–11/1892–4°*, *Kanz al-hidāyat* by M. Bāqir b. Sharaf al-Dīn Lāhaurī (Amritsar 1335/1917*), *Imam-i-Rabbani Mujaddid i Alf i Thani Shaikh Ahmad Sirhindi's Conception of Tawhid*, by B. A. Fārūqī, Lahore, date ? (*Luzac's Oriental List* 1940 p. 148).

[1] M. al-Bāqī, or M. Bāqī, or M. Bāqī bi'llāh, b. Qāḍī 'Abd al-Salām Uwaisī Naqshbandī was born at Kābul about 971/1563–4 or 972/1564–5 (*Z. al-m.* p. 5 penult.) and died at the age of forty or so in 1012/1603 at Delhi. His influence contributed much to the spread of the Naqshbandī order in India. It has been mentioned in the preceding note that his *rubā'īyāt* are extant with a commentary by his disciple, Aḥmad Sirhindī. A collection of his letters has also been preserved (cf. Rieu iii 1058*b*, Ivanow 1328(5), I.O. D.P. 1058(*b*). Urdu trans.: *Maktūbāt i sharīf i ḥaḍrat i Khwājah Bāqī bi 'llāh Dihlawī*, Lahore 1923*). According to the *Kalimāt al-ṣādiqīn* he wrote a commentary on some *sūrahs* of the *Qur'ān* and a *mathnawī*. The I.O. MS. D.P. 1095 is a copy of his *Kullīyāt*. See *Gulzār i abrār* no. 520; *Kalimāt al-ṣādiqīn* no. 120; *Safīnat al-auliyā'* p. 85 (no. 93); *Ḥaḍarāt al-quds*, at end of *ḥaḍrat* 1; *Riyāḍ al-auliyā'*; *Khazīnat al-aṣfiyā'* i pp. 605–7; Beale *Oriental biographical dictionary* under Muḥammad Bāqī; *Ḥayāt i bāqiyah* (in Urdu), Delhi [1905°].

Leningrad Univ. no. 305 (*Nasamāt fī manāqib al-mashāyikh al-Naqshbandīyah,* by M. H. b. Q. Salemann-Rosen p. 19. Cf. Semenov *Ukazatel'* p. 19, where a reference is given to Validov *Vostochnye rukopisi v Ferganskoi oblasti* (in *Zapiski Vostochn. Otd. Imp. Russ. Arkheol. Obshchestva,* xxii) pp. 306–8).

1317. On 22 Sha'bān 1042/22 February 1633 **Pīr Muḥammad Shaṭṭārī** b. 'Āqil Muḥammad Farkhārī and some friends of his were at the tomb of Saiyid al-Shuhadā' Shāh Ismā'īl Ghāzī 'Arabī and heard the story of the martyr from some of the guardians of the shrines at Kāntā-Duwār and Jalā-Maqām.[1] Impressed by the wonderful tale, his friends urged him to put it into writing and in response to their request he wrote the *Risālat al-shuhadā'* in Shāh-Jahān's reign (1037–69/1628–59).

Risālat al-shuhadā', a short (18 pp.) account of Shāh Ismā'īl, a Saiyid said to have gone from Mecca to Bengal in the reign of Bārbak Shāh (864–79/1459–74), for whom he defeated the rebel Rājah of Madāran and conquered Kāmrūp but by whose order he was beheaded on 14 Sha'bān 878/4 January 1474[2]: MS. found by G. H. Damant " in the possession of the Faqír in charge of Ismá'íl Ghází's tomb at Káṇṭá Dúár, Rangpúr".

Edition: *Notes on Sháh Ismá'íl Ghází, with* [the Persian text and] *a sketch of the contents of a Persian MS., entitled " Risálat ush-Shuhadá ", found at Káṇṭá Dúár, Rangpúr. By G. H. Damant* (in *JASB.* xliii (1874), pt. 1, pp. 215–39).

1318. **M. b. Jalāl Shāhī Riḍawī** is the author of a Ṣūfī tract entitled *Istiqāmat al-sharī'ah 'alā manhaj al-ḥaqīqah* (Ethé 2916 (1)).

[1] " There are four Dargáhs, or shrines, in Rangpúr, erected to the memory of Sháh Ismá'íl Ghází. They are all situate a few miles to the north-east of G'hoṛág'háṭ, in thánah Pírganj. The principal one is at Káṇṭá Dúár, a place marked in the survey maps at Chatra Hát, and as Katta Doar on Sheet 119 of the Indian Atlas. It is said to have been erected over his body. About three miles west is another at a place called Jalá Maqám. . . . These two dargáhs are under the care of the same faqīr, who has a large jágír and claims to be a descendant of one of the servants of Ismá'íl, who came with him from Arabia. The head of the saint is said to be buried at Káṇṭá Dúár, and his body at Madáran, in Jahánábád, west of Húglí " (*JASB.* 1874 p. 215).

[2] " The account given in the MS. corresponds most strangely in many particulars with the legend which Mr. Blochmann heard at Húglí (*see* Asiatic Society's Proceedings, April, 1870, page 117)."

al-As'ilah wa-'l-ajwibah, answers to seventeen questions received in 1042/1632–3 from S. M. Bhuwah concerning important dates in the lives of eminent *shaikhs* : **Ethé** 2916 (2).

1319. Mīr **'Alī Akbar** Ḥusainī **Ardistānī** dedicated his *Majma' al-auliyā'* to Shāh-Jahān, who reigned from 1037/1628 to 1068/1658.

Majma' al-auliyā', more fully *Maḥfil al-aṣfiyā' wa-majma' al-auliyā',* or chronogrammatically *Majma' i faiḍ* (= 1043/1633–4, the date of completion), lives of about 1,400 or 1,500 saints in a *muqaddimah* (on Ṣūfī technical terms), twelve *babs* ((1) the first four Caliphs, the Twelve Imāms, the *Ṣaḥābah,* the *Tābi'īn,* etc., 304 biographies, (2) Ḥasan Baṣrī and 142 of his order, (3) Ibrāhīm b. Adham and 62 of his order, (4) Ma'rūf Karkhī and 73 of his order, (5) Bāyazīd Bisṭāmī and 53 of his order, (6) Junaid Baghdādī and 89 of his order, (7) 162 Naqshbandīs and Turkish *shaikhs,* (8) 65 Qādirīs, (9) 64 Suhrawardīs, Kubrawīs and Chishtīs, (10) 277 Indian saints of Delhi, Gujrāt, etc., (11) 36 saints who were poets, (12) 38 female saints) and a *khātimah* (on the merits of the Prophet's family and the first four Caliphs with some account of al-Khiḍr and Ilyās) : **Ethé** 645 (A.H. 1043/1633, autograph), 646 (apparently a later redaction. *Muqaddimah* and *Bābs* 1–6 only), **Ivanow** 261 (*Bābs* 1–4 only. 18th cent.), **Bukhārā** Semenov 99.

1320. The *Manāqib al-ḥaḍarāt* is one of the authorities cited by M. Iḥsān in his *Rauḍat al-qaiyūmīyah,* where it is described as the work of M. Amīn, a *khalīfah* of Ādam Banūrī (see Ivanow-Curzon p. 87). This information is confirmed and amplified in the *Khazīnat al-aṣfiyā'* (I p. 632[9]), where the author is called Ḥājjī **M. Amīn Badakhshī.**

Manāqib al-ḥaḍarāt, or more fully *Manāqib i Ādamīyah u ḥaḍarāt i Aḥmadīyah,* lives of Naqshbandī saints, especially Aḥmad Fārūqī Sirhindī (for whom see p. 988 n. 5 *supra*), his sons, M. Sa'īd 'Umarī [1] and M. Ma'ṣūm,[2] his disciple Sh. Ādam Banūrī,[3]

[1] His second son, b. Sha'bān 1005/1597, d. 1070/1659–60. See *Zubdat al-maqāmāt* pp. 308–15, *Khazīnat al-aṣfiyā'* i pp. 638–9, Raḥmān 'Alī 190.

[2] His third son, b. 1007/1599 or 1009/1600–1, d. 1070/1659, or 1079/1668–9 or 1080/1669–70. See *Zubdat al-maqāmāt* pp. 315–26, *Khazīnat al-aṣfiyā'* i pp. 639–42 ; Raḥmān 'Alī p. 212.

[3] d. at al-Madīnah in 1053/1643. A collection of his sayings and letters entitled *Natā'ij al-Ḥaramain* is preserved at Peshawar (990B). See *Khazīnat*

and their disciples and contemporaries, in a *muqaddimah*, three *maṯlabs*, eleven *bābs* and a *khātimah* : **Ethé** 652 (defective and disarranged.[1] A.H. 1139–40/1726–8).

1321. Sulṭān M. **Dārā-Shukōh** [2] " Qādirī ", the eldest son of the Mogul Emperor Shāh-Jahān (1037–68/1628–58) and Mumtāz-Maḥall, was born at Ajmēr in Ṣafar 1024/March 1615. In Sha'bān 1042/Feb. 1633 he married Nādirah Bēgam, the daughter of his uncle, Sulṭān Parwēz. From 1043/1633, when he received his first *manṣab* (12,000/6,000) and the *sarkār* of Ḥiṣār as his fief, he was rapidly promoted and eventually reached unprecedented rank (60,000/40,000) in the State Service. He was appointed to several governorships (Allahabad in 1055/1645, the Panjāb in 1057/1647, Gujrāt (Gujarat) in 1059/1649, Multān and Kābul in 1062/1652), but these provinces were administered for him by deputies, and Lahore was the only provincial capital to which he ever paid a visit of any length. In 1063/1653 he was in command at the unsuccessful siege of Qandahār, which forms the subject of Rashīd Khān's *Laṭa'if al-akhbār* (see p. 574 *supra*). Although he had been recognized by Shāh-Jahān as heir to the throne, his claim was disputed in 1067/1657, when Shāh-Jahān fell ill, by his younger brothers, Shāh-Shujā', Aurangzēb and Murād-Bakhsh. He was twice defeated in battle by Aurangzēb, first at Samūgaṛh, near Āgrah, in Ramaḍān 1068/June 1658 and then at Ajmēr in Jumādā II 1069/March 1659. On 26 Dhū 'l-Ḥijjah 1069/14 September 1659 he was executed at Delhi by order of Aurangzēb, who had obtained from the *'ulamā'* a *fatwā* declaring him to be a *kāfir*.

al-aṣfiyā' i pp. 630–5. Banūr, some twenty miles from Sirhind, is now in the State of Patiala.

[1] The three *basmalahs* found by Ethé in the MS. (on foll. 1*b*, 40*b* and 189*b*) may be the beginnings of the *Manāqib al-ḥaḍarāt* and of two other works quoted therein. The *Natā'ij al-Ḥaramain* referred to on the margin of the first beginning is, as mentioned in the preceding note, a collection of Ādam Banūrī's sayings and letters. Ethé's suggested identification of M. Murād b. Ḥabīb Allāh b. Sa'dī (mentioned, perhaps as author, on the margin of the third beginning) with the Kashmīrī saint, M. Murād Naqshbandī (d. 1134/1722), is not possible, since the latter's father was M. Ṭāhir (see *Khazīnat al-aṣfiyā'* I p. 658).

[2] The words Dārā and Shukōh in this name form a compound idea (" Majes tic as Dārā," the ancient Persian king), and the second element is not, strictly speaking, separable from the first, but Manucci, Bernier and other Europeans speak of " Prince Dara ". Contemporary Indians may possibly have done the same in conversation.

Dārā-Shukōh and his sister Jahān-ārā were, according to the latter (see *OCM.* xiii/4 p. 16^{16-17}), the first of Tīmūr's line to set their feet upon the path of *Khudā-ṭalabī* and *Ḥaqq-jū'ī*. Dārā-Shukōh himself says (*Sakīnat al-auliyā'*, Urdu trans. p. 5^{3}) that *darwīshes* had always fascinated him and that much of his time had been spent in seeking them out. Then on the 10th,[1] or the 29th,[2] of Dhū 'l-Ḥijjah 1049, at the age of twenty-five, he had been admitted to the society of a saint (*ēk dōst i Khudā*[3] *kī ṣuḥbat mēṅ phunchā*) and had been treated by him with great kindness.[4] That which others used to obtain after a month he had obtained on the first night, and in a month that for which others needed a year. He had reached immediately and without austerities an aim usually attained only through years of severe discipline (*sālhā-sāl kē mujāhadoṅ aur riyāḍatōṅ sē*). Of Dārā-Shukōh's works the best known by far is the *Safīnat al-auliyā'* completed in 1049/1640, which may be described as a standard work of reference. Somewhat similar in content, but of narrower scope and much less known is the *Sakīnat al-auliyā'* completed in 1052/1642–3. The *Risālah i Ḥaqq-numā*, written in 1055/1645, is a small Ṣūfī tract.[5] The *Ḥasanāt al-'ārifīn*, composed in 1062/1652 is an annotated collection of ecstatic or paradoxical

[1] So Bānkīpūr viii p. 49.

[2] So Urdu trans. p. 5^{11}.

[3] So in the Urdu translation, but apparently not in the Persian original, since Rieu speaks of an "eminent master" and 'Abd al-Muqtadir of the "great master".

[4] The unnamed saint was of course Mullā Shāh. Rieu interprets Dārā-Shukōh's statements in this place as meaning that "he had received the initiation to the Ḳādirī order in A.H. 1049", but this is not expressly stated in the text (at any rate not in the Urdu translation). His admission to the Qādirī order seems to have occurred before this month with Mullā Shāh, since in the *Safīnat al-auliyā'* completed in Ramaḍāṅ 1049 he already describes himself as M. Dārā-Shukōh Ḥanafī Qādirī. According to his sister (*Ṣāḥibīyah*, Urdu trans. in *OCM.* xiii/4 p. 14^{17}) he was a *murīd* of Miyāṅ Mīr (*Mērē bhā'ī ḥaḍrat Miyāṅ-jīw sē nisbat i irādat rak'htē haiṅ*). In the *Safīnat al-auliyā'* he says only that he had visited Miyāṅ Mīr twice (p. 72^{12}: *īn faqīr dū bār ba-mulāzamat i īshān rasīdah*) and that one of these occasions was when at the age of twenty he was taken to the saint by Shāh-Jahān and through his intercession was cured of an illness which had baffled the physicians.

[5] Editions: Lucknow 1881°, 1883†, 1888†. English translation: *The Compass of Truth; or, Risala-i-Haqnuma. By Muhammad Dara Shikoh . . . Rendered into English by Rai Bahadur Śriśa Chandra Vasu*, Allahabad 1912°*. MSS.: Āṣafīyah i p. 416, Bānkīpūr xvi 1398, Ivaṅow Curzon 444 ii, 462 xix, Lahore Panjāb Univ. (*OCM.* VIII/4 p. 40). Description: Qanungo i pp. 141–3

utterances (*shaṭaḥāt* or *shaṭḥīyāt* [1]) ascribed to various mystics.[2] A work entitled *Rumūz i taṣawwuf*, which is described by Arberry as a catechism of Ṣūfī doctrine, was published with an Urdu translation at Lahore in [1923*]. Whether this is a genuine work of Dārā-Shukōh's and whether it contains a date are matters for investigation. The works of Dārā-Shukōh's last years are a remarkable series resulting from an interest in Hindu mysticism and a desire to reconcile Hinduism and Islām. Apparently the earliest literary outcome of this interest was not actually a work of his but a record of some seventy questions posed by him to the Hindu ascetic Bābā Lāl [3] and the answers given by the latter.[4] In 1065/1654–5 he completed the *Majma' al-*

---

[1] Cf. Dozy and *Ency. Isl.* under Shaṭḥ.
[2] Edition: Delhi 1309/1892°. MSS.: 'Alīgaṛh Subḥ MSS. p. 18, Āṣafīyah i p. 414 nos. 553, 685, 875, Berlin 1022, Būhār 179, Ivanow 1270, Ivanow Curzon 441 i, Lahore Panjāb Univ. (*OCM.* VIII/4 p. 42), Princeton 111, 130 (4). Urdu translation: Lahore [1921*]. Description: Qanungo i pp. 154–8.
[3] Bābā Lāl (spelt also La'l), or Lāl Dās, or Lāl Dayāl, as he is variously called in different MSS., is said by Huart and Massignon (p. 287) on the authority of the Urdu translation of the *Shaṭaḥāt*, i.e. the *Ḥasanāt al-'ārifīn*, (p. 44) to have been a Kabīr-pant'hī. Qanungo (I p. 336) doubts whether he was "a Kabirpanthi out and out". For information concerning him see H. H. Wilson's article, *Sketch of the religious sects of the Hindus*, in *Asiatic Researches* xvii (Calcutta 1832) pp. 294–8, Garcin de Tassy (mainly dependent on Wilson) i pp. 273–4, Qanungo i pp. 332–3, Garcin de Tassy *Mémoire sur les particularités de la religion musulmane dans l'Inde*, 2nd ed., Paris 1869, pp. 100–1 and Sujān Rāy *Khulāṣat al-tawārīkh* pp. 68–9 (under D'hyānpūr).
The text of these questions and answers translated from the "Hinduwī" by Chandarbhān "Barahman" (cf. p. 571 *supra*) and headed in the MSS. by various titles or quasi-titles, such as *Su'āl u jawāb i Dārā-Shukōh u Bābā Lāl*, *Jawāb u su'āl i Bābā La'l-Dās u Dārā-Shukoh*, *Nādir al-nikāt*, etc., has been published with a French translation by Cl. Huart and L. Massignon under the title *Les entretiens de Lahore* [*entre le prince impérial Dârâ Shikûh et l'ascète hindou Baba La'l Das*] in the *Journal asiatique*, tome CCIX (July–Dec. 1926) pp. 285–334. An edition (undated ?) is mentioned in the Āṣafīyah catalogue, i p. 444. For MSS., which show some differences of recension and some of which are only abstracts, see 'Alīgaṛh Subḥ. MSS. p. 14, Āṣafīyah i p. 444, Bānkīpūr xvi 1454, Bānkīpūr Suppt. ii 2267, Berlin 1081(2), Bodleian 1241(14), 1821, Brelvi-Dhabhar p. 73 no. 3, Browne Suppt. 776 (King's 14[1]), Rieu ii 841*b*, iii 1034*a*. According to Garcin de Tassy, i p. 274, there is an Urdu translation entitled *Risālah i aswilah u ajwibah i Dārā-Shukōh u Bābā Lāl*. An English translation of some extracts is given by Qanungo (i pp. 337–47).
[4] An indication of date is provided by the opening words quoted by Massignon (*op. cit.* p. 333) from a MS. acquired by W. Ivanow in 1926. According to Massignon they run as follows: *Su'ālāt i Dārā-Shukōh i shāh-zādah jawāb i Gōsā'īn* [sic lege] *Bābā Lāl sākin i KYTL* [read *Kait'hal ?*] *MḤRĀN* [read *Muḥarrirān ?*] *Ray Chandarbhān i Barahman munshī i shāh-zādah sih sih* [dittographed ?] *rūz dū* [read *dar ?*] *majlis shudah u sābiq Rāy Jādau Dās dar bayāḍ i khāṣṣ nawishtah būdand dar NYWLĀ* [read certainly *dar-īn-wilā*] *ba'd i fatḥ i Qandahār bāz ittifāq uftād.*

baḥrain,[1] in the preface [2] to which he says that in his intercourse with Hindu *faqīrs* he had ascertained that their divergence from the Ṣūfīs was merely verbal and that he had written the work with the object of reconciling the two systems. In 1067/1657 was completed at Delhi after six months' labour the *Sirr i akbar* or *Sirr al-asrār*, a translation of 50 [3] or 52 [4] Upanishads undertaken by Dārā-Shukōh with the help of some pandits of Benares.[5] These works were congenial to him because "although he had perused the Pentateuch, the Gospels, the Psalms, and other sacred books, he had nowhere found the doctrine of Tauḥīd, or Pantheism, explicitly taught, but in the Beds (Vedas) and more especially in the Upnikhats (Upanishads), which contain their essence".[6] Another work, the *Ṭarīqat al-ḥaqīqah*, described by Edwards as a tract in prose and verse on the Vēdānta philosophy, was published at Gūjrānwālah in [1895°*]. An Urdu translation by Aḥmad 'Alī Batālawī appeared at Lahore in [1923*]. A translation of the *Yōgavāsishṭ'ha* (*Tarjamah i Jōg Bāshisht*) made in 1066/1655–6 (by a certain Ḥabīb Allāh according to Ethé 2927) under the auspices of Dārā-Shukōh

[1] Edition with English translation: *Majma'-ul-baḥrain; or, The mingling of the two oceans . . . Edited . . . with English translation, notes and variants by M. Mahfuz-ul-Haq*, Calcutta 1929* (Bibliotheca Indica). MSS.: Āṣafīyah i p. 472, Aumer 351 (1), Bānkīpūr xvi 1452, Bodleian 1241 (13), 1820–1, Brelvi-Dhabhar p. x no. 9, Eton 36, Ivanow Curzon 681, Rieu ii 828*a*, 841*b*. Description: Qanungo pp. 143–6. Arabic translation: *Tarjamah i Majma' al-baḥrain* written before 1185/1771 by M. Ṣāliḥ b. al-Shaikh Aḥmad al-Miṣrī: Būhār Arab. Cat. 133.

[2] This preface occurs in one of the two B.M. MSS.

[3] So Rieu.

[4] So Qanungo i p. 147, Ivanow-Curzon 678.

[5] MSS.: Āṣafīyah ii p. 1540 nos. 1, 2, 52, Bānkīpūr xvi 1453, Bānkīpūr Suppt. ii 2083, Berlin 1077(2), Blochet I 216–17, Bodleian 1329–31, Būhār 107, Ethé 1976–82, Ivanow 1708, 1714(4), Ivanow-Curzon 678–9, Ivanow 2nd Suppt. 1093, Lindesiana p. 131 no. 340, Princeton 145, Rieu i 54–55*a*, ii 841*b*. Edition: *Sirr i akbar*, Benares 1909* (Pt. 1 (15 Upanishads) only. Ed. Brij Mōhan Lāl). Latin translation: *Oupnek'hat (id est, Secretum Tegendum): opus ipsa in India rarissimum, . . . ad verbum, e persico idiomate, samskreticis vocabulis intermixto, in latinum conversum . . . : studio et opera Anquetil Duperron*, Strasbourg 1801–2°*. German translation: *Das Oupnek'hat . . . Aus der sanskrit-persischen Uebersetzung des Fürsten Mohammed Daraschekoh in das Lateinische von Anquetil Duperron, in das Deutsche übertragen von F. Mischel*, Dresden 1882°. Descriptions: (1) *The unpublished translation of the Upanishads by Prince Dara Shukoh*, by Mahesh Das (in *Dr. Modi Memorial Volume*, Bombay 1930, pp. 622–38), (2) Qanungo i pp. 147–54.

[6] Rieu i p. 54, from Dārā-Shukōh's preface.

is preserved in several MSS.[1] There is also a translation of the *Bhagavad-gītā*, called in some MSS. by the title *Āb i zindagī*,[2] which is ascribed on very doubtful authority [3] to Dārā-Shukōh. According to Qanungo (i p. 139) the *Gulzār i ḥāl*, Walī Rām's translation of the *Prabōd'ha-chandrōdaya* (see p. 451 *supra*), was written " for the use of Dara Shukoh ". No authority is cited for this statement. In any case the *Gulzār i ḥāl* was not completed until 1073/1662–3, i.e. more than three years after Dārā-Shukōh's death.

Dārā-Shukōh wrote poetry in which he used the *takhallus* " Qādirī ". His *dīwān* is mentioned by " Sarkhwush ", who describes it as short, and also by Kishan Chand " Ikhlāṣ ". Ghulām-Sarwar Lāhaurī had seen a copy of it (*Khazīnat al-aṣfiyā'* i p. 174[15]), but it is now extremely rare.[4] Finally it may be noted that Dārā-Shukōh was a calligraphist. Two pages from an autograph MS. of his *Safīnat al-auliyā'* are reproduced in *OCM*. x/3, where they face p. 114, and other specimens of his writing are in existence.[5]

(1) ***Safīnat al-auliyā'***, completed on 27 Ramaḍān 1049/21 Jan. 1640 and devoted to short notices [6] of holy men, namely the Prophet (p. 17), the first three Caliphs (p. 19), the Twelve Imāms (p. 22), Salmān Fārisī (p. 30), Uwais Qaranī (p. 30), Ḥasan Baṣrī (p. 31), Qāsim b. M. b. Abī Bakr (p. 31), the four Imāms (Abū Ḥanīfah, etc., p. 32), Abū Yūsuf (p. 34), M. Shaibānī

[1] Bānkīpūr Suppt, ii 2080, Berlin 1077(1), Browne Pers. Cat. 35(2), Ethé 1972–4, 2927, Ross-Browne 194, Ivanow 1700, Ivanow-Curzon 680. Cf. Qanungo i pp. 159–60.

[2] Ethé 1949, Ivanow 1707, Rieu i 59*a*.

[3] To quote Ethé's words " In the British Mus. copy it is wrongly ascribed to Abû-alfaḍl ; the real translator was, as a note on fol. 1*a* in the present copy proves [!], prince Dârâ Shukûh ".

[4] The only copy traceable at present belongs to the private library of Khān Bahādur Maulawī Ẓafar Ḥasan, Superintendent, Archæological Survey, Northern Circle, Āgrah, who has published a description of it under the title *Manuscript copy of the Dīwān of Dārā Shikūh* in the *JRASB*., Letters, Vol. V, 1939, pp. 155–73. The statement of Massignon (*Textes inédits* i p. 256) that " Le dîwân de Dârâ Shikouh est à Londres (MS. Or. 9492) " is incorrect. The B.M. MS. Or. 9492 is the *dīwān* of " Dārā ", a poet of Fatḥ-'Alī Shāh's time. Dārā-Shukōh's *takhallus* was not " Dārā ", but " Qādirī ".

[5] On p. 172 of the article referred to in the preceding note Ẓafar Ḥasan speaks of " the specimens of his writing, still available ". Cf. p. 997[21] *infra*.

[6] Particularly valuable on account of " a comparative strictness in the chronological order and the full dates they give " (Ethé).

(p. 34), *shaikhs* of the QĀDIRĪ (previously Junaidī) order[1] (pp. 35–73, nos. 27–65[2]) from Ma'rūf Karkhī (d. 200/815) to Miyāṅ Mīr (d. 1045/1635), Khwājahs, i.e. NAQSHBANDĪS (previously Ṭaifūrīs) (pp. 73–85, nos. 66–94) from Abū Yazīd Bisṭāmī (d. 261/875) to Ṣāliḥ Khwājah Dahbīdī (d. 1048/1638 at Balkh), CHISHTĪS (pp. 86–102, nos. 95–119) from Khwājah 'Abd al-Wāḥid [b.] Zaid (d. 177/793) to Sh. Jalāl T'hānēsarī (d. 989/1582. Cf. p. 17 *supra*), KUBRAWĪS (pp. 102–9, nos. 120–39) from Abū Bakr Nassāj to Sulṭān Walad (d. 712/1312), SUHRAWARDĪS (pp. 110–19, nos. 140–59) from Mimshād Dīnawarī (d. 299/911–12) to Shāh-'Ālam (d. 880/1475 at Aḥmadābād[3]), miscellaneous *shaikhs* (*mashāyikh i mutafarriqah*, pp. 119–99, nos. 160–377) from Mālik [b.] Dīnār (d. 137/754–5) to Sh. Bilāwal Lāhaurī (d. 1046/1637), and holy women (pp. 199–216, nos. 378–411), i.e. the wives and daughters of the Prophet and some female saints from Zā'idah, 'Umar's slave-girl, to Bībī Jamāl Khātūn, Miyāṅ Mīr's sister, who was still alive in 1049 at the time of writing[4]: **Lahore** private library of Dīwān Anand Kumār, Reader in Biology in the Panjāb University (an autograph described by M. Shafī' in *OCM*. x/3 (May 1934) pp. 109–15), **Bānkīpūr** viii 673 (revised and corrected by the author), 674 (A.H. 1108/1697), **Lindesiana** p. 131 no. 164 (A.H. 1063/1652–3), no. 193 (A.D. 1701), **Rieu** i 356*b* (17th cent.), iii 976*b* (extracts only. *Circ.* A.D. 1850), **Blochet** i 432 (17th cent.), **Ethé** 647 (17th cent.), 648 (A.H. 1120/1709), 649 (A.H. 1179/1765), **Ross and Browne** 124 (A.H. 1151/1738–9), **I.O.** D.P. 666 (A.H. 1151/1739), **Āṣafīyah** i p. 320 no. 24 (4th yr. of Farrukh-siyar /1127–8/1715–16), no. 101 (A.H. 1113/1701–2), iii p. 164 no. 118, **Ivanow** 262 (A.H. 1137/1724–5 ?), **Rehatsek** p. 203 no. 54 (A.H. 1143/1730–1),

[1] At the end of the notice of Shāh Madār (no. 358, p. 188 = *OCM*. x/3 p. 115) the author says that of the people of India [i.e. presumably of those who belonged to Ṣūfī orders] half, mostly from the upper classes (*ashrāf*), were followers (*murīd*) of 'Abd al-Qādir, a quarter, mostly from the lower classes (*ajlāf*), followed Shāh Madār (see p. **1006** n. **2** *infra*), an eighth followed Mu'īn al-Dīn Chishtī (see p. **943** n. **3** *supra*) and an eighth Bahā' al-Dīn Zakarīyā' (see p. **970** n. **7** *supra*).

[2] These are the numbers assigned to the notices in Ethé's description of the I.O. MS. Ethé 647. In the Nawal Kishōr editions the notices are not numbered.

[3] Cf. *Mir'āt i Aḥmadī, khātimah* pp. 37–8, English trans. pp. 35–6.

[4] She died in 1057 (see p. **998** n. **4** *infra*).

Lahore Panjab Univ. Lib. (2 copies dated A.H. 1153/1740 and Samwat 1896), **Berlin** 17 (1), 576 (3).

List and epitome of the biographies: Ethé coll. 274–315.

Editions: **Āgrah** 1269/1853*, **Lucknow** 1872°, **Cawnpore** 1884†‡, 1318/1900°.

(2) *Sakīnat al-auliyā'*, an account of the great saint of Lahore, Miyāṅ, or Mīyāṅ [1], Mīr [2] and some of his disciples, especially Mullā Shāh,[3] completed in 1052/1642–3 [4]: **Bānkīpūr** viii 675 (18th cent.), **Ivanow** Curzon 73 (18th cent.), **Rieu** i 357 (A.H. 1276/1859).

[1] This Hindī word, meaning "lord" or "master", is a title of respect and not a part of the saint's name.

[2] Miyāṅ Mīr, or Shāh Mīr, whose real name was Mīr Muḥammad (*Sakīnat al-auliyā'*, Urdu trans., p. 19, '*Amal i Ṣāliḥ* iii p. 363 ult.), or Muḥammad Mīr (*Khazīnat al-aṣfiyā'* i p. 154[4]: *Shaikh M. Mīr al-mashhūr bi-Miyān-Mīr Bālā Pīr Qādirī Lāhaurī*), was a Fārūqī (not a Saiyid apparently) and was born at Sīwistān (i.e. Sehwan, in Sind) in 938/1531–2 (*Sakīnah*, Urdu trans., p. 19 ult.), or 957/1550 (*Safīnah* p. 70[10]), or 975/1567–8 (*Sakīnah*, Urdu trans., p. 75 ult.). He settled in Lahore (at the age of twenty-five according to *Khazīnah* i p. 154[14]) and had been living there for more than sixty years when he died on the 7th (*Safīnah* p. 72[19]), or the 17th (*Sakīnah*, Urdu trans., p. 74 ult.) of Rabī' I 1045/21st or 31st August, 1635 (so both *Safīnah* and *Sakīnah*) or in 1044/1634–5 (*Pādshāh-nāmah* i, 2, p. 331[1], '*Amal i Ṣāliḥ* iii p. 366[10]). His tomb to the east of Lahore at the place now called Miyāṅ Mīr is close to the military cantonment. The *jī* or *jīw* sometimes appended to the word Miyāṅ is a Hindī affix indicative of respect. See *Tūzuk i Jahāngīrī* p. 286 antepenult., Rogers and Beveridge's trans. ii p. 119; *Safīnat al-auliyā'* pp. 70–3 (no. 65); *Pādshāh-nāmah* i, 2, pp. 329–31; '*Amal i Ṣāliḥ* iii pp. 363–6; *Khazīnat al-aṣfiyā'* i pp. 154–60; Rieu i p. 358*a*; Beale *Oriental biographical dictionary* under Shāh Mīr (the *Ḍiyā' al-'uyūn*, however, is by Shāh Mīrzā (for whom see p. 54 *supra*), not Shāh Mīr); *Ency. Isl.* under Mīrāndjī (*sic* ?) (Hidayet Hosain).

[3] See p. 1009 n. 2 *infra*.

[4] This date occurs at the end of the preface (Urdu trans. p. 6[10]). At the beginning of the account of Bībī Jamāl Khātūn, the saint's sister, (Urdu trans. p. 101[4]) 1050 is mentioned as the current year. Two or three dates are later insertions. Thus the notice of Sh. 'Abd al-Wāḥid, which speaks of him in the present tense, ends with a statement that he died in 1056 (Urdu trans. p. 170[12]). Similarly Bībī Jamāl Khātūn, who is described as "now, in 1050, alive and well" (Urdu trans. p. 101[4]), is said to have died on Tuesday, 27 Rabī' I 1057 "after the writing of this book" (Urdu trans. p. 102 penult.). A reference to the *Safīnat al-auliyā'* occurs in the chapter headed *Bayān i faḍīlat i silsilah i Qādirīyah* (Urdu trans. p. 12[6]). Curiously enough the *Safīnat al-auliyā'* contains a reference (inserted either subsequently or in anticipation of a future event) to the *Sakīnat al-auliyā'*. It comes near the end of the notice of Miyāṅ Mīr and in the autograph described by M. Shafī' it runs as follows: *Chūn ba'd az-īn risāla'ī dar bayān i aḥwāl u auḍā' i ān-ḥaḍrat u pīr u murīdān i īshān nawishtah shud dar-īn kitāb ba-hamīn qadr iktifā numūd* (*OCM*. x/3 p. 111[11]). In the Nawal Kishōr text (p. 72[17]) *pīsh az-īn* takes the place of *ba'd az-īn*, and *risāla'ī* is expanded into *risāla'ī musammā ba-Sakīnat al-auliyā*.

Urdū translation [1]: *Urdū tarjamah i kitāb i Sakīnat al-auliyā'*, **Lahore** [*circ.* 1920 ?‡].

[Autobiographical statements (relating mainly to meetings with Ṣūfīs and visits to graves) in the *Safīnat al-auliyā'* (collected by M. Shafī' in *OCM.* x/3 pp. 110–15) and the *Sakīnat al-auliyā'*; other autobiographical statements in the preface to the *Sirr i akbar*; Manucci *Storia do Mogor*, tr. W. Irvine, i pp. 221–7, etc.; the travels of Bernier, Tavernier, etc.; contemporary and later histories of India; *Kalimāt al-shu'arā'* (Sprenger p. 113); *Hamīshah bahār* (Sprenger p. 128); *Ṣuḥuf i Ibrāhīm*; *Makhzan al-gharā'ib* no. 2083; *Tadhkirah i khwush-nawīsān* p. 54; *Riyāḍ al-'ārifīn* pp. 208–9; *Khazīnat al-aṣfiyā'* i pp. 174–5; Elliot and Dowson *History of India* vii pp. 220–32, 236–41, 242–6 (extracts from the *Muntakhab al-lubāb*); *Facsimiles of several Autographs of Jahángír, Sháhjahán, and Prince Dárá Shikoh, together with Notes on the Literary Character and the Capture and Death of Dárá Shikoh.—By H. Blochmann* (in *JASB.* xxxix, pt. 1 (1870) pp. 271–9); Beale *Oriental biographical dictionary* under Dara Shikoh; *Ency. Isl.* under Dārā Shikōh (H. Beveridge); *Dārā Shikoh as an author*, by Pandit Sheo Narain (in *Journal of the Panjab Historical Society*, ii (1913–14) pp. 21–38); *Court painters of the Grand Moguls*, by L. Binyon and T. W. Arnold, London 1921, pp. 25–29 and plates xx–xxii; *Un essai de bloc islamo-hindou au XVIIe siècle: l'humanisme mystique du prince Dârâ*, by L. Massignon and A. M. Kassim (in *Revue du monde musulman* lxiii (1926) pp. 1–14); *L'Inde mystique au moyen âge*, by Yūsuf Ḥusain, Paris 1929, last chapter; *Dara Shukoh. Vol. I. Biography.* [By] *Kalika-Ranjan Qanungo*, Calcutta [1935]. For portraits of Dārā-Shukōh see *Indische historische Porträts* by H. Goetz (in *Asia Major* ii (1925)) p. 238; *Court painters of the Grand Moguls* by Binyon and Arnold, plates xx–xxii; Rieu ii 780*b*, 781*b*, 785*b*; Ethé 1980 (?); etc.]

1322. **Jahān-ārā** Bēgam, sometimes called simply Begam Ṣāḥib[2] or Bēgam Ṣāḥibah [3] by contemporary historians, was the

[1] I have failed to trace an edition of the Persian text.
[2] e.g. *Pādshāh-nāmah* i, 1, p. 178[4], [7], *'Amal i Ṣāliḥ* i p. 80[13].
[3] Cf. *Ma'āthir al-umarā'* i p. 10[4].

second child of Shāh-Jahān and Mumtāz-Maḥall. She was born on 21 Ṣafar 1023/23 March 1614, almost exactly a year before her eldest brother, Dārā-Shukōh (for whom see pp. 992–9 *supra*). Devoted to her father, whom she attended in his captivity, and also to Dārā-Shukōh, she shared the latter's interest in Ṣūfism, and was initiated into the Qādirī order by his *pīr*, Mullā Shāh,[1] early in 1050/1650, when she and her father were on a visit to Kashmīr (*OCM.* xiii/4 (Aug. 1937) pp. 14–15). "Shāh's" opinion of her (" She has attained to so extraordinary a development of mystical knowledge that she is worthy of being my representative ") and her description of one of her own mystical experiences are quoted (from the *Nuskhah i aḥwāl i Shāhī*) by Macdonald in *The religious attitude and life in Islam*, p. 205,[2] and thence by Qanungo in *Dara Shukoh*, i pp. 351–2. In spite of her Qādirī connections she had a fondness for the Chishtī order [3]: in the preface to the *Mu'nis al-arwāḥ* she calls herself a votary (*murīdah*) of Mu'īn al-Dīn Chishtī and on her tomb she is described as a disciple of the saints of Chisht. She died unmarried in Ramaḍān 1092/1681 and was buried at Delhi in a tomb built by herself,[4] and still standing, to the south of the tomb of Niẓām al-Dīn Auliyā (for whom see p. 941 n. 5 *supra*). "The events of Jahánárá's life, such as they are, have suffered on the one hand from sentiment which adorns her 'with every virtue that a woman possesses'; and on the other by the court-tattle of Bernier which I need not repeat here." [5]

(1) ***Mu'nis al-arwāḥ***, a biography of Mu'īn al-Dīn Chishtī,[6] with notices of some of his disciples, completed in 1049/1640: **Brit. Mus.** (a MS. presented by W. Irvine, who

[1] See p. 18 *supra*, p. 1009 *infra*, and Additions and Corrections.

[2] As Qanungo points out, Macdonald (or rather von Kremer, since the former is only quoting the latter) calls her Fāṭimah through a misunderstanding of the complimentary title Fāṭimat al-Zamānī.

[3] Doubtless because Mu'īn al-Dīn Chishtī was (to quote Qanungo *Dara Shukoh* p. 104) " the patron saint of the house of Akbar ".

[4] For this tomb see S. Aḥmad Khān *Āthār al-ṣanādīd* (in Urdu), Delhi 1853, *Bāb* 3, p. 73; *The Indian antiquary* ii p. 120; Carr Stephen *The archæology . . . of Delhi* p. 108; etc.

[5] Carr Stephen *loc. cit.* For Peter Mundy's accusation against her see *The Indian antiquary* xliv pp. 24, 211.

[6] For whom see p. 943 n. 3 *supra*.

believed it to be an autograph),[1] **Rieu** i 357*b* (17th cent.), 357*a* (18th cent.), **Āṣafīyah** i p. 492 no. 770 (A.H. 1198/1783–4), no. 237 (A.H. 1320/1902–3), **Ivanow** Curzon 74 (18th cent.), **Bodleian** 372, **Eton** 38, **Lahore** Panjāb Univ. (see *OCM.* III/1 (Nov. 1926) p. 73).

Urdu translation[2] : **Lahore** [1908*].

(2) *Ṣāḥibīyah*, an account of Mullā S͟hāh (see p. 1009 n. 2 *infra*) written (completed ?) on 27 Ramaḍān 1051/30 December 1641 : **Aḥmadābād** Āpā-Rāō Bhōlā-Nāt'h Library (19 foll.).

Description and Urdu summary : *Jahān-ārā Bēgam kī ēk g͟hair-ma'rūf taṣnīf : Ṣāḥibīyah*, by M. Ibrāhīm (in *OCM.* xiii/4 (Aug. 1937) pp. 3–19).

[Autobiographical statements (relating almost entirely to the years 1049–50 and especially to her connexions with Mullā S͟hāh) at the end of the *Ṣāḥibīyah ; Pāds͟hāh-nāmah* i, 1, p. 94 and elsewhere ; *'Amal i Ṣāliḥ* i p. 80 and elsewhere ; *Ma'āt͟hir i 'Ālamgīrī* p. 213 ; N. Manucci *Storia do Mogor*, tr. W. Irvine, vol. i, London 1907, p. 217 (see also index) ; Carr Stephen *The archaeology and monumental remains of Delhi*, Ludhiana and Calcutta [1876] pp. 108–9 ; Rieu i 357 ; Beale *Oriental biographical dictionary*, 2nd ed., under Jahan Ara Begam ; *Jahān-ārā* (in Urdu), by Maḥbūb al-Raḥmān " Kalīm ", 'Alīgaṛh 1907* and 2nd ed. [1918*] ; *Persian letters from Jahān Arā, daughter of Shāh Jahān, . . . to Raja Budh Parkash of Sirmur*, by H. A. Rose (in *JASB.* 1911 pp. 449–78) ; *Ency. Isl.* under D͟jahānārā Bēgam (H. Beveridge) ; *Jahānārā*, by G. Yazdani (in *Journal of the Panjab Historical Society* ii/2 (Calcutta 1914) pp. 152–69, where many references are given) ; K. R. Qanungo *Dara Shukoh*, vol. i, biography, Calcutta [1935], p. 10 and elsewhere ; the afore-mentioned article by M. Ibrāhīm].

1323. S͟haik͟h **Badr al-Dīn** b. Ibrāhīm **Sihrindī** became a disciple of the great saint Aḥmad Sihrindī (for whom see p. 988 n. 5

[1] See Manucci *Storia do Mogor*, tr. W. Irvine, iv p. 423. According to M. Ibrāhīm (*OCM.* xiii/4 (Aug., 1937) p. 3 footnote) there is an autograph MS. of this work in the Lucknow [Public ?] Library.

[2] I have failed to trace an edition of the Persian text, although according to Ivanow the work " has been repeatedly lithographed in India, in the original Persian and in Hindustani translations ".

supra) in 1018/1609–10, remained in close association with him for seventeen years, and was present when he was washed after death. Among works of his own that he mentions are (1) *Wiṣāl i Aḥmadī*, on some miracles which occurred just before and after the saint's death, (2) *Karāmāt al-auliyā'*, in support of the belief that saints can perform miracles after death, (3) *Majma' al-auliyā'*,[1] biographies of 1,500 saints completed in 1044/1634–5, (4) a Persian translation of the *Futūḥ al-ghaib* of 'Abd al-Qādir al-Jīlānī, (5) *Maqāmāt i Ghauth al-thaqalain*, a Persian translation of the *Bahjat al-asrār*, a life of 'Abd al-Qādir by 'Alī b. Yūsuf al-Shaṭṭanūfī (see p. 933 *supra*), (6) a Persian translation of another life of 'Abd al-Qādir entitled *Rauḍat al-nawāẓir*, i.e. presumably the *Rauḍat al-nāẓir*, which Ḥ. Kh. ascribes to al-Fīrūzābādī (see Ahlwardt 10080–1, Brockelmann ii, p. 119, l. 2), (7) an unfinished Persian translation of the *'Arā'is al-bayān fī ḥaqā'iq al-Qur'ān*, a Ṣūfī *tafsīr* by Rūzbihān al-Baqlī (for which see Brockelmann i 414, *Sptbd.* i 735; *Catalogue of the Arabic MSS. in the Library of the India Office*, vol. ii, no. 1106). The last three were undertaken at the request of Sulṭān M. Dārā-Shukōh.

(1) **Sanawāt al-atqiyā'**, very brief biographies of distinguished persons, with special reference to the dates of their death, from the time of Adam to 1044/1634–5: **I.O.** D.P. 672 (A.H. 1085/1674).

(2) **Ḥaḍarāt al-quds**, biographies of Naqshbandī saints in two *daftars*, of which the first in one *ḥadrat* begins with Abū Bakr al-Ṣiddīq and ends with M. Bāqī (for whom see p. 989 n. 1 *supra*) and the second deals in *Ḥaḍarāt* ii–xii with Aḥmad Sihrindī, his life, sayings, miracles, children and disciples, completed not earlier than 1053/1643, since Ādam Banūrī's death, which occurred in that year (cf. p. 991 n. 3 *supra*), is mentioned: **I.O.** D.P. 630 (*Daftar* ii only. 17th cent.), **Tashkent Univ.** 70 (*Daftar* ii. A.H. 1248/1832), 70-*a* (*Daftar* ii apparently. A.H. 1257/1841).

[1] For a work of this title containing about the same number of biographies and completed in 1043/1633–4 by Mīr 'Alī Akbar Ḥusainī Ardistānī see p. 991 *supra*.

Urdu translation: by Khwājah Aḥmad Ḥusain Khān, **Lahore** 1923*].

1324. Probably soon after 1054/1644–5, the latest date mentioned in the work, an anonymous disciple wrote—

Fātiḥ al-qulūb, an account (32 foll.) of the life and miracles of the saint, calligrapher and poet Mīr 'Abd Allāh "Waṣfī" b. Mīr Muẓaffar Ḥusainī Tirmidhī, who received from Akbar or Jahāngīr the title of *Mushkīn-qalam* and who died in 1025/1616 or 1035/1626 [1]: **Ethé** 650.

1325. **Ilāh-diyah,**[2] or Allāh-diyah, b. Sh. 'Abd al-Raḥīm b. Sh. Bīnā Ḥakīm **Chishtī** 'Uthmānī, a descendant of Sh. Jalāl al-Dīn Pānīpatī,[3] was a disciple of Shāh A'lā Pānīpatī [4] and lived at Kairānah,[5] near Pānīpat. His grandfather, Sh. Bīnā, or Bhīnā,[6] was a noted surgeon of Akbar's time, and his paternal uncle, Muqarrab Khān,[7] Jahāngīr's surgeon and friend (cf. p. 196 *supra*), was Governor of Gujrāt, Bihār and Āgrah in Jahāngīr's reign and on his retirement in Shāh-Jahān's reign was given the *parganah* of Kairānah, his birthplace, as a *jāgīr*. Ilāh-diyah and his two brothers, Sh. Qāsim and Sh. Fuḍail, took part in Shāh-Jahān's march towards Kābul.

[1] See Badā'ūnī iii pp. 383–4 (cf. Sprenger p. 65); *Ā'īn i Akbarī* p. 115[5] (merely the name Mīr 'Abd Allāh in a list of calligraphists), Blochmann's trans. p. 103[7]; *Ṣuḥuf i Ibrāhīm*; *Makhzan al-gharā'ib* no. 2951; Rieu i p. 154; Beale *Oriental biographical dictionary* under 'Abdullah Tirmizi. For his son M. Ṣāliḥ "Kashfī" see pp. 214–15 *supra*.

[2] *diyah* (or *diyā*, as it is usually written) is a Hindī word meaning "given".

[3] d. 765/1363. See *Siyar al-aqṭāb*; *Mir'āt al-asrār, ṭabaqah* 22; *Sawāṭi' al-anwār* no. 26; *Khazīnat al-aṣfiyā'* i pp. 361–5.

[4] d. 1033/1624. See *Siyar al-aqṭāb* (last biography: summarized by Rieu, i p. 359*a*); *Khazīnat al-aṣfiyā'* i pp. 459–61.

[5] Kairānah, now in the Muẓaffarnagar District of the United Provinces, is about twenty miles east of Pānīpat, which is in the Karnāl District of the Panjāb. Muqarrab Khān "built many edifices" in Kairānah, "and laid out a beautiful garden with an immense tank" (*Ā'īn i Akbarī*, tr. Blochmann p. 544[1]). He also "constructed a mausoleum near the tomb of the renowned Saint Sharafuddín of Pánípat" (*op. cit.* p. 543 penult.).

[6] See Badā'ūnī *Muntakhab al-tawārīkh* iii p. 169; *Ā'īn i Akbarī* p. 234[11] (merely his name in the list of physicians), Blochmann's trans. p. 543.

[7] Ḥakīm Sh. Ḥasan, d. at Kairānah in 1056/1646, aged ninety. See *Memoirs of Jahāngīr*, tr. Rogers and Beveridge, p. 27 and elsewhere (see index); *Ma'āthir al-umarā'* iii pp. 379–81; *Ā'īn i Akbarī* tr. Blochmann pp. 543–4; Rieu iii p. 1086*a*, l. 3.

Siyar al-aqṭāb, begun in 1036/1626–7 completed in 1056/1646–7 and devoted to the lives of twenty-seven persons from 'Alī b. Abī Ṭālib to Shāh A'lā Pānīpatī, who form the author's spiritual pedigree and each of whom, according to the Chishtīs, became Quṭb al-aqṭāb: **Rieu** i 358*b* (17th cent.), **I.O.** D.P. 669 (A.H. 1019/1610 [!], perhaps a mistake for 1119/1707), **'Alīgaṛh** Subḥ. MSS. p. 60 no. 15 (A.D. 1867).

Editions: **Lucknow** 1877°*, 1881†, 1889†.

List of the saints: Rieu i p. 359.

1326. Abū 'l-'Abbās **M. Ṭālib.**

Maṭlab al-ṭālibīn, a history of the Jūybārī *shaikhs* written about 1056/1646: **Tashkent** A. A. Semenov's private library (A.H. 1235/1819–20. See Semenov *Kurzer Abriss* p. 6).

1327. In 1060/1650 was written—

Ḥikāyat[1] *al-ṣāliḥīn*, anecdotes of famous saints, stated to be a translation from the Arabic: **Browne** Suppt. 407 (A.H. 1217/1802–3. Corpus 228[6]), **Blochet** iv 2134 (A.H. 1228/1813).

1328. Mīr **Muḥammad Fāḍil,** called (*al-mad'ū bi-*) Maẓhar al-Ḥaqq, b. S. Aḥmad b. S. Ḥasan al-Ḥusainī al-Tirmidhī **al-Akbarābādī** died in Rabī' ii A.H. 1106/Nov.-Dec. 1694 (according to the chronograms given by his nephew at the end of the *Mukhbir al-wāṣilīn*). One of the opening sections of the *Mukhbir al-wāṣilīn* is in praise of Shāh-Jahān, who was on the throne when he began the work.

Mukhbir al-wāṣilīn (a chronogram = 1060/1650, the date of inception), a series of chronogrammatic poems containing the dates of the death of the Prophet, the first four Caliphs, the Twelve Imāms, numerous saints and a few other persons from the first century of Islām to A.H. 1105/1693–4 (often with the place of burial but usually little else except laudatory phrases): **Āṣafīyah** i p. 252 no. 756 (A.H. 1140/1727–8), no. 405, **Ivanow** 759 (A.H. 1151/1738–9), **Ivanow** Curzon 268 (19th cent.), **'Alīgaṛh** Subḥ. MSS. p. 16 no. 83, **Rieu** iii 1035*b* (extracts only. *Circ.* A.D. 1850).

[1] In the singular, not *Ḥikāyāt*.

Editions : **Calcutta** 1249/1833–4*, **Lucknow** (Muṣṭafā'ī Press) 1265/1849 (see Sprenger p. 489).

1329. **'Abd al-Raḥmān** b. 'Abd al-Rasūl b. Qāsim b. S͟hāh Bud'h 'Abbāsī 'Alawī **C͟his͟htī** was a descendant of the saint Aḥmad 'Abd al-Ḥaqq Rudaulawī,[1] and succeeded in 1032/1622, on his brother's death, to the headship of a local branch of the C͟his͟htī order at Rudaulī.[2] According to the *Mir'āt al-'ālam*, the author of which was a personal acquaintance, he lived at D'hanītī,[3] a village in the *sarkār* of Lucknow, and died there in 1094/1683 (see Rieu iii p. 973*a*). Among his works were (1) *Mir'āt al-mak͟hlūqāt*, a translation and Islamising explanation, written in 1041/1631–2, of a Sanskrit verse treatise on Hindu cosmogony in the form of a dialogue between Mahādēv and Pārbatī handed down by the Munī Bās͟his͟ht (Vāsishṭ'ha) (MSS. : Rieu iii 1034*a*, Āṣafīyah ii p. 1386, Bodleian 1823), (2) *Mir'āt al-ḥaqā'iq*, an abridged translation and Islamising explanation of the *Bhagavad-gītā* (MSS. : Rieu iii 1034*b*, Bombay Univ. p. 134, Āṣafīyah ii p. 1356), (3) *Nafas i Raḥmānī* (Edition : place ? 1307/1889–90. See Āṣafīyah i p. 494), (4) *Aurād i C͟his͟htīyah* (MS. : Āṣafīyah iii p. 24),

(5) *Mir'āt al-asrār*, biographies of numerous saints from the early days of Islām to Ḥusām al-Dīn Mānikpūrī (d. 853/1449), begun in 1045/1635–6, completed in 1065/1654 and divided into a preface (on Ṣūfism, the degrees of spiritual knowledge, the origin and contents of the work), a *muqaddimah* (on the *k͟hirqah i k͟hilāfat*, the four Pīrs, Ḥasan, Ḥusain, Kumail, Ḥasan Baṣrī, the fourteen *k͟hānawādahs*, and twelve of the forty derivative orders or *silsilahs*) and twenty-three *ṭabaqāt* devoted to successive generations of *s͟haik͟hs* : **Ivanow** 264 (A.H. 1088/1677–8), **Lindesiana** p. 118 no. 196 (*circ.* A.D. 1750), **Rieu** i 359*b* (A.H. 1189/1775), iii 973*b* (extracts only. *Circ.* A.D. 1850), **Bānkīpūr** viii 676 (A.H. 1220/1806), Suppt. ii 2074 (*Muqaddimah* only. 19th cent.), **Būhār** 89 (probably transcribed from Bānkīpūr viii 676. B.S. 1301/1894), **Āṣafīyah** iii p. 166 no. 167 (A.H. 1309/1891–2).

[1] See p. 968 n. 2 *supra*.
[2] Thirty-eight miles from Bārā Bankī in Oudh.
[3] Not confirmed.

List and epitome of the biographies : Bānkīpūr viii pp. 55–63.

(6) *Mir'āt i Madārī*, a life of the saint of Makanpūr,[1] Badī' al-Dīn surnamed Quṭb al-Madār and commonly called Shāh Madār,[2] written in 1064/1654 at Makanpūr and based mainly on the *Īmān i Maḥmūdī*, a biography by the saint's *khalīfah*, Qāḍī Maḥmūd Kintūrī,[3] and the *Laṭā'if i Ashrafī* (see Rieu iii 1042*a*, Ivanow 1214, etc.), whose author was a friend of Shāh Madār's : **Ivanow** 263 (A.H. 1146/1733–4), **Rieu** i 361*a* (18th cent.), iii 973*a* (19th cent.), **Bānkīpūr** viii 677 (18th cent.), **I.O.** D.P. 657(*c*), **Būhār** 88 (transcribed from the Bānkīpūr MS. in 1304/1886).

Urdū translation : *Thawāqib al-anwār li-maṭāli' Quṭb al-Madār*, by M. 'Abd al-Rashīd Ẓuhūr al-Islām, **Farrukhābād** 1328/1910*.

(7) *Mir'āt i Mas'ūdī*, a life of the legendary hero and martyr Sulṭān al-Shuhadā' Sālār Mas'ūd Ghāzī,[4] said to be based on a contemporary history by Mullā M. Ghaznawī, a

[1] A village 8 miles N.W. of Bilhaur and 40 miles from Cawnpore.

[2] Sh. Madār, " one of the most popular saints of India and the subject of the most fabulous legends " (Rieu), is said in the *Mir'āt i Madārī* to have been a Jew born at Aleppo in 715/1315, who visited Mecca, embraced Islām at al-Madīnah, migrated to India, and settled at Makanpūr, where he died in 840/1436 after spending thirty-five years of his life in Syria, forty at Mecca, al-Madīnah and al-Najaf and fifty in India. He was treated with great respect by Ibrāhīm Shāh Sharqī, who built his tomb. According to a pedigree quoted in the *Khazīnat al-aṣfiyā'* he was descended on his father's side from Abū Hurairah and on his mother's from 'Abd al-Raḥmān b. 'Auf (!). See *Akhbār al-akhyār* p. 164 ; *Gulzār i abrār* no. 60 ; *Kalimāt al-ṣādiqīn* no. 21 ; *Safīnat al-auliyā'* pp. 187–8 (no. 358) ; *Dabistān i madhāhib*, trans., New York 1937, p. 279 ; *Khazīnat al-aṣfiyā'* ii pp. 310–12 ; *Ā'īn i Akbarī*, tr. Jarrett, iii p. 370 ; Garcin de Tassy *Mémoire sur . . . la religion musulmane dans l'Inde* (2nd ed. Paris 1869) pp. 52–9 ; S. M. Amīr Ḥasan *Tadhkirat al-muttaqīn* (see p. 1052 *infra*) ; *Siyar al-Madār* (in Urdu), by Ẓahīr Aḥmad " Ẓahīrī ", Pt. i Lucknow 1900, Pt. ii Badāyūn 1920 ; *Cawnpore District Gazetteer* (Allahabad 1909) pp. 309–10 ; Ja'far Sharīf *Islam in India or the Qānūn-i-Islām*, tr. G. A. Herklots, revised W. Crooke, Oxford 1921, pp. 195–6 ; Bānkīpūr Cat. viii pp. 64–66 (where the *Mir'āt i Madārī* is summarized).

[3] Kintoor (officially so spelt) is a village near Bārā Bankī.

[4] An alleged nephew of Sulṭān Maḥmūd Ghaznawī, born at Ajmēr in 405/1014 and killed in battle against the Hindu idolaters in 424/1033 at Bahrā'ich, where his tomb is a celebrated place of pilgrimage. See *Safīnat al-auliyā'* p. 160 (no. 290) ; *Mir'āt al-asrār, ṭabaqah XII* ; *Khazīnat al-aṣfiyā'* ii pp. 217–24 ; Garcin de Tassy *Mémoire sur . . . la religion musulmane dans l'Inde* (2nd Ed., Paris 1869) pp. 72–9 ; *Ghazā-nāmah i Mas'ūd* (in Urdū), by 'Ināyat-Ḥusain Bilgrāmī, Cawnpore 1293/1876°* ; Rieu iii 1015; Beale *Oriental biographical dictionary* under Masa'ud Ghazi ; Ivanow 322 ; *Ency. Isl.* under Ghāzī Miyān (Hidayat Ḥusain), where some further references will be found.

servant of Sulṭān Maḥmūd: **Ivanow** Curzon 103 (A.H. 1233/1818), **Rieu** iii 1029*a* (*circ.* A.D. 1850), **'Alīgaṛh** Subḥ. MSS. p. 59 no. 6.

Abridged English translation by B. W. Chapman: **B.M.** MS. Add. 30776.

Extracts from Chapman's translation: Elliot and Dowson *History of India* ii pp. 513–49.

Abridged Urdu translation: *Khulāṣah i tawārīkh i Mas'ūdī*, by Akbar 'Alī b. M.-Bakhsh, [**Lucknow** ?] 1288/1871°.

Abridgment by the author himself: *Qiṣṣah i Sālār Mas'ūd i Ghāzī*: **Rieu** iii 1042*b* (*circ.* A.D. 1850).

[Autobiographical statements in *Mir'āt al-asrār* (summarized by Rieu and 'Abd al-Muqtadir) and *Mir'āt i Madārī*; *Sawāṭi' al-anwār* no. 29 (Ethé col. 336[22]).]

1330. **'Alā' al-Dīn M. Chishtī Barnāwī.**[1]

Chishtīyah i bihishtīyah, or ***Firdausīyah i qudsīyah***,[2] a large work on the saints of the Chishtī order completed perhaps in 1066/1655–6, the date of Prof. Maḥmūd Shērānī's MS. (such dates as 1069/1658–9, 1071/1660–1 and 1076/1665–6, which occur in Ivanow-Curzon 78, being presumably later insertions), and divided into a *muqaddimah*, twenty-eight *dhikrs* (of which the first twenty-one are short notices of the early saints, etc., from the Prophet to Naṣīr al-Dīn Chirāgh i Dihlī (cf. p. 942 n. 1 *supra*), while the twenty-second to the twenty-eighth are much longer notices of the local saints of Barnāwah and Rāprī,[3] namely Badr al-Dīn b. Sharaf al-Dīn Anṣārī (d. 788/1386), Naṣīr al-Dīn i Buzurg (d. 855/1452), 'Alā' al-Dīn i Buzurg (d. 875/1471), Pīr Būd'han (d. 29 Sha'bān in an unspecified year), Badr al-Dīn i Thānī (d. 949/1543), Farīd al-Dīn b. Bāyazīd b. Pīr Būd'han

[1] At the beginning of Professor Maḥmūd Shērānī's article mentioned below the name of this author is followed by the dates 1007 and 1088, presumably as those of his birth and death, but the authority for them is not specified.

[2] *Īn risālah īst musammā bi'sm i Firdausīyah* [*i qudsīyah?*] *ya'nī* [!] *nām i īn nuskhah Chishtīyah i bihishtīyah* etc. (Ivanow-Curzon 78, fol. 2). In the Āṣafīyah catalogue it is called *Chishtīyah i bihishtīyah musammā bah Firdausīyah i qudsīyah.*

[3] Rāprī is a village, once a large town, in the Shikōhābād *taḥṣīl* of the Mainpūrī District of the United Provinces. Barnāwah is not mentioned either in the Mainpūrī District Gazetteer or in the Imperial Gazetteer of India.

(d. 987/1579), Bahā' al-Dīn b. 'Alā' al-Dīn,[1] grandson of the preceding (d. 1038/1628), whose biography occupies more than half the work), a *k͟hātimah* (additional information concerning descendants of the foregoing *s͟haik͟hs*), and a *waṣl al-k͟hātimah* (eulogies of the C͟his͟htī order): **Lahore** Prof. Maḥmūd S͟hērānī's private library (A.H. 1066/1655–6, possibly autograph), **Ivanow** Curzon 78 (A.H. 1209/1795), **Āṣafīyah** i p. 412 no. 562 (A.H. 1258/1842).

1331. **Niẓām al-Dīn Aḥmad b. M. Ṣāliḥ** Ṣiddīqī Ḥusainī lived in the time of S͟hāh-Jahān and composed in 1060/1650 a work on poetical figures entitled *Majma' al-ṣanā'i'*.[2]

Karāmāt al-auliyā', on the miracles of saints in all periods of the history of Islam, completed in 1068/1658: **Ivanow** 265 (18th cent.), **Rieu** iii 974*a* (*circ.* 1850).

1332. **Tawakkul Bēg Kūlālī**[3] was a son of the *Qūs͟h-bēgī* to I'tiqād K͟hān, Governor of Kas͟hmīr. At the age of sixteen[4] he became a disciple of the Qādirī saint, Mullā S͟hāh Badak͟hs͟hī,[5] who was then resident in Kas͟hmīr, and he kept in touch with him, visiting him at intervals, until 1071/1660–1, when he saw his master for the last time. For a period anterior to 1053/1643–4 he was in the service of S͟hāh-S͟hujā', Governor of Bengal. In 1054/1644 he went with a letter of introduction from Mullā S͟hāh to Dārā-S͟hukōh (see p. 992 *supra*), who gave him the rank of *dū-ṣadī* and subsequently on several occasions sent him with messages to Mullā S͟hāh. After Aurangzēb's accession in 1069/1659 he obtained a post in the government service at Kāngrah.

[1] For S͟h. Bahā' al-Dīn Barnāwī, who was not only a saint but also a musician, see an Urdu article by Professor Maḥmūd S͟hērānī based mainly on the *C͟his͟htīyah i bihis͟htīyah* and entitled *Mak͟hdūm S͟haik͟h Bahā' al-Dīn Barnāwī* in the *OCM*. iii/4 (Aug. 1927) pp. 41–58, iv/1 (Nov. 1927) pp. 9–26, and v/4 (Aug. 1929) pp. 72–99. This article includes a summary of the information contained in the *C͟his͟htīyah i bihis͟htīyah* concerning the earlier *s͟haik͟hs* of Barnāwah.

[2] Lindesiana p. 205 no. 754, Ross and Browne 68, Ethé 2937–8, Bānkīpūr ix 850–2, xi 1098 liii, Būhār 263–4, Ivanow 1st Suppt. 788, Ivanow Curzon 176, Rieu ii 814*b*, 821*b*, iii 999*b*, Browne Suppt. 1144–5 (Corpus 23[1] and 28), Leyden v p. 160, etc.

[3] Meaning of this *nisbah* not ascertained. A Mīr Yūsuf Kūlālī is mentioned in 'Abd al-Ḥamīd's *Pāds͟hāh-nāmah* i, 2, p. 320[2].

[4] As Tawakkul Bēg says that he had availed himself of Mullā S͟hāh's teaching for forty years, this discipleship must have begun in, or about, 1031/1622.

[5] See p. 1009 n. 2 below.

It seems likely that he is identical with Tawakkul Bēg b. Tūlak Beg,[1] who in Shāh-Jahān's 26th regnal year, A.H. 1063/1653, was sent by Dārā-Shukōh, at that time *Ṣūbah-dār* of Kābul, to Ghaznīn as *Amīn* and *Waqā'i'-nawīs* and who at the request of Shamshēr Khān Tarīn, the *T'hānah-dār* of Ghaznīn, wrote the *Shamsher-Khānī*, an abridgment of Firdausī's *Shāh-nāmah* (see Rieu ii 539–40, Ethé 883–90, etc.).

Nuskhah i aḥwāl i Shāhī (a chronogram = 1077/1666–7), an account of Mullā Shāh [2] and his teachings: **Rieu** Suppt. 130 (early 19th cent.), **Āṣafīyah** iii p. 56 no. 349.

French summary: *Mollâ-Shâh et le spiritualisme oriental, par M. A. de Kremer* (in *Journal Asiatique*, vi^e série, tome xiii (1869), pp. 105–59).

[Autobiographical statements in the *Nuskhah i aḥwāl i Shāhī* (see Rieu and *Journal asiatique, loc. cit.*)]

1333. **'Abd Allāh [3] Khwēshgī [4] Qaṣūrī[5],** i.e. Ghulām-Mu'īn al-Dīn 'Abd Allāh known as al-Khalīfah al-Khwēshgī al-Chishtī (Ross-Browne 56), or " 'Abdallâh, known as 'Ubaid-allâh, with

[1] Rieu mentions that in one of the B.M. MSS. of the *Shamshēr-Khānī* he is called Tawakkul Muḥammad son of Tūlak Muḥammad al-Ḥusainī.

[2] Mullā, or Maulānā, Shāh, whose name was Shāh Muḥammad (Shāh being part of his name, not a title), though Miyāṅ Mīr used to call him Muḥammad Shāh (*Sakīnat al-auliyā'*, Urdu trans. p. 117², Bānkīpūr viii p. 50²), was born in Badakhshān A.H. 992/1584, settled in India in 1023/1614–15 and died at Lahore in 1072/1661. See pp. 18–19 *supra*; Jahān-ārā *Ṣāḥibīyah* (cf. p. 1001 *supra*); *Sakīnat al-auliyā'* foll. 86–118 (pp. 116–58 in the Urdu translation); *'Amal i Ṣāliḥ* iii pp. 370–2; *Tadhkirah i Naṣrābādī* p. 63; *Wāqi'āt i Kashmīr* pp. 161–2; *Riyāḍ al-shu'arā'* (cf. Bland in *JRAS.* 1848 p. 147); *Farḥat al-nāẓirīn* (passage quoted in *OCM.* iv/3 (May 1928) pp. 95–6); *Riyāḍ al-'ārifīn* pp. 161–2; Beale *Miftāḥ al-tawārīkh* (Āgrah 1849) pp. 401–2; S. M. Latif *Lahore: its history*, etc., pp. 59, 175–6, 178; *Ency. Isl.* Suppt. under Shāh Muḥammad; K.-R. Qanungo *Dara Shukoh. Vol. i. Biography* (Calcutta [1935]) pp. 348–58; *Jahān-ārā Bēgam kī ēk ghair-ma'rūf taṣnīf: Ṣāḥibīyah*, by M. Ibrāhīm (in *OCM.* xiii/4 (August 1937) pp. 3–19).

[3] It will be seen that his proper name was 'Abd Allāh but that he was known as 'Ubaid Allāh (or *vice versa*, since there is some disagreement in the MSS.). Similarly his father was properly called 'Abd al-Ḥaqq but was known as 'Abd al-Qādir.

[4] The name of an Afghān clan (cf. p. 661 n. 4 *supra*).

[5] Qaṣūr is 34 miles S.E. of Lahore. " The Afghâns of Qasûr belong mostly to the Khweshgî clan, whose eponym appears to have flourished in the eleventh century [A.D.] " (M. Shafī' in the article mentioned below). See also an article entitled *Shahr i Qaṣūr kē muta'alliq iqtibāsāt* by M. Shafī' in *OCM.* xiii/2 (Feb. 1937) pp. 92–8.

the epithet Khalîfah Ḥayy [read Khalīfah-jī] [1] bin 'Abd-alḥakk (known as 'Abd-alḳâdir al-khwîshî [*sic* ?] alćishtî) " (Ethé 1271), or " 'Abdu'l-lah Khalīfa-jī b. 'Abdi'l-Ḥaqq, known as 'Abdu'l-Qādir Khwīshagī " (Ivanow 273), or " 'Abdu'l-lah Khwīshagī Chishtī, surnamed Khalīfah, of Qaṣūr " (Ivanow 1294), or 'Ubaid Allāh known as (*al-ma'rūf bah*) 'Abd Allāh al-Khwēshgī al-Chishtī, who used the *takhallus* " 'Ubaidī " (*OCM.* iii/4 p. 21), was born at Qaṣūr (Ross-Browne 56) and it was there that in Shāh-Jahān's reign after finishing his studies (*taḥṣīl i 'ulūm sē farāghat pā-kar, OCM.* iii/4 p. 23[1]) he completed the first volume of his first commentary on Ḥāfiẓ, the *Baḥr al-firāsah,* which he had begun while still a student. The second and final volume was completed long afterwards at Bījāpūr (*OCM.* iii/4 p. 23[3]). From the preface to his second commentary, the *Khulāṣat al-baḥr,* also a production of his early life, it appears that " he was for a time attached to the Shaikh Maulânâ 'Abd-alrashîd (known as Muḥammad Rashîd) Yuwânjî and afterwards in the service of [2] Shaikh Pîr Muḥammad of Lakhnau " (Ethé 1271). In 1077/1666–7 he was at Aurangābād, where he had gone in the service of Dilēr Khān,[3] and it was there that he wrote the *Akhbār al-auliyā'* (*Islamic culture* iii/3 p. 453). In 1133/1720–1, Muḥammad Shah's second regnal year, he was again at Qaṣūr, evidently towards the end of a long life, and there he wrote his *Asrār i Mathnawī* at the instigation of two Khwēshgī chiefs, Ḥasan [Ḥusain ?] Khān and Sa'īd Khān (Ross-Browne 56). In the preface to his *Asrār i Mathnawī u anwār i ma'nawī,* a commentary on the first *daftar* of Rūmī's *Mathnawī* completed in 1133/1720–1 (MSS.: Ross-Browne 56 (A.H. 1133/1721, perhaps autograph), Sprenger 373 (Mōtī Maḥall)) he gives a

[1] The *jī* appended to the word *khalīfah* is the same Hindi affix indicative of respect that occurs, for example, in Miyān-jī (cf. p. 998 n. 2).

[2] Or rather, visited. Sh. Pīr Muḥammad Lak'hnawī died at Lucknow in 1080/1669–70 or 1082/1671–2. See *Khazīnat al-aṣfiyā'* i pp. 482–3 (where there is a quotation from the *Ma'ārij al-wilāyat* telling how 'Abd Allāh Khwēshgī on his way to Bengal [*ba-safar i Bangālah,* possibly with Dilēr Khān, who took part in the campaign of Mu'aẓẓam Khān Mīr Jumlah against Shāh-Shujā' at the beginning of Aurangzēb's reign] visited him at Lucknow, showed him the *Baḥr al-firāsah* and was invested by him with the Chishtī *khirqah*) ; *Tajallī i nūr* i pp. 81–2.

[3] i.e. Jalāl Khān Dāwud-za'ī, for whom see *Ma'āthir al-umarā'* ii pp. 42–56, Beveridge's translation pp. 495–505.

list of his earlier works, which is quoted verbatim by Sprenger. These are firstly three commentaries on the *dīwān* of Ḥāfiẓ, (1) *Baḥr al-firāsah* [in the preface of which Shāh-Jahān (A.H. 1037–68/1628–58) is praised. MSS.: Kapūrt'halah 123 (see *OCM*. iii/4 p. 21), Peshawar 1028], (2) *Khulāṣat al-baḥr fī 'ltiqāṭ al-durar*, a larger commentary (MSS.: Āṣafīyah (transcribed by Dārā-Shukōh, "who was a disciple of Sayyid Ādam Rasūl [1] of Māwarā' al-Nahr as would appear from the colophon." See Nadhīr Aḥmad 129), Ethé 1271), (3) *Jāmi' al-baḥrain* (no MSS. recorded), then (4) *Rāḥat al-ashbāḥ*, a commentary on the *Nuzhat al-arwāḥ* [of Ḥusain b. 'Ālim al-Ḥusainī] (no MSS. recorded), (5) *Makhzan al-ḥaqā'iq*, a commentary on the *Kanz al-daqā'iq*, (6) *Sharḥ i ḤRF* [*sic* ?] *i 'āliyāt*, and (7) *Ma'ārij al-wilāyat* "*kih dar bayān i mashāyikh i Hindūstān-ast.*" In this list he mentions neither the *Akhbār al-auliyā'* nor the two Ṣūfī works *Taḥqīq al-muḥaqqiqīn fī tadqīq al-mudaqqiqīn* (Ivanow 1294 (1)) and *Fawā'id al-'āshiqīn* (Ivanow 1294 (2)).

(1) ***Akhbār al-auliyā' min lisān al-aṣfiyā'***, an account of Khwēshgī and other saints written in 1077/1666–7 at Aurangābād and divided into six *bābs* ((1) *dar bayān i aḥwāl i Khwēshgiyān*, (2) *dar bayān i mashāyikh i sā'ir i Afghānān*, (3) *dar bayān i aḥwāl i nisā' i 'ārifāt*, (4) *dar nasab i Afghānān u sabab i āmadan az Bait al-Maqdis ba-Kūhistān*, (5) *dar aḥwāl i mashāyikh i Qaṣūr u nawāḥī i ān*, (6) *dar aḥwāl i īn aḥqar i 'ibād Allāh* (*'Abd Allāh Khwēshgī Chishtī*): **Ivanow** 273 (A.H. 1294/1877, transcribed at Qaṣūr for H. Blochmann).

This work is one of the sources of M. Shafī''s article *An Afghan colony at Qasur. I.* in *Islamic culture* iii/3 (July 1929) pp. 452–73.

(2) ***Ma'ārij al-wilāyat*** (*dar bayān i mashāyikh i Hindūstān*), mentioned by the author in the above-mentioned list of his own works and often quoted in the *Khazīnat al-aṣfiyā'* but not yet recorded in any published catalogue.

[Autobiography (without exact dates according to Ivanow p. 620) in *Bab* 6 of the *Akhbār al-auliyā'* (a biography based on

[1] Not identified. It is not clear why Dārā-Shukōh (presumably the well-known son of Shāh-Jahān and disciple of Mullā Shāh) should describe himself as a disciple of this person, who seems not to be mentioned in the *Safīnat al-auliyā'* or the *Sakīnat al-auliyā'*.

this chapter was to be included in Part II of M. Shafīʻ's article mentioned above, but no such second part seems to be traceable in *Islamic culture* from 1929 to 1937).

1334. Ḥāfiẓ **M. Saʻīd** b. Ḥāfiẓ [*sic ?*] began the *Rāḥat al-arwāḥ* in Rajab 1084/October 1673 and completed it in 1085/1674–5.

Rāḥat al-arwāḥ, a biography of Sh. ʻAzīz Allāh, who was born at Lahore on 3 Jumādā II 1047/23 Oct. 1637 and died on 20 Shawwāl 1084/28 Jan. 1674 : **Ethé** 651 (A.H. 1108/1696).

1335. S. **Zindah ʻAlī** al-Muftī wrote towards the end of the eleventh/seventeenth century.

Thamarāt al-mashāyikh, on Central Asian *shaikhs* of various orders : **Bukhārā** Central Library (A.H. 1277/1860–1. See Semenov *Kurzer Abriss* p. 7).

1336. For Sh. **Ḥusain b.** Sh. **Abdāl Zāhidī's** *Silsilat al-nasab i Ṣafawīyah*, which was dedicated to Shāh Sulaimān (reigned 1077–1105/1667–94) and which deals mainly with Ṣafī al-Dīn Isḥāq (cf. p. 939 *supra*) and mystics descended from him, see p. 318 *supra*.

1337. For **M. Baqā** " Baqā " Sahāranpūrī (b. 1037/1627–8, d. 1094/1683) and **Bakhtāwar Khān** (d. 1096/1685) see pp. 131–4 *supra*. Another of the works written by the former but by a " courteous fiction " ascribed to the latter is the *Riyāḍ al-auliyā'*.

Riyāḍ al-auliyā' (a chronogram = 1090/1679–80, the date of completion), lives of saints, etc., in four *chamans* ((1) the first four Caliphs, (2) the Imāms, (3) saints, (4) Indian saints) : **Rieu** iii 975*a* (A.D. 1851), **Āṣafiyah** i p. 320 no. 115, **Browne** Suppt. 728 (Corpus 126).

1338. In the only recorded copy of the *Adhkār al-aḥrār* all of the preface except the last 6½ lines is missing and the name of the author does not appear. He was, however, a disciple of Mīr Abū 'l-ʻUlā Naqshbandī Akbarābādī, and he completed his biography in Safar 1093/1682.

Adhkār al-aḥrār, an account of the saint Amīr Abū 'l-ʻUlā ibn Amīr Abī'l-Wafā' ibn Amīr ʻAbd al-Salām, or as he is called in the *Khazīnat al-aṣfiyā'* (i p. 636) Mīr Abū 'l-ʻUlā Naqshbandī

Akbarābādī, who was born in 990/1582 at Nārēlah near Delhi and who died on 9 Ṣafar 1061/1651 and was buried at Akbarābād (i.e. Āgrah): **I.O.** D.P. 576*a* (defective at beginning. 11th year of M. Shāh = A.H. 1142/1730).

1339. **M. Ṣādiq Shihābī** Sa'dī Qādirī wrote the *Manāqib i Ghauthīyah* at the request of his *murshid*, S. 'Abd al-Qādir b. S. 'Abd al-Jalīl al-Ḥasanī al-Ḥusainī Gharīb Allāh, who was a descendant and *khalīfah* of 'Abd al-Qādir al-Jīlānī at Aḥmadābād. The work cannot have been written earlier than the 17th century, since the *Takmīl al-īmān* of 'Abd al-Ḥaqq Dihlawī, who died in 1052/1642 (cf. p. 194 *supra*), is mentioned in the preface, nor later than 1160/1747, the date of Ivanow-Curzon 76.

Manāqib i Ghauthīyah, an account of 'Abd al-Qādir al-Jīlānī, called al-Ghauth al-a'ẓam (for whom see p. 933 n. 2 *supra*), divided into a *muqaddimah* and fifty or more [1] *manqabahs* and dealing with *manāqib* not contained in such well-known works as the *Bahjat al-asrār* (see p. 933 *supra*) and the *Takmilah* of al-Yāfi'ī (see p. 936 *supra*): **Ivanow** Curzon 76 (A.H. 1160/1747), **Ivanow** 268–70 (all 18th cent.), **Āṣafīyah** i p. 490 nos. 813 (A.H. 1179/1765–6), 428 (A.H. 1260/1844–5), ii p. 1556 no. 52, p. 1558 no. 43, **I.O.** D.P. 751B (*a*) (A.H. 1211/1797), 751A (A.H. 1248/1832), **Ethé** 1799, **Bānkīpūr** xvii 1589 (A.H. 1253/1837–8), **Būhār** 181 (19th cent.), **Lahore** Panjāb Univ. (see *OCM*. iii/1 p. 69), **Peshawar** 1014.

Edition: **Bombay** 1886†.

Urdu translation: *M. i Gh.*, **Lucknow** 1907* (2nd ed.).

1340. In 1109/1697–8 an anonymous author wrote—

Khawāriq al-sālikīn (a chronogram), some anecdotes of early Ṣūfīs of Kashmīr, etc.: **Ivanow** Curzon 79 (4) (foll. 106–15. Mid 19th cent.).

1341. **M. Būlāq** b. Sh. Abū M. Khālidī **Dihlawī** b. Sh. 'Alī Akbar was a descendant of the great saint Niẓām al-Dīn Auliyā (for whom see p. 941 n. 5 *supra*).

[1] Fifty followed by a *khātimah* and a *tadhyīl* (the last on 'Abd al-Qādir's pedigree and the more celebrated of his 49 children) in Ethé 1799, sixty-seven in I.O. D.P. 751B(*a*), ninety-one (the number of years in 'Abd al-Qādir's life) in I.O. D.P. 751A.

Maṭlūb al-ṭālibīn, a detailed biography of Niẓām al-Dīn Auliyā with short accounts of his relations, disciples and spiritual descendants and of the other Chishtī *pīrs* and the different branches of the Chishtī order, divided into seventeen *maṭlabs* and completed in 1111/1699–1700 : **Ethé** 653 (A.H. 1137/1724–5).

Urdu translation : *Shawāhid i Niẓāmī* (a chronogram = 1317/1899–1900), by M. Ḍāmin 'Alī, **Delhi** 1900°.

List of the saints : Ethé coll. 318–26.

Probably identical with the above-mentioned M. Būlāq is M. Bulāq [1] (spelt without *wāw*), who wrote the *Rauḍah i aqṭāb*.

Rauḍah i aqṭāb (a chronogram = 1124/1712), biographies of Quṭb al-Dīn Bakhtyār Ūshī Kākī (for whom see p. 943 n. 4 *supra*) and some saints buried near him : **Rieu** iii 974*a* (extracts only. *Circ.* A.D. 1850).

Editions : **Delhi** 1304/1887°, **Lahore** 1890†.

Urdu translation : *Rauḍah i aqṭāb*, **Delhi** 1892*.

1342. Sh. **Manṣūr b.** Shāh **Chānd Muḥammad** b. Shāh M. Mīr b. Shāh Ḥāmid b. Shāh 'Abd al-Qawī b. Shāh Chānd M. b. Shāh Ḥamīd al-Dīn known as Shaikh Chā'ildah was forty years old in 1119/1707–8, when he wrote the *Tuḥfat al-qāri'*.

Tuḥfat al-qāri', biographies of saints in three parts ((1) Ḥaḍrat i 'Abbās, (2) Shāh 'Alī Sarmast and how he settled in Gujrāt, (3) Shāh Chā'ildah (d. 7 Ṣafar 911/1515) and Qāḍī Maḥmūd Maḥbūb Allāh (d. 941/1534–5) and his sons) and two appendices ((1) Shaikh al-Islām Shāh Lār Muḥammad, (2) Shāh Jamāl Muḥammad (d. 985/1577–8)) : **Bombay** Fyzee 16 (A.H. 1261/1845).

1343. S. **Aḥmad b.** S. **Ḥusain Akbarābādī.**

Maqāmāt i ḥaḍrat i Shāh Naqshbandī, written in 1119/1707–8 : **Brelvi and Dhabhar** p. xliii no. 7 (defective at beginning).

1344. At the beginning of his notice of Sh. Sa'dī Lāhaurī the author of the *Khazīnat al-aṣfiyā'* mentions a certain Sh. **M. 'Umar**

[1] Edwards prefixes the title Sayyid to M. Bulāq's name, doubtless on the authority of a title-page, but the text of the work itself (to judge from Rieu and Blumhardt) seems to give no warrant for this. Rieu writes Muḥammad Yalāq, but this is presumably a corruption.

Pashāwarī who was a disciple and friend of Sh. Sa'dī and who wrote under the title *Jawāhir al-asrār* a biography of his master extending from his birth to the date of his death. Probably this Sh. M. 'Umar Pashāwarī is identical with M. 'Umar b. Ibrāhīm al-Nīshāpūrī [*sic ?*], who wrote the *Ẓawāhir al-sarā'ir*. Doubtless the work was written in the first half of the eighteenth century.

Ẓawāhir al-sarāsir [*sic*, for *al-sarā'ir* presumably], on the lives and teachings of Sa'dī Lāhaurī,[1] 'Abd al-Raḥmān Sulamī Nīshāpūrī, and S. Ādam Banūrī[2]: **Nadhīr Aḥmad** 40 (Shāh M. Muḥaddith's library, Rāmpūr).

1345. For Kāmwar Khān's *Haft gulshan i Muḥammad-Shāhī*, a history of India which extends to 1132/1719–20 and of which the seventh *gulshan* is devoted to Indian saints, see p. 459 *supra*.

1346. Sh. **Abū 'l-Faiyāḍ** Qamar al-Ḥaqq[3] **Ghulām-Rashīd,** born on 8 Rabī' al-Awwal 1096/12 Feb. 1685, was the son [? [4]], disciple and successor (*sajjādah-nishīn*) of Sh. Badr al-Ḥaqq M. Arshad b. M. Rashīd 'Uthmānī Jaunpūrī. In 1147/1734–5 his discourses were attended by Ghulām-Sharaf al-Dīn b. Imām al-Dīn, who has given an account of his life and teachings in the *Ganj i Faiyāḍī* (see p. 1022 *infra*). He died at Jaunpūr on 5 Ṣafar 1167/2 Dec. 1753. Among his works were an Arabic commentary on [his father's [?] Arabic grammar] the *Hidāyat al-naḥw*[5] and a Persian commentary on the *Qaṣīdah i Ghauthīyah*.[6]

Ganj i Arshadī, an account of the life and sayings of the above-mentioned Badr al-Ḥaqq M. Arshad b. M. Rashīd 'Uthmānī

[1] Sh. Sa'dī BLKHĀRĪ Mujaddidī Lāhaurī, a *khalīfah* of Sh. Ādam Banūrī, died in 1108/1696. See *Khazīnat al-aṣfiyā'* i pp. 647–53. BLKHĀRĪ is not a misprint for Bukhārī, since a chronogram for the date of his death requires the presence of the *lām*.

[2] Cf. p. 991 n. 3 *supra*.

[3] So Rieu iii 1013*a*.

[4] *Pisar u murīd u sajjādah-nishīn i Shāh Arshad ast* (*Tajallī i nūr* p. 74[8]). Browne in his description of the *Ganj i Faiyāḍī* describes him as the son of Shaikh Muḥibb Allāh. If this is a real discrepancy and Muḥibb Allāh is not merely a description of M. Arshad, the information derived from the *Ganj i Faiyāḍī* is likely to be correct.

[5] See p. 1016 n.1.

[6] A well-known Arabic *qaṣīdah* ascribed to 'Abd al-Qādir al-Jīlānī (see Brockelmann *Sptbd.* i p. 779 no. 44).

Jaunpūrī,[1] compiled in 1134–5/1721–3 from rough notes written by Sh. Shukr Allāh : **'Alīgaṛh** Subḥ. MSS. p. 19 no. 19, **Rieu** iii 1013*b* (preface, table of contents and extracts only. *Circ.* A.D. 1850).

[*Tajallī i nūr* i p. 74 (from the *Baḥr i zakhkhār*).]

1347. Mullā **Niẓām al-Dīn** M. **Sihālawī** [2] was the third son of Mullā Quṭb al-Dīn Sihālawī, a celebrated teacher who was murdered in 1103/1692 (cf. p. 1048 n. 3 *infra*). Having studied under Ghulām-Naqshband Lak'hnawī (cf. Brockelmann *Sptbd.* ii p. 611, Raḥmān 'Alī p. 158) and others, he, like his father, became famous in India as a teacher. He died in Jumādā I 1161/May 1748, and the scholarly tradition of the family was carried on by his son, Mullā 'Abd al-'Alī M. Baḥr al-'ulūm Lak'hnawī (for whom see Raḥmān 'Alī p. 122, *Ency. Isl.* under Baḥr al-'ulūm, Brockelmann *Sptbd.* ii p. 624). His works, nearly all commentaries or *ḥawāshī* on standard text-books, include (1) annotations on Ṣadrā's commentary on al-Abharī's *Hidāyat al-ḥikmah* (see Brockelmann *Sptbd.* i p. 840 antepenult.), (2) a commentary on Muḥibb Allāh al-Bihārī's *Musallam al-thubūt* (see Brockelmann *Sptbd.* ii p. 623, l. 5 *ab infra*), (3) *Ṣubḥ i ṣādiq*, a commentary on Ḥāfiẓ al-Dīn al-Nasafī's *Manār al-anwār* (see Brockelmann *Sptbd.* ii p. 264, l. 4 *ab infra*), (4) annotations on the *Shams i bāzighah* of Maḥmūd Jaunpūrī (see Brockelmann *Sptbd.* ii p. 621), (5) annotations on Jalāl al-Dīn Dawānī's commentary (*'Aqā'id i Jalālī*) on the *'Aqā'id* of 'Aḍud al-Dīn al-Ījī (see Brockelmann *Sptbd.* ii p. 292[12]).

Manāqib al-Razzāqīyah, a life of the author's *pīr*, the Qādirī saint, S. 'Abd al-Razzāq Bānsawī, who died on 6 Shawwāl

[1] M. Arshad, according to the *Tajallī i nūr* (i p. 73), was the son of Dīwān M. Rashīd [evidently the same person as 'Abd al-Rashīd Jaunpūrī, who died in 1083/1672 and whose works include the *Rashīdīyah*, well known in India : see Raḥmān 'Alī p. 119 ; *Tajallī i nūr* i p. 71 ; Būhār Arab. cat. p. 513 ; Brockelmann *Sptbd.* ii p. 621 ; etc.]. Born in 1041/1631–2, he became one of the best scholars of Jaunpūr as well as an influential Ṣūfī affiliated to the Chishtī, Suhrawardī and Qalandarī orders. The [anonymous] Arabic syntax entitled *Hidāyat al-naḥw* [for which see Ellis col. 637, Brockelmann i p. 305, *Sptbd.* i 535] was one of his works according to the *Tajallī i nūr*, which does not mention the titles of any other works by him. He died on 24 Jumādā II 1113/26 Nov. 1701 and was buried at Jaunpūr, near his father.

[2] *Sihālī* (*ba-kasr i sīn i muhmalah u hā-yi hawwaz u alif u lām i maksūr u yā-yi taḥtānī i ma'rūf*) *qaṣabah īst az tawābi' i Lak'hna'ū* (Raḥmān 'Alī p. 168).

1136/1724 at Bānsī in the Bastī District of the United Provinces[1]: **Bānkīpūr** xvii 1592, **I.O.** D.P. 729.

Edition: **Lucknow** 1896° (pp. 20).

[*Malfūẓ i Razzāqī* pp. 148–59; *Ma'āthir al-kirām* p. 220; *Subḥat al-marjān* pp. 94–5; *Ḥadā'iq al-Ḥanafīyah* p. 445; Raḥmān 'Alī p. 241; Alṭāf al-Raḥmān *Aḥwāl i 'ulamā' i Farangī Maḥall* (in Urdu), Lucknow [1907*] p. 77; Bānkīpūr xvii p. 78.]

1348. **Bahā' al-Ḥaqq al-Qādirī** cannot have lived earlier than the 17th century, since he several times quotes 'Abd al-Ḥaqq Dihlawī, who died in 1052/1642. If the Rāmpūr MS. is correctly described by Nadhīr Aḥmad as an autograph, he was living in 1138/1725–6.

Anīs al-Qādirīyah, an account of 'Abd al-Qādir al-Jīlānī with brief notices of some earlier saints: **Rāmpūr** (A.H. 1138/1725–6, autograph. See Nadhīr Aḥmad 31), **I.O.** D.P. 577 (18th cent.).

1349. **M. Ḥabīb Allāh** b. Shaikh Jahān **Akbarābādī** Dihlawī was born at Akbarābād [i.e. Āgrah] in 1082/1671–2. At the age of twelve he left his *maktab* and entered the *madrasah* of Malik al-'Ulamā' Sh. 'Aṭā' Allāh,[2] with whom he read the Arabic *'ulūm* until the age of twenty.[3] He then married and spent five years in straitened circumstances as a teacher at Delhi. Having entered the service of Zēb al-Nisā', Aurangzēb's daughter [who died in 1114/1702],[4] he was for a time engaged in translating the *Fatāwī i 'Ālamgīrī*.[5] Later in association with Muḥammad-

[1] An Urdu work on this saint is *Karāmāt i Razzāqīyah* by Nawwāb M. Khān Shāhjahānpūrī, Hardoi [1907*].

[2] A biography of this scholar, who seems not to be mentioned by Raḥmān 'Alī, is given in the *Dhikr i jamī' i auliyā' i Dihlī* (foll. 101*a*–103*b* in D.P. 594, foll. 85*a*–87*a* in D.P. 634).

[3] Reading *bist-sālagī* instead of the impossible *sī-sālagī*.

[4] For Z. al-N. see Jadunāt'h Sarkār's *Studies in Mughal India* pp. 79–90.

[5] *Chandī dar sarkār i Z. al-N. . . . tarjamah i Fatāwī i 'Ālamgīrī numūd.* There seem to be no extant MSS. of this translation undertaken at the instance of Zēb al-Nisā' and perhaps never completed. A translation of the *kitāb al-ḥudūd* and the *kitāb al-jināyāt* made at a much later date by Qāḍī 'l-quḍāt M. Najm al-Dīn Khān Kākōrawī, who died in 1229/1814 (see Raḥmān 'Ali pp. 233–5, Sprenger p. 166), was printed at Calcutta in 1813°*. For the Arabic original, compiled by Sh. Niẓām Burhānpūrī (cf. Raḥmān 'Alī p. 242) and others (five of whom are mentioned in Bānkīpūr xix p. 63), see Brockelmann ii p. 417, *Sptbd.* ii p. 604.

Yār Khān, the Governor of Delhi, he compiled a lexicographical work or works.[1] At the same time he wrote annotations (*ḥāshiyah*) on the *Qāmūs*.[2] Having composed a work entitled *Muzīl al-aghlāṭ* he submitted it to the Khān i Khānān,[3] and was taken into the service of Bahādur Shāh (1119–24/1707–12) with a *manṣab* of 150. An advantageous intimacy with the Wazīr al-Mulk [i.e. the Khān i Khānān] ensued.[4] After receiving the appointments of Lecturer to the Emperor and Librarian to the Khān i Khānān,[5] he accompanied the Imperial army to Ḥaidarābād [in the campaign of 1120/1708–9 against Kām-bakhsh, Bahādur Shāh's brother]. When they reached the Narbadā on the return journey, he wrote a *risālah i ḥurūf i sab'ah* [so D.P. 594, but for *sab'ah* D.P. 634 has *ṣīghah* (?)] and submitted it to the Emperor, who rewarded him with a *khil'at*, a present of 1,000 rupees, promotion to a *manṣab* of 400, and a *jāgīr*. In the reign of the *Shahīd i marḥūm* [i.e. Farrukh-siyar, 1124–31/1713–19] he became Keeper of the Treasury at Delhi and also Superintendent of the Holy Shrines.[6] At this time, he says, he undertook and completed his translation of the *Bahjat al-asrār* (for which see p. 933 *supra*, where it has been recorded that in the work itself the date of completion is given as 1133). At the beginning of Muḥammad Shāh's reign (1131–61/1719–48) he was appointed *wakīl i shar'ī* to the king and received the title of Khān.[7] At the time of writing the *Dhikr i jamī' i auliyā' i Dihlī* he was hoping to resign his *manṣab* and go on a *ḥajj*. In 1147/1735 he completed and dedicated to Muḥammad Shāh a Persian translation of the *Qāmūs* to which he gave the title *Qābūs* (MSS. : Āṣafīyah iii p. 618 nos.

[1] *u muddatī dar ṣuḥbat i M. Y. Kh. Nāẓim i Dār al-khilāfah tālīf i kitāb* [D.P. 634 has *kutub*] *i lughat mī-kard.*

[2] No MSS. of this *ḥāshiyah* seem to be recorded. His Persian translation of the *Qāmūs* is mentioned below.

[3] i.e. Mun'im Khān, who died in 1123/1711. See *Ma'āthir al-umarā'* iii pp. 667–77, Irvine *Later Mughals* i pp. 19, 36, 38, 125, etc.

[4] *u bā Wazīr al-Mulk muṣāḥabat u mu'āsharat numūdah fawā'id i bisyār girift.*

[5] *u ba-khidmat i tadrīs i ḥuḍūr sar-buland gardīd u dāroghagī i kitāb-khānah wa-ghairah khidamāt az sarkār i nawwāb i 'ālī-janāb yāft.* I do not feel sure that I have translated this correctly.

[6] *ba-khidmat i Amānat i Khizānah i 'āmirah i Dār al-khilāfat u Amānat i Mazārāt i mutabarrakah sar-buland gardīdah.*

[7] *u dar shurū' i 'ahd i mubārak ba-khidmat i wakālat i shar'ī i ḥaḍrat i Khidīw i Gaihān ba-iḍāfah i ṣadī u khiṭāb i khānī 'izz i imtiyāz yāft.*

373–4, Bodleian 1674, Būhār 253–4, Calcutta Madrasah 157–60, Rieu ii 511*a*, 511*b*). According to the *Tārīkh i Muḥammadī* (cited by Rieu. iii 1089*a*) he died at Delhi in 1160/1747.

Dhikr i jamī' i auliyā' i Dihlī (a chronogram = 1140/1727–8), lives of the saints of Delhi arranged according to the dates of their *a'rās*: **I.O.** D.P. 594 (18th cent.), 634 (A.H. 1242/1827), **Rieu** iii 975*b* (*circ.* A.D. 1850) and probably also **Āṣafīyah** i p. 316 ult. (*Tadhkirah i j. i a. i D.* Author not stated. A.H. 1180/1766–7).

[Autobiography in the *khātimah* to the *Dh. i j. i a. i D.*]

1350. **M. Akram** b. Sh. M. 'Alī b. Sh. Ilāh-bakhsh al-Ḥanafī al-**Barāsawī**,[1] a disciple of Sh. Saund'hā Safīdūnī,[2] by whom he was invested with the *khirqah i khilāfat* in 1111/1699–1700, began his *Sawāṭi' al-anwār* at Delhi in 1135/1722–3 and completed it in Muḥarram 1142/July–August 1729.

Sawāṭi' al-anwār, or *Iqtibās al-anwār*,[3] a large work on the saints of the Chishtī order in four chapters called *iqtibās* ((1) Muḥammad, the first four Caliphs and the Imāms, (2) from Ḥasan Baṣrī to 'Uthmān Hārūnī, (3) from Mu'īn al-Dīn Chishtī to M. b. 'Ārif b. Aḥmad 'Abd al-Ḥaqq Rudaulawī,[4] (4) from 'Abd al-Quddūs Gangōhī (cf. p. 967 *supra*) to the author's father), these chapters being subdivided into sections called *nūr* and, in the case of the third *iqtibās*, into subsections called *sāṭi'*, *lāmi'*, and *shu'ā'*: **Ethé** 654, **I.O.** D.P. 667.

Edition: *Iqtibās al-anwār*, **Lahore** 1895°* (pp. 349).

List and epitome of the biographies: Ethé coll. 327–39.

1351. M. **'Abd al-Rashīd** b. Nadhr-Muḥammad Qādirī **Kairānawī** was a disciple of Ḥājjī Shāh Fatḥ-Muḥammad Qādirī Kairānawī, called Miyān-jīw.[5] The latter, who was both the maternal uncle and the father-in-law of Nadhr-Muḥammad,

[1] Barās is a village situated a few miles west of Karnāl in the Panjāb.

[2] For Sh. Saund'hā see Ethé col. 338 no. 36, *Khazīnat al-aṣfiyā'* i p. 487. Safīdūn is now in the State of Jīnd.

[3] This is given as an alternative title in the author's preface according to the I.O. MSS., but as the sole title in the lithographed edition, which (1) omits from the author's preface his statement concerning the date of composition, (2) inserts after the preface a *muqaddimah* on Ṣūfism, the 14 main orders, etc. (3) differs elsewhere from the text of the I.O. MSS.

[4] For A. 'Abd al-Ḥaqq Rudaulawī see p. 968 n. 2 *supra*.

[5] This is an Indian title of respect (cf. p. 998, ll. 11 and 25, *supra*).

'Abd al-Rashīd's father, was born at Anbālah (i.e. Ambala in the Panjāb), received the *khirqah i khilāfat* from Sh. Muḥyī 'l-Dīn (so Rieu), or Sh. Yaḥyā (so 'Abd al-Muqtadir), Madanī at al-Madīnah, settled at Kairānah[1] and died there on 29 Rabī' al-Awwal 1130/2 March 1718.

(1) ***Taḥā'if i Rashīdīyah***, biographies (each headed *Tuḥfah*) of thirty-seven persons from the Prophet to Shāh Fatḥ-Muḥammad, who form the author's spiritual pedigree in the Qādirī order, begun in 1137/1724–5 and completed in 1143/1730–1: **Rieu** i 361*b* (A.H. 1146/1733).

List of the biographies: Rieu i p. 362*a*.

(2) ***Tārīkh i Qādirīyah***, a shorter work on the lives of the same persons, written in 1150/1737: **Rāmpūr** (A.H. 1193/1779. See Nadhīr Aḥmad 74), **Bānkīpūr** viii 678 (18th cent.).

List of the biographies: Bānkīpūr viii p. 67.

1352. Quṭb al-Dīn Aḥmad, known as (*al-ma'rūf bi-*) **Walī Allāh**, b. 'Abd al-Raḥīm b. Wajīh al-Dīn i Shahīd b. Mu'aẓẓam b. Manṣūr al-'Umarī al-Naqshbandī al-Muḥaddith **al-Dihlawī**, who was born in 1114/1703 and died in 1176/1762–3, has already been mentioned as the author of the *Fatḥ al-Raḥmān* (p. 21), *al-Fauz al-kabīr* (p. 22), the *Surūr al-maḥzūn* (p. 179) and the *Qurrat al-'ainain* (p. 219). Twenty of his works are mentioned by Brockelmann, and Hidāyat Ḥusain's list, which includes only "the most important" and omits "many pamphlets on religious subjects", enumerates seventeen. His life, spent in teaching and writing, was uneventful, but he exercised great influence in India as a theologian.

(1) ***Anfās al-'ārifīn***, on the lives, sayings and miracles of the author's kinsmen, teachers, etc., in three *qisms*, namely (**1**) *Bawāriq al-wilāyah*, on the author's father, 'Abd al-Raḥīm Dihlawī (d. 1131/1719. See Raḥmān 'Alī p. 119), (**2**) *Shawāriq al-ma'rifah*, on the author's paternal uncle, Abū 'l-Riḍā Muḥammad, (**3**) in five separately-titled and detachable *faṣls*, of which the first is *Imdād fī ma'āthir al-ajdād*, the second *al-Nubdhat al-ibrīzah* [*al-ibrīzīyah* ?] *fī 'l-laṭīfat al-gharīzah* [*al-gharīzīyah* ?] (*dar nashr i aḥwāl i Shaikh 'Abd al-'Azīz Dihlawī u aslāf u akhlāf*

[1] Kairānah is a town on the Jumna 31 miles S.W. of Muẓaffarnagar.

i īshān), the third *al-ʻAṯīyat al-Ṣamadīyah fī* ['l- ?] *anfās al-Muḥammadīyah* (*dar dhikr i manāqib . . . i ḥaḍrat i Shaikh Muḥammad al-PHLTĪ*), the fourth *Insān al-ʻain fī mashāyikh al-Ḥaramain*, and the fifth *al-Juz' al-laṯīf fī tarjamat al-ʻabd al-ḍaʻīf*, a brief autobiography extending to 14 Rajab 1145/ 31 Dec. 1732, the date of the author's return home from his pilgrimage to Mecca [1]: **I.O.** 3985 (only the *Imdād*. *Circ.* A.D. 1895).

Edition: *Anfās al-ʻārifīn*, **Delhi** 1315/1897* (pp. 196).

Edition and English translation of *Qism* iii, *faṣl* 5: *The Persian autobiography of Shāh Walīullah bin ʻAbd al-Raḥīm al-Dihlavī : its English translation and a list of his works. By Mawlavi M. Hidayat Husain* (in *JASB*. N.S. viii (1912) pp. 161–75).

Edition of *Qism III*, *faṣl* 5: *Saṯaʻāt maʻah . . . Juz' al-laṯīf* [**Delhi** 1890°].

(2) **al-Intibāh fī salāsil auliyā' Allāh,** an enumeration of the spiritual pedigrees of the author with incidental expositions of Ṣūfī practices and other matters, divided (in the I.O. MS.) under the headings *Muqaddimah* fol. 1*b*, *Silsilah i Ṣūfīyah i ʻulamā'* fol. 7*b*, *Silsilah i bishārah* fol. 8*b*, *Silsilah i Khwājah* [*sic*] *i Qādirīyah* fol. 10*b*, *Ṭarīqah i Naqshbandīyah* fol. 21*a*, *Ṭarīqah i Chishtīyah* fol. 42*a*, *Ṭarīqah i Kubrawīyah* fol. 55*a*, *Ṭarīqah i Madyanīyah* fol. 58*a*, *Ṭarīqah i Shādhilīyah* fol. 61*a*, *Ṭarīqah i Shaṭṭārīyah* fol. 62*a*: **Āṣafīyah** i p. 402 no. 584 (A.H. 1174/1760–1), **I.O.** D.P. 776 (late 18th cent.).

[1] This autobiography of five pages tells of his birth (4 Shawwāl 1114), his going to *maktab* (in his 5th year), his beginning to pray and fast, his circumcision, his finishing the *Qur'ān* and beginning to read Persian books (7th year), his reading the *Sharḥ i Mullā* [Jāmī on Ibn al-Ḥājib's *Kāfiyah*] (10th year), marriage (14th year), his introduction to the practices of the Ṣūfīs, especially the Naqshbandīs, as his father's disciple and his completion of the traditional course of studies (15th year), his father's death after giving him licence to accept *baiʻat* and give *irshād* (17th year), some twelve years of teaching, of progress in Ṣūfism, study of the books of the four *madhāhib* and acceptance of the *rawish i fuqahā-yi muḥaddithīn*, his departure for the pilgrimage (end of 1143), his visits to Mecca and Medina, his intercourse with the traditionist Sh. Abū Ṭāhir [M. b. Ibrāhīm al-Kurdī al-Madanī, d. 1145 : see *JASB*. 1912 p. 166], by whom he was admitted to several Ṣūfī orders (*khirqah i jāmiʻah i Sh. A. Ṭ. kih ḥāwī i jamīʻ i khiraq i Ṣūfīyah tuwān guft pūshīd*), his performance of the *ḥajj* at the end of this year, his departure for India (beginning of 1145) and his arrival home on 14 Rajab. Many of the books read by him in the course of his studies are specified.

Edition: **Delhi** 1311/1893–4 (see *JASB.* 1912 p. 168).

[To the biographical sources mentioned on p. 22 may be added *Khazīnat al-aṣfiyā'* ii p. 373; *Ḥayāt i Walī* (in Urdu. 360 pp.), by M. Raḥīm-Bakhsh, Delhi 1319/1901–2*; Bānkīpūr xiv pp. 134–5; Brockelmann *Sptbd.* ii pp. 614–5. For an anonymous work defending Walī Allāh against the charge that he had insufficient respect for the Imāms, see Bānkīpūr xvii 1619.]

1353. For the *Burhān al-futūḥ*, which was composed in 1148/1736–7 by M. 'Alī b. M. Ṣādiq Ḥusainī Nīshāpūrī Najafī Burhānpūrī, and of which the fifteenth *bāb* is devoted to notices of *ṣūfīs*, see p. 137 *supra.*

1354. **Ghulām-Sharaf al-Dīn**[1] b. Sh. Imām al-Dīn b. Sh. Karīm al-Dīn was the son of a daughter of Hidāyat Allāh Qādirī Rashīdī Arshadī Faiyāḍī Manērī. He was a disciple of Sh. Abū 'l-Faiyāḍ Ghulām-Rashīd (see p. 1015 *supra*), whose discourses he attended and noted down from 11 Muḥarram to 12 Ramaḍān 1147/13 June 1734 to 5 February 1735.

Ganj i Faiyāḍī, a biography of the above-mentioned Sh. Abū 'l-Faiyāḍ Ghulām-Rashīd with a collection of his letters and sayings: **Browne** Pers. Cat. 111 (A.H. 1150/1738), **Ivanow** Curzon 80 (18th cent.).

1355. **M. b. Yār-Muḥammad**[2] b. Rājī Kamman **Kōlawī** tells us that he was born on 2 Dhū'l-Ḥijjah 1098/9 October 1697.

Ashjār al-jamāl or alternatively *Akhbār al-jamāl,* short notices of prophets and saints including some Ṣūfīs of Kōl (i.e. 'Alīgaṛh), completed in 1151/1738: **Ivanow** Curzon 81 (defective. Late 18th cent.) = Nadhīr Aḥmad 57.

1356. M. **Qiyām al-Dīn,** commonly called (*'urf*) Qāḍī Khān, b. Abū 'l-Ḥasan Chishtī Fārūqī.

[1] Similar personal names consisting of the word Ghulām followed by the name of a saint are Ghulām-Jīlānī (cf. p. 697 *supra*), Ghulām-Hamadānī (p. 875 *supra*), Ghulām-Muḥyī 'l-Dīn (pp. 395, 670 *supra*), and Ghulām-Naqshband (cf. Brockelmann *Sptbd.* ii p. 611). The Sharaf al-Dīn referred to is evidently Sharaf al-Dīn Yaḥyā Manērī (for whom see p. **1049 n. 2**).

[2] Nadhīr Aḥmad gives the author's name as "Yār Md. B. Rājī Kamman", and this indeed appears to be the form in which the name first occurs in the MS., since Ivanow in quoting the opening words [*al-Ḥ. l.... ammā ba'd fa-qāla...* (*M. b.*) *Yār M. b. Rājī* . . .] brackets *M.b.* as though supplied from another place.

Ḥaqā'iq al-auliyā', written in 1154/1741–2: **Āṣafīyah** iii p. 100 no. 1293 (Precise subject not stated. A.H. 1154/1741–2).

1357. **M. Najīb Qādirī Nāgaurī** Ajmērī wrote his *Makhzan al-a'rās* in 1155/1742 and 1156/1743 (and possibly subsequent years) on the basis of a work by Sharaf al-Dīn b. Qāḍī Shaikh M. Nahrawālī.[1]

Makhzan al-a'rās, dates of the deaths of saints arrayed under the months: **Ivanow** 1631 (slightly defective at end. Late 18th cent.), 1632 (late 18th or early 19th cent.), **Ivanow** 1st Spt. 869 (early 19th cent.).

Edition (presumably of this work): *Kitāb i a'rās*, by M. Najīb Qādirī Nāgaurī, [**Āgrah**] 1300/1883°.

1358. Miyāṅ **Aḥmad b. Maḥmūd Uwaisī** Chanābī.

Laṭā'if i nafīsīyah[2] *dar faḍā'il i Uwaisīyah*, anecdotes of Uwais al-Qaranī,[3] written in 1156/1743: **Lahore** Panjāb Univ. Lib. (see *OCM*. viii/4 p. 42).

Edition: **Delhi** 1314/1896°.

Urdu translation: *Nasīm i Yaman fī ḥālāt i Uwais i Qaran*, by S. M. Ishfāq[4] Ḥusain Shāh Razzāqī, **Lahore** 1328/1910*.

1359. Abū 'l-Faiḍ Kamāl al-Dīn **M. Iḥsān** b. Ḥasan Aḥmad (d. 1149/1736) b. M. Hādī b. M. 'Abd Allāh b. Aḥmad Mujaddid i Alf i Thānī was a great-great-grandson of the celebrated Naqshbandī saint Aḥmad Sirhindī and was apparently a *khalīfah* of the saint in Oudh or Bengal.

Rauḍat al-qaiyūmīyah, begun before 1152/1739 but then interrupted until about 1154/1741 and containing in the concluding lines a reference to the reigning sovereign Muḥammad

[1] Nahrawālah = Pattan in Gujrāt.

[2] So called because "*maḍāmīn u ma'ānī i laṭīfah i nafīsah par mabnī hai*" (Urdu trans., p. 9, l. 5 from below).

[3] For Uwais al-Qaranī, who is said to have been killed at the Battle of Ṣiffīn (A.H. 37/657) or to have died at some other date (A.H. 18, 22, 32, etc.), see *Kashf al-maḥjūb*, tr. Nicholson, pp. 83–4; *Tadhkirat al-auliyā'* i pp. 15–24; *Haft iqlīm* pp. 19–22 (no. 1); *Majālis al-mu'minīn* pp. 120–1 (3rd biography in *Majlis* 4); *Safīnat al-auliyā'* p. 30 (no. 18); *Khazīnat al-aṣfiyā'* ii pp. 118–21; Caetani *Chronographia Islamica* i pp. 214 (A.H. 18) and 423 (A.H. 37), where other references will be found.

[4] Or Ashfāq in accordance with the usual, though corrupt, Indian pronunciation in such names as this.

Shāh (d. 1161/1748), though some later dates (e.g. 1164/1751) occur in the narrative, a detailed account of the lives (narrated laudably year by year) and miracles, etc., of the great saint Aḥmad Fārūqī Sirhindī, called here the first *qaiyūm* (*qaiyūm i awwal i īn ummat*), who died in 1034/1624 (see p. 988 n. 5 *supra*), and his first three successors (the second, third and fourth *qaiyūm*), namely, his (third) son, M. Ma'ṣūm called 'Urwat al-wuthqā (b. 1007/1599, d. 1079/1668),[1] M. Naqshband Ḥujjat Allāh (b. 1034/1625, d. 1114/1702), the son of the preceding, and M. Zubair (b. 1093/1682, d. 1152/1740), with an enormous number (probably more than two thousand) of short notices of their descendants and disciples, interspersed with incidental references to historical events, e.g. Nādir Shāh's invasion, which the author, an eye-witness, describes at some length : **Ivanow** Curzon 82 (A.H. 1218/1804).

1360. **M. Amān b. M. Yūsuf** b. M. Raḥīm seems to have followed the army of Niẓām al-Mulk Āṣaf-Jāh to Arcot [in 1156/1743]. He had visited the shrines of saints at Aurangābād, Gwalior and elsewhere.

Safīnat al-'ārifīn, notices of numerous holy men, mostly Indian, from the first four Caliphs to the end of the eleventh century of the Hijrah, the latest date being 1103/1692, the year of the death of S. Ḥasan Rasūl-numā[2] : **Rieu** i 362*b* (18th cent.).

1361. For the *Wāqi'āt i Kashmīr*, begun by M. A'ẓam in 1148/1735–6, completed in 1160/1747, and devoted largely to the lives of Kashmīrī saints, see p. 683 *supra*.

1362. Mīr **Ghulām-'Alī " Āzād " Bilgrāmī,** who was born at Bilgrām in 1116/1704 and died, doubtless at Aurangābād, in 1200/1786, has already been mentioned (pp. 855–66 *supra*) as the author of the *Khizānah i 'āmirah* and other works.

(1) ***Rauḍat al-auliyā',*** lives of ten saints buried at Rauḍah (" Rauza ", " Roza ", " Raoza "), or Khuldābād (cf. p. 858 n. 2

[1] Cf. p. 991 n. 2 *supra* and *Qaiyūm i thānī*, a short (48 pp.) Urdu biography by M. 'Aẓīm Fīrōzpūrī, Lahore [1905*].

[2] For whom see *Dhikr i jamī' i auliyā' i Dihlī* (I.O. D.P. 594 foll. 90*b*–92*a*) ; Khāfī Khān ii pp. 552–3 ; *Chahār gulshan* (I.O. 3944 fol. 23*a* ult.) ; *Āthār al-ṣanādīd* (in Urdu), *bāb* iii p. 74 ; *Khazīnat al-aṣfiyā'* i p. 180 margin. A collection of his sayings taken down by a disciple named Khalīl is preserved in an I.O. MS. (D.P. 590).

supra), namely Burhān al-Dīn M, called al-Gharīb al-Hānsawī [1] (p. 4), Muntajab al-Dīn Zarzarī Zar-bakhsh (p. 14), Ḥasan Dihlawī (p. 16), Rājū Qattāl (p. 18), Gēsū-darāz (p. 19), Farīd al-Dīn Adīb (p. 25), Khwājah Ḥusain b. Maḥmūd Shīrāzī (p. 26), Zain al-Dīn Dāwud b. Khwājah Ḥusain Shīrāzī (p. 26), Shāh Jalāl Ganj i Rawān (p. 41), Shāh Khāksār (p. 42), followed by brief notices of three rulers buried there (Aurangzēb, Niẓām al-Mulk Burhān Shāh, Niẓām al-Mulk Āṣaf-Jāh) and an autobiography of the author, who wrote the work in 1161/1748: **Āṣafīyah** iii p. 164 no. 148 (A.H. 1167/1753–4), i p. 320 no. 22 (A.H. 1232/1816–17), **Ethé** 655.

Edition: **Aurangābād** 1310/1892-3*.

Urdu translation by Saif Allāh Qādirī: *Tarjamah i R. al-a.*, **Ḥaidarābād** (see Ḥaidarābād Coll. p. 52, where neither the date of publication nor the name of the original author is mentioned).

(2) ***Ma'āthir al-kirām tārīkh i Bilgrām***, completed in 1166/1752–3 and divided into two *faṣls*, namely (1) lives of about eighty *fuqarā'*, i.e. saints and mystics, firstly those of Bilgrām and its neighbourhood and secondly those incidentally mentioned in the preceding biographies, (2) lives of about seventy *fuḍalā'*, i.e. learned men, firstly those of India and secondly those of Oudh and Bilgrām: **Āṣafīyah** i p. 348 no. 105 (A.H. 1180/1766–7), **Ethé** 682 (sent by the author to Richard Johnson in 1785), **I.O.** 3923 (*circ.* A.D. 1880?), **Bānkīpūr** viii 723 (early 19th cent.), **Rieu** iii 971*a* (A.H. 1266/1850), **Berlin** 603 (*Faṣl* 2 only).

Edition: **Ḥaidarābād** 1910 (with introduction by 'Abd al-Ḥaqq. See *OCM*. iii/2 (Feb. 1927) p. 33 footnote).

List of the biographies in *Faṣl* 2: Berlin pp. 567–8.

The *Sarw i āzād*, which is the second volume of this work, though for all practical purposes it may be regarded as independent, has already been dealt with (p. 864 *supra*).

[1] B. al-D. Gh., who is the person commemorated in the name of Burhānpūr, was a disciple of Niẓām al-Dīn Auliyā (cf. p. 941 n. 5) and died in 738/1337 (or thereabouts). See *Akhbār al-akhyār* pp. 93–4; *Haft iqlīm* no. 390; Firishtah ii pp. 400–1; *Safīnat al-auliyā'* p. 101 (no. 117); *Khazīnat al-aṣfiyā'* i pp. 346–8; *Nuzhat al-khawāṭir* pp. 143–4; Beale *Oriental biographical dictionary* under Burhan-uddin Gharib; etc.

1363. Ḥanīf al-Dīn **'Abd al-Qādir** b. Qāḍī S. M. S̲h̲arīf b. Qāḍī S. M. Ḥanīf **Kintūrī**[1] Nīs̲h̲āpūrī died in 1204/1789-90 (according to the Āṣafīyah catalogue).

Kuḥl al-jawāhir fī manāqib 'Abd al-Qādir, written in 1167/1753-4 : **Āṣafīyah** i p. 460 no. 633.

1364. For the *C̲h̲ahār guls̲h̲an* of Rāy C̲h̲aturman, which was completed in 1173/1759-60 and of which the fourth *guls̲h̲an* is devoted to Muslim and Hindu saints, see p. 472 *supra*.

1365. For the *Mir'āt i Aḥmadī*, which was completed by 'Alī Muḥammad K̲h̲ān in 1175/1761, and of which the *k̲h̲ātimah* contains *inter alia* accounts of the saints and Saiyids buried in, or near, Aḥmadābād, see pp. 729-31 *supra*.

1366. **M. Ṣādiq Kās̲h̲g̲h̲arī.**

Tad̲h̲kirah i K̲h̲wājagān, or *Tad̲h̲kirah i 'Azīzān*, a Turkī work on the lives of certain saints of Kās̲h̲g̲h̲ar, written in 1182/1768-9 : **Leningrad** Institut (see *Manuscrits turcs de l'Institut des Langues Orientales décrits par W. D. Smirnow* (St. Petersburg 1897) pp. 156-60. Cf. Semenov *Ukazatel* p. 15, where no MSS. are mentioned).

English epitome : *The history of the K̲h̲ojas of Eastern-Turkistān summarized from the Tazkira-i-K̲h̲wājagān of Muhammad Ṣādiq Kās̲h̲g̲h̲arī, by the late Robert Barkley Shaw . . . Edited with introduction and notes by N. Elias*. **Calcutta** 1897 (*Journal of the Asiatic Society of Bengal*, vol. lxvi, part 1, extra no.).

Persian version (?)[2] : MSS. ?

1367. **M. 'Ābid.**

Ḥālāt i Saiyid Sālār Mas'ūd G̲h̲āzī, an account, written in 1188/1774-5, [presumably of the Saiyid who is said to have founded G̲h̲āzīpūr (cf. p. 1060 n. 1 *infra*) rather than of the legendary hero who has already been mentioned (p. 1006 *supra*) as the subject of the *Mir'āt i Mas'ūdī*] : **Āṣafīyah** iii p. 362 no. 251 (A.D. 1831)?

---

[1] Presumably in reference to Kintūr, a village 21 miles N.E. of Bārah Bankī in Oudh.

[2] That the work exists in a Persian form is implied by its inclusion in Semenov's *Ukazatel*', but the inclusion may be inadvertent.

1368. S. **Ghulām-Ḥusain Khān** b. Hidāyat-'Alī Khān b. S. 'Alīm Allāh b. S. Faiḍ Allāh [1] **Ṭabāṭabā'ī** Ḥasanī, who was born at Delhi in 1140/1727–8, has already been mentioned (pp. 625–40) as the author of the *Siyar al-muta'akhkhirīn*, which he began in 1194/1780 and completed in 1195/1781.

Bishārat al-imāmah, a *mathnawī*, written before the *Siyar al-muta'akhkhirīn*,[2] on the lives of the author's ancestors, especially the miracles of his great-grandfather, S. Faiḍ Allāh Ṭabāṭabā'ī, and his grandfather S. 'Alīm Allāh Ṭabāṭabā, the latter of whom died at 'Aẓīmābād (i.e. Patna) in Sha'bān 1156/1743 [3]: **Bānkīpūr** Suppt. i 1991 (A.H. 1277/1860).

1369. "From various incidental allusions in his book it is possible to conclude that" a certain **Sabzawārī** (*khāk-sār i Sabzawārī*, as he calls himself) "wrote shortly after 1188/1774" (Ivanow). S. Qamar al-Dīn Aurangābādī (d. 1193/1779 or 1195/1781: cf. p. 22 *supra*), the subject of the 26th *sāniḥah*, and Mīr Ghulām-'Alī "Āzād" (d. 1200/1786: cf. p. 858 *supra*), the subject of the 27th, were still alive at the time of writing.

(*Sawāniḥ*), a work in 31 *sāniḥahs* on the saints buried or still living in or near Aurangābād (the first being Burhān al-Dīn Gharīb, who died in 738/1337, the last Miyāṅ Ghulām-Ḥusain, still living), with descriptions of their graves and of the city: **Ivanow** 285 (late 18th cent.), possibly also **Rehatsek** p. 197 no. 43 ("*Resáláh Sowáneh* . . . This little MS. contains the legends of the saints who lived during the time of Aurung-zyb, who amounted to about a dozen or so; it contains also a description of the city of Aurungábád, which he restored and looked upon with peculiar favour, and of the mausoleum of one of his Begums; it was composed during his lifetime,[4] but bears no date").

List of the biographies, etc.: Ivanow pp. 122–3.

[1] Cf. *Siyar al-muta'akhkhirīn* i p. 3^{13}, ii p. 374^{11} (Lucknow editions).

[2] The *B. al-i.* is mentioned in the *S. al-m.* ii pp. 523^{16}, 613^{13} (Lucknow editions).

[3] *S. al-m.* ii p. 613^{11-12} (Raymond's trans. (1926) ii p. 171).

[4] If this work was really written in Aurangzēb's lifetime, Ivanow 285 is presumably an expanded recension of it.

1370. **M. A'ẓam T'hattawī.**

Tuḥfat al-ṭāhirīn, an account of the saints buried at Tattah and on Maklī hill (cf. p. 1031[1] *infra*), written in 1194/1780: **Rieu** iii 1061*b* (extracts only).

1371. It was at the request of Ṭīpū Sulṭān (ruler of Mysore 1197–1213/1782–99: cf. pp. 767–72) that a certain **M. Sharīf** compiled the *Ṣaḥīfat al-a'rās*.

Ṣaḥīfat al-a'rās, or *Tārīkh i wafāt i buzurgān*, an almanac giving the names of the holy personages who died on each day of the Muḥammadan year: **Ethé** 2733, **Ivanow** 1634.

1372. Mīr Shihāb al-Dīn [1] "Niẓām", entitled **'Imād al-Mulk** [2] **Ghāzī al-Dīn Khān Fīrōz-Jang** [III], was a son of the Amīr al-Umarā' Ghāzī al-Dīn Khān Fīrōz-Jang [II, i.e. Mīr M. Panāh, d. 1165/1752 [3]] and a grandson of Niẓām al-Mulk Āṣaf-Jāh.[4] His mother was a daughter of I'timād al-Daulah Qamar al-Dīn Khān,[5] who became *Wazīr* to Muḥammad Shāh in 1136/1724 and died in 1161/1748. In the reign of Aḥmad Shāh (1161–7/1748–54) he was *Mīr Bakhshī* (Quartermaster General [6]) and subsequently *Wazīr*. He directed the military operations against Ṣafdar-Jang [7] and, with Marāṭ'hā help, against Sūraj Mal, the Jāṭ. In 1167/1754 he deposed Aḥmad Shāh and placed 'Ālamgīr II upon the throne. In 1169/1755 Mīr Mu'īn al-Mulk, Governor of the Panjāb,[8] who had perforce submitted to Aḥmad Shāh Abdālī, died, and his widow and her favourite Ādīnah Bēg Khān [9] seized the reins of government. 'Imād al-Mulk, desiring to restore the province to the empire, captured Lahore, where

[1] This name was borne also by his great-grandfather, who like him had the title Ghāzī al-Dīn Khān Fīrōz-Jang (but not 'Imād al-Mulk) and who died in 1122/1710. See *Ma'āthir al-umarā'* ii pp. 872–9, Beveridge's trans. pp. 587–92; Beale *Oriental biographical dictionary* under Ghazi-uddin Khan i.

[2] By the title 'Imād al-Mulk he is distinguished from his father and his great-grandfather, both of whom bore the title Ghāzī al-Dīn Khān Fīrōz-Jang.

[3] See *Ma'āthir al-umarā'* i pp. 361–2; *Khizānah i 'āmirah* pp. 49–50.

[4] Mīr Qamar al-Dīn. See *Ma'āthir al-umarā'* iii pp. 837–48; *Khizānah i 'āmirah* pp. 35–49.

[5] Mīr M. Fāḍil. See *Ma'āthir al-umarā'* i pp. 358–61.

[6] See *BSOS*. ix/1 p. 225.

[7] See *Ma'āthir al-umarā'* i pp. 365–8.

[8] He was a son of I'timād al-Daulah Qamar al-Dīn Khān and therefore a maternal uncle of 'Imād al-Mulk.

[9] Cf. p. 665 *supra*.

he left Ādīnah Bēg Khān in charge, removed Mughulānī Bēgam to Delhi and married her daughter. Aḥmad Shāh Abdālī at once marched on Lahore (A.H. 1170/1756), expelled Ādīnah Bēg Khān, and went on to Delhi, which he entered victoriously with 'Ālamgīr II and 'Imād al-Mulk in his train. 'Imād al-Mulk then took part on behalf of Aḥmad Shāh Abdālī in the operations of Jahān Khān against Sūraj Mal and in unsuccessful hostilities against Shujā' al-Daulah of Oudh. Aḥmad Shāh Abdālī, displeased with 'Imād al-Mulk, appointed Najīb al-Daulah *Amīr al-Umarā'* and left for Lahore. 'Imād al-Mulk marched from Farrukhābād against Najīb al-Daulah and with Marāṭ'hā help besieged him and 'Ālamgīr II in Delhi. In 1174/1760 the growing power of the Sik'hs and Marāṭ'hās brought Aḥmad Shāh Abdālī for the fourth time to India, and the Marāṭ'hās were defeated at Pānīpat. 'Imād al-Mulk, knowing that 'Ālamgīr II desired an Abdālī victory, had murdered him [8 Rabī' II 1173/29 Nov. 1759] on Aḥmad Shāh's approach.

The days of 'Imād al-Mulk's power were now over. For a time he stayed with Sūraj Mal [who died in 1177/1763], then with Aḥmad Khān Bangash [d. 1185/1771] at Farrukhābād, and he fought on the side of Shujā' al-Daulah of Oudh against the British. In 1187/1773 he went to the Deccan and received some land in Mālwah from the Marāṭ'hās. Then after living for a time at Sūrat he went on a pilgrimage to Mecca. In 1195/1781 according to the *Gulzār i Ibrāhīm* (cited in Sprenger p. 273) he was in Sind. Subsequently he was at the court of Tīmūr Shāh Abdālī (who reigned 1187–1207/1773–93), and in 1211/1797, when Zamān Shāh (1207–16/1793–1801) invaded the Panjāb, 'Imād al-Mulk is said to have been in his service. He died at Kālpī on 10 Rabī' II 1215/1 September 1800.[1]

'Imād al-Mulk, who originally used the *takhalluṣ* "Āṣaf" but abandoned it later for "Niẓām", wrote poetry in Persian, Urdu, Arabic and Turkī. His Persian *dīwān*, of which there are MSS. in the British Museum (Rieu ii 719*b*) and at Leningrad (Romaskewicz p. 9), was published in 1301/1883–4 (see Āṣafīyah iii p. 296, where the place of publication (presumably Ḥaidarābād) is not mentioned). A poem in praise of 'Alī (*Manqabat i*

[1] See *JASB*. xlviii/1 (1879) p. 130.

Niẓām dar madḥ i 'Alī) and a *qaṣīdah* are preserved in MS. (autograph ?) at 'Alīgaṛh (Subḥ. MSS. p. 37 nos. 7, 8). His *mathnawīs* included one on the miracles of Maulānā Fakhr al-Dīn (*Fakhrīyat al-Niẓām*), but no MSS. seem to be recorded.

Manāqib i Fakhrīyah, a biography of Maulānā M. Fakhr al-Dīn called Muḥibb al-Nabī Dihlawī,[1] written in 1201/1786–7: **I.O.** D.P. 728 (A.H. 1227/1812), **Lindesiana** p. 158 no. 741 (A.H. 1240/1824–5), **Āṣafīyah** i p. 490 no. 342 (A.H. 1312/1894–5).

Edition: **Delhi** 1315/1897*.

[*Khizānah i 'āmirah* pp. 50–4; *Ma'āthir al-umarā'* ii pp. 847–56; *Gulzār i Ibrāhīm;* Muṣḥafī *Tadhkirah i Hindī; Makhzan al-gharā'ib* no. 2922; *Majmū'ah i naghz* ii pp. 277–80; *Tadhkirah i Sarwar; Tadhkirah i khwush-nawīsān* p. 76; *'Iyār al-shu'arā'; Gulshan i bī-khār; Tārīkh 'Imād al-Mulk* (see p. 623 *supra*); *Naghmah i 'andalīb;* Sprenger p. 273; Garcin de Tassy ii pp. 476–7; W. Irvine *The Bangash Nawábs of Farrukhábád* (in *JASB.* xlviii/1 (1879)) pp. 128–30; Rieu ii 719–20, iii 1092*b*; Beale *Oriental biographical dictionary* under Ghazi-uddin Khan III.]

1373. Mīr **'Alī Shēr "Qāni'" Tattawī,** who was born in 1140/1727–8 and was still alive in 1202/1787–8, has already been mentioned (p. 656 *supra*) as the author of the *Tuḥfat al-kirām* and other works.

(1) *Mi'yār i sālikān i ṭarīqat* (a chronogram = 1202/1787–8), lives of saints from the time of Muḥammad to the close of the twelfth century of the Hijrah in twelve *mi'yārs* each devoted to a century: **Rieu** ii 847*b* (A.H. 1246/1830), **I.O.** 4396 (*circ.* A.D. 1852 probably).

[1] Fakhr al-Dīn Fakhr i Jahān Shāhjahānābādī Chishtī, as he is called in the *Khazīnat al-aṣfiyā'*, was the son and *khalīfah* of Sh. Niẓām al-Dīn Aurangābādī (cf. p. 1038[4] *infra*). Born at Aurangābād in 1126/1714, he migrated to Delhi at the age of twenty-five and died there in Jumādā II 1199/April–May 1785. See *Dhikr al-aṣfiyā'*; *Miftāḥ al-tawārīkh* p. 360; *Khazīnat al-aṣfiyā'* i pp. 498–505; Beale *Oriental biographical dictionary* under Fakhr-uddin (Maulana) (Beale's statement that he was styled Saiyid al-shu'arā' seems to be based on the fact that the chronogram on his tomb is followed by the words *min kalām S. al-sh. Fakhr al-Dīn Maqbūl i Ilāhī sanah i* 1199, but presumably the author of the chronogram was his disciple S. Fakhr al-Dīn "Mast", who is mentioned in the *Khazīnat al-aṣfiyā'* i p. 500[3]).

(2) ***Maklī-nāmah,*** accounts of the saints buried on Maklī hill [1] (beside Tattah): **Rieu** iii 1061*b* (extracts only).

1374. Autobiographical statements in the text of the *Baḥr i zakhkhār* show that the author, **Wajīh al-Dīn Ashraf,** lived at Lucknow and that he was writing the work in 1203/1788–9.

Baḥr i zakhkhār (beginning: *Ḥamd i bī-ḥadd Qadīmī rā*), a " vast compilation " (595 foll. in the very imperfect B.M. MS.) devoted to the lives of saints and mystics, mostly Indian and many contemporary with the author, divided into eight *lujjahs*, which are subdivided into *nahrs* and again into *maujs* (viz.[2] (**1**) Muḥammad's children and wives, the Caliphs and the Companions, (**2**) 'Alī, Fāṭimah, the Imāms, the *Tābi'īn*, traditionists, jurists and Qur'ān-readers, (**3**) (*a*) Ḥasan Baṣrī [3] and his disciples, (*b*) Chirāgh i Dihlī (cf. p. 942 n. 1 *supra*) and his disciples, (*c*) Sirāj al-Dīn 'Uthmān [4] and his order, (*d*) 'Alī Ṣābir,[5] etc., (**4**) (*a*) Ma'rūf Karkhī,[6] etc., (*b*) 'Abd al-Qādir Gīlānī (cf. p. 933 n. 2

[1] Cf. p. 1028[3] *supra.*

[2] The analysis which follows is based on the table of contents prefixed to the work in the B.M. MS. (foll. 1–70).

[3] Celebrated traditionist and ascetic, d. 110/728 at al-Baṣrah. See Ibn Qutaibah *Ma'ārif* p. 225; *Kashf al-maḥjūb*, tr. Nicholson p. 86; *Tadhkirat al-auliyā'* i pp. 24–40; Ibn Khallikān no. 155; *Haft iqlīm* p. 144 (no. 88); *Safīnat al-auliyā'* p. 31 (no. 19); *Khazīnat al-aṣfiyā'* i pp. 222–5; *Rauḍāt al-jannāt* pp. 208–11; *Ency. Isl.* under al-Ḥasan (unsigned); Caetani *Chronographia Islamica* p. 1396 (where many further references will be found); Massignon *Essai sur les origines du lexique technique de la mystique musulmane* pp. 152–79; *Der Islam* XIV (1925) pp. 1–75.

[4] One of Niẓām al-Dīn Auliyā's disciples, d. 758/1357. See *Maṭlūb al-ṭālibīn* (Ethé col. 324[22]); *Sawāṭi' al-anwār* (Ethé col. 333[6]); *Khazīnat al-aṣfiyā'* i pp. 357–8; *Nuzhat al-khawāṭir* (in Arabic) p. 77; etc.

[5] 'Alā' al-Dīn 'Alī b. Aḥmad Ṣābir Kalyarī, founder of the Ṣābirī branch of the Chishtī order and a disciple of Ganj i Shakar (for whom see p. 941 n. 4 *supra*), died in 690/1291 and is buried at Pīrān Kalyar, near Roorkee, in the Sahāranpūr District of the United Provinces. See *Akhbār al-akhyār* p. 69; *Sawāṭi' al-anwār* (Ethé col. 334 no. 24); *Khazīnat al-aṣfiyā'* i pp. 315–19; *Sawāniḥ i 'umrī i ḥaḍrat i Ṣābir . . . mukammal tārīkh i Pīrān Kalyar i sharīf* (in Urdu), by Sulṭān Maḥmūd b. Mushtāq Aḥmad Murādābādī, Murādābād [1911 ?]; *Tadhkirah i Ṣābirīyah ma'rūf bah Siyāḥat i Kalyar* (in Urdu), by Walī Aḥmad Khān, Badāyūṅ [1922]; etc.

[6] For M. al-K., a celebrated Ṣūfī who died in 200/815–16 and is buried at Baghdād, see *Kashf al-maḥjūb* tr. Nicholson pp. 113–15; *Tadhkirat al-auliyā'* i pp. 269–74; Ibn Khallikān no. 371; *Nafaḥāt* pp. 42–3; *Haft iqlīm* p. 105 (no. 38); *Majālis al-mu'minīn* p. 266; *Safīnat al-auliyā'* p. 35 (no. 27); *Khazīnat al-aṣfiyā'* i pp. 76–8; *Rauḍāt al-jannāt* iv pp. 216–17; *Ency. Isl.* under Ma'rūf (Nicholson); etc.

supra), and the Qādirīs, (*c*) Abū Najīb Suhrawardī,[1] etc., (*d*) Najm al-Dīn Kubrā,[2] (**5**) (*a*) saints of the Maghrib, (*b*) Qalandarīs, (*c*) martyrs, (*d*) Bāyazīd Bisṭāmī[3]; Bahā' al-Dīn Naqshband (cf. p. 948 n. 2 *supra*); Shaṭṭārīs; Shāh Madār (cf. p. 1006 *supra*), (*e*) Wais [i.e. Uwais] Qaranī (cf. p. 1023 *supra*), (**6**) saints of unknown affiliation, (**7**) ecstatics (*majdhūbān*), (**8**) female saints): **Rieu** iii 976*b* (*Lujjahs* 1–3 and first two sections of *Lujjah* 4, defective at end. *Circ.* A.D. 1850).

Edition of the portion relating to the Ṣābirīs: *Shu'bah* [= *Mauj* ?] *i siwum az nahr i duwum*[4] *i lujjah i siwum i kitāb i Baḥr i zakhkhār*, **Allahabad** 1313/1895* (51 pp.).

1375. M. **Na'īm Allāh Bahrā'ichī** Ḥanafī Naqshbandī, born in 1153/1740–1, doubtless at Bahrā'ich (65 miles north-east of Lucknow), was the son of Ghulām-Quṭb al-Dīn, commonly called (*'urf*) Malik Kālī (or Kālē ?), b. Malik Ghulām-Muḥammad. In 1171/1757–8 he went to Lucknow and pursued Arabic studies there. Subsequently he studied at Shāhjahānpūr, Bareilly, Delhi, Murādābād and elsewhere. In 1186/1772–3 he was initiated into the Naqshbandī order by M. Jamīl, one of Mīrzā Jān-i-Jānān "Maẓhar's" *khalīfahs*, who had come from Delhi to Lucknow. Not long afterwards he visited "Maẓhar" at Delhi and spent four months there. In 1189/1775–6 he returned to Delhi and remained in constant association with "Maẓhar"

[1] 'Abd al-Qāhir b. 'Abd Allāh, d. 563/1168 at Baghdād. See Ibn Khallikān (Cairo 1310) i p. 299; Subkī iv p. 256; *Nafaḥāt* p. 478; *Safīnat al-auliyā'* p. 103 (no. 122); *Khazīnat al-aṣfiyā'* ii p. 11; Brockelmann i p. 436, *Sptbd.* i p. 780; etc.

[2] Founder of the Kubrawī order, d. 618/1226 at Khwārazm. See *Tārīkh i Guzīdah* p. 789; Subkī v p. 11; *Nafaḥāt* p. 480; *Majālis al-'ushshāq* no. 19; *Haft iqlīm* no. 1401; *Majālis al-mu'minīn* p. 286 (*Majlis* 6); *Safīnat al-auliyā'* p. 103 (no. 124); *Riyāḍ al-'ārifīn* p. 239; *Khazīnat al-aṣfiyā'* ii p. 258; *Rauḍāt al-jannāt* p. 81; Browne *Lit. Hist.* ii pp. 491–4; *Ency. Isl.* under Nadjm al-Dīn (Berthels); Brockelmann i p. 440, *Sptbd.* i p. 786; *Doklady Akademii Nauk*, Leningrad 1924, series B, April-June, p. 36 (an article by Berthels on Kubrā's quatrains with biography and bibliography).

[3] Abū Yazīd Ṭaifūr b. 'Īsā al-Bisṭāmī, d. 261/875 or 264/878 at Bisṭām. See *Kashf al-maḥjūb* tr. Nicholson pp. 106–8; *Tadhkirat al-auliyā'* i pp. 134–79; Ibn Khallikān under Ṭaifūr; *Nafaḥāt* p. 62; *Majālis al-'ushshāq* no. 4; *Haft iqlīm* no. 836; *Majālis al-mu'minīn* p. 263; *Safīnat al-auliyā'* p. 73 (no. 66); *Riyāḍ al-'ārafīn* p. 46; *Khazīnat al-aṣfiyā'* i pp. 519–22; *Rauḍāt al-jannāt* pp. 338–41; *Ency. Isl.* under Bāyazīd (unsigned); Massignon *Essai sur les origines du lexique technique de la mystique musulmane* pp. 243–56; etc.

[4] This division seems to diverge from that of the B.M. MS.

for four years, receiving from him the *khirqah* and his *ijāzat* as a member of the Naqshbandī, Qādirī, Chishtī and Suhrawardī orders. Thenceforward he lived mainly in Lucknow. When he wrote his autobiography in 1208/1793–4, he had visited Delhi four times, the *bilād i Afāghinah* (i.e. probably Rohilkhand) several times and Pānīpat twice. He died at Bahrā'ich in 1218/1803–4.

(1) *Bishārāt i Maẓharīyah dar faḍā'il i ḥadarāt i ṭarīqah i Mujaddidīyah*[1] (beginning: *al-Ḥ. l. 'lladhī aẓhara fī mir'āt al-ḥudūth anwār al-qidam*), a life of the saint and poet Mirzā "Maẓhar",[2] founder of the Shamsīyah Maẓharīyah branch of the Naqshbandī order, with accounts of twelve other Naqshbandī *shaikhs* (the first Aḥmad Sirhindī, the last

[1] i.e. the branch of the Naqshbandī order founded by Aḥmad Sirhindī called Mujaddid i Alf i Thānī (for whom see p. 988 n. 1 *supra*).

[2] Mīrzā Shams al-Dīn Ḥabīb Allāh (cf. Rieu i 363*b*, where the information concerning his "real name" comes evidently from the *Bishārāt i Maẓharīyah*), or Mīrzā Jān-i-Jānān "Maẓhar" (*Jān-i-Jānān mutakhalliṣ bi- "Maẓhar" pisar i Mīrzā Jān "Jānī" takhalluṣ*, as he calls himself in the autobiographical preface to his *dīwān*) is said to have owed the name or nickname Jān-i-Jān (upon which Jān-i-Jānān is apparently a later improvement: cf. Sprenger p. 488) to a punning suggestion by Aurangzēb that Jān-i-Jān would be a suitable name for the new-born son of Mīrzā Jān, who was a *manṣabdār* in the Imperial service. He was born at Kālābāgh, Mālwah, in 1111/1699–1700 or 1113/1701–2 or thereabouts ("Maẓhar's" own statements on this subject seem to have varied: see *OCM*. xviii/1 pp. 37–8), but most of his life was spent at Delhi, where he was murdered by a Shī'ite fanatic in Muḥarram 1195/January 1781 (other dates, 1192, 1194, seem to have less good authority). Although "Maẓhar" wrote little in Urdu, his influence on the development of Urdu poetry is regarded as important. In Persian he is represented by (1) a *dīwān* of some 1,000 verses (Editions: Calcutta 1267/1851*, Cawnpore 1271/1855°*, Madras 1272/1855–6, Lahore [1922*]. MSS.: Āṣafīyah i p. 732, iii p. 294, Browne Suppt. 609–10, Edinburgh 321, Lindesiana p. 186, Blochet iii 1945, Bānkīpūr Suppt. i 1966, Ivanow 875–6, Ivanow-Curzon 745(4), Edinburgh New Coll. p. 9, etc.), (2) *Kharīṭah i jawāhir*, an anthology of single lines and a few *rubā'īs* selected [by "Maẓhar", not by M. 'Abd al-Raḥmān as stated in the B.M. and I.O. catalogues] from the works of many ancient and modern poets (Editions (appended to the *dīwān*): Cawnpore 1271/1855°*, Lahore [1922*]. MS.: I.O. D.P. 1328), (3) *Maktūbāt*, Ṣūfī letters compiled by M. Na'īm Allāh Bahrā'ichī (MSS.: 'Alīgaṛh Subḥ. MSS. p. 53 no. 13, p. 18 no. 12 (it is not clear from the catalogue whether the second MS. contains the same collection as the first)). See "Maẓhar's" brief autobiographical preface to his *dīwān* (quoted in Sprenger p. 488); *Maqāmāt i Maẓharī* (see p. 1035 *infra*); *Safīnah i Khwushgū* (see Bānkīpūr viii p. 111); *Nikāt al-shu'arā'*; *Sarw i āzād*; "Ḥairat" *Maqālāt al-shu'arā'* (Sprenger p. 159); *Gul i ra'nā*; *Gulzār i Ibrāhīm*; *'Iqd i Thuraiyā*; *Ṣuḥuf i Ibrāhīm*; *Khulāṣat al-afkār* no. 448; *Makhzan al-gharā'ib* no. 2693; *Majmū'ah i naghz* ii pp. 198–200; *Ṭabaqāt i sukhun*; *Nishtar i 'ishq*; *Natā'ij al-afkār*; *Khāzin al-shu'arā'* fol. 152*a* ult.; Sprenger p. 256 (information from several Urdu *tadhkirahs*); *Khazīnat al-aṣfiyā'* i pp. 784–7;

M. ʻĀbid Sunāmī[1]) and some forty-five of "Maẓhar's" *khulafā'* (the first Thanā' Allāh Pānīpatī (cf. *Khazīnat al-aṣfiyā'* i p. 689, Raḥmān ʻAlī p. 38, etc.) the last Nūr-Muḥammad Qandahārī), written in 1204/1789–90 at the suggestion of Mīr M. Māh Bahrā'ichī and divided into a *muqaddimah*, two *maqṣads* (subdivided into five and six *bābs* respectively), and a *khātimah*: **Rieu** i 363*a* (A.H. 1207/1792), **I.O.** 4431 (late 18th cent.).

(2) *Maʻmūlāt i Maẓharīyah*, "an account of the Maẓharī sect of Ṣūfīs with special reference to the doctrines of its founder Maẓhar Jān-jānān" (Arberry). Editions: **Cawnpore** 1284/1867*, **Lahore** 1893† (in both of these editions the *M. i M.* is followed by *Maḥbūb i ʻārifīn*, "a short tract on the duties of the mystic" (Arberry), by ʻAlī Rāstīnī).

(3) (*Aḥwāl i Naʻīm Allāh Bahrā'ichī*), a brief autobiography (beginning: *Baʻd i ḥamd u ṣalāt az faqīr Naʻīm Allāh ʻufiya ʻanhu birādar i girāmī-qadr Bakhsh Allāh wa-ghairah birādarān zāda qadruhum daryāband kih* . . .) written in 1208/1793–4 at the age of fifty-six: **I.O.** 4431 foll. 142*b*–145*b* (late 18th cent.).

[Autobiography mentioned above; statements in the *Bishārāt i Maẓharīyah* (summarized by Rieu); Raḥmān ʻAlī p. 243.]

1376. Shāh ʻAbd Allāh, commonly called (*al-mashhūr bi-*) **Ghulām-ʻAlī**, b. S. ʻAbd al-Laṭīf Mujaddidī ʻAlawī **Dihlawī** was born in 1158/1745 at Baṭālah in the Gūrdāspūr District of the Panjāb. At the age of thirteen he went to Delhi and associated with well-known Ṣūfīs like Fakhr al-Dīn Fakhr i Jahān (cf. p. 1030 n. 1 *supra*) and Khwājah Mīr "Dard". In 1180/1766–7 at the age of twenty-two he became a disciple of Mīrzā "Maẓhar" (cf. p. 1033[11] *supra*) and in due course received from him the *khirqah i khilāfat* of the four main orders. After "Maẓhar's" death Ghulām-ʻAlī succeeded him as superior of his community (*jā-nishīn u ṣāḥib-*

Garcin de Tassy ii pp. 297–300; Rieu i 363, iii 1086*a*; *Ḥadā'iq al-Ḥanafīyah* p. 453; Beale *Oriental biographical dictionary* under Jan Janan; Raḥmān ʻAlī p. 226; Saksēna *History of Urdu literature* pp. 49–51; *Ency. Isl.* under Maẓhar (Hidayet Hosain); T. Grahame Bailey *History of Urdu literature* p. 46; Bānkīpūr Suppt. i pp. 214–15; *OCM.* xviii/1 (Nov. 1941) pp. 27–43 (part of an Urdu article entitled *Tanqīd bar Āb i ḥayāt i Maulānā M. Ḥusain "Āzād"* by M. Maḥmūd Shērānī); etc.

[1] Sunām is now in the State of Patiala.

sajjādah i īshān shud). He died on 22 Ṣafar 1240/1824. Collections of his letters (*Makātīb i sharīfah*. Edition : Madras 1334/1916*) and of his utterances (*Durr al-ma'ārif*.[1] Edition : Delhi [1927*]) were made by his disciple Shāh Ra'ūf Aḥmad Muṣṭafā-ābādī (for whom see *Khazīnat al-aṣfiyā'* i p. 703, *Ḥadā'iq al-Ḥanafīyah* p. 472, Raḥmān 'Alī p. 66). The former is presumably the work *dar bāb i maktūbāt u maqāmāt i ān-janāb* referred to in the *Khazīnah* i p. 703 antepenult.

Maqāmāt i Maẓharī, or *Laṭā'if i khamsah*, "memoirs, with some letters, of Shams ul-Dīn Habīb Ullāh Maẓharī" [*sic*, but read Maẓhar] : **'Alīgaṛh** Subḥ. MSS. p. 18 no. 10 (?) (*Risālah dar ḥālāt i . . . Mirzā Jān i Jānān wa-ghairah*, by Shāh Ghulām-'Alī).

Edition : **Delhi** 1309/1892°, probably also [**Delhi**] Aḥmadī Press, 1269/1853* (a biography of "Maẓhar" epitomized from Maulawī Na'īm Allāh's work (see p. 1033 *supra*) by Ghulām-'Alī Mujaddidī 'Alawī, without title-page but beginning with the words *Īn risālah i sharīfah dar bayān i ḥālāt u maqāmāt i ḥaḍrat i Shams al-Dīn Ḥabīb Allāh . . .*).

Probably this author is the same as 'Abd Allāh *ma'rūf bah* Ghulām-'Alī who wrote

Karāmāt u irshādāt i Mujaddid i Alf i Thānī[2] : **Āṣafīyah** i p. 460 no. 288.

[*Khazīnat al-aṣfiyā'* i pp. 693–700 ; Raḥmān 'Alī p. 155.]

1377. Mullā **M. Ṣādiq Yārkandī.**

Majma' al-muḥaqqiqīn, a history of the Khwājahs of Kāshghar to 1208/1793–4 : no MSS. recorded ?

Eastern-Turkish translation by Mullā M. Sātqīn : MS. in private possession (see Semenov *Ukazatel'* p. 24, where a reference is given to Validov *Vostochnye rukopisi v Ferganskoi oblasti* (*Zapiski Vostochn. Otd. Imp. Russ. Arkheol. Obshchestva* xxii) p. 304).

1378. **Turāb 'Alī** b. M. Kāẓim Qalandarī 'Alawī **Kākōrawī**,[3] a descendant of Niẓām al-Dīn Qārī known as Sh. Bhīkan Kākō-

[1] So Arberry, but *Dār al-ma'ārif* according to the *Khazīnah*, the *Ḥadā'iq* and Raḥmān 'Alī.
[2] Cf. p. 988 n. 5 *supra*.
[3] Kākōrī is about eight miles due west of Lucknow.

rawī,[1] was born in 1181/1767–8 and died on 5 Jumādā I 1275/11 December 1858. Among his works were a *dīwān* (described by Raḥmān ʻAlī as *mashhūr*), *Maṭālib i rashīdī* (on ethics and Ṣūfism. Editions: Lucknow 1280/1863°, 1875°*, 1896†) and *Sharā'iṭ al-wasā'iṭ* ("on the duties and observances of Ṣūfī instructors and their disciples". Edition: Lucknow 1293/1876*). Of the *Maktūbāt i Shāh Mujtabā Lāharpūrī*,[2] compiled by him in 1224/1809, there is a MS. at Ḥaidarābād (Āṣafīyah i p. 484). To the south-east of the town of Kākōrī are the *dargāhs* of Shāh M. Kāẓim [3] and Shāh Abū Turāb, "in whose memory annual festivals are celebrated and a great fair is held, attended by large numbers of people from Lucknow and the neighbouring villages" (*Lucknow: a gazetteer*, by H. R. Nevill, Allahabad 1904, p. 191).

(1) *Kashf al-mutawārī fī ḥāl i Niẓām al-Dīn i Qārī*, a biography of the afore-mentioned Sh. Bhīkan. Edition: **Lucknow** 1318/1901°.

(2) *Uṣūl al-maqṣūd*, accounts of twelve Qalandarī *shaikhs*, the spiritual ancestors of the author,[4] written in 1225–6/

[1] Qārī Amīr Niẓām al-Dīn b. Amīr Saif al-Dīn, called Sh. Bhīkan, or Bhikārī, or Bhīk, was born in 890/1485 and died in 981/1573–4. According to Raḥmān ʻAlī he wrote works entitled *Manhaj* (*dar uṣūl i ḥadīth*), *Maʻārif* (*dar taṣawwuf*) and *Tarjamah i risālah i Mulhamāt i Qādirī*, the last being described as a translation of a work by S. ʻAbd al-Razzāq, one of ʻAbd al-Qādir al-Jīlānī's sons. See *Ṭabaqāt i Akbarī* ii p. 478 (only his name in a list); Badā'ūnī *Muntakhab al-tawārīkh* iii p. 24; Raḥmān ʻAlī p. 33.

[2] Shāh Mujtabā is the eighth of the *shaikhs* whose biographies are given in the *Uṣūl al-maqṣūd*.

[3] Shāh M. Kāẓim, Turāb ʻAlī's father, died in 1221/1806.

[4] In giving this account of his spiritual ancestors the author professes to follow the custom observed in the Chishtī affiliation. The twelve shaikhs are ʻAbd al-ʻAzīz Makkī, Khiḍr Rūmī, Najm al-Dīn Ghauth al-dahr, Quṭb al-Dīn Bīnā-dil Jaunpūrī (d. 925), M. Quṭb [Jaunpūrī], ʻAbd al-Salām [Jaunpūrī] (d. 976), ʻAbd al-Quddūs Jaunpūrī (d. 1052), Mujtabā Lāharpūrī (d. 1084), Fatḥ Jaunpūrī (d. 1118), Ilāh-diyah Aḥmad Lāharpūrī (d. 1147), Bāsiṭ ʻAlī Ilāhābādī (d. 1196) and M. Kāẓim (d. 1221), the author's father, of whom a very long and detailed account is given. "The work sheds no light on the origin and the history of the Qalandars and the flourishing period of their movement in India, where it acquired great importance. The author's more or less authentic information begins only with the x/xvi c., when Qalandarīs had finally degenerated, lost their importance, and when their different branches had become amalgamated with other Sufic orders which still flourished at that time, especially the Qādirīs and Chishtīs" (Ivanow). The *muqaddimah* to the *Tārīkh i maẓhar i buzurgān* (Bodleian 1997) contains a brief account of the Qalandarī order.

1810–11 and divided into twelve chapters called *aṣl*: **Ivanow** Curzon 83 (A.H. 1275/1858), **Bānkīpūr** viii 679 (latter half of 19th cent.).

Edition: place ? 1312/1894–5 (see Āṣafīyah i p. 316).

Lists of the biographies: (1) Ivanow-Curzon p. 88, (2) Bānkīpūr viii p. 69.

[*al-Rauḍ al-azhar* p. 190 onwards; *Mawāhib al-qalandar* p. 25⁸; Raḥmān 'Alī p. 36.]

1379. A certain "**Girāmī**" appears to be the author of the *Riyāḍ al-wāṣilīn.*

Riyāḍ al-wāṣilīn (a chronogram = 1229/1814), or *Tadhkirah i wāṣilān*, a metrical account of famous saints composed by order of M. Raḥīm Khān, of Khīwah (who reigned 1221–41/1806–25): **Leningrad** Mus. Asiat. (see *Mélanges asiatiques* vii (St. Petersburg 1876) p. 402).

1380. **Gul Muḥammad** Ma'rūfī Karkhī[1] Chishtī **Aḥmadpūrī** is described in a marginal note on p. 1 of the Delhi edition of his *Dhikr al-aṣfiyā'* as the eldest son of Ḥakīm Allāh-Yār Ma'rūfī Karkhī and as a resident of Aḥmadpūr Sharqīyah in the State of Bahāwalpūr. He is mentioned in the Bahāwalpūr State Gazetteer (p. 179) as a disciple and *khalīfah* of Khwājah M. 'Āqil, a saint buried at Kōṭ Miṭ'han[2] in the Ḍērah Ghāzī Khān District. According to the list of *a'rās* printed at the end of the *Dhikr al-aṣfiyā'* (p. 226) he died on 9 Muḥarram 1243/3 August 1827.

Dhikr al-aṣfiyā' fī takmilat Siyar al-auliyā' dar manqabat i Shams al-Hudā,[3] a continuation of the *Siyar al-auliyā'* of S. M. Kirmānī (see p. 943 *supra*) divided into a *muqaddimah* (on the *ḥilyah* of the Prophet and the dates of the death of the Chishtī saints down to Chirāgh i Dihlī),[4] two

[1] For Ma'rūf al-Karkhī see p. 1031 n. 6 *supra*.

[2] "The shrine of Muhammad Aqil Sáhib at Koṭ Miṭhan was in the old town of Koṭ Miṭhan, but when in S. 1919 both town and shrine were washed away by the Indus, the coffin containing the body of Muhammad Aqil Sáhib was disinterred and brought to the present shrine" (H. A. Rose *Glossary of the tribes and castes of the Punjab and North-West Frontier Province* i p. 599).

[3] So in the author's preface. On the title-page, however, we read "*Kitāb i maḥāmid-intisāb . . . al-mausūm bah Dhikr al-aṣfiyā ma'rūf Takmilah Siyar al-auliyā dar manqabat i Shams al-Hudā*, the words *Takmilah Siyar al-auliyā* being put in the boldest type.

[4] See p. 942 n. 1 *supra*.

bābs (on the lives of Kamāl al-Dīn 'Allāmah,[1] Sirāj al-Dīn b. Kamāl al-Dīn,[2] 'Alam al-Dīn M.,[3] Sh. Rājan,[4] Sh. JMN (Jumman ?),[5] Sh. Ḥasan M.,[6] Sh. M. b. Ḥasan M.,[7] Muḥyī 'l-Dīn Yaḥyā Madanī,[8] Kalīm Allāh Jahānābādī,[9] Niẓām al-Dīn Aurangābādī,[10] Fakhr al-Dīn b. Niẓām al-Dīn Aurangābādī,[11] Nūr-M. Mahārawī,[12] M. 'Āqil,[13] and their disciples) and a *khātimah* (on the *a'rās*). Edition: **Delhi** 1312/1894°*.

[*Dhikr al-aṣfiyā'* p. 208 foll.]

1381. Qāḍī M. **Irtaḍā 'Alī Khān** " Khwushnūd " **Gōpāmawī**[14] was born in 1198/1783–4. He was a pupil of Maulawī Ḥaidar 'Alī Sandīlī[15] and Maulawī M. Ibrāhīm Bilgrāmī. In 1225/1810–11 he went to Madrās, where his father, Muṣṭafā 'Alī Khān, was *Qāḍī*, and after his father's death he himself became *Qāḍī* of Madrās. He died in 1251/1835–6. Of his works Raḥmān 'Alī

[1] One of Chirāgh i Dihlī's disciples, d. 756/1355. See *Khazīnat al-aṣfiyā'* i p. 353; Raḥmān 'Alī p. 173.

[2] Son of the preceding, mentioned incidentally *Khazīnah* i p. 436[2] in the pedigree of Sh. Ḥasan M., whose great-great-grandfather he was.

[3] A disciple of Chirāgh i Dihlī, mentioned incidentally *Khazīnah* i p. 536[4].

[4] A disciple of the preceding, mentioned incidentally *Khazīnah* i p. 536[4] as Sh. Maḥmūd al-ma'rūf (i.e. known as) Sh. Rājan.

[5] A disciple of the preceding mentioned incidentally *Khazīnah* i p. 436[3] as Sh. Jamāl al-Dīn al-mashhūr (i.e. known as) Sh. JMN. Cf. *Mir'āt i Aḥmadī, khātimah*, p. 75[6], Eng. trans. p. 65[13], where there is another incidental mention. In the English trans. the surname is spelt Jumman. In the *Tadhkirat al-kirām* (Bānkīpūr Suppt. i 1783 fol. 146) there is a notice of a certain Shāh Jamāl Muḥammad alias Jumman.

[6] *Khalīfah* of the preceding, d. 980/1572–3 or 982/1575. See *Mir'āt i Aḥmadī, khātimah*, pp. 75–6, Eng. trans. pp. 65–6; *Khazīnah* i p. 436.

[7] Son of the preceding, d. 1040/1630. See *Mir'āt i Aḥmadī, khātimah*, pp. 76–9, Eng. trans. pp. 66–8.

[8] Grandson of the preceding, d. 1101/1689. See *Mir'āt i Aḥmadī, khātimah* pp. 79–83, Eng. trans. pp. 68–70.

[9] Disciple of the preceding, d. 1140/1727. See *Khazīnah* i pp. 494–5; *Ḥadā'iq al-Ḥanafīyah* pp. 438–9; Raḥmān 'Alī p. 172.

[10] Disciple of the preceding, d. 1142/1730. See *Khazīnah* i pp. 495–7.

[11] Son and *khalīfah* of the preceding, d. 1199/1785. See p. 1030 *supra*.

[12] Disciple of the preceding, d. 1205/1791. See p. 1045 n. 3.

[13] Disciple of the preceding, d. 1229/1814 and is buried at Kōṭ Miṭ'han. See *Khazīnah* i p. 507 antepenult.; H. A. Rose *Glossary of the tribes and castes of the Punjab* i p. 599. Cf. p. 1037 n. 2.

[14] Gōpāmau is a small town 14 miles north-west of Hardoi in Oudh.

[15] d. at Sandīlah (cf. p. 880 n. 4 *supra*) in 1225/1810. See Raḥmān 'Alī pp. 54–5. One of his pupils was the Shī'ite *Mujtahid*, S. Dildār 'Alī Lak'hnawī (for whom see Raḥmān 'Alī pp. 60–1, Brockelmann *Sptbd.* ii p. 852).

mentions (1) commentaries or *ḥawāshī* on Ṣadrā,[1] Mīr Zāhid Mullā Jalāl[2] and other text-books, (2) *Nafā'is i Irtaḍā'īyah*, (3) *Nuqūd al-ḥisāb*, (4) *risālah i Farā'iḍ*,[3] (5) *Sharḥ i qaṣīdah i Burdah*. For a MS. of his *Fatāwā* see Āṣafīyah ii p. 1062 no. 97.

(1) *Fawā'id i Sa'dīyah*, "lives of famous saints and Ṣūfīs." Edition: **Lucknow** 1885°.

(2) *Tuḥfah i A'ẓamīyah*,[4] catalogued under the heading *Tadhkirah i Fārisī*, but whether it is a *tadhkirah* of poets or saints is not stated: **Āṣafīyah** i p. 316 no. 96 (A.H. 1235/1819–20).

[*Ishārāt i Bīnish*; *Ṣubḥ i waṭan* pp. 65–8; *Ḥadīqat al-marām* p. 4; *Sham' i anjuman* p. 145; Raḥmān 'Alī p. 21; Brockelmann *Sptbd.* ii p. 854.]

1382. **Imām al-Dīn Khān** b. Ghulām-Ḥusain Khān b. Ghulām-Gīlānī Khān was a dependent of M. Amīr Khān [Nawwāb of Tōnk 1817–34: cf. pp. 690–1 *supra*].

Majma' al-karāmat (sing.), a life of Shāh Dargāhī Naqshbandī,[5] of Rāmpūr: **Nadhīr Aḥmad** 91 (A.H. 1236/1820–1. Ḥāfiẓ Aḥmad 'Alī Khān's library, Rāmpūr).

1383. **Niẓām al-Dīn Balkhī Mazārī** b. Mīr M. 'Azīz Anṣārī Mutawallī[6] was born on 1 Ramaḍān 1195/21 August 1781. At Balkh in 1213/1798–9 he met for the first time Shāh Faḍl i Aḥmad Ma'ṣūmī, a Naqshbandī *shaikh*, one of whose *khulafā'* he subsequently became. Among his writings were a *dīwān* and a biographical work entitled *Aḥsan al-tawārīkh fī dhikr al-'ulamā' wa-'l-fuqarā' wa-'l-mashāyikh*. No copies of these works seem to be recorded. His *Tuḥfat al-murshid* was completed at Balkh in Shawwāl 1240/May–June 1825.

[1] i.e. the commentary of Ṣadr al-Dīn M. b. Ibrāhīm al-Shīrāzī on the first *fann* of the second part (physics) of Athīr al-Dīn al-Abharī's *Hidāyat al-ḥikmah* (for which see Brockelmann i p. 464, *Sptbd.* i pp. 839–41).

[2] i.e. the annotations of Mīr M. Zāhid al-Harawī on the commentary of Jalāl al-Dīn al-Dawānī on the first part (logic) of al-Taftāzānī's *Tahdhīb al-manṭiq wa-'l-kalām* (for which see Brockelmann ii p. 215, *Sptbd.* ii pp. 302–4).

[3] *Furaiz-i-Irtazeeah: a treatise on the Mohammedan law of inheritance. By Moulavie Mohummud Irtaza Alee Khan Bahadur*, Madras, 1825*.

[4] Dedicated presumably to Nawwāb M. Ghauth Khān "A'ẓam", for whom see pp. 897–9 *supra*.

[5] Who died in 1226/1811. See *Khazīnat al-aṣfiyā'* i pp. 690–2.

[6] i.e. Warden of the alleged shrine of 'Alī at Balkh.

Tuḥfat al-murshid, on the life, sayings and devotional practices of Shāh Faḍl i Aḥmad Ma'ṣūmī, known as Ḥaḍrat-jīw [1] Ṣāḥib, who was born in 1151/1738–9 and died at Peshawar in 1231/1815–16 or 1232/1816–17. Edition: **Lahore** [1912*].

[Autobiography in *Tuḥfat al-murshid*, pp. 175–84.]

1384. M. **Abū 'l-Ḥayāt Qādirī P'hulwārī** [2] Bihārī wrote the *Tadhkirat al-kirām* in 1249/1833–4.

Tadhkirat al-kirām, biographies of forty-five Bihārī *shaikhs*, mostly of the 18th and early 19th century, the first being M. Wārith Rasūl-numā (b. 1084/1673, d. 1166/1753), the thirty-fifth M. 'Alī Akbar (d. 1247/1832) and the last Burhān al-Dīn (d. 1107/1696): **Ivanow** 1st Suppt. 772 (19th cent.), **Bānkīpūr** Suppt. i 1783 (19th cent.).

Edition: **Lucknow** [1880°].

Lists of the biographies: (**1**) Ivanow 1st Suppt. pp. 12–13, (**2**) Bānkīpūr Suppt. i pp. 46–7.

1385. Āqā **Taqī,** of Khōy, the author of the *Ādāb al-musāfirīn*, is doubtless identical with Taqī b. M., who in the *Dānishmandān i Ādharbāyjān* (p. 87) is described as one of the well known '*urafā*' of Khōy and is there stated to have written at Shīrāz in 1257/1841 a metrical commentary entitled *Nuqṭah i asrār* in about two thousand verses on the first verse of Rūmī's *Mathnawī*.

Ādāb al-musāfirīn, notices of Ṣūfī saints: **Browne** Suppt. 7 (A.H. 1256/1840–1).

1386. For the *Riyāḍ al-'ārifīn*, completed by Riḍā-Qulī Khān "Hidāyat" in 1260/1844 and devoted to notices of saints who were also poets, see p. 911 *supra*.

1387. The author of the *Makhzan i Aḥmadī* was "Sayyid Muḥammad 'Alî" according to the Bānkīpūr Catalogue, "**Muhammad 'Alī,** called [3] 'Alī" according to the Catalogue of Persian printed books in the British Museum. "A faithful

[1] For the affix *jīw* see p. 998[25] *supra*.

[2] Phulwārī is a village in the Patna Division of Bihār.

[3] In the terminology of the British Museum "called" is used to represent *mutakhalliṣ*, but also *mad'ū, ma'rūf, mashhūr, mulaqqab, mukhāṭab* and the like.

disciple of Aḥmad Shâh," he "spent most of his time in the company of his *Pîr*".[1]

Makhzan i Aḥmadī, completed in 1261/1845 and dedicated to Wazīr al-Daulah,[2] a life of S. Aḥmad Shāh [3] from

[1] On pp. 203–4 of his *Tadhkirah i 'ulamā' i Hind* Raḥmān 'Alī gives a biography of Maulawī [not Saiyid, be it noted] Muḥammad 'Alī Ṣadrpūrī b. Shaikh Ramaḍān 'Alī, a resident (*mutawaṭṭin*) of Ṣadrpūr in the parganah of Malīhābād near Lucknow. He was a Ṣūfī and a poet using the *takhalluṣ* "Muḥammad" [not "'Alī"]. Born early in the second decade of the thirteenth century of the Hijrah, he studied Ḥadīth and Tafsīr under Mirzā Ḥasan 'Alī Muḥaddith Lak'hnawī and entered the Naqshbandī Mujaddidī order of Ṣūfīs as a *murīd* of Maulawī Shāh Bishārat-'Alī Bahrā'ichī. He strove earnestly to promote fidelity to the *Sunnah* and to extirpate *bid'ah*, and was himself a man of deep piety. In 1258/1842 he went to Ṭōnk and entered the service of Wazīr al-Daulah Nawwāb Wazīr M. Khān [to whom the *Makhzan i Aḥmadī* is dedicated]. He died in Rajab 1289/1872 in the time of Nawwāb M. 'Alī Khān. Among the works of his which Raḥmān 'Alī mentions is [not *Makhzan i Aḥmadī* but] *Waqā'i' i Aḥmadīyah* (*dar ḥālāt i Saiyid Aḥmad i Mujāhid i Rāy Barēlī*). In spite of the discrepancies noted above it seems difficult to believe that M. 'Alī Ṣadrpūrī is not identical with the author of the *Makhzan i Aḥmadī* [which, we may note, "is intermixed with numerous poems and verses"].

[2] Wazīr al-Daulah Wazīr M. Khān succeeded his father Amīr Khān (for whom see pp. 690–1 *supra*) as Nawwāb of Ṭōnk in 1834 and died in 1864.

[3] S. Aḥmad Mujāhid Rāy-Barēlawī, as Raḥmān 'Alī calls him, or S. Aḥmad Barēlawī, as he is more commonly called, was the son of M. 'Irfān and belonged to the family of the Saiyids of the Rāy Barēlī *takyah* (*az khānadān i Sādāt i takyah i Rāy Barēlī*, Raḥmān 'Alī p. 81). In 1222/1807 he became a disciple of Shāh 'Abd al-'Azīz Dihlawī (for whom see pp. 24–5 *supra*) and assimilated the latter's puritanical views and hostility towards all "idolatrous" or superstitious innovations. On leaving Delhi he started a revivalist movement, in the course of which he "performed miracles and attracted a large number of followers", becoming "a terror to the Shî'ahs of Lucknow and Naṣîrâbâd". In 1821 he visited Calcutta and gained numerous adherents. In 1822 he made a pilgrimage to Mecca with his two chief disciples M. Ismā'īl Dihlawī (cf. *Ency. Isl.* under Ismā'īl al-Shahīd] and 'Abd al-Ḥaiy Dihlawī, who were respectively the nephew and the son-in-law of his old teacher, Shāh 'Abd al-'Azīz, and of whom the former expounded S. Aḥmad's doctrines in the Persian work *Ṣirāṭ al-mustaqīm* (Calcutta 1238/1823°). On 7 Jumādā II 1241/17 Jan. 1826 he set out from Rāy Barēlī with a view to conducting a *jihād* against the Sik'hs, whom he accused of oppressing the Muslims in the Panjāb, of prohibiting the *adhān* and the killing of cows. After inciting the people of Kābul and Qandahār, he with ten or twelve thousand adherents from India and Afghānistān attacked the Peshawar district. For some years he engaged Ranjīt Sing'h's forces with varying success until he was killed in battle at Bālākōṭ on 24 Dhū 'l-Qa'dah 1246/6 May 1831. His works include short tracts entitled *Tanbīh al-ghāfilīn* (Delhi 1285/1868*) and *Mulhimāt* [*sic*] *i Aḥmadīyah fī 'l-ṭarīq al-Muḥammadīyah* (Āgrah 1299/1882°). See *JASB.* i (1832) pp. 479–98 (cf. Beale *Oriental biographical dictionary*, London 1894, pp. 354–5); *The Indian Musalmans*, by W. W. Hunter, London 1871, pp. 12–18, 52–3, etc.; *Tawārīkh i 'ajībah* or *Sawāniḥ i Aḥmadī* (in Urdu), by M. Ja'far, Delhi 1891*, Sād'haurah [1914*]; Raḥmān 'Alī pp. 81–2; *Ḥayāt i ṭaiyibah* (in Urdu), by Mīrzā Ḥairat Dihlawī, Delhi 1895*; Buckland *Dictionary of Indian biography* p. 8; *Ency. Isl.* under Aḥmad b. Muḥammed 'Irfān (Blumhardt); Niẓāmī Badāyūnī *Qāmūs al-mashāhīr* (in Urdu) i pp. 314–15.

his birth at Rāy Barēlī[1] in Ṣafar[2] 1201/Nov.–Dec. 1786 to his return thither from Mecca in 1239/1823: **Bānkīpūr** xvi 1415 (A.H. 1263/1847).

Edition: **Āgrah** 1299/1882°.

1388. Miyāṅ **Khair Muḥammad** Munshī, by whom the MS. referred to below is signed at the end, may be the author of the biography.

(*Aḥwāl i Shāh Gul*[3] *Imām Chū*[4] *walad i Saiyid Aḥmad 'Alī Shāh Chū*) (beg. *Shāh-ṣāḥib S. A. 'A. Shāh Chū walad i Shāh Fatḥ Nūr Shāh*), a notice of Shāh Gul Imām, a Saiyid and *faqīr* of great sanctity, who settled at Ūchh (now in the state of Bahāwalpūr) and in Samwat 1810 (A.D. 1754) erected various buildings there, together with an account of his family extending to the death of his successor, S. Gul M. Shāh, in 1209/1794–5: **Rieu** iii 977*a* (foll. 9. A.H. 1267/1850).

1389. 'Abd al-'Alīm **Naṣr Allāh Khān** Aḥmadī Khwēshgī Khūrjawī, who died in 1299/1881, has already been mentioned as the author of the *Tārīkh i Dakan* (p. 757 *supra*) and the *Gulshan i hamīshah-bahār* (p. 904).

Bayāḍ i dil-gushā (probably intended to be a chronogram for 1268/1851–2 (though actually amounting to 1168), like four alternative titles (e.g. *Ma'lūmāt i Khwājagān*), which do in fact come to 1268), a detailed biography of the author's *pīr*, Shāh 'Abd al-'Alīm (b. Ākhūnd Jān Muḥammad, *B. i d.-g.* p. 21[5]) Lōhārawī[5] (d. 13 Muḥarram 1266/29 Nov. 1849: see *B. i d.-g.* p. 219 antepenult.) with shorter accounts of the latter's *pīr*, Shāh Iḥsān-'Alī Pāk-Pattanī, and of Ṣūfīs associated with them.

[1] Rāy (Rai, or Rae) Barēlī, the chief town of a district in Oudh 48 miles S.E. of Lucknow, is to be distinguished from Barēlī (officially Bareilly) in Rohilkhand.

[2] So *Makhzan i Aḥmadī*, but the *Ency. Isl.* gives the date 1 Muḥ. 1201/24 Oct. 1786.

[3] Rieu writes Kul, but Gul seems more probable.

[4] Perhaps a misreading of Jīw (for which see p. 998[25]).

[5] According to *B. i d.-g.* p. 22[6] Lōhārī, known as Lōhārī-Jalālābād, is in the District of Muẓaffarnagar "*az muta'alliqāt i Sahāranpūr*".

Edition: **Kōl** [i.e. 'Alīgaṛh. Probably A.H. 1268/1851–2 or 1269/1852–3].[1]

1390. **Faḍl Allāh b. Shaikh al-Mulūk** enjoyed the patronage of Mīr Ṭahmāsp b. Daulat-Shāh b. Fatḥ-'Alī Shāh, Governor of Fārs. Shortly after reaching Shīrāz from 'Irāq in 1272/1855–6 he wrote his *Ḍiyā' al-'ārifīn.*

Ḍiyā' al-'ārifīn, on the lives and sayings of 96 *'urafā'* who flourished in the first four centuries of Islām: **Rieu** Suppt. 102.

1391. Muftī M. **Ghulām-Sarwar** b. Muftī Ghulām-Muḥammad b. Muftī Raḥīm Allāh Quraishī Asadī al-Hāshimī al-**Lāhaurī** wrote the Urdu works *Guldastah i karāmāt*, on the life of 'Abd al-Qādir Jīlānī (Delhi 1867*, Lucknow 1875*, Lahore 1878*), *Akhlāq i Sarwarī* (Lahore 1288/1871°*, Lucknow 1878°), *Makhzan i ḥikmat*, moral tales and sayings (Lahore 1871°* [Lucknow] 1878°), *Dīwān i Sarwarī*, verses in praise of 'Abd al-Qādir Jīlānī (Lahore 1872°*, 1873*, 1292/1876°), *Na't i Sarwarī*, verses in praise of Muḥammad (Lahore 1290/1873°*, 1877*, Lucknow 1878°, 1880°), *Gulshan i Sarwarī*, ethics in verse (Lahore 1874*, Lucknow 1295/1878°), *Ḥadīqat al-auliyā'* (Lahore 1875*, Cawnpore 1877*, 1889*), *Bahāristān i tārīkh* or *Gulzār i shāhī*, a history of India followed by a sketch of English history (Lucknow 1877°*), *Tārīkh i Makhzan i Panjāb*, a gazetteer of the Panjāb (Lucknow 1877°*), *Zubdat al-lughāt* or *Lughāt i Sarwarī*, a dictionary of Arabic, Persian and other foreign words explained in Urdu (Lucknow 1294/1877°*), and *Dīwān i ḥamd i Īzadī* (Lucknow 1881°).

(1) *Khazīnat al-aṣfiyā'* (a chronogram = 1280), biographical notices of saints begun in 1280/1863–4, completed in 1281/1864–5 (but with some later additions) and divided into seven *makhzans* ((1) the Prophet, the first four Caliphs and the Imāms, not only the Twelve but also Abū Ḥanīfah, Mālik, Abū Yūsuf, Shaibānī, Shāfi'ī and Aḥmad b. Ḥanbal, vol. i p. 4,[2] (2) Qādirīs, vol. i p. 76, (3) Chishtīs, vol. i p. 222,

[1] The date 1270 given by Arberry has perhaps been taken inadvertently from a short pamphlet printed at the same press which comes next to the *Bayāḍ i dil-gushā* in the collectaneous India Office volume.

[2] The references are to the Cawnpore edition of 1914.

(4) Naqshbandīs, vol. i p. 516, (5) Suhrawardīs, vol. ii p. 2, (6) miscellaneous orders, vol. ii p. 118, (7) in four *ḥiṣṣahs* (*a*) the Prophet's wives, vol. ii p. 397, (*b*) his daughters, vol. ii p. 404, (*c*) saintly women, vol. ii p. 406, (*d*) deranged saints (*majānīn u majādhīb*), vol. ii p. 428).

Editions: **Lahore** 1284/1867–8 (pp. 1072, 18. See *JASB.* xxxix, pt. 1 (1870), p. 274 n.); **Lucknow** (Thamar i Hind Pr.) 1873*; **Cawnpore** (N.K.) 1312/1894*; 1902°; 1914‡.

(2) *Ganjīnah i Sarwarī*, or, chronogrammatically, *Ganj i tārīkh* (= 1284), chronograms for the birth and death of famous Muslims.

Editions: **Lahore** 1285/1868*, **Lucknow** (N.K.) 1877°*, 1307/1889*.

1392. **M. Ḥusain** b. M. Mas'ūd Chishtī Ṣābirī [1] Quddūsī [2] **Murādābādī,** a disciple of S. Amānat 'Alī Ḥusainī Chishtī,[3] completed his *Anwār al-'ārifīn* in 1286/1870.

Anwār al-'ārifīn, lives of numerous ancient and modern saints, especially of the Chishtī, Qādirī and Naqshbandī orders, including a number buried at Murādābād. Editions: **Barēlī** ("Bareilly") 1290/1873*, **Lucknow** 1876°*.

1393. **Ghulām-Muḥammad Khān Jhajjarī** became a disciple of Khwājah M. Sulaimān Chishtī Taunsawī [4] in 1255/1839.

Manāqib i Sulaimānī, a life of Khwājah M. Sulaimān Chishtī Taunsawī, written in 1255/1839–40, with a continuation

[1] For 'Alī Ṣābir see p. 1031 n. 5 *supra*.

[2] For 'Abd al-Quddūs Gangōhī see p. 967 *supra*.

[3] Perhaps Maulawī A. A. Chishtī, who lived at Amrōhah and died in 1280/1864. See *Khazīnat al-aṣfiyā'* i p. 515.

[4] M. S., born at Gargōjī, in the hill-country west of Taunsah in the Ḍērah Ghāzī Khān District of the Panjāb, was educated at the *madrasah* of Qāḍī M. 'Āqil (cf. p. 1038[6]) at Miṭ'hankōṭ and afterwards became a disciple of Nūr-Muḥammad Mahārawī (for whom see p. 1045 n. 3). He settled at Taunsah and died there on 7 Ṣafar 1267/12 December 1850. His grave is marked by a mausoleum erected by M. Bahāwal Khān III, Nawwāb of Bahāwalpūr 1825–52, who was one of his disciples. See *Manāqib al-maḥbūbain*; *Khazīnat al-aṣfiyā'* i p. 514; *Anwār al-'ārifīn*; *Qaṣr i 'ārifān*; Dera Ghazi Khan Gazetteer (1898) p. 54; Bahawalpur State Gazetteer (1904) p. 74; *Khātam i Sulaimānī* (in Urdu), by Ilāh-Bakhsh Khān Balōch, Lahore 1325/1907*; *Note on the shrine of Taunsa*, by D. C. Phillott (in *JASB.* 1908 pp. 21–9); Griffin and Massey *Chiefs and families of note in the Panjab*, revised ed., Lahore 1909–11, vol. ii p. 388; H. A. Rose *Glossary of the tribes and castes of the Panjab and North-West Frontier Province* i (Lahore 1919) pp. 602–3.

(*takmilah*) to the time of the saint's death, written in 1287/1870–1. Editions: **Delhi** [1871*], **Jhajjar** 1897†.

1394. Ḥāfiẓ **Aḥmad Yār,** a resident of Pākpattan, wrote a biography of K͟hwājah M. Sulaimān Taunsawī (cf. p. 1044 n. 4 *supra*) entitled *Manāqib i Sulaimānīyah.*[1] An abridgement of this, containing some additional information but devoted mainly to the saint's utterances (*malfūẓāt*), was made by **Yār-Muḥammad b. Tāj-Muḥammad,** who was himself one of the saint's associates.

Intik͟hāb i Manāqib i Sulaimānīyah. Edition: **Lahore** 1325/1907°*.

1395. **Aḥmad 'Alī K͟hairābādī** was a disciple of S͟hāh Sulaimān Taunsawī (for whom see p. 1044 n. 4 *supra*).

Qaṣr i 'ārifān, notices of Chis͟htī, Qādirī, Suhrawardī and Naqs͟hbandī saints to the time of S͟hāh Sulaimān Taunsawī: **Lahore** Panjab Univ. Lib. (A.H. 1291/1874, copied from an autograph. See *OCM.* iii/1 p. 73).

1396. **Najm al-Dīn Nāgaurī** is mentioned among the *k͟hulafā'* of K͟hwājah M. Sulaimān Taunsawī (for whom see p. 1044 n. 4 *supra*) on p. 84 of G͟hulām-Muḥammad K͟hān's *Manāqib i Sulaimānī,* where he is called Najm al-Dīn Jhunjhunuwī and described as a descendant of Sulṭān al-tārikīn Ḥamīd al-Dīn Nāgaurī (for whom see p. 6 *supra*) resident at Jhunjhunū.[2]

Manāqib al-maḥbūbain, lives of Nūr-Muḥammad Mahārawī,[3] his *k͟halīfah,* S͟hāh Sulaimān Taunsawī, and other Chis͟htī saints, followed by a short life of the author. Editions: [**Rāmpūr,** 1890?°], **Lahore** 1312/1895°.

[1] In his *Intik͟hāb* Yār-Muḥammad regularly calls this work *Manāqib i s͟harīfah.* The publisher calls it *Manāqib i Sulaimānīyah.*

[2] Jhunjhunū is "about 90 miles north-by-north-west of Jaipur city" (*Imperial Gazetteer of India, Provincial series, Rājputāna,* Calcutta 1908, p. 262). Nāgaur is in the State of Jōd'hpūr (cf. p. 5 n. 4 *supra*).

[3] This saint, surnamed Qiblah i 'ālam, has through his disciples "exercised a profound influence over the whole of the south-western Punjab" (Rose). Born in 1142/1730, he went to Delhi and obtained the *k͟hirqah i k͟hilāfat* from Fak͟hr al-Dīn Muḥibb al-Nabī (for whom see p. 1030[5] *supra*). He died in 1205/1791 and was buried at Chis͟htiyān, near Mahārān, in the State of Bahāwalpūr. See *K͟hazīnat al-aṣfiyā'* i pp. 506–8; *Bahawalpur State Gazetteer* (1904) pp. 176–8; H. A. Rose *Glossary of the tribes and castes of the Punjab and North-West Frontier Province* i (Lahore 1919) p. 533.

1397. Shāh **Ḍiyā' Allāh** Faḵẖrī Qādirī Ḥanafī died in 1292/ 1875–6 and was buried at Lahore.

Maktūb i Ḍiyā'ī (a chronogram = 1289/1872–3), or, as on the title-page but not in the preface, *Nasab-nāmah i kalān*, pedigrees of the Prophet and of fourteen Ṣūfī "families" with short biographical notes, followed by an account of the seventy-two Islāmic sects derived from the *Ghunyat al-ṭālibīn* of 'Abd al-Qādir al-Jīlānī (cf. Brockelmann i p. 435). Editions : **Lahore** 1289/1872°, 1293/1876*, 1296/1879*, 1309/1891°.

1398. Maulawī Abū Muḥammad **Ḥasan "Shi'rī" Qādirī** b. Ṣadr al-Dīn M., or Ḵẖwājah Ḥasan Kaul [or Kōl ?] " Shi'rī ", as he is called in the *Taḥā'if al-abrār*, was a Kaṣẖmīrī but spent most of his life as a trader in the Panjāb and Hindūstān. He died in 1298/1881 and was buried at Amritsar. He is the author of (1) a *dīwān* entitled *Dīwān i Shi'rī* or *Mir'āt al-ḵẖayāl* (Edition : Amritsar 1304/1887°), (2) a cosmography entitled *Zubdat al-aḵẖbār* (Edition : Amritsar 1282/1865°) and (3) a metrical *Chār darwīsh*.

Gulzār i Ḵẖalīl, a life of the Kaṣẖmīrī saint Ḵẖwājah M. Ḵẖalīl b. 'Abd al-Ghafūr Qādirī (b. 1175/1761, d. 1242/1827) followed by an account of the author's ancestors, completed in 1290/1873. Edition : **Lahore** 1291/1874*.

[*Gulzār i Ḵẖalīl* pp. 35–6 ; *Taḥā'if al-abrār* p. 351.]

1399. Maulawī Shāh **Taqī 'Alī** Qalandar **Kākōrawī** was the younger son of Shāh Turāb 'Alī Qalandar Kākōrawī (for whom see p. 1035 *supra*). He was born in 1213/1798–9 and after a life devoted to teaching at Kākōrī died on 17 Rajab 1290/10 September 1873.

al-Rauḍ al-azhar fī ma'āthir al-Qalandar, or *Laṭā'if al-adḥkār fī manāqib 'umdat al-aḵẖyār*, a detailed biography of the author's father, Shāh Turāb 'Alī, with some account of his spiritual ancestors, the Qalandarī order and other matters, divided into a *muqaddimah* (in three *faṣls*, of which the third is *dar ta'rīf i ahl i sulūk az firaq i Ṣūfīyah i Malāmatīyah u ḥikāyāt u kalimāt u iṣṭilāḥātaṣẖān*) and ten *laṭīfahs* ((1) on the Prophet, his parents, 'Alī b. Abī Ṭālib etc., (2) on the meaning of the word *qalandar*, etc., biography of 'Abd al-'Azīz Makkī, (3) biographies of ten shaikhs from Khiḍr Rūmī to Bāsiṭ 'Alī Ilāhābādī [the same ten as in the *Uṣūl al-maqṣūd*, p. 1036 *supra*], (4) biographies of Mas'ūd 'Alī Ilāhābādī and the author's grandfather M. Kāẓim (cf. p. 1036[10]), (5) on Shāh Turāb 'Alī and his 'Alawī pedigree, M. b. al-Ḥanafīyah, the meaning of the expression Āl i Nabī, etc., (6) *dar dhikr i mabādī i ḥāl i ān-ḥaḍrat*, (7) *dar bayān i maslak i ḥaḍrat i īshān dar uṣūl wa-ghair i ān*, (8) *dar dhikr i maslak i ḥaḍrat i walī-ni'mat dar ta'abbud u tanassuk* etc., (9) *dar dhikr i samā' i ghinā*, and (10) [supplied after the author's death by 'Alī Anwar Qalandar] *dar bayān i 'ishq u maḥabbat*). Edition: **Rāmpūr and Lucknow** 1331–6/1913–18[–19*] (with an introduction, *Mawāhib al-qalandar li-man yuṭāli' al-Rauḍ al-azhar*, on the life of Taqī 'Alī etc., completed in 1333/1915 by Shāh Ḥabīb Ḥaidar Qalandar, and a continuation, *Ḥauḍ al-Kauthar fī takmilat Rauḍ* [*sic*] *al-azhar*, completed in 1291/1874 by 'Alī Anwar Qalandar).

[*Mawāhib al-qalandar* p. 11 ult.–22; *al-Rauḍ al-azhar* pp. 707 ff.; Raḥmān 'Alī p. 37.]

1400. **'Alī Anwar** Qalandar b. 'Alī Akbar b. Ḥaidar 'Alī, who was born in 1269/1853, completed in 1291/1874 the *Ḥauḍ al-Kauthar fī takmilat Rauḍ* [*sic*] *al-azhar*, which has been mentioned above (p. 1047[15]).

(1) ***Intiṣāḥ 'an dhikr ahl al-ṣalāḥ***, biographies of famous Ṣūfīs with some account of the Ṣūfī orders: [**Lahore**] Majma' al-'ulūm Pr. [1877*] (pp. 120); **Lucknow** 1327/1910* (with a continuation (p. 164 onwards) entitled *al-Īḍāḥ fī tatimmat al-Intiṣāḥ* by M. Ḥabīb Ḥaidar. Pp. 214).

(2) ***Taḥrīr al-Anwar fī tafsīr al-Qalandar***, an account of the Qalandars: [**Lucknow**] 'Alawī Pr. 1290/1873°* (pp. 32).

[*Mawāhib al-qalandar* (cf. p. 1047[13] *supra*) pp. 20 ult., 22.]

1401. Maulawī **Walī Allāh** b. Mullā Ḥabīb Allāh b. Mullā Muḥibb Allāh Anṣārī **Lak'hnawī** Farangī-Maḥallī, one of the well-known family of *'ulamā'* who have taught for several generations at Farangī Maḥall,[1] Lucknow, died on 10 Ṣafar 1270/12 November 1853. Among his works were *'Umdat al-wasā'il*, on the *manāqib* of the saint S. 'Abd al-Razzāq Bānsawī (cf. p. 1016[28] *supra*), a commentary on the *Qur'ān* entitled *Ma'din al-jawāhir*, as well as commentaries and *ḥawāshī* on several standard text-books.

al-Aghṣān al-arba'ah li-l-shajarat al-ṭaiyibah, a life of the saintly Mullā Aḥmad Anwār al-Ḥaqq Farangī-Maḥallī [2] and other descendants of the celebrated teacher Quṭb al-Dīn Sihālawī,[3] the ancestor of the *'ulamā'* of Farangī Maḥall, Lucknow, in a *muqaddimah* (on the genealogy of Quṭb al-Dīn) and four *aṣls* devoted to the lives and descendants of Quṭb al-Dīn's four sons,[4] with additions by the author's son, M. In'ām Allāh, Deputy Collector, bringing the information down to 1296/1879. Edition: **Lucknow** 1298/1881*.

[Raḥmān 'Alī p. 252; Alṭāf al-Raḥmān *Aḥwāl i 'ulamā' i Farangī Maḥall* (in Urdu), Lucknow [1907*], p. 80.]

1402. Ḥājjī Mullā **M. Bāqir** b. M. Ismā'īl b. 'Abd al-'Aẓīm b. M. Bāqir Māzandarānī Kujūrī (*aṣl*[an]) **Ṭihrānī** (*maulid*[an] *wa-maskin*[an]).

Jannat al-na'īm wa-'l-'aish al-salīm fī aḥwāl Maulānā 'Abd al-'Aẓīm (so in the Arabic preface p. 3 ult., but *J. al-n. fī a. 'A. al-'A. 'alaihi 'l-salām wa-'l-takrīm*, in the Persian preface p. 10[2]), an account, written in 1296/1879 (see p. 6[15]), of the Imām-zādah 'Abd al-'Aẓīm b. 'Abd Allāh al-Ḥasanī (b. 'Alī b. Ḥasan b. Zaid b. Ḥasan b. 'Alī b. Abī Ṭālib.

[1] Cf. Raḥmān 'Alī p. 168: *Farangī Maḥall aknūn maḥallah īst az maḥallāt i shahr i Lak'hna'ū dār al-imārah i ṣūbah i Awad'h sābiq qiṭ'ah i zamīn būd kih dar-ān tājirī az Farangistān sukūnat dāsht az-īn wajh ān qiṭ'ah i zamīn ba-Farangī Maḥall shuhrat girift ba'd i murūr i aiyām ba-wajh i na-māndan i a'qāb i tājir i Farangī zamīn i madhkūrah dar nuzūl i shāhī dar-āmad ba'd i qatl i Mullā-yi shahīd* [i.e. Quṭb al-Dīn Sihālawī] *aulādashān jihat i qiyām i khwud jā-yi madhkūr mu'āf yāftand u dar-ān-jā hanūz aulād i sharīfash qiyām-padhīr and u ān mauqi' bah Farangī Maḥall shuhrat dārad.*

[2] A. A. al-Ḥ. F.-M. b. Aḥmad 'Abd al-Ḥaqq b. M. Sa'īd b. Quṭb al-Dīn Sihālawī died in 1236/1821. See Raḥmān 'Alī p. 13.

[3] Q. al-D. Sihālawī was murdered in 1103/1692. See *Ma'āthir al-kirām* i no. 24; *Subḥat al-marjān* p. 76; Raḥmān 'Alī p. 167; etc. Sihālī is a village near Lucknow (cf. p. 1016 n. 2 *supra*).

[4] For the third of these four sons, Mullā Niẓām al-Dīn M. Sihālawī, see pp. 1016–17 *supra*.

Cf. *J. al-n.* p. 479 antepenult.; *Rauḍāt al-jannāt* p. 356; *Muntahā 'l-maqāl* p. 179; etc.), who is said to have died at Raiy about A.H. 250/864 and whose shrine is at the place called after him Shāh 'Abd al-'Aẓīm, five or six miles south of Ṭihrān (cf. Browne *A year amongst the Persians* pp. 82, 158–61, etc.), together with notices of his ancestors and of some holy, learned or pious persons buried near Ṭihrān.

Edition: [**Ṭihrān**] 1296–8/1879–81* (pp. 548. Portrait of the author at end).

1403. **Ghulām-Naqī** b. M. Fatḥ-'Alī **Bilgrāmī** Chishtī Ṣābirī[1] was born on 17 Ramaḍān 1231/11 August 1816.

Manbahāt [*Munabbihāt* ?] *fī 'ilm al-amwāt*, biographies of well-known Indian saints, chiefly Chishtīs, and of a few poets, princes and noblemen, completed at the Jāmi' Masjid Madrasah, Ḥaidarābād, in 1298/1881: **Ivanow** Curzon 84 (autograph ?).

1404. **Amīn Aḥmad** "Thabāt" Firdausī.

(1) *Gul i bihishtī*, a metrical account of some Chishtī saints: [**Lucknow**] 1881° (242 pp.).

(2) *Gul i firdaus*, a metrical biography of Sharaf al-Dīn Aḥmad b. Yaḥyā Munyarī,[2] with interwoven notices of other Chishtī saints: **Lucknow** 1884° (266 pp.).

[1] Cf. p. 1031 n. 5.

[2] Sh. al-D. A. b. Y. Munyarī or Manērī, born at Manēr, a village in the Patna Division of the Province of Bihār, went to Delhi either before or shortly after the death of Niẓām al-Dīn Auliyā (for whom see p. 941 n. 5 *supra*) and became a disciple of Najīb al-Dīn Firdausī. After his return to Bihār he spent many years of seclusion and austerity in the Rajagriha hills. Later he settled outside the town of Bihār (now a place of pilgrimage called on his account Bihār Sharīf) and died there on 7 Shawwāl 772/1371 or 781/1380 or 782/1381. See *Akhbār al-akhyār* pp. 117–22; *Gulzār i abrār* no. 99; *Mir'āt al-asrār*, *ṭabaqah* 20, last biography; *Makhzan al-gharā'ib* no. 1143; *Khazīnat al-aṣfiyā'* ii pp. 290–2; Ḍamīr al-Dīn *Sīrat al-Sharaf* (cited in *Nuzhat al-khawāṭir* p. 10² and Bānkīpūr xvi p. 25); Rieu ii 402; Beale *Oriental biographical dictionary* under Sharaf-uddin Ahmad Ahia [*sic*] Maniri and also under Shah Sharaf-uddin; Raḥmān 'Alī p. 84; *Nuzhat al-khawāṭir* (in Arabic) pp. 8–10; Bānkīpūr xvi p. 25. Among his works were (1) *Maktūbāt*, well known Ṣūfī letters, of which there are three or four collections (MSS.: Āṣafīyah i p. 486 nos. 68, 69, 461, 683, 810, Bānkīpūr xvi 1361–5, xvii 1585, 1615, Brelvi-Dhabhar p. 72, Ethé 1843–7, Ivanow 1205–7, Ivanow-Curzon 756, Ivanow 1st Suppt. 855, Kapurthala (*OCM.* iii/4 (Aug. 1927) p. 10), Lahore (*OCM.* viii/3 (May 1932) p. 138), Leyden v p. 42 no. 2304, Peshawar 940*b*, Princeton 98. Editions: *Maktūbāt i ṣadī* [*sic* ?], [Arrah] 1287/1870* (vol. i only, pp. 165), *Maktūbāt*, Lucknow 1885° (pp. 400). Translation: *Letters from a Sûfî teacher, Shaikh Sharfuddîn Manerî or Makhdûm-ul-Mulk. Translated . . . by Baijnath Singh*, Benares

(3) *Rauḍat al-naʿīm*, metrical biographies of ʿAbd al-Qādir Jīlānī and other saints: S̲h̲araf al-ak̲h̲bār Pr. [**Lucknow**?] 1301/1883-4*.

1405. M. **Diyā' al-Raḥmān** S̲h̲āhqulīpūrī was a disciple of S. S̲h̲āh ʿAlī ʿAbd al-Qādir S̲h̲ams al-Qādirī called Murs̲h̲id ʿAlī Qādirī Bag̲h̲dādī ($aṣl^{an}$) Mēdnīpūrī ($maulid^{an}$), who was himself (see p. 13, l. 7 from foot) a disciple of S. Ṭufail ʿAlī Qādirī Razzāqī D̲h̲ākirī (d. 1251/1836 : see p. 187³), the nephew (*birādar-zādah*, p. 152⁸), son-in-law and successor of S. S̲h̲āh D̲h̲ākir ʿAlī.

Mud̲h̲ākarah i Quṭb al-ʿālamīn, or *Madārij i sanīyah i D̲h̲ākirīyah*, or *Ad̲h̲kār i baiyinah i Qādirīyah* (all chronograms = 1309/1891-2), a life of S. S̲h̲āh Abū 'l-Ḥasan M. D̲h̲ākir ʿAlī Qādirī Razzāqī Bag̲h̲dādī, called G̲h̲auth i T̲h̲ānī, a son of S. S̲h̲āh Abū M. ʿAbd Allāh al-Qādirī al-Bag̲h̲dādī and a descendant of ʿAbd al-Qādir al-Jīlānī, who was born at Bag̲h̲dād in 1111/1699-1700 (see p. 193), migrated to India in 1180/1766-7, settled at Mangalkōṭ, north of Bardwān in Bengal, and died there in 1192/1778, based on the *Risālah i D̲h̲ākirīyah* (a chronogram = 1232/1817) of an unnamed disciple of the *s̲h̲aik̲h̲* : **Cawnpore** (Aḥmadī Press) 1310/1893‡.

1406. Qāḍī S. **Imām al-Dīn Ḥasan K̲h̲ān,** Deputy Collector at Ajmēr, may be presumed to have written his *Muʿīn al-auliyā'* shortly before publication.

[1909*] (pp. 130)), (2) *Ajwibah* (MSS. : Bānkīpūr xvii 1569, Bombay Univ. p. 231 no. 151, Ivanow-Curzon 462 IV. Edition (?) : *Maktūbāt i jawābī*, Lucknow 1884°), (3) *Fawāʾid i Ruknī*, extracts from the *Maktūbāt* (MS. : Bānkīpūr xvii 1612). Edition: place ? 1328/1910 (Āṣafīyah iii p. 200)), (4) *Irs̲h̲ād al-sālikīn* (MSS. : Bānkīpūr xvii 1583, Ethé 1849, Ivanow-Curzon 462 iii), (5) *Maʿdin al-maʿānī*, a collection of *malfūẓāt* (MSS. : Āṣafīyah i p. 488 no. 70, Bānkīpūr xvi 1360, Ivanow-Curzon 425, Lahore (*OCM.* viii/3 (May 1932) p. 138), Vollers 902 (?)). (6) *Muk̲h̲k̲h̲ al-maʿānī*, a collection of *malfūẓāt*. Edition : Āgrah 1321/1904*. The name of his birthplace, officially spelt Maner (i.e. Manēr presumably), is spelt Munair in the Bānkīpūr catalogue (xvi p. 25) and Manīr (*bi-fatḥ al-mīm wa-kasr al-nūn*) in the *Nuzhat al-k̲h̲awāṭir* (p. 9¹), but the spelling Munyar (or Manyar ?) is attested, though perhaps only as a poetic licence, by several verses in the *S̲h̲araf-nāmah i Aḥmad i Munyarī*, a dictionary dedicated to his memory in 877/1472 or 878/1473 by a dweller at his shrine, Ibrāhīm Qiwām Fārūqī Bihārī (e.g. *Mug̲h̲īt̲h̲ i jahān sarwar i Munyar ast* * *kih k̲h̲āk i dar i rauḍah as̲h̲ ʿanbar ast* (quoted Ethé ii 3052), *Samī-yi Nabī Aḥmad i Munyarī* * *kih dārad ba-d-ū dīn i ḥaqq bartarī* (Sipahsālār Cat. ii p. 190), *Sarāpā kih mamlū zi durr i darī 'st* * *S̲h̲araf-nāmah i Aḥmad i Munyarī 'st*).

Mu'īn al-auliyā', a life of Mu'īn al-Dīn Chishtī Ajmērī,[1] his successors and his spiritual descendants: **Ajmēr** [1894°. Pp. 308].[2]

1407. Ṣāḥib-zādah **M. Ḥasan** b. 'Abd al-Raḥmān **Mujaddidī Naqshbandī,** a descendant of Aḥmad Sirhindī (for whom see p. 988 n. 5 *supra*), was resident at Amritsar in 1910.

Anīs al-murīdīn, a life of the author's father, Pīr 'Abd al-Raḥmān b. 'Abd al-Qaiyūm (b. 1244/1828–9, d. 1315/1897), written in 1316/1898–9. Edition: **Amritsar** 1328/1910*.

1408. **Ma'ṣūm 'Alī** b. Raḥmat-'Alī **Ni'mat-Allāhī al-Shīrāzī** (see *Ṭarā'iq al-ḥaqā'iq*, author's preface, l. 2), or Āqā-yi Ḥājjī Mīrzā Ma'ṣūm[3] *Nā'ib al-Ṣadr*, as "Furūghī" calls him in his prefixed *taqrīẓ* (so also on the title-page of Vol. I), or al-Ḥājj Ma'ṣūm 'Alī Shāh al-Ni'mat-Allāhī al-Shīrāzī, as he is called on the other title-pages, was the son of Ḥājjī Zain al-'Ābidīn known as (*ma'rūf bi-*) Ḥājjī Mīrzā Kūchak Nā'ib al-Ṣadr and surnamed (*mulaqqab bi-*) Raḥmat-'Alī Shāh (see "Furūghī's" *taqrīẓ* p. 5[8]). He was born at Shīrāz on 14 Rabī' al-Awwal 1270/15 Dec. 1853. In the course of extensive travels he visited various parts of Persia, 'Irāq, India, Turkistān and Turkey, meeting numerous men of learning and piety. His visit to Mecca and al-Madīnah he described in a *safar-nāmah* entitled *Tuḥfat al-Ḥaramain.*

Ṭarā'iq al-ḥaqā'iq, biographical notices of saints and mystics completed at Ṭihrān in Ṣafar 1318/1900 and divided into a *muqaddimah* (on Ṣūfism, etc.), six *waṣls* ((1) companions of 'Alī b. Abī Ṭālib, vol. ii pp. 2–27, (2) the *silsilah* of Ḥasan i Baṣrī, vol. ii pp. 27–39, (3) the *silsilah* of Kumail b. Ziyād, vol. ii pp. 39–51, (4) the *silsilah* of Ibrāhīm b. Adham, vol. ii pp. 51–68, (5) the *silsilah* of Bāyazīd i Bisṭāmī, vol. ii pp. 68–114, (6) the *silsilah* of Ma'rūf i Karkhī and its fourteen branches including the Ni'mat-Allāhī *shaikhs*, whose biographies are the

[1] For whom see p. 943 n. 3 *supra.*
[2] The Āṣafīyah Library has two copies of this work dated 1312 [i.e. 1894–5] which the catalogue [iii p. 166 nos. 131, 173] describes, probably by inadvertence, as manuscripts.
[3] His father calls him Muḥammad Ma'ṣūm in a note recording the date of his birth which is quoted in the *Ṭarā'iq al-ḥaqā'iq* iii p. 220 antepenult.

primary concern of the work, vol. ii pp. 114–311, vol. iii pp. 2–220) and a *khātimah* (an account of the author and some of his contemporaries, vol. iii pp. 220–354).

Edition: **Ṭihrān** 1316–19/1898–1901‡ (cf. Mashhad iii p. 137).

[Autobiography in *khātimah* to *Ṭarā'iq al-ḥaqā'iq*: *taqrīẓ* by M. Ḥusain "Furūghī" Iṣfahānī prefixed to vol. i: portrait following the *taqrīẓ*.]

1409. Ḥājjī Abū Muḥammad **Muḥyī 'l-Dīn "Miskīn"** b. Mullā M. Shāh Aḥmadī Kubrawī Ḥanafī Naqshbandī was born in 1282/1865–6. He was a pupil of Ḥājjī M. Yaḥyā, whom he accompanied in 1307/1889–90 on a pilgrimage to Mecca. In 1309/1891–2 he wrote a work entitled *'Ain al-jārī sharḥ Arba'īn al-Qārī*. When he wrote the preface to his *Taḥā'if al-abrār* he was resident in the district of Amīrākadal.

Taḥā'if al-abrār [so in the author's preface, but on the title-page *Tārīkh i kabīr i Kashmīr al-mausūm bah T. al. a. fī dhikr al-auliyā' al-akhyār*], a mainly biographical work on Kashmīr begun in 1310/1892–3, completed in 1321/1903–4 and divided into ten *taḥā'if* ((1) Saiyids, (2) *rīshīs*, i.e. anchorites [cf. p. 985 n. 3 *supra*], (3) *mashāyikh u ṣāliḥān*, (4) scholars, (5) *majdhūbān*, (6) poets, (7) sacred relics, (8) sulṭāns, (9) geography, (10) on the permissibility of certain foods and drugs). Edition: **Amritsar** 1321–2/1905°* (only the first seven *taḥā'if*, being the first of the two volumes).

[*Taḥā'if al-abrār* pp. 363–4.]

1410. Maulawī S. M. **Amīr Ḥasan Madārī Fanṣūrī** [1] b. Saiyid Shāh Ākhūn is described on the title-page of the *Tadhkirat al-muttaqīn* as a (still-living) *ra'īs* of Makanpūr.[2]

Tadhkirat al-muttaqīn (the title-page adds *fī aḥwāl khulafā' Saiyid Badī' al-Dīn*), biographies of Shāh Madār (for whom see p. 1006 n. 2 *supra*), his *khulafā'* and prominent members

[1] This *nisbah* indicates descent from Saiyid Abū Turāb Fanṣūr (d. 899/1494), Shāh Madār's immediate successor, whose biography is given on pp. 22–31 of the first volume of the *Tadhkirat al-muttaqīn*. The word Fanṣūr is not explained. For its use as a geographical name see *Ḥudūd al-'ālam*, tr. Minorsky, p. 87.

[2] A village 8 miles N.W. of Bilhaur and 40 miles from Cawnpore, owing its celebrity to the shrine of Shāh Madār.

of his order down to the author's time. Edition : **Cawnpore** 1315/1898* (vol. i) and 1322–3/1905* (vol. ii).

1411. APPENDIX

(1) *Adhkār al-adhkiyā' fī bayān manāqib mashāyikh al-ṭuruq* (beg. : *A'lā'i ajnās i ḥamd u sipās*) : **Cairo** p. 498 (A.H. 1126/1714).

(2) (*Aḥwāl Ibn al-Khafīf*), an Arabic biography of Abū 'Abd Allāh M. b. al-Khafīf al-Shīrāzī,[1] by his pupil Abū 'l-Ḥasan 'Alī b. M. al-Dailamī (cf. Brockelmann *Sptbd.* i p. 359 and R. Walzer in *JRAS* 1939 pp. 407–22) : no MSS. recorded.

Persian translation in thirteen *bābs* prepared by Rukn al-Dīn Yaḥyā b. Burhān al-Dīn b. Junaid at the request of an unnamed Atābak described as *Atābak i sa'īd i marḥūm i shahīd* : **Berlin** 605 (breaks off in *Bāb* x. 62 foll. Old), **Köprülü** 1589 foll. 379*a*–406*b*.

Extracts : Massignon *Recueil de textes inédits* p. 81.

(3) *Aḥwāl u aqwāl i ḥaḍrat i Saiyidnā 'Abd al-Qādir i Jīlānī* : **Āṣafīyah** i p. 396 no. 876 (A.H. 1232/1816–17).

(4) *Anecdotes of saints in the first three Islāmic centuries* (beginning : *al-Ḥ. l. R. al-'ā. . . . Thanā u sitāyish mar Khuday rā kih āfrīdgār i jahānast u āfrīdgār i hamah i jānwarān ast*) divided according to subject into twenty *bābs* (I. *Andar khwurdan i ḥalāl*, etc.) and written apparently in the fifth/eleventh century : **Rieu** Suppt. 393 (defective at end. 13th cent.).

(5) (*Ansāb i mashāyikh i Kashmīr*), genealogical tables and chains of spiritual succession relating to prophets and other holy persons, especially Kashmīrī saints, with occasional dates (of which 1101/1690 and 1128/1716 seem to be the latest) : **Ivanow** Curzon 79 (3).

(6) *Anwār al-Raḥmān li-tanwīr al-janān*, the life and

[1] For this saint, who died in 371/981–2, see *Kashf al-mahjūb* tr. Nicholson p. 158 ; 'Abd Allāh Anṣārī *Ṭabaqāt al-Ṣūfīyah* (Ivanow 234, no. 110) ; 'Aṭṭār *Tadhkirat al-auliyā'* ii pp. 124–31 ; *Haft iqlīm* no. 171 ; *Safīnat al-auliyā'* p. 110 (no. 144) ; Massignon *La passion d'al-Hallaj* pp. 363–4 ; Brockelmann *Sptbd.* i pp. 358–9 (where further references will be found).

teachings of S͟hāh 'Abd al-Raḥmān, by M. Nūr Allāh. Edition: **Lucknow** 1321/1903°*.

(7) *A'rās i buzurgān* (beginning, without preface, S͟hahr i Rabī' al-Awwal. 1. Wafāt yāft Saiyid al-Mursalīn) the Persian version of an Arabic obituary calendar relating to oly persons from the first Islāmic century onwards, especially to members of the Bā-'Alawī family (about whom particulars are given mainly on the authority of '*Iqd al-jawāhir wa-'l-durar* (Brockelmann ii p. 383, *Sptbd.* ii p. 516), *al-Nūr al-sāfir* (Brockelmann ii p. 419, *Sptbd.* ii p. 617) and similar works), composed evidently in India [1] and doubtless soon after 1160/1747 (the date of the latest death recorded, that of S. M. b. Ḥāmid b. 'Abd Allāh b. 'Alī Bā-'Alawī, of Malabar, p. 34, 27th Rajab) apparently by a son of S. S͟haik͟h b. 'Alawī b. 'Abd Allāh Bā-'Abbūd Bā-'Alawī (who on p. 28 is called *al-Saiyid al-jalīl al-'allāmah al-wālid* [2]), probably S. 'Alawī b. S͟haik͟h Bā-'Abbūd Bā-'Alawī, who is mentioned on p. 74 ult. as the author of the preceding biography and whose name occurs also on pp. 7[9] and 34[7] (as the subject of statements in the third person, however).

Edition: *The Á'aras-i-bozorgán, being an obituary of pious and learned Moslims from the beginning of Islám to the middle of the twelfth century of the Hijrah.* Edited [from a MS., containing also, it seems, the Arabic original, in the Library of the College of Fort William] [3] *by W. Nassau Lees, and Mawlawi Kabir al-Dín Ahmad.* Published by W. N. Lees. [**Calcutta**] 1855°* (pp. 91).

(8) *Asrār al-mas͟hāyik͟h*, by Bahā' al-Dīn b. Maḥmūd b. Mak͟hdūm Qāḍī Ḥamīd al-Dīn Nāgaurī [4] *al-ma'rūf bah* Rājah: **Āṣafīyah** iii p. 362 no. 192 (A.H. 1077/1666–7).

(9) *Badā'i' al-āt͟hār*, an account of the visit of 'Abd al-Bahā' to the United States in 1912, by Maḥmūd Zarqānī: **Bombay** 1332/1914°* (Vol. I only ?).

---

[1] For Indian saints the compiler's chief authority is the *Mir'āt al-asrār* (cf. p. 1005 *supra*).
[2] The last word is queried in the printed text.
[3] The MS. should presumably be now either in the library of the Royal Asiatic Society of Bengal or in that of the India Office, but it seems not to be traceable in the catalogues of those libraries.
[4] For Qāḍī Ḥ. al-D.N. see pp. 5–6 *supra*.

(10) *Bhagat-māl*: see *Bhakta-māla*.

(11) *Bhagat-nāmah*: see *Bhakta-māla*.

(12) *Bhakta-māla*, translations of Nābhājī's Hindī biographies of Vaishnava saints, (1) *Srī Bhagat-māl*, with introduction, marginal notes, and glossary, **Meerut** 1269/1853* (pp. 12, 6, 468, 50), (2) *Gangā-sāgar 'urf Bhagat-nāmah*, a metrical translation by Nat'han Lāl from Tulasī-Rāma's Urdu version, **Delhi** 1897° (18 pts.).

(13) *Dār al-asrār fī khawāriq Badī' al-Dīn Shāh Madār*[1]: **Peshawar** 1957 (9).

(14) *Dhikr i Khwājah 'Abd al-Khāliq i Ghujduwānī*[2]: **Leyden** v p. 232 no. 2641 (22 foll. A.H. 900/1494–5).

The same saint, who died in 575/1179–80, is the subject of **Rieu** ii 862*a* i (beginning *Az ān shaikh i rabbānī*. 18th cent.) and **Ethé** 1923 (1) (*Dhikr i Khwājah i Khwājahā Khwājah i jahān 'Abd al-Khāliq i Ghujduwānī*, beginning *Ān shaikh i 'alā 'l-iṭlāq*).

(15) *Dhikr i maqāmāt i Imām i A'ẓam* (i.e. presumably Abū Ḥanīfah): **Āṣafīyah** ii p. 1556 no. 44.

(16) *Ḍiyā' al-qulūb*, "a treatise on Ṣūfī orders," by Imdād Allāh Fārūqī: **Delhi** [1877 ?°*]; place ? 1914 (Āṣafīyah III p. 200); and in the *Kullīyāt i Imdādīyah*, **Cawnpore** 1315/1898°, pp. 127–81.

(17) *Durr al-dārain fī manāqib Ghauth al-Thaqalain*,[3] by S. Ghulām-'Alī Qādirī Mūsawī: **Āṣafīyah** iii p. 662 (author's name given as 'Alī al-Mūsawī).

Edition: place ? 1308/1890–1 (Āṣaf. ii p. 1556 nos. 16–17).

(18) *Gangā-sāgar*: see *Bhakta-māla*.

(19) *Genealogies of Shī'ite and Ṣūfī families*: **Lindesiana** p. 142 no. 789 (circ. A.D. 1750).

[1] Cf. p. 1006 n. 2 *supra*.

[2] See *Nafaḥāt al-uns* p. 431; *Rashaḥāt* p. 18; *Haft iqlīm* no. 1486; *Safīnat al-auliyā'* p. 76 (no. 76); *Khazīnat al-aṣfiyā'* i p. 532; *Ency. Isl.* under Ghudjduwānī (unsigned).

[3] The Ghauth al-Thaqalain is of course 'Abd al-Qādir al-Jīlānī (for whom see p. 933 n. 2).

(20) *Ḥālāt i ḥaḍrat i Shāh Balāwal i Lāhaurī*[1] (in Persian ?): no MSS. recorded. Urdu translation: *Urdū tarjamah i kitāb i Ḥ. i ḥ. Sh. B. L.*, **Lahore** [1923*].

(21) *Ḥālāt i Saiyid Muḥammad i Jaunpūrī*, a life of S. M. b. S. Bud'h Uwaisī Jaunpūrī, who claimed to be the Mahdī, founded a sect in Gujrāt[2] and died in 910/1504–5[3]: **Āṣafīyah** ii p. 848 no. 34 (A.H. 1267/1850–1).

(22) *Mathnawī i Ḥālāt i shahādat i Muḥammad Ghauth Qādirī*: **Āṣafīyah** i p. 468 no. 679 (A.H. 1240/1824–5).

(23) *Ḥālāt u karāmāt i ḥaḍrat i Shāh Ṣafī u Shāh Miyān u Shāh Ilhām-Allāh u Shāh Qudrat-Allāh*, by Shāh Faiḍ Allāh: **Āṣafīyah** iii p. 196 no. 1454.

(24) *Risālah i ḥasab u nasab i ḥaḍrat i Ḥāfiẓ M. 'Alī-Shāh Khairābādī*,[4] an autobiography: **Āṣafīyah** iii p. 362 no. 208 (A.H. 1310/1892–3).

(25) *Risālah i ḥasab u nasab i Makhdūm Abū'l-Fatḥ b. S. Niẓām al-Dīn Shanūzānī* (?) *al-MLKI al-Khurāsānī*, apparently an autobiography: **Āṣafīyah** iii p. 362 no. 208 (A.H. 1310/1892–3).

(26) *Ḥikāyāt al-ṣāliḥīn*, anecdotes in twenty *bābs* each containing ten *ḥikāyāt*, by 'Uthmān b. 'Umar called Kahf: Ḥ. Kh. iii p. 81 (beginning not quoted).

Arabic translation: **Lahore** 1298/1881° (pp. 108).

(27) *Ḥikāyāt i auliyā i ṣāliḥīn*: **Āṣafīyah** i p. 416 no. 639.

(28) *Intikhāb i tawārīkh al-Aghyār*, notices of S. M.

[1] S. Shāh B. b. S. 'Uthmān b. S. 'Īsā Qādirī Lāhaurī, was born at Shaikhūpūrah, became a disciple of S. Shams al-Dīn Qādirī Lāhaurī and died on 28 Sha'bān 1046/25 Jan. 1637. See *Safīnat al-auliyā'* p. 198 (no. 377); 'Abd al-Ḥamīd *Pādshāh-nāmah* i, 2 p. 334; *'Amal i Ṣāliḥ* iii p. 366; *Khazīnat al-aṣfiyā'* i pp. 161–3.

[2] See *Ency. Isl.* under Mahdawīs; Raḥmān 'Alī pp. 188–9; etc.

[3] See *Ẓafar al-wālih* (in Arabic) i pp. 34–6; *Ma'āthir al-umarā'* i pp. 124–5, Beveridge's translation pp. 116–7; Raḥmān 'Alī pp. 197–201; *Sawāniḥ i Mahdī i mau'ūd* (in Urdu), by S. Walī Sikandarābādī, Āgrah 1321/1903*; *Intikhāb i tawārīkh al-Aghyār* (no. (28) below); etc. For a work entitled *Ithbāt i madhhab i Saiyid Muḥammad Ṣāḥib i Jaunpūrī*, by Shihāb al-Dīn Mahdawī (d. circ. 1275/1858–9), see Āṣafīyah ii p. 1354 no. 50.

[4] Presumably the same person as the subject of the *Manāqib i Ḥāfiẓīyah* mentioned below (no. 48).

Jaunpūrī (see no. (21) above) and his followers (called *Ghair-mahdī* by their enemies: see *Ency. Religion and Ethics* vi p. 189). Edition: place ? date ? (Peshawar no. 1549).

(29) *'Iqd al-la'ālī'*, on the life and merits of Shāh Abū 'l-Ma'ālī,[1] by Maulawī Mushtāq Aḥmad Ṣābirī[2]: **Sād'haurah** 1331/1913*.

(30) *Kanz al-ansāb*, the genealogy of eminent saints and other famous men, by 'Abd al-Razzāq 'Aṭā Ḥusain: **Bombay** 1883° (pp. 344).

(31) *Karāmāt al-auliyā'*: **Āṣafīyah** i p. 460 nos. 706 (A.H. 1236/1820–1), 894.

(32) *Karāmāt i Qādir Walī*, in verse, by M. Najīb b. Aḥmad 'Alī. Edition: place ? 1267/1851 (Āṣafīyah ii p. 850).

(33) *Khulāṣat al-'ārifīn*: **Āṣafīyah** i p. 416 (2 copies).

(34) *Lam'at al-shams*, a metrical account of Shams al-Dīn [Tabrīzī ?] and of Ni'mat Allāh Walī (presumably N. A. W. Kirmānī. Cf. p. 952 n. 1 *supra*), by ?: **Āṣafīyah** ii p. 850 no. 50.

(35) *Maḥāmid i Ḥammādīyah*, a life of S. Shāh Ghulām-Muḥammad Qādirī *al-mukhāṭab min 'ind Rasūl Allāh bah* Ḥammād i Thānī, by Maulawī S. M. Burhān al-Dīn Khān. Edition: place ? 1308/1890–1 (Āṣafīyah iii p. 202 no. 1494).

(36) *Majmū'ah i fawā'id i 'Uthmānī*, life, letters, and sayings of M. 'Uthmān Damānī, by M. Akbar 'Alī Shāh Dihlawī: **Delhi** 1316/1899°.

(37) *Makhzan i 'irfānī*, "the life, sayings and writings of the Peshawari saint S. Amīr called Ḥaḍrat-jī," by Sulṭān M. Ajnālawī: **Amritsar** [1920*].

(38) *Malfūẓ i asrār al-makhdūmīn*, sayings of Shāh Karak Karawī and anecdotes concerning him, compiled by Karīm-Yār, Ra'īs of Yuhan: **Fatḥpūr** 1893°.

[1] Presumably Abū 'l-Ma'ālī b. S. M. Ashraf Chishtī Ṣābirī, of Anbahtah ("Ambahta") near Sahāranpūr, who was a disciple of M. Ṣādiq Gangōhī and a *khalīfah* of his son, M. Dāwud b. M. Ṣādiq Gangōhī Chishti, and who died in 1116/1704–5. See *Sawāṭi' al-anwār* (Ethé col. 338 no. 35 (*d*)), *Khazīnat al-aṣfiyā'* i pp. 485–6.

[2] Author of the Ṣūfī tract *Ḍābiṭah dar taḥṣīl i rābiṭah*, Ludiana 1893*.

(39) *Malfūẓ i Razzāqī*, the life and sayings of ʿAbd al-Razzāq Bānsawī (cf. p. 1016[28] *supra*), by M. Khān Razzāqī, edited by S. Ghulām-Jīlānī : **Lucknow** 1896°, [1905*].

(40) *Malfūẓāt i Ḥājjī Wārith ʿAlī Shāh*, life and sayings of W. ʿA. Sh., by Khudā-Bakhsh "Shāʾiq"[1]: Anwār i Muḥammadī Press [**Lucknow**] 1293/1876*.

(41) *Malfūẓāt i Shāh Mīnā* : see *Tuḥfat al-Saʿdīyah* below.

(42) *Malfūẓāt i Sharīfī*, life and sayings of Sharīf al-Dīn M. Chishtī : **Ambala** 1917* (with preface by Mushtāq Aḥmad Chishtī).

(43) *Manāqib al-aṣfiyāʾ*, lives of famous saints, by Shāh Shuʿaib Firdausī : **Calcutta** 1895° (152 pp.).

(44) *Manāqib i Amīr Kulāl*[2] : **Peshawar** 1003.

(45) (*Manāqib i auliyā i kirām*), short lives of saints (Luqmān i Ḥakīm, Jaʿfar i Ṣādiq, Uwais i Qaranī, etc.) : **Berlin** 589 (69 foll.).

(46) *Manāqib i Ghauthīyah*[3], **Peshawar** 1094 (1).

(47) *Manāqib i ḥaḍrat i Shaikh Jīw Khunuk* [?], by ʿAbd al-Ḥalīm : **Āṣafīyah** i p. 490 (A.H. 1177/1763–4).

(48) *Manāqib i Ḥāfiẓīyah*, a life of M. ʿAlī Khairābādī,[4] by Ghulām M. Hādī ʿAlī Khān Chishtī Kashmīrī : **Cawnpore** 1305/1888° (256 pp.).

(49) *Manāqib i mazārāt i Bukhārā-yi sharīf* : **Leningrad** Univ. 390 (Salemann-Rosen p. 17), possibly also **Peshawar** 999A (*Risālah i mazārāt i Bukhārā sharīf*).

(50) *Manāqib i Qādirīyah* : **Peshawar** 995.

[1] "Shāʾiq" is the author of a *Mathnawī* in six *daftars* published at Lucknow in 1294/1877°*.

[2] Presumably S. Amīr Kulāl, who died in 772/1370. See *Maqāmāt i Amīr Kulāl* (no. (51) below; perhaps another copy of the same work); *Nafaḥāt al-uns*; *Rashaḥāt* pp. 42–3; *Haft iqlīm* no. 1488; *Safīnat al-auliyāʾ* p. 77 (no. 81); *Khazīnat al-aṣfiyāʾ* i pp. 546–8.

[3] Whether this is the work of M. Ṣādiq Shihābī (see p. 1013 *supra*) does not appear from the catalogue.

[4] Probably identical with the subject of the (*Risālah i*) *ḥasab a nasab i . . . Ḥāfiẓ M. ʿAlī-Shāh Khairābādī* mentioned above (no. (24)).

(51) *Maqāmāt i Amīr Kulāl*[1] : Ḥ. Kh. vi p. 54, **Lahore** Panjāb Univ. Lib. (defective at end and disarranged. See *Oriental College Magazine*, vol. iii, no. 1 (Lahore, Nov. 1936) p. 70).

(52) *Maʻqūlāt* [*sic*] *i auliyā' Allāh*, sayings and biographies of saints (beginning *Wa-ʻan Abī 'l-Dardā'*) : **Ethé** 1895 (1).

(53) *Mazārāt i Bukhārā* : see *Manāqib i mazārāt i Bukhārā* (no. 49 above).

(54) *Mishkāt al-nubuwwah*, an account of the saints of Ḥaidarābād, etc., by S. ʻAlī : **Āṣafīyah** iii p. 166 no. 194.

(55) *Mukhbir al-auliyā'*, an account of Chishtī and other saints, most of them buried at Aḥmadābād, by Rashīd al-Dīn Maudūd Lālā [?] b. Sh. Aḥmad Chishti al-Fārūqī b. Sh. Ḥusām al-Dīn M. Farrukh al-Ṣūfī al-Chishtī, who was a native of Aḥmadābād and whose spiritual guide was S. M. Aḥsan al-Sijzī, the head of the Chishtī order : **Bombay** Fyzee 14 (19th cent.).

(56) *Munājāt i Khākī*, a metrical Naqshbandī pedigree, by Ḥakīm Qamar al-Dīn Siyālkōtī : **Lahore** [1911*].

(57) *Nāfiʻ al-sālikīn*, a life of M. Sikandar " Wāṣil " Khāliṣpūrī, by Sh. Dāwud Pūtrīk : **Bombay** 1310/1893° (appended to M. Sikandar's *Tuḥfat al-ʻulamā'*, for which see Ellis).

(58) *Nasab-nāmah i ḥaḍrat i S. Shāh Ismāʻīl i Bukhārī* : **Āṣafīyah** i p. 494 no. 123.

(59) *Nasab-nāmah i nāmī i shaikh-zādagān*, " genealogies of certain noted saints " : **Lucknow** 1876*.

(60) *Nasab-nāmah i Shāh Wajīh al-Dīn*[2], by S. Yaḥyā b. S. Ḥusain : **Bombay** Fyzee 15 (incomplete).

[1] For S. Amīr Kulāl see no. (44) above. According to *Rashaḥāt* p. 45, the author of the *Maqāmāt i Amīr Kulāl* was a grandson of Amīr Ḥamzah, Amīr Kulāl's second son (*dar Maqāmāt i Amīr Kulāl kih nabīrah i Amīr Ḥamzah ta'līf kardah*). This passage is probably the source of Ḥ. Kh.'s information. According to the *OCM*. the author's name does not occur in the preface. The cataloguer inferred from a passage on fol. 15 that Amīr Ḥamzah himself was the author.

[2] Presumably Wajīh al-Dīn ʻAlawī Gujrātī, a well-known scholar and mystic, who died in 998/1590 and whose grave at Aḥmadābād is marked by a beautiful tomb. See Badā'ūnī iii pp. 43–4 ; *Ma'āthir i Raḥīmī* iii pp. 17–18 ; *Safīnat al-auliyā'* p. 193 (no. 371) ; *Ma'āthir al-kirām* ; *Mir'āt i Aḥmadī, khātimah* pp. 68–70, Eng. trans. pp. 60–61 ; *Subḥat al-marjān* p. 45 ; *Majmūʻah i ḥālāt i ḥaḍrat i Shāh W. al-D. ʻA. G.* (" in Urdu, Persian, and Arabic "), by M. Yūsuf b. Aḥmad Khatkhatī, Shihābī Press, Bombay (see Ḥaidarābād Coll. p. 36) ; Raḥmān ʻAlī pp. 249–50 ; Brockelmann *Sptbd.* i p. 534 and elsewhere.

(61) *Nasā'im i Ghauthīyah*, a life of 'Abd al-Qādir al-Jīlānī (cf. p. 933 n. 2 *supra*) in eleven *nasīms* : **Ivanow** 271 (18th cent.), **Ethé** 1801 (n.d.). Abridgment : *Nasā'im al-Qādirīyah*, likewise in eleven *nasīms* : **Ethé** 1802 (A.H. 1154/1741), probably also **Āṣafīyah** ii p. 882 no. 79.

(62) *Nasā'im al-Qādirīyah* : see under *Nasā'im i Ghauthīyah* above.

(63) *Nawādir al-safar*, notices of 22 Chishtī saints with descriptions of their shrines, by Farīd al-Dīn : **Ivanow** 272 (defective at end ?. 18th cent.).

(64) *Qiṣṣah (Ḥālāt) i Sālār Mas'ūd i Ghāzī* [1], " a fiction of the wildest character " (Rieu), being one form of the legend of Sālār Mas'ūd (cf. p. 1006 *supra*) : **Ivanow** 322 (early 19th cent.), **Rieu** iii 1015*a* (A.D. 1850).

(65) *Rauḍat al-abrār*, lives of Kashmīrī saints, by Abū 'l-Ḥasan M., known as Muḥammad al-Dīn Qādirī Lāhaurī : **Jēlam** [i.e. Jihlam, Jehlam, or " Jhelum "] 1302/1885° (80 pp.).

(66) *Rauḍat al-auliyā'*, *tadhkirah i auliyā' i Bījāpūr*, by M. Ibrāhīm : **Āṣafīyah** iii p. 164 no. 169 (A.H. 1310/1892–3).

(67) *Rauḍat al-auliyā' fī aḥwāl al-aṣfiyā'*, a life of Muḥammad and brief notices of Naqshbandī saints, by M. Ḥusain b. M. Riḍā. Edition : **Amritsar** 1333/1915*.

(68) *Risālah i amīrīyah*, a life of Bahā' Allāh, by M. Muṣṭafā al-Baghdādī : see no. (73) below.

(69) *Risālah i Bahā'īyah fī maqāmāt i ḥaḍrat i Khwājah Bahā' al-Dīn*, by Abū l'-Qāsim b. M. b. Mas'ūd : **'Alīgaṛh** Subḥ. MSS. p. 12 no. 11 (A.H. 1062/1652).

(70) *Risālah i buzurgān i Samarqand* : **Bukhārā** Semenov 71.

(71) *Risālah dar ḥālāt i Shāh Pīr Muḥammad*, by Maulawī 'Aẓamat Allāh : **'Alīgaṛh** Subḥ. MSS. p. 62 no. 41.

[1] In the B.M. MS. the title is given as *Ḥālāt i Saiyid Sālār Mas'ūd i Ghāzī*. The attribution of the title Saiyid to Sālār Mas'ūd is perhaps due to a confusion with Saiyid Mas'ūd Ghāzī, the founder of Ghāzīpūr, who is said to have died in 767/1365–6. See *A short history of Syed Masud Gházi and his descendants*, by S. Ali Azhar, in the *Journal of the United Provinces Historical Society*, iii pp. 49–53.

(72) *Risālah i quṭbīyah i 'ishqīyah*, a panegyric in honour of the anonymous author's spiritual guide, Mihr 'Alī Shāh, followed by a metrical *silsilah* of Chishtī saints; **Lahore** [1916*].

(73) *al-Risālat al-tis'-'asharīyah*, a life of Bahā' Allāh, by Aḥmad Suhrāb, preceded by biographies of Sh. Aḥmad al-Aḥsā'ī and S. Kāẓim al-Rashtī and followed (p. 103) by the *Risālah i amīrīyah* of M. Muṣṭafā al-Baghdādī on the life of Bahā' Allāh: **Cairo** 1338/1919* (128 pp.).

(74) *Riyāḍ al-nūr ma'rūf bah Gulzār i surūr*, chronograms on the births and deaths of Muslim celebrities, especially Ṣūfīs, by M. Imām al-Dīn: **Lahore** 1333/1915*.

(75) *Sālik i ṭarīqat*, a list of famous *shaikhs* of various orders: **Lucknow** 1300/1883° (the first work in a *Majmū'ah i rasā'il* (50 pp.) containing also (2) *Rauḍat al-'ibrat*, (3) *Ḥadīqat al-masā'il*, and (4) *Ṣirāṭ al-jannah*).

(76) *Sawāniḥ i mukhtaṣar i Shāh Wājid 'Alī Qalandar*, by Maulawī M. Ikrām 'Alī Qalandar: **Calcutta** 1919* (with an Urdu translation entitled *Lawā'iḥ i naẓar*).

(77) *Sawāniḥ i Shāh Ni'mat Allāh Walī* (beg. *Bar ḍamīr i khwurshīd-iqtibās*), by Ṣun' Allāh Ni'mat-Allāhī, abridged, according to Nadhīr Aḥmad, from the *Jāmi' i Mufīdī* (see p. 352 *supra*) and therefore later than 1090/1679: **Nadhīr Aḥmad** 87 (W. Ivanow's collection. A.H. 1281/1864), perhaps also **Āṣafīyah** i p. 442 no. 815 ("*Silsilat al-'ārifīn*," author not named. Defective). Edition (?): *Sawāniḥ al-aiyām fī mushāhadāt al-a'wām mausūm ba-Silsilat al-'ārifīn*: **Bombay** 1307/1890°.

(78) *Sayings and miracles of Khwājah 'Alā' al-Dīn 'Aṭṭār*[1]: **Rieu** ii 862*b* (18th cent.).

(79) *Shaikh Aḥmad Bībī-Khānī*, a metrical biography by Ghulām-Muḥyī 'l-Dīn "Sanjī": **Lahore** 1924* (18 pp.).

(80) *Shajarah i 'āliyah i Naqshbandīyah*, a metrical Naqshbandī pedigree, by Ḥabīb Allāh Naqshbandī: **Ludhiana** 1888°.

[1] 'Alā' al-Dīn M. Bukhārī, one of the chief disciples of Bahā' al-Dīn Naqshband, died in 802/1400. See *Nafaḥāt al-uns* p. 448; *Rashaḥāt* pp. 79–90; *Haft iqlīm* no. 1490; *Safīnat al-auliyā'* p. 80 (no. 85); *Khazīnat al-aṣfiyā'* i pp. 551–3.

(81) *Shajarah i ʻāliyah i ṭarīqah i Qādirīyah i Mujaddidīyah*, a metrical pedigree down to M. Shēr, the author's *pīr*, by M. Yūsuf ʻAlī Qādirī : **Āgrah** 1322/1904*.

(82) *Shajarah i ansāb i pīrān i ṭarīqah i Naqshbandī i Mujaddidī khānadān i Maulānā* [Raḥīm-Bakhsh called] *M. Masʻūd Shāh*, in prose and verse : Ḥasanī Press [**Delhi** 1869*].

(83) *Shajarah i Chishtī u Qādirī u Qalandarī u Ṣābirī*, prose and verse pedigrees of the author, Ghulām-Bhīk [1], in several orders, with a panegyric on Maulawī Qādir-Bakhsh Sahāranpūrī : **Murādābād** [1912*].

(84) *Shajarah i khānadān i Naqshbandīyah*, followed by *Shajarah i khānadān i Qādirīyah*, metrical pedigrees by Abū 'l-Ḥasan Ṣiddīqī Nānautawī : **Āgrah** 1873*.

(85) *Shajarah i khānadān i Qādirīyah* : see no. (84) above.

(86) *Shajarah i mubārakah i Chishtīyah i Ṣābirīyah i Quddūsīyah i Muḥibbīyah i Muḥammadīyah*, followed (p. 20) by *Shajarah i sharīfah i manẓūmah i Qādirīyah*, a metrical pedigree by Shāh Ḥabīb Allāh Thānī Muḥibb-Allāhī : **Allahabad** [1926*].

(87) *Shajarah i mutabarrakah i manẓūmah* : see no. (90) below.

(88) *Shajarah i Naqshbandīyah*, a metrical pedigree of S. Imām ʻAlī : Fārūqī Press [**Delhi** 1874*].

(89) *Shajarah i Qādirī*, prose and verse pedigrees of Shāh Mardān, by Ghulām-Nabī : **Lahore** 1330/1912*.

(90) *Shajarah i Qādirīyah*, "a genealogy of the Qādirī order," followed (p. 5) by *Shajarah i mutabarrakah i manẓūmah*, "a metrical genealogy of certain saints of the same order, and (p. 10) by a similar work in Panjabi verse by Raḥīm-bakhsh" : **Lahore** [1879*].

(91) *Shajarah i sharīfah i manẓūmah i Qādirīyah*, by Shāh Ḥabīb Allāh Thānī Muḥibb-Allāhī : see no. (86) above.

[1] For proper names of this type see p. 1022 n. 1. For Sh. Bhīk see p. 1036 n. 1.

(92) *Shajarah i taiyibah* (on title-page: ... *Shajarah i 'āliyah i Naqshbandīyah*), " a genealogy of certain branches of the Naqshbandī order," by Ḥusain Allāh Ghaznawī. Followed (p. 5) by *Munājāt*, prayers of Shāh 'Abd Allāh Abū 'l-Khair (p. 6), an account of his death (p. 7), *Na't i nūrānī*, metrical devotions by Shāh Ḥusainī: **Ludhiana** [1923*].

(93) *Shajarah i taiyibah i khānadān i Chishtīyah*, " genealogies of various branches of the Chishtī order: Niẓāmīyah, Ṣafawīyah, Khādimīyah, and Khalīlīyah ": **Lucknow** 1920*.

(94) *Shajarah i taiyibah i Qādirīyah*, pedigree of Shāh 'Alī M. Lāhaurī: **Lahore** [1904*].

(95) *Shajarah i taiyibah i silsilah i 'āliyah i Naqshbandīyah*: **Lahore** [1889°].

(96) *Shajarah i taiyibah i silsilah i 'alīyah i Suhrawardīyah i ḥaḍarāt i Rafīqīyah*, " succession list of the Shaikhs of the Rafīkī order of Ṣūfīs, in verse, with a genealogical table of the posterity of Abū M. Shihāb ul-Dīn Kilīj down to the author," 'Abd al-Salām Rafīqī Nūrpūrī: **Lahore** [1899°].

(97) *Shajarahā-yi salāsil i Qādirīyah u Chishtīyah wa-ghairah*, metrical pedigrees, by M. Asad Allāh Khān and M. Ḥāfiẓ Allāh: **Jhajjar** [1897°].

(98) *Shajarat al-'ārifīn*, a brief metrical account of the family of Shāh M. Rafī' al-Zamān Ilāhābādī, by M. 'Alī " Ulfat ": **Allahabad** 1297/1880° (followed by selections from the *dīwān* of Shāh M. Ḥasan " Ashraf " Ilāhābādī [1]).

(99) *Shams al-ansāb*, on the genealogy of 'Abd al-Qādir Jīlānī, by M. Ma'ṣūm Sharīf Iṣfahānī: **Āṣafīyah** ii p. 1778 no. 110.

(100) *Sharḥ i ḥāl i auliyā*: **Lindesiana** p. 116 no. 790 (circ. A.D. 1650).

(101) *Silsilah i 'āliyah*, " an account of the Shaikhs of Kanbuh," by 'Ināyat Ḥusain b. Fatḥ Allāh, with supplements by Faiḍ Aḥmad b. Dildār Aḥmad: **Meerut** 1306/1889° (196 pp.).

(102) *Silsilah i 'alīyah*, a genealogy of Khwājah 'Ubaid

[1] A biography of " Ashraf " without dates is given in the *Khāzin al-shu'arā'* (fol. 46*b*). He was apparently alive at the time of writing (1260–5/1844–9).

Allāh Aḥrār (see p. 964 n. 3 *supra*) and his family, by 'Abd al-Ḥaiy b. Abū 'l-Fatḥ al-Ḥusainī, a descendant of Khwājah Aḥrār : **Tashkent** Univ. 74 (5).

(103) *Silsilah i 'āliyah i Chishtīyah i Fakhrīyah i Niẓāmīyah i Sulaimānīyah*, the spiritual pedigree of the author, M. Sulaimān : **Lahore** 1870*.

(104) *Silsilah i 'alīyah i Chishtīyah i Niẓāmīyah i Fakhrīyah i Sulaimānīyah i Laṭ īfīyah*, the spiritual pedigree of the author, Shāh 'Abd al-Laṭīf, successor of M. Sulaimān : **Tippera** 1917*.

(105) *Silsilah i Qādirīyah*, the spiritual pedigree of the author, 'Abd al-Ḥaqq Shāh : **Fīrōzpūr** [1918]*.

(106) *Silsilah i ṭarīqah i Naqshbandīyah*, by Ḍiyā' al-Dīn Khālid al-Mujaddidī al-Baghdādī : **Cairo** p. 415 (A.H. 1276/1860).

(107) *Silsilat al-la'ālī'*, spiritual genealogies of the Naqshbandī, Qādirī, Chishti and Suhrawardī orders, by Mu'īn al-Dīn "Thabāt" : **Lucknow** [1883°].

(108) *Sketch of the life of 'Abd al-Qādir al-Jīlānī* (cf. p. 933 n. 2 *supra*) written by Muḥsin at the request of Sh. M. b. Sh. M. Ashraf Lāhaurī : **Tashkent** Univ. 18 (3).

(109) *Spiritual pedigrees of Ṣūfic shaikhs of Kashmīr* : **Ivanow** Curzon 79.

(110) *Sulṭānī*, a metrical biography of Sulṭān al-'ārifīn Ḥamzah Makhdūmī [1] and his descendants, by Mullā Bahā' al-Dīn MTW Kashmīrī : **Lahore** [1933*].

(111) *Ṭabaqāt i mashāyikh i Nashbandīyah i Bukhārā* : **Leningrad** Univ. no. 854 (Salemann-Rosen p. 17).

(112) *Tadhakkur al-mashāyikh*, biographies of a few *shaikhs*, beginning with the affiliation of Nūr al-Dīn 'Abd al-Raḥmān b. M. al-Isfarāyinī (d. 639), by an anonymous Kubrawī *darwīsh* : **Blochet** i 159 (10) (A.H. 877/1472).

[1] i.e. presumably either Sh. Ḥamzah Kashmīrī (for whom see p. 975 n. 2 *supra*) or someone descended from him.

(113) *Ta<u>dh</u>kirah i ḥaḍrat i <u>Kh</u>wājah Mu'īn al-Dīn <u>Ch</u>i<u>sh</u>tī*:[1] **Āṣafīyah** ii p. 848.

(114) *Ta<u>dh</u>kirah i <u>Kh</u>wājagān i Naq<u>sh</u>bandīyah*: **Peshawar** 1015.

(115) *Ta<u>dh</u>kirah i Ṣūfīyah*, by Ra<u>sh</u>kī b. Dīwān Mannū Lāl Falsafī: **Āṣafīyah** i p. 318 no. 100 (defective at end).

(116) *Ta<u>dh</u>kirat al-auliyā'*, lives of Aḥmad Zain al-Dīn Aḥsā'ī,[2] Kāẓim b. Qāsim Ra<u>sh</u>tī,[3] and M. Karīm <u>Kh</u>ān Kirmānī,[4] by Ni'mat Allāh Riḍawī: **Bombay** 1313/1896° (pp. 143).

(117) (*fī Tārī<u>kh</u> i ajdād u farzandān u aṣḥāb i ḥaḍrat i Maulānā Jalāl al-Millah wa-'l-Dīn Muḥammad i Rūmī*): **Leyden** v p. 232 no. 2640 (22 foll. A.H. 900/1494–5).

(118) *Tarjamat Ibn al-<u>Kh</u>afīf*: see *Aḥwāl Ibn al-<u>Kh</u>afīf*.

(119) *<u>Th</u>amarāt al-quds*, biographies of saints and pious women, mostly of the <u>Ch</u>i<u>sh</u>tī order, by La'l Bēg: **Rāmpūr** (defective. See Na<u>dh</u>īr Aḥmad 84).

(120) *Tuḥfaḥ i Akmalīyah*, on the life and sayings of Akmal al-Dīn Bada<u>kh</u><u>sh</u>ī and his successors, by Abū M. Ḥasan b. Ḥāfiẓ Walī Allāh Kubrawī Ka<u>sh</u>mīrī: **Lahore** 1350/1932* (appended to the same author's mystical *mīmīyah* entitled *Mu<u>kh</u>bir al-asrār*).

(121) *Tuḥfah i nāznīn*, a biography in prose and verse of M. Saif al-Dīn Qādirī, by S. Bahā' al-Dīn M. Naq<u>sh</u>bandī Ka<u>sh</u>mīrī: **Lahore** [1920*].

(122) *Tuḥfat al-auliyā'*, a biography of S. 'Abd al-Wahhāb Ṣābirī called A<u>kh</u>ūn Panjū, by Maulawī Mīr Aḥmad <u>Sh</u>āh Riḍwānī Pa<u>sh</u>āwarī: **Lahore** 1321/1903*.

[1] For whom see p. 943 n. 3 *supra*.

[2] Founder of the <u>Sh</u>ai<u>kh</u>ī sect, d. 1242/1827. See Browne *Lit. Hist.* iv pp. 410–11, 421–2; Brockelmann *Sptbd.* ii pp. 844–5, and the authorities there cited.

[3] One of Aḥsā'ī's pupils. See Browne *op. cit.* iv p. 421; Brockelmann *Sptbd.* ii p. 845.

[4] One of Kāẓim Ra<u>sh</u>tī's pupils, d. 1288/1871. See Browne *op. cit.* iv. p. 421; Brockelmann *Sptbd.* ii p. 846.

(123) *Tuḥfat al-Sa'dīyah*[1] or (*Malfūẓāt i Shāh Mīnā*), on the life and teachings of Shāh Mīnā,[2] by Muḥyī 'l-Dīn b. Ḥusain Riḍawī Ḥusainī: **Ivanow** Curzon 70 (defective and damaged. Early 19th cent.), **Rāmpūr** (see Nadhīr Aḥmad 76).

Edition: *Malfūẓāt i . . . Mīnā*, **Hardoi** (1900°].

(124) *Waqā'i' i Shāh Mu'īn al-Dīn i Chishtī*,[3] by Bābū Lāl. Editions: **Lucknow** 1879°, 1881†, 1883† (cf. Āṣafīyah ii p. 850).

(125) *Ẓafar al-Islām*, a life of Mu'īn al-Dīn Chishtī (cf. p. 943 n. 3 *supra*), by S. Ẓafar 'Alī "Ẓafar": **Delhi** [1904*].

N. BIOGRAPHY: (c) AMBASSADORS

1412. For the embassies sent by Sulṭān Shāh-Rukh to China and India see pp. 295–6 *supra*.

1413. For the (*Tārīkh i Īlchī i Niẓām-Shāh*), by Khwurshāh b. Qubād al-Ḥusainī, which contains an account of the author's mission to Shāh Ṭahmāsp, see p. 113 *supra*.

1414. S. **Ghulām-'Alī Khān** was sent to Istānbūl in 1200/1786 by Ṭīpū Sulṭān of Mysore, (for whom see pp. 767–72 *supra*) in the vain hope of enlisting Ottoman support against the British. The instructions issued to him are preserved in a MS. at Calcutta (Ivanow 1677).

Waqā'i' i manāzil i Rūm, a diary of the journey to Istānbūl in 1200–1, completed on 19 Rabī' al-Awwal 1201/9 January 1787: **Ivanow** 1678 (foll. 123).

1415. **Quṭb al-Mulk** and **'Alī Riḍā** were sent as envoys to Ḥaidarābād by Ṭīpū Sultān, of Mysore, (for whom see pp. 767–72 *supra*). The instructions issued to them are preserved in a MS. at Calcutta (Ivanow 1679), which is dated 1217 Maulūdī[4] [circ. 1205/1790–1].

[1] This is the title given (incorrectly ?) by Nadhīr Aḥmad.
[2] For whom see p. 983 n. 3 *supra*.
[3] Cf. p. 943 n. 3 *supra*.
[4] For Ṭīpū's Maulūdī era see p. 772 n. 1 *supra*.

(*Rūz-nāmah i wukalā' i Ḥaidarābād*), a report on the above-mentioned mission, dealing chiefly with the expenses incurred on the journey : **Ivanow** 1680.

1416. In return for the mission of Captain (afterwards Sir) John Malcolm to Persia (in 1799–1801) Fatḥ-'Alī Shāh dispatched Ḥājjī Khalīl Khān Qazwīnī Malik al-Tujjār as his envoy to the Government of India. In 1802 Khalīl Khān was killed at Bombay in a quarrel between his servants and the Hindu soldiers provided as his bodyguard. To succeed him the Shāh appointed his relative [1] M. Nabī Khān Qazwīnī, who returned to Persia in January, 1807. An account of the mission of these two envoys was written by an unnamed grandson of the second. [*Rauḍat al-ṣafā-yi Nāṣirī* ix foll. 81*b*–82*a* (A.H. 1219) ; Watson *History of Persia* pp. 129–30 ; Sykes *History of Persia* ii p. 302].

Tārīkh i sifārat i Ḥājjī Khalīl Khān u M. Nabī Khān ba-Hindūstān 1802–1805 : **Bombay** 1886°.

1417. Ḥājjī Mīrzā **Abū 'l-Ḥasan** Khān b. Mīrzā M. 'Alī **Shīrāzī,** nephew and son-in-law [2] of the late Prime Minister Ḥājjī Ibrāhīm Khān Shīrāzī, left Ṭihrān on 22 Rabī' I 1224/7 May, 1809, accompanied by James Morier, on a mission to London of which the main purpose was to ascertain how the subsidy promised to Persia under the preliminary treaty of March, 1809, was to be paid (*Rauḍat al-ṣafā-yi Nāṣirī* ix fol. 95*b*, Watson *History of Persia* p. 163, Sykes *History of Persia* ii p. 308, etc.). On 18 July, 1810, he set sail on his return journey with Sir Gore Ouseley and Morier (*Rauḍat al-ṣafā'* ix fol. 99*a* penult., etc.). In 1815 he was sent as envoy to St. Petersburg (*R. al-ṣ.* ix fol 111*a* penult.) and in 1818 as envoy extraordinary to Great Britain (*R. al-ṣ.* ix fol. 116*a*). Subsequently he became Minister for Foreign Affairs, and he continued to hold this office until 1250/1834, the last year of Fatḥ-'Alī Shāh's reign (*R. al-ṣ.* ix fol. 171*a*).[3]

[1] A nephew (*hamshīrah-zādah*) according to Riḍā-Qulī Khān, a brother-in-law according to Sykes.

[2] *hamshīrah-zādah u dāmād* (*Rauḍat al-ṣafā-yi Nāṣirī* ix fol. 95*b* penult.).

[3] Mīrzā Mas'ūd Ādharbāyjānī was appointed Foreign Minister by Muḥammad Shāh shortly after his accession (*R. al-ṣ.* x fol. 6*b*, l. 24).

Ḥairat-nāmah i sufarā, a diary of the author's mission to England in 1224–5/1809–10, apparently left unfinished since both the recorded MSS. end before the departure from England: **Bānkīpūr** vii 630 (ends with 10 Ṣafar 1225/17 March, 1810. Written in 1228/1813 for Sir G. Ouseley), **Rieu** i 386*b* (spaces for the dates left blank. Early 19th cent.).

[*Rauḍat al-ṣafā-yi Nāṣirī*, passages specified above and others (e.g. ix fol. 147*b*, x fol. 42*a*); J. Morier *A journey through Persia, Armenia, and Asia Minor to Constantinople, in* . . . 1808 *and* 1809, London 1812, pp. 220–3, *A second journey through Persia* . . . *to Constantinople*, 1810–16, London 1818, appendix; W. Ouseley *Travels in various countries of the East*, i, London 1819, p. 2 *et passim*; W. Price *Journal of the British embassy to Persia*, London 1825; J. B. Fraser *A winter's journey (tâtar) from Constantinople to Tehran*, ii, London 1838, p. 3; *A memoir of . . . Sir Gore Ouseley . . . by the Rev. James Reynolds* (prefixed to G. Ouseley's *Biographical notices of Persian poets*, London 1846); Portrait by Sir W. Beechey at the India Office. A caricature of Abū 'l-Ḥasan Khān was drawn by J. Morier in his romance *The adventures of Hajji Baba, of Ispahan, in England*, London 1828, reprinted 1835, 1942.]

1418. Ḥusain Khān Muqaddam [1] Ajūdān-bāshī was descended from Āqā Khan Muqaddam, an *amīr* of Shāh Ṣafī's time (*Rauḍat al-ṣafā-yi Nāṣirī* x fol. 29*b*, l. 4). After a period in the service of the Nā'ib al-Salṭanah ['Abbās Mīrzā, d. 1249/1833: cf. p. 338 *supra* and corrections] he became an officer in the army and rose to the rank of Adjutant General. In 1254/1838 Muḥammad Shāh sent him on a special mission to Great Britain, France, and Austria in the hope of obtaining the recall of the British Minister at Ṭihrān, Sir John McNeill (*op. cit.* x fol. 29*b*, l. 20, Watson *History of Persia* pp. 324, 328–31, Sykes *History of Persia* ii p. 336). Having visited Istānbūl and Vienna he reached Paris on 1 Ṣafar 1255/16 April, 1839, and London shortly afterwards (*R. al-ṣ.* x fol. 30*a*, l. 20). Here he interviewed Lord Palmerston and was given a memorandum containing nine demands of the British Government. In 1258/1842 he was appointed Governor of

[1] A Turkish tribal name.

Yazd (*op. cit.* x fol. 30*a*, l. 25), and held this office for two years (*op. cit.* x fol. 30*b*, l. 1). Presumably it was about this time that the title of Niẓām al-Daulah was conferred upon him. In the early days of the Bābī movement he was Governor of Fārs and in that capacity he interviewed and imprisoned the Bāb at Shīrāz (*op. cit.* x fol. 35–36*a*, Watson pp. 349–51, Sykes p. 341, and the Bābī histories). In the disturbances which followed the death of Muḥammad Shāh (in 1264/1848) Ḥusain Khān was besieged in the fort of Karīm Khan's citadel until rescued by his supersessor, Bahrām Mīrzā (*op. cit.* x fol. 46*b*, l. 19 foll.).

According to Riḍā-Qulī Khān (*op. cit.* fol. 22*a* ult.) an account of Ḥusain Khān's mission to Europe was written by Mīrzā **'Abd al-Fattāḥ Garmrūdī,**[1] who accompanied the envoy as his deputy (*nā'ib*. Cf. fol. 30*a*, l. 11, where he is called Mīrzā Fattāḥ). It is not clear whether Chanykov's MS. contains this account or another.

Travels of Ḥusain Khān, Ajūdān-bāshī, in Germany [Austria ?], France, and England in 1254/1838 (beginning: *Khudāwandī-rā bandah īm*): **Chanykov** 116.

1419. Ḥājjī Mīrzā **Muḥammad Khān b. Fatḥ-'Alī Bēg Lawāsānī** was sent on a mission to Russia at the beginning of Nāṣir al-Dīn Shāh's reign [1264–1313/1848–96]. He was editor of the *dīwān* of "Nashāṭī" Khān Hazārjarībī published at [Ṭihrān [2]] in [1845 ?°].

Mir'āt al-arḍ, an account of the above-mentioned mission to Russia written in 1264/1848: **Majlis** 702.

[1] Cf. *Dānishmandān i Ādharbāyjān* p. 258, where it is stated that 'A. al-F. Garmrūdī Tabrīzī wrote (1) *Chahār faṣl*, an account of the Ajūdān-bāshī's mission, (2) *Shab-nāmah*, on the licentiousness of European life, and that numerous copies of both works are in existence.

[2] Cf. Browne *Press and poetry of modern Persia* p. 8: The well-known Mashhadí Asad Áqá "*Básma-chí*" ("the Printer") of Tabríz . . . also relates that Mírzá Ṣáliḥ of Shíráz, the *Wazír* of Ṭihrán, sent at great expense one Mírzá Asadu'lláh, of the province of Fárs, to St. Petersburg to learn the art of printing, and that on his return thence he founded at Tabríz, with the assistance of the late Áqá Riẓá, father of the above-mentioned Mashhadí Asad Áqá, a lithographic press, the first book lithographed at which was the Holy Qur'án in the hand-writing of Mírzá Ḥusayn the famous calligraphist. Five years later, at the Sháh's command, this press and its appurtenances were transferred to Ṭihrán, where the first book printed was the *Díwán* of Nisháṭí Khán the poet.

1420. For Riḍā-Qulī Khān "Hidāyat's" *Sifārat-nāmah i Khwārazm*, an account of his embassy to Khiva in 1267/1851, see p. 342 *supra*.

1421. Mīrzā **Ḥusain b. 'Abd Allāh Sarābī Tabrīzī.**

Makhzan al-asfār, an account of Farrukh Khān Kāshānī's [1] mission to Europe in the course of which he negotiated the Anglo-Persian treaty of March 1857 [2] at Paris and subsequently visited London: **Browne** Coll. K. 7 = Houtum-Schindler 38 (A.H. 1276/1860), **Mashhad** iii, *Faṣl* 14, MSS., p. 28 (*Makhzan al-waqā'i'*).

1422. Mushīr al-Daulah Mīrzā **Ja'far Khān** Ḥusainī, the son of Mīrzā Taqī Ḥusainī Wazīr i Tabrīzī, was, like Mīrzā M. Ṣāliḥ Shīrāzī (see p. 1148), one of the young Persians sent to England in 1230/1815 for the completion of their education. He spent four years in Europe, mainly in London (*Rauḍat al-ṣafā'* x fol. 27*b*, l. 1), and later, having specialized in Mathematics and Geometry, he wrote a book on arithmetic printed at Ṭihrān in 1263/1847 and known as the *Khulāṣat al-ḥisāb i Mushīr al-Daulah*. In 1252/1836–7 he was *Muhandis-bāshī i 'Asākir i Manṣūrah* when he was sent as Persian Ambassador to Istānbūl and in the course of his residence there he negotiated the commercial treaty of 1257/1841 with Belgium and the treaty of 1258/1842 with Spain. In 1260/1844 he was on his way to the Erzerum conference (see Watson *History of Persia* p. 365) when he fell ill at Tabrīz and was replaced as Persian Commissioner by Mīrzā Taqī Khān

[1] Amīn al-Mulk F. Kh. K. Khāzin i Sulṭānī was in the service of four Shāhs of Persia (*Rauḍat al-ṣafā-yi Nāṣirī* x fol. 107*b*, l. 26). In M. Ḥasan Khān's list of the successive Heads of Government Departments in Nāṣir al-Dīn Shāh's reign (*al-Ma'āthir wa-'l-āthār* pp. 15–29) he appears under the headings *Riyāsat i 'amalah i khalwat i khāṣṣah i humāyūnī* (p. 20*a*), *Idārah i ṣandūq-khānah i mubārakah* (*ibid.*), *Idārah i muhr i mubārak u khizānat i khātam i humāyūn* (p. 20*b*), *Idārah i ṣarf i jaib i mubārak* (*ibid.*), *Mukhāṭabīn i salām i 'āmm* (p. 22*b*), and *Pīshkhidmat-bāshiyān i ḥuḍūr i mubārak* (p. 23*a*). His appointment to the *Ṣāḥib-jam'ī i khāṣṣ* took place in 1270/1854 (*Rauḍat al-ṣafā'* x fol. 92*b*, l. 7 from foot). He must have been an elderly man at the time of his mission to Europe (for which see *Rauḍat al-ṣafā'* x fol. 107*b*, l. 21–109*a*, l. 5, fol. 122*a*, l. 18–123*a*, l. 2, fol. 128*a*, l. 1–129*b*, l. 17, fol. 130*a*, ll. 13–27, Watson *History of Persia* pp. 430, 456, 459, 461). A *Siyāḥat-nāmah* of Farrukh Khān is mentioned in Browne's *Press and poetry of modern Persia* p. 20*n*, as having been circulated in manuscript.

[2] The date 11 Dhū 'l-Qa'dah 1273/3 July 1857 given in the catalogue of the Browne collection as that of Farrukh Khān's departure from Ṭihrān is, of course, incorrect.

Farāhānī. In 1264/1848 he went to Baghdād and Muḥammarah to discuss the delimitation of the frontier between Persia and Turkey with representatives of Turkey, Russia, and Great Britain. The results of his investigations into the question of the frontier were recorded in a booklet, of which, according to M. ʿAlī "Tarbiyat", many copies are in existence. In 1275/1858–9 he was appointed President of the Dār al-Shūrā and in 1277/1860–1 he was sent as Envoy Extraordinary on a mission to England. He died at Mashhad after a period as *Mutawallī* of the Shrine of the Imām Riḍā (cf. *al-Maʾāthir wa-'l-āthār* p. 15).

(*Siyāḥat-nāmah i Jaʿfar Khān Mushīr al-Daulah*), an account of the above-mentioned journey to England in 1277/1860–1 : **Ṭihrān** 1277/1861 (in the *Rūz-nāmah i Daulat i ʿalīyah i Īrān* no. 513, 29 Rajab 1277/10 Feb., 1861. See *Dānishmandān i Ādharbāyjān* p. 345 penult.[1])

[*Rauḍat al-ṣafā-yi Nāṣirī* x fol. 27*a*, l. 4 from foot, fol. 56*a*, l. 24, 81*b*, l. 25 ; *Dānishmandān i Ādharbāyjān* pp. 344–7 (portrait).]

N. BIOGRAPHY : (*d*) CALLIGRAPHISTS AND PAINTERS

In the parts of this work devoted to the biography of poets and saints, attention has been drawn to a number of historical works containing biographical sections. Some of these contain notices of calligraphists (in addition to such poets as were also calligraphists), but no attempt is made here to give a complete list of such works.

In an article entitled *Khaṭṭ u khaṭṭāṭān*, which he contributed to the *OCM*. x/4 (Aug. 1934), pp. 3–72, Prof. M. Shafīʿ published extracts relating to calligraphists from (1) the *Khaṭṭ u sawād* of Majnūn b. Maḥmūd Rafīqī, (2) an unidentified general history, possibly the *Khulāṣat al-tawārīkh* of Aḥmad Ibrāhīmī (cf. p. 1074[19] *infra*), (3) the *Mirʾāt al-ʿālam* of Bakhtāwar Khān, (4) the *Khulāṣat al-makātīb* of Sujān Rāy and (5) the *Mirʾāt al-iṣṭilāḥ* of Anand Rām "Mukhliṣ". An index to the names of the

[1] *Sharḥ u tafṣīl i īn siyāḥat u māmūrīyat dar shumārah i 513 i Rūz-nāmah i D. i ʿa. i Ī. . . . nawishtah shudah ast.* M. ʿAlī "Tarbiyat" does not say that the account was written by Jaʿfar Khān himself.

calligraphists noticed in these extracts is given on p. 70 of M. S͟hafī''s article. Further information concerning the first three of these sets of extracts will be found below.

1423. The second chapter of Majnūn b. Maḥmūd al-Rafīqī's *K͟haṭṭ u sawād* (written after 909/1503–4 : see Bodleian 1369 (1) ; Rieu ii 531*b* ; Ivanow 1623 (1), 1624 ; Ethé 1763 (4), 2931) is devoted to very brief notices of calligraphists and has been published by M. S͟hafī' in *OCM*. x/4 (Aug. 1934), pp. 17–18. The whole work has been published by Yā-Sīn K͟hān " Niyāzī " in *OCM*. xi/2 (Feb. 1935), pp. 46–74.

1424. For the *Laṭā'if-nāmah*, which was written in 927/1521 by Sulṭān-Muḥammad " Fak͟hrī " b. " Amīrī " Harawī and of which the fifth *qism* of the ninth *majlis* is devoted to *arbāb i hunar*, including calligraphists and painters, see p. 792 *supra*.

1425. For the *Bābur-nāmah*, which contains brief notices of Sulṭān-'Alī Mas͟hhadī, the calligraphist, and Bihzād, the painter, (published in 'Abd al-Raḥīm's Persian translation by M. S͟hafī' in *OCM*. x/3 pp. 147–8), see pp. 529–35 *supra*.

1426. For M. Ḥaidar Dūg͟hlāt's *Tārīk͟h i Ras͟hīdī*, of which the second *daftar*, completed in 948/1541, contains biographies of scholars, poets, calligraphists, painters, etc., see pp. 274–5 *supra*. The Persian text of the whole of this biographical section has been published by C. Salemann in *Mélanges asiatiques* ix (St. Petersburg 1888) pp. 323–80 and by M. S͟hafī' in *OCM*. x/3 (Lahore, May 1934) pp. 150–70. An English translation of the notices of painters and gilders was published by T. W. Arnold under the title *Mīrzā Muḥammad Ḥaydar Dug͟hlāt on the Harāt school of painters* in the *BSOS*. v/4 (1930) pp. 671–4.

1427. **Dūst-Muḥammad** al-Kātib, as he calls himself (*Ḥālāt i hunarwarān* p. 8[8]), was according to his own statement (*op. cit.* p. 30[7]) one of the *kuttāb i kitāb-k͟hānah i s͟harīfah i a'lā 'illīyūn*. Probably he is identical with Dūst-Muḥammad Harātī, who is mentioned by Aḥmad Ibrāhīmī (cf. p. 1074 *infra*) and others [1] as

---

[1] Cf. *Paidāyis͟h i k͟haṭṭ u k͟haṭṭāṭān* p. 157. In a list of *nasta'līq*-writers who died in S͟hāh Ṭahmāsp's reign Iskandar Muns͟hī gives the name, but no further particulars, of Maulānā Dūst (so, not Dūst-Muḥammad) Harātī ('*Ālam-ārāy i 'Abbāsī* p. 124).

a calligraphist of Shāh Ṭahmāsp's time and who according to the former (see *BSOS*. x/1 p. 205 n. 2) was the king's favourite and was retained in his service when all the other calligraphists were dismissed.

(*Ḥālāt i hunarwarān* [1]), a sketch of the history of Muslim calligraphy and painting written as an introduction (*dībāchah*, p. 31[1]) to an album of ancient and modern paintings and specimens of calligraphy arranged and embellished by the author in 953/1546 at the command and for the library of Abū 'l-Fatḥ Bahrām Mīrzā [2] : **Istānbūl** Tōp Qapū Sarāy.

Edition : *A treatise on calligraphists and miniaturists, Ḥālāt i hunarwarān, by Dōst Muhammad, the Librarian of Behram Mirza (d. 1550), edited by M. Abdullah Chaghtai*, **Lahore** 1936‡.

1428. For the *Tuḥfah i Sāmī*, which was composed, at least partly, in or about 957/1550, and which contains notices of a number of calligraphists, painters, musicians, etc., see p. 798 *supra*. The notices of these calligraphists, painters, etc., extracted from the various parts of the *Tuḥfah i Sāmī* were published by M. Shafī' in an article entitled *Iqtibāsāt i Tuḥfah i Sāmī rāji' bah hunarwarān* in the *OCM*. x/2 (Feb. 1934) pp. 73–128 (the last two pages being an alphabetical index).

1429. For the *Mudhakkir i aḥbāb*, written in 974/1566–7 by " Nithārī " Bukhārī, from which extracts relating to seven poets who were also calligraphists have been published by Nawwāb Ṣadr Yār Jang in *OCM*. xi/2 (Feb. 1935) pp. 39–45, see p. 802 *supra*.

1430. Extracts relating to calligraphists from an unidentified general history [3] written apparently in the second half of the tenth/sixteenth century were published by M. Shafī' in *OCM*. x/4 (Aug. 1934) pp. 23–30.

[1] This title, which by chronogrammatic licence indicates 952 (instead of 953), is the invention of the editor, M. Abdullah Chaghtai.

[2] One of Shāh Ṭahmāsp's younger brothers. He died on 19 Ramaḍān 956/11 Oct. 1549 at the age of 33 and was buried at Mashhad (Ḥasan Rūmlū p. 342, Seddon's trans. p. 155).

[3] Possibly the *Khulāṣat al-tawārīkh* of Aḥmad Ibrāhīmī (for which see p. 1074[19]). According to the owner, Prof. Maḥmūd Shērānī, of Lahore, the title *Khulāṣat al-tawārīkh* was written on the back of the MS., from which both the beginning and the end are missing.

1431. Qāḍī **Aḥmad Ibrāhīmī** Ḥusainī [Qummī] b. Mīr Munshī Sharaf al-Dīn Ḥusain was the great-grandson of Ḥāfiẓ Qanbar Sharafī, an Abyssinian slave who was a calligraphist and poet in the service of Qāḍī Sharaf al-Dīn, Governor of Qum (*BSOS.* x/1 (1939) p. 200). His father, who "was successively *munshī* to Sām Mīrzā [1] in Harāt, scribe to the secretariat under the vakīl Aḥmad Beg Nūr Kamāl, and vazīr at the court of the famous Ibrāhīm Mīrzā, when that prince was governor in Mashhad" (*BSOS.* x/1 p. 201), received from Shāh Ṭahmāsp (A.H. 930–84/1524–76) the title of *Mīr Munshī* and died in 990/1582 at the age of seventy-six (*ibid.*). Qāḍī Aḥmad, when still a boy (*dar aiyām i ṣibā*, *BSOS.* p. 204 penult.), went in 964/1556–7 to Mashhad and remained there for eight years, during which time he received instruction in penmanship from Shāh Maḥmūd Zarrīn-Qalam Nīshāpūrī (d. 972/1564–5). Shāh Ismāʻīl II (A.H. 984–5/1576–8) instructed him to write a history extending from the accession of Shāh Ismāʻīl I (A.H. 907–30/1502–24) to the current reign (*ZDMG.* 89 p. 319), and this task he fulfilled by composing the fifth volume of the *Khulāṣat al-tawārīkh*,[2] which he completed down to 999/1590–1 [3] and dedicated to Shāh ʻAbbās (A.H. 985–1038/1587–1629). Other works of his, mentioned in the *Khulāṣat al-tawārīkh* but not yet recorded in any published catalogue, were *Majmaʻ al-shuʻarāʼ wa-manāqib al-fuḍalāʼ*, a *tadhkirah* of poets (*ZDMG.* 89 p. 317. Cf. *BSOS.* x p. 200), and *Jamʻ al-khiyār*, a *tadhkirah* in at least six volumes on the scholars and poets of Ādharbāyjān, Arabian ʻIrāq and ʻArabistān (*ZDMG.*, *loc. cit.*).

(*Tadhkirah i khwush-nawīsān u naqqāshān* [4]), written [*circ.* 1006/1597–8] about twenty years after the execution of Shāh Ṭahmāsp's daughter, Parī-Khān Khānum [3 Dhū 'l-Ḥijjah 985/11 Feb. 1578. See *ʻĀlam-ārāy i ʻAbbāsī* p. 162] and divided

[1] Cf. pp. 797–800 *supra*.

[2] A MS. of this fifth volume was acquired in 1895 by the Preussische Staatsbibliothek and has been described by W. Hinz in an article entitled *Eine neuentdeckte Quelle zur Geschichte Irans im 16. Jahrhundert* (*ZDMG.* 89/3–4 (1935) pp. 315–28). See also p. 1073 n. 3 *supra*.

[3] The Berlin MS., which is defective at the end, breaks off in the year 1592. Persian histories often extend beyond the limits indicated in their prefaces.

[4] Correct title unknown.

into three *faṣls* ((1) *th̲ulth̲*-writers, (2) *ta'līq*-writers, (3) *nasta'līq*-writers) and a *kh̲ātimah* (on a few of the most recent painters, illuminators, and other craftsmen): **London** (?) private library of Mrs. C. C. Edwards (84 foll., lacking introduction and a leaf or leaves at end), **Ḥaidarābād** private library of Āqā S. M. 'Alī (lacks a page or more of the introduction), **Moscow** Museum of Oriental Civilisations.

Edition: announced as in preparation by Miss Zahrā Dā'ī-zādah for the M.A. degree at Ḥaidarābād (cf. *BSOS*. x/1 (1939) p. 211).

Russian translation: *Kazi Ahmed. Traktat o kalligrafakh i khudozhnikakh .... Vvedenie, perevod i kommentarii Professora B. N. Zakhodera.* **Moscow** 1947.

Descriptions: (1) *Calligraphers and artists: a Persian work of the late 16th century. By C. C. Edwards* (with the text and translation of two extracts (S̲h̲āh Maḥmūd and Āqā Riḍā) and an index to the calligraphers and artists. In *BSOS*. x/1 (1939) pp. 199–211), (2) *Tad̲h̲kirah i kh̲wus̲h̲-nawīsān u naqqās̲h̲ān*, by Zahrā Dā'ī-zādah (in *Armag̲h̲ān* xix (1318)/5–6 pp. 344–5).

1432. For the *Ma'āt̲h̲ir i Raḥīmī*, which was completed in 1025/1616 by 'Abd al-Bāqī Nihāwandī, and of which the third volume is devoted to notices of contemporary celebrities including towards the end some calligraphists and painters, see p. 553 *supra*.

1433. For the *'Amal i Ṣāliḥ* of M. Ṣāliḥ Kanbō Lāhaurī, which was completed in 1070/1659–60 and which contains at the end of vol. ii notices of seven calligraphists (pp. 443–6), see pp. 580–1 *supra*.

1434. For the *Mir'āt al-'ālam*, which was composed in 1078/1667 ostensibly by Bak̲h̲tāwar K̲h̲ān but really by M. Baqā Sahāranpūrī and of which the first *numūd* of the *afzāyis̲h̲* is devoted to notices of calligraphists (published by M. S̲h̲afī' in *OCM*. x/4 (Aug. 1934) pp. 33–65), see p. 132 *supra*.

1435. For the *Tad̲h̲kirah i Ṭāhir i Naṣrābādī*, which was begun in 1083/1672–3 and of which the second *firqah* of the third *ṣaff* is devoted to calligraphists, see p. 820 *supra*. The Persian text of this second *firqah* was published by M. Shafī' on the basis of a British Museum MS. (Rieu i p. 368) in the *OCM*. xi/4 (Aug. 1935) pp. 154–9.

1436. Notices of some Sindī calligraphists from the third volume (p. 241 in the 1304 edition) of 'Alī-Shēr "Qāni'" Tattawī's *Tuḥfat al-kirām* (for which see p. 656 *supra*) have been published on the basis of an autograph MS. by M. Shafī' under the title *Khaṭṭāṭān i Sind* in *OCM*. xi/2 (Feb. 1935) pp. 131–4.

1437. Khalīfah Sh. **Ghulām-Muḥammad "Rāqim"** Haft-qalamī Akbar-Shāhī Dihlawī, a calligraphist of note in his time, is mentioned by "Qāsim" in his *Majmū'ah i naghz*, a *tadhkirah* composed in 1221/1806, as a young man who "twelve or thirteen years ago before going to Lucknow" had read with him the *Sharḥ i Shamsīyah* [i.e. Quṭb al-Dīn al-Rāzī's commentary on al-Kātibī's manual of logic entitled *al-Risālat al-Shamsīyah*] and the *Ḥāshiyah i Mīr* [i.e. the annotations of al-Saiyid al-Sharīf al-Jurjānī (see p. 36 *supra*) on the *Sharḥ al-Shamsīyah*], had submitted Urdu verses to him and who, having returned to Delhi, was at that time studying medicine under Mirzā Muḥammad "'Ishq". He must have been born some years before 1194/1780, since he was a pupil of the calligraphist M. Ḥāfiẓ Khān, who died in that year and, if the date A.H. 1261/1845 is not a later addition to the work mentioned as no. iii below, he must have lived to an advanced age.

I. (*Tadhkirah i khwush-nawīsān*) (beg. *ai qiṭ'ah i luṭf zīr-mashq i karamat*), chronologically arranged notices of celebrated calligraphists preceded by instructions in prose and verse concerning the choice of a pen, the making of ink, etc.: **Rieu** ii 532*a* (defective. A.D. 1863), **Ivanow** Curzon 86 (defective. Mid 19th cent.).

Edition: *The Tadhkira-i-khushnavīsān of Mawlānā Ghulām Muḥammad Dihlavī edited with prefaces, notes, and indices by M. Hidayet Husain*, **Calcutta** 1910°* (*Bibliotheca Indica*).

II. *Musawwadah i Tadhkirah i khaṭṭ u khwush-nawīsān az ibtidāy* [*sic*] *tā zamān i ākhir i sanah i 1239* (beg. *Ḥamdī kih qalam az taḥrīr i ān qāṣir ast*), a work of which the contents are "to some extent identical" with those of the preceding: **Rieu** ii

532*b* (incomplete and out of order. 19th cent.), **Rāmpūr** (see *Oriental College Magazine*, vol. vi, no. 2 (Lahore, Feb. 1930), pp. 113–14, where the work is called *Tadhkirat al-kātibīn*). Probably **Bānkīpūr** xi 1077, in which the preface, defective at the beginning, mentions a division into a *muqaddimah*, three [1] *bābs* and a *khātimah* and gives 1239/1823 as the date of completion, is another copy of this work or of this recension.

III. (*Risālah i mutaḍammin i ḥālāt i khwush-nawīsān i khuṭūṭ* [2]), notices of Indian calligraphists from the time of Akbar to that of Bahādur Shāh II divided into four *faṣls* ((1) nasta'līq writers, (2) shikastah and shafī'ā'ī writers, (3) naskhī and ṭughrā writers, (4) seal-engravers), the latest date mentioned being A.H. 1261/1845: **Rieu** iii 1033*a* (circ. A.D. 1850).

[*Majmū'ah i naghz* I 264; *Gulshan i bē-khār* 125; Sprenger p. 280 ult.; Garcin de Tassy ii p. 567.]

1438. Mīrzā **Sanglākh Khurāsānī,** surnamed (*mulaqqab*) Dānā-yi Īrān and Āftāb i Khurāsān, calligraphist, poet, and Ṣūfī, one of the celebrities of his time in Persia, excelled especially in the writing of *nasta'līq*. In the course of his travels, which are described at some length in the *Imtiḥān al-fuḍalā'*, he visited not only many parts of Persia but also Turkistān, 'Arabistān, Kurdistān, Turkey, and Egypt. At Istānbūl he made a prolonged stay. He died at Tabrīz in 1294/1877 at the age of one hundred and ten " approximately ". A poem of his in praise of Smyrna was published with a Turkish paraphrase (*Tarjamah i qaṣīdah i Sanglākh dar madḥ i Izmīr*) at Būlāq in 1261/1845°.

Imtiḥān al-fuḍalā', or *Tadhkirat al-khaṭṭāṭīn*, bombastic notices of calligraphists in four unnumbered parts ((1) ancient and modern calligraphists, (2) an account of Sanglākh's travels, dated 1288/1871, (3) Sanglākh's pupils, (4) Ottoman calligraphists), described on the title-page as the work of Sanglākh but written

[1] Only two *bābs* ((1) seventy calligraphists, mainly *nasta'līq*-writers, (2) thirty-six *shikastah*-writers) are mentioned in M. Shajā'at-'Alī Khān's description of the Rāmpūr MS.

[2] These are the opening words of the B.M. MS.

actually, as is not concealed, by his pupil, Munshī "Ghaibī": [**Tabrīz**] 1291/1874° (foll. 465, unpaginated. Described as Vol. I).

[*Imtiḥān al-fuḍalā'* (portrait facing 2nd title-page); *al-Ma'āthir wa-'l-āthār* p. 216.]

1439. Ḥājjī Mīrzā **'Abd al-Muḥammad Khān** Iṣfahānī **Īrānī** is, or was, editor of the illustrated weekly newspaper *Chihrah-numā* published from 1322/1904–5 onwards first for a short time at Alexandria and subsequently at Cairo.[1] In the preface to his *Paidāyish i khaṭṭ u khaṭṭāṭān*, of which he wrote the *khātimah* in Ramaḍān 1346/1928, he mentions works of his entitled *Amān al-tawārīkh* and *Fu'ād al-tawārīkh*.

Paidāyish i khaṭṭ u khaṭṭāṭān, a sketch of the history of writing from its beginning to the early 'Abbāsid period followed by (1) notices of Ibn Muqlah (p. 90), Ḥasan b. Muqlah (p. 107), Ibn Bawwāb (p. 109), and al-Bukhārī (p. 115), (2) more or less alphabetically arranged notices of 104 calligraphists, none of them, except Abū 'l-Faḍl Sāwajī (d. 1312/1894–5. P. 153, under Mīrzā), later than the first half of the 18th century, the first being Ibrāhīm Mīrzā Ṣafawī (p. 117) and the last Yaḥyā-yi Ṣūfī (7th/13th cent.), (3) *Sargudhasht i ijmālī i barkhī az khaṭṭāṭān i gum-nām* (p. 249), (4) *Sargudhasht i khwush-nawīsān i muta-'akhkhirīn u ma'āṣirīn*, containing after a brief historical introduction notices of 'Abd al-Wahhāb "Nashāṭ" (d. 1244/1829, P. 252), 'Alī Khān Amīn al-Daulah (p. 254), M. Ḥusain Mushkīn-qalam (d. 1330/1912. P. 256), Qāsim Āqā Tabrīzī (d. 1292/1875. P. 258), M. 'Alī b. Ḥusain 'Alī Bahā' (b. 1270/1853–4. P. 260) and Najīb Bēk Hawāwīnī: **Cairo** 1345–6/1927–8‡.

1440. APPENDIX

(1) ***Tārīkh i Kalām al-mulūk***[2] (*fī bayān ẓuhūr wa-ījād al-khaṭṭ wa-aḥwāl al-khaṭṭāṭīn.* Beginning of the first Cairo MS.: *Bi-dān-kih aṣl i khaṭṭ nuqṭah ast*), by Mīrzā Yūsuf al-Lāhijī: **Cairo** p. 500 (part only. Foll. 49), *ibid.* (the same part? Foll. 36. A.H. 1275/1858).

[1] Cf. Browne *Press and poetry of modern Persia* pp. 72–3.

[2] Two works with this title have already been mentioned (p. 337 *supra*). Whether the title has good authority in this case is not clear.

N. BIOGRAPHY : (*e*) COMPANIONS OF THE PROPHET

See also Traditionists, pp. 1136–8 *infra*, and Biography : General, pp. 1164 *seqq. infra*.

1441. **ʿUbaid Allāh b. ʿAbd Allāh al-Ḥusainī** known as (*al-mas͟hhūr bi-*) **Murs͟hid b. Aṣīl** was presumably the son of S. Aṣīl al-Dīn ʿAbd Allāh al-Ḥusainī (for whom see p. 184 *supra*). He tells us that he had long cherished the idea of waiting on the *Ṣaḥābīs* cited as authorities in the six collections, but that his intention could not be carried out until in S͟haʿbān 884/1479 it won the approval of the Amīr Niẓām al-Daulah wa-'l-Dīn ʿAlī-S͟hīr (for whom see pp. 789–95 *supra*).

(1) ***Tuḥfat al-faqīr al-ḥaqīr ilā ḥaḍrat al-Amīr al-Kabīr*** (beg. *al-Ḥ. l. 'l. jaʿala rijāla*), short notices [1] of the Prophet's contemporaries who are cited as authorities for traditions in the six canonical collections, in four *bābs* ((1) the *ʿAs͟harah i Mubas͟hs͟harah*, (2) persons best known by their *asmā'*, (3) persons best known by their *kunyahs*, (4) the Prophet's wives and daughters : **I.O.** D.A. 157 fol. 31–58 (17th cent.), **Rāmpūr** (see Nad͟hīr Aḥmad 78).

(2) ***Tuḥfah i Murs͟hidī*** (beg. *al-Ḥ. l. 'l-Muwaffiqi 'l-Muʿīn*), the same biographical notices arranged alphabetically : **Rāmpūr** (see Nad͟hīr Aḥmad 79).

1442. Other works :

(1) ***Aṣḥāb i kirām***, popular biographies of the Prophet's Companions, translated (from what language ?) by S. Riḍā ʿAlī-Zādah : **Lahore** 1344–5/1926–7* (2 vols).

(2) ***Manāqib al-Aṣḥāb wa-'l-Tābiʿīn***, by ʿAbd Allāh al-Naisābūrī. Anonymous Persian translation (beginning : *Ḥ. u sipās u sitāyis͟h lā'iq*) : **Cairo** p. 504 (A.H. 1274/1760–1).

[1] The information given relates to the name, or names, of each *Ṣaḥābī* and, if necessary, the spelling of them, the collections in which his traditions occur, the total number of traditions related by him, the number occurring in each collection, and the date of his death.

N. BIOGRAPHY: (*f*) FAMILIES, TRIBES, RACES

(1) AFGHĀNS

For some works containing genealogical information concerning the Afghāns and the Afghān tribes see pp. 393–407 *supra*. For the Bangash Nawwābs of Farrukhābād see pp. 693–4. For the Rohillas see pp. 694–8. For the Āfrīdīs and Khwēshgīs see pp. 1080[20] and 1083[13] *infra*.

1443. **Shēr Muḥammad Khān Gandah-pūr,**[1] who came of a well-known family resident at Kulāchī in the Ḍērah Ismā'īl Khān District of the Panjāb, visited many parts of Afghānistān in quest of the *nasab-nāmahs* and other genealogical, historical, and sociological information on which he based his *Khwurshīd i jahān*. He died in 1302/1885. Among his works were a *Safar-nāmah i Īrān u Turkistān* and a *risālah i kaifīyat i jam' i Qur'ān*.

Khwurshīd i jahān, a detailed work on the genealogies of the Afghān tribes and clans with information concerning their history and customs: **Lahore** 1894° (pp. 320. Cf. Peshawar 1546).

[Peshawar catalogue p. 291]

N. BIOGRAPHY: (*f*) FAMILIES, TRIBES, ETC.

(2) ĀFRĪDĪS

1444. **Qāsim 'Alī Khān Āfrīdī** b. Burhān (d. 1194/1780) b. Nēk-nām Khān (d. 1145/1732) was born on 20 Rajab 1183/19 Nov. 1769 and was the great-grandson of an Afghān who had settled in India and whose descendants were scattered in different parts of the country, ignorant of their family connexions and almost all ignorant of Pashtō. His home, for at any rate a large part of his life, was at Farrukhābād, but his career (as a soldier ?) took him to various parts of India and he saw service under Jaswant Rāō Hōlkar, Nawwāb Amīr Khān, Mīr Ja'far "Masīḥ" and others. In 1222/1807 he was appointed Superintendent of the Criminal Court Prison at Farrukhābād and in 1223/1808 Superintendent of the Civil Court Prison. According to a note in the Bānkīpūr MS. of his works he died on 15 Jumādā i 1241/26 Dec. 1825. In addition to the *Tuzuk i Āfrīdī* described below

[1] This is an Afghān tribal name (see *Ency. Isl.* under Afghānistān).

several other works of his are preserved in the Peshawar MS. 1910A (*Kullīyāt i Āfrīdī*) and in the similar MS. Bānkīpūr Suppt. ii 2245–50. These are (1) Sh̲afā'at i Āfrīdī, forty-one Persian poems, *qaṣīdahs* and *g̲h̲azals*, in praise of the Prophet, the Imāms and eminent *sh̲aik̲h̲s*, Bānkīpūr Spt. ii 2246 (foll. 60b–71a. Probably identical with the *Qaṣā'id i Āfrīdī*, Peshawar 1910A (4), described as in Persian and Pash̲t̲ō), (2) *Dīwān i Hindī*, *g̲h̲azals* in alphabetical order intermixed with some Persian *g̲h̲azals* and completed (according to the concluding verse) in Rajab 1216/Nov.–Dec. 1801, Bānkīpūr Spt. ii 2247 (foll. 72b–178a. Doubtless more or less identical with Peshawar 1910A(3) (*Dīwān i Āfrīdī ba-zabān i Urdū*)), (3) *Āfrīdī-nāmah*, a vocabulary of Persian words (the first of which is *Āfrīdī*) with Pash̲t̲ō, Kashmīrī, English, and Hindi translations, Bānkīpūr Spt. ii 2248 (foll. 179b–207a. Evidently identical with *Farhang i Āfrīdī*, Peshawar 1910A (5)), (4) *Dīwān i Pash̲t̲ō*, Bānkīpūr Spt. ii 2249 = Peshawar 1910A (2). (5) *Khwāb-nāmah*, *mustazāds* in Pash̲t̲ō, Bānkīpūr Spt. ii 2250 = Peshawar 1910 (4) (b). In addition to " Āfrīdī " or " Afrīdī " " Qāsim 'Alī " occurs in these poems as a *takh̲alluṣ*.

Tuzuk i Āfrīdī (so Peshawar), or **Risālah i Āfrīdī** (so Bānkīpūr), a family history and autobiography in twenty-one *bābs* completed in 1222/1807 with a twenty-second *bāb* (on the death of the author's brother, A'ẓam 'Alī Kh̲ān) added in 1225/1810 and a twenty-third added in 1239/1823 (concerning relatives about whom he had subsequently collected information): **Peshawar** 1910A (acephalous. Transcribed for the author in 1230/1815. Number of *bābs* not stated in the catalogue), **Bānkīpūr** Suppt. ii 2245 (probably autograph. Many additions and marginal notes).

N. BIOGRAPHY: (f) FAMILIES, TRIBES, ETC.

(3) BARMECIDES

1445. The anonymous history of the Barmecides published by 'Abd al-'Aẓīm Kh̲ān Garakānī is assigned by him on linguistic, stylistic and other grounds to the fourth/tenth or fifth/eleventh century.

(*Akhbār i Barāmikah*), beginning: *al-Ḥ. l. R. al-ʻā. wa-'l-ṣ. ʻalā khairi khalqihi M. wa-ālihi 'l-ṭāhirīn. Riwāyat kard Abū 'l-Qāsim b. Ghassān gird-āwarandah i akhbār i Āl i Barmak guft Barmak mardī būd az farzandān i wuzarā-yi mulūk i Akāsirah*: MS. in the possession of the editor mentioned below.

Edition: *Akhbār i Barāmikah* [so on title-page], or *Tārīkh i B.* [so on wrapper], **Ṭihrān** A.H.S. 1312/1935* (edited with a long introduction by Mīrzā ʻAbd al-ʻAẓīm Khān Garakānī [1]).

1446. **Ḍiyā' al-Dīn Baranī** has already been mentioned (pp. 505–8 *supra*) as the author of a *Tārīkh i Fīrōz-Shāhī* completed in 758/1357.

Akhbār i Barmakiyān (beginning *Ḥ. u thanā mar Khudā'ī rā kih ba-faḍl i khwīsh*), anecdotes of the Barmecides translated from the Arabic of Abū 'l-Qāsim M. al-Ṭā'ifī or Abū M. ʻAbd Allāh b. M. Lābarī (the latter apparently a writer of the third/ninth century: see Rieu), or both,[2] and dedicated to Fīrōz-Shāh [3]: **Ethé** 569 (A.H. 1097/1686), **I.O.** D.P. 363 (a) (small fragment only), **Rieu** i 333*b* (17th cent.), **Bodleian** 308 (seal dated 1124/1716), **Ivanow** Curzon 85 (A.H. 1285/1868).

Edition: place? 1280/1863–4 (Āṣafīyah i p. 222 no. 880), **Bombay** [1889°].

1447. **ʻAbd al-Jalīl** b. Niẓām al-Dīn Yaḥyā **Yazdī**.

Tawārīkh i Āl i Barmak, a history of the Barmecides begun in 762/1360, dedicated to Shāh Shujāʻ, the Muẓaffarid, and based

[1] ʻA. al-ʻA. Kh. "Qarīb" b. Mīrzā ʻAlī Akbar, born at Garakān in 1296/1879, went to Ṭihrān in 1311/1893–4 and studied French among other subjects. In 1317/1899–1900 he was appointed teacher in the Madrasah i ʻIlmīyah and since then he has taught the Persian language and literature in several of the schools and colleges of Ṭihrān. When Ishaque wrote his *Sukhunvarān* [circ. 1932] he was on the staff of the Madrasah i ʻĀlī i Niẓām (Military College). His works include (1) *Qawāʻid i Fārisī*, a Persian grammar in three volumes, (2) *Dastūr i zabān i Fārisī*, in four volumes, (3) *Farā'id al-adab*, an anthology with biographies of the authors, (4) an edition of *Kalīlah wa-Dimnah*, (5) an edition of the *Gulistān*. See Ishaque *Sukhanvarān* i pp. 219–24 (portrait), *Modern Persian poetry* pp. 9, 20, etc.

[2] Both of these persons are described in different places as *mu'allif i aṣl*, *mu'allif i awwal i īn kitāb*, *mu'allif i ʻArabī*, etc.

[3] The date "A.H. 755 = A.D. 1356" [*sic!*] given in the Bodleian catalogue as that of the completion of the work seems to be a *lapsus calami* for 757 [= 1356], which, however, is mentioned in Rieu's description [incorrectly for 758] as that of the *Tārīkh* [*i Fīrōz-Shāhī*], not of the *Akhbār i Barmakiyān*.

on material collected by the author's father: **Blochet** i 633 (late 15th cent.), 634 (A.H. 926/1520),

Extracts: C. Schefer, *Chrestomathie persane*, **Paris** 1883–5°*, ii pp. 1–54 (notes, etc., pp. 1–64 at other end).

N. BIOGRAPHY: (*f*) FAMILIES, TRIBES, ETC.

(4) BŌHORAHS

1448. **M. ʻAbbās** "Rifʻat" **S̲h̲īrwānī** has already been mentioned as the author of the *Tārīk̲h̲ i Āl i amjād* (p. 227), the *Sulṭān-nāmah* (p. 421) and the *Bāg̲h̲ i c̲h̲ahār-c̲h̲aman* (p. 738).

Qalāʼid al-jawāhir fī aḥwāl al-Bawāhir,[1] composed in 1287/1870–1. Edition: place? 1301/1883–4 (Āṣafīyah i p. 248).

N. BIOGRAPHY: (*f*) FAMILIES, TRIBES, ETC.

(5) K̲H̲WĒS̲H̲GĪS

1449. Some sources of information concerning the K̲h̲wēs̲h̲gī clan have already been mentioned in connection with Pīr Ibrāhīm K̲h̲ān K̲h̲wēs̲h̲gī (pp. 661–3) and ʻAbd Allāh K̲h̲wēs̲h̲gī (p. 1009). The former's *Sairistān*, which includes a short account of the K̲h̲wēs̲h̲gīs, is mentioned on p. 662.

1450. For ʻAbd al-ʻAlīm Naṣr Allāh K̲h̲ān K̲h̲wēs̲h̲gī see pp. 756–7.

N. BIOGRAPHY: (*f*) FAMILIES, TRIBES, ETC.

(6) NĀʼIṬĪS

1451. **G̲h̲ulām-ʻAbd al-Qādir** [2] **"Nāẓir"**, surnamed Qādir ʻAẓīm K̲h̲ān, b. G̲h̲ulām-Muḥyī 'l-Dīn "Muʻjiz" **Nāʼiṭī** S̲h̲āfiʻī was born in 1200/1786 and died in 1243/1827–8.

[1] For the Bohoras, or Bohrahs, a caste in Western India, mostly Ismāʻīlī S̲h̲īʻites in the Bombay Presidency, see *Ency. Isl.* under Bohorās (T. W. Arnold).

[2] For names of this type see p. 1022 n. 1 *supra*.

Gulistān i nasab, a genealogical work (124 foll.) on the Nā'iṭī (or Nā'iṭī) tribe or clan [1] completed in 1224/1809 and divided into three *bābs* ((1) *dar bayān i faḍīlat i qaum i Banū Nā'iṭ*, (2) *dar bayān i nasab i rāqim i suṭūr*, (3) *dar bayān i faḍīlat i aslāf i buzurgān i khwud*) and a *khātimah* (*dar bayān i tafṣīl i nasab u mustaqīm shudan i silsilah i aqārib i īn khānadān*) : **Ivanow** 1st Suppt. 774 (1) (circ. A.H. 1251–8/1835–42).

[*Ṣubḥ i waṭan* p. 168 ; *Ishārāt i Bīnish* ; *Gulzār i A'ẓam* pp. 360–1.]

1452. The manuscript containing the *Gulistān i nasab* just described contains also five short works on the Nā'iṭī tribe, three of them in Persian, one in Arabic, and one in Urdu.[2] Those in Persian are :—

(1) ***Aḥwāl al-qaum*** by M. Akram Khān : **Ivanow** 1st Suppt. 774 (2).

(2) ***Kashf al-nasab,*** by an anonymous author who refers to the *Gulistān i nasab* and M. Akram's work : **Ivanow** 1st Suppt. 774 (4).

(3) ***al-Nā'it*** (so spelt here, with tā' not ṭā', as also in M. Akram's work), by M. Sa'īd known as (*shahīr*) Ustād : **Ivanow** 1st Suppt. 774 (3) (A.H. 1251/1835).

Another Persian work relating to this tribe is

Qābūs li-mu'tariḍ ṣāḥib al-Qāmūs, " a refutation " by M. 'Abd al-Razzāq b. 'Alī Aḥmad Khān " of the claim put forward by Ghulām Dastgīr, in a work entitled *Qawānīn i Dastgīrī*, that the tribe of Nawāyat is descended from the Quraish " : **Madras** 1331/1913*.

[1] The Nā'iṭīs, Navāyat, Navayet, Nawā'it, who claim Arab descent, are a largely sea-faring tribe living on the coast of the Bombay Presidency and elsewhere in southern India : cf. Yule and Burnell *Hobson Jobson*, under Navait, Naitea, Nevoyat, etc. Among the best known members of the tribe are 'Alī b. Aḥmad al-Mahā'imī, author of the *Tabṣīr al-Raḥmān*, an Arabic commentary on the Qur'ān written in 831/1427–8 (see the *Catalogue of Arabic MSS. in the . . . India Office* ii no. 1142, Brockelmann *Sptbd.* ii p. 310) and Nawwāb 'Azīz-Jang (see p. 758 *supra*). See also p. 779 n.1.

[2] It has been mentioned on p. 758 that an Urdu *Tārīkh al-Nawā'iṭ* was written by Nawwāb 'Azīz-Jang, the former owner of Ivanow 1st Suppt. 774.

N. BIOGRAPHY : (*f*) FAMILIES, TRIBES, ETC.

(7) NAUBAKHTĪS

1453. **'Abbās Khān Iqbāl** Āshtiyānī, who in 1342/1924 [1] and A.H.S. 1312/1933–4 [2] was described as a *Mu'allim* in the *Dār al-Mu'allimīn* (Teachers' Training College) and in 1938 [3] as a Professor in the University of Ṭihrān, visited Europe for the first time in 1925 [4] and was here again thirteen years later, since his introduction to the *Ṭabaqāt al-shu'arā' al-muḥdathīn* was written at Paris in September, 1938. Among his works are *Tārīkh i mufaṣṣal i Īrān* (vol. i, Ṭihrān A.H.S. 1312/1933–4. See p. 242 *supra*), *Tārīkh i 'umūmī wa Īrān* (*Luzac's Oriental List* 1940 p. 107), and *Tārikh i tamaddun i jadīd* (*Luzac's Oriental List* 1942 p. 9), as well as biographies of 'Abd Allāh b. al-Muqaffa, (see p. 1088 *infra*) and Qābūs b. Washmgīr (p. 1088 *infra*). Persian and Arabic [5] works edited by him include (1) Rashīd al-Dīn Waṭwāṭ's *Ḥadā'iq al-siḥr*, Ṭihrān A.H.S. 1308/1929*, (2) the *Bayān al-adyān* of Abū 'l-Ma'ālī M. Ḥusainī, Ṭihrān A.H.S. 1312/1933*, (3) the *dīwān* of Hātif Iṣfahānī, Ṭihrān A.H.S. 1312/1934‡, (4) the *Tabṣirat al-'awāmm fī ma'rifat maqālāt al-anām*, Ṭihrān A.H.S. 1313/1934*, (5) the *Tajārib al-salaf* (cf. p. 81 *supra*), Ṭihrān A.H.S. 1313/1934*, (6) Ibn Shahrāshūb's *Ma'ālim al-'ulamā'* (A.), Ṭihrān A.H. 1353/1934*, (7) al-Tha'ālibī's *Tatimmat al-Yatīmah* (A.), Ṭihrān A.H. 1353/1934‡, (8) the *Ṭabaqāt al-shu'arā' al-muḥdathīn* of Ibn al-Mu'tazz (A.), London 1939 (Gibb Memorial Series).

Khānadān i Naubakhtī [6] (*Les Naubakht, leur biogrphhie, leurs œuvres politiques, littéraires et intellectuels ; histoire sommaire des principales sectes musulmanes jusqu'au Ve siècle de l'Hégire ; secte Imamienne et ses premiers théologiens ; liste alphabétique des différentes sectes chiites ; abrégé de leurs doctrines et références*

[1] *Qābūs i Washmgīr*, title-page.
[2] *Tārīkh i mufaṣṣal i Īrān*, title-page.
[3] *Ṭabaqāt al-shu'arā' al-muḥdathīn*, introduction, at end.
[4] *Op. cit.* introduction p. xxviii.
[5] Marked (A) in the list which follows.
[6] For the Āl i Naubakht see Massignon *La passion d'al Hallâj* pp. 142–59 ; *Die Sekten der Schî'a von al-Ḥasan ibn Mūsā an-Naubaḫtī herausgegeben von H. Ritter*, Istanbul 1931, introduction. For Abū Sahl Ismā'īl b. 'Alī Ibn Naubakht, the denouncer of al-Ḥallāj, see also *Rauḍāt al-jannāt* p. 31 ; *Tanqīḥ al-maqāl* i p. 139 ; Brockelmann *Sptbd.* i p. 319 ; etc.

bibliographiques les concernant : avec table généalogique) : **Ṭihrān** A.H.S. 1311/1933* (see *Luzac's Oriental List* 1933 p. 13 and a review by R. Levy in *JRAS.* 1935 pp. 739–40).

[Portrait in *Qābūs i Washmgīr*, frontispiece.]

N. BIOGRAPHY : (*f*) FAMILIES, TRIBES, ETC.

(8) APPENDIX

1454. (1) *Nasab-nāmah i Sādāt i Bārhah*[1] : **Āṣafīyah** ii p. 1778 no. 119 (A.H. 1314/1896–7).

(2) *Tārīkh i Imām-zādahā i Shaft u Fūman u Kahdam wa-ghairuhā* : **Leningrad** Mus. Asiat. (see *Mélanges asiatiques* iv (1863) p. 499).

N. BIOGRAPHY : (*g*) KINGS

1455. **M. b. 'Alī** b. M. b. al-Ḥasan al-Kātib **al-Samarqandī** (so Leyden iii p. 14), or Bahā' al-Dīn[2] M. b. 'Alī b. M. b. Ḥusain[3] al-Ẓahīr[4] al-Kātib al-Samarqandī (cf. Rieu ii p. 748*b*, *al-Muẓaffarīyah* p. 255) is said by 'Aufī,[5] who calls him Ẓahīr al-Dīn . . . M. b. 'A. al-Samarqandī al-Kātib, to have been for a time (*muddatī*) Minister (*ṣāḥib-dīwān i inshā'*) to Qilich Ṭamghāch Khān. His *A'rāḍ al-siyāsah* is dedicated to " Abū 'l-Muẓaffar Qilich Ṭamghāch Khāqān b. Jalāl al-Dīn ", i.e. according to Barthold (*Turkestan* p. 18) Qilich Ṭamghāch Khān Mas'ūd b. 'Alī (cf. *op. cit.* pp. 334, 336).[6] His *Sindbād-nāmah*,[7]

[1] For the Bārhah Saiyids see Blochmann's translation of the *Ā'īn i Akbarī* pp. 390–5 ; W. Irvine *Later Mughals* i pp. 201–2 ; Blumhardt *Catalogue of Hindustani manuscripts in the . . . India Office* p. 22 ; etc.

[2] *Sindbād-nāmah*, B.M. MS. Or. 255 fol. 11*b* (quoted by Rieu) : *mī-gūyad muqarrir i īn kalimāt . . . al-ṣadr al-ajall al-auḥad malik al-udabā' wa-'l-kuttāb Bahā' al-Dīn sa'd al-Islām ṣāḥib al-naẓm wa-'l-nathr mu'jiz al-bayānain mafkhar al-lisānain . . . M. b. 'A. b. M. b. 'Umar al-Ẓahīrī al-Kātib al-Samarqandī.*

[3] So in the R.A.S. MS. It will be noticed that the B.M. MS. has 'Umar, probably a corruption.

[4] So in the R.A.S. MS., while the B.M. MS. has al-Ẓahīrī.

[5] *Lubāb al-albāb* i p. 91.

[6] He " ascended the throne, judging from his coins, in 558/1163. In 560/1165 he restored the city walls of Bukhārā on a foundation of baked bricks . . . " (Barthold *Turkestan* p. 336). For the word Ṭamghāch see M. Qazwīnī's remarks in his edition of the *Chahār maqālah*, notes, pp. 92–4, English translation p. 102.

[7] This work is in prose, not in " prosaic Persian verses ", as stated by Barthold (*Turkestan*, London 1928, p. 18). P.S. It is now accessible in the edition published at Istānbūl in 1948 by Ahmed Ateş.

of which there are MSS. at the British Museum (Rieu ii 748) and the Royal Asiatic Society (see S. Oldenburg's article *O persidskoi prozaicheskoi versii* "*Knigi Sindbāda*" in *al-Muẓaffarīyah : Sbornik statei uchenikov . . . bar. V. R. Rozena*, St. Petersburg 1897, pp. 255–8) begins with a long eulogy of the same monarch, who is there called Rukn al-Dīn . . . Quṯlugh Bilgā [Bēg ? [1]] Abū 'l-Muẓaffar Qilich Tamghāch Khān b. Qilich Qarā-Khān and is described as having vanquished his foes in Tūrān in the year fifty-six (i.e. 556/1161. See Rieu ii p. 748*a*). A third work, *Sam' al-Ẓahīr fī jam' al-Ẓahīr*, is mentioned by 'Aufī (cf. *Haft iqlīm* and Ḥ. Kh., both probably dependent on 'Aufī).

A'rāḍ al-siyāsah fī aghhrāḍ al-ri'āsah, biographies of 74 persons, nearly all kings,[2] from Jamshīd to Sanjar, "largely anecdotal in character, and of little interest on the whole, with the exception of the narrative of contemporary events during the reign of Qilich-Ṭamghāch-Khān inserted at the end of the book" (Barthold *Turkestan* p. 28) : Ḥ. Kh. i p. 368 (*Aghrāḍ al-siyāsah*), **Leyden** iii p. 14 no. 927 (A.H. 948/1541–2), **Āṣafīyah** ii p. 1218 no. 107, **Āyā Ṣōfyah** 2844.

Extracts (contemporary events) : Barthold *Turkestan v epokhu mongolskago nashestviya*, **St. Petersburg** 1900°* i, Teksty, pp. 71–2.

[*Lubāb al-albāb* i pp. 91–2 ; *Haft iqlīm* no. 1422 ; Rieu ii p. 748.]

1456. For the *Futūḥāt i Fīrōz-Shāhī* see p. 509 *supra*.

For the *Bābur-nāmah*, or Memoirs of Bābur, see pp. 529–35 *supra*.

For the "autobiography" of Shāh Ṭahmāsp see pp. 305–6 *supra*.

For the *Jahāngīr-nāmah* or *Tūzuk i Jahāngīrī* see pp. 556–60 *supra*.

For Mīrzā Jawān-bakht's account of his escape from Delhi see p. 624 *supra*.

For the autobiography of Ṭīpū Sulṭān see p. 770 *supra*.

For the autobiography of Shāh Shujā' al-Mulk see p. 401 *supra*.

For Nāṣir al-Dīn Shāh Qājār's diaries of his journeys to Europe and elsewhere see pp. 341–2 *supra*.

[1] Cf. Barthold *Turkestan* p. 336 n. 1.

[2] Among the others are Ptolemy (al-Ḥakīm), Plato, Aristotle, and Abū Muslim.

For the autobiography of ‘Abd al-Raḥmān Khān, Amīr of Afghānistān, see p. 406.

For Muẓaffar al-Dīn Shāh Qājār's diary of his visit to Europe in 1900 see p. 347 *supra*.

1457. **‘Abbās Khān Iqbāl** Āshtiyānī (see p. 1085 *supra*).

Qābūs i Washmgīr i Ziyārī : *zindagānī i ‘ilmī u adabī i ū* : **Berlin** 1342/1924‡ (Intishārāt i Īrānshahr, i).

N. BIOGRAPHY: (*h*) MUNSHĪS

1458. For the *Riyāḍ al-afkār* completed in 1268/1852 by Wazīr ‘Alī “ ‘Ibratī ” ‘Aẓīmābādī see p. 900 *supra*.

See also the subsection Biography : (*j*) Officials.

N. BIOGRAPHY: (*j*) OFFICIALS (MINISTERS OF STATE, MILITARY OFFICERS, ETC.)

1459. It has been convincingly demonstrated by M. Qazwīnī [1] that Muḥammad i munshī, the author of the *Nafthat al-maṣdūr*, is the same person as **M. b. Aḥmad** b. ‘Alī b. M. al-munshī **al-Nasawī**,[2] who in 639/1241–2 wrote the Arabic *Sīrat al-Sulṭān Jalāl al-Dīn Mankubirnī* (for which see Brockelmann i p. 319, *Sptbd.* i p. 552). Born at Kharandiz [? [3]], a fort near Nasā for many generations in the possession of his family, he was for some time

[1] In a pamphlet of forty pages printed with a preface of three pages by ‘Abbās Iqbāl at the Maṭba‘ah i Majlis, Ṭihrān, in 1308/1929* under the title *Maqāla'ī tārīkhī u intiqādī az ḥaḍrat i ‘allāmah i ustād Āqā-yi Mīrzā M. Khān Qazwīnī dar bāb i nuskhah i Nafthat al-maṣdūr ta'līf i Nūr al-Dīn Muḥammad i munshī*.

[2] Qazwīnī's main evidence is provided by a series of parallel passages, which could not conceivably have been written by two different persons (*Maqālah* pp. 9–15).

[3] This place, spelt Khrndr or the like (with incomplete punctuation) in the very old Paris MS. of the *Sīrat Jalāl al-Dīn* (and perhaps identical with the Kharāndīz described by Yāqūt as being, he thought, in Khurāsān), is mentioned several times in the *Sīrah* (pp. 30, 53, 57–8, 60–1), and more than once as the author's birthplace and home (e.g. p. 30 : *qal‘at Kharandiz masqaṭ ra'sī wa-mansha' asāsī*). In the *Nafthat al-maṣdūr*, on the other hand, a place spelt ZYDR is mentioned twice (pp. 34[2] and 63[7]), in the latter case as the author's birthplace (*turbat i aṣlī*). M. Qazwīnī's suggestion that Zaidar may be merely a corruption of Kharandiz will probably commend itself to most students. In any case it was doubtless on the strength of the second passage that “ Hidāyat ” appended the *nisbah* Zaidarī to the author's name. See Qazwīnī's *Maqālah* pp. 17–21.

in the service of the local rulers, the Āl i Ḥamzah (to use the name suggested by Qazwīnī for the dynasty), and about the year 621/1224 was sent by one of them, Nuṣrat al-Dīn Ḥamzah b. M. b. M. b. ʿUmar b. Ḥamzah, on a mission to Sulṭān Ghiyāth al-Dīn, the brother of the Khwārazm-Shāh Sulṭān Jalāl al-Dīn Mankubirnī.[1] Before he could carry out his mission Sulṭān Ghiyāth al-Dīn was defeated at Ray by his brother, and M. Nasawī, proceeding to the latter's camp near Hamadān, was taken into his service. In 622/1225, at Marāghah he was appointed to the office of secretary (*kātib al-inshā'*), and thenceforward he was in constant attendance on the Sulṭān in his campaigns. After the conquest of Akhlāṭ in 627/1230 he was sent on a mission to the Malāḥidah of Alamūt. In the following year the Sulṭān was severely defeated near Āmid by the Mongols, but escaped from the battlefield only to be killed by Kurds near Maiyāfāriqīn. Nasawī escaped in a different direction and with two or three others reached Āmid, where he was imprisoned for three months by the Ortuqid Malik Masʿūd. Thence he went successively to Mārdīn, Irbil, Urūmiyah, Khōy, Pergerī (Muḥarram 629/Oct. 1231) and finally after great hardships, to Maiyāfāriqīn. There he settled under the protection of Malik Muẓaffar Shihāb al-Dīn Ghāzī, the Aiyūbid, and it was there that he wrote the *Nafthat al-maṣdūr* four years later.

(***Nafthat al-maṣdūr***[2]) (beg. *Dar īn-muddat kih talāṭum i amwāj i fitnah*), an account of the author's adventures in four months of 628/1231 between his separation from Sulṭān Jalāl al-Dīn at Āmid and his arrival at Maiyāfāriqīn : **Ṭihrān** two modern MSS. in private ownership (see Mujtabā Mīnuwī's footnote on p. 2 of M. Qazwīnī's *Maqālah*).

Edition : *Kitāb i Nafthat al-maṣdūr* . . .[3] *ta'līf i Khwājah*

[1] For whom see *Ency. Isl.* under Djalāl al-Dīn Mangubartī (an unsigned article of which the authorship is acknowledged by Brockelmann, *GAL. Sptbd.* i p. 552).

[2] This expression, meaning " complaint of one's misfortunes ", " *dard i dil*," occurs twice in the text (p. 31[7] : *az nafthat al-maṣdūrī kih mahjūrī ba-d-ān rāḥatī tuwānad yāft*, and p. 58[10] : *Bi-yā tā ba-sar i nafthat al-maṣdūr i khwīsh bāz shawīm kih īn muṣībat nah az ān qabīl ast kih ba-bukā u ʿawīl dar muddat i ṭawīl ḥaqq i ān tuwān gudhārd*) and forms a convenient and appropriate title, though there is no reason to suppose that the author intended it to serve as such (see M. Qazwīnī's *Maqālah* p. 21).

[3] The words omitted (*fī futūr zamān al-ṣudūr wa-zamān ṣudūr al-futūr*) are apparently an arbitrary addition based on the title of Anūshirwān b. Khālid's memoirs (see p. 255 *supra* and M. Qazwīnī's *Maqālah* pp. 23–5).

Nūr al-Dīn [1] *Muḥammad Zaidarī* [2] *Khurāsānī . . . bā muqaddimah i marḥūm Riḍā-Qulī Khān Hidāyat i Ṭabarī Lalah-bāshī.* **Ṭihrān** A.H.S. 1307–8 [3]/1928–9‡ (*Shirkat i ṭab' i kitāb.* Pp. 105, of which 2–26[3] are devoted to the introduction, written in 1281/1864–5, by " Hidāyat ").

1460. Of unknown authorship is :—

Nasā'im al-asḥār, biographies of *wazīrs* completed in Ṣafar 725/1325 and used extensively by the author of the *Āthār al-wuzarā'* : **Āyā Sōfyah** 3487 (see Viqār Aḥmad Hamdānī's remarks on this work in *JRAS.* 1938 p. 563).

1461. **Saif al-Dīn Ḥājjī b. Niẓām al-Faḍlī** (or al-'Uqailī ?) was in the service of Khwājah Qiwām al-Dīn Niẓām al-Mulk Khwāfī, who became Governor of Qum and Rai in 873/1468–9, was appointed Wazīr by Sulṭān Ḥusain in 875/1470–1 and was deposed in 892/1487.

Āthār al-wuzarā', notices of celebrated *wazīrs*, composed in 883/1478–9, dedicated to Niẓām al-Mulk Khwāfī and divided into two *maqālahs* ((1) in twelve *bābs* devoted to the *wazīrs* of particular dynasties, namely (*a*) Pre-Islāmic kings of Persia, (*b*) the first four Caliphs, (*c*) Umaiyads, (*d*) 'Abbāsids, (*e*) Sāmānids, (*f*) Ghaznawids, (*g*) Buwaihids, (*h*) Saljūqids, (*j*) Khwārazm-Shāhs, (*k*) Chingiz Khān and his descendants, (*l*) Muẓaffarids and Ghōrids, (*m*) Tīmūrids to Abū Sa'īd, (2) on Khwājah Qiwām al-Dīn, apparently imperfect in all the MSS.) : **Bānkipūr** viii 654 (A.H. 1044/1634), **Rieu** Suppt. 101 (17th cent.), iii 969*b* (A.H. 1239/1824), **Āṣafīyah** iii p. 92 no. 1059 (defective at both ends), **Bodleian** 347 (n.d.), **Browne** Pers. Cat. 109, **Ethé** 621, **Majlis** 619 (4).

1462. Ghiyāth al-Dīn surnamed (*mulaqqab*) **Khwānd-Amīr,** who died probably in 942/1535–6, has already been mentioned as the author of the *Ma'āthir al-mulūk* (p. 102 *supra*), the *Khulāṣat*

[1] The author himself does not mention his *laqab*, but Juwainī in the *Jahān-gushā* (ii p. 153) speaks of Nūr al-Dīn munshī as the Sulṭān Jalāl al-Dīn's *munshī* and the *mudabbir* of his kingdom. It was doubtless this passage or a similar passage in some later historian that " Hidāyat " had in mind when he called our author Nūr al-Dīn. See Qazwīnī's *Maqālah* pp. 16–17.

[2] See p. 1088 n. 3 above.

[3] 1307 on the title-page, 1308 on the cover, and [A.H.] 1341 [*sic* ? = 1922–3] in the lithographer's colophon.

al-akhbār (*ibid.*), the *Ḥabīb al-siyar* (p. 104), the *Humāyūn nāmah* (p. 536), and the *Makārim al-akhlāq*, a panegyric on Mīr 'Alī Shīr (p. 795).

Dastūr al-wuzarā' (a chronogram = 915/1509–10 [1]), lives of eminent *wazīrs* arranged—apart from the first two, Āṣaf and Buzurjmihr—under dynasties from the Umaiyads to the Tīmūrids, the last being ministers of Sulṭān Ḥusain [2] : Ḥ. Kh. iii p. 228, **Bodleian** 87 (A.H. 965/1558), **Chanykov** 66 (A.H. 974/1566), **Berlin** 604 (A.H. 1013/1604), **Rieu** i 335*a* (A.H. 1036/1627), **Ivanow** 212 (A.H. 1222/1807–8), **Browne** Coll. J. 11 (12) (A.H. 1268/1852), **Bukhārā** Semenov 70, **Flügel** ii 1204, **Leningrad** Mus. Asiat. (see *Mélanges asiatiques* iv (St. Petersburg 1863) p. 54).

Edition : **Ṭihrān** A.H.S. 1317/1938‡ (ed. Sa'īd Nafīsī).

Extracts : [Faḍl Isfarāyinī, Aḥmad Maimandī and Ḥasanak, Ghaznawid *wazīrs*] Elliot *Bibliographical index* . . . , Calcutta 1849, *muntakhabāt* pp. 25–7.

Translation of the same extracts : Elliot *Bibliographical index* pp. 117–20 ; Elliot and Dowson *History of India* iv pp. 148–53.

List of the biographies : *Wiener Jahrbücher*, Bd. 74 Anz.-Bl. pp. 1–4 (Hammer).

1463. For the memoirs of Asad Bēg Qazwīnī, which extend from 1011/1602 to 1014/1605 see p. 554 *supra*.

[1] Not 906 as stated in the third note on p. 8 of the printed edition. This chronogram, as the author tells us in his preface (p. 8), indicates the date of completion. The work must have been begun several years earlier, since Abū 'l-Fatḥ Sulṭān Ḥusain Bahādur Khān (d. 911/1506) is spoken of in the preface as a living sovereign (p. 5). It is dedicated to one of his *wazīrs*, whose name, not mentioned in the British Museum MS., is given in the printed edition (p. 6) as Kamāl al-Millah wa-l-Dunyā wa-'l-Dīn Khwājah Maḥmūd [*sic* ?]. According to Sa'īd Nafīsī, whose edition is based on two MSS. belonging respectively to 'Abbās Iqbāl (undated) and 'Abd al-Raḥīm Khalkhālī (A.H. 1010), the work exists in two forms (*dū riwāyat*), of which the first, composed in 906 [a date based apparently on his miscalculation of the chronogram], is represented by 'Abbās Iqbāl's MS., while the second, containing twelve additional biographies at the end and completed after 914 (the latest date mentioned) and before 916 (the date of the death of Shaibānī Khān, who is three times mentioned towards the end as a living ruler), is represented by 'Abd al-Raḥīm Khalkhālī's MS. It is at any rate a fact that the final biographies are not the same in all MSS.

[2] Darwīsh Aḥmad (d. 912/1507) is the last *wazīr* in the printed edition, which contains—on the basis of 'Abd al-Raḥīm Khalkhālī's MS.—biographies of some contemporary *wazīrs* apparently absent from most of the MSS. According to the catalogues, Bodleian 87 and Rieu i 335*a* end with Majd al-Dīn M. (printed ed., pp. 400–18), Flügel ii 1204 and Ivanow 212 with Afḍal al-Dīn M. Kirmānī (printed ed., pp. 433–41).

1464. For the *Ma'āthir i Raḥīmī*, completed in 1025/1616 by 'Abd al-Bāqī Nihāwandī, see p. 553 *supra*.

1465. Sh. **Farīd** b. Sh. Ma'rūf **Bhakkarī.**[1]

Dhakhīrat al-khawānīn, lives of Indian nobles from the time of Akbar to 1060/1650, dedicated to Nawwāb Shāyistah Khān [2] and divided into three chapters ((1) Akbar's, (2) Jahāngīr's, and (3) Shāh-Jahān's contemporaries): **Ḥaidarābād** Prof. 'Abd al-Ḥaqq's private library (foll. 230, one leaf missing at end. Bears a librarian's note of 1069/1659 or 1169/1756. See M. Abdulla Chughtai's description in *Islamic culture* ix/3 (July, 1935) pp. 411–22, where information is given concerning a number of nobles associated with the arts, especially building).

Almost the whole of this work seems to have been incorporated with little alteration in the *Ma'āthir al-umarā'*. In Shāh-nawāz Khān's preface (vol. i p. 8[3], Beveridge's trans. p. 7) it is referred to in the words *Agar-chih dar-īn waqt kitābī mausūm ba-Dhakhīrat al-khawānīn taṣnīf i Shaikh Ma'rūf Bhakkarī mutaḍammin i aḥwāl i umarā ba-naẓar rasīd u akthar i maṭālib i ān ḍamīmah i īn nuskhah gardīd līkin chūn binā-yi ān bar akhbār i samā'ī i mukhālif i taḥqīq i ahl i īn fann būd u ma'khadh i īn nuskhah kutub i mu'tabarah i thiqāt ast rujḥānī badīhī u mazīyatī ẓāhir bar-ān mutaḥaqqaq u thābit gasht*. It will be noticed that here, apparently by inadvertence, the author of the *Dhakhīrat al-khawānīn* is called Sh. Ma'rūf Bhakkarī.[3] The same thing occurs in the apparently spurious preamble of Ivanow 215, in which Sh. Ma'rūf Bhakkarī is made to speak as though the work contained

[1] M. Abdulla Chughtai's summary of the preface to the *Dhakhīrat al-khawānīn* (*Islamic culture* ix/3 (July, 1935) p. 412) begins with the sentence "After offering praise to the Almighty God and asking blessings on the Prophet, Sheykh Farîd son of Sheykh Ma'rûf *Sadr Sarkar Bhakkar* (District Officer of Bhakkar) says that volumes have been devoted by historians to accounts of the former and the present Sultans". It appears from the *Ma'āthir al-umarā*, iii p. 75, that a Sh. Ma'rūf, presumably Sh. Farīd's father, was *Ṣadr* of Bhakkar shortly after 1007/1598–9. Consequently the words quoted above do not necessarily mean that Sh. Farīd was himself *Ṣadr* of Bhakkar, though he may of course have held the same post as his father.

[2] Mīrzā Abū Ṭālib Shāyistah Khān Amīr al-Umarā' died in 1105/1694. See *Ma'āthir al-umarā'* ii pp. 690–706; Beale *Oriental biographical dictionary* under Shaista Khan.

[3] He is called Sh. Farīd Bhakkarī in *Ma'āthir al-umarā'* ii p. 788 and also in 'Abd al-Ḥaiy's preface.

in the MS. were the *Dhakhīrat al-khawānīn*, whereas it appears to be a defective copy of the *Ma'āthir al-umarā'*.[1]

1466. **Ṣadr al-Dīn M.** "Fā'iz" **b. Zabardast Khān** is the author of poetical works in Persian and Urdu, including a Persian *mathnawī* dated 1134/1721–2, which are preserved with some Persian *ruqa'āt* in the Bodleian MS. 1177 (*Kullīyāt i Fā'iz*). The Urdu *mathnawī* describing a bang-seller has been translated into French by Garcin de Tassy (i pp. 436–8). He wrote a short astronomical (or astrological?) work entitled *Najm al-Ṣadr* (MS.: Panjāb Univ. Lib. (dated 1135/1723 and probably autograph). See *OCM*. x/3 p. 106) and doubtless also the treatise on gardening entitled *Zīnat al-basātīn* (MS.: Panjāb Univ. Lib. See *OCM*. x/1 (Nov. 1933) p. 99, where the date of transcription, given as "probably 1032", should perhaps be read 1132).

Irshād al-wuzarā', short notices of celebrated viziers written (according to Elliot *History of India* iv p. 148) in Muḥammad Shāh's reign (1131–61/1719–48) and divided into twelve *maqālahs* devoted for the most part to particular dynasties, the last being concerned with the viziers of the Indian Tīmūrids: **Rieu** i 338*b* (foll. 65, breaking off in the notice of Dhū 'l-Faqār Khān b. Asad Khān, vizier to Jahāndār Shāh. 18th cent.), iii 1014*b* (extracts only. Circ. A.D. 1850), 1046*a* (extract only).

1467. Early in 1160/1747 **Mīran** [? [2]] **Lāl** wrote:

Tadhkirah i aḥwāl i Saiyid M. Khān (beginning *Az ān-jā kih pīsh-gāh i Dāwar i ḥaqīqī*), an account of the career of a contemporary official: **Ivanow** Curzon 159 (7) (foll. 301*b*–317. A.H. 1207/1792–3).

The same official's career, especially the events of 1160–1/1747–8, is the subject of another short tract with the same title but of unstated authorship (beginning *Īn sipihr i lu'bat-bāz rā rasmī ast qadīm*): **Ivanow** Curzon 159 (3) (foll. 249–256*b*. A.H. 1207/1792–3).

1468. M. **'Abbās Khān "'Abbās" Afghānī** b. M. Ziyārat Allāh

[1] The biographies are alphabetically arranged, without any grouping in three chapters, and include a life of Amīr Khān Sind'hī, a noble of Aurangzēb's time.

[2] As the second consonant is unpointed, the name could be read Mitran, Manran, etc.

died in 1188/1774 according to Nadhīr Aḥmad, who gives a reference to *Akhbār al-ṣanādīd*,[1] part i, pp. 373–5.

Ḥālāt i 'Abbās Khān, an autobiography: **Rāmpūr** Ḥāfiẓ Aḥmad 'Alī Khān's library (see Nadhīr Aḥmad 66).

Extracts: *Akhbār al-ṣanādīd, loc. cit.*

1469. Rāy **Kēwal Rām**, son of Rag'hunāt'h Dās, describes himself as an Aggarwālah by caste and a resident of Kāsnah in the *ṣūbah* (province) of Delhi.

Tadhkirat al-umarā', concise notices of Indian nobles (khāns from *nuh-hazārī* to *dū-ṣadī*, untitled *amīrs* from *shash-hazārī* to *hazārī*, Hindū *zamīndārs*, and Deccan *amīrs* from *haft-hazārī* to *pānṣadī*) who served under Akbar and his successors to the death of Aurangzēb [A.H. 1119/1707], completed in 1140/1727–8 (so Bodleian 258), or 1184/1770–1 [2] (so Rieu i 339 and Sprenger, MSS. of the late Sir H. Elliot (*JASB.* xxiii (1854) p. 239), or 1194/1780 (so Ethé 629, Ivanow 216, and Elliot *History of India* viii p. 192), and divided into two *bābs* ((1) Muslims, in two *faṣls*, (*a*) those who bore the title *khān*, with a *dhail* devoted to those who bore such other titles as Amīr al-umarā', Amīn al-Daulah, and I'timād al-Daulah, (*b*) those without official titles, such as Ibrāhīm Mīrzā, Sh. Ibrāhīm, Sh. Abū 'l-Faḍl, Ḥakīm Abū 'l-Fatḥ, (2) Hindūs, in two *faṣls*, (*a*) those who bore the titles Rānā, Mahārājah, Rājah, Rāō, Rāwat, Rāwal, Rāy-Rāyān, or Rāy, (*b*) Rājpūts and others without these titles): **Rieu** i 339*a* (A.H. 1195/1781), ii 876*b* (18th cent.), iii 971*b* (circ. A.D. 1850), **Ivanow** 216 (probably defective in middle. Late 18th cent.), **Bodleian** 258, **Ethé** 629.

1470. For the *Ṭahmās-nāmah*, the memoirs of Ṭahmās Khān, written in 1193/1779, see p. 625 *supra*.

1471. **Shāh-nawāz Khān Aurangābādī**, i.e. Mīr **'Abd al-Razzāq** b. Mīr Ḥasan 'Alī Ḥusainī Khwāfī **Aurangābādī**, entitled Nawwāb

[1] Presumably an Urdu work, but not traceable in the Urdu catalogues of the British Museum, India Office, Āṣafīyah Library, or the Subḥān Allāh collection at 'Alīgaṛh. From the number of pages in part i it would appear to be a much larger work than Sir Saiyid Aḥmad's *Āthār al-ṣanādīd* (cf. p. 485 *supra*), the first part of which in the Lucknow edition of 1876 has only 98 pages.

[2] Ethé's argument that the date 1184 is impossible in view of the fact that a former owner's seal on fol. 1*a* of Bodleian 258 bears the date 1181 is of course invalid, since seals were often used long after the dates inscribed on them.

Ṣamṣām al-Daulah Shāh-nawāz Khān Ṣamṣām-Jang, the descendant of a Saiyid who had migrated from Khwāf to India in Akbar's reign, was born on 28 Ramaḍān 1111/20 March 1700 at Lahore,[1] where his father had died fifteen days before at the age of nineteen.[2] His grandfather, M. Kāẓim Khān,[3] who died in 1135/1722–3, had been appointed *Dīwān* of Lahore and subsequently of Multān by Aurangzēb, but many of his relations were resident in Aurangabad,[4] and there Mīr 'Abd al-Razzāq settled in the year in which the Amīr al-Umarā' Ḥusain 'Alī Khān went to the Deccan [i.e. in 1127/1715].

In his twenties[5] he entered the service of Nawwāb Niẓām al-Mulk Āṣaf-Jāh (the first of the " Niẓāms " of Ḥaidarābād) and in 1145/1732–3 he was appointed *Dīwān* of Barār (" Berar "). In 1155/1742[6] he was dismissed for taking part in the rebellion of Nāṣir-Jang, Āṣaf-Jāh's second son, who had been vice-gerent during his father's absence in the north,[7] and he had five years of leisure, which he devoted to the compilation of his great work, the *Ma'āthir al-umarā'*. In 1160/1747 Āṣaf-Jāh reappointed him *Dīwān* of Barār. In 1161/1748 Nāṣir-Jang succeeded his father

[1] So according to " Āzād ", *Ma'āthir al-umarā'* i p. 18¹. Shāh-nawāz Khān himself (*M. al-u.* iii p. 721¹⁶) does not say expressly that he was born at Lahore, though he says that his father died there and that he was born fifteen days afterwards. Rieu (on what authority ?) says that he was born at Multān.

[2] So according to Shāh-nawāz Khān (*M. al-u.* iii p. 721¹⁴). " Āzād " says twenty (*M. al-u.* i p. 16¹⁸).

[3] For his life see *M. al-u.* iii pp. 715–21.

[4] Shāh-nawāz Khān's great-grandfather, Mīrak Mu'īn al-Dīn Aḥmad entitled Amānat Khān (for whose life see *M. al-u.* i pp. 258–68, Beveridge's trans. pp. 221–30), was appointed *Dīwān* of the Deccan in Aurangzēb's 22nd year (1089/1678) and died in 1095/1684. The same office was held by his son, Mīr 'Abd al-Qādir Diyānat Khān, his grandson, 'Alī Naqī Diyānat Khān, and his great-grandsons, Mīrak M. Taqī Wizārat Khān and Mīr M. Ḥusain Khān Yamīn al-Daulah Manṣūr-Jang.

[5] *M. al-u.* i p. 6⁵ : *dar 'asharah i thālithah i sinīn i nadāmat-qarīn . . . zamānah ba-kashākash i mulāzim-pīshagī afkand.*

[6] *M. al-u.* i p. 6¹⁴.

[7] Muḥammad Shāh summoned Āṣaf-Jāh to help him against the Marāṭ'hās, who in 1737 suddenly appeared on the outskirts of Delhi. Āṣaf-Jāh was outgeneralled by them near Bhōpāl in 1738 and, without any actual fighting, obtained peace by ceding the province of Mālwah. These events were followed by Nādir Shāh's invasion. Āṣaf-Jāh was one of the commanders at the Battle of Karnāl in 1739 and took a prominent part in the subsequent negotiations with Nādir Shāh. See *De Voulton's Noticia. Translated . . . by L. Lockhart* (in *BSOS.* iv/2 (1926) pp. 223–45) ; L. Lockhart *Nadir Shah* pp. 124, 132–3, 136, 139–42, 148, and the various authorities cited by Lockhart.

and made Shāh-nawāz Khān *Dīwān* of the Deccan, i.e. Prime Minister.

Nāṣir-Jang's succession, however, was contested by a nephew, Muz̤affar-Jang, who sought French help to further his designs. On Nāṣir-Jang's assassination in December 1750, Dupleix, the Governor of Pondicherry, installed Muz̤affar-Jang as *Ṣūbah-dār* of the Deccan and provided him with a bodyguard of French troops and sepoys under the command of M. Bussy.[1] Muz̤affar-Jang, however, was murdered in February, 1751, and his uncle, Ṣalābat-Jang, was proclaimed *Ṣūbah-dār* by Bussy, who now made French influence predominant at Aurangābād, Ṣalābat-Jang's capital. In 1165/1752 Ṣalābat-Jang appointed Shāh-nawāz Khān *Ṣūbah-dār* of Ḥaidarābād, but he was soon dismissed at Bussy's instance. In 1167/1753, again at Bussy's instance, he was appointed Prime Minister [2] with the rank of a *haft-hazārī* and the title of Ṣamṣām al-Daulah.

Shāh-nawāz Khān now made an effort to terminate the French predominance in the Niz̤ām's dominions, and at his advice Ṣalābat-Jang dismissed Bussy. Bussy, however, marched on Ḥaidarābād, took up a strong position in which he withstood a siege for nearly two months and was then reinstated by Ṣalābat-Jang. In 1170/1757 Shāh-nawāz Khān's downfall was precipitated by his failure to satisfy the demands of the army, whose pay was much in arrear. Rising against him, they obtained his dismissal and he fled to Daulatābād with his family and nearly five hundred followers. His property was confiscated and troops were sent to besiege him. His friend Ghulām-ʻAlī " Āzād ", one of the few who remained faithful to the fallen minister, exerted himself on his behalf and eventually secured his return to favour. Shortly afterwards, however, Ḥaidar-Jang, Bussy's right-hand man, seized an opportunity of putting him under arrest and five weeks later, on 3 Ramaḍān 1171/11 May 1758, he was murdered by one of Bussy's Hindu soldiers. With other members of his family he lies buried to the south of Aurangābād.

[1] Charles Joseph Patissier, Marquis de Bussy-Castelnau (1718–85), for whom see Buckland's *Dictionary of Indian biography*, p. 64.

[2] *Nawwāb Ṣamṣām al-Daulah rā ba-ʻat̤ā-yi khilʻat i wakālat i mut̤laq i khwud . . . bar-nawākht. U ū muddat i chahār sāl ba-manṣab i wakālat i mut̤laq pardākht* (*M. al-u.* i p. 21^{14-17}).

His *tadhkirah*, the *Bahāristān i sukhun*, has already been mentioned (p. 854 *supra*). His *munsha'āt* are highly praised by Ghulām-'Alī " Āzād ", who expresses regret that they had never been collected (*Ma'āthir al-umarā'* i p. 36[8]). A small collection of them (87 foll.) is preserved in an acephalous MS. at Bombay (Bombay Univ. p. 110 no. 39).

Ma'āthir al-umarā', biographies of Indian nobles from the reign of Akbar to the author's time (*pānṣadīs* and upwards in Akbar's reign, *sih-hazārīs* and upwards thereafter to the middle of Aurangzēb's reign, thenceforward *panj-hazārīs* or *haft-hazārīs*) arranged in groups alphabetically according to the initial letter of the title and within these groups chronologically according to the dates of death, begun in 1155/1742 (author's preface p. 6[14], Beveridge's trans. p. 6[18]), worked at for five years (" Āzād's " preface p. 11[4], Beveridge's trans. p. 10[1]), neglected then for some twelve years (" Āzād's " preface p. 11[8], Beveridge's trans. p. 10[6]) and still unfinished at the author's death, after which the MS. was lost until eventually recovered a year or more later [1] in fragments and incomplete by the author's friend Ghulām-'Alī " Āzād " Bilgrāmī (cf. pp. 855–66 *supra*), who prepared an edition extant in several MSS., but soon superseded by the greatly enlarged edition of Mīr 'Abd al-Ḥaiy, the author's son.[2]

I. Ghulām-'Alī " Āzād's " edition, containing a preface by the editor (beg. *Ḥamd i Shāhanshāhī*), his life of the author (beg. *Nawwāb Ṣamṣām al-Daulah . . . Nām i aṣlī i ū Mīr 'Abd al-Razzāq ast*), the author's preface (beg. *al-Ḥ. l. wa-salām 'alā 'ibādihi*), and a series of biographies (two hundred and thirty-four in Bodleian 166, two hundred and sixty in Morley 101–2,

[1] *Ba'd i yak sāl i kāmil az shahādat i muṣannif* (" Āzād's " preface p. 11 ult.). 'Abd al-Ḥaiy says *Ba'd az chand sāl qadrī ajzā ba-dast āmad* (p. 3[12]).

[2] Ṣamṣām al-Mulk (previously for a time Ṣamṣām al-Daulah) Mīr 'Abd al-Ḥaiy " Ṣārim " Aurangābādī was born in 1142/1727–30. In 1162/1749 Nāṣir-Jang (cf. p. 1095[15, 19]) appointed him to a *manṣab*, conferred upon him the title of Khān and made him *Dīwān* of Barār (" Berar "). In the time of Ṣalābat-Jang (cf. p. 1096[10]) he became Governor (*Nāẓim*) of Aurangābād and Commandant of the fort of Daulatābād. His father's downfall (in 1170/1757) involved him too, but Niẓām-'Alī (cf. p. 750[2]) restored him to favour and appointed him *Dīwān* of the Deccan. He was with Niẓām-'Alī's army before the fort of Kaulās, when he fell ill and died on 15 Jumādā 'l-Ūlā 1196/28 April 1782. It has already been mentioned (p. 854) that he completed his father's *tadhkirah*, the *Bahāristān i sukhun*. See *Ma'āthir al-umarā'* iii pp. 973–9 (a brief autobiography); *Khizānah i 'āmirah* pp. 296–7 ; *Sawāniḥ i Dakan* ; Rieu i pp. 340*b*, 342*a*.

two hundred and eighty-seven in Bānkīpūr 655) beginning with Adham Khān Kōkah, ending with Yāqūt Khān Ḥabashī, and including three (S. ʻAbd Allāh Khān Quṭb al-Mulk, Nawwāb Āṣaf-Jāh, and Nawwāb Niẓām al-Daulah Nāṣir-Jang) added by the editor from his *Sarw i Āzād* (for which see p. 864 *supra*): **Lindesiana** p. 219 no. 824 (circ. A.D. 1770. Not described in the catalogue as "Āzād's" edition, but if the conjectural date is correct it can be nothing else), **Madrās** i 444 (A.H. 1192/1778), **Ethé** 622 (A.H. 1199/1785), 623 (A.H. 1203/1789), 624–5, **R.A.S.** P. 104–5 = Morley 101–2 (A.H. 1204/1789), P. 106–7 (A.H. 1261/1845), **Ivanow** 213 (A.H. 1221/1806–7), 215 (some differences, for which see Ivanow's description. The beginning partly spurious), **Lahore** Panjab Univ. Lib. (A.H. 1244/1828. See *Oriental College Magazine*, vol. iii, no. 1 (Lahore, Nov. 1926), p. 68), **Bānkīpūr** viii 655 (287 biographies. 19th cent.), **Bodleian** 166 (234 biographies), 167 ("quite modern").

II. ʻAbd al-Ḥaiy's edition, begun in 1182/1768–9 some time after the recovery of further fragments of the author's MS., completed in 1194/1780 and containing ʻAbd al-Ḥaiy's preface (beg. *Sitāyish i bī-karān*), the author's preface, "Āzād's" preface, "Āzād's" life of the author, a list of the biographies (in which the many added by ʻAbd al-Ḥaiy are marked with a Q as an abbreviation for *Ilḥāq*), the series of biographies, seven hundred and thirty [1] in number according to a statement prefixed by ʻAbd al-Ḥaiy to his list, the first being Ismāʻīl Bēg DWLDĪ, the last Yalangtōsh Khān, and finally a *khātimah* devoted to a brief autobiography of the editor and specimens of his poetry: **Ethé** 627 (apparently autograph first brouillon, lacking seventy-two leaves between foll. 4 and 5 and containing about three hundred and seventy-one biographies), 626 (containing, without preface or *khātimah*, a series of biographies beginning with Ismāʻīl Bēg DWLDĪ and ending with Yalangtōsh Khān, perhaps ʻAbd al-Ḥaiy's biographies separately copied. Received by Richard Johnson from Mīr M. Ḥusain at Ḥaidarābād in 1788),

[1] On this approximately correct number see Beveridge's remarks in his translation p. 32 n. 1. As he says, however, "the number of the biographies contained in the three volumes [sc. of the printed edition] is considerably more than 726, for most of the notices end with accounts of the sons and grandsons of the subject of the biography."

I.O. 3903–5 (transcribed probably in 1886), **Rieu** i 339*b* (A.H. 1196/1782) 341*b* (two copies, both dated 1196/1782), 342*a* (two 18th-cent. copies), **Blochet** i 639–40 (late 18th cent.), 641 (late 18th cent.), **Ivanow** 214 (18th cent.), **R.A.S.** P. 108 = Morley 103 (A.H. 1242/1826), **Bānkīpūr** viii 656–7 (19th cent.), **Āṣafīyah** i p. 252 no. 520 (from *dāl* to *mīm*).

Edition (of 'Abd al-Ḥaiy's recension) : *The Maásir-ul-umará by Nawāb Samsámud-Dowla Shah Nawáz Khan . . . Edited . . . by Maulaví 'Abd-ur-Rahím (and Maulaví Mirzá Ashraf 'Alí).* **Calcutta** 1888 [1887]–91°* (3 vols. Bibliotheca Indica).

English translation (rearranged) : *The Maaṣiru-l-umarā* [fasc. 7 *The Maāthir-ul-umarā*], *being biographies of the Muḥammadan and Hindu officers of the Timurid sovereigns of India from 1500 to about 1780* A.D. *by Nawāb* [fasc. 7 *Nawwāb*] *Ṣamṣāmu-d-Daula Shah Nawāz Khān and his son 'Abdul Ḥaqq* [*sic*, but correctly on fasc. 7 *'Abdul-Ḥayy*]. . . . *Translated by H. Beveridge* . . . [fasc. 7 adds *and revised, annotated and completed by Baini Prashad, D.Sc., F.R.A.S.B.*]. **Calcutta** 1911– °*, *in progress* [fasc. 1–6, 600 pp., published in 1911–14°*, and fasc. 7, pp. 601–840, published in 1941°*, form " Vol. I " and contain the biographies of those persons whose names or titles,[1] when transliterated, begin with the letters A–L, the first being 'Abd al-'Azīz Khān Bahādur (Persian text, vol. ii p. 836), and the last Luṭf Allāh Khān Ṣādiq (Persian text, vol. iii p. 177). Bibliotheca Indica.]

[*Ma'āthir al-umarā'* iii pp. 721–8 (an autobiography appended to the biography of his grandfather, M. Kāẓim Khān), i pp. 14–40 (a biography prefixed to the work by the editor, Ghulām-'Alī " Āzād ". English translations of this biography have appeared in the *Quarterly Oriental Magazine* (Calcutta 1825) p. 269 onwards and in Beveridge's translation of the *M. al-u.* pp. 12–32) ; *Khizānah i 'āmirah* pp. 62–3 (in the account of Ṣalābat-Jang) ; contemporary European writers such as Orme and Dupleix ;

[1] Some persons entered in the original under their titles are entered by Beveridge under their names and *vice versa*. Thus Ḥaidar-Qulī Khān Mu'izz al-Daulah will be found under M in the original but under H in the translation. The original not infrequently departs from the best usage in entering persons under such prefixed titles as Shaikh, Ḥakīm, Mīr, and Qāḍī. Beveridge's arrangement is occasionally affected by eccentricities of transliteration, e.g. Ekatāz Khān (the only entry under E !).

Mir'āt al-ṣafā' (B.M. Add. 6540) foll. 103–4, etc.; Persian histories of Ḥaidarābād; M. Wilks *Historical sketches of the south of India*, i (London 1810) pp. 382, 387, 389; J. Grant Duff *History of the Mahrattas* (1826), revised edition, Oxford 1921, vol. i pp. 434, 460, 463, 476, 486–7, 494–9, 500; H. G. Briggs *The Nizam* (London 1861) i pp. 124–33; Elliot and Dowson *History of India* viii pp. 187–91; Rieu i p. 340; Buckland *Dictionary of Indian biography* p. 385; Bānkīpūr catalogue viii pp. 11–12; *Ency. Isl.* under Ṣamṣām al-Dawla (H. H. Schaeder); *Pictorial Hyderabad compiled ... by K. Krishnaswamy Mudiraj*, Hyderabad 1929, vol. i pp. 183–4; etc.]

1472. Nawwāb **'Alī Ibrāhīm Khān** died in 1208/1793–4 (see pp. 700–2 *supra*).

Declaration concerning his governorship [*sic?*] *of Benares*: **Rieu** Suppt. 405A (see p. 701 *supra*).

1473. For the *Ḥairat-nāmah i sufarā'* of Mīrzā Abū 'l-Ḥasan Shīrāzī, Persian envoy in London, and afterwards Minister for Foreign Affairs, see p. 1068 *supra*.

1474. **M. Riḍā "Najm" Ṭabāṭabā** (see pp. 148–9 *supra*).

Notice of Shāh-nawāz Khān [Dihlawī],[1] *Shāh-'Ālam's Wazīr*: **Rieu** iii 1018*b* viii (A.D. 1849).

1475. Rājāyān-rājah Rājah **Chandū La'l** "Shādān" Mahārājah Bahādur has already been incidentally mentioned in this work (pp. 252, 754). A member of a family claiming descent from Rājah Tōdar Mal, Akbar's Finance Minister, he was born in 1766 and, like his paternal uncle before him, became *Kaṛōṛgīr* of the town of Ḥaidarābād in the time of Mīr Niẓām-'Alī Khān (A.H. 1175–1218/1761–1803). In 1221/1806 Mīr-'Ālam (for whom see pp. 750–2) obtained the Niẓām's sanction for his appointment as *Peshkār* (*Mīr-'Ālam Rājah Chandū La'l rā bah pēshkārī i khwēsh az pēshgāh i Ḥuḍūr i pur-nūr sarfarāz u sarbuland u mumtāz gardānīdah, Gulzār i Āṣafīyah* p. 101[13]). After the death of Mīr-'Ālam in 1223/1808 Munīr al-Mulk was appointed *Dīwān*, but the administration of the state was in the hands of Chandū

[1] For Shāh-nawāz Khān Dihlawī see p. 146 *supra*. He is, of course, to be distinguished from Shāh-nawāz Khān Aurangābādī (for whom see pp. 1094–1100 *supra*).

La'l, its virtual ruler (*Gulzār i Āṣafīyah* p. 105 penult.[1]). In 1235/1820 the title of Mahārājah Bahādur was conferred upon him (*G. i Ā.* p. 109[10]), in the time of Mīr Farkhundah 'Alī Khān (1829–57) he received the additional title of Rājāyān-rājah (*G.i Ā.* p. 234[10]), and on 15 April 1845 he died.

He was the author of *dīwāns* in Persian and Urdu and was a generous patron of letters. Some information about his lavish benefactions will be found in the *Gulzār i Āṣafīyah*, pp. 234[12]–36.

One of his descendants was Mahārājah Sir Kishun Pershad [i.e. Kishan Parshād], G.C.I.E., "Hereditary Peshkar and President of the Executive Council of the State [of Ḥaidarābād]," who was born in 1864 and died on 13 May 1940 (see *Who was Who* 1929–40 under Kishun Pershad).

'Ishrat-kadah i āfāq, in three *fuṣūl*[2] ((1) *dar aḥwāl i khānadān i Āṣafīyah . . .* [*bā ?*] *nabdhī az aḥwāl i ābā wa-ajdād i kirām i khwud*, (2) *dar dhikr i ghazalīyāt u rubā'īyāt u afrādī kih bī mashīyat u fikr sar-zad i khāmah . . . gardīdah*, (3) *dar dhikr i ḥikāyāt i 'ajībah u nikāt i gharībah*) : **I.O.** 4386.

Edition : place ? [presumably **Ḥaidarābād**] 1325/1907 (see Āṣafīyah iii p. 6 no. 264).

[*Gulzār i Āṣafīyah* pp. 233–6, 101, 109, and elsewhere ; Briggs *The Nizam* i pp. 149–54 ; Garcin de Tassy iii pp. 90–2 ; Buckland *Dictionary of Indian biography* p. 79 ; Niẓāmī Badāyūnī *Qāmūs al-mashāhīr* (in Urdu) i p. 191 ; Saksena *History of Urdu literature* p. 201 ; K. Krishnaswamy Mudiraj *Pictorial Hyderabad* i p. 196 (portrait, p. 195) ; see also p. 252 n.1 *supra*.]

1476. **Ḥasan Chelebī "Shaidā"** was evidently a dependent of Dāwud Pāshā, Governor of Baghdād.[3]

Durrat al-tāj wa-ghurrat al-ibtihāj, described as the fourth volume of the *Khamsah i Dāwud-Shāhī* and devoted mainly to

[1] Cf. *op. cit.* 234[2] : *Dar dīwānī i Munīr al-Mulk Bahādur az pēshgāh i khudāwand i ni'mat ḥaḍrat i Maghfirat-manzil* [i.e. Sikandar-Jāh, 1803–29] . . . *ba-darajah i buland i arjmand i mukhtārī i umūr i riyāsat u wakālat i Angrēz Bahādur . . . ma'mūr gashtah.*

[2] The subjects of the three *fuṣūl* are given here in the author's own words as quoted in the 1938 catalogue of the Ibrāhīmī Bookshop (Maktabah i Ibrāhīmīyah), Ḥaidarābād, Deccan, p. 46. According to Saksena "He also wrote a book entitled *Ishrat Qada* [*sic*] *Afaq* in which he narrates the incidents of his life, the history of his family, and his own services in the Nizam's dominions."

[3] See *Ency. Isl.* under Dā'ūd Pasha.

a metrical chronicle of Dāwud Pāsẖā's movements and the daily occurrences at his residency from Rajab 1236/April 1821 to Ramaḍān 1237/May–June 1822 (foll. 56–212), but also to six prose tracts (foll. 5–55) and the author's *dīwān* (foll. 213–77) : **Rieu** Suppt. 356 (A.H. 1237/1822).

1477. An as yet unidentified author born at Iṣfahān on 16 Jumādā 1197/19 May 1783, who traces his descent to Ḥājjī Qiwām al-Dīn Sẖīrāzī, of Sẖāh Sẖujā''s time [A.H. 760–86/ 1359–84], and mentions brothers named Mīrzā 'Alī Akbar, Mīrzā 'Alī Riḍā, and Fatḥ Allāh Kẖān, and a great-uncle named 'Abd al-Raḥīm Kẖān, began in Dẖū 'l-Ḥijjah 1239/Aug. 1824 at the request of some friends to note down the events of his life and thus produced an autobiography, from which it appears that he held various positions in the reign of Fatḥ-'Alī Sẖāh.

Autobiography (beginning : *Bas bi-gardīd u bi-gardad rūzgār dil ba-dunyā dar na-bandad hūsẖyār*), divided into four *bābs* ((1) *dar kaifīyat i nasab*, (2) *az zamān i wilādat ilā awān i magẖḍūb sẖudan az sulṭan i jahāniyān* . . . , (3) *dar inḥirāf i mizāj i mubārak i sulṭānī* . . . , (4) *tafṣīl i aḥwāl ba'd az siyāsat u yāsā* . . .) and followed by (1) Mīrzā Kūcẖak [" Wiṣāl "] Sẖīrāzī's poetical description of an earthquake at Sẖīrāz some years before the composition of the autobiography, fol. 53*a*, (2) a concise account of the ancient Persian kings (*guftār dar dẖikr i mukẖtaṣarī az waqā'i' i auḍā' u aḥwāl i mulūk i pasandīdah-sẖiyam i 'Ajam* . . . , foll. 61*a*–139) : **Ethé** 706 (transcribed A.H. 1253/1837 by Abū 'l-Qāsim b. 'Abd-al-Riḍā Qazwīnī).

1478. Mīrzā **M. Ja'far** b. Mīrzā M. Kẖān, better known as M. Jān, was the grandson of Nawwāb Mīrzā Mahdī 'Alī Kẖān Bahādur Ḥasẖmat-Jang Kẖurāsānī, whose father, Mīrzā M. Ṣādiq Kẖān, was *Ḥakīm-bāsẖī* to the Persian court after the murder of Nādir Sẖāh.

Majmū'ah i Ja'farī, a biography of the above-mentioned Nawwāb Mīrzā Mahdī 'Alī Kẖān (b. 1168/1755, sent to Turkey as envoy by Sẖāh-Rukẖ Mīrzā, invited to India by Nawwāb Dẖū 'l-Faqār al-Daulah Najaf 'Alī Kẖān [1] [d. 1196/1782, cf. pp. 474 n., 624], reached Sūrat in 1193/1779, Sẖāhjahānābād in 1195/1781,

---

[1] More commonly called Najaf Kẖān.

and ʻAẓīmābād in 1198/1783–4, entered the E.I. Co.'s service, was given an appointment in the Customs and Revenue Department at G͟hāzīpūr, became a friend of Jonathan Duncan, Collector of Benares, who later, when Governor of Bombay, invited him thither and sent him on a mission to Fatḥ-ʻAlī S͟hāh, was granted a pension by the Marquis Wellesley and died on 17 Rabīʻ II 1219/5 July 1804): **Bombay** Univ. p. 148.

1479. **S͟hafīʻ al-Dīn Ḥasan** b. Niʻmat Allāh al-Mūsawī **al-S͟hūs͟htarī** completed in Ṣafar 1259/March 1843:—

Muʻtamadīyah, a life of Muʻtamad al-Daulah Minūc͟hihr K͟hān (cf. p. 902 n. 1): **Berlin** 31 (8) (A.H. 1259/1843), 31 (1) (a few additions (*mulḥaqāt*) only).

1480. ʻAbd al-ʻAlīm M. **Naṣr Allāh K͟hān** K͟hwēs͟hgī **K͟hūrjawī,** who died in 1299/1881, has already been mentioned (pp. 756–7) as the author of a *Tārīk͟h i Dakan.*

Jāmiʻ i Fatḥ-K͟hānī (a chronogram = 1263/1847), a biography of the author's maternal uncle, Fatḥ K͟hān b. Ṣadr K͟hān, who was born in 1193/1779 and died in 1262/8 Nov. 1846 after serving as *Taḥṣīldār* at Niẓāmābād (Aʻẓamgaṛh District) and elsewhere, with much autobiographical information: **Delhi** 1848*.

Urdu translation by Pandit Dayā Nāt'h " Ārām " Dihlawī: *Jāmiʻ i Fatḥ-K͟hānī,* **Delhi** 1849*.

1481. S. **Ḥaidar Ḥusain K͟hān** b. M. Ḥusain K͟hān **S͟hāhjahānābādī** wrote in 1264/1848:—

Tārīk͟h i aḥwāl i Islām K͟hān Mas͟hhadī[1]: **Āṣafīyah** iii p. 94 no. 1135.

1482. Mubāriz al-Daulah **Pīr Ibrāhīm K͟hān** K͟hwēs͟hgī Qaṣūrī has already been mentioned (pp. 661–3 *supra*) as the author of a history of Bahāwalpūr.

Sairistān, a brief account of the author's visit to England in 1851–2 together with a short history of his tribe.

Edition: [**Multān** according to M. S͟hafīʻ, **Bahāwalpūr** according to Edwards] 1854°.[2]

[1] For a biography of this *amīr* of S͟hāh-Jahān's time see *Maʼāt͟hir al-umarāʼ* i pp. 162–7. Cf. p. 567 *supra.*

[2] In the B.M. catalogue this work is mistakenly entered under " Mubāriz ul-Daulah, *Nawab of Bahawalpur* "

Description (by M. S̲h̲afī‘) : *Islamic culture* iii no. 3 (July 1929) pp. 454, 472.

1483. S̲h̲. **Aḥmad 'Alī " Rasā " Lak'hnawī** was a *taḥṣīldār* in British India until 1857.

D̲h̲ikr i yārān i zamān, an autobiography with accounts of the author's contemporaries : **Āṣafīyah** ii p. 848 no. 39 (A.H. 1276/1859–60, autograph).

1484. APPENDIX.

(1) *Ḥālāt i Āṣaf-Khānān*, short accounts of four persons entitled Āṣaf K̲h̲ān, viz., (1) K̲h̲wājah 'Abd al-Majīd Harawī, who became Ā. K̲h̲. in Akbar's fifth year, (2) K̲h̲wājah G̲h̲iyāt̲h̲ al-Dīn 'Alī Qazwīnī, who became Ā. K̲h̲. in Akbar's eighteenth year, (3) Ja'far Bēg, who became Ā. K̲h̲. in Akbar's twentieth year, and (4) Abū 'l-Ḥasan b. I‘timād al-Daulah : **Edinburgh** 413 (A.H. 1161/1748).

(2) (*Tārīk̲h̲ i Mīrzā Mas‘ūd*), a history of 'Abbās Mīrzā Nā'ib al-Salṭanah : see p. 338 *supra*.

N. BIOGRAPHY : (*k*) ORIENTALISTS.

1484A. **Abū 'l-Qāsim Sahāb.**

Farhang i khāwar-s̲h̲ināsān dar s̲h̲arḥ i ḥāl u k̲h̲idamāt i dānis̲h̲mandān i Īrān-s̲h̲inās u mustas̲h̲riqīn, notices of some 570 orientalists (based in some cases on information supplied by themselves) with about sixty portraits : **Tihrān** A.H.S. 1317/ 1938 (375 pp.)

N. BIOGRAPHY : (*l*) PHILOSOPHERS,

PHYSICIANS, ETC.

[See also BIOGRAPHY : GENERAL.]

1485. Abū Sulaimān M. b. Ṭāhir b. Bahrām al-Manṭiqī al-Sijzī (or al-Sijistānī), a philosopher of the 4th/10th century (see M. Qazwīnī *Abû Sulaimân Manṭiqî Sidjistânî*, Publications de la Société des Etudes Iraniennes [Paris] no. 5, 1933 ; Brockelmann *Sptbd.* i pp. 377–8 ; etc.) wrote in Arabic a work entitled Ṣiwān al-ḥikmah (the Repository of philosophy) on the

Greek (and some Islāmic ?) philosophers and their ideas. Of this work no complete copy is known to exist, but extracts from it are preserved in at least four MSS. (Bas͟hīr Āg͟hā 494 foll. 1–95, Murād 1408 (incorrectly 1431 in the *daftar*) foll. 1–88, Köprülü 902 foll. 1–123, Leyden ii p. 292 no. 888 foll. 1–73, and probably also Uri (Bodleian) p. 121 no. 484 [1]).

A supplement to this work was written between 553/1158 [2] and 565/1169–70 [3] by Ẓahīr al-Dīn Abū 'l-Ḥasan **'Alī b. Zaid al-Baihaqī,** who has already been mentioned (pp. 353–4 *supra*) as the author of a *Tārīk͟h i Baihaq*.

Tatimmat Ṣiwān al-ḥikmah,[4] an Arabic work on the lives and sayings of 111 philosophers, physicians, mathematicians, etc., many of them contemporary or nearly contemporary with the author, the first being Ḥunain b. Isḥāq and the last Ismā'īl al-Jurjānī, author of the *D͟hak͟hīrah i K͟hwārazms͟hāhī* : **Murād** 1408 (*b*) (A.H. 639/1241–2), **Bas͟hīr Āg͟hā** 494 (*b*) (A.H. 689/1290), **Leyden** ii p. 292 no. 888 (*b*) (A.H. 692/1293), **Köprülü** 902 (14th cent.), **Mas͟hhad** iii, *fṣl* 14, MSS., no. 24, **Ahlwardt** ix no. 10052 (18th cent.), and probably **Uri** p. 121 no. 484.

Edition of the Arabic text : *Tatimma Ṣiwān al-ḥikma of 'Alī b. Zaid al-Baihaḳī, edited by Mohammad Shafī'. Fasciculus I* [5]*— Arabic text.* **Lahore** 1351/1935‡. (For a review by M. Krause see *Der Islam* 24/1 (1937) pp. 90–2).

Extract : *The earliest account of 'Umar Khayyām.*[6] By E. D. R[oss] and H. A. R. G[ibb] (in *BSOS.* v/3 (1929) pp. 467–70, with English translation, pp. 470–3).

Translations of the same extract : **(1)** [German] *Zu 'Omer-i-Chajjâm. Von G. Jacob und E. Wiedemann* (in *Der Islam* iii/1 (1912) pp. 42–7). **(2)** [English] see above under Extract.

Description and discussion : *Abû Sulaïmân Manṭiqî Sidjistânî,*

[1] Cf. M. Plessner's observations on all these MSS. in *Islamica* iv/4 (1931) pp. 534–8.

[2] The date of the death of Abū Bakr b. 'Urwah mentioned on p. 141[7].

[3] The date of Baihaqī's death.

[4] This title, though not mentioned in the work itself, is that by which the author designates the work in his *Mas͟hārib al-tajārib* (quoted in Yāqūt *Irs͟hād al-arīb* v p. 212[9]).

[5] Fasc. II is the Persian translation mentioned below. Fasc. III containing the " introduction, etc. " may perhaps not yet have appeared.

[6] S͟hahrazūrī's account is an abridged reproduction of Baihaqī's with the addition of three Arabic poems and two rubā'īs.

savant du IVe siècle de l'Hégire. Par M. Muḥammad Khan Qazvînî (Publications de la Société des études iraniennes [Paris], no. 5, 1933), pp. 1–7, etc.

Persian translation : *Durrat al-akhbār wa-lum'at al-anwār*, written probably about 730/1330 [1] and dedicated to Sulṭān Abū Sa'īd's *Wazīr*, Khwājah Ghiyāth al-Dīn M. b. Khwājah Rashīd al-Dīn Faḍl Allāh (d. 736/1336) by an as yet unidentified author who appended biographies of Shihāb al-Dīn [Yaḥyā b. Ḥabash] Qatīl al-Suhrawardī, Fakhr al-Dīn al-Rāzī, Naṣīr al-Dīn M. al-Ṭūsī and Rashīd al-Dīn Faḍl Allāh : **Lahore** Panjāb Univ. Lib.

Editions : (**1**) *Tārīkh al-ḥukamā' al-musammā bah D. al-a. w. l. al-a.* (ed. M. Shafī'. In *OCM*. v/2 (**Lahore** Feb. 1929) *ḍamīmah*, pp. 1–56, v/3 (May 1929) *ḍamīmah*, pp. 57–80, vi/1 (Nov. 1929) *ḍamīmah*, pp. 81–152). (**2**) *Tatimma Ṣiwān al-ḥikma of 'Alī b. Zaid al-Baihaḳī, edited by Moḥammad Shafī' . . . Fasciculus II—Persian version*, **Lahore** 1350/1935‡ (Panjab University Oriental Publications Series, no. 20. Title on Persian title-page as in *OCM.*). (**3**) **Ṭihrān** (see *Luzac's Oriental List* 1940, no. 1, p. 15, where the date is not mentioned).

1486. 'Alī b. Yūsuf **al-Qifṭī** was born in 568/1072 at Qifṭ in Upper Egypt and died at Aleppo in 646/1248 [Brockelmann i p. 325, *Sptbd.* i p. 559 ; *Ency. Isl.* under Ibn al-Ḳifṭī (Mittwoch) and al-Ḳifṭī (Brockelmann)].

Ikhbār al-'ulamā' bi-akhbār al-ḥukamā' : no MSS. recorded (?).[2]

Arabic abridgment : *al-Muntakhabāt wa-'l-multaqaṭāt min kitāb Ta'rīkh al-ḥukamā'*, written in 647/1249–50 by M. b. 'Alī b. M. al-Khaṭībī al-Zauzanī : **Ahlwardt** ix 10053–4, **Cureton-Rieu** p. 684, **Flügel** ii 1161–2, **Leyden** 2nd ed. ii (1) p. 130, etc. (see Brockelmann).

[1] The period of Ghiyāth al-Dīn's vizierate is referred to near the end (1935 ed. p. 133⁹) as *īn muddat i dū sih sāl*, which may not be meant quite literally. The precise date of Ghiyāth al-Dīn's appointment does not seem to be recorded, but it followed the killing of Dimashq Khwājah on 5 Shawwāl 727/24 Aug. 1327 (*Guzīdah*, trans. p. 150).

[2] As MSS. of the "Grundwerk" Brockelmann gives "Halet 619 (622*h*), Mešh. xiv, 5". The first words of Mashhad iii, *faṣl* 14 p. 5 no. 14 [*Ta'rīkh al-ḥukamā'*, beginning *al-Ḥ. l. al-Qadīm al-Azal* (*sic*)] suggest that it is a copy of Shahrazūrī's *Nuzhat al-arwāḥ*.

Edition of the Arabic abridgment: *Ibn al-Qifṭī's Ta'rīḫ al-Ḥukamā'. Auf Grund der Vorarbeiten Aug. Müller's herausgegeben von Prof. Dr. J. Lippert.* **Leipzig** 1903°*.

Persian translation of the abridgment: *Tarjamah i Ta'rīkh al-ḥukamā'*, written in the time of Shāh Sulaimān Ṣafawī (A.H. 1077–1105/1666–94) by an anonymous translator and dedicated to Mīrzā M. Ibrāhīm, *Mustaufī i Mamālik i Īrān*: **Majlis** 536 (A.H. 1099/1688), 535, **Mashhad** iii, *fṣl.* 14, MSS., no. 10 (A.H. 1296/1879), **Vatican** Pers. 133 (Rossi p. 137).

1487. Shams al-Dīn M. b. Maḥmūd **al-Shahrazūrī** al-Ishrāqī, who completed his *Rasā'il al-Shajarat al-Ilāhīyah fī 'ulūm al-ḥaqā'iq al-Rabbānīyah* (cf. Brockelmann i p. 469, *Sptbd.* i p. 851) in 680/1282 (as appears from Weisweiler's description of the Tübingen MS.[1]), wrote also *al-Rumūz wa-'l-amthāl al-lāhūtīyah fī 'l-anwār al-mujarradat al-malakūtīyah* (*fī ma'rifat al-nafs wa-'l-rūḥ*. See Escurial (Derenbourg) i 696, Vatican (Levi della Vida) 299,[2] etc.) as well as commentaries on two works of Shihāb al-Dīn Yaḥyā b. Ḥabash al-Suhrawardī al-Maqtūl (d. 587/1191), namely, *Sharḥ Ḥikmat al-ishrāq* (MSS. Yeñī 767, Sarāy, Aḥmad III 3230, Lālah-lī 2525. See Ritter in *Der Islam* 24/3–4 (1937) p. 278) and *al-Tanqīḥāt fī sharḥ al-Talwīḥāt* (MSS.: Köprülü 880, 'Āṭif 1588, Nūr i 'Uthmānīyah 2693–4. See Ritter *loc. cit.* p. 273).

Nuzhat al-arwāḥ wa-rauḍat al-afrāḥ,[3] an Arabic work on the lives and especially the sayings of about 34 Pre-Islāmic "philosophers" from Adam to Galen and about 77 Post-Islāmic from Ḥunain b. Isḥāq to Yaḥyā b. Ḥabash al-Suhrawardī, based mainly, it seems,[4] on the *Mukhtār al-ḥikam* of Mubashshir

[1] "Am Schluss findet sich die Angabe, dass der Verfasser das Werk am 23. Dū'l-Ḥiğğa680/1282 vollendet habe."

[2] "La sottoscrizione a f. 77v in data 611 è certamente falsa." This date, which is quoted in the Leyden catalogue (iii p. 345) and was inadvertently taken by Sachau for the date of the Leyden MS. of the *Nuzhat al-arwāḥ*, was one of the bases for his conclusion that that work was written after 586 [the date of Yaḥyā Suhrawardī's death: Alhwardt read the same date as 587] and before 611.

[3] This title, not mentioned in the work itself, is inscribed on some of the MSS. and is that by which the work was known to the Persian translator and to Ḥājjī Khalīfah. A variant, which transposes the two halves (*R. al-af. wa-n. al-ar.*), seems to be based on the sole authority of the Leyden MS.

[4] For al-Shahrazūrī's unacknowledged debt to the *Mukhtār al-ḥikam* see Leyden iii p. 344. The extent to which he has reproduced the *Tatimmat Ṣiwān al-ḥikmah* can be judged from M. Shafī''s textual notes to his edition of that work.

b. Fātik (Brockelmann i p. 459, *Sptbd.* i p. 829) and the *Tatimmat Ṣiwān al-ḥikmah* (see p. 1105 *supra*), of which latter a large part has been incorporated: Ḥ. Kh. vi p. 321, **Ahlwardt** 10056 (A.H. 782/1380), 10055 (circ. A.H. 1100/1688), **I.O.** 4613 (15th cent. See *JRAS.* 1939 p. 383), **Cureton-Rieu** p. 601 (A.H. 995/1587), p. 688 (A.H. 996/1658), **Leyden** iii p. 343 (undated, but modern), **Mashhad** iii, *fṣl* 14, MSS., p. 77 (5) no. 14 (cf. p. 1106, n. 2, *supra*), etc. (see Brockelmann i p. 469, *Sptbd.* i p. 851).

Persian translation: *Tarjamah i Taʼrīkh al-ḥukamāʼ*, begun in 1011/1602–3 by Maqṣūd ʻAlī Tabrīzī [1] at the request of Sulṭān Salīm Shāh [who succeeded to the throne in 1014/1605 as the Emperor Jahāngīr]: **Ethé** 614 (pt. 1 dated Āgrah A.H. 1019/1610, pt. 2, in a different hand, undated), 615 (A.H. 1039/1630, collated with an autograph at Āgrah), 616 (A.H. 1041/1631–2), 617, **Ivanow** 274 (A.H. 1033 (?)/1623–4), **Rieu** Suppt. 100 (A.H. 1088/1677), **Lahore** Panjāb Univ. Lib. (A.H. 1120/1708. See *OCM.* iii/1 p. 68), **Lindesiana** p. 191 no. 435 (?) [2] (circ. A.D. 1770), **Browne** Suppt. 232 (King's 97), **Būhār** 94 (defective. 19th cent.), **Āṣafīyah** i p. 224 no. 247, **Tashkent Univ.** 68 (1).

Abridgment: *Intikhāb i Tārīkh al-ḥukamāʼ* (beg.: *Sipās u sitāyish Ḥakīmī rā kih awwal i bī-awwal-ast*), written in 1054/1644 (*intikhāb* is a chronogram) for presentation to ʻAbd Allāh Quṭb-Shāh by an unknown author,[3] a resident of Muḥammadābād,[4] who wrote also the ethico-theological *Risālah i*

[1] M. ʻA. T., of whom a biography containing no mention of the *Tarjamah i Taʼrīkh al-ḥukamāʼ* is given on pp. 59–60 of the first *qism* (*aḥwāl i ʻulamā u fuḍalā*) of the *khātimah* to the *Maʼāthir i Raḥīmī* (completed in 1025/1616: cf. pp. 552–3 *supra*), is described there as an incomparable Ṣūfī, a scholar and a man of austere piety. In spite of his unworldly character he was prevailed upon by ʻAbd al-Raḥīm Khān (Governor of Gujarat: cf. p. 533 *supra*) to accept the life of a courtier and official and served him for many years (*muddat-hā dar silsilah i ʻalīyah i īn sipahsālār mulāzim u jāgīrdār būd*). He became *Ṣadr* of the province of Gujarāt, but eventually through the intrigues of an enemy was dismissed and imprisoned in the fortress of Gwalior.

[2] " Translated from the Arabic by ʻAzīzī."

[3] Ethé 618 is described as an abridgment or extract from Maqṣūd ʻAlī's translation " made by Munshî Mîr Sayyid Ṣadr-aldîn bin Mîr Muḥammad Ṣâdiḳ bin Mîr Muḥammad Amîn ". " On the . . . first page Mr. Richard Johnson states that he has received this little book from Munshî Ṣadr aldîn (that is, from the compiler himself), being an extract from his common-place book, A.D. 1778." A note at the end of Berlin 71 (1) describes the work as *jamʻ kardah i Saiyid Ṣadr al-Dīn az kutub i muʻtabar*. It may be doubted whether S. Ṣadr al-Dīn's contribution to the work extended beyond copying it into his commonplace book All the manuscripts begin with the words given above.

[4] I.e. doubtless Bīdar, now in the state of Ḥaidarābād

kalām (Bānkīpūr Spt. ii 2298, Calcutta Madrasah 180 (2), Būhār 210) and the ethico-political *Akhlāq i bādshāhī* (a chronogram = 1055. Bānkīpūr Spt. ii 2299, Calcutta Madrasah 180 (3), Bodleian 1469, Browne Suppt. 30 (King's 7), Ivanow 1391, I.O. 4625 (2)): **Bānkīpūr** viii 651 (LIST OF BIOGRAPHIES. 18th cent.), Suppt. i 1778, Suppt. ii 2297 (18th cent.), **Calcutta** Madrasah 180 (1) (late 17th cent.), probably also **Ivanow** 275 (A.H. 1100 (?)/1688–9), **Ethé** 618 (not later than A.D. 1788), **Berlin** 71 (1) ("rec[d] Juny [Jany ?] 1797 from Moonshy Sudder ul Deen"), **Rieu** ii p. 834 no. xix (foll. 166–70: evidently only a fragment or a drastic abridgment. Late 17th cent.).

1488. Ḥā[jjī ?] Ḥmd [= Aḥmad or Muḥammad ?] b. 'Alī b. al-Ḥājj Jamāl al-Dīn Ḥusain **al-Anṣārī,** a son of Zain al-Dīn 'Alī al-'Aṭṭār, the author of the *Ikhtiyārāt i Badī'ī*, a well-known work on materia medica, was born at Shīrāz in 760/1359. He had spent forty years in attendance upon his father, who died in 806/1403–4, and he had written works entitled *Miftāḥ al-kunūz*, on medicaments, *Dastūr al-muta'ākilīn*,[1] on sweetmeats, *Tuḥfat al-mulūk*, on intoxicating drinks, *Dastūr al-zirā'ah*, on agriculture, *Dastūr al-su'adā'*, on the sayings of sages, and some shorter treatises. [Autobiographical statements in the notice of his father at the end of the MS. described below.]

Unidentified work, of which the first *qism* is divided into two *ḥarfs* ((1) on the value of learning. Notices of Pre-Islāmic philosophers, (2) meagre accounts of the lives and sayings of Muslim philosophers, beginning with Muḥammad and 'Alī and ending (according to the preface)[2] with 'Alā' al-Dīn Manṣūr, a physician whose brother 'Izz al-Dīn Mas'ūd is stated to have died in 813/1410–11 and one of his nephews in 817/1414–15, the latest date mentioned): **Rieu** ii 873*a* (a fragment containing *Qism* I and possibly a part of *Qism* II. Beg. *Qism i awwal dar faḍīlat i 'ilm u ḥikmat u tawārīkh i ḥukamā* . . . 18th cent.).

1489. Mullā **Aḥmad** b. Naṣr Allāh **Tattawī,** who was murdered at Lahore in 996/1588, has already been mentioned (p. 119 *supra*) as the chief author of the *Tārīkh i alfī*.

[1] *al-muta'akkilīn* according to Rieu, but this seems improbable.
[2] The last notice is in fact that of the author's father.

Khulāṣat al-ḥayāt, on the lives [1] and sayings of philosophers, written at the request of [Ḥakīm] Abū 'l-Fatḥ b. 'Abd al-Razzāq [Gīlānī, one of Akbar's physicians [2]] and divided, according to the preface, into a *fātiḥah* (5 introductory discourses), two *maqṣads* (on Pre-Islāmic and Islāmic philosophers respectively), and a *khātimah* (*dar bayān i madhāhib i millatain*), but probably left unfinished, since no MS. hitherto described extends beyond Socrates in *Maqṣad* i: **Upsala** Zetterstéen 390 ("Theil I". A.H. 1037/1628), **Bānkīpūr** Suppt. i 1779 (A.H. 1078/1668), **I.O.** D.P. 639 (*Fātiḥah* and *Maqṣad* i. 17th cent.), **Āṣafīyah** i p. 318 no. 33, **Ivanow** Curzon 497 (*Fātiḥah* and *Maqṣad* i, defective and much damaged. Early 19th cent.), **Majlis** 541 (ends with Socrates), **Rieu** iii 1034*b* (description and some extracts only. A.D. 1851).

1490. **'Abd al-Sattār b. Qāsim Lāhaurī** has already been mentioned (pp. 164–5) as collaborator with Jerome Xavier (d. 1617) in the translation of the latter's biographies of Christ and the Twelve Apostles into Persian and (p. 287) as epitomator of Sharaf al-Dīn 'Alī Yazdī's *Ẓafar-nāmah*.

Thamarat al-falāsifah (presumably identical with the "*Aḥwāl i Farangistān*", Rieu iii p. 1077*a*), an account of Greece and Rome and of the lives (doubtless more especially the sayings) of the Greek and Roman philosophers (cf. Sir E. Maclagan *The Jesuits and the Great Mogul*, London 1932, p. 218): **Mashhad** iii p. 78 ("*Tadhkirat al-ḥukamā'*". Not later than A.H. 1145/1732–3), **Lindesiana** p. 177 no. 445 (A.H. 1185/1771), **Browne** Suppt. 770 ("*Samar al-falāsifah*", A.H. 1197/1783, King's 222), **B.M.** Or. 5893 (see Maclagan *op. cit.* p. 218), **Āṣafīyah** i p. 346 nos. 118 (A.H. 1236/1820–1), 169, **Patiala** Victoria Library (see Maclagan *op. cit.* p. 218).

1491. Ḥakīm al-Mamālik Mīrzā **'Alī-Naqī b. Ismā'īl,** physician to Nāṣir al-Dīn Shāh Qājār, had a knowledge of French and had

[1] The contents of *Maqṣad* i give this work little claim to be regarded as biographical but, as in the earlier works of this kind, the biographical element would doubtless have been greater in the portion dealing with Islāmic times.

[2] See *Ā'īn i Akbarī* tr. Blochmann pp. 424–5; *Ma'āthir al-umarā'* i pp. 558–62, Beveridge's trans. pp. 107–10; Beale *Oriental biographical dictionary* under Abul-Fath Gilani.

studied medicine and other subjects abroad (doubtless in France). He was also a poet.

Rūz-nāmah i Ḥakīm al-Mamālik : **Ṭihrān** 1286/1869–70 (see Āṣafīyah iii p. 350. Apparently identical with the *Ruz-nāmah* describing Nāṣir al-Dīn Shāh's visit to Khurāsān in 1867. See p. 341 *supra* and Additions and Corrections *infra*).

[*al-Ma'āthir wa-'l-āthār* p. 194.]

1492. Appendix.

(1) *Aḥwāl i ḥukamā'*, "biographical notices and sayings of ancient philosophers," the first Idrīs, the last two Ibn Sab'īn and Abū Naṣr M. b. M. al-Turk : **Bānkīpūr** Suppt. i 1986 foll. 83*a*–98*b*.

(2) *Tadhkirat al-ḥukamā'* : **Rehatsek** p. 77 no. 16 (A.H. 1211/1796–7. "The book is not scarce, and may be had in the bazar." Probably therefore it is one of the works mentioned above.)

N. BIOGRAPHY : (*m*) PLACES (I.E. INHABITANTS OF PARTICULAR TOWNS, PROVINCES, OR COUNTRIES [1])

(1) ĀDHARBĀYJĀN

1493. **M. 'Alī Khān " Tarbiyat "** Tabrīzī, recently (A.H.S. 1314/ 1935–6),[2] a Deputy in the Majlis, was presumably the proprietor of the Tarbiyat Library, which " lasted from A.H. 1316 to 1326 (= A.D. 1898–1908) ", serving as a centre " of distribution and interchange for most of the Persian, Arabic, and Turkish papers published in Persia " and maintaining " epistolary and other relations with the chief educational centres ".[3] Under the management of that Library appeared in 1320–1/1903–4 the fortnightly scientific magazine *Ganjīnah i funūn*,[4] which

[1] References have been given to a number of works already described which may be regarded as dealing with the biography of particular localities. Such references could be multiplied, especially by the inclusion of works dealing with single saints.

[2] See the first title-page of the *Dānishmandān i Ādharbāyjān* and Ḥasan Isfandiyārī's *taqrīẓ*.

[3] *The press and poetry of modern Persia* p. 1.

[4] *Op. cit.* p. 130.

published "Tarbiyat's" work *Hunar-āmūz*.[1] The date of the closure of the Library (1908) is doubtless the year in which "Tarbiyat" went into exile at Istānbūl,[2] from which place he sent to E. G. Browne, apparently in 1912, the manuscript of his work *Waraqī az daftar i tārīkh i maṭbū'āt i Īrānī u Fārisī*, which the latter translated, enlarged, and published under the title *The press and poetry of modern Persia* (Cambridge 1914). 'Abd al-'Azīz "Jawāhir al-Kalām" mentions him as the founder of two libraries, the Public Library (*Kitāb-khānah i 'Umūmī*) at Tabrīz (about 7,000 volumes) and his own private library of about 5,000 volumes. A work of his entitled *Zād u būm*, a geography of Persia, is mentioned in *The press and poetry of modern Persia*, p. 163 no. 123.

Dānishmandān i Ādharbāyjān, a biographical dictionary of celebrities, mainly poets and scholars: **Ṭihrān** A.H.S. 1314/1935–6. (For a review by Minorsky see *BSOS*. ix/1 (1937) pp. 251–3).

[Browne *The press and poetry of modern Persia*, pp. ix, 1–2, 130, 163, etc.; 'Abd al-'Azīz "Jawāhir al-Kalām" *Kitāb-khānahā-yi Īrān* [Ṭihrān], A.H.S. 1311/1932–3, pp. 91–2; Ḥasan Isfandiyārī's *taqrīẓ* prefixed to the *Dānishmandān i Ādharbāyjān*].

N. BIOGRAPHY: (*m*) PLACES (2) AḤMADĀBĀD

1494. For the *Mir'āt i Aḥmadī*, which was completed by 'Alī Muḥammad Khān in 1175/1761, and of which the *khātimah* contains *inter alia* accounts of the saints and Saiyids buried in, or near, Aḥmadābād, see pp. 729–31 *supra*.

1495. For the *Mukhbir al-auliyā'* of Rashīd al-Dīn Maudūd Lālā, which is concerned mainly with saints buried at Aḥmadābād, see p. 1059 *supra*.

N. BIOGRAPHY: (*m*) PLACES (3) AMRŌHAH

1496. It was in 1296/1879 that Saiyid M. **Āl i Ḥasan** b.

[1] *Ibid.*
[2] *Op. cit.* pp. x, 2 n. 1, 6.

S. Naḏẖīr Aḥmad b. S. Imām al-Dīn Aḥmad Maudūdī Amrōhawī completed his :—

Nukẖbat al-tawārīkẖ, on the saints and other celebrated men of Amrōhah,[1] in a *muqaddimah* ((*a*) genealogical information concerning the patriarchs, etc., the Prophet and his family, (*b*) a sketch of the history of Amrōhah), four *bābs* ((1) the Saiyids, (2) the Ṣẖaikẖs, (3) the Muḡẖuls and Afḡẖans, (4) the Kambōhs and Kalāls) and a *kẖātimah* (further saints, etc., *manṣabdārs*, the author's teachers and friends). Edition : **Amrōhah** 1880°*.

N. BIOGRAPHY : (*m*) PLACES (4) AURANGĀBĀD

1497. For the (*Sawāniḥ*) of Sabzawārī, written shortly after 1188/1774 and dealing with the saints of Aurangābād, see p. 1027 *supra*.

N. BIOGRAPHY : (*m*) PLACES (5) BAIHAQ

1498. For the *Tārīkẖ i Baihaq*, which was completed in 563/1168 by 'Alī b. Zaid al-Baihaqī and which is mainly biographical, see p. 354 *supra*.

N. BIOGRAPHY : (*m*) PLACES (6) BALḴH

1499. For the *Faḍā'il i Balkẖ*, an Arabic work which was completed in 610/1213 and translated into Persian at some date later than 676/1278 and of which the third section contains biographies of seventy famous *ṣẖaikẖs* of Balkẖ and its neighbourhood, see p. 1296 *infra*.

1500. For the *Tārīkẖ i mazārāt i Balkẖ* of M. Ṣāliḥ b. Amīr 'Abd Allāh (A.H. 1006/1598), see p. 981 *supra*, where another work (?) of the same kind is mentioned.

N. BIOGRAPHY : (*m*) PLACES (7) BARNĀWAH

1501. For the *Chiṣẖtīyah i bihiṣẖtīyah* of 'Alā' al-Dīn M. Barnāwī, which was written about 1066/1655–6 and deals more especially with the Chiṣẖtīs of Barnāwah and Rāprī, see p. 1007 *supra*.

[1] Amrōhah is an old town 19 miles W.N.W. of Murādābād. Several of the celebrities mentioned by Āl i Ḥasan are mentioned also in the official *Gazetteer of Moradabad* (Allahabad, 1911).

N. BIOGRAPHY: (*m*) PLACES (8) BENARES

1502. For the *Riyāḍ al-wifāq* (a chronogram = 1229/1814) of Dhū 'l-Faqār 'Alī Khān "Mast", which is concerned mainly with contemporaries of the author connected with Calcutta and Benares, see p. 885 *supra*.

N. BIOGRAPHY: (*m*) PLACES (9) BHAKKAR (BHAK'HAR)

1503. For the *Manba' al-ansāb*, an account of the Saiyids of Bhak'har written by S. Mu'īn al-Ḥaqq some time after 830/1426–7 and enlarged probably about the close of the 10/16th century by S. 'Alī Ghaḍanfar, see p. 949 *supra*. The *Taḥrīr al-mu'taqid* (p. 946) and the *Ḥālāt i Shāh 'Uthmān Akbar* (p. 952) are concerned with the same family.

N. BIOGRAPHY: (*m*) PLACES (10) BIHĀR

1504. For the *Tadhkirat al-kirām* of M. Abū 'l-Ḥayāt P'hulwārī, which was written in 1249/1833–4 and deals with Bihārī *shaikhs*, see p. 1040 *supra*.

1505. S. M. **Jawād Ḥusain.**

Tārīkh i Ḥasan, a short history of Islām in India, followed by notices of the Saiyids of Bihār: **Cawnpore** 1329/1912*.

N. BIOGRAPHY: (*m*) PLACES (11) BĪJĀPŪR

1506. For the *Rauḍat al-auliyā'*, a *tadhkirah* of the saints of Bījāpūr, by M. Ibrāhīm, see p. 1060 *supra*.

N. BIOGRAPHY: (*m*) PLACES (12) BILGRĀM

1507. In 1110/1698–9 (according to the Āṣafīyah catalogue) S. **Junaid** b. S. Darwēsh M. Ḥātim **Bilgrāmī** composed his

Junaidīyah or *Nasab-nāmah i sādāt i Bilgrām u Bārhah*, on the genealogy of the Saiyids of Bilgrām [1] and Bārhah [2]: **Rieu** iii

[1] The genealogies of the Saiyids of Bilgrām form the subject of an Urdu work, *Rauḍat al-kirām shajarah i Sādāt i Bilgrām* (236 pp.), by S. Waṣī al-Ḥasan (Gōrak'hpūr 1920).

[2] Cf. p. **1086** n. **1** *supra*.

1021*b* (extracts only? Circ. A.D. 1850), **Āṣafīyah** ii p. 1778 no. 115 (A.H. 1309/1891–2).

1508. For the *Ma'āthir al-kirām tārīkh i Bilgrām* completed in 1166/1752–3 by Ghulām-'Alī " Āzād " Bilgrāmī, see p. 1025 *supra*. For the same author's *Sarw i āzād*, which includes some biographies of Bilgrāmīs, see p. 864 *supra*.

1509. **Ghulām-Ḥasan " Thamīn "** Ṣiddīqī Farshūrī[1] **Bilgrāmī** has already been mentioned (p. 620 *supra*) as the author of an account of Aḥmad Shāh Abdālī's third invasion of India written in 1197/1783 at the request of Jonathan Scott.

Sharā'if i 'Uthmānī, biographies of eminent Bilgrāmīs belonging to the 'Uthmānī clan, composed in 1179/1765–6 and written primarily to correct alleged mis-statements in " Āzād's " *Ma'āthir al-kirām* [which was completed in 1166/1752–3 : see p. 1025 *supra*] : **Ivanow** 277 (many blank spaces. A.D. 1875), **I.O.** 3913, **Āṣafīyah** iii p. 164 no. 202.

1510. For the *Tabṣirat al-nāẓirīn*, composed in 1182/1768 by Mīr S. Muḥammad b. 'Abd al-Jalīl Bilgrāmī and dealing mainly with events in the lives of Bilgrāmī Saiyids, see p. 713 *supra*.

1511. Other works :—

(1) *Musajjalāt fī ta'rīkh al-quḍāt*, on the Qāḍīs of Bilgrām, by Qāḍī Aḥmad Allāh Bilgrāmī, commonly known as (*'urf*) M. 'Uthmān b. Qāḍī M. Iḥsān, who, according to Raḥmān 'Alī (p. 15), was Qāḍī of Bilgrām until 1196/1782 : **I.O.** 3913*b*.

(2) *Naẓm al-la'ālī fī nasab āl 'Alā' al-Dīn al-'ālī*, or, chronogrammatically, *Subḥat al-durr wa-'l-yawāqīt*, on the genealogy of the Saiyids of Bilgrām, by S. M. b. S. Ghulām-Nabī b. al-Saiyid al-shahīd al-musammā bi-'l-Arshad : **Āṣafīyah** iii p. 720.

N. BIOGRAPHY : (*m*) PLACES
(13) BUKHĀRĀ ETC.

1512. For the *Kitāb i Mullā-zādah*, which was written probably

[1] In the bibliography to the unsigned article on Bilgrām in the *Ency. Isl.* this word is [correctly ?] spelt Firshawrī. FRSHWR (vocalization ?) is an old form of the name Peshawar (cf. 'Iṣāmī *Futūḥ al-salāṭīn* p. 401, l. 7863 (also ll. 7866, 7870), *Ṭabaqāt i Akbarī* i p. 37[3]), but this may have nothing to do with Ghulām-Ḥasan's *nisbah*.

in the 9th/15th century by Aḥmad b. Maḥmūd called (*madʻū*) Muʻīn al-fuqarā' and which contains notices of s̲h̲aik̲h̲s and others buried at Buk̲h̲ārā, see p. 953 *supra*.

1513. For the *Manāqib i mazārāt i Buk̲h̲ārā-yi s̲h̲arīf* see p. 1058 *supra*.

For the *Ṭabaqāt i mas̲h̲āyik̲h̲ i Naqs̲h̲bandīyah i Buk̲h̲ārā* see p. 1064 *supra*.

1514. For the *Mud̲h̲akkir i aḥbāb* (a chronogram = 974/1566–7) of " Nit̲h̲ārī ", which contains notices of 275 poets who lived in Buk̲h̲ārā or its dependencies after the time of Mīr ʻAlī-S̲h̲īr, see p. 802 *supra*.

1515. **ʻAbd al-Karīm b. Maḥmūd Qāḍī** b. Nūr al-Dīn M. Qāḍī, known as Qāḍī **Ik̲h̲tiyār,** began in 1009/1600–1 :—

'Awālim al-asrār fī g̲h̲arā'ib al-asfār (beginning: *Majmūʻah i ʻAwālim al-a. fī g̲h̲. al-a. az ṣādirāt i ʻawālim i āfāqī . . . u bayān i aḥwāl i akābir i mahrūsah i Buk̲h̲ārā*), an interesting account of travels in Transoxiana and K̲h̲urāsān, to Kābul, etc., together with biographies of distinguished men, s̲h̲aik̲h̲s, poets, and others, who lived at Buk̲h̲ārā in the author's time : **Ethé** 2723.

1516. For the *Tārīk̲h̲ i Jahāngīrī*, which was begun in 1034/ 1625 by " Muṭribī " al-Aṣamm al-Samarqandī and which deals with poets of Transoxiana, see p. 814 *supra*.

1517. For the *Tārīk̲h̲ i Mīr Saiyid S̲h̲arīf Rāqim*, a collection of chronograms relating to kings, divines, men of letters, etc., who flourished in Central Asia from the birth of Tīmūr in 736/1336 to 1054/1644–5, see p. 377 *supra*.

1518. For the *Maṭlab al-ṭālibīn* of Abū 'l-ʻAbbās M. Ṭālib, which was written about 1056/1646 and deals with Jūybārī s̲h̲aik̲h̲s, see p. 1004 *supra*.

1519. For the *T̲h̲amarāt al-mas̲h̲āyik̲h̲* of S. Zindah ʻAlī, which was written towards the end of the eleventh/seventeenth century and deals with Central Asian s̲h̲aik̲h̲s of various orders, see p. 1012 *supra*.

1520. For the *Tuḥfat al-aḥbāb* of Raḥmat Allāh " Wāḍiḥ ",

which deals with Central Asian poets of the nineteenth century, see p. 916 *supra*.

1521. For the *Afḍal al-tadhkār*, notices of Central Asian poets of the nineteenth century written in 1322/1904 by "Afḍal" Makhdūm i Pīrmastī, see p. 917 *supra*.

N. BIOGRAPHY : (*m*) PLACES (14) CALCUTTA

1522. For the *Riyāḍ al-wifāq* (a chronogram = 1229/1814) of Dhū 'l-Faqār 'Alī Khān "Mast", which is concerned mainly with contemporaries of the author connected with Calcutta and Benares, see p. 885 *supra*.

N. BIOGRAPHY : (*m*) PLACES (15) THE CARNATIC

1523. For the *Guldastah i Karnāṭak* (a chronogram = 1210/1795–6) of "Rā'iq", see p. 890 *supra*.

1524. For the *Ṣubḥ i waṭan*, completed in 1257/1841, ostensibly by Nawwāb M. Ghauth Khān, see p. 898 *supra*.

1525. For the *Ishārāt i Bīnish* (a chronogram = 1265/1848–9), see p. 904.

N. BIOGRAPHY : (*m*) PLACES (16) CHITTAGONG

1526. **'Abd al-'Alī Islāmābādī** b. Minnat 'Alī was born in 1262/1846, presumably at Chittagong. Educated at the Calcutta Madrasah, he was appointed Professor of Persian in that institution and subsequently became Professor of Arabic in the Hoogly Madrasah.

Ṣaḥīfat al-a'māl wa-mir'āt al-aḥwāl, a history of Islāmābād (i.e. Chittagong) and its famous men : **Āgrah** [1889°] (pp. 276).

[Raḥmān 'Alī p. 124 ; M. Idrīs p. 47.]

N. BIOGRAPHY : (*m*) PLACES (17) DAULATĀBĀD

1527. For the *Rauḍat al-auliyā'*, which was written in 1161/1748 by Mīr Ghulām-'Alī "Āzād" Bilgrāmī and which is concerned with ten saints buried in the cemetery called Rauḍah or Khuldābād near Daulatābād, see p. 1024 *supra*.

N. BIOGRAPHY: (*m*) PLACES (18) THE DECCAN

1528. For the *Tuḥfat al-shu'arā'*, written in 1165/1751–2 by Afḍal Bēg Khān Qāqshāl Aurangābādī and dealing with poets of the Deccan who flourished under Niẓām al-Mulk I, see p. 849 *supra*.

N. BIOGRAPHY: (*m*) PLACES (19) DELHI

1529. For the *Kalimāt al-ṣādiqīn*, completed in 1023/1614 by M. Ṣādiq Kashmīrī Hamadānī and dealing with saints buried at Delhi, see p. 985 *supra*.

1530. For the *Rauḍah i aqṭāb* (a chronogram = 1124/1712) of M. Bulāq, which is concerned with Quṭb al-Dīn Bakhtyār Kākī and some saints buried near him, see p. 1014 *supra*.

1531. For the *Dhikr i jamī' i auliyā' i Dihlī* (a chronogram = 1140/1727–8) of M. Ḥabīb Allāh Akbarābādī, see p. 1019 *supra*.

1532. Nawwāb **Dargāh-Qulī Khān Sālār-Jang** Mu'taman al-Daulah [afterwards Mu'taman al-Mulk] b. Khānadān-Qulī Khān b. Naurōz-Qulī Khān was the great-great-grandson of Khānadān-Qulī Khān Dhū 'l-Qadr Turkmān Būrbūr, who settled in India in the reign of Shāh-Jahān. Born in 1122/1710 at Sangamnēr,[1] at which place his father was for a time *Waqā'i'-nigār* (*Khizānah* p. 222 antepenult.), he entered the service of Nawwāb Niẓām al-Mulk Āṣaf-Jāh and at the age of twenty became one of the Nawwāb's suite. He accompanied Āṣaf-Jāh to Delhi [in 1150/1737] and while there wrote the *Risālah i Sālār-Jang*. In the reign of Nawwāb Ṣalābat-Jang [1164–75/1750–62] he was given the rank of *Shash-hazārī*, the title of Mu'taman al-Daulah, and the Governorship (*Ṣūbah-dārī*) of Aurangābād. Nawwāb Niẓām-'Alī [1175–1217/1762–1802] promoted him to the rank of *Haft-hazārī* and conferred upon him the *Māhī-marātib* and the title of Mu'taman al-Mulk. In 1179/1765 he was dismissed from the Governorship of Aurangābād, and on 18 Jumādā I 1180/22 October 1766 he died.

(***Risālah i Sālār-Jang***), or (***Ābādī i Dihlī***), (beg. *Waqtī*

[1] Presumably SNGMYR (*Khizānah* p. 223[1]) should be so emended. Sangamnēr is 49 miles N.W. of Aḥmadnagar.

kih Nawwāb Dargāh-Qulī Khān . . . ba-rafāqat i Nawwāb Niẓām al-Mulk), an account of Delhi, its buildings, pleasure-grounds, festivals, etc., and its contemporary *shaikhs*, poets, singers, and dancers: **Rieu** ii 858*b* (apparently either A.H. 1192/1778 or 1200/1786), **Rehatsek** p. 218 no. 11 (A.H. 1214/1799), **Ross and Browne** 240 (transcribed from the preceding MS. in 1280/1864).

[*Khizānah i ʿāmirah* pp. 221–4; *Ḥadīqat al-ʿālam* ii p. 283 (summarized in Rieu ii p. 858*b*).]

N. BIOGRAPHY: (*m*) PLACES (20) FĀRS

1533. For "Furṣat's" *Āthār i ʿAjam*, which contains numerous notices of celebrities connected with Fārs and other parts of south-western Persia, see p. 353 *supra*.

N. BIOGRAPHY: (*m*) PLACES (21) GUJRĀT (GUJARAT)

1534. For the *Gulzār i abrār* completed in, or about, 1022/1613 by M. Ghauthī and containing biographies of saints, many of whom were Gujrātīs, see p. 984 *supra*.

1535. For the *Makhzan i shuʿarāʾ* (a chronogram = 1268/1851–2), which is a *tadhkirah* of the Urdu poets of Gujrāt by Nūr al-Dīn "Fāʾiq", see p. 904 *supra*.

See also PLACES (2) AHMADĀBĀD above.

N. BIOGRAPHY: (*m*) PLACES (22) ḤAIDARĀBĀD

1536. For the *Mishkāt al-nubuwwah*, an account of the saints of Ḥaidarābād, by S. ʿAlī, see p. 1059 *supra*.

See also PLACES (18) THE DECCAN.

N. BIOGRAPHY: (*m*) PLACES (23) HARĀT

1537. For the *Maqṣad al-iqbāl al-sulṭānīyah* of ʿAbd Allāh b. ʿAbd al-Raḥmān al-Ḥusainī see p. 356 *supra*. Presumably this is the same work as *Mazārāt i Harāt* by ʿA. A. b. ʿA. al-R. Ḥusainī, Harāt A.H.S. 1310/1931–2 [Lescot].

N. BIOGRAPHY: (*m*) PLACES (24) INDIA

1538. The Arabic work *Subḥat al-marjān fī āthār Hindustān* written in 1177/1763–4 by Mīr Ghulām-ʿAlī "Āzād" Bilgrāmī has already been described (pp. 859-60 *supra*). It can relevantly be mentioned here, since the second *faṣl*, containing biographies of Indian scholars, has been translated into Persian (see p. 860[23] *supra*).

1539. M. ʿAbd al-S̲h̲akūr commonly called **Raḥmān ʿAlī** b. Ḥakīm S̲h̲ēr ʿAlī [1] was born in 1244/1829 at Aḥmadābād Nārah. After his father's death he was brought up by an elder brother at Fatḥpūr. In 1267/1851 he went to the Central Indian State of Rēwān (otherwise Rewa), where the eldest son of the Hindu Rājah, disliking his name ʿAbd al-S̲h̲akūr, changed it to Raḥmān ʿAlī. Having held various offices, including those of Civil Judge and Magistrate of the First Class, he became in 1284/1867-8 a member of the Council of the State. In 1887 he received from the Government of India the title of K̲h̲ān Bahādur. He wrote a number of works, most of them in Urdu.

Tad̲h̲kirah i ʿulamāʾ i Hind, or *Tuḥfat al-fuḍalāʾ fī tarājim al-kumalāʾ*, biographies of ancient and modern Indian scholars: Edition : **Lucknow** 1894°*.

[Raḥmān ʿAlī pp. 258-61 ; M. Idrīs p. 26.]

N. BIOGRAPHY: (m) PLACES (25) ISTĀNBŪL

1540. For the *Ḥujjat al-abrār*, a *mat̲h̲nawī* completed in 996/1588 by S. Murs̲h̲id and dealing with the orders of dervishes at Istānbūl and their heads, see p. 976 *supra*.

N. BIOGRAPHY: (m) PLACES (26) JĀʾIS

1541. For ʿĀbid Ḥusain's *Tārīk̲h̲ i Jāʾis* see p. 713 *supra*.

N. BIOGRAPHY: (m) PLACES (27) JAUNPŪR

1542. **K̲h̲air al-Dīn M. Ilāhābādī,** who died about 1827 (see pp. 520-2 *supra*), has already been mentioned as the author of works entitled *ʿIbrat-nāmah* (see p. 641 *supra*), *Jaunpūr-nāmah* (see p. 698 *supra*), *Guwāliyār-nāmah* (see p. 736 *supra*) and *Tuḥfah i tāzah* (p. 702).

---

[1] For a notice of Ḥakīm S̲h̲ēr ʿAlī see Raḥmān ʿAlī p. 89.

Tadhkirat al-ʿulamā', completed on 25th September, 1801 (15 Jumādā I A.H. 1216), and containing biographies of 28 scholars connected with Jaunpūr together with that of the author, which forms the *Khātimah*: **Ivanow** 203 (19th cent.), **I.O.** 4028 (transcribed in 1903 from the preceding MS.).

Edition with English translation: *Tazkirat-ul-ʿUlama, or, A memoir of the learned men (of Jaunpur) by Mawlana Khair-ud-Din Muhammad of Jaunpur, edited . . . with English translation, notes, etc., by Muhammad Sana Ullah*, **Calcutta** 1934‡.

1543. Munshī **M. Mahdī** b. Khalīl Aḥmad was the head of an old family, which had held the zamīndārī of Mariahu (Maṛiyāhū, Madiyāhū, or Mandiyāhū) near Jaunpūr and the hereditary office of *Qāḍī* since the time of Akbar. He was *Taḥṣīldār* at Mariahu during the Mutiny and protected the treasury and records. He was still living in 1888.

Tadhkirah i Mahdī or (*mulaqqab bah*) *Baḥr al-marām*,[1] a metrical autobiography: **Allahabad** 1888°*.

[*Jaunpūr District Gazetteer* 1908, p. 104.]

1544. S. **Nūr al-Dīn** "Zaidī" **Ẓafarābādī** Jaunpūrī indicates by a chronogram that 1881 was the year in which he composed the first part of his *Tajallī i nūr*.

Tajallī i nūr or (*maʿrūf bah*) *Tadhkirah i mashāhīr i Jaunpūr*, biographies of the famous men of Jaunpūr in three *shigarf-nāmahs* ((1) saints and mystics, (2) scholars and poets, (3) amīrs).

Edition: Pt. I, **Jaunpūr** 1889*, Pt. II, **Jaunpūr** 1900°*. It seems possible that Part III (amīrs) was never written.

See also PLACES (43) ẒAFARĀBĀD.

N. BIOGRAPHY: (m) PLACES (28) KĀSHGHAR

1545. For the *Tadhkirah i Khwājagān*, A Turkī work written in 1182/1768–9 by M. Ṣādiq Kāshgharī, see p. 1026 *supra*.

1546. For the *Majmaʿ al-muḥaqqiqīn*, a history of the Khwājahs of Kāshghar to 1208/1793–4 by M. Ṣādiq Yārkandī, see p. 1035 *supra*.

[1] This is what the author himself calls the work in the last line.

N. BIOGRAPHY: (*m*) PLACES (29) KASHMĪR

1547. For the *Rīshī-nāmah* of Bābā Naṣīb Kashmīrī, who died in 1047/1637, see p. 985 *supra.*

1548. For the *Rīshī-nāmah* of "Bahā" see p. 986 *supra.*

1549. For the *Khawāriq al-sālikīn* (a chronogram = 1109/1697–8), anecdotes of early Ṣūfīs of Kashmīr, etc., by an anonymous author, see p. 1013 *supra.*

1550. For the *Wāqi'āt i Kashmīr* (a chronogram = 1148/1735–6) of M. A'ẕam, which is devoted mainly to biographies of the saints, poets, and scholars of Kashmīr, see p. 683 *supra.*

1551. For the *Taḥā'if al-abrār*, which was completed in 1321/1903–4 by Muḥyī 'l-Dīn "Miskīn" and which deals mainly with saints and other celebrities of Kashmīr, see p. 1052 *supra.*

1552. For the *Rauḍat al-abrār* of Muḥammad al-Dīn Lāhaurī see p. 1060 *supra.*

For spiritual pedigrees of certain *shaikhs* of Kashmīr see pp. 1053 (5) and 1064 (109) *supra.*

N. BIOGRAPHY: (*m*) PLACES (30) KHURĀSĀN

1553. For the *Maṯla' al-shams* of M. Ḥasan Khān Marāghī, which includes notices of Khurāsānī celebrities, see p. 356 *supra.*

N. BIOGRAPHY: (*m*) PLACES (31) KŌL

1554. For the *Ashjār al-jamāl* of M. b. Yār-Muḥammad Kōlawī, which includes notices of some Ṣūfīs of Kōl, see p. 1022 *supra.*

N. BIOGRAPHY: (*m*) PLACES (32) LUCKNOW

1555. For *al-Aghṣān al-arba'ah*, Walī Allāh Lak'hnawī's life of Aḥmad Anwār al-Ḥaqq Farangī-Maḥallī and other descendants of Quṯb al-Dīn Sihālawī, the ancestor of the 'ulamā' of Farangī Maḥall, see p. 1048 *supra.*

N. BIOGRAPHY : (*m*) PLACES (33) MURĀDĀBĀD

1556. For the *Anwār al-ʿārifīn* of M. Ḥusain Murādābādī, which includes notices of some Ṣūfīs buried at Murādābād, see p. 1044 *supra*.

N. BIOGRAPHY : (*m*) PLACES (34) RĀPRĪ

1557. For the *Chishtīyah i bihishtīyah* of ʿAlāʾ al-Dīn M. Barnāwī, which was written about 1066/1655–6 and deals more especially with the Chishtīs of Barnāwah and Rāprī, see p. 1007 *supra*.

N. BIOGRAPHY : (*m*) PLACES (35) SAMARQAND

1558. For *al-Qand fī maʿrifat ʿulamāʾ Samarqand*, see p. 371 *supra*.

For a *Risālah i buzurgān i Samarqand* see p. 1060 *supra*.

N. BIOGRAPHY : (*m*) PLACES (36) SHĪRĀZ

1559. Muʿīn al-Dīn Abū ʾl-Qāsim **Junaid** b. Najm al-Dīn Abī ʾl-Fatḥ Maḥmūd al-ʿUmarī **al-Shīrāzī** was the son of a devout Ṣūfī and preacher who died in 740/1339–40 and the great-grandson of Ṣadr al-Dīn al-Muẓaffar b. M. al-ʿUmarī al-ʿAdawī, author of the *Marmūzāt al-ʿishrīn* (Ḥ. Kh. v p. 500) and many other works, who died in 688/1289. He was himself a *khaṭīb* and must have lived to a very advanced age.

Shadd al-izār fī ḥaṭṭ al-auzār ʿan zuwwār al-mazār, usually called *Hazār mazār*, an Arabic work on the celebrated men buried at Shīrāz written probably in 791/1389, the latest date mentioned : Ḥ. Kh. iv p. 16, **Rieu** Arabic Suppt. 677 (19th cent.), **Majlis** 559.

Persian translation : *Multamas al-aḥibbā khāliṣ min al-riyāʾ* made by the author's son ʿĪsā b. Junaid al-ʿAdawī : **Rieu** i 346*b* (18th cent.).

N. BIOGRAPHY : (*m*) PLACES (37) SHŪSHTAR

1560. For the *Tadhkirah i Shūshtarīyah* of S. ʿAbd Allāh b. Nūr al-Dīn Shūshtarī, which includes notices of celebrated men connected with Shūshtar, see p. 365 *supra*.

1561. **ʿAbd al-Laṭīf** b. Abī Ṭālib b. Nūr al-Dīn b. Niʿmat Allāh al-Ḥusainī al-Mūsawī **al-Shūshtarī**, a Nūrī Saiyid and the nephew of ʿAbd Allāh b. Nūr al-Dīn Shūshtarī (for whom see p. 365 *supra*), was born in 1172/1758–9. After visiting S͟hīrāz, Kirmāns͟hāhān, and Bag͟hdād he left Baṣrah in 1202/1787–8 for Bengal. In 1211/1796–7 he went to Lucknow and in 1214/1799–1800 to Ḥaidarābād, where in 1215–16/1800–2 he wrote his *Tuḥfat al-'ālam*, dedicated to Mīr-'Ālam (for whom see pp. 750–2 *supra*). In 1216/1801–2 he went to Bombay, where he met Abū Ṭālib K͟hān Landanī (for whom see pp. 144–6 *supra*), and in 1219/1804–5 he returned to Ḥaidarābād, where he died in 1220/1806 (see Rieu Suppt. 84 ii).

Tuḥfat al-'ālam, a narrative of the author's life and travels preceded by an account of S͟hūs͟htar, of some neighbouring places and of the Nūrī Saiyids and followed, in some MSS., by an appendix, *Dhail al-Tuḥfah*, written in 1219/1804–5 at the request of Āqā Aḥmad b. M. 'Alī Bihbahānī (for whom see p. 1130 *infra*): **Būhār** 95 (autograph (?), A.H. 1214/1799 (?)), **Edinburgh** 85 (A.H. 1222/1807) **Bodleian** 323 (A.H. 1229/1814), **Bānkīpūr** Suppt. i 1777 (A.H. 1229/1814), **Ivanow** Curzon 98 (defective at both ends. Contains part of the *Dhail*. Early 19th cent.), **Rieu** i 383a (contains the *Dhail*. Early 19th cent.), Suppt. 84 ii (contains the *Dhail*. A.H. 1258/1842), **Leningrad** Univ. 1101 (A.H. 1255/1839. See Romaskewicz p. 4), **I.O.** 4624 (A.H. 1258/1842. See Arberry in *JRAS*. 1939 p. 389), **Ross and Browne** 238 (circ. A.D. 1864), **Blochet** i 646 (contains the *Dhail*. 19th cent.), **Āṣafīyah** i p. 232 no. 634, **Berlin** 98 (contains the *Dhail*), **Majlis** 685 (?), **Rehatsek** p. 69 no. 5.

Editions: **Bombay** 1263/1847 (cf. Rieu i 383b, Zenker i p. 61, and Mas͟hhad iii p. 118. In the last work Ḥaidarābād is given as the place of printing); **Ḥaidarābād** n.d.°; place ? 1297/1880 (Āṣaf. i p. 232 no. 870).

Analyses of the work: (1) Rehatsek pp. 70–1. (2) Rieu i pp. 383–4.

List of 21 poets and theologians whose biographies are given in the work: Ivanow-Curzon p. 101.

N. BIOGRAPHY: (*m*) PLACES (38) SINANDIJ

1562. For the *Ḥadīqah i Amān-Allāhī*, notices of the poets of Sinandij completed in 1265/1848–9 by 'Abd Allāh "Raunaq", see p. 903 *supra*.

N. BIOGRAPHY: (*m*) PLACES (39) SIND

1563. For the *Ḥadīqat al-auliyā'* completed in 1016/1607–8 by 'Abd al-Qādir b. Hāshim, see p. 983 *supra.*

1564. For the *Maqālāt al-shu'arā'* (a chronogram = 1174/1760–1) of 'Alī Shēr " Qāni' " Tattawī see p. 854 *supra.*

1565. For the same author's *Tuḥfat al-kirām* (a chronogram = 1180/1766–7), the third volume of which is concerned to a large extent with celebrities of Sind, see p. 656 *supra.*

1566. For the same author's *Maklī-nāmah* see p. 1031 *supra.*

1567. For the *Tuḥfat al-ṭāhirīn*, written in 1194/1780 by M. A'ẓam T'hattawī, see p. 1028 *supra.*

N. BIOGRAPHY: (*m*) PLACES (40) TABRĪZ

1568. For the *Rauḍah i aṯhār* of " Ḥashrī " Tabrīzī see p. 982 *supra.*

N. BIOGRAPHY: (*m*) PLACES (41) ṬIHRĀN

1569. For the *Jannat al-na'īm* of M. Bāqir Ṭihrānī, see p. 1048 *supra.*

N. BIOGRAPHY: (*m*) PLACES (42) YAZD

1570. For the *Jāmi' i Mufīdī*, which in its third *mujallad* contains numerous notices of famous men of Yazd, see p. 352 *supra.* M. Mufīd Mustaufī wrote also —

An autobiographical memoir " very rich in words and poor in facts " extending over the years 1077–85/1666–75 (beg.: *Ḥ. u s. i bī-qiyās Mālik al-mulkī rā kih rif'at*): **Bodleian** 423 (91 foll.).

1571. For the *Tārīkh i Yazd* of 'Abd al-Ḥusain " Āyatī ", which was completed in 1317/1938–9 and which contains biographies of many Yazdī celebrities, especially poets, see p. 1294 *infra.*

1572. S. **Muḥammad 'Alī b. S. Ja'far Yazdī** after twenty years of unprofitable study in his birthplace Yazd and twenty years of wandering in Persia, Turkey, Arabia, Turkistan, and the Deccan settled in 1226/1811 at Sūrat. He had spent nearly twenty years in service under British patrons (Wm. Forbes, Judge at Sūrat, J. Romer, J. Sutherland [1]) when in 1244/1827 he completed his *Mīzān al-akhlāq* and dedicated it to Sir John Malcolm, the Governor of Bombay.

Mīzān al-akhlāq, a record of the author's life and a eulogy of British rule in India: **Rieu** i 388 (A.H. 1244/1827).

N. BIOGRAPHY: (*m*) PLACES (43) ẒAFARĀBĀD

1573. S. **'Abd al-Aḥad** b. S. Barakat 'Ali **Ẓafarābādī** was living in 1914 and himself corrected the proofs of his *Maẓhar al-aḥadīyah*.

Maẓhar al-aḥadīyah fī bayān al-ansāb [*sic*] ***al-sādāt al-Zaidīyah***, on the genealogy of the Zaidī Saiyids of Ẓafarābād (4¾ miles S.E. of Jaunpūr) from Ādam to the author's time.

Edition: **Jaunpūr** 1914°*.

N. BIOGRAPHY: (*n*) SHĪ'ITES

1574. Qāḍī S. **Nūr Allāh** "Nūrī" [2] b. S. Sharīf b. S. Nūr Allāh Ḥusainī Mar'ashī **Shūshtarī** was born at Shūshtar [3] in 956/1549 (?).[4] In early manhood (*fī mabādi' al-shabāb* [5]) he went

[1] For the last-named see Buckland's *Dictionary of Indian biography*.

[2] *Dar fann i shā'irī kamāl i qudrat u mahārat dāsht takhalluṣ i wai Nūrī būd dar jawāb i qaṣīdah i S. Ḥasan i Ghaznawī qaṣīda'ī guftah kih īn chand bait az ānjāst: Shukr i Khudā kih nūr i ilāhīst rahbaram*, etc. (*Riyāḍ al-shu'arā'* as quoted in *Nujūm al-samā'* p. 12.) The author of the *Nujūm al-samā'* goes on to say *Rāqim al-ḥurūf rā bisyārī az ash'ār i ābdār i ān sulālat al-akhyār ba-naẓar rasīdah.* Cf. Badā'ūnī iii p. 137[16]: *ṭab' i naẓmī dārad u ash'ār i dil-nishīn mī-gūyad.* No *dīwān* or other collection of his poems seems to be recorded in the catalogues, but the list of his works in the *Nujūm al-samā'* includes a *dīwān i qaṣā'id* (p. 16 antepenult.) and a *dīwān i ash'ār* (p. 17[7]).

[3] *Majālis al-mu'minīn* p. 31, l. 10 from foot (*dar ān-diyār i faiḍ-āthār maulid i īn khāksār ast*), *Iḥqāq al-ḥaqq, khātimah*, quoted in *Nujūm al-samā'* p. 10 (*idh ba'da mā rakibtu ghārib al-ightirāb fī mabādi' al-shabāb li-taḥṣīl al-ḥikam wa-takmīl al-fuyūḍ wa-'l-ni'am min waṭanī Shūshtar al-maḥrūsah ilā 'l-Mashhad al-muqaddasat al-Riḍawīyat al-ma'nūsah ramānī zamānī ilā 'l-Hind al-manḥūsah qāmat tilka 'l-shauhā' al-ma'yūsah 'alā 'zdiyād ghammī*, etc.).

[4] *Nujūm al-samā'* p. 13[2], *Shahīd i thālith* p. 4. It is not clear whether this date has good authority.

[5] See the passage from the *Iḥqāq al-ḥaqq* quoted in n. 3 above. Mirzā M. Hādī says, on the authority of a note in an old MS. of the *Maṣā'ib al-Nawāṣib*, that he went to Mashhad in 979/1571–2. In that year he must have reached the age of twenty-three, if 956 is the correct date for his birth.

to Ma͟shhad and he subsequently settled in India. He was there apparently in 992/1584, if not earlier, since his work *al-Jalālīyah*[1] completed in that year (I.Ḥ. 775) is stated by I'jāz Ḥusain to have been written in the time of Jalāl al-Dīn M. Akbar Bahādur, Sulṭān of Delhi, a statement based doubtless on the author's own words. In Rajab 993/July 1585 [2] he began at Lahore his best known work, the *Majālis al-mu'minīn*. In 995/1587 he wrote and dedicated to the K͟hān i K͟hānān 'Abd al-Raḥīm K͟hān[3] *al-'As͟harat al-kāmilat al-K͟hān-i-K͟hānānīyah* (I.Ḥ. 2116).

It must have been in 994/1586 or 995/1587[4] that Akbar, to whom he had been presented by Ḥakīm Abū 'l-Fatḥ Gīlānī,[5] appointed him, though a S͟hī'ite, *Qāḍī* of Lahore in place of the aged S͟h. Mu'īn, who after falling down through infirmity in the imperial *darbār* had been retired and who died in 995/1587.[6] 'Abd al-Qādir Badā'ūnī speaks in high praise of his integrity as a judge, his strict control of corrupt *muftīs* and *muḥtasibs*, and his personal piety and learning. His last years seem to have been spent in Āgrah, since it was there that he completed his *Iḥqāq al-ḥaqq* in 1014/1605 and there that he was flogged to death by order of Jahāngīr on 18 Jumādā ii 1019/7 Sept. 1610. Authorities disagree concerning the precise reason for his execution. According to the *Amal al-āmil* (p. 73[6]) he was put to death *bi-sabab ta'līf Iḥqāq al-ḥaqq*, and this may well be correct. Not only does that work indicate a fanatical hatred of Sunnism, but as Horovitz has shown, it contains at least one passage which Jahāngīr might have considered personally offensive. The statement in the *Riyāḍ al-s͟hu'arā'* that the cause of his undoing was the evidence of his S͟hī'ism provided by the *Majālis al-mu'minīn* is highly improbable. As Horovitz observes, his

[1] Presumably so called in allusion to Akbar's *laqab*.

[2] Cf. Rieu i p. 338*a*, where it is recorded that "at the end [of Add. 23,541, Rieu i p. 337*a*] is a marginal note, apparently transcribed from the author's autograph, stating that the work had been commenced in Lahore, in Rajab, A.H. 993, and completed on the 23rd of Zulka'dah, A.H. 1010".

[3] For whom see pp. 533 and 553 *supra*.

[4] Akbar reached Lahore on 27 May, 1586 (see *Akbar-nāmah* tr. Beveridge iii p. 748) and he was there until 1589 (*ibid.* pp. 817–18).

[5] For whom see p. 1110[2] *supra*. He was a brother of Ḥakīm Humām, who has been mentioned on p. 119 *supra*.

[6] Badā'ūnī iii p. 96.

Shī'ism was no secret [1] and would in itself have been no sufficient ground for execution.[2] Another account says that he incurred Jahāngīr's wrath by a disparaging remark about the latter's patron saint Sh. Salīm Chishtī.[3] In any case Nūr Allāh is regarded by the Shī'ites as a martyr and those in India call him *al-Shahīd al-thālith*.[4]

Of his numerous works the lists given in the *Nujūm al-samā'* and in M. Hādī's *Shahīd i thālith* contain 89 and 109 titles respectively. They include a number of *ḥawāshī* on well-known text-books, but few of them seem to have become popular. Concerning those mentioned by Brockelmann (*Sptbd.* ii pp. 607–8) it may be noted that the *Maṣā'ib al-nawāṣib* (I.H. 2954) is preserved also at the India Office (Arab. MSS. Cat. ii no. 2158) and a Persian translation of it by M. Ashraf at Mashhad (I *fṣl.* i no. 260), the *Iḥqāq al-ḥaqq* (I.H. 111) also at the India Office (Arab. MSS. Cat. ii no. 2149), the British Museum (Ellis-Edwards p. 8), Bānkīpūr (x 623), and the R.A.S.B. (Ashraf 'Alī, Arab. Cat. p. 23. 3 copies), and a Persian translation of it at Bānkīpūr (xiv 1332), and the *Ḥāshiyah 'alā tafsīr al-Baiḍāwī* also at Calcutta (A.S.B. Govt. Coll. 1903–7 p. 16). The *Sirāj al-qulūb wa-'ilāj al-dhunūb* mentioned by Brockelmann as a work of Nūr Allāh's is by Zain al-Dīn al-Ma'barī (cf. Sarkis *Dictionnaire encyclopédique de bibliographie arabe* col. 1762). Nūr Allāh's annotations on the fifth *maqṣad* (*al-Imāmah*) of al-Qūshjī's commentary (*al-Sharḥ al-jadīd*, Brockelmann i p. 509[17], *Sptbd.* i p. 926[12]) on Naṣīr al-Dīn al-Ṭūsī's *Tajrīd al-'aqā'id*) are preserved at the India Office (Loth 471 xv). Badā'ūnī describes Nūr Allāh as *ṣāḥib i taṣānīf i lā'iqah*, but he specifies only a *tauqī'* "beyond all praise"

[1] Cf. Badā'ūnī iii p. 137 : *agarchih Shī'ī-madhhab ast.*

[2] There were, of course, many Shī'ites among the prominent men of Jahāngīr's time in India.

[3] Cf. *JASB.* 1875 p. 116.

[4] That the third place among the martyrs was still regarded as vacant by some at least of the Shī'ites of Persia in the 19th century is shown by the fact that the title *Shahīd i thālith* was given to Ḥājjī Mullā M. Taqī Burghānī, who was assassinated by a Bābī in 1848 (see *Qiṣaṣ al-'ulamā'* p. 19 seq. ; *Nujūm al-samā'* pp. 407–11 ; *Aḥsan al-wadī'ah* pp. 30–5 ; *Tārīkh i jadīd* pp. 274–80 ; Browne *Lit. Hist.* iv p. 421 ; Brockelmann *Sptbd.* ii p. 829 ; etc.). For the *Shahīd i awwal* see *Majālis al-mu'minīn* p. 249 ; *Lu'lu'atā 'l-Baḥrain* pp. 142–8 ; Brockelmann i 108, *Sptbd.* ii p. 131 and for the *Shahīd i thānī* p. *infra.* In the *Nujūm al-samā'*, p. 330, the title *Shahīd i rābi'* is given to Mīrzā M. Mahdī b. Hidāyat Allāh Mūsawī Iṣfahānī Mashhadī.

(*kih az ḥaiyiz i ta'rīf u tauṣīf bīrūn-ast*) on the undotted [1] *tafsīr* of " Faiḍī ".

Majālis al-mu'minīn, begun in Rajab 993/1585 at Lahore and completed on 23 Dhū 'l-Qa'dah 1010/1602,[2] biographies of eminent Shī'ites (including a number who according to the author passed as Sunnites though they were really Shī'ites practising *taqīyah*) divided into a *fātiḥah* (on the term Shī'ah) and twelve *majālis* ((1) places with Shī'ite associations, p. 11, (2) some Shī'ite tribes and families, p. 52, (3) Shī'ite contemporaries of the Prophet, p. 66, (4) Shī'ites of the next generation (Tābi'ūn), p. 118, (5) Shī'ite scholars of the succeeding generations, p. 141, (6) Ṣūfīs, p. 255, (7) philosophers, p. 329, (8) Shī'ite kings and Shī'ite dynasties, p. 354, (9) governors, generals, etc., p. 420, (10) *wazīrs* and calligraphists,[3] p. 433, (11) Arab poets, p. 458, (12) Persian poets, p. 496) : I.H. 2738, **I.O.** D.P. 745 (A.H. 1016/1608), 732 (breaks off in *Majlis* v. A.H. 1051/1641–2 (earlier part only)), **Ethé** 704 (n.d.), 2829 ii (fragments), **I.O.** 3834, 3869, **Lindesiana** p. 207 no. 363 (circ. A.D. 1600), **Bānkīpūr** vii 720 (A.H. 1045/1635), 721 (18th cent.), **Berlin** 601 (A.H. 1051/1641), 602 (defective), **Leningrad** Univ. 1039 (A.H. 1052/1642–3. See Romaskewicz p. 13), **Mashhad** iii p. 100 (A.H. 1054/1644–5), **Majlis** 556 (A.H. 1058/1648), **Rieu** i 337*a* (17th cent.), 338*a* (17th cent.), 338*a* (17th cent.), 338*b* (17th cent.), **Ivanow** 276 (1st 5 *majālis*. 17th cent.), 1st Suppt. 773 (last 6 *majālis*. A.H. 1077/1667), **Bodleian** 367 (n.d.), 368 (A.H. 1102/1690) 369 (n.d.), 370 (n.d.), **Blochet** i 429 (A.H. 1104/1692), 430 (defective at end. 17–18th cent.), **Edinburgh** 244 (A.H. 1157/1744, copied from a MS. of 1028/1618), **As'ad** 1280, **'Umūmīyah** 5148.

Editions : **Ṭihrān** 1268/1852° (unpaginated), 1299/1881–2‡.

[1] *Tauqī'ī bar tafsīr i muhmal i Sh. Faiḍī nawishtah.* Several orientalists have misunderstood the word *muhmal* and spoken of the " worthless " *tafsīr* of " Faiḍī ". The peculiarity of " Faiḍī's " *tafsīr*, the *Sawāṭi' al-ilhām* (Brockelmann ii p. 417, *Sptbd.* ii p. 610), is that it consists entirely of words containing no dotted (*manqūṭ*) letters. His *Mawārid al-kilam wa-silk durar al-ḥikam* is another specimen of this kind of composition.

[2] The authority for these dates is a marginal note " apparently transcribed from the author's autograph " at the end of the B.M. MS. Add. 23, 541. Mirzā M. Hādī gives 990/1582 as the date of composition, and so does E. G. Browne (on what authority ?).

[3] The calligraphists are Ibn al-Bawwāb (p. 456), Mīr 'Alī Tabrīzī, Sulṭān-'Alī Mashhadī and Mīr 'Alī Mashhadī.

[Biography of his grandfather, S. Nūr Allāh b. M.-Shāh Shūshtarī, in *Majālis al-mu'minīn* pp. 223–5; brief autobiographical passage in *Iḥqāq al-ḥaqq*, *khātimah* (quoted in Goldziher's *Beiträge zur Literaturgeschichte* (see below) pp. 486–8, *Nujūm al-samā'* pp. 10–11, *Shahīd i thālith* (see below) pp. 26–30); *Ā'īn i Akbarī* p. 234 (only his name in a list), Blochmann's trans. p. 545 (where a few facts are added from unspecified sources); *Ṭabaqāt i Akbarī* ii p. 468 (only *Imrūz* [i.e. in 1002 presumably] *ba-qaḍā-yi Lāhaur mashghūlast u ba-diyānat u amānat u faḍā'il u kamālāt ittiṣāf dārad*); Badā'ūnī *Muntakhhab al-tawārīkh* iii 137–8; *Mir'āt al-'ālam* (among the *'ulamā'* at the end of *Ārāyish* vii); *Amal al-āmil* p. 73; *Riyāḍ al-shu'arā'* (the passage, or parts of it, quoted in *Nujūm al-samā'* pp. 12–13, 14–16, and thence, so far as the account of the martyrdom is concerned, in *Der Islam* iii pp. 66–7); *Tadhkirah i Shūshtar* p. 36; *Khulāṣat al-afkār* no. 290; *Makhzan al-gharā'ib* no. 2821; *Rauḍāt al-jannāt* iv pp. 222–3; *Nujūm al-samā'* pp. 9–17; I. Goldziher *Beiträge zur Literaturgeschichte der Śî'â und der sunnitischen Polemik* (Sitzungsberichte der K. Akademie der Wissenschaften [zu Wien], phil.-hist. Classe, 78. Bd., Vienna 1874) pp. 486–513 (on the *Iḥqāq al-ḥaqq* mainly. A review of the *Beiträge* was published in *ZDMG*. 29 (1876) pp. 673–81 by O. Loth, who added some details); Rieu i 337; Raḥmān 'Alī p. 245; *Taqijja, von J. Horovitz* (in *Der Islam* iii (1912) pp. 63–7, where the text of 'Alī-Qulī Khān "Wālih's" account of the martyrdom is quoted from the *Nujūm al-samā'*); *Shahīd i thālith*, an Urdu biography by Mirzā M. Hādī "'Azīz" Lak'hnawī, Lucknow 1916* (photograph of the tomb as frontispiece); *Ṣaḥīfah i nūr*, an Urdu biography by S. Ṣaghīr Ḥasan "Shams" Zaidī Wāsiṭī, Delhi 1919*; Būhār Arabic Cat. pp. 124–7; Bānkīpūr viii pp. 161–2; *Ency. Isl.* under Nūr Allāh (Hidayet Hosain); Brockelmann *Sptbd.* ii pp. 607–8.]

1575. **Aḥmad b. M. 'Alī** b. M. Bāqir al-Iṣfahānī commonly called (*al-mashhūr bi-*) **al-Bihbahānī**,[1] a member of the Majlisī family which produced several famous Shī'ite theologians,[2] was

[1] The first syllable of this *nisbah* is vocalized with a *kasrah* on the margin of *Rauḍāt al-jannāt* p. 123.

[2] For the most famous of these, M. Bāqir b. M. Taqī al-Majlisī, see pp. 196–8 *supra*; Brockelmann *Sptbd.* ii pp. 572–4.

born at Kirmān<u>sh</u>āhān in 1191/1777. His father, a bitter enemy of the Ṣūfīs, whom he denounced in his *Risālah i <u>Kh</u>airātīyah* (Rieu i p. 33*b*), was " the chief priest of Kermanshah ", whom Sir John Malcolm met in 1800 (*History of Persia*, London 1829, ii pp. 271, 297–8) and who died in 1216/1801–2 (see *Mir'āt al-aḥwāl i jahān-numā, Maṭlab* 4 ; *Rauḍāt al-jannāt* iv pp. 121–2 ; *Qiṣaṣ al-'ulamā'* p. 157, in the notice of his father). Aḥmad b. M. 'Alī had visited the Mesopotamian sanctuaries and various towns in Persia before leaving Ma<u>sh</u>had in 1219/1804–5 on the journey which took him via Bandar i 'Abbās, Ṣuḥār, and Masqaṭ to Bombay in Ṣafar 1220/1805. From Bombay he went to Ḥaidarābād (Deccan) and, among other places, Calcutta (1221/1806), Mur<u>sh</u>idābād, 'Aẓīmābād (Patna), Faiḍābād (Fyzabad) (1222/1807), Lucknow, Faiḍābād again (1223/1808), 'Aẓīmābād again, Mur<u>sh</u>idābād again, Jahāngīrnagar (i.e. Dacca) and again 'Aẓīmābād, where he wrote his autobiography in 1224–5/1809–10. A list of his own works, nineteen in number, is given in the *Mir'āt al-aḥwāl i jahān-numā* (*Maṭlab* v, *maqṣad* 2, near the end) and is quoted in the Bānkīpūr Catalogue (vii pp. 184–5). Of the *Tuḥfat al-muḥibbīn* (no. 9, composed at Faiḍābād) and the *Tanbīh al-<u>gh</u>āfilīn* (no. 15, composed at Lucknow in 1222/1807 = I.Ḥ. 709, on the *a<u>kh</u>bārīs* and *'ulamā'* suspected of Ṣūfism) there are MSS. at Bānkīpūr (xiv nos. 1321 and 1322). The *Risālah i wilādat u wafāt i <u>Ch</u>ahārdah Ma'ṣūm* (= no. 12 (?), I.Ḥ. 1542) is preserved at Calcutta (Ivanow 2nd Suppt. 1063 (2)). A later work, the *Sabīl al-najāt* completed at 'Aẓīmābād in 1225/1810 or 1226/1811 and dedicated to M. 'Alī <u>Kh</u>ān Qājār, is preserved at Calcutta in two copies (Ivanow 1128 and Ivanow-Curzon 392).

Mir'āt al-aḥwāl i jahān-numā, an account of the author's ancestors and relations, of his own life and travels, and of the persons whom he met, completed (so far as the first *mujallad*, the only one extant,[1] is concerned) in 1225/1810 at 'Aẓīmābād [i.e. Patna], dedicated to M. 'Alī <u>Kh</u>ān Qājār [Fatḥ-'Alī <u>Sh</u>āh's eldest son, d. 1237/1821 [2]] and divided into five *maṭlabs*

[1] It will be observed that in this volume the narrative is carried down to the time of composition.

[2] 26 Ṣafar 1237. See *Rauḍat al-ṣafā-yi Nāṣirī* ix fol. 124*b*, l. 21.

((1) M. Taqī b. Maqṣūd ʿAlī Majlisī[1] and his descendants, (2) M. Bāqir b. M. Taqī Majlisī,[2] (3) M. Ṣāliḥ b. Aḥmad Māzandarānī,[3] pupil and son-in-law of M. Taqī, (4) M. Bāqir b. M. Akmal Iṣfahānī Bihbahānī,[4] grandson of M. Ṣāliḥ and grandfather of the author, (5) the author's memoirs in three *maqṣads*, (*a*) from his birth to his landing at Bombay, (*b*) his life in India, (*c*) account of Europe and the English) and a *Khātimah* (advice to kings and rulers and a sketch of Persian history from the decline of the Ṣafawīs to the author's time): **Rieu** i 385*a* (A.H. 1225/1810), Suppt. 131 (A.H. 1281/1864, containing on the margins of foll. 69–79 some additional notices written in Nāṣir al-Dīn Shāh's reign by M. Ṣādiq b. S. M. Mahdī b. Amīr S. ʿAlī), **Bānkīpūr** vii 628 (lacking the sketch of recent Persian history at end of *Khātimah*. 19th cent.) 629 (A.H. 1225/1810–11), **Būhār** 96 (A.H. 1225/1810–11), **I.O.** D.P. 748 (not later than A.H. 1226/1811), **I.O.** 3941 (defective at both ends and damaged. 19th cent.), **Ivanow** 278 (A.H. 1227/1812), 2nd Suppt. 935 (lacks *Maqṣad* 3 of *Maṭlab* v and *Khātimah*. Mid-19th cent.), **Āṣafīyah** i p. 252 no. 195, **Nadhīr Aḥmad** 71 (S. Zain al-ʿĀbidīn, Murshidābād).

[Rieu i pp. 385–6; *Nujūm al-samāʾ* pp. 382–6 (based on the *Mirʾāt al-aḥwāl*); Bānkīpūr vii pp. 180–5.]

1576. In 1231/1816 an anonymous author dedicated to Ghāzī al-Dīn Ḥaidar, King of Oudh,

Āʾīnah i ḥaqq-numā, notices of contemporary Shīʿite scholars, especially S. Dildār ʿAlī,[5] his teachers and pupils and some persons who visited Lucknow in his time: **I.O.** D.P. 259 (*b*), **Āṣafīyah** ii p. 1330, iii p. 182, **Bānkīpūr** Suppt. ii 2062 (19th cent).

1577. **M. ʿAlī b. Ḥājjī M. Ḥasan** known as Hindī went from Persia to India in 1193/1779 and returned home after an absence of thirty-seven years, fifteen of which were spent in the service

[1] Cf. *Luʾluʾatā ʾl-Baḥrain* pp. 49–50; *Rauḍāt al-jannāt* pp. 129–31; *Qiṣaṣ al-ʿulamāʾ* pp. 181–3; Browne *Lit. Hist.* iv p. 409.

[2] See pp. 196–8 *supra*; Brockelmann *Sptbd.* ii pp. 572–4.

[3] Cf. *Rauḍāt al-jannāt* p. 331, *Qiṣaṣ al-ʿulamāʾ* pp. 179–80; *Nujūm al-samāʾ* p. 106; Brockelmann *Sptbd.* ii p. 578.

[4] Cf. *Rauḍāt al-jannāt* pp. 123–4, *Qiṣaṣ al-ʿulamāʾ* pp. 157–61; Brockelmann *Sptbd.* ii p. 504.

[5] For whom see Raḥmān ʿAli p. 60; Brockelmann *Sptbd.* II p. 852.

of Nawwāb Āṣaf al-Daulah (Nawwāb-Wazīr of Oudh 1189–1212/1775–97) and those from 1227/1812 onwards (evidently, therefore, only two or three) in that of the Governor General.[1]

Majmaʿ al-nuqūl, stories of persons who honoured the memory of al-Ḥusain by means of *taʿziyahs*, pilgrimages to Karbalā', and lamentation (*taʿziyah-dārān u zawwārān u giryah-kunandagān i Saiyid al-Shuhadā'*): **Berlin** 1020.

1578. Mīrzā M. **Ḥaidar-Shukōh** b. Mīrzā M. Kām-bakhsh Bahādur b. Mīrzā M. Sulaimān-Shukōh b. Muḥammad Shāh, apparently a great-grandson of the Mogul Emperor Muḥammad Shāh (1131–61/1719–48), flourished in the third quarter of the 13th/19th century.

Majmūʿah i Ḥaidar-Shukōh (beginning: *Fātiḥah i kull i kalām . . . ammā baʿd īn Shīʿī i maurūthī M. Ḥaidar-Shukōh b. Mīrzā M. Kām-bakhsh*, etc.), memoirs, correspondence (some of the letters being dated 1270/1853–4), and a declaration of allegiance to Shīʿism, which, according to the author, was the faith of the earlier Indian Tīmūrids: **Ivanow** 2nd Suppt. 930 (21 foll., defective at end. Late 19th cent.).

1579. **M. b. Sulaimān** b. M. Rafīʿ b. ʿAbd al-Muṭṭalib b. ʿAlī **al-Tunakābunī**[2] was born in 1234/1818–19 or 1235/1819–20.[3] His father, a scholar and physician, was for some years in attendance on Muḥammad-Qulī Mīrzā, Governor of Māzandarān. It is stated in the Mashhad catalogue (iii p. 142) on the authority of Ḥājj S. M. (Mujtahid i) Tunakābunī that M. b. Sulaimān died in 1308/1890–1. His works, of which he gives a list in the *Qiṣaṣ al-ʿulamā'*, amounted to more than two hundred. Of these *al-Fawā'id fī uṣūl al-dīn*, a *manẓūmah*, was published at Ṭihrān in 1283/1866–7 (*Aḥsan al-wadīʿah* i p. 122[10]), the *Mawāʿiẓ al-muttaqīn* at [Ṭihrān] in 1297/1880°, and the *Sabīl al-najāt* in the same volume as the *Qiṣaṣ al-ʿulamā'* at [Ṭihrān] in 1304/1886° and 1309/1891‡. In his list of his works are mentioned an

[1] *Ḥākim i Gawarnar MHRĀ Nā'ib i Kanpūnī Angrēz Bahādur*, which Pertsch interprets as meaning Lord Moira who, however, as Pertsch points out, did not reach India until 1228/1813.

[2] For Tunakābun, the most westerly district of Māzandarān (capital Khurramābād), see Rabino *Mázandarán and Astarábád* pp. 21–4, 105–7, etc.

[3] *Qiṣaṣ al-ʿulamā'*, 1309 ed., p. 61[11]: *u maulid i īn faqīr dar sanah i hazār u duwīst u sī u chahār yā sī u panj būdah.*

alphabetically arranged *Tadhkirat al-'ulamā'* (*Qiṣaṣ al-'ulamā'* p. 69[19]. Cf. p. 7[14]), a work entitled *Karāmāt al-'ulamā'* (*op. cit.* p. 69[20]) and an autobiography entitled *Mudhakkir al-ikhwān* (*op. cit.* p. 72[3]).

Qiṣaṣ al-'ulamā', notices of 153 ancient and modern Shī'ite scholars completed 17 Rajab 1290/10 Sept. 1873, arranged *ba-tartīb i ijāzāt u tartīb i azminah u a'ṣār* and beginning with the author's teacher S. Ibrāhīm Qazwīnī: **Āṣafīyah** i p. 348 nos. 114–5 (A.H. 1301/1883–4).

Editions: [**Persia** ?] 1296/1879°; [**Ṭihrān**] 1304/1886° (followed by (1) M. b. Sulaimān Tunakābunī's *Sabīl al-najāt*, (2) S. Murtaḍā's *Tabṣirat al-'awāmm*); [**Ṭihrān**] 1308–9/1891‡ (followed by the same two works on p. 350 and p. 358 respectively); **Bombay** or Lucknow (?) 1306/1888–9 (cf. *Aḥsan al-wadī'ah* i p. 122[6], Browne *Lit. Hist.* iv p. 354); **Tabrīz** 1320/1902–3 (cf. *Aḥsan al-wadī'ah* i p. 122[6]).

Description: *A traveller's narrative written to illustrate the episode of the Báb edited . . . and translated . . . by E. G. Browne*, ii (Cambridge 1891) pp. 197–8.

Urdu translation by Mīr Nādir 'Alī "Ra'd": *Qiṣaṣ al-'ulamā'*, **Ḥaidarābād** 1340–1/1921–3*.

[*Qiṣaṣ al-'ulamā'*, 1308–9 ed., pp. 58–74; *al-Ma'āthir wa-'l-āthār* p. 157; *Aḥsan al-wadī'ah* i pp. 121–3.]

1580. Maulawī Mīrzā **Muḥammad 'Alī** (so on the title-page and in the three prefixed *taqārīẓ*) al-Kashmīrī *aṣlan* *thumma* 'l-Lak'hnawī (so in the third *taqrīẓ*, p. iv, l. 3) or, as he calls himself in the preface, Muḥammad b. Ṣādiq b. Mahdī, was a pupil of S. M. 'Abbās Shūshtarī[1] and an old friend of S. Ḥāmid Ḥusain.[2]

Nujūm al-samā' fī tarājim al-'ulamā', lives of Shī'ite scholars of the eleventh (p. 4), twelfth (p. 157), and thirteenth

[1] *wa-huwa mimman qara'a 'alaiya ba'da 'l-kutubi 'l-adabīyah wa-shaṭran min kitābī Rawā'iḥ al-Qur'ān fī faḍā'il umanā' al-Raḥmān* (first *taqrīẓ*, p. i, l. 5 from foot). M. 'A. Sh. is the author of a *mathnawī* entitled *Mann u salwā* (I.H. p. 564. Editions: [Delhi ?] 1263/1847°, Amrōhah 1894°) and other works.

[2] S. Ḥ. Ḥ. Mūsawī Nīshāpūrī Lak'hnawī wrote the large Shī'ite work *'Abaqāt al-anwār fī imāmat al-A'immat al-aṭhār*, of which the British Museum has a number of parts published from 1293/1876 to 1314/1896 (Edwards col. 243). Cf. *al-Ma'āthir wa-'l-āthār* p. 168.

(p. 313) Islāmic centuries, begun in 1286/1869–70 [1] at the request of S. Ḥāmid Ḥusain [2] and divided, according to the preface, into three *najms*, one for each century, and a *khātimah*, of which the subject is not stated: **Lucknow** 1303/1886° ("Vol. I (*jild i awwal*)," apparently the only one published, consisting of 424 pages and ending with Muftī S. Muḥammad-Qulī Khān b. S. M. Ḥusain b. S. Ḥāmid Ḥusain, who died at Lucknow in 1260/1844).[3]

1581. **'Abd al-'Azīz "Jawāhir al-Kalām"** is the author of *Kitāb-khānahā-yi Īrān* (Firdausī Press [Tihrān] A.H.S. 1311/1932–3), at the end of which is printed a list of other works by the same author. These are (1) *Āthār al-Shī'at al-Imāmīyah* (see below), (2) a Persian translation of Ibn Khaldūn's *Muqaddimah* (described as having been sent to the Persian Ministry of Education in the hope that it would be published), (3) a commentary [doubtless in Arabic] on the *Kifāyat al-uṣūl* of Mullā M. Kāẓim Khurāsānī [4] (in three volumes, of which half of the first volume is described as having been lithographed at Tihrān), (4) *Nahj al-faṣāḥah*, a collection of the Prophet's short speeches, sayings etc., modelled on the *Nahj al-balāghah* (unfinished), (5) philosophical and other essays published in periodicals at Cairo, Bairūt and Istānbūl. According to a statement on the back cover of the *Kitāb-khānahā-yi Īrān* the author had collected much material for two further works, namely (6) *Tārīkh i Tihrān* and (7) *Kitāb i makhṭūṭāt i Īrān*, on the Arabic and Persian MSS. in the libraries of Persia.

Āthār al-Shī'at al-Imāmīyah rāji' ba-'aqā'id u afkār u adwār i siyāsī u adabī u tārīkh i bilād u mamālik u āthār i adabī u māddī u sharḥ i ḥāl i mardumān i nāmī i 'ilmī u siyāsī i Shī'ah az ibtidā-yi tashkīl i īn firqah tā 'aṣr i ḥāḍir ... in twenty volumes, of which only two are described at the end of the *Kitāb-khānahā-yi Īrān* as having been printed, namely vol. iii (in Arabic [Tihrān

[1] A prefixed *taqrīẓ* by S. Ḥāmid Ḥusain is dated 1290/1873, but the printed text contains quotations from the *Qiṣaṣ al-'ulamā'* (e.g. pp. 410^{10}, 412^{9}, 415^{6}), which were doubtless inserted some years later than 1290.

[2] *wa-qad ṣannafa bi'ltimāsī kitāban rā'i'an* as Ḥāmid Ḥusain says in his *taqrīẓ*, p. ii antepenult.

[3] There is nothing to show whether or not this is the end of the third *najm*.

[4] Cf. Brockelmann *Sptbd.* ii p. 799; Browne *Lit. Hist.* iv p. 371.

1342/1924‡ (according to the title-page, but 1348 [1929–30] according to the cover)] and also in a Persian translation, *shāmil i ḥālāt i salāṭīn u farmānrawāyān i Shīʻah az ibtidā-yi Islām tā kunūn*) and vol. iv (*shāmil i ḥālāt i kāffah i wuzarā' u umarā' i īn firqah*), the latter (biographies of wazīrs arranged chronologically under the dynasties and then (*Bāb* 2, p. 125) biographies of amīrs similarly arranged) having been printed in a Persian translation at the Maṭbaʻah i Majlis [**Tihrān**] in A.H.S. 1307/1928–9‡. From the colophon of vol. iv it appears that the subject of vol. v is the history of modern Persia from Qājār times to the present.

1582. Other works :—

(1) ***Kākh i dil-āwīz yā Tārīkh i Sharīf i Raḍī***,[1] by S. ʻAlī Akbar Burquʻī Qummī (in, and offprinted from, *Armaghān* xix/5–6 (Murdād 1317/1938) pp. 357–71, xix/7 (Mihr 1317) pp. 451–8, xix/8 (Ābān 1317) pp. 505–12, xix/9–10 (Ispand 1317) pp. 593–608 (cf. *Luzac's Oriental List* 1940 p. 107)).

(2) ***Risālah dar faḍīlat i ʻilm u ʻulamā'***, a short treatise written not earlier than 1052/1642 (Shāh Ṣafī being referred to as dead) by M. Muqīm al-Ḥusainī al-Astarābādī [2] on the spiritual advantages of theological learning, with eulogies of some famous Shīʻite divines and especially an encomiastic biography of M. Bāqir Dāmād (d. 1040/1630–1 or 1041/1631–2. See Brockelmann *Sptbd.* ii p. 579 and the authorities there cited) : **Ivanow** Curzon 705 (late 18th cent.).

(3) ***Risālah dar sabab i shahādat i Shahīd i Thānī***, on the death of Zain al-Dīn al-ʻĀmilī [3] at Istānbūl : **Ivanow** 1st Spt. 827(6) (A.H. 1252/1837).

N. BIOGRAPHY : (*o*) TRADITIONISTS

1583. For the *Tuḥfat al-faqīr al-ḥaqīr* and the *Tuḥfah i Murshidī* of ʻUbaid Allāh b. ʻAbd Allāh al-Ḥusainī known as

[1] For whom see *Ency. Isl.* under al-Sharīf al-Raḍī (Krenkow), Brockelmann I p. 82, *Sptbd.* I pp. 131–2.

[2] Presumably identical with M. Muqīm b. Jamāl al-Dīn Ḥusain al-Ḥusainī al-Astarābādī, who wrote for " Quṭb-Shāh " a *Risālah fī 'l-maʻād* (I.Ḥ. 1523).

[3] Cf. *Lu'lu'atā 'l-Baḥrain* pp. 25–31 ; etc.

Murshid b. Aṣīl, the former of which was written in 884/1479, see p. 1079 *supra*.

1584. Muḥammad, entitled **Khawāṣṣ Khān,** Ḥanafī Qādirī Qurashī Madanī[1] Bījāpūrī was a contemporary of the Mogul Emperor Farrukh-siyar.

Muhimmat al-muḥaddithīn (a chronogram = 1128/1716), a short biographical dictionary of Ḥanafī traditionists: **Āṣafīyah** i p. 348 (= Nadhīr Aḥmad 95).

1585. **Walī Allāh** b. 'Abd al-Raḥīm **Dihlawī** was born in 1114/1703 and died in 1176/1762–3 (see pp. 20–22, 179, 219, 1020–22 *supra*).

Āthār al-muḥaddithīn: **Āṣafīyah** i p. 346 no. 81 (A.H. 1174/1760–1).

1586. **'Abd al-'Azīz** b. Walī Allāh **Dihlawī,** who was born in 1159 [2]/1746 and died in 1239/1824, has already been mentioned as the author of the *Fatḥ al-'Azīz* (p. 24) and the Arabic work *Sirr al-shahādatain* (p. 223).

Bustān al-muḥaddithīn, a bibliography of works on the Traditions with biographies of their authors: **Bānkīpūr** viii 652 (mid 19th cent.).

Editions: **Delhi** [12]93/1876°*, **Lahore** [1884*], [1893°].

1587. Nawwāb M. **Ṣiddīq Ḥasan Khān,** who was born at Bareilly in 1248/1832 and died at Bhōpāl in 1890, has already been mentioned as the author of the *Ifādat al-shuyūkh bi-miqdār al-nāsikh wa-'l-mansūkh* (p. 27), the *Iksīr fī uṣūl al-tafsīr* (p. 28) and the *Sham' i anjuman* (p. 913).

Itḥāf al-nubalā' al-muttaqīn bi-iḥyā' ma'āthir al-fuqahā' al-muḥaddithīn, a bibliography of works on the Traditions followed by biographies of traditionists: **Cawnpore** 1289/1872* (446 pp.).

1588. Other works:

(1) *Kitāb al-dīn al-mubīn fī sharḥ uṣūl al-ḥadīth wa-bayān aḥwāl al-mashāhīr min al-muḥaddithīn,* one (evidently

[1] So Nadhīr Aḥmad. The Āṣafīyah catalogue calls him Imtinān [*sic ?*] Khawāṣṣ Khān Ḥanafī Qādirī Bījāpūrī.

[2] Ghulām-Ḥalīm, the pseudonym adopted by him in the *Tuḥfah i Ithnā-'Asharīyah,* is a chronogram indicating this year.

the first)[1] of the twenty-four volumes of the *Rauḍāt i Shāhī* (a work *mutaḍammin i aḥwāl i buzurgān u dar aḥādīth u tafsīr wa-ghairah* according to Raḥmān 'Alī) composed in 1077/1666–7 by S. M. Ja'far Badr i 'Ālam Aḥmadābādī Gujrātī b. S. Jalāl al-Dīn M. Maqṣūd i 'Ālam, who was born in 1023/1614 and died in 1085/1675 (see Raḥmān 'Alī p. 214): **Nadhīr Aḥmad** 85 (M. 'Alī Ḥusain's library, Ḥaidarābād. A.H. 1077/1667, apparently autograph).

(2) *Silsilat al-'asjad fī dhikr mashāyikh al-sanad.* Edition: place ? date ? (Āṣafīyah i p. 346).

N. BIOGRAPHY: (*p*) TRAVELLERS, PILGRIMS, TOURISTS

See also Ambassadors, pp. 1066–71 *supra*

1589. Ḥakīm Abū Mu'īn **Nāṣir** "Ḥujjat" **ibn Khusrau** Qubādiyānī Marwazī, born in Dhū 'l-Qa'dah 394/Aug.–Sept. 1004 apparently at Qubādiyān, was by profession an official in the revenue department. In Rabī' ii 437/Oct.–Nov. 1045, when Chaghrī Bēg Dāwud b. Mīkā'īl b. Saljūq was *Amīr* of Khurāsān, Nāṣir went on revenue business from Marw to Panj-dīh, near Marw al-Rūd, and from there to Jūzjānān. Here he dreamt a dream which caused him to abandon the practice of drinking and undertake a pilgrimage to Mecca. Returning to Marw he resigned his official appointment and set out on the journey which he has described in his *Safar-nāmah*. In Egypt, then flourishing under Fāṭimid rule, he came in contact with Ismā'īlī theologians, and presumably it was there that he became a convert to the Ismā'īlī creed. At this time or later he was appointed *ḥujjat* or leader of propaganda for Khurāsān. Some time after his return, however, his religious views or his propagandist activities met with disapproval from the authorities and he was forced to leave Balkh. He seems to have gone for a time to

[1] According to the colophon (quoted by Nadhīr Aḥmad) it is followed "*fī 'l-sifr al-thānī*" by "*al-kitāb al-thānī wa-huwa 'l-musammā bi-kitāb al-mu'jizāt wa-'l-āyāt al-baiyināt.*"

Māzandarān, but eventually he settled at Yumgān (or Yamkān ?) in the mountains of Badakhshān, and there he died and was buried probably in, or about, 481/1088.

Among his works were (**1**) a *dīwān* (Editions : Tabrīz 1280/1864°, Tihrān A.H.S. 1304–7/1925–8 (*Dīwān i ash'ār i Ḥakīm ... Nāṣir b. Khusrau ... ba-inḍimām i Rūshanā'ī-nāmah ... u Sa'ādat-nāmah* ... with introduction, notes and indexes by Mujtabā Mīnuwī). Selections : (*a*) *Auswahl aus Nâṣir Chusrau's Ḳaṣîden* [with translation]. *Von ... H. Ethé* (in *ZDMG*. 36 (1882) pp. 478–508) : (*b*) *Kürzere Lieder und poetische Fragmente aus Nâçir Khusraus Dîvân. Von H. Ethé* (in *Nachrichten der Gesellschaft der Wissenschaften*, Göttingen 1882, pp. 124–52). (**2**) *Rūshanā'ī-nāmah*, a philosophical poem (Editions : (1) *Nâṣir Chusrau's Rûśanâinâma ... oder Buch der Erleuchtung in Text und Uebersetzung, nebst Noten und kritisch-biographischem Appendix. Von H. Ethé* (in *ZDMG*. 33 (1879) pp. 645–65, 34 (1880) pp. 617–42) : (2) Berlin 1341/1923* (*Safar-nāmah i Ḥakīm N. i Kh. ba-inḍimām i Rūshanā'ī-nāmah u Sa'ādat-nāmah*. A reprint of Ethé's text) : (3) Tihrān A.H.S. 1304–7/1925–8 (see above under *dīwān*) : (**3**) *Sa'ādat-nāmah*, a didactic poem (Editions : (1) *Le Livre de la Félicité ..., par Nâçir ed-Dîn ben Khosroû* [with a French translation] *par E. Fagnan* (in *ZDMG*. 34 (1880) pp. 643–74 : (2) Berlin 1341/1923* (see above under *Rūshanā'ī-nāmah*) : (3) Tihrān A.H.S. 1304–7/1925–8 (see above under *dīwān*). Emendations : *ZDMG*. 36 (1882) pp. 96–114 : (**4**) *Zād al-musāfirīn*, a prose handbook of Ismā'īlī theology and metaphysics (Edition : Berlin 1341/1923* (ed. M. Badhl al-Raḥmān)) : (**5**) *Wajh i dīn* (Edition : Berlin 1343/1925* (with preface by T. Īrānī)).

(*Safar-nāmah i Ḥakīm Nāṣir i Khusrau*), an account of a journey which started from Jūzjānān on 6 Jumādā II 437/19 Dec. 1045 and during which the author visited among other places Shāburqān, Marw, Nīshāpūr, Qūmis (i.e. Bisṭām), Dāmghān, Simnān, Qazwīn, Tabrīz (where he met " Qaṭrān "), Vān, Akhlāṭ, Bitlīs, Arzan (Erzerum), Maiyāfāriqīn, Āmid, Aleppo, Ma'arrat al-Nu'mān (where he met Abū 'l-'Alā'), Ḥamāh, Tripoli, Bairūt, Sidon, Tyre, Acre, Ḥaifā, Jerusalem, Mecca (to which he made four pilgrimages), Damascus, Jerusalem again, Egypt (where he stayed two or three years) and finally the Ḥijāz, the Yemen, Laḥsā, Qaṭīf, Baṣrah, Arrajān, Iṣfahān, Nā'īn, Ṭabas, Tūn, Sarakhs and Marw (26 Jumādā II 444/23 Oct. 1052): **Rieu** i 379 (A.H. 1102/1691), iii 979*a* (abstract only. Circ. A.D. 1850), **Blochet** i 644 (A.D. 1874), 645 (A.H. 1296/1878), **Ivanow** 279 (A.H. 1292/1875).

Editions: **Paris** (Vienne printed) 1881°* (*Sefer Nameh, relation du voyage de Nassiri Khosrau . . . , publié, traduit et annoté par C. Schefer.* Publications de l'École Spéciale des Langues Orientales Vivantes, Série ii, vol. 1), **Delhi** 1882°* (*Safar-nāmah i Ḥakīm Nāṣir i Khusrau.* With a biographical preface by M. Alṭāf Ḥusain "Ḥālī"), **Bombay** 1309/1892°, **Ṭihrān** 1312/1894–5 (*Siyāḥat-nāmah.* See Mashhad, fṣl. 14, ptd. bks., no. 130), [**Ṭihrān** ?] 1314/1896–7 (with the *dīwān*: see Ghanī-zādah's *muqaddimah* to the 1341 edition, p. *dāl*, and Taqī-zādah's *muqaddimah* p. NB n.), **Berlin** 1341/1923*.

French translation: see Editions above.

Russian translation: *Safar-name. Kniga puteshestviya* [translation and introduction by E. E. Berthels] **Leningrad** [1] (or Moscow ? [2]) 1933.

Translations of extracts: (**1**) *An account of Jerusalem translated . . . from the Persian text of Násir ibn Khusru's* [*sic*] *Safar-námah. By . . . Major A. R. Fuller* (in *JRAS.* 1873 p. 142 *et seqq.*). (**2**) *Diary of a journey through Syria and Palestine by Nâsir-i-Khusrau, in* 1047 A.D. *Translated . . . and annotated by G. le Strange.* **London,** 1888° (Palestine Pilgrims' Text Society).

[Autobiographical statements in his works especially the *Safar-nāmah* and the *dīwan* (most fully discussed in S. Ḥasan Taqī-zādah's *muqaddimah* to the 1304–7 edition of the *dīwān* and very briefly summarised in C. N. Seddon's review, *JRAS.* 1930 pp. 671–4. A spurious autobiography (of which an abridgment is printed in the Tabrīz edition of the *dīwān*) is the source of incorrect and legendary information given in the *Khulāṣat al-ash'ār*, the *Haft iqlīm*, the *Ātash-kadah* and elsewhere (cf.

[1] So *Ency. Isl.* under Nāṣir-i-Khusraw.
[2] So Harrassowitz's *Litterae orientales* 58 (April 1934) p. 22.

Browne *Lit. Hist.* ii pp. 218–20)); Zakarīyā' al-Qazwīnī *Āthār al-bilād* (in Arabic) pp. 328–9 (s.v. Yumgān. Cf. Browne *Lit. Hist.* ii p. 218); *Tārīkh i Guzīdah* p. 826; *Bahāristān, Rauḍah* 6, 8th notice; Daulat-Shāh pp. 61–4; *Khulāṣat al-ash'ār*; *Haft iqlīm* no. 863; *But-khānah* no. 3; *Mir'āt al-khayāl* pp. 27–8 (no. 7); *Ātash-kadah* pp. 187–[194] (no. 425 (under Iṣfahān). Based on the spurious autobiography. Summarized by Bland in *JRAS.* vii (1843) pp. 360–1); *Majma' al-gharā'ib* no. 2711; Sprenger pp. 428–9; *Majma' al-fuṣaḥā'* i pp. 607–33; *Rauḍāt al-jannāt* iv p. 223; Rieu i pp. 379–81; H. Ethé *Nasir Khusrau's Leben, Denken und Dichten* (in *Travaux . . . du Congrès international des orientalistes à Leyde,* vol. ii, Leyden 1884); *Náṣir-i-Khusraw, poet, traveller and propagandist. By E. G. Browne* (in *JRAS.* 1905 pp. 313–52); Browne *Lit. Hist.* ii pp. 218–46; M. Ghanī-zādah's *muqaddimah* to the 1241 edition of the *Safar-nāmah; Ency. Isl.* under Nāṣir-i Khusraw (Berthels); S. Ḥasan Taqī-zādah's *muqaddimah* to the 1304–7 edition of the *dīwān* (very briefly summarised in C. N. Seddon's review, *JRAS.* 1930 pp. 671–4)].

1590. Sh. Abū 'l-Faiḍ "**Faiḍī**" b. Mubārak was born at Āgrah in 954/1547 and died there in 1004/1595 (see p. 540 *supra*).

A short account of the pilgrimage of Rafī' al-Dīn Shāh Abū Turāb (cf. p. 727 *supra*) *to Mecca in* 986/1578 *and his return in* 987/1579 *with the Qadam i Rasūl* (beginning: *Qadam i qalam dar ṭaiy i masālik i maḥāmid i Ilāhī kūtāh ast*): **Bānkīpūr** Suppt. i 1995 vii (foll. 68*b*–70*a*. 18th cent.).

1591. For the *'Awālim al-asrār fī gharā'ib al-asfār,* begun in 1009/1600–1 by Qāḍī Ikhtiyār, see p. 1116 *supra.*

For the *Baḥr al-asrār,* which concludes with an account of Maḥmūd b. Amīr Walī's extensive travels from 1034/1624–5 onwards, see p. 375 *supra.*

1592. **Ṣafī b. Walī Qazwīnī** has already been mentioned as the author of the *Zēb i tafāsīr* (p. 19 *supra*) and the *Tuḥfat al-akhyār* (p. 130 *supra*).

Anīs al-ḥujjāj, an account of a journey to Mecca and

Medina in 1087–8/1676–7 after the completion of the *Zēb i tafāsīr* : **Rieu** iii 980*a* (defective and disarranged. Circ. A.D. 1850).

1593. **M. Mufīd** Mustaufī b. Najm al-Dīn Maḥmūd Bāfqī Yazdī has already been mentioned as the author of the *Jāmi' i Mufīdī*, begun at Baṣrah in 1082/1671 and completed at Multān in 1090/1679 (see p. 352 *supra*), and of the *Mukhtaṣar i Mufīd*, begun in the Deccan in 1087/1676–7 and completed at Lahore in 1091/1680–1 (see p. 237 *supra*). The fifth *maqālah* of the third *mujallad* of the former work is devoted to an account of the author's life and travels.

A memoir (beg. *Ḥamd u sipās i bī-qiyās Mālik al-mulkī rā kih rif'at i sarā-pardah i 'aẓamatash*), "very rich in words and poor in facts", extending over the years 1077–85 but dealing mainly with the author's journey to India (Iṣfahān, Baghdād, Baṣrah, Sūrat, Shāhjahānābād, Ḥaidarābād, Sārangpūr, Burhānpūr, Aurangābād, Golconda) in 1081–5 : **Bodleian** 423.

1594. For Anand Rām "Mukhliṣ's" account of his journey from Delhi to Muktēsar in 1156/1743 (?), see p. 613 *supra* and the additions and corrections relating to that page.

For the *Bayān i wāqi'* of Khwājah 'Abd al-Karīm b. 'Āqibat-Maḥmūd Kashmīrī, who entered Nādir Shāh's service at Delhi in 1151/1739, reached Qazwīn with him in 1154/1741, travelled thence to 'Irāq, Syria and Arabia, returned to Delhi in 1156/1743 and wrote an account of these travels and of contemporary history to 1198/1784, see pp. 326–7 *supra*.

1595. **I'tiṣām al-Dīn** b. Sh. Tāj al-Dīn, of Tājpūr (described by him as in the Nadiyah District [of Bengal]), began his official career as a *munshī* under Ja'far 'Alī Khān ["Mīr Ja'far", Nawwāb-Nāẓim of Bengal 1170–4/1757–60 and again 1763–5. Cf. pp. 628, 630 *supra*]. On the accession of Mīr Qāsim [in 1174/1760. Cf. p. 630 *supra*] he entered the service of Major Yorke and took part in the campaign against the Rājah of Bīrbhūm. He later fought on the British side against Mīr Qāsim [in 1177/1763. Cf. p. 631 *supra*]. Then after a short period in the service of General Carnac [1765–6] he entered that of Shāh-'Ālam. In 1180/1767, when Captain Archibald Swinton came to

England with a letter from Shāh-ʿĀlam to George III, Iʿtiṣām al-Dīn accompanied him.[1] He embarked at Hijilī [2] on 9 Shaʿbān 1180/10 January 1767 [3] and returned to Bengal in 1183/1769 after an absence of two years and nine months.[4] In 1189/1775 he was sent to Poonah to help in the negotiations of the East India Company with the Marāṭ'hās.

Shigarf-nāmah i wilāyat, or *Wilāyat-nāmah*, an account written in 1199/1785 of the author's voyage to England in 1180/1767 and of his experiences there, but not of his return journey, which brought him back to Bengal in 1183/1769: **Rieu** iii 981*b* (A.D. 1810), i 383*a* (A.H. 1227/1812), **I.O.** D.P. 685 (Samwat 1869/1812), 595 (A.H. 1231/1816), **I.O.** 4021, **Āṣafīyah** iii p. 350 no. 94 (A.H. 1230/1815), ii p. 836 no. 25, **Bodleian** 1854, **Ivanow** Curzon 96 (19th cent.).

Urdu translation: **R.A.S.** H.2.

Abridged Urdu and English translations: *Shigurf namah i Velaët, or Excellent intelligence concerning Europe; being the travels of Mirza Itesa modeen, in Great Britain and France. Translated from the original Persian manuscript into Hindoostanee, with an English version and notes, by J. E. Alexander* [5] [and

[1] Cf. *Bengal: past and present*, vol. 45 (1933) p. 135, where the following extract from Captain Swinton's diary is quoted from p. 105 of the *Swinton family records* (Edinburgh 1908, privately printed): In the end of the year 1765 the Emperor Shah Alam requested the English Army to conduct him to Delhy, and assist in placing him on the throne of his Fathers, but as Lord Clive could not promise him that, he resolved with Lord Clive's approbation to send a letter to the King of Great Britain to solicit his assistance. As I was about to return to Europe and was well known to the King of Hindostan, the Vizier Monyr ul Dowla requested me to be the bearer of it. This I mentioned to Lord Clive who readily consented: accordingly in December, 1765, the letter was delivered to Lord Clive, and the same time put into my hand by his Lordship. . . . He also requested me to carry a Munshy to Europe with me in case it should be thought proper to send an answer in the Persian language. Having obtained Lord Clive's consent, I engaged the Munshy to go to Europe. Monyr ul Dowlah [so] however insisted on paying Rs. 2,000 towards his charges.

[2] Cf. W. Foster's *Early travels in India 1583–1619* p. 25 n. 1: "Hijili, on the west side of the Hūgli river, at the mouth of the Rāsulpur river. It was for a long time a place of importance, as cargoes were landed there for transport up the Hūgli, but was gradually washed away."

[3] This date does not seem to tally with the statement in Captain Swinton's diary (if correctly reproduced) that Shāh-ʿĀlam's letter was delivered to him in December 1765.

[4] This would imply that he returned in, or about, the beginning of Jumādā I 1183/September 1769.

[5] Sir James E. Alexander 1803–85: see the *Dictionary of national biography* and Buckland *Dictionary of Indian biography*.

Munshī Shamshēr Khān: cf. Garcin de Tassy iii pp. 109–10]. **London** 1827°*.

[Autobiographical statements, summarized in Rieu i 383, Bodleian, and Buckland's *Dictionary of Indian biography*].

1596. Mīr **M. Ḥusain** b. 'Abd al-Ḥasanī [read perhaps 'Abd al-Ḥusain] **al-Iṣfahānī.**

(Risālah i aḥwāl i mulk i Farang u Hindūstān), an account of a journey in 1188/1774 via Calcutta to Lisbon and London and of a year's residence in the latter place, followed by a sketch of European astronomy: **Rehatsek** p. 19 no. 33, p. 99 no. 51.

1597. [Mīr] **Jamāl al-Dīn Ḥusain b.** Mīr [? [1]] **Aḥmad al-Ḥusainī al-Mūsawī** b. Mīr Ibrāhīm b. Mīr Amīn al-Dīn b. Mīr Jamāl al-Dīn Ḥusain b. Mīr Fakhr al-Dīn Ḥasan [2] b. Mīrzā 'Imād al-Dīn Ḥusain surnamed (*al-mulaqqab*) Injū b. Mīr Sharaf al-Dīn Rāhūlī [3] was evidently the great-great-grandson of the author of the *Farhang i Jahāngīrī* [4] (not, as Pertsch seems to have supposed, the author of the *Farhang i Jahāngīrī* himself).

Brief memoirs (beg. *al-Ḥ. l. 'l. ta'abbada lahu*), divided into a *muqaddimah*, a *faṣl* and a *khātimah* and dealing mainly with persons met by the author on his travels, especially on a journey to Mecca and Medina: **Berlin** 13 (7) (only 9 or 10 leaves. Defective at end).

1598. **Ghulām-Muḥammad Khān,** who may possibly be identical with the author of the *Nawādir al-qiṣaṣ* (p. 1147),

[1] Queried by Pertsch for some reason unspecified.

[2] Ḥusain according to Pertsch.

[3] *Sic?* Read perhaps Rāhūyī.

[4] Mīr J. al-D. Ḥu. b. Fakhr al-Dīn Ḥa. Injū, a member of a Shīrāzī Saiyid family, went to the Deccan and eventually became *Wakīl*, or Prime Minister, to Murtaḍā Niẓām-Shāh (reigned 972–96/1565–88). Entering Akbar's service in the 30th regnal year (993–4), he held high positions both in his reign and in that of Jahāngīr and died at Āgrah in 1035/1625–6 (according to the *Tārīkh i Muḥammadī*, cited by Rieu iii p. 1088*b*). See *Burhān i ma'āthir* pp. 397[7], 452[22], 453[1], 454[5], 456[3], 456 antepenult., 567[4]; *Ā'īn i Akbarī* p. 226*b* no. 164 (only his name in a list of *Nuh-ṣadīs*), Blochmann's trans. p. 450; *Memoirs of Jahāngīr*, tr. Rogers and Beveridge, i 46 and elsewhere; *The Embassy of Sir T. Roe to India . . . edited by Sir W. Foster*, new ed., Oxford, 1926, pp. 209–12; *Ma'āthir al-umarā'* iii pp. 358–60 (quoted and translated in Blochmann's *Contributions to Persian lexicography* (*JASB.* 37 (1868)) pp. 66–8, translated in *Ā'īn i Akbarī*, tr. Blochmann, pp. 450–1); Rieu ii pp. 496–7.

undertook his travels of 1196–1201/1782–7 at the request of Warren Hastings, the Governor-General of India.

Account of a journey in and beyond northern India, especially of the part from Shāhjahānābād [i.e. Delhi] to Kābul and Qandahār with reports on contemporary historical events : **Ethé** 2725 (defective at end).

1599. S. Shāh **'Azīz Allāh Bukhārī,** " Moonshy to Sir John Murray, Bart.",[1] was in the 68th year of his age in Ramaḍān 1209/March 1795, when he wrote at Calcutta for his employer " Seven alphabets with the combinations of all the letters in each " (Rieu ii 533). Berlin 997 and 1084 are MSS. transcribed by him for Sir J. Murray in 1210/1796.

Reminiscences of a journey from Farrukhābād in 1201/ 1786–7 (beg. *Huwa 'l-Muta'ālī. Rūzī dar siyāḥat i īn bī-biḍā'at dar aiyām i bī-kārī kih kamāl i bī-qarārī-st dar sanah i 1201*), written in 1203/1789 at the request of Sir J. Murray [2] : **Berlin** 15 (1) (4 foll.).

It appears from the opening words of the reminiscences just mentioned that 'Azīz Allāh Bukhārī was unemployed in 1201/ 1786–7 and it may be conjectured that his employment by John Murray began not earlier than that year. If so, it must have been someone else who accompanied Murray and at his request kept a diary of his journey from Calcutta to Rāmpūr and back in the period 25 June 1783 to 1 January 1784.

Diary of a journey made in the company of John Murray from Calcutta along the Ganges via Mīrzāpūr, Allahabad, Cawnpore, Farrukhābād and Āgrah to Rāmpūr and back by

[1] John Macgregor Murray, who was Military Secretary to the Commander-in-Chief in the Rohilla War (1774) and subsequently First Secretary and Member of the Military Board, became a Lieutenant-Colonel in 1787, was created a Baronet in 1795, retired in 1798 and died in 1822 (see *East India Military Calendar* London 1823, vol. ii p. 461 ; Rieu i 409*b*). Two volumes containing respectively Persian letters received by him in the years 1788–96 and Persian letters sent by him in the same period to various Indians of rank are described in Rieu i p. 410. Two volumes described in Rieu i pp. 409*b* and 410*a* contain miscellaneous papers collected by him on the history and administration, land-tenure and revenue of Bengal and Bihar, etc.

[2] In his description of this MS. (Berlin p. 52) Pertsch does not say that Sir John Murray was present on this journey, but he says so, perhaps erroneously, later in the catalogue (p. 380).

another route (Barēlī etc.), beginning *Dar bayān i ān-kih ba-mūjab i farmūdah i khudāwand i ni'mat* and containing not only dates of arrival and departure etc. but also information about topography, local customs, industry, trade, revenue, history and other matters: **Berlin** 361 (apparently the original draft. 139 foll.), 362 (A.H. 1204/1790, fair copy by S. Shāh 'Abd al-Laṭīf. 203 foll.).

1600. Maulawī **Rafī' al-Dīn** b. Farīd al-Dīn Khān **Murādābādī,** a pupil of Walī Allāh Dihlawī (see pp. 20–2, 179, 219, 1020–22, *supra*) and an associate of 'Abd al-'Azīz Dihlawī (see pp. 24, 223), died at Murādābād on 15 Dhū 'l-Ḥijjah 1218/27 March 1804. Several works of his (*Tārīkh i Afāghinah, Tadhkirat al-mashāyikh, Suluww al-ka'īb bi-dhikr al-ḥabīb, Qiṣar al-āmāl bi-dhikr al-ḥāl wa-'l-ma'āl, Kanz al-ḥisāb, Sharḥ i Arba'īn i Nawawī, Tarjamah i 'Ain al-'ilm, Ḥālāt al-Ḥaramain* and others) are mentioned without specification of the language by Ṣiddīq Ḥasan, Ghulām-Sarwar and Raḥmān 'Alī.

(*Ḥālāt al-Ḥaramain*),[1] an account of a journey from Murādābād to Mecca and Medina in 1201–3/1786–8: **Bānkīpūr** vii 626 (19th cent.).

[*Itḥāf al-nubalā'* p. 251; *Ḥadā'iq al-Ḥanafīyah* p. 463; Raḥmān 'Alī p. 66.]

1601. **M. Baqā** is described by Major Yule [2] in a manuscript note as " my friend Muhummud Buqqa ".

Short account of the author's journey from Cawnpore to Benares and back through Jaunpūr and Partābgaṛh to Lucknow from 23 April to 8 October 1798 with descriptive and historical notes on the places visited: **Rieu** ii 841*b* (late 18th cent.).

1602. **'Alī b. Mīrzā Khairāt-'Alī.**

Manāzil i ḥajj, a short account of a pilgrimage from Persia to the Shī'ite shrines in Mesopotamia and thence to Mecca and Medina, written in 1214/1799 and dedicated to Muḥammad Mīrzā b. Ḥusain, grandson of Shāh Ṭahmāsp II: **Ivanow** 287 (early 19th cent.).

[1] No title is mentioned in the preface.
[2] William Yule, father of Sir Henry Yule.

1603. **Ghulām-Muḥammad Khān** left his birthplace, Sirhind, at the age of twelve and [in course of time ?] wandered eastwards in pursuit of learning and a livelihood. He seems to have been for a time in the service of Shujā‘ al-Daulah (*Nawwāb-Wazīr* of Oudh 1167–88/1754–75), and he was wounded at the battle of Baksar (" Buxar ", A.H. 1178/1764). In 1214/1799, when Colonel John Collins [1] was sent from Farrukhābād to Jaipūr in pursuit of Wazīr-‘Alī, the fugitive *Nawwāb-Wazīr* of Oudh,[2] Ghulām-Muḥammad Khān was veterinary surgeon to his detachment. The surrender of Wazīr-‘Alī by the Mahārājah of Jaipūr seems to have made an unfavourable impression on him, since in writing the *Nawādir al-qiṣaṣ* at the request of his fourteen-year-old son Faḍl i Ḥusain " his main object was to disparage the court of Jaipūr ".

Nawādir al-qiṣaṣ, narratives and notes relating to Lahore, Qaṣūr, Kashmīr, Tibet, Multān, Siyālkōṭ, Bilāspūr (Sirhind) etc., Delhi, Jaipūr, Qāsim ‘Alī Khān [Mīr Qāsim : cf. p. 630 *supra*], the Rōhēlahs of Kaṭ'hēr and Najīb Khān [cf. p. 694 *supra*], the Jāts, Farrukhābād [cf. p. 693], the Marāṭ'hās and the battle of Pānīpat [cf. pp. 398, 620–1], Shujā‘ al-Daulah's wars with the Rōhēlahs, etc. : **Rieu** iii 981*b* (circ. A.D. 1854, said to have been transcribed from an autograph).

1604. For the *Masīr i Ṭālibī fī bilād i Afranjī*, Abū Ṭālib Khān's narrative of his journey to Europe in 1213–18/1799–1803, see p. 878 *supra*.

1605. Ra'īs al-Umarā' Ḥāfiẓ M. **‘Abd al-Ḥusain** Karbalā'ī Hindī **Karnātakī** is doubtless identical with the Nawwāb Ra'īs al-Umarā' who in the period 1 Sha‘bān 1234/26 May 1819 to 17 Rabī‘ I 1236/23 Dec. 1820 made a pilgrimage from Karbalā' via Ṭihrān to Mashhad, of which an account (*Tadhkirat al-Riḍā* ?) was written by S. Muḥibb Ḥusain Khān b. Ja‘far al-Mūsawī (Berlin 360). He completed on 21 Shawwāl 1233/24 Aug. 1818 :

Tadhkirat al-ṭarīq fī maṣā'ib ḥujjāj Bait al-‘Atīq, an account of a pilgrimage from Karbalā' to Mecca and al-Madīnah

[1] For whom see Buckland *Dictionary of Indian biography* p. 89.

[2] He was wanted for the murder of George Frederick Cherry (for whom see Buckland *op. cit.* p. 80).

in the period 26 Shawwāl 1230/1 Oct. 1815 to 17 Jumādā I 1232/ 4 April 1817 : **Berlin** 359.

1606. Ḥājjī **M. Ḥusain Khān** b. Bāyram 'Alī Khān succeeded to the princedom of Merv in 1202/1787–8, his father having died while repelling an invasion of Shāh Murād, the Sulṭān of Bukhārā. For some years the son continued hostilities but, having made peace, he accepted an invitation to Bukhārā and was treacherously detained there with his chief supporters while Shāh Murād took possession of Merv and deported to Bukhārā nearly one thousand families.[1] After seven years' detention M. Ḥusain Khān escaped to Shahr i Sabz and went from there to Khujand, Khōqand, Yārkand, Khutan, Chitrāl, Wakhān, Kāfiristān, Jalālābād, Kābul, Ghaznī, Qandahār, Isfizār, Ṭabas and eventually to Ṭihrān. It was there that he met Sir Gore Ouseley and he had been living there for eighteen years as the guest of Fatḥ-'Alī Shāh when at the age of fifty-odd years he wrote his brief account of his wanderings.

Translation : *Narrative of the travels of Haji Muhammed Hussein Khan, Prince of Marv, written in* 1818 [2]*; translated from the original,*[3] *which the Prince wrote at the request of Sir Gore Ouseley* (in *Biographical notices of Persian poets . . . by the late . . . Sir Gore Ouseley, Bart.*, **London** 1846, pp. 332–51).

1607. **M. Ṣāliḥ** b. Ḥājjī Bāqir Khān **Shīrāzī,** known as (*al-shahīr bi-*) Kāzarānī [*sic*], who accompanied Sir Gore Ouseley's embassy from Iṣfahān to Ṭihrān in 1812 and had been attached to the service of Colonel D'Arcy,[4] was one of five Persians sent by the Prince Qā'im-maqām ['Abbās Mīrzā b. Fatḥ-'Alī Shāh] to England in 1815 under the guardianship of Colonel D'Arcy for the purpose of gaining proficiency in European subjects (English, French, Latin and Natural Science in his case). He is

[1] " An almost mortal blow was dealt it at the end of the 18th century when the Amīr of Bukhārā Shāh Murād destroyed the dam on the Murghāb and drove away almost all the inhabitants of Merw." (*Ency. Isl.*, Suppt., under Merw al-Shahidjān (Jakoubovsky)).

[2] Sir Gore Ouseley left Persia in 1814. M. Ḥusain Khān's account of his wanderings was sent to him by letter.

[3] The original does not seem to be among the Ouseley MSS. described by Ethé in the Bodleian catalogue.

[4] Attached to Sir G. Ouseley's mission in 1810, he subsequently entered the Persian service.

identified by Rieu, doubtless correctly, with "Mirza Salih, one of the public secretaries of H.M. the Shah of Persia, who has been employed on a diplomatic mission in this country" and who, according to an unsigned article (*Persian newspaper and translation*) in the *JRAS*. v (1839) pp. 355–71, was editor of a Ṭihrān newspaper "undertaken a few years since".[1] Presumably also he is the same person as "Mírzá Ṣáliḥ of Shíráz, the *Wazír* of Ṭihrán", who, according to Browne's *Press and poetry of modern Persia* p. 8, sent at great expense one Mírzá Asadu'lláh, of the province of Fárs, to St. Petersburg to learn the art of printing, and . . . on his return thence . . . founded at Tabríz, with the assistance of the late Áqá Riẓá . . . a lithographic press, the first book lithographed at which was the Holy Qur'án in the handwriting of Mírzá Ḥusain the famous calligraphist." A collection of Persian dialogues (*Su'āl u jawāb*) composed by him for Sir Gore Ouseley, probably in 1812, is preserved in MS. at Oxford (Bodleian 1857) and is doubtless the same as the *Persian dialogues . . . with an English translation by W. Price* published at Worcester in 1822° and reissued in W. Price's *Grammar of the three principal Oriental languages, Hindoostanee, Persian, and Arabic . . . to which is added a set of Persian dialogues . . . by Mirza Mohammed Saulih, of Shiraz . . . with an English* [and French] *translation* (London, Worcester printed, 1823°*).

(1) ***Account of a journey from Iṣfahān to Ṭihrān*** [with Sir Gore Ouseley's embassy ?], "containing topographical and historical information about these two towns and the places lying between," and "dated at the end, A.H. 1227, the 11th of Jumâdâ I = A.D. 1812, 23rd of May": **Bodleian** 1856 (40 foll.).

(2) ***(Siyāḥat-nāmah i M. Ṣāliḥ i Shīrāzī)***, in four *faṣls* ((1) circumstances leading to the author's departure, (2) his journey from Tabrīz (10 Jumādā II 1230/19 April 1815) through Erivan, Tiflis, Moscow, St. Petersburg and thence by sea, (3)

[1] The specimen described in the *JRAS*., "lithographed on two large folios, printed on one side only" and "surmounted by the Persian emblem of the Lion and Sun", began with the headings *Akhbār u waqā'i' i shahr i Muḥarram al-Ḥarām 1253 * Dar Dār al-Khilāfah i Ṭihrān inṭibā' yāftah * Akhbār i mamālik i sharqīyah.* The second part of the paper, devoted to European news, is headed *Akhbār i mamālik i gharbīyah.* This newspaper seems not to be mentioned in Browne's *Press and poetry of modern Persia.*

his arrival in England (29 Shawwāl 1230/4 October 1815) and his stay there, (4) his return journey by sea to Istānbūl and thence by land towards Persia from 2 Shawwāl 1234/4 July 1819 to Ṣafar 1235/Nov.–Dec. 1819, at which point the MS. breaks off with an account of his stay at Erzerum : **Rieu** i 387*b* (presented by the author to George Willock).

1608. In 1237/1822 S. **M. b. Aḥmad al-Ḥasanī** completed—

Risālah i S. M. b. A. al-Ḥ., a brief account of the author's journey to Kurdistān with Claudius James Rich [1] : **Leningrad** Mus. Asiat. (see *Mélanges asiatiques* ii (St. Petersburg 1852–6) p. 54).

1609. **Zain al-'Ābidīn** b. Iskandar **Shīrwānī** Ni'matallāhī, born at Shamākhī on 15 Sha'bān 1194/1780, was taken as a child of five to Karbalā', where he received his education. Finding his teachers biased and narrow-minded, he started at the age of seventeen on a long series of travels in search of knowledge and enlightenment, associating with scholars, mystics and others. Among the places visited by him were 'Irāq, various parts of Persia, Kābul, where he became the disciple of a celebrated *murshid* named Ḥasan 'Alī Shāh, Peshawar, which he left after the death of Ḥasan 'Alī Shāh in 1216/1801, Delhi, Bengal, the Deccan and other places in India, Ṭukhāristān, Turkistān, Southern Arabia, Abyssinia, the Ḥijāz, Egypt, Syria, Asia Minor, Greece, Constantinople and Morocco. Having returned to Persia, he went to Ṭihrān and was at first well received but later, having been traduced by enemies to Fatḥ-'Alī Shāh, he went successively to Hamadān, Shīrāz and Kirmān. Returning to Shīrāz in 1236/1820, he married and decided to settle there, but, having been declared an infidel by the *mujtahids*, he fled to Yazd. Thence he went to Iṣfahān. Shortly afterwards he returned to Shīrāz and taking his wife to Qūmishah settled there in 1237/1821. He died in 1253/1837. This remarkable man was both intelligent and broad-minded. His works contain varied and interesting information.

(1) *Riyāḍ al-siyāḥah*, a geographical work interspersed

[1] For C. J. Rich (1787–1821) see the *Dictionary of national biography*, Rieu iii p. xi, etc.

with much biographical and historical information, of which the first volume (on Persia) was completed at Qūmis͟hah in 1237/1821–2 and the second (on extra-Persian countries which the author had visited or about which he had received information) in 1242/1827: **Chanykov** 115 (autograph. See *Mélanges asiatiques* i (St. Petersburg 1849–52) p. 556), **Leningrad** Mus. Asiat. (A.H. 1258/1842. See *Mélanges asiatiques* ii, p. 57), **Rieu** Suppt. 139 (vol. ii only. Before A.H. 1246/1830), **Cairo** p. 531 ("*Risālah manqūlah min kitāb Riyāḍ al-siyāḥah awwaluhā Dar c͟higūnagī* (*sic lege*) *i taqsīm i zamīn ba-ḥukm i ḥukamā i ḥikmat.* A.H. 1240/1824–5).

Edition: **Iṣfahān** 1329/1911 (see Harrassowitz's *Bücher-Katalog* 430 (1931) no. 897).

Extract: Dorn (B.) *Muhammedanische Quellen zur Geschichte der südlichen Küstenländer des Kaspischen Meeres*, iv (St. Petersburg 1858°*) pp. 455–67.

(2) ***Bustān al-siyāḥah***, an alphabetically arranged geographical dictionary interspersed with much biographical and historical information completed at S͟hīrāz in 1247/1832: **Rieu** Suppt. 140 (lacks the four chapters which in the 1310/1892–3 edition precede the *Sair* (see Browne *Lit. Hist.* iv p. 451). Apparently A.H 1248/1832), **D.M.G.** 17 (only 19 of the 28 *guls͟hans*. Circ. A.H. 1250/1834–5), **Leningrad** Pub. Lib. (see *Mélanges asiatiques* iii (St. Petersburg 1859), p. 732).

Editions: **Ṭihrān** 1310/1892–3 (see Browne *Lit. Hist.* iv p. 450 n. 3); 1315/1898°; **S͟hīrāz** 1342/1923–4 (see Harrassowitz's *Bücher-Katalog* 430 (1931) no. 896).

Description: Browne *Lit. Hist.* iv, pp. 450–2.

(3) ***Ḥadā'iq al-siyāḥah***, an earlier and shorter recension of the *Bustān al-siyāḥah* completed at S͟hīrāz in 1242/1827: **Rieu** Suppt. 141 (A.H. 1273/1857), **Blochet** i 673 (A.H. 1274/1857–8).

The "*Risālah fī bayān aḥwāl al-jānī* [*I*]*bn Iskandar Zain al-'Ābidīn al-S͟hirwānī*" (**Cairo** p. 531. A.H. 1240/1824–5) may be a part of the *Riyāḍ al-siyāḥah* or a short independent autobiography.[1]

[1] The opening words are given as *al-Ḥamdu lillāhi Rabbi 'l-'ālamīn.*

[*Ḥadā'iq al-siyāḥah*, preface ; *Bustān al-siyāḥah*, preface and under Shamākhī ; *Mélanges asiatiques*, tome iii (1857–9), pp. 50–9 (Lettre de M. Khanykov à M. Dorn) = *Bulletin histor-phil. de l'Acad. des Sciences*, tome xiv, N. 16 ; *Rauḍat al-ṣafā-yi Nāṣirī* ix foll. 166*b*, l. 19, 171*b*, p. 4, x foll. 5*b*, l. 14, 7*a*, l. 19, and elsewhere ; Rieu Suppt. pp. 99–102 ; Browne *Lit. Hist.* iv pp. 450–2 ; *Dānishmandān i Ādharbāyjān* pp. 169–71.]

1610. **'Alī Mirzā** " Maftūn " b. Mirzā Abū Ṭālib **Dihlawī** (*mutawaṭṭan*^{an}) **'Aẓīmābādī** (*maskin*^{an}).

Zubdat al-akhbār fī sawāniḥ al-asfār, an account of pilgrimages to Mecca and Mashhad in 1241–3/1825–7 dedicated to Amīn al-Daulah Nāṣir-Jang [*Wazīr* to the King of Oudh, dismissed in 1263/1847. Cf. Rieu iii, p. 963*a*] and divided into three *muḥīṭs* subdivided into *anhār* ((1) 'Aẓīmābād by boat to Bārh, Bhāgalpūr, Rājmaḥall, Hūglī, Calcutta, thence to Ceylon, Mokhā, Jiddah, Medina and Mecca, (2) Jiddah to Muscat, Shīrāz, Kāzarūn, Iṣfahān, Kāshān, Naṣrābād, Qumm, Ṭihrān, Simnān, Dāmghān, Nīshāpūr, Mashhad, (3) return journey to Ṭihrān etc.) : **Bānkīpūr** vii 631 (*Muḥīṭ* i. Written in 1246/1831 by the author's brother, Mirzā Amīr 'Alī), 632 (*Muḥīṭ* ii. A.H. 1249/1833, autograph).

1611. M. **Qādir Khān** " **Munshī** " Bīdarī has already been mentioned as the author of the *Tārīkh i Āṣaf-Jāhī* (p. 755), the *Tawārīkh i farkhundah* (*ibid.*), and the *Tārīkh i Qādirī* (p. 748).

Sair i Hind u gulgasht i Dakan, composed in 1247/1831–2 : **Āṣafīyah** i p. 242 nos. 754 (A.H. 1254/1838), 286.

1612. Nawwāb M. **Muṣṭafā Khān** " Shēftah " and " Ḥasratī " who was born at Delhi in, or about, 1806 and who died in 1869, has already been mentioned (pp. 895–6 *supra*) as the author of the *Gulshan i bī-khār*.

Targhīb al-sālik ilā aḥsan al-masālik, or *Rah-āward*, an account of a pilgrimage to Mecca and Medina in 1254–6/1839–41.

Edition : place ? 1283/1866–7 (Āṣafīyah ii p. 836, Peshawar 1941).

Urdu translation by S. Zain al-'Ābidīn : *Sirāj i munīr*, place ? 1910.

1613. **Yūsuf Khān Gilīm-pōsh.**

Tārīkh i Yūsufī, an account of a journey from Ḥaidarābād to Europe, especially England, in 1828, composed in 1259/1843 and dedicated to Queen Victoria: **Ivanow** 289 (late 19th cent.).

1614. The anonymous Frenchwoman who speaks in the first person in the *Rūz-nāmah i safar i Shīrāz* seems to have been a teacher in the service of the Shāh,[1] though Boré, the former owner of the MS., has written thereon a note saying that she went to Persia to trade in jewellery.

Rūz-nāmah i safar i Shīrāz, account of a journey in 1251/1835–6 from Ṭihrān to Shīrāz and from Shīrāz to Iṣfahān, "évidemment rédigé par un mirza persan sur les notes ou d'après les souvenirs de la voyageuse": **Blochet** i 649 (1st half of 19th cent.).

1615. Nawwāb Riḍā-Qulī Mīrzā[2] Nā'ib al-Iyālah [Deputy Governor of Fārs], Nawwāb **Najaf-Qulī Mīrzā** "Wālī", Governor of Kūhgīlūyah and Bihbahān as well as "a well known Persian and Arabic scholar, an excellent poet, and consulted as an oracle on many subjects, being exceedingly fond of literature", and Ḥusām al-Daulah Taimūr Mīrzā,[3] "a celebrated warrior, horseman, and hunter," who "governed Bushir for many years and had seen many English who visited the Persian Gulf", are respectively the first, the third, and the fifth of the seventeen sons of the Farmān-farmā Ḥusain-'Alī Mīrzā b. Fatḥ-'Alī Shāh enumerated in the *Rauḍat al-ṣafā-yi Nāṣirī* (x fol. 5*a*, ll. 17, 21, 23). When their father the Governor of Fārs was defeated in his attempt to supplant his brother Muḥammad Shāh and to seize the throne after the death of Fatḥ-'Alī Shāh [19 Jumādā II 1250/23 October 1834], they managed to escape from Shīrāz (*op. cit.* x fol. 4*b*, l. 7 from foot) and after visiting England in the summer

[1] *Chūn īn kamīnah i namak-khwārah i daulat-khwāh i Shāhanshāh i gītī-panāh madām i mu'allim kih zan i Farangsīs-am* (quoted by Blochet from fol. 1*b*).

[2] Cf. p. 907 n. 6.

[3] Spelt "Taymoor Meerza" by As'ad Y. Khaiyāṭ, and "Timour Meerza" by J. B. Fraser. "Teymur" and "Taymur" are given in the *Farhang i Nafīsī* as the ways of pronouncing the name of the founder of the Tīmūrid dynasty (Tamerlane). Taimūr Mīrzā, best known as the author of the *Bāz-nāmah i Nāṣirī*, died in 1291/1874 (according to Phillott's introduction to his translation of the *Bāz-nāmah*).

of 1836 settled in Baghdād. An account of these events was written by Najaf-Qulī Mīrzā and a copy of it was obtained from him, or from one of his brothers, at Baghdād by As'ad Ya'qūb Khaiyāṭ,[1] a Syrian Christian who had been for more than five years Principal Interpreter to the British Consul General at Damascus and had accompanied the princes as their interpreter. Another account of the visit was written by their British *mihmāndār*, James Baillie Fraser,[2] under the title *Narrative of the residence of the Persian princes in London in 1835* [*sic*[3]] *and 1836, with an account of their journey from Persia and subsequent adventures* (2 vols., London 1838).

English translation: *Journal of a residence in England, and of a journey from and to Syria, of their Royal Highnesses Reeza Koolee Meerza, Najaf Koolee Meerza, and Taymoor Meerza, of Persia, to which are prefixed some particulars respecting modern Persia, and the death of the late Shah. Originally written in Persian, by H.R.H. Najaf Koolee Meerza, son of Prince Firmân Firmân* [*sic*], *grandson of H.M. Fathali Shah, the late Emperor of Persia; and translated, with explanatory notes, by Assaad Y. Kayat. In two volumes. Printed for private circulation only.* **London** 1839°*.

[A portrait of the three princes forms the frontispiece to Fraser's *Narrative*.]

1616. Ḥājj Mīrzā **'Alī Khān** Marāghī, entitled Ḥājib al-Daulah and later **I'timād al-Salṭanah,** was the father of M. Ḥasan Khān Marāghī I'timād al-Salṭanah (for whom see pp. 154–5 *supra*). From the latter's list of successive Heads of Government Departments in Nāṣir al-Dīn Shāh's reign (*al-Ma'āthir wa-'l-āthār* pp. 15–29) it appears that he became Minister of Justice in 1278/1861–2 (*op. cit.* p. 16*b*) and Minister of *Waẓā'if* in the nineteenth year of the reign (i.e. in 1282/1865–6. *Op. cit.* p. 17*b*). Other offices held by him are mentioned without dates in the aforesaid list under the headings *Idārah i Farrāsh-khānah u Ḥijābat i Daulat* (p. 19*a*), *Idārah i Bannā'ī i Dīwān i*

[1] Cf. Fraser's *Narrative* i p. 58.

[2] For whom see the *Dictionary of national biography* and Buckland's *Dictionary of Indian biography*.

[3] The princes did not reach England until 1836.

A'lā (p. 21*b*),[1] *Idārah i Bāghāt i Mubārakah i Daulatī* (p. 22*a*) and *Idārah i Khāliṣajāt i Dīwānī* (p. 23*b*). He was at different times Governor of 'Arabistān and Khūzistān (*op. cit.* p. 31*b*), Luristān (*op. cit.* p. 32*a*) and Gīlān (*ibid*). According to the Mashhad catalogue he died in 1285/1868–9.

(*Safar-nāmah i Ḥājj Mīrzā 'Alī Khān i Marāghī*),[2] an account of a journey to Mecca written in 1263/1847: **Mashhad** iii p. 90 (A.H. 1306/1888–9).

1617. Mubāriz al-Daulah **Pīr Ibrāhīm Khān** Khwēshgī Qaṣūrī, who was born at Qaṣūr in 1794 and died in 1856, has already been mentioned (pp. 661–3 *supra*) as the author of a history of Bahāwalpūr.

(1) *Autobiography* (in Persian ?): see p. 663 *supra*.

(2) *Sairistān*, an account of a visit to England in 1851–2 together with a brief history of his tribe: **Multān**[3] 1854° (pp. 237).

1618. **Khudā-dād Khān** b. Rāḍō Khān Tarīn has already been mentioned (p. 659 *supra*) as the author of the *Lubb i tārīkh i Sind'h* completed in 1318/1900.

Waqā'i' al-sair i Jaisalmēr, an account of a tour to Jaisalmēr in 1859: **Karāchī** 1875*.

1619. Maulawī Abū Rajā **M. Zamān Khān** Shāhjahānpūrī, *Mudarris* in a *madrasah* at Ḥaidarābād and one of the instructors who educated Mīr Maḥbūb 'Alī Khān (Niẓām of Ḥaidarābād, b. 1866, succeeded his father 1869, d. 1911), wrote an Urdu work *Hadīyah i Mahdawīyah* (Editions: Cawnpore 1867*, 1877*) in refutation of the teachings expounded in four tracts by S. 'Īsā, commonly called ('*urf*) 'Ālim Miyān, Mahdawī Ḥaidarābādī, the leader of the Mahdawī sect (cf. p. 1056 no. (21)). On 6 Dhū 'l-Ḥijjah 1292/3 Jan. 1876 he was murdered in a mosque at Ḥaidarābād by an alleged Mahdawī. According to Niẓāmī Badāyūnī an annual '*urs* is celebrated at his tomb in the court of his *madrasah*.

[1] Cf. *Rauḍat al-ṣafā-yi Nāṣirī* x fol. 141*a* (fifth page from end) ult.

[2] Called *Safar-nāmah* simply in the Mashhad catalogue, but it is not clear whether this is a formal title or a description.

[3] So M. Shafī' in *Islamic culture* iii/3 pp. 454, 472 (cf. p. 662 *supra*).

Dāstān i jahān, an account of a journey to Egypt, Syria, and Mesopotamia in 1283/1866 (pp. 3–92 = *Kitāb* i), followed by a geography of the world (pp. 92–309 = *Kitāb* ii), a history of Jerusalem (pp. 309–360 = *Kitāb* iii) and a history of the Ottoman Sulṭāns (pp. 360–92 = *Kitāb* iv): **Badāyūn** [1906°, 1911*].

[Raḥmān 'Alī pp. 188–90; Niẓāmī Badāyūnī *Qāmūs al-mashāhīr* (in Urdu) ii pp. 191–2 (evidently based mainly on Raḥmān 'Alī or on some common source).]

1620. For Nāṣir al-Dīn Shāh's diaries of his journeys in Europe and Asia see pp. 341–2.

1621. Ḥājjī **Ḥabīb Punnōchhī.**

Manāzil al-safar i ḥajj, a metrical account of a pilgrimage in 1287–8/1870–1: **Lahore** 1875* (24 pp.).

1622. Nawwāb M. **Kalb-'Alī Khān** succeeded his father, Yūsuf 'Alī Khān, as Nawwāb of Rāmpūr in 1865. He was a member of Lord Lytton's Council and was created G.C.S.I. He died in 1887 and was succeeded by his son Mushtāq 'Alī Khān. His works include (1) *Shigūfah i khusrawī*, addresses, prefaces and other compositions, Rāmpūr 1287–9/1870–3°*, and (2) *Tarānah i gham*.

Qindīl i Ḥaram, an account in rhymed prose of a pilgrimage in 1872: **Rāmpūr** 1290/1873°*.

[*Nigāristān i sukhun* pp. 128–30; *Būstān i Awad'h* p. 188; *Who's who in India*, 1911; Rām Bābū Saksēna *A history of Urdu literature* pp. 177–9; portrait in the Urdu translation of R. B. Saksēna's work.]

1623. For the diary of M. Ḥasan Khān Marāghī I'timād al-Salṭanah, describing his journey with Nāṣir al-Dīn Shāh from Tiflīs to Ṭihrān in 1290–1/1873–4, see p. 344 *supra*. The journey on which he accompanied Nāṣir al-Dīn Shāh to Mashhad in 1300/1882 is described in the *Maṭla' al-shams* (for which see p. 356 *supra*).

1624. **Farhād Mīrzā** b. 'Abbās Mīrzā b. Fatḥ-'Alī Shāh, who died in 1888, has already been mentioned in connexion with the works *Qamqām i zakhkhār* (p. 204 *supra*) and *Jām i Jam* (p. 155).

Hidāyat al-sabīl wa-kifāyat al-dalīl, diary of a pilgrimage to Mecca in 1292–3/1875–6 : **Shīrāz** 1294/1877* (362 pp.), **Ṭihrān** 1294/1877° (385 pp.).

1625. **Sulṭān-Murād Mīrzā** Ḥusām al-Salṭanah is the eleventh of the twenty-six sons of ʿAbbās Mīrzā b. Fatḥ-ʿAlī Shāh enumerated by Riḍā-Qulī Khān (*Rauḍat al-ṣafā'* ix, fol. 166*a*, l. 11). He held at different times the governorships of several towns [1] and provinces,[2] but he is more especially associated with Khurāsān, of which province he was Governor at least five times (*al-Ma'āthir wa-'l-āthār* pp. 29*b*, 30*a*). It was he who dealt with the rebellion of the Sālār (M. Ḥasan Khān b. Allāh-Yār Khān Qājār Dawālū) and besieged him in Mashhad after the death of Muḥammad Shāh (Watson *History of Persia* pp. 368, 380, 383–4). He was for a time Minister of War (*al-Ma'āthir wa-'l-āthār* p. 16).

Dalīl al-anām fī sabīl ziyārat Bait Allāh al-ḥarām, the journal of a pilgrimage to Mecca in 1297/1880 : **Majlis** *693 (A.H. 1323/1905).

[*Rauḍat al-ṣafā-yi Nāṣirī* ix foll. 155*a*, l. 17, 166*a*, l. 11, x foll. 18*b*, l. 2, 58*b* antepenult., 71*b*, l. 19, 91*b*, l. 7, 113*b*, l. 16, 118*b*, l. 17, 120*a*, l. 15, and elsewhere.]

1626. Ḥājjī **Pīr-zādah Nā'īnī.**

Safar-nāmah i Ḥājjī Pīr-zādah i Nā'īnī, an account of a journey to Paris, Istānbūl and Cairo in 1303/1885–6 : **Majlis** 695 (A.H. 1321/1903).

1627. Nawwāb Mīr **Lā'iq ʿAlī Khān** ʿImād al-Salṭanah Sir **Sālār-Jang** [II], K.C.I.E., elder son of the great Prime Minister of Ḥaidarābād, Nawwāb Mīr Turāb ʿAlī Khān Sir Sālār-Jang [I], G.C.S.I., was born at Ḥaidarābād in 1862 [3] or 1863,[4] and was educated with Mīr Maḥbūb ʿAlī Khān (b. 1866, succeeded his

[1] e.g. Iṣfahān (*al-Ma'āthir wa-'l-āthār* p. 21a penult.), Yazd (*ibid.* p. 33*a*), Kirmānshāh (*ibid.*, p. 35*a*).
[2] e.g. Fārs (*al-M. wa-'l-ā.* p. 21*a*), Kurdistān (*ibid.* p. 32*a*).
[3] So Buckland.
[4] 1280/1863 according to Niẓāmī Badāyūnī.

father as Niẓām in 1869, d. 1911). After his father's death in 1883 he was appointed Secretary to the Council of Regency and in 1884 he became Prime Minister. Having resigned in April 1887 owing to differences with the Niẓām, he visited England and was created K.C.I.E. He died in July 1889. His son, Mīr Yūsuf 'Alī Khān (Sālār-Jang III), was Prime Minister in 1912–14.

The travels in Europe of Nawab Mir Laik Ali Khan Imadul Saltana Sir Salar Jang Bahadur (*Waqā'i' i musāfarat* etc.[1]) : **Bombay** 1305/1888°.

[Buckland *Dictionary of Indian biography* p. 371 ; Niẓāmī Badāyūnī *Qāmūs al-mashāhīr* (in Urdu) i p. 278.]

1628. S. **M. Riḍā b.** Muftī S. **Dildār Ḥusain** Hāshimī was Mīr Munshī to Amīr al-Daulah Sa'īd al-Mulk Rājah M. Amīr Ḥasan Khān Mumtāz-Jang,[2] Rājah of Maḥmūdābād (near Sītāpūr in Oudh), whom he accompanied on the journey described in his *Dalā'il al-ẓafar*.

Dalā'il al-ẓafar fī tadhkirat al-safar, an account of a journey in 1306/1889 to the Shī'ite sanctuaries of Mesopotamia.

Edition : **Lucknow** [1893°*].

1629. **Maḥmūd Ṭarzī** b. Ghulām-Muḥammad Khān Ṭarzī, a descendant of Sardār Raḥm-dil Khān, brother of Amīr Dōst-Muḥammad Khān (who reigned 1242–80/1826–63), was born at Ghaznī in 1285/1870. In the reign of 'Abd al-Raḥmān Khān (1296–1319/1879–1901. Cf. pp. 405–6 *supra*) his father, having been accused of high treason and banished from Afghānistān, settled with all his family at Damascus, and here Maḥmūd married a Syrian wife. After the father's death the family was pardoned by Ḥabīb Allāh Khān (1319–37/1901–19) and Maḥmūd returned to Kābul, where in 1329/1911 he founded the fortnightly newspaper, *Sirāj al-akhbār*, " the ancestor of all the present periodical publications in Afghanistan " (Bogdanov). In 1919 after the accession of his son-in-law, Amān Allāh Khān

[1] In the Āṣafīyah catalogue (ii p. 836) the work is called *Safar-nāmah i Sālār Jang i marḥūm*, but this cannot be the actual title.

[2] b. 1849, succeeded his father 1858: see Sir R. Lethbridge *The Golden Book of India* pp. 331–2.

(1919–29), he was appointed Minister of Foreign Affairs. In 1922 he became Afghān Minister to France and Belgium, but in 1924 he was reappointed Minister of Foreign Affairs. In 1927 he went to France on leave for the sake of his health.

He played a prominent part in the literary renaissance which occurred in the reign of Ḥabīb Allāh Khān. Among his works are (1) *Rauḍah i ḥikam*, "moral, literary and political essays" (Arberry), Kābul 1331/1913*, (2) *Az har dahan sukhanī u az har chaman samanī*, a commonplace book in prose and verse, Kābul 1331/1913*, (3) *Adab dar fann* or *Maḥmūd-nāmah*, a small collection of odes (45 pp.), Kābul 1331/1913* (I.O. V.T. 3754*a*), (4) *Tārīkh i muḥārabah i Rūs u Zhāpān* (see p. 430 *supra*), as well as the following translations of the Turkish versions of novels by Jules Verne, (5) *Siyāḥat dar jaww i hawā* (= *Robur le Conquérant* = *A clipper of the clouds*), Kābul 1331/1913*, (6) *Jazīrah i pinhān* (= *L'île mystérieuse*), Kābul 1332/1914* (vol. i), (7) *20,000 farsakh siyāḥat dar zīr i baḥr* (= *Vingt mille lieues sous les mers*), Kābul 1332/1914*. According to Bogdanov he "found time to translate (from the Arabic and Turkish versions) several novels by Victor Hugo and most of the novels by Jules Verne". Few of these seem to have reached Europe.

Siyāḥat-nāmah i sih qiṭʻah i rūy i zamīn dar 29 rūz, an account of a journey in Asia, Europe and Africa in 1308/1890–1: **Kābul** 1333/1915* (674 pp.).

[L. Bogdanov *Notes on the Afghan periodical press* (in *Islamic culture* iii/1 (Jan. 1929) pp. 126–52) p. 127 n. 2.]

1630. Colonel **Shāh Bēg Khān** b. Raḥmān Bēg b. Yūsuf Bēg Shughnānī was born in 1288/1871, his father being *Aq-saqāl* of some villages in Shughnān. In 1301/1884 he was taken to Kābul and became a protégé of the Amīr ʻAbd al-Raḥmān, who arranged for the continuance of his education and subsequently gave him employment at court. After his return from his first pilgrimage he was appointed by the Amīr Ḥabīb Allāh to membership of the Common Council (p. 117[7]: *dar jumlah i mimbarān i Shūrā-yi ʻĀmm*) and six months later to the Privy Council (*sharaf i bār-yābī i Shūrā-yi Khāṣṣ nīz ʻaṭā farmūdand*). Later he became Afghān Minister in Bombay.

Safar i aiyām i sa'īdah bā nikāt i mufīdah (so at top of p. 1 and in the preface, but on the cover *Safar-nāmah i Ḥijāz . . . mushtamil-bar ḥālāt i S. i a. i s. . . .*), accounts of pilgrimages from Kābul to Mecca in 1320–1/1903 and 1322–3/1904–5 (pp. 19–34), together with extracts (*nikāt i mufīdah*) from the *Anwār i Suhailī* and elsewhere (pp. 35–116) and a biography of the author (pp. 8–19), the whole accompanied by an Urdu translation by the editor, M. Fāḍil Khān b. M. Ḥusain, *Mīr Munshī* to the Afghān Legation : **Lahore** [1915*].

[Biography referred to above. Portrait frontispiece. Portrait of the translator at end.]

1631. Other works :—

(1) *Adventures of Columbus, Discoverer of America. Translated by Mirza Mahommad Munshi.* (*Aḥwāl i Kristōfar Kulambas*) : **Calcutta** 1910*.

(2) *Aḥwāl i Kristōfar Kulambas* : see *Adventures, etc.*, above.

(3) *Armaghān i Hindūstān*, by S. Luṭf-'Alī Shāh Maudūdī Chishtī. Edition : place ? 1311/1893–4 (Āṣafīyah ii p. 836).

(4) *Fawā'id al-nāẓirīn*, an account of al-Ṭā'if and Mecca translated from J. L. Burckhardt's *Travels in Arabia* (London 1829, vol. i p. 101—vol. ii p. 87) by M. Najm al-Dīn : **Rieu** iii 993*b* (A.H. 1254/1838 ?).

Edition : *Fowaid oon Nazireen, or Travels of the late Mr. John Lewis Burckhardt on the Hedjaz, as far as Mecca. Abridged and translated into Persian by Robert Neave, Esq., and arranged for the press by Nuzmood Deen Mahomud*, **Calcutta** 1832°*.

(5) *Guldastah i Ḥakīm mausūm bah Safar i Ḥijāz*, an account of a pilgrimage by 'Abd Allāh Khān " Ḥakīm " Kāndilī : **Lahore** 1322/1904*.

(6) *Guldastah i Ingilistān*, a short account in prose and verse of a visit to London, by S. 'Abd Allāh b. M. : **Calcutta** 1271/1854°*.

(7) *'Ibrat al-nāẓirīn safar-nāmah i 'Irāq* : **Āṣafīyah** ii p. 836.

(8) *Nuh sāl dar Amrīkah*, by 'Abd Allāh Dashtī : **Ṭihrān**, date ? (see *Luzac's Oriental List* 1934 p. 107).

(9) *Rūz-nāmah i Mīrzā M. Shafī' Gushtāsb Māzandarānī* (Travels? cf. no. 14 below): **Leningrad** Univ. 866*b* (Salemann-Rosen p. 16).

(10) *Rūz-nāmah i safar i Mīrzā Naṣīr Allāh Sulṭān*: **Leningrad** Univ. 407 (Salemann-Rosen p. 16).

(11) *Rūz-nāmah i safar i Piṭirburgh*, by Mīrzā Mas'ūd: **Leningrad** Univ. 680 (Salemann-Rosen p. 16).

(12) *Safar i Ḥijāz*. See *Guldastah i Ḥakīm*.

(13) *Safar-nāmah i janāb i Qāḍī Taqī Muttaqī*, the travels of Q.T.M., of Ambala, by S. Amīn Allāh b. M. Munīr: **Ambala** [Anbālah], [1909*].

(14) *Safar-nāmah i Mīrzā M. Shafī' Gushtāsb Māzandarānī* (cf. no. 9 above): **Leningrad** Univ. 866*a* (Salemann-Rosen p. 16).

(15) *Safar-nāmah i Mūsyū Farānsīsī*: **Āṣafīyah** ii p. 836.

(16) *Safar-nāmah i Qum*, by Mīrzā Ghulām-Ḥusain Afḍal al-Mulk: **Majlis** 697 (A.H. 1324/1906).

(17) *Safar-nāmah (Mimwār) i Sar Antwān Sharlī u Sar Rubart Sharlī*, a translation made by Ḥājj 'Alī-Qulī Khān Sardār i As'ad: **Ṭihrān** 1330/1912 (see Mashhad iii p. 136).

(18) *Safar-nāmah i Wāmbirī*, a translation made in 1302/1884–5 by Āwānus[1] Masīḥī b. Ustād Ibrāhīm Zargarbāshī (cf. no. (22) below) from the French version of A. Vámbéry's *Travels in Central Asia, being the account of a journey from Teheran . . . performed in* 1863 (London 1864): **Majlis** 698 (ends in *Faṣl* xv).

(19) *Sarbāz i Pārsī*, an account of travels in Persia by Khalīl Wazīr: **Bombay** A.H.S. 1311/1933* (96 pp.).

(20) *Sawāniḥ i safar al-Ḥijāz*: **Leningrad** Univ. 1141*i* (Romaskewicz p. 10).

(21) *Siyāḥat i Turāb*, by Turāb 'Alī: **Lindesiana** p. 228 no. 349 (circ. A.D. 1820).

(22) (*Siyāḥat-nāmah*), a translation made in 1890 by Āwānus Khān (cf. no. (18) above) from a French version of H. M. Stanley's *In darkest Africa* (London 1890): **Majlis** 699 (A.H. 1308/1890–1).

[1] For this name cf. p. 841 n. 1 *supra*.

(23) ***Siyāḥat-nāmah***, account of an expedition sent in Nāṣir al-Dīn Shāh's reign to extend the telegraph to Iṣfahān, Yazd, Kirmān and the ports of the Persian Gulf: **Majlis** 700.

(24) ***Ṭalīʿah i shams***, a translation by Ibrāhīm Khān Ṣaḥḥāf-bāshī of an account of Christopher Columbus: **Mashhad** 1327/1909 (see Mashhad 14, ptd. bks., no. 139).

(25) ***Tuḥfat al-bāṣirīn***, a diary of a pilgrimage by M. ʿAlī b. M. Qāsim: **Karāchī** 1858°.

(26) ***Tūshah i rāh***, a *mathnawī* describing a journey from Kashmīr to India and meetings with persons of distinction by M. Anwar Shāh "Anwar"[1]: **Lahore** 1874* (18 pp. Cf. Arberry p. 306).

N. BIOGRAPHY: (*q*) WOMEN

1632. For the memoirs of Gulbadan Bēgam see p. 539 *supra*.

1633. For the *Jawāhir al-ʿajāʾib* of "Fakhrī" b. "Amīrī" Harawī see p. 797 *supra*.

1634. **Gaston Bruit** composed his account of Bībī Juliyānā[2] at the request of Colonel Jean-Baptiste Joseph Gentil,[3] who had come to India in 1165/1752, twenty-two years before the date of composition, and had married Bībī Juliyānā's great-grand-niece.

Aḥwāl i Bībī Juliyānā, an account of a Portuguese woman who was taken captive in childhood, apparently at Hūglī, by Shāh-Jahān's forces and who, having in course of time entered the service of Prince M. Muʿaẓẓam (Shāh-ʿĀlam Bahādur Shāh), rose to an influential position in his household and died (according to the *Tārīkh i Muḥammadī* cited by Rieu) at Delhi

[1] Another work by the same author is *Manẓūm i Anwar*, poems in praise of Kalb-ʿAlī Khān, Nawwāb of Rāmpūr (for whom see p. 1156 *supra*), Amritsar 1293/1876°* (220 pp.).

[2] For whom see Gentil's *Mémoires sur l'Indoustan* pp. 367–80; J. A. Ismael Garcias *Uma doña portuguesa na corte do Grão Mogol*, Nova Goa 1907: E. Maclagan *The Jesuits and the Great Mogul*, London 1932, pp. 181–9; etc.

[3] For whom see Buckland *Dictionary of Indian biography* p. 161. He was at this time in the service of Shujāʿ al-Daulah, the *Nawwāb-Wazīr* of Oudh and "was most generous in helping less fortunate fellow countrymen, and enrolled a body of them to serve under the Nawab.". He was born at Bagnols in 1726 and died there in 1799. His collection of Persian MSS. is now in the Bibliothèque Nationale.

in Rabī' I 1147/August 1734: **Rieu** ii 822*a* (late 18th cent.), **Browne** Suppt. 16 (King's 20).

French translation: *Histoire de Donna Juliana* (*Ahwál-i Bíbí Julyáná*). *Traduite d'un manuscrit persan de la bibliothèque du King's College, Cambridge ... Par Edward Henry Palmer* (in, and offprinted from, *Nouvelles annales des voyages*, tome ii, May 1865, pp. 161–84).

1635. For a biography of Bēgam Samrū see p. 692 *supra*.

1636. For the verses by poetesses contained in the *Zubdat al-mu'āṣirīn* of Mīr Ḥusain al-Ḥusainī see p. 889 *supra*.

1637. For the *Nuql i majlis*, notices of poetesses composed in 1241/1825–6 by Maḥmūd Mīrzā Qājār, see p. 888 *supra*.

1638. For S͟hāh-Jahān Bēgam's history of Bhōpāl, the *Tāj al-iqbāl*, see p. 734 *supra*.

1639. For the *Ak͟htar i tābān* or *Tad͟hkirat al-nisā'* of Abū 'l-Qāsim Muḥtas͟ham and the *Tad͟hkirat al-k͟hawātīn* of M. b. M. Rafī' S͟hīrāzī see p. 916 *supra*.

1640. For the *Ḥadīqah i 'is͟hrat* of Durgā-Pars͟hād "Mihr" Sandīlī see p. 917 *supra*.

1641. M. Ḥasan K͟hān Marāg͟hī, entitled **Ṣanī' al-Daulah** and afterwards **I'timād al-Salṭanah**, died at Ṭihrān in 1896 (see pp. 154–5 *supra*).

K͟hairāt ḥisān,[1] lives of eminent Muslim women, in 3 vols. Edition: [**Ṭihrān**,] 1304/1887°–1307/1889°.

1642. For an anonymous *Tad͟hkirat al-nisā'* on Indian poetesses see p. 923 *supra*.

1643. Other works:—

(1) *Aḥwāl i Bānū ... Mumtāz-Maḥall*[2]: **Lindesiana** p. 111 no. 351 (A.D. 1844).

(2) *K͟hulāṣah i aḥwāl i Bānū Bēgam*: **Lahore** Panjāb Univ. Lib. (see *OCM*. ii/4 (Lahore, August 1926) p 53).

[1] Cf. *Qur'ān* lv 70.

[2] For other accounts of Mumtāz-Maḥall see the works relating to Āgrah and the Tāj Maḥall in the geographical and topographical section of this work.

N. BIOGRAPHY: (*r*) GENERAL AND MISCELLANEOUS

1644. M. b. Manṣūr b. Saʿīd . . . b. Abī Bakr al-Ṣiddīq al-Taimī al-Qurashī, surnamed (*al-mulaqqab*) **Mubārak-Shāh** known as (*maʿrūf bi-*) **Fakhr i Mudabbir,** as he calls himself ("*Tārīkh*", ed. Ross, p. 62[3], *Ādāb al-ḥarb*, preface [1]), was descended on his mother's side from the *amīr* Bilgā-tagīn, the father-in-law of Sulṭān Maḥmūd Ghaznawī (Rieu ii p. 488*a*). Fifteen years after the defeat of Khusrau Shāh by ʿAlāʾ al-Dīn Ghōrī [i.e. in or about 565/1169–70, since according to Ibn al-Athīr, *Kāmil* xi p. 108, Khusrau Shāh was defeated in 550/1155] he was in Multān and was then a mere youth (*kūdakī*, Rieu *ibid.*). "Several other references to Multān make it probable that it was his native place" (Rieu, *ibid.*). After the defeat of Khusrau Malik by Muʿizz al-Dīn M. b. Sām [in 582/1186] Mubārak-Shāh went to Lahore and caused a search to be made for title-deeds and other family papers long inaccessible to him. His family pedigree having been found and taken to Lahore, he conceived the idea of working out genealogical tables of the Prophet and the ʿAsharah i Mubashsharah, one of whom was his ancestor Abū Bakr. This led to further study and eventually after more than thirteen years of research he completed a volume of genealogical tables, which earned the warm commendation of his erudite father, the pupil of many great scholars of Ghaznah ("*Tārīkh*", p. 70[5]) and the master of more than twenty branches of learning (*ibid.* p. 68[10]). In the autumn of 602/1206, when Muʿizz al-Dīn M. b. Sām was in Lahore, he was told about these tables and asked to see them, but before they could be shown to him he left Lahore and was murdered on his way to Ghaznah. When his successor, Quṭb al-Dīn Aibak, entered Lahore, he too was told about Mubārak-Shāh's tables. The author was presented and the tables, or some of them, were read to the Sulṭān, who expressed his approval and gave orders that they should be transcribed and bound for the royal library. A later work by this author, the *Ādāb al-ḥarb wa-'l-shajāʿah* (so Rieu ii p. 487 and Ivanow 1608),

[1] In the latter place the name, as quoted by Rieu, is Sharīf M. [b.] Manṣūr [b.] Saʿīd . . . Quraishī *mulaqqab bi-*Mubārak-Shāh *maʿrūf bi-*Fakhr i Mudabbir.

or *Ādāb al-mulūk wa-kifāyat al-mamlūk* (so in Ethé 2767), seems to be undated, but it is dedicated to Sulṭān Īltutmish, who reigned at Delhi from 607/1210 to 633/1236.[1] In both of these works he speaks of himself as an infirm old man (*pīr i ḍaʻīf*, " *Tārīkh* " p. 62[3]).

(*Shajarah i ansāb i Mubārak-Shāhī*),[2] 137 genealogies relating to the Prophet, the ʻAsharah i Mubashsharah, the Muhājirūn, the Anṣār, the Prophets mentioned in the *Qur'ān*, the Ghassānids, the Tabābiʻah, Pre-Islāmic and Islāmic poets, the Pre-Islāmic Persian kings, the Umaiyads and ʻAbbasids, Arab tribes, the Umarā' of Umaiyad and ʻAbbāsid times, the Ṭāhirids, Ṣaffārids, Sāmānids, Subuktagīnids, Ghōrids and others, preceded by an introduction containing some historical information about the last Ghōrids and their first successors in India as well as a number of pages in description and praise of the Turks: **Ellis Coll.** M. 253 (16th cent.).

Edition of the introductory matter and of the account of Adam and Eve and their immediate descendants (i.e. foll. 1–48*a* and 50*b*–55*b* out of 125): *Taʻríkh-i* [*sic*] *Fakhru'd-Dín Mubárakshâh, being the historical introduction to the Book of Genealogies of Fakhru'd-Dín Mubárakshâh Marvar-rúḍí* [*sic* [3]] *completed in* A.D. *1206. Edited from a unique manuscript by E. Denison Ross*, **London** 1927* (R.A.S., Forlong Fund).

Description with an abridged translation of most of the introductory portion: *The genealogies of Fakhr-ud-Dín Mubárak Sháh*. [Signed E. Denison Ross. In *ʻAjab-nāmah: a volume of oriental studies presented to E. G. Browne*, Cambridge, 1922, pp. 392–413].

[1] The title Nāṣir Amīr al-Mu'minīn appended to the name of Īltutmish in the preface (see Rieu ii p. 488*a*, Ethé col. 1493) would imply, if really a part of the author's text, that the work was completed late in the reign. Some fifty pages of extracts relating to the Ghaznawids have been published with English translation and prefatory remarks by Miss Iqbāl M. Shafīʻ in *Islamic culture* for April 1938.

[2] No formal title is given to the work by the author, but he refers to it as *īn shajarah* (e.g. pp. 68[8], 69[8], 73[2]), *ān shajarah i ansāb* (p. 71 penult.), *īn shajarah u* [*sic ?*] *ansāb* (p. 62[8]).

[3] As indicated below, F. al-D. M.-Sh. Marwarrūdhī seems to be a different person from the author of this work.

Elucidation of Mubārak-Shāh's statements concerning the Turks: *On Mubarakshah Ghuri* [*sic*]. *By Ahmet-Zeki Validi* (in *BSOS*. vi/4 (1932) pp. 847–58. Pp. 856^{27}–858 are devoted to a description of the *Raḥīq al-taḥqīq* of Fakhr al-Dīn M.-Sh. Ghōrī, who, as indicated below, seems to be a different person).

In spite of some curious resemblances it seems impossible to identify Fakhr al-Dīn Mubārak-Shāh Qurashī (M. b. Manṣūr) with Fakhr al-Dīn Mubārak-Shāh Marwarrūdhī. The latter, according to Ibn al-Athīr (*al-Kāmil*, ed. Tornberg, xii p. 160 ult.), was Fakhr al-Dīn Mubārak-Shāh b. al-Ḥasan [so in Tornberg's text, not b. Abī 'l-Ḥasan, as Ross states] al-Marwarrūdhī, a good Arabic and Persian poet, the owner of a guest-house containing books for the learned and chess-boards for the ignorant [evidently therefore a rich man], who stood high in the regard of Ghiyāth al-Dīn the Great, Lord of Ghaznah and Harāt, and who died in Shawwāl 602/May-June 1206 [1] [i.e. several years before Mubārak-Shāh Qurashī can have died]. According to the *Ṭabaqāt i Nāṣirī* (p. 28^{8}, where he is called Malik al-kalām Maulānā Fakhr al-Dīn Mubārak-Shāh Marwarrūdhī) he wrote *in verse* a genealogy of the Ghōrids (*nisbat-nāmah i īn salāṭīn i nāmdār rā dar silk i naẓm kashīdah*). Minhāj i Sirāj had himself in 602/1205–6 [i.e. at, or about, the age of thirteen: see p. 68 *supra*] seen a copy of this metrical genealogy in the *ḥaram* of Māh i Mulk, Ghiyāth al-Dīn M. b. Sām's daughter, who told him [*Ṭabaqāt* p. 69^{7-13}] that the work was originally dedicated to Sulṭān 'Alā' al-Dīn Ḥusain Jahānsūz [who died in 551/1156 [2]] but was put aside by the author in an unfinished state until eventually completed with a new dedication to Ghiyāth al-Dīn M. b. Sām [d. 599/1202]. In the *Haft iqlīm* (no. 516, Ethé col. 415. Text quoted by Ross in *Ta'ríkh-i Fakhru'd-Dín*, introd., pp. iii–v) there is a notice of a certain Fakhr al-Dīn Mubārak-Shāh, who, though placed under Marw i Shāhjān, is evidently the same person as Fakhr

[1] Ibn al-Athīr's words are: *wa-fīhā fī Shawwāl tuwuffiya Fakhr al-Dīn Mubārak Shāh b. al-Ḥasan al-Marwarrūdhī wa-kāna ḥasan al-shi'r bi-'l-Fārisīyah wa-'l-'Arabīyah wa-lahu manzilah 'aẓīmah 'inda Ghiyāth al-Dīn al-kabīr ṣāḥib Ghaznah wa-Harāh wa-ghairihimā wa-kāna lahu dār ḍiyāfah fīhā kutub wa-shiṭranj fa-'l-'ulamā' yuṭāli'ūn al-kutub wa-'l-juhhāl yal'abūn bi-'l-shiṭranj.*

[2] Mubārak-Shāh Qurashī, if a *kūdak* in 565 (see p. 1164^{11}), cannot have been much more than a child in 551.

al-Dīn Mubārak-Shāh Marwarrūdhī. He is described as *Ṣadr i Saḥbān-bayān i daryā-banānī*,[1] an intimate friend of Sulṭān Ghiyāth al-Dīn Ghōrī and a dispenser of lavish hospitality.[2] Amīn Rāzī quotes two verses from a *qaṣīdah* of his in praise of Malik Saif al-Dīn Ghōrī [who died in 558/1162 [3]]. Finally Mubārak-Shāh Marwarrūdhī is probably identical with the poet Mubārak-Shāh Ghūrī, who according to the *Ḥabīb al-siyar* (Bombay ed. ii p. 155, translated by Ross in *'Ajab-nāmah* p. 394) wrote verses in praise of Ghiyāth al-Dīn [Ghōrī] as well as the astronomical work *al-Madkhal al-manẓūm fī baḥr al-nujūm*,[4] and who, as Ahmet-Zeki Validi has shown (*BSOS*. vi/4 pp. 856–8), completed in Muḥarram 584/March 1188 the metrical work on ethics *Raḥīq al-taḥqīq* (*min kalām Fakhr al-Dīn Mubārak-Shāh Ghōrī*. MS.: Āyā Ṣōfyah 4792).

1645. Shams al-Dīn A. b. M. b. Ibrāhīm b. Abī Bakr **Ibn Khallikān** al-Barmakī al-Irbilī al-Shāfi'ī was born at Arbela in 608/1211 and died at Cairo, as a professor in the Madrasat al-Amīnīyah, in 681/1282. His Arabic biographical dictionary, the *Wafayāt al-a'yān wa-anbā' abnā' al-zamān*, was begun at Cairo in 654/1256 and completed in 672/1274. The Arabic text has been published at Göttingen (ed. F. Wüstenfeld) in 1835–50, at Paris (only as far as no. 678, ed. MacGuckin de Slane) in 1838–42, at Būlāq in 1275/1859° and 1299/1882°, at Cairo in 1299/1882° and 1310/1892‡ and at [Ṭihrān ?] in 1284/1867°. An English translation by MacGuckin de Slane was published in the Oriental Translation Fund Series, Paris and London, 1842–71°. [See Brockelmann i pp. 326–8, *Sptbd*. i p. 561; *Ency. Isl.* under Ibn Khallikān; etc.]

The following Persian translations are extant:—

(1) ***Manẓar al-insān fī tarjamat Wafayāt al-a'yān***, an abridged translation begun in 893/1487 and completed in 895/1489 by Yūsuf b. Aḥmad b. M. b. 'Uthmān b. 'Alī b. Aḥmad al-Shujā' al-Sijzī or al-Sanjarī for Maḥmūd Shāh Bēgaṛah of

[1] I have conjecturally emended the text printed by Ross.

[2] *Finā' i suddah i ū maḥaṭṭ i raḥl i afāḍil u marji' u ma'āb i amāthil mī būd.*

[3] In 565, as we have noted above, Mubārak-Shāh Qurashī was a *kūdak*.

[4] Cf. Ḥ. Kh. v p. 472, where the author's name is corrupted into Mubārak 'Ūdhī.

Gujrāt (reigned 863–917/1458–1511): **Rieu** ii 809*a* (latter half of the work. 16th cent.), i 334*a* (A.H. 1012/1603), 335*a* (16th cent.), **Bānkīpūr** viii 719 (A.H. 1018/1609).

(2) (*Tarjamah i Wafayāt al-aʻyān*) an incomplete (?)[1] translation made for Sulṭān Salīm I (A.H. 918–26/1512–20) by [ʻAbd al-] Kabīr b. Uwais b. M. al-Laṭīfī (i.e. Ẓahīr al-Dīn al-Ardabīlī al-Ḥanafī known as (*al-shahīr bi-*) Qāḍī-zādah),[2] who completed the first part (nos. 1–204) at Istānbūl on 5 Dhū 'l-Qaʻdah 926/17 Oct. 1520 and the second part (nos. 205–453) in 928/1521–2; Ḥ. Kh. vi p. 455, **Browne** Suppt. 1359 (Pt. I, autograph, A.H. 926/1520, Pt. II, transcribed from an autograph, A.H. 1019/1610–11. King's 110), **Majlis** 538 (Pt. I, A.H. 926/1520), **Bodleian** 361 (Pts. I–II, A.H. 1197/1783).

1646. For the *Bahjat al-tawārīkh*, which was completed in 861/1456–7 by Shukr Allāh b. Shihāb al-Dīn Aḥmad al-Rūmī and which is largely biographical (the 13 *bābs* being devoted respectively to (1) cosmography, geography and ethnology, (2) the Pre-Islāmic prophets, (3) Muḥammad's genealogy, (4) his birth, life, etc., (5) his wives, children, and other relations, (6) his ten principal associates, (7) his other companions, (8) the Twelve Imāms, (9) the famous *shaikhs*, (10) the ancient philosophers, (11) the Pre-Islāmic Persian kings, (12) the Umaiyad and ʻAbbāsid Caliphs, (13) the Ottoman Sulṭāns), see p. 91 *supra*.

1647. For the *Tārīkh i Ṣadr i jahān*, which was written at least partly in 907/1501–2 by Faiḍ Allāh b. Zain al-ʻĀbidīn Banbānī and which contains biographies of poets, Companions of the Prophet, scholars, etc., see p. 110 *supra*.

[1] According to the translator's statement (see Ḥ. Kh. vi p. 455[5], Bodleian col. 193) he had translated half of the work when Salīm died. It will be observed that the two parts extant in manuscript contain 453 of the 865 biographies. At that point presumably the work was discontinued.

[2] Kabīr b. Uwais was deported from Tabrīz to Istānbūl by Salīm after the battle of Chāldirān [in 920/1514] and was granted a stipend of eighty dirhams a day. His account of Salīm's campaigns of 922–3/1516–17, which included the conquest of Egypt, has already been mentioned (p. 417 *supra*). In 930/1524 he was put to death at Cairo with Aḥmad Pāshā " al-Khā'in ". See *al-Shaqā'iq al-Nuʻmānīyah*, Cairo 1310, i p. 506, Rescher's trans. p. 289; *Shadharāt al-dhahab* viii p. 173; *Dānishmandān i Ādharbāyjān* pp. 249–50; *Majālis al-nafā'is* tr. Qazwīnī pp. 396–7.

1648. **Abū Bakr b. Hidāyat Allāh Ḥusainī** wrote his *Riyāḍ al-khulūd* in 989/1581.

Riyāḍ al-khulūd, on the lives and sayings of amīrs, scholars, and divines : **Majlis** 549 (A.H. 1316/1898–9).

1649. **Amīn** [ibn] Aḥmad **Rāzī** [1] was born at Rai,[2] of which town his father, Khwājah Mīrzā Aḥmad,[3] a favourite of Shāh Ṭahmāsp, was for some years *Kalāntar*. Khwājah M. Sharīf "Hajrī" Rāzī,[4] *Wazīr* successively of Khurāsān, Yazd and Iṣfahān, was his paternal uncle, and I'timād al-Daulah (Ghiyāth Bēg b. M. Sharīf), Nūr-Jahān's father and Jahāngīr's *Wazīr*, was his first cousin. That Amīn Rāzī was resident in India when he wrote the *Haft iqlīm* is shown by incidental references to Akbar and his court, such, for example, as the statement that "Ṭarīqī" Sāwajī (*Haft iqlīm* no. 1011 : cf. Badā'ūnī iii p. 263) was for about fifteen years *mulāzim i īn dargāh*.

Haft iqlīm, biographical notices of about 1560 poets, saints, scholars, and other celebrities completed in 1002/1593–4 [5] and arranged geographically under their towns or countries, of which in many cases geographical accounts are given : Ḥ. Kh. vi p. 501 no. 14411, **Sipahsālār** ii p. 485 no. 1123 (A.H. 1025/1616), nos. 1124–5, **Bodleian** 416 (A.H. 1039/1630), 417 (A.H. 1075/1665), 418 (A.H. 1199/1785), 419 (3rd and 5th *iqlīms* only. N.d.), 420 (4th *iqlīm* only. N.d.), MS. Pers. c. 24 (A.H. 1052/

[1] At the beginning of the preface to the *Haft iqlīm* he calls himself Amīn i Aḥmad i Rāzī. The *iḍāfat* has commonly been ignored by Orientalists and the name read as Amīn Aḥmad, but we know on Amīn's own authority that his father's name was Aḥmad and the presence of the *iḍāfat* is made clear in the chronogrammatic *rubā'ī* at the end of the preface. It runs as follows :—

Īn nuskhah kih hast hamchu firdaus nikū
Tā mū na-shawī darū nah bi-shkāfī mū.
Gar az tu kasī su'āl i tārīkh kunad,
Taṣnīf i Amīn i Aḥmad i Rāzī gū.

[2] *Shahr i Rai kih maulid u mansha' i īn faqīr ast* (Bombay Univ. p. 72).

[3] *Haft iqlīm* no. 1117.

[4] "Hajrī" (this vocalisation seems more probable than "Hijrī" hitherto favoured by Orientalists) died in 984/1576–7. See *Haft iqlīm* no. 1114; *Makhzan al-gharā'ib* no. 3051 ; etc. For his *dīwān* see Bānkīpūr ii 244 and Ethé 1440.

[5] The chronogram indicating this date is quoted in note 1 on p. 1169. As Ethé pointed out (I.O. Cat. col. 498), the mention of Muḥammad III (acc. 1003/1595) in the list of Ottoman Sultans shows that some parts of the *Haft iqlīm* are later than 1002, but Browne's statement (*Lit. Hist.* iv p. 448) that it was "composed in 1028/1619" is doubtless a mistake.

1642), **Oxford** Ind. Inst. MS. Whinfield 20 (defective. N.d.), **Cairo** p. 509 (A.H. 1052/1643), **Rieu** i 335*b* (17th cent.), 336*b* (A.H. 1059/1649), 337*a* (17th cent.), 337*a* (the first two-thirds of the work. 17th cent.), iii 970*a* (A.H. 1261/1845), Suppt. 138 (17th cent.), **Leningrad** Univ. 1134 (A.H. 1066/1655-6. See Romaskewicz p. 15), 1154 (*vid. ibid.*), **Blochet** 642 (A.H. 1068/1657–8), 643 (A.H. 1094/1683), **Ethé** 724, 725 (A.H. 1089/1678), 726 (defective, beginning in 3rd *iqlīm*. A.H. 1093/1682), **I.O.** 4541 (A.H. 1006/1597–8 or 1106/1694–5 ? date indistinct), **Bānkīpūr** vii 636 (17th cent.), **Āṣafīyah** iii p. 162 no. 190 (17th cent.), i p. 232 no. 465, **Ivanow** 282 (A.H. 1166/1752–3), 283 (A.D. 1871), Curzon 706 (19th cent.), **Lindesiana** p. 113 no. 712 (extracts only. Circ. A.D. 1750), **Majlis** 456 (A.H. 1273/1856–7), **Būhār** 100 (19th cent.), **Bombay** Univ. 36 (portion only, corresponding to nos. 985–1558 in Ethé's description), **Browne** Pers. Cat. 110, **Browne** Coll. K. 5 (13) = Houtum-Schindler 39, K. 4 (= I.O. 4541 above), **Eton** 56 (imperfect), **Kapurthala** 49 (see *Oriental College Magazine* vol. iii/4 (Lahore, Aug. 1927) p. 19), **Lahore** Panjab Univ. Lib. (2 copies. See *Oriental College Magazine*, vol. iii, no. 1 (Lahore, Nov. 1926), p. 68).

Edition : *Haft Iqlîm, or the geographical and biographical encyclopaedia of Amîn Aḥmad Râzî. Edited by E. Denison Ross and . . . ʻAbdul Muqtadir* (*Fasc.* 2. *Edited by A. H. Harley and ʻAbdul Muqtadir. Fasc.* 3. *Edited by A. H. H., ʻA. M. and M. Mahfuz-ul Haq*), **Calcutta** 1918°* (Fasc. 1), 1927°* (Fasc. 2), 1939 (Fasc. 3). These three fasciculi, which form " vol. i ", extend to " Partawī " of Shīrāz (no. 260 in Ethé's enumeration).

Abridgment : *Intikhāb i Haft iqlīm* by Faiḍ Allāh " Himmat " Anṣārī Jaunpūrī, dedicated to Wajīh al-Dīn ʻAlī Khān Bahādur : **Ethé** 727.

Extracts : (**1**) [on Māzandarān, Gīlān, etc.] B. Dorn *Muhammedanische Quellen zur Geschichte der südlichen Küstenländer des Kaspischen Meeres*, **St. Petersburg** 1850–8°*, Theil iv pp. 88–100, (**2**) [on Turkistān] *Description . . . de Boukhara par Mohammed Nerchakhy, suivie de textes relatifs à la Transoxiane. Texte persan publié par C. Schefer*, Paris 1892°*, pp. 243–91, (**3**) [on Africa] *Documents persans sur l'Afrique publiés et traduits par C. Huart* (in *Recueil de mémoires orientaux. Textes et traductions publiés . . .*

à l'occasion du XIVe Congrès International des Orientalistes réuni à Alger avril 1905. Publications de l'École des Langues Orientales Vivantes, V^e série, vol. 5, **Paris** 1905°*, pp. 104-14 (text), 114-30 (trans.)). For one or two other extracts see Edwards.

Translations of extracts : (**1**) [on Kāshghar (French)] *Notice de l'ouvrage persan qui a pour titre Matla-assaadeïn . . . Par M. Quatremère* (in *Notices et extraits des manuscrits de la Bibliothèque du Roi* . . . tome xiv (**Paris** 1843°*)), pp. 474–89. (**2**) [on Africa] see Extracts (3) above.

Lists and epitomes of the biographies : (**1**) Ethé coll. 381–499, (**2**) [nos. 985–1558 only, i.e. from " Qudsī " Tafrishī to Amīr Aḥmad Ḥājjī of Kāshghar] Bombay Univ. pp. 68–107.

1650. M. Ṣādiq, the author of the *Ṭabaqāt i Shāhjahānī*, who mentions a brother of his, Mullā M. Yūsuf Kashmīrī Hamadānī (d. 1033/1623–4) among the poets of Jahāngīr's reign, may be regarded as certainly identical with **M. Ṣādiq Hamadānī,** the author of the *Kalimāt al-ṣādiqīn* (see p. 985 *supra*), who in the *Tārīkh i Muḥammadī* is called Maulānā Ṣādiq Kashmīrī (see Rieu iii p. 1096*b*). From the *Ṭabaqāt i Shāhjahānī* Rieu ascertained that the author was born about 1000/1591–2, that he spent his life in Delhi, studied under Sh. Fā'iḍ (d. 1022/1613), and was a favourite disciple of Sh. 'Abd al-Ḥaqq Dihlawī (for whom see pp. 194–5, 978–80 *supra*). The author of the *Kalimāt al-ṣādiqīn*, who often refers to Sh. 'Abd al-Ḥaqq Dihlawī as *ḥaḍrat i makhdūmī*, mentions a maternal grandfather, Ḥājjī M. Hamadānī, who went to Multān and finally settled in Delhi, where he died in 1006/1597 (Bānkīpūr viii pp. 34–5). He speaks of an earlier work of his entitled *Silsilat al-ṣādiqīn* and expresses a hope of being able to write a *Ma'āthir i Jahāngīrī* (*ibid.* p. 35).

Ṭabaqāt i Shāhjahānī, lives of 871 celebrities who lived under Tīmūr and his successors, divided into ten *ṭabaqāt* ((1)) Tīmūr, 770–807/1369–1405, (2) Mīrān-Shāh and Shāh-Rukh, 807–50/1405–47, (3) Mīrzā Sulṭān-Muḥammad and Ulugh Bēg, 850–3/1447–9, (4) Abū Sa'īd, 854–73/1450–69, (5) 'Umar Shaikh, 873–99/1469–94, (6) Bābur, 900–37/1495–1530, (7) Humāyūn, 938–63/1531–56, (8) Akbar, 963–1014/1556–1605, (9) Jahāngīr, 1014–37/1605–27, (10) Shāh-Jahān, from 1037/1627 to the date of composition, which is not specified in the preface, though 1046/1636–7 is mentioned early in *Ṭabaqah* 10 as the current year), each *ṭabaqah* being subdivided into three *bābs* ((1) Saiyids and saints, (2) scholars, physicians and men of letters (*'ulamā'*, *ḥukamā'*, *fuḍalā'*), (3) poets): **Āṣafīyah** i p. 246 no. 721 (before A.H. 1156/1743), **Ethé** 705 (n.d.), **Rieu** iii 1009*b* (19th cent.).

1651. For the *Ṣubḥ i ṣādiq*, which was completed in 1048/1638–9 by Mirzā M. Ṣādiq b. M. Ṣāliḥ Iṣfahānī and of which the third *mujallad* is devoted to celebrated men of the first eleven centuries, see p. 126 *supra*. The same author's *Shāhid i ṣādiq* (for which see p. 125 *supra*) contains some biographical matter (e.g. *Bāb* iii, *faṣl* 79, which is devoted to " notices of remarkable events and of the death of celebrated men in chronological order from the Hijrah to A.H. 1042 " (Rieu ii p. 776), and the *khātimah*, which is " an alphabetical list of proper names of places and men, with fixation of their spelling, and short notices " (*ibid.*)).

1652. For the *Mir'āt al-'ālam*, which was composed in 1078/1667 ostensibly by Bakhtāwar Khān but really by M. Baqā Sahāranpūrī and which contains biographies of celebrities, see p. 132 *supra*.

1653. Mīrzā Nūr al-Dīn M. " **'Ālī** " b. Ḥakīm Fatḥ al-Dīn Shīrāzī, entitled **Ni'mat Khān** and **Dānishmand Khān,** who died at Delhi in 1122/1710, has already been mentioned as the author of the *Waqā'i' i Ḥaidarābād* (p. 590 *supra*) and other works.

Rāḥat al-qulūb (beg. *Āfrīn Sukhan-āfrīnī rā kih dar ṣalā-yi thanāyash*), satirical notices of some contemporaries, whose names are indicated by means of riddles: **Rieu** ii 796*a* (18th cent.), **Edinburgh** 375 (1) (18th cent.).

1654. For the *Farḥat al-nāẓirīn*, which was completed in 1184/1770–1 by M. Aslam Parasrūrī and of which the *khātimah* is devoted to geography, the lives of scholars, saints and poets, and the family of Shujā' al-Daulah, see p. 140 *supra*.

1655. For the *Ḥadīqat al-aqālīm*, which was written mainly in 1192–6/1778–82 by Murtaḍā Ḥusain Bilgrāmī and which, like the *Haft iqlīm*, consists largely of geographically arranged biographies, see p. 142 *supra*.

1656. For the *Lubb al-siyar u jahān-numā*, which was compiled in 1208/1793–4 by Mīrzā Abū Ṭālib Khān Iṣfahānī and of which the third *bāb* contains biographies of philosophers, Companions of the Prophet, scholars, poets, etc., see p. 145 *supra*.

1657. For the *Zubdat al-gharā'ib*, which was composed in 1231/1816 by M. Riḍā "Najm" Ṭabāṭabā and of which the fifth volume contains lives of philosophers, saints, poets, etc., see p. 148 *supra*.

1658. For the *Yādgār i Bahādurī*, which was completed in 1249/1833–4 by Bahādur Sing'h b. Hazārī-Mal, and of which the third *sāniḥah* contains *inter alia* biographies of philosophers, saints (Muslim and Hindu), scholars, poets and others, see p. 149 *supra*.

1659. Mâulawī S. **Ashraf al-Dīn Aḥmad** b. Nawwāb Wazīr al-Sulṭān S. M. Amīr 'Alī Khān Bahādur, who was born in 1855 and received the title of Khān Bahādur in 1893, has already been mentioned (p. 724 *supra*) as the author of the *Ṭabaqāt i Muḥsinīyah* (Calcutta 1889*). In addition to the *Nau ratan* referred to there he wrote some essays on education published under the title *Chār dīwār* at Calcutta in 1894*.

Dur-dānah i khayāl, an autobiography: **Lucknow** (N.K.) 1889*.

1660. According to M. 'Alī "Tarbiyat"[1] as translated by E. G. Browne in *The Press and poetry of modern Persia*, pp. 165–6, the *Nāmah i dānishwarān i Nāṣirī* was "compiled by a committee of scholars consisting of Mírzá Abu'l-Faẓl of Sáwa, Mīrzā Hasan of Ṭálaqán,[2] 'Abdu'l-Wahháb of Qazwín,[3] known

[1] For whom see p. 1111 *supra*.

[2] In the British Museum catalogue the *Nāmah i dānishwarān* [vol. i only] is entered under Ḥusain [*sic*], Ṭaliqānī, to whom also the *Lisān al-'Ajam*, a Persian grammar of 172 pp. published at Bombay in 1317/1899°, is there ascribed. According to the Bombay Quarterly Catalogue (1900, 4th quarter) the author of the *Lisān al-'Ajam* was Mīrzā Ḥasan b. M. Taqī Ṭālaqānī. The other collaborators in the *Nāmah i dānishwarān* are not mentioned by Edwards, but the Āṣafīyah catalogue (i p. 348) gives the four names—Mīrzā Abū 'l-Faḍl Sāwī, Mīrzā Ḥasan Ṭālaqā'ī [*sic*], Mullā 'Abd al-Wahhāb Qazwīnī and Mullā M. Mahdī.

[3] He died in Muḥarram 1306/Sept. 1888. See *al-Ma'āthir wa-'l-āthār* p. 161; *Bīst maqālah i Qazwīnī*, pt. 1, p. 5.

as " Mullá Áqá ", and Muḥammad called al-Mahdí.[1] This work, which was not completed, is a detailed Dictionary of Biography of the notable and eminent persons, men of letters, divines, philosophers, mystics, etc., who were most celebrated in Islám, and contains accounts of their biographies, adventures, characteristics and writings. Its publication was begun in A.H. 1296 (= A.D. 1879) under the supervision of 'Alí-qulí Mírzá *I'tiẓádu's-Salṭana.*[2] On his death in A.H. 1298 (= A.D. 1881), after the publication of two volumes,[3] the editorial committee made over the supervision to Muḥammad Ḥasan Khán *I'timádu's-Salṭana,*[4] so that the last five volumes (iii–vii) were published as appendices to the Year Books (*Sál-náma*) of A.H. 1318, 1319, 1321, 1322, and 1323 (= A.D. 1900–5)."

Nāmah i dānishwarān i Nāṣirī, a large unfinished dictionary of learned men, vol. i (beginning with Ibn Bābawaih [5] and ending with Abū Isḥāq Ibrāhīm b. Aḥmad b. M. Ṭabarī [6]) [**Ṭihrān**] 1296/1879°, vol. ii (beginning with Abū 'l-Baqā' 'Abd Allāh b. al-Ḥusain al-'Ukbarī [7] and ending with Ibn Abī 'l-'Azāqir, i.e. M. b. 'Alī al-Shalmaghānī [8]) **Ṭihrān** 1312/1894 (cf. Browne *Lit. Hist.* iv p. 447 and Āṣafīyah i p. 348 no. 57), vols. iii–vii appended to the *Sāl-nāmahs* specified above.

1661. **M. Ḥasan Khān** Marāghī, entitled **Ṣanī' al-Daulah** and afterwards **I'timād al-Salṭanah,** who died at Ṭihrān in 1896, has already been mentioned several times (pp. 154, 225, 246, 344, 356, 362, 429). His work *al-Ma'āthir wa-'l-āthār* is mentioned on p. 344, but, since it contains a considerable amount of biography, it deserves further attention and more precise description here.

al-Ma'āthir wa-'l-āthār, memorabilia of the first forty

[1] Shams al-'Ulamā' Sh M. Mahdī Qazwīnī 'Abd-al-Rabb-ābādī, who died at Ṭihrān on 24 Dhū 'l-Ḥijjah 1331/24 November 1913. See *Bīst maqālah i Qazwīnī*, pt. 1, p. 8, and the periodical *Yādgār* V/3, p. 60.
[2] Cf. p. 238 *supra.*
[3] The second volume did not appear until 1312 (see below).
[4] Cf. pp. 154–5 *supra.*
[5] Cf. p. 209 *supra.*
[6] A Mālikī who died at Baghdād in 393/1003.
[7] Cf. Brockelmann i 282, *Sptbd.* i p. 495. He died in 616/1219.
[8] Burnt at Baghdād as a heretic in 322/934. Cf. *Tusy's List of Shy'ah books* p. 305 ; *Shadharāt al-dhahab* ii p. 293 ; Brockelmann *Sptbd.* I p. 189 n. 1.

years of Nāṣir al-Dīn S͟hāh's reign, written in 1306/1888–9 and divided into sixteen chapters ((1) on the S͟hāh's personal appearance, mental and spiritual gifts, etc., p. 4, (2) his children and grandchildren, p. 11, (3) the mothers of his children, p. 13, (4) list of high officials, p. 15, (5) list of provincial governors, p. 29, (6) list of wars, rebellions, riots, punitive expeditions, etc., p. 37, (7) buildings erected, repaired or decorated, parks and gardens laid out, etc., p. 53, (8) social reforms, innovations, discoveries, etc., p. 91, (9) the S͟hāh's journeys in Persia and elsewhere, p. 132, (10), biographies of scholars, divines, writers, physicians, etc., p. 135, (11) list of persons honoured with the *Nis͟hān i Timt͟hāl i Humāyūn*, p. 227, (12) list of titles conferred, p. 230, (13) the national revenue of 1268/1851–2 compared with that of 1303/1885–6, p. 242, (14) contemporary rulers in all parts of the world, p. 245, (15) diplomatic representatives of foreign countries in Ṭihrān, p. 253, (16) a year-by-year record of remarkable events outside Persia, p. 257), to all of which is appended a separately paginated list of officials in the ministries at Ṭihrān and in the offices of the provincial governments, etc. : **Tihrān** 1306–7/1889°*. (Pp. 294, 62. The date 1306 is given on the title-page, but 8 Muḥarram 1307 in the colophon on p. 294.)

1662. Ḥājj S͟h. **'Abbās** b. M. Riḍā **Qummī** is described as *marḥūm* on the title-page of the Tihrān edition of the *Hadīyat al-aḥbāb*.

Hadīyat al-aḥbāb fī d͟hikr al-ma'rūfīn bi-'l-kunā wa-'l-alqāb wa-'l-ansāb, short alphabetically arranged notices of ancient and modern S͟hī'ite and Sunnite scholars, poets, etc., composed in 1349/1930–1 (according to the Sipahsālār catalogue i p. *Yā-Alif*) and divided into three *bābs* ((1) names beginning with Abū, (2) names beginning with Ibn, (3) *nisbahs*, surnames, descriptions, etc.) : **Najaf** 1349/1930–1 (Sipahsālār cat., *loc. cit.*) ; **Tihrān** A.H.S. 1329/1950‡ (281 pp.).

1663. Ḥājī Mīrzā **Yaḥyā** "Yaḥyā" b. S. Hādī **Daulatābādī,** well known as a writer, an educationist and a prominent figure in the Persian revolution, was born at Daulatābād in 1281/1864–5. In the second volume of M. Ishaque's *Sukhanvarān-i-Īrān dar 'aṣr-i-ḥāẓir*, published in 1937, it was stated that for some years he had been resident in Belgium and was acting as guardian to the Persian students in that country. In the same author's *Modern Persian poetry*, published in 1943, the date of his death is given as 1318 (!), possibly a misprint for 1361/1942, since his son in his preface to the *Ḥayāt i Yaḥyā* speaks of the eighty years of his life. Among his published works is *Urdībihisht* (vol. i only, Tihrān A.H.S. 1304/1925*, a collection of his poems).

Ḥayāt i Yaḥyā, an autobiography in four volumes : **Tihrān** A.H.S. 1328/1950–, *in progress* (the date is that of the editor's preface to vol. ii, the only volume so far published. Title on cover : *Tārīkh i mu'āṣir yā Ḥayāt i Yaḥyā*).

[Browne *The press and poetry of modern Persia* pp. 54, 102, 157, *Lit. Hist.* iv pp. 225, 307 ; D. J. Irani *Poets of the Pahlavi regime* pp. 668B–690 (portrait) ; M. Ishaque *Sukhanvarān-i-Īrān* ii pp. 416–22 (portrait), *Modern Persian poetry* pp. 9, 17, 87, 165, etc. ; Ḥabīb Allāh Mukhtārī *Tārīkh i bīdārī i Īrān* p. 28 (portrait).]

1664. Mīrzā **Muḥammad b. 'Abd al-Wahhāb** b. 'Abd al-'Alī **Qazwīnī**, whose father has already been mentioned (p. 1173) as one of the compilers of the *Nāmah i dānishwarān*, was born at Ṭihrān on 15 Rabī' al-Awwal 1294/30 March 1877, and it was at Ṭihrān that he received an education in the usual subjects of the traditional Islāmic curriculum. Of all these subjects the Arabic *adabīyāt*, and especially Arabic grammar, appealed to him most strongly (*Bīst maqālah i Qazwīnī*, pt. 1, p. 6 : *Az miyān i īn hamah 'ulūm i mutadāwalah na-mī-dānam ba-chih sabab az hamān ibtidā-yi amr shauqī shadīd ba-adabīyāt i 'Arab girībān-gīr i man shud tā akthar i aiyām i ṣibā u shabāb dar shu'ab i mukhtalifah i īn fann ba-khuṣūṣ naḥw ṣarf gardīd u 'umr i girān-māyah dar ishtighāl ba-ism u fi'l u ḥarf gudhasht u aknūn kih ta'ammul i aiyām i gudhashtah mī-kunam u bar 'umr i talaf-kardah ta'assuf mī-khwuram bāz yakī az bihtarīn i tafrīḥāt i man muṭāla'ah i Sharḥ i Raḍī u Mughnī 'l-labīb ast kih barā-yi man aḥlā min waṣl al-ḥabīb ast ! Al-'ādah ka-'l-ṭabī'at al-thāniyah*). Apart from his teachers in various *madrasahs* he came into close contact with several persons of culture and distinction, such as Sh. Hādī Najmābādī, S. Aḥmad " Adīb " Pīshāwarī, Shams al-

'ulamā' Sh. M. Mahdī Qazwīnī 'Abd-al-Rabb-ābādī (cf. p. 1174, n. 1, *supra*) and M. Ḥusain Khān " Furūghī " Iṣfahānī (cf. p. 240 *supra*). One of the sons of the last-named, M. 'Alī Khān Dhakā' al-Mulk (cf. p. 241 *supra*), became his pupil in Arabic, his instructor in French and soon his intimate friend. For some years too he gave instruction in Arabic grammar to the two sons of Sh. Faḍl Allāh Nūrī (who was crucified at Ṭihrān on 13 Rajab 1327/31 July 1909). In 1322/1904 at the suggestion of his brother, Mīrzā Aḥmad Khān, who was then in London, he came to see the manuscripts of the British Museum, and he remained in London for nearly two years. In 1324/1906, having accepted the invitation of the Trustees of the E. J. W. Gibb Memorial to prepare an edition of the *Tārīkh i Jahān-gushāy i Juwainī* (for which see p. 261 *supra*), he moved to Paris, where several good manuscripts of that work are preserved. At the end of 1333/1915, when it became impossible for him to continue his work in Paris (*ba-'ilalī kih īn-jā mauqi' i dhikr i ān nīst dīgar barāy i man dar Pārīs ba-hīch wajh idāmah i kārhā'ī kih ba-dast dāshtam mumkin na-būd*), he welcomed the proposal of his old friend, Ḥusain-Qulī Khān Nawwāb, the newly appointed Persian Minister to Germany, that they should travel together through Switzerland to Berlin. There he and the other members of the Persian colony, among whom were S. Ḥasan Taqī-zādah (cf. p. 241[28] *supra*), S. M. 'Alī Khān Jamāl-zādah, Mīrzā Maḥmūd Khān Ghanī-zādah, Mīrzā Ḥusain Kāẓim-zādah, M. 'Alī Khān Tarbiyat (cf. p. 1111 *supra*) and Mīrzā Ibrāhīm Pūr-Dāwud (cf. Browne *Press and poetry of modern Persia* pp. xviii, 289), suffered hardships which some of them mitigated by engaging in propagandist activities (cf. Browne *Lit. Hist.* iv p. 483). When the war came to its end, Qazwīnī was eager to resume his work on the *Tārīkh i Jahān-gushāy i Juwainī*, but travel from one European country to another was difficult in those days and it was not until 16 Jumādā II 1338/8 January 1920 that he again reached Paris. His return had been facilitated by his old friend M. 'Alī Khān " Furūghī " (cf. p. 241 *supra*), one of the Persian delegates to the Peace Conference, who soon afterwards was instrumental in obtaining for him a modest stipend from the Persian Government. He was by this time recognized as by far the most learned and critical of living Persians in historical and linguistic matters.[1] In 1939 he returned to Persia and accepted an invitation to teach in the University of Ṭihrān. He died on 6 Khurdād 1328/28 Rajab 1368/27 May 1949. In addition to several well-known volumes of the Gibb Memorial Series edited by him with copious learned notes his works include articles contributed to Persian periodicals. Twenty of these have been collected and published under the title *Bīst maqālah i Qazwīnī*[2] (pt. i, Bombay [1928*], pt. ii, Ṭihrān A.H.S. 1313/1934*).

(1) ***Maqāla'ī tārīkhī u intiqādī . . . dar bāb i nuskhah i Nafthat al-maṣdūr . . .***[3]: see p. 1088, n. 1.

(2) ***Sharḥ i ḥāl i Abū Sulaimān i Manṭiqī i Sijistānī***[4] (French title: *Abû Sulaimân Manṭiqî Sidjistânî . . .*), Chalon-sur-Saone 1352/1933 (46 pp. Publications de la Société des Études Iraniennes et de l'Art Persan, 5).

(3) ***Wafayāt i mu'āṣirīn,*** alphabetically arranged biographies of the author's contemporaries, begun in the periodical *Yādgār* iii/3, continued in the succeeding issues of that volume, then interrupted for reasons explained in iv/3 pp. 73–4, resumed in v/1–2 (Sept.–Oct. 1948) pp. 89–110 (letters Z and S), v/3 pp. 51–72 (Sh[5]), v/4–5 pp. 63–91 (Ṣ–Ẓ), v/6–7 pp. 122–8 (part of 'Ain), v/8–9 pp. 66–72 ('Ain continued), interrupted at that point by the author's death[6] and concluded in v/10 pp. 44–54 by a life of Qazwīnī himself [unsigned, but presumably by the editor, 'Abbās Iqbāl].

[1] "Mais le premier qui commença à étudier l'histoire de la Perse d'une manière critique fut Moḥammad b. 'Abdu 'l-Wahhāb Ḳazwīnī, auteur qui s'acquit une haute autorité scientifique, même parmi les savants de l'Occident. La recherche et l'analyse critique des documents historiques persans (*isnād*) furent le domaine principal de son activité scientifique. . . . Son hypercriticisme et sa pédanterie ne lui permirent, jusqu'à présent, de composer aucun grand ouvrage digne de lui." (F. Machalski, *Quelques remarques sur l'état actuel de l'historiographie persane*, in *Rocznik Orientalistyczny* xv (1939–49) p. 100.)

[2] This is actually the title of Pt. I only, Pt. II being called *B.m. az maqālāt i tārīkhī u intiqādī u adabī bi-qalam i . . . Muḥammad Khān Qazwīnī.*

[3] This *maqālah* is not included in the *Bīst maqālah i Qazwīnī.*

[4] Cf. p. 1104 *supra* and *Bīst maqālah i Qazwīnī* ii pp. 102–23 (in an article on the *Tatimmat Ṣiwān al-ḥikmah*).

[5] Including Shams al-'Ulamā' M. Ḥusain Qarīb Garakānī.

[6] It is highly desirable that these biographies should be published as an independent work, with or without any further biographies for which Qazwīnī may have left materials, especially as the first three volumes of *Yādgār* seem to be now unprocurable.

[Autobiography in *Bīst maqālah i Qazwīnī*, pt. i (Bombay [1928]) pp. 5–23; *Yādgār* v/8–9 pp. 1–8 (portrait frontispiece), v/10 pp. 44–5; *The Times* 4.6.49; *BSOAS*. xiii/2 (1950) pp. 547–50 (an obituary by Mojtabā Mīnovī); Īraj Afs͟hār *Nat͟hr i Fārsī i muʻāṣir* pp. 57–66 (portrait).]

1665. **ʻAbd Allāh Mustaufī** was born according to Machalski (*Rocz. Or.* xv p. 106[3]) in "1294 h. (1875)", i.e. presumably either in 1292/1875 or in 1294/1877.

S͟harḥ i zindagānī i man yā Tārīk͟h i ijtimāʻī u idārī i daurah i Qājārīyah, a history of Qājār times incorporating autobiographical memoirs and a highly interesting picture of Persian domestic and social life: **Ṭihrān** A.H.S. 1324/1945–6 onwards (cf. p. 1288 *infra*).

Description of vols. i–ii: F. Machalski *Quelques remarques sur l'état actuel de l'historiographie persane* (in *Rocznik Orientalistyczny* xv (1939–49)) pp. 105–7.

1666. **Īraj Afs͟hār.**

Nat͟hr i Fārsī i muʻāṣir: muntak͟habātī az bihtarīn i āt͟hār i muwarrik͟hīn u muḥaqqiqīn i nāmī i Īrān az ṣadr i mas͟hrūṭīyat tā muʻāṣir [with short biographies [1] and portraits]. **Ṭihrān** A.H.S. 1330/1951 (to be followed by a similar volume on novelists, etc., and dramatists by Saʻīd Nafīsī).

1667. Other biographical works:—

(1) *Abraham Lincoln; sa vie et son œuvre*, by K͟hān Bahādur Mīrzā Muḥammad (for whom see under *Dūstdārān i bas͟har* below): **Berlin** A.H. 1343/1924 (Publications Iranschähr, no. 8. See the R.A.S.'s *Catalogue of printed books*, p. 278).

(2) *Ad͟hkār al-kirām al-bararah fī manāqib Imām Dār al-Hijrah*, a biography of Mālik b. Anas, by Maulawī S. M. Jalāl al-Dīn: **Madrās** 1310/1893* (116 pp.).

(3) *Aḥwāl i Amīr ʻAṭā' Allāh Jaʻfarī Zainabī*, an account of A. ʻA. A., who migrated from Delhi to Bengal [sc. Bihār], became *Wazīr* to S͟hēr S͟hāh at Sahasrām ("Sasseram" in Bihār) and eventually settled at P'hulwārī, near Patna,

[1] Unfortunately too late in their arrival to be used adequately in the present survey.

by Shāh Nūr al-Ḥaqq: **Bānkīpūr** Suppt. ii 2272 (A.H. 1298/1881).

(4) *Aḥwāl i aulād u jāydād i Saiyid Aḥmad Sāndawī*, "compiled by 'Alī Naqī Khān, under instructions from the Governor-General of India, to clear up certain complications which had arisen in regard to the disposal of the estate in Oudh in the possession of the descendants of Sayyid Aḥmad Sāndwī": **Edinburgh** 89 (159 foll., with a large map of Fatḥ-ganj. A.H. 1230/1814).

(5) *Aḥwāl i Sar Jamshēd-jī Jījī-bhā'ī*, a metrical biography of Sir Jamsetjee Jejeebhoy [probably the first Baronet of that name (1783–1859),[1] but the B.M. catalogue does nor make this clear], by Farāmarz Naurōz-jī Kuṭār: **Bombay** A.Y. 1264/1895° (63 pp.).

(6) *Armaghān i aḥbāb* (*Tadhkirah i mashāhīr mausūm bah A. i a.*), brief biographies of poets, kings, and other celebrities, mainly Persian, by Shams al-'Ulamā' Maulawī M. Ḥusain [b. M. Sirāj al-Dīn], Professor, Mission College, Lahore,[2] whose preface is dated 1 November 1890 and who compiled in 1906 a work entitled *al-'Ajā'ib* (see index): **Lahore** 1890° (68 pp.); 1917* (116 pp.); **Sād'haurah** 1893° (64 pp.).

(7) *al-Aslāf*, a biographical dictionary of famous men, ancient Greeks and Muslims, prophets, etc., by M. Shajā'at 'Alī Khān: **Badāyūn** 1916* (114 pp.).

[1] See Buckland's *Dictionary of Indian biography* p. 223; *D.N.B.* under Jeejeebhoy; *Ency. Brit.*, 11th ed., *ibid.*

[2] In spite of the British Museum catalogue this person (still alive when the 1917 edition was published) is clearly different from Shams al-'Ulamā' M. Ḥusain "Āzād" b. M. Bāqir (b. Delhi 1827, 1828 or 1830, d. Lahore 22.1.1910), who was Professor of Arabic in the Government College, Lahore (1870 ?–1889), wrote some Persian and Urdu readers for the Panjāb Education Department, and whose name is illustrious in the history of Urdu literature. For his life and works (which include Urdu works on Persian literature) see Prāg Narāyan Bhārgava *Ṣaḥīfah i zarrīn* (in Urdu), Lucknow 1902, Panjab section, p. 8; *Civil and military Gazette* [a newspaper], Lahore, 23.1.1910, p. 10*b*; Rām Bābū Saksēna *History of Urdu literature* pp. 219–22, 274–9, *Tārīkh i adab i Urdū* [Urdu translation of the preceding work], Lucknow [1929], *ḥiṣṣah i nathr*, pp. 46–52 (portrait facing p. 50); *Maulānā M. Ḥusain Āzād* [a short Urdu biography, 48 pp.] by Ṭālib Ilāhābādī, Allahabad 1931; T. Grahame Bailey *History of Urdu literature* pp. 87, 96; *Shams al-'Ulamā' Maulānā M. Ḥusain "Āzād"*, by Āghā M. Bāqir [his grandson] (in *OCM*. xv/2 (Feb. 1939), *ḍamīmah*, pp. 41–118 (portrait facing p. 41)); etc.

(8) *Chahār ā'īn i Maḥbūbī*, by Maulawī Abū 'l-Faiḍ Najm al-Dīn b. Aḥmad 'Alī 'Abbāsī Chirīyākōtī [who died in 1306/1888–9 : see Raḥmān 'Alī pp. 235–6] : **Āṣafīyah** iii p. 162 no. 145 (under *Tadhkirah i fārisī*, but without further indication of the subject, which may not be biographical. A.H. 1334/1915–16).

(9) *Dūstdārān i bashar*, biographies of famous philanthropists, male (vol. i) and female (vol. ii,[1] of which the preface is dated Masqaṭ, 28 Ṣafar 1330 [1912]), by [Mīrzā] Muḥammad [b. Aḥmad,[2] Munshī], M.R.A.S.[3], Order of the Lion and the Sun (2nd Class), Nishān i 'Ilmī (3rd Class) : **Bombay** [printed, but published at Najaf] 1914† (138 pp. Vol. i only ?) ; **Berlin** (Kāvayānī Pr.) 1343/1925* (the date of vol. ii, which alone is in the I.O. Library).

(10) *Faḍl i Ṣafdarī*, on the merits of 'Alī b. Abī Ṭālib, by M. Najm al-Dīn Qādirī : **Ārah** [" Arrah "], Nūr al-Anwār Pr., 1294/1877* (pp. 8, 76).

(11) *al-Far' al-nāmī min al-aṣl al-sāmī*, on *ansāb* (according to *Ma'āthir i Ṣiddīqī* iv, appended *fihrist i kutub*, p. 14), by Ṣiddīq Ḥasan Khān (for whom see pp. 27–8, 913, 1137) : **Bhōpāl** (so *M. i Ṣ.*, without date) 1301/1883–4 (so Āṣafīyah ii p. 1556, without place, but Sarkīs and Brockelmann say India 1291 : there may, therefore, be two editions).

(12) *Jaur [u] jafā* (?), love-story of the author, M. Riḍā, son of the late Amīr M. Zamān Khān Durrānī Fufalzai, and a dancing-girl named Murād-Bakhsh at Ḍērah Ghāzī Khān [once seat of the Durrānī Governors], written in 1221/1806 : **Rieu** i 384*b* (cf. iii 1087*a*. 36 PICTURES).

[1] Vol. iii is described as in the press in a list of Kāvayānī publications at the end of the Berlin ed. of vol. ii.

[2] So in the *Ṭulū' i tamaddun*.

[3] Khān Bahādur Āghā Mīrzā Muḥammad, C.I.E., The Sheikh's Market, Ashar, Basrah, Iraq, appears in the lists of Members published in the *JRAS*. from 1924 to 1932. On the title-page of the *Dūstdārān i bashar*, vol. ii, are mentioned the titles of nineteen works by him, including *Aḥwāl i Kristōfar Kulambas* (cf. p. 1160 *supra*), *Ṭulū' i tamaddun* (cf. p. 157 *supra*), *Inshā' i a'lā*, *Inshā' i jadīd*, *Zabān i Ingilīsī*, *Aḥwāl i Gārfīld*, *Tārīkh i Ālmān* and *Ḍarb al-amthāl i fārsī*. His portrait forms the frontispieces to S. Aḥmad Kasrawī's *Nāmhā-yi shahrhā u dīhhā-yi Īrān*, *daftar* i (Ṭihrān A.H.S. 1308/1929–30) and *daftar* ii (Ṭihrān A.H.S. 1309/1930–1). Kasrawī made his acquaintance in the course of his visit to 'Irāq and Khūzistān (cf. p. 366 *supra*).

(13) *Jawāhir i arba'ah*. Edition: place ? date ? (Āṣafīyah i p. 346, under *Tarājim i Fārisī*, but without further indication of the subject).

(14) *Kār-nāmah i suturgān i shurafā i Pārsiyān i mamlakat i Hindūstān*, biographies of eminent Parsees, by Āmūzandah Shērmand Īrānī: [**Poona** 1917*] (48 pp.).

(15) *Kitāb i Ṣubḥī*, an autobiographical apologia, composed (so far as pt. i is concerned) A.H.S. 1312/1933 [1] by Faiḍ Allāh Muhtadī *ma'rūf ba-* Ṣubḥī, who after some years as a Bahā'ī missionary became private secretary to 'Abd al-Bahā' (d. 28.11.1921 [2]) at Ḥaifā and who has much to say about the history of Bahā'ism and its leading personalities: **Ṭihrān** A.H.S. 1312/1933–4‡ (*Daurah* i. 216 pp.).

(16) *Maṭla' al-anwār*, by M. Shafī' Khān al-Wazīr [b. ?] 'Abd al-Bāqī al-Sharīf al-Baghdādī: **Āṣafīyah** ii p. 1556 (*Manāqib*) no. 9.

(17) *Maẓhar al-ḥaqq* (*Taḥqīq al-ansāb al-mashhūr bi'sm i tārīkhī Maẓhar al-ḥaqq* [= 1284/1867–8]), on the races and genealogies of Indian Muslims (Shaikhs, Saiyids, Mughals, Pat'hāns, etc.), by 'Abd al-Razzāq Kalyānawī: N.K. [**Lucknow**] 1292/1875°*.

(18) *Miftāḥ al-jannah*, by Mullā M. *al-shahīr bah* Zanjānī. Edition: 1290/1873 (Āṣafīyah ii p. 1556 (*Manāqib*) no. 10).

(19) *Mir'āt al-kaunain*, by Ghulām-Nabī Firdausī. Edition: place ? 1312/1894–5 (Āṣafīyah i p. 324).

(20) *Mi'yār al-faḍā'il li-khilāfat al-akhyār wa-'l-radhā'il*, " a Persian version of a work (originally written in Arabic) on the exploits of famous Muslim champions " (Arberry), by Maulawī Nasīm Ḥasan: **Amrōhah** 1334/1917* (308 pp.).

(21) *Nasab-nāmah*, by Faḍl Allāh Shihāb al-Dīn b. al-Qāḍī Ḥasan: **Cairo** p. 529.

(22) *Niẓām al-ansāb*, written in 1307/1889–90 (vol. i) and 1310/1892–3 (vol. ii) by S. M. Manṣūr 'Alī " Khirad " Naqawī al-Bukhārī b. S. Zain al-'Ābidīn Shikārpūrī: **Āṣafīyah** iii p. 720 (A.H. 1307 and 1310).

[1] Five years (p. 4[4]) after the circulation, in 1307/1928 (p. 2, l. 5 from foot), of an attack on his orthodoxy and character.

[2] For an obituary notice by E. G. Browne see *JRAS*. 1922 pp. 145–6.

(23) *Qur'ān* [sic, possibly for *Qirān*] *al-su'adā*, by M. Ḥusainī Madanī Aurangābādī : **Āṣafīyah** i p. 322 no. 18 (under the heading *Taḏẖkirah*).

(24) *Risālah fī bayān nasl al-mulūk wa-'l-aṣẖrāf min Ādam :* **Leningrad** Univ. 384 (Salemann-Rosen p. 17).

(25) *Risālah i ḏẖikr i muġẖanniyān i Hindūstān*, composed in Aḥmad Ṣẖāh's fifth regnal year (A.H. 1165-6) by 'Ināyat Ḵẖān " Rāsiḵẖ " (fl. 1163/1750 : see Ethé 411) : **Bānkīpūr** xvii 1734 (15 foll. 19th cent.).

(26) *Riyāḍ i laṭīf*, *Reyaz-i-Latif*, *or Biographical sketches of the Persian authors for the use of* . . . *candidates of the Universities, Calcutta, Bombay, Madras, Panjab and Allahabad*, by Abū 'l-Munīf M. Laṭīf: **Calcutta** 1904°* (64 pp.).

(27) *Safīnah i Raḥmānī*, by Ḥāfiẓ 'Abd al-Raḥmān " Ḥairat ". Edition: place ? 1884 (Āṣafīyah i p. 320).

(28) *Ṣaḥā'if i ṣẖarā'if*, composed in 1231/1816 by M. 'Askarī Ḥusainī Bilgrāmī : **Āṣafīyah** i p. 322 no. 19 (autograph).

(29) *Ṣẖajarah i ṭaiyibah*, by Ġẖulām-'Alī " Āzād " Bilgrāmī : see p. 862 (12) *supra*.

(30) *Ṣẖams al-manāqib*, by M. 'Alī Ḵẖān " Surūṣẖ " Iṣfahānī (d. 1285/1868–9 : see *Majma' al-fuṣaḥā'* ii pp. 184–95) : [**Ṭihrān**] 1301/1884 (122 foll. See Karatay p. 121).

(31) *Ṣẖarḥ i ḥāl i 'Abd Allāh b. al-Muqaffa'*, by 'Abbās Iqbāl (cf. p. 1085 *supra*) : **Berlin** 1926* (Intiṣẖārāt i Īrānṣẖahr, 15).

(32) *Ṣẖarḥ i ḥāl i Kulunil Muḥammad Taqī Ḵẖān* (*Colonel Mohamed Taghi Khan* (*Biography of*) by some of his friends and admirers [Riḍā-zādah " Ṣẖafaq "[1] and others]) : **Berlin** 1927* (Intiṣẖārāt i Īrānṣẖahr, 20).

---

[1] Dr. Ṣādiq Ḵẖān R.-z. " Ṣẖafaq ", Professor of Modern Philosophy in the University of Ṭihrān, was born at Tabrīz in 1310/1892–3 and was in 1328/1910 owner and editor of the Tabrīz weekly newspaper *Ṣẖafaq* (Browne *The press and poetry of modern Persia* p. 111). Subsequently he studied at Robert College, Istānbūl, and at the University of Berlin. His works include a *Tārīḵẖ i adabīyāt i Īrān barāy i dabīristānhā* [Ṭihrān A.H.S. 1321/1942] and a *Farhang i Ṣẖāhnāmah* (Luzac's *OL*. 1942 p. 10). See Raṣẖīd Yāsamī *Adabīyāt i mu'āṣir* p. 59 (portrait) ; D. J. Irani *Poets of the Pahlavi regime* pp. 345–348B (portrait) ; Ishaque *Sukhanvarān-i-Īrān* ii pp. 241–6 (portrait), *Modern Persian poetry* pp. 10 n. 3, 11, 26 ; Mahdī Mujtahidī *Rijāl i Āḏẖarbāyjān* pp. 97–99 ; *Tārīḵẖ i jarā'id u majallāt i Īrān* iii p. 74 ; Iraj Afṣẖār *Naṯẖr i Fārsī i mu'āṣir* pp. 138–44 (portrait).

(33) _Sharh i ḥāl u āthār i Saiyid Jamāl al-Dīn i Asadābādī_ [1] (French title: Seyed Djemal-ud-Din Afghani. Par son neveu M. Lutfullah Khan [Asadābādī] avec quelques appendices par des savants différents) : **Berlin** 1926* (tom. i. 128 pp. Intisẖārāt i Īrānsẖahr, 13); **Tabrīz** A.H.S. 1326/1947-8 (an augmented edition. See Yādgār iv/1-2 p. 127).

(34) _Sharh i ḥāl u iqdāmāt i Shaikh Muḥammad i Khiyābānī_ [2] (Cheikh Mohammad Khiabani. Sa biographie et son activité politique et sociale. Par ses amis et ses admirateurs [Riḍā-zādah " Sẖafaq " [3] and others]. **Berlin** 1926* (Intisẖārāt i Īrānsẖahr, 14).

(35) _Tadhkirah i Allāhī,_ a biography of Muẓaffar 'Alī Sẖāh Allāhī, of Āgrah, by M. Abū 'l-Ḥasan Farīdābādī: **Lucknow** 1887° (122 pp.).

(36) _Tadhkirat al-akhyār,_ brief notices of Prophets, Imāms, kings and philosophers, by 'Alī Akbar Sẖarīf Gīlānī: **Lahore** Panjāb Univ. (A.H. 1224/1809. See OCM. viii/4 (Aug. 1932) p. 45).

(37) _Taḥqīq al-ansāb :_ see _Maẓhar al-ḥaqq_ above.

(38) _Tarānah i gham,_ a panegyric in rhymed prose on Maulānā M. 'Abd al-Rasẖīd, by M. Kalb-'Alī Khān, Nawwāb of Rāmpūr (cf. p. 1156): [**Rāmpūr**] 1289/1872°*.

(39) _Tārīkh i jāwīd,_ short biographical notices and portraits of Persian officers killed on active service : **Ṭihrān** (Ministry of War) A.H.S. 1325/1946-7 (vol. i, covering the years 1320-5), 1326 (vol. ii, covering the years 1300-26), 1327 (vol. iii, additional biographies for the years 1300-27).

(40) _Tarīq al-bukā',_ stories of saints and martyrs, by Mullā M. Ḥusain " Giryān " Sẖahrābī: **Bombay** 1343/1925*.

---

[1] Born 1254/1838-9, died at Istānbūl 9 March 1897. See Zaidān _Masẖāhīr al-sẖarq_ ii pp. 54-66, Ta'rīkh ādāb al-lughat al-'arabīyah iv pp. 312-13 ; Browne _The Persian revolution_ pp. 2-30, etc. (portrait frontispiece); _Ency. Isl._ under Djamāl al-Dīn (Goldziher); _Armaghān_ xii (A.H.S. 1310/1931-2) pp. 586-601 (an article by Ṣifāt Allāh Jamālī); Brockelmann _Sptbd._ iii pp. 311-15; etc. A biography of 96 pp. published at Tihrān is mentioned in _Luzac's OL._ 1951 p. 32, where the title is given as " Seyed Jamal Afgani " and the author's name is not mentioned.

[2] Cf. Ḥabīb Allāh Mukhtārī _Tārīkh i bīdārī i Īrān_ p. 54 (portrait); M. Ṣadr Hāsẖimī _Tārīkh i jarā'id u majallāt i Īrān_ ii p. 106 (portrait).

[3] Cf. p. 1183 n. _supra._

(41) *Yādgār i Hindī*, " Poems in Persian entitled Yadgar-i-Hindee, containing a brief account of the great prophets, kings, rulers, and philosophers of the world by Rai Kunhya Lall " i.e. Kanhaiyā Lāl " Hindī " (for whom see p. 674 *supra*) : **Lahore** 1290/1873°*.

(42) *Zindagānī i Mānī*, by Malik al-Shu'arā' [" Bahār " presumably. Cf. p. 1291[17]] : **Ṭihrān** (see *Luzac's O.L.* 1938 p. 186).

(43) *Zubdat al-'ulūm*, by 'Iwaḍ Ḥiṣārī [1], a collection of legends and traditions of Muḥammad, his Companions, celebrated scholars, saints, etc., with an account of the miracles of 'Abd al-Qādir al-Jīlānī and a description of Heaven and Hell : **Bodleian** 334 (n.d.).

O. SOME MISCELLANEOUS HISTORICAL WORKS

1668. (1) *al-'Ajā'ib*, accounts of marvellous events in the reigns of Akbar and Jahāngīr extracted from the *Iqbāl-nāmah i Jahāngīrī* (cf. p. 561 *supra*), by Shams al-'ulamā' Maulawī M. Ḥusain [b. M. Sirāj al-Dīn [2]], Professor, Mission College, Lahore, whose preface is dated 16 Muḥarram 1324/12 March 1906 and who is described as *marḥūm* on the title-page of the 1924 edition [but who was still alive in 1917, when an edition of his *Armaghān i aḥbāb* was published (see p. 1180 *supra*) : **Lahore** [1906*] (38 pp.) ; 1924* (36 pp.). English translation : *The curiosities of Indian history. Being an English translation of Al-'Ajaib . . . by K. M. Maitra* : **Lahore** 1922* (55 pp.).

(2) *Chār chaman*, by 'Abd al-Wadūd : **Āṣafīyah** iii p. 100.

(3) *Ḍiyā' i qamar*, composed in 1305/1887–8 by Ākhund Shēr Ḥasan Khān : **Āṣafīyah** i p. 246 no. 627.

(4) *Ḥaqq al-Sulṭān*, on the merits of the Ottoman dynasty, by M. Nuṣrat 'Alī : **Delhi** (Nuṣrat al-Maṭābi') 1295/1878* 184 pp.).

[1] Who was a protégé of a certain Khwājah Bāqī Jān Ghiyāth al-Millah wa-'l-Dunyā wa-'l-Dīn [ibn ?] 'Imād al-Dīn.

[2] A *marthiyah* on the compiler's father by Maulawī 'Azīz al-Dīn, calligraphist to the Nawwāb of Bahāwalpūr, is appended to *al-'Ajā'ib* (p. 36 in the 1924 edition).

(5) *Ḥilyat al-ʻadhrā'* stories of the Prophets for children, by M. ʻAbd al-Ḥalīm "Sharar"[1]: **Lucknow** 1921* (100 pp.).

(6) *Jahān-nāmah*, a metrical sketch of general and Indian history composed in the reign of Aurangzēb not earlier than 1099/1688 by "Fanā'ī", a disciple of Sh. Luqmān b. Sh. ʻUthmān Khalīl Sulaimānī: **Rieu** ii 701*b* (*Jild* i only, on the Creation, the Prophets, etc., from Adam to Luqmān and the early kings of Persia. Late 17th cent.).

(7) *Jang-nāmah i Mashriqī*, by Bhawānī Parshād "Mashriqī" Kāyast'h, a resident of Qinnauj: **Āṣafīyah** iii p. 100 no. 1134 (A.H. 1208/1793–4).

(8) *Kitāb-khānah i Iskandarīyah*, a translation by S. M. Taqī Fakhr Dā'ī Gīlānī of an Urdu pamphlet by M. Shiblī Nuʻmānī[2] in rebuttal of the allegation that the library at Alexandria was destroyed by ʻUmar: **Ṭihrān** A.H.S. 1315/1936–7* (67 pp. See Harrassowitz's *Litterae orientales*, Oct. 1938 p. 14).

(9) *Laṭā'if al-tawārīkh*, a sketch, mainly catechetical, of Oriental history (Chaldæa, Media, Persia, Macedonia, Carthage, Egypt, Arabia, etc.), mostly ancient and mediæval, but in the case of Egypt brought down to 1914, by Āqā Mīrzā Ḥājjī Āqā[3] b. Ḥājjī Abū 'l-Ḥasan Kāzarūnī, Principal of the Madrasah i Khazʻalīyah at Muḥammarah: **Bombay** 1332–3/1915* (*Daurah* i. 272 pp.).

[1] A well-known Urdu novelist, historian and journalist (1860—December 1926). See R. B. Saksena *History of Urdu literature* pp. 334–41; T. Grahame Bailey *History of Urdu literature* p. 91.

[2] b. 1857, d. 18 Nov. 1914, the author of several well-known biographical, historical and other works in Urdu (e.g. *al-Ma'mūn*, *Sīrat al-Nuʻmān* [i.e. Abū Ḥanīfah], *al-Fārūq*, *al-Ghazālī*, *Sīrat al-Nabī*, *Shiʻr al-ʻAjam*, *al-Kalām*) as well as of some Persian poetry. Of the five parts of his *Shiʻr al-ʻAjam* at least three have been translated into Persian by M. Taqī Fakhr-Dā'ī Gīlānī ((1) *Luzac's OL.* 1938 p. 10, (2) *LOL.* 1948 p. 68, (5) *LOL.* 1939 p. 179). See *Ency. Isl.* under Shiblī (A. Ṣiddīqī); R. B. Saksena *History of Urdu literature* pp. 287–94; T. Grahame Bailey *History of Urdu literature* pp. 88–9; R. P. Bhajiwalla *Mauláná Shibli and Umar Khayyám*, Surat 1932, pp. 19–50 (portrait); Brockelmann *Sptbd.* ii p. 862; translator's preface to Persian trans. of *Shiʻr al-ʻAjam*, vol. i; etc.

[3] Ā.M.Ḥ.Ā., so on the title-page: M. Ḥ. Ā. Kāzarūnī on the cover, but in the Quarterly Catalogue (Bombay 1917 (1)) he is called Aghá Mirzá Háji Ráza [*sic*] Kazráni [*sic*].

(10) *Maʿārif i shattā*, composed in 1306/1888–9 by S. M. Manṣūr ʿAlī " Khirad " Naqawī Bukhārī Shikārpūrī : **Āṣafīyah** iii p. 110 (A.H. 1306/1888–9).

(11) *Mukhtaṣar i tārīkh i Rūsiyah*, translated [from a Turkish original ?] by S. Riḍā ʿAlī-zādah : **Lahore** 1345/1927* (Mufīd i ʿāmm Pr. 122 pp.).

(12) *Muntakhab al-tawārīkh*, by Abū 'l-Barakāt b. M. Naṣr Allāh : **Lindesiana** p. 107 no. 401 (A.H. 1111/1699).

(13) *Nuskhah i Dhakā*, composed in 1265/1849 by Ghulām-Aḥmad Maḥmūd " Dhakā ", a resident of Ṭēkmāl : **Āṣafīyah** iii p. 102.

(14) *Shams al-madhāhib*, composed in 1251/1835–6 by Munshī M. Qādir Khān (cf. p. 748) : **Āṣafīyah** i p. 246 no. 851 (A.H. 1251/1835–6. Under *Tārīkh*, but without further indication of the subject).

(15) *Sharaf-nāmah*, by M. Auliyā Nāʾiṭī entitled (*al-mukhāṭab bah*) Ḥāfiẓ-Yār-Jang : **Āṣafīyah** i p. 246 no. 530.

(16) *Tanbīh al-sālikīn*, by Ḥasan ʿAlī b. S. ʿAlī known as (*al-shahīr bi-*) Mīrzā Buzurg Ṭabīb Shīrāzī : **Āṣafīyah** i p. 234 no. 692.

(17) *Tārīkh i adabīyāt i Īrān*, by Jalāl al-Dīn " Sanā " Humāʾī Iṣfahānī[1] : **Tabrīz** 1348/1929–30* (vols. i–ii only (from the beginnings to the Mongol conquest). Pp. 332 ; 408).

(18) *Tārīkh i badāyiʿ* (a chronogram = 1298), or *Tarjamah i Ḥaqāʾiq al-kalām fī taʾrīkh al-Islām*, a translation by Iskandar Efendī, *ṣāḥib-imtiyāz i* " *Akhbār i Dār al-Khilāfah* ", of the Turkish work of ʿAbd al-Laṭīf Ṣubḥī Pāshā (d. 1303/1886 : see Babinger *Geschichtsschreiber der Osmanen* p. 369) : **Istānbūl** 1298/1880‡ (vol. i only (from Muḥammad to ʿAlī). 301 pp. Maḥmūd Bey's Pr. Cf. Karatay p. 166).

[1] Born 1317/1899–1900 at Iṣfahān. See D. J. Irani *Poets of the Pahlavi regime* pp. 336–9 (portrait) ; Ishaque *Sukhanvarān-i-Īrān* ii pp. 214–19 (portrait), *Modern Persian poetry* pp. 12, 30 ; Burqaʿī *Sukhanwarān i nāmī i muʿāṣir* pp. 124–6 (portrait) ; Īraj Afshār *Nathr i Fārsī i muʿāṣir* pp. 205–11 (portrait).

(19) *Tārīkh i Iskandarī*, by Ṭāhir b. Ḥasan b. 'Alī b. Mūsā al-Ṭūsī : **Āṣafīyah** i p. 222 no. 429 (defective at end).

(20) *Tārīkh i milal i mashriq*, a revised and enlarged edition of the work of Seignobos, by M. 'Alī Khān Dhakā' al-Mulk [" Furūghī " : cf. p. 241] : **Ṭihrān** 1327/1909 (Mashhad cat. iii p. 121).

(21) *Tārīkh i Qipchāqī* [1] : **Leningrad** Univ. no. 964*c* (A.H. 1238/1822–3. Romaskewicz p. 4).

(22) *Tārīkh i 'umūmī*, Pt. i (the ancient world) by M. 'Alī Khān, **Lahore**, Mufīd i 'āmm Pr., A.H.S. 1306/1928* (440 pp.), Pt. ii (the middle ages) by Abū 'l-Ḥasan Arjmand Sāwajī and M. Ḥusain Khān, **Lahore** A.H.S. 1305/1927* (571 pp.).

(23) *Tārīkh i 'umūmī i qurūn i wusṭā*, by 'Abd al- Ḥusain Shaibānī : **Ṭihrān** [1932*–], *in progress* [?].

(24) *Tārīkh i Yahūd*, by Parwīz Rāhbar : **Ṭihrān** 1946 (see Probsthain's *Orientalia nova*, 2 (1946–8) p. 28).

(25) *Tuḥfah i A'ẓamīyah*,[2] by Badr al-Daulah, Muftī of Madrās (cf. pp. 222 and 482 *supra*) : **Āṣafīyah** ii p. 876 (" *Siyar i Fārsī* ") nos. 111 (A.H. 1236/1820–1), 24 (A.H. 1259/1843).

[1] Possibly = *Tārīkh i Qipchāq-Khānī* (for which see p. 136).
[2] For a work of this title described as by Irtaḍā 'Alī Khān see p. 1039.

ADDITIONS AND CORRECTIONS

P. xviii, l. 10. *Read* Nagrāmī. For Nagrām, a village near Lucknow, see Raḥmān 'Alī p. 124[16], where the name is spelled out.

I. QUR'ĀNIC LITERATURE. A. TRANSLATIONS AND COMMENTARIES

P. 2, l. 22. [*Tarjamah i Tafsīr i Ṭabarī*]. Also **Ṭihrān** National Museum (vols. i–iv and vi (last). A.H. 606–8/1209–11. From the shrine of Sh. Ṣafī at Ardabīl. See A. Romaskewicz's article *Persidski "tafsīr" Tabarī* in *Zapiski Kollegii Vostokovedov* v (1930) pp. 801–6), **Mashhad** i, *fṣl.* 3, MSS., no. 19 (S. xxiii 58–xxxiv 19), **Āṣafīyah** iii p. 230 no. 572.

P. 2 ult. al-Mufaqqih is apparently a corruption of al-Mutafaqqih.

P. 3, l. 2. Among the MSS. of old commentaries as yet unidentified are **Fātiḥ** 301 (S. xlix–lxiv. A.H. 630. Language archaic. Translation of xliv 1 begins *Ai girawandagān pīshī makunīt bar Muḥammad.* Magnificent MS.) [Ritter, *OLZ.* 1928 col. 1123], **Browne** Coll. A. 2 (probably composed in 5th/11th cent. S. xxxviii 20–xcv. 13th cent.) and **Blochet** iv 2211 (S. vii–x. An isolated volume of a large commentary (in 14 or 15 vols. ?). Early 13th cent.). A fragment of 46 leaves (S. ii 61–146) from an old *tafsīr* has been described with some extracts and an exposition of its linguistic features in an Urdu article (*Qur'ān Pāk kī ēk qadīm tafsīr*) contributed by Prof. Maḥmūd Shērānī (probably the owner of the fragment) to *OCM*. viii/3 (May 1932) pp. 1–96.

P. 3, l. 11. [*Tafsīr al-Sūrābādī*]. Also **Brit. Mus.** (S. xix–xxv. A.H. 535/1140–1. See *British Museum Quarterly* vi/2 (1931) p. 55). For a MS. dated 684/1285 of the first quarter of this commentary in the private library of the late M. 'Alī Khān "Tarbiyat" (cf. p. 1111 *supra*) at Tabrīz see 'Abd al-'Azīz Jawāhir al-Kalām's *Kitāb-khānahā-yi Īrān*, [Ṭihrān] A.H.S. 1311, p. 91, and Mahdī Bayānī's article *Sargudhasht i hasht qarn i yak nuskhah i khaṭṭī i Qur'ān* in the periodical *Payām i nau* i/7 (Ṭihrān [1945]) p. 45.

P. 3, l. 30. [*Tāj al-tarājim*]. Also **Fātiḥ** 302 foll. 1–127 and 280–528 (S. xviii–cxiv. A.H. 506/1112–13. See Ritter in *OLZ*. 1928/12 col. 1123), **Sipahsālār** i pp. 78–80 no. 138 (S. xix–cxiv. 15th cent.).

P. 4, l. 1. [Abū Naṣr etc.]. According to the editor's Arabic preface in the MS. Fātiḥ 303 the author's name is A. N. Aḥmad b. al-Ḥasan b. Aḥmad al-Daranī (?) and he is there said to have died in 549 [1154–5]. According to the copyist's colophon his surname [*Beiname*] is Zāhid, not Zāhidī. [Ritter, *OLZ*. 1928/12 col. 1123]. Among the forms in which the name occurs are Saif al-Dīn A. N. b. A. b. Ḥusain b. Sulaimān Drwājkī (Mas͟hhad cat.), A. N. b. A. b. al-Ḥusain b. A. b. S. Darwājakī or Wardājakī (Ivanow Curzon 332) and A. N. A. b. al-Ḥasan b. A. Sulaimānī al-Rārwhkī (Bānkīpūr xiv p. 2). The words *Qāla 'l-S͟haik͟h al-Imām al-Zāhid* recur fairly often in the text (Ivanow Curzon 333).

P. 4, l. 3. [*Tafsīr i Zāhidī*]. The work is so called in some of the colophons (e.g. Ivanow Curzon 332, 333, Bānkīpūr xiv 1112–13). According to the already cited Arabic editorial preface in Fātiḥ 303 the title is *Laṭā'if al-tafsīr* [Ritter, *OLZ*. 1928/12 col. 1123]. Other MSS. : **Mas͟hhad** i, *fṣl.* 3, MSS., no. 26 ("*Tafsīr i Saif al-Dīn*". Apparently complete. A.H. 829/1425–6), **Fātiḥ** 303 (S. i–xviii. A.H. 877/1472–3. See Ritter, *OLZ*. 1928/12 col. 1123).

P. 4, l. 7. **Bānkīpūr** Pers. Hand-list 1121–2 = **Bānkīpūr** xiv 1112–13.

P. 4, l. 10. *Insert :*

5*a*. **Ras͟hīd al-Dīn** Abū 'l-Faḍl **Aḥmad b. M.** b. Aḥmad b. Mihrpazd **al-Maibudī** al-Yazdī.

Kas͟hf al-asrār wa-'uddat al-abrār (beg. *K͟hair kalimāt al-s͟hukr*), a large commentary begun in 520/1126, based in part on the concise *tafsīr* [1] of 'Abd Allāh al-Anṣārī (for whom see pp. 924–7 *supra*) and having the comments on each verse arranged in three *naubats* ((1) a literal Persian translation,

[1] Cf. the words quoted in the Mas͟hhad catalogue from the preface : *C͟hūn nusk͟hah i tafsīr Abī Ismā'īl 'Abd Allāh b. M. b.* [*sic*] *Anṣārī rā dīdam kih dar kamāl i ījāz ast k͟hwāstam Fārisī kunam* . . . . For Anṣārī's *tafsīr* see p. 925 *supra*.

(2) explanation of the sense, variant readings, occasion of the revelation, legal application, traditions and anecdotes, (3) Ṣūfī explanation) : Ḥ. Kh. v p. 202 no. 10674 (incorrect), **As'ad** 146 (S. xxvi–cxiv, described as vols. 7 and 8. A.H. 726), 145 (S. i–xvii. A.H. 889), **Nūr i 'Uthmānīyah** 474 (S. vi–x. Early 8th/14th cent.), 444 (S. iv 147–ix 119, described as vol. 3. 8th/14th cent. ?), **Yeñi** p. 80 no. 43 (complete. Written for the *Wazīr* Faṣīḥ al-Dīn Aḥmad Pāshā and bearing the seal of Bāyazīd II) [Ritter, *OLZ*. 1928/12 col. 1123], **Mashhad** i, *fṣl.* 3, MSS., nos. 176 (S. i–ii 193), 30 (S. xxi 6–xxv), **Sipahsālār** i p. 148 no. 209 (S. vi–ix, 13th cent.).

P. 4, l. 20. **Bānkipūr** Pers. Hand-list 1137–9 = **Bānkipūr** xiv 1114–16 (first two leaves missing).

P. 4, l. 21. [*Rauḍ al-jinān*]. Also **Mashhad** i, *fṣl.* 3, MSS., nos. 129–36 (of which 134 (S. xxxiii–xlviii) and 136 (S. lxxiv–cix) are dated 556/1161 and 557/1162 respectively), **Majlis** ii 811 (vols. i–x (out of 20 vols.). A.H. 1058/1648), **Sipahsālār** i pp. 129–34 no. 194 (S. xii–xvii), **'Alīgaṛh** Subḥ. MSS. p. 6 no. 11 ("*juzw i thānī*").

Edition : **Ṭihrān** (Maṭba'ah i Majlis) A.H. 1323/1905–6 (vol. i, i.e. S. i–iv 61 and vol. ii, i.e. S. iv 62–ix), A.H.S. 1313–15/1934–6 (vols. iii–v, i.e. S. x–cxiv). According to the Sipahsālār catalogue Muẓaffar al-Dīn Shāh gave orders in 1319/1901–2 for the printing of this work and at the time of his death (Dhū 'l-Qa'dah 1324/Jan. 1907) "vols. i–ii" and 173 pages of "vol. iii", i.e. more than ten of the author's twenty *mujallads*, had been printed. In Riḍā Shāh's reign the printing was resumed and completed (cf. Mashhad iv p. 491, Majlis ii p. 27[16]).

P. 5, l. 6. [*Tafsīr i Baṣā'ir i Yamīnī*]. "The Tafsīr described by me in the first catalogue as No. 956 is apparently *not* identical with Rosen 45. But it *is* identical, as Professor Houtsma has written, with Leyden iv, 45 (No. 1710) . . ." [W. Ivanow, in a letter.]

P. 5, l. 9. [*Tafsīr i Baṣā'ir i Yamīnī.*] **Bāyazīd** 68 should be deleted, since that MS. (217 foll. 8th/14th cent. ?) contains the *Baṣā'ir al-naẓā'ir*, an introduction to the *Qur'ān* and a Qur'ānic glossary, by Abū 'l-Faḍā'il M. b. al-Ḥusain al-Mu'īnī [Ritter, *OLZ*. 1928, col. 1123]. Other MSS. : **Mashhad** i, *fṣl*. 3, MSS., nos. 12–13 (1st half only. A.H. 610/1213) and probably **Leyden** iv p. 45 no. 1710 (S. xviii–xxxiv 32. N.d. See the correction to p. 5, l. 6).

P. 6, l. 1. [Qāḍī Ḥamīd al-Dīn Nāgaurī.] His tomb is near that of Bakhtyār Kākī. For the inscription, which gives 695/1296 as the date of his death, see Beale *Miftāḥ al-tawārīkh* (1867) p. 73.

P. 6, l. 7. [Qāḍī Ḥ. al-D. Nāgaurī.] Also *Ā'īn i Akbarī* tr. Jarrett p. 367 ; *Gulzār i abrār* no. 20 ; *Kalimāt al-ṣādiqīn* no. 5 ; *Riyāḍ al-'ārifīn* (A.H.S. 1316) p. 104.

P. 6, l. 15. [Sh. Ḥamīd al-Dīn Nāgaurī.] Also *Ā'īn i Akbarī* tr. Jarrett p. 367 ; *Gulzār i abrār* no. 50 ; *Makhzan al-gharā'ib* no. 566.

P. 7, l. 12. [*al-As'ilah wa-'l-ajwibah.*] Āyā Ṣōfyah 1033*a* and 69*b* are dated 826 and 885 respectively. Ā.Ṣ. 71 belonged to the library of Bāyazīd II (886–918). The words " (probably also 66) " should be deleted : Ā.Ṣ. 66 contains the Ḥurūfī commentary described in the addendum to p. 7, l. 25. [Ritter, *OLZ*. 1928 col. 1123.]

P. 7, l. 13. [*al-As'ilah wa-'l-ajwibah*]. Also **Nāfidh Pāshā** 108 (modern). [Ritter.] *Delete* (also 98 ?). Fātiḥ 98 is the Ḥurūfī commentary described in the addendum to p. 7, l. 25.

P. 7, ll. 15–25. These lines should be deleted. For the *Kashf al-asrār wa-'uddat al-abrār* (erroneously ascribed by Ḥ. Kh. to al-Taftāzānī) see the addendum to p. 4, l. 10.

P. 7, l. 25. *Insert* :

12*a*. (*Tafsīr i Ḥurūfī*) (beg. *Ibtidā* (5 times) *khilqat az īn-jā nah az aurāq*), a curious Ḥurūfī commentary stated to have been composed in 796/1394 : **Āyā Ṣōfyah** 66 (bears seal of Bāyazīd II (886–918)), **Fātiḥ** 98 (same seal), probably also **Kamānkash** 230 (acephalous. A.H. 914). [Ritter, *OLZ*. 1928 col. 1123.]

P. 8, l. 4. [*Tafsīr i M. Pārsā.*] This work was composed at

Bukhārā in 820, as appears from the author's colophon in As'ad 84 (A.H. 1059). [Ritter, *OLZ*. 1928 col. 1124.]

P. 8, l. 7. Delete the note of interrogation. [Ritter, *ibid.*]

P. 8, l. 16. *Delete* probably. [Ritter, *ibid.*]

P. 8, l. 20. [M. Pārsā.] Also *Khazīnah i ganj i Ilāhī* (Sprenger p. 84); *Haft iqlīm* no. 1492; Rieu ii p. 863; Ethé no. 1855; Brockelmann *Sptbd.* ii pp. 282–3.

P. 9, l. 3. [Ni'mat Allāh Walī.] Also *Khazīnah i ganj i Ilāhī* (Sprenger p. 86); *Ātash-kadah* no. 250; *Khazīnat al-aṣfiyā'* i pp. 114–15; Bānkīpūr ii pp. 10–11. Photograph of his tomb (erected in 840 by Aḥmad Shāh Bahmanī) in Sykes *History of Persia* ii, facing p. 156.

P. 9, l. 7. Charkh is a small place on the road from Kābul to Ghaznī and is nearer to the former than to the latter.

P. 9, ll. 15–16. [*Tafsīr i Ya'qūb i Charkhī.*] Fātiḥ 299 and As'ad 88 are dated 924 and 933. [Ritter, *OLZ*. 1928 col. 1124.]

P. 9, l. 17. Yeñī p. 79 no 22 should be deleted, since it contains a small (20 foll.) anonymous commentary on the *Fātiḥah* (beg. *Fātiḥah i futūḥāt i Ilāhī*) with an appendix on the *khawāṣṣ* of the *sūrah*. [Ritter, *ibid.*] Other MSS.: **Lahore** Panjāb Univ. (2 copies, one dated 1089–91/1678–80. See *OCM*. xi/2 p. 77), **Ivanow** 2nd Suppt. 988 (late 18th cent.), **Bānkīpūr** xiv 1156 (18th cent.), **Nāfidh Pāshā** 59 (A.H. 1234/1818–19. See Ritter, *OLZ*. 1928 col. 1124), **Blochet** iv 2212 (A.H. 1239–42/1823–7), **Vatican** Pers. 158 (A.H. 1270/1853. Rossi p. 151), **'Alīgaṛh** Subḥ. MSS. p. 6.

P. 9, l. 20. Also **Bombay** 1308/1890–1 (Mashhad i, *fṣl.* 3, ptd. bks., no. 8).

P. 10, ll. 9–10. [*Baḥr i mawwāj.*] **Bānkīpūr** Pers. Hand-list 1105–8, 1109 and 1110–11 = **Bānkīpūr** xiv 1117–20 (complete, A.H. 1265/1849), 1121 (S. xxxviii–cxiv. A.H. 1101/1689–90) and 1122–3 (S. i–xviii. 17th cent.).

P. 10, l. 11. [*Baḥr i mawwāj.*] *Read* **Nūr i 'Uthmānīyah** 234 (S. i–xii. A.H. 984), 235 (S. xiii–cxiv. A.H. 984). [Ritter, *OLZ*. 1928 col. 1124.]

P. 10, l. 12. [*Baḥr i mawwāj.*] Also **'Alīgaṛh** Subḥ. MSS. p. 5 nos. 1–2 (S. xxxvi–cxiv. A.H. 1087/1676–7), p. 6 no. 26 (defective).

P. 10, l. 15. *Akhbār al-akhyār* (Delhi 1332) pp. 180–1.

P. 10, l. 16. [Shihāb al-Dīn Daulatābādī.] Also *Khazīnat al-aṣfiyā'* i pp. 390–2.

P. 10, l. 28. [*al-Muḥammadīyah* or *Tafsīr i Muṣannifak.*] Correct title: *k. al-Shifā' fī tafsīr kalām Allāh al-munazzal min al-samā'*. It was begun in 862 (not 863) and completed in 866. [Ritter, *OLZ*. 1928 col. 1124.]

P. 11, ll. 1–5. [*Tafsīr i Muṣannifak.*] *Read* **Fātiḥ** 636 (S. i. Author's brouillon presented in 863), **Bāyazīd** 260 (S. i, 307 foll., of which 1–234*a* are autograph), 261 (S. lxxvii–cxiv. A.H. 1123), **Āyā Ṣōfyah** 285 (S. lxxvii–cxiv. After A.H. 1000). [Ritter, *OLZ*. 1928 col. 1124.]

P. 11, l. 7. [Muṣannifak.] Also *Ency. Isl.* under al-Bisṭāmī (Huart).

P. 11, ll. 8–17. These lines should be deleted, since Salīmīyah 49 contains a part (S. i and lxxviii–cxiv. A.H. 974) of Kāshifī's *Mawāhib i 'alīyah* (for which see p. 12). [Ritter, *OLZ*. 1928 col. 1124.]

P. 11, l. 22. **Bānkīpūr** Pers. Hand-list 1128 = **Bānkīpūr** xiv 1139.

P. 11, l. 25. **Bānkīpūr** Pers. Hand-list 1123–6 = **Bānkīpūr** xiv 1140–3 (1140 and 1141 of 17th cent., 1142 dated 1104, 1143 19th cent.).

P. 11, l. 28. [*Tafsīr i Sūrah i Yūsuf.*] Also **Mashhad** iv p. 438 nos. 335 (A.H. 986/1579), 336, **Bānkīpūr** Suppt. ii 2056 (A.H. 1098/1687), **Majlis** ii 789 (early 19th cent.), **Lahore** Panjāb Univ. (A.H. 1273/1856–7. See *OCM*. xi/2 p. 77).

P. 11, l. 30. [*Tafsīr i Sūrah i Yūsuf.*] Also **Lucknow** 1309/1891–2 (under the title of *Tafsīr i nuqrah-kār*.[1] See Mashhad iv p. 481).

P. 12, l. 3. [Mu'īn al-Dīn Farāhī.] Also *Majālis al-nafā'is* (tr. Fakhrī ed. Ḥikmat p. 94, ed. 'Abd Allāh om. (p. 159[12]), tr. Qazwīnī ed. Ḥikmat p. 269); *Tārīkh i Rashīdī* (quoted in *Mélanges asiatiques* ix p. 348); *Gulzār i abrār* no. 233. For some of his descendants see *Ma'āthir al-umarā'* iii p. 117.

[1] Possibly with the intention of ascribing the work to S. 'Abd Allāh *al-ma'rūf bi-* Nuqrah-kār (cf. Ḥ. Kh. iv p. 534[3], Brockelmann i p. 305[24], *Supptbd.* ii pp. 14[29], **21**).

P. 12, l. 10. *Read* 910/1504–5.

P. 12, l. 14. **Bānkīpūr** Pers. Hand-list 1131–2 = **Bānkīpūr** xiv 1124–5.

P. 12, l. 18. [*Jawāhir al-tafsīr.*] Also Yeñī 19 (S. i–iv. A.H. 967, transcribed from an autograph), **Qarah Muṣṭafā** 100 (S. i–iv. A.H. 1031), **Nūr i 'Uthmānīyah** 279 (S. i–iv. A.H. 1062 ?), [Ritter, *OLZ.* 1928 col. 1125], **Mashhad** i, *fṣl.* 3, MSS., nos. 75–77 (of which 75 is dated 979/1571–2), iv p. 432, nos. 317 (S. i. A.H. 1118/1706), 318 (S. i), **Majlis** ii 808 (A.H. 983/1575–6) **Sipahsālār** i p. 113, nos. 171 (S. i–iv 81. 16th cent.), 172 (S. i–iii), **Āṣafīyah** iii p. 230 (beautiful MS.), **Leningrad** Univ. (Salemann-Rosen p. 14).

P. 12, ll. 23–4. Nūr i 'Uthmānīyah 279 and Yeñī 19 are the *Jawāhir al-tafsīr* (see the Additions to p. 12, l. 18, above) : Bāyazīd 145 is the *Mawāhib i 'alīyah.* [Ritter, *OLZ.* 1928 col. 1125.] Tashkent 8 (17th cent.) is the *Mawāhib i 'alīyah*, as the opening words show.

P. 12, penult. [Mu'īn al-Dīn Farāhī.] For a Persian abridgment, *Khulāṣah i Baḥr al-durar*, see *OCM.* xi/2 (Feb. 1935) p. 76 (Lahore, Panjāb Univ. A.H. 1213/1798).

P. 12, l. 32. [*Mawāhib i 'alīyah.*] **Bānkīpūr** Pers. Hand-list 1145–56 = **Bānkīpūr** xiv 1126–37.

P. 13, l. 9. [*Mawāhib i 'alīyah.* Editions.] Also **Ṭihrān** A.H.S. 1317/1938 (2 vols. See Mashhad cat. iv p. 503).

P. 13, l. 21. *Insert* : A Ṣūfī commentary on Sūrah xii divided into sixty *fuṣūl* and entitled *Jāmi' al-sittīn* (beg. *al-Ḥ. l. al-Khāliq al-Akbar*) is described briefly in **Sipahsālār** i pp. 100–1 no. 163 (defective. 19th cent.), where it is stated that according to the [spurious ?] preface the subject matter was taken down by a number of hearers from the dictation of Ḥusain Kāshifī, who then furnished the work with a preface. It seems probable that this commentary is identical with the *Jāmi' laṭā'if al-basātīn* recorded below (p. 29 (10). See also Additions and corrections, p. 1210).

P. 13, l. 24. [Ḥusain Kāshifī.] Also *Majālis al-nafā'is* (tr. Fakhrī, ed. Ḥikmat p. 93, ed. 'Abd Allāh p. 158, tr. Qazwīnī, ed. Ḥikmat p. 268) ; *Khazīnah i ganj i Ilāhī* (Sprenger p. 74) ; *Khazīnat al-aṣfiyā'* ii pp. 326–7.

P. 13, l. 24. *Insert*:

20*a*. **'Imād** [al-Dīn] M. [b. Maḥmūd] **Ṭārumī,** born at Ṭārum, migrated to Gujrāt and died there in 941/1534–5. [*Ẓafar al-wālih* (in Arabic) i p. 246.]

Risālah i firdausīyah, a commentary (dealing with *īmān* and *taubah*) on Sūrah vi 159 (" . . . *yauma ya'tī ba'ḍu āyāti Rabbika* . . .), written by order of Shams al-Dīn Abū 'l-Naṣr Muẓaffar Shāh [II] b. Maḥmūd Shāh [of Gujrāt, A.H. 917–32/1511–26]: **Mashhad** iv p. 440 no. 340 (defective at end).

P. 13, l. 25. [Abū 'l-Fatḥ al-Ḥusainī.] Mīr Abū 'l-Fatḥ Sharafī Sharīfī Ḥusainī 'Arab-Shāhī b. S. M. b. Makhdūm b. S. Sharīf Jurjānī (cf. p. 36 *supra*), a pupil of 'Iṣām al-Dīn Ibrāhīm [b. M. b. 'Arab-Shāh] al-Isfarā'īnī (cf. Brockelmann *Sptbd.* ii p. 571), was educated in Transoxiana but settled eventually at Ardabīl, where he died in 976/1568–9 (see Ḥasan Rūmlū ed. Seddon p. 443[9], Seddon's trans., p. 192). He was a convert to Shī'ism, his father having been an Anti-Shī'ite (Mashhad cat. i, *fṣl.* 1, MSS., nos. 180, 271). Among his works, of which several are mentioned by Ḥasan Rūmlū, was an Arabic commentary, *Miftāḥ al-lubāb*, composed in 955/1548 (Mashhad i, *fṣl.* 1, MSS., nos. 180, 271, I. Ḥ. 1772), on *al-Bāb al-ḥādī-'ashar* (cf. Brockelmann *Sptbd.* i p. 707[22]). Although a *ḥāshiyah bar Tahdhīb i manṭiq* (in addition to a *ḥāshiyah bar Kubrā* [1]) is mentioned by Ḥasan Rūmlū among Mīr Abū 'l-Fatḥ's works, it seems at least doubtful whether he can be identical (as is stated in the Mashhad catalogue, i, *fṣl.* 3, MSS., p. 18[5], and the Sipahsālār catalogue, i p. 129[2]) with Mīr Abū 'l-Fatḥ S. M. b. Abī Sa'īd al-Ḥusainī known as Tāj i Sa'īdī, who annotated and completed Dawānī's unfinished commentary on Taftāzānī's *Tahdhīb al-manṭiq* (Mashhad i, *fṣl.* 2, MSS., no. 34, I'jāz Ḥusain 858) and who, according to those catalogues, was a pupil of Qāḍī-zādah i Rūmī [2] and died in 950 (or, according to I. Ḥ., about 950).

[1] Cf. Ivanow Curzon 513, Ḥ.Kh. iii p. 446[7].

[2] Qāḍī-zādah's death is mentioned in the *Zīj* of Ulugh Bēg, who died in 853/1449. Mīr Abū 'l-Fatḥ Sharīfī cannot therefore have been a pupil of his.

P. 13, l. 32. [*Tafsīr i Shāhī.*] Also **Mashhad** i, *fṣl.* 2, MSS., nos. 49–51 (three copies, one dated 974/1566–7), **Sipahsālār** i p. 129 no. 193.

P. 14, l. 9. **Bānkīpūr** Pers. Hand-list 1112–13 = **Bānkīpūr** xiv 1144–5.

P. 14, ll. 12–13. [*Tarjamat al-khawāṣṣ.*] **Bashīr Āghā** 37, 38 and 39 contain respectively Sūrahs i–xvii (quite modern, though dated 882 (!)), xix–xxxv (defective at end. N.d.) and xxxvi–cxiv (defective at beginning. A.H. 1113). 37 is certainly Zawārī's commentary, 38 possibly so, 39 probably so. [Ritter, *OLZ.* 1928 col. 1125.] Also **Mashhad** i, *fṣl.* 3, MSS., nos. 15–18 (all defective. 18 dated 1020/1611–12), iv p. 412 no. 263, **Lahore** Panjāb Univ. (" Pt. I " dated 1089/1678–9, " Pt. II " dated 1061/1651. See *OCM.* xi/2 (Feb. 1935) p. 76), **Majlis** ii 798 (S. xix–cxiv. A.H. 1074/1663–4), 797 (S. i–xvii. A.H. 1083/1672–3), 796 (S. i–xviii. 17th cent.).

P. 14 ult. For al-Faḍl al-Ṭabarsī see *Tārīkh i Baihaq* pp. 242–3, where the date of his death is given as 523.

P. 15, l. 10. [*Tarjamah i tafsīr i Imām Ḥasan i ʻAskarī.*] This is the *Āthār al-akhyār* (not *al-akhbār*) mentioned p. 29 *infra* : see Mashhad iv p. 401, where a slightly defective MS. of 1265/1849 is described.

P. 15, l. 16. *Insert* :

22*a*. S. **ʻAzīz Allāh** Ḥusainī wrote in 967/1559–60 for Shāhzādah Sulṭānum Ṣafawīyah [1] an Arabic commentary on Sh. Ṭūsī's *Uṣūl i dīn* (Mashhad i *fṣl.* 1, MSS., no. 194). For the same princess he wrote in Persian—

Tafsīr i Kalimah i Tahlīlīyah: **Mashhad** i, *fṣl.* 3, MSS., no. 59 (A.H. 963/1555–6).

P. 15, l. 33. [Ibn Ṭā'ūs.] Also *Qiṣaṣ al-ʻulamā'* p. 315 ; Brockelmann i p. 498, *Sptbd.* i pp. 911–13.

P. 15, l. 38. For the *ʻUddat al-dāʻī* see also Gotha Arab. cat. ii no. 771 (1) (?), I.Ḥ. 2110, Brockelmann *Sptbd.* ii p. 210.

P. 15 ult. [Ibn Fahd.] Also *Majālis al-mu'minīn* p. 249 penult. ; *Qiṣaṣ al-ʻulamā'* p. 336 ult. *For* Brockelmann i 498 *read* Brockelmann *Sptbd.* ii p. 210.

[1] Daughter of Shāh Ismāʻīl, b. 925, d. 969 (see Ḥasan Rūmlū p. 418, Seddon's trans. p. 182).

P. 16, l. 9. [*Manhaj al-ṣādiqīn.*] Also **Mashhad** iv p. 456 nos. 381 (acephalous, S. xxv (end only)–xxxv. A.H. 983/1575), 380 (S. xix–xxv, defective at end. Same hand. According to the catalogue the composition of this volume, the fourth, was completed on 28 Muḥarram 982), i, *fṣl.* 3, MSS., no. 213 (S. iv–viii), **Sipahsālār** i pp. 177–8 nos. 239 (S. ix–xviii = *Jild* iii. N.d.), 240 (S. xxxvi–lv. N.d.).

P. 16, l. 11. [*Manhaj al-ṣādiqīn.* Editions.] Also **Tabrīz** 1314/1896–7 (see Mashhad iv p. 502 and Harrassowitz's *Bücher-Katalog* 415 (1928) no. 3319, the latter of which gives Ṭihrān as the place of publication).

P. 16, l. 19. **Bānkīpūr** Pers. Hand-list 1133–6 = **Bānkīpūr** xiv 1146–9.

P. 16, l. 21. [*Khulāṣat al-Manhaj.*] Also **Mashhad** i, *fṣl.* 3, MSS., nos. 119–28 (one of which is dated 989/1581), **Sipahsālār** i pp. 123–7 nos. 186–9 (of which 187 is dated 1067/1656–7), **Majlis** ii 809 (A.H. 1114–15/1702–4), **Ellis Coll.** M. 113 (A.H. 1128/1716), **Ivanow** 2nd Suppt. 989 (S. i–vi. A.H. 1153/1740), **'Alīgaṛh** Subḥ. MSS. p. 6 nos. 16 (S. i–xix. A.H. 1251/1835–6), 17 (S. xix–cxiv), **Bānkīpūr** Suppt. ii 2057 (last *juz'* (?) A.H. 1255/1839), **Caetani** 25.

P. 17, l. 17. [Fakhr al-Dīn Sammākī.] Also Ḥasan Rūmlū p. 490 (his death on 9 Dhū 'l-Qa'dah 984/28 Jan. 1577), Seddon's trans. p. 209 ; Brockelmann *Sptbd.* ii p. 587.

P. 17, l. 36. [Jalāl al-Dīn T'hānēsarī.] Also *Akhbār al-akhyār* p. 285 ; *Ṭabaqāt i Akbarī* ii p. 473 ; *Akbar-nāmah* iii p. 341, Beveridge's trans. iii p. 500 ; *Gulzār i abrār* no. 560.

P. 18, l. 26. *Insert* :

27*a*. **'Abd al-Ḥaqq** b. Saif al-Dīn al-Turk **al-Dihlawī** al-Bukhārī died in 1052/1642–3 (see pp. 194, 978, etc., *supra*).

Tafsīr i Āyat al-Nūr (S. xxiv 35) ; **Rieu** ii 863*a* (18th cent.).

27*b*. Shāh [1] **Qāḍī Yazdī.**

Tafsīr āyāt al-aḥkām, completed in 1021/1612 for Sulṭān Muḥammad Quṭb-Shāh (A.H. 1020–35/1612–26) :

[1] It is not clear whether this word is here a title or part of the name. In the former case the *Tafsīr āyāt al-aḥkām* may possibly be an early work of Mīrzā Qāḍī b. Kāshif al-Dīn Yazdī, who died at Ardabīl in 1075/1664–5 (see Rieu ii 844*a*).

I.Ḥ. 518 (*Tarjamat āyāt al-aḥkām*), 612 (*Tafsīr ā. al-a.*), 1765 (*Sharḥ ā. al-a.*), **Āṣafīyah** iii p. 230 no. 436.

27*c*. **Aḥmad b. Zain al-'Ābidīn** al-'Alawī **al-'Āmilī** al-Iṣfahānī, a cousin (*ibn khālah, Rauḍāt al-jannāt* p. 116[15]) and pupil of M. Bāqir Dāmād (who died in 1041/1631–2 : see Browne *Lit. Hist.* iv p. 406) and the recipient of an *ijāzah* written in 1018/1609–10 by Bahā' al-Dīn al-'Āmilī (I.Ḥ. 23), is best known as the author of two anti-Christian works (neither of them mentioned by I.Ḥ.), *al-Lawāmi' al-rabbānīyah fī radd al-shubah al-Naṣrānīyah* completed in 1031/1621 (MSS. : Browne Pers. Cat. 7, 8, Blochet i 54, Edinburgh 372, Vatican 22) and the *Miṣqal i ṣafā dar tajliyah i Ā'īnah i ḥaqq-numā* completed in 1032/1622 (MSS. : Blochet i 52, 53, Mashhad i, *fṣl.* 1, nos. 256, 257, Rieu i 28*b*, Vatican 72 (5)). He wrote also *Kashf al-ḥaqā'iq fī sharḥ Taqwīm al-īmān*, annotations (in Arabic) on the *Taqwīm al-īmān* of M. Bāqir Dāmād (I.Ḥ. 853, Mashhad i, *fṣl.* 1, MSS., no. 222) and *Miftāḥ al-Shifā' wa-'l-'urwat al-wuthqā*, annotations on the *ilāhīyāt* of the *Shifā'* of Ibn Sīnā (I.Ḥ. 3034).

Laṭā'if i ghaibī (beg. *Ba'd az ḥamd i Mubdi'ī kih sab'ah i mu'allaqāt*), a commentary on those verses of the *Qur'ān* relating to the person and attributes of God and other points of dogma,[1] begun in 1033/1623–4 and dedicated to I'timād al-Daulah Abū 'l-Ḥasan : **Bodleian** 1819 (transcribed from an autograph), **Mashhad** i, *fṣl.* 3, MSS., no. 181 (defective at end).

27*d*. **Yūsuf Miṣrī.**

'Iqd i gauhar, a metrical commentary written in 1035/1625–6 for Shāh 'Abbās I : **Princeton** 447 foll. 1–23*b* (beginning only. A.H. 1123/1711).

27*e*. **Mu'izz al-Dīn Ardistānī** b. Ẓahīr al-Dīn Mīr Mīrān al-Ḥusainī.

Tafsīr i Sūrah i Hal atā [i.e. S. lxxvi presumably], completed in 1044/1634 at the suggestion of M. b. Khātūn

[1] This account of the subject of the work is based on that given in the Mashhad catalogue. In the Bodleian catalogue it is described as "a rich collection of traditions, with Persian paraphrase and detailed explanation".

(cf. p. 51[2] *supra*) and dedicated to 'Abd Allāh Quṭb-Shāh : **Mashhad** i, *fṣl.* 3, MSS., no. 55 (apparently autograph).

P. 19, l. 15. [Mullā Shāh.] See also p. 1009, n. 2, *supra* ; *Pādshāh-nāmah* i, 1, p. 333, ii p. 754 ; *Hamīshah bahār* (Sprenger p. 128) ; Khāfī Khān i p. 549.

P. 19, l. 16. *Insert* :

28*a*. Bahā' al-Dīn M. b. Tāj al-Dīn Ḥasan al-Iṣfahānī, surnamed **al-Fāḍil al-Hindī,** died at Iṣfahān in 1137/1725 (see p. 217 *supra*).

al-Baḥr al-mawwāj, a translation and commentary: **Majlis** ii 790 (no preface. 18th cent.).

P. 19, l. 19. *Insert* :

29*a*. **Bahā' al-Dīn** M. b. Shaikh-'Alī Sharīf **Lāhījī.**

Tarjamat al-Qur'ān, a Shī'ite translation and commentary completed at Patnah [?] in 108– (perhaps 1086 : corruptly in the colophon as quoted " *min sanati wa-thamānīna wa-alf* ") : **Mashhad** iv p. 414 nos. 267 (S. ii 4–xvii), 268 (S. xviii–cxiv. A.H. 1260 (?)/1844).

P. 19, l. 23. [*Zēb i tafāsīr.*] Cf. *Ma'āthir i 'Ālamgīrī* p. 539.

P. 20, l. 11. *Insert* :

32*a*. **M. Riḍā b. M. Mahdī** b. M. Bāqir **Sabzawārī.**

Tarjamat al-Sulṭānī, an annotated translation of Sūrah xviii (*al-Kahf*) completed in 1115/1704 at the request of Shāh Sulṭān-Ḥusain Ṣafawī : **Mashhad** iv p. 413 no. 264 (ornate MS.).

P. 20, l. 20. [*Mawā'id al-Raḥmān.*] Presumably identical with the (apparently untitled) translation prepared by order of Nādir Shāh, which is preserved in **Blochet** iv 2210 (written circ. A.D. 1740 for Nādir Shāh's library). For the Bombay lithograph see also Mashhad iv p. 502.

P. 20, l. 25. [Jamāl al-Dīn Khwānsārī.] Also " Ḥazīn's " *Tadhkirat al-aḥwāl* p. 53 penult., Belfour's trans. p. 59 ; *Nujūm al-samā'* p. 191.

P. 20, l. 27. *Insert* :

34*a*. **Zain al-'Ābidīn Birādar " Dīwān ",** presumably a Dak'hanī, since he wrote verses in Dak'hanī Urdū, is the author of a commentary (apparently in Persian) on Muḥibb Allāh Bihārī's *Sullam al-'ulūm* (see Brockelmann ii p. 421,

Sptbd. ii p. 622), which he completed in 1150/1737–8 and which is preserved together with his *dīwān* (*Dīwān i Dīwān*) and thirty-five other works, mostly short tracts, in an India Office MS.

(1) ***Fuyūḍāt al-Fātiḥah***, a commentary on Sūrah i : **Ethé** 1700 (1).

(2) ***Ḥāshiyah i risālah i Fuyūḍāt al-Fātiḥah***, notes on the preceding : **Ethé** 1700 (2).

P. 20 ult. [Ḥusain Khwānsārī.] Also *Ātash-kadah* (Bodleian 384 no. 434).

P. 21, l. 4. [*Fatḥ al-Raḥmān.*] Also **Bānkīpūr** xvii 1655 (*Muqaddamah* only. A.H. 1251/1835), 1654 (?) (*Muqaddamah fī qawānīn al-tarjamah*), **Alīgaṛh** Subḥ. MSS. p. 6 no. 14. **Bānkīpūr** Pers. Hand-list 1140–1 = **Bānkīpūr** xiv 1157–8.

P. 22, l. 4. [*al-Fauz al-kabīr.*] For a description of this work see Zubaid Aḥmad *The contribution of India to Arabic literature* pp. 28–31.

P. 22, l. 5. [*al-Fauz al-kabīr.* MSS.] Also **Bānkīpūr** xvii 1601.

P. 22, l. 9. [*al-Fauz al-kabīr.* Editions.] Also **Cairo** 1346/1927–8 (as an appendix to M. Munīr's *Irshād al-rāghibīn fī 'l-kashf 'an āy al-Qur'ān al-mubīn.* See *Der Islam* xix p. 74 no. 168).

P. 22, l. 12. For the *Fatḥ al-Khabīr* see Zubaid Aḥmad *The contribution of India to Arabic literature* pp. 19–20.

P. 22, l. 19. [Walī Allāh Dihlawī.] Also *Khazīnat al-aṣfiyā'* ii p. 373 ; *Ḥayāt i Walī* (in Urdu. 360 pp.), by M. Raḥīm-Bakhsh, Delhi 1319/1901–2* ; Bānkīpūr xiv p. 134 ; Brockelmann *Sptbd.* ii pp. 614–15 ; Zubaid Aḥmad *The contribution of India to Arabic literature* pp. 19–20, 246, etc. For an anonymous work defending Walī Allāh against the charge that he had insufficient respect for the Imāms see Bānkīpūr xvii 1619.

P. 23, l. 3. [Qamar al-Dīn Aurangābādī.] Also Brockelmann *Sptbd.* ii p. 616 ; Zubaid Aḥmad *The contribution of India to Arabic literature* p. 314.

P. 23, l. 3. *Insert* :

36*a*. Āqā M. **Hāshim** "Hāshim" b. Mīrzā Ismā'īl **Shīrāzī** Dhahabī was a *mustaufī* in the service of the Zands, but resigned in order to lead the life of a Ṣūfī. He became the disciple, son-in-law and ḵẖalīfah of S. Quṭb al-Dīn Nairīzī, one of the maṣẖāyiḵẖ of the Silsilah i Ḏẖahabīyah i Kubrawīyah. He died in 1199/1785 and was buried in the Ḥāfiẓīyah at S̱ẖīrāz. [*Riyāḍ al-ʻārifīn* pp. 624-6; *Ṭarāʼiq al-ḥaqāʼiq* iii p. 98; Maṣẖhad cat. iv pp. 501-2].

Manāhil al-taḥqīq, a commentary on the words "*A-lā ilā ʼllāhi tasīru ʼl-umūr*" (Sūrah xlii 53) containing Ṣūfī reflexions on *mabdaʼ* and *maʻād*: **Ṭihrān** 1323/1905 (followed by a Ṣūfī tract, *risālaʼī dar sulūk*, by Mīrzā Abū ʼl-Qāsim known as (*maʻrūf bi-*) Mīrzā Bābā Ḏẖahabī S̱ẖīrāzī. See Maṣẖhad iv p. 501 no. 286).

P. 23, ll. 24-6. [*Laṭāʼif al-tafsīr*.] "Die Zuweisung des Werkes an Naḥīfī lässt sich aus dem Codex ohne weiteres nicht rechtfertigen. Offenbar die Kladde des Verfassers. Der eigentliche Text scheint fol. 3*b* zu beginnen:

بسمله ... المناجاة الرحمانية اى معبود شاهان و اى مسجود پادشاهان

Nähere Untersuchung war mir nicht möglich." [Ritter, *OLZ*. 1928 col. 1125.]

P. 23, l. 30. [*Durr al-naẓīm*.] Presumably identical with the *Durr i naẓīm i Ḵẖāqānī* (beg. *Jāmiʻtarīn kalāmī*) written by Mullā M. Riḍā "Kauṯẖar" Hamadānī for Fatḥ-ʻAlī S̱ẖāh, of which a MS. (pt. 1 only, on the verses relating to *tauḥīd*, in a *muqaddamah*, five *aṣl*s and a *ḵẖātimah*. A.H. 1223/ 1808-9) is described in Maṣẖhad iv p. 439 no. 338. Edition (pts. 1 and 2): **Ṭihrān** (see Maṣẖhad iv p. 488. Probably the edition of 1279).

P. 24, l. 15. **Bānkīpūr** Pers. Hand-list 1142-4 = **Bānkīpūr** xiv 1159-61.

P. 24, l. 17. [*Fatḥ al-ʻAzīz*.] Also **ʻAlīgaṛh** Subḥ. MSS. p. 5 no. 8 (S. lxvii-cxiv), **Ivanow** 2nd Suppt. 990 (S. lxxviii-cxiv. 19th cent.).

P. 24, ll. 22-6. [*Fatḥ al-ʻAzīz*. Editions.] Also **Delhi** 1267/1851 (Bibl. Orient. Sprengeriana 449-50, Zenker ii 1069). An edition of 1264/1848 is recorded (without specification of the place of publication) in Āṣafīyah iii p. 230 no. 441.

P. 24, l. 31. ['Abd al-'Azīz Dihlawī.] Also *Khazīnat al-aṣfiyā'* ii pp. 388–9 ; Brockelmann *Sptbd.* ii p. 615.

Insert :

40*a*. **Ḥusain Riḍā** b. 'Alī b. Ya'qūb **Afshār**.

Tafsīr i 'Alawī, a Shī'ite commentary written in 1202/ 1787–8 : **Calcutta Madrasah** 108–9 (A.H. 1207–8/1792–4).

P. 24 footnote. Ghulām-Ḥalīm is the chronogrammatic pseudonym used by 'Abd al-'Azīz in his *Tuḥfah i Ithnā-'Asharīyah*, whether or not it was (as Raḥmān 'Alī implies) the *nām i tārīkhī* given to him by his father. Cf. Blochmann *Contributions to Persian lexicography* (in *JASB.* 37/1 (1868)) p. 63 : *nám i tārīkhī*, an additional name which parents give their children, in order to remind them of the year in which they were born—a very necessary thing in the East, where few people know their correct age.

P. 25, l. 7. [*Risālah i shaqq al-qamar.*] For a lithographed edition (pp. 16. As'ad al-akhbār Pr., Āgrah, 1268/1852) see Arberry p. 435.

P. 25, l. 9. [Rafī' al-Dīn Dihlawī.] Also *Fihrist i muṣannafāt i Maulānā Shāh Rafī' al-Dīn Dihlawī* (in Urdu), by M. Shafī' (in *OCM.* ii/1 (Nov. 1925) pp. 42–9).

P. 25, l. 9. *Insert* :

41*a*. **M. Bāqir** (*mashhūr bah*) **Nawwāb** b. M. Lāhījānī (by origin) Iṣfahānī (by residence), the author of a Persian translation of the *Nahj al-balāghah* (Sipahsālār ii pp. 17–19), wrote his *Tuḥfat al-Khāqān* in 1230/1815 at the request of Fatḥ-'Alī Shāh.

Tuḥfat al-Khāqān, a commentary in which the expositions are classified under the headings (1) *qiṣaṣ*, (2) *aḥkām*, (3) *ma'ārif*, (4) *mawā'iẓ* and (5) *mawā'īd* : **Sipahsālār** i pp. 97–8 no. 161 (vol. i only, on the verses relating to the Prophets and the Imāmate. Possibly autograph), **Majlis** ii p. 8 no. 794 (vol. i only. A.H. 1230/1815).

P. 25, l. 24. **Bānkīpūr** Pers. Hand-list 1101 = **Bānkīpūr** xiv 1168.

P. 26, l. 3. [M. Sa'īd Aslamī.] Also *Ḥadīqat al-marām* (in Arabic) p. 3.

P. 26, l. 4. More fully S. Rajab 'Alī Khān Bahādur Ḥusainī Ḥasanī Naqawī Bhakkarī Dihlawī Lāhaurī (see Mashhad iv p. 492, where the Lahore edition of the *Sirr i akbar* is described).

P. 26, l. 6. More fully *K. al-gh. 'an wujūh āyāt Hal atā* (see Mashhad iv p. 495).

P. 26, l. 27. *Read Ḥaḍrat-Shāhī.*

P. 26 antepenult. [M. Ḥasan Amrōhawī.] Also *Nukhbat al-tawārīkh* p. 63.

P. 26 antepenult. *Insert*:

47*a*. **Ḥaidar 'Alī Faiḍābādī,** a dogmatic theologian and an Anti-Shī'ite controversialist, spent the last few years of his life at Ḥaidarābād in receipt of a stipend from the Niẓām and he died there about 1890. His *Muntahā 'l-kalām* was published at [Lucknow] in 1282/1865 (cf. Edwards col. 240).

Fuyūḍāt i Ḥaidarīyah, a *tafsīr*: **Āṣafīyah** iii p. 230 nos. 573–8 (6 vols.).

[Raḥmān 'Alī p. 55.]

P. 27, l. 2. *Read* Qinnaujī.

P. 27, l. 32. *Read* Qinnaujī.

P. 27, l. 17. 29 Jumādā ii 1307/20 Feb. 1890 is the date given in the *Ma'āthir i Ṣiddīqī* iii p. 200[2].

P. 27, l. 30. [*Ifādat al-shuyūkh.*] This work is a treatise on the abrogating and abrogated verses of the *Qur'ān*, not a *tafsīr*.

P. 28, l. 23. Also Brockelmann *Sptbd.* ii pp. 859–61.

P. 28, l. 27. *Insert*:

48*a*. **M. Bāqir Bawānātī,** surnamed Ibrāhīm Jān Mu'aṭṭar, an eccentric poet, who had "travelled through half the world" and had "been successively a Shī'ite Muhammadan, a dervish, a Christian, an atheist, and a Jew" before elaborating his own "Islamo-Christianity", was resident in London for some years as an old man and there had E. G. Browne as a pupil in Persian. Having left London towards the end of 1884 he lived for a time at Bairūt and returned thence to Persia, where he died about 1890. His *Shumaisah i Landanīyah*, a *qaṣīdah* of 366 verses, was published in London (with a similar poem, the *Sudairah i nāsūtīyah*) in 1882*. Twenty-nine verses from the former poem were printed with an English translation by E. G. Browne in *The press and poetry of modern Persia*, pp. 168–74.

Rauḍāt i Landanī u fauḥāt i anjumanī kināyat az Qur'ān i Mu'aṭṭar, a metrical commentary composed in 1883 on twenty-six sūrahs believed by the commentator to have been revealed in the first year of the Prophet's mission : **Browne** Coll. A. 3 (autograph).

[Browne *A year amongst the Persians* pp. 12–15. Portrait in *The press and poetry of modern Persia*, facing p. 168.]

48*b*. Ḥasan b. M. Bāqir Iṣfahānī, surnamed (*mulaqqab*) **Ṣafī 'Alī-Shāh** and, as a poet, calling himself " Ṣafī ", was an eminent member of the Ni'mat-Allāhī order.[1] Devoted from boyhood to the society of Ṣūfīs, he went at the age of twenty from Iṣfahān to visit Mīrzā Kūchak [2] at Shīrāz, was accepted by him as a disciple and later accompanied him to Kirmān. In 1280/1863–4 he went by way of India on a pilgrimage to Mecca. On his return to India he stayed there for four years and published at Bombay a metrical work entitled *Zubdat al-asrār* (*dar asrār i shahādat*), which he had begun at Kirmān on the suggestion of Mīrzā Kūchak. He then went to Karbalā' and from there to Yazd, but in consequence of disagreements with the *ahl i ḥāl u qāl* he returned to India, intending to spend the rest of his life in the Deccan. After two years, however, he went back to Persia and settled in Tihrān, where he died on 24 Dhī-Qa'dah 1316/5 April 1899. In addition to the *Zubdat al-asrār* and the *tafsīr* works by him entitled *'Irfān al-ḥaqq*, *Baḥr al-ḥaqā'iq* and *Mīzān al-ma'rifah* are mentioned in the *Ṭarā'iq al-ḥaqā'iq* (iii p. 204[34]).

Tafsīr i Ṣafī, a metrical (*mathnawī*) Ṣūfī commentary on the whole of the *Qur'ān* begun in 1306/1888–9 and completed in 1308/1890–1 : **Ṭihrān** 1308/1890–1 (see Mashhad iv p. 474).

[*al-Ma'āthir wa-'l-āthār* (quoted in the *Ṭarā'iq al-ḥaqā'iq*) ;

[1] According to a brief autobiography summarised in the *Ṭarā'iq al-ḥaqā'iq* he was born on 3 Sha'bān 1251/24 Nov. 1835, but this date is inconsistent with the statement that he was twenty years old (*dar bīst-sālagī*) when he became a disciple of Mīrzā Kūchak [who died in 1262/1846].

[2] For Mīrzā Kūchak " Wiṣāl " see Browne *Lit. Hist.* iv p. 316.

Ṭarā'iq al-ḥaqā'iq iii p. 204; Rashīd Yāsimī *Adabīyāt i mu'āṣir* p. 66 (portrait); Mashhad cat. iv p. 474.]

48*c*. Ākhūnd Mullā **Ḥusain** b. 'Alī **Sijāsī** Zanjānī.

Wasīlat al-najāh, a commentary on the Sūrah i Wa-'l-shams (xci), begun on 2 Dhī-Ḥijjah 1321/19 Feb. 1904: **Tabrīz** 1323/1905 (see Mashhad iv p. 504).

48*d*. **Zain al-'Ābidīn Khān Kirmānī.**

Ajwibat al-masā'il, explanations of certain Qur'ānic verses in answer to questions from Ḥājj Mīrzā 'Alī Akbar Āqā-yi Jaurābchī Tabrīzī, completed in 1339/1921; **Tabrīz** 1344/1925–6 (appended to the same author's *Tanzīh al-anbiyā'* and *Tamyīz al-auṣiyā'*. See Mashhad iv p. 463).

48*e*. Sh. **Asad Allāh "Shams" Gulpāyagānī** was living at the time when his *Asrār al-'ishq* was published.

Asrār al-'ishq, a Ṣūfī *mathnawī* in explanation of the Sūrah i Yūsuf (xii): **Iṣfahān** 1343/1924–5 (Mashhad IV p. 464).

48*f*. S. **Ḥusain b. Naṣr Allāh** b. Ṣādiq Mūsawī **'Arab-Bāghī.**

(1) *Īqān dar awāmir u nawāhī i Qur'ān*, a translation of the Qur'ānic verses containing commands and prohibitions, completed in 1345/1927: **Urūmiyah** 1346/1927–8 (see Mashhad iv p. 466).

(2) *Manāhij al-mu'minīn*, an exposition of the Qur'ānic verses relating to the Prophet's family, divided into eighteen *manāhij* and a *khātimah* and completed in 1358/1939 (see Mashhad iv p. 501, where the date and place of publication are not mentioned but a reference is given to the [not yet published ?] section of the catalogue dealing with *Akhbār* under *Manāhij al-'ārifīn*).

48*g*. **'Abbās 'Alī Kaiwān Qazwīnī.**

Tafsīr i Kaiwān: **Ṭihrān** 1350/1931–2 (pts. 1–3, extending to S. iv 109. See Mashhad iv p. 480).

48*h*. S. M. 'Aṣṣār, i.e. S. M. b. Maḥmūd Ḥusainī Tihrānī Lawāsānī *ma'rūf bi-* **'Aṣṣār** *mutakhalliṣ bah* "Āshuftah", was born at Tihrān in 1264/1848 or 1265/1849 and died at Mashhad on 9 Muḥarram 1356/22 March 1937 (see Mashhad iv p. 22[18]). Autograph MSS. of several works by him are preserved at Mashhad.

Nāsikh al-tafāsīr, a commentary of which the first volume (probably the only one ever written) was begun in 1351/1932 and completed towards the end of 1355/1936–7 : **Mashhad** iv p. 457 no. 383 (S. i–xxxix 6. Autograph).

48*j*. **Muḥsin 'Imād** *mudarris i* **Ardabīlī** *mutakhalliṣ bi-* " Ḥālī."

Āyāt al-raj'ah, a commentary on the verses bearing on the doctrine of *raj'at*, completed in 1357/1938 : **Tihrān** A.H.S. 1318/1939–40 (see Mashhad iv p. 462).

48*k*. S. **Kāẓim** [b. S. M.] **'Aṣṣār** is described in the Mashhad catalogue as a Professor in the University of Tihrān.

Tafsīr [*i Saiyid Kāẓim i 'Aṣṣār*], exegetical lectures from a Ṣūfī standpoint delivered in the Mu'assasah i Wa'ẓ u Khiṭābah in the years A.H.S. 1315 and 1317 and extending only to the verse *Māliki yaumi 'l-dīn* [*az āyah i Māliki yaumi 'l-dīn tajāwuz na-kardah*] : **Tihrān** A.H.S. 1315–17/1936–9 (see Mashhad iv p. 468).

48*l*. Ḥājj Sh. **Sharī'at** b. Ḥājj Sh. Ḥasan b. Mīrzā Riḍā-Qulī **Sanglajī**, having studied Law, Theology, Philosophy and Ṣūfism under eminent instructors in Tihrān, spent four years in the prosecution of his studies at Najaf. He died at Tihrān on 9 Muḥarram 1363/5 Jan. 1944 at the age of fifty-three.

Kilīd i fahm i Qur'ān, on some preliminary matters relating to *tafsīr* (*kitāb barkhī maṭālib i muqaddamātī i tafsīr ast*) : **Tihrān** 1361/1942 (see Mashhad iv p. 495).

48*m*. Sh. **Muḥammad** (b. Ḥājj Sh. Ḥasan) **Sanglajī Tihrānī**.

(1) *Tafsīr i Sūrah i Ḥamd u Ikhlāṣ*, a concise commentary on Sūrahs i and cxii completed in 1361/1942 : **Tihrān** (Tābān Pr.) (see Mashhad iv p. 472, where the date of publication [not later than A.H.S. 1323/1944, the date of purchase] is not stated).

(2) *Tafsīr i Sūrah i Ḥamd*, a later edition of the first of the above-mentioned commentaries : **Tihrān** (Majlis Pr.) A.H.S. 1325/1946–7 (see Mashhad iv p. 472).

48*n*. **'Aṭā' Allāh Shihāb-pūr** is described in the Mashhad catalogue as a contemporary author.

Āyāt i Dhū 'l-Qarnain, a commentary on the verses relating to Dhū 'l-Qarnain: **Tihrān** A.H.S. 1323/1944 (2nd ed. Anjuman i Tablīghāt i Islāmī. See Mashhad iv p. 462).

48*o*. Sh. **M. Bāqir Kamara'ī.**

Kānūn i ḥikmat i Qur'ān, a commentary on Sūrah xxxi (Luqmān) completed on 20 Ādhar-māh 1323 [*sic*, but this seems to be a misprint for 1322 [1]]: **Tihrān** 1323/1945 (see Mashhad iv p. 494).

48*p*. Sh. M. **Khāliṣī-zādah.**

Tafsīr i Qur'ān: **Tihrān** A.H.S. 1323/1945 (*muqaddamah*. See Mashhad iv p. 479).

48*q*. **Khalīl b. Abū Ṭālib Kamara'ī** was born in 1317/1899–1900. Having received his early education at Khwānsār and elsewhere, he went in 1337/1918–19 to Sulṭānābād and from 1340/1921–2 to 1354/1935–6 he studied and taught at Qum. Since A.H.S. 1314/1935–6 he has been resident in Tihrān.

Tafsīr i Sūrah i Nūr: **Tihrān** A.H.S. 1324–5/1945–6 (pts. 1–2, of which the second, completed in 1365/1946, extends to verse 35 (36), "*Allāhu nūr al-samāwāt.*" See Mashhad iv p. 473).

P. 29 (2). The *Anīs al-murīdīn wa-rauḍat al-muḥibbīn*, written at Balkh in 475/1082–3, is in forty *majālis* and forms part of the *Tāj al-qiṣaṣ* (see p. 159 *supra* and Bānkīpūr vi p. 75). **Bānkīpūr** Pers. Hand-list 1103 = **Bānkīpūr** xiv 1111 (A.H. 1001/1592–3).

P. 29, l. 3. *Insert*:

(2*a*). *Anīs* (or *Uns*) *al-murīdīn wa-shams al-majālis* (beg. *al-Ḥ. l. 'l. abdaʻa wujūd al-insān* . . ., some lines after which there follows (in Ethé 1778 at any rate: see *JRAS.* 1929 p. 103) a Persian doxology beginning *Ḥ. u sp. mar Ṣāniʻī rā kih bulbul i khwash-nawā-yi balāghat*): a Ṣūfī exposition of the Qur'ānic story of Joseph, ascribed incorrectly (see R. Levy's article in *JRAS.* 1929 pp. 103–6) to ʻAbd Allāh Anṣārī (for whom see pp. 924–7 *supra*):

[1] According to the Mashhad catalogue the work was published in Isfand 1323 and purchased in Farwardīn 1324.

Ḥ. Kh. i p. 453 (reading *Uns*), **Ethé** 1778 (A.H. 1013/1605), **Mashhad** iv p. 408 no. 255 (defective at both ends), **Browne** Coll. D. 7 (modern).

P. 29 (3). [*Aṣdaq al-bayān fī qiṣaṣ al-Qur'ān wa-mawā'iẓ al-Raḥmān*]. **Bānkīpūr** Hand-list 1102 = **Bānkīpūr** xiv 1151 (S. vii–xviii. Described on a fly-leaf as the second quarter of the *Ḥadā'iq al-tafsīr*, but the title given above occurs in a (spurious ?) preface. The work contains references to the *Yūsuf u Zalīkhā* of Jāmī, who is described as "deceased". A.H. 1038/1629).

P. 29 (4). [*Āthār al-akhyār* (so, not *al-akhbār*, in the Mashhad cat., doubtless correctly).] Also **Mashhad** iv p. 401 no. 230 (slightly defective. A.H. 1265/1849. According to the catalogue this is the translation made by 'Alī b. Ḥasan al-Zawārī (cf. p. 15[11] *supra*)).

P. 29, l. 8. *Insert*:

(4*a*). ***Āyāt al-wilāyah***, a commentary by Mīrzā Abū 'l-Qāsim Dhahabī Shīrāzī on 1001 verses regarded as referring to the Prophet's family: **Tihrān** 1323/1905 (2 vols. See Mashhad iv pp. 462–3).

P. 29, l. 9. [*Baḥr al-asrār*.] Also **Mashhad** iv p. 409 nos. 256 (A.H. 1278/1862), 257. Edition: **Kirmān** 1329/1911 (see Mashhad iv p. 466). According to the Mashhad catalogue, which refers to *Bustān al-siyāḥah* p. 483 and *Ṭarā'iq al-ḥaqā'iq* iii [p. 93], Mīrzā M. Taqī b. M. Kāẓim Kirmānī *mulaqqab bi-* Muẓaffar 'Alī-Shāh died in 1215/1800–1 and was buried outside the East Gate of Kirmānshāhān.

P. 29 (6). The *Baḥr al-ma'ānī* is a commentary on S. lxxviii–cxiv. **Bānkīpūr** Hand-list 1104 = **Bānkīpūr** xiv 1153. The former writes *al-mad'ū bi-* KhWĀWND Miyān, the latter *al-mad'ū bi-* KhWND Miyān (transliterated Khund Miân).

P. 29, l. 15. *Insert*:

(7*a*). ***Fātiḥah u ma'nā-yi ān***, a translation by 'Abbās Rāsikhī of M. 'Abduh's *Tafsīr Sūrat al-Fātiḥah wa-mushkilāt al-Qur'ān* (for which see Brockelmann *Sptbd.* iii p. 320): **Rasht** [A.H.S. 1325/1946 (?), that being the year in which the translator presented the work to the Mas͟hhad library. See Mas͟hhad iv p. 494].

P. 29, l. 17. Ṭā-Hā Quṭb al-Dīn Qādirī Kairānawī [1] (not Katānawī) is the subject of the penultimate biography in the *Taḥā'if i Ras͟hīdīyah* and the *Tārīk͟h i Qādirīyah* (see p. 1020 *supra*). Presumably he lived in the second half of the 17th century.

P. 29 (9). Read *Istiqṣā' al-ifḥām* (with dotted ḥ) . . . *fī jawāb Muntahā 'l-kalām*. The work is a reply to the Anti-S͟hī'ite *M. al-k.* ([Lucknow] 1282/1865°) of Ḥaidar 'Alī Faiḍābādī (cf. p. 1204 *supra*) and doubtless has no very strong claim to appear in this section. Another edition: 1276/1859–60 (Āṣafīyah ii p. 1330 where the place of publication [probably Lucknow] is not mentioned).

P. 29 (10). [*Jāmi' laṭā'if al-basātīn.*] **Bāyazīd** 287, dated 841 and containing 317 foll., begins *Sipās mar K͟hud͟hāwandī rā kih Āfrīd͟hgār u Qādir i bar kamāl-ast . . . c͟hunīn gūyad K͟hwājah i Imām Tāj al-Dīn Saif al-Naẓar Jamāl al-Ayimmah Abū Bakr Aḥmad b. M. b. Yazīd al-Ṭūsī.* **Bāyazīd** 288 is an Arabic *ḥās͟hiyah* on Baiḍāwī (*daftar* incorrect). **As'ad** 94 (43 foll., undated) begins *Qāl al-Saiyid al-Imām Tāj al-Dīn Saif al-Naẓar Imām Aḥmad b. M. b. Zaid al-Ṭūsī Nīkūtarīn i 'ilmhā pand u ḥikmat-ast.* It deals with Sūrah xii but could not at the most be more than a mere abridgment of the work contained in Bāyazīd 287. [Ritter, *OLZ.* 1928 col. 1125.] The title as given by Ivanow is *Kitāb sittīn jāmi'u'l-laṭā'if (wa') l-basātīn.* **Ivanow** 1241 (late 15th or early 16th cent.) begins *Sp. mar K͟hudāwandī rā kih Qādir i bar kamāl ast.* Probably another MS. of this work is **Sipahsālār** i pp. 100–1 no. 163 (see Additions and corrections p. 1195, *ad* p. 13, l. 21).

P. 29, l. 27. *Insert*:

(10*a*). ***Jawāhir al-īmān***, a translation of the *tafsīr* ascribed to the 11th Imām, al-Ḥasan al-'Askarī, (cf. p. 29 (4) *supra* and the Additions and corrections, p. 1209) by Āg͟hā M. Bāqir Yazdī. Edition: 1320/1902–3 (see Āṣafīyah iii p. 230, where the place of publication is not stated).

[1] For Kairānah see p. 1020, n.1 *supra*.

P. 29 (11). **Peshawar** 155 (*sic lege*) is described as a 15th cent. MS.

P. 29 (12). [*Jalā'* [1] *al-adhhān.*] Also **Mashhad** i, *fṣl.* 3, MSS., nos. 78 (S. i–xxxv. A.H. 972/1564–5), 79 (S. vii–xxxv. A.H. 1010/1601–2), 80 (S. xxxvi–cxiv. A.H. 1011/1602–3), **Majlis** ii 803 (S. ii 148–vi (?). A.H. 1009/1600–1), 804 (S. vii–xvii. A.H. 1011/1602–3), 805 (S. xix–xxxv. 17th cent.), 806 (S. xxxvi–cxiv. A.H. 1069/1658–9), 807 (S. i–xvii. 17th cent.), **Sipahsālār** i pp. 101–6 nos. 164 (S. i–xviii (?). A.H. 1038/1628–9), 165 (?) (S. xix–cxiv. A.H. 1093/1682. The cataloguer gives reasons for doubting whether this volume is a part of the *Jalā' al-adhhān*).

P. 30, l. 3. *Insert*:

(12*a*). *al-Kalām al-aʻlā fī tafsīr Sūrat al-Aʻlā bi-aḥādīth al-Muṣṭafā*, by Maulawī Mushtāq Aḥmad Ḥanafī Chishtī Amēṭ'hawī.[2] Edition: **Ḥaidarābād** (Āṣafīyah iii p. 230, where the date is not mentioned).

P. 30 (14). Asʻad 145 and 146 are the *Kashf al-asrār wa-ʻuddat al-abrār* of Rashīd al-Dīn A. b. M. Maibudī (see p. 1190, *ad* p. 4, l. 10). [Ritter, *OLZ*. col. 1124[24].]

P. 30 (15). The *Lawāmiʻ al-tanzīl* was begun in 1296/1879 according to Mashhad i, *fṣl.* 3, ptd. bks., no. 35 (vol. i. A.H. 1301/1883–4).

P. 30, l. 14. *Insert*:

(15*a*). *Lubb al-fawā'id*: **ʻAligaṛh** Subḥ. MSS. p. 6 no. 25.

P. 30 (18). [*Majmaʻ al-biḥār.*] For Muẓaffar ʻAlī Niʻmatallāhī see the Additions and corrections to p. 29 (5). Another MS.: **Mashhad** iv p. 450 no. 364 (A.H. 1268/1852). According to the Mashhad catalogue this is a prose version of the same author's *Baḥr al-asrār*, a Ṣūfī commentary on Sūrah i (cf. p. 29 (5) *supra* and the Additions and corrections p. 1209).

Edition: [**Persia**] 1323/1905 (title incorrectly given as *Jāmiʻ al-biḥār* at beginning. See Mashhad iv p. 496).

P. 30 (19). **Bānkīpūr** Pers. Hand-list 1129 = **Bānkīpūr** xiv 1169 (vol. iii, apparently the last, in 136 chapters. 19th cent.). Neither the author's name nor the title occurs in

[1] This vocalisation is more probable than *Jilā'*.
[2] For Amēṭ'hī see p. 474, n.4 *supra*.

the text of the Bānkīpūr MS., but in several places a later hand has written *Tafsīr i Maẓhar al-Ḥaqq.* " The arrangement is that all the verses relating to a particular subject, such as prayer, the reading of the Qurân, etc., are grouped in a chapter, and then commented on."

P. 30, l. 23. *Insert* :

(19*b*.) ***Miftāḥ al-'irfān fī tartīb suwar al-Qur'ān,*** probably by M. Bāqir Bawānātī (for whom see p. 1204 *supra*) : **Browne** Coll. Y. 9 (4).

P. 30, l. 28. *Insert* :

(20*a*.) ***Mubīn,*** a concise commentary in the nature of a literal translation, by Nūr al-Dīn M. birādar-zādah i Faiḍ : **Mashhad** i, *fṣl.* 3, MSS., no. 182 (A.H. 1274/1857–8).

P. 31 (22). [***al-Mustakhlaṣ***]. See Additions to p. 36, l. 2 (p. 1215 *infra*).

P. 31, l. 5. *Insert* :

(24*a*.) (***Qiṣṣah i Yūsuf***), an anonymous commentary beginning *al-Ḥ. l. R. al-'ā. wa-'l-'āqibatu . . . Faṣl. Bi-dān-ki īn kitāb jam' kardah āmad dar bayān i qiṣṣah i Yūsuf* : **Skutari** Hudā'ī 77 (A.H. 849). [Ritter, *OLZ.* 1928 col. 1126[7].] Probably also **Bānkīpūr** xiv 1171 (19th cent. Cf. p. 33 (61) and Additions).

(24*b*.) (***Qiṣṣah i Yūsuf***), in 57 chapters, perhaps translated from an Arabic original : **Blochet** i 395 (acephalous, beginning in Ch. XII. A.H. 898/1492).

P. 31, l. 11. *Insert* :

(27*a*.) ***Risālah i nūrīyah,*** a commentary on the *Āyah i nūr* (S. xxiv 35), by Ḥājj M. Raḥīm Khān Kirmānī. Edition : place ? date ? (see Mashhad iv p. 488).

(27*b*.) ***Risālah i Qalandarīyah,*** on S. xxxv 1 : **Cambridge** Trin. Coll. R. 13, 45 (19) (Palmer p. 115).

P. 31 (33). S. Nāṣir al-Dīn M. **Abū 'l-Manṣūr** Dihlawī b. S. M. 'Alī b. S. Fārūq 'Alī, noted in his day as an Anti-Christian controversialist, was born at Nāgpūr, where his father was *Mīr Munshī* to the British Residency. When Raḥmān 'Alī wrote about him (presumably in, or shortly before 1894), he had reached the age of sixty-four and was resident in Delhi, engaged in the composition of his Persian *tafsīr.*

Raḥmān 'Alī mentions the titles of twenty-eight other works by him, most of them, if not all, presumably in Urdu and many of them replies to the works of Indian and other Christians (see also the index to Blumhardt's catalogue of Hindustani books in the India Office Library under Muḥammad Abū al-Manṣūr). [*Kalimat al-ḥaqq*, an Urdu biography, by M. Nuṣrat 'Alī, Delhi 1870*, 1876* ; *'Ain al-yaqīn*, an Urdu account of his writings, by S. Mahdī Ḥasan, Delhi 1873* ; Raḥmān 'Alī p. 232.]

P. 31, l. 25. *Insert* :

(33*a*.) ***Tafsīr al-Qur'ān***, a translation by S. M. Taqī Fakhr-Dā'ī Gīlānī of S. Aḥmad Khān's Urdu translation and commentary (for which see p. 486, l. 5 *supra*) : **Ṭihrān** (pt. 1 (to Sūrah ii 80), apparently undated but presented by the publishers to the Mashhad Library A.H.S. 1318/1939–40. See Mashhad iv p. 479).

(33*b*.) ***Tafsīr fī ma'nā 'l-tauḥīd***, on the last (30th) section : **Princeton** 79 (acephalous. A.H. 1264/1848).

P. 32, l. 5. *Insert* :

(36*a*.) ***Tafsīr i Āyat al-Kursī*** (beg. *al-Ḥ. l. 'l. anzala 'alā 'abdihi 'l-kitāb . . . Ba'd az imlā-yi ṣaḥā'if i ilāhī*), a Sunnī commentary written apparently in the 10th/16th century and divided into a *muqaddamah*, two *maqālahs* and a *khātimah* : **Majlis** ii 802 (A.H. 962/1555).

P. 32 (37). Delete the query after al-Majlisī. The work is dedicated to Shāh Sulaimān Ṣafawī. **Bānkipūr** Pers. Hand-list 1114 = **Bānkipūr** xiv 1154 (19th cent.).

P. 32 (42). The *Tafsīr i Dalīl al-Raḥmān* is a large Shī'ite commentary begun in Rajab 1214/1799 in Shāh-'Ālam's reign. **Bānkipūr** Pers. Hand-list 1115–20 = **Bānkipūr** xiv 1162–7.

P. 32 (43) should be deleted. **Nūr i 'Uthmānīyah** 444 is the *Kashf al-asrār wa-'uddat al-abrār* of Rashīd al-Dīn A. b. M. Maibudī (see p. 1190 *supra*, Additions to p. 4, l. 10). [Ritter, *OLZ*. 1928 col. 1124[27].]

P. 32 (47), an Arabic work, should be deleted. [Ritter, *OLZ*. 1928 col. 1125.]

P. 33, l. 17. *Insert*:

(57*a*.) ***Tafsīr i Sūrah i Wa-'l-ḍuḥā*** (xciii), by M. 'Alī Qādirī: **Āṣafīyah** iii p. 230 no. 513 (A.H. 1130/1718).

P. 33 (60). **As'ad** 101, dated 1028, is defective at the beginning (first words: *u bayān ba-ṣaub i Sūrah i Āl i 'Imrān mutawajjih shud*). [Ritter, *OLZ*. 1928, col. 1125.]

P. 33 (61). ***Tafsīr i Sūrah i Yūsuf*** (beg. *al-Ḥ. l. R. al-'ā. . . . Bi-dān-kih īn kitāb jam' kardah āmad dar bayān i Yūsuf b. Ya'qūb . . . bā āyathā-yi Qur'ān.* Cf. p. 1212 *supra*, (24*a*), Additions to p. 31 l. 5): **Bānkīpūr** Pers. Hand-list 1127 = **Bānkīpūr** xiv 1171 (19th cent.).

P. 33 (62). ***Tafsīr i Sūrah i Yūsuf*** (beg. *Ḥamd i bī-ḥadd u bī-nihāyat u madḥ i bī-'add u bī-ghāyat ḥaḍrat i jalāl*), a Shī'ite work: **Chelebī 'Abd Allāh** 19 (A.H. 667). [Ritter, *OLZ*. 1928 col. 1125.]

P. 33, l. 24. *Insert*:

(64*a*) ***Tafsīr i Sūrah i Yūsuf***: **Lindesiana** p. 222 no. 537 (circ. A.D. 1750).

(64*b*) ***Tafsīr i Sūrah i Yūsuf***, by Miyāṅ [1] Jān Muḥammad b. Abū Sa'īd Anṣārī Jāland'harī [2]: **Lahore** Panjāb Univ. (A.H. 1277/1860. See *OCM*. xi/2 p. 77).

P. 34 (69) should be deleted. Qarah Muṣṭafā 100 (A.H. 1031) is the *Jawāhir al-tafsīr* (for which see p. 12 *supra* and Additions and corrections p. 1195). [Ritter, *OLZ*. 1928 col. 1125[6].]

P. 34, l. 6. *Insert*:

(69*a*) ***Tarkīb al-Qur'ān*** (beg. *Naḥmaduka 'llāhumma yā man alhamanā . . . Bar alwāḥ i ṣāfiyah*), grammatical analysis and Persian translation of the *Qur'ān* by an anonymous Shī'ite apparently of the Ṣafawī period: **Majlis** ii 800 (S. i–ii only. With a marginal commentary by another Shī'ite apparently contemporary with the author. A.H. 1120/1708).

P. 34 (70). The *Tauḍīḥ* (beg. *Ḥamd ān Khudā'ī rā kih bi-firistād bar Paighāmbar i mā Qur'ān i muzhdah-dihandah*) is a concise anonymous commentary based on the *Kashshāf*, the *Tafsīr i Zāhidī* (see p. 4 *supra* and Additions, p. 1190),

[1] Cf. p. 998, n.l.

[2] Jāland'har = "Jullundur" in the Panjāb.

Dīnawarī, etc. Other MSS. : **Bānkīpūr** xiv 1150 [= no. (72) below. 16th cent.], **Mashhad** i, *fṣl.* 3, MSS., no. 32 (old).

P. 34 (72). **Bānkīpūr** Pers.Hand-list 1130 = **Bānkīpūr** xiv 1150. This is the same work as no. (70) above.

P. 34, l. 14. *Insert* :

(73a) ***'Urwat al-muttaqīn,*** a Shī'ite commentary on the *Āyat al-Kursī* (S. ii 256) and the two succeeding verses, by M. b. Ḥaidar 'Alī *ma'rūf bi*-Ashraf Warnūsfādarānī : **Mashhad** iv p. 443 no. 346 (acephalous).

P. 35, l. 2. *Insert* : (9) **Mashhad** i, *fṣl.* 3, MSS., no. 34 (beg. Basmalah *Āghāz kardam ba-nām i Khudāwand i Rūzī-dihandah i Āmurzandah Al-Ḥamdu li-llāhi* . . . Old), (10) **Mashhad** i, *fṣl.* 3, MSS., no. 43 (defective at both ends. The author quotes Persian verses by Sa'dī and others. Old).

P. 35, l. 15. **Vatican** 20 (55) = **Vatican** Pers. 55 (Rossi p. 81. Cf. Vatican Pers. 51, Rossi p. 77).

I. QUR'ĀNIC LITERATURE. B. GLOSSARIES

P. 35 penult. [*Tarājim al-a'ājim.*] Of the Āyā Ṣōfyah MSS. only 4665 is the *T. al-a.* 4664*a* and 4666*a* are the *Mustakhlaṣ* of Ḥāfiẓ al-Dīn Bukhārī [see Additions, p. 1215[32]]. The rest of those two MSS. is devoted to a commentary on a *qaṣīdah* of Dhū 'l-Rummah. [Ritter, *OLZ.* 1928 col. 1125.]

P. 35 ult. *Read* **Fātiḥ** 5177 (the number given in the *defter* is incorrect). [Ritter, *ibid.*]

P. 36, l. 2. *Insert* :

50*a*. **Ḥāfiẓ al-Dīn** Abū 'l-Faḍl M. b. M. b. Naṣr **Bukhārī** was born at Bukhārā in 615/1218 and died there in 693/1294 (see *al-Jawāhir al-muḍī'ah* ii pp. 121–2, *al-Fawā'id al-bahīyah* p. 199).

al-Mustakhlaṣ (beg. *al-Ḥ. l. wa-salām 'alā 'ibādihi 'lladhīna 'ṣṭafā 'alā 'l-khuṣūṣ wa-'l-khulūṣ*), a Qur'ānic glossary : **Āyā Ṣōfyah** 4664*a* (A.H. 757), 4666*a* (A.H. 772), 4837*a*, **Fātiḥ** 645*a*. [Ritter, *OLZ.* 1928 col. 1125, *ad* p. 31 no. 22.]

P. 37, l. 7. 'Āshir p. 175 no. 428 (dated 925) is 'Ādil Shīrāzī's alphabetical rearrangement of the work. [Ritter, *OLZ.* 1928 col. 1126.]

P. 37, l. 8. [*Tarjumān al-Qur'ān.*] Also **'Alīgaṛh** Subḥ. MSS. p. 56 no. 15 (A.H. 952 ?), **Mas͟hhad** iii, *faṣl.* 11, MSS., no. 9.

P. 37, l. 13. 'Ādil S͟hīrāzī (cf. Ritter *OLZ.* 1928 col. 1126) wrote Persian metrical paraphrases of 'Alī's *Ṣad kalimah* (see Sipahsālār ii pp. 68–72; Bodleian 1432–4; etc.) and of the *Nat͟hr al-la'ālī'* (Krafft p. 182 no. 478, probably also Berlin 9 foll. 12*b*–15*b* and de Slane 2770 fol. 135*b seq.* Edition: Ṭihrān 1306/1888–9 (see Sipahsālār ii p. 69[11])) as well as a commentary on Abū 'l-Fatḥ Bustī's *qaṣīdah* [*al-nūnīyah* presumably] (MS. in the possession of S. Naṣr Allāh Taqawī. See Sipahsālār ii p. 69[5]).

P. 37, l. 14. [*Tarjumān al-Qur'ān.* 'Ādil's rearrangement.] Also **'Ās͟hir** p. 175 no. 428 (beg. *Bi-dān aiyadaka 'llāh kih tarjumān ta'rīb i tar-zafān-ast u dar wai sih lug͟hat ast.* A.H. 925). [Ritter, *OLZ.* 1928 col. 1126[17]], probably also **Āyā Ṣōfyah** 85 (contains no mention of author, but opening words agree with 'Ās͟hir p. 175 no. 428. Undated. Ritter, *OLZ.* 1928 col. 1126[11]).

Insert:

(3) anonymous epitome rearranged alphabetically; **Ellis Coll.** M. 84 (3) (probably A.H. 1101/1690).

P. 37, l. 18. [al-Jurjānī.] Also Bānkīpūr Arab. Cat. v p. 86; Brockelmann *Sptbd.* ii p. 305.

P. 37, ll. 19–27. These lines should be deleted. Āyā Ṣōfyah 85 (undated) contains no mention of the author, but the opening words (which agree with those of 'Ās͟hir p. 175 no. 428) seem to show that it is the *Tarjumān al-Qur'ān* of al-Jurjānī [as rearranged by 'Ādil S͟hīrāzī]. [Ritter, *OLZ.* 1928 col. 1126[11].]

P. 38, l. 19. Āyā Ṣōfyah 4837 (1) should be deleted. This is the *Mustak͟hlaṣ* of Ḥāfiẓ al-Dīn Buk͟hārī (see Additions p. 1215, *ad* p. 36, l. 2). [Ritter, *OLZ.* 1928 col. 1125, *ad* p. 31 (22).]

P. 38, l. 24. [*K͟hulāṣah i Mustak͟hlaṣ al-ma'ānī.*] Also **Lindesiana** p. 178 no. 498 (circ. A.D. 1650).

P. 38, l. 25. **Bānkīpūr** Pers. Hand-list 1164 = **Bānkīpūr** xiv 1174.

P. 38 ult. *Insert*:

(6*a*) ***Risālah i lug͟hāt al-Qur'ān ba-Fārisī*** (beg. *wa-ba'du* *fa-innī tarjamtu lughāt al-Qur'ān 'alā abwāb mufaṣṣalah bi-'l-ḥurūf al-mu'jamah*) : **Majlis** 607 (1) (16th cent. ?).

(6b) *Tarjamah i lughāt i Qur'ān* (beg. *Sūrat al-Nās. al-Qaul guftan*) : **Sipahsālār** i pp. 185–6 no. 251 (16th cent.).

P. 39, l. 1. *Read* (7) *Tarjumān al-Qur'ān* (beg. *al-Ḥ. l. 'l. arsala 'l-rusul*) : **Berlin** 232 (8) (fragment), **Majlis** 54.

I. QUR'ĀNIC LITERATURE. C. PRONUNCIATION AND VARIANT READINGS

P. 39, l. 18. [*Kashf al-amānī . . .*] "Nr. 58 (3) (926h.) 379 foll. ist ein selbständiges Buch, wenn auch auf der *Šāṭibīje* beruhend. Anfang :

. . . اما بعد حمد الله على نواله

[Ritter, *OLZ.* 1928 col. 1126.]

P. 39, l. 21. "Nr. (5) ist eine *Terjeme*, kein *Šarḥ*." [Ritter, *OLZ.* 1928 col. 1126.]

P. 39 (6). Kamānkash 15 bis (undated) contains (1) the *Shāṭibīyah* with interlinear Persian translation beginning *Āghāz kardam ba-kalimah i Bi-smi 'llāh jam' al-awwal naqīḍ al-ākhir*. [Another MS. : **'Atīq Wālidah** 20*a* (old naskhī of 7th–8th/13th–14th cent.)], (2) a Persian tract of 9 foll. on *tajwīd* beginning *al-Ḥ. l. 'l. taqaddasa 'an al-aulād wa-'l-ajnād*, (3) a Persian work on the interpretation of dreams (*al-bāb al-awwal fī adab al-mu'abbir wa-tamyīz al-ru'yā*). [Ritter, *OLZ.* 1928 col. 1126.]

P. 39, l. 23. *Insert* :

(6a) *Sharḥ i Shāṭibīyah*, dedicated to Fatḥ-'Alī Shāh and his heir apparent 'Abbās Mīrzā (cf. p. 338 n. 3 *supra*) by M. Qāsim b. Muḥsin b. 'Alī Ḥusainī Tabrīzī : **Majlis** ii 812.

P. 39, l. 26. **Bānkīpūr** Pers. Hand-list 1167 = **Bānkīpūr** xiv 1175.

P. 40, ll. 5–9. In Majlis ii p. 31[14] the name is given as M. b. Maḥmūd b. M. b. Aḥmad b. 'Alī Sharīf Samarqand [ī?] Hamadānī 'l-aṣl "Ḥāfiẓ" takhalluṣ. The Vatican catalogue (p. 93) adds to the *nisbahs* al-Baghdādī (by residence).

Cf. Brockelmann *Sptbd.* i p. 727. He wrote also in Arabic *al-Qaṣīdat al-fā'iḥah fī tajwīd al-Fātiḥah* (Ḥ. Kh. iv p. 545, Vatican Pers. 70 (3), Rossi p. 93).

P. 40, l. 10. *al-Mabsūṯ fī 'l-qirā'at* [*sic*] *al-sab' wa-'l-maḍbūṯ min idā'at al-ṯab'* is the form in which the title occurs in the preface of the Majlis MS. The work is divided into three *kitābs*, of which the second and third are in Arabic. Opening words: *al-Ḥ. l. 'l. adhāqa qulūb.* Other MSS.: **Vatican** Pers. 70 (4) (A.H. 754/1353. Rossi p. 93), **Majlis** ii 817 (A.H. 865/1460–1), **Mashhad** ii, *fṣl.* 7, MSS., no. 38 (A.H. 1019/1610–11).

P. 40, l. 11. *Read* Aḥmad Allāh.

P. 40, l. 12. *al-Multaqaṯ min ma'ānī Ḥirz al-amānī fī tajrīd al-tajwīd* is the full title according to Majlis ii p. 39. The work is a *qaṣīdah* in forty-four verses. Opening words: *al-Ḥ. l. 'l. anzala 'l-Qur'āna tanzīl*^{an}. Another MS.: **Majlis** ii 821–2 (with a metrical commentary by the author in 400 verses. In the same hand as Majlis ii 817, which is dated 865/1460–1).

P. 40, l. 15. *Insert*:

(3) (*Risālah dar ikhtilāf i Abū Bakr b. 'Abbās u Ḥafṣ dar qirā'at*) (beg. *al-Ḥ. l. 'l. j. ṣudūranā khazā'in*): **Mashhad** ii, *fṣl.* 7, MSS., no. 13.

P. 40, l. 16. The "*kitāb i qirā'at*" (beg. *al-Ḥ. l. R. al-'ā. . . . I'lam hadāka 'llāh*) by *bandah i ḍa'īf Samarqandī* is in ten *bābs*.

P. 40, ll. 25–6. [*Farā'id al-fawā'id.*] **Bānkīpūr** Pers. Hand-list 1168 (*b*) = **Bānkīpūr** xiv 1180 foll. 71–133. Also **'Alīgaṛh** Subḥ. MSS. p. 5 (A.H. 1079/1668–9).

P. 41, l. 4. **Bānkīpūr** Pers. Hand-list 1168 = **Bānkīpūr** xiv 1180 (A.H. 1145/1733).

P. 41, l. 8. Another commentary on al-Jazarī's *Muqaddimah* is *Taisīr al-bayān fī tajwīd al-Qur'ān*: **Āṣafīyah** iii p. 748.

P. 41, l. 11. *Khulāṣat al-tanzīl fī adā' al-ḥurūf li-l-tartīl* is the full title according to Palmer. Opening words: *Ai ba-nām i Tu iftitāḥ i kalām.* Also **'Alīgaṛh** Subḥ. MSS. p. 5 (A.H. 1079/1668–9), **Cambridge** Trinity R. 13. 45 (16) (Palmer p. 114) and apparently also **Mashhad** ii, *fṣl.* 7, MSS., nos.

12 (*Risālah dar makhārij al-ḥurūf*, by Ibn 'Imād, written in 809 [so, not 803] and beginning as above. A.H. 1017/1608–9), 41 (*Manẓūmah dar tajwīd*, by Ibn 'Imād, beginning as above).

P. 41, l. 15. [Ṭāhir Iṣfahānī.] Cf. Brockelmann *Sptbd.* ii p. 274.

P. 41, l. 17. [*Durr al-farīd.*] Also **Mashhad** ii, *fṣl.* 7, MSS., no. 10 (A.H. 1018/1609–10).

P. 41, l. 18. *Manhal al-'aṭshān fī rasm aḥruf al-Qur'ān* (so Ritter, *OLZ.* 1928 col. 1126, and also Peshawar 1095).

P. 41, l. 19. **'Umūmī** 208, dated 878, contains (1) *Manhal al-'aṭshān* . . . (beg. *Ḥ. u sp. i bī-ḥadd u q. Pādshāhī rā*), (2) the same author's *Nihāyat al-itqān fī tajwīd al-Qur'ān* (so according to the colophon. Beg. *A. b. chunīn gūyad faqīr i ḥaqīr i jānī Ṭāhir i Ḥāfiẓ i Iṣfahānī kih īn mukhtaṣar mushtamil ast bar qā'ida'ī u ḍābiṭa'ī chand dar tajwīd u taṣḥīḥ i Qur'ān i 'Aẓīm*). Possibly identical with p. 48 (7). [Ritter, *OLZ.* 1928 col. 1126.]

P. 41, ll. 20–21. **Āyā Ṣōfyah** 44 (undated) is an anonymous work on *tajwīd*, the ascription of which to Ṭāhir is quite arbitrary. It begins *Ḥ. i bī-ḥ. u thanā-yi lā-yu'add Khudāwandī rā sazad kih nuqūsh i ḥurūf i jawāhir i Qur'ān bar lauḥ i qalb.* [Ritter, *OLZ.* 1928 col. 1126.]

P. 41, ll. 22–3. **'Umūmī** 213 (A.H. 894) contains (1) a monograph on Ḥamzah's reading, especially his treatment of the *hamz*, beginning *Chunīn gūyad faqīr i ḥaqīr i jānī Ṭāhir b. 'Arab* [so : cf. Ḥ. Kh. iv p. 546[6]] *b. Ibrāhīm al-Iṣfahānī kih ba'ḍī az dūstān . . . bayān i madhhab i Ḥamzah b. Ḥabīb al-Zaiyāt i Kūfī rā dar waqf bar hamz* . . ., (2) *Nihāyat al-itqān fī tajwīd al-Qur'ān.* [Ritter, *OLZ.* 1928 col. 1126.]

P. 41, l. 25. **Mashhad** ii, *fṣl.* 7, MSS., no. 11 (acephalous) is a *Risālah dar wuqūf* described in the catalogue as by M. Ṭāhir Ḥāfiẓ Iṣfahānī.

P. 41, l. 30. **Bānkīpūr** Pers. Hand-list 1171–2 = **Bānkīpūr** xiv 1177–8.

P. 42, l. 3. [*Qawā'id al-Qur'ān.*] Also **Mashhad** ii, *fṣl.* 7, MSS., no. 27 (A.H. 930 [*sic* ?]), **Majlis** ii 815 (17th cent.), **Blochet** iv 2213, **Peshawar** 1953 (5), **Princeton** 448 (fragments), 450 (fragment).

P. 42, l. 9. [*Tuḥfah i Shāhī.*] Also **Mashhad** ii, *fṣl.* 7, MSS., no. 5 (A.H. 1087/1676–7), **Princeton** 447 (A.H. 1123/1711), **Blochet** iv 2169 (A.H. 1133/1721).

P. 42, ll. 11–12. **Bānkīpūr** Pers. Hand-list 1170 = **Bānkīpūr** xiv 1181 (beg. *al-Ḥ. l. R. al-ʻā. . . . chunīn gūyad aqallu ʻibādi 'llāh wa-aḥwajuhum ilā ʻafwi 'llāh.* Divided into a *muqaddamah*, twelve *faṣls* and a *khātimah*).

P. 42, l. 12. Also by ʻImād al-Dīn al-Astarābādī is :—

Risālah dar qirā'at i ʻĀṣim (beg. *Ḥ. i bī-ḥ. u sp. i bī-q.*), in the manner of the *Shāṭibīyah* ("*īn risālah ba-ṭarīq i Shāṭibīyah ast*") : **Mashhad** ii, *fṣl.* 7, MSS., no. 16.

P. 42, l. 27. [*Maqṣūd al-qāri'.*] Also **Lahore** Panjāb Univ. (A.H 1275/1858–9. See *OCM.* xi/2 p. 78).

P. 43, l. 2. [*Maqṣūd al-qāri'.*] *Read* Editions : **Bombay** (Ḥaidarī Pr.) 1290/1873* (in *Majmūʻah : al-Bayān al-jazīl* . . ., a collection of nine short Urdu, Persian and Arabic works on the *Qur'ān* and its recitation, the first being *al-Bayān al-jazīl li-l-tartīl*, in Urdu, the second *M. al-q.* 92 pp.) ; **Lucknow** (Asadī Pr.) 1290/1873°* (in *Majmūʻah* : *al-B. al-j. li-l-t.*, *M. al-q.* . . . ; another edition of the same, or perhaps nearly the same, collection. 72 pp.) ; (Majmaʻ al-ʻulum Pr.) 1293/1876* (72 pp.) ; (N.K.) 1886† (a similar *majmūʻah.* 62 pp.) ; (Dilpadhīr Pr.) 1308/1891° (in *Majmūʻah i bīst rasā'il i qirā'at*, the first nine (?) being those contained in the *Majmūʻah : al-Bayān al-jazīl* . . . 108 pp.) ; (Qādirī Pr.) 1895† (the same twenty works. 108 pp.).

P. 43, l. 5. *Insert* :

69*a*. S. **Qāsim b.** Mīr **Nūr Allāh.**

Maṭlaʻ al-shams, a metrical work written in 1045/1635–6 at Ḥaidarābād : **Mashhad** ii, *fṣl.* 7, MSS., no. 32.

P. 43, l. 6. Saiyid Abū 'l-Qāsim *mutakhalliṣ bi*-Qārī says in his preface that he wrote in the reign of Shāh ʻAbbās i Thānī i Ṣafawī (see Majlis ii p. 39).

P. 43, l. 7. [*Naẓm al-la'ālī* . . .]. Also **Majlis** ii, p. 39 no. (819) (*Manẓūma'ī dar tajwīd*). No formal title is mentioned in the Majlis catalogue, which, however, quotes a verse in which *Naẓm i la'ālī* occurs as a chronogram (= 1061 or 1062).

The work is metrical, consists of 89 verses and begins *Ai kalām az intiẓām i nām i dhātat bar niẓām.* Perhaps it is identical with the *Naẓm i la'ālī* published on the margin of S. Ḥasan Lak'hnawī's *Rashḥah i faiḍ* (see p. 1222 *infra*).

P. 43, l. 9. Mullā Muṣṭafā Qārī Tabrīzī Shī'ī Imāmī according to the Sipahsālār catalogue.

P. 43, l. 13. [*Tuḥfat al-qurrā'.*] According to Majlis ii p. 10 the work was begun at Mecca, completed at al-Madīnah and after the author's return to Persia was shown to Mullā M. Bāqir Khurāsānī, one of the *'ulamā'* of Iṣfahān, who made some additions.

P. 43, l. 15. [*Tuḥfat al-qurrā'.*] *For* (13) *read* (1–3). Also **Sipahsālār** i p. 184 no. 250 (A.H. 1072/1661–2), **Majlis** ii 795 (A.H. 1087/1676), **Mashhad** ii, *fṣl.* 7, MSS., no. 6 (A.H. 1088/1677), **'Alīgaṛh** Subḥ. MSS. p. 5 (A.H. 1122/1710), and possibly **Ivanow** 1st Suppt. 818 (defective). Edition: **Bombay** 1302/1884–5 (Āṣafīyah iii p. 154).

P. 43, l. 17. The *Irshād al-qārī'* (beg. *Ai Fātiḥah i muṣḥaf i ḥamdat tauḥīd*), was begun at the tomb of 'Alī, completed in 1078/1668 at the shrine of Ḥusain and dedicated to Maulānā M. Bāqir. **Bānkīpūr** Pers. Hand-list 1165 = **Bānkīpūr** xiv 1179.

P. 43, l. 20. [*Ḥilyat al-qārī'.*] Also **Āṣafīyah** iii p. 154 no. 128.

P. 44, l. 8. *Insert* :

76*a*. In 1180/1766–7 at Ḥaidarābād was written :—

(*Risālah dar tajwīd*) : **Rehatsek** p. 195 no. 42.

P. 44, ll. 12–13. This entry should be deleted. The *Mukhtaṣar al-tajwīd*, though described in the List as Persian, is an Urdu work written in 1242 and published at Delhi in 1285*, when the author was still alive.

P. 44, l. 16. *Insert* :

79*a*. **Mukhtār** A'mā **Iṣfahānī**.

Mukhtār al-qurrā', written in 1240 (but see further on) : **Mashhad** ii, *fṣl.* 7, MSS., nos 33–4 (the latter dated 1230 !), **Majlis** ii p. 35 nos. 818–19 (A.H. 1274/1857–8).

P. 44, l. 18. *Insert* :

80*a*. S. **Maḥmūd b. 'Abd Allāh** Mūsawī **Dizfūlī**.

(1) *Qawā'id al-tajwīd fī tartīl al-Qur'ān al-Majīd,*

begun in 1238/1822–3, completed in 1239/1823–4 and divided into a *muqaddamah*, twelve *bābs* and a *khātimah*: **Majlis** ii 813 (A.H. 1240/1824–5).

(2) *Tuḥfat al-ikhlāṣ*, an abridgment of the preceding work, completed in 1244/1828–9, divided similarly and dedicated to the Shāh-zādah Ḥusām al-Salṭanah: **Majlis** ii 793 (same hand).

(3) *Mukhtaṣar al-tajwīd*, completed in 1240/1824–5 and divided into ten *faṣls*: **Majlis** ii p. 36 no. 814 (same hand).

80*b*. S. **M. b. Mahdī Ḥusainī** dedicated to Muḥammad Shāh Qājār (A.H. 1250–64/1834–48) a Qur'ānic concordance (with a Persian preface) entitled *Kashf al-āyāt i Muḥammad-Shāhī* (a chronogram = 1251/1835–6), which has been published at Tabrīz [date? See Mashhad ii, *fṣl.* 7, ptd., bks., no. 2] and, appended to the *Tafsīr al-Jalālain*, at Ṭihrān in 1276/1859–60 [see Ellis ii col. 160, Mashhad iv p. 495].

Maẓāhir i Maḥmūdīyah: **Ṭihrān** 1264/1848 (see Mashhad ii, *fṣl.* 7 (*Tajwīd*), ptd. bks., no. 3, where the precise subject is not stated).

80*c*. S. **Ḥasan Lak'hnawī.**

Rashḥah i faiḍ, composed in 1264/1848. Edition: **Lucknow** (Āṣafīyah iii p. 154 no. 132, where the date is not mentioned. With *Naẓm i la'ālī* (cf. p. 43⁷?) on margin).

80*d*. **M. b. Asad Allāh** b. 'Alī-Riḍā Qāri' **Māzandarānī.**

Maẓamir [*sic*, apparently for *Maẓāhir*] *i Muḥammadīyah*, dedicated to Nāṣir al-Dīn Shāh: **Mashhad** ii, *fṣl.* 7, MSS., no. 40.

P. 45, l. 5. [Sa'd Allāh Murādābādī.] Also Bānkīpūr ix pp. 57–8.

Insert:

81*a*. **Maḥmūd b. M.** 'Alawī Fāṭimī Ḥasanī Ḥusainī Ḥāfiẓ **Tabrīzī** was Warden of the tomb of the Walī-'ahd and Nā'ib al-Salṭanah [i.e. presumably 'Abbās Mīrzā: cf. p. 338 n. 3 *supra*, *Ency. Isl.* under 'Abbās Mīrzā] as well as Instructor and Head of the *Ḥuffāẓ*, *Qurrā'*, *Ṣudūr* and *Khuṭabā'* at the shrine of the Imām Riḍā [at Mashhad]. He was the author of an Arabic work entitled *Jawāhir al-Qur'ān*, which was published at Tabrīz in 1287/1870–1 with a marginal Persian translation by the author (cf. Brockelmann *Sptbd.* ii p. 830, where the date given for his death, 1270/1853, seems to be incorrect).

Mafātīḥ al-tanzīl, on *tajwīd* and other matters relating to the *Qur'ān*, in a *muqaddamah*, twelve *bābs* and a *khātimah*, but perhaps never continued beyond the tenth *bāb*, which was completed in 1297/1880: **Majlis** ii 820 (*Muqaddamah* and *Bābs* i–x).

P. 45, l. 10. *Insert*:

(1*a*). *Baḥr al-nūr*, on the *qirā'āt i Sab'ah* in eight *bābs* and a *khātimah*, by 'Alī b. Ḥasan 'Alī Kūsārī (cf. p. 45, l. 18): **Majlis** ii 791 (part of the first *faṣl* and a fragment of the *khātimah*. Circ. A.H. 1117/1705–6 ?).

P. 45, l. 15. *Ḥall i mutashābih i mamzūj* is a chronogram = 882/1477–8.

P. 45, l. 16. **Bānkīpūr** Pers. Hand-list 1169 = **Bānkīpūr** xiv 1176.

P. 45, l. 19. [*Ḥayāt al-fu'ād.*] Beg. *al-Ḥ. l. al-'Alī 'l. rafa'a ahlahu.* Also **Majlis** II p. 22 no. 792 (lacunae. A.H. 1117/1705–6. Title given here as *Ḥayāt al-qulūb*). For another work by the same author, *Baḥr al-nūr*, see Additions to p. 45, l. 10.

P. 45, l. 25. [*Qaṣīdah* by 'Izz al-Dīn M.] **Decourdemanche** ii S.P. 1673 (12) = **Blochet** iv 2213, fol. 161*b* (author's name given as Émir 'Izz ed-Din ibn Mohammed ibn Béha ed-Din el-Djouri). **Decourdemanche** ii S.P. 1673 (6) = **Blochet** iv 2213 fol. 79*b*. Another MS. of M. Ṣādiq's commentary: **Ethé** ii 3058 (9) (A.H. 1135/1722).

P. 46, l. 7. *Insert*:

(10*a*). *Khulāṣat al-qirā'ah*, by M. Mu'min b. 'Abd al-Karīm Qāri' (who quotes Bahā' al-Dīn al-'Āmilī (d. 1030/1621)): **Sipahsālār** i p. 186 no. 252.

(10*b*). *Khulāṣat al-tajwīd*, anonymous: **Blochet** iv 2213 fol. 162*b*.

P. 46, l. 17. *Insert*:

(15*a*). *Majma' al-gharā'ib*, by Dūst-Muḥammad b. Yādgār: **Leningrad** Univ. no. 556 (Salemann-Rosen p. 18).

(15*b*). *Marta' al-ghizlān*, on *tajwīd*, composed in 1212/

1797–8 by Ḥaidar: **Lahore** Panjāb Univ. (A.H. 1275/1858. See *OCM*. xi/2 p. 77).

(15c). ***Minhāj al-nashr fī 'l-qirā'āt al-'ashr***, by Ḥusain b. 'Uthmān: **I.O.** 4594 (17th cent. See *JRAS*. 1939 p. 376).

P. 46, l. 18. *Insert*:

(16a). ***Mukhtaṣar***, by M. b. 'Alī b. M. al-Ḥusainī [possibly identical with no. (17) and with p. 48 (5)]: **'Alīgaṛh** Subḥ. MSS. p. 5.

P. 46 (17) [*Mukhtaṣar fī bayān* . . .]. See the preceding addition.

P. 46, l. 21. *Insert*:

18a. ***Nūr i sarmadī az mishkāt i Muḥammadī***. Edition: 1261/1845 (Āṣafīyah iii p. 154 no. 129, where the place of publication is not stated).

P. 46, ll. 29–30. *Delete* (22) ***Taisīr al-qārī*** etc. This is evidently Nūr al-Ḥaqq Dihlawī's commentary on al-Bukhārī's *Ṣaḥīḥ*.

P. 47 (26). [*Tuḥfat al-ḥuffāẓ*.] Also **Mashhad** ii, *fṣl*. 7, MSS., no. 4.

P. 47, l. 9. *Tuḥfat al-Raḥmānī dar tajwīd i Qur'ānī* (so " in the conclusion "), a short tract in five chapters. **Bānkīpūr** Pers. Hand-list 1166 = **Bānkīpūr** xiv 1182.

P. 47 (28). [*Zīnat al-qārī'*.] Also **Lahore** Panjāb Univ. (A.H. 1224/1809–10. See *OCM*. xi/2 p. 78), **Bānkīpūr** xvii 1561. The opening words given in the different catalogues vary considerably.

P. 48 (5). Possibly identical with the *Mukhtaṣar fī bayān tajwīd al-Furqān*, p. 46 (17) (see also Additions and corrections to p. 46, l. 18).

P. 48, l. 24. *Insert*:

(12) ***Risālah i tajwīd*** (beg. *al-Ḥ. l. 'l. faḍḍala 'l-'ilma fī 'l-a'ṣār*), metrical, with an Arabic preface in prose, by 'Abd Allāh b. Aḥmad Bāyazīd al-Kultānī: **Bānkīpūr** Suppt. ii 2215 (19th cent.).

(13) ***Risālah dar 'ilm i tajwīd***, in twelve *bābs*, by Aḥmad b. Ḥusain, a descendant of Burair (or Barīr ?) b. Khuḍair (or Khaḍīr ?) Hamadānī: **Majlis** 66 (A.H. 753/1352).

(14) ***Risālah i tajwīd*** (beg. *al-Ḥ. l. al-'Alī al-'Aẓīm alladhī*

nazzala 'l-Kitāb), by Ḥāfiẓ G͟hulām-Muṣṭafā : **Bānkīpūr** Suppt. ii 2214 (19th cent.).

(15) *Risālah i tajwīd* (beg. *al-Ḥ. l. R. al-ʿā. . . . a. b. īn risālah īst muk͟htaṣar dar bayān i ḍarūrīyāt*), in a *muqaddamah*, eight *faṣls* and a *k͟hātimah*, by M. Muḥsin b. Samīʿ : **Sipahsālār** i p. 187 no 253 (A.H. 1228/1813).

P. 49, l. 12. *Insert* :

(10) *Risālah dar qirāʾat* (beg. *al-Ḥ. l. R. al-ʿā. Bidān-kih barāy i tartīb i adāʾ i naẓm i Qurʾān*), composed probably towards the end of the 8th/14th century: **Sipahsālār** i pp. 187–8 no. 254 (A.H. 1046/1636–7).

(11) *Risālah fī tajwīd al-Qurʾān* (beg. *al-Ḥ. l. R. al-ʿā. al-Malik al-ʿAllām wa-jāʿil al-nūr wa-ʾl-ẓalām*) : **Princeton** 80 (A.H. 1083/1672, said to have been transcribed from a MS. written at Simnān in 876/1471–2).

(12) Several untitled works : **Blochet** iv 2213.

(13) Salemann-Rosen p. 15 no. 406.

P. 49, l. 26, no. (6). Cf. **Rehatsek** p. 195 no. 42.

P. 49, l. 27. *Insert* :

(8) *Wuqūf i Kalām Allāh i S͟harīf* (beg. *Baʿd az-ān āram bayānī az wuqūf*): **Lahore** Panjāb Univ. (A.H. 1275/1858. See *OCM.* xi/2 p. 78).

I. QURʾĀNIC LITERATURE. E. INDEXES, CONCORDANCES, ETC.

P. 51, l. 2. M. ʿAlī Karbalāʾī is the subject of a brief notice in the *Nujūm al-samāʾ*, p. 134, where, however, there is little information beyond some words about *al-Wāḍiḥah* (for which see Brockelmann *Sptbd.* ii p. 610).

P. 51, ll. 6–11. Full title : *Hādiyah i Quṭb-S͟hāhī dar istik͟hrāj i āyāt i kalām i ilāhī*. [Ritter, *OLZ.* 1928 col. 1126 penult.] Also **Āṣafīyah** iii p. *bāʾ*, no. 112. Bāyazīd 14, Nūr i ʿUt͟hmānīyah 135 and Salīmīyah 7 are copies of the *Hādiyah i Quṭb-S͟hāhī*. [Ritter, *OLZ.* 1928, col. 1127.]

P. 51, l. 14. Muṣṭafā K͟hān Kās͟hī (*kih s͟hīʿah īst* [read *s͟huʿbah īst* ?] *az ulūs i Afāg͟hinah*, *Maʾāt͟hir al-umarāʾ* iii p. 637) was in the service of Prince M. Aʿẓam, Aurangzēb's third son and became his intimate friend and counsellor, but by order of Aurangzēb, who distrusted him, he was dismissed and sent on a pilgrimage to Mecca. The rest of his life was spent in seclusion at Aurangābād. See Khāfī Khān ii pp. 439–43 ; *Ma'āthir al-umarā'* iii pp. 637–9.

P. 51, l. 18. **Bānkipūr** Pers. Hand-list 1162–3 = **Bānkipūr** xiv 1172–3.

P. 51, l. 20. [*Nujūm al-Furqān.*] Other editions : **Ṭihrān** 1274/1857–8 (Mashhad i, *fṣl.* 3, ptd. bks., no. 51) ; **Lucknow** 1886†.

P. 51, l. 27. Delete the full stop after 1795–6.

P. 51, l. 30. For M. b. Khātūn see also Ṭāhir Naṣrābādī p. 159.

P. 52, ll. 1–2. 'Umūmī 190 (dated 1088) deals with the division of the text into tenths and fifths and begins *al-Ḥ. l. R. al-'ā. ḥamd*[an] *dā'im*[an] *li-rubūbīyatihi . . . a.b. bi-dān-kih Imām . . . Tāj al-Dīn MṢDR* [*Muṣaddar* ?] *Bukhārī dar-īn nuskhah dhikr i āyāt u a'shār u akhmās kardah ast u har sūrah rā guftah ast kih chand 'ushr ast u 'adad i a'shār ba-ḥisāb i handasah nawishtah ast.* [Ritter, *OLZ*. 1928 col. 1127.]

P. 52, l. 26. *Insert* :

87*a*. Ṣadr al-'ulamā' Mīrzā **'Abd al-Muḥammad** b. Shams al-'ulamā' Ḥājj Mīrzā Fatḥ-'Alī **Lāhījānī**.

Manẓūmah i nūrānīyah, a metrical list of the sūrahs, etc., completed in 1341/1922 : **Ṭihrān** 1341/1922–3 (see Mashhad iv p. 502).

I. QUR'ĀNIC LITERATURE. F. TALISMANIC VIRTUES

P. 53, l. 18. [*al-Durr al-naẓīm.*] *Insert* :

Persian translation completed in 926/1519–20 by Aḥmad b. Ḥājjī M. al-Sakkākī al-Ṭabasī : **Priceton** 77 (17th cent.), **Majlis** ii 799 (A.H. 1249/1833–4).

P. 53, l. 27. ['Abd al-'Alī's work on the *Khawāṣṣ al-Qur'ān.*] Also **Ivanow** 1st Suppt. 909 (acephalous. Early 19th cent.), **Lahore** Panjāb Univ. (see *OCM*. xi/2 p. 76, where the title is given as *Jauhar al-Qur'ān*).

New edition in which the verses are arranged in the same order as in the *Qur'ān* : *Khizānat al-asrār* (beg.

al-Ḥ. l. 'l. anzala 'l-Q. 'alā 'abdihi li-yakūna . . .), prepared in 962/1554–5 by Maẓhar al-Dīn M. al-Qārī' b. Bahā' al-Dīn 'Alī and divided into twenty chapters : **Būhār** 192 (defective at end and elsewhere. 17th cent.).

P. 53, n. 1. For 'Abd al-'Alī Birjandī see also *Haft iqlīm* no. 830 ; Brockelmann *Sptbd.* ii p. 591. According to the Ma<u>sh</u>had cat., iii, *fṣl.* 17, MSS., no. 115, he died in 934.

P. 54, l. 19. [*Ḍiyā' al-'uyūn.*] Also **Ivanow** 1st Suppt. 911 (late 18th cent.), 2nd Suppt. 1096 (1) (defective).

P. 54, l. 22. *al-Mir'āt al-'iyānīyah* was composed for Prince Bāyazīd b. Sulaiman [I]. Ā.Ṣ. 407 is a " Dedikations-exemplar ". [Ritter, *OLZ.* 1928, col. 1127.]

P. 54 ult. For the *<u>Kh</u>awāṣṣ al-Qur'ān* of al-Tamīmī see also Brockelmann *Sptbd.* ii p. 985.

P. 55, l. 3. M. b. M. Sabzawārī is presumably identical with M. b. <u>Sh</u>. M. b. Sa'īd al-Harawī, author of the *Baḥr al-<u>gh</u>arā'ib* (Edition : place ? 1299/1882 (Āṣafīyah i p. 54 no. 213, under Ad'iyah)) and with M. b. <u>Sh</u>. M. Harawī, author of the *Waẓā'if al-ṣāliḥīn* (MS. : Āṣafīyah i p. 64 no. 18 (A.H. 1272/1855–6), under Ad'iyah).

P. 55, l. 3. *Read* **Bānkīpūr** xvi 1427 (18th cent.).

P. 55, l. 5. [*Tuḥfat al-<u>gh</u>arā'ib.*] Also **'Alīgaṛh** Subḥ. MSS. p. 20 no. 18, **Āṣafīyah** i p. 54 no. 147.

P. 55, l. 5. *Insert* :

Urdu translation (?) : *Tuḥfat al-<u>gh</u>arā'ib*, by M. b. <u>Sh</u>. M. Arḍ Bīlī [*sic*, presumably for Ardabīlī] : 1305/1887–8 (Āṣafīyah i p. 66, where the place of publication is not mentioned).

P. 55, l. 7. **Āyā Ṣōfyah** 424 is ascribed to the Imām <u>Sh</u>āfi'ī. [Ritter, *OLZ.* 1924 col. 1127.]

P. 55, l. 19. *Insert* : (19) **Princeton** 71 (2) (S. xxxvi), 71 (3) (S. lxxiii).

I. QUR'ĀNIC LITERATURE. G. FĀL-NĀMAHS

P. 55 ult. [*Fal-nāmah i Ja'far al-Ṣādiq.*] Also **Ivanow** 1st Suppt. 913–14, 2nd Suppt. 1096 (6), **Edinburgh** New Coll. p. 11, **Upsala** Zetterstéen 395 (6), **Ethé** 3075.

I. QUR'ĀNIC LITERATURE. H. MISCELLANEOUS WORKS

P. 57, l. 22. *Insert*:

99*a*. Sh. **M. Riḍā b. Asad Allāh Yazdī.**

Rajā' al-ghufrān fī muhimmāt al-Qur'ān, completed in 1331/1913: **Shīrāz** 1331/1913 (see Mashhad iv p. 488).

99*b*. S. **Mahdī Badā'i'-nigār** " Lāhūtī " Tafrīshī.

Badā'i' al-bayān fī jāmi' [*sic* ?] *al-Qur'ān*, a concise introduction to the *Qur'ān* completed in 1346/1927: **Ṭihrān** A.H.S. 1319/1940–1 (see Mashhad iv p. 466).

P. 57, l. 26. *Insert*:

(1*a*) *Ghāyat al-taḥqīq*, on the number of sūrahs, their occasion, the number of verses, letters and *rukū'āt* in them, etc., by Niẓām al-Dīn al-Banārasī: **Blochet** iv 2155 (17th cent.).

(1*b*) *I'jāz i Qur'ān u balāghat i Muḥammad*, a translation of Muṣṭafā Ṣādiq al-Rāfi'ī's *I'jāz al-Qur'ān wa-'l-balāghat al-Nabawīyah* (Brockelmann *Sptbd.* iii p. 75) by 'Abd al-Ḥusain b. al-Dīn [*sic* ?]: **Ṭihrān** A.H.S. 1320/1941–2 (see Mashhad iv p. 465).

P. 57, ll. 27–8. This entry should be deleted. The *'Ilm al-kitāb* by Khwājah Mīr " Dard " does not deal with the *Qur'ān* but is a commentary on the author's Ṣūfī work *Wāridāt* (see Bānkīpūr xvi 1408).

P. 58, l. 2. *Insert*:

(5*a*) *Maẓhar al-tibyān fī tarjamat al-Itqān*, a translation of al-Suyūṭī's *Itqān* (see Brockelmann ii p. 154, *Sptbd.* ii p. 179) made by S. 'Alī Akbar b. Murtaḍā Ṭabāṭabā'ī Yazdī, *Mudarris* in the Madrasah i Manṣūrīyah at Shīrāz (cf. *Fārs-nāmah i Nāṣirī* i p. 97), by request of Mu'tamad al-Daulah Farhād Mīrzā (for whom see p. 204 *supra*): **Mashhad** iv p. 454 no. 376 (pt. 1 only. A.H. 1298/1881).

P. 58, l. 12. *Insert*:

(9*a*) *Tārīkh i Qur'ān*, a translation by Abū 'l-Qāsim Saḥāb (cf. p. 1104 *supra*) of the (unpublished ?) *Ta'rīkh al-Qur'ān* of Abū 'Abd Allāh Zanjānī (Professor in the University of Ṭihrān, b. A.H. 1309/1891–2, d. A.H.S. 1320/1941): **Ṭihrān** A.H.S. 1317/1938–9 (see Mashhad iv p. 467).

II. A. GENERAL HISTORY

P. 63, l. 22. [*Tarjamah i Tārīkh i Ṭabarī.*] Also **Bānkipūr** Suppt. I 1744 (A.H. 1012/1604), **Caetani** 31 (A.H. 1034/1624), **Aumer** 361 (in the *Ergänzungsheft.* A.H. 1038/1628–9), **Leningrad** Pub. Lib. (3 copies. See *Mélanges asiatiques* iii (St. Petersburg 1859) p. 726), **Majlis** 231.

P. 64, ll. 12–13. [*Tarjamah i Tārīkh i Ṭabarī.*] A copy of Dubeux's translation preserved in the Cambridge University Library contains pp. 1–368, breaking off abruptly in the account of the Exodus. [J. D. Pearson, in a letter.] The copies at the British Museum and the India Office contain only pp. 1–280.

P. 66, l. 9. [*Zain al-akhbār.*] Another edition : **Ṭihrān** A.H.S. 1315/1936–7 [R. Lescot, *B.E.O.I.F. de Damas* vii-viii p. 281].—" Some extracts from Gardīzī's chapter on the Turks have been re-edited and translated by Marquart in his *Das Volkstum d. Komanen* (1914) and some more translations by the said author lie in MS. in the library of the Istituto biblico pontificale in Rome." [Minorsky, *BSOS.* viii p. 256.]

P. 66, l. 28. *Insert* :

(**4**) [The chapter on India (English)] *Gardīzī on India. By V. Minorsky* (in *BSOAS.* xii/3–4 (1948) pp. 625–40).

P. 67, l. 20. [*Mujmal al-tawārīkh wa-'l-qiṣaṣ.*] Also **Istānbūl** Prof. M. Fuad Köprülü (A.H. 751/1350. See *Die Welt des Islams* 12 (1930–1) p. 104 and *JRAS.* 1938 p. 563), **Heidelberg** P. 118 (circ. A.D. 1500. See *Zeitschrift für Semitistik* 6/3 (1928) p. 233). Edition : **Ṭihrān** A.H.S. 1318/1939–40 (ed. Malik al-Shu'arā' " Bahār ").

P. 68, l. 21. *For* Niyāltigīn *read* Yināl-tigīn. [Minorsky, *BSOS.* viii/1 (1935) p. 257].—l. 22. *Read* Uchh.

P. 69, l. 24. [*Ṭabaqāt i Nāṣirī.*] Also **Leningrad** Asiat. Mus. (a good old MS. See Barthold's article *O nekotorykh vostochnykh rukopisakh* in *Prilozhenie k. prot. X. zasyed. Otd. Istor. Nauk i Fil. Ross. Akad. ot* 17 *Sent.* 1919 *g.*, pp. 923–30. Cf. *Islamica* iii p. 316), **Blochet** iv 2327 (*Ṭabaqahs* xvii–xxii. 17th cent.).

P. 70, l. 2. [*Ṭabaqāt i Nāṣirī.*] Russian translation of extracts relating to the Golden Horde : *Sbornik materialov otnosyashchikhsya k istorii Zolotoi Ordy.* ii [1] : *Izvlecheniya iz persidskikh sochinenii sobrannye V. G. Tizengauzenom i obrabotannye A. A. Romaskevichem i S. L. Volinym,* **Leningrad** 1941 (Akademiya Nauk SSSR, Institut Vostokovedeniya), pp. 13–19.

P. 70, l. 3. [Minhāj Jūzjānī.] Also *Ẓafar al-wālih* (in Arabic) by 'Abd Allāh M. al-Makkī ed. E. D. Ross, London 1910–28 (see index).

P. 70, l. 9. Also *'Ahd i Shamsī kā ēk mu'arrikh shā'ir,* by Āghā 'Abd al-Sattār Khān (in *OCM.* xiv/3 (May 1938) pp. 11–24).

P. 71, l. 4. [*Niẓām al-tawārīkh.*] Also **Princeton** 53A (early 14th cent.), **Blochet** iv 2162 (1) (A.H. 1081/1670).

P. 71, l. 9. Another edition : **Ṭihrān** A.H.S. 1313/1931 [Lescot, *B.E.O.I.F. de Damas* vii–viii p. 281].

Pp. 71–2. [*al-Majmū'at al-Rashīdīyah.*] For other MSS. see Brockelmann *Sptbd.* ii p. 273.

P. 72, l. 10. *For* ancien fonds, persan 107 *read* **Blochet** iv 2217. Ancien fonds, persan 107 (= Blochet iv 2154) is a volume containing *inter alia* the same attestations of the orthodoxy of Rashīd al-Dīn's works as occur in de Slane 2324. Cf. Krafft 148.

P. 72, l. 11. [*Munsha'āt i Rashīdī.*] Edition : *Mukātabāt i Rashīdī,* **Lahore** 1947 (ed. M. Shafī'. See the list of abbreviations prefixed to M. Shafī''s edition of the *Maṭla' i sa'dain,* vol. ii, pts. 2–3, Lahore 1949). For an account of six of these letters (nos. 12, 29, 43, 34, 52 and 47) see *Letters of Rashīd al-Dīn Faḍlullāh relating to India,* by M. Shafī' (in the *Woolner commemoration volume,* Lahore 1940, pp. 236–40). Reasons for doubting the genuineness of the collection have been given by R. Levy in an article entitled *The Letters of Rashīd al-Dīn Faḍl-Allāh* in *JRAS.* 1946 pp. 74–8.

P. 73, l. 14. [*Dhail i Jāmi' al-tawārīkh.*] Extracts relating to the Golden Horde have been published on the basis of

[1] Vol. i, containing extracts from Arabic authors, was published by Tiesenhausen (d. 15.2.1902) at St. Petersburg in 1884.

Blochet i 255 and a Leningrad MS. (Institut Vostokovedeniya D 66 (a)) with a Russian translation in *Sbornik materialov otnosyashchikhsya k istorii Zolotoi Ordy, II . . .* **Leningrad** 1941 (cf. p. 1230 *supra*) pp. 243–7 (trans. pp. 139–43).

P. 73, l. 33. [*Jāmi' al-tawārīkh*. MSS.] Also **Blochet** iv 2279 (most of vol. ii. A.H. 830/1426/7), 2280 (part of vol. i, viz. the account of the Mongol tribes and of Chingiz Khān's ancestors and the greater part of the life of Chingiz Khān. 16th cent.).

P. 76, l. 9. [*Jāmi' al-tawārīkh*. Extracts.] *Add*:

(1a) [part of (?) *Faṣl* 1 of *Bāb* 1 of vol. i (on the origin of the Turkish tribes)]. *Das Kudatku Bilik des Jusuf Chass-Hadschib aus Bälasagun. Theil I. Der Text in Transscription herausgegeben von . . . W. Radloff.* **St. Petersburg** 1891, pp. xiv–xxviii (Persian text with German translation by C. Salemann).

P. 76, l. 16. [*Jāmi' al-tawārīkh*. Extracts.] *Insert*:

(2a) Reprint of the bare Persian text from Blochet's edition: **Ṭihrān** A.H.S. 1313/1934–5.—l. 29. *Read* ancêtres.

P. 76, n. 1. For replies to Blochet's condemnation of Berezin's edition see Barthold's review mentioned on p. 78[5] *supra* and Minorsky's remarks in *BSOS*. viii/1 (1935) p. 256.

P. 77, l. 6. [*Jāmi' al-tawārīkh*. Extracts.] *Insert*:

(7) [the reigns of Abāqā, Tikūdār, Arghūn and Gaikhātū from vol. i, *Bāb* 2] *Ta'rīḫ-i-mubārak-i-Ġāzānī des Rašīd al-Dīn Faḍl Allāh Abī-l-Ḫair. Geschichte der Ilḫāne Abāġā bis Gaiḫātū* (1265–1295). *Kritische Ausgabe . . . von Karl Jahn.* **Prague** 1941 (Abhandlungen der Deutschen Gesellschaft der Wissenschaften und Künste in Prag, phil.-hist. Abteilung, i.Heft).

(8) [The reign of Ghāzān, from vol. i, *Bāb* 2.] *Geschichte Ġāzān-Ḫān's aus dem Ta'rīḫ-i-mubārak-i-Ġāzānī des Rašīd al-Dīn Faḍlallāh . . . herausgegeben . . . von Karl Jahn.* **London** 1940 (Gibb Memorial, N.S. xiv).

(9) *The account of the Ismā'īlī doctrines in the* Jāmi' al-Tawārīkh *of Rashīd al-Dīn Fadlallāh. By R. Levy* (in *JRAS*. 1930 pp. 509–36 (Persian text with English translation)).

P. 77, l. 28. [*Jāmiʿ al-tawārīkh*. Translations.] *Add* :

(**8**) [English translation of extracts concerning the Ismāʿīlī doctrines] *The account of the Ismāʿīlī doctrines in the* Jāmiʿ al-Tawārīkh *of Rashīd al-Dīn Faḍlallāh. By R. Levy* (in *JRAS*. 1930 pp. 509–36. With the Persian text).

(**9**) [Russian translation of passages relating to the Golden Horde] *Sbornik materialov otnosyashchikhsya k istorii Zolotoi Ordy. II* . . . **Leningrad** 1941 (cf. p. 1230 *supra*) pp. 27–79.

(**10**) [Russian translation extending from the reign of Hulāgū to that of Ghāzān] *Sbornik letopisei. Tom III*[1]. *Perevod s persidskago A.K. Arendsa, pod redaktsiyei* (†) *A. A. Romaskevicha* [who had the largest share in the work], *E. E. Bertelsa i A. Y. Yakobovskago*. **Leningrad** 1946 (Akademiya Nauk SSSR. 340 pp. The translation, in the preparation of which seven MSS. were consulted, was ready before the war). [Minorsky, in a letter.]

P. 78, l. 19. [Rashīd al-Dīn.] Also *Durrat al-akhbār* (*takmilah*) pp. 126–30 ; *Dastūr al-wuzarāʾ* pp. 315–21.

P. 79, l. 6. [*Zubdat al-tawārīkh*.] For a description see Blochet *Introduction à l'histoire des Mongols* pp. 140–57.

P. 79, l. 20. [Nīkpay's history.] *Insert* :

Extracts relating to the Sāmānids derived from al-ʿUtbī's *Yamīnī : Description topographique et historique de Boukhara par Mohammed Nerchakhy . . . Texte persan publié par* C. Schefer, **Paris** 1892°*, pp. 111–22.

P. 80, l. 5. [*Rauḍat ūlī 'l-albāb*.] Also **Tashkent** Univ. 56 (A.H. 1275/1858–9).

P. 80, l. 6. *Delete* : **ʿĀshir** p. 114 no. 254.

P. 80, ll. 7–8. Nūr i ʿUthmānīyah 3088 is Maḥmūd al-Ījī's history (see *PL*. p. 211) and should be deleted. [Rypka, *Archiv Orientální* x/1–2 (1938) p. 359.]

P. 81, l. 18. Hindūshāh b. Sanjar completed at Tabrīz in 707/1308 the Arabic work *Mawārid al-adab* (for which see Brockelmann ii p. 192, *Sptbd.* ii p. 256). For the scanty

[1] Vol. i, according to the original plan, was to contain the introduction on the Turkish and Mongol tribes (cf. p. 76[3] *supra*), vol. ii the history of Ogedey etc. (= Blochet) and vol. iv a commentary and indexes, but at the moment there is no question of completing the work.

autobiographical information obtainable from the *Tajārib al-salaf* see the editor's introduction to the Ṭihrān edition and *Dānishmandān i Ādharbāyjān* p. 399. Kīrān (evidently an arabicised form of Gīrān, since the *nisbah* is spelt al-Jīrānī in the preface to the *Mawārid al-adab*) is described in the *Nafthat al-maṣdūr* p. 42 n. and the *Dānishmandān i Ādharbāyjān* p. 399 n. as a town between Tabrīz and Bailaqān. For a place of this name near Iṣfahān see Samʿānī fol. 147*a* (where it is spelt Jairān) and *Tāj al-ʿarūs* iii p. 116, l. 8 *ab infra*.

P. 81, l. 21. [*Tajārib al-salaf*.] Edition: *T. al-s. . . . ta'līf i Hindūshāh . . . Ṣāḥibī Nakhjuwānī . . . bi-taṣḥīḥ u ihtimām i ʿAbbās Iqbāl*, **Ṭihrān** A.H.S. 1313/1934. Extract [life of Niẓām al-Mulk]: *Siasset Namèh . . . Texte persan édité par C. Schefer. Supplément*, pp. 1–21.

P. 83, l. 16. [*Tārīkh i Guzīdah*.] Also **Blochet** iv 2282 (A.H. 989/1581), **Tashkent** Univ. 59 (defective. 17th cent.). **Leningrad** Asiat. Mus. (at least two in addition to the MS. of 847/1443 mentioned on p. 82: see *Mélanges asiatiques* ii (1852–6) p. 56 (a MS. of 1244/1828), iv (1860–3) p. 54), Pub. Lib. (at least two copies: see *Mélanges asiatiques* iii (1859) p. 727, vi (1873) p. 93), **Caetani** 13 (A.H. 1296/1878).

P. 83, ll. 32–4. *Delete the entry* (**3**).

P. 84, l. 21. [*Tārīkh i Guzīdah*.] *Add*:

(**7**) [Russian translation of passages relating to the Golden Horde] *Sbornik materialov* . . . (cf. p. 1230 *supra*), ii . . . **Leningrad** 1941 pp. 90–8 (Persian text pp. 219–27).

P. 85, l. 15. Ethé 22 is dated 1127/1715.

P. 85, l. 20. *Insert*:

112*a*. **Abū Bakr al-Quṭbī al-Aharī.**

Tārīkh i Shaikh Uwais, a general history dedicated to Sulṭān Shaikh Uwais, the Jalā'ir, who reigned 756–76/1355–74: **Leyden** v p. 228 no. 2634 (defective. N.d.).

Extracts relating to the Golden Horde: *Sbornik materialov* . . . (cf. p. 1230 *supra*) ii . . ., **Leningrad** 1941 pp. 228–31 (Russian translation pp. 99–103).

P. 86, l. 10. [*Firdaus al-tawārīkh.*] *Insert*:
Extract (passage on the Great Lur): *Chèref-Nâmeh ou Fastes de la Nation Kourde . . . Traduits . . . par F. B. Charmoy* (cf. *PL.* p. 368[4]) i/2 pp. 328–37.

P. 86, l. 12. *For* an unknown author *read* **Mu'īn al-Dīn Naṭanzī** (cf. Daulat-Shāh p. 371[15]).

P. 86, l. 15. *Read*: (1) *A general history* to A.H. 815/1412 (called by Barthold "The Anonym of Iskandar", but subsequently (in *Comptes-rendus de l'Acad. des Sciences de l'U.R.S.S.*, 1927, pp. 115–16)[1] identified by him as the work of Mu'īn al-Dīn Naṭanzī).

P. 86, l. 22. *Insert*:
Extracts relating to the Golden Horde: *Sbornik materialov* . . . (cf. p. 1230 *supra*) ii . . . **Leningrad** 1941 pp. 232–42 (Russian translation pp. 126–38).

P. 86, l. 22. *Insert*:
(2) *Muntakhab al-tawārīkh i Mu'īnī*, a sketch of general history to the end of Tīmūr's reign presented to Mu'īn al-Dunyā wa-'l-Dīn Abū 'l-Fatḥ Shāh-Rukh Bahādur at Harāt on 22 Rajab 817/1414 and shown by Barthold ("*Yeshche ob anonyme Iskendera*" in *Bulletin de l'Acad. des Sciences de l'U.R.S.S.*, 1929 pp. 165–80) to be virtually identical, apart from the change of dedication,[2] with the "Anonym of Iskandar": **Blochet** iv 2283 (transcribed from an autograph and corrected by the author).
French translation of extracts: *Les exploits d'Emîrzâdé 'Omar Cheikh fils de Timour, à Kachghar, en Ferghana et en Mongolie*, by L. Zimin (in *Revue du Monde Musulman*, 28 (Paris, 1914) pp. 244–58).

P. 86, l. 23. In a passage translated by W. Hinz (*ZDMG.* 90/2 (1936) pp. 376–7) from the Leningrad MS. (see below) the author calls himself Ja'farī b. M. al-Ḥusainī and uses "Ja'farī" as his *takhalluṣ*.

[1] Cf. *BSOS.* viii/1 (1935) p. 256 (Minorsky) and *ZDMG.* 90/2 (1936) pp. 361–3.

[2] ". . . its only difference is that all the passages referring to the former dedicatee Iskandar have been abridged and his title reduced from *ḥaḍrat-i Sulṭān* to *amīr-zāda*" (Minorsky, *BSOS.* viii/1 (1935) p. 257. Cf. Hinz, *ZDMG.* 90/2 (1936) pp. 362–3).

P. 86, l. 26. [*Tārīkh i Ja'farī.*] Also **Leningrad** Pub. Lib., Pers. nov. ser. 201 (defective at both ends. 16th cent. See W. Barthold's article *Novy istochnik po istorii Timuridov* in *Zapiski Instituta Vostokovedeniya* v (Leningrad 1936) pp. 5–42 and W. Hinz's summary of the article in *ZDMG.* 90/2 (1936) pp. 373–98).

P. 87, l. 19. For the spelling of the name Kart see p. 354, n. 1.

P. 87, n. 1. For other MSS. see K. Bayānī's preface to his edition of the *Dhail i Jāmi' al-tawārīkh.*

P. 88, l. 8. [*Majmū'ah i Ḥāfiẓ i Abrū.*] Also **Blochet** iv 2284 (apparently the *Dhail i Jāmi' al-tawārīkh*, the history of the Muẓaffarids, the *Ẓafār-nāmah* and the *Dhail i kitāb i Ẓafar-nāmah.* Circ. A.D. 1530. Mistakenly described by Blochet as the last part of the *Zubdat al-tawārīkh*).

P. 88, l. 10. [*Majmū'ah i Ḥāfiẓ i Abrū.*] *Insert*:

Edition of 2(*h*): *Dhail i Jāmi' al-tawārīkh i Rashīdī ta'līf i Shihāb al-Dīn 'Abd Allāh . . . al-mad'ū bi-Ḥāfiẓ i Abrū . . . Bakhsh i nukhustīn* [pt. 2 is the French translation] *bā muqaddamah u ḥawāshī u ta'līqāt i Duktur Khān-Bābā Bayānī.* **Ṭihrān** 1317/1939‡.

Translation of the years 703–58/1303–57[1] from 2 (*h*): *Ḥâfiẓ-i Abrû. Chronique des Rois Mongols en Iran. Texte persan édité et traduit par K. Bayani . . .* II. *Traduction et notes.* **Paris** 1936‡ (reviewed by Minorsky in *BSOS.* ix/1 (1937) pp. 235–6).

Edition of 2(*k*): *Continuation du Ẓafarnāma de Niẓāmuddīn Šāmī par Ḥāfiẓ-i Abrū éditée d'après les manuscrits de Stamboul par Felix Tauer* (in *Archiv Orientální*, vi (**Prague** 1934) pp. 429–65).

P. 88 ult. [*Majma' al-tawārīkh.*] Majlis 257 contains *Rub'* ii. For some other MSS. see K. Bayānī's preface to his edition of the *Dhail i Jāmi' al-tawārīkh* pp. *lām–alif-tā.*

P. 89, l. 3. [*Majma' al-tawārīkh.* Extracts.] *Add*:

(2) *Safar-nāmah i Chīn sanah 1419* '[*Īsawī*] *tā sanah 1422* '[*Īsawī*] *ya'nī maḍmūn u muḥaṣṣal i rūz-nāmchah i Khwājah Ghiyāth al-Dīn i naqqāsh īlchī i Bāysunghur Mīrzā b. Shāh-Rukh . . . kih Ḥāfiẓ i Abrū dar Zubdat al-tawārīkh*

[1] The first date expressly mentioned in the narrative (p. 14^{16}) is 706.

darj numūdah [edited with notes and index by M. Shafī'] (in the *Oriental College Magazine*, vol. vii, no. 1 (Lahore, Nov. 1930), pp. 1–66).

(**3**) *A Persian embassy to China ; being an extract from Zubdatu't Tawarikh of Hafiz Abru. Translated* [and edited] *by K. M. Maitra.* **Lahore** 1934*.

P. 89, l. 10. [*Majma' al-tawārīkh*. Descriptions.] *Add* :

(**4**) Barthold *Turkestan*, London 1928, pp. 55–6.

P. 89, l. 13. The Persian text of the passage in the *Mujmal i Faṣīḥī* is quoted in Rosen Institut p. 325.

P. 89 ult. [*Tārīkh i khairāt*.] Cf. W. Hinz, *ZDMG*. 90/2 (1936) pp. 363–5.

P. 90, l. 3. *Read* Būndēlk'haṇḍ.

P. 90, l. 4. For Yūsuf Bud'h (if that is the correct spelling) see *Sawāṭi' al-anwār* (Ethé col. 332) ; *Gulzār i abrār* no. 160 ; *Khazīnat al-aṣfiyā'* i pp. 383–4 ; Raḥmān 'Alī p. 256 ; Rieu, iii p. 1079*a* ; Bānkīpūr xvi p. 49 ; etc.

P. 90, l. 13. *Read either* **Khwāfī** *without the article or* **al-Khawāfī**, *that being the Arabic form of the word.*

P. 91, l. 14. [*Jāmi' al-tawārīkh i Ḥasanī*.] Also **Ṭihrān** National Lib. (A.H. 880/1475–6. See p. 5 of Mahdī Bayānī's introduction to his edition of the *Badā'i' al-azmān*).

P. 91, l. 24. *Read* 861/1456–7.

P. 91, l. 27. For a MS. of the *Manhaj* (so ?) *al-rashād* see Leyden iv p. 299 no. 2110.

P. 92, l. 2. *Read* Ergänzungsheft.

P. 92, l. 22. For Burhān al-Dīn Khāwand-Shāh see *Haft iqlīm* no. 1494.

P. 92, l. 25. According to *Ḥabīb al-siyar* iii, 3, p. 339[16], Mīr Khwānd died on 2 Dhī Qa'dah 903. Rajab seems to be a slip of Rieu's.

P. 93, l. 3. [*Rauḍat al-ṣafā'*.] The *khātimah* was written in 900/1494–5 according to a statement (" in most copies ") at the end of the article on Khwārazm (Rieu iii p. 1079*b*). Other MSS. : **Princeton** 462 (vol. i A.H. 909/1503–4), 463–7 (three more copies of vol. i and two of vol. iii), 55 (vol. vi), **Tashkent Univ.** 62 (A.H. 977/1569), **Aumer** 202 (*Khātimah*. A.H. 994/1586), **Bānkīpūr** Suppt. i 1745 (vol.

iv. A.H. 997/1588–9), **Blochet** iv 2286–90, etc.—l. 14.
Read Nau<u>dh</u>ar.

P. 95, l. 27. *Read* 1265–6 *instead of* 1266 *and* 1853–7° *instead of* 1853–6°. " 2 vols." is doubtless correct as regards the B.M. and I.O. copies, but the ten unpaginated *jilds* are separable and are not always bound in two.

P. 96, l. 19. [*Rauḍat al-ṣafā'*.] The extract published by Mitscherlich in 1814 relates to the kings of Nīmrūz, the descendants of Ṭāhir b. M. b. Ṭāhir b. <u>Kh</u>alaf. [A. G. Ellis, orally.]

P. 97, l. 6. [*Mirchondi Historia Seldschukidarum*.] In the Cambridge University Library there is another issue published at Giessen in 1838 (in libraria J. Rickeri) identical with the previous issue except for the title-page. [J. D. Pearson, in a letter.]

P. 98, l. 28. [*Rauḍat al-ṣafā'*.] For an Eastern-Turkish translation made by M. Yūsuf, called al-Rājī, b. Qāḍī <u>Kh</u>wājam-birdī al-<u>Kh</u>uwārazmī in the reign of Abū 'l-<u>Gh</u>āzī M. Amīn <u>Kh</u>wārazm-<u>Sh</u>āh (A.H. 1261–71/1845–55) see *Mélanges asiatiques* vii (St. Petersburg 1876) p. 411.—l. 4 *ab infra*. Amberes = Antwerp.

P. 99, l. 29, no. (13). For the meaning of " the Ṭāhirids " in this case see p. 1237 [7–10] *supra*.

P. 100, l. 34. [Mīr <u>Kh</u>wānd.] Also *Laṭā'if-nāmah* pp. 159–60.

P. 101, l. 13. *Read* 887/1482.

P. 101, l. 30. [<u>Kh</u>wānd-Amīr.] According to the *Sanawāt al-atqiyā'*, fol. 282a, he died in 946.

P. 102, l. 4. The India Office MS. is D.P. 435B.

P. 103, l. 2. [*<u>Kh</u>ulāṣat al-a<u>kh</u>bār*.] Also **Caetani** 10, **Leningrad** Mus. Asiat. (see *Mélanges asiatiques* ii (St. Petersburg 1852–6) p. 57).

P. 104, l. 15. [*Ḥabīb al-siyar*.] See Rieu iii 1079b : " In an appendix found in some copies only, and quoted at length in Mir'āt i Jahān-numā, fol. 345, <u>Kh</u>wānd-Amīr records his journey to India, A.H. 934, and his introduction to Bābar, A.H. 935. He adds that he accompanied the emperor on his expedition to Bengal, working on the road, as circumstances and his enfeebled health would allow, at his great history, and that he completed the work (or its final revision) at a place near the confluence of the Siru with Ganges (in the month of Sha'bān, A.H. 935 ; see Bābar's Memoirs, p. 411). A translation of the main part of that appendix is to be found in Elliot's History of India, vol. iv, pp. 143, 155."

P. 105 antepenult. *Read* 1063/1652–3.

P. 106, l. 16. [*Ḥabīb al-siyar.*] Also **Blochet** iv 2291 (complete. A.H. 1010/1601–2), **Princeton** 56 (*Iftitāḥ* and vol. i. 18th cent.).—l. 20. According to Dorn (*Mélanges asiatiques* vi (St. Petersburg 1873) p. 119) the Ṭihrān edition omits "mehrere gerade für Russland interessante Capitel".

P. 107, l. 24. [*Ḥabīb al-siyar.*] *Insert* :

(**10**) [Life of Niẓām al-Mulk] *Siasset Namèh . . . Texte persan édité par C. Schefer . . . supplément*, pp. 22–48.

(**11**) *Rijāl i kitāb i Ḥabīb al-siyar az ḥamlah i Mughūl tā marg i Shāh Ismā'īl i Awwal*, **Ṭihrān** A.H.S. 1324/1945–6 (ed. 'Abd al-Ḥusain Nawā'ī. Supplement to the periodical *Yādgār*, Year 1. Cf. *Oriens* iii/2 (1950) p. 330).

P. 108, no. (**14**). Cf. L. Bouvat *L'empire mongol* (2ème *phase*), Paris 1927, p. 163 n. 2 : "La notice de Sultân Hoseïn Baykara occupe les pp. 239–283 du t. iii de Khondémir ; M. H. Ferté en a traduit la première partie, allant jusqu'à la page 254 . . ."

P. 109, l. 1. [Khwānd-Amīr.] Also *Laṭā'if-nāmah* p. 157 ; *Akbar-nāmah* i p. 120, Beveridge's trans. i p. 281.

P. 109, l. 9. 'Abd al-Karīm al-Namīdīhī is doubtless identical with the author whose name Horn spells 'Abd al-Karīm Namīdahī and whose work *Kanz al-ma'ānī* is preserved at Istānbūl in the 'Āshir Efendī Library (no. 884. See Horn *Pers. Hss.* p. 501 no. 952).

P. 110, l. 5. [Faiḍ Allāh Banbānī.] For further information about him and his works, which include the *Majma' al-nawādir* completed in 903/1497–8, see an Urdu article entitled *Majma' al-nawādir* by M. Iqbāl in *OCM*. xv/4 (Aug. 1939) pp. 98–106. Cf. Brockelmann *Sptbd.* ii p. 610.—l. 14. *Read* 86*b*.

P. 111, l. 12. For Naqīb Khān see p. 118, n. 1.

P. 111, l. 24. [*Lubb al-tawārīkh.*] Also **Ellis Coll.** M. 244 (A.H. 967/1559–60), M. 245 (defective. 17th cent.), **Vatican** Pers. 16 (A.H. 986/1578. Rossi p. 42), **Blochet** iv 2177 (2) (18th cent.).

P. 112, l. 8. Vatican 48 = Vatican Pers. 16 (A.H. 986/1578. Rossi p. 42). *Insert*:

Editions: (**1**) **Bombay** 1302/1884 (264 pp. See Fahmi Edhem Karatay *Istanbul Üniversitesi Kütüphanesi Farsça Basmalar Kataloğu* p. 192). (**2**) [**Ṭihrān**] A.H.S. 1314/1936 ‡ (ed. S. Jalāl al-Dīn Ṭihrānī. 264 pp.).

P. 112, l. 21. *Insert*:

French translation: **Paris** Bibl. Nat. fonds français 19027 (see Blochet iv 2177).

P. 113, l. 4. *For* 134 *read* 129–34.

P. 113, l. 17. [*Tārīkh i Ibrāhīmī.*] Also **Leningrad** Mus. Asiat. (see Semenov *Ukazatel'* p. 30).—l. 21. *Insert*:

130*a*. A history entitled *Takmilat al-akhbār*, of which no MSS. seem to be recorded in the published catalogues of libraries, is cited several times as an authority in the *Dānishmandān i Ādharbāyjān*, on p. 76 of which it is said to have been composed in 997 [*sic*, but read 967/1559] and dedicated to Shāh Ṭahmāsp's daughter Parī Khān Khānum by Khwājah 'Alī mulaqqab bah Zain al-'Ābidīn ma'rūf bah 'Abdī Bēg b. 'Abd al-Mu'min Ṣadr al-Dīn Shīrāzī, who at first used "Nuwīdī" and later "'Abdī" as his *takhalluṣ*. [P.S. Of this history, a general history to 967/1559 with a section on the Ṣafawīs, there is a MS., defective at the end, in the possession of Prof. B. N. Zakhoder according to his statement on p. 7 of his translation of Qāḍī Aḥmad's "*Traktat o kalligrafakh i khudozhnikakh*" [cf. p. 1074 *supra*]. V. Minorsky, in a letter.]

P. 114, l. 14. *Read* no. 1330 (portion only).—l. 16. *For* 133 *read* 134*b*.

P. 114, l. 24. [Khwur-Shāh b. Qubād.] Also *Ency. Isl.* under Niẓām-Shāhī (Minorsky).

P. 115, l. 16. I.O. 3939 is dated 1074/1664.

P. 115, l. 28. [*Nigāristān.*] Also **Madras** 319 (A.H. 1015/1606), **Ellis Coll.** M. 120 (A.H. 1043/1633), **Oxford** Ind. Inst. MS. Whinfield 48 (A.H. 1070/1659), **Heidelberg** P. 222 (A.H. 1102/1690. PICTURES. See *ZDMG.* 91/2 (1937) p. 376), **Blochet** iv 2292 (late 17th cent.), **Tashkent Univ.** 39 (A.H. 1274/1857–8), **Ivanow** 1st Suppt. 776 (A.H. 1300/1883 ?).

P. 116, l. 10. *Read* 999/1591.

P. 116, l. 15. [*Nusakh i jahān-ārā.*] *Insert*:

Text and Russian translation of passages relating to the Golden Horde: *Sbornik materialov* . . . (cf. p. 1230 *supra*) II . . . **Leningrad** 1941, pp. 269–71, 210–12.—l. 21. Also (**3**) Elliot *Bibliographical index* pp. 136–8.

P. 116, l. 24. [Aḥmad Ghaffārī.] Also *Safīnah i Khwushgū* ii no. 204; *Makhzan al-gharā'ib* no. 205; *Tadhkirah i khwush-nawīsān* pp. 82–3.

P. 118, l. 3. [Muṣliḥ al-Dīn Lārī.] Also Ḥasan Rūmlū xii p. 454, Seddon's trans. p. 197; *Tārīkh i Ma'ṣūmī* p. 204; Brockelmann *Sptbd.* ii p. 620.

P. 118, l. 20. *Insert*:

134*a*. **'Abd Allāh Kābulī.**

Tadhkirat al-tawārīkh, written in 990/1582: **Bukhārā** Semenov 46.

P. 118, l. 35. [Naqīb Khān.] Also *Ṭabaqāt i Akbarī* ii p. 450: *Iqbāl-nāmah* pp. 75–6.

P. 119, l. 16. [Fatḥ Allāh Shīrāzī.] Also *Ma'āthir al-umarā'*, Beveridge's trans. pp. 543–6.—l. 17. *Delete the word* Mīr.—l. 18. [Ḥakīm Humām.] Also *Haft iqlīm* no. 1219; *Ma'āthir al-umarā'* i pp. 563–5.—l. 22. [Ḥakīm 'Alī Gīlānī.] Also *Haft iqlīm* no. 1214; *Ma'āthir al-umarā'* i pp. 568–73, Beveridge's trans. pp. 180–4; Brockelmann *Sptbd.* ii p. 626.—l. 40. [Aḥmad Tattawī.] Also *Muntakhab al-tawārīkh* iii pp. 168–9.

P. 120, l. 36. [Āṣaf Khān (Ja'far Bēg).] Also *Tadhkirah i Naṣrābādī* pp. 53–5; *Ma'āthir al-umarā'*, Beveridge's trans. pp. 282–7.

P. 121, l. 26. [*Tārīkh i alfī.*] Also **Bombay** Univ. 93 (from Riḥlat 505 to a little after Shāh Ṭahmāsp's death), **Madras** 286

(A.H. 501–840. N.d.). See also *Discovery of a portion* [how much is not stated, but the pages reproduced deal with Ma'mūn, Mu'taṣim and Wāthiq] *of the original illustrated manuscript* [" in large folio size " with " magnificent miniatures on each leaf "] *of the Tarikh-i-alfi written for the Emperor Akbar* (*in the collection of Mr. Ajit Ghose, Calcutta*), by M. Maḥfūẓ al-Ḥaqq (in *Islamic culture* v/3 (July 1931) pp. 462–71, with reproductions of two pages).

P. 121, l. 5 *ab infra*. Read *al-ghuṣaṣ*.

P. 122, l. 20. [" Wuqū'ī."] Also *Nafā'is al-ma'āthir* (Sprenger p. 54) ; *Haft iqlīm* no. 763. There seems to have been some confusion between M. Sharīf " Wuqū'ī " Nīshāpūrī and " Wuqū'ī " Tabrīzī [see *Nafā'is al-ma'āthir* (Sprenger p. 54), *Haft iqlīm* no. 1346, *Dānishmandān i Ādharbāyjān* pp. 394–5]. *Insert* :

136*a*. Sh. **Kabīr b. Munawwar Lāhaurī**, a scholar of Akbar's reign, accompanied Murtaḍā Khān (Sh. Farīd Bukhārī, d. 1025/1616) to the siege of Kāngrah in 1025/1616 and died at Aḥmadābād in 1026/1617 or 1027/1618 [Badā'ūnī iii p. 106 ; *Ṭabaqāt i Shāh-Jahānī* ; *Mir'āt al-'ālam* ; *Ā'īn i Akbarī* tr. Blochmann p. 547 ; Rieu iii p. 1097*a*].

Tārīkh i Murtaḍā 'l-dahr, a (general ?) history composed in 1006/1597–8 : **Rieu** iii 1037*b* (extracts only. Circ. A.D. 1850).

P. 122, l. 28. [Ṭāhir M. Sabzawārī.] For abridged paraphrases of the *Mahābharata* and of two other Sanskrit works made by him at Akbar's request see Rieu iii 1043*a*, Ethé 1955.

P. 123, l. 7. [*Rauḍat al-ṭāhirīn*.] Also **I.O.** 4588 (defective. A.H. 1131/1719. See *JRAS*. 1939 p. 374), **Bānkīpūr** Suppt. i 1749 (defective. 18th cent.) 1748 (A.H. 1228/1813).

P. 123 ult. [Ḥasan Bēg Khākī.] Also *Akbar-nāmah* iii p. 834 ; *Makhzan al-gharā'ib* no. 721.

P. 124, l. 28. [*Tārīkh i Ḥaidarī*.] *Add* :

(**3**) [Passages relating to the Golden Horde] *Sbornik materialov* . . . (cf. p. 1230 *supra*) ii . . . **Leningrad** 1941 pp. 272–4 (Russian trans. pp. 213–15).

P. 126, l. 7. [*Ṣubḥ i ṣādiq*.] *For* ten centuries *read* eleven centuries.

—l. 18. Also **'Alīgaṛh** Subḥ. MSS. p. 57 no. 10 (vol. ii. A.H. 1159/1746), **Vatican** Pers. 93–7 (vols. ii–iii. A.H. 1196/1782. Rossi p. 109).—ll. 20–1. *Tadhkirah i Ṭāhir i Naṣrābādī* p. 64 in the Ṭihrān edition (his father, M. Ṣāliḥ, p. 452).

P. 128, l. 12. The *Mīzān al-ḥaqq* is in Turkish, not Arabic. l. 32. [*Taqwīm al-tawārīkh.*] Also **Blochet** iv 2293 (mid 17th cent.).

P. 130, l. 10. [*Afṣaḥ al-akhbār.*] Also **Rieu** iii 1017*b* (extracts only. Circ. A.D. 1850).—l. 17. *Insert*:

147*a*. **M. Afḍal Husainī.**

Zubdat al-tawārīkh (beg. *Ba'd az sp. u st. i Parwardgār i 'ālamiyān u durūd i nā-ma'dūd i ḥaḍrat i Saiyid al-Mursalīn*), a concise general history, including a detailed account of the Ṣafawīs, to A.H. 1063/1652, similar in contents and arrangement to the *Z. al-t.* of Kamāl Khān [1] [and possibly a plagiarism]: **Bānkīpūr** Suppt. i 1750 (19th cent.).

147*b*. **M. Barārī** Ummī b. M. Jamshēd b. Jabbārī Khān b. Majnūn Khān Qāqshāl is the author of a scientific encyclopædia entitled *'Uqūl i 'asharah*, which he completed in 1084/1673–4 (see Bānkīpūr ix 914, Berlin 97, Bodleian 1495, Būhār 222, Flügel i 27, Ivanow 1500 (2), Ivanow Curzon 485, Lindesiana p. 193 no. 714). His great-grandfather and his grandfather were both grandees of Akbar's time (see *Ā'īn i Akbarī* tr. Blochmann pp. 369–70, *Ma'āthir al-umarā'* iii pp. 207–11).

Mujmal i mufaṣṣal, a concise general history to A.H. 1037/1628 (Shāh-Jahān's accession), transcribed from the original drafts in 1065/1655 (according to a statement near the beginning of Ivanow 43) but not completed apparently until 1079/1668, since that is given as the date of the second volume (on the Persian and Indian Tīmūrids): **Bodleian** 101 (defective at beginning and concluding with A.H. 1020/1611. Identified by Ivanow), 242 (vol. ii only. A.H. 1079/1668 (?), apparently autograph), **Ivanow** 43 A.H. 1100/1688–9, transcribed for the author), **Madras** i 317 (A.H. 1171/1757–8).

[1] The opening words of Kamāl Khān's work are *Ba'd az ḥamd u thanā-yi P. u d. i bī-pāyān bar Aḥmad i Mukhtār.*

P. 131, l. 1. M. Yūsuf " Wālih " was subsequently appointed to the *wizārat i sarkār i tūp-khānah i mubārakah.*

P. 131, l. 20. [*Khuld i barīn.*] *Insert*:

Extract (Shāh Ṣafī's reign from the sixth year onwards): *Dhail i Tārīkh i 'Ālam-ārāy i 'Abbāsī ta'līf i Iskandar Bēg Turkmān . . . u M. Yūsuf i mu'arrikh ba-taṣḥīḥ i Suhailī i Khwānsārī*, **Tihrān** A.H.S. 1317/1938–9 (Iskandar Bēg's account of Shāh Ṣafī's first five years (see *PL.* p. 314) followed (p. 146[8]) by the narrative of the remainder of the reign from the *Khuld i barīn* on the basis of a MS. in the Kitāb-khānah i Millī i Malik. Cf. *BSOS.* x/2 (1940) p. 540).

P. 131, l. 22. [M. Yūsuf " Wālih."] Also *Tadhkirah i Naṣrābādī* i p. 82.

P. 132, l. 27. [*Mir'āt al-'ālam.*] Also **Bānkīpūr** Suppt. i 1751 (19th cent.).

P. 133, l. 6. [*Mir'āt al-'ālam.*] *Insert*:

Extracts (lives of calligraphists, painters, etc.): *OCM.* x/4 (Aug. 1934) pp. 33–65 (ed. M. Shafī'). Description etc. by Maulawī Ṣiddīq Ḥusain: *OCM.* v/1 (Nov. 1928) pp. 7–8.

P. 133, l. 14. [*Mir'āt i jahān-numā.*] Also **Ellis Coll.** M. 259 (A.H. 1142/1729–30).

P. 133, l. 30. [*Mir'āt i jahān-numā.*] Another description: *OCM.* v/1 (Nov. 1928) pp. 8–22 (an article by Maulawī Ṣiddīq Ḥusain).

P. 135, l. 10. [*Jannāt al-firdaus.*] Also **Ellis Coll.** M. 246 (with a continuation to A.H. 1244/1828–9 by Tajammul Ḥusain. Early 19th cent.).

P. 136, l. 8. [*Tārīkh i Qipchāq-Khānī.*] See also Validov *O sobr. rkp. v Bukh. khan.* pp. 258–9.

P. 136, l. 15. M. Muḥsin calls himself *Mustaufī i sarkār i faiḍ-āthār*, which may perhaps mean that he was *Mustaufī* of the estates of the Mashhad sanctuary (see Minorsky's commentary to the *Tadhkirat al-mulūk*, p. 146). " It may be added that Muḥammad Muḥsin in his *Zubdat al-tavarīkh* (f. 205*b*) states that in 1132/1720 he was in attendance on the Nāẓir of the Cathedral Mosque of Mashhad and enjoyed the rank of vazīr ' in the same department ' . . ." (Minorsky, *ibid.*).

P. 137, l. 20. *Read* **M. 'Ali** b. M. Ṣādiq Ḥusainī Nīshāpūrī Najafī **Burhānpūrī**.

P. 138, l. 10. [*Mir'āt al-ṣafā'*.] Also **Ellis Coll.** M. 258 (A.H. 1176/1762–3, apparently autograph).—l. 13. *Read* **Āṣafīyah** iii.

P. 138, l. 17. The *Tārīkh i rāḥat-afzā*, a history of the Tīmūrids from 736/1335–6 to 1173/1759–60, the date of compilation, was published in 1947 at Ḥaidarābād (Deccan) with an Urdu preface by S. Khwurshēd 'Alī. [J. D. Pearson, in a letter.]

P. 138, l. 27–P. 139, l. 11. [*Tuḥfat al-kirām*.] See the amended account of this work on p. 656 *infra*.

P. 139, l. 26. [*Jām i jahān-numā*.] Also **Bānkīpūr** Suppt. i 1752–3 (A.H. 1018 [*sic* ! Read 1180 ?]. Described as autograph).

P. 140, l. 21. *Read* 1182/1768–9.

P. 141, l. 9. [*Farḥat al-nāẓirīn*.] Also **Kapūrt'halah** 35 (see *OCM*. iii/4 (Aug. 1927) p. 16).

P. 141, ll. 25–6. *Read* : and the *Muntakhab al-tawārīkh* of Ḥasan Bēg Khākī (see p. 123 *supra*) very deficient.

P. 141, penult. and ult. [*Tārīkh i Muḥammadī*.] If Rieu's statement that the author completed this work in 1190 is based only on the fact that the necrologies in the B.M. MS. end with that year, it should not be accepted without further evidence. In I.O. 3980 the necrologies extend to 1208. Doubtless the copyists or owners of different MSS. continued the series of dates to their own times.

P. 141 ult. [*Tārīkh i Muḥammadī*.] I.O. 3889 and 3890 contain only the necrologies. I.O. 3980 contains only the preface and the necrologies from 1150 to 1208.

P. 142, l. 3. [M. b. Mu'tamad Khān.] See also the autobiography of his cousin " Āshōb " (MS. : I.O. 4034) fol. 14*b*.

P. 142, l. 23. **Rehatsek** p. 99 no. 52 (*Risālah i Kaptān Jōnātan* [*sic*] *dar aḥwāl i Farang* " composed A.H. 1211 ") seems to be a later version of Jonathan Scott's account of Europe.

P. 143, l. 16. Mavī = MWY, the vocalisation being conjectural.

P. 143, l. 25. [*Jām i jahān-numā*.] Also **Rieu** iii 1051*a* (extracts only).

P. 144, l. 19. *Read*: **I.O.** 3994 (reigns of Farrukh-siyar, Rafī' al-Darajāt etc. and M. Shāh, probably from the *B. al-m.*[1] A.D. 1891), 3983 (Nādir Shāh and Aḥmad Shāh Durrānī. A.D. 1895), 3883 (reigns of Aḥmad Shāh and 'Ālamgīr II, probably from the *B. al-m.* 18th cent.).

P. 145, l. 32. [*Khulāṣat al-afkār.*] The preface and *khātimah* are summarized in *JRAS.* 1848 pp. 154–7.

P. 146, l. 2. [Abū Ṭālib Khān.] Also *Dānishmandān i Ādharbāyjān* pp. 243–4.

P. 146, ll. 5, 10. " *Ardalān* is a better form for *Ardilān* (p. 146), in spite of the *E.I.* " (Minorsky, *BSOS.* viii/1 (1935) p. 257[17]).

P. 146, l. 14. *Read* **Dihlawī.**

P. 146, l. 27. [*Mir'āt i āftāb-numā.*] Also **Bodleian** 121 (n.d.), **Ellis Coll.** M. 373 (early 19th cent.).

P. 147, l. 12. [" Bandah " Tabrīzī.] Although apparently his name is written Riḍā (رضا) in the B.M. MS. Rieu i 135 (cf. Browne Coll. G. 16 and Majlis 258, but not Rieu Suppt. 39), the biographers seem to be unanimous in calling him Mīrzā (M.) Raḍī.

P. 147, l. 30. [" Bandah " Tabrīzī.] Also *Tadhkirah i Muḥammad-Shāhī* (Rieu Suppt. 124) fol. 183*a*; *Rauḍat al-ṣafā-yi Nāṣirī* vol. ix, eleventh page from end; *Dānishmandān i Ādharbāyjān* pp. 70–1; Berthels *Ocherk istorii persidskoi literatury* p. 82.

P. 148, l. 12. Ṭabāṭabā, not Ṭabāṭabā'ī, seems to be the form preferred by M. Riḍā himself.

P. 148, l. 27. [*Zubdat al-gharā'ib.*] Also **Ellis Coll.** M. 280 (vol. i. A.H. 1238/1823).

P. 150, l. 13. Mirzā Jahāngīr and Mirzā Bābur were sons of M. Akbar Shāh (cf. Blumhardt's *Catalogue of Hindustani MSS. in the . . . India Office* p. 93).—l. 15. *Read* Hamīrpūr *with undotted h.*

[1] So far as Indian Tīmūrid history is concerned the *B. al-m.* and the *Tārīkh i Muẓaffarī* (cf. *PL.* p. 522) are practically identical (see Bānkīpūr vii p. 108, l. 5 *ab infra*).

P. 150, l. 21. *Insert*:

184*a*. Faiḍ i Ḥaqq Chishtī Qādirī, known as (*'urf*) **M. Faiḍ Allāh** Munshī, entitled (*mukhāṭab*) **Faḍl i 'Alī Khān** Ṣiddīqī Āṣaf-Jāhī has already been mentioned (*PL.* i p. 753) as the author of histories entitled *Waqā'i' i Dakan* and *Gauhar i shāhwār*.

Khizānah i Rasūl-Khānī, a general history to A.H. 1251/1835, the date of completion, with a special history of the Quṭb-Shāhs and Niẓāms, dedicated to Nawwāb Ghulām-Rasūl Khān: **Bānkipūr** Suppt. i 1755 (A.H. 1296/1879).

P. 151, ll. 1–18 should follow ll. 28–31.

P. 151, l. 18. There is a portrait of T. W. Beale in the possession of the Royal Asiatic Society of Bengal (see *JASB*. 1925 p. xcvi).

P. 151, l. 28. M. Ṣādiq "Akhtar" i.e. doubtless M. Ṣ. "A." Hūglawī, for whom see pp. 707–8.

P. 151, l. 31. *Insert*:

188*a*. Rājah **Kundan Lāl "Ashkī"** b. Mannūn Lāl "Falsafī" Dihlawī was the author of an encyclopædia entitled *Nuzhat al-nāẓirīn* (Lindesiana p. 172), of the *Zīj i Ashkī* composed in 1231/1816 (Āṣafīyah i p. 814) and of the Arabic work *al-Qisṭās* composed at Delhi in 1237/1821–2 at the age of twenty-four [1] (Brockelmann *Sptbd.* iii p. 1312, Zubaid Aḥmad *The contribution of India to Arabic literature* p. 383).

Muntakhab i Tanqīḥ al-akhbār,[2] "historical tables" (general or Indian?): Sulṭān al-maṭābi' [**Lucknow**? [3]] 1267/1851*.

P. 152, l. 3. *Read* 1853–7°. For a description of the *Rauḍat al-ṣafā-yi Nāṣirī* see *A traveller's narrative written to illustrate the episode of the Bâb, edited . . . and translated . . . by E. G. Browne*, ii (Cambridge 1891) pp. 188–92.

P. 152, l. 8. [S. Ilāhi Bakhsh.] An account of this author and his *Kh. i j-n.* is given in an appendix to M. 'Ābid 'Alī Khān's

[1] If he was twenty-four in 1237, he must have been only eighteen in 1231, the date given for the composition of his *Zīj*.

[2] For a volume of a work entitled *Tanqīḥ al-akhbār* see p. 157. A work of that title is ascribed to Rājah Kundan Lāl in the Urdu dictionary *Jāmi' al-lughāt* (under Kundan La'l).

[3] For a Sulṭān al-maṭābi' at Lucknow see Arberry pp. 288, 452 and 518.

Memoirs of Gaur and Pandua, Calcutta 1931 (cf. *JRAS*. 1933 pp. 169–71).

P. 153, l. 8. M. Taqī " Sipihr " died on 17 Rabīʿ ii 1297 [29 March 1880] according to *al-Maʾāt͟hir wa-'l-āt͟hār* p. 188*a*, l. 2.

P. 153, l. 10. [*Nāsik͟h al-tawārīk͟h.*] The words " published (originally, it appears) in 14 volumes " should be deleted. According to the volumes preserved in the Cambridge University Library (about which information has kindly been supplied by Mr. J. D. Pearson) and the descriptions in the Mas͟hhad catalogue (vol. iii, *fṣl.* 14, nos. 193–207, where, however, nothing is said about a division into *kitābs* and a continuous numeration is given to the *jilds*) the work is divided as follows :—

Kitāb I (from Ādam to the Hijrah) in two *jilds* ((**1**) " *kih maʿrūf ast ba-Hubūṭ* " (M [1]), to the birth of Christ, **Ṭihrān** 1273/1857 (C[2], probably also BM.), 1285/1868–9 (*Ency. Isl.* under Sipihr), 1306/1888–9 (M., Ā [3]), 1321/1903 (C), (**2**) to the Hijrah, **Ṭihrān** [1860 ? °], 1285/1868–9 (*Ency. Isl.* under Sipihr), 1310/1892–3 (Ā), 1320/1902 (C), published also, it seems, in two parts (*a*) " *mas͟hhūr ba-Aḥwālāt i ḥaḍrat i ʿĪsā* " (M), 2nd ed. **Ṭihrān** 1303/1885–6 (M), (*b*) " *kih mutaʿalliq ast ba-tārīk͟h i ḥaḍrat i k͟hatmī-martabat* " (M), i.e. Muḥammad's life [to the Hijrah presumably], 2nd ed. **Ṭihrān** 1301/1883–4 (M).

Kitāb II, from the Hijrah to the author's time, but only the following *jilds* seem to have been published, (**1**) [called vol.[4] 3 in M] Muḥammad, from the Hijrah to his death, 1st ed. **Ṭihrān** 1285/1868–9 (M), 1310/1892–3 (Ā) 1314/1896–7 (C), (**2**) [" vol. 4 ", M] the first three Caliphs, **Ṭihrān** 1280/1863–4 (" 1st ed. ", M), 1305/1888 (date of index. C), 1306/1888–9 (identical with the preceding ? Ā), (**3**) [" vol. 5 ", M] ʿAlī, n.d. ? (Ā), 1319/1901–2 (C), 1323/1905–6 (M), (**4**) [" vol. 6 ", M) Fāṭimah, 1308/1890–1 (Ā); 1319/1901 (C); **Tabrīz** 1320/1902–3 (M), (**5**) [" vol. 7 ", M] Ḥasan, **Ṭihrān**

[1] M = Mas͟hhad catalogue.
[2] C = Cambridge University Library.
[3] Ā = Āṣafīyah catalogue.
[4] The letter *jīm*, apparently an abbreviation for *jild*, rather than *juz'*, in this catalogue.

1302/1884–5 (M), 1309/1891–2 (C), (**6**) ["vol. 8", M] Ḥusain, place? 1307/1889–90 (Ā), **Bombay** 1309/1892 (M, C (?)), (**7**) ["vol. 9", M] Zain al-ʻĀbidīn, pt. 1,[1] "**Persia**" 1313/1895–6 (Āṣafīyah iii p. 110 no. 1530, where a copy (apparently of this volume) is called *N. al-t.* (*takmilah*), *jild i awwal* and ʻAbbās-Qulī K͟hān is given (incorrectly?) as the author), **Qafqāz** 1324/1906 (M), (**8**) ["vol. 10", or *Mis͟hkāt al-adab i Nāṣirī*, M] Zain al-ʻĀbidīn, pt. 2, composed in 1304/1886–7, by ʻAbbās-Qulī K͟hān (cf. *PL.* p. 227), **Ṭihrān** 1316/1898–9 (M), "**Persia**" 1322/1904 (Āṣafīyah iii p. 110 no. 1530, where this volume (apparently) is called *N. al-t.* (*takmilah*), *jild i duwum*), (**9**) ["vol. 11", M] Bāqir, pt. 1, composed (in 1315 according to Āṣafīyah cat.) by ʻAbbās-Qulī K͟hān, **Ṭihrān** 1315/1897–8 (M), "**Persia**" 1318/1900–1 (Āṣafīyah iii p. 110 no. 1532, where this volume (apparently) is called *N. al-t.* (*takmilah*) *jild i awwal*), (**10**) ["vol. 12", M] Bāqir, pt. 2, compiled (by ʻAbbās-Qulī K͟hān) in 1324 (so M)[2] under the superintendence (*ba-ihtimām*) of ʻAin al-Daulah, **Majlis** 563 ("*N. al-t. Mutammim i jild i duwum i aḥwāl i . . . M. Bāqir.*" 338 foll.). Edition: **Ṭihrān** 1324/1906 (M. Cf. Āṣafīyah iii p. 110 no. 1533, where this volume is called *N. al-t.* (*takmilah*), *jild i duwum*, and ʻAbbās-Qulī K͟hān is given as the author. Cf. *PL.* i p. 227), together with the *Tārīk͟h i Qājārīyah* ("*az mujalladāt i N. al-t.*") in three *jilds* (1) the early Qājārs to Fatḥ-ʻAlī S͟hāh, (2) Muḥammad S͟hāh, (3) Nāṣir al-Dīn S͟hāh, **Ṭihrān** 1273/1856–7 (C. Only *Jild* 1 has this date: the other *jilds* have copyists' names but no date), 1304/1886–7 (C, Ā), 1315/1897–8 (M, C), **Tabrīz** 1319/1901–2 (M, C. Date in all three vols. Cf. *PL.* i p. 343).

P. 154, l. 14. (M. Taqī "Sipihr".] Also *al-Maʼāt͟hir wa-'l-āt͟hār* pp. 187–8.

P. 155, l. 9. [Iʻtimād al-Salṭanah.] Also Browne *The Persian revolution* p. 405; *Dānis͟hmandān i Ād͟harbāyjān* pp. 43–5;

[1] According to the Mas͟hhad catalogue, iii, *fṣl.* 14, ptd. bks., p. 41, M. Taqī "Sipihr" wrote eight (complete) volumes of the *N. al-t.* and half of the biography of Zain al-ʻĀbidīn.

[2] At the end of Majlis 563 the author gives 1323 as the date of the completion of the *baqīyah i jild i duwum i aḥwāl i . . . M. Bāqir.*

Tārīkh i jarā'id i pp. 311–12. Portraits in Feuvrier *Trois ans à la cour de Perse*, Paris [circ. 1894 ?], pp. 49, 80.

P. 155. *Insert*:

(3*a*) *Khulāṣat al-tawārīkh*, by M. b. Yūsuf Miftāḥ al-Mulk: **Ṭihrān** 1325/1907. [R. Lescot, *B.E.O.I.F. de Damas*, vii–viii, p. 281].

P. 156, l. 9. *Insert*:

(9*a*) *Muntakhab al-tawārīkh i Muẓaffarī*, by Ibrāhīm Khān Ṣadīq [Ṣiddīq ?] al-Mamālik: **Ṭihrān** 1323/1905 [R. Lescot, *ibid.*]. [P.S. See an article by Jahāngīr Qā'im-maqāmī in *Yādgār* IV/1–2 (1947) pp. 19–34.]

P. 156, l. 13. *Insert*:

(10*a*) *Rāḥat al-qulūb*, a sketch of general history, with a special history of Bengal to 1207/1792–3, the date of composition, by M. Rāḥat: **Bānkīpūr** Suppt. i 1754 (A.D. 1840).

(10*b*) *Rāḥat al-qulūb*, by Faiḍ Allāh Khān: **Lindesiana** p. 136 no 420 (A.H. 1134–40/1721–8).

P. 156, ult. [*Subḥat al-akhyār*.] Also **Philadelphia** Lewis Coll. 37.

P. 157, l. 6. *Insert*:

(13*a*) *Tārīkh i 'umūmī dar qarn i hafdahum u hizhdahum*, by Naṣr Allāh Khān "Falsafī"[1]: **Ṭihrān** A.H.S. 1316/1937–8 [R. Lescot, *B.E.O.I.F. de Damas* vii–viii, p. 281].

(13*b*) *Tārīkh i 'umūmī dar qarn i nūzdahum u bīstum*, by the same: **Ṭihrān** A.H.S. 1310/1931–2 [R. Lescot, *ibid.*].

(13*c*) *Tārīkh i 'umūmī i qurūn i wusṭā*, by 'Abd al-Ḥusain Shaibānī, 3 vols. **Ṭihrān** A.H.S. 1312–15/1933–7*. [R. Lescot, *ibid.*].

P. 157, l. 10. The date is 1329–43 according to Harrassowitz's *Bücher-Katalog* 430 no. 933.

P. 158, l. 4. [Ethé 120.] **Bānkīpūr** Suppt. i 1747 (17th cent.) seems to be another copy.

[1] b. Ṭihrān A.H. 1319/1901–2 (see Ishaque *Modern Persian poetry* pp. 12, 31; Īraj Afshār *Nathr i Fārsī i mu'āṣir* pp. 225–31 (portrait)). Cf. p. 1283[12] *infra*.

II. History, etc. B. The Prophets, etc.: (*a*) *Qiṣaṣ al-anbiyā'*

P. 160, l. 14. *Read* **Āṣafīyah** ii p. 880 no. 55. l. 15. [*Qiṣaṣ al-anbiyā'.*] Also **Edinburgh** New Coll. p. 7. l. 22. [*al-Bashāghirī.*] This *nisbah*, used of a different person, is spelt Pashāghirī in *Rashaḥāt* p. 215 (*az qaryah i PSHĀGHR būdah and kih dīhī buzurg ast az wilāyat i Samarqand miyān i sharq u shamāl u az-ānjā tā shahr duwāzdah farsang ast*). l. 32. [*Kashf al-ghawāmiḍ.* Al-Ṣābūnī's abridgment.] A MS. at Cairo (Catalogue, 2nd ed., v p. 265) is mentioned by Brockelmann (*Sptbd.* ii p. 262).

P. 161, l. 10. [*Maqāṣid al-auliyā'.*] "Opus . . . Sultano e gente Selgukidarum 'Abû-l-Muzaffer . . . dedicatum est" (Mehren). l. 12. **Decourdemanche** S.P. 1852 = **Blochet** iv 2295 (late 17th cent.). Another MS.: **'Alīgaṛh** Subḥ. MSS. p. 60 no. 19 (old).

P. 162, l. 18. [*Zarātusht-nāmah.*] Also **Bombay** Univ. p. 331 (A.Y. 1164/1794–5), **Brelvi-Dhabhar** p. xxix no. 16.

P. 162, l. 27. For Abū 'l-Ḥasan b. al-Haiṣam al-Būshanjī see Brockelmann *Sptbd.* i p. 592, probably also *Haft iqlīm* no. 616.

P. 162, l. 29. M. b. As'ad b. 'Abd Allāh al-Ḥanafī al-Tustarī, an author of Ūljāytū's time, wrote an abridgment of the *Jawāmi' al-ḥikāyāt* (*Muntakhab i Jāmi'* [*sic*] *al-ḥikāyāt*, as Khwānd-Amīr calls it) in 723/1323 (MS. (?): Vatican Pers. 71 (2) = Rossi p. 94). See *Tārīkh i Guzīdah* p. 811; *Ḥabīb al-siyar* iii, 1, p. 113; Niẓām al-Dīn *Introduction to the Jawámi'u 'l-Ḥikáyát* pp. 31[19], 123[20]; H. W. Duda *Ferhād und Schīrīn* p. 180.

P. 162, l. 31. *Read* J. 21 (12).

P. 162, l. 31. [al-Būshanjī's *Qiṣaṣ al-anbiyā'.*] *Insert*:

Extract: *A parallel to the story in the* Mathnawí *of Jalálu 'd-Dín Rúmí, of the Jewish king who persecuted the Christians. By E. G. Browne* (in *Islamica* ii/1 (Leipzig 1926) pp. 129–34).

P. 162 antepenult. Read (*Tārīkh i Mūsawī*). Other quasi-titles are *Qiṣṣah i Mūsā* and *Mūsā-nāmah*.

P. 163, l. 3. *Read* **Madras** i 299, 300, 531.

P. 164, l. 16. [*Mir'āt al-quds.*] Also **Vatican** Pers. 48 (defective. 18th cent. Rossi p. 75).

P. 165, l. 26. [*Dāstān i aḥwāl i Ḥawāriyān.*] Also **Vatican** Pers. 81 (17th cent. Rossi p. 99).

P. 168, l. 21. *Insert*:

(4*a*) ***Anīs al-murīdīn wa-shams al-majālis***, an account of Joseph in fourteen *majālis* incorrectly ascribed to the celebrated 'Abd Allāh Anṣārī of Harāt, who died in 481/1088 (see *Ency. Isl.* under Anṣārī, Brockelmann i 433, *Rauḍāt al-jannāt* 450, *Haft iqlīm*, no. 619, *Safīnat al-auliyā'* p. 165 (no. 300) and the authorities cited in the *Ency. Isl.* and in *J.R.A.S.*, 1929, p. 105): Ḥ.Kh. i, no. 1339, **Ethé** 1778 (A.H. 1013/1605), **Browne** Coll. D. 7 (modern). For a discussion of the authorship see *A prose version of the Yūsuf and Zulaikha legend, ascribed to Pīr-i Anṣār of Harāt. By Reuben Levy* (in *J.R.A.S.*, 1929, pp. 103–6).

P. 170, no. (34). [*Qiṣaṣ al-anbiyā'.*] MSS.: **I.O.** D.P. 698A (A.H. 1063/1651), 698B, 698C, 700.

P. 171, l. 21. *Insert*:

(41*a*) ***Qiṣṣah i Yūsuf***, in 57 chapters: **Blochet** i 395 (lacking preface and Ch. i–ix. A.H. 898/1492).

(41*b*) ***Qiṣṣah i Yūsuf***, by Qāḍī S. . . . 'Alī Amīr-al-Zamānī: **Blochet** iv 2125 (*Majālis* 4–38 with lacunæ. 15th cent.).

P. 171, no. (42). [*Tadhkirat al-anbiyā'*, by Ghulām-Muḥammad.] Possibly also **Rehatsek** p. 190 (n.d.).

P. 172, l. 14. *Insert*:

(2) History of Alexander the Great in prose: **Blochet** iv 2374 (A.H. 1115/1704).

II. HISTORY, ETC. B. THE PROPHETS, ETC.: (*b*) MUḤAMMAD.

P. 173, l. 13. [*Tarjamah i Siyar al-Nabī.*] Also **'Alīgaṛh** Subḥ. MSS. p. 61 nos. 33–5 (A.H. 985/1577–8).

P. 173, l. 20. *For* in al-Ruṣāfah *read* or al-Ruṣāfah. "According to Le Strange, *Baghdad during the Abbasid Caliphate*, p. 189, the two were identical." [R. Levy, *JRAS.* 1936 p. 524].

P. 175, l. 6. [*Tarjamah i Shamā'il al-Nabī*, completed in 988.] Also **Manchester** Rylands Lib. no. 133.

P. 175, l. 10. [*Shamā'il al-Nabī.*] *Insert* :

(6) By " 'Allāmah Niẓām al-Dīn " : **Āṣafīyah** iii p. 270 no. 967 (extending to the *Bāb al-kuḥl*).

(7) Verse translation dedicated to Akbar by Ḥāfiẓ [M. b. Bāqir] Harawī, who wrote also a Persian prose translation entitled *Khaṣā'il* : **Princeton** 58 (17th cent.).

P. 175, l. 17. [*Sharaf al-Nabī.*] See Niẓámu'd-Dín *Introduction to the Jawámi'u'l-Ḥikáyát*, G.M.S., London, 1929, p. 87, where it is pointed out that Rieu Arabic Suppt. 509 lacks nearly half of the ninety chapters and that Blochet i 371 contains only sixty-one of them.

P. 176, ll. 2–3. [*Tarjamah i Sharaf al-Nabī.*] For Blochet i 371 see the preceding note.

P. 176, l. 18. Abu Bakr b. M. Bharūchī is the author of a Persian translation of *al-Ḥiṣn al-ḥaṣīn* (Brockelmann ii p. 203, *Sptbd.* ii, p. 277) completed in 910/1505 for Sulṭān Maḥmūd Shāh [Bēgarah] of Gujrāt (MSS. : Ethé 2641, Ivanow 992).

P. 176, l. 19. [*al-Shifā'*]. *Insert* :

Commentary by Shihāb Efendī : **Āṣafīyah** iii p. 270 no. 932.

P. 176, l. 21. [*al-Ṭabarsī.*] The common pronunciation and the usual explanation (that the word is equivalent to Ṭabaristānī or Ṭabarī) appear to be incorrect, since according to his contemporary 'Alī b. Zaid al-Baihaqī (*Tārīkh i Baihaq*, p. 242) al-Faḍl b. al-Ḥasan came originally from ṬBRS (apparently like Ṭabrish (*Tārīkh i Qum* pp. 78, 117, etc.) an Arabicised form of Tafrish, for according to Baihaqī ṬBRS is *manzilī miyān i Qāshān u Iṣfahān*) and the correct pronunciation would therefore seem to be Ṭabrasī or Ṭabrisī (see Aḥmad Bahmanyār's discussion of the word in his edition of the *Tārīkh i Baihaq*, pp. 347–53).

P. 177, l. 10. [*Tarjamah i Makārim al-akhlāq*, completed in 1064.] Also **Bānkīpūr** xiv 1219, **Ivanow** 2nd Suppt. 1021.

P. 177, l. 13. *Add* :

(5) [*Tarjamah i*] *Makārim al-akhlāq*, probably one of those already mentioned : **Lindesiana** p. 109 no. 680 (A.H. 1180/1766–7).

P. 177, l. 14. *Insert*:

218*a*. Quṭb al-Dīn Abū 'l-Ḥasan **Sa'īd b. Hibat Allāh al-Rāwandī** died in 573/1177–8.

al-Kharā'ij wa-'l-jarā'iḥ, fī 'l-mu'jizāt (in Arabic), on the miracles of Muḥammad and the Imāms (see I.Ḥ. 1046, Brockelmann *Sptbd.* i p. 624).

Persian translation: *Kifāyat al-mu'minīn*, by M. Sharīf al-Khādim: **Āṣafīyah** iii p. 662.

P. 177, l. 15. For 'Abd al-Salām al-Andarasfānī see Brockelmann *Sptbd.* i p. 624.

P. 177, l. 32. For biographies of Kamāl al-Dīn Khwārazmī see *PL.* pp. 973[13], 974[9], [20]. Cf. *Laṭā'if-nāmah* p. 17; *Majālis al-mu'minīn* pp. 321–9.

P. 178, l. 12. [*al-Maqṣad al-aqṣā.*] Also **Heidelberg** P. 434 (16th cent. See *Zts. f. Semit.* x/1–2 (1935) p. 85).

P. 179, l. 4. [*Surūr al-maḥzūn.*] MSS.: **Princeton** 60 (A.H. 1256/1840), **'Alīgaṛh** Subḥ. MSS. p. 60 no. 14.

P. 179, l. 15. [Sa'īd al-Kāzarūnī.] For other works by him see Brockelmann *Sptbd.* ii p. 262.

P. 179, l. 18. [Sa'īd al-Kāzarūnī.] Also *Haft iqlīm* p. 209 (no. 166).

P. 180, l. 26. [*Sufar al-sa'ādah.*] The authority for vocalizing *Sufar* with *ḍammah* is Gotha 33, dated 884, in which the *sīn* is repeatedly so vocalized.

P. 181, l. 6. [*Sufar al-sa'ādah.*] Also **Princeton** 81 (A.H. 1261/1845), 82 (extracts. 18th cent.).

P. 181, ll. 12–15. [*Sufar al-sa'ādah.* Arabic trans.] For other MSS. and editions see Brockelmann *Sptbd.* ii p. 235.

P. 181, l. 19. *The words* (corrected by the author himself) *should be deleted.*

P. 182, l. 13. *Read* 8th/14th century.

P. 182, ll. 17–19. [Ḥasan b. Ḥusain Sabzawārī.] *Delete the words in square brackets.* By Blochet the dedicatee is described, no doubt correctly, as " l'un des souverains sarbédarides du Khorasan, Nizam ed-Din Yahya ibn Shams ed-Din Khadjè Karabi,[1] qui regna de 753 à 759 de l'hégire (1352–

[1] *Sic*, but Karrāb *bar wazn i ḍarrāb* is, or was, a village three parasangs from Khusraujird (see *Tārīkh i Baihaq*, ed. Bahmanyār, p. 343).

1358 . . ."). Ḥasan Sabzawārī must therefore have been an author of the 8th/14th century.

P. 182, l. 19. [*Rāḥat al-arwāḥ.*] Also **Blochet** iv 2296 (A.H. 930/1523–4), **Ivanow** 2nd Suppt. 1041 (2) (A.H. 1125/1713).

P. 182, l. 25. [*Bahjat al-mabāhij.*] *Read* 578A. I.O.D.P. 578B (*sic lege*) breaks off in the *faṣl* on al-Bāqir.

P. 183, l. 19. *Read* : S. **Muḥammad b. . . . Ja'far . . . Makkī.**

P. 184, l. 6. [M. b. Ja'far Makkī.] Also *Akhbār al-akhyār* pp. 136–41.

P. 185, l. 6. [*al-Tuḥfat al-Salāmīyah.*] Also **Āṣafīyah** iii p. 380 no. 184 (A.H. 1252/1836–7).

P. 186, l. 3. [*Bayān i ḥaqā'iq i aḥwāl i Saiyid al-Mursalīn.*] Also Sprenger 296 (A.S.B.), **Leningrad** Univ. 1175c (*Miṣbāḥ al-a.* only. Romaskewicz p. 14), 1198 (*F. al-a.* only. Romaskewicz p. 11), **Majlis** ii 1135 (1) (*F. al-a.* only. Late 15th cent.), 1132 (1) (*F. al-a.* A.H. 1235/1820), 1132 (2) (fragment of *F. al-a.* A.H. 1252/1836–7).

P. 186, l. 7. [Pīr Jamāl.] Also Ilāhī (Sprenger p. 74) ; *Ātashkadah* no. 362 ; *Riyāḍ al-'ārifīn*, 2nd ed., pp. 85–91.

P. 187, l. 15. [*Shawāhid al-nubuwwah.*] Also **Blochet** iii 1676 (A.H. 895/1490, from an autograph), iv 2300 (3) (A.H. 968/1561), **Browne** Coll. B. 4 (before A.H. 970/1562–3), **Princeton** 85 (16th cent.), **Lahore** Panjāb Univ. (A.H. 1010/1601–2 (?). See *OCM.* viii/3 (May 1932) p. 142), **'Alīgaṛh** Subḥ. MSS. p. 15 no. 69, p. 16 no. 80, **Ivanow** 612 (1).

P. 187, l. 18. *Read* **Bombay** 1288/1872 (see Karatay p. 36).

P. 187, l. 19. [*Shawāhid al-nubuwwah.*] *Insert* :

Description : Browne *Lit. Hist.* iii p. 513.

P. 188, l. 27. [*Ma'ārij al-nubuwwah.*] Also **Tashkent Univ.** 13 (A.H. 896/1490–1, from an autograph), **Blochet** iv 2298 (*Rukns* iii–iv and *Khātimah*. Early 16th cent.) **Berlin** 545 (A.H. 998/1589–90), 546, 547 (*Muqaddimah* and *Rukns* i–ii. A.H. 1066/1655), **Ellis Coll.** M. 286 (A.H. 1004/1596), M. 285, **'Alīgaṛh** Subḥ. MSS. p. 59 nos. 2–3, p. 61 no. 31.

P. 188 antepenult. [*Dalā'il i nubuwwat.*] Also **Lindesiana** p. 259 no. 112, **Upsala** 310.

P. 189, ll. 16–19. [*Rauḍat al-aḥbāb.*] Ethé's account of the divisions of this work has been provisionally accepted here and the contents of other MSS. have been described in accordance therewith, but possibly a further examination of good old MSS. might lead to some modification of Ethé's statements.

P. 191, l. 16. [*Rauḍat al-aḥbāb.*] Also **Blochet** iv 2300 (1) (*Maqṣad* i only. A.H. 968/1561), 2299 (16th cent.), **Vatican** Pers. 111 (*Maqṣad* ii. A.H. 977/1569. Rossi p. 120), **'Alīgaṛh** Subḥ. MSS. p. 57 no. 5 (A.H. 999/1590–1), p. 56 no. 4, **Brelvi and Dhabhar** p. 62 no. 1 (*Maqṣad* i. A.H. 1084/1673–4).

P. 191, l. 20. [*Rauḍat al-aḥbāb.* Turkish trans.] MS.: **Heidelberg** T 417 (see *Zts. f. Semit.* x/1–2 (1935) p. 84).

P. 192, l. 5. [Jamāl al-Ḥusainī.] Also *Ḥadā'iq al-Ḥanafīyah* pp. 368–9; Brockelmann *Sptbd.* ii p. 262.

P. 193, l. 12. The word Ganā'ī (or Kanā'ī, whichever is the correct spelling) is explained as meaning *nawīsandah* in the *Wāqi'āt i Ka<u>sh</u>mīr* p. 66 (cf. p. 143).

P. 193, l. 26. Read: *Muntak<u>h</u>ab al-tawārīk<u>h</u>* iii pp. 142–9, 259–60, 403⁶.

P. 193, l. 28. Read: *Wāqi'āt i Ka<u>sh</u>mīr* pp. 110–11.

P. 193, l. 30. [Ya'qūb "Ṣarfī".] Also *Ā'īn i Akbarī* p. 250, Blochmann's trans. pp. 581–2; *Ḥadā'iq al-Ḥanafīyah* p. 394.

P. 193, l. 32. [*Maṭāli' al-anwār.*] It is pointed out by <u>Sh</u>. 'Abd al-Qādir i Sarfarāz (Bombay Univ. cat. p. 18) that the *M. al-a.* was one of the works used by M. Bihāmad-<u>Kh</u>ānī for his *Tārīk<u>h</u> i Muḥammadī* (cf. p. 90 *supra*) and must therefore have been composed before 842/1438–9. That it is later than 700/1300–1 seems to be shown by a reference to Ṣig<u>h</u>nāqī's commentary on the *Hidāyah* (Brockelmann i p. 377²¹, *Sptbd.* i, p. 644, l. 9 *ab infra*), which occurs on fol. 90*a* in the I.O. MS. D.P. 741.

P. 194, l. 3. Full title: *Maṭāli' al-anwār fī tarjamat al-ā<u>th</u>ār.*

P. 194, l. 6. [*Maṭāli' al-anwār.*] Also **Lahore** Panjāb Univ. (A.H. 1011/1602–3. See *OCM.* viii/3 (May 1932) p. 142), **Bombay** Univ. p. 18 (A.H. 1210/1796).

P. 194, l. 7. *Read* 1122/1710.

P. 194, l. 18. 'Abd al-Ḥaqq Dihlawī seems usually to call himself

'A al-Ḥ. b. S. al-D. al-Turk [not al-Turkī] al-Dihlawī al-Bukhārī, but in a note appended to his commentary on the *Mishkāt* (Rieu i p. 14*b*) he calls himself 'A. al-Ḥ. b. S. al-D. al-Dihlawī *waṭan*[an] al-Bukhārī, *aṣl*[an] al-Turkī *nasab*[an] . . .

P. 195, l. 3. [*Madārij al-nubuwwah.*] Also **Princeton** 84 (extracts only).

P. 195, l. 4. *For* [**Lucknow** ?] *read* [**Madrās**].

P. 195, ll. 6–11. ['Abd al-Ḥaqq Dihlawī.] The *Ḥilyah* (beg. *Bi-smi 'llāh wa-'l-ḥ. l. 'alā jūdihi.* Other MSS. : **Rieu** ii 863*b*, **I.O.** D.P. 654A) was extracted by the author from the *Madārij al-nubuwwah* just after its completion. The (*Ādāb i libās i Rasūl*) (beg. *Ba'd i ḥ. u st. i Ilāhī*) appears to be independent. Other MSS. : **Ivanow** 1st Suppt. 923 (3) (late 18th cent.), **Bānkīpūr** Suppt. ii 2169 (19th cent.).

P. 195, l. 13. 'Abd al-Ḥaqq Dihlawī's list of his works has been published also by Hidāyat Ḥusain in *JASB.* xxii (1926) pp. 43–60. Another MS. : **Āṣafīyah** iii p. 34.

P. 195, l. 27. ['Abd al-Ḥaqq Dihlawī.] Also *Ṭabaqāt i Akbarī* ii p. 464 ; *Gulzār i abrār* no. 571 ; *Tūzuk i Jahāngīrī* p. 282, l. 5 *ab infra*, English trans. ii p. 111 ; *'Amal i Ṣāliḥ* iii pp. 384–5 ; *Muntakhab al-lubāb* i pp. 239–40, ii p. 551 ; *Safīnah i Khwushgū* no. 321 ; *Subḥat al-marjān* pp. 52–3 ; Elliot *Bibliographical index* pp. 273–6 ; *Ḥadā'iq al-Ḥanafīyah* p. 409 ; Brockelmann *Sptbd.* ii p. 603.

P. 196, l. 16. [" Masīḥ " Kairānawī.] Also *Kalimāt al-shu'arā'* (Sprenger p. 114) ; *Safīnah i Khwushgū* no. 688.

P. 197, l. 1. The *Zād al-ma'ād* is classed among M. Bāqir's Persian works, though the actual prayers are in Arabic.

P. 197, l. 3. [List of M. Bāqir's works.] Also **Ivanow** 2nd Suppt. 1039 and probably **'Alīgaṛh** Subḥ. MSS. p. 3.

P. 197, l. 12. [*Ḥayāt al-qulūb.*] **I.O.** D.P. 632B contains vol. ii only.

P. 197, l. 15. [*Ḥayāt al-qulūb.*] Also **Edinburgh** New Coll. p. 7.

P. 197, l. 29. *Insert* :

Continuation : *Ṣaḥīfat al-muttaqīn wa-manhaj al-yaqīn* (*dar dhikr i imāmat takmilah i Ḥ. al-q.*), by Raḍī al-Dīn M. b. M. Naṣīr birādar-zādah i 'Allāmah i Majlisī : I.Ḥ. 2060 (where the author is called M. Raḍī b. M. N. al-Majlisī and the work is stated to have been composed in the reign of Shāh Sulṭān-Ḥusain), **Āṣafīyah** iii p. 380 no. 261 (A.H. 1212/1797–8).

P. 198, l. 1. **Jalā'** should probably be read rather than **Jilā'**.

P. 198, l. 9. [*Jalā' al-'uyūn.*] Also **Bānkīpūr** Suppt. i 1758 (damaged. A.H. 1107/1696), **'Alīgaṛh** Subḥ. MSS. p. 59 no. 1.

P. 198, l. 30. [M. Bāqir Majlisī.] Also *al-Faiḍ al-qudsī fī aḥwāl al-Majlisī*, a detailed biography (in Arabic apparently) by Ḥusain Nūrī Tabarsī (19th century: see Brockelmann ii p. 832), which according to Majlis ii p. 53 n. 2 has been printed at the beginning of the *Biḥār al-anwār*; Brockelmann *Sptbd.* ii pp. 572–4.

P. 199, l. 9. [Ḥakīm M. Kāẓim.] Also Zubaid Aḥmad *The contribution of India to Arabic literature* p. 386.

P. 199, l. 10. *Read* Qinnaujī.—l. 14. *Read* Qinnauj.

P. 200, l. 24. [*Ḥamlah i Ḥaidarī.*] Also **'Alīgaṛh** Subḥ. MSS. p. 39 no. 22 (A.H. 1137/1724–5), p. 57 no. 7, **I.O.** D.P. 631 (with Najaf's continuation).

P. 201, l. 2. *Read* 175.

P. 201, l. 4. According to Sprenger the *Ḥamlah i Ḥaidarī* was "lithographed at Lucnow, A.H. 1268, 2 vols. folio 238 and 329 pp. of 50 bayts". The 1267 edition has 238 and 333 pages. It is without any continuation.

P. 201, ll. 11–17. ["Bādhil."] Also *Ma'āthir al-umarā'* iii p. 940; Sprenger no 153; *Nujūm al-samā'* p. 220.

P. 201, l. 17. *Insert*:

250*a*. **'Abd al-Aḥad** b. M. Sa'īd b. Aḥmad **Sirhindī** died in 1142/1729–30. He was a grandson of the celebrated saint Aḥmad Sirhindī (for whom see *PL.* p. 988 n. 5). His father, Sh. M. Sa'īd, surnamed Khāzin al-raḥmah, was born in 1005/1597 (see *Ḥaḍarāt al-quds*; I.O. D.P. 630, fol. 99*a*) and died in 1070/1659–60 (see *Khazīnat al-aṣfiyā'* i 639, where he is called Aḥmad Sa'īd).

Khazā'in i nubuwwat[1] (a chronogram = 1126/1714), a short biography of Muḥammad: **I.O.** D.P. 636 (18th cent.).

[*Khazīnat al-aṣfiyā'* i p. 662.]

[1] *Khazā'in al-nubuwwat* in the MS., but the title is said to be a chronogram and in this form it would give a date later than the author's death.

P. 202, l. 3. The bracket after Tīmūrids should be a comma.

P. 202, l. 20 *et seq.* For ʿAbd al-Raḥīm Ṣafīpūrī's works see Brockelmann *Sptbd.* ii p. 853.

P. 203, l. 10. *Insert*:

Mīr **ʿAlī** b. Ḥāfiẓ M. ʿAlī **Riḍawī Dihlawī.**

Māʾidah i pur-t̲h̲imār tarjamah i Nuzul al-abrār, "biographical notes concerning the Prophet and the Shīʿite Imāms," being a translation made in 1252/1836–7 of the *N. al-a.* [" by abu-Ṭālib al-Makkī †386 [A.D. 996]," according to the Princeton catalogue, possibly the anonymous work of this title which was published at [Bombay] in [1880] and which is described in Ellis ii p. 447 as " biographies of the Caliph ʿAlī, his wife Fāṭimah and his two sons al-Ḥasan and al-Ḥusain "], to which the translator has added a concluding chapter on the Twelve Imāms based on Jāmī's *S̲h̲awāhid al-nubuwwah*: **Princeton** 61 (A.H. 1280/1863).

P. 203, ll. 23–6. [ʿAlī Akbar " Bismil ".] Also *Madāʾiḥ al-Muʿtamadīyah* (Rieu Suppt. 127) fol. 57*a*; *Riyāḍ al-ʿārifīn* pp. 423–4; *Ṭarāʾiq al-ḥaqāʾiq* iii p. 156.

P. 204, l. 24. [Farhād Mīrzā.] Also *Majmaʿ al-fuṣaḥāʾ* i pp. 46–52; *al-Maʾāt̲h̲ir wa-'l-āt̲h̲ār* p. 195; Rieu Suppt. p. 221; Berthels *Ocherk istorii persidskoi literatury* pp. 102–3.

P. 205, l. 5. *Insert*:

(5*a*) ***Jām i gītī-numā***, a metrical account of the Prophet's expeditions, by M. b. Ismāʿīl K̲h̲wānsārī. Edition: **Ṭihrān** 1303/1885–6 (Āṣafīyah iii p. 100).

P. 205, l. 11. *Insert*:

(7*a*) *Kunūz al-rumūz*, on the merits and exploits of Muḥammad in forty *maqāmahs*, by Ḥusām b. M. al-Mas̲h̲s̲h̲āṭī: **Gotha** 4 (2) (A.H. 889/1484).

(7*b*) *Laṭāʾif al-ak̲h̲bār fī siyar al-Muk̲h̲tār*, by S̲h̲. Ibrāhīm b. Ismāʿīl Tattawī: **Āṣafīyah** iii p. 380 no. 275 (Pt. I only).

P. 205, l. 27. *Insert*:

(15*a*) *Miʿrāj-nāmah*: **Ivanow** 1st Suppt. 837 (1) (A.H. 1134/1722).

(15*b*) *Miʿrāj-nāmah* (beg. *ʿAun mī-k̲h̲wāhad dilam az K̲h̲āliq* *i Jān-āfrīn*), metrical, by a certain "'Aṭṭār": **Blochet** ii 1050 (4).

P. 205, l. 29. *Insert*:

(16*a*) ***Muʿjizāt i Ān-Ḥaḍrat ṣlʿm muntakhab az kutub i siyar***, by S. Nūr 'Alī al-mukhāṭab bah Qudrat-Jang b. Qādir al-Daulah Bahādur: **Āṣafīyah** iii p. 380.

P. 206, ll. 15–17. *Read*: (22) ***Nathr al-jawāhir***, a translation by S. 'Alīm Allāh b. 'Atīq Allāh Ḥusainī Jāland'harī [1] (d. 1202/1787–8) of the Arabic *Naẓm al-durar wa-'l-marjān* (cf. Bānkīpūr Arab. cat. xv 1033, Āṣafīyah ii p. 874, Brockelmann *Sptbd.* ii p. 603), a life of Muḥammad completed in 1091/1680 by Auḥad al-Dīn Mīrzā Jān (or **Khān**) Brkī Jāland'harī. Edition: **Lahore** 1902°.

P. 206, l. 18. *Read*: ***Naẓm al-durar wa-'l-marjān.***

P. 206, l. 21. *Insert*:

(24*a*) ***Nūr-nāmah***: **Bānkīpūr** xvii 1660 (*Aṣl* vii only, on the Miʿrāj. 1127 *Faṣlī*).

(24*b*) ***Risālāh dar bayān i khilqat i Nūr i Muḥammadī***: **Āṣafīyah** iii p. 380.

P. 206, l. 28. *Insert*:

(27*a*) ***Shamā'il-nāmah***; **Blochet** iv 2219 (19th cent.).

(27*b*) ***Shamā'il-nāmah***, metrical: **Āṣafīyah** iii p. 380 no. 191 (A.H. 1277/1860–1).

P. 207, l. 4. *Insert*:

(32*a*) ***Taṣwīr i balāghat*** (*ḥilyat al-Nabī*), by Nawwāb 'Azīz-Jang (for whom see p. 758). Edition: place ? 1340/1921–2 (Āṣafīyah iii p. 380).

(32*b*) ***Tawallud-nāmah***: **Ivanow** 1st Spt. 837 (2) (A.H. 1134/1722).

P. 207, l. 6. *Read* 1847°, [1869*], 1877*.

P. 207, l. 9. *Insert*:

(35) ***Wasīlat al-faqīr sharḥ asmā' al-Rasūl al-Bashīr***, by M. Hāshim b. ['Abd ?] al-Ghafūr Sind'hī: **Āṣafīyah** iii p. 380.

P. 207, ll. 14–15. Delete these lines. See p. 185.

[1] i.e. of "Jullundur" in the Panjāb. According to *Khazīnat al-aṣfiyā'* i p. 505 and Raḥmān 'Alī p. 147 he was a disciple of Shāh Abū 'l-Maʿālī and a *khalīfah* of S. Bhīk'h.

P. 207, l. 18. *Insert*:

(4) Work on the Prophet's birth in 9 sections: **Blochet** iv 2350 (15th cent.).

(*c*) Early Caliphs and Imāms

P. 207, l. 20 sq. [Ibn A'tham.] Cf. Brockelmann *Sptbd.* i p. 220. According to the Mashhad cat., iii, *fṣl.* 14, MSS. no. 11, the *Futūḥ* was composed in 204/819–20.

P. 208, l. 10. M. b. Aḥmad b. Abī Naṣr b. Aḥmad al-Mustaufī al-mulaqqab al-Raḍī al-Kātib according to the preface of Browne Coll. G. 1 (1).

P. 208, l. 19. [al-Mābarnābādī.] For Mābīzhanābād (spelling and vocalization uncertain, but zh, not r, seems to be correct) see *Tārīkh i jahan-gushā-yi Juwainī* ii p. 134[19], with Qazwīnī's note, and *Tatimmat Ṣiwān al-ḥikmah*, Arabic text, ed. M. Shafī', p. 158[4]. It was evidently near Khwāf.

P. 208, l. 22. [*Futūḥ i Ibn i A'tham.*] Also **Browne** Coll. G. 1 (1) (defective at both ends and extending to 'Uthman's murder), G. 1 (2) (from 'Uthmān's murder to al-Ḥusain's death. A.H. 924/1518).

P. 209, l. 16. [Ibn A'tham.] Also Brockelmann i p. 516, *Sptbd.* i p. 220.

P. 209, l. 32. [*Tuḥfah i Malikī.*[1]] Also **Āṣafīyah** iii p. 270 (A.H. 1230/1815).

P. 210, l. 11. *Insert*:

(**3**) ***Tarjamah i 'Uyūn akhbār al-Riḍā***, a translation made at Mashhad in 1075/1664–5 by M. Ṣāliḥ b. M. Bāqir Qazwīnī: **Sipahsālār** i p. 225 no. 290.

P. 210, l. 25. [*Tarjamat al-manāqib.*] The date 938 is that given in the *Rauḍāt al-jannāt*, but the translator's colophon as quoted in the Sipahsālār catalogue i p. 229[12] gives 968. No date is mentioned in the Bānkīpūr and Aberystwyth catalogues.

P. 210, l. 29. [*Tarjamat al-manāqib.*] Also **Āṣafīyah** iii p. 662, **Sipahsālār** i p. 228 no. 294 (late 18th cent.).

[1] In spite of Arabic grammatical rules this is doubtless the correct form of the title.

P. 210 ult. [al-Irbilī.] Also *Āthār al-Shī'at al-Imāmīyah* iv p. 165; Brockelmann *Sptbd.* i p. 713.

P. 211, l. 5. [*Aḥsan al-kibār.*] It appears from a statement on fol. 95*b* (seven lines from the beginning of *Bāb* 5) in I.O. MS. D.P. 573 that in 728/1327–8 the author, having returned from Sulṭānīyah to Iṣfahān and thence to Fīrūzān, became resident in the last place and began to write the *Aḥsan al-kibār* in 739/1338–9.

P. 211, l. 7. **I.O.** D.P. 573 contains only the first twelve of the seventy-eight *bābs.*

P. 211, l. 19. *Read* 109A.

P. 211, l. 21. [*Manāqib al-Sādāt.*] Also **Ivanow** Curzon 371 (A.H. 1103/1691), **'Alīgaṛh** Subḥ. MSS. p. 16 no. 82, **Mashhad** i, *fṣl.* 14, MSS., no. 35 (defective at end). This work is a Sunnī *arba'īn* with Persian translation and commentary and is misplaced in this section. The title does not occur in the text.

P. 212, l. 26. [*Rauḍat al-shuhadā'.*] Also **Tashkent Univ.** 73 (16th cent.), **Blochet** iv 2301 (defective. Late 16th cent.), **Princeton** 457 (A.H. 1080/1669–70), **Vatican** Pers. 159 (1) (A.H. 1105/1693. Rossi p. 152), **Bānkīpūr** Suppt. i 1757 (A.H. 1240/1825), **'Alīgaṛh** Subḥ. MSS. p. 57 no. 8 (A.H) 1243/1827–8), no. 9, p. 56 nos. 1–2 (A.H. 1251–2/1835–7), **Ethé** 159, **Āṣafīyah** iii p. 102 no. 1161, p. 104 nos. 1163, 1516.

P. 212, l. 28. [*Rauḍat al-shuhadā'.* Editions.] Also **Bombay** 1285/1868–9 (Āṣafīyah iii p. 104).

P. 213, l. 4. [*Dah majlis.*] Also **I.O.** D.P. 656 (A.H. 1159/1746), 646 (A.H. 1223/1808), **Blochet** iv 2305 (A.H. 1245/1829–30), **Bombay** Univ. p. 245 no. 167, **Āṣafīyah** iii p. 102 (metrical), **T.C.D.** 1590.

P. 213, l. 8. [*Ḥadīqat al-su'adā'.*] Also **Dresden** p. 84 no. 80 (Wolfenbüttel), **R.A.S.** T 6 (?) (*Sa'ādat-nāmah*).

P. 213, l. 27. For Sifarghābād, evidently a village near Jām, cf. *JRAS.* 1917 p. 355[11], where it is spelt اسفرغابد, and p. 335[15], where a person named Akhī 'Alī اسفرغابدی

is mentioned. These passages occur in the biography of Aḥmad i Jām edited by W. Ivanow (cf. *PL.* p. 950).

P. 214, l. 19. The *Aḥwāl al-A'immah al-Ithnai-'ashar*, as the author calls it in his *Ta'līf qalb al-alīf*, was completed in 1010/1601–2 and based mainly on the *Faṣl al-khiṭāb* of M. Pārsā (for whom see *PL.* pp. 7–8). The opening words are *Sp. i bī-andāzah Āfrīdgārī rā.* Other MSS.: **Rieu** ii 863*b* ult. (18th cent.), **Bānkīpūr** xvii 1736 (18th cent.), probably also **Āṣafīyah** iii p. 662 (*Faḍā'il i A. i I.-'a.*, composed in 1008 (*sic* ?). Author not stated [1]).

P. 214, l. 26. [M. Ṣāliḥ " Kashfī ".] For " Subḥānī " the *'Amal i Ṣāliḥ* has " Sujān " (a Hindī word meaning " well-informed ", " wise ", " intelligent " : cf. *PL.* p. 453 n. 2), which is much more probable.

P. 215, l. 4. The date of I.O. 4425 is 1067/1656.

P. 215, l. 13. *Read*: *Pādshāh-nāmah* ii 505 etc.; *'Amal i Ṣāliḥ* iii p. 444.

P. 215, l. 26. [A work on the Imāms.] This work was completed in 1058/1648. Other MSS.: **Būhār** 117 (A.H. 1081/1670–1), 118–19, **I.O.** D.P. 307A, **Rieu** i 32*b*.

P. 216, l. 16. *Read* 1295/1878°.

P. 217, l. 22. [al-Fāḍil al-Hindī.] Also " Ḥazīn " *Tadhkirat al-aḥwāl* p. 130, Belfour's trans. p. 143; *Nujūm al-samā'* p. 211.

P. 217, l. 5 *ab infra.* [An anonymous author.] In the preface of Ivanow 2nd Suppt. 1042 he gives his name as M. Riḍā b. M. Mu'min al-Imāmī al-Khātūnābādī al-mudarris. The work was begun in 1125/1713 and completed in 1127/1715.

P. 218, ll. 1–4. [*Jannāt al-khulūd.*] Tables giving the names of God with explanations, the names and brief accounts of the ancient Prophets, Muḥammad, the Imāms, Caliphs, some eminent Shī'ites, holy days, anniversaries and festivals, prayers, etc. Other MSS.: **Ellis Coll.** M. 279 (A.H. 1259/1843), **Ivanow** 2nd Suppt. 1042 (A.H. 1267/1851), **Mashhad**

[1] 'Abd al-Ḥaqq's name does not appear in the preface to the *A. i A. i I.-'a*, but his *takhalluṣ* " Ḥaqqī " occurs in a *rubā'ī* at the end. No title is mentioned in the preface.

iii, *fṣl.* 14, MSS., no. 26. Editions: **Ṭihrān** 1264/1848°, 1268/1852°. It has repeatedly been printed according to the Mashhad catalogue.

P. 218, l. 10. Read *Dil-gushā-nāmah.*

P. 218, l. 16. *Insert*:

282*a*. **M. Mashhadī.**

Ansāb al-aṯhār, lives of the Panj Tan and the Imāms, completed in 1146/1733–4: **Madras** 437.

P. 219, l. 7. [*Qurrat al-'ainain.*] Also **Bānkīpūr** xiv 1288.

P. 220, ll. 5–8. [*Muḥarriq al-qulūb.*] Also **Blochet** iv 2297 (A.H. 1234/1819). Other editions: place? 1284/1867–8 (with Ḥasan Yazdī's *Muhaiyij al-aḥzān* (cf. *PL.* p. 231) on margin. See Mashhad i, *fṣl.* 4, ptd. bks., no. 127); **Persia** 1294/1877 (see Āṣafīyah iii p. 108).

P. 220, l. 9. [M. Mahdī Nirāqī.] Also *Nujūm al-samā'* p. 319; Brockelmann *Sptbd.* ii p. 824.

P. 221, l. 4. More fully M. Ikrām al-Dīn b. Niẓām al-Dīn b. Muḥibb al-Ḥaqq.

P. 221, l. 6. The *Sa'ādat al-kaunain* is based mainly on the Arabic *Miftāḥ al-najā' fī manāqib Āl al-'Abā'* of M. b. Mu'tamad Khān (see *PL.* p. 141).

P. 221, l. 16. [*Ḥamlah i Ḥaidarī.*] *Read* on the lives of Muḥammad and 'Alī.

P. 221, l. 26. [Bamūn 'Alī "Rājī".] Also *Majma' al-fuṣaḥā'* ii pp. 147–50.

P. 221, l. 29. *Muḥīṭ al-'azā'* (i.e. presumably "the ocean of mourning") is doubtless the correct reading.

P. 222, l. 15. [*Riyāḍ al-shahādah.*] Also **Ellis Coll.** M. 263 (A.H. 1244/1826).

P. 222, l. 30. [*Mātam-kadah.*] For an edition without place or date of publication (282 pp.) see Harrassowitz's *Bücher-Katalog* 430 (1912) no. 821.

P. 223, l. 3. [Ṣibghat Allāh.] See also *PL.* p. 482.

P. 223, l. 6. [*Dāstān i gham.*] Another edition: A.H. 1311/1893–4 (Āṣafīyah i p. 240 no. 298, where the place of publication is not mentioned).

P. 223, l. 16. ['Abd al-'Azīz Dihlawī.] *Read*: (i) *Sirr al-shahādatain.*

P. 223, l. 21. [Salāmat Allāh "Kashfī".] See also *Sham' i anjuman* pp. 405–6.

P. 223, l. 21. [*Taḥrīr al-shahādatain.*] MS.: **'Alīgaṛh** Subḥ. MSS. p. 60 no. 8, probably also **Bānkīpūr** xvii 1624 (*Tarjamah i Sirr al-shahādatain*, without preface or translator's name, but transcribed at Cawnpore (Salāmat Allāh's place of residence) in 1259/1843).

P. 223, l. 27. ['Abd al-'Azīz Dihlawī.] *Insert*:

(2) *Qirān al-sa'dain i dhū 'l-nūrain dar dhikr i shahādat i Imām Ḥusain*: **Āṣafīyah** iii p. 106 no. 1021 (defective at end).

P. 223, l. 28. For M. Ṣāliḥ Burghānī, who was a brother of the *Shahīd i Thālith*, M. Taqī Burghānī (for whom see the next addendum), and who died at Karbalā' on a date apparently unrecorded, see *Qiṣaṣ al-'ulamā'* pp. 74–6; *Nujūm al-samā'* pp. 416–17; *Aḥsan al-wadī'ah* i pp. 35–8.

P. 224, l. 2. *Insert*:

300*a*. **M. Taqī** b. M. **Burghānī** Qazwīnī, called *Shahīd i Thālith*, was born at Burghān, near Ṭihrān, and settled at Qazwīn, where he was murdered in 1264/1848 by Bābīs, who resented his *takfīr* (see p. 1128 n. 4 *supra*).

Majālis al-muttaqīn, composed in 1258/1842, dedicated to Muḥammad Shāh Qājār and evidently of rather miscellaneous contents, since according to the *Nujūm al-samā'* p. 409[10] *mushtamil ast bar mawā'iẓ u ḥikam u ḥall i aḥādīth u tafsīr i āyāt u taṭbīq i ān ba-maṣā'ib i Saiyid al-Shuhadā' 'm balkih 'umdah i maqṣūdash dar ān-kitāb dhikr i maṣā'ib i ān-ḥaḍrat ast.*[1] Edition: **Persia** 1270/1854° (cf. Āṣafīyah iii p. 108 no. 1015. According to *Aḥsan al-wadī'ah* i p. 33[12], where it is inadvertently called *Majālis al-mu'minīn*, it has been lithographed several times (*mirār*^{an}) in Persia).

300*b*. Mullā **M. b. 'Alī Akbar Khurāsānī** known (*al-mashhūr*) as Firishtah, is described as *marḥūm* on the title-page of his *Mātam-kadah*.

Mātam-kadah, on the Imāms, etc., begun in 1261/1845

[1] In the Āṣafīyah catalogue, therefore, it occurs in the section *Tārīkh i fārisī*, whereas Edwards describes it as "a work on Shī'ah doctrine and morals".

and divided, according to the preface, into fourteen *mātam-kadahs* and a *khātimah* [but probably left unfinished]: **Calcutta** 1270/1854 (*Mātam-kadahs* i–iv (Muḥammad, Fāṭimah, 'Alī, Ḥasan) only. Imāmīyah Pr. Pp. 413, misprinted 414. SOAS.).

P. 224, l. 6. *Insert*:

301*a*. "**Rājī**" (evidently, if the date given below is correct, a different person from Bamūn 'Alī "Rājī" Kirmānī, who, as stated on p. 221 *supra*, died some years before 1270).

Ḥaqā'iq, or, according to the heading, *Tārīkh i Muḥammadī* (beg. *Ḥaqā'iq-shināsān i rāh i hudā*), a long metrical biography of Muḥammad, completed in 1270/1853–4, dedicated to Nāṣir al-Dīn Shāh and divided into 291 *'unwāns*: **Ivanow** 2nd Suppt. 987 (A.H. 1272/1856).

301*b*. In 1270/1853–4 Maulawī S. **Najaf 'Alī** and **Ṣafdar 'Alī** b. Ḥaidar 'Alī Riḍawī (cf. p. 25 *supra*) wrote their *Tadhkirat al-aṣfiyā'* at the suggestion of Nawwāb Dilēr al-Daulah Dilāwar al-Mulk Mīrzā M. 'Alī Khān Fīrōz-Jang.

Tadhkirat al-aṣfiyā': **Āṣafīyah** iii p. 380 no. 186 (under *Siyar i fārisī*, but the precise subject is not stated. A.H. 1270/1853–4).

P. 226, l. 29. *Read* broker (*dallāl*).

P. 226 ult. [A. b. M. al-Yamanī al-Shirwānī.] Also Sarkis *Dictionnaire encyclopédique de bibliographie arabe* coll. 1120–1; *Dānishmandān i Ādharbāyjān* p. 31.

P. 227, l. 3. [M. 'Abbās "Rif'at" Shirwānī.] Also *Ṣubḥ i gulshan* pp. 180–2.

P. 227, ll. 8–11. [*Aḥwāl i ḥaḍrat i Bāqir*, or rather, to judge from Edwards's quotation from the title-page, *Sharḥ i aḥwāl i . . . ḥaḍrat i Bāqir*.] For this work, written in continuation of the *Nāsikh al-tawārīkh*, see the Additions to p. 153.

P. 227, l. 14. [*Ṭirāz al-mudhahhab i Muẓaffarī*.] Also [**Ṭihrān**] 1315/1898 (see Karatay p. 186).

P. 228, l. 9. Ismā'īl Khān "Sarbāz" was a poet of Nāṣir al-Dīn Shāh's reign (see *al-Ma'āthir wa-'l-āthār* p. 207).

P. 228, l. 31. [*Bait al-aḥzān.*] Another edition: **Persia** 1325/1907 (Āṣafīyah iii p. 94, where 1262 is given as the date of composition).

P. 229, l. 5. *Insert*:

(13*a*) *Dhikr i shahādat i ḥaḍrat i Imām Ḥusain mausūm bah Ṣaḥīfah i dhahabīyah*, by M. 'Abd al-Qādir b. Mīrān S. Ḥasan b. S. M. al-Ḥusainī al-Qādirī: **Āṣafīyah** iii p. 102 (A.H. 1165/1752).

P. 229, l. 9. [*Durr baḥr al-manāqib.*] Also **Blochet** iv 2302 (doubtless the abridgment, though Blochet describes it as the *B. al-m.* Circ. A.D. 1525), **Majlis** ii 831 (A.H. 1046/1636–7).

P. 229, l. 13. *Read* Mashhad, *fṣl.* 4, ptd., bks., no. 112.

P. 229, l. 15. *Insert*:

(16*a*) *Faḍl i Ṣafdarī*, on the merits of 'Alī, by M. Najm al-Dīn Qādirī: **Arrah** 1294/1877*.

(16*b*) *Gham-namah i ḥaḍrat i Imām Ḥusain*, composed in the time of Nawwāb M. Ghauth Khān of the Carnatic (1842–55) by Ghulām-Yaḥyā Naqawī Ḥusainī[1]: **Āṣafīyah** iii p. 106.

P. 230, l. 12. [*Kanz al-ansāb.*] Also [**Ṭihrān?**] 1297/1880‡.

P. 230, l. 12. *Insert*:

(23*a*) *Kanz al-gharā'ib fī qiṣaṣ al-'ajā'ib*, on the history and merits of the first four Caliphs, al-Ḥasan and al-Ḥusain, by Najm al-Dīn Qāsim b. M. Madhmakīnī (?): **Blochet** iv 2141 (A.H. 882/1478).

(23*b*) *Kanz al-maṣā'ib*, by S. M. Ḥasan al-Ḥusainī al-shahīr bah Āqā Khān: **Āṣafīyah** iii p. 108.

P. 230 (25). For Ja'far Shūshtarī, who died in 1303/1885, see *Aḥsan al-wadī'ah* i pp. 92–9, where it is stated that the *Khaṣā'iṣ al-Ḥusainīyah* has been lithographed more than once in Persia.

P. 230, l. 17. *Insert*:

(25*a*) *Khulāṣat al-akhbār* (subject ?), by S. M. Mahdī b. S. M. Ja'far al-Mūsawī. Edition: **Persia** 1282/1865–6 (Āṣafīyah iii p. 380).

[1] A pupil of Irtaḍā 'Alī Khān (for whom see p. 1038 *supra*).

P. 230, l. 29. *Insert*:

(30a) ***Manāqib i Maʻṣūmīn***, by ʻAbd al-Khāliq b. ʻAbd al-Karīm Yazdī Mashhadī. Edition: **Persia** 1313/1895–6 (Āṣafīyah iii p. 662).

P. 231, l. 4. [*Muhaiyij al-aḥzān.*] Also 1284/1867–8 (place? On margin of Mahdī Nirāqī's *Muḥarriq al-qulūb* (cf. p. 220 *supra*). See Mashhad i, *fṣl.* 4, ptd. bks., no. 127).

P. 231, l. 22. *Insert*:

(38a) ***Mukhtār-nāmah***: **Ellis Coll.** M. 54 (18th cent.).

P. 232, l. 13. *Insert*:

(48a) ***Nukhbah i Sipihrī*** (subject?), by ʻAbd al-Raḥīm b. Abī Ṭālib Tabrīzī. Edition: 1322/1904–5 (place? See Āṣafīyah iii p. 380). [P.S. According to Browne *Press and poetry* p. 161 this is a life of the Prophet abridged from the *Nāsikh al-tawārīkh.*]

P. 233, l. 10. *Insert*:

(58a) ***Safīnah i Ahl i Bait***, dates of birth and death, compiled in the reign of ʻAlī ʻĀdil-Shāh [1]: **Āṣafīyah** iii p. 104 no. 997 (A.H. 1331/1913).

(58b) ***Ṣaḥīfah i dhahabīyah*** (*Dhikr i shahādat i ḥaḍrat i Imām Ḥusain mausūm bah Ṣ. i dh.*), by M. ʻAbd al-Qādir b. Mīrān S. Ḥasan b. S. M. Ḥusainī Qādirī: **Āṣafīyah** iii p. 102 (A.H. 1165/1752).

P. 233, l. 29. *Insert*:

(63a) ***Tadhkirat al-Sādāt***, the names, surnames, dates of birth and death and similar matters connected with Muḥammad, Fāṭimah and the Twelve Imāms, by Aḥmad b. Maḥmūd Muḥammadī Akbarābādī: **Allahabad** 1880*.

(63b) ***Tadhkirat al-shuhadā'***, lives of Muḥammad, Abū Bakr, Fāṭimah, ʻUmar, ʻUthmān, ʻAlī, al-Ḥusain and al-Ḥasan, by M. Ḥusain b. Bāqī Bukhārī: **Blochet** iv 2303 (19th cent.).

P. 233 (65) [*Tārīkh i ʻUmarī.*] Also **Āṣafīyah** iii p. 96 no. 999 (where the work is called *T. i ʻU. al-maʻrūf bah Ḥiṣār al-Islām* and the author's (translator's) name is given as M. Ḥusain [b.] ʻUmar [b.] M. [b. ?] ʻAbd al-Salām Harawī).

[1] The two Sulṭāns of this name reigned 965–87/1557–79 and 1070–97/1660–86 respectively.

P. 233 ult. *Insert* :

(65*a*) *Tarjīḥ al-faḍā'il* (subject ?): **Āṣafīyah** iii p. 662 (under *Manāqib*).

P. 234, l. 2. M. Ibrāhīm "Jauharī" died in 1253/1837–8 (see S. Jalāl al-Dīn Ṭihrānī's *Iṣfahān* (in *Gāh-namah i 1312* (cf. p. 263[16] *supra*) p. 135)).

P. 234, l. 6. *Insert* :

(66*a*) *Tuḥfat al-abrār dar dhikr i ḥālāt i A'immah i akhyār*, a short work in a *muqaddamah*, twelve *bābs* and a *khātimah* : **Vatican** Pers. 12 (2) (17th cent. Rossi p. 39).

P. 234, l. 18. Naurūz 'Alī Bisṭāmī is described in *al-Ma'āthir wa-'l-āthār* (p. 214) as a scholar (*'ālim*) and preacher (*wā'iẓ*) resident at Mashhad.

P. 234, l. 19. *Insert* :

(69*a*) *Wasā'il i Muẓaffarī*, *dar maṣā'ib*, by 'Alī al-'Alawī al-Yazdī b. Murtaḍā al-Ṭabāṭabā'ī. Edition : **Ṭihrān** 1320/1902–3 (Āṣafīyah iii p. 112).

P. 234, l. 26. *Insert* :

(72) *Zubdat al-akhbār dar faḍā'il u manāqib i Aṭhār*, by M. Qāsim b. M. Sharīf : **Āṣafīyah** iii p. 662.

C. History of Persia : (*a*) General

P. 238, l. 1. 'Alī-Qulī Mīrzā was *Wazīr i 'Ulūm*, the first person to be so called (*al-Ma'āthir wa-'l-āthār* p. 193*b* antepenult.). He was *Mudīr* of the Dār al-Funūn from 1272/1855–6 until his death in 1298/1880 (*op. cit.* p. 19) and *Wazīr i Tijārah* and *Wazīr i Ṣanā'i'* from the fourteenth year of Nāṣir al-Dīn Shāh's reign (*ibid.*). He died on 10 Muḥarram 1298/13 December 1880.

P. 238, l. 18. ['Alī-Qulī Mīrzā.] Also *Majma' al-fuṣaḥā'* i p. 41 (under his *takhalluṣ* "Fakhrī"); *al-Ma'āthir wa-'l-āthār* pp. 193–4; *Ṭarā'iq al-ḥaqā'iq* iii p. 278. For a portrait see Rieu Suppt. 412 (vi).

P. 239, l. 19. Jalāl al-Dīn, the fifty-fifth son of Fatḥ-'Alī Shāh, was eight years old at his father's death (*Majma' al-fuṣaḥā'* i p. 21).

P. 239, n.1. For a portrait of Mānekjī see Feuvrier *Trois ans à la cour de Perse*, Paris [circ. 1894 ?], p. 273.

P. 240, l. 11. [*Nāmah i khusrawān.*] Also **Lucknow** 1931* ("Part 1, dealing with the Sāsānian dynasty" (Arberry). Ed. Ṣābir 'Alī Khān). See also Browne *Lit. Hist.* ii p. 6.

P. 240, l. 20. The name of "Furūghī's" father was given incorrectly as M. 'Alī on the authority of the British Museum catalogue, in which works by more than one "Furūghī" are grouped under the heading "Muḥammad Ḥusain ibn Muḥammad 'Alī, called Furūghī and Adīb i Iṣfahānī". M. Ḥasan Khān Marāghī, who was an intimate friend of Mīrzā M. Ḥusain Adīb i Iṣfahānī mashhūr bi-laqab i Furūghī, says that he was the son of M. Mahdī Arbāb (*al-Ma'āthir wa-'l-āthār* p. 189). He mentions that at the time of writing he was Director of the Dār al-Ṭibā'ah i Khāṣṣah (the Royal Press) and of the Dār al-Tarjamah and that his *dīwān* was then in the press.

P. 240, l. 28. M. Ḥusain Khān "Furūghī" died in 1325/1907 (*Bīst maqālah i Qazwīnī*, pt. 1, p. 8 n.2). P.S. Exact date: 15 Ramaḍān/22 October.

P. 241, l. 5. ["Furūghī's" *Tārīkh i Īrān.*] Also **Ṭihrān** 1318/1900–1. [R. Lescot, *Bull. E.O.I.F. de Damas*, vii–viii p. 281.]

P. 241, l. 8. [M. Ḥusain "Furūghī".] Also *al-Ma'āthir wa-'l-āthār* p. 189; *Tārīkh i jarā'id* . . . ii pp. 122–4.

P. 241, l. 18. M. 'Alī Khān Furūghī was born in 1873 (so *The Times*) or 1875 (so *Indo-Iranica*) and died on 26–27 November 1942 (obituary notice in *The Times* of 1.12.42; portrait in *Indo-Iranica* i/2 (Calcutta, Oct. 1946), facing p. 37). See also Īraj Afshār *Nathr i Fārsī i mu'āṣir* pp. 67–74 (portrait).

P. 242, l. 20. *Insert*:

(7*a*) ***Tārīkh i Īrān,*** by M. Ḥasan Khān I'timād al-Salṭanah (for whom see pp. 154–5 *supra*): **Ṭihrān** 1293/1876. [R. Lescot, *Bull. E.O.I.F. de Damas* vii–viii, p. 281.]

P. 242, l. 30. *Insert*:

(11*a*) ***Tārīkh i pādshāhān i 'Ajam,*** metrical, by Mīrzā Ṣadīq [Ṣādiq ?] Qā'im-maqām: **Ṭihrān** 1324/1906. [R. Lescot, *ibid.*].

P. 243, l. 4. [*Tārīkh i Shaikh Uwais.*] This is a general history and is misplaced here. Extracts relating to the Golden

Horde: *Sbornik materialov* . . . ii . . . **Leningrad** 1941 (cf. p. 1230 *supra*) pp. 228–31 (Russian translation, pp. 99–103).

C. HISTORY OF PERSIA: (*b*) PRE-ISLAMIC DYNASTIES

P. 245, l. 17. [*Tajārib al-umam.*] This is evidently a translation of the Arabic work *Nihāyat al-arab fī akhbār al-Furs wa-'l-'Arab,* which was described by E. G. Browne in *JRAS.* 1900 pp. 195–259. [N. C. Sainsbury and, independently, A. J. Arberry, in letters.] Cf. Brockelmann *Sptbd.* i p. 235. There is another MS. (dated 811/1409) in the possession of Mr. Wilfred Merton. According to that MS. the ruler for whom the translation was made was Nuṣrat al-Dīn Aḥmad [Atābak of Luristān from 696/1296 to 733/1333. Cf. p. 81[12] *supra*]. The translator's name does not appear in the text but on the title-page the work is ascribed to Ḥamd Allāh Mustaufī. The names Aiyūb b. Qirrīyah, 'Abd Allāh b. al-Muqaffa' and "Atābak i sa'īd Sa'd b. Zangī" occur in their correct forms. In view of this new information the Āyā Ṣōfyah MS. cannot be regarded as an autograph. [A. J. Arberry, in a letter.]

P. 247 antepenult. For a MS. containing forty-two of these fictitious letters see Majlis 772, where they are called *Ṣad khiṭābah* and where it is stated that they appear to have been printed in the eleventh or twelfth year of the Calcutta newspaper *Ḥabl al-matīn.*

P. 248, l. 7. The *Nāmah i bāstān* was completed at Trebizond in 1313/1895–6 (see Browne *The Persian Revolution* p. 409).

P. 248, l. 15. [*Sālār-nāmah.*] Another edition: **Kirmān** 1316/1898–9. [R. Lescot, *Bull. E.O.I.F. de Damas* vii–viii p. 281.]

P. 249, l. 20. [Ḥasan Pīrniyā.] Cf. V. Minorsky in *Acta Orientalia* xvi p. 49 n.2: "Comme travail populaire il faut signaler l'histoire du monde ancien en trois volumes de Ḥasan-khān Pīrniyā (ex-Mušīr al-daula, mort le 23 novembre 1935); c'est une vue d'ensemble très méritoire basée sur les bonnes sources européennes." See also Īraj Afshār *Nathr i Fārsī i mu'āṣir* pp. 50–6.

P. 249, l. 25. *Insert*:

(3a) ***Īrān-nāmah***, by Mīrzā ʿAbbās b. M. ʿAlī Sostarī [Shushtarī ?]: **Mysore** 1925. [R. Lescot, *Bull. E.O.I.F. de Damas* vii–viii p. 282.]

(3b) ***Jang-hā-yi haft-ṣad-sālah i Īrān u Rūm***, by Colonel Ghulām-Ḥusain Muqtadir: **Ṭihrān** A.H.S. 1315/1936–7. [R. Lescot, *ibid*.].

P. 249, l. 30. *Insert*:

(6) ***Qushūn-kashī ba-mamālik i Tūrān***, a study of the *Shāh-nāmah* from the strategic point of view, by Jamīl Qūzānlū: **Ṭihrān** A.H.S. 1310/1931–2. [R. Lescot, *ibid*.]

(7) ***Tārīkh i niẓāmī i jang i ʿArab bā ʿAjam***, by Jamīl Qūzānlū: **Ṭihrān** A.H.S. 1311/1932–3. [R. Lescot, *ibid*.]

(8) ***Tārīkh i niẓāmī i jang i Īrān u Makidōniyah***, by Jamīl Qūzānlū: **Ṭihrān** A.H.S. 1311/1932–3. [R. Lescot, *ibid*.]

(9) ***Tārīkh i pādshāhān i ʿAjam yā Siyāq al-tawārīkh***: anonymous: **Ṭihrān** 1292/1875. [R. Lescot, *ibid*.]

(10) ***Yād-dāsht-hā-yi Khusrau i awwal Anūshīrwān***, by Ibrāhīm-Zādah Ṣafawī: **Ṭihrān** 1310/1892–3. [R. Lescot, *ibid*.]

(11) ***Yazdgird i siwwum***, anonymous: **Ṭihrān** A.H.S 1312/1933–4. [R. Lescot, *ibid*.]

C. History of Persia: (c) The Ghaznawids

P. 252, n. 1. For Chandū Lāl see pp. 1100–1.

P. 253, l. 27. [*Tārīkh i Baihaqī*.] Also **Ellis Coll.** M. 21 (A.H. 1281/1864–5).

Other editions: (**3**) **Ṭihrān** A.H.S. 1319/1940 (vol. i, 600 pp. corresponding to the first 614 out of the 868 pages of the Calcutta edition, edited with textual notes by Saʿīd Nafīsī), 1326/1947 (vol. ii, pp. 601–968 i.e. the remainder of the text and the explanatory notes on pp. 1–39), *in progress*. (**4**) **Tihrān** A.H.S. 1324/1945 (ed. Ghanī and Faiyāḍ).

P. 254, l. 20. [Abū 'l-Faḍl Baihaqī.] The passage in the *Tārīkh i Baihaq* occurs on pp. 175–8 in Aḥmad Bahmanyār's edition and is quoted in M. Shafīʿ's edition of the *Tatimmat Ṣiwān al-ḥikmah*, fasc. 1, pp. 179–83. See also *Āthār i gum-shudah i Abū 'l-Faḍl i Baihaqī*, by Sa'īd Nafīsī, Ṭihrān A.H.S. 1315/1936‡.

C. HISTORY OF PERSIA: (*d*) THE SALJŪQIDS

P. 255, l. 12. [Anūshirwān b. Khālid.] Also *Dastūr al-wuzarā'* pp. 210–11.

P. 260, l. 14. [*al-Tawassul ilā 'l-tarassul.*] Also Ḥ. Kh. ii p. 463, **Yenī** 1000, **Nūr i 'Uthmānīyah** 4300.

C. HISTORY OF PERSIA: (*e*) THE MONGOLS

P. 262, l. 25. [*Tārīkh i Jahān-gushāy i Juwainī.*] Also **Ellis Coll.** M. 214 (vol. i and part of vol. ii. 16th cent.), M. 215 (vol. i and large part of vol. ii. 18th cent.).

P. 263, l. 14. *Read* (**3**).—l. 19. *Delete the full stop after the word* Khān.

P. 264, l. 20. [*Tārīkh i Jahān-gushāy i Juwainī.* Translations of extracts.] *Add*:

(**6**) [On the Golden Horde. (Russian.).] *Sbornik materialov* . . . ii . . ., **Leningrad** 1941 (cf. p. 1230 *supra*), pp. 20–24.

P. 267, ll. 1–7. [*Tārīkh i Uljāytū Sulṭān.*] "The question of Qāshānī's authorship is studied by Barthold in his review of Blochet's book, in *Mir Islama*, i, 1, 1912, pp. 56–107 . . ." [Minorsky, *BSOS.* ix/1 (1937) p. 254).

P. 267, l. 14. "The most detailed description of Aqsarā'ī's history now available is found in Barthold's *O nekotorikh vostoch. rukopisakh Konstantinopol'a, Zapiski*, xviii (1908), pp. 0124–0137 (numerous quotations)." [Minorsky, *ibid.*] P.S. See p. 1305 *infra*.

P. 267, l. 27. [Waṣṣāf.] For a MS. at Cairo containing selections from his poems and prose works [presumably in Arabic] see Brockelmann *Sptbd.* ii p. 53.

P. 269, l. 23. [*Tārīkh i Waṣṣāf.*] Also **Ivanow** 1st Suppt. 757 (lacks vol. v. A.H. 1246/1831, **Ellis Coll.** M. 418–M. 421.

P. 269, l. 4 *ab infra.* Also **Bombay** 1241/1826 (707 pp. See Karatay p. 1).

P. 269 antepenult. *Read* 1314/1896–7*.

P. 270, l. 18. [*Tārīkh i Waṣṣāf.*] *Insert*:

Russian translation of passages relating to the Golden Horde:

Sbornik materialov . . . ii, Leningrad 1941 (cf. p. 1230 *supra*), pp. 80–89.

P. 272, l. 22. [*Shajarat al-Atrāk*. Extracts.] *Add* :

(**2**) [Passages relating to the Golden Horde.] *Sbornik materialov* . . . ii . . . **Leningrad** 1941 (cf. p. 1230 *supra*) pp. 262–8 (with Russian translation, pp. 202–9).

P. 273, l. 13. [Ulugh Bēg.] Also *Laṭā'if-nāmah* p. 207.

P. 274, ll. 12–13. *For* no. 83 (" Diwan des Ahmad Jasawi " [sic]) *read* no. 88 (Geschichte von Fīrūz Šāh in Versen (Mesnewi) [sic]).

P. 274, l. 15. See *Ein türkisches Werk von Haydar-Mirza Dughlat. Von Ahmet-Zeki Validi* (in *BSOS*. viii/4 (1937) pp. 985–9).

P. 274, l. 16. [*Tārīkh i Rashīdī*.] As the *T. i R.* is not concerned with the Mongols of Persia, it is inappropriately placed here and should be regarded as transferred to the subsection on KĀSHGHAR (p. 392 *infra*).

P. 274, l. 17. The correct date seems to be 953 (see Ethé 2848 and Ross's translation).

P. 275, l. 30. [*Tārīkh i Rashīdī*. Translations of extracts.] *Add* :

(**3**) *Mīrzā Muḥammad Ḥaydar Dughlāt on the Harāt school of painters*, [an English translation] *by T. W. Arnold* (in *BSOS*. v/4 (1930) pp. 671–4).

C. HISTORY OF PERSIA : (*f*) THE MUẒAFFARIDS

P. 277, l. 19. [*Mawāhib i Ilāhī*.] Also **Ellis Coll.** M. 287 (autograph ? 14th cent.).
Edition : **Tihrān** 1326/1947 (" vol. i ", about half of the work. Ed. Sa'īd Nafīsī).

C. HISTORY OF PERSIA : (*g*) THE TĪMŪRIDS

P. 278, l. 13. [*Rūz-nāmah i ghazawāt i Hindūstān*.] See the remarks of W. Hinz in *ZDMG*. 90/2 (1936) pp. 358–9.

P. 278, l. 33. " It is a question whether Shanb-i-Ghāzān (p. 278) is correct ; Rizā Qulī Khān in the Farhang-i-Nāṣirī spells the word Shumb." [C. N. Seddon, *JRAS*. 1938 p. 569.]

P. 279, l. 27. [Niẓām Shāmī's *Ẓafar-namah*.] Russian translation of passages relating to the Golden Horde : *Sbornik materialov* . . . ii . . . , **Leningrad** 1941 (cf. p. 1230 *supra*), pp. 104–25.

P. 279 antepenult. Read *Ẓafar-nāmah* iv p. 248.

P. 281, ll. 4–5. **Houtum-Schindler** 54 (3) = **Browne** Coll. R. 1 (3) (abridged or incomplete. 19th cent.).

P. 281, l. 32. [*Malfūẓāt i Tīmūrī.*] Also **Calcutta Madrasah** 176 (3) (17th cent.), **'Aligarh** Subḥ. MSS. p. 60 no. 12 (A.H. 1252/1836–7), **Tashkent Univ.** 65 (A.H. 1303/1885–6).

P. 282, l. 8. *Add* :

(**5**) *Tūzuk i Tīmūrī u Tūzuk i Napōliyōn*, **Bombay** 1308/1890–1 [R. Lescot, *Bull. E.O.I.F. de Damas*, vii–viii, p. 282].

P. 283, l. 4. [*Malfūẓāt i Ṣāḥib-Qirān.*] **Ellis Coll.** M. 257 (18th cent.).

P. 284, l. 24. [Sharaf al-Dīn's *Ẓafar-nāmah.*] Also **Rāmpūr** (A.H. 843/1439–40. See *OCM.* ii/2 (Feb. 1926) p. 12), **Princeton** 54 (A.H. 872/1467–8. PICTURES by Bihzād), **Tashkent Univ.** 63 (A.H. 1112/1700–1), **Leningrad** Univ. 1122* (Romaskewicz p. 10).

P. 286, l. 4. **Dorn** A.M. p. 375 = **Dorn** 295.

P. 286, l. 26. [*Ẓafar-nāmah.* Extracts.] *Add* :

(**2**) [the *dībāchah* and the first few lines of the *muqaddamah*] *OCM.* xv/4 (Aug. 1939), *ḍamīmah*, pp. 3–28 (ed. M. Shafī').

(**3**) [Passages from the *muqaddamah* relating to the Golden Horde] *Sbornik materialov* . . . ii . . . **Leningrad** 1941 (cf. p. 1230 *supra*) pp. 248–50.

P. 287, l. 6. [*Ẓafar-nāmah.* Translations of extracts.] *Add* :

(**4**) [Passages relating to the Golden Horde (Russian).] *Sbornik materialov* . . . ii . . . **Leningrad** 1941 (cf. p. 1230 *supra*) pp. 144–89.

P. 288, l. 8. *Read* : *Mir'āt al-khayāl* p. 67 (no. 51).

P. 288, l. 14. [Sharaf al-Dīn 'Alī Yazdī.] Also *Riyāḍ al-'ārifīn* pp. 363–4 ; " Āyatī " *Tārīkh i Yazd* pp. 295–6.

P. 289. [*Tīmūr-nāmah i Hātifī.*] Also **Majlis** ii 905 (A.H. 957/1550), **Vatican** Barb. Orient. 104 (1) (A.H. 967/1559–60. Rossi p. 159), **Ellis Coll.** M. 141 (A.H. 976/1568–9), **Blochet** iii 1536 (A.H. 978/1571), **Sipahsālār** ii 1154 (A.H. 980/1572–3), 1152–3 (both mid 10th/16th cent.), **Philadelphia** Lewis Coll. p. 53 (A.H. 991/1583), **Calcutta Madrasah** 145 (early 18th cent.), **Rāghib** 1095 (n.d. See Duda *Ferhād und Schīrīn* p. 181).

P. 290, l. 8. *Read* **Madras** I 101.

P. 290, l. 10. [*Ẓafar-nāmah i Hātifī.* Editions.] Also **Lucknow** 1896‡ (2nd ed.).

P. 290, ll. 14–25. [" Hātifī."] Also *Laṭā'if-nāmah* pp. 105–6 ; *Khulāṣat al-afkār* no. 304.

P. 290, l. 20. *Khulāṣat al-kalām* (Bodleian 390) no. 76 = Bānkīpūr viii 705 no. 56 (p. 146).

P. 290, l. 32. *Insert* :

(2*a*) *Tārīkh i Ṣāḥib-Qirān Amīr Tīmūr Kūrkān* (beg. *Ḥ. u sp. u sh. u st. ḥaḍrat i Pādshāhī rā tuwānad būd*), composed in 1124/1712 (the same date as the preceding work) by an author who calls himself " Rumūz " [*sic* ?] : **Tashkent Univ.** 58 (A.H. 1261–5/1845–9. Cf. Kahl pp. 17–18).

P. 291, ll. 1–8. The " Anonym of Shāh-Rukh " is identical with Tāj al-Salmānī's history [W. Hinz, *Quellenstudien zur Geschichte der Timuriden* (*ZDMG*. 90/2 (1936)) pp. 367–8]. The B.M. MS. contains two-fifths of the work. [Hinz, *ibid*., p. 369 penult.]

P. 291, l. 8. Read : *ta'līf*.

P. 291, ll. 9–12. Tāj al-Salmānī went from Shīrāz to Tīmūr at Samarqand in 800/1397–8. For the little autobiographical information given by him in his history see W. Hinz, *ZDMG*. 90/2 (1936) pp. 368–9. He is doubtless the same person as the calligraphist Khwājah T. al-S., of Iṣfahān, who is described as the first to write *Ta'līq* with elegance or even as its inventor [Majnūn Rafīqī *Khaṭṭ u sawād*, *Bāb* ii (*OCM*. x/4 (Aug. 1934) p. 18) ; Aḥmad Ibrāhīmī *Khulāṣat al-tawārīkh* (?), *Qism* ii, at end (*OCM*. x/4 (Aug. 1934) p. 29) ; Idem, (*Tadhkirah i khwush-nawīsān*) (cf. p. 1074 *supra*), Zakhoder's trans. p. 89].

P. 291, ll. 13–18. *Read* :

(*Dhail i Ẓafar-nāmah*) or (*Tārīkh i Tāj i Salmānī*), an untitled history of the end of Tīmūr's reign and the early years of Shāh-Rukh's (to 811/1409) : Ḥ. Kh. iv p. 176 l. 3, **Lālā Ismā'īl** 304 = Tauer 414 (very slightly defective at beginning. A.H. 988/1580. See W. Hinz *ZDMG*. 90/2 (1936) pp. 367–73), **Rieu** i 180*b* (beg. *Afḍal i ḥ. u sp. u akmal i sh. i bī-q*. About two-fifths of the work, lacking nearly all of the *sabab i ta'līf i kitāb* and extending to the defeat of Pīr Muḥammad by Khalīl in Ramaḍān 808/Feb. 1406. 15th cent. Cf. W. Hinz *ZDMG*. 90/2 (1936) pp. 357–8, 366–71), **Āyā Ṣōfya** 3028–9 (?) (see W. Hinz *ibid*. p. 367 n. 3, where these two MSS. are described on the authority of Aḥmad Zakī Valīdī as a further copy (so, not two copies) of Tāj i Salmānī's history. In the *defter* they do indeed appear as *Tārīkh i Tīmūr* by Tāj al-Salmānī, but Tauer describes these MSS. (nos. 409 and 401 in his list) as copies of Sharaf al-Dīn Yazdī's *Ẓafar-nāmah* (cf. p. 285 *supra*) and, to judge by the number of leaves (586 and 366), this would seem to be correct), **Fātiḥ** 4305 = Tauer 415 (about three-quarters of the work. 12th/18th cent.).

P. 291, l. 18. Insert here article 364 (*Mu'izz al-ansāb*) from p. 298.

P. 292, l. 22. " Qāsimī " died in 982/1574–5 (see Ḥasan Rūmlū p. 462[1], Seddon's trans. p. 201).

P. 293, l. 5. [" Qāsimī."] Also *Mai-khānah* pp. 141–52 ; *Haft āsmān* pp. 136–8.

P. 294, l. 10. [*Maṭla' i sa'dain*.] Also **Ellis Coll.** M. 14 (*Daftar* ii. A.H. 970/1563), M. 12 (apparently A.H. 807–30 from *Daftar* ii. 17th cent.), M. 13 (*Daftar* i. 18th cent.).

P. 295, l. 4. [*Maṭla' i sa'dain*.] The publication of M. Shafī''s [first] edition was resumed in *OCM*. xiv/2 (Feb. 1938), pp. 193–224, and continued in succeeding issues, but this edition may be regarded as superseded by M. Shafī''s second edition, of which the first volume (*Jild* ii, *juz'* 1. A.H. 807–33. Pp. 655 [?]) was published at **Lahore** in 1360/1941 [Information concerning this volume from V. Minorsky, in a letter] and the second volume (*Jild* ii, *juz'* 2–3. A.H. 833–75. Pp. 621–1558) at the same place (Gīlānī Press) in 1368/1949‡. A volume of indexes is in preparation.

P. 295 ult. Also in *A Persian embassy to China ; being an extract from Zubdatu't-tawarikh of Hafiz Abru* [*sic*]. *Translated* [and edited] *by K. M. Maitra*. Lahore, 1934*.

P. 296, l. 3. [*Maṭla' i sa'dain*. Extracts.] *Add* :

(**7**) [Passages relating to the Golden Horde.] *Sbornik materialov* . . . ii . . . **Leningrad** 1941 (cf. p. 1230 *supra*) pp. 251–61.

P. 297, l. 22. [*Maṯla' i sa'dain*. Translations of extracts.] *Add*: (**14**) [Passages relating to the Golden Horde. (Russian.)] *Sbornik materialov* . . . ii . . . **Leningrad** 1941 (cf. p. 1230 *supra*), pp. 190–201.

P. 298. [*Mu'izz al-ansāb*.] Article 364 should follow article 361 on p. 291.

C. History of Persia: (j) The Āq-Quyūnlū.

P. 300, l. 4. *Insert*:

369*a*. **Jalāl al-Dīn** M. b. As'ad Ṣiddīqī **Dawānī**, well known as the author of the *Akhlāq i Jalālī*, was born at Dawān, near Kāzarūn, in 830/1426–7, became *Qāḍī* of Fārs and Professor in the Dār al-Aitām madrasah at Shīrāz and died in 908/1502–3 (see *Majālis al-nafā'is* (tr. Fakhrī ed. 'Abd Allāh p. 229, ed. "Ḥikmat" p. 141, tr. Qazwīnī ed. "Ḥikmat" p. 309; Ḥasan Rūmlū p. 71, Seddon's trans. p. 31; *Majālis al-mu'minīn* p. 347 (4th biography from end of *Majlis* vii); *Haft iqlīm* i p. 209 (no. 167); *al-Fawā'id al-bahīyah* p. 89 n. 2; *Ency. Isl.* under Dawwānī (Brockelmann); Brockelmann ii p. 217, *Sptbd.* ii p. 306; etc.).

'Arḍ-nāmah, an account of a parade held by Sulṭān Khalīl in 881/1476 near Band i Mīr or Band i Amīr ("a short distance to the south of the ruins of Persepolis", Minorsky) in Fārs, when he was Governor of the province on behalf of his father Ūzūn Ḥasan, including a list of civil and military officers in Fārs and interesting statistical data: **I.O.** D.P. 952 (*d*) (A.H. 900/1495), **Bānkīpūr** Suppt. ii 2120 (A.H. 1077/1667), **Ḥamīdīyah** 1438 (in the *Kullīyāt* of Dawānī).

Edition: *Milli tatabbu'lar mejmu'asi, jild* ii, *say* 5, **Istānbūl** 1331/1913, pp. 273–305 (corrections, pp. 385–6. Edited by Kilisli Rif'at. See *BSOS*. x/1 (1939) p. 141 n. 1).

Abridged translation with notes: *A civil and military review in Fārs in 881/1476. By V. Minorsky* (*BSOS*. x/1 (1939) pp. 141–78).

P. 300, l. 5. *Read* Rūzbihān.

P. 300, l. 24. *Read Mīhmān-nāmah*.

P. 301, l. 2. *Read* 915/1509.

P. 301, ll. 7–9. [*Tārīkh i 'ālam-ārāy i Amīnī.*] These three lines should be deleted. The two Cairo MSS., though described in the catalogue (evidently through a misuse of Ḥ. Kh.) as the *'Ālam-ārāy* of Faḍl Allāh, are parts of the *'Ālam-ārāy i 'Abbāsī* (see p. 310 *infra*), as the opening words show. "The Eton MS. described as *Tārīkh-ı 'Ālam-ārā* in fact consists of two quite distinct volumes: Vol. i is the first of the *Afḍal al-tawārīkh* by Faḍlī Iṣfahānī, of which the Br. Mus. MS. described in Rieu, Supp. p. 56 (Professor Storey's 385) forms the immediate continuation; Vol. ii is the second part of Iskandar Munshī's *'Ālam-ārā* down to the year 1023." [V. Minorsky, *BSOS.* ix/1 (1937) p. 254.]

C. History of Persia: (*k*) The Ṣafawids.

P. 301, l. 19. ["Banā'ī."] "I have little doubt that Bannā'ī is the correct form of the *nisba*. In words like *saqqā*, *nakhkhās*, etc., Persian verse writers often drop the *tashdīd* for metrical reasons." [R. A. Nicholson, in a letter.] In an Edinburgh MS. containing a selection of "Banā'ī's" *ghazals* (New Coll. Or. (Pers.) 35 (*b*)) the form with *tashdīd* seems never to occur.

P. 302, l. 17. [*Dīwān i Banā'ī.*] Also Bānkīpūr Suppt. i 1879, Blochet iii 1769.

P. 303, l. 3. *Tuḥfah i Sāmī*, Ṭihrān ed., pp. 98–100.

P. 303, l. 11. ["Banā'ī."] Also *Zapiski Vost. Otd. Russ. Arkh. Obshch.* xix p. 0164 seqq. (an article by Samoilovich referred to by Barthold in *Mir-Ali-Shir* p. 160); Barthold *Herāt* tr. Hinz, pp. 85–6.

P. 303, l. 19. [*Shāh-nāmah i Hātifī.*] Also **Rāghib** 1095 (see Duda *Ferhad und Schirin* p. 181).

P. 304, l. 11. [(*Tārīkh i Shāh Ismā'īl*).] "Many of the facts reported in the anonymous 376 have been utilized in Ḥasan-i Rūmī's *Aḥsan al-tawārīkh*" [Minorsky, *BSOS.* ix/1 (1937) p. 254]. See also *BSOS.* x/4 (1942) p. 1026, where in a review of Ghulām Sarwar's *History of Shāh Ismā'īl Ṣafawī* Minorsky remarks "As regards the sources, he establishes two interesting facts with regard to the anonymous B.M. Or. 3248, which the lamented Sir E. D. Ross studied in his thesis (published in *JRAS.*, April 1896) : (1) he contradicts the idea that Or. 3248 is identical with the *Futūḥāt* of Ṣadr al-Dīn Harawī, and (2) suggests that the real author's name appears in a marginal note as Bījan. The note has been mutilated at the bookbinder's and cannot be read entirely, but the suggestion merits our attention."

P. 304, l. 4 from foot. [*Tārīkh i Maḥmūd b. Khwānd-Amīr.*] Also **Ellis Coll.** M. 232 (A.H. 1047/1637).

P. 305, l. 12. [*Shāh-nāmah i Ismā'īl.*] Also **Blochet** iii 1828 (A.H. 993/1585 or thereabouts), **Majlis** ii 1103 (A.H. 1060/1650), **Madrās** 129, 257 (*b*).

P. 305, l. 17. [*Shāh-nāmah i Ṭahmāsp.*] Also **Madrās** 129, 257 (*b*).

P. 305 ult. "The origin of Shāh Tahmāsp's Memoir was first and fully discussed and established by Zhukovsky in *Zap.* vi, 1891, pp. 377–383." [Minorsky, *BSOS.* ix/1 (1937) p. 254.]

P. 306, l. 3. [*Tadhkirah i Shāh Ṭahmāsp.*] Also **Ellis Coll.** M 375 (A.H. 1289/1872).

P. 306, l. 12. *Read* 1343/1924 * (See Arberry p. 509).

P. 306, l. 25. Ḥasan Rūmlū was born at Qum in 937/1530–1 according to his own statement (*Aḥsan al-tawārīkh* p. 238^{17}, Seddon's trans. p. 110).

P. 307, l. 16. [*Aḥsan al-tawārīkh.*] Also **Ellis Coll.** M 138 (vol. xii. Mainly 17th cent.), M 445 (vol. xii).

P. 308, l. 14. *Insert* :

382*a*. Qāḍī **Aḥmad Ibrāhīmī** Husainī [Qummī] b. Mīr Munshī Sharaf al-Dīn has already been mentioned (p. 1074 *supra*) in connexion with his *tadhkirah* of calligraphists and painters composed about 1006/1597–8.

Khulāṣat al-tawārīkh, a work[1] of which the fifth and last volume[2] contains a history of the Ṣafawīs undertaken by order of Shāh Ismā'īl II (A.H. 984–5/1576–8),

[1] To quote the author's words as summarised by W. Hinz : "ein neues Werk (*nosḫä-yĕ tāzä*) über die Geschichte der ṣafavīdischen Herrschaft und der Fürsten dieses Hauses . . . , zugleich mit einem Überblick über die den 'Alīden anhangenden Herrscher in einer Reihe von Bänden vom Beginn der Schöpfung bis zum Aufkommen des jetzigen Herrscherhauses.

[2] Possibly the only volume ever written.

"completed" down to 999/1590–1, dedicated to Sh̲ā̲h̲
'Abbās and extending to 1592 in the Berlin MS., which is
defective at the end : **Berlin** Preussische Staatsbibliothek
2°, 2202, **Majlis** (see *Oriens* 3/1 (1950) p. 159).
Description : *Eine neuentdeckte Quelle zur Geschichte Irans
im 16. Jahrhundert. Von Walther Hinz* (in *ZDMG.* 89/3–4
(1935) pp. 315–28).

P. 308, l. 32. [(*Tārīkh̲ i 'Abbāsī*).] Also **Madrās** 295 (?) (a fragment of 86 pp. Not identified in the catalogue, but beginning with the same words). A German translation by W. Hinz was described by him in *ZDMG.* 89/3–4 (1935) p. 315 n.2 as nearly completed in manuscript.

P. 308 penult. The author of the *Afḍal al-tawārīkh̲* is Faḍlī Iṣfahānī. [Minorsky, *BSOS.* ix/1 (1937) p. 254.]

P. 309, l. 3. [*Afḍal al-tawārīkh̲*.] Also **Eton** 172 (*a*) (vol. i, of which Rieu Suppt. 56 is the immediate continuation). [Minorsky, *ibid.*]

P. 309, ll. 11–14. [*Jang-nāmah i Kish̲m̲*.] **Vatican** p. 27 no. 66 = **Vatican** Pers. 30 (A.H. 1032/1622. Rossi p. 56). An earlier edition (?) : " *Gengnamé Kesciem, poemetto persiano c. nota di L. Bonelli*. Torino (1886) " (Harrassowitz's Bücher-Katalog 352 (1912) no. 1525).

P. 310, l. 4. Iskandar probably died in 1043/1633–4, having dealt with the first five years of Sh̲ā̲h̲ Ṣafī's reign in his *Dh̲ail i Tārīkh̲ i 'Ālam-ārāy i 'Abbāsī* (see p. 314 *supra* and the Additions and Corrections p. 1281).

P. 312, l. 19. [*Tārīkh̲ i 'Ālam-ārāy i 'Abbāsī*.] Also **Cairo** p. 505 (two copies of *Ṣaḥīfah* i, one dated A.H. 1001/1592–3, wrongly described in the catalogue as copies of the *Tārīkh̲ i 'Ālam-ārāy i Amīnī*), **Eton** 173 (*Ṣaḥīfah* ii, *Maqṣad* i to A.H. 1023/1614. See Minorsky *BSOS.* ix/1 (1937) p. 254. Wrongly described in the catalogue), **Madrās** 297 (*Ṣaḥīfah* ii), **Lincei** (see *Rendiconti* 1912 p. 116), **Caetani** 24 (A.H. 1256/1840).

P. 313, l. 7. [Iskandar Munsh̲ī.] Also *Makh̲zan al-g̲h̲arā'ib* no. 1069.

P. 313, l. 28–P. 314, l. 27. " In the previous fascicle (p. 313, No. 391) Professor Storey gave expression to the view that the history of the Safavid Sh̲ā̲h̲-Ṣafī by Muḥammad Ma'ṣūm b.

Khwājagī (Aumer 31) may be identical with the *Khulāṣat al-siyar* which Dorn, *As. Mus.*, p. 382, described as the continuation of Iskandar-munshi's *'Ālam-ārā*. Some light on the question is now thrown by Romaskevich (*Materialï po istorii Turkmen*, ii, 1928, p. 12) who confirms the view that Muhammad Ma'ṣūm's biography is found in the MS. (a detail overlooked by Dorn). The only point still obscure is how much of the book belongs respectively to Iskandar-munshī and Muḥammad B. Ma'ṣūm. In the introduction of the book it is stated that when Iskandar-munshi brought his *'Ālam-ārā* to completion, he was requested to extend his famous annals over the reign of Shah 'Abbās I's successor, Ṣafī I. After some hesitation, the aged historian (then 70 years old) started on this new work, which he began by describing the accession of Ṣafī I and by a paragraph on the education which 'Abbās I gave to the future 'Abbās II. The style of the work does not allow to discriminate between its two parts but, as Ṣafī I ruled 14 years, while Muhammad b. Ma'ṣūm says that he wrote the history of his 10 years, it would seem, Professor Romaskevich remarks, that the first four years of this shah (namely 1038–1042/1628–32) were written by Iskandar-munshi. If so, the famous historian must have lived to the age of 74 years, at least. The *Khulāṣat al-siyar* stops at the accession of 'Abbās II (1052/1642), but M. b. Ma'ṣūm records his appointment as vazīr to the governor of Qarabāgh (Ganja) Murtaḍa-quli khan Ziyād-oghlï, in the fourth year of 'Abbas II. M. b. Ma'ṣūm's previous employment recorded by Professor Storey : *ishrāf-i iṣṭabl-i nāmvār* points only to his employment as mushrif (" controller ") in the administration of the Amīrakhor-bāshī (the real Master of the Horse !)." [Minorsky, *BSOS*. x/2 (1940) p. 540.]

P. 314, l. 6. *Read* **Aumer** 231 (A.H. 1074/1663–4).

P. 314, l. 17. Edition of Iskandar Bēg's own continuation : *Dhail i Tārīkh i 'Ālam-ārāy i 'Abbāsī ta'līf i Iskandar Bēg Turkmān . . . u M. Yūsuf i mu'arrikh ba-taṣḥīḥ i Suhailī Khwānsārī*, **Tihrān** A.H.S. 1317–18/1938–9 (Iskandar probably died in 1043, having dealt with the first five years of Shāh Ṣafī.

The editor has completed the reign (p. 146[8] onwards) from the *Khuld i barīn* (see *PL.* p. 131) on the basis of a MS. in the Kitāb-khānah i Millī i Malik).

P. 316, l. 7. [*'Abbās-nāmah.*] Also **Madrās** 293 (A.H. 1184/1771), **Ellis Coll.** M 406 (18th cent.), M 405 (A.H. 1284/1868–9), **Leningrad** Univ. 1031 (Romaskewicz p. 4).

P. 316, l. 17. *Tadhkirah i Naṣrābādī*, Ṭihrān ed., pp. 17–20.

P. 317, l. 3. " Iwāghlī is undoubtedly Ev-oghlï (of this name there is a village to the north-east of Khoy, and four villages in Transcaucasia ; the term seems to correspond to the Ottoman *ev-oghlan*)." [Minorsky, *BSOS*. ix/1 (1937) p. 255. Cf. *BSOS*. x/4 (1942) p. 1028[1].]

P. 317, l. 19. [*Majma' al-inshā'.*] Possibly also **Lindesiana** p. 109 no 834 (*Murāsalāt i pādshāhān*, by Ibn Abū 'l-Qāsim Iṣfahānī. Iṣfahān, A.H. 1096/1684).

P. 317 ult. [Walī-Qulī Shāmlū.] See *Tadhkirah i Naṣrābādī* pp. 93–4.

P. 318, l. 21. *Read* Description.

P. 318, l. 30. Read *Yasāwul*. [Minorsky, *BSOS*. ix/1 (1937) p. 255.]

P. 319, l. 14. *Insert* :

399*a*. ***Tārīkh i sulṭānī***, an anonymous history of the Ṣafawids, the last date mentioned being 1163/1750 : **Ellis Coll.** M 59 (A.H. 1205/1790).

P. 319, l. 30. [*Majma' al-tawārīkh.*] *Read* **I.O.** 3750 (circ. A.D. 1906). *Insert* :

Edition : **Ṭihrān** A.H.S. 1328/1950 (ed. 'Abbās Iqbāl).

P. 319 ult. Read *nisbah*.

P. 320, l. 13. [*Fawā'id i Ṣafawīyah.*] Also **Ellis Coll.** M 23 (continued to A.H. 1231. Early 19th cent.).

P. 320, l. 7 from foot. *Zabūr i Āl i Dāwud* is without doubt the correct reading. ['Abbās Iqbāl's introduction to the *Majma' al-tawārīkh* (see addendum to p. 319, l. 30 *supra*), p. *dāl* n. 3.]

P. 321, l. 16. Read *dār al-salṭanah i Tabrīz*.

P. 321, l. 29. [*Tārīkh i pādshāhān i Ṣafawīyah.*] Presumably identical with **Madras** i 294, a history of the Ṣafawids to

Sulṭān-Ḥusain beginning *Subḥāna 'llāhi dhī 'l-mulk wa-'l-malakūt.*

P. 321, l. 15. *Insert*:

(1*a*) ***Makātīb i zamānah i salāṭīn i Ṣafawīyah,*** by 'Abd al-Ḥusain b. Adham Naṣīrī Ṭūsī: **Āṣafīyah** iii p. 110 no. 1214, **Blochet** iv 2338, **D.M.G.** 69 (2) (preface only).

P. 321, l. 30. *Insert*:

(5) ***Sharḥ i tāj-gudhārī i Shāh Sulaimān i Ṣafawī,*** by Chardin, tr. 'Alī-Riḍā Khān. Edition: **Ṭihrān** (date? See Mashhad iii, *fṣl.* 14, ptd. bks., no. 135).

(6) ***Tārīkh i rawābiṭ i Īrān u Urōpā dar daurah i Ṣafawīyah,*** by Naṣr Allāh "Falsafī"[1]: Vol. i. **Ṭihrān** A.H.S. 1316/1937–8. [R. Lescot, *Bull. E.O.I.F. de Damas*, vii–viii p. 282. Cf. *Luzac's Oriental list* 1938 p. 9.]

C. HISTORY OF PERSIA: (*l*) NĀDIR SHĀH

P. 322, l. 16. Mahdī Khān was appointed "Historiographer" in 1736 according to Catholicos Abraham (Brosset's trans. p. 312, cited by Minorsky, *Tadhkirat al-mulūk*, comm. p. 121[24]).

P. 322, l. 21. Read *Mabānī 'l-lughah.*

P. 323, l. 24. [*Tārīkh i Nādirī.*] Also **Philadelphia** Lewis Coll. p. 64 (A.H. 1187/1773), **Strassburg** 17 (defective), **Edinburgh** New Coll. p. 6. Other editions: **Tabrīz** 1264/1848 (R. Lescot, *Bull. E.O.I.F. de Damas*, vii–viii p. 282), **Bombay** 1309/1892 (*ZDMG*. 85 (1931) p. *20* no. 19033).

P. 324, l. 27. [*Durrah i nādirah.*] Also **Heidelberg** p. 367 (A.H. 1252/1836. See *Zts. f. Semit.* x/1–2 (1935) p. 97), **Leningrad** Univ. 1091 (A.H. 1255/1839–40. Romaskewicz p. 6).

P. 324, l. 28. *Read* 1854–5*.

P. 324 penult. [*Durrah i nādirah.* Editions.] Also **Tihrān** A.H.S. 1324/1945 (abridged and printed as pp. 7–60 of a volume entitled *Nādir Shāh*, which contains also (pp. 61–130) the *Tadhkirat al-aḥwāl* of "Ḥazīn", similarly abridged).

P. 325, ll. 22 and 23. Read *Akademii.*

[1] b. A.H. 1319/1901 at Ṭihrān. See D. J. Irani *Poets of the Pahlavi regime* pp. 515–41 (portrait); M. Ishaque *Sukhanvarān i Īrān* i pp. 414–17 (portrait facing p. 412), *Modern Persian poetry* pp. 12, 21. Cf. p. 1249[23] *supra*.

P. 326, l. 15. [Note on the Persian invasions of India.] Also **Bānkīpūr** Suppt. ii 2240.

P. 326, ll. 30, 31. These two lines should be transposed.

P. 328, l. 4. *Read* Malcolm's.

P. 328, l. 7. *Read* Khudāwandī.

P. 328, l. 20. *Insert*:

(11*a*) ***Nādir Shāh,*** by S. M. 'Alī, Professor, Niẓām's College, Ḥaidarābād. Edition: 1332/1914 (place? See Āṣafīyah iii p. 110).

P. 329, l. 4. *Insert*:

(14*a*) ***Tārīkh i niẓāmī i jang i Īrān u Hind,*** by Jamīl Qūzānlū: **Ṭihrān** A.H.S. 1307/1928–9 [R. Lescot, *Bull. E.O.I.F. de Damas* vii–viii p. 282].

P. 329 ult. See also *Note on James Fraser* . . ., by W. Irvine, in *JRAS.* 1899 pp. 214–20.

C. History of Persia: (*m*) The Zands

P. 330, l. 32. [*Mujmal al-tārīkh i ba'd-i-Nādirīyah.*] Also **Ellis Coll.** M 22 (A.H. 1245/1829).

P. 331, l. 3. [*Mujmal al-tārīkh*. . . .] Another edition: *Mujmal al-tawārīkh i pas az Nādir*, **Ṭihrān** (date? See *Luzac's Oriental list* 1942 p. 9).

P. 331, l. 22. *Insert*:

Edition: *Tārīkh i Gītī gushā*, **Ṭihrān** A.H.S. 1317/1938–9 (with continuations by 'Abd al-Karīm b. 'Alī Riḍā al-Sharīf (p. 276) and M. Riḍā Shīrāzī (p. 374). Edited by Sa'īd Nafīsī).

P. 332, l. 11. [*Tārīkh i Zandīyah.*] Also **Leningrad** Univ. 1136 (Romaskewicz p. 4).

C. History of Persia: (*n*) The Qājārs

P. 333, l. 15. *For* M. Nadīm "Nadīm" *read* Mīrzā M. "Nadīm".

P. 333, l. 26. [M. "Nadīm".] Also *Rauḍat al-ṣafā-yi Nāṣirī* ix fol. 178b (fifth page from end).

P. 334, l. 10. [*Shahanshāh-nāmah.*] Also **Majlis** ii 1104, **Āṣafīyah** iii p. 106 no. 1538 (?) (*Fatḥ-nāmah i Ghāzī*. A different recension? Defective), **Bānkīpūr** Suppt. i 1989 (1) (selections only), **Heidelberg** p. 249 (circ. A.D. 1850. See *Zts. f. Semit.* x/1–2 (1935) p. 94).

P. 334, l. 26. [" Ṣabā " Kāshānī.] Also *Rauḍat al-ṣafā-yi Nāṣirī* ix, 8th page from end ; Berthels *Ocherk istorii persidskoi literatury* pp. 82–6.

P. 335, l. 4. *Read* **Madrās** i 316 (A.H. 1245/1829–30).

P. 335, l. 30. ['Abd al-Razzāq Dunbulī.] Also *Rauḍat al-ṣafā-yi Nāṣirī* ix, 7th page from end ; *Dānishmandān i Ādharbāyjān* pp. 353–7.

P. 336, l. 19. [M. Ṣādiq " Humā ".] Also *Rauḍat al-ṣafā-yi Nāṣirī* ix, 9th page from end.

P. 336, l. 31. [*Tārīkh i Ṣāḥib-qirānī.*] Also **Leningrad** Univ. 1142 (Romaskewicz p. 4).

P. 336 ult. [Maḥmūd Qājār.] Also *ZDMG.* 45 (1891) p. 403 (Vambéry. Cf. p. 888 *supra*). *Insert* :

428*a*. **M. Mahdī Iṣfahānī**, known as al-Muḥibb.

Ḥikāyāt al-salāṭīn, a history of the Zands and of the Qājārs to Fatḥ-'Alī Shāh, a compilation from sources for the most part already known : **Edinburgh** New Coll. p. 6.

P. 337, l. 12. [*Tārīkh i Dhū 'l-Qarnain.*] Also **Leningrad** Univ. 1164* (Romaskewicz p. 4).

P. 337, l. 23. [" Khāwarī " Shīrāzī.] Also *Rauḍat al-ṣafā-yi Nāṣirī* ix, 7th page from end.

P. 337, l. 32. [M. Taqī 'Alī-ābādī.] Also *Rauḍat al-ṣafā-yi Nāṣirī* ix fol. 175*b* ult. (11th page from end).

P. 338, l. 24. [Abū 'l-Qāsim Farāhānī.] Also *Rauḍat al-ṣafā-yi Nāṣirī* x fol. 5*a* antepenult. ; *Ṭarā'iq al-ḥaqā'iq* ii p. 123.

P. 338, ll. 25–29. For Riḍā-Qulī Mīrzā's journey see pp. 1153–4.

P. 338, l. 30. *Read* Fatḥ-'Alī's second and eldest surviving son.

P. 339, l. 3. *Read* **'Aḍud.**

P. 339, l. 11. Jahāngīr Mīrzā was made Governor of Sāliyān in 1243/1827–8 (*Rauḍat al-ṣafā-yi Nāṣirī* ix fol. 137*a*). For a reference to the *Tārīkh i nau* see *R. al-ṣ. i N.* ix fol. 139*a*.

P. 339, l. 15. [*Tārīkh i nau.*] Edition : **Ṭihrān** A.H.S. 1327/1949 (see *Oriens* iv/1 (1951) p. 187).

P. 340, l. 4. [*Nuqṭat al-kāf.*] *Insert* :

Commentary on E. G. Browne's introduction to his edition :

Risālah i Saiyid Mahdī i Dahajī[1]: **Browne** Coll. F. 57 (vol. i only. Autograph. Cf. Browne *Materials for the study of the Bábí religion* pp. 231–3 and 237).

P. 340, l. 9. [Mīrzā Jānī Kāshānī.] Also *Ency. Isl.* under Kāshānī (T. W. Haig).

P. 340, ll. 25–7. The Persian original of 'Abd al-Aḥad Zanjānī's reminiscences is Browne Coll. F. 25 (6).

P. 341, l. 6. *Read* *Rūz-nāmah.* This is apparently the untitled edition of the Ḥakīm al-Mamālik's journal (see p. 1111 *supra*, Mashhad cat. iii, *fṣl.* 14, ptd. bks., no. 122, where it is called *Safar-nāmah i Khurāsān*, and Āṣafīyah iii p. 250 no 98, where it is called *Rūz-nāmah i Ḥakīm al-Mamālik*).

P. 342, l. 13. *Read* *'Irāq.*

P. 342, l. 13. [*Safar i 'Irāq.*] Edition: **Ṭihrān** 1311/1893–4 (see Mashhad iii, *fṣl.* 14, ptd. bks., no. 120).

P. 342, l. 15. [Nāṣir al-Dīn Shāh.] Also Zaidān *Mashāhīr al-sharq* (in Arabic) pp. 133–5.

P. 342, l. 20. *Read* 1273/1856.

P. 342, l. 24. *Read* Langues.

P. 342 antepenult. *Read* 1853–7°.

P. 343, l. 8. [*Tārīkh i Qājārīyah.*] See also the Additions and Corrections to p. 153 *supra.*

P. 343, l. 23. For Farrukh Khān see also p. 1070, n.1.

P. 344, l. 8. *Insert*:

443*a*. **Aḥmad b. Abū 'l-Ḥasan Sharīfī Shīrāzī.**

(*Tārīkh i Qājārīyah*), a history of Persia from 1212/1805 to 1286/1869: MS. in the possession of Khān Bahādur Āghā Mīrzā Muḥammad, C.I.E. Description with English translation of some extracts: *Some new notes on Babiism.* By Kh. B. Ā. M. M., C.I.E. (in *JRAS.* 1927, pp. 443–70).

P. 344, l. 21. *Read* ending with Tihrān (spelt with tā, not ṭā).

P. 344, l. 25. [*al-Ma'āthir wa-'l-āthār.*] For a more adequate description see pp. 1174–5.

P. 344, l. 27. [*al-Ma'āthir wa-'l-āthār.*] *Read*:

Edition: [**Ṭihrān**] 1306–7/1889°* (the date 1306 is given on

[1] Dahaj is near Shahr i Bābak.

the title-page, but 8 Muḥarram 1307 in the colophon on p. 294).

P. 345, l. 24. [*Tārīkh i jadīd.*] Also **Browne** Coll. Sup. 7 (transcribed by Browne from Browne Coll. F. 55 and collated with Rieu Suppt. 15).

P. 346, l. 24. *Insert*:—

447*a*. Shāh-zādah **'Abbās Mīrzā Mulk-ārā** b. Muḥammad Shāh Qājār was born in Rajab 1255/Sept.–Oct. 1839 and was thus eight years younger than his brother Nāṣir al-Dīn Shāh (for whom see pp. 340–2 *supra*). Being regarded by the latter as an enemy and as a potential claimant to the throne, he was banished to Baghdād towards the end of 1268/1852 and it was not until the end of 1294/1877 that he received permission to return to Persia. Nāṣir al-Dīn Shāh then conferred upon him the title of Mulk-ārā and appointed him Governor of Zanjān. Subsequently he held the Governorships of Qazwīn and Gīlān. Having resigned in 1313/1895–6, he was sent as Envoy Extraordinary to congratulate the Tsar Nicholas II on his accession [which occurred in November 1894]. After the assassination of Nāṣir al-Dīn Shāh [1 May 1896] he was again sent to Russia. In 1314/1896 he was appointed Minister of Justice and in 1316/1898–9 he died at Ṭihrān and was buried at Qum.

(*Sharḥ i ḥāl i 'Abbās Mīrzā Mulk-ārā*), an autobiography extending to the author's return from Russia in 1314/1896: MS. in the possession of Dr. Qāsim Ghanī (cf. p. 919 *supra*) transcribed from an autograph.

Edition: [**Ṭihrān**] A.H.S. 1325/1946 (ed. 'Abd al-Ḥusain Nawā'ī. With an introduction by 'Abbās Iqbāl (cf. p. 1085 *supra*). Nashrīyāt i Anjuman i Nashr i Āthār i Īrān, no. 1).

P. 347, l. 3. *Read* 1915°*.

P. 347, l. 23. [*Tārīkh i bīdārī i Īrāniyān.*] The place and date are Ṭihrān 1328 [1910] according to Berthels *Ocherk istorii persidskoi literatury* p. 202.

P. 348, l. 6. *Insert*:

(5) *Dawn-breakers, The; Nabīl's*[1] *narrative of the*

[1] "Nabīl" Zarandī died in 1892 (see Browne *Lit. Hist.* iv pp. 151 n., 187 n., etc.).

early days of the Bahá'í revelation . . . Translated from the original Persian and edited by Shoghi Effendi : **New York** (Kingsport, Tennessee, printed) 1932* (685 pp.).

(6) *Fārs u jang i bain al-milal*, by Rukn-zādah Ādamīyat : **Ṭihrān** A.H.S. 1312/1933*.

(7) *Inqilāb u taḥawwul i Ādharbāyjān*, the history of Sattār Khān,[1] etc., by Ḥusain Farzād : **Ṭihrān** (see *Luzac's O.L.* 1946 p. 104, where the date is not mentioned).

(8) *Īrān u Ingilīs*, by Mahdī Mujtahidī : A.H.S. 1326/1947 (see the same author's *Rijāl i Ādharbayjān*, fly-leaf at end).

(9) *Julūs i Muẓaffarī*, on the events connected with the accession of Muẓaffar al-Dīn Shāh : **Majlis** 678.

(10) *Kitāb i sabz i bī-ṭarafī i Īrān* : **Ṭihrān** 1336–7/1917–19 (2 vols. See R. Lescot, *Bull. E.O.I.F. de Damas* vii–viii p. 282).

(11) *Mukhtaṣarī az zindagānī i siyāsī i Sulṭān Aḥmad Shāh Qājār*, by Ḥusain Makkī : **Ṭihrān** A.H.S. 1323/1944–5 (see an unsigned review in the periodical *Sukhan*, Yr. ii/2 (Bahman 1323) p. 152).

(12) *Rawābiṭ i Napōliyōn u Īrān*, by 'Abbās Mīrzā : **Ṭihrān** n.d. [R. Lescot, *Bull. E.O.I.F. de Damas* vii–viii p. 282.]

(13) *Taḥawwulāt i siyāsī i niẓām i Īrān*, by Qā'im-maqāmī : **Ṭihrān** A.H.S. 1326/1947 (see Probsthain's *Orientalia nova* 2 (1946–8) p. 27).

(14) *Tārīkh i ijtimā'ī u idārī i daurah i Qājār*, by 'Abd Allāh Mustaufī[2] : **Ṭihrān** A.H.S. 1324/1945 onwards. (vol. i, 728 pp., Probsthain's *Orientalia nova* 1 (1944–6) p. 16, "Part 2" (= vol. ii ?), 720 pp., *Luzac's O.L.* 1945 p. 79, vol. iii, pt. 2 (1300–4), 539 pp., Probsthain's *Orientalia nova* 2 (1946–8) p. 28, *Luzac's O.L.* 1948 p. 12.) Cf. p. 1179 *supra*.

(15) *Tārīkh i inqilāb i mashrūṭīyat i Īrān*, by Mahdī Malik-zādah, in 7 vols. : **Ṭihrān** A.H.S. 1328/1949– , *in progress* (vol. i 1328, vol. ii 1329).

[1] For whom see Browne *History of the Persian revolution*; *Yādgār* v/1–2 pp. 96–99 (a biography by M. Qazwīnī); *Rijāl i Ādharbāyjān* pp. 85–7.

[2] A work by this author entitled *Inqilāb i Farānisah* is mentioned in Yāsimī's *Adabīyāt i mu'āṣir* p. 113.

(16) *Tārīkh i jang i Ingilīs u Īrān* (mentioned, without author's name or date, in the list of the *Intishārāt i majallah i Yādgār* on the back cover of the *Simṭ al-'ulā*).

(17) *Tārīkh i jarā'id u majallāt i Īrān,* an alphabetical dictionary of newspapers and periodicals, by M. Ṣadr Hāshimī : **Iṣfahān** A.H.S. 1327/1948– *in progress* (vol. i (*Alif*), 351 pp., vol. ii (*Bā'* to *Rā'*), 339 pp., A.H.S. 1328/1950).

(18) *Tārīkh i mashrūṭah i Īrān* by S. Aḥmad Kasrawī Tabrīzī (for whom see pp. 242, 366 *supra*) : **Ṭihrān** (2nd ed. See *Luzac's O.L.* 1942 p. 9, where the date is not mentioned, and Mahdī Mujtahidī's *Rijāl i Ādharbāyjān* p. 129).

(19) *Tārīkh i rawābiṭ i siyāsī i Īrān ba-dunyā,* by Najaf-Qulī Mu'izzī[1] (Ḥusām al-Daulah) : **Ṭihrān** (See *Luzac's Oriental list* 1946 p. 105, where the date is not mentioned.)

(20) *Tārīkh i rawābiṭ i siyāsī i Īrān u Ingilīs dar qarn i nūzdahum i mīlādī,* by Maḥmūd i Maḥmūd : **Ṭihrān** (vol. i. See *Luzac's Oriental list* 1950 p. 38 (date not mentioned), vol. ii, see *LOL.* 1950 p. 59 (date not mentioned).)

(21) *Wāqi'āt i dū-sālah yā Tārīkh i bad-bakhtī i Īrān,* by Ḥājjī Āqā Shīrāzī : **Ṭihrān** 1330/1912 [R. Lescot, *Bull. E.O.I.F. de Damas* vii–viii p. 282].

(22) *Yāddāshthā'ī az zindagānī i khuṣūṣī i Nāṣir al-Dīn Shāh,* by Dūst-'Alī Khān Mu'aiyir al-Mamālik (b. Dūst-Muḥammad Khān Mu'aiyir al-Mamālik), whose mother was 'Iṣmat al-Daulah, a daughter of Nāṣir al-Dīn Shāh : [**Ṭihrān**, 1946 ?] (188 pp.).

C. History of Persia : (o) Riḍā Shāh Pahlawī (b. 16.3.1878, acc. 12.12.1925, d. 26.7.1944) and his Dynasty

P. 348, l. 8. 'Abd Allāh Khān Amīr Ṭahmāsb, having skilfully pacified Ādharbāyjān, was appointed Minister of War by Riḍā Shāh Pahlawī and subsequently Minister of Roads. He was murdered by Lurs on the road between Khurramābād

[1] Works by this author entitled *Tārīkh i Amrīkā* and *Sukhanwarān i 'aṣr i Pahlawī* are mentioned in Yāsimī's *Adabīyāt i mu'āṣir* p. 113.

and Burūjird, when on a visit of inspection. See Ḥabīb Allāh Mukhtārī's *Tārīkh i bīdārī i Īrān* pp. 349⁹-351 (portrait).

P. 348, l. 12. *Insert*:

452a. M. R. **Hazār**.

Daurān i Pahlawī : <u>Sh</u>irāz A.H. 1336/1917–18. [R. Lescot, *Bull. E.O.I.F. de Damas* vii–viii p. 282.]

452b. Ḥabīb Allāh "**Naubakht**", *nigārandah i majallah i Qushūn*, was born at <u>Sh</u>īrāz in 1284/1905. Among his publications are the educational works *Qānūn i fikr* and *'Ilm i ṭabā'i'*.

(1) *Shāhanshāh i Pahlawī* : Ṭihrān n.d. (Pt. i, years 1301-8/1923–30. Pp. 320, 7). [Minorsky, *BSOS*. ix/1 (1937) p. 254; R. Lescot, *Bull. E.O.I.F. de Damas* vii–viii p. 282; *Dharī'ah* iii p. 259.]

(2) *Shāh-nāmah*, or *Pahlawī-nāmah*, a history of Persia, in verse, from the fall of the Sāsānians to the beginning of the Pahlawī dynasty in six parts : vol. i (= pts. 1–3) Ṭihrān [1932*] (cf. *Luzac's O.L.* 1933 p. 14).
[Irani *Poets of the Pahlavi regime* pp. 619–25; Yāsimī *Adabīyāt i mu'āṣir* pp. 99, 113, 116; Ishaque *Modern Persian poetry* pp. 105, 112, 116; M. Ṣadr Hā<u>sh</u>imī *Tārīkh i jarā'id u majallāt i Īrān* ii pp. 32–6 (portrait).]

452c. **Ja'far Saiyāḥ**.

Pahlawī-nāmah, in verse : Ṭihrān A.H.S. 1313/1934–5. [R. Lescot, *Bull. E.O.I.F. de Damas* vii–viii p. 282.]

452d. **Ḥabīb Allāh Mukhtārī** Mukhtār al-Salṭanah, the son of Karīm <u>Kh</u>ān Mukhtār al-Salṭanah Sardār i Manṣūr, has held various military commands and administrative appointments connected with the Persian army (for some details see *Tārīkh i bīdārī i Īrān* p. [923] and for a portrait *op. cit.* p. 1).

Tārīkh i bīdārī i Īrān, a history of Persia under the Pahlawī dynasty to 1946 preceded by a summary account of the last thirty years of Qājār rule : Ṭihrān 1326/1947 (923 pp. Many illustrations).

452*e*. Other works [1]:—

(1) ***Pīsh-rafthā-yi Īrān***, by Sa'īd Nafīsī (cf. p. 918 *supra*): **Ṭihrān** (see *Luzac's O.L.* 1939 p. 177, where the date is not mentioned).

(2) ***Az Shahrīwar tā fāji'ah i Ādharbāyjān u Zanjān***, on the events of A.H.S. 1320/1941 and the following years, by Ḥusain Kūhī Kirmānī: **Ṭihrān** n.d. [1947. See Probsthain's *Orientalia nova* 2 (1946–8) p. 27 no. 424].

(3) ***Siyāsat i daulat i Shūrawī dar Īrān az 1296*** [1917–18] ***tā 1306*** [1927–8], by M. 'A. Manshūr Garakānī: **Ṭihrān** A.H.S. 1326/1948‡ (vol. i).

(4) ***Tārīkh i bīst-sālah i Īrān***, by Ḥusain Makkī: **Ṭihrān** A.H.S. 1323–4/1944–5 (vol. i: the coup d'état of 1299, vol. ii: the change of dynasty. See Probsthain's *Orientalia nova*, i (1944–6) p. 16). Cf. p. 1349 *infra*.

(5) ***Tārīkh i mukhtaṣar i aḥzāb i siyāsī i Īrān***, by Malik al-Shu'arā' "Bahār" [2]: **Ṭihrān** A.H.S. 1323/1944 (vol. i (the fall of the Qājār dynasty). See *Luzac's O.L.* 1945 p. 6, where the date is not mentioned, Probsthain's *Orientalia nova* 1 (1944–6) p. 15, and a review by B. Ṣ. in the periodical *Sukhan*, Yr. ii/2 (Bahman 1323/1945) p. 151). Cf. Machalski in *Rocz. Orient.* xv pp. 107–8.

C. History of Persia: (p) Qum

P. 349, l. 7. *Insert*:

Description: *An account of the Tārīkhi Qumm, by Ann K. S. Lambton* (in *BSOAS*. xii/3–4 (1948) pp. 586–96).

P. 349, l. 8. *Read* Sh. **M. 'Alī b. Ḥusain** b. 'Alī b. Bahā' al-Dīn, a resident of Qum.

P. 349, ll. 8–9. *For* wrote in 1302/1884–5 *read* began in 1325/1907.

[1] No attempt has been made to deal at all fully with the publications of contemporary Persian historians, which scarcely fall within the scope of the present work.

[2] Mīrzā M. Taqī, the son of M. Kāẓim "Ṣabūrī" Kāshānī, was born at Mashhad in 1304/1886–7. See Browne *The press and poetry of modern Persia* pp. 260–89 (portraits), etc., *Lit. Hist.* iv p. 345; D. J. Irani *Poets of the Pahlavi regime* pp. 196–226 (portrait); M. Ishaque *Sukhanvarān-i-Īrān* i pp. 358–403 (portrait), *Modern Persian poetry* pp. 10, 24, etc.; Rashīd Yāsimī *Adabīyāt i mu'āṣir* pp. 30–32 (portrait).

P. 349, l. 10. The title, not formally mentioned in the preface, is given on the title-page as *Tārīkh i Qum musammā bi-Anwār al-Mushaʿshaʿīn*. P. 2 is headed *Hādhā jild* [*sic*] *al-awwal min kitāb Anwār al-Mushaʿshaʿīn fī sharāfat al-Qum* [*sic*] *wa-'l-Qummīyīn* . . . In the first of the publisher's two colophons the work is called *Tārīkh i Qum* and in the second *Anwār al-Mushaʿshiʿīn* [*sic*]. The volume is described by the author as vol. i. There is a copy in the Cambridge University Library.

P. 349, l. 11. *Insert*:

454*a*. S. **ʿAlī Akbar "Kāshif"** b. S. Raḍī **Burqaʿī** Qummī, already mentioned as the author of the *Kākh i dilāwīz* (p. 1136 *supra*), was born at Qum in A.H.S. 1278/1899–1900 (see *Sukhanwarān i nāmī i muʿāṣir*, by his son, S. M. Bāqir Burqaʿī, p. 190).

Rāhnumā-yi Qum, "History and Geography of Qum": **Ṭihrān** (see *Luzac's O.L.* 1939 p. 177, where the date is not mentioned).

C. History of Persia: (*q*) Iṣfahān

P. 349, l. 22. *Read* al-ʿAlawī al-Āwī *according to the printed text, p. 1 penult.*

P. 349, l. 25. [*Maḥāsin i Iṣfahān.*] *Insert*:

Edition of the Persian translation: *T. i M. i I.*, **Ṭihrān** A.H.S. 1328/1949‡ (ed. ʿAbbās Iqbāl).

P. 349, l. 3 from foot. M. Mahdī Arbāb b. M. Riḍā Iṣfahānī, the father of M. Ḥusain Khān "Furūghī" (see *PL.* p. 240 and the corrigenda to that page) died in 1314/1896–7 (see ʿAbd al-Karīm Jazī's *Rijāl i Iṣfahān* p. 232).

P. 350, l. 5. [*Niṣf i jahān.*] Also **London** S.O.A.S. Per. 28 (A.H. 1315/1897). *Insert*:

456*a*. **Ḥasan** b. ʿAlī b. Maḥmūd **Jābirī Anṣārī** Iṣfahānī was born in 1287/1870–1 and was still alive [in 1950 ?] when S. Muṣliḥ al-Dīn Mahdawī gave a brief account of him in his preface to ʿAbd al-Karīm Jazī's *Rijāl i Iṣfahān* (p. *hā*). His works amount to more than twenty.

(1) *Nīm-jahān*, a concise history of Iṣfahān composed in 1333/1915 and containing at the end biographies of its

celebrities together with a sketch of universal history ("*wa-fī dhailihi ta'rīkh 'umūmī nāfi' mufīd*", *Dharī'ah* iii p. 233[4]). Edition : 1333/1915 (see *Dharī'ah* iii p. 232, where the place of publication, doubtless Iṣfahān, is not mentioned).

(2) ***Tārīkh i niṣf i jahān u hamah i jahān,*** probably identical with the preceding or a new edition of it : **Iṣfahān** n.d. [R. Lescot *Bull. E.O.I.F. de Damas*, vii–viii p. 282].

(3) ***Tārīkh i Iṣfahān u Rai*** (mentioned by S. Muṣliḥ al-Dīn Mahdawī, *loc. cit.*, without specification of the date and place of publication).

456*c*. Mīr S. **'Alī Janāb** b. M. Bāqir b. M. Ḥusain (Mīr S. 'A. b. M. B. b. M. Ḥ. *al-mushtahir bi*-Janāb) was born at Iṣfahān in 1287/1870–1 and died at Tihrān in Shawwāl 1349/Feb.–March 1931 (see 'Abd al-Karīm Jazī *Rijāl i Iṣfahān*, editor's preface, p. *dāl*).

al-Iṣfahān [*sic*], an account, historical, topographical, statistical, etc., begun in Shawwāl 1342/May 1924 : **Iṣfahān** A.H.S. 1303/1924‡ (vol. i only. Cf. *Dharī'ah* iii p. 233).

456*d*. **Ḥusain Nūr Ṣādiqī** was born on 24 Shawwāl 1328/29 October 1910 (see 'Abd al-Karīm's *Rijāl i Iṣfahān*, editor's preface, p. *wāw*).

Iṣfahān : **Ṭihrān** "1938" (see Harrassowitz's *Litterae orientales* Oct. 1938 p. 15 and *Luzac's O.L.* 1938, p. 71).

P. 350, l. 15. *Insert* :

C. History of Persia : (*r**) Yazd

457*a*. **Aḥmad b. Ḥusain b. 'Alī** al-Kātib wrote in the reign of Jahān-Shāh [of the Qarā-Quyūnlū, A.H. 839–72/1435–67].

Tārīkh i jadīd, extending to 862/1458 : **Majlis** (not in the published catalogues, but see "Āyatī's" *Tārīkh i Yazd* p. 17[20]).

Edition : *T. i j. i Yazd* : **Yazd** A.H.S. 1317/1938‡.

457*b*. **M. Mufīd** Mustaufī b. Najm al-Dīn Maḥmūd Bāfqī **Yazdī** (see p. 352 *supra*).

Jāmi' i Mufīdī (see p. 352, where this work is erroneously placed, since Yazd, though anciently in Fārs and so treated, for example, in the *Fārs-nāmah* and by Yāqūt, has for some centuries been regarded as a part of ʻIrāq i ʻAjamī).

457*c*. **M. Ṭāhir Mālmīrī.**

Tārīkh i Shuhadā i Yazd : **Cairo** 1342/1923–4 [R. Lescot, *Bull. E.O.I.F. de Damas* vii–viii p. 283].

457*d*. **ʻAbd al-Ḥusain "Āyatī"** (formerly "Āwārah") b. Ḥājj Sh. M. was born at Taft in 1288/1871. In 1320/1902–3 he became a convert to Bahāism and for a number of years he travelled extensively as a missionary of that faith. In 1923 he published at Cairo a history entitled *al-Kawākib al-durrīyah fī ma'āthir al-Bahā'īyah*,[1] but he later abandoned Bahāism and published a three-volume attack on it under the title *Kashf al-ḥiyal*. The monthly periodical *Namakdān* founded by him in 1929 was edited by him until its discontinuance in 1935.

Tārīkh i Yazd (on the wrapper, but not on the title-page, is added *yā Ātash-kadah i Yazdān*), completed A.H.S. 1317/1938–9 : **Yazd** A.H.S. 1317/1938–9.

[Autobiography in *Tārīkh i Yazd* p. 277 (portrait) ; M. Ishaque *Sukhanvarān-i-Īrān* ii pp. 8–14 (portrait), *Modern Persian poetry* pp. 9, 18, 41, 196, etc.]

457*e*. **Aḥmad Ṭāhirī.**

Tārīkh i Yazd : **Ṭihrān** (See *Luzac's O.L.* 1939 p. 75, where the date is not mentioned.)

C. History of Persia : (*s*) Fārs

P. 351, l. 27. [*Shīrāz-nāmah.*] Also **I.O.** 4615 (A.H. 1075/1665. See *JRAS*. 1939 p. 384), **Ellis Coll.** M. 183 (A.H. 1287/1871).

P. 351, l. 28. Dorn 305 and Dorn A.M. p. 374 are the same MS.

P. 352, ll. 4–25. [*Jāmiʻ i Mufīdī.*] This article is misplaced : see the addenda to p. 350, l. 15.

P. 353, l. 18. [*Fārs-nāmah i Nāṣirī.*] *Insert* :

Abridged translation of the two sections relating to the tribes in the final chapter : *Hajji Mirza Hasan-i-Shirazi on the*

[1] An Arabic translation from the (doubtless unpublished) Persian : see Brockelmann *Sptbd.* ii p. 847 $^{11-13}$, where the date is given as 1343/1924.

nomad tribes of Fars in the Fars-nameh-i-Nasiri. By D. Austin Lake (in *JRAS*. 1923 pp. 209–31).

P. 353, l. 19. M. Naṣīr "Furṣat" b. "Bahjat" Ḥusainī Shīrāzī entitled (*mulaqqab*) Furṣat al-Daulah was born in 1271/1854–5 according to Majlis 323, where a collection of his poems (*Ash'ār i Furṣat*) is described. Cf. Ishaque *Modern Persian poetry* pp. 33 n., 82, where the date of his death is given as 1339/1920. A collection of his poems, *Dabistān al-furṣah*, was published at Bombay in 1334/1916* with a biography by Ibrāhīm Adīb "Sākit". Presumably he is identical with the Furṣat Shīrāzī whose *Āthār i salāṭīn i 'aẓīm al-sha'n i 'ahd i qadīm i bāstān i mamlakat i Īrān* was published at Ṭihrān in 1354/1935 (see Harrassowitz's *Litterae Orientales*, Oct. 1938 p. 10 no. 823).

P. 353, l. 21. *For* south-eastern *read* south-western.

P. 353, l. 22. *Insert*:

465*a*. **Rukn-zādah "Ādamīyat".**

Fārs u jang i bain al-milal: **Ṭihrān** A.H.S. 1312/1933*.

C. HISTORY OF PERSIA : (*t*) KHURĀSĀN

P. 353, l. 27. ['Alī b. Zaid Baihaqī.] The correct date of his birth is 493 (see *Tārīkh i Baihaq*, editor's preface, p. YB).

P. 354, l. 4. A fragmentary MS. of the *Wishāḥ Dumyat al-qaṣr* preserved in the Chelebī Ḥusain Library at Brusa was described by O. Rescher in *ZDMG*. 68 (1914) p. 52.

P. 354, l. 17. [*Tārīkh i Baihaq*.] Edition: **Ṭihrān** A.H.S. 1317/1937‡ (ed. Aḥmad Bahmanyār. With prefaces by the editor and by M. Qazwīnī).

Extracts: (**1**) [concerning the author's family] *OCM*. ix/2 (Feb. 1933) pp. 107–20 (ed. M. Shafī'). (**2**) [concerning the Niẓām al-Mulk and his family] *OCM*. v/1 (Nov. 1928) pp. 76–80, v/2 (Feb. 1929) pp. 85–94 (ed. M. Shafī').

P. 354, l. 18. ['Alī b. Zaid Baihaqī.] The reference to the *Kharīdat al-qaṣr* [*sic lege*] should be deleted. The person whose biography occurs in that work, and to whom 'Imād al-Dīn erroneously ascribes the *Wishāḥ Dumyat al-qaṣr* is Sharaf al-Dīn 'Alī b. al-Ḥasan al-Baihaqī, of whom there is a notice in the *Tārīkh i Baihaq*, pp. 225–6. See M. Shafī''s remarks in *Islamic culture* vi/4 (Oct. 1932) pp. 595–6.

P. 354, l. 19. ['Alī b. Zaid Baihaqī.] Also *The author of the oldest biographical notice of 'Umar Khayyam & the notice in question*, by M. Shafī' (in *Islamic culture* vi/4 (Oct. 1932) pp. 586–623); M. Shafī''s introduction to his edition of the *Tatimmat Ṣiwān al-ḥikmah* (cf. p. 1106 *supra*); Brockelmann *Sptbd.* i pp 557–8; M. Qazwīnī's preface to the *Tārīkh i Baihaq*, Ṭihrān A.H.S. 1317/1937.

P. 355, l. 2. [*Tārīkh i Mulūk i Kart.*] Also **Kābul** State Library (see *Journal asiatique*, Jan. 1924, p. 150). [Minorsky, *BSOS*. ix/1 (1937) p. 255.]

P. 355, l. 25. [*Rauḍāt al-jannāt.*] Also **Ellis Coll.** M. 288 (A.H. 1073/1663).

P. 356, l. 11. [*Maqṣad al-iqbāl al-Sulṭānīyah.*] Presumably this is the same work as

Mazārāt i Harāt, by 'Abd Allāh b. 'Abd al-Raḥmān Ḥusainī: **Harāt** A.H.S. 1310/1931–2 (with a supplement by 'Ubaid Allāh Abū Sa'īd Harawī). [R. Lescot, *Bull. E.O.I.F. de Damas*, vii–viii p. 283.]

P. 356, l. 31. *Read* 1301/1884°*–1303/1886°*.

P. 356, l. 24. *Insert*:

471*a*. Other works relating to Khurāsān :—

(1) *Āthār i Harāt*,[1] by Khalīl Afghān: **Harāt** A.H.S. 1309–10/1930–2 (3 vols.). [R. Lescot, *Bull. E.O.I.F. de Damas* vii–viii p. 283.]

(2) *Faḍā'il i Balkh*,[1] an anonymous translation made at the request of the Qāḍī *Majlis i 'ālī Ṣadr i kabīr* Fakhr al-Dīn Abū Bakr 'Abd Allāh b. Abū 'l-Farīd al-Balkhī (but this name, written in place of a name erased, may not be genuine) from an Arabic work in three sections ((1) traditions concerning the superiority of Balkh, (2) a description of the town, (3) biographies of seventy celebrated *shaikhs* connected with the neighbourhood) completed at Balkh on 1 Ramaḍān 610/14 January 1214 by the Shaikh al-Islām Abū Bakr b. 'Abd Allāh [b.] 'Umar b. Dāwud al-Wā'iẓ Ṣafī al-Dīn al-Balkhī (but this name, occurring

[1] Both Harāt and Balkh are of course now in Afghānistān.

in the translator's preface, has likewise been written in place of a name erased) : **Blochet** i 519 (lacks last six " sections " (biographies ?). Late 15th cent.). Edition of Sections i and ii : Schefer *Chrestomathie persane*, tome i (3).

(3) *Tārīkh i inqilāb i Ṭūs*, by M. Ḥasan Harawī : **Mashhad** 1339/1920–1. [R. Lescot, *Bull. E.O.I.F. de Damas*, vii–viii p. 283.]

(4) *Tārīkh i mazārāt i Balkh*, written in the reign of 'Abd al-Mu'min Khān b. 'Abd Allāh Khān Uzbak [A.H. 1006–7/1598–9] by M. Ṣāliḥ b. Amīr 'Abd Allāh b. Amīr 'Abd al-Raḥmān : **Kābul** National Library (see A. Z. Validi in *Journal asiatique*, Jan.–March 1924 p. 150). [Minorsky, *BSOS*. ix/1 (1937) p. 255.]

(5) *Tārīkh i muḥāṣarah u fatḥ i Harāt*, on the taking of Harāt by the Persians in the Anglo-Persian War, by Mīrzā Ibrāhīm Badā'i'-nigār : **Ṭihrān** 1273/1856–7. [R. Lescot, *Bull. E.O.I.F. de Damas* vii–viii p. 283.]

(6) *Tārīkh i wāqi'ah i Mashhad i Muqaddas*, on the bombardment of Mashhad by the Russians, anonymous : **Mashhad** 1330/1912. [R. Lescot, *ibid.*]

C. History of Persia : (*u*) Kirmān

P. 357, l. 16. [*Badā'i' al-azmān.*] *Insert* :

Incomplete reconstruction of the work from quotations in the *Jāmi' al-tawārīkh i Ḥasanī* (cf. p. 91 *supra*) and M. b. Ibrāhīm's *Tārīkh i Saljūqiyān i Kirmān* (cf. p. 358 *supra*) : *Tārīkh i Afḍal yā Badā'i' al-azmān fī waqā'i' Kirmān . . . farāham āwardah i Duktur Mahdī Bayānī*, **Ṭihrān** A.H.S. 1326/1948 (Intishārāt i Dānish-gāh i Ṭihrān, 15).

P. 358, l. 7. [*Simṭ al-'ulā.*] Edition : **Ṭihrān** A.H.S. 1328/1949 (ed. 'Abbās Iqbāl with help from M. Qazwīnī).

P. 359, l. 22. *Insert* :

476*a*. Major **Sykes** (i.e. presumably Sir Percy Sykes, b. 1867, d. 11.6.1945,[1] who became British Consul for Kirmān and Persian Balūchistān in 1894 and who is best known for his *History of Persia* (2 vols., London 1915, 2nd ed. 1921,

[1] For obituary notices see *The Times* 12.6.1945 ; *Luzac's O.L.* 1945 p. 28 ; etc.

3rd ed. 1930), of which the first volume (at least) has appeared in a Persian translation [1] (see *Luzac's O.L.* 1945 p. 79)).

Tārīkh i Kirmān, translated by Mīr Naṣr Allāh Khān Nawwāb Shīrāzī from the unpublished English original: **Kirmān** 1322/1904–5. [R. Lescot, *Bull. E.O.I.F. de Damas* vii–viii p. 283.]

C. HISTORY OF PERSIA: (*w*) ṬABARISTĀN

P. 360, l. 16. [Ibn Isfandiyār's *Tārīkh i Ṭabaristān*.] Edition: **Ṭihrān** A.H.S. 1320/1941–2 (Pt. 1. 331 pp. Cf. *Luzac's O.L.* 1942 p. 66, 1947 p. 39).

P. 360 ult. Cf. also *Acta Orientalia* x (1931) pp. 45–55 (Christensen).

C. HISTORY OF PERSIA: (*x*) GĪLĀN

P. 363 ult. [*Tārīkh i Gīlān*.] Another edition: **Rasht** A.H.S. 1315/1936–7. [R. Lescot, *Bull. E.O.I.F. de Damas* vii–viii p. 283.]

C. HISTORY OF PERSIA: (*z*) KHŪZISTĀN

P. 365, l. 18. [*Tadhkirah i Shūshtarīyah*.] Also **Ellis Coll.** M. 9 (A.H. 1322/1904).

P. 366, l. 13. *Insert*:

488*a*. S. **Ṣadr al-Dīn Ẓahīr-al-Islām-zādah Dizfūlī.**

Shakaristān dar tārīkh i sih-hazār-sālah i Khūzistān: **Ṭihrān** A.H.S. 1308/1929–30. [R. Lescot, *Bull. E.O.I.F. de Damas* vii–viii p. 283.]

P. 366, l. 21. S. Aḥmad Kasrawī was murdered in Ṭihrān towards the end of A.H.S. 1324/1945–6. See *Rijāl i Ādharbāyjān*, by Mahdī Mujtahidī, pp. 126–31, 223–4, and, for a portrait, the frontispiece to *Maqālāt i Kasrawī* (*Essays from Kasrawi, collected by Y. Zoka*), pt. 1 (Ṭihrān A.H.S. 1327/1948).

P. 366, l. 24. [*Tārīkh i pānṣad-sālah i Khūzistān*.] "On the rare sources utilized by Kasravī in his book on Khūzistān see my review in *BSOS*. viii 4, p. 1173." [Minorsky, *BSOS*. ix/1 (1937) p. 255.]

[1] His *Ten thousand miles in Persia* (London 1902) has been translated by Ḥusain Sa'ādat Nūrī under the title *Hasht sāl dar Īrān yā dah hazār mīl sair dar kishwar i Shāhanshāhī* (2 vols. Iṣfahān and Ṭihrān A.H.S. 1315–16/1936–7. See Harrassowitz's *Litterae orientales* April–July 1939 p. 18).

P. 366, l. 25. *Insert :*

C. HISTORY OF PERSIA : (*aa*) THE BAKHTYĀRĪS

489*a*. **'Abd al-Ḥusain Khān Lisān al-Salṭanah** Malik al-Mu'arrikhīn.

(1) *Tārīkh i Bakhtyārī,* a history covering the years 1004–1299/1692–1882 composed in 1327/1909 by order of Ḥājjī 'Alī-Qulī Khān Sardār i As'ad Wazīr i Jang b. Ḥusain-Qulī Khān Īlkhānī Bakhtyārī : Maṭba'ah i Mīrzā 'Alī Aṣghar [place ?] n.d. (Camb. Univ. Lib. Moh. 591.A.3).

(2) *Khulāṣat al-a'ṣār fī ta'rīkh al-Bakhtiyār :* **Ṭihrān** 1333/1915. [R. Lescot, *Bull. E.O.I.F. de Damas* vii–viii p. 283.]

C. HISTORY OF PERSIA : (*bb*) ĀDHARBĀYJĀN

489*b*. **'Abd al-Razzāq** Bēg b. Najaf-Qulī Khān **Dunbulī** died in 1243/1827–8 (see p. 334 *supra*).

Tārīkh i Danābilah (cf. p. 334 penult. and *BSOS*. ix/1 (1937) p. 254, where Minorsky remarks " Under ' local histories ' Ādharbāyjān ought to be represented by the history of the Dunbulī rulers of Khoy and Tabrīz by 'Abd al-Razzāq Dunbulī . . . ", but no MSS. or editions seem to be recorded in the catalogues. According to *Dharī'ah* iii p. 253 the title of the work is *Riyāḍ al-jannah*).

489*c*. **Nādir Mīrzā** b. Badī' al-Zamān b. M.-Qulī b. Fatḥ-'Alī Shāh **Qājār** wrote a work on Persian cookery (title ?) and another entitled *Nawādir i Nādirī* on Arabic proverbs (see *Dānishmandān i Ādharbāyjān* p. 367 ; Īraj Afshār *Nathr i Fārsī i mu'āṣir* pp. 12, 14–16 (portrait)).

Tārīkh u jughrāfiyā-yi dār al-salṭanah i Tabrīz : **Ṭihrān** [A.H. 1323 (1905) according to Īraj Afshār, but according to Minorsky (*Acta Orientalia* xxi (1951) p. 122) the work, edited in 1905 [1323] by " Sipihr " [cf. *PL*. p. 227], was not published until circ. 1940].

489*d*. Ḥājjī **M. Bāqir.**

Tārīkh i inqilāb i Ādharbāyjān u balwā-yi Tabrīz : **Tabrīz** 1326/1908. [R. Lescot, *Bull. E.O.I.F. de Damas* vii–viii p. 283.]

489*e*. S. Aḥmad **Kasrawī Tabrīzī** (see pp. 366, 1298 *supra*).
(1) *Tārīkh i hijdah-sālah i Ādharbāyjān :* **Tabrīz** A.H.S. 1314–16/1935–8. [R. Lescot, *ibid.*]
(2) *Shahriyārān i gum-nām* (see p. 242 (5) *supra*).

D. History of Kurdistān

P. 369, ll. 22–4. "The histories of the vālīs of Ardalān are in Persian : *Ḥadīqa-yi Nāṣirī* by 'Alī-Akbar (towards A.H. 1310) and the history of Mastūra (= Māh-sharaf khānum). Of the latter I possessed a copy which was said to be an autograph ; the MS. was stolen from me in Tehran." [Minorsky, *BSOS*. ix/1 (1937) p. 255.]

"Māh-i-Sharaf Khānūm, connue en poésie sous le *takhalloṣ* de Mastūre fī'l-wāqi' (elle aurait laissé un diwan de 20,000 vers), morte en 1264 à 44 ans, est l'auteur d'une histoire des émirs d'Ardelan, composée en 1247. Un manuscrit de cet ouvrage est conservé dans la bibliothèque du Dr. Sa'īd Khān (Téhéran). Il est daté de 1339. Les premières pages manquent." [R. Lescot, *Bull. E.O.I.F. de Damas* vii–viii p. 283.]

"Mīrzā 'Alī Akbar Monshī Vaqā'i' Negār, *Ḥadīqe-i-nāṣerīye*. Histoire des émirs d'Ardelan composée en 1309 lunaire. Le Dr. Sa'īd Khān en possède une copie executée en 1316." [R. Lescot, *ibid.*]

P. 369, l. 24. *Insert* :
494*a*. **'Alī Aṣghar Hamadānī.**
Kurdistān : **Tabrīz** 1312/1894–5. [R. Lescot, *ibid.*]

E. History of Central Asia : (1) Bukhārā, etc.

P. 370, l. 12. [*Tārīkh i Bukhārā.*] Also **Tashkent Univ.** 68 (2) (A.H. 1304/1886–7).

P. 370, l. 20. [*Tārīkh i Bukhārā.*] Another edition (of M. b. Zufar's abridgment) : **Tihrān** [1939] (preface dated Isfandmāh 1317 [1939]. Ed. Mudarris Riḍawī. 128 (not 178) pp. Cf. *Luzac's OL*. 1939 p. 75).

P. 371, l. 23. [*Qandīyah.* Persian trans.] Also **Upsala** Zetterstéen 402 (defective).

P. 371, l. 33. *Read* "**Banā'ī**". Cf. p. 1278 *supra*.

P. 372, l. 14. *Read* Bābur's.

P. 372, l. 25. *Read* ***Mīhmān-nāmah.***

P. 373, ll. 1–15. [" Wāṣifī ", *Badā'i' al-waqā'i'.*] See an article by A. N. Boldyrev in the *Trudy* of the Oriental Section of the Hermitage Museum at Leningrad, vol. ii (1940) pp. 203–70, in which " Wāṣifī's " memoirs are studied in detail and from which it appears that " Wāṣifī ", a professional poet, was born at Harāt in 889/1485 and lived there until April 1512, when he went to Central Asia. [Minorsky, in a letter.]

P. 374, ll. 12–15. [" Mushfiqī."] Also *Ṭabaqāt i Akbarī* ii p. 497 ; *Ātash-kadah* no. 724 ; *Khulāṣat al-afkār* no. 442.

P. 374, l. 24. " The terms ' pompous and verbose ' hardly do justice to Ḥāfiẓ Tanish's history, which has been highly praised by many scholars." [Minorsky, *BSOS.* ix/1 (1937) p. 255.]

P. 375, l. 5. [*Sharaf-nāmah i shāhī.*] Also **Ellis Coll.** M. 408 (18th cent.).

P. 378, l. 3. *Read* P. 162.

[*Tārīkh i Rāqimī.*] Also **Tashkent Univ.** 57 (A.H. 1244/1828–9).

P. 380, l. 2. *Read* etc.) and.

P. 380, l. 17. [*Tadhkirah i Muqīm-Khānī.*] Also **Tashkent Univ.** 61 (A.H. 1225/1810), **Leningrad Univ.** 964*b* (A.H. 1238 ? See Romaskewicz p. 5), **Caetani** 4.

P. 382, l. 27. [*Tārīkh i Badakhshān.*] Another MS. : **Kābul** National Library (see A. Z. Validi in *Journal asiatique,* Jan.-March 1924, p. 150). [Minorsky, *BSOS.* ix/1 (1937) p. 255].

P. 384, l. 25. [A history of the Manghits.] This MS. is in the Asiatic Museum (see *Islamica* iii/3 (1927) p. 316).

P. 385, l. 9. *Read* Semenov.

P. 387, l. 21. Wapkandi. Possibly Wābkanawī (from Wābkanah, 3 farsakhs from Bukhārā : see Barthold *Turkestan* p. 132).

E. History of Central Asia : (2) Farghānah

P. 391, l. 3. *Read* **Shighā'ul.** [Minorsky, *BSOS.* ix/1 (1937) p. 255[23].] Cf. Minorsky in *BSOS.* ix/1 (1937) p. 243 : " . . . *Shiqā'ul,* or *Shighā'ul,* a Turkish rank = Pers.

mihmāndār, "master of ceremonies," cf. Budagov *Slovar'* p. 668."

P. 391, l. 18. *Read* 385).

P. 392, l. 8. This entry should be deleted. For Eton 175 see p. 534, l. 21.

E. History of Central Asia: (3) Kāshghar

P. 392, l. 9. *Insert*:

541*a*. M. **Ḥaidar Dūghlāt** died in 958/1551 (see pp. 273–6 *supra*).

Tārīkh i Rashīdī: see pp. 274–5 *supra*.

P. 392, l. 25. Read *v* xvi *v*.

P. 392 penult. The *Tadhkirah i Khwājagān* of M. Ṣādiq Kāshgharī, being apparently a Turkī work on the lives of certain Central-Asian saints, should be deleted. See *Manuscrits turcs de l'Institut des Langues Orientales décrits par W. D. Smirnov* St. Petersburg 1897) pp. 156–60. Even if it exists also in Persian, the work should appear under Biography, not History.

F. History of Afghānistān

P. 393. [*Tārīkh i Khān-i-Jahānī*.] Also **Kapūrt'halā** 36 (not an autograph. See M. Shafī' in *OCM*. iii/4 (Aug. 1927) p. 18), **Āṣafīyah** iii p. 94 no. 1073 (defective). For some further MSS. as well as for descriptions of some of those already mentioned see the article by S. M. Imām al-Dīn in *Islamic culture* referred to below (p. 1302, l. 29).

P. 393 ult. [*Tārīkh i Khān-i-Jahānī*.] *Insert*:

Edition: in preparation by S. M. Imāmu'd-Dīn (see *Islamic culture* xxii/3 (July 1948) p. 294). Description: *The Tārīkh Khān-i-Jahānī-wa-Makhzan-i-Afghānī*, by S. M. Imamuddin (in *Islamic culture* xxii/2 (April 1948) pp. 128–42, xxii/3 (July 1948) pp. 280–94).

P. 394. [*Makhzan i Afghānī*.] Also **Princeton** 57 (A.H. 1159/1746), **Āṣafīyah** iii p. 108 no. 1052. For some further MSS. as well as for descriptions of some of those already mentioned see the article by S. M. Imāmu'd-Dīn referred to above (p. 1302, l. 29).

P. 394, l. 16. *Read* (A.H. 1181/1767–8. Christ's).

P. 395, l. 5. *Insert:*

544*a*. "The manuscripts of some historical works in Persian by Khushḥāl Khān Khaṭak[1] have been discovered by Miss Khadijah Begam Feroz ud-Din and are discussed in her (unpublished) Lahore thesis on the "Life and Works of the Illustrious Khushḥāl Khān, Chief of the Khaṭaks". [G. Morgenstierne, *AO.* xvii p. 239.]

P. 395, l. 15. *Read* Mannū.

P. 395 ult. [*Tārīkh i Aḥmad-Shāhī.*] Also **Ellis Coll.** M. 233 (apparently complete. Late 18th cent.).

P. 396, l. 9. "The expression 'Yūsuf-zai (i.e. Bāyazīd Anṣārī)' . . . is not correct" [G. Morgenstierne, *Acta Orientalia* xvii p. 238.]

P. 396, l. 16. Read *Tawārīkh.*

P. 396, l. 18. "According to Darmesteter, Chants populaires des Afghans, p. clxxxv, the Tārīkh i Ḥāfiẓ-Raḥmat (No. 551) was written in 1770." [G. Morgenstierne, *AO.* xvii p. 238.] If this is correct, the date of I.O. 3733 cannot be A.H. 1176.

P. 397, l. 16. [*Khulāṣat al-ansāb.*] Also **Ellis Coll.** M. 130 (early 19th cent.).

P. 398, l. 15. [*Bhāō-nāmah.*] Also probably **Blochet** iv 2331 fol. 136 (?) (late 18th cent.). According to the *Cambridge History of India* iv p. 591 "the original MS. has now been discovered by Sir Jadunath Sarkar and a revised translation appeared in the *Indian historical quarterly*, 1934".

P. 399, l. 16. *Insert:*

557*a*. (***Tārīkh i Aḥmad Shāh***), without preface or title: **Blochet** iv 2382 (18th cent.).

P. 399, l. 5 from foot. [*Ḥusain-Shāhī.*] *Insert:*

Fragment of an early draft (?): **I.O.** 4035.

P. 400, l. 15. *Read* Durrānīs.

P. 401, l. 30. For a short account of Akbar Khān (d. 1849) see Buckland's *Dictionary of Indian biography* p. 9.

[1] Warrior and poet, b. 1022/1613, imprisoned for seven years at Gwalior by Aurangzēb, d. "A.D. 1691, in the 78th year of his age". (Blumhardt *Catalogue of the Marathi . . . Pushtu, and Sindhi manuscripts in . . . the British Museum* p. 15 (based on Raverty's *Selections from the poetry of the Afghans*); *Ency. Isl.* under Khushḥāl Khān (R. B. Whitehead); etc.)

P. 401 ult. [*Akbar-nāmah.*] Also **Ellis Coll.** M. 133 (late 19th cent.).

P. 402, l. 9. [*Ẓafar-nāmah i Kābul.*] Also **Ellis Coll.** M. 331 (late 19th cent.).

P. 403, l. 27. [*Tārīkh i Aḥmad.*] Probably also **Āṣafīyah** iii p. 94 no. 1317 (described as *Tārīkh i Durrānī*, by Ḥājjī [*sic* ?] 'Abd al-Karīm).

P. 404, l. 13. *Insert :*

570*a*. S. **Badr al-Dīn** was a resident of Aḥmadnagar.

Kaifīyat i jang i Kābul (beg. *Aḥwālāt i safar i Kābul kih jam'īyat i Ingilīs*), a short (9 foll.) account of the British march to Kābul and the battle of Lahore with the Sik'hs, ending with 21 April 1845 : **Bombay** Univ. p. 228.

P. 404, l. 22. *Read* composition, and.

P. 405, l. 8. *Read* Editions.

[*Fatḥ-nāmah i Kāfiristān.*] The date of the first edition is given by Arberry as 1313 (1896).

P. 406, ll. 14–17. [Amīr 'Abd al-Raḥmān's autobiography.] There were apparently two editions of the Persian retranslation, (1) **Lahore-Mashhad** 1319/1901–2 (title : *Tāj al-tawārīkh* etc. 2 vols. See Semenov *Ukazatel'* p. 10) ; (2) **Bombay,** Faiḍ-rasān Press, 1322/1904 (title : *Tāj al-tawārīkh* etc. 2 vols. Pp. 244 ; 220. See F. E. Karatay *Istanbul Üniversitesi Kütüphanesi Farsça Basmalar Kataloğu* p. 5. Described by C. N. Seddon (*JRAS.* 1938 p. 569) as " a lithographed edition prepared by M. Ja'far Mawlā and M. Ḥusain Lārī, A.H. 1322 ".[1])

P. 406, l. 22. [Amīr 'Abd al-Raḥmān Khān.] Also Zaidān *Mashāhīr al-sharq* (in Arabic) i pp. 142–52 ; *Who was who 1897–1915* p. 2.

[1] These two persons, however, are not mentioned as the translators but as those by whose order (*farmāyish*) and under whose superintendence (*ihtimām*) the work was printed. Ghulām-Murtaḍā Khān is described (vol. ii, *khātimah* p. 219) as the *mu'allif u mutarjim* of the book, and it is stated that he completed the translation at the end of Dhī Qa'dah 1319. Mīrzā 'Abd al-Raḥmān Khān was assistant translator of vol. i, and, having died just after the completion of that volume, was succeeded by Ḥusain 'Alī Shīrāzī. There is a copy of the Bombay edition in the Cambridge University Library.

P. 406, l. 29. *Insert:*

576*a*. **Maḥmūd Ṭarzī** was born in 1285/1870 (see *PL.* pp. 1158–9).

Sirāj al-tawārīkh, a detailed history of the Afghāns: **Kābul** (vol. i (only ?). Date ? See Peshawar cat. p. 291).

P. 407, l. 5. *Read* Ṣafawids): **Rieu.** —— l. 25. *Insert*:

(11*a*) (*Tārīkh i Badakhshān*), a history of the years 1068–1223/1658–1808: **Kābul** National Library (see A. Z. Validi in *Journal asiatique*, Jan.–March 1924, p. 150). [Minorsky, *BSOS*. ix/1 (1937) p. 255]. See also p. 382 *supra*.

P. 407 ult. For some works relating to Balkh, Harāt, etc., now in Afghānistān, see the section History of Persia: Khurāsān.

G. History of Asia Minor and Turkey

P. 408. "On Ibn Bībī see now Duda, *ZDMG*. [N.F.], Band 14 [89], Heft 3/4 [1935], p. 19." [Minorsky, *BSOS*. ix/1 (1937) p. 255.]

P. 410, ll. 6–13. Schefer's *Quelques chapitres* occupy pp. 1–102 of the first volume of the *Recueil de textes et de traductions*.

P. 410, l. 13. [*Mukhtaṣar i Saljūq-nāmah.*] *Insert:*

Russian translation of extracts relating to the Golden Horde: *Sbornik materialov* . . . ii . . . Leningrad 1941 (cf. p. 1230 *supra*) pp. 25–6.

P. 410, l. 17 (579). [*Tārīkh i āl i Saljūq.*] *Insert*:

Facsimile with Turkish translation: *Histoire des Seldjoukides d'Asie Mineure par un anonyme depuis l'origine de la dynastie jusqu'à la fin du regne de Sultan Alâ-ed-Din Keikoubad IV. fils de Soleimanshah.* 765/1364. *Texte persan publié d'après le MS. de Paris par Prof. Dr. Feridoun Nâfiz Uzluk.* **Ankara** 1952 (*Tārīkh i āl i Selchūq dar Ānāṭōlī.* Pp. 95, 80. Anadolu Selçuklulari gününde Mevlevi Bitikleri, 5: Anadolu Selçuklulari Devleti Tarihi, iii).

P. 410, l. 22. *Read* Caliphs.

P. 410, l. 24. [Aqsarā'ī's history.] Edition: *Musāmarat al-akhbār*[1] *wa-musāyarat al-akhyār ta'līf i Maḥmūd* . . . *al-*

[1] *al-aḥbār?*

Aqsarā'ī . . . bā muqaddamah u taṣḥīḥ u ḥawāshī i Duktur 'Uthmān Tūrān, **Ankara** 1944 (Türk Tarih Kurumu Yayınlardan iii. seri, no. 1). [V. Minorsky, in a letter.]

P. 411 antepenult. [*Bāyazīd-nāmah.*] The author is Maḥmūd "Niẓāmī" Malik-zādah. [F. Babinger, in a letter.]

P. 413, l. 12. Read *Hasht bihisht.*

P. 415. [*Hasht bihisht.*] Also **Ellis Coll.** M. 186 (*Katībahs* i–vi. 18th cent.), M. 187 (*K.* vi–viii. 19th cent.), **Bombay Univ.** 35 (part of *K.* vii).

P. 416, l. 5. [*Dhail i Hasht bihisht.*] The author's son, i.e. Abū 'l-Faḍl M. Daftarī (cf. p. 71[17] *supra* and p. 416[17] *infra*).

P. 416, l. 7. For *''llāha* read *'llāha.*

P. 416, l. 10. *Read* Tauer 525.

P. 417, l. 4. *For* may be *read* is. Aẓhar al-Dīn ; so Ḥ. Kh., but Ẓahīr al-Dīn is correct. For Kabīr b. Uwais see p. 1168 n. 2 *infra.*

P. 420, ll. 6–8. [*Shahanshāh-nāmah i . . . Sulṭān Murād Khān.*] For the illustrations in the Yildiz MS. see Edhem and Stchoukine *Les manuscrits orientaux illustrés de la Bibliothèque de l'Université de Stamboul*, Paris 1933, pp. 3–6.

P. 420, l. 20. [*Futūḥāt al-'Ajam.*] Also **Rieu** ii 665*a*.

P. 420, l. 28. [*Fatḥ-nāmah i Khūnkār i Rūm.*] Also **Ethé** 859 (2).

P. 421, l. 9. Ibrāhīm Efendī, i.e. Dr. Ibrāhīm b. Najjār according to F. E. Karatay *Istanbul Üniversitesi Kütüphanesi Farsça Basmalar Kataloğu* p. 84.

P. 421, l. 17. *Read* 600.

P. 422, l. 1. [*Tārīkh i Āyā Ṣōfyah.*] For a short anonymous tract on the foundation of the Ā.Ṣ. see Blochet iii 1976 fol. 177 (A.H. 947/1540–1).

P. 422, l. 17. *Insert:*

(3) ***Tārīkh i Rūm u Farang,*** a history of Turkey and Europe, by ' Abd al-' Azīz Dihlawī (for the best-known person of this name see pp. 24–5 *supra*) : **Ellis Coll.** M.2. (incomplete. Autograph ?).

H. History of Caucasia

P. 423, l. 27. *Read* Alikhanov-Avarski. [Minorsky, *BSOS.* ix/1 (1937) p. 255.] l. 28. Read *Alikhanova-Avarskogo.*

P. 425, l. 6. Read *Alikhanova-Avarskogo.*

P. 426, l. 19. "Bacharly is a German transcription from Russian for Bahārlī." [Minorsky, *BSOS.* ix/1 (1937) p. 255.]

P. 426, l. 24. ['Abbās-Qulī Āg͟hā.] Also *Dānis͟hmandān i Ād͟har-bāyjān* pp. 305–6; *Abbaskulu ağa Bakihanli,* by M. F. Köprülü (in *Türk amaci* i (1942–3) pp. 145–50. Cf. *Oriens* i/2 (1948) p. 346).

J. History of Arabia

P. 427, l. 25. [*Ak͟hbār i ḥasīnah.*] Also **Ivanow** Curzon 90 (18th cent.).

P. 428, l. 5. [*Jad͟hb al-qulūb.*] Also **Ellis Coll.** M. 4 (A.H. 1109/1697–8), **Princeton** 64 (18th cent.), **'Alīgaṛh** Subḥ. MSS. p. 61 no. 36 (pt. i only), **Peshawar** 1462 (3), 1437.

P. 428, l. 9. *Insert:*

(1*b*) *Īrān i kunūnī u K͟halīj i Fārs,* by Ismā'īl Nūr-zādah Būs͟hahrī: **Tihrān** (216 pp. See *Luzac's OL.* 1946 p. 104).

P. 428, l. 12. *Insert:*

(2*a*) *Mafātīḥ al-adab fī tawārīk͟h al-'Arab,* by M. 'Alī Sadīd al-Salṭanah: place ? n.d. [R. Lescot, *Bull. E.O.I.F. de Damas* vii–viii p. 283*b*.]

P. 428, l. 14. *Insert:*

(3*a*) *Naft u marwārīd,* by M. 'A. Mans͟hūr Garakānī: (cf. p. 1291 no. (3)) **Tihrān** 1946 (189 pp. See Probsthain's *Orientalia nova* 2 (1946–8) p. 27 no. 425; *Luzac's OL.* 1946 p. 105 (title given as *Siyāsat i Ingilīs dar K͟halīj i Fārs u jug͟hrāfiyāyi jazā'ir i Baḥrain*), 1947 p. 101).

(3*b*) *Naẓarī bah Īrān u K͟halīj i Fārs,* by Nūr-zādah (i.e. presumably Ismā'īl N.-Z. Būs͟hahrī mentioned above under (1*b*)): **Tihrān** (128 pp. See *Luzac's OL.* 1945 p. 79, 1946 p. 6).

P. 428, ll. 18–21. [*Short account of the Wahhābī incursions.*] Published by R. B. Serjeant and G. M. Wickens in *Islamic culture* xxiii/4 (Oct. 1949) pp. 308–9.

K. History of Europe and America

P. 429, l. 6. *Insert:*

[England.] ***Tārīkh i guzīdah i Farīdūn Malkum,*** by Farīdūn Malkum [son of Prince Malkom Khān Nāẓim al-Daulah (for whom see Browne *The press and poetry of modern Persia* pp. 18–19, etc., *Lit. Hist.* iv pp. 463, 468)]: **Paris** 1324/1908 (407 pp. See F. E. Karatay *Istanbul Üniversitesi Kütüphanesi Farsça Basmalar Kataloğu* p. 52; Browne *The press and poetry of modern Persia* p. 162).

P. 429, ll. 7, 10. *Read* ***Ingilistān.***

P. 430, l. 7. Read *Piṭr.* [Minorsky, *BSOS.* ix/1 (1937) p. 255.]

P. 430, l. 21. For the name Āwānus cf. p. 841 n. 1 and E. Rossi's *Elenco dei manoscritti persiani della Biblioteca Vaticana* p. 80, where the transcription Oannes [presumably an Armenian name [1]] is suggested with a query.

P. 430, l. 23. *Insert:*

[Russia.] ***Ā'īnah i Sikandarī,*** a biography of Alexander III (b. 1845, acc. 1881, d. 1894), by Ḥasan Khān I'timād al-Salṭanah (cf. p. 154 *supra*): **Mashhad** iii, *fṣl.* 14, MSS., no. 4 (A.H. 1313/1895–6).

[Russia.] ***Qaiṣar-nāmah*** a *mathnawī* on the Russo-Turkish war, by 'Azīz al-Dīn "'Azīz" (so Āṣafīyah) or "'Azīzī" (so Edwards) Lak'hnawī: [**Cawnpore**] 1296/1879°.

P. 430, l. 24. Read ***Piṭr*** [cf. correction to l. 7 *supra*].

P. 430, l. 30. The *Mīkādō-nāmah* is a verse according to Arberry.

P. 430 antepenult. For Maḥmūd Ṭarzī see p. 1158 *infra.*

P. 430 ult. The date as given by Arberry is 1334–5/1916–17*.

L. History of China and Japan

P. 431, l. 10. For Surkhkat see Barthold *Turkestan* pp. 120 n. 6, 131.

P. 431, l. 22. For 'Alī Akbar Khiṭā'ī see *Islam Ansiklopedisi* under Alî Ekber (A. Zeki Velidi Togan); P. Kahle *Eine islamische Quelle über China um 1500* (in *Acta Orientalia* xii/2).

[1] That Āwānus is an Armenian name seems highly probable. An Armenian called "Agha Wanus" was in the service of the Bēgam Samrū (see Brajendranath Banerji *Begam Samru* p. 67).

P. 432, l. 12. The *Mīkādō-nāmah* is in verse according to Arberry.

P. 432 penult. For Maḥmūd Ṭarzī see p. 1158 *infra*.

P. 432 ult. The date, as given by Arberry, is 1334–5/1916–17*.

M. History of India: (*a*) General

P. 435, l. 24. Also *Life and work of Khwāja Nizāmuddīn Ahmad Bakhshī. By Baini Prashad* (in *JASB.*, Letters, iv/4 (1938) pp. 769–94).

P. 435, l. 31. *Read* مفاعلن.

P. 436, l. 24. The hemistich *Wa-awwalu arḍ^in* etc. is quoted in the *Tāj al-ʿarūs* under TMM and is there ascribed to Raqqāʿ or Raffāʿ b. Qais al-Asadī. Cf. Lane *s.v.* ʿaqqa, *Irshād al-arīb* ii p. 12, Ibn Baṭṭūṭah iv p. 327.

P. 437, l. 15. [ʿAbd al-Qādir Badāʾūnī.] Of the dates given for his death 1024/1615 must be nearest to the truth, if the reference to the death of "Ẓuhūrī" and "Malik" Qummī is not a later insertion in the notice of "Ẓuhūrī" in the *Muntakhab al-tawārīkh* iii p. 269.

P. 438, l. 27. For the *Baḥr al-asmār* see *ʿAbd al-Qādir Badāʾūnī and the Kathā-sarit-sāgara*, by C. A. Storey (in *Woolner commemoration volume*, Lahore 1940, pp. 249–50).

P. 441, l. 19. [Nūr al-Ḥaqq Dihlawī.] "Mashriqī" was his *takhallus*.

P. 442, l. 6. [Nūr al-Ḥaqq Dihlawī.] Another passage from the *Farḥat al-nāẓirīn* giving a brief notice of N. al-Ḥ. "Mashriqī" as a poet is quoted in *OCM*. iv/4 (Aug. 1928) p. 105.

P. 451, l. 10. *Read* 1877°* *and delete* 1887°.

P. 452, l. 18. [*Rājāwalī*.] Also **Madrās** i 276 (?) (described as *Aḥwāl i rājagān* by ʿAbd al-Karīm b. Ilyās, but the opening words agree with those of the *Rājāwalī*). A similar work is **Madrās** i 292 (*Tārīkh i rājagān*, beginning *Ḥamd u thanāy Muqaddirī rā kih qudratash*).

P. 453, l. 16. [*Lubb al-tawārīkh i Hind*.] Also **Ellis Coll.** M. 351 (A.H. 1105/1094).

P. 455, l. 20. [*Khulāṣat al-tawārīkh*.] Also **Ellis Coll.** M. 392 (18th cent.).

P. 470, l. 3. [*Muntakhhab al-lubāb.*] Also **Madrās** i 318 (vol. iii. A.H. 1197/1783), **Ellis Coll.** M. 220 (vol. ii. 18th cent.).

P. 477, l. 21. [Lachhmī Narāyan "Shafīq".] Another work of his is the *Nakhlistān*, a collection of tales written in 1218/1803–4 (MSS.: Rehatsek p. 233 no. 56, Ross-Browne 253).

P. 478, l. 4. [*Ḥaqīqat-hā-yi Hindustān.*] Also **Rehatsek** p. 104 no. 60, **Madrās** i 533 (A.D. 1936).

P. 478, l. 24. [*Ṣaḥīḥ al-akhbār.*] Also **Rieu** iii 1052*a* (extracts only).

P. 481, l. 16. [*Chahār chaman.*] Also **Ellis Coll.** M. 91 (?) (*Chahār gulshan* (*sic* ?)).

P. 485, l. 6 from foot. *Insert a second bracket after* 1860–1.

P. 486, l. 5. [*Tafsīr al-Qur'ān.*] The first part (to S. ii v. 80) of a Persian translation by S. M. Taqī Fakhr-Dā'ī Gīlānī has been published in Tihrān (presumably in or shortly before A.H.S. 1318/1939–40, the date of presentation to the Mashhad library. See Mashhad iv p. 479).

P. 487, l. 24. [*Jām i Jam.*] Also **Ellis Coll.** M. 390.

P. 488, l. 20. [S. Aḥmad Khān.] Also *Eminent Mussalmans* (anon., pub. Natesan, Madras, 1926) pp. 1–37; L. Bevan Jones *The people of the mosque*, London, 1932 pp. 208–11; W. C. Smith *Modern Islām in India*, Lahore 1943, pp. 6–23; J. M. S. Baljon *The reforms and religious ideas of Sir Sayyid Aḥmad Khân*, Leyden 1949.

M. History of India: (*b*) Sulṭāns of Delhi

P. 494. [*Tāj al-ma'āthir.*] Also **Leningrad** Univ. 1157 (A.H. 987/1579), 1093 (A.H. 1288/1871–2. See Romaskewicz p. 4).

P. 500. [*Qirān al-sa'dain.*] Also **Leningrad** Univ. 1114*a* (A.H. 982/1574–5. See Romaskewicz p. 11), 1172 (A.H. 1041/1631–2 ?), **Majlis** ii 1129 (17th cent. ?), **Vatican** Pers. 153 (A.H. 1257/1841. Rossi p. 149), **Edinburgh** New Coll. p. 8.

P. 500, l. 28. *Read* **Madrās** i 131 (A.H. 1173/1760).

P. 501, l. 19. Also (**4**) *Sharḥ i Qirān al-sa'dain*, by "'Afwī" Dihlawī: **'Alīgaṛh** Subḥ. MSS. p. 48 no. 3 (A.H. 1157/1744).

P. 502, ll. 15–18. [*Khazā'in al-futūḥ.*] For a review of this edition, with numerous corrections, by " Sh. " [= M. Shafī' ?] see *OCM*. xi/4 (Aug. 1935) pp. 105–19.

P. 502 antepenult. DWL, according to the poet (cf. Rieu ii p. 612*b*), is to be pronounced like the plural of *daulat*, possibly therefore Diwal, which, of the plurals of *daulat*, is nearest in sound to Dēval, if that was the first element in the name of the Rājah's daughter.

P. 502 ult. *Read* : The pronunciation Khiḍr occurs occasionally in the poem, but much less frequently than Khaḍir.

P. 503, l. 22. [*Duwal Rānī Khaḍir Khān.*] Also **Majlis** ii 934 (A.H. 989/1581).

P. 503, l. 6 from foot. *Read* **Madrās** i 111.

P. 504, l. 13. [*Nuh sipihr.*] *Insert* :

Edition : **Oxford Univ. Press** 1950 (ed. M. Waḥīd Mirzā. Islamic Research Association Series, 12).

P. 504, ll. 22–4. [*Tughluq-nāmah.*] For a review by M. Shafī' see *OCM*. x/2 (Feb. 1934) pp. 148–51 and for corrections of the text of this edition see an Urdu article by M. Waḥīd Mirzā in *OCM*. xi/1 (Nov. 1934) pp. 116–46.

P. 505. [Khusrau Dihlawī.] Also Jāmī *Bahāristān*, near end of *Rauḍah* vii ; *Riyāḍ al-'ārifīn* pp. 112–15 ; *Nuzhat al-khawāṭir* pp. 38–41 ; Raḥmān 'Alī p. 57 ; Berthels *Ocherk istorii persidskoi literatury* pp. 39–43.

P. 507, l. 26. [*Tārīkh i Fīrōz-Shāhī.*] Also **Ellis Coll.** M. 101 (early 19th cent.), **Madrās** i 298 (defective).

P. 508. [Ḍiyā' al-Dīn Baranī.] Also *Kalimāt al-ṣādiqīn* no 61 ; *Maṭlūb al-ṭālibīn* (Ethé col. 325) ; *Nuzhat al-khawāṭir* p. 64.

P. 509, l. 8. Another edition : *Futūḥāt-i-Fīrūzshāhī* [Persian text edited from a transcript of a MS. belonging to 'Alīgaṛh Muslim University]. *By N. B. Roy* (in *JRASB.*, Letters, vol. vii/1 (1941) pp. 61–89).

P. 509, l. 11. Another translation : *The victories of Sulṭān Fīrūz Shāh of Tughluq Dynasty* (752–90 *h.*). *English translation of Futūḥāt-i-Fīrūz Shāhī. By N. B. Roy* (in *Islamic culture* 15/4 (Oct. 1941) pp. 449–64).

P. 509, l. 15. [Fīrōz Shāh Tughluq.] Also *Nuzhat al-khawāṭir* pp. 110–13.

P. 509, l. 20. [*Sīrat i Fīrōz-Shāhī.*] *Insert*:
Extracts: (**1**) *A memoir on Kotla Firoz Shah, Delhi. By J. A. Page . . . with* [the Persian text and] *a translation of* [an extract, viz. foll. 91*b*–105*b* in the Bānkīpūr MS., from] *Sirat-i-Firozshahi by Moh. Hamid Kuraishi.* (Memoirs of the Archæological Survey of India, no. 52 (Delhi 1937) pp. 3–25 (text), 33–42 (translation).) (**2**) *Jajnagar expedition of Sulṭān Fīrūz Shāh—English translation and text of an extract from 'Sīrat-i-Fīrūz Shāhī'. By N. B. Roy* (in *JRASB.*, Letters, viii/1 (1942) pp. 57–98).

P. 513, l. 23. Ḥasnū: so Rieu, but presumably Ḥasanū (i.e. Ḥasan with the diminutive termination -ū) is correct.

P. 516, l. 11. [*Tārīkh i salāṭīn i Afāghinah.*] *Insert*:
Edition: *Tārīkh-i-Shāhī (also known as Tārīkh-i-Salāṭīn-i-Afāghina) of Aḥmad Yādgār . . . Edited by M. Hidayat Hosain.* **Calcutta** 1939 (Bibliotheca Indica, no. 257. Cf. *JRAS.* 1939 p. 684).

M. History of India: (*c*) The Tīmūrids (1) General

P. 519 antepenult. [*Malāḥat i maqāl.*] Also **Lahore** Panjāb Univ. (defective. See *OCM.* ix/1 p. 23).

P. 520, l. 16. For the names Ṣūfī Ṣan'ān and Mirzā Bābā cf. *Ḥabīb al-siyar* iii, 3, p. 342 (Sh. Ṣūfī 'Alī) and *'Ālam-ārāy i 'Abbāsī* p. 122 (Mīrzā Bābā).

P. 524, l. 1. [Apūrva Krishna, or, to use the Hindī forms, Apūrb Kishan.] "Kunwar," Apūrb Kishan's *takhalluṣ*, is a Hindī word meaning "prince".

P. 527, l. 29. ["Ghālib."] Also *Āthār al-ṣanādīd* (cf. p. 485), Lucknow 1876, pt. 4, pp. 74–82; *Madhhab i Ghālib* (in Urdu), a discussion of "Ghālib's" religious views, by S. Aulād Ḥusain "Shādān" Bilgrāmī (in *OCM.* viii/3 (May 1932) pp. 123–9); *Ghālib kē jadīd tadhkirōṅ par ēk naẓar*, by S. M. 'Abd Allāh (in *OCM.* xv/4 (Aug. 1939) pp. 3–25).

P. 529, l. 12. *Insert*:
(2*a*) ***Tārīkh i bādshāhān i Dihlī***, by Akbar 'Alī b. S. M. 'Alī al-Bukhārī.
Edition: place ? 1273/1856–7 (Āṣafīyah iii p. 94).

M. History of India : (c) The Tīmūrids (2) Bābur

P. 531 ult. Read *JASB*.

P. 532, l. 24. (Zain al-Dīn Khwāfī.] Also Raḥmān 'Alī p. 68.

P. 533, l. 11. *Read* Bihrōz.

P. 534, l. 23. [*Wāqi'āt i Bāburī*.] Also **Madrās** i 301.

M. History of India : (c) The Tīmūrids (3) Humāyūn

P. 536, l. 11. *Insert* :

Edition : *Qānūn-i-Humāyūnī (also known as Humāyūn Nāma) of Khwāndamīr. Edited by M. Hidayat Hosain.* **Calcutta** 1940 (Bibliotheca Indica, no. 260. See *JRAS*. 1941 p. 96).

P. 537 ult. For the Bayāt tribe see also Malcolm *History of Persia* ii, London, 1829, p. 140 n.4.

P. 538, l. 19. [*Tārīkh i Humāyūn*.] No formal title is given to the book by the author, who refers to it as *īn tadhkirah* and *īn mukhtaṣar*. The title given to the work by Ethé seems to come from the copyist's colophon, where it is called *Tawārīkh i ḥaḍrat i Humāyūn Bādshāh* (Hidayat Hosain's edition p. 378). *Insert* :

Edition : *Tadhkira-i-Humāyūn wa Akbar of Bāyazīd Biyāt* [*sic*]. *Edited by M. Hidayat Hosain.* **Calcutta** 1941* (Bibliotheca Indica, 264).

P. 538, l. 22. According to Hidayat Hosain (preface, p. vii) Prof. Banārsi Prasād Saksēna published "in the same *Journal*" [i.e. apparently the *Allahabad University Studies*] in 1939 (History Section, pp. 1–82) the translation of another part (unspecified) of the Memoirs. "The translation of about one-third of the work still remains to be published."

P. 538, l. 29. [Bāyazīd Bayāt.] Also *Journal of Indian history*, iv/1–3 (Madras 1926) pp. 43–60 (an account of the author and his work by B. P. Saksēna. See Hidayat Hosain's preface, p. vii).

M. History of India : (c) The Tīmūrids (4) Akbar

P. 540, l. 5. Read "**Faiḍī**".

P. 542, l. 8 from foot. [*Mukātabāt i 'Allāmī, daftar* iv.] See also the corrections to p. 543, ll. 1–2.

P. 542 antepenult. [*Ruqa'āt i Abū 'l-Faḍl.*] *For* Editions *read* An edition.

P. 543, l. 1. [*Ruqa'āt i Abū 'l-Faḍl.*] *Read* was published at Calcutta in 1238* of the Bengali (Faṣlī) era.

P. 543, ll. 1–2. The words " and at Cawnpore in 1872* " should be deleted. The work published by Nawal Kis͟hōr at Cawnpore in 1876* (not 1872) and reprinted at least three times under the title *Ruqa'āt i Abū 'l-Faḍl* is the work referred to above as the fourth *daftar* of the *Mukātabāt i 'Allāmī.*

P. 543, l. 11. Read *Akbarī.*

P. 544 ult. [*Akbar-nāmah.*] The Chester Beatty MS. is presumably the subject of the Roxburghe Club's *Chronicle of Akbar the Great. A description* [by Sir Thomas Arnold and J. V. S. Wilkinson] *of a manuscript of the Akbar-nama illustrated by the court painters* (Oxford 1937. Impl. folio, with coloured frontispiece and 33 plates, 5 of which are coloured. See Bernard Quaritch's Catalogue No. 562 (1939) p. 4, where a copy was offered at £25, and Luzac's Supplement No. 6 (March 1941) p. 2).

P. 546. [*Akbar-nāmah.*] Also **Vatican** Pers. 90–92 (*Daftar* i, pt. 2, and *Daftar* ii. Rossi p. 107), 109 (*Daftar* i, pt. 1. Rossi p. 119).

P. 546 penult. *Read* **Madrās** i 281–4.

P. 547, l. 16. [*Akbar-nāmah.*] This translation is by W. Erskine.

P. 547, l. 25. [*Akbar-nāmah.*] *Insert* :

Description of a MS. : see addendum to p. 544 ult.

P. 550, l. 29. [*Ā'īn i Akbarī.* English translations.] *Insert :*

The Ā'īn-i Akbarī . . . Translated . . . by H. Blochmann . . . Second edition, revised by D. C. Phillott, **Calcutta** 1927–39. *'Ain* [*sic*]*-i-Ākbari* [*sic*] *. . . Vol. iii . . . Translated . . . by Colonel H. S. Jarrett . . . revised and further annotated by Sir Jadu-Nath Sarkar,* **Calcutta** 1948 (Bibliotheca Indica). Vol. ii, the first of Jarrett's two volumes, seems to have been omitted from this re-edition. Blochmann's volume contains the first two of the five *daftars,* " vol. iii " contains the last two.

P. 551, l. 13. Maulawī M. Najaf 'Alī K͟hān Jhajjarī *al-muk͟hāṭab bah* Tāj al-'ulamā', son of a Qāḍī of Jhajjar (i.e., according to M. Idrīs, the place of that name near Rohtak) was in the service of M. 'Alī Khān, Nawwāb of Ṭōnk, from whom in 1295/1878 he received instructions to write commentaries in Arabic, Persian and Urdu on each of the three poems, *Bānat Su'ād*, *Qaṣīdah i Burdah* and *Qaṣīdah i Amālī*. Among his many works in Arabic, Persian and Urdu were *Takmilah i Ṣaulat i Fārūqī* (cf. *PL.* p. 616) in 50,000 verses and commentaries on the *Maqāmāt* of Ḥarīrī (in words consisting entirely of undotted letters), the *Dīwān* of Mutanabbī, the *Ḥamāsah* and the *Dasātīr*. See Raḥmān 'Alī p. 236, M. Idrīs p. 91. Both of these authors, the latter of whom completed the *Taṭyīb al-ikhwān* in 1313/1895, speak of Najaf 'Alī Khān as still alive.

P. 551, l. 14. Jhajar seems to be an obsolete English spelling for Jhajjar.

P. 551, l. 18. [Abū 'l-Faḍl.] Autobiography also in *Mukātabāt i 'Allāmī*, *daftar* 3 (according to Bombay Univ. p. 282).

P. 553, l. 3. According to the printed text of the *Ma'āthir i Raḥīmī* (vol. iii p. 1698 penult.) the date of collation was 1026. The note relating to this is followed by another dated 1031.

P. 553, l. 27. *Read* Āqā Bābā.

P. 554, l. 24. B. W. Chapman [Rieu iii 980*a*, l. 2] seems to be a mistake for R[obert] B[arclay] Chapman (see Rieu iii, preface p. xxiv).

P. 554 antepenult. S. Amīr Ḥaidar "Amīr" b. S. Nūr al-Ḥusain b. Mīr Ghulām-'Alī "Āzād" Bilgrāmī was born in 1165/1751–2 and was only three years old when his father was accidentally drowned. Educated first at Bilgrām by his relative S. M. "Shā'ir" Bilgrāmī (for whom see p. 712 *supra*) and after his death [in 1185/1772] by his grandfather Ghulām-'Alī "Āzād" (for whom see pp. 855–66 *supra*) at Aurangābād, he returned to Bilgrām after the latter's death [in 1200/1786] and was subsequently appointed *Muftī* to the '*Adālat i Kull*, or Supreme Court, in the Presidency of Bengal. On p. 4 of his *Persian moonshee* (London 1801) Gladwin expresses acknowledgments to "Mowlawy Ameer Hyder, Mufty to the Sudder Nizamut and Dewanny Adawlats" [i.e. the Supreme Courts of Criminal and Civil Justice].

P. 555, l. 28. [S. Amīr Ḥaidar Bilgrāmī.] Also *Mi'rāj al-khayāl*; *Khāzin al-shu'arā'* fol. 45*b* (where the biography in Walī Allāh's *Tārīkh i Farrukhābād* is summarized); *Ṣubḥ i gulshan* p. 39; Maqbūl Aḥmad *Ḥayāt i Jalīl* (cf. p. 712 n. *supra*) ii p. 174 note 132.

P. 556, l. 6. [*Nāfi' al-ṭālibīn*.] Also **Ivanow** Curzon 135 (A.D. 1797–8).

M. HISTORY OF INDIA: (*c*) THE TĪMŪRIDS (5) JAHĀNGĪR

P. 561, l. 5. *Read* the first two rarer.

P. 561, l. 32. [*Iqbāl-nāmah i Jahāngīrī*.] For a discussion of the pictures in the Philadelphia MS. see an article entitled *Late Mughul illustrations to the Iqbāl-Nāmah* by M. A. Simsar and W. Norman Brown in *JAOS*. 58/2 (June 1938).

P. 561 penult. This note should be deleted.

P. 562, l. 13. *Read* p. 60 no. 21 (vol. ii).

P. 562, l. 15. *Read* p. 52), **Madrās** i 278–80.

P. 562, l. 18. [*Iqbāl-nāmah i Jahāngīrī*.] Also **Brelvi and Dhabhar** p. xiii (A.H. 1137/1724–5. Wrongly described in the catalogue as the *Ma'āthir i Jahāngīrī*), **Rehatsek** p. 76 no. 12.

P. 563, ll. 17–19. [*Ma'āthir i Jahāngīrī*.] **Brelvi and Dhabhar** p. xiii and **Rehatsek** p. 76 no 12 should be deleted. These are evidently copies of the *Iqbāl-nāmah* (as is shown by the opening words quoted in the former catalogue).

M. HISTORY OF INDIA: (*c*) THE TĪMŪRIDS (6) SHĀH-JAHĀN

P. 565, l. 24. *Read* Young)].

P. 567, l. 24. Read *Tadhkirah i Ṭāhir i Naṣrābādī* p. 227.

P. 568. [*Ẓafar-nāmah i Shāh-Jahānī*.] Also **Leningrad** Univ. 1063*a* (A.H. 1082 ? Romaskewicz p. 11).

P. 569, ll. 2–3. Read *'Amal i Ṣāliḥ* iii pp. 397–401.

P. 569, l. 8. Read *Wāqi'āt i Kashmīr* p. 150.

P. 571, ll. 6–7 from foot. [*Chār chaman i Barahman*.] *Read* **Madrās** i 315 and 336*a* (both *Qawā'id al-salṭanat i Shāh-Jahān*). Also **Madrās** i 306 (*Chār chaman*. A.H. 1134/

1721–2), **Ellis Coll.** M. 79 (*Ch. ch.* Early 19th cent.), 80 (A.H. 1241/1826), **Rehatsek** p. 66 no. 17 (apparently *Ch. ch.*), presumably also **Lahore** Panjāb Univ. (*Q. al-s. i Sh-J.* A.H. 1249–50/1834. See *OCM.* vii/4 (Aug. 1931) p. 69).

P. 572, l. 4. [*Guldastah i Chār chaman.*] Also **Blochet** iv 2328 (early 18th cent.).

P. 572, l. 8. Read *'Amal i Ṣāliḥ* iii pp. 434–5, 443.

P. 572, l. 18. [" Barahman ".] Also *Sham' i anjuman* p. 92.

P. 573, ll. 12–13. [" Kalīm."] Read *'Amal i Ṣāliḥ* iii pp. 402–4; *Tadhkirah i Ṭāhir i Naṣrābādī* (Sprenger p. 90; Ṭihrān ed. pp. 220–3).

P. 573, l. 27. Read *Īzadī.*

P. 577, l. 2. *Read* Rieu i 260, iii 934*b*.

P. 580, l. 10. Read *muṣaḥḥiḥ*.

P. 580, l. 13 from foot. [*'Amal i Ṣāliḥ.*] Possibly also **Eton** 190 (see addendum to p. 598, l. 17).

P. 580, ll. 8–9 from foot. *Read* 1912–39°*.

P. 581 ult. *Insert*:

(3) ***Iqbāl-nāmah i Dhū 'l-Faqār-Khānī,*** an account of Nawwāb Dhū 'l-Faqār Khān's expedition against Ma'ṣūm Khān, composed in 1068/1657–8 " during the reign of Aurangzeb " at the request of Mirzā M. Ṭāhir: **Calcutta Madrasah** 182 (2) (A.H. 1069/1658–9).

P. 582, l. 19. [*Tārīkh i Shāh-Shujā'ī.*] For some remarks on this history see J. Sarkar *History of Aurangzib* ii p. 303.

M. HISTORY OF INDIA: (c) THE TĪMŪRIDS (7) AURANGZĒB

P. 583, l. 27. [*Tārīkh i Āshām.*] The date is given (incorrectly) by Edwards as 1264 [1847] and by Arberry more correctly as 1265/1848–9. The year occurs both on the title-page and in the colophon. In the latter place the day of the month, 1 Rajab, is added. Consequently the correct date is 1265/1849°*.

P. 586, l. 19. [*'Ālamgīr-nāmah.*] Also **Ellis Coll.** M. 268 (18th cent.).

P. 586, l. 24. *Read* **Madrās** i 311 (A.H. 1133/1720), 312, 313.

P. 588, l. 3. [*Futūḥāt i ʿĀlamgīrī.*] Cf. also Sarkar *History of Aurangzib* ii p. 305.

P. 589, l. 7. [*Dilgushā.*] Cf. also Sarkar *History of Aurangzib* ii p. 304.

P. 590, l. 14. *Read* [1873 ?°].

P. 590, l. 20. Niʿmat Khān's *tafsīr*, the *Niʿmat i ʿuẓmā*, has been mentioned on p. 20 *supra*.

P. 590, l. 22. Read *jihād i Ḥaidarābād*.

P. 591, l. 18. *Read* **Madrās** i 273–4.

P. 592, l. 8. [*Jang-nāmah.*] Also **Lahore** Panjāb Univ. Lib. (A.H. 1256/1840. See *OCM*. vii/3 (May 1931) p. 62).

P. 593, l. 25. A.H. 1180 is an " owner's date ".

P. 593, l. 34. *Insert*:

English translation: *Maāsir-i-ʿĀlamgiri . . . of Sāqi Mustʿad* [*sic*] *Khan. Translated . . . and annotated by Sir Jadunath Sarkar . . .* **Calcutta** 1947 (Bibliotheca Indica).

P. 594, l. 5. *Read* 936*b*, 1083*b*.

P. 594, l. 21. For the meaning of Maʿmūrī see *Maʾāthir al-umarāʾ* iii p. 376, where it is stated that Muẓaffar Khān Mīr ʿAbd al-Razzāq Maʿmūrī was by descent a Saiyid of Maʿmūrābād " *kih mauḍiʿī-st az Najaf i Ashraf* ".

P. 597, l. 1. [*Aḥkām i ʿĀlamgīrī.*] " The volume contains not fully written out letters but only a precis of the points which the Emperor dictated to his secretary for inclusion in the letters. But they are not so brief and obscure as the contents of 31 [i.e. the *Kalimāt i ṭaiyibāt*]. The persons addressed are usually named. The contents refer to the last decade of Aurangzib's reign. I have used the Rampur State Library MS., a fine copy which must have belonged to the Delhi Palace Library, and collated it with the Khuda Bakhsh MS., a neatly written copy of the 18th century. No other MS. of it is known to exist." (Jadunath Sarkar *History of Aurangzib* ii (Calcutta 1912) p. 310.)

P. 598, l. 11. For the *Aurang-nāmah* (composed in 1072/1661–2) see a description entitled *An unpublished contemporary history of Aurangzeb's accession in verse* by M. Abdulla Chughtai in *Islamic culture* vi/1 (Jan. 1932) pp. 157–60, where the date of the Āṣafīyah MS. is given as 1116/1704.

P. 598, l. 17. Margoliouth writes *Gulshān*. The date of composition (1070) suggests that this is a MS. of the *'Amal i Ṣāliḥ* (see p. 580 *supra*).

P. 598 antepenult. *For* his *read* the.

M. History of India: (c) The Tīmūrids (8) The 18th Century

P. 600, l. 27. *Read* **Browne** Suppt. 189 (n.d. King's 47).

P. 602, l. 11. *Read* Ḥaidarābād.

P. 603, l. 16. *Read* 1127.

P. 606, l. 14. *Read* death, to.

P. 607, l. 2. *Read* 19 June 1707.

P. 609, l. 7 from foot. For *infra* read *supra*.

P. 610 antepenult. " Some 200 Sanskrit and Zend MSS." (Buckland.) The Fraser MSS. in the Bodleian include a considerable number in Persian (see Ethé's *Catalogue of the Persian . . . manuscripts in the Bodleian Library, Pt. II*, coll. 1373–6).

P. 611, l. 13. [*Mir'āt i wāridāt.*] *Read* **Rieu** i 275*b* (*Ṭabaqah* i. Late 18th cent.).

P. 612, l. 6. [Anand Rām.] Ānanda, with a long *ā* in the first syllable, is the Sanskrit form, but in Hindī the first syllable can be shortened and this shortened form seems to be used by most Indian writers in speaking of " Mukhliṣ ".

P. 612, l. 26. *Delete* I.O. D.P. 491 (*e*).

P. 613, l. 11. *Insert*:

(8*a*) *Rāḥat al-afrās*, on farriery (MSS.: Lindesiana p. 113, Rāmpūr (Nadhīr Aḥmad 260)).

P. 613, ll. 12–23. *Read*:

(9) ***Badā'i' i waqā'i'***, memoirs of the author's life and of contemporary events in northern India, written at different dates [1] and incorporating three or four sections ((1) the account of Nādir Shāh's invasion [2] (beg. *Wāqi'ah*

[1] A.H. 1152 and the 29th regnal year [A.H. 1159] are mentioned as dates of composition on foll. 116 and 234 of the Panjāb University MS.

[2] The title *Tadhkirah i Anand Rām Mukhliṣ* given by Elliot (and Sarkār) to this part (and the two succeeding parts ?) of the work came doubtless from Nawwāb Ḍiyā' al-Dīn Khān's MS., but it may have no good authority. The extracts translated from that MS. by Perkins for Elliot relate only to Nādir Shāh's invasion, but there is nothing to show whether the last words of Perkins's translation were the end of the MS.

īst nādir) = foll. 114*b*–169*b* in the Panjāb Univ. MS., (2) *Aḥwāl i sīzdah-rūzah safar i Gaṛh Muktēsar* [in Dhū 'l-Qa'dah 1156 [1]] = foll. 180*a*–192*b* in the Panjāb Univ. MS., (3) *Aḥwāl i safar i Bingaṛh* [2] [in Muḥ.-Jum. I 1158 [3]] = foll. 193*a*–229 in the Panjāb Univ. MS.) and (4) *Nuskhah i sawāniḥ i aḥwāl*, on events in the Panjāb from Jumādā II 1158/ July 1745 to Jumādā II 1161/June 1748 = foll. 229*b*–243*a* in the Panjāb Univ. MS.), which may have originated as separate tracts: **Lahore** Panjāb Univ. (286 foll., beginning with events of 1145 and ending with 1161, the only complete copy hitherto recorded. See M. Shafī''s detailed description mentioned below), **Rāmpūr** (= Nadhīr Aḥmad 61, beg. *Aḥwāl i mutawajjih shudan i . . . M. Shāh . . . samt i Gaḍh Muktēsar . . . Bīst u sīwum i Muḥarram al-Ḥarām sāl i 1158.* A.H. 1158/1745, autograph), **'Alīgaṛh** Muslim Univ. Akh. 112 (71 foll., containing only the account of Nādir Shāh's invasion, the *Nuskhah i sawāhiḥ i aḥwāl*, and the *Aḥwāl i sīzdah-rūzah i safar i Gaḍh Muktēsar*. See M. Shafī's article p. 89), **Delhi** K.B.Ẓafar Ḥasan's private library (complete ? See Aẓhar 'Alī's edition p. 41[8]), **Ethé** 2724 (the journey to Muktēsar in 1156 only. 16 foll. Description on fol. 1*a*: *Waqā'i' i sair i Gangā*).

Edition of the account of the march to Bingaṛh: *Safar-nāmah i Mukhliṣ . . . ba-taṣḥīḥ u taḥshiyah i . . . Saiyid Aẓhar 'Alī*, **Rāmpūr** 1946 (*Silsilah i maṭbū'āt i Kitāb-khānah i Riyāsat i Rāmpūr*, no. 7. Persian text (108 pp.) with Urdu introduction (140 pp.), notes and indexes).

Description of the work with a full list of the headings and an edition of the *Nuskhah i sawāniḥ i aḥwāl*: *Iqtibās az Badā'i' i waqā'i'*, by M. Shafī' (in *OCM*. xviii/1 (Nov. 1941) pp. 89–124).

[1] i.e. Dec.–Jan. 1743. W. Irvine gives the date as 1747, which would correspond to 1160.

[2] A journey " undertaken with the object of shooting and hunting as well as to punish one 'Alī Muḥammad Rohilla " (Nadhīr Aḥmad). The route led first to Muktēsar, but this journey is quite different from that to Muktēsar fair in 1156.

[3] The 27th and (from 1 Rabī' ii) 28th years of Muḥammad Shāh's reign. The date 1150/1737 given by Nadhīr Aḥmad is obviously a slip, since his quotation from the Persian text gives 1158.

Description of a portion of the work (from a MS. belonging to Nawwāb Ḍiyā' al-Dīn Khān of Lōhārū) with 22 pp. of translated extracts: Elliot and Dowson *History of India* viii 76–98.

English translation of the account of the pilgrimage to Muktēsar: see p. 613, ll. 20–3.

P. 613, l. 24. [Anand Rām "Mukhliṣ."] Also *Majmū'ah i naghz* ii p. 176; S. Aẓhar 'Alī's introduction to the *Safar-nāmah* pp. 7–39.

P. 617. Nos. 5 (*Sawāniḥ i aḥwāl i Āshōb*) and 6 (*Tārīkh i shahādat i Farrukh-siyar* . . .) are of course in prose and should not have been included in a list of poetical works by "Āshōb".

P. 620, l. 3. Farshūrī, or rather, it would seem, Farshaurī (or Firshaurī ?) i.e. connected with Peshawar. Cf. *Ṭabaqāt i Akbarī* i p. 37[3] (*Pashāwar kih dar kutub i salaf bah Bikrām u PRSWR u FRSHWR mashhūr ast*); "'Iṣāmī" *Futūḥ al-salāṭīn* p. 410, l. 7863: *Shunīdam kih khwad ham ba-Lāhaur mānd Sarān i sipah rā ba-FRSHWR rānd* (cf. ll. 7866, 7870); 'Abd al-Ḥaiy Lak'hnawī *Nuzhat al-khawāṭir* (in Arabic) p. 146[13] (*M. b. M. al-Junaidī . . . al-FRSHWRĪ . . . wulida bi-madīnat Pashāwar*); Yule and Burnell *Hobson Jobson* under Peshawar. Yāqūt spells the name Farshābūr.

P. 621, l. 30. Shākir Khān was born at Pānīpat in 1128/1716 according to his own statement in his encyclopædia *Ḥadīqah i ḥādiq i ganjīnah i Ṣādiq* (Ethé 2228, Bānkīpūr Suppt. ii 2022).

P. 624, l. 9. For James Browne (not Brown) see p. 665 *infra*.

P. 624, l. 17. *Read* Kōl, and.

P. 625, l. 3. According to "Rangīn's" Persian preface to his *Dīwān i rēkhtah* (Blumhardt *Catalogue of Hindustani manuscripts in the . . . India Office*, no. 185) Ṭahmās Bēg Khān reached India at the age of seven with Nādir Shāh's invading army. He eventually became a *haft-hazārī*.

P. 625, l. 9. The words "who created him a Khān" should be deleted. It was Tīmūr Shāh who raised him to the rank of khān, changing his original name of Tīmūr to Ṭahmās Khān.

P. 625 penult. *Tawallud* : so in the printed texts. Perhaps *maulid* should be read. Read *dār al-k͟hilāfah i*.

M. HISTORY OF INDIA : (*d*) 19TH CENTURY

P. 643, l. 6. [" Az̤farī."] For the Persian translation of the *Maḥbūb al-qulūb* see an article entitled '*Alī-S͟hēr kī ēk kitāb kā qalamī nusk͟hah ya'nī Marg͟hūb al-fu'ād tarjamah i Maḥbūb al-qulūb* [in the Panjāb Univ. Lib.], by S. M. 'Abd Allāh in *OCM*. xi/4 (Aug. 1935) pp. 41-8.

P. 643, l. 15. [" Az̤farī."] For his *Mīzān i Turkī*, a Turkī grammar, see Madrās i 459 (A.H. 1209/1794-5, autograph).

P. 643, l. 20. [*Wāqi'āt i Az̤farī*.] Read **Madrās** i 450 (A.H. 1243/ 1828), 451.

P. 643, l. 28. [" Az̤farī."] Also *OCM*. xi/4 (Aug. 1935) pp. 41-8 (in the article referred to above).

P. 644, l. 9. [*S͟hāh-'Ālam-nāmah*.] Also **Ellis Coll.** M. 293 (slightly defective at end).

P. 646. Faḍl i 'Az̤īm " 'Az̤īm " K͟hairābādī was a son of Maulawī Faḍl i Imām K͟hairābādī (for whom see Raḥmān 'Alī p. 162) and an elder brother of the well known scholar Faḍl i Ḥaqq K͟hairābādī (for whom see Raḥmān 'Alī p. 164, Brockelmann *Sptbd*. ii p. 854). The brief and dateless notices of him given in the *S͟ham' i anjuman* (p. 328) and the *Ṣubḥ i guls͟han* (p. 288) do not mention the titles of any of his works.

P. 647, l. 10. For " Farānsū " see an article entitled *Urdū kā Jarman s͟hā'ir " Farānsū " aur us kī taṣnīfāt* by S. M. 'Abd Allāh in *OCM*. xx/3 (May 1944) pp. 3–30, where information is drawn from MSS. (apparently not autographs [1]) of " Farānsū's " works in the Panjāb University Library. His name as given by himself (but not without some later corruption) is Farānsū KWYN [2] walad i Jān [3] Kārlīw [4] KWYN (*Masarrat-afzā*, preface, and *Guldastah i ḥusn u 'is͟hq*, preface, *OCM*. xx/3 p. 5, l. 4 from foot, and

---

[1] Except perhaps one MS. of the *dīwān* (*OCM*. xx/3 p. 25[6]).
[2] This is evidently the name which appears elsewhere as Gūst, Gūstīn, Akden, etc. If Gādlīb had not occurred by its side in these MSS., it might have been supposed to be itself a corruption of Götlīb.
[3] i.e. John.
[4] Apparently a corruption of Gādlīb.

p. 20[11]), Farānsū KWYN . . . nām i wālid Jān Kādlīb[1] KWYN (*Mir'āt i ḥusn u 'ishq*, colophon, *OCM*. xx/3 p. 5[8]) Farāsū Gādlīb KWYN (*Gulbun i tamannā*, preface, *OCM*. xx/3 p. 22 penult.). In "Shōr's" *Waqā'i' i Ghadr* it is stated that Misṭar Farānsis کوئنس [Kō'ins ?] died suddenly of old age in July 1861 (*OCM*. xx/3 p. 7 ult., quoting from an article on "Farānsū" by Pyārē Lāl "Shākir" Mīraṭ'hī in the *sāl-nāmah* of the *Adabī dunyā* (Lahore) for 1939). The correct form of the surname could probably be ascertained by examination of the Indian newspapers for July 1861. His father went to India from Poland at the age of sixteen or seventeen and married a Frenchwoman, to whom Farānsū KWYN was born at Shāhjahānābād on 15 March 1777 (*Mir'āt i ḥusn u 'ishq*, colophon, *OCM*. xx/3 p. 5). He became a Captain in the service of the Bēgam Samrū (for whom see p. 691 *infra*) and after her death (in 1836) went to Harchandpūr, where he suffered grievously at the time of the Mutiny.

P. 647, l. 25. [*Fatḥ-nāmah i Angrēz.*] A defective MS. beginning with the "capture of Benares" and ending with the title only of the section "Return of the government to Calcutta" is in the Phillipps collection (cf. p. 1325[28] *infra*). [G. M. Wickens, in a letter.]

P. 649, l. 2. For Nawwāb Amīr 'Alī see also the *Chār dīwār* of his son S. Ashraf al-Dīn Aḥmad (Calcutta 1894*).

M. History of India : (*f*) Sind

P. 650. [*Chach-nāmah.*] According to C. N. Seddon (*JRAS*. 1941 p. 172) the title of the Arabic original was *Minhāj al-dīn wa-'l-mulk.*

P. 651, l. 2. *Insert:*

Edition : *Fatḥ-nāmah i Sind* (*Chach-nāmah*) *by 'Alī ibn Ḥāmid . . . al-Kūfī. Edited by Dr. 'Umar ibn Muḥammad Dāūdpōtā*, **Ḥaidarābād**, Deccan, [Delhi printed] 1939 (Persian MSS. Society Series, no. 3. For a review by C. N. Seddon see

[1] i.e. presumably Gādlīb = Gottlieb.

JRAS. 1941 pp. 171–2. The wording of the title-page may not be precisely as given above).

P. 652, l. 30. [*Tārīkh i Ma'ṣūmī.*] Also **I.O.** 4563 (2) (A.H. 1242/1826. See *JRAS.* 1939 p. 356).

P. 652 penult. For *Sazzid* read *Sayyid.*

P. 653, l. 31. [*M. Ma'ṣūm "Nāmī".*] Also *Islamic culture* ix/3 (July 1935) p. 417 (a notice from the *Dhakhīrat al-khawānīn* translated by M. Abdulla Chughtai); *OCM.* xiii/4 (Aug. 1937) pp. 90–110 (the inscription on his tomb and some other inscriptions connected with him and his family in an article entitled *Sind'h kē ba'ḍ kitbē* by M. Shafī').

P. 654, l. 19. [*Bēg-Lār-nāmah.*] Also **Ellis Coll.** M. 185 (A.H. 1233/1817).

P. 656, l. 5. *For* Mount Maklī *read* Maklī hill.[1]

P. 656, l. 6. [*Tuḥfat al-kirām.*] An autograph MS. (doubtless in private possession) was used by M. Shafī' for his article *Khaṭṭāṭān i Sind* (cf. p. 1076[8] *infra*) in *OCM.* xi/2 (Feb. 1938) pp. 131–4.

P. 656, l. 16. **I.O.** 4535 was formerly **I.O.** MSS. Per. D. 4.

P. 656, l. 19. [*Tuḥfat al-kirām.*] *Insert*:

Extract relating to the calligraphists of Sind (= vol. iii p. 241 in the lithograph): *OCM.* xi/2 (Feb. 1935) pp. 131–4 (ed. M. Shafī').

P. 659, l. 30. *Insert*:

(3) **Tārīkh i Sind,** an anonymous epitome to 1207/1792–3: **I.O.** 4563 (1) (A.H. 1242/1826. See *JRAS.* 1939 p. 356).

M. History of India: (*g*) Bahāwalpūr

P. 663, l. 15. *Read* p. 472.

M. History of India: (*h*) The Panjāb

P. 664, l. 26. *Read probably* [? Hindie].

P. 667, l. 14. *Read* 294*a*); Amar.

P. 668, l. 2. [*Aḥwāl i firqah i Sik'hān.*] Also **Ellis Coll.** M. 224 (A.H. 1224/1809).

[1] On Maklī hill, two miles N.W. of Tattah, is a vast necropolis covering an area of six square miles.

P. 669, l. 8. *For* wich whas *read* which was.

P. 672, l. 10. *Insert* :

Analysis : *A notice of the 'Umdatu 't-tawarikh. By the late E. Rehatsek* (in *The Indian antiquary* xxiii (1894) pp. 57–72).

P. 672, l. 21. Jamūn : so Rieu (iii p. 955), but Jammūn in K͟hwājah 'Abd al-Majīd's Urdu dictionary *Jāmi' al-lug͟hāt*.

P. 674, l. 34. For the Sit'hānah and Malkah campaign see also W. W. Hunter *The Indian Musalmans*, London, 1871, pp. 1–43 (cf. G. F. I. Graham *Life and work of Syed Ahmed Khan*, London 1885, pp. 228–9, etc.) ; *The Punjaub and North-West Frontier of India. By an old Punjaubee*, London 1878 pp. 47–61 ; R. R. Sethi *Events leading to the Ambela Expedition, 1863* (in *Bengal : past and present*, 46/1 (July–Sept. 1930) pp. 14–22).

M. History of India : (*j*) Kas͟hmīr

P. 679, l. 16. [*Rāja-taraṅgiṇī*.] For S͟hāh-Muḥammad S͟hāhābādī's translation see *Ā'īn i Akbarī* tr. Blochmann p. 106.

P. 680, l. 24. [Ḥaidar Malik.] According to the *Wāqi'āt i Kas͟hmīr*, p. 125, the title given to Ḥaidar Malik was Ra'īs al-Mulk i C͟hag͟hatā'ī.

P. 682, l. 12. [Narāyan Kaul's *Tārīk͟h i Kas͟hmīr*.] Also **Ellis Coll.** M. 299 (" with the continuation of Pandit Bīrbal." A.H. 1267/1851), M. 298 (with the continuation to 1262/1846).

P. 684, l. 4. [M. A'ẓam.] Also *Ḥadā'iq al-Ḥanafīyah* p. 450.

P. 684, l. 22. [*Gauhar i 'ālam*.] An undated MS. (367 foll., $8\frac{1}{4} \times 6\frac{1}{2}$ in., 15 or 16 ll.) formerly in the collection of Sir Thomas Phillipps (1792–1872) and now in another private collection contains both the sixth *ṭabaqah* and the *k͟hātimah* (marvels, etc., to the number of forty-five) and brings the history down to 1191/1777. [G. M. Wickens, in a letter.]

P. 685, l. 6. *Read* Paklī *instead of* Paglē.

P. 685, l. 14. [*Majma' al-tawārīk͟h*.] Also **Ellis Coll.** M. 317 (*Majmū'at* [so, fol. 7] *al-tawārīk͟h*. Samwat 1927/1870), M. 316 (19th cent.). See also the addendum to p. 682, l. 12.

P. 686, l. 25. [*Gulzār i Kas͟hmīr*.] MS. : **Ellis Coll.** M. 225 (mid 19th cent.).

P. 687, l. 19. *Insert*:

(5*a*) *Mūjaz al-tawārīkh*, a sketch of the history of Kashmīr in tabular form, by M. Saif al-Dīn Kashmīrī: **Amritsar** (Khādim i Panjāb Press) 1324/1907* (*Tārīkh i jadwalī i Kashmīr mausūm bah M. al-t.* 28 pp.).

M. History of India: (*m*) Rājpūtānah

P. 688, l. 16. *Read* 1825.

P. 689, l. 28. *Insert*:

893*a*. Pandit **Shankar Nāt'h "Nādir"** (A.D. 1826).

Jangnāmah i Bharatpūr, or *Nuṣrat u Ẓafar*, an account of Durjan Sāl's deposition: **Lahore** Panjāb Univ. (A.H. 1260/1841. See *OCM*. vii/4 p. 68).

P. 690, l. 5. For Francis Gottlieb "Farānsū" see the addenda to p. 647 *supra*.

M. History of India: (*t*) The Rohillas

P. 694, l. 14. [The Rohillas.] According to M. Longworth Dames's article on Ḥāfiẓ Raḥmat Khān in the *Ency. Isl.* "the name Rohilla (properly Rōhēlā) or Highlander" is an Eastern Pandjābī adjective from *rōh* "a hilly country". In Khwājah 'Abd al-Majīd's Urdu dictionary *Jāmi' al-lughāt* (iii p. 248) the word is spelt Rŏhīlā with *ī* not *ē* and with a short first syllable. Presumably that is the correct pronunciation in Urdu.

P. 694, l. 15. Ghulām-Muḥyī 'l-Dīn[1] S. 'Abd al-Laṭīf is the author of three mystical works, (1) *Laṭā'if i Laṭīfī*, (2) *Risālah i taufīq* and (3) *Miftāḥ al-asrār*, which are preserved in an India Office MS. (I.O. 4570. See *JRAS*. 1939 p. 360). For another work of his, *Dār al-khuld*, a collection of letters mainly on Ṣūfī subjects, see Ivanow 415. He died in 1194/1780 (see *Guldastah i Karnātak* (Ivanow 1st Suppt. p. 8); *Ṣubḥ i waṭan* 76).

P. 694, l. 23. Nūr al-Dīn Ḥusain was at one time an officer in the household of 'Imād al-Mulk Ghāzī al-Dīn Khān (for whom see pp. 1028–30 *supra*) and later became *Munshī*

[1] For names of this type consisting of the word *ghulām* followed by the name of a saint cf. p. 1022, n. 1.

and trusted diplomatic agent to Sir Charles Malet, the British Resident at Poona [Jadunath Sarkar in *Islamic culture* x/4 (Oct. 1936) p. 648].

P. 695, l. 28. [*Tārīkh i faiḍ-bakhsh.*] Also **Ellis Coll.** M. 294 (18th cent.).

P. 696, l. 6. *Insert*:

912*a*. **Bihārī Lāl** Munshī.

Lives of (1) ***Najīb al-Daulah,***[1] (2) ***Ḍābiṭah Khān,***[2] (3) ***'Alī Muḥammad Khān, Ḥāfiẓ Raḥmat Khān,***[3] ***Dūndē Khān***[4] ***and other Rohillas,*** written in 1787 at Camp Fatḥgaṛh for Captain "Ustar":[5] MS. discovered (at some place unspecified) by Jadunath Sarkar.

Translation of the first section: *Najib-ud-daulah, Ruhela chief. A unique Persian manuscript.* [Translated in part by] *Jadunath Sarkar* (in *Islamic culture* x/4 (Oct. 1936) pp. 648–58).

P. 698, l. 5. [*Durr i manẓūm.*] Also **Princeton** 59 (but this MS. of 15 foll. is apparently a fragment from the beginning of the poem, since it is described as "a poetical description of the nocturnal journey of the Prophet and of his personal appearance").

History of India: (*u*) Jaunpūr

P. 699, l. 5. *Read* 1899°*.

M. History of India: (*w*) Benares

P. 702, l. 2. *Insert*:

922*a*. Another account of Chait Sing'h's rebellion is contained in Sanbhau Lāl's *Miftāḥ i khazā'in* (a chronogram = 1197/1783. See Rieu iii 1016*b*, 1026*a*, 1056*b*).

P. 702, l. 10. [*Tuḥfah i tāzah.*] Also **Ellis Coll.** M. 221 (A.H. 1238/1821).

[1] Cf. p. 694 $^{25-29}$.
[2] Cf. p. 695 ^{15}.
[3] Cf. p. 696 $^{8-11}$.
[4] Cf. p. 646 n. 5 and n. 6.
[5] Believed by Sarkār to be "a copyist's error for *Istur* = *Stuart,* meaning that Col. Stuart who was kidnapped by the Sikhs when hunting near Anupshahar and afterwards released for a ransom through the mediation of Begam Samru in 1788". But if "Ustar" was a captain in 1787, he is unlikely to have been a colonel in 1788.

M. History of India: (*aa*) Oudh

P. 704, l. 4. *Insert*:

930*a*. For the *Waqā'i' i Shujā'ī* see p. 625 *supra*.

P. 706, l. 19. [*'Imād al-sa'ādat*.] Also **Ellis Coll.** M. 126 (19th cent.).

P. 707, l. 19. An edition of the *Ṣubḥ i ṣādiq* was lithographed at Meerut in 1292/1875* (26 pp.). Sprenger's description of this work as an autobiography is incorrect, since it is a string of reflections in ornate prose and verse on the trials of human life and the wickedness of contemporary humanity.

P. 708, l. 2. [Ṣādiq Khān "Akhtar".] Also Garcin de Tassy i p. 184 (where his father's name is given as Qāḍī M. La'l and where he is said to have been still alive in 1854); *Mi'rāj al-khayāl* (Ivanow Curzon p. 67); *Khāzin al-shu'arā'* fol. 46*a*, l. 4; R. B. Saksēna *History of Urdu literature* p. 122 (where it is stated that, having lost the favour of Wājid 'Alī Shāh, he left Lucknow and became a *Taḥṣīldār* at Etawah, where he died in 1858); T. Grahame Bailey *History of Urdu literature* p. 67.

P. 708, l. 4. John Doeswell Shakespeare: so Rieu, but J. Dowdeswell Shakespear is correct (cf. W. W. Hunter *The Thackerays in India* p. 147).

P. 708, l. 6. 'Abd al-Aḥad "Rābiṭ" b. M. Fā'iq, a resident of Amēṭ'hī, was a "Sarishtedar" in the office of the British Resident at Lucknow and died at Amēṭ'hī in 1268/1851–2 (see M. Taqī Aḥmad's translation, p. 1 n., where no authority is mentioned). P.S. See *Nigāristān i sukhan* p. 28.

P. 708, l. 14. [*Waqā'i' i dil-padhīr*.] *Insert*:

Translation: *Tarikh Badshah Begam* (*a Persian manuscript on the history of Oudh*) *translated by Muhammad Taqi Ahmad* [from a MS. formerly in the possession of "the late Maharajah of Balrampur"]. **Allahabad** 1938 (cf. *JRAS*. 1939 p. 351).

P. 708, ll. 18–19. *Read* iii 1052*b* (extracts only), 1053*b* (extracts only. Circ. A.D. 1850).

P. 709, l. 15. *For* A.H. 1197/1782–3 *read* on 23 Muḥarram 1197/29 December 1782 (see *OCM*. iii/3 (May 1927) p. 49).

P. 710, l. 2. [Ratan Sing'h "Zakhmī".] Also *Ṣubḥ i gulshan* p. 189, where the date of his death is given as 1267 [1850–1].

P. 712 ult. ['Abd al-Jalīl Bilgrāmī.] Also *Safīnah i Khwushgū* (Bānkīpūr viii p. 97) ; *Khulāṣat al-kalām* (Bkp. viii p. 143).

P. 713, l. 16. [M. b. 'Abd al-Jalīl Bilgrāmī]. Also *Khizānah i 'āmirah* pp. 284–6.

P. 713, l. 18. *Read* 1929, ii pp. 159–63.

P. 713, l. 22. *For* village *read* small town.

M. Ḥistory of India : (*bb*) Bengal and Orissa

P. 714, l. 28. [*Bahāristān i Ghaibī.*] *Read* **Gauhati** 1936 (see *JRAS.* 1937 p. 581 and Sir R. Burn's review in *JRAS.* 1941 pp. 70–2).

P. 717, l. 13. [*Tārīkh i Mahābat-Jang.*] Also **Ellis Coll.** M. 429 (A.H. 1185/1772).

P. 724, l. 20. [*Ṭabaqāt i Muḥsinīyah.*] *Read* 57 foll.) : **Calcutta** 1889*.

P. 724, n. 2. There was a portrait of Ḥājjī M. Muḥsin in Room 195 at the India Office and a reproduction of it in *Bengal : past and present*, v p. 159.

P. 725, l. 6. For Munnī (not Manī) Bēgam see *Amīr-nāmah* p. 32 and Beale's *Oriental biographical dictionary* p. 280.

M. History of India : (*cc*) Gujrāt

P. 728, l. 3. *Insert* :

Urdu translation : *Tarikh-i-Gujrat. By Abu Turab Vali. Translated . . . into Urdu, with introduction, by Shabeah* [*sic* ?] *Ahmad.* **Allahabad** 1945 (see Probsthain's *Orientalia nova* i (1944–6) no. 614 and *Luzac's OL.* 1945 p. 58, in which latter place the language of the translation is not specified).

P. 728, l. 15. *Read* **Sikandar ibn** M. **Manjhū.**

P. 729, l. 8 from foot. Read *Aḥmadābād i Gujrāt.*

M. History of India : (*ff*) Bhōpāl

P. 734, l. 2. [Shāh-Jahān Bēgam.] *Read* "Shīrīn", afterwards "Tājwar". See *Ḥayāt i Shāh-Jahānī*, tr. Ghosal, p. 241. In her Persian poetry, however, she seems to have called herself "Shāh i Jahān", which is given as her *takhalluṣ* in the *Sham' i anjuman*, the *Nigāristān i sukhan* and the *Ṣubḥ i gulshan*.

P. 734, ll. 14–15. For these and other works see *Ḥayāt i Shāh-Jahānī*, tr. Ghosal, pp. 241–6.

P. 734, l. 30. [Shāh-Jahān Bēgam.] Also *Nigāristān i sukhan* pp. 45–7 ; *Ṣubḥ i gulshan* pp. 217–20 ; *Hayat-i-Shahjehani, life of . . . Nawab Shahjehan Begum . . ., by Her Highness Nawab Sultan Jehan Begum . . . Translated by B. Ghosal.* Bombay 1926.

M. History of India : (*hh*) Gwalior

P. 735, l. 19. *Read* **Ḥiṣārī.**

M. History of India : (*jj*) Būndēlk'hand

P. 737, l. 26. Read ***Wāqi'ah i Jhōjhār Sing'h.***

M. History of India : (*kk*) The Deccan

P. 739, l. 17. *Insert* :

(4*a*) ***Tūdah i ṭūfān i Machhlī-bandar,*** an account of an inundation at Masulipatam (cf. no. (1) above) in 1281/1864–5, by Qādir Muḥyī 'l-Dīn : **Āṣafīyah** iii p. 100.

M. History of India : (*ll*) The Bahmanids

P. 740, l. 21. ['Alī b. 'Azīz Allāh Ṭabāṭabā.] *Insert* :

[*Haft iqlīm* no. 1147 ?]

M. History of India : (*mm*) Aḥmadnagar

P. 741, l. 13. [*Fatḥ-nāmah i Shōlāpūr.*]

Edition : *Conquest of Sholāpūr by Burhān Niẓām Shāh I (914–961 A.H., 1508–1553) as described by Shāh Ṭāhir. By M. Hidayat Hosain* (in *JRASB.*, Letters, v/1 (1939) pp. 133–53).

P. 741, l. 18. [Shāh Ṭāhir Dak'hanī.] Also *Haft iqlīm* no. 1305 ; *Khazīnah i ganj i Ilāhī* (Sprenger p. 80[20]) ; *Hamīshah bahār* (Sprenger p. 125) ; *Safīnah i Khwushgū* no. 70 ; *Khulāṣat al-afkār* no. 162 ; *Makhzan al-gharā'ib* no. 1453 (?) ; article by Hidayat Hosain in the Denison Ross *Festschrift.*

P. 742, l. 5. The *Jāmiʻ al-ʻulūm* was completed on 14 Muḥarram 1173/8 Sept. 1759 according to Brockelmann *Sptbd.* ii p. 628.

M. History of India : (*nn*) Bījāpūr

P. 743, l. 33. [*Futūḥāt i ʻĀdil-Shāhī.*] Also **Ellis Coll.** M. 119 (17th cent.).

P. 743 penult. [" Fuzūnī ".] Also *Ṣubḥ i gulshan* p. 317.

P. 743 penult. *Insert* :

1015*a*. **M. Ẓuhūr ibn** Maulawī **Ẓuhūrī** was presumably a son of the poet " Ẓuhūrī " Turshīzī (who died in 1025/1616 or thereabouts : see Browne *Lit. Hist.* iv p. 253 ; *Ency. Isl.* under Ẓuhūrī (Huart) ; Bānkīpūr cat. iii pp. 32–4 ; etc.).

Muḥammad-nāmah, on the reign of Muḥammad ʻĀdil-Shāh : **Ellis Coll.** M. 282 (A.H. 1183/1769–70), **Kapurthala** 31 (24 year of Shāh-ʻĀlam (A.H. 1196–7). See *OCM.* iii/4 (Aug. 1927) p. 15).

P. 744, l. 1. " The University Library of Belfast possesses an incomplete history of Bījāpūr (especially of the Khāqān-i Sikandar-iqbāl = Muḥammad, 1035–70/1626–60 ?), beginning: *shukr-va-sipās-va sitāyish-i bī-qiyās ḥaḍrat-i pādshāh-i ʻalal-iṭlāq*. It must be identical with Abul-Qāsim's *Guldasta-yi gulshan-i rāz*, Browne Coll. H. 17 (13) which begins *ḥamd-va-sipās-i bi-qiyās* " [Minorsky, *BSOS.* x/2 (1940) p. 540]. This identification seems improbable, since the opening words of the *Guldastah i gulshan i rāz* (?) (this title comes merely from a fly-leaf) are *Ḥ. u sp. i bī-qiyās mar dhāt i mustajmaʻ i jamīʻ i ṣifāt i kamāl.*

P. 744, l. 16. [*Tārīkh i ʻAlī ʻĀdil-Shāh.*] Also **Madrās** i 213 (*a*) (*Tārīkh i ʻĀdil-Shāh*, by Nūr Allāh . . . , described as a history of Ibrāhīm ʻĀdil-Shāh, presumably therefore the earlier part (84 pp. only) of the *T. i ʻA. ʻĀ.-Sh.*).

M. History of India : (*pp*) Ḥaidarābād

P. 749, l. 3. [*Tārīkh i futūḥāt i Āṣafī.*] Probably also **Madrās** i 127 (*Mathnawī i Futūḥāt i Āṣafī.* " Author, Asafi." Beg. *Ba-nām i Shahanshāh i mulk i baqā*).

P. 751, l. 1. [Mīr-ʻĀlam.] For this form of title cf. Mīrzā-yi ʻālamiyān Mīrzā M. Shafīʻ (*ʻĀlam-ārāy i ʻAbbāsī* p. 568[9]).

P. 751, l. 34. *For* be *read* he.

P. 752. l. 9. *Read* Early.

P. 752, l. 9. *Read* 1266/1850°*.

P. 752, l. 26. [Mīr-'Ālam.] Also *A memoir of Sir Salar Jang, G.C.S.I.*, by Syed Hossain Bilgrami, Bombay 1883, pp. 9–12.

P. 752, l. 28. *Read* Ḥaidarābād 1930 (see *JRAS.* 1933 pp. 194–6).

P. 754, l. 33. For C̲h̲andū Lāl see pp. 1100–1 *infra.*

P. 756, l. 3. [*Gulzār i Āṣafīyah.*] For an autograph MS. in the private library of Maulawī 'Umar Yāfi'ī [presumably at Ḥaidarābād] see *Islamic culture* xxii/4 (Oct. 1948) p. 400.

P. 756, n. 1. On p. 111 the 2nd of Muḥarram 1260 is called *al-ān.*

P. 757, l. 2. For the *Bayāḍ i dil-gus̲h̲ā*, incorrectly described here (on the authority of Steingass's card-catalogue) as an anthology, see p. 1042 *infra.*

P. 757, l. 15. [Naṣr Allāh K̲h̲ān.] Also *Guls̲h̲an i hamīs̲h̲ah-bahār* pp. 92–4 (autobiography. Cf. p. 904 *infra*); *Ṣubḥ i guls̲h̲an* p. 519.

P. 758, l. 18. For the Nā'iṭī tribe see pp. 1083–4 *infra* and *Ma'āt̲h̲ir al-umarā'* iii p. 562 (Beveridge's trans. i p. 164).

P. 758, l. 29. [Nawwāb 'Azīz-Jang.] Also a short autobiography prefixed to the *Kullīyāt i naẓm i Wilā* (Ḥaidarābād 1328/1910*).

P. 759, l. 6. *Insert*:

(2a) ***Gazēṭīr i ḍil' i Ēlgandal,*** composed in 1289 *Faṣlī* [A.H. 1297/1880 ?] by Mānik-S̲h̲āh Bābūjī, formerly 2nd Ta'alluqdār of the Elgandal District: **Āṣafīyah** iii p. 102 (A.H. 1297/1880).

P. 759, l. 25. For the *Tārīk̲h̲ i rāḥat-afzā* see p. 1244 *supra* (addendum to p. 138, l. 17).

P. 759, l. 29. [*Waqā'i' i s̲h̲ūris̲h̲ i Afg̲h̲ānīyah.*] It is not clear whether the Ḥaidarābād referred to is Ḥaidarābād, Sind, or Ḥaidarābād, Deccan.

P. 759, l. 33. *Insert*:

(12) *Waṣīyat-nāmah i Nawwāb Āṣaf-Jāh Bahādur*: **Bodleian** 2020.

M. History of India: (qq) The Marāṭ'hās

In spite of the preference of certain Orientalists for the form *Marhaṭṭah* (with a doubled *ṭ*) it appears doubtful whether this form is even permissible in Urdu and in the Persian of India. At any rate the usual Urdu pronunciation seems to be with a single *ṭ*. In 'Abd al-Majīd's *Jāmi' al-lughāt* (an Urdu dictionary) *Marhaṭā* and *Marhaṭah* are given as the Urdu spellings and *Marhaṭṭā* as a Hindī spelling. Another pronunciation (the only one mentioned in the *Farhang i Āṣafīyah*) is *Marahṭā* or *Marahṭah*. Presumably therefore the spelling *Marhaṭṭah* should be corrected on pp. 760 (ll. 17, 20), 762 (ll. 7, 13, 14), 763 (l. 16) and 764 (ll. 18, 24).

P. 763, l. 7. *Read* Ghulām-Ṣamadānī.

P. 763, l. 10. [*Bisāṭ al-ghanā'im.*] *Insert*:
English translation by Colonel J. W. Watson: **Ethé** ii 3018 marg.

P. 764, l. 21. [*Aḥwāl i Bhā'ō Marhaṭah.*] *For* Circ. A.D. 1808 (?) *read* 2 copies, one dated 1197/1783.

P. 764, l. 25. [*Aḥwāl i ḥasab u nasab i Janūbiyān.*] Also **Ellis Coll.** M. 47.

M. History of India: (ss) Mysore

P. 769, l. 7. *Read* Persian.

P. 770, l. 2. *Delete* this.

P. 771, l. 10. *Read* **Letters.**

P. 771, l. 18. For a transcript of Ethé 3001 see Blochet iv 2119.

P. 771, l. 19. Read *infra cit.*

P. 772, l. 22. Read *Tippoo.*

P. 775, l. 4. *Read* [*sic*, for 1844].

P. 775, l. 10. Read *Kirdgār kārsāz i rūzgār.*

P. 776, l. 5. In the Calcutta Madrasah catalogue, p. 105, the *Kār-nāmah i Ḥaidarī* is spoken of as a work of 'Abd al-Raḥīm Gōrak'hpūrī (who went to Afghānistān with Mountstuart Elphinstone and W. Fraser, translated some English mathematical works into Persian and died in Calcutta).

P. 776, l. 17. *Read* Calcutta 1854.

P. 777, l. 7. Read *Srī-Rang-Paṭan* [with a single *ṭ*. Dr. Khiḍr 'Alī Khān, orally].

P. 777, l. 8. *Insert*:

(8) *Tārīkh i Ṭīpū Sulṭān* (beg. *Sulṭān i nash'atain*): **Madrās** i 288.

(9) *Waqā'i' i Ḥaidarī* (beg. *Shāyistah-tarīn kalāmī*), a brief history of Ḥaidar 'Alī and Ṭīpū: **Madrās** i 320–1.

M. History of India: (*uu*) The Carnatic

P. 778, l. 13. *Read* 1162/1749.

P. 778, l. 26. *Insert*:

Edition: *Anwar Nāma of Abjadi. Edited by Muhammad Husain Mahvi.* **Madrās** 1944 (Madras Univ. Islamic Series, no. 8. See *JRAS*. 1946 p. 210).

P. 779, l. 9. *Read* **Madrās** i 304.

P. 779, l. 14. [*Tūzuk i Wālā-Jāhī.*] Part ii of Nainar's translation was published in 1939 (see *JRAS*. 1940 p. 398, 1942 p. 71).

P. 780, l. 17. [*Sawāniḥāt i mumtāz.*] Also **Madrās** i p. 546 no. 535, p. 486 no. 447 (A.H. 1350/1931,[1] probably transcribed from the preceding MS.).

P. 780, l. 33. *Insert*:

(1*a*) *Bahār i A'ẓam-Jāhī*, an account of Nawwāb A'ẓam-Jāh's journey to Nagūr and back in 1238/1822–3 by Ghulām-'Abd al-Qādir "Nāẓir" entitled Qādir 'Aẓīm Khān (for whom see p. 1083): **Madrās** i 529 (A.H. 1239/1823–4, autograph).

(1*b*) *Sharaf-nāmah*, or *Tārīkh i Ḥafīẓ-Allāh-Khānī*, a history of the Nawwābs of the Carnatic from 'Aẓīm al-Daulah to Ghulām-Ghauth, by M. Auliyā, entitled Ḥafīẓ Allāh Khān: **Madrās** i 530 (A.H. 1354/1935).

N. Biography: (*a*) Poets

P. 784, l. 22. *Insert*:

1091*a*. For the *Badā'i' al-waqā'i'* of "Wāṣifī" see p. 373.

P. 790, n. 1. [*Dīwān i Fānī.*] Also **Majlis** ii 1035 (between 901/1495–6 and 906/1500–1).

P. 794, l. 4. *Read* pp. 155–7); *Tuḥfah.*

[1] The words "Appearance, old" in the description of the MS. are presumably a *lapsus calami* for "Appearance, new".

P. 796 penult. Shujā' Bēg Arghūn, or Amīr Shāh-Shujā' Arghūn was not another son of Dhū 'l-Nūn but the same person as Shāh-Bēg Arghūn (see *Ency. Isl.* under Arghūn dynasty of Sind, Firishtah ii p. 620 penult.).

P. 799, l. 14. [*Tuḥfah i Sāmī.*] Also **Vatican** Pers. 106 (A.H. 977/1569 or 997/1588. Rossi p. 116), **Ellis Coll.** M. 367 (A.H. 1026/1617).

P. 805, l. 12. *Insert*:

1105*a*. Ṣādiq Bēg "**Ṣādiqī**" **Afshār**, poet and painter, was born at Tabrīz in 940/1533–4 and became Librarian to Shāh 'Abbās (985–1038/1587–1629). According to the *Dānishmandān i Ādharbāyjān* he prepared in 1010/1601–2 at Iṣfahān a collected edition of his works in Persian and Turkī prose and verse, which included a Persian *mathnawī* entitled *Fatḥ-nāmah i 'Abbās i nāmdār* as well as the *Majma' al-khawāṣṣ*. For his *Ḥazzīyāt*, a small Persian work on Ṣūfism, see Berlin 12 (7), Bodleian 1243 (2) and *Dānishmandān i Ādharbāyjān* p. 213 (10).

Majma' al-khawāṣṣ, dateless Turkī notices of contemporary poets composed [*circa* 1000/1592 [1]] in the reign of Shāh 'Abbās (985–1038/1587–1629) and divided into eight *majma's* ((1) kings, p. 7, (2) princes, p. 21, (3) nobles of Turkish race (*arkān i salṭanat az Turkān*), p. 29, (4) nobles of Persian race, p. 39, (5) sons of Turkish and Persian nobles, p. 63, (6) Saiyids, p. 74, (7) Turkish poets who wrote in Turkish, Persian and Arabic, p. 102, (8) contemporary Persian poets, p. 131), and a *khātimah* (verses by the author): Ḥ. Kh. ii p. 263, v p. 401, **Istānbūl** Univ. Lib. 4085 (A.H. 1016/1607–8), 4097 (A.H. 1037/1627–8), **Nūr i 'Uthmānīyah** 3720 (A.H. 1021/1612), **Gotha** Turkish cat. p. 139 no. 168.

Edition with Persian translation: *Tadhkirah i Majma' al-khawāṣṣ ba-zabān i Turkī i Chaghatāy ta'līf i Ṣādiqī i Kitābdār u tarjamah i ān ba-zabān i Fārsī ba-khāmah i Duktur 'Abd al-Rasūl Khayyām-pūr mu'allim i Dānish-gāh i Tabrīz*, **Tabrīz** A.H.S. 1327/1948–9 (327 pp.).

[1] At the end of the work there is a chronogram for the circumcision of Ṣafī Mīrzā in 1003.

List of the 342 [1] poets in the Gotha MS.: Gotha Turkish cat. pp. 140–8.

[Autobiographical statements collected in editor's preface, pp. *ḥā* to *yā*; *Ta<u>dh</u>kirah i Naṣrābādī* pp. 39–40; *'Ālam-ārāy i 'Abbāsī* p. 127; *<u>Kh</u>ulāṣat al-kalām* no. 39; *Ma<u>kh</u>zan al-<u>gh</u>arā'ib* no. 1299; *<u>Sh</u>am' i anjuman* p. 256; *Dāni<u>sh</u>-mandān i Ā<u>dh</u>arbāyjān* pp. 212–13; *Arma<u>gh</u>ān* xii pp. 15–21, 185–99.]

P. 826, l. 16. Read *ra'nā*.

P. 830, l. 18. Lakzī is the Arabic form (cf. Sam'ānī fol. 495, l. 19, Suyūṭī *Lubb al-Lubāb* p. 230, *Tāj al-'arūs* iv p. 78, l. 5 from foot) and it may possibly be used also in Persia, but the word is spelt Lagzī in the *Farhang i Niẓām*.

P. 839, l. 26. [*Munta<u>kh</u>ab i Majma' al-nafā'is.*] Also **Ellis Coll.** M. 50 (early 19th cent.).

P. 842, n. 1–n. 5. The number 1 has been erroneously assigned to two of these notes.

P. 842, n. 3. The spelling Sīwistān may be incorrect. Yāqūt writes Sīwastān.

P. 848, l. 4. [*Ta<u>dh</u>kirat al-aḥwāl.* Editions.] Also **Ṭihrān** A.H.S. 1324/1945 (abridged by Muḥammadī and published under the title *Safar-nāmah i Shai<u>kh</u> Muḥammad 'Alī Ḥazīn* as pp. 61–130 (last) of the volume entitled *Nādir <u>Sh</u>āh*, of which pp. 7–60 are an abridgment of M. Mahdī's *Durrah i Nādirī* [*sic*]).

P. 848, l. 30. [" Ḥazīn."] A brief note by " Ḥazīn ", in Arabic, on the teachers whose lectures he attended and on the books studied by him is preserved in Ivanow 1778 (3).

P. 856, ll. 8 and 14. The spelling Sīwistān may be incorrect. Yāqūt writes Sīwastān.

P. 859, l. 13. [*Subḥat al-marjān.*] Cf. Zubaid Aḥmad *The contribution of India to Arabic literature* pp. 180–2.

P. 860, l. 22. *For* (12) *read* (11).

P. 860, l. 28–p. 861, l. 23. For " Āzād's " *dīwāns* see also Zubaid

[1] The number is 333 in the Istānbūl MSS. used by 'Abd al-Rasūl <u>Kh</u>aiyām-pūr (see his preface p. *zāy*, n. 1). According to the *Dāni<u>sh</u>mandān i Ā<u>dh</u>arbāyjān* the number of biographies is 480 [presumably in a later edition].

Aḥmad *The contribution of India to Arabic literature* pp. 213–19, 428.

P. 861, l. 29. [*Maẓhar al-barakāt.*] See also Zubaid Aḥmad *The contribution of India to Arabic literature* p. 428.

P. 863, l. 9 from foot. The spelling Sīwistān may be incorrect. Yāqūt writes Sīwastān.

P. 871, l. 26. [*Ātash-kadah.*] Also **Majlis** ii 886 (A.H. 1217/1802–3), **Ellis Coll.** M. 231 (ornate MS. Late 18th cent.).

P. 872, l. 27. [*Tadhkirah i Isḥāq.*] Also **Majlis** ii 897 (A.H. 1217/1802–3).

P. 875, l. 8. [*Anīs al-aḥibbā'.*] Also **Majlis** ii 893 (A.H. 1203/1788–9).

P. 877, l. 6. [*Gulzār i Ibrāhīm.*] For an autograph MS. of the second half (*sīn* to *yā'*) in the private library of Maulawī 'Umar Yāfi'ī [presumably at Ḥaidarābād] see *Islamic culture* xxii/4 (Oct. 1948) p. 403.

P. 877, l. 10. [*Gulzār i Ibrāhīm.* Urdu trans.] According to *Islamic culture* xxii/4 (Oct. 1948) p. 403 " Later in 1212 A.H. Mirza 'Alī Luṭf translated a selection of it in Urdu. This was published by Muhammad 'Abdullah Khān (late Nazim of the Āṣafia Library) with a foreword by Maulvi 'Abdul Ḥaq, B.A., in 1906, as Gulshan-i-Hind. Some time back the Tadhkira was corrected and edited by Dr. Zore [i.e. " Zōr "] and was published by the Anjuman-i-Tarraqi [*sic*]-i-Urdu, and forms No. 72 of its publication series."

P. 884, l. 2. Read *Ṣād i daftar i ashwāq* (a chronogram = 1187/1773. See Rieu ii 723*b*).

P. 884, l. 6. [*Bāgh i gulhā-yi ḥusn.*] Also **Rieu** ii 723*b* ii (A.H. 1191/1777). The work, however, does not belong to this section : it contains " descriptions of the various points of female beauty, in ornate prose, with appropriate verses, partly due to the author, partly to other poets not named " (Rieu).

P. 884, l. 18. [" 'Ishq."] Also Garcin de Tassy ii p. 45 ; Rieu ii 723*b*.

P. 887, l. 16. [*Anjuman i Khāqān.*] Also **Majlis** ii 892.

P. 888, l. 16. *Insert*:

1195*a*. S. Ḥasan (or Ḥusain ?) "**Thamar**" **Nā'īnī** is mentioned briefly in the *Anjuman i Khāqān* as one of the Ṭabāṭabā'ī Saiyids of Nā'īn. He is mentioned also in the *Bayān i Maḥmūd*.

Tadhkirah i Thamar i Nā'īnī, notices of forty panegyrists of Ḥājj M. Ḥusain Khān Niẓām al-Daulah Iṣfahānī, who succeeded Mīrzā Shafī' as Ṣadr i A'ẓam and who died in 1238/1822–3, in a *muqaddamah*, two *bābs* and a *khātimah*: **Majlis** ii 898 (lacks *Muqaddamah* and perhaps part of *Khātimah*. Autograph ?).

P. 889, l. 30. ['Abd al-Razzāq Bēg Dunbulī.] *Insert*:

(1*a*) *Ḥadā'iq al-udabā'*, twenty-three *ḥadīqahs* dedicated in 1232/1817 to 'Abbās Mīrzā Nā'ib al-Salṭanah and dealing, in the words of the cataloguer, with "*munsha'āt u muṭāraḥāt i shu'arā-yi 'Arab u 'Ajam u faṣāḥat u balāghat i aqwāl i ānān u siyāsat i mulūk u ādāb i wuzarā' u uṣūl i dīn u akhlāq u tawārīkh u lughāt u ghair az īnhā*": **Majlis** ii 915 (a large fragment (322 foll.) containing biographies of Persian poets and selections from their Arabic poems. Autograph ?).[1]

P. 890, l. 19. [" Rā'iq."] Also *Sham' i anjuman* p. 181.

P. 893, l. 1. [*Tadhkirat al-salāṭīn*.] For the Majlis MS. see now **Majlis** ii 894.

P. 894, l. 7. [*Tadhkirah i Muḥammad-Shāhī*.] Also **Majlis** ii 902 (A.H. 1249/1833–4), 903 (A.H. 1251/1835–6).

P. 896. [Muṣṭafā Khān "Shēftah".] Also *Āthār al-ṣanādīd* (cf. p. 485 *supra*), Lucknow 1876, pt. 4, pp. 110–11.

Pp. 900–1. The first of the two articles numbered 1212, which is out of chronological order and duplicates 1217, was left undeleted through a misunderstanding.

P. 902, l. 28. [*Madā'iḥ al-Mu'tamadīyah*.] Also **Majlis** ii 1192 (autograph ?).

P. 912, l. 13. [*Majma' al-fuṣaḥā'*.] Another edition: [**Ṭihrān**, n.d.] (657 pp. See F. E. Karatay *Istanbul Üniversitesi Kütüphanesi Farsça Basmalar Kataloğu*, p. 151).

[1] A (complete ?) MS. of this work was seen by the cataloguer in the library of the late Thiqat al-Islām.

P. 913, l. 10. *Insert*:

1225*a*. "**Kāẓim**" wrote at least part of his *tadhkirah* at Zanjān.

Tadhkirah i Kāẓim, notices of a few poets and poetesses, nearly all ancient, composed in 1286–7/1869–70: **Majlis** ii 901 (307 foll. A.H. 1286–7, autograph).

P. 915, l. 2. Nawwāb Shams al-'Ulamā' 'Alī Ḥasan Khān is mentioned incidentally in S. Najīb Ashraf Nadwī's *Muqaddamah i ruqa'āt i 'Ālamgīr* (in Urdu), A'ẓamgaṛh [1930*] p. 108[3], where he is described as Nāẓim i Nadwah, Lak'hna'ū [i.e. presumably Director (?) of the educational society Nadwat al-'Ulamā' founded at Lucknow in 1894 or of the school maintained by that society or both (see R. B. Saksēna *History of Urdu literature* p. 290)]. In the autobiography printed under the *takhalluṣ* "Salīm" (evidently a *takhalluṣ* still earlier than "'Āshiqī" mentioned above) in the *Ṣubḥ i gulshan*, pp. 208–11, it is stated that he was born on 4 Rabī' al-Ākhir 1283/16 August 1866 at Bhōpāl. He was thus twelve years old when he published that work and must have received a great deal of assistance from the collaborator mentioned in his preface, Maulawī S. M. Yūsuf 'Alī, *Kārpardāz i āstānah i 'alīyah i walī-'ahd i riyāsat.*

P. 916, l. 19. *Insert*:

1231*a*. **Ibrāhīm b. Mahdī.**

Tadhkirah i majdīyah, poems by members of Nāṣir al-Dīn Shāh's court and high officials, with notices of the authors and portraits: **Ṭihrān** 1302/1885° (52 foll.); 1303/1885–6 (81 pp. See Karatay p. 84).

1231*b*. From statements made here and there in his *tadhkirah* it appears that "**Mumaiyiz**" was at one time auditor at Nihāwand (*sālī kih bandah ma'mūr bi-ta'dīl i Nihāwand būdam,*[1] p. 209), that in 1250/1834–5 he was at Tabrīz (p. 184), that in 1262/1846 he was staying in Tihrān (p. 114) and that in 1299/1881–2 he saw Mūsā Khān "Sarhang" and took down some verses of his.

[1] From these words the cataloguer infers that he "*maqām i ta'dīl i mālīyāt yā mumaiyizī dāshtah*".

Tadhkirah i Mumaiyiz, notices of contemporary poets: **Majlis** ii 904 (A.H. 1306/1888–9, apparently autograph).

P. 918, l. 3. *Insert*:

1235*a*. **'Alī Aṣghar "Ḥikmat"** b. Ḥishmat al-Mamālik Aḥmad 'Alī Mustaufī, member of a distinguished medical family and on his mother's side the grandson of Ḥasan Fasā'ī (see p. 353 *supra*), was born at Shīrāz on 23 Ramaḍān 1310/10 April 1893 and was educated at the American High School [in Ṭihrān] and the University of Paris. He has been Professor of Persian Literature in the University of Ṭihrān since 1931 and was Minister of Foreign Affairs in the cabinet of 1948. He had previously held several other ministries, including that of education. Among his works are didactic *mathnawīs* and translations of plays by Shakespeare. His edition of two translations of the *Majālis al-nafā'is* has already been mentioned (pp. 792–3 *supra*).

Jāmī, *mutaḍammin i taḥqīqāt dar tārīkh i aḥwāl u āthār i manẓūm u manthūr i khātam al-shu'arā Nūr al-Dīn 'Abd al-Raḥmān i Jāmī*: **Tihrān** 1320/1942 (413 pp.).

[Rashīd Yāsimī *Adabīyāt i mu'āṣir* pp. 41–4 (portrait); M. Ishaque *Modern Persian poetry* pp. 11, 26, etc.; Ḥabīb Allāh Mukhtārī *Tārīkh i bīdārī i Īrān* pp. 270–1 (portrait); *International Who's who* 1950 under Hekmat; Īraj Afshār *Nathr i Fārsī i mu'āṣir* pp. 132–7 (portrait)].

P. 918, l. 12. Sa'īd Nafīsī is one of the Professors of Persian Literature in the University of Ṭihrān (see *The world of learning* 1950). Also *Tārīkh i jarā'id u majallāt i Īrān* iii pp. 70–1 (portrait); Īraj Afshār *Nathr i Fārsī i mu'āṣir* pp. 169–92 (portrait).

P. 919, l. 4. "Rashīd" Yāsamī is Professor of the History of Īrān in the University of Ṭihrān (see *The world of learning*, 1950, where Yāsamī is so spent (officially ?)). See also Berthels *Ocherk istorii persidskoi literatury* pp. 167–9; S. M. Bāqir Burqa'ī *Sukhanwarān i nāmī i mu'āṣir* pp. 89–93 (portrait); Īraj Afshār *Nathr i Fārsī i mu'āṣir* pp. 149–56 (portrait).

P. 920, l. 11. [Qāsim Ghanī.] Also Īraj Afshār *Nathr i Fārsī i mu'āṣir* pp. 193–204 (portrait).

P. 920, l. 26. B. al-Z. Furūzān-far is Professor of the History of Persian Literature in the University of Ṭihrān (see *The world of learning* 1950).

P. 921, l. 7. [Badī' al-Zamān Furūzān-far.] Also Burqa'ī *Sukhanwaran i nāmī i mu'āṣir* pp. 22–4 (portrait. His name is given here as M. Ḥasan B. al-Z. F.-f.); Īraj Afshār *Nathr i Fārsī i mu'āṣir* pp. 212–14 (portrait).

P. 921, l. 25. *Insert*:

1240*a*. S. **Ḥusain Shajarah "Bīnā"** b. 'Abd al-Rasūl Shajarah was born at Iṣfahān in 1318/1900–1.

(1) *Shakhṣīyat i Maulawī*, on Jalāl al-Dīn Rūmī and his work: **Ṭihrān** A.H.S. 1316/1937–8.

(2) *Taḥqīq dar rubā'īyāt u zindagānī i Khaiyām*: **Ṭihrān** (see *Luzac's Oriental List* 1942 p. 11, where the date is not mentioned).

[Ishaque *Sukhanvarān-i-Īrān* ii pp. 220–4 (portrait), *Modern Persian poetry* pp. 12, 30.]

P. 922, l. 9. ["Ḥabīb" Yaghmā'ī.] Also D. J. Irani *Poets of the Pahlavi regime* p. 271; Burqa'ī *Sukhanwarān i nāmī i mu'āṣir* p. 57 (portrait).

P. 922, l. 13. *Insert*:

1242*a*. S. **M. Bāqir Burqa'ī** is the son of S. 'Alī Akbar "Kāshif" Burqa'ī Qummī.[1]

Sukhanwarān i nāmī i mu'āṣir, alphabetically arranged notices of poets who were alive in A.H.S. 1300/1920–1 or later years, with a final notice of the earlier poet "Amīrī" (M. Ṣādiq Adīb al-Mamālik, for whom see Browne *Lit. Hist.* iv pp. 346–9): [**Ṭihrān** A.H.S. 1329/1950–1 (date of preface).] (Mu'assasah i Maṭbū'ātī i Amīr i Kabīr.)

P. 922, l. 17. *Insert*:

(1*a*) *Ḥayāt i Sa'dī*, translated from the Urdu of Alṭāf Ḥusain "Ḥālī"[2] by S. Naṣr Allāh "Surūsh": **Tihrān**

[1] For whom see *Sukhanwarān i nāmī i mu'āṣir* pp. 190–6, where it is stated that he was born at Qum A.H.S. 1278/1899–1900 and where twelve published works of his are mentioned. For one of these works, the *Kākh i dil-āwīz*, see p. 1136 *supra*. Another is the *Rāhnumā-yi Qum*.

[2] For "Ḥālī" (1837–1914) see pp. 488–7, 527[23] *supra*; R. B. Saksēna *History of Urdu literature* pp. 210–19, 279–82; T. Grahame Bailey *History of Urdu literature* pp. 88, 94.

A.H.S. 1316/1937 (see *Luzac's OL.* 1938 p. 127 and Harrassowitz's *Litterae orientales* July 1938 p. 9).

P. 922, l. 20. *Insert*:

(2*a*) ***Iqbāl i Lāhaurī*,**[1] *shā'ir i Pārsī-gūy i Pākistān. Baḥth dar aḥwāl u afkār i ū nigārish i Mujtabā Mīnuwī.*[2] **Ṭihrān** A.H.S. 1327/1948–9 (*Az intishārāt i majallah i Yaghmā.* 75 pp.).

P. 922, l. 19. For Aḥmad "Suhailī" b. Ghulām-Riḍā Khān Khwānsārī (b. A.H.S. 1291/1912–13 at Tihrān, Librarian of the Kitāb-khānah i Millī i Malik [3] and editor of the *Dhail i Tārīkh i 'Ālam-ārāy i 'Abbāsī*) see Burqa'ī *Sukhanwarān i nāmī i mu'āṣir* pp. 127–8 (portrait).

P. 922, l. 25. *Insert*:

(4*a*) ***Sa'dī-nāmah*,** essays (and some poems) on Sa'dī by M. Qazwīnī, 'Abbās Iqbāl, Furūzān-far and others, mostly Professors in the University of Ṭihrān: **Ṭihrān** A.H.S. 1316/1938‡ (nos. 11–12 of the periodical *Ta'līm u tarbiyat*, vol. (year) vii, but published also as an independent work).

P. 923, l. 1. *Read* notices.

N. BIOGRAPHY: (*b*) SAINTS, MYSTICS, ETC.

P. 926, ll. 1–9. The Mashhad and Sipahsālār MSS. are evidently portions of the *Kashf al-asrār wa-'uddat al-abrār* of Rashīd al-Dīn Aḥmad b. M. Maibudī (see p. 1190 *supra*, addendum to p. 4, l. 10).

P. 927, l. 25. *Insert*:

1245*a*. **Abū Bakr Muḥammad al-Khaṭīb**, i.e. Abū Bakr M. b. 'Abd al-Karīm b. 'Alī b. Sa'd al-Khaṭīb, died in 502/1109.

[1] For "Iqbāl" (1875–1938) see T. Grahame Bailey *History of Urdu literature* pp. 103–4; etc., etc.

[2] Born in 1320/1902–3 at Tihrān, now Professor in the Faculty of Adabīyāt at Tihrān: see Īraj Afshār *Nathr i Fārsī i mu'āṣir* pp. 215–24 (portrait).

[3] For an account of this library, collected by Ḥājj Ḥusain Āqā Malik [al-Tujjār, who was still alive in A.H.S. 1318/1939, when "Suhailī" Khwānsārī wrote his preface to the *Dhail i Tārīkh i 'Ālam-ārāy i 'Abbāsī*], see 'Abd al-'Azīz Jawāhir al-Kalām's *Kitāb-khānahā-yi Īrān* (cf. *PL.* p. 1135[10]), pp. 79–85, where it is described as the most important of the libraries of Persia at the present time. In *The world of learning* and the *Index generalis* it is called the Hadji Malek Library.

(*Aḥwāl al-Shaikh Abī Isḥāq al-Kāzarūnī*),[1] an Arabic biography of A. I. al-K. (for whom see p. 936, n. 1, *Der Islam* xix p. 18 *sqq*. (M. F. Köprülü and P. Wittek) and *Ency. Isl.*, suppt., under Kāzerūnī (Wittek)): no MSS. recorded.

Persian translations (expanded): (1) ***Firdaus al-murshidīyah fī asrār al-ṣamadīyah***, completed in 728/1327 by Maḥmūd b. 'Uthmān: **Āyā Ṣōfyah** 3254.

Edition: *Die Vita des Scheich Abū Isḥāq al-Kāzarūnī in der persischen Bearbeitung von Maḥmūd b. 'Uṯmān, herausgegeben und eingeleitet von F. Meier*, **Leipzig** 1948 (Bibliotheca Islamica, 14).

(2) ***Marṣad al-aḥrār ilā siyar al-murshid al-abrār***, composed circ. 750/1349 by Rajā' Muḥammad b. 'Abd al-Raḥmān b. 'Abd al-Raḥīm al-Kāzarūnī surnamed (*al-mulaqqab bah*) 'Alā' [al-Dīn], apparently one of the saint's disciples: **A. Chester Beatty's** private library (A.H. 830/1427).

Description: *The biography of Shaikh Abū Isḥāq al-Kāzarūnī. By A. J. Arberry* (in *Oriens* 3/2 (1950) pp. 163–82).

P. 933 ult. ['Abd al-Qādir Jīlānī.] Also M. A. Ayni and F. J. Simore-Munir *Seyyid Abd-al-Kadir Guilani, un grand saint de l'Islam*, Paris 1938 (Les grandes figures de l'Orient, vi. See *Luzac's OL*. 1939 p. 21); *Saiyedena Hazrat Ghaus-ul-Azam*, by Saiyed Abdus Salik, Calcutta (see *Luzac's OL*. 1939 pp. 118, 126).

P. 936, n. 1. [Abū Isḥāq Kāzarūnī.] Also p. 1343[1-19]; *Der Islam* xix p. 18 *sqq*. (M. F. Köprülü and P. Wittek); *Ency. Isl.*, suppt., under Kāzerūnī (Wittek).

P. 941, n. 2. [Mīr (i ?) Khwurd.] Cf. also *Ātash-kadah* no. 189: "Mîr Khurd, with the takhalluṣ Malâlî, brother of Mîr Kalân of Sabzwâr."

P. 942, l. 7. [Niẓām al-Dīn Auliyā kī bastī.] See *A guide to Niẓāmu-d Dīn*, by Maulvi Zafar Hasan, Calcutta 1922 (Memoirs of the Archæological Survey of India, no. 10).

P. 945, l. 26. [*Safar-nāmah i Makhdūm i Jahāniyān*.] **Berlin** 536 (2) (58 foll. A.H. 1236/1821. "Allerhand fabelhafte

[1] The title, if it has one, is not mentioned in Arberry's article, the source of most of the information given here.

Erzählungen von meist fabelhaften Ländern," beginning with the Masjid i Aqṣā) seems to be a part of this work.

P. 948, n. 1. ['Alā' al-Dīn 'Aṭṭār.] Also p. 1061 (78) *infra*; *Ḥabīb al-siyar* iii, 3, p. 87.

P. 950, l. 4. [*Khulāṣat al-maqāmāt.*] For a work entitled *Maqāmāt i Aḥmad i Jām* by Muḥammad al-Ishasnawī see Ellis Coll. M. 266 (16th cent.).

P. 954, l. 28. [*Nafaḥāt al-uns.*] Also **Ellis Coll.** M. 209 (A.H. 901/1496).

P. 957, l. 13. [*Ḥāshiyah i Nafaḥāt al-uns.*] Also **Majlis** ii 914 (A.H. 1036/1626–7).

P. 964, n. 2. The abridgment seems to be the *Tuḥfah i Khānī* (see Ivanow Curzon 648).

P. 965, l. 19. M. Ḥusain b. M. Hādī is the author of several medical works, which include the *Majma' al-jawāmi'*, composed in 1185/1771–2, and the well-known *Makhzan al-adwiyah*, and of a commentary on Muḥsin Kāshī's *Kalimāt i maknūnah* (Brockelmann *Sptbd.* ii p. 584).

P. 978 ult. He usually calls himself al-Turk (not al-Turkī) but nevertheless in a note at the end of his commentary on the *Mishkāt* he calls himself 'A. al-Ḥ. b. S. al-D. al-Dihlawī *waṭan^{an}* al-Bukhārī *aṣl^{an}* al-Turkī *nasab^{an}* al-Ḥanafī *madhhab^{an}* al-Ṣūfī *mashrab^{an}* al-Qādirī *ṭarīqat^{an}* (see Rieu i p. 14).

P. 979, l. 10. [*Akhbār al-akhyār.*] Also **Ellis Coll.** M. 5 (A.H. 1168/1755), M. 6 (18th cent.).

Editions: also [**Bombay**] Hāshimī Pr., 1280/1864 (310 pp. See F. E. Karatay, Istanbul Univ. cat. p. 3).

P. 989, l. 21. [Aḥmad Sirhindī.] Also *Gulzār i asrār al-Ṣūfīyah* (Ethé 1901), *Bāb* iv, and probably *Manāqib i Aḥmadīyah u maqāmāt i Sa'dīyah*, by M. Maẓhar al-Dīn Fārūqī, Delhi 1847 (see F. E. Karatay, Istanbul Univ. cat. p. 127).

P. 991, n. 3. [Ādam Banūrī.] Also *Gulzār i asrār al-Ṣūfīyah* (Ethé 1901), *Bāb* iv; S. Shams Allāh Qādirī *Qāmūs al-a'lām* (in Urdu), pt. 1 (Ḥaidarābād 1935), col. 12.

P. 1015, n. 1. [Sa'dī Lāhaurī.] Also *Gulzār i asrār al-Ṣūfīyah* (Ethé 1901), *Bāb* iv.

P. 1038, l. 9. The first element in the name of this author seems to have been, not Irtiḍā', as might have been expected, but Irtaḍā (ارتضى), the third person singular of the perfect tense. It will be noticed that on the title-page of his "*Furaiz-i-Irtazeeah*", printed at Madrās in his lifetime (see p. 1039, n. 3), his name is spelt Irtaza Alee.

P. 1048, l. 18. M. Bāqir Wā'iẓ Māzandarānī died in 1313/1895–6 according to Mashhad iii, *fṣl.* 14, ptd. bks., no. 61. It seems that Māzandarānī, rather than Ṭihrānī, should be in thick type.

P. 1053, l. 17. *Insert*:

(3*a*) ***Aḥwālāt i marḥūm Shaikh Aḥmad b. Zain al-Dīn al-Aḥsā'ī***,[1] by M. Ṭāhir.
Edition: place ? 1310/1892–3 (Āṣafīyah iii p. 362).

P. 1054 (9). The *Badā'i' al-āthār* is in two volumes according to the *Kitāb i Ṣubḥī* p. 141[2], where there is some information about Maḥmūd Zarqānī.

P. 1055, l. 8. *Insert*:

(12*a*) ***Bisṭām u Bāyazīd i Bisṭāmī***, by Iqbāl Yaghmā'ī: **Ṭihrān** (see *Luzac's OL.* 1938 p. 183).

P. 1055, l. 19. Imdād Allāh, a prominent Ṣūfī resident at T'hānah Bhawan (18 miles N.W. of Muẓaffarnagar), emigrated to Mecca at the time of the Indian Mutiny and was still there, lecturing on Rūmī's *Mathnawī* in the Ḥaram i Sharīf, when Raḥmān 'Alī wrote a notice of him on pp. 28–9 of his *Tadhkirah i 'ulamā' i Hind* [published in 1894].

P. 1055 ult. *Insert*:

(19*a*) ***Ghazzālī-nāmah***, a life of al-Ghazzālī, by Jalāl [al-Dīn Khān "Sanā"] Humā'ī[2]: **Ṭihrān** (see *Luzac's OL.* 1940 pp. 63, 108).

P. 1056 (26). [*Ḥikāyāt al-ṣāliḥīn.*] MS. (without title and author's name but divided as described by Ḥ. Kh.): **Rieu** Suppt. 393 (beg. *Th. u st. mar Khudāy-rā kih Āfrīdgār i jahān-ast u Āfrīdgār i hamah jānwarān ast.* Breaks off towards end of second *ḥikāyat* in *Bāb* xx. 153 foll. 13th cent.). "The author

[1] Cf. pp. 1061 (73), 1063 (99*a*) [Additions], 1065 (116).
[2] For whom see p. 1187 n. *supra*.

was a Sunni, living apparently in the fifth century of the Hijrah " (Rieu).

P. 1057, l. 24. *Insert*:

(36a) *Makhzan al-a'rās*, by Sh. Sharaf al-Dīn [b. ?] Qāḍī Sh. M. Shahrawānī: **Āṣafīyah** iii p. 106 (A.H. 1156/1743).

(36b) *Makhzan al-wilāyah wa-'l-jamāl li-ḥuṣūl al-ma'rifah wa-'l-kamāl*, an account of Chishtī Niẓāmī *shaikhs*, by M. Wilāyat 'Alī Khān: **Lucknow** 1300/1883° (on title-page 1286. 164 pp.).

P. 1058, l. 11. *Insert*:

(43a) *Manāqib i Aḥmadīyah u maqāmāt i Sa'dīyah*,[1] by M. Maẓhar al-Dīn Fārūqī: **Delhi** 1847 (288 pp. See F. E. Karatay *Istanbul Üniversitesi Kütüphanesi Farsça Basmalar Kataloğu* p. 127).

P. 1060, l. 10. *Insert*:

(63a) *Naẓm al-durar fī silk al-siyar*, a life of S. Amīr, a Naqshbandī saint, by Ṣafī Allāh called Mullā-yi Bāndah[2]: **Delhi** [1888°] (332 pp.).

P. 1063, l. 9 from foot. *Insert*:

(99a) (*Sharḥ i ḥāl al-Shaikh Aḥmad* [*b.*] *Zain al-Dīn al-Aḥsā'ī*)[3]: **Bombay** n.d. (Browne *Materials for the study of the Bábí religion* p. 194).

P. 1065, l. 4. *Insert*:

(114a) *Tadhkirah i Shāh-'Ālam*,[4] by S. 'Abd al-Raḥmān, commonly called ('*urf*) Shāh Buddah [BDH ?]: **Āṣafīyah** i p. 318.

P. 1065, l. 7. *Read* Aḥmad [b.] Zain al-Dīn.

P. 1065, l. 9. *Insert*:

(116a) *Tadhkirat al-qubūr*, on the saints and other celebrities buried at Iṣfahān, by 'Abd al-Karīm b. Mahdī Iṣfahānī: **Iṣfahān** 1324/1906 [R. Lescot, *Bull. E.O.I.F. de Damas* vii–viii p. 282]. See also p. 1353 *infra*.

[1] The combination of *Aḥmadīyah* in the title with Fārūqī in the name of the author suggests that this work is concerned with Aḥmad Fārūqī Sirhindī (for whom see p. 988 *supra*) and presumably with Sa'dī Lāhaurī (for whom see p. 1015, n. 1, *supra*).

[2] i.e., presumably, of Bāndah (" Banda ") in Būndēlk'hand.

[3] Cf. pp. 1053 (3a) [Additions], 1061 (73), 1065 (116).

[4] The work may possibly relate to the Gujrātī saint Shāh-'Ālam [d. 880/1475 see *Gulzār i abrār* (Ivanow 259) no. 183 and p. 997[11] *supra*].

P. 1065, l. 17. *Insert* :

(119a) ***Tiqṣār juyūd al-aḥrār min tidhkār junūd al-abrār***, biographies of Ṣūfīs, by Nawwāb M. Ṣiddīq Ḥasan Khān (d. 1890 : see p. 27 *supra*) : **Bhōpāl** 1295/1878 (295 pp. See F. E. Karatay Istanbul Univ. cat. p. 131).

P. 1066, l. 8. *Insert* :

(124a) ***Wāqi'āt i Rashīdī***, an account of various spiritual experiences of the author, Maulawī M. Rashīd al-Dīn Khān : **Lucknow** 1923* (with Urdu translation by Taqī Ḥaidar Qalandar).

N. BIOGRAPHY : (d) CALLIGRAPHISTS AND PAINTERS

P. 1077, l. 27. [Sanglākh.] For works by S. entitled *Burj i zawāhir* (Istānbūl 1276/1859, 176 pp.) and *Durj i zawāhir* (*sic* ; read *jawāhir* ? Cairo 1272/1855, 147 pp.), see F. E. Karatay *Istanbul Üniversitesi Kütüphanesi Farsça Basmalar Kataloğu*, p. 161.

P. 1078, l. 2. [*Imtiḥān al-fuḍalā'*.] Other editions : **[Persia]** 1288/1871 (2 vols. See F. E. Karatay, *op. cit.* p. 161) ; **Istānbūl** 1291/1874 (104 pp. [*sic* ?]. *Vid. ibid.*).

P. 1078, l. 4. [Sanglākh.] Also *Yādgār* v/1–2 pp. 106–8 (biog. by M. Qazwīnī).

P. 1078, ll. 5–11. 'Abd al-Muḥammad Khān Īrānī died at Cairo on 5 Ābān-māh A.H.S. 1314/27 October 1935 (see M. Ṣadr Hāshimī *Tārīkh i jarā'id u majallāt i Īrān* ii p. 197, where a biography and a portrait (p. 198) will be found). For a work of his entitled *Zardusht i bāstānī u falsafah i ū* (212 pp.) see Harrassowitz's *Litterae orientales* 57 (Jan. 1934) p. 15, where the place and date of publication are given (doubtless incorrectly [1]) as Teheran 1933.

N. BIOGRAPHY : (f) FAMILIES, TRIBES, ETC. (2) ĀFRĪDĪS

P. 1081, ll. 16–18. [Qāsim 'Alī Khān " Āfrīdī "]. For his Pashtō *dīwān* see also Blumhardt *Catalogue of the Marathi, . . . Pushtu, and Sindhi manuscripts in . . . the British Museum* pp. 23–4 nos. 38–9.

[1] The same place and date are given on the same page for the publication of the *Paidāyish i khaṭṭ u khaṭṭāṭān*.

P. 1081, l. 30. *Insert*:

N. BIOGRAPHY: (*f*) FAMILIES, TRIBES, ETC. (2*a*) THE BAKHTYĀRĪS

1444*a*. **ʻAbd al-Ḥusain Khān Lisān al-Salṭanah** Malik al-mu'arrikhīn.

(1) *Tārīkh i Bakhtyārī*,[1] covering the period 1004–1299/1692–1882 and composed in 1327/1909 by command of Ḥājjī ʻAlī-Qulī Khān Sardār i Asʻad Wazīr i Jang: Maṭbaʻah i Mīrzā ʻAlī Aṣghar [**Ṭihrān**? n.d.].

(2) *Khulāṣat al-aʻṣār fī ta'rīkh al-Bakhtiyār*: **Ṭihrān** 1333/1914–15. [R. Lescot, *Bull. E.O.I.F. de Damas* vii–viii p. 283.]

N. BIOGRAPHY: (*f*) FAMILIES, TRIBES, ETC. (6) NĀ'IṬĪS

P. 1084, n. 1. For the Nā'iṭī tribe see also *Ma'āthir al-umarā'* iii p. 562, Beveridge's trans. i p. 164.

N. BIOGRAPHY: (*f*) FAMILIES, TRIBES, ETC. (7) NAUBAKHTĪS

P. 1086, l. 4. [ʻAbbās Iqbāl, b. 1314/1896–7.] See Īraj Afshār *Nathr i Fārsī i muʻāṣir* pp. 157–68 (portrait).

N. BIOGRAPHY: (*f*) FAMILIES, TRIBES, ETC. (8) APPENDIX

P. 1086, l. 8. *Insert*:

(1*a*) *Risālah dar ḥāl i āmadan i Sādāt i Mutaʻallawī [Mustaʻlawī?] dar Sind*: **Āṣafīyah** iii p. 756.

(1*b*) *Shajarah i khānadān i Bambah*, a pedigree of certain descendants of the Caliph ʻUthmān, compiled by Mīr M. ʻAlī Muẓaffarābādī and edited by Khudā-bakhsh Bambah: **Rāwal Pindī** 1338/1920* (Shāntī Steam Press. 30 pp.).

N. BIOGRAPHY: (*g*) KINGS

P. 1088, l. 8. *Insert*:

1457*a*. **Mujtabā Mīnovī**[2] and **Ṣādiq Hidāyat**.

Māziyār (English title: *Māziyār*. (1) *His life and activi*

[1] This title is given in the preface.
[2] Cf. p. 1342 n.2 *supra*.

ties. (2) *A historical drama in 3 acts*) : **Ṭihrān** A.H.S. 1312/1933* (128 pp.).

N. BIOGRAPHY : (j) OFFICIALS

P. 1088, ll. 17–19. [*Sīrat al-Sulṭān Jalāl al-Dīn Mankubirnī.*] For a Persian translation by M. 'Alī Khān "Nāṣiḥ"[1] published at Ṭihrān (presumably in 1945) see *Luzac's OL.* 1946 p. 6.

P. 1100, l. 15. *Insert* :

1472*a*. Mīrzā **Muḥammad b. Abī 'l-Qāsim** was ten years old at the time of his father's death early in 1142/1729. He was appointed *Kalāntar* of Fārs in 1170/1756 by Karīm Khān Zand and he died at Iṣfahān in 1200/1786.

(*Rūznāmah i Mīrzā Muḥammad*), an autobiography extending to the year 1199/1785 ; **Ṭihrān** National Library (A.H. 1299/1882), Prof. Sa'īd Nafīsī's private library (A.H. 1324/1906), Royal Library.

Edition : *Rūznāmah i Mīrzā Muḥammad Kalāntar i Fārs*, **Ṭihrān** A.H.S. 1325/1946 (ed. 'Abbās Iqbāl (cf. p. 1085 *supra*). Supplement to the periodical *Yādgār*, year 2).

P. 1104, l. 7. *Insert* :

1483*a*. **Ḥusain Makkī** (pseud. **Farīdūn Ādamīyat**[2]) has already been mentioned as the author of the *Tārīkh i bīst-sālah i Īrān*[3] (p. 1291 *supra*) and of *Mukhtaṣarī az zindagānī i siyāsī u khuṣūṣī i Sulṭān Aḥmad Shāh Qājār*[4] (p. 1288 *supra*).

Amīr i Kabīr[5] *u Īrān yā waraqī az tārīkh i siyāsī*

[1] Born at Ṭihrān in 1316/1898–9 : see Ishaque *Sukhanvarān-i-Īrān* ii pp. 341–9 (portrait), *Modern Persian poetry* pp. 12, 29 ; Irani *Poets of the Pahlavi regime* pp. 598–9 ; M. Bāqir Burqa'ī *Sukhanwarān i nāmī i mu'āṣir* pp. 220–2 (portrait).

[2] Cf. F. Machalski in *Rocz. Orient.* xv (1939–49) p. 101, where the names are reversed (Ādamīyat Farīdūn), and Maḥmūd Farhād Mu'tamad's *Sipahsālār i A'ẓam* p. 5 n.

[3] Vol. i, *Kūditā-yi 1299*, Ṭihrān A.H.S. 1323/1944, vol. ii, *Muqaddamāt i taghyīr i salṭanat*, Ṭihrān A.H.S. 1324/1945 (cf. Machalski, *loc. cit.*, p. 102).

[4] Cf. Machalski, *loc. cit.*, p. 103 [1].

[5] M. Taqī Farāhānī, Nāṣir al-Dīn Shāh's first Prime Minister, who was put to death by his order on 9 January 1852 (see Watson *History of Persia* pp. 364 *sqq.*, 398–406 ; Browne *Lit. Hist.* iv pp. 152–3 ; Sykes *History of Persia*, 3rd ed., ii pp. 339–40, 344–5 ; Ḥallāj *Tārīkh i nahḍat i Īrān* p. 20 (portrait)).

i Īrān, a Ṭihran University doctoral dissertation published originally under the pseudonym Farīdūn Ādamīyat : **Ṭihrān** A.H.S. 1323–4/1944–5 (3 vols. See Machalski, *Rocz. Orient.*, xv p. 101, n. 2) ; 2nd edition, **Ṭihrān** (see *Luzac's OL.* 1951 p. 30, where the title is given as *Amīr i Kabīr : ba-munāsabat i ṣadumīn sāl i qatl i Amīr i Kabīr* and the number of pages as 326. Presumably this is the same work as that called *Zindagī i Mīrzā Taqī Khān Amīr i Kabīr* in the select list of publications of the *Mu'assasah i Maṭbū'ātī i Amīr i Kabīr* printed on the back cover of S. M. Bāqir Burqa'ī's *Sukhanwarān i nāmī i mu'āṣir*).

Description : F. Machalski *Quelques remarques sur l'état actuel de l'historiographie persane* (in *Rocznik Orientalistyczny* xv (1939–49)) pp. 101–2.

1483*b*. **Mahdī Mujtahidī** (cf. p. 1352 *infra*).

Tārīkh i zindagānī i Taqī-zādah[1] : **Ṭihrān** A.H.S. 1322/ 1944 (see the same author's *Rijāl i Ādharbāyjān*, fly-leaf at end).

1483*c*. **Maḥmūd Farhād Mu'tamad.**

Tārīkh i siyāsī i daurah i ṣadārat i Mīrzā Ḥusain-Khān Mushīr al-Daulah Sipahsālār i A'ẓam, an account of Mīrzā Ḥusain Khān b. Nabī Khān, who was Sipahsālār i A'ẓam from Rajab to Sha'bān 1288/Sept.-Nov. 1871 and Prime Minister from Nov. 1871 to 1290/1873 : **Ṭihrān** A.H.S. 1325 [–6/1947‡].

N. BIOGRAPHY : (*l*) PHILOSOPHERS, PHYSICIANS, ETC.

P. 1105, l. 23. [*Tatimmat Ṣiwān al-ḥikmah.* Arabic text.] Another edition : *Ta'rīkh ḥukamā' al-Islām*, **Damascus** 1946 (Arab. Academy. Ed. M. Kurd 'Alī. See *JRAS.* 1948 p. 72).

P. 1108, l. 15. [*Nuzhat al-arwāḥ.* Maqṣūd 'Alī's trans.] Also **Ellis Coll.** M. 238 (17th cent.).

P. 1108, l. 19. [*Nuzhat al-arwāḥ.*] Another Persian translation : *Kanz al-ḥikmah tarjamah i N. al-a.* **Ṭihrān** A.H.S. 1316/ 1938 (a modern translation by Ḍiyā' al-Dīn Durrī. 2 vols. See *Oriens* iii/2 (1950) p. 330).

[1] Cf. p. 241[28] *supra* ; Īraj Afshār *Nathr i Fārsī i mu'āṣir* pp. 75–86 (portrait).

P. 1108, l. 19. [*Tarjamah i Ta'rīkh al-ḥukamā'*.] Āṣafīyah i p. 346 no. 102 is a work of this title composed, according to the catalogue, in 1152/1739–40. If this date is correct, the work must be different from Maqṣūd 'Alī's translation of Shahrazūrī.

P. 1111, ll. 3–6. [*Rūz-nāmah i Ḥakīm al-Mamālik*.] See the addendum to p. 341, l. 6, and also M. Ṣadr Hāshimī *Tārīkh i jarā'id u majallāt i Īrān* ii pp. 327–9.

P. 1111, l. 6. ['Alī Naqī Ḥakīm al-Mamālik.] Also Browne *Press and poetry of modern Persia* p. 91 ; M. Ṣadr Hāshimī *op. cit.* p. 328, where a reference is given to *Yādgār* iii/1.

P. 1111, l. 6. *Insert* :

1491*a*. Dr. **Maḥmūd Najmābādī.**

Sharḥ i ḥāl u maqām i Muḥammad i Zakarīyā i Rāzī pizishk i nāmī i Īrān : **Ṭihrān** (396 pp. See *Luzac's OL.* 1939 p. 76).

1491*b*. Dr. **Qāsim Ghanī** was born in 1316/1898–9 at Sabzawār (see p. 919 *supra* and Īraj Afshār *Nathr i Fārsī i mu'āṣir* pp. 193–204 (portrait)).

Ibn i Sīnā : **Ṭihrān** (see *Luzac's OL.* 1937 p. 208).

1491c. **'Alī Akbar Khān "Dih-khudā"**, or "Dakhau", Qazwīnī was born at Ṭihrān in 1297/1880 and is well known as the author of *Amthāl u ḥikam* (4 vols., Ṭihrān A.H.S. 1310/1931–2) and of the enormous *Lughat-nāmah* now in progress, to say nothing of his other claims to fame.

Zindagānī i Abū Raiḥān al-Bīrūnī : **Ṭihrān** (see *Luzac's OL.* 1946 p. 43).

[Browne *Lit. Hist.* iv pp. 469–82, *Press and poetry of modern Persia* pp. 190, 200–4 (portrait) ; Berthels *Ocherk istorii persidskoi literatury* pp. 125–6 ; D. J. Irani *Poets of the Pahlavi regime* pp. 277–80 (portrait) ; Ishaque *Sukhanvarān-i-Īrān* i pp. 84–91 (portrait), *Modern Persian poetry* pp. 10, 21, etc. ; Rashīd Yāsimī *Adabīyāt i mu'āṣir* pp. 50–2 (portrait) ; Burqa'ī *Sukhanwarān i nāmī i mu'āṣir* pp. 77–9 (portrait) ; Īraj Afshār *Nathr i Fārsī i mu'āṣir* pp. 93–6 (portrait).]

N. Biography: (*m*) Places (1) Ādharbāyjān

P. 1112, l. 7. M. ʻAlī Khān "Tarbiyat" died on 26 Dai 1318/-January 1940 (see Mahdī Mujtahidī *Rijāl i Ādharbāyjān* p. 31).

P. 1112, l. 21. *Insert*:

1493*a*. **Mahdī Mujtahidī** is the author of a work entitled *Īrān u Ingilīs* (see p. 1288 *supra*).

(1) *Rijāl i Ādharbāyjān dar ʻaṣr i mashrūṭīyat*: [**Ṭihrān**] A.H.S. 1327/1948‡.

(2) *Tārīkh i zindagānī i Taqī-zādah*: see p. 1350 *supra*.

N. Biography: (*m*) Places (12) Bilgrām

P. 1115, l. 6. For "Āzād's" *Shajarah i ṭaiyibah* see p. 862 (12) *supra*.

N. Biography: (*m*) Places (19) Delhi

P. 1119, l. 8. [Dargāh-Qulī Khān.] Also *Shamʻ i anjuman* p. 148.

P. 1119, l. 12. *Insert*:

N. Biography: (*m*) Places (20*a*) Gīlān

1533*a*. **Ḥasan Shams Gīlānī**, the son of a well-known *khaṭīb*, Ḥājj Iʻtimād, was born at Rasht on 29 Ṣafar 1343/29 September 1924 and educated at Rasht, Qum and Najaf.

Tārīkh i ʻulamāʼ u shuʻarā-yi Gīlān, composed A.H.S. 1325/1946 and divided into a *muqaddamah* (autobiography, p. 4), two *faṣls* ((1) on Gīlān and its towns, p. 21, (2) scholars, poets, etc., of Gīlān, p. 29) and a *khātimah* (on the poets of Qum, p. 134): **Ṭihrān** A.H.S. 1327–8/1949‡ (152 pp.).

N. Biography: (*m*) Places (24) India

P. 1120, l. 19. *Insert*:

1539*a*. Other works:—

(1) *Mukhtaṣar i siyar i Hindūstān*, a short dictionary of celebrities who were born or flourished in India, by M. Waḥīd Allāh Sabzawārī: **Delhi** 1270/1854° (95 pp.), apparently also **Āgrah** 1892† (Ḥaidarī Pr.).

N. BIOGRAPHY: (*m*) PLACES (24*a*) IṢFAHĀN

1539*b*. Ākhund Mullā **'Abd al-Karīm b. Mahdī Jazī** [1] [or Gazī] Iṣfahānī died on 13 Dhū 'l-Ḥijjah 1339/18 August 1921.

Tadhkirat al-qubūr, on the celebrities buried at Iṣfahān: **Iṣfahān** 1324/1906. [R. Lescot *Bull. E.O.I.F. de Damas* vii–viii p. 282]; A.H.S. 1328/1949–50 (title: *Rijāl i Iṣfahān yā Tadhkirat al-qubūr*. 2nd ed., with notes and additions by the author's son S. Muṣliḥ al-Dīn Mahdawī. 260 pp.).

1539*c*. S. **Jalāl al-Dīn Ṭihrānī**, a teacher of astronomy and mathematics, has published editions of several Persian and Arabic texts (cf. pp. 263[16], 349[6,19] *supra* and, for a list, *Gāh-nāmah i 1314* pp. 2–3), some of them as appendices to his almanacs for the years A.H.S. 1310–14/1931–6.

Iṣfahān, mainly on its buildings and the celebrities buried there: **Ṭihrān** A.H. 1351/A.H.S. 1311/1933 (in *Gāh-nāmah i 1312* pp. 76–160).

P. 1123, l. 4. *Insert*:

N. BIOGRAPHY: (*m*) PLACES (33*a*) QUHISTĀN

1556*a*. Sh. Ḍiyā' al-Dīn **M. Ḥusain " Āyatī "** Khurāsānī.

Bahāristān dar tārīkh u tarājim i rijāl i Qā'ināt u Quhistān, completed in 1364/1945: **Ṭihrān** A.H.S. 1327/1948–9‡ (393 pp.). Cf. p. 923 (9).

P. 1125, l. 11. *Insert*:

N. BIOGRAPHY: (*m*) PLACES (39*a*) ṬABARISTĀN

1555*a*. **'Abbās Shāyān** is *Ra'īs i idārah i āmār u thabt i aḥwāl i Tihrān* (see *Māzandarān*, vol. ii, title-page, and, for a portrait, vol. ii p. 199).

Māzandarān,, vol. ii (contemporary celebrities of Māzandarān) **Ṭihrān** A.H.S. 1327/1949 (199 pp.).[2]

[1] Gaz (or, in its arabicised form, Jaz) is a village in the *bulūk* of Barkhwār, north of Iṣfahān.

[2] Vol. i (geography and history) has been printed (according to vol. ii p. 199) but may not yet have reached Europe, vol. iii is to deal with tribes, local customs, supplementary biographies, etc.

N. Biography: (*n*) Shī'ites

P. 1128, l. 7. For Arabic works by Nūr Allāh Shūshtarī see also Zubaid Aḥmad *The contribution of India to Arabic literature* pp. 237–8, 255, 275–6, 323–5, 348, 405.

P. 1129, l. 25. [*Majālis al-mu'minīn.*] Also **Ellis Coll.** M. 313 (A.H. 1093/1682), 314 (1st half. 19th cent.).

P. 1132, n. 5. For S. Dildār 'Alī see also *Nujūm al-samā'* pp. 346–51 and *Kashf al-ḥujub* (in Arabic, by I'jāz Ḥusain Kintūrī), editor's preface, p. 4, n. 1.

P. 1133. [*Majmū'ah i Ḥaidar-Shukōh.*] Cf. *Risālah i Ḥaidarī dar 'aqā'id i salāṭīn i Tīmūrī* ("*dar bayān i nadhr gudharānīdan i 'alam ba-dargāh i ḥaḍrat i 'Abbās 'm.*"), by Shāhzādah M. Ḥ.-Sh. b. Mīrzā M. K.-b. Edition: Lucknow (date? with the mathnawī *Shaukat i Ḥaidarī.* Āṣafīyah iii p. 102).

P. 1134, l. 23. [M. b. Sulaimān Tunakābunī.] Also *Tārīkh i 'ulamā u shu'arā-yi Gīlān* p. 58, where the date of his death is given as 28 Jumādā II 1302.

P. 1135, l. 9. "Jawāhir al-Kalām": so on the title-pages of the *Āthār al-Shī'at al-Imāmīyah* and the *Kitāb-khānahā-yi Īrān*, but Jawāhir-kalām on the title-page of the *Fihrist i Kitāb-khānah i 'Umūmī i Ma'ārif* (Pt. i, A.H.S. 1313, Pt. ii, A.H.S. 1314).

N. Biography: (*o*) Traditionists

P. 1137, l. 21. [*Bustān al-muḥaddithīn.*] Also **Delhi**, Mujtabā'ī Pr., 1898 (132 pp. See F. E. Karatay, Istanbul Univ. cat. p. 3).

N. Biography: (*p*) Travellers, etc.

P. 1154, l. 11. [Journey of the Persian princes.] *Insert*:
Persian text [?]: see p. 338, l. 25, *supra.*

P. 1160 antepenult. *Insert*:

(7*a*) ***Musāfarat i Tiflīs***, by Mīrzā Taqī Khān: **Leningrad** Univ. 1120 (A.H. 1288/1871. Romaskewicz p. 14).

(7*b*) ***Musāfir***, an account in verse of a visit to Afghānistān in October 1933, with poems written on that occasion, by

M. Iqbāl Lāhaurī, the well-known Urdu and Persian poet: **Lahore**, Gīlānī Electric Pr., 1934* (59 pp.).

P. 1161, l. 10. **Ambala**: so Arberry, but according to the U.P. Quarterly Catalogue (1909/1) the book, published by a resident of Ambala, was printed at the Mas͟hriq al-'Ulūm Press, **Bijnaur**.

N. BIOGRAPHY: (*q*) WOMEN

P. 1163, l. 4 from foot. *Insert*:

(3) *Taṣwīr i 'ibrat*, a biography of Bībī K͟hūrī Jān, by M. 'Abd al-Qādir K͟hān: **Madrās** 1922* (92 pp.).

N. BIOGRAPHY: (*r*) GENERAL AND MISCELLANEOUS

P. 1168, n. 2. [Kabīr b. Uwais.] Also *Majālis al-nafā'is* tr. S͟hāh-Muḥammad Qazwīnī pp. 396–7.

P. 1170, l. 9. [*Haft iqlīm.*] Also **Ellis Coll.** M. 41 (A.H. 1089/1678. Now in Cambridge Univ. Lib.), M. 42, M. 43.

INDEX OF TITLES

(*Ābādī i Dihlī*) 1118
'*Abbās-nāmah* 315, 1282
'*Abd-Allāh-nāmah* = *Sharaf-nāmah i Shāhī* 374, 1301
Abraham Lincoln 1179
Account of the Battle of Paniput 398, 1303
Account of the four Afghān tribes 399
Account of the Wahhābī incursions 428(5), 1307
Ādāb al-musāfirīn 1040
Ādāb i libās i Rasūl 195, 1256
Adabīyāt i mu'āṣir 919
Adhkār al-adhkiyā' 1053
Adhkār al-aḥrār 1012
Adhkār al-kirām al-bararah 1179
Adhkār i baiyinah i Qādirīyah 1050
'*Ādil-nāmah* 743
Adventures of Columbus 1160
Afḍal al-tadhkār 917
Afḍal al-tawārīkh, by Afḍal al-Mulk Shīrāzī 347 ; by Faḍlī Iṣfahānī 308, 1278, 1280
Afḍal-nāmah 759
Afghān wa Kābul wa Bukhārā . . . Khānlarīniñ aḥwāl 383
Afṣaḥ al-aḥwāl 168
Afṣaḥ al-akhbār 130, 1242
Afsānah i Bhartpūr 689
Afsānah i shāhān 516
Aghrāḍ al-siyāsah 1087[17]
al-Aghṣān al-arba'ah 1048
Aḥkām al-muḥibbīn 185[27]
Aḥkām i 'Ālamgīrī, by Ḥamīd al-Dīn Khān (?) 597 ; by 'Ināyat Allāh Khān 596, 1318
Aḥmad-nāmah 620
Aḥsan al-ḥadā'iq 25
Aḥsan al-kibār 211, 1261
Aḥsan al-qaṣaṣ, by 'Abd al-'Aẓīm 168 ; by Iḥsān Allāh 204 ; by M. b. Maḥmūd Khāwand Shāh 196 ; by Mu'īn al-Dīn Farāhī 11, 1194 ; by Mu'īn al-Dīn Juwainī [*sic*] 28
Aḥsan al-qaṣaṣ wa-dāfi' al-ghuṣaṣ 121
Aḥsan al-siyar, by Barkhwurdār Turkmān 535 ; by " Ḥādhiq " 199
Aḥsan al-tawārīkh, by Ḥasan Bēg Khākī (= *Muntakhab al-tawārīkh*) 123 ; by Ḥasan Bēg Rūmlū 307, 1279 ; by M. b. M. Taqī Sārū'ī 332
Aḥwāl al-A'immat al-Ithnai-'ashar 214, 1262
Aḥwāl al-khawāqīn 610
Aḥwāl al-qaum 1084
Aḥwāl al-Shaikh Abī Isḥāq al-Kāzarūnī 1343
Aḥwāl i A'immah i Ithnā-'ashar 214, 1262
Aḥwāl i āmadan i Marhaṭah-hā dar Hindūstān 764, 1333
Aḥwāl i Amīr 'Aṭā' Allāh Ja'farī 1179
Aḥwāl i Asad Bēg 554
Aḥwāl i aulād u jāydād i S. Aḥmad Sāndawī 1180
Aḥwāl i Bābā Nānak 677
Aḥwāl i Bānū . . . Mumtāz-Maḥall 1163
Aḥwāl i Bhāō Marhaṭah 620, 1333
Aḥwāl i Bībī Juliyānā 1162
Aḥwāl i Dīnā Bēg Khān 665
Aḥwāl i firqah i Sik'hān 668, 1324
Aḥwāl i gharaq i Machhlī-bandar 739
Aḥwāl i ḥaḍrat i Bāqir 227, 1265
Aḥwāl i Ḥaidar 'Alī Khān 767
Aḥwāl i ḥasab u nasab i Janūbiyān 764, 1333
Aḥwāl i ḥukamā' 1111
Aḥwāl i Humāyūn Pādshāh 539
Aḥwāl i Ibn al-Khafīf 1053
Aḥwāl i Ibn i Yamīn 919
Aḥwāl i 'imārāt i Mustaqarr al-Khilāfah 693
. . . *Aḥwāl* . . . *i* . . . *Jalāl al-Dīn i Rūmī* 921
Aḥwāl i jang i Marhaṭah 762
Aḥwāl i . . . Kamāl al-Dīn i Khwārazmī 974
Aḥwāl i Kashmīr 682
Aḥwāl . . . i Khwājū 918
Aḥwāl i Kristōfar Kulambas 1160 (1)
Aḥwāl i Mād'haujī Sīnd'hiyah 737
Aḥwāl i Mahārājah Sawā'ī Rānā Chhatar Sing'h 737
Aḥwāl i mulk i Farang u Hindūstān 1144
Aḥwāl i mulk i Kurg 777
(*Aḥwāl i Na'īm Allāh i Bahrā'ichī*) 1034
Aḥwāl i Nawwāb Burhān al-Mulk 713
Aḥwāl i Nawwāb Ḥaidar 'Alī Khān 767
Aḥwāl i qal'ah i Guwāliyār 736
Aḥwāl i rājah i Sōlāpūr 776
Aḥwāl i rājahā i Jaipūr 691
Aḥwāl i rājahā i Maisūr 774
Aḥwāl . . . i Rūdakī 918
Aḥwāl i Rūzbihān 934
Aḥwāl i safar i Bingaṛh 1320[4]
Aḥwāl i salāṭīn i Bījāpūr 745

Aḥwāl i Sar Jamshēd-jī Jījī-bhā'ī 1180
Aḥwāl i sarkār i Gāykwār 732
Aḥwāl i Shāh Gul Imām Chū 1042
Aḥwāl i shahr i Akbarābād 693
Aḥwāl i shāh-zādagī i Shāh-Jahān 565
Aḥwāl i . . . Sh. Bahā'ī 918
Aḥwāl i Sīwand 353
Aḥwāl i sīzdah-rūzah i safar i Gaṛh Muktēsar 1320[2]
Aḥwāl u aqwāl i . . . 'Abd al-Qādir i Jīlānī 1053
Aḥwālāt i marḥūm Sh. Aḥmad . . . al-Aḥsā'ī 1345
Aḥwālāt i salāṭīn i Rūm 422
Aḥwāl-nāmah i Ḥaidar Nā'ik 776
Aḥwāl-nāmah i Karnūl 766
'Ain al-bukā' 219
'Ain al-jinān 598
Ā'īn i Akbarī 549, 1314–15
Ā'īn i 'Ālam-Shāhī 640
Ā'īnah i ḥairat-numā 648
Ā'īnah i ḥaqq-numā 1132
Ā'īnah i Sikandarī, by Āqā Khān Kirmānī 248 ; by M. Ḥasan Khān 1308
al-'Ajā'ib 1185
'Ajā'ib al-qiṣaṣ 167
'Ajā'ib al-tajwīd 45
'Ajā'ib al-wāridāt 721
Ajmal al-tawārīkh 239
Ajwibat al-masā'il 1206
Akbar-nāmah, by Abū'l-Faḍl 543, 1314 ; by "Faiḍī" b. Mubārak 540[9] ; by "Ḥamīd" 401, 1304 ; by Ilāh-dād "Faiḍī" Sirhindī 552 ; by "Qāsim" 402, 1304
Akhbār al-akhyār 979, 1344
Akhbār al-anbiyā' 168
Akhbār al-aṣfiyā' 983
Akhbār al-auliyā' 1011
Akhbār al-jamāl 1022
Akhbār al-Madīnah 428
Akhbār al-nawādir 472
Akhbār al-ṣidq 719
Akhbār i Barāmikah 1082
Akhbār i Barmakiyān 1082
Akhbār i Bukhārā 386
Akhbār i ḥasīnah 427, 1307
Akhbār i Jahāngīrī 568
Akhbār i Maḥabbat 473
Akhbār i Nādir Shāh i Afshār 327
Akhbār i waqā'i' i Nādir Shāh u Farrukh-siyar 327
Akhbārāt i Hind 488
Akhlāq al-Nabī 204
Akhtar i tābān 916
'Alāmāt i Nujūm al-Furqān 51, 1226
'Ālamgīr-nāmah, by Ḥātim Khān, 587 ; by M. Kāẓim 586, 1317
'Amal i Ṣāliḥ 580, 1317
Amārāt al-Kalām al-Raḥmānī 51
Āmīn i khatm al-Qur'ān 57
Amīr i Kabīr u Īrān 1349
Amīr-nāmah, by Amīr 'Alī 648 ; by Basāwan La'l 691
Anbiyā-nāmah 168
Anfa' al-akhbār 125
Anfās al-'ārifīn 1020
Anīs al-aḥibbā' 874, 1337
Anīs al-'āshiqīn 890
Anīs al-ḥujjāj 1141
Anīs al-murīdīn, by M. Ḥasan Mujaddidī 1051
Anīs al-murīdīn wa-rauḍat al-muḥibbīn, by Abū Naṣr Aḥmad Bukhārī 29, 159[17], 1208
Anīs al-murīdīn wa-shams al-majālis 1208, 1251
Anīs al-Qādirīyah 1017
Anīs al-ṭālibīn 948
Anjuman i Khāqān 887, 1337
"*Anonym of Iskandar*" 86, 1234[8], 1234[24]
"*Anonym of Shāh-Rukh*" 291, 1275[14]
Ansāb al-aṭhār 1263
Ansāb al-salāṭīn 391
Ansāb i mashāyikh i Kashmīr 1053
Ansāb i Ṭālibiyīn 228
(*al-Risālat*) *al-ansābīyah* 233
Ansāb-nāmah 230
Anwār al-adhkiyā' 932[33]
Anwār al-'ārifīn 1044
Anwār al-Musha'sha'īn 1292[3]
Anwār al-Raḥmān 1053
Anwār al-shahādah 227
Anwār al-'uyūn fī asrār al-maknūn 968
Anwar-nāmah 778, 1334
A'rāḍ al-siyāsah 1087
'Arafāt al-'ārifīn (or *al-'āshiqīn*) 810
A'rās i buzurgān 1054
Ārāyish i maḥfil 456
'Arḍ-nāmah 1277
Arghūn-nāmah = *Tarkhān-nāmah* 655
Armaghān i aḥbāb 1180
Armaghān i Hindūstān 1160
Āṣaf-nāmah, by "Mauzūn" 704
Āṣaf-nāmah = *Tuzuk i Āṣafī* 750
Aṣaḥḥ al-tawārīkh = *Tārīkh i khairāt* 89, 1236
Asās al-īmān 228
Asās al-'ulūm 38
Asās i riyāsat i Karnāṭak 780
Aṣdaq al-bayān 29, 1209

Aṣḥāb i kirām 1079
Ashjār al-jamāl 1022
Ashraf al-tawārīkh 483
Ashraf al-'unwān 407
Ashraf-nāmah 647
Āshūb-nāmah i Hindūstān 581
al-As'ilah wa-'l-ajwibah, by Aqsarā'ī 7, 1192; by M. b. Jalāl Shāhī Riḍawī 991
al-Aslāf 1180
Āsmān i sukhan 788[30]
'Aṣr i sa'ādat 204
Asrār al-'ishq 1206
Asrār al-makhdūmīn 1057
Asrār al-mashāyikh 1054
Asrār al-shahādah, by 'Abbās 'Alī 228 (4); by Ismā'īl Khān " Sarbāz " 228 (5)
Asrār al-shahādah = *Sirr al-shahādatain* 223
Asrār al-tauḥīd 929
Ātash i bī-dūd 675
Ātash-kadah, by " Ādhar " 871, 1337; by " Jauharī " 228
Ātash-kadah i Yazdān = *Tārīkh i Yazd*, by " Āyatī " 1294
Āthār al-akhyār (var. *al-akhbār*) 29, 1197, 1209
Āthār al-muḥaddithīn 1137
Āthār al-mulūk wa-'l-anbiyā' 155
Āthār al-Shī'at al-Imāmīyah 1135
Āthār al-wuzarā' 1090
Āthār i Aḥmadī 192
Āthār i 'Ajam 353, 1295
Āthār i Harāt 1296
Āthār i Ja'farī 352
Āthār i Shāh-Jahānī 568
al-'Aṭīyat al-Ṣamadīyah 1021[1]
Aurang-nāmah 598, 1318
Auṣāf al-Āṣaf 704
Auṣāf-nāmah i 'Ālamgīrī 587
Autobiography of Shujā' al-Mulk 401
'Awālim al-asrār 1116
al-Awāmir al-'alānīyah 409
Awīmāq i Mughul 528
Āyāt al-raj'ah 1207
Āyāt al-wilāyah 1209
Āyāt i Dhū 'l-Qarnain 1208
Āyīn i Akbarī 549, 1314–15
Āyinah i bakht 132
Az Parwīz tā Chingīz 241
Az Shahrīwar tā fāji'ah i Ādharbāyjān u Zanjān 1291
A'ẓam al-ḥarb 606
A'ẓam-nāmah 587
'Aẓīm al-tawārīkh 482
Bābur-nāmah 530
Badā'i' al-āthār 1054, 1345
Badā'i' al-azmān fī waqā'i' Kirmān 357, 1297
Badā'i' al-bayān 1228
Badā'i' al-waqā'i' 373, 1301
Badā'i' i waqā'i', by " Mukhliṣ " 1319
Badī' al-afkār 889
Badr al-ahillah 168
Badr i musha'sha' 228
Bādshāh-nāmah by 'Abd al-Ḥamīd Lāhaurī 575; by Amīnā Qazwīnī 567; by Jalālā Ṭabāṭabā'ī 565; by " Kalīm " Hamadānī 572; by Ṣādiq Khān 577; by Yaḥyā Kāshī 569
Bāgh i chahār-chaman 738
Bāgh i gulhā-yi ḥusn 884, 1337
Bāgh i ma'ānī 855
Bahādur-Shāh-nāmah 600
Bahār i A'ẓam-Jāhī 1334
Bahāristān dar tārīkh u tarājim i rijāl i Qā'ināt u Quhistān 1353
Bahāristān i Ghaibī 714, 1329
Bahāristān i Shāhī 679
Bahāristān i sukhun 854
Bahjat al-asrār 933
Bahjat al-mabāhij 182, 1254
Bahjat al-tawārīkh 91
Baḥr al-ansāb, by ?, 228; by S. M. b. Ja'far Makkī 184; = *Kanz al-ansāb* 229, 1266
Baḥr al-asrār, by Maḥmūd b. Amīr Walī, 375; by Muẓaffar 'Alī [Shāh], 29, 1209
Baḥr al-durar dar aḥwāl i Mūsā 168
Baḥr al-ifāḍat 706
Baḥr al-la'āli', by ? 246; by 'Alī Akbar " Bismil " 203
Baḥr al-ma'ānī 29, 1209
Baḥr al-manāqib 229
Baḥr al-marām 1121
al-Baḥr al-mawwāj, by al-Fāḍil al-Hindī 1200
Baḥr al-mawwāj by M. 'Alī Khān Anṣārī 144, 1245
Baḥr al-nūr 1223
Baḥr al-sa'ādat 708, 1328
Baḥr al-tawārīkh 155
Baḥr al-'ulūm al-Islāmīyah 23
Baḥr al-zakhkhār, by M. Riḍā " Najm " Ṭabāṭabā'ī 148–9, 488, 523
Baḥr i gham 223
Baḥr i mawwāj, by Iḥsān Allāh " Mumtāz " 168; by Shihāb al-Dīn Daulatābādī 10, 1193

Bahr i zakhkhār 1031
Baḥth dar āthār u afkār u aḥwāl i Ḥāfiẓ 920
Bait al-aḥzān 228, 1266
Balāghat-nāmah 244
Balwand-nāmah = *Tuḥfah i tāzah* 702, 1327
Bansāwalī i buzurgān i Mahārājah D'hīrāj Sawā'ī Pratāp Sing'h 690
Barakāt al-Aḥmadīyat al-bāqiyah 988
Baring-namah 648
Barsing'h-charitra 738
Baṣā'ir al-naẓā'ir 1192 [1]
al-Baṣā'ir fī'l-tafsīr 5, 1191
Basātīn al-salāṭīn 745
Baṣīrat-nāmah dar gudhārish i istīlā-yi Afghān bar Iṣfahān 321, 335
Bawāriq al-wilāyah 1020
Bayāḍ i dil-gushā 1042
Bayāḍ i mukālamah i Shāh Ṭahmāsp bā īlchiyān 305
Bayān i aḥwāl i . . . M. Qāḍī 973
Bayān i ansāb i Ṭālibīyīn 228
Bayān i ba'ḍ i ḥawādithāt i Bukhārā u Khuwāqand u Kāshghar 386
Bayān i ḥaqā'iq i aḥwāl i Saiyid al-Mursalīn 185, 1254
Bayān i jang i Āṣaf-Jāh kih dar Barār wāqi' shudah 752
Bayān i kaifīyat i muḥārabah u muṣālaḥah i Muḥammad Shāh bā Nādir Shāh 327
Bayān i wāqi' 326
(*Bāyazīd-nāmah*), by " 'Ārif " 418
Bāyazīd-nāmah, by Maḥmūd " Niẓāmī " Malik-zādah 411, 1306
Bazm i Khāqān 892, 1338
Bazm i khayāl 480
Bazm i sukhan 915
Bazm i wiṣāl 922
Bazm u razm 411
Bazm-ārāy 805
Bēg-Lār-nāmah 654, 1324
Bēring-nāmah 648
Bhagat-māl 1055
Bhagat-nāmah 1055
Bhakta-māla 1055
Bhāō-nāmah 398, 1303
Bidā'ah i muzjāh 365
Bidāyat al-maḥabbat 185
Biḥār al-anwār 216
Bilqīs u Sulaimān 169
Bī-naẓīr 854
Biographical sketch of Shah Soojah 401
Bisāṭ al-ghanā'im 762, 1333
Bishārat al-imāmah 1027
Bishārāt i Maẓharīyah 1033
Bisṭām u Bāyazīd i Bisṭāmī 1345
Burhān al-futūḥ 137
Burhān i Awad'h 713
Burhān i ma'āthir 740
Bustān al-muḥaddithīn 1137, 1354
Bustān al-siyāḥah 1151
Būstān i Awad'h 712
But-khānah 807

Chach-nāmah 650, 1323
Chahār ā'īn i Maḥbūbī 1181
Chahār bāgh (= *Naghmah i 'andalīb*) 901
Chahār chaman 481, 1310
Chahār faṣl 1069, n. 1
Chahār gulshan 472
Chahār gulzār i Shujā'ī 476
Chamanistān i shu'arā' 867
Chār bāgh i Panjāb 673
Chār chaman, by 'Abd al-Wadūd 1185; by Daulat Rāy 481, 1310; by " 'Ishq " (= *Bāgh i gulhā-yi ḥusn*) 884, 1337
Chār chaman i Barahman 571, 1316
Chinese chronicle 80
Chingīz-nāmah 299
Chirāgh i Panjāb 673
Chishtīyah i bihishtīyah 1007
Couronnement de Soleimaan Troisiéme, Roi de Perse, by Chardin, 1283[8]

Dah majlis 212–13, 1261
Dakhmah i shāhān 383
Dalā'il al-nubuwwah 175, 1252
Dalā'il al-ẓafar 1158
Dalā'il i nubuwwat i Muḥammadī 188, 1254
Dalīl al-anām 1157
Ḍamīmah i Gulistān i Raḥmat 697
Ḍamīmah i Ma'āthir i Maḥmūd-Shāhī 726
Dānishmandān i Ādharbāyjān 1112
Dar aḥwāl i Sīwand 353
Dār al-asrār 1055
Darband-nāmah 423
Darband-nāmah i jadīd 426
Dāstān i aḥwāl i Ḥawāriyān 165, 1251
Dāstān i Akbar Bādshāh 540
Dāstān i gham 223, 1263
Dāstān i ghazwah i Ḥunain 221
Dāstān i jahān 1156
Dāstān i Karbalā' 229
Dāstān i Masīḥ 163, 1251
Dāstān i San Pēdrō 165
Dāstān i Sulaimān 169

Dāstān i turk-tāzān i Hind 491
Dastanbūy 647
Dāstānhā i Īrān i qadīm 249
Dastūr al-'amal 459
Dastūr al-'amal (?) 472
Dastūr al-wuzarā' 1091
Dastūr i fā'iḍ al-nūr 195, 1256
Dastūr i shahriyārān 319
Daurah i mukhtaṣar i tārīkh i Īrān 241
Daurān i Pahlawī 1290
Dawal Rānī Khiḍr Khān 502, 1311
Dawn-breakers, The 1287
Dhail i Hasht bihisht 416, 1306
Dhail i Tārīkh i 'ālam-ārāy i 'Abbāsī 314, 1281
Dhail i Ẓafar-nāmah, by Ḥāfiẓ i Abrū 87–8, 279, 1235; by Tāj al-Salmānī 291, 1275
Dhakhīrat al-khawānīn 1092
Dhakhīrat al-'uqbā 229
Dhikr al-aṣfiyā' 1037
Dhikr al-mulūk 441
Dhikr al-siyar 642
Dhikr i aḥwāl i Nādir Shāh 327
Dhikr i jamī' i auliyā' i Dihlī 1019
Dhikr i Khwājah 'Abd al-Khāliq i Ghujduwānī 1055
Dhikr i maqāmāt i Imām i A'ẓam 1055
Dhikr i Mīr 851
Dhikr i mughanniyān i Hindūstān 1183
Dhikr i yārān i zamān 1104
al-Dhirwat al-'ulyā 183
Dil-gushā, by Bhīm Sēn 588, 1318; by 'Ināyat Allāh Kanbō 578
Dil-gushā-nāmah 218
(*Kitāb*) *al-Dīn al-mubīn* 1137
Dīwān i muntakhab 853
Ḍiyā' al-'ārifīn 1043
Ḍiyā' al-mu'minīn 204
Ḍiyā' al-qulūb, by a disciple of Khwājah Isḥāq 981; by Imdād Allāh Fārūqī 1055
Ḍiyā' al-tafāsīr 29
Ḍiyā' al-'uyūn 54, 1227
Ḍiyā' i qamar 1185
Durar al-akhbār 382
Durar al-tījān 246
Dur-dānah i khayāl 1173
Durj al-durar 184
Durr al-dārain 1055
Durr al-farīd 41, 1219
al-Durr al-naẓīm, by Ibn al-Khashshāb, abridged by al-Yāfi'ī 53, 1226; by M. Riḍā Hamadānī,[1] 23, 1202
Durr baḥr al-manāqib 229, 1266
Durr i bī-bahā 202
Durr i manẓūm 698, 1327
Durr i naẓīm i Khāqānī 1202
Durrah i nādirah 324, 1283
Durrat al-akhbār 1106
al-Durrat al-farīdah 42
Durrat al-tāj wa-ghurrat al-ibtihāj 1101
Dūstdārān i bashar 1181
Duwal Rānī Khaḍir Khān 502, 1311

Faḍā'il al-A'immah 229, 1266
Faḍā'il al-'ārifīn 233
Faḍā'il i A'immah i Ithnā-'ashar 214, 1262
Faḍā'il i Balkh 1296
Faḍl i Ṣafdarī 1181, 1266
al-Fakhrī 81, 1233
Falak-āshūb 617
Fāl-nāmah 55–6, 1227
Fāl-nāmah i Qur'ānī 56
al-Far' al-nāmī 1181
Faraḥ-bakhsh 706
Faraḥ-bakhsh i jān 738
Faraḥ-nāmah i Fāṭimī 218
Farā'id al-fawā'id 40, 1218
Farāzistān 246
Farhang i khāwar-shināsān 1104
Farhang i Mīr Saiyid 'Alī 36
Farḥat al-'ālam 202
Farḥat al-nāẓirīn 140, 1244
Farrukh-nāmah 604
Farrukhsiyar-nāmah, by ? 606; by M. Aḥsan "Ījād" 604; by S. Qāsim, 608[11]
Fārs u jang i bain al-milal 1288
Fārs-nāmah 350
Fārs-nāmah i Nāṣirī 353, 1294
Fatḥ al-abwāb 185, 1254
Fatḥ al-'Azīz 24, 1202
Fatḥ al-futūḥ 501
Fatḥ al-Mannān 53
Fatḥ al-Raḥmān 21, 1201
Fatḥ-nāmah, by Ḥusām Allāh 395, 618; by M. 'Aẓīm al-Dīn Tattawī 657; by Musāfir 717; by Ṣūbadār Khān 658; by Ṭāhir Dak'hanī 741, 1330
Fatḥ-nāmah=*Chach-nāmah* 650, 1323; = *Miftāḥ al-futūḥ* 501
Fatḥ-nāmah i Angrēz 647, 1323

[1] For whom see *Ṭarā'iq al-ḥaqā'iq* iii p. 117 sqq.

Fatḥ-nāmah i Ḥaidarī 384
Fatḥ-nāmah i Kāfiristān 405, 1304
Fatḥ-nāmah i Khūnkār i Rūm 420, 1306
Fatḥ-nāmah i Nādir Shāh 327
Fatḥ-nāmah i Nūr-Jahān Bēgam 563
Fatḥ-nāmah i Ṣafdarī 615
Fatḥ-nāmah i Ṣāḥib-qirānī 287
Fatḥ-nāmah [*i Shaibānī Khān*] 372
Fatḥ-nāmah i Shōlāpūr 1330
Fatḥ-nāmah i Sind = *Chach-nāmah* 650, 1323
Fatḥ-nāmah i Ṭīpū Sulṭān 773
Fatḥīyah i 'ibrīyah (or *'ibratīyah*) 582
Fātiḥ al-qulūb 1003
Fātiḥ dar Fātiḥah 45
Fātiḥah u ma'nā-yi ān 1209
al-Fauz al-kabīr 22, 1201
Fawā'id al-nāẓirīn 1160
Fawā'id i Sa'dīyah 1039
Fawā'id i Ṣafawīyah 320, 1282
Fihris al-tawārīkh 342
Fihrist i rājahā i Maisūr 774
Fihrist i sūrahā i Kitāb Allāh 52
Fihrist i Tīmūrīyah 529
Firdaus al-murshidīyah 1343
Firdaus al-tawārīkh 86, 1234
Firdausīyah 1196
Firdausīyah i qudsīyah 1007
Forgotten rulers, The 242
Frere-namah 658
Frīr-nāmah 658
Futūḥ al-'Arab 431
Futūḥ al-mujāhidīn (or *al-mushāhidīn*) 956
Futūḥ al-salāṭīn 433
Futūḥ i Ibn i A'tham 208, 1260
Futūḥāt al-'Ajam 420, 1306
Futūḥāt i 'Ādil-Shāhī 743, 1331
Futūḥāt i 'Ālamgīrī, by Īsar Dās 587, 1318; by Ma'ṣūm (?) 582; by Ra'fat 588
Futūḥāt i Āṣafī 605, 748, 1331
Futūḥāt i Bāburī 534
Futūḥāt i Fīrōz-Shāhī 509, 1311
Futūḥāt i humāyūn 308
Futūḥāt i Salīm Shāh Khān 417
Futūḥāt-nāmah i Ṣamadī 664
Futūr zamān al-ṣudūr 255
Fuyūḍāt al-Fātiḥah 1201
Fuyūḍāt i Ḥaidarīyah 1204

Gangā-sāgar 1055 (12)
Ganj i Arshadī 1015
Ganj i dānish 242
Ganj i Faiyāḍī 1022
Ganj i ma'ānī 727
Ganj i shāygān, by Ṭāhir " Shi'rī " 905
Ganj i tārīkh 1044
Ganjīnah (*Tārīkh i G.*) 131
Ganjīnah i Sarwarī 1044
Gauhar i 'ālam 684 1325
Gauhar i shāhwār 753
Gauhar-nāmah i 'ālam 684, 1325
Gazēṭīr i ḍil' i Ēlgandal 1332
Genealogies of Fakhr-ud-Dín Mubárak Sháh 1165
George-námah 645
G'hakkar-nāmah = *Kai-Gauhar-nāmah* 675
Gham-nāmah i Imām Ḥusain 1266
Ghāyat al-himmah 220
Ghāyat al-taḥqīq 1228
Ghazā i Sulaimānī 418
Ghazā-nāmah i Rūm 412
Ghāzān-nāmah 271
Ghazawāt al-Sulṭān Salīm 417
Ghazzālī-nāmah 1345
Gul i bihishtī 1049
Gul i bī-khazān 692
Gul i firdaus 1049
Gul i Raḥmat 697
Gul i ra'nā 867
Gulāb-nāmah 686
Guldastah 811
Guldastah i Chār chaman i Barahman 572, 1317
Guldastah i gulshan i rāz 744
Guldastah i Ḥakīm 1160
Guldastah i Ingilistān 1160
Guldastah i Karnātak 890
Guldastah i maḥabbat 707
Gulistān i bī-khazān (in Urdu) 896[22]
Gulistān i Hind 491
Gulistān i hunar [given by Suhailī Khwānsārī (*Dhail i Tārīkh i 'Ālam-ārāy i 'Abbāsī* (cf. p. 1281 *supra*), *muqaddamah* p. 2, n. 1) as the title of Qāḍī Aḥmad's work on calligraphists and painters] 1074
Gulistān i Iram, by 'Abbās-Qulī 426
Gulistān i nasab 1084
Gulistān i Raḥmat 696
Gulshan, by M. Ṣāliḥ 598, 1319
Gulshan al-mulūk 385
Gulshan i bī-khār 896
Gulshan i farhang 169
Gulshan i hamīshah-bahār 904
Gulshan i Ibrāhīmī 446
Gulshan i jang 763
Gulshan i Maḥmūd 887
Gulshan i murād 331
Gulzār i abrār 984

Gulzār i Āṣafīyah 755, 1332
Gulzār i A'ẓam 899
Gulzār i Ibrāhīm 877, 1337
Gulzār i Ibrāhīm (?) 701
Gulzār i Kashmīr 686, 1325
Gulzār i Khalīl, by Ḥasan "Shi'rī" 1046
Gulzār i surūr 1061 (74)
Guwāliyār-nāmah 735–7

Ḥabīb al-siyar 104, 1237–8
Ḥadā'iq al-ḥaqā'iq 12[1]
Ḥadā'iq al-shu'arā' 901
Ḥadā'iq al-siyāḥah 1151
Ḥadā'iq al-udabā' 1338
Ḥaḍarāt al-quds 1002
Hādī i tajwīd 45
Ḥadīqah i Aḥmadī 732
Ḥadīqah i Amān-Allāhī 903
Ḥadīqah i 'ishrat 917
Ḥadīqah i Nāṣirī 1300
Ḥadīqat al-'ālam 751
Ḥadīqat al-aqālīm 142
Ḥadīqat al-auliyā' 983
Ḥadīqat al-ḥaqā'iq 391
Ḥadīqat al-Hind 732
Ḥadīqat al-Iram [*sic*] 386
Ḥadīqat al-ṣafā' 140
Ḥadīqat al-salāṭīn 747
Ḥadīqat al-su'adā' 213, 1261
Ḥādithah i Nādir-Shāhī 328
Hādiyah i Quṭb-Shāhī 51, 1225
Hadīyat al-aḥbāb 1175
Haft āsmān 906
Haft gulshan i Muḥammad-Shāhī 459
Haft iqlīm 1169, 1355
Ḥaidar-nāmah 384
Ḥairat-nāmah i sufarā' 1068
Ḥālāt al-Ḥaramain 1146
Ḥālāt i 'Abbās Khān 1094
Ḥālāt i Akbarābād 693
Ḥālāt i Asad Bēg 554
Ḥālāt i Āṣaf-Khānān 1104
Ḥālāt i hunarwarān 1073
Ḥālāt i jang i Malkah u Sit'hānah 674
Ḥālāt i Nādir Shāh, by Amar, 618; by Malcolm 328
Ḥālāt i Saiyid Muḥammad i Jaunpūrī 1056
Ḥālāt i Saiyid Sālār Mas'ūd i Ghāzī 1026
Ḥālāt i Sālār Mas'ūd i Ghāzī 1060 (64)
Ḥālāt i . . . Shāh Bilāwal i Lāhaurī 1056
Ḥālāt i Shāh Pīr Muḥammad 1060 (71)
Ḥālāt i Shāh 'Uthmān Akbar 952
Ḥālāt i shahādat i Muḥammad Ghauth Qādirī 1056
Ḥālāt i wālā ḥaḍrat i Amīr 'Abd al-Raḥmān 406, 1304
Ḥālāt u karāmāt i . . . Shāh Ṣafī etc. 1056
Ḥālāt u sukhanān i . . . Abū Sa'īd . . . b. Abī 'l-Khair 928
Ḥall i mutashābih i mamzūj 45, 1223
Ḥamalāt i Ḥaidarī 776
Ḥamīd-Khānī = *Tārīkh i Ḥamīd Khān* 774
Hamīshah bahār 826
Ḥamlah i Aḥmadī 206
Ḥamlah i Ḥaidarī, by "Bādhil" 199, 1257; by "Rājī" 221
Ḥamlah i Ḥusainī 224
Ḥaqā'iq, by "Rājī" 1265
Ḥaqā'iq al-akhbār i Nāṣirī 344
Ḥaqā'iq al-auliyā' 1023
Ḥaqā'iq al-kalām 1187
Ḥaqā'iq al-tafsīr 1209[7]
Ḥaqā'iq i sarkār i Gāykwār 732
Ḥaqīqat i binā u 'urūj i firqah i Sik'hān 677
Ḥaqīqat i Musalmān i Bangālah 722
Ḥaqīqat i rājahā i Ujjain 737
Ḥaqīqat i sarkār i Gāykwār 732
Ḥaqīqat-hā-yi Hindustān 477, 1310
Ḥaqq al-Sulṭān 1185
Ḥasab u nasab i . . . Ḥāfiẓ M. 'Alī-Shāh Khairābādī 1056 (24)
Ḥasab u nasab i Makhdūm Abū 'l-Fatḥ b. S. Niẓām al-Dīn Shanūzānī (?) 1056 (25)
Ḥasb al-irshād 707
Ḥāshiyah i Nafaḥāt al-uns, by 'Abd al-Ghafūr Lārī 956, 1344; by M. Dihdār "Fānī" 957[18]
Ḥashmat i Kashmīr 685
Hasht bihisht, by Idrīs Bidlīsī 413, 1306; Turkish translation of the *Manāqib al-'ārifīn* 938[12]
Hasht chaman 483[13]
Ḥauḍ al-Kauthar 1047[15]
Ḥayāt al-fu'ād 45, 1223
Ḥayāt al-qulūb 197, 1256
Ḥayāt i Fakhr i kā'ināt 205
Ḥayāt i Sa'dī 1341
Ḥayāt i Yaḥyā 1176
Hazār mazār 1123
Hidāyat al-ma'rifat 185
Hidāyat al-sabīl 1157
Ḥikāyāt al-salāṭīn 1285
Ḥikāyat [sing.] *al-ṣāliḥīn* 1004
Ḥikāyāt al-ṣāliḥīn, by 'Uthmān b. 'Umar called Kahf 1056, 1345

Ḥikāyāt i auliyā i ṣāliḥīn 1056
Ḥikāyat i Muḥammad i Ḥanafīyah 229
(*Ḥilyah i Rasūl*) 195[6], 1256[8]
Ḥilyah i Shāh-Jahān 570
Ḥilyat al-'adhrā' 1186
Ḥilyat al-'ārifīn 975
Ḥilyat al-qārī' 43, 1221
Ḥirz al-amānī 39, 40, 1217–18
Ḥiṣār al-Islām = *Tārīkh i 'Umarī* 233 (65), 1267
Ḥiṣār i Nāy 922
Ḥiṣaṣ al-atqiyā' 161
Ḥishmat i Kashmīr 685
Histoire de l'Asie centrale 383
Histoire de l'Empire de Russie sous Pierre-le-Grand 430
Historia S. Petri 165
Historia Sinensis 80
History of England, by Davis 429
History of Nadir Shah, by James Fraser 329
History of the fortress of Gwalior 737
Ḥujjat al-abrār 976
Ḥujjat al-sa'ādah 225
Humayūn-nāmah, by Gulbadan 539; by Khwānd-Amīr 536, 1313; by ? 529; by ? 539
Humāyūn-Shāhī 537
Ḥusain-Shāhī 399, 1303

Ibn i Sīnā 1351
'Ibrat al-nāẓirīn 1160
'Ibrat i arbāb i baṣar 715
'Ibrat-nāmah, by Kāmrāj 607; by Khair al-Dīn M. Ilāhābādī 641; by M. b. Mu'tamad Khān 606; by M. Qāsim " 'Ibrat " 607; by Sōhan La'l Sūrī 672
'Ibrat-nāmah u 'Umdat al-tawārīkh, by 'Alī al-Dīn 673
Īḍāḥ al-ma'ānī 39
Ifādat al-shuyūkh 27, 1204
Iftitāḥ i sulṭānī 598
Iḥyā' al-mulūk 365
Ījāz al-ma'ānī 39
I'jāz al-Qur'ān wa-'l-balāghat al-Nabawīyah 1228
Ījāz al-siyar 711
I'jāz i Muṣṭafawī 215
I'jāz i Qur'ān u balāghat i Muḥammad 1228
Ikhbār al-'ulamā' bi-akhbār al-ḥukamā' 1106
Ikhtināq i Īrān 347
al-Ikmāl li-ma'rifat al-rijāl 371
Iksīr al-tawārīkh 210
Iksīr fī uṣūl al-tafsīr 28
'Imād al-sa'ādat 706, 1328
Imdād fī ma'āthir al-ajdād 1020
Imtiḥān al-fuḍalā' 1077, 1347
In darkest Africa 1161 antepenult.
Inqilāb u taḥawwul i Ādharbāyjān 1288
Insān al-'ain 1021[3]
Inshā' i Abū 'l-Faḍl = *Mukātabāt i 'Allāmī* 542, 1313, 1314[9]
al-Intibāh fī salāsil auliyā' Allāh 1021
Intikhāb al-tawārīkh 479
Intikhāb i Jahāngīr-Shāhī 564
Intikhāb i Ka'bah i 'irfān 811
Intikhāb i Manāqib i Sulaimānīyah 1045
Intikhāb i Muntakhab (*i tawārīkh*) 127
Intikhāb i tafsīr i Sūrah i Muzzammil 29
Intikhāb i tawārīkh al-Aghyār 1056
Intiṣāḥ 'an dhikr ahl al-ṣalāḥ 1047
Intiẓām i rāj i A'ẓamgaṛh 703
Īqān dar awāmir u nawāhī i Qur'ān 1206
Iqbāl i Lāhaurī 1342
Iqbāl-nāmah, by ? 705
Iqbāl-nāmah. Tārīkh i Humāyūn Pādshāh (?) 539
Iqbāl-nāmah i Dhū- 'l-Faqār-Khānī 1317
Iqbāl-nāmah i Jahāngīrī 561, 1316
Iqbāl-nāmah i sa'ādat-āyāt 661
'Iqd al-la'ālī' 1057
'Iqd al-'ulā 357
'Iqd i gauhar 1199
'Iqd i Thuraiyā 876
Iqtibās al-anwār 1019
Īrān i bāstānī 249
Īrān i kunūnī u Khalīj i Fārs 1307
Īrān i qadīm 249
Īrān u Ingilīs 1288
Īrān-nāmah 1271
Irshād al-qārī' 43, 1221
Irshād al-tafsīr 3
Irshād al-wuzarā' 1093
Iṣfahān, by Ḥusain Nūr Ṣādiqī 1293
Iṣfahān, by Jalāl al-Dīn Ṭihrānī 1353
al-Iṣfahān 1293
Ishārāt i Bīnish 904
'Ishrat-kadah i āfāq 1101
Iskandar-nāmah, by ? 169; by 'Abd Allāh 276, 372
Ismā'īl-nāmah 303, 1278
'Iṣmat al-anbiyā' 160
Istiqṣā' al-ifḥām 29, 1210
Istīṣāl i Sādāt i Bārhah 619
Itḥāf al-nubalā' al-muttaqīn 1137

al-Itqān 1228
'*Iyār al-shu'arā'* 891
Izhār al-sa'ādah 223

Jāddat al-'āshiqīn 974
Jadhb al-qulūb 427, 1307
Jadwal i mubīn 45
Jahāndār-nāmah 603
Jahāngīr-nāmah 556
Jahān-gushāy i Nādirī 322, 1283
Jahān-nāmah, by "Fanā'ī" 1186; by "Mushfiqī" 374
Jalā' [or *Jilā'*] *al-adhhān*, by Ḥusain b. Ḥasan Kāzarūnī 29, 1211; by Mu'īn al-Dīn Karawī 56
Jalā' (or *Jilā'*) *al-'uyūn* 198, 1257
Jām i gītī-numā, by M. b. Ismā'īl Khwānsārī, 1258
Jām i jahān-numā, by Mahārat Khān 139, 1244; by Qudrat Allāh "Shauq" 143, 1244
Jām i jahān-numā-yi Sāsānī 147, l. 5 from foot
Jām i Jam, by Aḥmad Khān 487, 1310; by Farhād Mīrzā (tr). 155
Jām i Jamshīd (*Takmilat al-shu'arā'*) 877
Jāmī, by "Ḥikmat" 1340
Jāmi' al-ansāb 85
Jāmi' al-ashyā' 483[13]
Jāmi' al-bayān = *Tafsīr i Ṭabarī* 2, 1189
Jāmi' al-fawā'id 839
Jāmi' al-sittīn 1195[26]
Jāmi' al-tawārīkh, by Faqīr Muḥammad 150; by Rashīd al-Dīn Faḍl Allāh 72, 1230–2; by S. M. Bukhārī 387; = *Tārīkh i Baihaqī* 253, 1271
Jāmi' al-tawārīkh i Ḥasanī 91, 1236
al-Jāmi' fī ta'rīkh Banī Subuktigīn 253, 1271
Jāmi' i Fatḥ-Khānī 1103
Jāmi' i Mufīdī 352, 1293
Jāmi' i Ṭaiyibī 205
Jāmi' i tārīkh i āl i Subuktigīn = *Tārīkh i Baihaqī* 253, 1271
Jāmi' laṭā'if al-basātīn (= *k. i Sittīn*) 29, 1210
Jāmi' mufradāt al-Qur'ān 38
Janam-sāk'hī 664
Jang i bain-al-milalī 429
Jang i Islām Khān 567
Janghā-yi haft-ṣad-sālah i Īrān u Rūm 1271
Jang-nāmah, by Aḥmad Khān "Ṣūfī" 205, 229; by Ni'mat Khān "'Ālī" 592, 1318
Jang-nāmah i Bharatpūr, by D'hōnkal Sing'h 689[1]; by Shankar Nāt'h "Nādir" 1326
Jang-nāmah i Dakan 649
Jang-nāmah i Ḥusainī 229
Jang-nāmah i Kishm 309, 1280
Jang-nāmah i Mashriqī 1186
Jang-nāmah i M. Mu'aẓẓam Shāh u A'ẓam Shāh, by 'Aṭā' Allāh 600
Jang-nāmah i Nawwāb Ghulām-Muḥammad Khān 698
Jannāt al-firdaus 135, 1243
Jannāt al-khulūd, by M. Riḍā b. M. Mu'min Khātūnābādī 218, 1262
Jannat al-na'īm 1048
Jārj-nāmah 645
Jarūn-nāmah 309
Jauhar i ṣamṣām 325, 614
Jaunpūr-nāmah 698
Jaur [*u*] *jafā* 1181
Jawāhir al-'ajā'ib 797
Jawāhir al-akhbār 118
Jawāhir al-asrār 1015[2]
Jawāhir al-īmān 1210
Jawāhir al-Qur'ān, by Ghulām-Aḥmad and S. 'Alī 51; by ? 38
Jawāhir al-tafsīr, by Majd al-Dīn Khāṣṣah Shīrāzī 29
Jawāhir al-tafsīr li-tuḥfat al-Amīr 12, 1195
Jawāhir al-ta'rīkh 428
Jawāhir al-tawārīkh 298
Jawāhir i 'Abbāsīyah 661
Jawāhir i arba'ah 1182
Jawāhir i Farīdī 986
Jawāhir i Shāhī 537
Jawāhir-nāmah 671
Jilā' [or *Jalā'*] *al-adhhān*, by Ḥusain b. Ḥasan Kāzarūnī 29, 1211; by Mu'īn al-Dīn Karawī 56
Jilā' (or *Jalā'*) *al-'uyūn* 198, 1257
Jirjīs i razm 764
Journal of a residence in England 1154, 1354
Journal of Nadir Shah's transactions in India 328
Julūs i Muẓaffarī 1288
Junaidīyah 1114
al-Juz' al-laṭīf 1021

Ka'bah i 'irfān 811
Kaifīyat i aḥwāl i Ḍabiṭ-Jang 759
Kaifīyat i aḥwāl i Tēgh-Jang 759

Kaifīyat i jang i Kābul 1304
Kaifīyat i Mūsī Bhūshī 759
Kaifīyat i Nawwāb Ḥaidar-Jang 759
Kaifīyat i rāhī shudan i . . . Nādir Shāh ba-samt i Hindūstān 328
Kaifīyat i Sirmūr 677
Kai-Gauhar-nāmah 675
Kākh i dil-āwīz 1136
al-Kalām al-a'lā 1211
Kalām al-mulūk, by M. Taqī 'Alī-ābādī 337 ; by ? 337 ; by ? 1078
Kalimāt al-ṣādiqīn 985
Kalimāt al-shu'arā' 822
Kalimāt i Yūsufī 30
Kāmil al-tajwīd 45
Kānūn i ḥikmat i Qur'ān 1208
Kanz al-ansāb, ascribed to Abū Mikhnaf 229, 1266 ; by 'Abd al-Razzāq 'Aṭā Ḥusain 1057
Kanz al-gharā'ib 1266
Kanz al-ḥikmah 1350
Kanz al-jawāhir al-sanīyah 417
Kanz al-laṭā'if 46
Kanz al-maṣā'ib 1266
Kanz al-qurrā' 46
Kanz i maḥfūẓ 493
Karāmāt al-auliyā', by Niẓām al-Dīn Aḥmad 1008 ; by ?, 1057
Karāmāt i Qādir Walī 1057
Karāmāt u irshādāt i Mujaddid i Alf i Thānī 1035
Karbalā i mu'allā 230
Kār-nāmah, by " Āshōb " 617
Kār-nāmah (?) (metrical Indian history) 493
Kār-nāmah i Guwāliyār 736
Kār-nāmah i Ḥaidarī 776, 1333
Kār-nāmah i suturgān i shurafā i Pārsiyān 1182
Kashf al-amānī 39, 1217
Kashf al-anwār 216
Kashf al-asrār wa-'uddat al-abrār 1190
Kashf al-āthār 933
Kashf al-gharā'ib 428
Kashf al-ghawāmiḍ 160, 1250
Kashf al-ghiṭā' 'an wujūh āyāt Hal atā 26, 1204
Kashf al-ghummah 210, 1260
Kashf al-mutawārī 1036
Kashf al-nasab 1084
Kāshif al-akhbār 149
Kāshif al-niqāb 210, 1260
Kawā'if i ḍil' i Gōrak'hpūr 703
Khair al-bayān 814
Khairāt ḥisān 1163
Khāl[i]ṣah-nāmah 667
Khānadān i Naubakhtī 1085
Kharābāt (= *Mai-khānah*), by Ḥasan b. Luṭf Allāh 814
al-Kharā'ij wa-'l-jarā'iḥ 1253
Khaṣā'iṣ al-Ḥusainīyah 230, 1266
Khātimah i Rūz-nāmchah i humāyūn 337
Khātimat al-khiṭāb 57
Khatm i Sūrah i An'ām 57
Khawāriq al-sālikīn 1013
Khawāriqāt 976
(*Khawāṣṣ i āyāt*) 53–4, 1226
Khawāṣṣ i sūrahā-yi Qur'ān 54
Khazā'in al-futūḥ 502, 1310
Khazā'in i nubuwwat 1257
Khāzin al-shu'arā' 903
Khazīnah i ganj i Ilāhī 816
Khazīnat al-aṣfiyā' 1043
Khiṭāy-nāmah 432
Khizānah i 'āmirah 864
Khizānah i Rasūl-Khānī 1246, 739
Khizānat al-asrār 1226
Khulāṣah az ḥāl i jang i Kābul 402
Khulāṣah i aḥwāl al-shu'arā' 808[2]
Khulāṣah i aḥwāl i Bānū Bēgam 1163
Khulāṣah i aḥwāl i Gauṛh 723
Khulāṣah i Baḥr al-durar 1195[19]
Khulāṣah i bayān i āmadan i Nādir Shāh Pādshāh bah Shājahānābād 328
Khulāṣah i maqāl 316
Khulāṣah i Mustakhlaṣ al-ma'ānī 38, 1216
Khulāṣah i tārīkh i anbiyā' 169
Khulāṣah i tārīkh i pādshāhān i 'Ajam 237
Khulāṣah i tawārīkh i 'Abbāsīyah 661
Khulāṣah i tawārīkh i Mas'ūdī 1007[7]
Khulāṣat al-afkār 878
Khulāṣat al-a'jāb 396
Khulāṣat al-akhbār, by 'Iṣmat Allāh 401 ; by Khwānd-Amīr 102, 1237 ; by M. Mahdī b. Ja'far 1266
Khulāṣat al-anbiyā' 169
Khulāṣat al-ansāb 397, 1303
Khulāṣat al-'ārifīn 1057
Khulāṣat al-a'ṣār fī ta'rīkh al-Bakhtiyār 1299
Khulāṣat al-ash'ār 803
Khulāṣat al-ḥayāt 1110
Khulāṣat al-Hind 478
Khulāṣat al-kalām 877
Khulāṣat al-mafākhir 936
Khulāṣat al-Manāqib, abridgment of *Manāqib al-'ārifīn*, 938 ; biography of S. 'Alī Hamadānī 946
Khulāṣat al-Manhaj 16, 1198
Khulāṣat al-maqāmāt 950, 1344

Khulāṣat al-Nafaḥāt, by Jalāl 958[14]; by Maḥmūd b. Ḥasan Āmulī 958[20]
Khulāṣat al-Nawādir 45
Khulāṣat al-qirā'ah 1223
Khulāṣat al-qirā'āt 43
Khulāṣat al-rusūm 46
Khulāṣat al-siyar (?) 314, 1281[1], [23]
Khulāṣat al-tajwīd 1223
Khulāṣat al-tanzīl 41, 1218
Khulāṣat al-tawārīkh, by Aḥmad Ibrāhīmī 1279; by Kalyān Sing'h 721; by Miftāḥ al-Mulk (M. b. Yūsuf) 1249; by Sujān Rāy 454, 1309; by ? 242
Khulāṣat al-tawārīkh i Kashmīr 685
Khulāṣat al-Wafā 427, 1307
Khulāṣat Jawāhir al-Qur'ān 36
Khuld i barīn 131, 1243
Khwurshīd i jahān 1080
Khwurshīd i jahān-numā 152, 1246
Kifāyat al-mu'minīn 1253
Kilīd i fahm i Qur'ān 1207
Kisrā-nāmah 249
Kitāb i a'rās 1023
Kitāb i Fārigh i Gīlānī 214
Kitāb i mu'jizāt 182, 1254
Kitāb i Mullā-zādah 953
Kitāb i Qum 348, 1291
Kitāb i sabz i bī-ṭarafī i Īrān 1288
Kitāb i sittīn 1210[26]
Kitāb i Ṣubḥī 1182
Kitāb-khānah i Iskandarīyah 1186
Kuḥl al-jawāhir 1026
Kunūz al-rumūz 1258
Kurdistān 1300

Lamaḥāt min nafaḥāt al-quds 983
Lam'at al-shams 1057
Laṭā'if al-adhkār 1046
Laṭā'if al-akhbār, by Rashīd Khān 574
Laṭā'if al-akhbār fī siyar al-Mukhtār 1258
Laṭā'if al-khayāl, by M. b. M. Dārābī 818
Laṭā'if al-tafsīr, by Naḥīfī [?] 23, 1202
Laṭā'if al-tafsīr = *Tafsīr i Zāhidī* 4, 1190
Laṭā'if al-tawārīkh 1186
Laṭā'if i ghaibī 1199
Laṭā'if i khamsah 1035
Laṭā'if i nafīsīyah 1023
Laṭā'if-nāmah 792
Lawāmi' al-anwār 211
Lawāmi' al-tanzīl 30, 1211
Lettre de Tansar au roi de Tabaristan 360
Life and times of Hafiz of Shiraz 922
Life of Abdur Rahman 406, 1304
Lisān al-dhākirīn 230
Lubāb al-albāb 783
Lubb al-fawā'id 1211
Lubb al-lubāb, by Muḥammad-Qulī Qājār 134
Lubb al-siyar u jahān-numā 145
Lubb al-tawārīkh, by M. A'ẓam 684; by Yaḥyā Qazwīnī 111, 1239; by ? 685
Lubb al-tawārīkh i Hind 453, 1309
Lubb i 'Ain al-bukā' 219
Lubb i lubāb 833
Lubb i tārīkh i Sind 659
Lughāt al-Qur'ān, 38
Lughat i Waṣṣāf 270
Lum'at al-tafsīr 30

Mā lā budd li-l-arīb 270
Ma'ālimāt al-asrār 26
al-Ma'ārif 155
Ma'ārif i shattā 1187
Ma'ārij al-'irfān 58
Ma'ārij al-nubuwwah 187, 1254
Ma'ārij al-wilāyat 1011
Ma'āthir al-Bāqirīyah 891
Ma'āthir al-khawāqīn 298
Ma'āthir al-kirām 1025
Ma'āthir al-mulūk 102
Ma'āthir al-umarā' 1097
Ma'āthir i 'Ālamgīrī 593, 1318
Ma'āthir i Āṣafī 750
Ma'āthir i Jahāngīrī 563 (delete Brelvi and Dhabhar p. xiii and Rehatsek p. 76 no. 12: these are MSS. of the *Iqbāl-nāmah*), 1316
Ma'āthir i Maḥmūd-Shāhī, by 'Abd al-Karīm Hamadānī 725–6; by 'Abd al-Khāliq Sar-birahnah 726; by 'Alī Kirmānī 735
Ma'āthir i Quṭb-Shāhī i Maḥmūdī 747
Ma'āthir i Raḥīmī 553, 1315
Ma'āthir i sulṭānīyah 335, 1285
al-Ma'āthir wa-'l-āthār 1174
Mabāhij al-muhaj 182
al-Mabsūṭ wa-'l-maḍbūṭ 40, 1218
Madā'iḥ al-Mu'tamadīyah 902, 1338
Maḍārib al-mushakkikīn 205
Madārij al-nubuwwah 194, 1256
Madārij i sanīyah i Dhākirīyah 1050
Madḥ i Abū'l-Manṣūr Sikandar-Jāh 759
Madhāq i sukhan 922
Ma'din al-asrār 46
Ma'din al-sa'ādat 520

Ma'din al-ṣulaḥā' 221
Ma'din i akhbār i Aḥmadī (or *Jahāngīrī*) 124
Madīnat al-anbiyā' 169
Madīnat al-'ilm 199
Mafātīḥ al-adab fī tawārīkh al-'Arab 1307
Mafātīḥ al-'Ajam 245
Mafātīḥ al-ri'āsat 523
Mafātīḥ al-tanzīl 1223
al-Maghāzī, by al-Wāqidī 173
Maghāzī 'l-Nabī, by "Ṣarfī" 193
Maḥāmid i Ḥammādīyah 1057
Maḥāsin al-ādāb 177
Maḥāsin i Iṣfahān 349, 1292
Maḥbūb al-rāghibīn 56
Maḥbūb al-siyar 758
Maḥbūbīyah 954
Maḥfil al-aṣfiyā' 991
Māh-nāmah 754
Mā'idah i pur-thimār 1258
Mā'idat al-fawā'id 591
Mai-khānah, by 'Abd al-Nabī 813; by Ḥasan b. Luṭf Allāh 814
Majālis al-aḥzān 230
Majālis al-mulūk 237
Majālis al-mu'minīn 1129, 1354
Majālis al-muttaqīn 1264
Majālis al-nafā'is 791
Majālis al-salāṭīn 450
Majālis al-'ushshāq 961
Majālis i Saiyid al-Shuhadā' 230
Majāmi' al-akhbār 122
Majd al-Dīn i Hamgar i Shīrāzī 918
Majma' al-akhbār, by Harsuk'h Rāy 147; by Khwush-ḥāl Chand 136[27]
Majma' al-ansāb, by M. b. 'Alī Shabānkāra'ī, 85; by Nūr al-Dīn M., 194
Majma' al-auliyā', by 'Alī Akbar Ardistānī 991; by Badr al-Dīn Sirhindī 1002[7]
Majma' al-biḥār 30, 1211
Majma' al-fuṣaḥā' 911, 1338
Majma' al-gharā'ib 1223
Majma' al-ḥasanāt 169
Majma' al-hudā 163
Majma' al-inshā' 317, 1282
Majma' al-karāmat 1039
Majma' al-khawāṣṣ 1335
Majma' al-manāqib 230
Majma' al-muḥaqqiqīn 1035
Majma' al-mulūk, by Ḥaidar Wazīrōf Darbandī 249; by M. Riḍā "Najm" 148
Majma' al-nafā'is 839
Majma' al-nuqūl 1133
Majma' al-qawā'id 46
Majma' al-salāṭīn 490
Majma' al-shu'arā' i Jahāngīr-Shāhī 813
Majma' al-tawārīkh, by Bīrbal Kāchar 685, 1325; by Ḥāfiẓ i Abrū 88, 1235–6; by Ḥaidar Rāzī 124[14]; by M. Khalīl 319, 1282
Majma' i faiḍ 991
Majma' i Maḥmūd 888[4]
Majma'ah i kātibīn 387
Majmū'ah i 'awālim al-asrār 1116
Majmū'ah i bist rasā'il i qirā'at 43, 46 (15), 48 (3), 49 (2) (3), 50 (*g*) (*i*) (*j*)
Majmū'ah i faiḍ 692
Majmū'ah i fawā'id i 'Uthmānī 1057
Majmū'ah i Fīrōz-Shāhī 46
Majmū'ah i Ḥāfiẓ i Abrū 87, 1235
Majmū'ah i Ḥaidar-Shukōh 1133, 1354
Majmū'ah i 'ishq 884, 1337
Majmū'ah i Ja'farī 1102
Majmū'ah i Mīr M. Amīn 379
Majmū'ah i Mīrzā-Mahdī-Khānī 519
Majmū'ah i naghz 882
Majmū'ah i shu'arā', by "Sirāj" 853
Majmū'ah i tārīkh i shāhanshāhān 607
Majmū'at al-tawārīkh = *Majma' al-tawārīkh* 1325[34]
Makārim al-akhlāq, by Khwānd-Amīr 795; by Ṭabarsī 176, 1252
Makārim al-karā'im 177
Makātīb i zamānah i salāṭīn i Ṣafawīyah 1283[4]
Makhāzin al-Qādirīyah 974
Makhāzin al-taqwā 385
Makhzan al-a'rās, by M. Najīb 1023; by Sharaf al-Dīn . . . Shahrawānī [*sic* ?] 1346 (cf. 1023[6])
Makhzan al-asfār 343, 1070
Makhzan al-bukā' 223
Makhzan al-futūḥ 644
Makhzan al-gharā'ib 881
Makhzan al-jawāhir 151
Makhzan al-waqā'i' 1070
Makhzan al-wilāyah wa-'l-jamāl 1346
Makhzan i Afghānī 393–4, 1302
Makhzan i Aḥmadī 1041
Makhzan i 'irfānī 1057
Makhzan i nikāt 853
Makhzan i shu'arā' 904
Maklī-nāmah 1031
Maktūb i Ḍiyā'ī 1046
Maktūbāt i Amīr i Bukhārā 387
Malāḥat i maqāl 519, 1312
Malfūẓ i asrār al-makhdūmīn 1057 (38)

Malfūẓ i Razzāqī 1058
Malfūẓāt i Aḥmad i Maghribī 953
Malfūẓāt i Ḥājjī Wārith ʻAlī Shāh 1058
Malfūẓāt i Ṣāḥib-qirān 283, 1274
Malfūẓāt i Shāh Mīnā 1066 (123)
Malfūẓāt i Sharīfī 1058
Malfūẓāt i Tīmūrī 280, 1274
Mālik al-mamālik 387
Maʻmūlāt i Maẓharīyah 1034
Manāhij al-muʼminīn 1206
Manāhij al-ṭālibīn 85
Manāhil al-taḥqīq 1202
Manāqib al-ʻārifīn 937
Manāqib al-aṣfiyāʼ 1058
Manāqib al-Aṣḥāb wa-ʼl-Tābiʻīn 1079
Manāqib al-ḥaḍarāt 991
Manāqib al-khulafāʼ 213
Manāqib al-maḥbūbain 1045
Manāqib al-Razzāqīyah 1016
Manāqib al-sādāt 211, 1261
Manāqib i Ādamīyah u ḥaḍarāt i Aḥmadīyah 991
Manāqib i Aḥmadīyah 1346
Manāqib i Amīr Kulāl 1058
Manāqib i anbiyāʼ (?), by M. Ṣādiq 166
Manāqib i . . . Bukhārā 387
Manāqib i dabīrīyah 233
Manāqib i Fakhrīyah 1030
Manāqib i Ghauthīyah, by M. Ṣādiq Shihābī 1013 ; by ? 1058
Manāqib i ḥaḍrat i Khudāwandgār 935[19]
Manāqib i Ḥāfiẓīyah 1058
Manāqib i Jalāl al-Dīn i Rūmī 935
Manāqib i Maʻṣūmīn 1267
Manāqib i Maulānā Isḥāq 981
Manāqib i mazārāt i Bukhārā-yi sharīf 1058
Manāqib i Murtaḍawī 214
Manāqib i . . . Niʻmat Allāh Walī 952
Manāqib i Qādirīyah 1058
Manāqib i . . . Shaikh Jīw Khunuk (?) 1058
Manāqib i Sulaimānī 1044
Manāzil al-futūḥ 398
Manāzil al-safar i ḥajj 1156
Manāzil i ḥajj 1146
Manbaʻ al-ansāb 949
Manbahāt fī ʻilm al-amwāt 1049
Manhaj al-ṣādiqīn 16, 1198
Manhal al-ʻaṭshān 41, 1219
Manthūr i Multaqaṭ i Ḥirz al-amānī 40[14]
Manẓar al-insān 1167
Manẓar al-qāriʼ 46
Manẓūmah i nūrānīyah 1226
Maqālah i shakhṣī saiyāḥ 346
Maqālaʼī tārīkhī u intiqādī 1088, n. 1, 1178
Maqālāt al-auliyāʼ 932[29]
Maqālāt al-shuʻarāʼ, by "Ḥairat", 855 ; by "Qāniʻ", 854
Maqāmāt i Aḥmad i Jām 1344
Maqāmāt i Amīr Kulāl 1059
Maqāmāt i Khwājah Naqshband (= *Anīs al-ṭālibīn*) 948
Maqāmāt i . . . Makhdūm i Aʻẓam 973
Maqāmāt i Maẓharī 1035
Maqāmāt i Saiyid Atāʼī 987
Maqāmāt i . . . Shāh Naqshbandī 1014
Maqāṣid al-auliyāʼ 161, 1250
al-Maqṣad al-aqṣā fī tarjamat al-Mustaqṣā 178, 1253
Maqṣad al-iqbāl al-Sulṭānīyah 356 1296
Maqṣad al-ṭālib 205
Maqṣūd al-qāriʼ 42, 1220
Maʻqūlāt [sic ?] i auliyāʼ Allāh 1059
Mardum i dīdah 830
Marghūb al-qāriʼ 46, 1224 ("*Risālah i tajwīd*", but the opening words agree)
Marghūb al-ṭālibīn 56
Maʻrifat al-qirāʼah 43
Marṣad al-aḥrār 1343
Marsūm al-khaṭṭ 50
Martaʻ al-ghizlān 1223
Mashāriq al-tawārīkh 192
Masīr i Ṭālibī 878
Maṣṭabah i Kharāb 897
Matāʻ al-īmān 57
Maṭāliʻ al-anwār 194, 1255
Mātam-kadah, by M. b. ʻAlī Akbar 1264 ; by Qurbān "Bīdil" 222, 1263
Mathnawī dar fatḥ i Bangālah 567
Mathnawī i Ṭaiyib Allāh 524[27]
Maṭlaʻ al-anwār 1182
Maṭlaʻ al-shams, by M. Ḥasan Khān Marāghī 356 ; by Qāsim b. Nūr Allāh 1220
Maṭlaʻ i saʻdain 293, 1276–7
Maṭlab al-ṭālibīn, by M. Ṭālib, 1004
Maṭlūb al-qāriʼ 40
Maṭlūb al-ṣāliḥīn 56
Maṭlūb al-ṭālibīn 1014
Maulūd al-Muṣṭafā 179–80
Maulūd al-Nabī, by Pīr M. Ḥaḍrat 205 ; by Saʻīd Kāzarūnī 179–80
Maulūd i Barzanjī 205
Maulūd i ḥaḍrat i Risālat-panāh i Muḥammadī 186

Mawāhib al-qalandar 1047[13]
Mawāhib al-Raḥmān 25
al-Mawāhib al-sanīyah 939[12]
Mawāhib i 'alīyah 12, 1195
Mawāhib i Ilāhī 277, 1273
Mawā'id al-Raḥmān 20, 1200
Maẓāhir al-anwār 224
Maẓāhir i Maḥmūdīyah 1222
Maẓāhir i Muḥammadīyah 1222
Māzandarān 1353
Mazārāt i Bukhārā sharīf 1058 (49)
Mazārāt i Harāt 1296
Maẓhar al-aḥadīyah 1126
Maẓhar al-Ḥaqq (*Tafsīr i M. al-Ḥ.*) 30, 1211
Maẓhar al-ḥaqq (*Taḥqīq al-ansāb*), by 'Abd al-Razzāq Kalyānawī 1182
Maẓhar al-tibyān 1228
Māziyār 1348
Memoirs of Khojeh Abdulkurreem 327
Miftāḥ al-futūḥ 501
Miftāḥ al-'irfān 1212
Miftāḥ al-jannah 1182
Miftāḥ al-qulūb 155
Miftāḥ al-Qur'ān 58
Miftāḥ al-ṭālibīn 973, 974[14]
Miftāḥ al-tawārīkh 151
Miḥakk al-sulūk 135
Mīhmān-nāmah i Bukhārā 372, 1301]
Mihr i nīm-rūz 527
Mīkādō-nāmah 430, 1309
Minhāj al-dīn wa-'l-mulk = *Chach-nāmah* 650, 1323
Minhāj al-nashr 1224
Mi'rāj al-khayāl 899
Mi'rāj-nāmah, by "'Aṭṭār" 1258; by Mu'īn al-Dīn Farāhī [?] 189; by "Shujā'ī", 205; by various unknown authors 205, 1258
Mir'āt al-adwār 117
Mir'āt al-aḥwāl i jahān-numā 1131
Mir'āt al-'ālam 132, 1243
Mir'āt al-arḍ 1069
Mir'āt al-ashbāh i salāṭīn i āsmān-jāh 528
Mir'āt al-asrār 1005
Mir'āt al-buldān i Nāṣirī 344
Mir'āt al-futūḥ 389
Mir'āt al-'iyānīyah 54, 1227
Mir'āt al-kaunain 1182
Mir'āt al-khayāl 824
Mir'āt al-madhāhib 215
Mir'āt al-Qāsān 350
Mir'āt al-quds 163, 1251
Mir'āt al-ṣafā' 138, 1244
Mir'āt al-wajh 407
Mir'āt al-zamān 432
Mir'āt i āftāb-numā 146, 1245
Mir'āt i Aḥmadī 729
Mir'āt i daulat i 'Abbāsī 660
Mir'āt i jahān-numā 133, 1243
Mir'āt i Kāshān 350
Mir'āt i Madārī 1006
Mir'āt i Mas'ūdī 1006
Mir'āt i Sikandarī 728
Mir'āt i wāridāt 611, 1319
Miṣbāḥ al-arwāḥ 185, 1254
Miṣbāḥ al-'āshiqīn 30
Miṣbāḥ al-sārī 421
Mishkāt al-adab i Nāṣirī 1248[8]
Mishkāt al-nubuwwah 1059
Mi'yār al-faḍā'il 1182
Mi'yār i sālikān i ṭarīqat 1030
Mīzān al-akhlāq 1126
Mīzān al-Furqān 58
Mīzān i dānish 473
Mubīn 1212
Mudhākarah i Quṭb al-'ālamīn 1050
Mudhakkir i aḥbāb 802
Mufarriḥ al-qulūb, by M. "Nadīm" 333; = *Mukhtār-nāmah* 231 (40).
Mufīd al-qurrā' 43
Mufīd al-tajwīd 46
Muhaiyij al-aḥzān 231, 1267
al-Muḥammadīyah 10, 1194
Muḥammad-Khānī 693
Muḥammad-nāmah 1331
Muḥammad-Shāh-nāmah 609, 619 (the same work ?)
Muḥārabah i ghaḍanfarī 200, 201
Muḥārabah i Kābul 402, 1304
Muḥārabah i Kābul u Qandahār 403
Muḥarriq al-qulūb 220, 1263
Muhimmat al-muḥaddithīn 1137
Muḥīṭ al-'azā' (*sic lege*) 221
al-Muḥīṭ al-a'ẓam 30
Mu'īn al-auliyā' 1051
Mu'izz al-ansāb 298
Mujalladāt i Abū 'l-Faḍl i Baihaqī 253, 1271
al-Mu'jam fī āthār mulūk al-'Ajam 243
Mūjaz al-tawārīkh 1326
Mu'jizāt i Ān-Ḥaḍrat 1259
Mu'jizāt wa-ḥikāyāt Maulāya . . . Amīr al-Mu'minīn 231
Mujmal al-tārīkh i ba'd-i-Nādirīyah 330, 1284
Mujmal al-tawārīkh wa-'l-qiṣaṣ 67, 1229
Mujmal i Faṣīḥī 90
Mujmal i mufaṣṣal 1242
al-Mujtabā fī sīrat al-Muṣṭafā 184
al-Mujtanā min kitāb al-Mujtabā 184
Mukāshafāt i 'Alī Akbar Wahbī 958[2]

Mukātabāt i 'Allāmī 542, 1313, 1314[9]
Mukātabāt i Rashīdī 1230[24]
Mukhbir al-auliyā' 1059
Mukhbir al-wāṣilīn 1004
Mukhtār al-akhbār 740
Mukhtār al-qurrā' 1221
Mukhtār-nāmah, by 'Aṭā' Allāh b. Ḥusām 233 (56); by M. Ḥusain Nā'īnī 233 (63); by M. Ṣādiq "Āzād" 218; by Salmān Fālī 214; various works 231, 1267
Mukhtaṣar, by M. b. 'Alī b. M. Ḥusainī, on *tajwīd* 1224; by ?, on the Imāms 231
Mukhtaṣar al-tajwīd 1222
Mukhtaṣar al-tawārīkh 156
Mukhtaṣar al-tawārīkh i Sulaimānī 156 (11), 1249
Mukhtaṣar fī bayān tajwīd al-Furqān 46
Mukhtaṣar i Mufīd 237
Mukhtaṣar i Saljūq-nāmah 409, 1305
Mukhtaṣar i Sharḥ i lughat i Waṣṣāf 270
Mukhtaṣar i siyar i Hindūstān 1352
Mukhtaṣar i tārīkh i Rūsiyah 1187
Mukhtaṣar i tārīkh i 'Uthmānīyah 421
Mukhtaṣar i Tīmūr-nāmah 290
Mukhtaṣar i Yūl 478
Mukhtaṣar tārīkh i Islām 156
Mukhtaṣar tārīkh i Kashmīr 687
Mukhtaṣar tārīkh i 'umūmī 156
Mukhtaṣarī az zindagānī i siyāsī i Sulṭān Aḥmad Shāh i Qājār 1288
Mulakhkhaṣ 577
Mulakhkhaṣ al-tawārīkh 639
Mulāqāt i Nānak 664
Multamas al-aḥibbā' 1123
Multaqaṭ al-tawārīkh 384
Multaqaṭ i Ḥirz al-amānī 40, 1218
Munabbihāt fī 'ilm al-amwāt 1049
Munājāt i Khākī 1059
Mu'nis al-arwāḥ 1000
Munsha'āt i Muntajab al-Dīn Badī' 259
Munsha'āt i Rashīdī 72, 1230
Muntakhab al-akhbār 205
Muntakhab al-ash'ār, by "Mubtalā", 829
Muntakhab al-badā'i' 134
Muntakhab al-ḥasanāt 210
Muntakhab al-lubāb 468, 1310
Muntakhab al-manāqib 206
Muntakhab al-tajwīd 46
Muntakhab al-tawārīkh, by 'Abd al-Qādir Badā'ūnī 439; by Abū 'l-Barakāt 1187; by Ḥasan Bēg Khākī 123; by Jagjīwan Dās 458; by M. Ḥakīm Khān Tūrā 389; by M. Yūsuf Aṭakī 127; by Sadāsuk'h 481
Muntakhab al-tawārīkh i Mu'īnī 1234
Muntakhab al-tawārīkh i Muẓaffarī 1249
Muntakhab i aḥwālāt i zain al-bilād i Aḥmadābād 732
Muntakhab i Ḥākim 829
Muntakhab i Majma' al-nafā'is 839, 1336
Muntakhab i Tanqīḥ al-akhbār 1246
Muntakhab i tawārīkh i Baḥrī 742
Muntakhab i tawārīkh i khānadān i Bhōnslah 764
Muntakhab i tawārīkh i Salājiqah 409
al-Muntaqā 179
Munyat al-fuḍalā' 81
Muqaddimah i Shāh-'Ālam-nāmah 641
al-Muqaddimat al-Jazarīyah 40, 41
Muraqqa' i Karbalā 428
Murūj al-dhahab 156
Musāfarat i Tiflīs 1354
Musāfarat-nāmah, by Nāṣir al-Dīn Shāh 341
Musāfir 1354
Musajjalāt fī ta'rīkh al-quḍāt 1115
Musāmarat al-akhbār [*al-aḥbār* ?] = *Tārīkh i Karīm i Aqsarā'ī* 267, 1272, 1305
Mūsā-nāmah = *Tārīkh i Mūsawī*, by Mu'īn al-Dīn Farāhī 162; by ? 169
Muṣībat-nāmah, by M. Baqā Wārith 232
al-Mustakhlaṣ 31, 1215
Mustakhlaṣ al-ma'ānī 38
al-Mustaqṣā 177
Mu'tamadīyah 1103
Muẓaffar-nāmah 718

Nabī-nāmah 206
Nādir al-zamānī 136
Nādir Shāh, by S. M. 'Alī 1284
Nādir-nāmah, by M. Kāẓim 325; = *Bayān i wāqi'*, by 'Abd al-Karīm Kashmīrī 326
Nafaḥāt al-uns 954, 1344
Nafā'is al-'arā'is 161
Nafā'is al-ma'āthir 801
Nāfi' al-sālikīn 1059
Nāfī' al-ṭālibīn 555, 1316
Naft u marwārīd 1307
Nafthat al-maṣdūr 1089
Naghmah i 'andalīb 901
al-Nā'it 1084

Najaf-nāmah 624
Najāt al-qārī' 44
Najīb-nāmah, by " Dhauqī " 694
Najm al-tawārīkh 134
Nāmah i bāstān 248, 1270
Nāmah i dānishwarān i Nāṣirī 1174
Nāmah i khusrawān 239, 1269
Nāmah i Shāh Salīm 417
Naql i Jamshēd Khān 748
Nasab al-ansāb 493
Nasab-nāmah 1182
Nasab-nāmah i Afāghinah 400
Nasab-nāmah i a'immah i ma'ṣūmīn 232
Nasab-nāmah i Jārējah 733
Nasab-nāmah i khawānīn i Durrānī 407
Nasab-nāmah i nāmī i shaikh-zādagān 1059
Nasab-nāmah i rājahā i Maisūr 774
Nasab-nāmah i Rasūl i maqbūl 206
Nasab-nāmah i Sādāt i Bārhah 1086
Nasab-nāmah i Sādāt i Bilgrām u Bārhah 1114
Nasab-nāmah i . . . S. Shāh Ismā'īl i Bukhārī 1059
Nasab-nāmah i Sarwar i anbiyā 206
Nasab-nāmah i Shāh Wajīh al-Dīn 1059
Nasab-nāmah i shahryārī 746
Naṣā'iḥ of Aurangzēb 598
Nasā'im al-asḥār 1090
Nasā'im al-maḥabbah 955 penult.
Nasā'im al-Qādirīyah 1060 (61)
Nasā'im i Ghauthīyah 1060
Nasamāt al-quds 989
Nashr [*sic* ?] *al-jawāhir* 387
Nāsikh al-tafāsīr 1207
Nāsikh al-tawārīkh 153, 1247
Nasīm i Yaman 1023
Nasl al-mulūk wa-'l-ashrāf min Ādam 1183
Natā'ij al-afkār 900
Nathr al-jawāhir, a translation by 'Alīm Allāh Ḥusainī Jāland'harī of the *Naẓm al-durar wa-'l-marjān* of Auḥad al-Dīn Jāland'harī 206, 1259 (probably also 387); by 'Alī Mullā [*sic ?*] Ḥasanī [*sic ?*], 387 [but see p. 1259]
Nathr i Fārsī i mu'āṣir 1179
Naubahār 880
Nauḥat al-aḥzān 215
Nauras-nāmah 446
Nawādir al-akhbār 682
Nawādir al-bayān 45
Nawādir al-qiṣaṣ 1147
Nawādir al-safar 1060
Naẓārat al-Sind 659
Naẓarī bah Īrān u Khalīj i Fārs 1307
Naẓm al-durar fī silk al-siyar 1346
Naẓm al-durar wa-'l-marjān 1259[9]
Naẓm al-jawāhir 25
Naẓm al-la'ālī fī nasab āl 'Alā' al-Dīn al-'ālī 1115
Naẓm al-la'ālī fī tajwīd kalām al-Muta'ālī 43, 1220
Naẓm al-mulūk 605
Naẓm al-shuhadā' 227
Naẓm i ḥāsim 44
Naẓm i khwush-bayān 50
Nigāristān, by Aḥmad Ghaffārī 114, 1240
Nigāristān i Āṣafī 755
Nigāristān i Dārā 889
Nigāristān i sukhan 914
Nigār-nāmah i Hind 399
Nihāyat al-arab fī akhbār al-Furs wa-'l-'Arab 1270[6]
Nihāyat al-bayān 58
Nihāyat al-ḥikmat 185
Nihāyat al-itqān 1219[12], 1219[28]
Nihāyat al-mas'ūl 180
Nihāyat al-su'ūl 232
Nikāt al-shu'arā' 851
Ni'mat i 'uẓmā 20
Nīm-jahān 1292
Nisbat-nāmah i shahryārī 746
Niṣf i jahān fī ta'rīf i Iṣfahān 350, 1292
Nishān i Ḥaidarī 774
Nishtar i 'ishq 886
Niẓām al-ansāb 1182
Niẓām al-tawārīkh 70, 1230
Nizhād-nāmah i pādshāhān i Īrānī-nizhād 239
Note on the Persian invasions of India, by " Ḥazīn " 615, 1284
al-Nubdhat al-ibrīzīyah 1020
Nuh sāl dar Amrīkah 1160
Nuh sipihr 504, 1311
Nujūm al-Furqān 51, 1226
Nujūm al-samā' 1134
Nukhbah i Sipihrī 1267
Nukhbat al-akhbār 151
Nukhbat al-tawārīkh 1113
Nuql i majlis 888
Nuqṭat al-kāf 339, 1285
Nūr al-abṣār 232
Nūr al-'ain 501
Nūr al-akhbār 206
Nūr al-īmān 203
Nūr al-karīmatain 22
Nūr al-shuhadā' 232

Nūr al-'ulūm 928
Nūr al-'uyūn 179, 1253
Nūr i sarmadī 1224
Nūrīyah 1212
Nūr-nāmah 1259
Nusakh i jahān-ārā 116, 1240
Nuskhah i aḥwāl i Shāhī 1009
Nuskhah i Dhakā 1187
Nuskhah i dil-gushā 588, 1318
Nuskhah i jāmi'ah i murāsalāt i ūlū 'l-albāb 317, 1282
Nuskhah i sawāniḥ i aḥwāl, by "Mukhliṣ" 1320[5]
Nuṣrat al-fatrah 255
Nuṣrat u ẓafar 1326
Nuzhat al-arwāḥ wa-rauḍat al-afrāḥ 1107, 1350
Nuzhat al-ḍamā'ir 698
Nuzul al-abrār 1258

Ōymāq i Mughul 528

Pādāsh i kirdār 642
Pādshāh-nāmah by 'Abd al-Ḥamīd Lāhaurī 575; by Amīnā Qazwīnī 567; by Jalālā Ṭabāṭabā'ī 565; by "Kalīm" Hamadānī 572; by Ṣādiq Khān 577; by Yaḥyā Kāshī 569
Pahlawī-nāmah, by Ja'far Saiyāḥ, 1290; by Naubakht, 1290
Paidāyish i khaṭṭ u khaṭṭāṭān 1078
Paighāmbar-nāmah 196
Pand-nāmah i Jahāngīrī 559
Persian Gulf, The, 428
Personal observations on Sindh 659
Pīsh-rafthā-yi Īrān 1291
Poets and poetry of modern Persia 921
Poets of the Pahlavi regime 917

Qābūs i Washmgīr i Ziyārī 1088
Qābūs li-mu'tariḍ ṣāḥib al-Qāmūs 1084
Qaḍāyā-yi salāṭīn i Dakan 738
Qaiṣarī-nāmah 649
Qaiṣar-nāmah 1308
Qalā'id al-jawāhir fī aḥwāl al-Bawāhir 1083
Qalā'id al-jawāhir fī manāqib al-shaikh 'Abd al-Qādir 972
Qamqām i zakhkhār 204
al-Qand 371, 1300
Qandīyah 371, 1300
Qānūn i Humāyūnī = *Humayūn-nāmah* 536, 1313
Qānūn-nāmah i Chīn i Khiṭā 432
Qarnīyah i Shāh-Jahān Bādshāh 577[30]
al-Qaṣīdat al-Shāṭibīyah 39, 40, 1217–18
Qaṣr i 'ārifān 1045
al-Qaul al-mujīd 42
Qaul i faṣl 46
Qawā'id al-Qur'ān 41, 1219
Qawā'id al-salṭanat i Shāh-Jahān 571, 1316–1317
Qawā'id al-tajwīd 1221
Qawānīn, Risālah i, 356
Qawānīn i Ḥafṣīyah 44
Qindīl i Ḥaram 1156
Qirān al-sa'dain 499, 1310
Qirān al-sa'dain i dhū 'l-nūrain 1264
Qirān al-su'adā 1183
Qiṣaṣ al-anbiyā' by A. b. M. al-Arfajnī [?] 159; by Allāh-Yār Khān 169; by al-Būshanjī (tr. M. b. As'ad Tustarī) 162, 1250; by Isḥāq Nīshāpūrī 160, 1250; by al-Kisā'ī 161; various works 170
Qiṣaṣ al-anbiyā' wa-siyar al-mulūk 158
Qiṣaṣ al-Khāqānī 317
Qiṣaṣ al-mursalīn 171
Qiṣaṣ al-'ulamā' 1134
Qiṣaṣ i anbiyā' i kirām 171
Qiṣaṣ i Ḥusainī 387
Qiṣaṣ i tawārīkh i anbiyā' 171
Qiṣṣah i Amīr al-mu'minīn Ḥasan u Ḥusain 232
Qiṣṣah i Ḥaidar 'Alī Khān 767
Qiṣṣah i Iskandar i Dhū 'l-Qarnain 171
Qiṣṣah i Mi'rāj 189
Qiṣṣah i Mukhtār 231
Qiṣṣah i Mūsā = *Tārīkh i Mūsawī* 162, 1250–1
Qiṣṣah i Sālār Mas'ūd i Ghāzī 1007[9], 1060
Qiṣṣah i Shīr i mardān 'Alī 232
Qiṣṣah i Sulaimān 171
Qiṣṣah i Sulaimān b. Dāwud 171
Qiṣṣah i Yūsuf (various works) 31, 171, 1212, 1251
Qum-nāmah 348, 1291
Qur'ān al-su'adā 1183
Qurrat al-'ain 58
Qurrat al-'ainain 219, 1263
Qushūn-kashī ba-mamālik i Tūrān 1271
Quṭbīyah sharḥ i Shāṭibīyah 39
Quṭb-numāy i 'ālam 751 n., 752[6]

Raghā'ib al-albāb 46
Rah-āward = *Targhīb al-sālik* 1152

Rāḥat-afzā 138, 759, 1244
Rāḥat al-arwāḥ, by M. Sa'īd 1012
Rāḥat al-arwāḥ wa-mu'nis al-ashbāḥ 182, 1254
Rāḥat al-mu'minīn 31
Rāḥat al-qulūb, by Faiḍ Allāh Khān, 1249; by M. Rāḥat 1249; by Ni'mat Khān "'Ālī" 1172
Rāḥat al-ṣudūr 256
Raḥīm-nāmah 676
Rāhnumā-yi Qum 1292
Rajā' al-ghufrān 1228
Rāja-taraṅgiṇī 679, 1325
Rājāwalī 452, 1309
Rāj-darshanī 687
Rāj-sōhāwalī 478
Ranjīt-nāmah 675
Ranjīt-Sing'h-nāmah 670
Rashaḥāt i 'ain al-ḥayāt 964
Rashḥah i faiḍ 1222
al-Rauḍ al-azhar fī ma'āthir al-Qalandar 1046
Rauḍ al-jinān 4, 1191
Rauḍ al-rayāḥīn 935
Rauḍah i aqṭāb 1014
Rauḍah i aṭhār 982
Rauḍat al-abrār 1060
Rauḍat al-aḥbāb 189, 1254–5
Rauḍat al-a'immah 232
Rauḍat al-ansāb 387
Rauḍat al-aṣḥāb 213
Rauḍat al-auliyā', by "Āzād" Bilgrāmī 1024; by M. Ibrāhīm 1060
Rauḍat al-auliyā' fī aḥwāl al-aṣfiyā' 1060
Rauḍat al-Ḥusainīyah 222
Rauḍāt al-jannāt fī auṣāf madīnat Harāt 355, 1296
Rauḍāt al-jinān wa-jannāt al-janān 975
Rauḍat al-khulafā' 232
Rauḍat al-ma'ārib 9
Rauḍat al-mujāhidīn 233
Rauḍat al-muttaqīn 167
Rauḍat al-Nabī 199
Rauḍat al-na'īm 1050
Rauḍat al-qaiyūmīyah 1023
Rauḍat al-Riḍwān 387
Rauḍat al-ṣafā' 92, 1236–7
Rauḍat al-ṣafā-yi Nāṣirī 151, 342, 1246
Rauḍat al-Ṣafawīyah 313
Rauḍat al-salāṭīn 797
Rauḍat al-sālikīn 959
Rauḍat al-shuhadā' 212, 1261
Rauḍat al-ṭāhirīn 122, 1241
Rauḍāt i Landanī 1205
Rauḍāt i Shāhī 1138[1]
Rauḍat ūlī 'l-albāb 79, 1232
Rawābiṭ i Napōliyōn u Īrān 1288
Rawā'iḥ al-Muṣṭafā 225
Razmistān 480
Récit du couronnement du roi de Perse Soliman III 1283[8]
Rijāl i Ādharbāyjān 1352
Rijāl i Iṣfahān 1353
Risālah dar faḍīlat i 'ilm u 'ulamā' 1136
Risālah dar ḥāl i āmadan i Sādāt i Muta'allawī dar Sind 1348
(*Risālah dar ikhtilāf i Abū Bakr b. 'Abbās u Ḥafṣ*) 1218
Risālah dar qirā'at i 'Āṣim 1220
Risālah dar sabab i shahādat i Shahīd i Thānī 1136
Risālah i Afghānān 395
Risālah i Āfrīdī 1081
Risālah i Alif Lām Mīm 31
Risālah i amīrīyah 1060
Risālah i Bahā'īyah 1060
Risālah i buzurgān i Samarqand 1060
Risālah i Dhākirīyah 1050[18]
Risālah i firdausīyah 1196
Risālah i Ghaibī 387
Risālah i Ḥaidarī dar 'aqā'id i salāṭīn i Tīmūrī 1354
Risālah i Idh qāla Yūsufu li-abīhi 31
Risālah i Ikhlāṣ 9
Risālah i Khāqānīyah 337
Risālah i lughāt al-Qur'ān 1216
Risālah i mufrad i Ḥamzah 41, 1219
Risālah i Muḥammad Shāh i Khān i Daurān 614
Risālah i Mullā-zādah 953
Risālah i Nānak Shāh 666
Risālah i nūn i quṭnī 47 (24)
Risālah i nūrīyah 1212
Risālah i Qalandarīyah 1212
Risālah i qawānīn 356
Risālah i quṭbīyah i 'ishqīyah 1061
Risālah i Rūḥ 31
Risālah i Ṣāḥib-numā 673
Risālah i S. Mahdī i Dahajī 1286
(*Risālah i Sālar-Jang*) 1118
Risālah i shaqq al-qamar 25[6], 1203
Risālah i Sipah-sālār 935
Risālah i tadābīr i Shāh u Wazīr 333
al-Risālat al-ansābīyah 233
Risālat al-shuhadā' 990
al-Risālat al-tis'-'asharīyah 1061
Rīshī-nāmah, by "Bahā" 986; by Naṣīb 985
Riyāḍ al-abrār 31
Riyāḍ al-afkār 900

Riyāḍ al-ʻārifīn 911
Riyāḍ al-auliyā', by M. Baqā Sahāranpūrī (ostensibly by Bakhtāwar Khān) 1012
Riyāḍ al-auliyā' (?), by Muʻīn al-Dīn Minbarī (?) 977
Riyāḍ al-firdaus 237
Riyāḍ al-fuṣaḥā' 876
Riyāḍ al-jannah 1299 [22]
Riyāḍ al-khulūd 1169
Riyāḍ al-mulūk 649
Riyāḍ al-nūr 1061
Riyāḍ al-Raḥmān 757
Riyāḍ al-salāṭīn 718
Riyāḍ al-shahādah 222, 1263
Riyāḍ al-shuʻarā' 832
Riyāḍ al-shuhadā' 233
Riyāḍ al-siyāḥah 1150
Riyāḍ al-uns 206
Riyāḍ al-wāṣilīn 1037
Riyāḍ al-wifāq 885
Riyāḍ i laṭīf 1183
Rulers of Baroda 733 (4)
Ruqaʻāt i Abū 'l-Faḍl 542, 1314
Ruqʻat al-qāri' 44
Russia 430
Russian supremacy in Central Asia, 388
Rūz i raushan 915
Rūz-nāmah, by M. Ḥasan Khān Marāghī 344; by Nāṣir al-Dīn Shāh 341–2
Rūz-nāmah i ghazawāt i Hindūstān 278, 1273
Rūz-nāmah i Ḥakīm al-Mamālik 1111, 1286[8]
Rūz-nāmah i Īrān, by M. Ḥasan Khān Marāghī 344
(*Rūz-nāmah i Mīrzā Muḥammad*) 1349
Rūz-nāmah i Mīrzā M. Shafīʻ Gushtāsb i Māzandarānī 1161
Rūz-nāmah i safar i Mīrzā Naṣīr Allāh Sulṭān 1161
Rūz-nāmah i safar i Piṭrburgh 1161
Rūz-nāmah i safar i Shīrāz 1153
Rūz-nāmah i waqā'iʻ i . . . Ḥaidarābād 590
Rūz-nāmah i wukalā' i Ḥaidarābād 1067
Rūz-nāmah i yaumīyah 345
Rūz-nāmchah i darbār i . . . Ghāzī al-Dīn Ḥaidar 708
Rūz-nāmchah i Ranjīt Sing'h 668
Rūz-nāmchah i Shāh-ʻĀlam 644

Saʻādat al-kaunain 221, 1263
Sāʻāt i nahḍat i ʻĀlamgīr Pādshāh 598
Sabīkat al-dhahab al-ibrīz 52
Ṣad khiṭābah 1270
Saʻdī-nāmah 1342
Saʻdīyah 976
Safar i aiyām i saʻīdah 1160
Safar i farkhundah-athar i ḥaḍrat i Pādshāh i ʻālam 418
Safar i Ḥijāz = *Guldastah i Ḥakīm* 1160
Safar i ʻIrāq 342, 1286
Safar-nāmah, by Muẓaffar al-Dīn Shāh 347; by Nāṣir al-Dīn Shāh 341
Safar-nāmah i Ḥakīm Nāṣir i Khusrau 1139
Safar-nāmah i ʻIrāq 1160 (7)
Safar-nāmah i Khurāsān, by Ḥakīm al-Mamālik 1111, 1286[11]
Safar-nāmah i Makhdūm i Jahāniyān 945, 1343
Safar-nāmah i Mīrzā M. Shafīʻ Gushtāsb i Māzandarānī 1161
Safar-nāmah i mubārak i shāhanshāhī, by Muẓaffar al-Dīn Shāh 347
Safar-nāmah i Mukhliṣ 1320[23]
Safar-nāmah i Mūsyū Farānsīsī 1161 (15)
(*Safar-nāmah i Najaf-Qulī Mīrzā*) 338 (433) (?), 1154
Safar-nāmah i Pīr-zādah i Nā'īnī 1157
Safar-nāmah i Piṭrōgrād 387
Safar-nāmah i Qāḍī Taqī Muttaqī 1161, 1355
Safar-nāmah i Qum 1161
Safar-nāmah i Riḍā-Qulī Mīrzā 338[25], 1154 (?)
Safar-nāmah i Sālār-Jang 1158
Safar-nāmah i Sar Antwān Sharlī 1161
Safar-nāmah i Wāmbirī 1161
Safīnah i Ahl i Bait 1267
Safīnah i Hindī 882
Safīnah i ʻishrat 855
Safīnah i Khwushgū 827
Safīnah i Raḥmānī 1183
Safīnat al-ʻārifīn 1024
Safīnat al-auliyā' 996
Safīnat al-Maḥmūd 888
Safīnat al-shuʻarā', Fahīm's Turkish translation of Daulat-Shāh 787; a work composed in 1170/1756–7 866
Ṣafwat al-akhbār 101
Ṣafwat al-ṣafā' 939
Ṣaḥā'if i sharā'if 1183
Ṣāḥibīyah 1001
Ṣaḥīfah i dhahabīyah 1266, 1267

Ṣaḥīfah i iqbāl 609
Ṣaḥīfah i wālā-qadrī 648
Ṣaḥīfat al-a'māl 1117
Ṣaḥīfat al-a'rās 1028
Ṣaḥīfat al-muttaqīn 1256
Ṣaḥīḥ al-akhbār 478, 1310
Sa'īd-nāmah 778
al-Saif al-māḍī 206
Sair i Hind u gulgasht i Dakan 1152
Sairistān 1103, 1155
Saiyid al-sādāt 233
Sakīnat al-auliyā' 998
Sālār-nāmah 248, 1270
Salāṭīn i Barōdah 733
Sālik i ṭarīqat 1061
Salīm-Khān-nāmah 419
Salīm-nāmah, by "Adā'ī" 417; by Idrīs Bidlīsī 416; by Luqmān 419
Saljūq-nāmah 409[2]
Sanawāt al-atqiyā' 1002
Sarbāz i Pārsī 1161
Sargudhasht i Nawwāb Najīb al-Daulah 695
Sargudhasht i rājahā i A'ẓamgaṛh 703
Sarw i āzād 864
Ṣaulat i Fārūqī 616
Ṣaulat i Ṣafdarī 200, 201
Ṣawāmi' al-malakūt 54
(*Sawāniḥ*), by Sabzawārī 1027
Sawāniḥ al-aiyām 1061 (77)
Sawāniḥ i aḥwāl, by "Āshōb" 617, 1321; by "Ḥazīn" 847, 1336; by "Mukhliṣ" 1320[5]
Sawāniḥ i Akbarī 555
Sawāniḥ i Dakan 749
Sawāniḥ i gharā'ib 719
Sawāniḥ i mukhtaṣar i Shāh Wājid 'Alī Qalandar 1061
Sawāniḥ i safar al-Ḥijāz 1161
Sawāniḥ i Shāh Ni'mat Allāh Walī 1061
Sawāniḥāt i mumtāz 780, 1334
Sawāniḥāt i salāṭīn i Awad'h 711
Sawāṭi' al-anwār 1019
Shadd al-izār 1123
Shāh i tafāsīr 19
Shāh-'Ālam-nāmah, by Ghulām-'Alī Khān 640; by Munnā Lāl 644, 1322
Shāhanshāh i Pahlawī 1290
Shahanshāh-nāmah, by Aḥmad Tabrīzī 271; by "Banā'ī" 302; by "Mulhamī" 421; by "Ṣabā" 334, 1284; composed in Shāh Sulaimān's reign 319
Shahanshāh-nāmah i Sulṭān Muḥammad 420
Shahanshāh-nāmah i . . . Sulṭān Murād Khān 420, 1306
Shāh i tafāsīr 19
Shāh-Jahān-nāmah, by 'Ināyat Khān "Āshnā" 577; by Jalāl Ṭabāṭabā'ī 565; by M. Ṣāliḥ Kanbō, 580; by Ṣādiq Khān 577; by ? 573
Shāh-nāmah, by Bihishtī Mashkūkī 420; = *Pahlawī-nāmah,* by Naubakht, 1290
Shāh-nāmah i Aḥmadī 397
Shāh-nāmah i Dakan 605
Shāh-nāmah i Hātifī 303, 1278
Shāh-nāmah i Hind, by Apūrb Kishan "Kunwar" 524; = *Razmistān* = *Bazm i khayāl,* by "Khwushdil" 480 ult.
Shāh-nāmah i Ismā'īl 305, 1279
Shāh-nāmah i munawwar-kalām 608
Shāh-nāmah i Nādirī 328
Shāh-nāmah i Qāsimī 305, 1279
Shāh-nāmah i Ṭahmāsp 305, 1279
Shāh-nāmah [i Tūrān-Shāh] 359
Shahriyārān i gum-nām 242
Shāh-Rukh-nāmah 292
Shaibānī-nāmah 372
Shaikh Aḥmad Bībī-Khānī 1061
Shajā'at al-Ḥusainī 225
Shajarah . . . (various "pedigrees") 1061–3
(*Shajarah i ansāb i Mubārak-Shāhī*) 1165
Shajarah i khānadān i Bambah 1348
Shajarah i ṭaiyibah, by "Āzād" Bilgrāmī 862 (12); by M. 'Alī Khān Nawwāb i Daulah 233
Shajarah i Turk 387
Shajarat al-'ārifīn 1063
Shajarat al-Atrāk 272, 1273
Shakaristān 1298
Shakhṣīyat i Maulawī 1341
Shām i gharībān 867
Sham' i anjuman 913
Sham' i maḥfil i sukhan 905
Shamā'il al-Nabī 174, 1252
Shamā'il i Nabawī 174
Shamā'il-nāmah 1259
Shams al-ansāb 1063
Shams al-ḍuḥā 233
Shams al-madhāhib 1187
Shams al-manāqib 1183
Shams al-tawārīkh 150
Sharaf al-Muṣṭafā 175, 1252
Sharaf al-Nabī 175, 1252

Sharaf al-sādāt = Manāqib al-sādāt 211, 1261
Sharaf al-nubuwwah 175, 1252
Sharaf-nāmah, by Ghulām-Ḥusain Khān 635[10]; by Ḥafīẓ Allāh Khān (M. Auliyā) 1187, 1334; by Sharaf Khān Bidlīsī, 367
Sharaf-nāmah i Muḥammad Shāh 609
Sharaf-nāmah i shāhī 374, 1301
Sharā'if i 'Uthmānī 1115
Sharḥ al-ṣudūr bi-tafsīr Āyat al-Nūr, by 'Abd al-Ḥaqq Dihlawī 1198 (?)
Sharḥ al-wāṣilīn 185
Sharḥ Fātiḥat al-Kitāb, by Ni'mat Allāh Walī 8
Sharḥ i Aḥadīyah, by 'Abd al-Aḥad "Rābiṭ" Amēṭ'hawī[1] (not by 'Abd Allāh, as stated in OCM.) 591
Sharḥ i aḥwāl i . . . ḥaḍrat i Bāqir 227, 1265
Sharḥ i aḥwāl i Marhaṭah 760
Sharḥ i aḥwāl i Nāṣir i Khusrau 922
(Sharḥ i ḥāl al-Shaikh Aḥmad . . . al-Aḥsā'ī) 1346
(Sharḥ i ḥāl i 'Abbās Mīrzā Mulk-ārā) 1287
Sharḥ i ḥāl i 'Abd Allāh b. al-Muqaffa' 1183
Sharḥ i ḥāl i Abū Sulaimān i Manṭiqī 1178
Sharḥ i ḥāl i auliyā' 1063
Sharḥ i ḥāl i Kulunil M. Taqī Khān 1183
Sharḥ i ḥāl i Yaghmā 922
Sharḥ i ḥāl u āthār i S. Jamāl al-Dīn i Asadābādī 1184
Sharḥ i ḥāl i iqdāmāt i Sh. M. i Khiyābānī 1184
Sharḥ i ḥāl u maqām i Muḥammad i Zakarīyā i Rāzī 1351
Sharḥ i nasab i Ardalān 369
Sharḥ i Qaṣīdat al-Shāṭibīyah 39 (6), 1217
Sharḥ i Qirān al-sa'dain, by 'Abd al-Rasūl Qāsim 501; by "'Afwī" 1310; by Khair Allāh "Muhandis" 501; by Nūr al-Ḥaqq Dihlawī 501
Sharḥ i Shāṭibīyah, by M. Qāsim Tabrīzī 1217
Sharḥ i suwar i arba'ah 31
Sharḥ i tāj-gudhārī i Shāh Sulaimān i Ṣafawī 1283

[1] Edition: Lucknow 1271/1854–5 (Āṣafīyah ii p. 1528).

Sharḥ i waqā'i' u sawāniḥ i dār al-salṭanah i Tabrīz 321
Sharḥ i Waṣṣāf 270
Sharḥ i zindagānī i man, by 'Abd Allāh Mustaufī 1179
Shāristān 246
Shash fatḥ i Kāngrah 566
al-Shāṭibīyah 39, 40, 1217–18
Shaukat i 'Arab 233
Shawāhid al-nubuwwah 186, 1254
Shawāhid i Niẓāmī 1014[6]
Shawāriq al-ma'rifah 1020
Shēr-Sing'h-nāmah 671
Shifā' al-qulūb 31
al-Shifā' bi-ta'rīf ḥuqūq al-Muṣṭafā 176, 1252
al-Shifā' fī tafsīr kalām Allāh al-munazzal min al-samā' = al-Muḥammadīyah = Tafsīr i Muṣannifak 11, 1194
Shigarf-nāmah i wilāyat 1143
Shihābī 742
Shīr u shakkar 668
Shīr-Sing'h-nāmah 671
Shīrāz-nāmah 351, 1294
Short account of the Wahhābī incursions 428 (5), 1307
Shujā' i Ḥaidarī 687
Sifārat-nāmah i Khwārazm 342
Sifr al-sa'ādah 181[7]
Ṣifwat al-akhbār 101
Ṣifwat al-ṣafā' 939
Sikandar-Shāhī 39
Silk al-bayān 46
Silsilah . . . (various works) 1063–4
Silsilah i 'āliyah 1063 (101)
Silsilah i 'alīyah 1063 (102)
Silsilah-nāmah i Khwājagān i Naqshband 975
Silsilat al-'ārifīn (on Ni'mat Allāh Walī) 1061 (77); (on 'Ubaid Allāh Aḥrār) 967
Silsilat al-'asjad 1138
Silsilat al-nasab i Ṣafawīyah 318
Silsilat al-salāṭīn 381
Simṭ al-'ulā 358, 1297
Sīrah i Sh. Abū Isḥāq i Kāzarūnī 936 n. 1, 1343
Sirāj al-sālikīn 981
Sirāj al-tawārīkh, by Faiḍ-Muḥammad 406; by Maḥmūd Ṭarzī 1305; by M. b. Ḥusain [b. ?] Luṭf Allāh 101; by Nūr-Muḥammad 482; a title (incorrectly ?) assigned to the 'Aẓīm al-tawārīkh 482 n. 1
al-Ṣirāṭ al-mustaqīm, by al-Fīrūzābādī 180

Sīrat al-Nabī, by M. b. 'Abd Allāh b. 'Umar 178
Sīrat al-Sulṭān Jalāl al-Dīn Mankubirnī 1349
Sīrat i Fīrōz-Shāhī 509, 1312
Sīrat Rasūl Allāh, by Ibn Hishām 172
Sīrat-nāmah i Shaikh Rūzbihān 934
Sirr al-shahādatain 223, 1263–4
Sirr i akbar 26
Sittīn (*Kitāb i s.*) 29 (10), 1210
Ṣiwān al-ḥikmah 1104 ult.
Siyāḥat i Turāb 1161
Siyāḥat-nāmah 1161–2
Siyāḥat-nāmah i Ja'far Khān Mushīr al-Daulah 1071
Siyāḥat-nāmah i sih qiṭ'ah i rūy i zamīn 1159
Siyāq al-tawārīkh 1271
Siyar al-aqṭāb 1004
Siyar al-'ārifīn 970
Siyar al-auliyā' 943
Siyar al-muta'akhkhirīn 635
Siyar al-Nabī, by Ibn Isḥāq 173, 1251; by Muḥyī Ḥiṣārī 183; by Sa'īd Kāzarūnī 179; by ? 185
Siyar i 'Afīfī 180
Siyar i Muḥammadī 949
Siyar i Nabawī, by 'Abd al-Awwal Jaunpūrī 193
Siyāsat al-amṣār 69
Siyāsat i daulat i Shūrawī dar Īrān 1291
Strangling of Persia 347
Ṣubḥ i gulshan 915
Ṣubḥ i khandān = *Yad i baiḍā'* 863
Ṣubḥ i ṣādiq 126, 1241–2
Ṣubḥ i waṭan 898
Subḥān-Qulī-nāmah 378
Subḥat al-akhyār (or *al-akhbār*) 156, 1249
Subḥat al-durr wa-'l-yawāqīt 1115
Subḥat al-marjān 859–60, 1336
Sufar al-sa'ādah 180, 1253
Ṣuḥuf i Ibrāhīm 877
Sukhan u sukhanwarān 920
Sukhanwarān i Īrān dar 'aṣr i ḥāḍir 921
Sukhanwarān i nāmī i mu'āṣir 1341
Sulaimān-Bāgh 681
Sulaimān-nāmah, by 'Abd al-Raḥmān "Ghubārī" 418; by Abū 'l-Faḍl Daftarī 416
Sulālat al-siyar 148
Sulṭān al-ḥikāyāt 711
Sulṭān al-tawārīkh, by Ratan Sing'h 709; by Zain al-'Ābidīn Shūshtarī 773
Sulṭānī 1064
Sulṭān-nāmah 421
Ṣūrat i ḥāl 874
Surūr al-arwāḥ 31
Surūr al-maḥzūn 179, 1253
Surūr al-mu'minīn, by M. 'Alī al-Kāẓimī 224; by M. Ḥusain Nā'īnī 233

al-Ṭabaqāt al-Maḥmūd-Shāhīyah 109
Ṭabaqāt al-shu'arā', by Qudrat Allāh "Shauq" 877
Ṭabaqāt al-Ṣūfīyah 926
Ṭabaqāt i Akbarī 433
Ṭabaqāt i Akbar-Shāhī 433
Ṭabaqāt i mashāyikh i Naqshbandīyah i Bukhārā 1064
Ṭabaqāt i Muḥammad b. Sa'd 174
Ṭabaqāt i Muḥsinīyah 724 (where the place and date of publication, Calcutta 1889*, have accidentally been omitted), 1329
Ṭabaqāt i Nāṣirī 68, 1229
Ṭabaqāt i Shāhjahānī 1171
Ṭabaqāt i sukhun 884
Tabjīl al-Tanzīl 31
Tabṣirah i anwār 201
Tabṣirat al-khawāriqāt i Gēsū-darāz 976
Tabṣirat al-nāẓirīn 713
Tadābīr i Shāh u Wazīr 333
Tadhakkur al-mashāyikh 1064
Tadhkirah i aḥwāl i Saiyid M. Khān 1093
Tadhkirah i Akhtar 885
Tadhkirah i Āl i Dāwud 320, 1282
Tadhkirah i 'Alī i Ḥusainī i Gardēzī 852
Tadhkirah i Allāhī 1184
Tadhkirah i Anand-Rām "Mukhliṣ" 613, 1319, n. 2
Tadhkirah i Āṣafī = *Tuzuk i Āṣafī* 750
Tadhkirah i 'Azīzān 392, 1026, 1302
Tadhkirah i bī-naẓīr 854
Tadhkirah i Bīnish = *Ishārāt i Bīnish* 904
Tadhkirah i Bughrah-Khānī 388
Tadhkirah i Darwīsh Nawā 895
Tadhkirah i dil-gushā 888
Tadhkirah i Fārsī 876
Tadhkirah i Gak'harān 676
Tadhkirah i ghadr i Hind 648
Tadhkirah i Hindī, by "Muṣḥafī" 876

Tadhkirah i Humāyūn u Akbar = *Tārīkh i Humāyūn* 538, 1313
Tadhkirah i Ḥusainī 833
Tadhkirah i Isḥāq 872[25], 1337
Tadhkirah i 'Ishqī 880
Tadhkirah i Kātib 885
Tadhkirah i Kāẓim 1339
Tadhkirah i Khwājagān 392, 1026, 1302
Tadhkirah i Khwājagān i Naqshbandīyah 1065
Tadhkirah i khwush-nawīsān 1076
Tadhkirah i khwush-nawīsān u naqqāshān 1074
Tadhkirah i Mahdī 1121
Tadhkirah i majdīyah 1339
Tadhkirah i masarrat-afzā 873
Tadhkirah i mashāhīr i Jaunpūr 1121
Tadhkirah i mubārakah i Nāṣirī 346
Tadhkirah i Muḥammad-Shāhī 894, 1338
Tadhkirah i . . . Mu'īn al-Dīn Chishtī 1065
Tadhkirah i mukhtaṣar dar ḥāl i Rēkhtah-gōyān i Hind 922
Tadhkirah i Mumaiyiz 1340
Tadhkirah i Muqīm-Khānī 380, 1301
Tadhkirah i muṣannifīn i Dihlī 195[16]
Tadhkirah i muta'akhkhirīn i shu'arā' i Fārs 922
Tadhkirah i Nawā 895
Tadhkirah i Nirmal 753
Tadhkirah i Nudrat 828
Tadhkirah i Qāsim (= *Majmū'ah i naghz*) 882
Tadhkirah i Sarwar 883
Tadhkirah i Shāh-'Ālam 1346
Tadhkirah i Shāh Ṭahmāsp 305, 1279
Tadhkirah i shaqq al-qamar 206
Tadhkirah i Shōrish 868
Tadhkirah i shu'arā', by "Ghanī" Farrukhābādī 923
Tadhkirah i shu'arā' i Qā'ināt 923 (cf. 1353[21])
Tadhkirah i Shūrish 868
Tadhkirah i Shūshtarīyah 365, 1298
Tadhkirah i Ṣūfīyah 1065
Tadhkirah i sukhun-āfrīnān i Hindī-zabān 868
Tadhkirah i Ṭāhir i Naṣrābādī 820
Tadhkirah i Thamar i Nā'īnī 1338
Tadhkirah i Ṭūr i Kalīm 914
Tadhkirah i 'ulamā' i Hind 1120
Tadhkirah i wāṣilān = *Riyāḍ al-wāṣilīn* 1037
Tadhkirah i Yūsuf 'Alī Khān 868
Tadhkirah u tabṣirah 923
Tadhkirat al-aḥwāl, by "Ḥazīn" 847, 1336
Tadhkirat al-a'immah 198
Tadhkirat al-akhyār 1184
Tadhkirat al-anbiyā' 171, 1251
Tadhkirat al-anbiyā' wa-'l-umam 171 (43)
Tadhkirat al-aṣfiyā' 1265
Tadhkirat al-auliyā', by "'Aṭṭār" 930; by M. Qāḍī 967; by Ni'mat Allāh Riḍawī 1065
Tadhkirat al-bilād wa-'l-ḥukkām 765
Tadhkirat al-ḥukamā' 1111
Tadhkirat al-kātibīn 1077[3]
Tadhkirat al-khaṭṭāṭīn = *Imtiḥān al-fuḍalā'* 1077, 1347
Tadhkirat al-khawātīn 916
Tadhkirat al-kirām 1040
Tadhkirat al-ma'ṣūmīn 218
Tadhkirat al-mu'āṣirīn 848
Tadhkirat al-mulūk, by M. Muẓaffar Khwāfī 242; by Rafī' al-Dīn Shīrāzī 743; by Yaḥyā Khān 471; by ? 493
Tadhkirat al-muttaqīn 1052
Tadhkirat al-nisā' = *Akhtar i tābān* 916; anon. 923
Tadhkirat al-qubūr 1353
Tadhkirat al-Riḍā [?] 1147[30]
Tadhkirat al-sādāt 217, 1267
Tadhkirat al-salāṭīn, by Abū 'l-Qāsim Nūr Muḥammad 493; by Sulṭān-Muḥammad Qājār 892, 1338
Tadhkirat al-salāṭīn i Chaghatā 517
Tadhkirat al-shu'arā', by Daulat-Shāh 785; by Ṣiddīq Khān 923 (13); by "'Urūj" 923 (12)
Tadhkirat al-shu'arā' i Subḥān-Qulī-Khānī 825
Tadhkirat al-shuhadā' 1267
Tadhkirat al-ṭarīq 1147
Tadhkirat al-tawārīkh 1240
Tadhkirat al-'ulamā' 1121
Tadhkirat al-umarā', by Kēwal Rām 1094; by J. Skinner 688
Tadhkirat al-wāqi'āt 536
al-Tadwīn fī aḥwāl jibāl Sharwīn 362
Tafḍīḥ al-ghāfilīn 705
Tafrīḥ al-'imārāt 693
Tafṣīl i aḥwāl i 'urūj u khurūj i rājahā u sardārān i Dak'han 760
Tafsīr al-Muṣṭafawī 23
Tafsīr al-Sūrābādī 3, 1189
Tafsīr fī ma'nā 'l-tauḥīd 1213
Tafsīr i Abū Bakr b. 'Umar b. Abī 'l-Faḍl 31
Tafsīr i 'Alawī 1203

Tafsīr i 'Alī 'Aẓīm Khān 32
Tafsīr i Amīnī 19
Tafsīr i asrār al-Fātiḥah 32
Tafsīr i 'Atīq i Sūrābādī 3, 1189
Tafsīr i āyāt al-aḥkām 1198
Tafsīr i Āyat al-Kursī, by Fakhr al-Dīn Sammākī 17; by M. Bāqir Majlisī 32 (37), 1213; by Nūr al-Dīn M. 17; by ? 32 (38); by ? 1213
Tafsīr i Āyat al-Nūr 1198
Tafsīr i Āyat al-sharīfah i Istikhlāf 32
Tafsīr i 'azīz 32
Tafsīr i 'Azīzī 24
Tafsīr i Baṣā'ir i Yamīnī 5, 1191
Tafsīr i Dalīl al-Raḥmān 32 (42), 1213
Tafsīr i Ḥaḍrat-Shāhī 26
Tafsīr i Ḥasan i 'Askarī 15, 29, 1197, 1209, 1210
(*Tafsīr i Ḥurūfī*) 1192
Tafsīr i Ḥusainī 12, 1195
Tafsīr i Kaiwān 1206
Tafsīr i Kalimah i Tahlīlīyah 1197
Tafsīr i Kāzarūnī = Jalā' al-adhhān 29, 1211
Tafsīr i Maẓhar al-Ḥaqq 30, 1211
Tafsīr i Mubārak-Shāh 32, 1213
Tafsīr i Muḥammad Pārsā 8, 1192
Tafsīr i Muṣannifak 10, 1194
Tafsīr i Nuqrah-kār 1194[29]
Tafsīr i Pārah i 'Amma, by Ḥamīd al-Dīn Nāgaurī 6
Tafsīr i qasamhā i Qur'ān i Majīd 32
Tafsīr i Qur'ān, by M. Khāliṣī-zādah 1208
Tafsīr i Ṣafī 1205 (cf. 32)
Tafsīr i Saif al-Dīn = Tafsīr i Zāhidī 1190
Tafsīr i Saiyid Kāẓim i 'Aṣṣār 1207
Tafsīr i Shāh 19
Tafsīr i Shāhī 13, 1197
Tafsīr i Sūrābādī 3, 1189
Tafsīr i Sūrah i Fātiḥah, by Mu'īn al-Dīn Farāhī 11, 1194
Tafsīr i Sūrah i Hal atā 1199
Tafsīr i Sūrah i Ḥamd, by M. b. Ḥasan Sanglajī, 1207
Tafsīr i Sūrah i Ikhlāṣ, by M. b Ḥasan Sanglajī 1207
Tafsīr i Sūrah i Innā a'ṭaināka 33
Tafsīr i Sūrah i Muzzammil, by Ghulām-Jīlānī 33; by Ṭā-Hā Quṭb al-Dīn 29 (8)
Tafsīr i Sūrah i Nūr, by Khalīl Kamara'ī 1208
Tafsīr i Sūrah i Wa-'l-ḍuḥā 1214
Tafsīr i Sūrah i Wa-'l-tīn 17
Tafsīr i Sūrah i Yā-Sīn, by 'Ubaid Allāh Khān 33 (58); by ? 33 (59)
Tafsīr i Sūrah i Yūsuf, by Jān Muḥammad Jāland'harī 1214; by Mu'īn al-Dīn Farāhī 11, 1194; several works 33, 1214
Tafsīr i Sūrat al-Fātiḥah, by 'Ābid Ḥusain 32 (46); by 'Ubaid Allāh Khān 32 (48)
Tafsīr i Sūrat al-Muddaththir 33
Tafsīr i Sūrat al-Mulk 33
Tafsīr i Sūrat al-Muzzammil 33 (53)
Tafsīr i Sūrat al-Naba', by 'Abd al-Raḥīm Samarqandī 33 (54); by Ḥammāmī-zādah 33 (55)
Tafsīr i Sūrat al-Qadr 33
Tafsīr i Sūrat al-Tauḥīd 33
Tafsīr i Sūrat al-Wāqi'ah 19
Tafsīr i Ṭabarī 2, 1189
Tafsīr i tadhkirat al-anbiyā' wa-'l-umam 171
Tafsīr i Thamāniyah 8
Tafsīr i wajīz 26
Tafsīr i Ya'qūb i Charkhī 9, 1193
Tafsīr i Zāhidī 4, 1190
Tafsīr i Zawārī 14, 1197
Tafsīr Sūrat al-Fātiḥah wa-mushkilāt al-Qur'ān 1209 antepenult.
Tafsīrāt i karīmah 33
Taḥā'if al-abrār 1052
Taḥā'if i Rashīdīyah 1020
Taḥawwulāt i siyāsī i niẓām i Īrān 1288
Tahawwur-nāmah 717
Ṭahmās-nāmah 625
Taḥqīq al-ansāb 1182
Taḥqīq dar rubā'iyāt u zindagānī i Khaiyām 1341
Taḥrīk al-shifāh bi-auṣāf Wālā-Jāh 780
Taḥrīr al-anwar 1047
Taḥrīr al-mu'taqid 946
Taḥrīr al-shahādatain 223, 1264
Taisīr al-bayān fī tajwīd al-Qur'ān 1218
Tāj al-iqbāl 734
Tāj al-ma'āthir 494, 1310
Tāj al-qiṣaṣ 159, 1208[25]
Tāj al-tarājim 3, 1190
Tāj al-tawārīkh, Amīr 'Abd al-Raḥmān's autobiography 406 n.2, 1304; by M. b. Rafī' Shīrāzī 492; by M. Sharīf, 382
Tajallī i nūr 1121
Tajārib al-salaf 81, 1233
Tajārib al-umam 245, 1270
Tajribat al-aḥrār 335

Tajrīd fī aḥkām al-tajwīd 47
Tajwīd i Aḥmadī 47 (24)
Tajwīd i lā-yanfakk 50
Tajwīd i Muḥammadī 47
Tajziyat al-amṣār 267, 1272
al-Takmīl 44
Takmilah i Akbar-nāmah 547
Takmilah i Ḥamlah i Ḥaidarī 200, 201
Takmilat al-akhbār 1239
Takmilat al-laṭā'if 159
Takmilat al-shu'arā' Jām i Jamshīd 877
Takmilat Rauḍ al-rayāḥīn 936
Ṭalī'ah i shams 1162
Ta'līf i Muḥammadī 202
Ta'līf qalb al-alīf 195[15], 1256
Tamaddun i Islāmī 157
Tanbīh al-sālikīn 1187
Tanmīq i shigarf 738
Tanqīḥ al-akhbār, by Kundan Lāl [?] 1246, n. 2 ; by M. Māh 135
Tanqīḥ al-akhbār fī āthār al-adwār 157
Tansar's epistle to Goshnasp 360
Tanwīr al-'ain 207
Tanwīr al-dujā 34
Taqwīm al-tawārīkh 128, 1242
Ṭarā'iq al-ḥaqā'iq 1051
Tarājim al-a'ājim 35, 1215
Tarānah i gham 1184
Targhīb al-Furqān 56
Targhīb al-sālik 1152
Ta'rīkh al-ḥukamā' 1107 (Qifṭī) ; 1108 (Shahrazūrī), 1350–1
Ta'rīkh al-Qāḍī Burhān al-Dīn = *Bazm u razm* 411
Ta'rīkh al-rusul wa-'l-mulūk = *Tārīkh i Ṭabarī* 61, 1229
Ta'rīkh al-salāṭīn 520
Ta'rīkh al-tamaddun al-Islāmī 157
Ta'rīkh ḥabībī wa-tadhkirat murshidī 952
Tārīkh i 'Abbāsī, by Jalāl i Munajjim 308, 1280
Tārīkh i 'Abbāsīyah, by 'Alī Shēr "Qāni'" 656
Tārīkh i 'Abd Allāh Khān 374
Tārīkh i Abū 'l-Khair-Khānī 110
Tārīkh i adabīyāt i Īrān, by "Sanā" Humā'ī 1187
Tārīkh i 'Aḍudī 339
Tārīkh i Afḍal 357, 1297
Tārīkh i Afghān 404
Tārīkh i Afghānistān 401
Tārīkh i Aḥmad 403, 1304
(*Tārīkh i Aḥmad Shāh*) 1303
Tārīkh i Aḥmad-Shāhī, by Maḥmūd b. Ibrāhīm 395, 1303 ; by M. 'Alī Khān Anṣārī 621 ; by ? 621
Tārīkh i aḥwāl, by "Ḥazīn" 847, 1336
Tārīkh i aḥwāl i Islām Khān Mashhadī 1103
Tārīkh i ajdād u farzandān u aṣḥāb i . . . Jalāl . . . al-Dīn M. i Rūmī 1065 (117)
Tārīkh i Akbarī 541
Tārīkh i Āl i amjād 227
Tārīkh i āl i Muẓaffar 277, 1273
Tārīkh i āl i Qājār 333
Tārīkh i āl i Saljūq, anon. 410, 1305
(*Tārīkh i āl i Saljūq dar mamālik i Rūm*), abridgment of Ibn i Bībī 409
Tarīkh i āl i Subuktigīn = *Tārīkh i Baihaqī* 253, 1271
Tārīkh i 'ālam-ārāy i 'Abbāsī 310, 1280
Tārīkh i 'ālam-ārāy i Amīnī 301, 1278
Tārīkh i 'Ālamgīr i Thānī 622
Tārīkh i 'Ālamgīrī, by 'Abd al-Ḥaiy, 599 ; by Aḥmad-Qulī Ṣafawī 599
Tārīkh i alfī 120, 1240
Tārīkh i 'Alī 'Ādil-Shāh 744, 1331
Tārīkh i 'ālī fī silk al-la'ālī 624, 1321
Tārīkh i 'Alī-Wirdī Khān 717, 1329
Tārīkh i Amīr Maḥmūd 304, 1279
Tārīkh i Amīr Ma'ṣūm 382
Tārīkh i Amjadīyah 757
Tārīkh i Āṣaf-Jāhī 755
Tārīkh i Āshām 582, 1317
Tārīkh i Awad'h 710
Tārīkh i Āyā Ṣōfyah, anon. 1306 ; by Aḥmad Jīlānī 422
Tārīkh i A'ẓamgaḍh 703
Tārīkh i A'ẓamī 683
Tārīkh i 'Azīzī 390
Tārīkh i Bābil u Nīnawā 344
Tārīkh i Badakhshān 382, 1301, 1305
Tārīkh i badāyi' 1187
Tārīkh i bad-bakhtī i Īrān = *Wāqi'āt i dū-sālah* 1289 (21)
Tārīkh i bādshāhān i Dihlī 1312
Tārīkh i Bahāwal Khān 660
Tārīkh i Bahāwalpūr 662
Tārīkh i Baihaq 354, 1295
Tārīkh i Baihaqī 253, 1271
Tārīkh i Bakhtyārī 1299
Tārīkh i Banākatī 79, 1232
Tārīkh i Bangālā 715
Tārīkh i Baṣrah 428
Tārīkh i Bēgam Samrū 692
Ṭārīkh i Bharatpūr, by Ānand Rāy 690 ; by Faḍl i 'Aẓīm 689

Tārīkh i Bharōch 733
Tārīkh i bīdārī i Īrān 1290
Tārīkh i bīdārī i Īrāniyān 347, 1287
Tārīkh i binā i Ḥaidarābād 759
Tārīkh i bīst u shash sāl i salṭanat i Aliksāndar i duwum 430
Tārīkh i bīst-sālah i Īrān 1291
Tārīkh i Bukhārā 370, 1300
Tārīkh i Chaghatāy 611
Tārīkh i Chīn 432
Tārīkh i Dakan, by 'Abd al-'Alīm Naṣr Allāh Khān 757; by Amjad Ḥusain (= *Tārīkh i Amjadīyah*) 757; by Munnā Lāl 739
Tārīkh i Danābilah 1299
Tārīkh i daulat i Rum 430
Tārīkh i Dāwudī 515
Tārīkh i Dhū'l-Qarnain 337, 1285
Tārīkh i dil-afrūz 754
Tārīkh i Dilēr-Jangī 766
Tārīkh i dil-gushā, by Bhīm Sēn 588, 1318; by 'Ināyat Allāh 578
Tārīkh i faiḍ-bakhsh 695, 1327
Ta'rikh-i Fakhru'd-Dín Mubárakshāh 1165
Tārīkh i Faraḥ-bakhsh 706
Tārīkh i Farānisah 429
Tārīkh i Farrukhābād 694
Tārīkh i Farrukhsiyarī 606
Tārīkh i fārsi fī wilādat al-Sulṭān . . . Shāh Ṭahmāsp 321
Tārīkh i Fatḥ-'Alī Shāh i Qājār 332
Tārīkh i Firishtah 446
Tārīkh i Fīrōz-Shāhī, by Ḍiyā' al-Dīn Baranī 507, 1311; by Shams i Sirāj 511
Tārīkh i Frānsah 429
Tārīkh i futūḥ i Shām 233
Tārīkh i futūḥāt i Āṣafī, by "Ījād" 605, 1331
Tārīkh i Ganjīnah 131
Tārīkh i Gauhar i shāhwār 753
Tārīkh i Ghāzānī 72, 1231–2
Tārīkh i Ghāzīpūr 702
Tārīkh i Gīlān 363, 1298
Tārīkh i Gīlān u Dailamistān 362
Tārīkh i Gītī-gushāy 331, 1284
Tārīkh i Gōrak'hpūr 703
Tārīkh i Gujrāt 727, 1329
Tārīkh i guzīdah 82, 1233
Tārīkh i guzīdah i Farīdūn Malkum 1308
Tārīkh i ḥabībī 952
Tārīkh i Ḥafīẓ-Allāh-Khānī 1334
Tārīkh i Ḥāfiẓ-Raḥmat-Khānī 396
Tārīkh i Ḥaidarī 124, 1241
Tārīkh i hajdah-sālah i Ādharbāyjān 1300
Tārīkh i ḥākimān i Hind 450
Tārīkh i Ḥamīd Khān 774
Tārīkh i Ḥaqqī 441
Tārīkh i Harāt 354, 1296
Tārīkh i Ḥasan 1114
Tārīkh i Hazārah 676
Tārīkh i hijdah-sālah i Ādharbāyjān 1300
Tārīkh i Hind, by Jawāhir La'l 489; by Khwurshēd 'Alī 489; = *Chach-nāmah* 650, 1323
Tārīkh i Hindī (?), by Bakhtāwar Khān (?) 517
Tārīkh i Hindī, by Rustam 'Alī 471
Tārīkh i Hindūstān, by ? 488
Tārīkh i Hinrī 150
Tārīkh i Humāyūn 538, 1313
Tārīkh i Humāyūnī = *T. i Ibrāhīmī* 113, 1239
Tārīkh i Ibrāhīmī 113, 1239
Tārīkh i ijtimā'ī u idārī i daurah i Qājārīyah 1179, 1288
Tārīkh i Īlchī i Niẓām-Shāh 113
Tārīkh i 'Imād al-Mulk 623
Tārīkh i Imām-zādahā i Shaft u Fūman . . . 1086
Tārīkh i Impirāṭūrān i Ālmān u Pāphā i Rūm 429
Tārīkh i Ingilistān 429
Tārīkh i inkishāf i Yangī-Dunyā 429
Tārīkh i inqilāb i Ādharbāyjān 1299
Tārīkh i inqilāb i mashrūṭīyat i Īrān 1288
Tārīkh i inqilāb i Ṭūs 1297
Tārīkh i Irādat Khān 602
Tārīkh i Īrān, by Malcolm 242; by M. Ḥasan Khān Marāghī 1269; by M. Ḥusain Khān "Furūghī" 241, 1269
Tārīkh i Iṣfahān 349, 1292
Tārīkh i Iṣfahān u Rai 1293
Tārīkh i Iskandar 430
Tārīkh i Iskandar i Dhū-'l-Qarnain 171
Tārīkh i Iskandarī 1188
Tārīkh i Jadīd 345, 1287
Tārīkh i jadīd [*i Yazd*] 1293
Tārīkh i Ja'farī 86, 1235
Tārīkh i jahān-ārā 336
Tārīkh i Jahāngīr 284, 1274
Tārīkh i Jahāngīrī, by "Muṭribī" 814
Tārīkh i Jahāngīrnagar 723
Tārīkh (*Tawārīkh*) *i Jahāngīr-Shāhī* 560

Tārīkh i Jahān-gushāy i Juwainī 261, 1272
Tārīkh i Jahān-gushāy i Nādirī 322, 1283
Tārīkh i Jā'is 713
Tārīkh i Jān Muḥammad 666
Tārīkh i jang i Farānisah bā Rūs 429
Tārīkh i jang i Ingilīs u Īrān 1289
Tārīkh i jarā'id u majallāt i Īrān 1289
Tārīkh i Jaunpūr 698
Tārīkh i jāwīd 1184
Tārīkh i Jhang Sayāl 676
Tārīkh i Jūgal Kishōr 474
Tārīkh i kabīr i Kashmīr = *Taḥā'if al-abrār* 1052
Tārīkh i Kalām al-mulūk 1078
Tārīkh i Kār-nāmah (?) 493
Tārīkh i Kāshghar 393
Tārīkh i Kashmīr, by Ḥaidar Malik 680; by Ḥasan (Ḥusain ?) b. 'Alī 680; by M. Ḥaidar 687; by Narāyan Kaul 682, 1325; by ? 687
Tārīkh i Kashmīr i A'ẓamī 683
Tārīkh i kathīrah 377
Tārīkh i khairāt 89, 1236
(*Tārīkh i khānadān i Tīmūrīyah*) 299
Tārīkh i Khānī 363
Tārīkh i Khān-Jahānī 393, 1302
Tārīkh i Khiṭāy u Khutan 431
Tārīkh i khudā-dādī 770
Tārīkh i Kirmān 1298
Tārīkh i Mā warā' al-Nahr 386
Tārīkh i madfūnīn i Balkh 981
Tārīkh i Madīnah 427
Tārīkh i Mahābat-Jang 717, 1329
Tārīkh i Maḥmūd b. Khwānd-Amīr 304, 1279
Tārīkh i Maḥmūd-Shāhī 726
Tārīkh i Mālwā 735
Tārīkh i mamālik i Hind 475
Tārīkh i Manghitīyah 388
Tārīkh i Manṣūrī 721
Tārīkh i Manṭiqī 242
Tārīkh i Mānukchī (*sic*) 345 ult.
Tārīkh i Marhaṭah 762
Tārīkh i mashrūṭah i Īrān 1289
Tārīkh i Mas'ūdī = *Tārīkh i Baihaqī* 253, 1271
Tārīkh i Ma'ṣūmī 652, 1324
Tārīkh i mazārāt i Balkh 981, 1297
Tārīkh i milal i mashriq 1188
Tārīkh i Mīr Saiyid Sharīf Rāqim 377
Tārīkh i Mīrzā Shāh-Maḥmūd i Churās 392
Tārīkh i Mu'aẓẓamābād 702
Tārīkh i Mubārak-Shāhī 512
Tārīkh i Mufaḍḍalī 135
Tārīkh i mufaṣṣal i Īrān, by 'Abbās Iqbāl 242
Tārīkh i Muḥammad 'Ārif i Qandahārī 541
Tārīkh i Muḥammadī, by M. Bihāmad-Khānī 90; by M. b. M. Taqī Sārū'ī 332; by M. b. Mu'tamad Khān 141, 1244; by "Rājī" (= *Ḥaqā'iq*) 1265
Tārīkh i Muḥammad-Shāhī, by Ghulām-Ḥusain 619; by Khwush-ḥāl Chand 136
Tārīkh i muḥārabah i Rūs u Zhāpān 430
Tārīkh i muḥāṣarah u fatḥ i Harāt 1297
Tārīkh i Muḥtasham 708
Tārīkh i Mu'īnī i Muẓaffarī 277, 1273
Tārīkh i mukhtaṣar dar waqā'i' i fatḥ i Qusṭanṭīnīyah 422
Tārīkh i mukhtaṣar i aḥzāb i siyāsī i Īrān 1291
Tārīkh i mukhtaṣar i Ḥaidarābād 759
Tārīkh i mulk-ārā 333
Tārīkh i mulk i Āshām 582, 1317
Tārīkh i Mulūk i Kart 354, 1296
Tārīkh i muntaẓam i Nāṣirī 154
Tārīkh i muraṣṣa' 394
Tārīkh i Murtaḍā 'l-dahr 1241
Tārīkh i Mūsawī 162, 1250–1
Tārīkh i Muẓaffarī, by M. 'Alī Khān Anṣārī 522; by Mu'īn Yazdī 277, 1273
Tārīkh i Muẓaffar-Shāhī (?), by "Qāni'ī" 727; by ? 725
Tārīkh i Nabawī 203
Tārīkh i Nabī, by Iḥsān Allāh 204
Tārīkh i Nādir-al-zamānī 136
Tārīkh i Nādirī, by 'Abd al-Karīm Kashmīrī (= *Bayān i wāqi'*) 326; by Fraser 329; by M. Mahdī 322, 1283
Tārīkh i nahḍat i Īrān 348
Tārīkh i Nāṣir-Shāhī 735
Tārīkh i nau 339, 1285
Tārīkh i Nauras-nāmah 446
Tārīkh i nisbat i Afghānī 407
Tārīkh i niṣf i jahān u hamah i jahān 1293
Tārīkh i niyābat i 'Aẓīm-Jāh 780
Tārīkh i niẓāmī i jang i 'Arab bā 'Ajam 1271
Tārīkh i niẓāmī i jang i Īrān u Hind 1284
Tārīkh i niẓāmī i jang i Īrān u Makidōniyah 1271
Tārīkh i Nuṣrat-Jangī 723

Tārīkh i pādshāhān i 'Ajam, by Ṣadīq [Ṣādiq ?] Qā'im-maqām, 1269 ; by ? 242 (10), 242 (11)
Tārīkh i pādshāhān i 'Ajam yā Siyāq al-tawārīkh 1271
Tārīkh i pādshāhān i Dihlī 1312
Tārīkh i pādshāhān i Ṣafawīyah 321, 1282
Tārīkh i Panjāb, by Būṭī Shāh 670
Tārīkh i Panjāb tuḥfat^{an} *li-l-aḥbāb* 673
Tārīkh i pānṣad-sālah i Khūzistān 366, 1298
Tārīkh i Piṭr 430
Tārīkh i qadīm i Yūnān 429
Tārīkh i Qādirī 748
Tārīkh i Qādirīyah 1020
Tārīkh i Qaiṣar i Rūm 421
Tārīkh i Qājārīyah, by Aḥmad Sharīfī Shīrāzī 1286 ; by M. Taqī " Sipihr " 153, 343, 1248
Tārīkh i Qandahārī = Laṭā'if al-akhbār 574
Tārīkh i Qipchāqī 1188
Tārīkh i Qipchāq-Khānī 136, 1243
Tārīkh i Qum, by Ḥasan Qummī 348, 1291 ; by M. 'Alī b. Ḥusain 349, 1291–2
Tārīkh i Qur'ān 1228
Tārīkh i Quṭb-Shāhī 748
Tārīkh i rāḥat-afzā 138, 759, 1244
Tārīkh i rājahā i Hind 450
Tārīkh i Rāqimī 377, 1301
Tārīkh i Rashīdī 274, 1273
Tārīkh i rawābiṭ i Īrān u Urōpā dar daurah i Ṣafawīyah 1283
Tārīkh i rawābiṭ i siyāsī i Īrān ba-dunyā 1289
Tārīkh i rawābiṭ i siyāsī i Īrān u Ingilīs 1289
Tārīkh i Rūm u Farang 1306
Tārīkh i Rūs 430
Tārīkh i Rūyān 361
Tārīkh i sa'ādat i jāwīd 479
Tārīkh i Ṣadr i Jahān 110
Tārīkh i Ṣāḥib-qirān 1275
Tārīkh i Ṣāḥib-qirānī 336, 1285
Tārīkh i saiyāḥ 321
Tārīkh i salāṭīn i Afāghinah 516, 1312
Tārīkh i salāṭīn i Dihlī 493
Tārīkh i salāṭīn i Gujrāt 733
Tārīkh i salāṭīn i Manghitīyah 383
Tārīkh i salāṭīn i Sāsānī 249
Tārīkh i salāṭīn i 'Uthmānī 422
Tārīkh i Salīmī = Jahāngīr-nāmah 556
Tārīkh i Salīm-Shāhī = Jahāngīr-nāmah 556
Tārīkh i Saljūqiyān i Kirmān 358
Tārīkh i Shāh 'Abbās i Thānī 315, 1282
Tārīkh i Shāh Ismā'īl i Ṣafawī 304, 1278
Tārīkh i shahādat i 'Abd Allāh Khān 388
Tārīkh i shahādat i Farrukh-siyar u julūs i Muḥammad Shāh 617, 1321
Tārīkh i Shāh-'Ālam, by Munnā Lāl 644, 1322
Tārīkh i Shāh-'Ālam Bahādur-Shāh 600
Tārīkh i Shāhanshāhī, by M. Khalīl 604
Tārīkh i shāhanshāhī i . . . Riḍā Shāh Pahlawī 348
Tārīkh i Shāhī = Tārīkh i salāṭīn i Afāghinah 516, 1312
Tārīkh i Shāhīyah i Nīshāpūrīyah 709
Tārīkh i Shāh-Rukh 87
Tārīkh i Shāh-Rukhī 391
Tārīkh i Shāh-Shujā'ī 582, 1317
Tārīkh i Shaikh Uwais 1233, 1269
Tārīkh i Shākir-Khānī 622
Tārīkh i Sharīf i Raḍī 1136
Tārīkh i Shauqī 392
Tārīkh i Shēr-Shāhī 513
Tārīkh i Shuhadā i Yazd 1294
Tārīkh i sifārat i Ḥājjī Khalīl Khān . . 1067
Tārīkh i Sind, anon., 1324 ; by M. Ma'ṣūm 652, 1324
Tārīkh i Sīstān 364
Tārīkh i siyāsī i daurah i ṣadārat i Mīrzā Ḥusain Khān Mushīr al-Daulah 1350
Tārīkh i Sōraṭ'h 731
Tārīkh i Subḥān-Qulī Khān 379
Tārīkh i ṣughrā 388
Tārīkh i Sulaimānī 172
Tārīkh i Sulṭān i Ghāzī 422
Tārīkh i Sulṭān-Muḥammad-Quṭb-Shāhī 747
Tārīkh i Sulṭān Saiyid Amīr Naṣr Allāh 385
Tārīkh i Sulṭānī, anon. 1282 ; by Ḥasan b. Murtaḍā 134 ; by Sulṭān-Muḥammad Khān 404 ; = *Tārīkh i . . . Amīr Naṣr Allāh* 385
Tārīkh i Ṭabarī 61, 1229
Tārīkh i Ṭabaristān 360, 1298
Tārīkh i Ṭabaristān u Rūyān u Māzandarān 361
Tārīkh . . . i Tabrīz 1299

Tārīkh i Ṭāhir i Waḥīd 315, 1282
Tārīkh i Ṭāhirī, by Ṭāhir M. Sabzawārī 122, 1241; by Ṭāhir M. "Nisyānī" Tattawī 655
Tārīkh i Ṭahmāsīyah 320
Tārīkh i tawallud u wafāt i pādshāhān 157
Tārīkh i Thābit 460
Tārīkh i Tīmūrī 287
Tārīkh i Ṭīpū Sulṭān 1334
Tārīkh i Turkumānīyah 299
Tārīkh i 'Ubaid Allāh Khān 379
Tārīkh i 'ulamā' u shu'arā-yi Gīlān 1352
Tārīkh i Ūljāytū Sulṭān 267, 1272
Tārīkh i 'Umarī 233, 1267
Tārīkh i 'umūmī 1188
Tārīkh i 'umūmī dar qarn i hafdahum u hizhdahum 1249
Tārīkh i 'umūmī dar qarn i nūzdahum u bīstum 1249
Tārīkh i 'umūmī i qurūn i wusṭā 1249
Tārīkh i wafāt i buzurgān 1028
Tārīkh i Walī 388
Tārīkh i waqā'i' u sawāniḥ i Afghānistān 404
Tārīkh i wāqi'ah i Mashhad i Muqaddas 1297
Tārīkh i Wāqidī 174
Tārīkh i Waṣṣāf 267, 1272
Tārīkh i Wazīr 'Alī 705
Tārīkh i Yādgār 755
Tārīkh i Yahūd 1188
Tārīkh i Yamīnī 251
Tārīkh i Yazd, by 'Abd al-Ḥusain "Āyatī" 1294; by Aḥmad Ṭāhirī 1294
Tārīkh i Yūnān 430
Tārīkh i Yūsufī 1153
Tārīkh i Zandīyah, by 'Alī Riḍā Shīrāzī 332, 1284; by M. Ṣādiq "Nāmī" = *Tārīkh i Gītī-gushāy* 331, 1284; by ? 331
Tārīkh i zindagānī i Taqī-zādah 1350
Tārīkh u jughrāfiyā-yi dār al-salṭanah i Tabrīz 1299
Tārīkh-nāmah i Rāqim 377
Ṭarīq al-bukā' 1184
al-Ṭarīq al-qawīm 181, 1253
Tarjamah i Aḥwālāt i Salāṭīn i Rūm 422
Tarjamah i Amīnī 251
Tarjamah i Āyat al-Kursī 34
Tarjamah i kaifīyat i nasab-nāmah i Rājah i Satārah-wālah 763
Tarjamah i lughāt i Qur'ān 1217
Tarjamah i Maḥāsin i Iṣfahān 349, 1292
Tarjamah i Manāqib i thawāqib 938[33]
Tarjamah i Maulūd i Muṣṭafā 180
Tarjamah i Qaṣīdah i Shāṭibīyah 39 (5), 1217
Tarjamah i Siyar al-Nabī 173, 1251
Tarjamah i Tafsīr i Ṭabarī 2, 1189
Tarjamah i Takmilah 936[24]
Tarjamah i Tamaddun i Islāmī 157, 1249
Tarjamah i Ta'rīkh al-ḥukamā' 1107 (Qifṭī) 1108 (Shahrazūrī) 1350–1
Tarjamah i Tārīkh i Yamīnī 252
Tarjamah i Yamīnī 251
Tarjamat al-asrār 201
Tarjamat al-jarīdah 39
Tarjamat al-khawāṣṣ 14, 1197
Tarjamat al-manāqib 210, 1260
Tarjamat al-mufīd 41
Tarjamat al-Qur'ān, by Bahā' al-Dīn Lāhijī 1200
Tarjamat al-Sulṭānī 1200
Tarjamat al-Takmilah 936[13]
Tarjamat Ibn al-Khafīf. See *Aḥwāl i Ibn al-Khafīf* 1053
Tarjīḥ al-faḍā'il 1268
Tarjumān al-Qur'ān, by al-Jurjānī 37, 39 (8) [I.O. D.A. 984 is Jurjānī's work] 1216; by al-Zauzanī 38; beg. *al-Ḥ. l. 'l. arsala 'l-rusul* 39 (7), 1217
Tarjumān i balāghat 244
Tarkhān nāmah 655
Tarkīb al-Qur'ān 1214
Tartīb i zībā, by Ṣāliḥ Nāẓim 53; = *Hādiyah i Quṭb-Shāhī* 51, 1225
Tasalluṭ i Ṣāḥibān i Angrēz 688
Tasliyat al-ikhwān 264
Taṣwīr i balāghat 1259
Taṣwīr i 'ibrat 1355
Tatabbu' u intiqād i aḥwāl u āthār i Salmān i Sāwajī 919
Tatimmat Ṣiwān al-ḥikmah 1105, 1350
Tauḍīḥ (beg. *Ḥ. ān Khudā'ī rā kih bi-firistād*) 34 (70), 34 (72), 1214
Tauḍīḥ [?] (different from the preceding) 34 (71).
Tauḍīḥ al-Rashaḥāt 965[19]
Tawallud-nāmah 1259
Tawārīkh i 'Abbāsiyān 657
Tawārīkh i Afāghinah 396
Tawārīkh i Aḥmad-Khānī 693
Tawārīkh i Āl i Barmak 1082
Tawārīkh i āl i Saljūq 409
Tawārīkh i Bangālā 715
Tawārīkh i Dwmṛī 683

Tawārīkh i Farangistān 429
Tawārīkh i farkhundah 755
Tawārīkh i haft kursī 744
Tawārīkh i Ḥaidarī 767
Tawārīkh i Jahāngīr-Shāhī, by Walī Sirhindī 560
Tawārīkh i Jawāhir i 'Abbāsīyah 661
Tawārīkh i khwurshīd i jahān 407
Tawārīkh i manẓūmah 390
Tawārīkh i Marhaṭah 762
Tawārīkh i mulk i Hazārah 676
Tawārīkh i Quṭb-Shāh 746
Tawārīkh i Raḥmat-Khānī 396
Tawārīkh i Rājagān i Hindūr 678
Tawārīkh i Shāh-Jahānī 577
Tawārīkh i Shahrukhīyah 391
Tawārīkh i tāzah-nawā'ī 659
al-Tawassul ilā 'l-tarassul 260, 1272
Thamarat al-falāsifah 1110
Thamarāt al-mashāyikh 1012
Thamarāt al-quds 1065
Thawāqib al-anwār 1006
Thawāqib al-manāqib i auliyā' Allāh 938
Tīmūr-nāmah, by "Hātifī" 289, 1274–5; by ? 290
Tīmūr-nāmah i Mufaḍḍalī 517
Ṭīpū-nāmah 773
Tiqṣār juyūd al-aḥrār 1347
Ṭirāz al-akhbār 126
Ṭirāz al-mudhahhab i Muẓaffarī 227, 1265
Tragica vertentis belli Persici historia 321, 335
Traveller's narrative 346
Travels in Arabia, by J. L. Burckhardt 1160 (4)
Travels in Central Asia, by A. Vámbéry 1161 (18)
Travels in Europe of . . . Sir Salar Jang 1158
Ṭūfān al-bukā' 234
Tughluq-nāmah 504, 1311
Tuḥfah i Akbarī 753
Tuḥfah i Akbar-Shāhī 513
Tuḥfah i Akmalīyah 1065
Tuḥfah i A'ẓamīyah, by Badr al-Daulah 1188; by Irtaḍā 'Alī Khān 1039
Tuḥfah i Malikī 209, 1260
Tuḥfah i Murshidī 1079
Tuḥfah i nadhrīyah 47
Tuḥfah i nāznīn 1065 (121)
Tuḥfah i Qāsimī 982
Tuḥfah i Rasūlīyah 207
Tuḥfah i sāmī, by S. Muẓaffar Kābulī 276; by Sām Mīrzā 798, 1335
Tuḥfah i shāhī, by 'Abd al-'Aẓīm Sāmī (?) 388; by 'Imād al-Dīn Astarābādī 42, 1220
Tuḥfah i Shāh-Jahānī 581
Tuḥfah i tāzah 702, 1327
Tuḥfat al-abrār, by Muṣṭafā b. Ibrāhīm Tabrīzī 43
Tuḥfat al-abrār dar dhikr i ḥālāt i A'immah i akhyār 1268
Tuḥfat al-aḥbāb 916
Tuḥfat al-aḥibbā' 191
Tuḥfat al-akhawain 234
Tuḥfat al-akhyār 130
Tuḥfat al-'ālam 1124
Tuḥfat al-auliyā' 1065
Tuḥfat al-bāṣirīn 1162
Tuḥfat al-dhākirīn 234
Tuḥfat al-faqīr al-ḥaqīr 1079
Tuḥfat al-fuḍalā' 1120
Tuḥfat al-gharā'ib 54, 1227
Tuḥfat al-Hind 471
Tuḥfat al-ḥuffāẓ 47, 1224
Tuḥfat al-ikhlāṣ 1222
Tuḥfat al-Khānī 381
Tuḥfat al-Khāqān, by M. Bāqir Nawwāb 1203
Tuḥfat al-Khāqān fī rasm al-Qur'ān 50
Tuḥfat al-kirām 656, 1324
Tuḥfat al-majālis 217
Tuḥfat al-mu'minīn 34
Tuḥfat al-murshid 1040
Tuḥfat al-murshidīn 935
Tuḥfat al-Qādirīyah 978
Tuḥfat al-qāri' 1014
Tuḥfat al-qurrā' 43, 1221
Tuḥfat al-Raḥmānī 47, 1224
Tuḥfat al-Riḍawīyah 234
Tuḥfat al-Sa'dīyah 1066
al-Tuḥfat al-Salāmīyah 185, 1254
Tuḥfat al-shu'arā' 849
Tuḥfat al-su'adā' 983
Tuḥfat al-ṭāhirīn 1028
Tuḥfat al-tawārīkh i Khānī 390
Ṭulū' i tamaddun u ikhtirā'āt i 'aẓīm 157
Ṭūr i Kalīm 914
Tūshah i rāh 1162
Tuzuk i 'Abd al-Raḥmān 406[18]
Tuzuk i Āfrīdī 1081
Tuzuk i Āṣafī 750
Tūzuk i Bāburī 530
Tūzuk i Jahāngīrī 556
Tūzuk i Tīmūrī 280, 1274
Tūzuk i Wālā-Jāhī 779, 1334
Tuzūkāt i Tīmūrī 280, 1274

'Ubaid-Allāh-nāmah 379
Ulūs i arba'ah i Chingīzī 272
'Umdah i muntakhabah (= *Tadhkirah i Sarwar*) 883
'Umdat al-tawārīkh 672, 1325
'Ummān al-bukā' 224
Uns al-murīdīn wa-rauḍat al-muḥibbīn 29 (2), 1208
Uns al-murīdīn wa-shams al-majālis 1208, 1251
'Unwān al-Qur'ān 53
al-'Urāḍah fī'l-ḥikāyat al-Saljūqīyah 258
'Urafāt al-āshiqīn 810
'Urūj u khurūj i Aḥmad Shāh 397
'Urwat al-muttaqīn 1215
Uṣūl al-maqṣūd 1036
'Uyūn akhbār al-Riḍā 209, 1260
'Uyūn al-athar 178

Wāḍiḥ al-bayān 38
Wafāt-nāmah 207
Wafayāt al-a'yān 1167
Wafayāt i mu'āṣirīn 1178
Walī-nāmah 932[1]
Waqā'i' al-sair i Jaisalmēr 1155
Waqā'i' al-zamān 563
Waqā'i' i Bāburī 530
Waqā'i' i Bangālah 725
Waqā'i' i Dakan, by Faiḍ i Ḥaqq 753
Waqā'i' i Dak'han, by ? 581
Waqā'i' i D'hōnkal Sing'h 689
Waqā'i' i dil-padhīr 708, 1328
Waqā'i' i Gulkundah 590
Waqā'i' i Ḥaidarābād 590
Waqā'i' i Ḥaidarī 1334
Waqā'i' i Ḥawāriyān i duwāzdah-gānah 165, 1251
Waqā'i' i Hōlkar 733
Waqā'i' i jang i Bahādur [*Shāh*] *Shāh-'Ālam ghāzī u M. A'ẓam Shāh* 600
Waqā'i' i Kūhistān 646
Waqā'i' i Mahābat-Jang 714
Waqā'i' i manāzil i Rūm 1066
Waqā'i' i Mīmīyah 340
Waqā'i' i musāfarat, by Nāṣir al-Dīn Shāh 341
Waqā'i' i musāfarat i Sālār-Jang 1158
Waqā'i' i Nādirī 329
Waqā'i' i Nawwāb Khān (?) 598
Waqā'i' i Ni'mat Khān i 'Ālī 590
Waqā'i' i sa'ādat 779
Waqā'i' i Shāh Mu'īn al-Dīn i Chishtī 1066
Waqā'i' i Shujā'ī 625
Waqā'i' i shūrish i Afghānīyah 759
Waqā'i' i Sōraṭ'h 731
Waqā'i' i tasalluṭ i Rūsiyā bar Āsiyā 388
Waqā'i' i tasalluṭ i Ṣāḥibān i Angrēz Bahādur dar mulk i Miyān i Dō-āb 688
Waqā'i' i wafāt i Fatḥ-'Alī Shāh u safar-nāmah i Riḍā-Qulī Mīrzā 338
Wāqi'ah i Jhōjhār Sing'h 737
Wāqi'ah i kharābī i Dihlī 329
Wāqi'āt al-nādirāt = *Khāzin al-shu'arā'* 903
Wāqi'āt i 'Ālamgīrī, by 'Āqil Khān (?) 584; by Ma'ṣūm (?) 582
Wāqi'āt i Aẓfarī 643, 1322
Wāqi'āt i Bāburī 530, 1313
Wāqi'āt i Durrānī 403
Wāqi'āt i dū-sālah 1289
Wāqi'āt i Jahāngīrī = *Jahāngīr-nāmah* 556
Wāqi'āt i Kashmīr, by Ḥusain Qārī (?) 680; by M. A'ẓam 683
Wāqi'āt i Mushtāqī 513
Wāqi'āt i Rashīdī 1347
Wāqi'āt i Tīmūrī 280, 1274
Wāridāt i Qāsimī 721[6]
Wasā'il i Muẓaffarī 1268
Wasīlat al-faqīr 1259
Wasīlat al-najāt, by Ḥusain b. 'Alī Sijāsī 1206; by M. Ḥusain 234; by M. Mubīn 220; by Naurūz 'Alī 234
Wasīlat al-qabūl 34
Wāsiṭat al-'iqd 599
Waṣīyat-nāmah, by Aurangzēb 599
Waṣīyat-nāmah i Nawwāb Āṣaf-Jāh 1332
Wazīr-nāmah 712
Wilāyat-nāmah 1143
Wird al-murīdīn 975

Xavāṣṣ-i-āyāt 54, 1226

Yad i baiḍā' 863
Yāddāshthā'ī az zindagānī i khuṣūṣī i Nāṣir al-Dīn Shāh 1289 (22)
Yād-dāsht-hā-yi Khusrau i awwal Anūshīrwān 1271
Yādgār i Bahādurī 149
Yādgār i Hindī 1185
Yādgār i Makk'han La'l 755
Yaghmā-yi Biyābānak 923
al-Yamīnī 250
Yazdgird i siwwum 1271
Yūsufīyah 172

Zabūr i Āl i Dāwud 320, 1282
Zād al-ākhirah, by Fatḥī Ḥusainī 166
Zād al-mudhakkirīn 5
Zād al-muttaqīn 979
Ẓafar al-Islām 1066
Ẓafar al-ẓafar 647 1323
Ẓafar-nāmah, by 'Alī b. Mulūk 412; by Faḍl i 'Aẓīm 689; by Ghulām-Muḥyī 'l-Dīn Khān 618; by Ḥamd Allāh 82; by " Hātifī " (= *Tīmūr-nāmah*) 289, 1274–5; by Niẓām Shāmī 279; by Sharaf al-Dīn Yazdī 284, 1274; by Sulṭān-Aḥmad 288
Ẓafar-nāmah i Aḥmadābād 540
Ẓafar-nāmah i Akbarī 402, 1304
Ẓafar-nāmah i 'Ālamgīrī, by 'Āqil Khān (?) 584
Ẓafar-nāmah i Kābul 402, 1304
Ẓafar-nāmah i Kāngrah 566
Ẓafar-nāmah i Khudā-Yār-Khānī 390
Ẓafar-nāmah i Ranjīt Sing'h, by Amar Nāt'h 669; by Kanhaiyā Lāl " Hindī " 675
Ẓafar-nāmah i Shāh-Jahānī 568, 1316
Ẓafar-nāmah i waqā'i' i Ghadr 648
Zain al-akhbār 65, 1229
Zarātusht-nāmah 162, 1250
Ẓawāhir al-sarāsir (?) 1015
Zēb al-tawārīkh 692
Zēb i tafāsīr 19, 1200
Zīb al-tawārīkh 692
Zīb i tafāsīr 19, 1200
Zīnat al-madā'iḥ 884
Zīnat al-qāri' 47
Zīnat al-tawārīkh, by 'Azīz Allāh 134; by M. Raḍī [*sic lege*] " Bandah " Tabrīzī 147
Zīnat al-zamān 492
Zindagānī i Abū Raiḥān al-Bīrūnī 1351
Zindagānī i Mānī 1185
Zīwar [*sic*, for *Zabūr*] *i Āl i Dāwud* 320, 1282
Zubdat al-akhbār, by Amar Sing'h " Khwush-dil " 480; by Khwush-ḥāl Chand (= *Tārīkh i Muḥammad-Shāhī, Maqālah* ii) 137; by M. Qāsim b. M. Sharīf 1268
Zubdat al-akhbār fī sawāniḥ al-asfār 1152
Zubdat al-āthār 933, 980
Zubdat al-gharā'ib 148, 1245
Zubdat al-maqāmāt 988
Zubdat al-mu'āṣirīn 889
Zubdat al-Nuṣrah 255
Zubdat al-qirā'ah 47
Zubdat al-taṣānīf 172
Zubdat al-tawārīkh, by 'Abd al-Karīm 639; by 'Abd Allāh Qāshānī 79, 1232; by Kamāl Khān 130; by M. Afḍal 1242; by M. Muḥsin 136; by Nūr al-Ḥaqq Dihlawī 441; by Ḥaidar Rāzī (= *Tārīkh i Ḥaidarī*) 124
Zubdat al-tawārīkh i Bāysunghurī 88[17]
Zubdat al-tawārīkh i Sinandijī 146
Zubdat al-'ulūm 1185
Ẓuhūrīyah i Ṣafawīyah 428
Zulāl al-ṣafā 178

INDEX OF AUTHORS, SUBJECTS,[1] ETC.

A‘azz al-Dīn M. 478
Abā Rafī‘ al-Dīn Aḥmad “ Ghāfil ” 682
Abarqūhī (‘Abd al-Salām b. ‘Alī) 180[13]
Abarqūhī (Khusrau b. ‘Ābid) 85, 1234
‘Abbās (Mīr) 57 (1)
‘Abbās b. M. ‘Alī Shūshtarī 1271[2]
‘Abbās b. M. Riḍā Qummī 1175
‘Abbās ‘Alī 228 (4)
‘Abbās ‘Alī Kaiwān Qazwīnī 1206
‘Abbās Iqbāl Āshtiyānī 1085, 242 (9), 1088, 1183 (31), 1348
‘Abbās Khān “ ‘Abbās ” b. M. Ziyārat Allāh 1093
‘Abbās Khān Sarwānī 513
‘Abbās Mīrzā *Rawābiṭ i Napōliyōn u Īrān* 1288
‘Abbās Mīrzā b. Fatḥ-‘Alī Shāh 338 (434), 1285
‘Abbās Mīrzā Mulk-ārā 1287
‘Abbās Rāsikhī 1209 antepenult.
‘Abbās Shāyān 1353
‘Abbās “ Ṭūṭī ” Māzandarānī 227
‘Abbās Yazdī 249 (4)
‘Abbās-Qulī Āghā “ Qudsī ” Bādkūbī 425, 1307 ; *Gulistān i Iram* 426 ; *Kashf al-gharā’ib* 428
‘Abbās-Qulī Khān “ Sipihr ” *Aḥwāl i ḥaḍrat i Bāqir* 227, 1265 ; *Mishkāt al-adab i Nāṣirī* 1248[8] ; *Nāsikh al-tawārīkh* (continuations) 1248[6, 9, 14, 17, 23] ; *Tadhkirah i mubārakah i Nāṣirī* 346 ; *Ṭirāz al-mudhahhab i Muẓaffarī* 227, 1265
‘Abd al-Aḥad (Amīr of Bukhārā) 387 (13)
‘Abd al-Aḥad b. Barakat ‘Alī Ẓafarābādī 1126
‘Abd al-Aḥad b. M. Sa‘īd Sirhindī 1257
‘Abd al-Aḥad “ Rābiṭ ” b. M. Fā’iq Amēṭ’hawī 708, 1328 ; *Sharḥ i Aḥadīyah* 591 (²) ; *Waqā’i‘ i dil-padhīr* 708, 1328.
‘Abd al-Aḥad Zanjānī 340[26], 1286
‘Abd al-‘Alī b. Minnat ‘Alī Islāmābādī 1117
‘Abd al-‘Alī b. M. b. Ḥusain 53, 1226[31]–1227
‘Abd al-‘Alī Birjandī 53 n.1, 1227[5]
‘Abd al-‘Alīm b. Jān Muḥammad Lōhārawī 1042[24]
‘Abd al-‘Alīm M. Naṣr Allāh Khān. See Naṣr Allāh Khān Khwēshgī
‘Abd al-Awwal Zaidpūrī 192
‘Abd al-‘Aẓīm b. ‘Abd Allāh Ḥasanī 1048[25]
‘Abd al-‘Aẓīm Ḥusainī Iṣfahānī 168 (2)
‘Abd al-‘Aẓīm Khān Garakānī 1082 n.1
‘Abd al-‘Aẓīm Sāmī [?] 388 (19)
‘Abd al-‘Azīz b. Ardashīr Baghdādī 410[27]
‘Abd al-‘Azīz b. Shēr Malik Wā‘iẓī 951
‘Abd al-‘Azīz b. ‘Uthmān Jasrī 159
‘Abd al-‘Azīz b. Walī Allāh Dihlawī 24, 1203 ; *Bustān al-muḥaddithīn* 1137, 1354 ; *Fatḥ al-‘Azīz* 24, 1202 ; *Qirān al-sa‘dain i dhū ’l-nūrain* 1264 ; *Sirr al-shahādatain* 223, 1263–4
‘Abd al-‘Azīz [b. Walī Allāh ?] Dihlawī *Tārīkh i Rūm u Farang* 1306
‘Abd al-‘Azīz Ḥiṣārī 183
‘Abd al-‘Azīz “ Jawāhir al-Kalām ” 1135, 1354
‘Abd al-‘Azīz Makkī 1036 n.4, 1047[1]
‘Abd al-Bahā’ b. Bahā’ Allāh 346, 1054 (9), 1182 (15)
‘Abd al-Bāqī Nihāwandī 552, 1315
‘Abd al-Bāqī “ Sa‘dī ” 415[31]
‘Abd al-Bāqī Sharīf Riḍawī 793[22]
‘Abd al-Fattāḥ Fūmanī 363, 1298
‘Abd al-Fattāḥ Garmrūdī 1069
‘Abd al-Ghafūr *Ẓafar-nāmah i Khudā-Yār-Khānī* 390
‘Abd al-Ghafūr Lārī 956 n.5, 1344
‘Abd al-Ghanī “ Ghanī ” Farrukhābādī 923 (8)
‘Abd al-Ḥaiy *Tārīkh i ‘Ālamgīrī* 599 (11)
‘Abd al-Ḥaiy b. ‘Abd al-Razzāq Aurangābādī 1097 n.2

[1] The subjects include most of the persons mentioned as the subjects of biographical works or notices. Some persons who are neither authors nor “ subjects ” have been included for special reasons as well as a few places and words.

(²) Author’s name incorrectly given as ‘Abd Allāh in the *OCM*. Edition : Lucknow 1271/1854–5 (Āṣafīyah ii, p. 1528).

'Abd al-Ḥaiy b. Abū 'l-Fatḥ Ḥusainī 1064[1]
'Abd al-Ḥaiy Dihlawī 38
'Abd al-Ḥaiy Gardēzī 65, 1229
'Abd al-Ḥakīm (Khwājah) 752
'Abd al-Ḥakīm Dihlawī 26
'Abd al-Ḥakīm " Ḥākim " Lāhaurī 829
'Abd al-Ḥakīm Khān (Khwājah) 664
'Abd al-Ḥalīm 1058 (47)
'Abd al-Ḥalīm " Sharar " 1186 (5)
'Abd al-Ḥamīd (M.) A'ẓamgaṛhī 174[4], 174[18]
'Abd al-Ḥamīd Lāhaurī 574
'Abd al-Ḥaqq Dihlawī 194, 1256, 1344; (*Ādāb i libās i Rasūl*) 195, 1256; *Aḥwāl al-A'immah al-Ithnai-'ashar* 214, 1262; *Akhbār al-akhyār* 979, 1344; *Dhikr al-mulūk* 441; *Faḍā'il al-A'immah al-Ithnai-'ashar* 214, 1262; (*Ḥilyah i Rasūl*) 195, 1256[8]; *Jadhb al-qulūb* 427, 1307; *Madārij al-nubuwwah* 194, 1256; *Sharḥ i Sufar al-sa'ādah* 181; *Tafsīr i Āyat al-Nūr* 1198; *Ta'līf qalb al-alīf* 195[15], 1256; *Tārīkh i Ḥaqqī* 441; *al-Ṭarīq al-qawīm* 181; *Zād al-muttaqīn* 979; *Zubdat al-āthār* 933, 980
'Abd al-Ḥaqq " Ḥādhiq " 674
'Abd al-Ḥusain b. 'Abd al-Raḥīm (known as Mīrzā Āqā Khān Kirmānī) 246, 1270
'Abd al-Ḥusain b. Adham Naṣīrī 1283[4]
'Abd al-Ḥusain b. 'Azīz Allāh Shūshtarī 365
'Abd al-Ḥusain b. — al-Dīn 1228[19]
'Abd al-Ḥusain " Āyatī " (formerly " Āwārah ") 1294
'Abd al-Ḥusain Karnātakī 1147
'Abd al-Ḥusain Khān Lisān al-Salṭanah 1299
'Abd al-Ḥusain Shaibānī 1249
'Abd al-Jalīl b. Yaḥyā Yazdī 1082
'Abd al-Jalīl Bilgrāmī 712 n.1, 1329
'Abd al-Kabīr b. Uwais (Ẓahīr al-Dīn al-Ardabīlī) 1168[6], 1355, 416 penult.
'Abd al-Karīm (Maulawī) 639[18]
'Abd al-Karīm b. 'Alī Riḍā Ishtihārdī *Tārīkh i Gītī-gushāy* 331, 1284; *Zīnat al-tawārīkh* 147
'Abd al-Karīm b. 'Āqibat-Maḥmūd Kashmīrī 326
'Abd al-Karīm b. Ismā'īl Bukhārī 382
'Abd al-Karīm b. Mahdī Jazī 1353
'Abd al-Karīm b. Maḥmūd Qāḍī 1116
'Abd al-Karīm b. M. Namīdīhī 109, 1238[26]
'Abd al-Karīm 'Alawī 402; *Muḥārabah i Kābul u Qandahār* 403; *Tārīkh i Aḥmad* 403, 1304; *Tārīkh i Panjāb* 673
'Abd al-Karīm Hamadānī 725 n., 726
'Abd al-Karīm " Nadīm " Bukhārī 382
'Abd al-Khāliq b. 'Abd al-Raḥīm [var. 'Abd al-Karīm] Yazdī Mashhadī *Bait al-aḥzān* 228 (11), 1266; *Manāqib i Ma'ṣūmīn* 1267
'Abd al-Khāliq Ghujduwānī 1055 (14)
'Abd al-Khāliq Pūnī (?) 726
'Abd Allāh *Tārīkh i Dāwudī* 515
'Abd Allāh (*Amīr*) 276 (1)
'Abd Allāh (*Maulawī*) 206 (27)
'Abd Allāh b. 'Abd al-Laṭīf Dihlawī (= Ghulām-'Alī Dihlawī) 1034
'Abd Allāh b. 'Abd al-Raḥmān. See Aṣīl al-Dīn Ḥusainī 184, 356, 1296
'Abd Allāh b. Aḥmad b. Bāyazīd Kalyānī [in the Bkp. cat. Kultānī] *Marghūb al-qāri'* 46 (15), 1224 (" *Risālah i tajwīd* ", but the opening words agree)
'Abd Allāh b. 'Alī Qāshānī 78, 267, 1232, 1272
'Abd Allāh b. Faḍl Allāh (Waṣṣāf) Shīrāzī 267, 1272
'Abd Allāh b. Ḥabīb Allāh Turshīzī 329
'Abd Allāh b. Luṭf Allāh (Ḥāfiẓ i Abrū) 86, 279, 1235–6
'Abd Allāh b. M. (S.) 1160 (6)
'Abd Allāh b. M. Anṣārī 924–7, 1190[32], 1208 antepenult., 1251[9]
'Abd Allāh b. M. Lābarī 1082[15]
'Abd Allāh b. al-Muqaffa' 245[4], 1183 (31)
'Abd Allāh b. al-Muqanna' 245[4]
'Abd Allāh b. Nūr al-Dīn Shūshtarī 365, 1298
'Abd Allāh b. 'Umar Baiḍāwī 70, 1230
'Abd Allāh Anṣārī Harawī 924–7, 1190[32], 1208 antepenult., 1251[9]
'Abd Allāh Dashtī 1160 (8)
'Abd Allāh " Hātifī " 288, 303, 1274–5, 1278
'Abd Allāh Kābulī 1240
'Abd Allāh Khān Amīr Ṭahmāsb 348, 1289
'Abd Allāh Khān " Ḥakīm " 1160 (5)
'Abd Allāh Khwēshgī Qaṣūrī 1009
'Abd Allāh Makkī 428 (5), 1307
'Abd Allāh Mushtāq 203

'Abd Allāh Mustaufī 1179, 1288 (14)
'Abd Allāh Naisābūrī 1079[28]
'Abd Allāh "Raunaq" Kurdistānī 903
'Abd Allāh "Shihāb" Turshīzī 329
'Abd Allāh "Waṣfī" 1003[6]
'Abd Allāh "Wāṣifī" 215[11]
'Abd Allāh "Yaqīn" 460
'Abd al-Laṭīf (Shāh) 1064 (104)
'Abd al-Laṭīf b. 'Abd Allāh 'Abbāsī 807 n.5 ; *But-khānah* 807
'Abd al-Laṭīf b. Abī Ṭālib Shūshtarī 1123
'Abd al-Laṭīf b. 'Alī Bīrjandī 171 (35)
'Abd al-Laṭīf "Alṭaf" 905
'Abd al-Laṭīf (S.) See "Dhauqī"
'Abd al-Laṭīf "Laṭīf" 620
'Abd al-Laṭīf Ṣubḥī 1187 (18)
'Abd al-Majīd (Raḍī al-Dīn Abū'l-Khair) 42
'Abd al-Malik b. Hishām 172, 1251
'Abd al-Malik b. M. Khargūshī 175, 1252
'Abd al-Muḥammad b. Fatḥ-'Alī Lāhijānī 1226
'Abd al-Muḥammad Khān Īrānī 1078, 1347
'Abd al-Nabī b. 'Abd al-Rasūl Aḥmadnagarī 741
'Abd al-Nabī b. Khalaf Fakhr al-Zamānī 811
'Abd al-Qādir b. Ḥasan Ḥusainī Qādirī 1266, 1267
'Abd al-Qādir b. Hāshim Ḥusainī 983
'Abd al-Qādir b. M. Sharīf Kintūrī 1026
'Abd al-Qādir Badā'ūnī 435, 679[18], 1309
'Abd al-Qādir Jīlānī 933[15], 936[9], 941[3], 972[26], 974[4], 978[9], 1017[14], 1050[1], 1053 (3), 1055 (17), 1060 (61), 1063 (99), 1064 (108), 1185 (43), 1343.
'Abd al-Qādir Khān (M.) 1355
'Abd al-Qādir Khān Āqah Bāsh Qājār 528
'Abd al-Qādir Khān Jā'isī 622 ; *Ḥashmat i Kashmīr* 685 ; *Tārīkh i 'Imād al-Mulk* 623
'Abd al-Quddūs Gangōhī 967
'Abd al-Quddūs Jaunpurī 1036 n.4, 1047[3]
'Abd al-Raḥīm (S.) 759 (2)
'Abd al-Raḥīm b. 'Abd al-Karīm Ṣafīpūrī 202, 1258
'Abd al-Raḥīm b. Abī Ṭālib Tabrīzī (i.e. Taliboff, d. 1318/1910 : see Browne *Press and poetry* 22, 106, 156, 161, Berthels *Ocherk* p. 117, *Dānishmandān i Ādharbāyjān* p. 254, Īraj Afshār *Nathr i Fārsī i mu'āṣir* p. 25) 1267
'Abd al-Raḥīm b. Bairam Khān 533, 553[4], 1313
'Abd al-Raḥīm b. M. Bāqir ("Munṣif") 889
'Abd al-Raḥīm b. Naṣr Allāh 'Alawī 34 (74)
'Abd al-Raḥīm b. Wajīh al-Dīn Dihlawī 1020[30]
'Abd al-Raḥīm Gōrak'hpūrī 1333[31]
'Abd al-Raḥīm Khān Shīrāzī 431[3]
'Abd al-Raḥīm "Munṣif" 889
'Abd al-Raḥīm Samarqandī 33 (54)
'Abd al-Raḥīm "Suhail" Dunbulī Kāshānī 350
'Abd al-Raḥmān (Shāh) 1054[1]
'Abd al-Raḥmān b. 'Abd Allāh ("Ghubārī") 418
'Abd al-Raḥmān b. 'Abd al-Qaiyūm (Pīr) 1051[7]
'Abd al-Raḥmān b. 'Abd al-Rasūl Chishtī 1005
'Abd al-Raḥman b. Aḥmad. See Jāmī
'Abd al-Raḥmān b. Burhān al-Dīn 41[1]
'Abd al-Raḥmān b. M. Idrīsī 371
'Abd al-Raḥmān b. M. Isfarāyinī 1064 (112)
'Abd al-Raḥmān b. Yūsuf 43
'Abd al-Raḥmān Dihlawī (Shāh-nawāz Khān) 146, 1100[20], 1245
'Abd al-Raḥmān "Ghubārī" 418
'Abd al-Raḥmān "Ḥairat" 1183 (27)
'Abd al-Raḥmān Khān (Amīr of Afghānistān) 405, 1304
'Abd al-Raḥmān Pānīpatī 47 (25)
'Abd al-Raḥmān Sulamī Nīshāpūrī 1015[9]
'Abd al-Raḥmān *'urf* Shāh Buddah [Bud'h ?] 1346[24]
'Abd al-Rashīd (M.) 1184 (38)
'Abd al-Rashīd (M.) Kairānawī 1019
'Abd al-Rasūl Khaiyām-pūr 1335, l. 5 from foot
'Abd al-Rasūl Qāsim 501[17]
'Abd al-Ra'ūf, dedicatee of a work on *tajwīd*, 49[1]
'Abd al-Razzāq b. 'Abd al-Nabī 753
'Abd al-Razzāq b. Ḥasan 'Alī. See Shāh-nawāz Khān 1094 ; 853
'Abd al-Razzāq b. Najaf-Qulī Dunbulī 334, 1285 ; *Baṣīrat-nāmah* 321, 335 ; *Ḥadā'iq al-udabā'* 1338 ;

Ma'āthir i Sulṭānīyah 335; *Nigāristān i Dārā* 889; *Riyāḍ al-jannah* 1299[22]; *Tajribat al-aḥrār* 335; *Tārīkh i Danābilah* 1299
'Abd al-Razzāq 'Aṭā Ḥusain 1057 (30)
'Abd al-Razzāq Bānsawī 1016[28], 1058 (39)
'Abd al-Razzāq Kalyānawī 1182 (17)
'Abd al-Razzāq Samarqandī 293, 1276–7
'Abd al-Salām *Mukhtaṣar al-tawārīkh* 156 (8)
'Abd al-Salām b. 'Alī Abarqūhī 180[13]
'Abd al-Salām b. M. Andarasfānī 177, 1253[9]
'Abd al-Salām Jaunpūrī 1036 n.4, 1047[3]
'Abd al-Salām Rafīqī Nūrpūrī 1063 (96)
'Abd al-Ṣamad b. Afḍal M. 983
'Abd al-Ṣamad Khān (Saif al-Daulah Dilēr-Jang) 664[16]
'Abd al-Sattār b. Qāsim Lāhaurī 164[1]; 287[24]; *Thamarat al-falāsifah* 1110
'Abd al-Shakūr b. 'Abd al-Wāsi' Tattawī 127[24]
'Abd al-Shakūr b. Shēr 'Alī 1120[5]
'Abd al-Wadūd 1185 (2)
'Abd al-Wahhāb b. 'Alī Ashraf Shīrāzī 151
'Abd al-Wahhāb b. Manṣūr Khān 811[16]
'Abd al-Wahhāb b. M. Ghauth Shāfi'ī 232 (48)
'Abd al-Wahhāb b. M. Hamadānī 938[24]
'Abd al-Wahhāb b. Walī Allāh al-Muttaqī 979[23]
'Abd al-Wahhāb 'Ālamgīrī b. S. Manṣūr Khān 811[16]
'Abd al-Wahhāb "Iftikhār" Daulatābādī 854
'Abd al-Wahhāb "Qaṭrah" 150
'Abd al-Wahhāb Qazwīnī 1173[27]
'Abd al-Wahhāb Ṣābirī 1065 (122)
'Abd al-Wāḥid b. M. 167
'Abd al-Wāḥid ("Shāhidī"?) Bilgrāmī 931[30]
'Abd al-Walī (Maulawī) 388 (20)
'Abd al-Wāsi' 58 (12)
'Abd al-Wāsi' (Niẓām al-Dīn) Shāmī 278, 1273
"'Abdī" 937[1]
'Abdī Bēg Shīrāzī 1239[24]
'Abduh (M.) 1209 antepenult.
'Ābid (M.) 1026
'Ābid Ḥusain (Maulawī) 32 (46)
'Ābid Ḥusain (S.) Sahasrāmī 713
Abīwardī ('Alī b. Maḥmūd) 959
Ābīzī (M. b. M.) 959[11]
"Abjadī" (M. Ismā'īl Khān) 778, 1334
'Abshamī (Tāj al-Dīn) 965 n.1
Abū 'Abd Allāh Zanjānī 1228 antepenult.
Abū 'Alī b. Sīnā 1351[20]
Abū Bakr b. 'Abd Allāh Balkhī 1296 penult.
Abū Bakr b. Hidāyat Allāh Ḥusainī 1169
Abū Bakr b. M. Bharūchī 176[18], 1252[16]
Abū Bakr b. 'Umar b. Abī 'l-Faḍl 31 (34)
Abū Bakr Isḥāq b. Tāj al-Dīn Multānī 36
Abū Bakr al-Khaṭīb 1342
Abū Bakr Quṭbī (?) Aharī 1233, 1269
Abū Dharr Salmān Fālī 214
Abū Isḥāq Kāzarūnī 936[1], 1343
Abū Kalījār (Jamāl al-Dīn Ibrāhīm) 184[26]
Abū 'l-Ashraf M. 180[14]
Abū 'l-Barakāt b. M. Naṣr Allāh 1187 (12)
Abū 'l-Faḍā'il Mu'īnī 1192[2]
Abū 'l-Faḍl b. Mubārak 541, 1313–15
Abū 'l-Faḍl Baihaqī 252, 1271
Abū 'l-Faḍl Maibudī Yazdī 1190
Abū 'l-Faḍl Ma'mūrī 594
Abū 'l-Faḍl Pazdawī (*sic*, for A. 'l-F. A. b. M. Maibudī Yazdī) 30 (14), 1190, 1211
Abū 'l-Faḍl Sāwī 1173[26]
Abū 'l-Faiḍ b. Mubārak. See "Faiḍī"
Abū 'l-Faiyāḍ Ghulām-Rashīd *Ganj i Arshadī* 1015; his biography, *Ganj i Faiyāḍī*, by Ghulām-Sharaf al-Dīn 1022
Abū 'l-Fatḥ (Rukn al-Dīn) 954
Abū 'l-Fatḥ b. Niẓām al-Dīn Shanūzānī (?) 1056 (25)
Abū 'l-Fatḥ al-Ḥusainī 1196; *Ṣafwat al-ṣafā'* (revised edition) 940; *Tafsīr i Shāhī* 13, 1197
Abū 'l-Fatḥ Ibrāhīm Sulṭān b. Shāh-Rukh 283[13], 284[10], 287[15], 932[2]
Abū 'l-Futūḥ Rāzī 4, 1191
Abū 'l-Ghāzī Bahādur Khān 387 (14)
Abū 'l-Ḥasan b. al-Haiṣam al-Būshanjī 162, 1250[19]
Abū 'l-Ḥasan b. Ibrāhīm Qazwīnī 319, 1282

Abū 'l-Ḥasan b. M. Amīn Gulistānah 330, 1284
Abū 'l-Ḥasan b. Mu'izz al-Dīn M. Ghaffārī Kāshānī 331
Abū 'l-Ḥasan Arjmand Sāwajī 1188 (22)
Abū 'l-Ḥasan (M.) Farīdābādī 1184 (35)
Abū 'l-Ḥasan Khān b. M. 'Alī Shīrāzī 1067
Abū 'l-Ḥasan Kharaqānī 927–8
Abū 'l-Ḥasan " Khurram " Shīrāzī 225
Abū 'l-Ḥasan Ṣiddīqī Nānautawī 1062 (84)
Abū 'l-Ḥasan Ṭabarī 245
Abū 'l-Ḥayāt Qādirī P'hulwārī 1040
Abū 'l-'Iṣmat M. Ma'ṣūm Samarqandī 33 (49)
Abū 'l-Jūd Makhzūmī 181[9], 1253
Abū 'l-Khair Khān Uzbak 110[28]
Abū 'l-Ma'ālī (S. Shāh) 679 n.3
Abū 'l-Ma'ālī (Shāh) 1057 (29)
Abū 'l-Ma'ālī b. Raḥmat Allāh 977
Abū 'l-Ma'ālī M. " Muslimī " 977
Abū 'l-Maḥāsin Ḥusain b. Ḥasan Kāzarūnī 29 (12), 1211
Abū 'l-Makārim b. 'Alā' al-Mulk Jāmī 950
Abū 'l-Manṣūr M. b. M. 'Alī 31 (33), 1212
Abū 'l-Munīf M. Laṭīf 1183 (26)
Abū 'l-Qāsim b. Ghassān 1082[3]
Abū 'l-Qāsim b. Ḥusain Riḍawī Qummī 30 (15), 1211
Abū 'l-Qāsim b. M. b. Mas'ūd 1060 (69)
Abū 'l-Qāsim b. Raḍī al-Dīn Mūsawī Shūshtarī (Mīr-'Ālam) 750, 1331–2
Abū 'l-Qāsim Dhahabī Shīrāzī 1209[17]
Abū 'l-Qāsim Ḥaidar Bēg Ēv-oghlī (*sic lege*) 317, 1282
Abū 'l-Qāsim Ḥusainī 743
Abū 'l-Qāsim Khān Nāṣir al-Mulk 329 (14)
Abū 'l-Qāsim M. al-Ṭā'ifī 1082[14]
Abū 'l-Qāsim Muḥtasham 916
Abū 'l-Qāsim Nūr-Muḥammad 493 (4)
Abū 'l-Qāsim " Qārī " 43, 1220
Abū 'l-Qāsim Qāshānī 78, 267, 1232, 1272
Abū 'l-Qāsim " Qāsim " 882
Abū 'l-Qāsim Saḥāb 1104, 1228, l. 5 from foot
Abū 'l-Qāsim Simnānī *Sulālat al-siyar* 148 ; *Tārīkh i Ṭabarī* 65
Abū 'l-Qāsim " Thanā'ī " Farāhānī 338, 1285
Abū 'l-Raiḥān al-Bīrūnī 1351[26]
Abū 'l-Riḍā Muḥammad 1020[32]
Abū 'l-Sharaf Jarbādhaqānī 251[12]
Abū 'l-'Ulā Naqshbandī Akbarābādī 1012 ult.
Abū Manṣūr M. b. M. 'Alī 31 (33), 1212
Abū Mikhnaf 229 (20–23), 1266
Abū Naṣr al-Bukhārī. See Bukhārī
Abū Naṣr Darwājakī (?) 1190
Abū Rafī' al-Dīn Aḥmad " Ghāfil " 682
Abū Sa'īd b. Abī 'l-Khair 928[24], 929[13]
Abū Sulaimān Manṭiqī Sijistānī 1104, 1350
Abū Ṭālib Findariskī 200
Abū Ṭālib Ḥusainī Turbatī 280, 1274
Abū Ṭālib Iṣfahānī. See Abū Ṭālib Khān
Abū Ṭālib " Kalīm " Hamadānī 572
Abū Ṭālib Khān Iṣfahānī 144, 1245 ; *Khulāṣat al-afkār* 878 ; *Lubb al-siyar* 145 ; *Masīr i Ṭālibī* 878 ; *Tafḍīḥ al-ghāfilīn* 705
Abū Ṭālib Landanī. See Abū Ṭālib Khān Iṣfahānī
Abū Ṭālib al-Makkī 1258[9]
Abū Turāb b. Aḥmad Riḍawī *Farḥat al-'ālam* 202 ; *Quṭb-numā-yi 'ālam* 751 n., 752[6] (cf. Rieu i p. 325*a*)
Abū Turāb Walī 727, 1141, 1329
Achwerdi = Ḥaqq-wirdī 166
" Adā'ī " Shīrāzī 417
Ādam Banūrī 991 n.3, 1015[10], 1344
Ādamīyat (Farīdūn) 1349
Ādamīyat (Rukn-zādah) 1288 (6)
" Ādhar " (Luṭf-'Alī Bēg) 868, 1337
Ādhar Kaiwān 245 n.2
Ādharbāyjān 940 n.3, 1111, 1288 (7), 1299, 1352
'Ādil b. 'Alī Shīrāzī 37, 1215–16
'Ādil-Shāhs 742–6, 1331
Ādīnah Bēg 665[1]
'Adlī 425[21]
'Aḍud al-Daulah Sulṭān Aḥmad 339
Afāḍ [?] al-Dīn (M.) Ḥasanī 44[10]
" Afḍal " (M. Afḍal) 666
Afḍal (M.) Bukhārī 282, 1274
Afḍal al-Dīn Kirmānī 357, 1297
Afḍal al-Mulk (Ghulām-Ḥusain) Shīrāzī *Afḍal al-tawārīkh* 347 ; *Safar-nāmah i Qum* 1161 (16)
Afḍal Bēg Khān Qāqshāl Aurangābādī 849
Afḍal (M.) Ḥusainī 1242
Afḍal Khān 394[23]
" Afḍal " Makhdūm i Pīrmastī 917
Afghān saints 393[25], 982[30], 1011[21]

Afghānistān 383[9], 393–407, 1302–5
Afghāns, The, 1080, 759[29]
'Afīf [al-Dīn] b. Nūr [al-Dīn] Kāshānī 193, 1255
'Afīf b. Sa'īd Kāzarūnī 179
Aflākī 937
" Āfrīdī " (Qāsim 'Alī Khān) 1080, 1347
Āfrīdīs, The, 1080, 1347
Afṣaḥ (M. Bāqir Tabrīzī) 130, 1242
Afshār (Īraj) 1179
" Afsōs " (Shēr 'Alī) 456
" 'Afwī " Dihlawī 1310, l. 4 from foot
Āghā (Mīr) 46 (19)
Āghā Jān (Mīrzā M.) 528
al-Aghājī ('Alā' al-Dīn Aḥmad b. Ṭughā Mīrak) 171[16]
Āgrah 692
Aharī (Abū Bakr Quṭbī) 1233, 1269
Aḥmad b. 'Abd al-Aḥad Sirhindī. See Aḥmad Sirhindī.
Aḥmad b. 'Abd al-Raḥīm Dihlawī. See Walī Allāh Dihlawī.
Aḥmad b. 'Abd al-Ṣabūr Balkhī 682
Aḥmad b. Abī 'l-Fatḥ Iṣfahānī 121
Aḥmad b. Abī 'l-Ḥasan Jāmī 950[4], 1344[6]
Aḥmad b. Abī 'l-Ḥasan Sharīfī Shīrāzī 1286
Aḥmad b. Abī 'l-Khair Shīrāzī 351, 1294
Aḥmad b. Aḥmad Bukhārī. See Bukhārī
Aḥmad b. Aḥmad Jīlānī 422 (2)
Aḥmad [or Muḥammad ?] b. 'Alī Anṣārī 1109[12]
Aḥmad b. A'tham 207, 1260
Aḥmad b. Bahbal Kanbō 124
Aḥmad b. Faḍl Allāh Khūzānī Iṣfahānī 126
Aḥmad b. Ḥāmid (Bakhshū Miyāṅ) 732
Aḥmad b. Ḥāmid Kirmānī 357, 1297
Aḥmad b. Ḥasan Astarābādī 192
Aḥmad b. Ḥasan Dardājikī 4 n.1, 1190
Aḥmad b. Ḥasan Sulaimānī Zāhidī 4, 1190
Aḥmad b. Ḥusain Akbarābādī 1014
Aḥmad b. Ḥusain Hamadānī 1224, l. 4 from foot
Aḥmad b. Ḥusain b. 'Alī *Tārīkh i jadīd* 1293
Aḥmad b. Jalāl al-Dīn Khwājagī Kāsānī 973[8]
Aḥmad b. Maḥmūd Muḥammadī Akbarabādī 217, 1267
Aḥmad b. Maḥmūd Ṣābūnī 160, 1250[9]
Aḥmad b. Maḥmūd Uwaisī Chanābī 1023
Aḥmad b. Mīr Munshī Ḥusainī 1074, 1279
Aḥmad b. M. *Khulāṣat al-Manāqib* 938[20]
Aḥmad b. M. . . . Ibn Khallikān 1167
Aḥmad b. M. called Mu'īn al-fuqarā' 953
Aḥmad b. M. 'Alī Bihbahānī 1130
Aḥmad b. M. Arfajnī [?] 159
Aḥmad b. M. Ghaffārī 114, 1240
Aḥmad b. M. 'Irfān Rāy-Barēlawī 1041 n.3
Aḥmad b. M. Maibudī 1190
Aḥmad b. M. Muqīm Harawī 433, 1309 ; *Ṭabaqāt i Akbarī* 433 ; *Tārīkh i alfī* 119, 1240–1
Aḥmad b. M. Pazdawī (*sic*, for A. b. M. Maibudī Yazdī) 30 (14), 1190, 1211
Aḥmad b. M. Qubāwī 370[1], 1300
Aḥmad b. M. Sakkākī Ṭabasī 1226[28]
Aḥmad b. M. Ṣāliḥ Ṣiddīqī Ḥusainī 1008
Aḥmad b. M. Ṭūsī 29 (10), 1210[19]
Aḥmad b. M. Yamanī Shirwānī 226 n.1, 916[12], 1265[25]
Aḥmad b. Naṣr Allāh Tattawī 119, 1240 ; *Khulāṣat al-ḥayāt* 1110 ; *Tārīkh i alfī* 120, 1240
Aḥmad b. Rukn al-Dīn Kūhgīlū'ī 43, 1221
Aḥmad b. Sa'd al-Dīn 'Alāra'ī 388 (15)
Aḥmad b. Ṭughā Mīrak al-Aghājī 171[16]
Aḥmad b. Yaḥyā Manērī 1049 n.2
Aḥmad b. Zain al-'Ābidīn al-'Āmilī 1199
Aḥmad 'Abd al-'Azīz Nā'iṭī. See 'Azīz-Jang (Nawwāb)
Aḥmad 'Abd al-Ḥaqq Rudaulawī 968[14]
Aḥmad Aḥsā'ī. See Aḥsā'ī
Aḥmad 'Alī b. Shajā'at-'Alī 905
Aḥmad 'Alī b. Yūsuf 'Alī Faiḍābādī 523
Aḥmad 'Alī Chishtī Niẓāmī 956[17]
Aḥmad 'Alī Gōpāmawī 776[10]
Aḥmad 'Alī " Khādim " Sand'hīlawī 880 n.4
Aḥmad 'Alī Khairābādī 1045
Aḥmad 'Alī Khān Sandīlawī 880
Aḥmad 'Alī Murādābādī 698
Aḥmad 'Alī " Rasā " Lak'hnawī (d. 20 Shawwāl 1292/19 Nov. 1875 :

see Sham' *i anjuman* p. 178 ult.) 1104
Aḥmad Allāh Bilgrāmī 1115[22]
Aḥmad Anwār al-Ḥaqq Farangī-Maḥallī 1048[8]
Aḥmad (S.) Barēlawī = Aḥmad b. M. 'Irfān Rāy-Barēlawī 1041 n.3
Aḥmad Bēg " Akhtar " 885
Aḥmad Bēg Khān Iṣfahānī 126
Aḥmad Bībī-Khānī 1061 (79)
Aḥmad Fārūqī. See Aḥmad Sirhindī
Aḥmad " Ghāfil " Balkhī 682
Aḥmad Hulāgū (or Halākū) " Kharāb " Qājār 897
Aḥmad Ḥusain (S.) 58 (5)
Aḥmad i Jām 950[4], 1344[6]
Aḥmad i K'haṭṭū 952 n.5
Aḥmad Ibrāhīmī *Khulāṣat al-tawārīkh* 1279 ; (*Tadhkirah i khwush-nawīsān u naqqāshān*) (1) 1074
Aḥmad Jāmī (or Aḥmad i Jām) 950[4], 1344[6]
Aḥmad Kasrawī Tabrīzī. See Kasrawī
Aḥmad Khān (S.) 483, 1310 ; *Jām i Jam* 487, 1310 ; *Tafsīr al-Qur'ān* 1213
Aḥmad Khān Bangash 693[20]
Aḥmad Khān " Ṣūfī " 169 (8), 205 (7), 206 (19)
Aḥmad Maghribī. See Aḥmad i K'haṭṭū
Aḥmad Munshī 159[30]
Aḥmad Qummī. See Aḥmad Ibrāhīmī
Aḥmad Sāndawī 1180[3]
Aḥmad Shāh Durrānī (or Abdālī) 331[3], 383[11], 395, 397–9, 403, 473 n.5, 617[8], 618, 620–1, 864[24], 1303–4
Aḥmad Shāh Qājār 1288 (11)
Aḥmad Shāh [Rāy-Barēlawī] 1041[4]
Aḥmad Shāh Riḍwānī Pashāwarī 1065 (122)
Aḥmad Sirhindī 988[18], 991[31], 1024[4], 1035[22], 1344, 1346 n.1
Aḥmad " Suhailī " Khwānsārī 1342[8]
Aḥmad Suhrāb 1061 (73)
Aḥmad Tabrīzī 270
Aḥmad Ṭāhirī 1294
Aḥmad Yādgār 515, 1312
Aḥmad Yār Pāk-Pattanī 1045
Aḥmad Yasawī 977[2]

(1) Title given as *Gulistān i hunar* by Suhailī Khwānsārī in *Dhail i Tārīkh i 'Ālam-ārāy i 'Abbāsī* (cf. p. 1281 *supra*), *muqaddamah*, p. 2, n. 1.

Aḥmadābād 1112, 1059 (55). See also Gujrāt
Aḥmad-bakhsh " Yak-dil " Chishtī Lāhaurī 668[24]
Aḥmadnagar 125[6], 740–2, 1330–1
Aḥmadpūr 1037[19]
Aḥmad-Qulī Ṣafawī 599 (12)
Aḥrār (Khwājah) 964[5], 967[6], 973[7], 1063 (102)
Aḥsā'ī (Aḥmad b. Zain al-Dīn) 1061 (73), 1065 (116), 1345[11], 1346[20]
Aḥsan (Miyāṅ) 200[15], 201[7]
Aḥsan Allāh Khān (Ḥakīm) 528[2]
Aḥsan Allāh Khān " Thāqib " 675
Aiyūb b. Fihr (*read* b. [al-]Qirrīyah) 245[2], 1270[16]
'Ajā'ib Sing'h Sūraj 666[2]
" 'Ājiz " (Narāyan Kaul) 681, 1325
Ajnālawī [?] (Sulṭān-Muḥammad) 1057 (37)
Ajōd'han 941 n.4
Akbar 299[10], 540–56, 1313–16
Akbar 'Alī b. M. 'Alī Bukhārī 1312 penult.
Akbar 'Alī b. M.-Bakhsh 1007[8]
Akbar 'Alī Shāh Dihlawī (M.) 1057 (36)
Akbar Khān 401[31], 1303
Akbarābādī (Aḥmad b. Maḥmūd) 217, 1267
" Akbarī " (Amar Nāt'h) 668
Akhḍarī (?) 46 (14)
" Akhtar " (Aḥmad Bēg Gurjī) 885
" Akhtar " (M. Ṣādiq Khān) 151, 707, 1246, 1328
Akmal al-Dīn Badakhshī 1065 (120)
Akram (M.) Barāsawī 1019
Akram Khān (M.) 1084[14]
Āl i Ḥasan b. Nadhīr Aḥmad Amrōhawī 1112
A'lā Pānīpatī 1003 n.4, 1004[3]
'Alā' al-Daulah " Kāmī " Qazwīnī 800
'Alā' al-Daulah Pīr 'Alī 183[10]
'Alā' al-Dīn 'Aṭā Juwainī 260, 1272
'Alā' al-Dīn 'Aṭṭār 948[1], 1061 (78), 1344[3]
'Alā' al-Dīn " Ghaibī " Iṣfahānī 714, 1329
'Alā' [al-Dīn] Kāzarūnī 1343[13]
'Alā' al-Dīn M. (Khwājah) 258n.
'Alā' al-Dīn M. (Muftī) 687 (6)
'Alā' al-Dīn M. Chishtī Barnāwī 1007
'Alā' [al-Dīn] Qazwīnī Hilālī 85
'Alā' al-Mulk Tūnī 575 n. 1
A'lam (Sharaf al-Dīn) 376, 1301
'Alam al-Dīn M. 1038[2]
'Alam al-Hudā (S. Murtaḍā) 230[4], 1266

'Alāra'ī (Aḥmad b. Sa'd al-Dīn) 388 (15)
" 'Alawī " or " 'Ulwī " 598 (5)
'Alawī b. Shaikh Bā-'Abbūd Bā-'Alawī 1054[16]
Alexander the Great 169 (11), (12), 171 (38), (45), (46), 1251[29], etc.
Alexander III, of Russia, 1308[17]
Alexandria 1186 (8)
" 'Ālī " See Ni'mat Khān
'Alī ('Imād al-Dīn) Astarābādī 42, 1220
'Alī (Qamar al-Dīn) Ḥusainī Nāṣirī 833[4]
'Alī (S.) (**1**) 52[25], (**2**) 1059 (54)
'Alī (S., Qāḍī i Lashkar) 51–2
'Alī (Sharaf al-Dīn) Yazdī 283, 1274
'Alī b. 'Abd al-Mu'min Shīrāzī 1239
'Alī b. Abī 'l-Qāsim Ḥā'irī 30 (15)
'Alī b. Abī Ṭālib 207–35 (*passim*), 1181 (10)
'Alī b. Aḥmad Ṣābir Kalyarī 1031 n.5
'Alī b. 'Azīz Allāh Ṭabāṭabā 739, 1330
'Alī b. Dastgīr 489[8]
'Alī b. Ḥāmid Kūfī 650, 1323
'Alī b. Ḥasan 'Alī Kūsārī 45[18] 1223[11]
'Alī b. Ḥasan Zawārī. See Zawārī
'Alī b. Ḥusain Kāshānī 321[25]
'Alī b. Ḥusain Kāshifī 962
'Alī b. Ḥusain Qazwīnī Hilālī 85
'Alī b. Ḥusām al-Dīn al-Muttaqī 979 n.3
'Alī b. Ibrāhīm Baghdādī 229 (14), 1266
'Alī b. 'Īsā Irbilī 210, 1260–1
'Alī b. Ja'far Iṣfahānī 230 (29)
'Alī b. Jamāl al-Islām Yazdī 278, 1273
'Alī b. Khairāt-'Alī 1146
'Alī b. Maḥmūd Abīwardī Kūrānī 959
'Alī b. Maḥmūd Ḥusainī 805
'Alī b. Maḥmūd Kirmānī 734
'Alī b. M. 'Alī Riḍawī Dihlawī 1258
'Alī b. M. Bāqir, known as Janāb, 1293
'Alī b. M. Dailamī 1053[8]
'Alī b. M. Jurjānī 36, 1216
'Alī b. M. Khatlānī (Khuttalānī ?) 44
'Alī b. M. Shāhrūdī Bisṭāmī Harawī 10, 1194
'Alī b. Murtaḍā 'Alawī Yazdī 1268
'Alī b. Shams al-Dīn Lāhijī 362
'Alī b. Shihāb al-Dīn Hamadānī, 946[24] ; *Farhang i Mīr S. 'Alī* 36
'Alī b. Ṭaifūr Bisṭāmī *Tarjamah i Makārim al-akhlāq* 177 ; *Tuḥfah i Malikī* 209, 1260
'Alī b. Ṭufail 'Alī Khān Bilgrāmī 721
'Alī b. Yūsuf Qifṭī 1106
'Alī b. Yūsuf Shaṭṭanūfī 933
'Alī b. Zaid Baihaqī 353, 1295–6 ; *Tārīkh i Baihaq* 354, 1295; *Tatimmat Ṣiwān al-ḥikmah* 1105, 1350
'Alī Akbar b. Asad Allāh 958[4]
'Alī Akbar b. Murtaḍā Ṭabāṭabā'ī Yazdī 1228[28]
'Alī Akbar " Bismil " Shīrāzī [(1)] 203, 888, 1258
'Alī Akbar Burqa'ī Qummī 1341 n.1 ; *Kākh i dil-āwīz* 1136 ; *Rāhnumā-yi Qum* 1292
'Alī Akbar Ḥusainī Ardistānī 991
'Alī Akbar Khān " Dih-khudā " 1351
'Alī Akbar Khiṭā'ī 431, 1308
'Alī Akbar Munshī Waqā'i'-nigār 1300[7, 20]
'Alī Akbar Sharīf Gīlānī 1184 (36)
'Alī al-Dīn b. Khair al-Dīn Lāhaurī 673
'Alī Anwar Qalandar 1047
'Alī Aṣghar b. Maudūd Chishtī 986
'Alī Aṣghar Hamadānī 1300
'Alī Aṣghar " Ḥikmat " 1340
'Alī 'Askarī ('Āqil Khān) 584
'Alī Astarābādī 42, 1220
'Alī 'Aẓīm Khān 32 (25)
'Alī-Bakht " Aẓfarī " 642, 1322
'Alī Ghaḍanfar (S.) 949
'Alī Gīlānī 119, 1240
'Alī Ḥā'irī (S.) 30 (15)
'Alī Ḥasan Khān 914, 1339[7]
'Alī Ḥusainī Gardēzī 852
'Alī Ḥusainī Qazwīnī (Nawwāb Nuṣrat-Jang) 723
'Alī Ibrāhīm Khān " Khalīl " 700 ; Account of Chait Sing'h's rebellion 701 ; Declaration concerning his " governorship " of Benares, 1100 ; *Gulzār i Ibrāhīm* 877, 1337 ; History of the Marāṭ'hā wars 761 ; *Khulāṣat al-kalām* 877 ; *Ṣuḥuf i Ibrāhīm* 877
'Alī Janāb b. M. Bāqir 1293
'Alī Kabīr b. 'Alī Ja'far Ilāhābādī 902 ; *Iẓhār al-sa'ādah* 223 ; *Khāzin al-shu'arā'* 903
'Alī Khān b. Aḥmad Khān Naṣr al-Aṭibbā' 430[2]
'Alī Khān Marāghī 1154
'Alī Kūsārī 45, 1223[11]
'Alī Mirzā " Maftūn " 1152

(1) b. 1187/1773–4, d. 1263/1847 (see *Ṭarā'iq al-ḥaqā'iq* iii p. 156).

'Alī M. Khān [Aḥmadābādī] 729
'Alī M. Khān Rōhēlah 649[12], 1327[9]
'Alī M. Lāhaurī 1063 (94)
'Alī Mullā [*sic*] Ḥasanī 387 (8). See 'Alīm Allāh b. 'Atīq Allāh Ḥusainī 1259[8]
'Alī Muqaddam 923 (14)
'Alī al-Mūsawī 1055 (17)
'Alī Naqī b. Ismā'īl (Ḥakīm al-Mamālik) 1110, 1286[9], 1351[6, 9]
'Alī Naqī Burūjirdī 219
'Alī Naqī Ḥā'irī 206 (24)
'Alī Naqī Khān 1180[4]
'Alī al-Qārī' 45 (5), 1223[11]
'Alī Qunduzī 390
'Alī Riḍā' of Mysore, 1066
'Alī Riḍā b. 'Abd al-Karīm Shīrāzī 332, 1284
'Alī Riḍā Khān 1283[9]
'Alī Riḍā Qarāḥiṣārī 932[23]
'Alī Riḍā " Rā'iq ". See " Rā'iq "
'Alī Sarmast 1014[22]
'Alī Shēr " Qāni' " 138; *Maklī-nāmah* 1031; *Maqālāt al-shu'arā'* 854; *Mi'yār i sālikān i ṭarīqat* 1030; *Tārīkh i 'Abbāsīyah* 656; *Tuḥfat al-kirām* 656, 1324
'Alī Shīr " Nawā'ī ", 789, 1334; *Majālis al-nafā'is* 791; *Nasā'im al-maḥabbah* 955 penult.
'Alī Yazdī 283, 1274
'Alī-Bakht " Aẓfarī " 642, 1322
'Alīgaṛh (Kōl) 692, 1022[25]
'Alīm b. Raḥīm Tāshkandī 391
'Alīm Allāh b. 'Atīq Allāh Ḥusainī Jāland'harī 1259[8] (probably also 387 (8))
'Alīm Allāh Ṭabāṭabā 1027[9]
'Ālim Shaikh 'Azīzān (1) 983
'Alī-Qulī " Iqbāl " Chulāwī Māzandarānī 333
'Alī-Qulī Khān Sardār i As'ad 1161 (17)
'Alī-Qulī Khān " Wālih " Dāghistānī 830
'Alī-Qulī Mīrzā 238, 1268; *Tārīkh i waqā'i' u sawāniḥ i Afghānistān* 404
'Alī-Shāh (M.) Khairābādī 1056 (24)
'Alī-Yār b. Kāẓim 424[16]

(1) Cf. *Tārīkh i Rāqimī*, Rosen Institut p. 136[4]; Āṣafīyah ii 1116, iii 444; Shams Allāh Qādirī *Qāmūs al-a'lām* (in Urdu), pt. 1, Ḥaidarābād 1935, coll. 61[7], 71–2[2]

'Alī-zādah (Riḍā) 156 (6) (7), 204 (3), 205 (5), 1079 (1), 1187 (11)
'Allāf (Ḥāfiẓ) 932[2]
Allāh-diyah b. 'Abd al-Raḥīm Chishtī 1003
Allāh-Yār b. Muḥammad-Yār Uzbak Balkhī 587
Allāh-Yār Bilgrāmī 142
Allāh-Yār Khān b. Ḥāfiẓ Raḥmat Khān 396[11]
Allāh-Yār Khān Ghilza'ī 169 (20)
Allāhī (Muẓaffar 'Alī Shāh) 1184 (35)
" Alṭaf " ('Abd al-Laṭīf) 905
Altī-Parmaq 188, 1254
Alwar 691[19]
Amān Allāh " Amānī " Ḥusainī 812 n.1
Amar, of Chandēṛī, 618
Amar Nāt'h " Akbarī " 668
Amar Sing'h " Khwush-dil " 479
Ambassadors 1066
America, 428–9, 1160 (8)
Amēṭ'hī 474 n.4
al-Amīn (Faḍl Allāh b. Rūzbihān) 300, 372, 1278
Amīn b. Aḥmad Rāzī 1169, 1355
Amīn Aḥmad " Thabāt " Firdausī 1049
Amīn al-Daulah Nāṣir-Jang 1152[12]
Amīn al-Dīn Ḥusain Khān 642
Amīn Allāh b. M. Munīr 1161 (13)
Amīn (M.) Ṣiddīqī 'Alawī Ḥusainī 19
Amīnā " Ātashī " 743
Amīnā Qazwīnī 566
Amīr (Munshī) 767[2]
Amīr (S) [Naqshbandī] 1346[16]
'Āmir [b. Sharāḥīl] Sha'bī 244
Amīr al-Dīn Aḥmad (Amr Allāh) Ilāhābādī 873
Amīr 'Alī Khān 648, 1323; *Amīr-nāmah* 648; *Bēring-nāmah* 648; *Wazīr-nāmah* 712
Amīr 'Alī Riḍawī 703
Amīr-al-Zamānī 1251[23]
Amīr Bēg " Amīr " Banārasī 901
Amīr Bēg Junābadī 313 n.1
Amīr Ḥaidar Bilgrāmī 554, 1315–16
Amīr Ḥasan Khān (M.), Rājah of Maḥmūdābād, 1158[13]
Amīr Ḥasan Madārī Fanṣūrī 1052
Amīr i Kabīr (M. Taqī Farāhānī) 1349
Amīr Khān " Anjām " 827[11], 843[7]
Amīr Khān (Nawwāb of Tōnk) 691[1]
Amīr [i ?] Khwurd 941[5]
Amīr Pashāwarī (S.) 1057 (37)
Amīr-Ṭahmāsb (also Amīr-Ṭahmāsbī ?) 348, 1289

Amjad Ḥusain (Abū 'l-Fatḥ Ḍiyā' al-Dīn M.) 757
Amr Allāh Ilāhābādī 873
Amrōhah 1112
Āmulī (Maḥmūd b. Ḥasan) 958[21]
Anand Rām " Mukhliṣ " 612, 1319–21
Ānand Rāy 689
Ānand-rūp 473
Andarasfānī ('Abd al-Salām b. M.) 177, 1253[9]
Angrēzābādī (Ilāhī Bakhsh) 152, 1246
" Anīs " (Mōhan La'l) 874, 1337
Anṣārī ('Abd Allāh) 924, 1190[32], 1208 antepenult., 1251[9]
Anṣārī (Aḥmad (?) b. 'Alī) 1109
Anṣārī (Ḥasan b. 'Alī Jābirī) 1292
Anṣārī (M. 'Alī Khān, *q.v.*)
Anūshah M. 388[3]
Anūshirwān b. Khālid Kāshānī 254, 1272
Anwār al-Ḥaqq (Aḥmad) 1048[8]
Anwar Shāh (M.) (**1**) 57, (**2**) 1162 (26)
Āpīz (?) 959 n.2
Āpīzī (M. b. M.) 959[11]
Apostles 165[6]
Apūrb Kishan (Apūrva Krishna) 524, 1312
Āqā (Ḥājjī) b. Abī 'l-Ḥasan Kāzarūnī 1186 (9)
Āqā Khān (Mīrzā) 905[7]
Āqā Khān (M. Ḥasan Ḥusainī) 1266[27]
Āqā Khān Kirmānī 246, 1270
Āqā Khān Muqaddam 1068[23]
Āqah Bāsh 528
'Āqil Khān " Rāzī " 584
Āq-quyūnlū 300, 1277–8
Aqsarā'ī (M. b. M.) 7, 1192
Aqsarā'ī (Maḥmūd b. M.) 410, 1272, 1305
Aqṭāshī (M. Awwābī) 423
Arabia 426, 1160 (4), 1307 (and in the section Travellers, etc. (pp. 1138–62) *passim*)
Ardalān 146[10], 367[14], 369, 1300[6]
Ardistānī (Mu'izz al-Dīn) 1199
Arfajnī [?] (Aḥmad b. M.) 159
" 'Ārif " 418
'Ārif Chelebī 966[9]
Arjmand Sāwajī 1188 (22)
Arshad (M.) b. M. Rashīd 'Uthmānī Jaunpūrī 1015
" Ārzū " (Sirāj al-Dīn 'Alī Khān) 834
Asad Allāh 422 (8)
Asad Allāh (S., called Mīr Nawwāb) 740
Asad Allāh Khān (M.) 1063 (97)
Asad Allāh Khān " Ghālib " 525, 647, 1312
Asad Allāh " Shams " Gulpāyagānī 1206
Asad Anwar 774[10]
Asad Bēg Qazwīnī 553
Asad Khān Lārī 744 n.1
As'ad Ya'qūb Khaiyāṭ 1154[3], [19]
Āṣaf-Jāh (Nawwāb) *Waṣīyat-nāmah* 1332
Āṣaf-Jāhī dynasty of Ḥaidarābād 748–59
Āṣaf Khān (**1**) 'Abd al-Majīd Harawī 1104[10], (**2**) Abū 'l-Ḥasan 1104[14], (**3**) Ghiyāth al-Dīn 'Alī 1104[11], (**4**) Ja'far Bēg 120[1], 1104[13], 1240
Aṣḥāb al-Nabī 1079
'Āshiq 'Alī Khān 229 (13)
" 'Āshiqī " (Ḥusain-Qulī Khān) 885
" Ashkī " (Kundan Lāl) 1246, probably also 1065 (115)
" Āshnā " (M. Ṭāhir 'Ināyat Khān) 577
" Āshōb " (M.-Bakhsh) 616, 1321
Ashraf (Wajīh al-Dīn) 1031
Ashraf al-Dīn Aḥmad *Dur-dānah i khayāl* 1173 ; *Ṭabaqāt i Muḥsinīyah* 724, 1329
" Ashraf " Ilāhābādī 1063 (98)
Ashraf Khān b. Dūndē Khān 646
Ashraf Warnūsfādarānī 1215
Asia Minor and Turkey 408, 1305
al-Aṣīl (Shams al-Dīn) 155
Aṣīl al-Dīn Ḥusainī *Durj al-durar* 184, *Maqṣad al-iqbāl al-Sulṭānīyah* 356, 1296 ; *al-Mujtabā* 184, *al-Mujtanā* 184
" Asīr " (Muẓaffar 'Alī Khān) 230 (24)
al-'Askarī (al-Ḥasan) 29 (4), 1197, 1209, 1210
'Askarī (Mīr) Khwāfī 584[10]
'Askarī (M.) Bilgrāmī 1183 (28)
Aslam (M.) " Mun'imī " 684, 1325
Aslam (M.) Parasrūrī 140, 1244
Aṣma'ī 245[6]
Assam 547[21], 567[19], 582–3, 1317
'Aṣṣār (Kāẓim b. M.) 1207
'Aṣṣār (M. b. Maḥmūd Tihrānī) 1206
Astarābādī (Aḥmad b. Ḥasan) 192
Astarābādī ('Imād al-Dīn 'Alī) 42, 1220
Astarābādī (M. b. 'Abd al-Karīm) 177
'Aṭā b. M. Juwainī 260, 1272
'Aṭā' Allāh *Jang-nāmah* . . . 600
'Aṭā' Allāh b. Faḍl Allāh Ḥusainī 189, 1254–5

'Aṭā' Allāh b. Ḥusām 233 (56)
'Aṭā' Allāh Dihlawī 1017 n.2
'Aṭā' Allāh Ja'farī 1179 (3)
'Aṭā' Allāh " Nudrat " 828
'Aṭā' Allāh Shihāb-pūr 1207
'Aṭā Ḥusain ('Abd al-Razzāq) 1057 (30)
Aṭā M. Shikārpūrī 659
Atā'ī (S.) 987
Aṭakī (M. Yūsuf) 127[5]
" Ātashī " (M. Ḥakīm Amīnā) 743
'Atīq b. M. Sūrābādī 3, 1189
'Atīqān 939 n.1
Ātmān Rām 168
" 'Aṭṭār " *Mi'rāj-nāmah* 1258–9
'Aṭṭār ('Alā' al-Dīn) 948[1], 1061 (78), 1344[3]
" 'Aṭṭār " (Farīd al-Dīn) *Tadhkirat al-auliyā'* 930
'Aufī (M. b. M.) 781
Auḥad al-Dīn 'Abd Allāh Balyānī 808 n.3
Auḥad al-Dīn Mīrzā Jān [var. Khān] Jāland'harī 1259[12]
Auḥadī (Taqī b. Mu'īn al-Dīn M.) 808
Auliyā (M.) Nā'iṭī 1187 (15), 1334[26]
Auliyā' Allāh Āmulī 361
Aurangābād 1027[20]. See also Khuldābād
Aurangzēb 582–99, 1317–19
Āwānus b. Ibrāhīm Zargar-bāshī 1161 (18), probably also 430[21], 1161 (22), 1308
Āwānūs Khalīfah 841[3], 1308
Āwānus Khān, probably identical with Āwānus b. Ibrāhīm Zargar-bāshī 430[21], 1161 (22), 1308
" Āwārah " ('Abd al-Ḥusain) 1294
Awwābī (M.) Aqṭāshī 423
Āyā Ṣōfyah 422 (2), (7)
" Āyatī " ('Abd al-Ḥusain) 1294
" Āyatī " (M. Ḥusain Khurāsānī) 1353
" Āzād " (Ghulām-'Alī) Bilgrāmī 855, 1336–7 ; *Khizānah i 'āmirah* 864 ; *Ma'āthir al-kirām* 1025 ; *Rauḍat al-auliyā'* 1024 ; *Sarw i āzād* 864 ; *Shajarah i ṭaiyibah* 862 (12) ; *Subḥat al-marjān* 859–60 ; *Yad i baiḍā* 863
" Āzād " (M. Ḥusain) 1180 n.2
" Āzād " (M. Ṣādiq) *Dil-gushā-nāmah* 218 ; *Mukhtār-nāmah* 218 ; *Takmilah i Ḥamlah i Ḥaidarī* 200
A'ẓam (M.) Kashmīrī 683, 1325
" A'ẓam " (M. Ghauth Khān) 897
'Aẓamat Allāh (Maulawī) 1060 (71)
A'ẓamgaṛh 703
" Aẓfarī " ('Alī-Bakht Gūrgānī) 642, 1322
Aẓhar al-Dīn Ardabīlī [properly Ẓahīr al-Dīn Ardabīlī] 417, 1168[6], 1306[15], 1355
" 'Aẓīm " (M. Faḍl i 'Aẓīm [Khairābādī] 646, 689, 1322
'Aẓīm al-Dīn b. M. Faiḍ al-Dīn DLWY 766
'Aẓīm al-Dīn Ḥusainī Shīrāzī Tattawī 657
'Aẓīm-Jāh (Ghulām-Muḥammad 'Alī) 780
'Aẓīm-Nawāz Khān 222, 482, 1188 (25), 1263
'Azīz b. Ardashīr Astarābādī 410
'Azīz b. M. Riḍā Marghīlānī 390
'Azīz al-Dīn " 'Azīz " and/or " 'Azīzī " 1308[22]
'Azīz Allāh 134
'Azīz Allāh Bukhārī 1145
'Azīz Allāh Ḥusainī 1197
'Azīz Allāh Lāhaurī 1012[6]
'Azīzān 'Ālim Shaikh 983 (see also 'Ālim Shaikh 'Azīzān above)
'Azīz-Jang (Nawwāb) 758, 1332 ; *Maḥbūb al-siyar* 758 ; *Taṣwīr i balāghat* 1259

Bā-'Alawī family, The, 1054 (7)
Bābū Lāl 1066 (124)
Bābūjī (Mānik-Shāh) 1332[27]
Bābur 529–36
Badā'i'-nigār (Ibrāhīm) 1297[16]
Badā'i'-nigār (Mahdī Tafrīshī) 1228
Badakhshān 382[23], 685[5], 1301, 1305
Badā'ūnī ('Abd al-Qādir) 435, 679[18], 1309
" Bādhil " (M. Rafī') 199, 1257
Bad'hrah (Ganēsh Dās) 672, 676, 687
" Badī' " (M. Ḥasan Khān) 428 (6)
Badī' (Muntajab al-Dīn) Juwainī 260
Badī' al-Dīn called Shāh Madār 1006[3], 1032[4], 1052[30], 1055 (13)
Badī' al-Zamān b. Masīḥ al-Zamān 52[30]
Badī' al-Zamān Furūzān-far 920, 1341
Badī' al-Zamān Rashīd Khān 573
Badr al-Daulah 'Aẓīm-Nawāz Khān 222[32], 482[17], 1188 (25), 1263
Badr al-Dīn (Mīr) 765[16]
Badr al-Dīn b. 'Abd al-Salām Kashmīrī 387 (11)
Badr al-Dīn b. Ibrāhīm Sihrindī 1001
Badr al-Dīn Aḥmadnagarī 1304

Badr al-Ḥaqq M. Arshad 1015[26], 1016 n.1
Badr i 'Ālam (M. Ja'far) 1138[4]
Bādshāh Bēgam 708[9], 1328
Baghdādī (M. b. al-Mu'aiyad) 260, 1272
Bāghistān 964 n.3
Bahā' al-Dīn (Khwājah) 1060 (69)
Bahā' al-Dīn b. 'Alā' al-Dīn Barnāwī 1008[1]
Bahā' al-Dīn b. Maḥmūd b. Ḥamīd al-Dīn Nāgaurī 1054 (8)
Bahā' [al-Dīn] b. Maḥmūd b. Ibrāhīm 30 (20)
Bahā' al-Dīn b. Sa'd al-Dīn 206[1]
Bahā' al-Dīn 'Āmilī 918 (4)
Bahā' al-Dīn " Bahā " 986
Bahā' al-Dīn Ḥasan Khān " 'Urūj " 923 (12)
Bahā' al-Dīn Kāzarūnī 183[9]
Bahā' al-Dīn MTW Kashmīrī 1064 (110)
Bahā' al-Dīn M. b. al-Mu'aiyad Baghdādī 260, 1272
Bahā' al-Dīn M. b. Shaikh-'Alī Lāhijī 1200
Bahā' al-Dīn M. Iṣfahānī (al-Fāḍil al-Hindī) 217, 1200, 1262
Bahā' al-Dīn M. Naqshbandī Kashmīrī 1065 (121)
Bahā' al-Dīn Naqshband 948[5], 973[5], probably also 1060 (69)
Bahā' al-Dīn Zakarīyā' Multānī 970 n.7
Bahā' al-Ḥaqq Qādirī 1017
Bahā' Allāh 1060 (68), 1061 (73)
Bahādur 'Alī Ḥusainī 584[5]
Bahādur-Jang (Raushan al-Daulah) 780 (2)
Bahādur Sing'h 149
" Bahā'ī " (Bahā' al-Dīn 'Āmilī) 918 (4)
" Bahār " (M. 'Alī Iṣfahānī) 902, 1338
" Bahār " (M. Taqī Kāshānī) 1185 (42), 1291 (5)
Bahāwalpūr 659–63
Bahman Mīrzā b. 'Abbās Mīrzā Qājār 893, 1338
Bahman Mīrzā Bahā' al-Daulah b. Fatḥ-'Alī Shāh 894 n.3.
Bahmanids 739–40, 1330
Bahrā'ich 1032[13]
Bahrām b. Farhād 245
Bahrām Mīrzā (Abū 'l-Fatḥ) 111[16]
Baiḍāwī ('Abd Allāh b. 'Umar) 70, 1230
Baihaq 354
Baihaqī (Abū 'l-Faḍl M. b. al-Ḥusain) 252, 1271
Baihaqī ('Alī b. Zaid) 353, 1295–6; *Tārīkh i Baihaq* 354, 1295; *Tatimmat Ṣiwān al-ḥikmah* 1105, 1350
Bairam Khān 553[7]
Bakhshish-'Alī Faiḍābādī 639[9]
Bakhshū Miyāṅ 732
Bakhtāwar Khān 132, 517, 1012, 1243
Bakht-Mal 666
Bakhtyār (Quṭb al-Dīn) 943 n.4, 987[1], 1014[12]
Bakhtyārīs 1299, 1348
Bālā Pīr 407 (12), 998[16]
Bālāg'hāt 765–6
Bālah-Chanī [?] 168 (4)
Bālakī [?] (M. Amīn) 125[1]
Bal'amī (M. b. M.) 61, 1229
Balāwal (Bilāwal ?) Lāhaurī 1056 (20)
Bālihī [?] (M. Amīn) 125[1]
Balkh 380[6], [32], 581[6], 981[1], [4], 1113, 1296, 1297
Balkhī (M. b. Abī Bakr) 977[7]
Ballabgaṛh 677[8], [12]
Bāl-mukund 715 [23–24]
Baltistān 687 (4)
Balyān 809 n.1
Bām al-Dīn (Bābā) 985[22]
Bambah family 1348[24]
Bamūn 'Alī " Rājī " Kirmānī 221, 1263
" Banā'ī " (Shīr 'Alī) Harawī 301, 1278; *Shāhanshāh-nāmah* 302; *Shaibānī-nāmah* 372
Banākatī (Fakhr al-Dīn) 79, 1232
Banbānī (Faiḍ Allāh) 109, 1238[31]
" Bandah " (M. Raḍī) Tabrīzī 147, 1245
Bandah-nawāz. See Gēsū-darāz
Bāng [?] La'l b. Tarang [?] La'l 733
Bangash Nawwābs 693–4, 649[10]
" Bannā'ī " 301, 1278
Banūrī (Ādam) 991 n.3, 1015[10], 1344
Banwālī-Dās " Walī " 450, 1309
" Baqā " Sahāranpūrī 131, 1012, 1243
Bāqī (Khwājah M.) or Bāqī bi-'llāh (M.) 989[1], 1002[27]
Bāqī Jān Ghiyāth al-Dīn 1185 n.1
Bāqir (Imām) 1248[12], [17]
Bāqir (M.) Ṭihrānī 1048, 1345[6]
Bāqir 'Alī Khān Bukhārī 150
Bāqir Ḥusain Khān " Rā'iq ". See " Rā'iq "
Bāqir " Khādim " 167
Baqlī (Rūzbihān) 934[13]

Baqqālī (M. b. Abī'l-Qāsim Khwārazmī) 35, 1215
"Barahman" (Chandar-bhān) 570, 1316–17
Barāmikah 1081–3
Baranī. See Ḍiyā' al-Dīn Baranī
Barār ("Berar") 757[23]
Barārī (M.) 1242
Barāsawī (M. Akram) 1019
Barghamawī (Kamāl) 244[22]
Bārhah Saiyids 619 (4), 1086 n.1, 1114[26]
Barhārī (spelling ?) 232 (55)
Baring (Thomas George, 1st Earl of Northbrook) 648[28]
Barkhwurdār Turkmān 535
Barmecides, The, 1081
Barnāwah 1007 n.3
Barnāwī ('Alā' al-Dīn M.) 1007
Baroda 732[28], 733[4]
Barsing'h (Bīrsing'h, Narsing'h ?) Dēō 738[3]
Barzanjī 205 (10)
Basāwan La'l "Shādān" 690
Bashāghirī (M. b. Yaḥyā) 160, 1250
Bāsiṭ 'Alī Ilāhābādī 1036 n.4, 1047[2]
Baṣrah 428 (6)
Bawānātī (M. Bāqir) 1204, 1212[8]
Bayāt 537 n.2, 1313[11]
Bāyazīd Bayāt 537, 1313
Bāyazīd Bisṭāmī 1032 n.3, 1051[30], 1345[18]
Beale (Thomas William) 151, 1246
Bēgdilī 868 n.
Benares 699, 1100[14], 1114, 1327
Bengal 714–25, 1249[14], 1329
Berar (Barār) 757[23]
Bhagwān Dās "Hindī" 881
Bhagwān-Dās Shīvpūrī [correctly Shēōpūrī ?] 644
Bhak'harī (or Bhakkarī) Saiyids 949, 1114
Bhakkarī (Farīd b. Ma'rūf) 1092
Bharatpūr 688–90, 1326
Bharūch ("Broach") 733[7]
Bharūchī (Abū Bakr b. M.) 176[18], 1252[16]
Bhawānī Parshād "Mashriqī" 1186 (7)
Bhīk, or Bhīkan, or Bhik'hārī (1) (spelt also Bhikārī), Kākōrawī 1036 n.1
Bhīm-Sēn b. Rag'hū-Nandan-Dās 588, 1318
Bhōpāl 734, 1329
Bhuwah (S. M.) 991[2]
Bībī-Khānī (Aḥmad) 1061 (79)
"Bīdil" (Qurbān b. Ramaḍān Bādashtī) *Mātam-kadah* 222, 1263
"Bīdil" (i.e. M. Kirmānshāhānī: see *Dharī'ah* iii p. 433 no. 1568) *Tuḥfat al-dhākirīn* 234 (68)
Bidlīsī (Idrīs b. 'Alī) 412, 1306
Bidlīsī (M. b. Idrīs) 71[17], 416[5, 17] 1306
Bidlīsī (Sharaf Khān) 366
Bihāmad-Khānī (M.) 90
Bihār 1114
Bihbahānī (Aḥmad b. M. 'Alī) 1130
Bihbahānī (M. Bāqir b. M. Akmal) 1132[3]
Bihishtī Mashkūkī 420
"Bihishtī" Shīrāzī 581
Bījan (1) 318 (2) 1279[5]
Bījāpūr 742–6, 1060 (66), 1331
Bilāwal (Balāwal ?) Lāhaurī 1056 (20)
Bilgrām 713[5, 9], 862 (12), 864[8], 1025[16], 1114–15, 1352
Bilgrāmī ('Abd al-Jalīl) 712 n., 1329
Bilgrāmī ('Abd al-Wāḥid) 931[30]
Bilgrāmī (Aḥmad Allāh) 1115[22]
Bilgrāmī ('Alī b. Ṭufail 'Alī Khān) 721
Bilgrāmī (Allāh-Yār) 142
Bilgrāmī (Amīr Ḥaidar) 554, 1315–16
Bilgrāmī (Ghulām-'Alī "Āzād"). See "Āzād"
Bilgrāmī (Ghulām-Ḥasan) 620, 1115
Bilgrāmī (Ghulām-Naqī) 1049
Bilgrāmī (Ilāh-Yār or Allāh-Yār) 142
Bilgrāmī (Junaid) 1114
Bilgrāmī (M. b. 'Abd al-Jalīl) 712, 1329
Bilgrāmī (M. b. Ghulām-Nabī) 1115[27]
Bilgrāmī (M. b. Pīr M. Fārūqī) 199[17]
Bilgrāmī (M. 'Askarī) 1183 (28)
Bilgrāmī (M. 'Uthmān) 1115[23]
Bilgrāmī (M. Ẓahīr al-Dīn) 56
Bilgrāmī (Pasand 'Alī) 200[16]
"Bīnā" (S. Ḥusain Shajarah) 1341
Bīnā-dil (Quṭb al-Dīn) Jaunpūrī 1036 n.4, 1047[3]
"Bīnā'ī" (probably incorrect spelling for Banā'ī = Bannā'ī) 301, 1278
Bindrāban 452, 1309
Bindrāban Dās "Khwushgū" 826
Bingaṛh 1320[4]
"Bīnish" (S. Murtaḍā) *'Aẓīm al-tawārīkh* 482[25]; *Ishārāt i Bīnish* 904
Bīrbal Kāchar 685, 1325[22, 33]
Bīrjand, poets of, 923 (9), 1353[21]
Bīrjandī ('Abd al-'Alī) 53 n.1, 1227
Bīrjandī ('Abd al-Laṭīf) 171 (35)
Bīrsing'h Dēō 738[3]

(1) Cf. p. 640 n.1 *supra.*

(1) b. 1187/1773–4, d. 1263/1847 (see *Ṭarā'iq al-ḥaqā'iq* iii p. 156).

Dāghistān 423–6
Daidūzamī (M. b. Ḥasan) 161[27]
Dailamī ('Alī b. M.) 1053[8]
Dalīl al-Raḥmān 32 (42), 1213
Dalpat Rāy 519, 1312
Dalpat Sing'h (Rāō) 519[17], 1312
Dāmād (M. Bāqir) 1136[23]
Ḍāmin 'Alī (M.) 1014[7]
Danābilah 1299[16]
Dānishmand Khān. See Ni'mat Khān
Daqqāq (Abū 'Alī) 808 n.4
Dārā-Shukōh (M.) 574[14], 992–9
Dārābī (M. b. M.) 817
Daranī (?) (Abū Naṣr) 1190
Darband 423–6
Dardājikī [?] (Aḥmad b. Ḥasan) 4 n.1, 1190
Dargāhī (Shāh) Naqshbandī 1039[16]
Dargāh-Qulī Khān Sālār-Jang 1118, 1352
Darwājakī [?] (Abū Naṣr) 1190
Darwīsh Maḥmūd al-Maulawī 938[34]
Dashtakī (Aṣīl al-Dīn 'Abd Allāh) 184, 356, 1296
Dashtakī (Jamāl al-Dīn 'Aṭā' Allāh) 189, 1254–5
Dashtī ('Abd Allāh) 1160 (8)
Daulat Rāy b. 'Izzat Rāy 659
Daulat Rāy Kāyat'h Saksēnah 481
Daulat-Shāh 784
Daulat Sing'h 765
Daulatābād 1117
Daulatābādī. See Shihāb al-Dīn
Davis *History of England* 429
Dawānī (Jalāl al-Dīn) 1277
Dāwud b. Ḥusain Shīrazī 1025[5]
Dāwud b. M. Banākatī 79, 1232
Dāwud Chūnī-wāl 978[1]
Dāwud Khākī 975
Dāwud Pāshā 1102[1]
Dāwud Pūtrīk 1059 (57)
Dayā-Rām Paṇḍit 668
Deccan, The, 738–9, 1118, 1330 (see also the names of separate parts of the Deccan)
Delhi 1118, 1352
Dērah Ismā'īl Khān 677 ult.
Derbend 423–6
" Dhakā' " (1) (Khūb Chand) 891
" Dhakā " (or " Dhukā ") (Ghulām-Aḥmad Maḥmūd) 1187 (13)

(1) Possibly " Dhukā " (" Sun "), as Sprenger supposed, but the *Jāmi' al-lughāt* (an Urdu dictionary) gives " Dhakā " as this poet's *takhalluṣ*.

Dhakā' (2) al-Mulk (M. 'Alī Khān) 241, 1188 (20), 1269
Dhakā' (2) al-Mulk (M. Ḥusain Khān) 240, 249, 1269
Dhākir 'Alī b. 'Abd Allāh Qādiri 1050[12]
" Dhauqī " (Ghulām-Muḥyī 'l-Dīn S. 'Abd al-Laṭīf, d. 1194/1780 : see Ivanow 1st Suppt. p. 8) 694, 1326
" Dhikrī " (Taqī al-Dīn Kāshī) 803
D'hōnkal Sing'h 688
" Dhukā." See " Dhakā "
Dhukā' al-Mulk. See Dhakā' al-Mulk
Dhū 'l-Faqār al-Daulah Najaf Khān 474 n.3, 624[15], 880[21]
Dhū 'l-Faqār 'Alī Khān " Mast " 885
Dhū 'l-Faqār Khān 1317[21]
D'hūnd'hār 690[24]
D'hūndū-jī Wāg'h (" Dhundia Wagh ") 776 (5)
Dihdār (M.) " Fānī " 957 n.
" Dih-khudā " ('Alī Akbar) 1351
Dihkhwāraqānī (Yūsuf) 215
Dildār 'Alī (S.) 1132[26], 1354[7]
Dilēr Khān Bahādur Dilēr-Jang 766[21]
Dīn Muḥammad Khurāsānī 298
Dīnā Bēg Khān 665
Dīnshāh Jījībhā'ī Īrānī 917
" Dīwān " (Zain al-'Ābidīn Birādar) 1200
Ḍiyā' al-Dīn Baranī 505, 1311 ; *Akhbār i Barmakiyān* 1082 ; *Tārīkh i Fīrōz-Shāhī* 507, 1311
Ḍiyā' al-Dīn Durrī 1350 antepenult
Ḍiyā' al-Dīn Khālid Mujaddidī Baghdādī 1064 (106)
Ḍiyā' al-Dīn M. (Amjad Ḥusain) 757
Ḍiyā' al-Dīn M. Ḥusain " Āyatī " 923 (9), 1353
Ḍiyā' Allāh Fakhrī 1046
Ḍiyā' al-Raḥmān Shāhqulīpūrī 1050
Dunbulī 334 n.
Dūṅdē (M. Ṣalāḥ) 952[6]
Dūṅdē Khān Lāl-Khānī 646[23]
Dūṅdē Khān Rōhēlah 1327[10]
Dūnī-chand Bālī 675
Durgā Dās 855
Durgā-Parshād " Mihr " Sandīlī 491 ; *Būstān i Awad'h* 712 ; *Gulistān i Hind* 491 ; *Ḥadīqah i 'ishrat* 917
Durrī (Ḍiyā' al-Dīn) 1350 antepenult.
" Durrī " Shūshtarī 828[5]
Dūst-'Alī Khān Mu'aiyir al-Mamālik 1289 (22)

(2) Or Dhukā' ?

Dūst-Muḥammad b. Yādgār 1223 antepenult.
Dūst-Muḥammad [Harātī ?] 1072

Ēlgandal 1332[26]
Ēlichpūr 757[24]
Elliot (F. A. H.) 733 (4)
England 429, 1068[2], 1069[18], 1070[8], 1070[12], 1071[12], 1103[31], 1143[8], 1144[8], 1150[1], 1153[3], 1154[12], 1155[14], 1158[4], 1160 (6), 1288 (8), 1289 (16), 1289 (20), 1308[3]
Europe 429–31, 1069[12], 1070[6], 1157[26], 1159[23], 1306 antepenult., 1308
Ēv-oghlī (Ḥaidar Bēg) 317, 1282
Exoos 432

al-Fāḍil al-Hindī 217, 1200, 1262
Fāḍil Khān "Rāwī" 886, 1337
Faḍl Allāh b. Abī 'l-Khair. See Rashīd al-Dīn
Faḍl Allāh b. Rūzbihān 300, 1278; *Mihmān-nāmah i Bukhārā* 372; *Tārīkh i 'ālam-ārāy i Amīnī* 301, 1278
Faḍl Allāh b. Shaikh al-Mulūk 1043
Faḍl Allāh Ḥusainī Qazwīnī 243
Faḍl Allāh "Jahānī" b. Asad Allāh 936[4]
Faḍl Allāh "Khāwarī" Shīrāzī 337, 1285
Faḍl Allāh Shihāb al-Dīn 1182 (21)
Faḍl Bēk Ūshī 382[29]
Faḍl i Aḥmad Ma'ṣūmī 1040[2]
Faḍl i 'Alī b. Maḥmūd Iṣfahānī 221
Faḍl i 'Alī Khān Ṣiddīqī Āṣaf-Jāhī 1246
Faḍl i 'Aẓīm "Aẓīm" [Khairābādī] 646, 1322; *Afsānah i Bhartpūr* 689; *Waqā'i' i Kūhistān* 646; *Ẓafar-nāmah* (*Tārīkh i Bharatpūr*) 689
Faḍl i Imām Khairābādī 252[6]
Faḍl i Rabbī 722
Faḍlī Iṣfahānī *Afḍal al-tawārīkh* 308, 1280
Fahīm Sulaimān 787[24]
Faiḍ Aḥmad b. Dildār Aḥmad 1063 (101)
Faiḍ Allāh (M.) = Faiḍ i Ḥaqq Ṣiddīqī 753, 1246 [and 739 (*Khizānah i Rasūl-Khānī*)]
Faiḍ Allāh (Shāh) 1056 (23)
Faiḍ Allāh Banbānī 109, 1238[31]
Faiḍ Allāh "Himmat" Anṣārī Jaunpūrī 1170[28]
Faiḍ Allāh Khān 1249[17]
Faiḍ Allāh Khān (Nawwāb) 695[18, 23], 697[12], 698[3]
Faiḍ Allāh Ṣubḥī 1182 (15)
Faiḍ Allāh Ṭabāṭabā'ī 1027[8]
Faiḍ-Bakhsh b. Ghulām-Sarwar 706
Faiḍ i Ḥaqq Ṣiddīqī Chishtī *Gauhar i shāhwār* 753; *Khizānah i Rasūl-Khānī* 1246, 739; *Waqā'i' i Dakan* 753
"Faiḍī" (Abū 'l-Faiḍ b. Mubārak) 540; Account of the pilgrimage of Shāh Abū Turāb 1141; (*Ẓafar-nāmah i Aḥmadābād*) 540
"Faiḍī" (Ilāh-dād Sirhindī) 537[20], 551
"Fā'iḍī" Kirmānī 788[33]
Faiḍ-M. b. Sa'īd M. Mughūl 406
Faiḍ-M. Panjābī 33 (66)
"Fā'iq" (Nūr al-Dīn) 904
Fakhr al-Dīn b. Niẓām al-Dīn Aurangābādī Dihlawī 1030[5], 1038[5]
Fakhr al-Dīn Banākatī 79, 1232
Fakhr al-Dīn Ḥusain 528
Fakhr al-Dīn Mubārak-Shāh 1164
Fakhr al-Dīn Muḥibb al-Nabī 1030[5], 1038[5]
Fakhr al-Dīn Sammākī Astarābādī 17, 1198
Fakhr al-Udabā' (Ḥaidar 'Alī) 156 (10)
Fakhr i Jahān Dihlawī 1030[5], 1038[5]
Fakhr i Mudabbir 1164
"Fakhrī" b. "Amīrī" *Jawāhir al-'ajā'ib* 797; *Laṭā'if-nāmah* 792; *Rauḍat al-salāṭīn* 797
"Falsafī" (Naṣr Allāh) 1249[23], 1283[12]
Families, tribes, etc., 1085, 1347
"Fanā'ī" 1186 (6)
"Fānī" ('Alī-Shīr) 789, 1334
"Fānī" (M. Dihdār) 957[19]
Fanṣūrī 1052
Faqīr Muḥammad 149
Fārābī (Maḥmūd b. Aḥmad) 161, 1250
Farāhī. See Mu'īn al-Dīn Farāhī
Farāmarz Naurōz-jī Kuṭār 1180 (5)
Farangī Maḥall 1048 n.1
"Farāsū" (or rather "Farānsū"?) 647, 1322–3; *Fatḥ-nāmah i Angrēz* (*Ẓafar al-ẓafar*) 647, 1323; History of Bharatpūr 690
Farghānah 388–92, 1301–2
Farhād Mīrzā 204, 1258; *Hidāyat al-sabīl* 1157; *Jām i Jam* 155; *Qamqām i zakhkhār* 204

Farhād Mu'tamad (Maḥmūd) 1350
Farhād Qandahārī (M.) 34 (73)
Farīd b. Ma'rūf Bhakkarī 1092
Farīd al-Dīn *Nawādir al-safar* 1060 (63)
Farīd al-Dīn Adīb 1025[3]
Farīd al-Dīn Aḥmad 733 (4)
Farīd al-Dīn Khān 759 (9)
Farīd al-Dīn Mas'ūd Ganj i Shakar 941 n.4, 944[1], 987[2]
Farīdābād (Ballabgaṛh) 677[8, 12]
Farīd-Nawāz-Jang (Nawwāb) 759 (9)
Farīdūn b. Aḥmad Sipah-sālār 935
Farīdūn Ādamīyat 1349
Farīdūn Malkum 1308[4]
" Fārigh " Gīlānī 214
al-Fāriyābī (Maḥmūd b. Aḥmad) 161, 1250
Farrukh Khān Kāshānī 1070 n.1
Farrukhābād 693–4, 649[10]
Fārs 350–3, 1294–5
Farshaurī (Firshaurī, Farshūrī ?) 620[3], 1115[7], 1321[13]
Farzād (Ḥusain) 1288 (7)
Farzand 'Alī Ḥusainī 639[17]
Fasā'ī (Ḥasan Shīrāzī) 353, 1294
Faṣīḥ Khwāfī 90
al-Fatḥ b. 'Alī al-Bundārī 255
Fatḥ Jaunpūrī 1036 n.4, 1047[3]
Fatḥ Khān b. Ṣadr Khān 1103[17]
Fatḥ-'Alī Ḥusainī Gardēzī 852
Fatḥ-'Alī Khān " Ṣabā " Kāshānī 333, 1284–5
Fatḥ Allāh (Mīrzā) 387 (4)
Fatḥ Allāh b. Shukr Allāh Kāshānī 15, 1198
Fatḥ Allāh Shīrāzī 118 ult., 1240
Fatḥ-Muḥammad Kairānawī 1019[28], 1020[8]
Fatḥ-M. Khān 47 (24)
Fatḥī Ḥusainī 166
Fattāḥ Garmrūdī 1069[14]
" Fidā'ī " (Naṣr Allāh Khān) 490
Findariskī (Abū Ṭālib) 200[6]
Firdausī (Ghulām-Nabī) 1182
Firishtah (M. b. 'Alī Akbar Khurāsānī) 1264
Firishtah (M. Qāsim Hindū-Shāh) 442
Fīrōz b. Rajab 508
Fīrōz Shāh Tughluq 508, 1311
Firshaurī (Farshaurī, Farshūrī ?) 620[3], 1115[7], 1321[13]
Fīrūz b. Kāwūs 644
Fīrūzābādī (M. b. Ya'qūb) 180, 1253
France 429, 1069[18]
Fraser (James) 610 n.2; *History of Nadir Shah* 329 (14)
" Fuḍūlī " 213, 1261
Fūman, The Imām-zādahs of, 1086
" Furṣat " (M. Naṣīr) 353, 1295
" Fursī " 746
" Furūghī " (M. 'Alī Khān) 241, 1188 (20), 1269
" Furūghī " (M. Ḥusain Khān) 240, 1269; *Tārīkh i Īrān* 241, 1269; *Tārīkh i salāṭīn i Sāsānī* 249
Furūzān-far (Badī' al-Zamān) 920, 1341
" Fuzūnī " (Hāshim Bēg Astarābādī) 743, 1331

Gak'hars 675–6
Ganēsh Dās Bad'hrah 672; *Chār bāgh i Panjāb* 673; *Chirāgh i Panjāb* 673; Notice of Rājah Jaipāl and the Gak'har tribe 676; *Rāj-darshanī* 687; *Risālah i Ṣāḥib numā* 673
Gangōhī ('Abd al-Quddūs) 967
Ganj i Rawān (Jalāl) 1025[6]
Ganj i Shakar 941 n.4, 944[1], 987[2]
Ganjah 314[5]
Garakānī ('Abd al-'Aẓīm Khān) 1082 n.1
Garakānī (M. 'A. Manshūr) 1291 (3), 1307[25]
Garakānī (M. Ḥusain) 1178 n.5
Gardēzī ('Abd al-Ḥaiy) 65, 1229
Gardēzī (Fatḥ-'Alī Ḥusainī) 852
Gardēzī Saiyids 852 n.1
Garmrūdī ('Abd al-Fattāḥ) 1069
" Gauhar " (Ghulām-Ṣamadānī Khān) 763
Gauṛ 724[1]
Gāzargāhī (Ḥusain) 960
Gazī ('Abd al-Karīm b. Mahdī) 1353
Germany 429, 1069[17]
Gēsū-darāz (S. M. b. Yūsuf Ḥusainī) 949[31], 976[4], 1025[3]
Ghaffārī (Aḥmad b. M.) 114, 1240
" Ghāfil " (Abā Rafī' al-Dīn Aḥmad Balkhī) 682
Ghaib Allāh Wapkandi 387 (12)
" Ghaibī " ('Alā' al-Dīn Iṣfahānī) 714, 1329
" Ghaibī " (Munshī) 1078[1]
" Ghālib " (Asad Allāh Khān) 525, 1312; *Dastanbūy* 647; *Mihr i nīm-rūz* 527
Ghanī (Qāsim) 919, 1340, 1351
" Ghanī " Farrukhābādī 923 (8)
Ghauth (M.) b. M. Fā'iq 649 (4)
Ghauth (M.) Guwāliyārī 834 n.7

Ghauth (M.) Qādirī 1056 (22)
Ghauth i Thānī 1050[13]
Ghauth Khān (Nawwāb M.) 897
Ghauth M. Khān (Nawwāb) 490
Ghauthī Manduwī 984
Ghāzī al-Dīn Khān Fīrōz-Jang [III] 623[26], 1028–30
Ghāzīpūr 702
Ghaznawids 250, 1271
Ghazzālī 1345[27]
Ghiyath al-Dīn (Bāqī Jān) 1185 n.1
Ghiyāth al-Dīn b. Humām al-Dīn (Khwānd-Amīr) 101, 1237–8
Ghiyāth al-Dīn 'Alī Yazdī 278, 1273
Ghiyāth al-Dīn M. Jāmī 157 (2)
Ghōr 685[6]
"Ghubārī" ('Abd al-Raḥmān) 418
Ghujduwānī ('Abd al-Khāliq) 1055 (14)
Ghujduwānī (Maḥmūd b. 'Alī) 973
Ghulām-'Abd al-Qādir Nā'iṭī 1083, 1334
Ghulām-Aḥmad (Qāḍī of Seringapatam) 51
Ghulām-Aḥmad Maḥmūd "Dhakā" ("Dhukā" ?) 1187 (13)
Ghulām-'Alī b. 'Abd al-Laṭīf Dihlawī 1034
Ghulām-'Alī "Āzād" Bilgrāmī. See "Āzād"
Ghulām-'Alī Jahāngīrnagarī 224
Ghulām-'Alī Khān (S.) 1066
Ghulām-'Alī Khān b. Bhik'hārī Khān 640
Ghulām-'Alī Khān Naqawī 705; *'Imād al-sa'ādat* 706, 1328; *Nigār-nāmah i Hind* 399
Ghulām-'Alī Qādirī Mūsawī 1055 (17)
Ghulām-Bāsiṭ Amēṭ'hawī 474
Ghulām-Bhīk 1062 (83)
Ghulām-Ḍāmin 779, 1334
Ghulām-Ḥaḍrat 702
Ghulām-Ḥalīm (= 'Abd al-'Azīz Dihlawī) 1203
Ghulām-Hamadānī "Muṣḥafī" 875
Ghulām-Ḥasan 773
Ghulām-Ḥasan b. Ghulām-Ḥusain Rātmanā'ī [?] 868
Ghulām-Ḥasan "Thamīn" Bilgrāmī 620; Account of Aḥmad Shāh Abdālī's third invasion 620; *Sharā'if i 'Uthmānī* 1115
Ghulām-Ḥasan Zaidī 699; Account of Calcutta 724; Account of Jaunpūr 699
Ghulām-Ḥusain 774[10]
Ghulām-Ḥusain Afḍal al-Mulk Shīrāzī 347, 1161 (16)
Ghulām-Ḥusain Khān b. M. Bāqir Khān 755, 1332
Ghulām-Ḥusain Khān b. M. Himmat Khān *Dhikr al-siyar* 642; History of Benares 699
Ghulām-Ḥusain Khān "Jauhar" 754
Ghulām-Ḥusain Khān Ṭabāṭabā'ī 625; *Bishārat al-imāmah* 1027; *Siyar al-muta'akhkhirīn* 635; *Tārīkh i Muḥammad-Shāhī* (?) 619
Ghulām-Ḥusain Muqtadir 1271[6]
Ghulām-Ḥusain "Salīm" Zaidpūrī 718
Ghulām-Jīlānī 31 (29), 33 (52)
Ghulām-Jīlānī "Rif'at" Rāmpūrī 697, 1327
Ghulām-Muḥammad *Tadhkirat al-anbiyā'* 171 (42), 1251 (?)
Ghulām-Muḥammad b. Ṭīpū Sulṭān 775, 1333
Ghulām-Muḥammad 'Alī 'Aẓīm-Jāh 780
Ghulām-Muḥammad Dihlawī 1076
Ghulām-Muḥammad-Ghauth Khān 897
Ghulām-Muḥammad Hādī 'Alī Khān 1058 (48)
Ghulām-Muḥammad Khān b. Faiḍ Allāh Khān (Nawwāb) 698[6]
Ghulām-Muḥammad Khān Jhajjarī 1044
Ghulām-Muḥammad Khān "Khabīr" Khaṭak 233 (62)
Ghulām-Muḥammad Khān [Sirhindī] *Nawādir al-qiṣaṣ* 1147
Ghulām-Muḥammad Khān [Sirhindī ?] Account of a journey in and beyond northern India 1144
Ghulām-Muḥammad Qādirī (S.) 1057 (35)
Ghulām-Muḥammad "Rāqim" 1076
Ghulām-Muḥyī'l-Dīn *Futūḥāt-nāmah i Ṣamadī* 664
Ghulām-Muḥyī 'l-Dīn (Būṭī Shāh Lūd'hiyānī) 670
Ghulām-Muḥyī 'l-Dīn "Dhauqī" 694, 1326
Ghulām-Muḥyī 'l-Dīn "'Ishq" 883, 1337
Ghulām-Muḥyī 'l-Dīn Khān 618
Ghulām-Muḥyī 'l-Dīn Pīr-zādah 745[1]
Ghulām-Muḥyī 'l-Dīn Qaṣūrī 207 (33)
Ghulām-Muḥyī 'l-Dīn S. 'Abd al-Laṭīf (died 1194/1780: see Ivanow 1st Suppt. p. 8) 694, 1326

Ghulām-Muḥyī 'l-Dīn "Sanjī" 1061 (79)
Ghulām-Murtaḍā called Ṣāḥib Ḥaḍrat 745
Ghulām-Murtaḍā Khān 406[19], 1304 n.1
Ghulām-Muṣṭafā (Ḥāfiẓ) 1225[1]
Ghulām-Muṣṭafā T'hānēsarī 23
Ghulām-Nabī (1) 169 (13), (2) 1062 (89)
Ghulām-Nabī Firdausī 1182
Ghulām-Naqī Bilgrāmī 1049
Ghulām-Qādir Khān Jā'isī 622, 684
Ghulām-Qādir Khān Rōhēlah 640[18], 642[9], 643[17]
Ghulām-Rashīd 1015, 1022
Ghulām-Riḍā Khān 759
Ghulām-Ṣamadānī Khān "Gauhar" 763
Ghulām-Sarwar Lāhaurī 1043
Ghulām-Sharaf al-Dīn b. Imām al-Dīn 1022
Ghulām-Yaḥyā Naqawī 1266
Ghulām-Zain al-'Ābidīn 739, 759[2]
Gīlān 233 (57), 362–3, 1298, 1352
Gilīm-pōsh (Yūsuf Khān) 1153
"Girāmī" 1037
Gīrānī (Hindū-Shāh) 81, 1232
Gird'hārī 703
"Giryān" (M. Ḥusain) 1184 (40)
Gīsū-darāz 949[31], 976[4], 1025[3]
Gîsûdâs (?) 738 n.1
Gōhad 737[15]
Gōkul Chand 691
Gōkul Prasād 639[13]
Golconda 746–8
Gōpāmau 1038 n.14
Gōrak'hpūr 702
Gottlieb (Francis) 647, 690, 1322–3
Greece 429–30
Griboyedov 338[13]
Gujarat (Gujrāt) 109[28], 725–33, 1119, 1329
Gul Imām Chū [Imām-jīw ?] (Shāh) 1042[10]
Gul Muḥammad Ma'rūfī Aḥmadpūrī 1037
Gul M. Shāh 1042[14]
Gulāb Sing'h (Mahā-rājah) 686[28]
Gulbadan Bēgam 538
"Gulshan" Jaunpūrī 873
Gushtāsb (M. Shafī') Māzandarānī 1161 (9), 1161 (14)
Gwalior 735–7
Ḥabīb Allāh Akbarābādī *Dhikr i jamī' i auliyā' i Dihlī* 1019; *Kashf al-āthār* 933
Ḥabīb Allāh Mukhtārī 1290
Ḥabīb Allāh Naqshbandī 1061 (80)
Ḥabīb Allāh Naubakht 1290
Ḥabīb Allāh Qinnaujī 199
Ḥabīb Allāh Thānī Muḥibb-Allāhī 1062 (86)
Ḥabīb Ḥaidar Qalandar 1047[15]
Ḥabīb Punnōchhī 1156
Ḥabīb Yaghmā'ī 921, 1341
"Ḥādhiq" ('Abd al-Ḥaqq) 674
"Ḥādhiq" (M. Kāẓim) 198, 1257; *Aḥsan al-siyar* 199; *Faraḥ-nāmah i Fāṭimī* 218
Hādī 'Alī Khān Chishtī Kashmīrī 1058 (48)
Hadji Malek Library 1342 n.3
Ḥaḍrat Shāh (S.) Rāmpūrī 26[22, 27]
Ḥaḍrat-jī(w) 1040[2], 1057 (37)
"Ḥāfiẓ" Shīrāzī 920[7], 922 (3)
Ḥāfiẓ al-Dīn Bukhārī 31 (22), 1215
Ḥāfiẓ Allāh (M.) 1063 (97)
Ḥafīẓ Allāh Khān (M. Auliyā) 1187[16], 1334[26]
Ḥāfiẓ i Abrū 86, 279, 1235–6
Ḥāfiẓ-Yār-Jang (= Ḥafīẓ Allāh Khān) 1187 (15), 1334[26]
Ḥaidar *Marta' al-ghizlān* 1223–4
Ḥaidar (Kamāl al-Dīn) 710
Ḥaidar (M.) 687 (8)
Ḥaidar b. 'Alī Rāzī 124, 1241
Ḥaidar b. M. Khwānsārī 172 (50)
Ḥaidar 'Alī Faiḍābādī 1204
Ḥaidar 'Alī Fakhr al-Udabā' 156 (10)
Ḥaidar 'Alī Sandīlī 1038[10]
Ḥaidar Bēg Ēv-oghlī (*sic lege*) 317, 1282
Ḥaidar Dūghlāt 273, 1273
Ḥaidar Ḥasan Ilāhābādī 922 (4)
Ḥaidar Ḥusain Khān Shāhjahānābādī 1103
Ḥaidar Ḥusainī Āmulī 30 (21)
Ḥaidar Malik 680, 1325
Ḥaidar-Jang (Nawwāb) 759 (5)
Ḥaidar-Shukōh 1133, 1354
Ḥaidar Wazīrōf Darbandī *Darband-nāmah i jadīd* 426; *Majma' al-mulūk* 249
Ḥaidarābād 748–59, 1059 (54), 1331–2
"Ḥairat" ('Abd al-Raḥmān) 1183 (27)
"Ḥairat" (Ismā'īl) 242 (7), 328 (7)
"Ḥairat" (Qiyām al-Dīn Akbarābādī) 854
"Ḥairatī" Tūnī 182[28]

Ḥā'irī ('Alī b. Abī 'l-Qāsim) 30 (15)
Ḥājib al-Daulah ('Alī Khān Marāghī) 1154
Ḥājjī (= Ḥājjī M. Kashmīrī ?) 175[3]
Ḥājjī Āqā b. Abū 'l-Ḥasan Kāzarūnī 1186 (9)
Ḥājjī Khalīfah 127, 1242
"Ḥākim" ('Abd al-Ḥakīm Lāhaurī) 829
"Ḥakīm" ('Abd Allāh Khān) 1160 (5)
"Ḥakīm" (M. Taqī Khān) 242 (3), 386
Ḥākim b. 'Imād Nāgaurī 38
Ḥakīm al-Mamālik ('Alī-Naqī) 1110, 1286[9], 1351[6, 9]
Ḥakīm Khān Tūrā 388
Halākū "Kharāb" Qājār 897
"Ḥālī" (Alṭāf Ḥusain) 1341
"Ḥālī" (Muḥsin 'Imād Ardabīlī) 1207
Ḥallāj (Ḥ. Mudīr) 348
Hamadānī ('Alī b. Shihāb al-Dīn) 946[24]; *Farhang i Mīr S. 'Alī* 36
Hamadānī (Ḥusain) 345, 1287
"Hamand Am" 407 (2)
Ḥamd Allāh Mustaufī 81, 1233
Hamgar (Majd al-Dīn) 918 (3)
Ḥāmid b. Faḍl Allāh "Jamālī" 968
Ḥamīd Allāh (M.) 922 (3)
Ḥamīd Allāh "Ḥamīd" Kashmīrī 401, 1304
Ḥāmid Ḥusain (S.) 29 (9), 1210
Ḥāmid Kabīr 954[5]
Ḥamīd Khān 774
Ḥamīd al-Dīn Khān 597[12]
Ḥamīd al-Dīn Nāgaurī 5, 1192, 1054 (8)
Ḥamīd al-Dīn Siwālī Nāgaurī 6, 971[3], 1192
Ḥammād i Thānī 1057 (35)
Ḥammāmī-zādah 33 (55)
Ḥamzah Kashmīrī 975[19, 28], 986[2, 16]
Ḥamzah Makhdūmī 1064 (110)
Handālawī [?] 986[20]
Ḥanīf (Ibrāhīm) 270
Ḥanīf al-Dīn 'Abd al-Qādir Kintūrī 1026
Hanīrām (?) b. D'hanīrām 478
"Ḥaqīrī" 598 (2), 1318
Ḥaqq-wirdī 166
Harāt 354–6, 1119
Harawī (M. b. Bāqir) 1252[6]
Harawī (M. b. M.) 55, 1227
Harawī (M. Ḥusain [b.] 'Umar [b.] M. [b. ?] 'Abd al-Salām) 233 (65), 1267 antepenult.
Har-Charan-Dās 475
Harnām Sing'h 479
Harsuk'h Rāy 147
Hārūn, pl. near Nīshāpūr, 943[22]
Ḥasan (Khwājah) 171 (43)
Ḥasan b. 'Alī b. Ḥasan Qummī 348[23], 1291
Ḥasan b. 'Alī Jābirī Anṣārī Iṣfahānī 1292
Ḥasan [Ḥusain ?] b. 'Alī Kashmīrī 680
Ḥasan b. 'Alī Yazdī KTHNWI 227
al-Ḥasan b. al-Faḍl al-Ṭabarsī 176, 1252
Ḥasan b. Ḥasan [b. ?] 'Abd al-Malik Qummī 348 ult., 1291
Ḥasan b. Ḥasan Shīrāzī 353, 1294
Ḥasan b. Ḥusain Sabzawārī 182, 1253
Ḥasan b. Luṭf Allāh Ṭihrānī Rāzī 814
Ḥasan b. M. b. Ḥasan Qummī 348, 1291
Ḥasan b. M. 'Alī Yazdī Ḥā'irī 231 (32), 1267
Ḥasan b. M. Bāqir Iṣfahānī 1205
Ḥasan b. M. Taqī Ṭālaqānī 1173 n.2
Ḥasan b. Murtaḍā Ḥusainī 134
Ḥasan b. Mūsā Aḥmadābādī 984[11]
Ḥasan b. Ni'mat Allāh Shūshtarī 1103
Ḥasan b. Ṣadr al-Dīn M. Kashmīrī 1046
Ḥasan b. Shihāb Yazdī 91, 1236
Ḥasan b. Walī Allāh Kubrawī Kashmīrī 1065 (120)
Ḥasan 'Alī (S.) 157 (1)
Ḥasan 'Alī (Shams al-Dīn 'Alī Khān) 210[4]
Ḥasan 'Alī b. 'Alī Shīrāzī 1187 (16)
Ḥasan 'Alī Shāh [Kābulī ?] 1150[20, 21]
Ḥasan 'Alī Shāh [= Ṣafī 'Alī Shāh] 32 (45), 1205
Ḥasan 'Askarī *Tafsīr*, (**1**) M. Bāqir Yazdī's translation (*Jawāhir al-īmān*) 1210, (**2**) Zawārī's translation (*Āthār al-akhyār*) 15, 29, 1197, 1209
Ḥasan Baṣrī 1031 n.3, 1051[27]
Ḥasan Bēg Khākī 123, 1241; *But-khānah* 807[16]; *Muntakhab* (or *Aḥsan*) *al-tawārīkh* 123
Ḥasan Bēg Rūmlū 306, 1279
Ḥasan Chelebī "Shaidā" 1101
Ḥasan Dihlawī 1025[2]
Ḥasan Fasā'ī 353, 1294
Ḥasan Kaul "Shi'rī" 1046[11]
Ḥasan Khān Manṭiq al-Mulk 242 (8)
Ḥasan Lak'hnawī (S.) 1222
Ḥasan Muḥammad (Sh.) 1038[3]
Ḥasan "Nithārī" Bukhārī 802

Ḥasan Niẓāmī 493, 1310
Ḥasan Pīr-niyā 249 (1)–(3), 1270
Ḥasan Rasūl-numā (S.) 1024[23]
Ḥasan Rūmlū 306, 1279
Ḥasan Shams Gīlānī 1352
Ḥasan "Shi'rī" Kashmīrī 1046
Ḥasan Taqī-zādah 241 (1), 1350[16]
Hāshim (M.) b. 'Abd al-Ghafūr Sind'hī (d. 1174/1760–1 : see Raḥmān 'Alī p. 253), 1259 (35)
Hāshim b. Ismā'īl Shīrāzī 1201
Hāshim b. M. Qāsim Badakhshānī 987
Hāshim Bēg "Fuzūnī" Astarābādī 743, 1331
Hāshim Kishmī 988[3]
Hāshim Mīrzā 320, 1282
Hāshimī (M. Ṣadr) 1289 (17)
Hāshimī (Tāj b. M.) 37[11]
Hashmat al-Daulah W. A. Brooke 685[2]
"Ḥashrī" Tabrīzī 982
"Hātifī" Jāmī *Ismā'īl-nāmah* = *Shāh-nāmah* 303, 1278; *Tīmūr-nāmah* 289, 1274–5
Ḥātim Khān 587
Hazār (M. R.) 1290
Hazārah 676[19]
Hazār-fann (Ḥusain) 432[4]
"Ḥazīn" (M. 'Alī Jīlānī) 840, 1336; Note on Persian invasions of India 615, 1284; (*Tadhkirat al-aḥwāl*) 847, 1336; *Tadhkirat al-mu'āṣirīn* 848
"Hidāyat." See Riḍā-Qulī Khān
Hidāyat (Ṣādiq) 1348
"Ḥikmat" ('Alī Aṣghar) 1340
"Ḥikmat" (Muḥibb 'Alī Khān) [*Faraḥ-nāmah i Fāṭimī*] 218; *Ṣaulat i Ṣafdarī* 200–1
Hilālī ('Alī b. Ḥusain) 85
Hindālawī [?] 986[20]
"Hindī" (Bhagwān Dās) 881
"Hindī" (Kanhaiyā Lāl) 674, 1185 (41)
Hindūr 678 (13)
Hindūshāh b. Sanjar 81, 1232–3
Hīrām (?) b. D'hanīrām 478
Hīrāman b. Gird'har-Dās 735
Ḥiṣār Fīrōzah 677 (5)
Ḥiṣārī ('Iwaḍ) 1185 (43)
Ḥiṣārī (Jalāl [al-Dīn]) 735, 737
Ḥiṣārī (M.-Qulī Mughūl) 533
Ḥiṣārī (Muḥyī [al-Dīn] 'Abd al-'Azīz) 183
Hōlkar (Jaswant Rāō) 733[27]
Hoogly (Hūglī) 724[19], 1329
Ḥujjat Allāh. See Naqshband (M.) b. M. Ma'ṣūm Sirhindī
Hulāgū "Kharāb" Qājār 897
"Humā" (M. Ṣādiq Marwazī) 335, 884, 1285
Humā'ī (Jalāl al-Dīn "Sanā") *Ghazzālī-nāmah* 1345; *Tārīkh i adabīyāt i Īrān* 1187
Humām b. 'Abd al-Razzāq Gīlānī 119[1], 1240
Humāyūn 536–40, 1313
Hunza 688
Hurmūz 109[12, 18], 309[15], 359[1]
Ḥusain (Quṭb al-Dīn) [really Kamāl al-Dīn Ḥusain Khwārazmī ?] 974[20]
Ḥusain (Sharaf al-Dīn) 974 n.5.
Ḥusain b. 'Abd Allāh Sarābī Tabrīzī 343, 1070
Ḥusain b. Abdāl Zāhidī 318
Ḥusain b. Aḥmad [Injū] 1144
Ḥusain b. 'Alī Kāshifī. See Kāshifī
Ḥusain [Ḥasan ?] b. 'Alī Kashmīrī 680
Ḥusain b. 'Alī Rāzī (Abū 'l-Futūḥ) 4, 1191
Ḥusain b. 'Alī Sijāsī Zanjānī 1206
Ḥusain b. Ghiyāth al-Dīn Maḥmūd Ṣaffārī *Iḥyā' al-mulūk* 365; *Khair al-bayān* 814
Ḥusain b. Ḥasan "Fārigh" Gīlānī 214
Ḥusain b. Ḥasan Jurjānī Kāzarūnī 29 (12), 1211
Ḥusain b. Ḥasan Khwārazmī 177, 973[13], 974[10], 1253[11], probably also 974[21] (Sh. "Quṭb al-Dīn Ḥusain")
Ḥusain b. Ḥusain Sarakhsī 976
Ḥusain b. Ismā'īl BRHĀRĪ 232 (55)
Ḥusain b. Maḥmūd Ṣaffārī *Iḥyā' al-mulūk* 365; *Khair al-bayān* 814
Ḥusain b. Maḥmūd Shīrāzī 1025[4]
Ḥusain b. Manṣūr b. Bāyqarā (Sulṭān) 959
Ḥusain b. M. b. Abī 'l-Riḍā Ḥusainī 'Alawī Āwī 349, 1292
Ḥusain b. M. Ja'farī [Ibn i Bībī ?] 408, 1305
Ḥusain b. M. Khwānsārī 20 n.2, 1201
Ḥusain b. Naṣr Allāh 'Arab-Bāghī 1206
Ḥusain b. Ṣābir Sindī 972
Ḥusain b. Shāh Murād 385
Ḥusain b. 'Uthmān 39 (2), 1224[3]
Ḥusain 'Alī Khān Kirmānī *Nishān i Ḥaidarī* 774; *Tadhkirat al-bilād wa-'l-ḥukkām* 765
Ḥusain 'Alī Shīrāzī 406[12], 1304 n.1

Ḥusain 'Alī Shīrāzī (identical with the preceding ?) 430[31], 1308
Ḥusain Allāh [*sic* ?] Ghaznawī 1063 (92)
Ḥusain Farzād 1288 (7)
Ḥusain Gāzargāhī [or rather, it seems, Kāzargāhī] 960
Ḥusain Hamadānī 345, 1287
Ḥusain Hazār-fann 432
Ḥusain Ḥusainī 889
Ḥusain Kāshgharī 32 (40)
Ḥusain Kāshifī. See Kāshifī
Ḥusain Kāzargāhī 960
Ḥusain Khān b. Nabī Khān 1350[22]
Ḥusain Khān Lōhānī 777
Ḥusain Khān Muqaddam Ajūdān-bāshī 1068
Ḥusain Khān Mushīr al-Daulah 1350[21]
Ḥusain Khān Sarābī Tabrīzī 343
Ḥusain Kūhī Kirmānī 1291 (2)
Ḥusain Makkī. See Makkī
Ḥusain " Nawā " Kāshānī 894
Ḥusain Nūr Ṣādiqī 1293
Ḥusain Nūrī Ṭabarsī (cf. Brockelmann *Sptbd.* ii p. 832) 228 (7)
Ḥusain Qārī 680
Ḥusain Qazwīnī (or Tabrīzī) 974
Ḥusain Riḍā b. 'Alī Afshār 1203
Ḥusain Shajarah " Bīnā " 1341
Ḥusain Shīrāzī Karbalā'ī 404[4]
Ḥusain Tabrīzī (or Qazwīnī) 974
Ḥusain " Thuraiyā " Ṭihrānī 352
Ḥusain-Dōst " Ḥusainī " Sanbhalī *Mukhtaṣar i Tīmūr-nāmah* 290; *Tadhkirah i Ḥusainī* 833
Husain-Qulī Khān " 'Āshiqī " 885
" Ḥusainī " (Ḥusain-Dōst Sanbhalī) 290, 833
" Ḥusainī " [Pashāwarī] 982
" Ḥusainī " (S. Luqmān ?) 419[25]
Ḥusām b. M. Mashshāṭī 1258[29]
Ḥusām al-Dīn (Munshī) 760
Ḥusām al-Dīn Guwāliyārī 693
Ḥusām Allāh 395
Ḥuwaizī (M.) 158
Hyderabad. See Ḥaidarābād

'Ibād Allāh *'Ajā'ib al-tajwīd* 45
'Ibād Allāh *Multaqaṭ al-tawārīkh* 384
Ibn al-Balkhī 350
Ibn al-Khafīf 1053[7]
Ibn al-Khashshāb 53, 1226
Ibn al-Muqaffa' 1183 (31)
Ibn al-Niẓām al-Ḥusainī 257
Ibn al-Qirrīyah 245, 1270[16]
Ibn al-Tāj 36
Ibn al-Ṭiqṭaqā 80, 1232–3
Ibn A'tham Kūfī 207, 1260
Ibn Bābawaih, 209, 1260
Ibn i Bazzāz 939
Ibn i Bībī 408, 1305
Ibn Funduq 353, 1105, 1295–6
Ibn i Ḥasan 713 penult.
Ibn Hishām 172, 1251
Ibn i 'Imād 41, 1218
Ibn i Isfandiyār 359, 1298
Ibn Isḥāq 172, 1251
Ibn i Khafīf 1053[7]
Ibn Khallikān 1167
Ibn i Mu'īn i Abarqūhī 85, 1234
Ibn Qutaibah 155
Ibn Saiyid al-Nās 178, 1253
Ibn i Shihāb i Yazdī 91, 1236
Ibn i Sīnā 1351[20]
Ibn i Yamīn 919
Ibn i Zarkūb i Shīrāzī 351, 1294
Ibrāhīm (Jamāl al-Dīn Abū Kālījār) 184[25]
Ibrāhīm [b. Najjār, Turkish Surgeon at Bairūt] 421, 1306[24]
Ibrāhīm b. 'Abd Allāh (" 'Iyānī ") 168
Ibrāhīm b. Adham 1051[29]
Ibrāhīm b. Ismā'īl Tattawī 1258[32]
Ibrāhīm b. Jalāl al-Dīn [Saljūqī ?] 161[10], 1250[13]
Ibrāhīm b. Jarīr 113, 1239
Ibrāhīm b. Mahdī 1339
Ibrāhīm b. Najjār 421[9], 1306[24]
Ibrāhīm b. Rūzbihān 934
Ibrāhīm b. Shahryār (Abū Isḥāq) Kāzarūnī 936[1], 1343
Ibrāhīm b. Taufīq Shīrāzī 742
Ibrāhīm Badā'i'-nigār 1297[16]
Ibrāhīm Darwīsh Bukhārī 33 (56)
Ibrāhīm Efendī 421, 1306[24]
Ibrāhīm Ḥanīf 270
Ibrāhīm Jān Mu'aṭṭar 1204[27], 1212[8]
Ibrāhīm Khān Ṣadīq [Ṣiddīq ?] al-Mamālik 1249[8]
Ibrāhīm Khān Ṣaḥḥāf-bāshī 1162 (24)
Ibrāhīm Khān Shīrāzī 333[3]
Ibrāhīm " Mulhamī " 420
Ibrāhīm Qazwīnī 423
Ibrāhīm Qummī 157 (14)
Ibrāhīm Sirhindī 119
Ibrāhīm Sulṭān b. Shāh-Rukh 283[13], 284[10], 287[15], 932[2]
Ibrāhīmī (Aḥmad) 1074, 1279
Ibrāhīm-zādah Ṣafawī 1271 (10)
" 'Ibrat " (M. Qāsim Lāhaurī) 607
" 'Ibratī " 'Aẓīmābādī 899
" Idrākī " Bēg-Lārī Tattawī 654, 1324

Idrīs b. 'Alī Bidlīsī 412, 1306
Idrīsī ('Abd al-Raḥmān b. M.) 371
Ifāḍ [Afāḍ ?] al-Dīn (M.) Ḥasanī 44[10]
" Iftikhār " Daulatābādī 854
Iḥsān-'Alī Pāk-Pattanī 1042[27]
Iḥsān Allāh " Mumtāz " 168 (7)
Iḥsān Allāh [" Mumtāz " ?] Lak'hnawī 204 (1)
" Ījād " (M. Aḥsan) *Farrukhsiyar-nāmah* 604 ; *Futūḥāt i Āṣafī* 748, 1331
I'jāz Ḥusain 428 (3)
Ījī (Maḥmūd b. M.) 211
" Ikhlāṣ " (Kishan Chand) 826
Ikhtiyār (Qāḍī) 1116
Ikrām al-Dīn b. Niẓām al-Dīn 221, 1263
Ikrām 'Alī Qalandar (M.) 1061 (76)
Ilāh-dād " Faiḍī " Sirhindī 537[20], 551
Ilāh-diyah b. 'Abd al-Raḥīm Chishtī 1003
Ilāh-diyah Aḥmad Lāharpūrī 1036 n.4, 1047[3]
" Ilāhī " Hamadānī 815
Ilāhī Bakhsh Angrēzābādī 152, 1246
Ilāh-Yār Bilgrāmī 142
Ilāh-Yār Khān b. Ḥāfiẓ Raḥmat Khān 396[11]
Īlchī i Niẓām-Shāh 113, 1239
Ilhām Allāh (Shāh) 1056 (23)
Iltifāt Ḥusain Khān 754
'Imād al-Dīn 'Alī Astarābādī 42, 1220
'Imād al-Dīn al-Kātib al-Iṣfahānī 255
'Imād [al-Dīn] Ṭārumī 1196
'Imād al-Mulk Ghāzī al-Dīn Khān Fīrōz-Jang [III] 623[26], 1028–30
Imām b. Aḥmad Kujābī 46 (12)
Imām al-Dīn (M.) 1061 (74)
Imām al-Dīn Ḥasan Khān 1050
Imām al-Dīn Ḥusainī Chishtī 399, 1303
Imām al-Dīn Khān b. Ghulām-Ḥusain Khān 1039
Imām al-Dīn Sh. Kabīr 407 (12)
Imām 'Alī (S.) 1062 (88)
Imām-Qulī Khān, Bēglarbēgī of Fārs, 309[4, 16]
Imām-zādahs of Shaft, etc., 1086[9]
Imdād Allāh Fārūqī 1055 (16), 1345[20]
Imtinān [*sic* ?] Khawāṣṣ Khān 1137
In'ām 'Alī 704
'Ināyat Allāh [b.] Muḥibb 'Alī 548[1]
'Ināyat Allāh Kanbō 578
'Ināyat Allāh Khān Kashmīrī 595, 1318
'Ināyat-Ḥusain b. Fatḥ Allāh 1063 (101)
'Ināyat-Ḥusain " of Mahrard " 149
'Ināyat Khān (M. Ṭāhir " Āshnā ") 577
'Ināyat Khān " Rāsikh " 1183 (25)
Indian celebrities 1352
Indian scholars 1119
Indore 733
Injū (Jamāl al-Dīn Ḥusain) 1144 n.4.
" Iqbāl " ('Alī-Qulī Chulāwī) 333
" Iqbāl " (M. Iqbāl Lāhaurī) 1342[4], 1355[1]
Iqbāl Yaghmā'ī 1345[18]
Irādat Khān " Wāḍiḥ " 601
Īraj Afshār 1179
Īrānī ('Abd al-Muḥammad Khān) 1078, 1347
Īrānī (Ā. Sh.) 1182 (14)
Īrānī (Dīnshāh J.) 917
Irbilī ('Alī b. 'Īsā) 210, 1260–1
Irtaḍā 'Alī Khān Gōpāmawī 1038, 1344 ult.
'Īsā b. Junaid 'Adawī 1123[28]
" 'Iṣāmī " 433
Īsar-Dās Nāgar 587, 1318
Iṣfahān 349, 1292, 1353
Iṣfahānī (Ḥāfiẓ) 47 (1) (but see p. 1219, addendum to p. 41, ll. 20–21)
Iṣfahānī ('Imād al-Dīn M. b. M.) 255
Isfarāyinī ('Abd al-Raḥmān b. M.) 1064 (112)
Isfarāyinī (Ṭāhir b. M.) 3, 1190
Isfarghābad 1261 antepenult.
Isfizārī (Mu'īn al-Dīn) 355, 1296
Isḥāq (M.) 921
Isḥāq (Ṣafī al-Dīn) 318[9], 939[15]
Isḥāq b. [Makhdūm i A'ẓam] Aḥmad 981[8, 16]
Isḥāq b. Ibrāhīm Nīshāpūrī 159, 1250
Isḥāq b. Tāj al-Dīn Multānī 36
Isḥāq Bēg " 'Udhrī " 872[25], 1337
Isḥāq Qārī 975
Ishaque (M.) 921
Ishasnawī (M.) 1344[6]
" 'Ishq " (Ghulām-Muḥyī 'l-Dīn) 883, 1337
" 'Ishqī " (M. Wajīh b. Ghulām-Ḥusain " Mujrim ") 880
" 'Ishrat " Siyālkōṭī *Shāh-nāmah i Aḥmadī* 397 ; *Shāh-nāmah i Nādirī* 328
Iskandar b. Manjhū 728, 1329
Iskandar b. 'Umar Shaikh 86[13]
Iskandar Bēg Munshī 309, 1280–1
Iskandar Efendī 1187 (18)
Iskandar Khān b. Imām-Qulī Khān 276 (1)

Islām Khān Mashhadī 567[18], 1103[26]
Islāmābād (= Chittagong) 1117
Ismā'īl [b. ?] Ibrāhīm 429[8]
Ismā'īl b. M. Taqī Zanjānī 216
Ismā'īl Bukhārī (S. Shāh) 1059 (58)
Ismā'īl Ghāzī 'Arabī 990
Ismā'īl " Ḥairat " 242 (7), 328 (7)
Ismā'īl Khān Mujāhidī 429[19]
Ismā'īl Khān " Sarbāz " Burūjirdī 228 (5), 1265
Ismā'īl Nūr-zādah Būshahrī 1307[18, 30]
'Iṣmat Allāh b. M. Aslam 401
Istānbūlī dervishes 977[1]
I'tiḍād al-Salṭanah 238, 404, 1268
I'timād al-Salṭanah ('Alī Khān Marāghī) 1154
I'timād al-Salṭanah. See M. Ḥasan Khān Marāghī
I'tiṣām al-Dīn b. Tāj al-Dīn 1142
'Iwaḍ Ḥiṣārī 1185 (43)
'Iwaḍ M. b. Rūzī M. 390
Īwāghlī, or rather Ēv-oghlī, (Abū 'l-Qāsim Ḥaidar) 317, 1282
'Iyāḍ b. Mūsā 176, 1252
" 'Iyānī " (Ibrāhīm b. 'Abd Allāh) 168
'Izz al-Dīn (Ḥāfiẓ) 47 (2)
'Izz al-Dīn M. (or 'I. al-D. b. M.) Jūrīdī (or Jūrī) 45, 1223
'Izzat 'Alī Riḍawī 232 (54)

Jādēv Mīr 733[16]
Ja'far (M.) 1102
Ja'far b. Ḥusain Shūshtarī 230 (25), 1266[29]
Ja'far b. M. Ḥusainī 86, 1234–5
Ja'far Badakhshī (Nūr al-Dīn) 946
Ja'far Bēg (Āṣaf Khān) 120[1], 1104[13], 1240
Ja'far Khān Ḥusainī (Mushīr al-Daulah) 1070
Ja'far Khān Khūrmūjī 343, 352
Ja'far Khān Naṣīrī 649[13]
Ja'far al-Ṣādiq 55, 1227
Ja'far Saiyāḥ 1290
Ja'far Shāh Riḍawī 65[14]
" Ja'farī " b. M. Ḥusainī 86, 1234–5
Jagat Sing'h (Mahārājah of Ūdaipūr) 519[21, 31]
Jagat Sing'h (Rājah, of Mau) 677 (9)
Jagjīwan Dās 458
Jahānābād (= Shāhjahānābād ?) 824 n.3
Jahānābād (w. of Hūglī) 990 n.1
Jahānābādī (Kalīm Allāh) 1038[4]
Jahān-ārā Bēgam 999
Jahāndār Shāh (Jawān-bakht) 624
Jahān-gasht 945[7] (see also Jalāl al-Dīn Bukhārī)
Jahāngīr Mīrzā Qājār 339, 1285
Jahāngīr Pādshāh 556–64, 1316
Jahāngīr-nagar (= D'hākah, " Dacca ") 723[8, 18]
" Jahānī " (Faḍl Allāh b. Asad Allāh) 936[4]
Jai Kishan Dās Mihrah 455[23]
Jaipūr 519[25, 31], 690[24], 691[21-22], 1147[14]
Jā'is 713
Jaisalmēr 1155[20]
Jalāl (probably S. Jalāl Harawī) 958[17]
Jalāl Ganj i Rawān 1025[5]
Jalāl Ḥiṣārī *Guwāliyār-nāmah* 735; *Wāqi'ah i Jhōjhār Sing'h* 737
Jalāl M. b. 'Abbādī [?] Kāzarūnī 935[32]
Jalāl i Munajjim 308, 1280
Jalāl al-Dīn (S. M.) 1179 (2)
Jalāl al-Dīn b. Fatḥ-'Alī Shāh 239, 1268–9
Jalāl al-Dīn Bukhārī (S.) 944, 954[3], 971[5], 1343
Jalāl al-Dīn Dawānī 1277
Jalāl al-Dīn Humā'ī 1187 (17), 1345[27]
Jalāl al-Dīn Mankubirnī 1088[17], 1349[4]
Jalāl al-Dīn M., Munajjim, Yazdī 308, 1280
Jalāl al-Dīn Pānīpatī 1003[11]
Jalāl al-Dīn Rūmī 921[2], 935[7], 937[14], 1065 (117), 1341
Jalāl al-Dīn " Sanā " Humā'ī 1187 (17), 1345[27]
Jalāl al-Dīn Ṭabāṭabā'ī 565
Jalāl al-Dīn Tabrīzī 971 n.7
Jalāl al-Dīn T'hānēsarī 17, 1198
Jalāl al-Dīn Ṭihrānī (S.) 1353
Jalālā Ṭabāṭabā'ī 565
Jāland'harī ('Alīm Allāh) 1259[8]
Jāland'harī (Auḥad al-Dīn Mīrzā Jān [var. Khān]) 1259[12]
Jāland'harī (Jān M.) 1214[19]
Jamāl [al-Dīn] b. Jalāl al-Dīn Shīrāzī 655
Jamāl [al-Dīn] Ardistānī 185, 1254
Jamāl al-Dīn Asadābādī 1184 (33)
Jamāl al-Dīn 'Aṭā' Allāh 189, 1254–5
Jamāl al-Dīn Ḥusain [Injū] 1144
Jamāl [al-Dīn] Ḥusainī Dashtakī Shīrāzī 189, 1254–5
Jamāl al-Dīn Ibrāhīm (Abū Kālījār) 184[25]

Jamāl al-Dīn Khwānsārī 20, 1200
Jamāl al-Dīn Qāshānī 78, 267, 1232, 1272
Jamāl [al-Dīn] Sājī 5
Jamāl Muḥammad (Shāh) 1014[25]
" Jamālī " Ardistānī 185, 1254
" Jamālī " Dihlawī 968
Jamālī b. Ḥasan Shūshtarī *Futūḥāt al-'Ajam* 420, 1306
Jāmī ('Abd al-Raḥmān b. Aḥmad) 954–9, 1340 ; *Nafaḥāt al-uns* 954, 1344 ; *Shawāhid al-nubuwwah* 186, 1254
Jāmī (Abū 'l-Makārim b. 'Alā al-Mulk) 950
Jāmī (Aḥmad b. Abī 'l-Ḥasan) 950[4], 1344[6]
Jāmī (Ghiyāth al-Dīn M.) 157 (2)
Jamīl Qūzānlū 1271 (6)–(8), 1284[11]
Jammū 687
Jān (Mīrzā) 932[33]
Jān i 'Ālam Shīrīn-raqam 690
Jān i Jānān (Mīrzā) 1033[18], 1035[12]
Jān M. b. Abī Sa'īd Anṣārī Jāland'harī 1214[19]
Jān M. b. Mūsā Khān 666[20]
Jān M. Khān Ma'rūfānī 660
Janāb ('Alī b. M. Bāqir) 1293
Jānī Kāshānī 339, 1285–6
Japan 432, 1309
Jār Allāh 949[20]
Jarbādhaqānī (Nāṣiḥ b. Ẓafar) 251
Jārchī-bāshī 886 penult.
Jārējas 733
Jarūn 309[15]
al-Jasrī ('Abd al-'Azīz) 159
Jaswant Rāō Hōlkar 733[27]
Jaswant Rāy " Munshī " 777
" Jauhar " (Ghulām-Ḥusain Khān) 754
Jauhar Āftābchī 536
" Jauharī " *Ātash-kadah* (?) 228 (6)
" Jauharī " (M. Ibrāhīm b. M. Bāqir Harawī [not Marwī] 234 (66), 1268
Jaunpūr 698, 1016 n.1, 1120
Jaunpūrī (S. M.) 1056 (21) and (28)
Jawād Ḥusain (S. M.) 1114
Jawāhir al-kalām, or Jawāhir-kalām, ('Abd al-'Azīz) 1135, 1354
Jawāhir La'l Akbarābādī 489
Jawān-bakht (Mīrzā) 624
Jazarī (M. b. M.) 40, 1218
Jazī ('Abd al-Karīm b. Mahdī) 1353
Jejeebhoy (Jamsetjee) 1180 (5)
Jesus Christ 163 penult., 172 (1), 197[25], 1247[21]
Jews 1188 (24)
Jhang Sayāl 676[25]
Jhōjhār Sing'h Būndēlah 737[26]
Jhunjhunū 1045 n.2
Jījī-bhā'ī (Jamshēd-jī) 1180 (5)
Johnson (Richard) 767n.
Jūgal Kishōr 474
Juliyānā (Bībī) 1162
Jumman (Sh.) 1038[2]
Jūnāgaṛh 731[27]
Junaid b. Maḥmūd Shīrāzī 1123
Junaid b. M. Ḥātim Bilgrāmī 1114
Jūrī (?), or Jūrīdī, ('Izz al-Dīn M. b. Bahā' al-Dīn) 45 (7), 1223[24]
Jurjānī ('Alī b. M.) *Tarjumān al-Qur'ān* 37, 39 (8) [I.O. D.A. 984 is Jurjānī's work], 1216
Jurjānī (Ḥusain b. Ḥasan Kāzarūnī) 29 (12), 1211
Juwainī ('Alā' al-Dīn 'Aṭā) 260, 1272
Juwairī (M.) 158
Jūybārī (M.) 374[29]
Jūybārī saints 374[29], 976[9], 1004[11]
Jūzjānī 68, 1229–30

Kabīr (Sh.) 407 (12)
Kabīr b. Munawwar Lāhaurī 1241
Kabīr b. Uwais (Ẓahīr al-Dīn al-Ardabīlī) 1168 n.2, 1306[15], 1355 ; *Ghazawāt al-Sulṭān Salīm* 417 ; *Tarjamah i Wafayāt al-a'yān* 1168
Kābulī ('Abd Allāh) 1240
Kāfiristān 405[6]
Kahdam, The Imām-zādahs of, 1086
Kahf ('Uthmān b. 'Umar) 1056 (26), 1345
Kai-Kā'ūs b. Kai-Khusrau 162, 1250
Kai-Khusrau b. Kā'ūs Fārisī 169 (10)
Kaidarī (M. b. Ḥusain) 181
Kairānah 1003 n.5, 1020[4]
Kairānawī (M. 'Abd al-Rashīd) 1019
Kairānawī (Sa'd Allāh " Masīḥ ") 196, 1256
Kaiwān ('Abbās 'Alī Qazwīnī) 1206
Kākī 943 ult.
Kākōrī 1035 n.3
Kalān Bukhārī 42
Kalb-'Alī Khān (Nawwāb) 1156, 1184 (38)
Kalhaṇa 678
" Kalīm " (Abū Ṭālib Hamadānī) 572
Kalīm Allāh Jahānābādī 1038[4]
Kallū (Mīrzā) 479[4]
Kalyān Sing'h b. Shitāb Rāy 719
Kalyānī. See 'Abd Allāh b. Aḥmad b. Bāyazīd
Kalyar 1031 n.5

Kamāl (Khwājah) 983
Kamāl al-Dīn 'Allāmah 1038[1]
Kamāl al-Dīn Ḥaidar 710
Kamāl al-Dīn Ḥusain Kāzargāhī 960
Kamāl al-Dīn Ḥusain Khwārazmī 177, 973[13], 974[10], 1253[11], probably also 974[21] (Sh. " Quṭb al-Dīn Ḥusain ")
Kamāl al-Dīn Maḥmūd Andujānī (apparently the same person as Maḥmūd Ghujduwānī 973) 974[11]
Kamāl Allāh Ṣiddīqī 201
Kamāl Barghamawī 244[22]
Kamāl Khān Munajjim 130
Kambō(h). See Kanbō(h)
Kāmgār Ḥusainī 563, 1316
" Kāmī " Qazwīnī 800
" Kāmī " Shīrāzī 563
Kāmrāj b. Nain-Sing'h 606
Kāmwar Khān (M. Hādī) *Haft gulshan i Muḥammad-Shāhī* 459; *Tadhkirat al-salāṭīn i Chaghatā* 517
" Kāmyāb " (Qurbān-'Alī Pāzawārī) 224
Kan'ānī (M. Yūsuf) 127[5]
Kanbō, or Kanbōh, 124 n., 968 n.3, 1063 (101), 1113[7]
Kāngrah 566[11]
Kanhaiyā Lāl " Hindī " 674, 1185 (41)
Kānjī-Mal 481
Kāṇṭā Dūār 990[10]
Kaptān (Fatḥ-'Alī Khān) 901[33]
Karak Karawī (Shāh) 1057 (38)
Karam-'Alī *Muẓaffar-nāmah* 718
Karam-'Alī *Tārīkh i Mālwā* 735[14]
Karāmat 'Alī Dihlawī 251 ult.
Karbalā' 428 (3)
al-Karīm (Maḥmūd b. M.) al-Aqsarā'ī 267, 1272, 1305
Karīm Khān Kirmānī 1065 (116)
Karīm-Yār 1057 (38)
Karnātak 777–80, 1117
Karnūl 766[3, 28]
Karrāb 1253 n.
Kārtānī (M. b. Aḥmad) 178
Kāsānī (Aḥmad b. Jalāl al-Dīn) 973[8]
Kāshān 350
Kāshānī ('Abd Allāh b. 'Alī) 78, 267, 1232, 1272
Kāshānī ('Afīf b. Nūr) 193, 1255
Kāshānī (Jamāl al-Dīn) 78, 267, 1232, 1272
Kāshānī (Shams al-Dīn) 266
" Kashfī " (M. Salāmat Allāh) 223, 1264
" Kashfī " (M. Ṣāliḥ) 214, 1262; *I'jāz i Muṣṭafawī* 215; *Manāqib i Murtaḍawī* 214 [for editions (Bombay 1269/1852–3 and Tihrān 1273/1856) see Mashhad V pp. 332–3]
Kāshghar 386[6], 392–3, 1026[15], 1035[27], 1302
" Kāshī " (M. Yaḥyā) 569
Kāshī (Muṣṭafā Khān) 1225, l. 4 from foot
" Kāshif " ('Alī Akbar Burqa'ī) 1136[14], 1292
" Kāshifī " *Ghazā-nāmah i Rūm* 412
Kāshifī ('Alī b. Ḥusain) 962
Kāshifī (Ḥusain b. 'Alī) 12, 1195; *Jāmi' al-sittīn* 1195[26]; *Jawāhir al-tafsīr* 12, 1195; *Mawāhib i 'alīyah* 12, 1195[15, 16, 21–24]; *Rauḍat al-shuhadā'* 212, 1261
Kāshī-Rāj 398, 1303
Kashmīr 678–87, 1325–6; 1013[29], 1052[18], 1053 (5), 1060 (65), 1064 (109), 1122
Kashmīrī (Ḥājjī M.) 175[3]
Kasrawī (S. Aḥmad K. Tabrīzī) 366, 1298; *Shahriyārān i gum-nām* 242 (5); *Tārīkh i hijdah-sālah i Ādharbāyjān* 1300; *Tārīkh i mashrūṭah i Īrān* 1289; *Tārīkh i pānṣad-sālah i Khūzistān* 366, 1298
Kathnawī (vocalisation ?) 227
Kātib (M. 'Alī) 884
Kātib Chelebī 127, 1242
Kāyat'h (= Kāyast'h) 471 n.3
Kāzargāhī (Ḥusain) 960
Kāzarūnī (Abū Isḥāq) 936[1], 1343
Kāzarūnī (Abū 'l-Maḥāsin Ḥusain b. Ḥasan) 29 (12), 1211
Kāzarūnī ('Afīf b. Sa'īd) 179
Kāzarūnī ('Alā' [al-Dīn]) 1343[13]
Kāzarūnī (Bahā' al-Dīn) 183[6]
Kāzarūnī (Ḥājjī Āqā) 1186 (9)
Kāzarūnī (Jalāl al-Dīn M.) 935[33]
Kāzarūnī (Nūr al-Dīn M.) 186
Kāzarūnī (Rajā' M. b. 'Abd al-Raḥmān) 1343[13]
Kāzarūnī (Sa'īd b. Mas'ūd) 179, 1253
" Kāẓim " (A.H. 1286) *Tadhkirah i Kāẓim* 1339
Kāẓim (M.), *Wazīr* of Marw, 325
Kāẓim b. M. 'Aṣṣār 1207
Kāẓim b. Qāsim Rashtī 1061 (73) 1065 (116)
Kēch Makrān 732[32]
Kēshav Dās (Kēsō Dās) 738
Kēwal Rām 1094
" Khabīr " (Ghulām-M. Khān Khaṭak) 233 (62)
" Khādim " (Bāqir) 167

Khāfī Khān 460, 1310
Khair al-Dīn Ḥasan Ghulām-Ḍāmin 779, 1334
Khair al-Dīn M. Ilāhābādī 520, 736; Account of affairs in Oudh (1188–9) 704; *Balwand-nāmah*, 702 1327; *Guwāliyār-nāmah* 736; *'Ibrat-nāmah* 641; *Jaunpūr-nāmah* 698; *Tadhkirat al-'ulamā'* 1121; *Tuḥfah i tāzah* 702, 1327
Khair Allāh " Muhandis " 501[14]
Khair Muḥammad Munshī 1042
Khair M. Pashāwarī 32 (36)
Khairābādī (Aḥmad 'Alī) 1045
Khairābādī (Faḍl i 'Aẓīm) 646, 689, 1322
Khairābādī (Faḍl i Imām) 252[6]
Khairābādī (M. 'Alī) 1058 (48)
Khairābādī (M. 'Alī-Shāh) 1056 (24)
" Khaiyām " ('Umar) 1296[4], 1341[13]
Khaiyām-pūr ('Abd al-Rasūl) 1335, l. 5 from foot.
Khaiyāṭ (As'ad Ya'qūb) 1154[3, 19]
Khākī (Dāwud) 975
Khākī (Ḥasan Bēg) 123, 807[16], 1241
Khāksār (Shāh) 1025[6]
Khālid (Ḍiyā' al-Dīn) Mujaddidī Baghdādī 1064 (106)
Khalīfah (title of a Christian dignitary) 841 n.1
Khalīfah-jī 1010[1]
" Khalīl " ('Alī Ibrāhīm Khān) 700, 761, 877, 1337
Khalīl b. Abū Ṭālib Kamara'ī 1208
Khalīl (M.) b. Dāwud Mīrzā 319, 1282
Khalīl Afghān 1296
Khalīl Allāh Khān 677 (2), (3), (5)
Khalīl Khān Qazwīnī 1067[6]
Khalīl Wazīr 1161 (19)
Khāliṣī-zādah (M.) 1208
Khānah-zād Khān (Amān Allāh) 812 n.1
Khān i Daurān (M. 'Āṣim) 614,[13, 29], 618[8]
Khān i Jahān (Sardār Khān) 666[19]
Khān i Jahān Lōdī 393[24]
Khān i Zamān Khān (Amān Allāh) 812 n.1
Khān i Zamān Khān (Khwājah Ghulām-Ḥusain Khān) 755
" Kharāb " (Aḥmad Hulāgū Qājār) 897
K'harakpat Rāy 839
Kharaqānī (Abū 'l-Ḥasan) 927–8
Khargūshī ('Abd al-Malik b. M.) 175, 1252
Khaṭībī (M. b. 'Alī) 1106[28]
Khatlānī [Khutlānī, Khuttalānī ?] ('Alī b. M.) 44
K'haṭṭū 952 n.5
Khātūnābādī. See M. Riḍā b. M. Mu'min
Khāwand Miyāṅ 29 (6), 1209[30]
" Khāwarī " (Faḍl Allāh Shīrāzī) 337, 1285
Khawāṣṣ Khān Bījāpūrī 1137
Khāzin al-raḥmah 1257[30]
Khiḍr b. Khiḍr Āmidī 65[9]
Khiḍr Rūmī 1036 n.4, 1047[2]
" Khirad " (M. Manṣūr 'Alī) 1182 (22); 1187 (10)
Khiyābānī (M.) 1184 (34)
Khōjah Mullā 300[7]
Khōqand 383[10], 386[5], 388[24], 389–92
Khūb Allāh Ilāhābādī 220[29], 903[8]
Khūb Chand " Dhakā " [" Dhukā " ?] 891
Khudā-bakhsh Bambah 1348[26]
Khudā-bakhsh " Shā'iq " 1058 (40)
Khudā-dād Khān 659; *Lubb i tārīkh i Sind* 659; *Waqā'i' al-sair i Jaisalmēr* 1155
Khuldābād, or Rauḍah 858 n.2, 1024[31]
Khūnd Miyān 29 (6), 1209[31]
Khunuk (?) (Shaikh Jīw) 1058 (47)
Khurāsān 353–6, 1295–7
Khūrī Jān (Bībī) 1355[9]
Khūrjah 756 n.5
" Khurram " Shīrāzī 225
Khusrau b. 'Ābid Abarqūhī 85, 1234
Khusrau b. M. b. Minūchihr 369
Khusrau Dihlawī 495, 1310–11
Khuttalān 947[1]
Khuttalānī [?] ('Alī b. M.) 44
Khūzānī (Aḥmad b. Faḍl Allāh) 126[24]
Khūzistān 237[21], 365–6, 1298
Khwāfī (Faṣīḥ) 90
Khwājagī Kāsānī 973[9]
Khwājah Mīr b. 'Imād al-Dīn M. 228 (8)
Khwājah Mullā 300[7]
Khwājah Pāshā 932[20]
Khwājah Shāh b. S. Aḥmad Khwārazmī 932[11]
Khwājah-zādah (Walī Sirhindī) 560[3]
Khwājam-Qulī Bēg Balkhī 136
Khwājū 396[16]
Khwājū Kirmānī 918[26]
Khwānd (Mīr) 92, 1236–7
Khwānd-Amīr 101, 1237–8; [*Āthār al-mulūk wa-'l-anbiyā'* 155;] *Dastūr al-wuzarā'* 1091; *Ḥabīb al-siyar* 104, 1237–8; *Humāyūn-nāmah*

536, 1313; *Khulāṣat al-akhbār* 102, 1237; *Ma'āthir al-mulūk* 102; *Makārim al-akhlāq* 795
Khwānsārī (Ḥusain) 20 n.2, 1201
Khwānsārī (Jamāl al-Dīn) 20, 1200
Khwānsārī (M. b. Ismā'īl) 1258[25]
Khwārazmī (Kamāl al-Dīn Ḥusain) 177, 973[13], 974[10], 1253[11], probably also 974[21] (Sh, "Quṭb al-Dīn Ḥusain")
Khwēshgīs 1083
Khwurd (Mīr) 941 (cf. 1343[29])
Khwurshāh b. Qubād Ḥusainī 113, 1239
Khwurshēd 'Alī 489
"Khwush-dil" (Amar Sing'h) 479
Khwush-gū (Bindrāban Dās) 826
Khwush-ḥāl Chand 136
Khwush-ḥāl Guwāliyārī 736[9]
Khwush-ḥāl Khān Khaṭak 1303[4]
Khwush-waqt Rāy 667, 1324
Kings 1086, 1348
Kintūr 1006 n.3, 1026 n.1
Kintūrī ('Abd al-Qādir b. M. Sharīf) 1026
Kintūrī (Maḥmūd) 1006[6]
al-Kīrānī (Hindū-Shāh) 81, 1232
Kirmān 357–9, 1297–8
Kirmānī (M. b. Mubārak) 941
Kirpā-Rām (Dīwān) 686, 1325
al-Kisā'ī 161
Kishan Chand "Ikhlāṣ" 826
Kishan-Dayāl 483
Kishm 309[11]
Kishm (in Badakhshān) 988 n.3
Kishwarī (Naẓar b. Ḥasan) 192[21]
Kitāb-khānah i Millī i Malik 1342 n.3
Kōch Bihār 547[21]
Kōch Hājō 547[21], 567[19]
Kōl 692, 1022[25]
Kōtah 691[25]
Kripā-Rām. See Kirpā-Rām 686, 1325
Krusinski (J. T.) 335[22]
Kubrā (Najm al-Dīn) 1032 n.2
al-Kūfī ('Alī b. Ḥāmid) 650, 1323
Kūhgīlūyah 237[21]
Kūhī (Ḥusain) Kirmānī 1291 (2)
Kujābī (Imām b. Aḥmad) 46 (12)
Kul Imām (Shāh) 1042[10]
Kulāl (Amīr) 1058 (44), 1059 (51)
Kūlālī 1008[15]
Kultānī. See 'Abd Allāh b. Aḥmad b. Bāyazīd Kalyānī
Kumail b. Ziyād 1051[28]
Kundan Lāl "Ashkī" 1246, probably also 1065 (115)
Kundurī. See Kaidarī 181
"Kunwar" (a Hindī word meaning "prince", "a rājah's son"), the *takhalluṣ* of Apūrb Kishan 524, 1312
Kūrānī ('Alī b. Maḥmūd) 959
Kurdistān 366–9, 1300
Kurg 777
Kurjī Jādēv Mīr 733
Kūsārī (M., or 'Alī, b. Ḥasan 'Alī) 45[18], 1223[11]
Kuṭār (F. N.) 1180 (5)
Kutubī [?] (Maḥmūd) 277

Lābarī ('Abd Allāh b. M.) 1082[15]
Lachhmī Narāyan (Munshī) 695
Lachhmī Narāyan "Shafīq" 476, 1310; *Bisāṭ al-ghanā'im* 762, 1333; *Chamanistān i shu'arā'* 867; Description of Ḥaidarābād 750; *Gul i ra'nā* 867; *Ḥaqīqat-hā-yi Hindustān* 477, 1310; *Ma'āthir i Āṣafī* 750; *Shām i gharībān* 867; *Tanmīq i shigarf* 738
Lagzī 1336[10]
Lāharpūrī (Mujtabā) 1036[7], 1036 n.4, 1047[3]
Lāhijī (Bahā' al-Dīn M. b. Shaikh-'Alī) 1200
Lāhijī (Yūsuf) 1078[31]
"Lāhūtī" Tafrishī 1228
Lā'iq 'Alī Khān Sālār-Jang 1157
Lakzī 1336[10]
Lāl, or Lāl Dās, or Lāl Dayāl, (Bābā) 994 n.3
La'l Bēg 1065 (119)
Lāl Rām 470
Lāl-jī b. Sītal Parshād 711
Lāmi'ī *Futūḥ al-mujāhidīn* 956[5]
Land'haurah 692
Lār Muḥammad (Shāh) 1014[25]
Lārī ('Abd al-Ghafūr) 956 n.5, 1344
Lārī (Muṣliḥ al-Dīn) 116, 174, 1240
"Laṭīf" ('Abd al-Laṭīf) 620
Laṭīf (Abū 'l-Munīf M.) 1183 (26)
Laṭīf al-Dīn (Bābā) 985[22]
Laṭīfī ('Abd al-Kabīr b. Uwais) 416, 1168[6], 1355
Lawāsānī (M. Khān b. Fatḥ-'Alī Bēg) 1069
Lincoln (Abraham) 1179 (1)
Lisān Allāh (Shāh-M. Badakhshī) 18[29]
Lisān al-Mulk 153
Lisān al-Salṭanah 1299
Lōhārī 1042 n.5
Lucknow 1048[11]
Luqmān b. Ḥusain 'Āshūrī Ḥusainī 418, 1306

Luqmān b. ʻUthmān Khalīl Sulaimānī 1186 (6)
Lutf-ʻAlī Bēg " Ādhar " 868, 1337
Luṭf-ʻAlī Mīrzā Qājār 340
Luṭf-ʻAlī Shāh Maudūdī 1160 (3)
Luṭf Allāh [b. ?] Aḥmad 48 (3)
Luṭf Allāh Aḥmad 205 (5)
Luṭf Allāh Chūstī 981[27]
Luṭf Allāh Khān (M.) Asadābādī 1184 (33)
Luṭf Allāh M. " Muhandis " 788[31]
Mābarnābādī. See Mābīzhanābādī
Mābīzhanābādī (M. b. Aḥmad) 208, 1260
Machhlī-bandar 739[4], 1330
Madār (Shāh) 1006, 1032[4], 1052[30], 1055 (13)
Madāran 990 n.1
Mād'hau Sing'h (Mahārājah of Jaipūr) 519[26, 31]
Mād'haujī Sīnd'hiyah 737[3]
Madhmakīnī (?) (Qāsim b. M.) 1266[25]
Māfarrūkhī 349, 1292
" Maftūn." See ʻAbd al-Razzāq b. Najaf-Qulī
" Maftūn " (ʻAlī Mirzā) 1152
Maghnīsāwī (Maḥmūd) 191, 1255
Māh (M.) 134 ult.
Māh i Shaʻbān i Biyābānī 946[10]
Maḥabbat Khān b. Faiḍ-ʻAṭā Khān 473
Mahādajī Sīnd'hiyah 737[4]
Mahārat Khān 139, 1244
Mahārawī (Nūr-Muḥammad) 1038[6], 1045[23]
Maḥbūb Aḥmad 56 (3)
Maḥbūb Allāh (Maḥmūd) 1014[24]
Mahdawīs 759, l. 6 from foot, 1056 n.2, 1057[1], 1155[29]
Mahdī b. Abī Dharr Nirāqī 219, 1263
Mahdī (M.) b. Khalīl Aḥmad 1121
Mahdī ʻAlī " Imāmī " 707[5]
Mahdī ʻAlī Khān (Nawwāb Mīrzā) 1102[33]
Mahdī Badā'iʻ-nigār Tafrīshī 1228
Mahdī Dahajī 1286[1]
Mahdī Ḥusain Nāṣirī 923 (10)
Mahdī Khān b. M. Naṣīr Astarābādī 322, 1283
Mahdī Khān Ṣafawī 519 ; *Ḍiyā' al-ʻuyūn* 54, 1227 ; *Majmūʻah i Mīrzā-Mahdī-Khānī* 519 ; *Qaḍāyā-yi salāṭīn i Dakan* 738
Mahdī Malik-zādah 1288 (15)
Mahdī Mujtahidī 1288 (8), 1350, 1352
Mahdī Najafī Kashmīrī 205 (8)
" Mahdī Samad b. ʻAli 'l-Hādi " 493[3]
" Mahjūr " (S. M. Ḥusain) 340[20]
Maḥmūd b. ʻAbd Allāh Dizfūlī 1221
Maḥmūd b. ʻAbd Allāh Nīshāpūrī 747 ; *Ma'āthir i Quṭb-Shāhī i Maḥmūdī* 747 ; *Tārīkh i Turkumānīyah* 299
Maḥmūd b. Aḥmad al-Fāriyābī 161, 1250
Maḥmūd b. ʻAlī Ghujduwānī (apparently the same person as Kamāl al-Dīn Maḥmūd Andujānī 974) 973
Maḥmūd b. Amīr Walī 375
Maḥmūd b. Fatḥ-ʻAlī Shāh. See Maḥmūd Mīrzā Qājār
Maḥmūd b. Ḥasan Āmulī 958[21]
Maḥmūd b. Ibrāhīm Ḥusainī 395, 1303
Maḥmūd b. Khwānd-Amīr 304, 1279
Maḥmūd i Maḥmūd 1289 (20)
Maḥmūd b. M. Aqsarā'ī 267, 1272, 1305
Maḥmūd b. M. Ījī 211
Maḥmūd b. M. Rāwandī 175
Maḥmūd b. M. Tabrīzī 1222
Maḥmūd b. ʻUmdat [?] al-Jalīl 373, 1301
Maḥmūd b. ʻUthmān 1343[6]
Maḥmūd Andujānī (apparently the same person as Maḥmūd b. ʻAlī Ghujduwānī) 974
Maḥmūd Chirāgh i Dihlī 942 n.1
Maḥmūd " Dhakā " (" Dhukā " ?) 1187 (13)
Maḥmūd Farhād Muʻtamad 1350
Maḥmūd " Ilāhī " 815
Maḥmūd Kutubī [?] 277
Maḥmūd Maghnīsāwī 191, 1255
Maḥmūd Maḥbūb Allāh (Qāḍī) 1014[24]
Maḥmūd Malik-zādah 1306[4]
Maḥmūd al-Maulawī (Darwīsh) 938[34]
Maḥmūd Mīrzā Qājār 336, 1285 ; *Gulshan i Maḥmūd* 887 ; *Majmaʻ i Maḥmūd* 888[4] ; *Nuql i majlis* 888 ; *Safīnat al-Maḥmūd* 888 ; *Tārīkh i Ṣāḥib-qirānī* 336, 1285
Maḥmūd Mūsawī 399
Maḥmūd Mūyīnah-dūz 970 n.6
Maḥmūd Najmābādī 1351
Maḥmūd Nāṣir al-Dīn b. Jalāl al-Dīn Bukhārī 954[4]
Maḥmūd " Niẓāmī " Malik-zādah *Bāyazīd-nāmah* 411, 1306
Maḥmūd Qājār. See Maḥmūd Mīrzā Qājār
Maḥmūd Ṭarzī 1158 ; *Sirāj al-tawārīkh* 1305 ; *Siyāḥat-nāmah i sih qiṭʻah i rūy i zamīn* 1159 ; *Tārīkh i muḥārabah i Rūs u Zhāpān* 430[34]

Maḥmūd " Wāṣifī " 373, 1301
Maḥmūd Zarqānī 1054 (9), 1345[16]
Maḥmūdābād (M. Amīr Ḥasan Khān, Rājah of) 1158[14]
Maḥmūd-Jang (M. Khair al-Dīn Khān) 780[24]
Māh-sharaf Khānum " Mastūrah " 1300[8, 12]
Mahtāb Sing'h 676
Maibudī (Rashīd al-Dīn Aḥmad b. M.) 1190
Maistre de la Tour [" M. M. D. L. T."] 775
Maisūr 767–77, 1333–4
Majd al-Dīn Hamgar 918 (3)
Majd al-Dīn Khāṣṣah Shīrāzī 29 (11)
Majlisī (M. Bāqir b. M. Taqī) 196–8, 1132[2], 1256–7 ; *Biḥār al-anwār* 216 ; *Ḥayāt al-qulūb* 197, 1256 ; *Jalā' al-'uyūn* 198, 1257 ; *Khawāṣṣ i sūrahā-yi Qur'ān* 54 ; *Tadhkirat al-a'immah* 198 ; *Tafsīr i Āyat al-Kursī* 32 (37), 1213[25]
Majlisī (M. Taqī b. Maqṣūd 'Alī) 1132[1]
Majlisī (Raḍī al-Dīn M. b. M. Naṣīr) 1256
Majnūn (Mīr) 44[2]
Makanpūr 1006[2], 1052[28]
Makhdūm i A'ẓam (i.e. Aḥmad b. Jalāl al-Dīn Khwājagī Kāsānī) 973[10] [according to the *Tārīkh i Rāqimī*, Rosen Institut p. 128[5], he died in 949/1542–3]
Makhdūm i Jahāniyān 944, 954[3], 971[5], 1343
" Makīn " (M. Fākhir) 874 n.2.
Makk'han La'l 755
al-Makkī (Abū Ṭālib) 1258[9]
Makkī (Ḥusain) *Amīr i Kabīr u Īrān* 1349 ; *Mukhtaṣarī az zindagānī i siyāsī i Sulṭān Aḥmad Shāh i Qājār* 1288 ; *Tārīkh i bīst-sālah i Īrān* 1291
Makkī (M. b. Ja'far) 183, 1254
Maklī hill 656[4], 1028[3], 1031[2], 1324 n.
Malcolm (John) *History of Persia* (1) 242 (7), 328 (7)

(1) A translation (*Tārīkh i Hind*) of Sir J. Malcolm's " *History of India* " appears in the catalogue of Persian books in the Library of the India Office, but one of the volumes so described (306.30.E.2) proves on inspection to be the *Tārīkh i Īrān* and an examination of the others would doubtless yield a similar result.

Malik al-Kuttāb Shīrāzī. See M. b. M. Rafī'
Malik al-Tujjār (Ḥājj Ḥusain Āqā) 1342 n.3
Malik al-Tujjār (Khalīl Khān Qazwīnī) 1067[6]
Mālik b. Anas 1179 (2)
Malik-zādah (Mahdī) 1288 (15)
Malik-zādah (Maḥmūd " Niẓāmī ") 1306[4]
Malkah 674, 1325
Malkum (Farīdūn) 1308[4]
Mālmīrī (M. Ṭāhir) 1294
Mālwah 734–5
Ma'mūrī (1) (Abū 'l-Faḍl) 594, 1318
Māndū 727[4]
Mānekjī Līmjī Hōshang Hātaryā 239n., 240[2], 246[21], 345[11], 1268 penult.
Manērī (Sharaf al-Dīn) 1049 n.2
Mangalkōt 1050[17]
Mānī (Manes) 1185 (42)
Manī Bēgam, incorrect spelling for Munnī Bēgam, 725[6], 1329
Mānik Chand 692
Mānik-Shāh Bābūjī 1332[27]
Mankubirnī (Jalāl al-Dīn) 1088[17], 1349[4]
Mann Allāh b. 'Alī Allāh M. Ḥusainī 976
Mannū (Mīr) 618 n.2
Mannū Lāl b. Bahādur Sing'h 643
Manshūr Garakānī (M. 'A.) 1291 (3), 1307[25]
Manṣūr b. Chānd Muḥammad 1014
Manṣūr 'Alī (S. M.) *Ma'ārif i shattā* 1187 ; *Niẓām al-ansāb* 1182
Manṣūr 'Alī Khān Nuṣrat-Jang 721[26]
Manṭiq al-Mulk (Ḥasan Khān) 242 (8)
Maqṣūd 'Alī Tabrīzī 1108, 1350
Maqṣūdābād 643[2]
Marāṭ'hās 760–5, 864[24], 1333
Mardān (Shāh : or Shāh-Mardān ?) 1062 (89)
Mardān 'Alī Khān " Mubtalā " 829
Marghīlān 390[15]
Marhaṭah. For the spelling see 1333
Maṛiyāhū 1121[11]
Ma'rūf Bhakkarī 1092 n.1
Ma'rūf Karkhī 1031 n.6, 1051[31]

(1) For this *nisbah* see *Ma'āthir al-umarā'* iii p. 376, where it is stated that Muẓaffar Khān Mīr 'Abd al-Razzāq Ma'mūrī was by descent a Saiyid of Ma'mūrābād " *kih mauḍi'ī-st az Najaf i Ashraf* ".

Marw 1148[4]
Mashhadī (M.) 1263
Mashkūkī (Bihishtī) 420
" Mashriqī " (Bhawānī Parshād) 1186 (7)
" Mashriqī " (Nūr al-Ḥaqq) 441, 1309
Mashshāṭī (Ḥusām b. M.) 1258[29]
" Masīḥ " (Sa'd Allāh Kairānawī) 196, 1256
Masītā (Mirzā) 479
" Mast " (Dhū 'l-Faqār 'Alī Khān) 885
" Mastūrah " (Māh-sharaf Khānum) 1300[8, 12]
Mas'ūd (Mīrzā) 1161 (11)
Mas'ūd b. 'Alī al-Ṣarrāf 160
Mas'ūd b. Sa'd b. Salmān 922[18]
Mas'ūd 'Alī Ilāhābādī 1047[4]
Mas'ūd Ganj i Shakar 941 n.4, 944[1], 987[2]
Mas'ūd Ghāzī (Saiyid) 1060n.
Mas'ūd Ghāzī (Sālār) 1006, 1060 (64)
Mas'ūd Ghāzī (Saiyid Sālār, presumably identical with one of the preceding) 1026[27]
al-Mas'ūdī *Murūj al-dhahab* 156 (10)
Mas'ūdī b. 'Uthmān Kūhistānī 110
Masulipatam 739[4], 1330
Ma'ṣūm (M.), i.e. Sharaf al-Dīn Ḥusain 974 n.5
Ma'ṣūm (M.) b. Aḥmad Sirhindī 991[32], 1024[7]
Ma'ṣūm b. Ḥasan b. Ṣāliḥ 582, 1317
Ma'ṣūm (M.) b. Khwājagī Iṣfahānī 313, 1280 ult., 1281
Ma'ṣūm (M.) " Nāmī " 651, 1324
Ma'ṣūm (M.) Sharīf Iṣfahānī 1063 (99)
Ma'ṣūm 'Alī b. Raḥmat-'Alī Ni'mat-Allāhī Shīrāzī 1051
Mat'hurā 692[21]
Matw [vocalisation ?] (Bahā' al-Dīn) Kashmīrī 1064 (110)
Maudūd Lālā (?) (Rashīd al-Dīn) 1059 (55)
Maulūdī era 772 n.1
" Mauzūn " 704
Māzandarān 359–62, 1298, 1353
Māzandarānī (M. Ṣūfī) 806
Mazārī 1039[19]
" Maẓhar " (Shams al-Dīn Ḥabīb Allāh) 1033[11], 1035[10]
Maẓhar al-Dīn Fārūqī 1346[12]
Maẓhar al-Dīn M. b. Bahā' al-Dīn 'Alī 1227[2]
Maẓhar al-Ḥaqq *Saiyid al-sādāt* 233 (59)
Maẓhar al-Ḥaqq [possibly the title of the work not the author's name] *Tafsīr i Maẓhar al-Ḥaqq* 30, 1211
Maẓhar al-Ḥaqq (M. Fāḍil) Akbarābādī 1004
Maẓhar 'Alī Khān " Wilā " 514
Māziyār 1348 antepenult.
Midḥat Bahārī Ḥusāmī 935[21]
Miftāḥ al-Mulk (M. b. Yūsuf) 1249[4]
Mihr 'Alī Shāh 1061 (72)
Mihrpazd 1190[29]
Mīm 952
Mīnā Lak'hnawī 983 n.3, 1066 (123)
Minhāj [al-Dīn] Jūzjānī 68, 1229–30
Minūchihr Khān 902[20], 1103[10]
Mīnuwī (Mujtabā) 1342 n.2, 1348
Mīr (Khwājah) 228 (8)
Mīr (Miyāṅ) 998[7]
" Mīr " (M. Taqī) 849
Mīr Āghā 46 (19)
Mīr-'Ālam 751, 1331–2
Mīr Dād 396[7], 982[29] (same person ?)
Mīr-Jumlah (Mīr M. Sa'īd) 582[30]
Mīr-Jumlah Bahādur Tarkhān (S. 'Ubaid Allāh Khān) 32 (48), 33 (57)
Mīr Khān, Ṣūbah-dār of Kābul, 585[4]
Mīr Khān b. Zain al-Dīn Jāmī 213
Mīr Khwānd 92, 1236–7
Mīr [i ?] Khwurd 941[6] (cf. 1343[29])
Mīrak (M.) 237
Mīran Lāl 1093
Mīran-jān (1) (M.) Ilāhābādī 902–3; *Iẓhār al-sa'ādah* 223; *Khāzin al-shu'arā'* 903
Mīrzā Bēg b. Ḥasan Junābadī 313
Mīrzā Jān 932[33]
Mīrzā Khān [var. Jān] Jāland'harī 1259[12]
Mīrzā-zādah 270[16]
Miyāṅ (pronounced also Mīyāṅ) 998 n.1
Miyāṅ (Shāh) 1056 (23)
Miyāṅ-jī(w) 998[25], 1010 n.1, 1019[29]
Mōhan (Lālah) 668
Mōhan La'l " Anīs " 874, 1337
Mōhan Sing'h 733
Moideen Peerzadah 744
Mongols 260–77, 1272–3
Mōtī Rām Guwāliyārī 736
MTW [vocalisation ?] (Bahā' al-Dīn) Kashmīrī 1064 (110)
Mu'aiyir al-Mamālik 1289 (22)
Mu'allim i Yazdī 277
Mu'aẓẓam Shāh (Pīr) 396
Mu'aẓẓamābād = Gōrak'hpūr 702

(1) Mīran, with a short a in the second syllable.

Mubārak Allāh " Wāḍiḥ " 601
Mubārak-Shāh (M. b. Manṣūr b. Sa'īd) 1164
Mubāriz al-Daulah Pīr Ibrāhīm Khān 661
Mubāriz al-Mulk (Ḍābiṭ-Jang) 759 (3)
al-Mubarqa' (Mūsā) 228 (7)
Mubīn (M.). See M. Mubīn
" Mubtalā " (Ghulām-Muḥyī 'l-Dīn) 883
" Mubtalā " (Mardān 'Alī Khān) 829
Mudīr Ḥallāj (Ḥ) 348
Mufaḍḍal b. Sa'd Māfarrūkhī 349, 1292
Mufaḍḍal Khān *Tārīkh i Mufaḍḍalī* 135; *Tīmūr-nāmah i Mufaḍḍalī* 517
Mufīd (M.). See M. Mufīd
Mughanniyān 1183 (25)
Mughūlistān 274[17]
Muhallab b. M. b. Shādī 67[9]
Muḥammad *Manāqib i Bukhārā* 387 (7)
Muḥammad *Mukhtaṣar fī bayān tajwīd al-Qur'ān* 46 (17)
Muḥammad (Ḥājjī) *Tajwīd i Muḥammadī* 47 (24)
Muḥammad (Mīrzā, fl. 1126/1714) *Jannāt al-firdaus* 135, 1243
Muḥammad (Mīrzā, fl. 1920) *Abraham Lincoln* 1179; *Aḥwāl i Kristōfar Kulambas* 1160 (1); *Dūstdārān i bashar* 1181; *Ṭulū' i tamaddun* 157
M. b. 'Abbādī (?) Kāzarūnī 935[33]
M. b. 'Abd al-Jabbār 'Utbī 250
M. b. 'Abd al-Jalīl Bilgrāmī 712, 1329
M. b. 'Abd al-Jalīl Ṣā [di ?] qī 45
M. b. 'Abd al-Jalīl Samarqandī 371, 1300
M. b. 'Abd al-Karīm Astarābādī 177
M. b. 'Abd al-Karīm al-Khaṭīb 1342
M. b. 'Abd Allāh Bukhārī 47 (32)
M. b. 'Abd Allāh Nīshāpūrī (probably = Maḥmūd b. 'Abd Allāh Nīshāpūrī) 299, 747
M. b. 'Abd Allāh b. Maḥmūd 39 (3), 1217
M. b. 'Abd Allāh b. 'Umar 178
M. b. 'Abd al-Wahhāb Qazwīnī 1176
M. b. Abī Bakr Jāmī Balkhī 977[7]
M. b. Abī 'l-Qāsim *Malfūẓāt i Aḥmad i Maghribī* 952–3
M. b. Abī 'l-Qāsim Baqqālī Khwārazmī 35, 1215
M. b. Abī 'l-Qāsim, Kalāntar of Fārs, 1349
M. b. Abī Zaid Warāmīnī 211, 1261
M. b. 'Adnān Surkhakatī 431, 1308
M. [Bēg] b. Aḥmad [Bēg Mīrzā] 368[7]
M. b. Aḥmad (Munshī). See Muḥammad (Mīrzā)
M. b. A. Dausī Zawārī (Sabzawārī ?) 55, 1227
M. b. Aḥmad al-Ḥasanī [or rather al-Ḥusainī, al-Munshī' al-Baghdādī] (1) 1150
M. b. Aḥmad Kārtānī (?) 178
M. b. Aḥmad Mābarnābādī [or rather Mābīzhanābādī (?)] 208[18], 1260
M. b. Aḥmad Mustaufī Harawī 208, 1260
M. b. Aḥmad Nasawī 1088, 1349
M. b. Aḥmad Nīshāpūrī 4 ult., 1191–2
M. b. Aḥmad Sinānī 40[14]
M. b. 'Alī (Maẓhar al-Dīn) 1227
M. b. 'Alī Akbar Khurāsānī 1264
Muḥammad [or Aḥmad ?] b. 'Alī Anṣārī 1109[12]
M. b. 'Alī Ḥusainī 48 (5)
M. b. 'Alī . . . Ibn Bābawaih 209, 1260
M. b. 'Alī b. M. Ḥusainī 1224[7]
M. b. 'Alī Kāshānī (i.e. Taqī Kāshī) 803
M. b. 'Alī Khaṭībī Zauzanī 1106[28]
M. b. 'Alī Rāwandī 256
M. b. 'Alī Samarqandī 1086
M. b. 'Alī Shabānkāra'ī 84
M. b. As'ad Dawānī 1277
M. b. As'ad Tustarī 162, 1250[22]
M. b. Asad Allāh Māzandarānī 1222
M. b. Bahā' al-Dīn Jūrīdī 45 (7), 1223
M. b. Bāqir Harawī 1252[6]
M. b. Bud'h Uwaisī Jaunpūrī 1056 (21)
M. b. Burhān al-Dīn Samarqandī (= M. Qāḍī) 966, 973[21]
M. b. Faḍl Allāh Mūsawī 89, 1236
M. b. Fatḥ-'Alī Bēg Lawāsānī 1069
M. b. Ghāzī 932[27]
M. b. Ghulām-Nabī [Bilgrāmī] 1115[27]
M. b. Ḥabīb Allāh Iṣfahānī 194
M. b. Ḥaidar 'Alī Warnūsfādarānī 1215
M. b. Ḥasan 'Alī Kūsārī 45, 1223[11]
M. b. Ḥasan Daidūzamī 161[27]
M. b. al-Ḥasan b. Isfandiyār 359, 1298

(1) Cf. *Itinerary of al-Munshi al-Baghdady . . . written in* 1237 *A.H.* = 1822 *A.D.* . . . *Translated* [into Arabic] *from the Persian original by Abbas al-Azzawi* [al-'Azzāwī], Baghdād 1367/1948. This work, presumably identical with the *risālah* preserved in Leningrad, is entirely geographical.

M. b. Ḥasan Iṣfahānī (al-Fāḍil al-Hindī) 217, 1200, 1262
M. b. al-Ḥasan Manduwī 984
M. b. Ḥasan M. 1038[3]
M. b. Ḥasan Sanglajī 1207
M. b. al-Ḥusain Baihaqī 252, 1271
M. b. Ḥusain [b. ?] Luṭf Allāh 101
M. b. Ḥusain Kaidarī 181
M. b. Ḥusain Muʻīnī 1192[2]
M. b. Ḥusain Qazwīnī 975
M. b. Ḥusain Sājī 5
M. b. Ḥusain Sammākī Astarābādī 17, 1198
M. b. Ibrāhīm 358
M. b. Idrīs Bidlīsī 71, 416, 1306
M. b. ʻĪsā al-Tirmidhī 174, 1252
M. b. Isḥāq 172, 1251
M. b. Isḥāq (Shams al-Dīn) Qādirī 973
M. b. Ismāʻīl Khwānsārī 1258[25]
M. b. Jaʻfar Makkī 183, 1254
M. b. Jaʻfar Narshakhī 369, 1300
M. b. Jalāl Shāhī Riḍawī 990
M. b. Jarīr. See Ṭabarī
M. b. al-Khafīf al-Shīrāzī 1053[8]
M. b. Khalīl Qūnawī 412 n.1
M. b. Khātūn ʻĀmilī 51[2], 1226[11]
M. b. Khāwand-Shāh 92, 1236–7
M. b. Khwājagī 29 (6), 1209[30]
M. b. Luṭf Allāh b. Abī Saʻīd (?) 928[20]
M. b. Mahdī Ḥusainī 1222
M. b. Maḥmūd Khāwand-Shāh 195
M. b. Maḥmūd Makhzūmī 181, 1253
M. b. Maḥmūd Nīshāpūrī 4, 1191–2
M. b. Maḥmūd Samarqandī 40, 1217
M. b. Maḥmūd Shahrazūrī 1107, 1350
M. b. Maḥmūd Ṭārumī 1196
M. b. Maḥmūd Ṭihrānī (ʻAṣṣār) 1206
M. b. Manṣūr b. Saʻīd (surnamed Mubārak-Shāh) 1164
M. b. al-Mu'aiyad Baghdādī 260, 1272
M. b. Mubārak Kirmānī 941
M. b. Mubārak Qazwīnī 793[6]
M. b. M. (Altī-Parmaq) 188, 1254
M. b. M. ʻAlī (Abū Manṣūr) 31 (33), 1212
M. b. M. Aqsarā'ī 7, 1192
M. b. M. ʻAufī 781
M. b. M. Dārābī 817
M. b. M. Ḥāfiẓī Bukhārī (M. Pārsā) 7, 1193
M. b. M. b. Naṣr (Ḥāfiẓ al-Dīn Bukhārī) 31 (22), 1215
M. b. M. . . . b. al-Niẓām 257
M. b. M. (ʻImād al-Dīn) al-Iṣfahānī 255
M. b. M. Kāẓim (" Nadīm ") 333, 1284
M. b. M. Naṣīr Majlisī 1256 antepenult.
M. b. M. Mustaufī Harawī 208[10], 1260
M. b. M. Rafīʻ Malik al-Kuttāb Shīrāzī 492 ; *Iksīr al-tawārīkh* 210 ; *Mir'āt al-zamān* 432 ; *Tadhkirat al-khawātīn* 916 ; *Tārīkh i Ingilistān* 429 ; *Tārīkh i qadīm i Yūnān* 429 ; *Zīnat al-zamān* 492
M. b. M. Sabzawārī 54, 1227
M. b. M. Ṣadrī 54, 1227
M. b. M. Sarfarāzī 55[1], 1227
M. b. M. Taqī Sārū'ī 332
M. b. M. al-Yaʻmarī (Ibn Saiyid al-Nās) 178, 1253
M. b. M. Zauzanī 38
M. b. al-Munawwar 929
M. b. Muʻtamad Khān 141, 1244 ; *ʻIbrat-nāmah* 606 ; *Tārīkh i Muḥammadī* 141, 1244
M. b. Pīr M. Fārūqī Bilgrāmī 199[17]
M. b. Raḥmat Allāh (Abū 'l-Maʻālī) 977
M. b. Rustam b. Qubād. See M. b. Muʻtamad Khān
M. b. Ṣādiq b. Mahdī 1134[27]
M. b. Shaikh-ʻAlī Lāhijī 1200
M. b. Sulaimān Tunakābunī 1133, 1354
M. b. Ṭāhir Manṭiqī Sijistānī 1104, 1350
M. b. ʻUmar al-Wāqidī 173
M. b. Yaḥyā Bashāghirī 160, 1250
M. b. Yaḥyā Tādifī 972
M. b. Yaʻqūb Fīrūzābādī 180, 1253
M. b. Yār-Muḥammad Kōlawī 1022
M. b. Yūsuf Ḥusainī. See Gēsū-darāz
M. b. Yūsuf Iṣfahānī 45 (4)
M. b. Yūsuf Miftāḥ al-Mulk 1249[4]
M. b. Yūsuf al-Ẓahīr 40
M. b. Zabardast Khān 1093
M. b. Zakarīyā' Rāzī 1351[14]
M. b. Zufar b. ʻUmar 370[4], 1300
M. ʻAbbās Khān Afghānī 1093
M. ʻAbbās " Rifʻat " Shīrwānī 226, 1265 ; *Bāgh i chahār-chaman* 738 ; *Qalā'id al-jawāhir fī aḥwāl al-Bawāhir* 1083 ; *Sulṭān-nāmah* 421 ; *Tārīkh i Āl i amjād* 227 ; *Tārīkh i Qaiṣar i Rūm* 421
M. ʻAbd al-Ḥakīm Dihlawī 26
M. ʻAbd al-Ḥamīd Aʻẓamgaṛhī 174[4], 174[18]
M. ʻAbd al-Karīm ʻAlawī 402, 1304
M. ʻAbd al-Qādir b. Ḥasan Ḥusainī Qādirī 1266, 1267

M. ʻAbd al-Qādir Khān Āqah Bāsh Qājār 528
M. ʻAbd al-Raḥmān (ʻAbd Allāh Mushtāq) 203
M. ʻAbd al-Rashīd Kairānawī 1019
M. ʻAbd al-Rashīd Ẓuhūr al-Islām 1006[13]
M. ʻAbd al-Razzāq b. ʻAlī Aḥmad Khān 1084
M. ʻAbd al-Shakūr b. Shēr ʻAlī 1120[5]
M. ʻAbduh 1209 antepenult.
M. ʻĀbid 1026
M. Abū 'l-Ḥasan Farīdābādī 1184 (35)
M. Abū 'l-Ḥayāt Qādirī P'hulwārī 1040
M. Abū Turāb Riḍawī 202
M. "Adā'ī" Shīrāzī 417
M. Afḍal "Afḍal" 666
M. Afḍal Bukhārī 282, 1274
M. Afḍal Ḥusainī 1242
M. Afḍal "Sarkhwush" 821
M. Āghā Jān 528
M. Aḥsan (Muftī) 41
M. Aḥsan Allāh Khān (Ḥakīm) 528[2]
M. Aḥsan Allāh Khān "Thāqib" 675
M. Aḥsan "Ījād" 604; 748, 1331
M. Akbar ʻAlī Shāh Dihlawī 1057 (36)
M. Akram Barāsawī 1019
M. Akram Khān 1084
M. Āl i Ḥasan Amrōhawī 1112
Muḥammad al-Dīn Qādirī Lāhaurī 1060 (65)
M. ʻAlī (S.) Professor, Niẓām's College, 1284[7]
M. ʻAlī b. Ḥusain Qummī 349, 1291
M. ʻAlī b. Jaʻfar Yazdī 1125
M. ʻAlī b. M. Fāḍil 221
M. ʻAlī b. M. Ḥasan Hindī 1132
M. ʻAlī b. M. Ḥusain b. ʻAlī b. Bahā' al-Dīn 349, 1291
M. ʻAlī b. M. Qāsim 1162 (25)
M. ʻAlī b. M. Ṣādiq Nīshāpūrī Burhānpūrī 137, 1244
M. ʻAlī b. M. Zawārī *Ma'āthir al-Bāqirīyah* 891
M. ʻAlī b. Mūsā Kāẓimī 224
M. ʻAlī b. Ramaḍān ʻAlī Ṣadrpūrī 1041 n.1
M. ʻAlī Akbar 1040[11]
M. ʻAlī "Bahār" Iṣfahānī 902, 1338
M. ʻAlī Bihbahānī 705
M. ʻAlī Burhānpūrī 137, 1244
M. ʻAlī "Ḥazīn". See "Ḥazīn".
M. ʻAlī Karbalā'ī 51, 1225[25]
M. ʻAlī Kashmīrī Lak'hnawī 1134
M. ʻAlī Kātib i Ṣafawī 884
M. ʻAlī Khairābādī 1058 (48)
M. ʻAlī Khān 1188 (22)
M. ʻAli Khān Anṣārī *Baḥr al-mawwāj* 144, 1245; *Tārīkh i Aḥmad-Shāhī* 621; *Ta'līf i Muḥammadī* 202; *Tārīkh i Muẓaffarī* 522
M. ʻAlī Khān "Furūghī". See "Furūghī".
M. ʻAlī Khān "Nāṣiḥ" 1349[5]
M. ʻAlī Khān Nawwāb i Daulah 233 (60)
M. ʻAlī Khān "Surūsh" 1183 (30)
M. ʻAlī Khān "Tarbiyat" 1111, 1352
M. ʻAlī Muẓaffarābādī 1348[26]
M. ʻAlī Qādirī 1214[2]
M. ʻAlī Sadīd al-Salṭanah 1307[21]
M. ʻAlī [Ṣadrpūrī] 1040
M. ʻAlī Sāmānī 949
M. ʻAlī-Shāh Khairābādī 1056 (24)
M. ʻAlī "Ulfat" 1063 (98)
M. ʻAlī Zawārī *Ma'āthir al-Bāqirīyah* 891
M. ʻAlīm b. Jān Muḥammad 134
M. ʻAlīm b. M. Mūsā Ilāhābādī 220
M. Amān b. M. Yūsuf 1024
M. Amīn b. Abī'l-Ḥusain Qazwīnī 566
M. Amīn b. Daulat M. Bālakī (?) 125
M. Amīn b. Khalīl Qūnawī 412
M. Amīn b. Mīrzā Zamān Bukhārī 378
M. Amīn Badakhshī 991
M. Amīn Balkhī 682 n.
M. Amīn "Ḥashrī" Tabrīzī 982
M. Amīn Ṣadr Kāshgharī 382
M. Amīn Ṣiddīqī ʻAlawī Ḥusainī 19
M. Amīr Ḥasan Madārī Fanṣūrī 1052
M. Anwar Shāh (**1**) 57, (**2**) 1162 (26)
M. ʻĀqil 1038[6], 1044 n.4
M. ʻĀrif b. M. Sharīf Arzanat-al-Rūmī 393[4]
M. ʻĀrif Qandahārī 541
M. Arshad b. M. Rashīd ʻUthmānī Jaunpūrī 1015[26]
M. Ashraf Khān b. Dūṅdē Khān 646
M. ʻAskarī Bilgrāmī 1183 (28)
M. Aslam b. M. Ḥafīẓ Parasrūrī 140, 1244
M. Aslam "Munʻimī" 684, 1325
M. Auliyā Nā'iṭī 1187 (15), 1334[26]
M. Awwābī Aqṭāshī 423[18]
M. Aʻẓam b. Khair al-Zamān Kashmīrī 683, 1325
M. Aʻẓam b. M. Ṣāliḥ Asadī Hāshimī 660
M. Aʻẓam T'hattawī 1028
M. ʻAẓīm al-Dīn DLWY 766
M. ʻAẓīm al-Dīn Ḥusainī Shīrāzī Tattawī 657

M. Badī' (Rashīd Khān) 573
M. Badī' b. Mīrzā Badakhshī 387 (10)
M. Badī' b. M. Sharīf Samarqandī 825
M. Bakhtāwar Khān. See Bakhtāwar Khān 132, 517, 1012, 1243
M. Baqā (friend of W. Yule) 1146
M. Baqā Sahāranpūrī *Āyinah i bakht* (?) 132; *Mir'āt al-'ālam* 132, 1243; *Mir'āt i jahān-numā* 133, 1243; *Riyāḍ al-auliyā'* 1012
M. Baqā Wārith 232 (44)
M. Bāqī (Khwājah) 989[1], 1002[27]
M. Bāqir (Ḥājī) 1299
M. Bāqir b. M. Akmal Bihbahānī 1132[3]
M. Bāqir b. M. 'Alī 973
M. Bāqir b. M. Ismā'īl Māzandarānī Ṭihrānī 1048, 1345[6]
M. Bāqir b. M. Taqī. See Majlisī.
M. Bāqir Afṣaḥ Tabrīzī 130, 1242
M. Bāqir 'Alī Khān 150
M. Bāqir Bawānātī 1204, 1212[8]
M. Bāqir Burqa'ī 1341
M. Bāqir Dāmād 1136[23]
M. Bāqir Kamara'ī 1208
M. Bāqir Kujūrī 1048, 1345[6]
M. Bāqir Māzandarānī 1048, 1345[6]
M. Bāqir Mūsawī Ḥusainī 891[16]
M. Bāqir Nawwāb Lāhijānī 1203
M. Bāqir Yazdī 1210 antepenult.
M. Barārī Ummī b. M. Jamshēd 1242
M. Bashīr Lak'hnawī 648
M. Bēg b. Aḥmad Bēg Mīrzā 368[7]
M. Bhuwah (S.) 991[2]
M. Bihāmad-Khānī 90
M. Bukhārī 387 (3)
M. Būlāq Dihlawī 1013
M. Burhān al-Dīn Khān (S.) 1057 (35)
M. Dhākir 'Alī b. 'Abd Allāh Qādirī 1050[12]
M. Dihdār " Fānī " 957[19]
M. Dihlawī (S.) 58 (8)
M. Ḍiyā' al-Raḥmān Shāhqulīpūrī 1050
M. Fāḍil Akbarābādī 1004
M. Fāḍil Khān " Rāwī " Garrūsī 886, 1337
M. Faḍl *Wāsiṭat al-'iqd* 599 (15)
M. Faḍl i 'Aẓīm. See Faḍl i 'Aẓīm " 'Aẓīm " [Khairābādī] 646, 689, 1322
M. Faḍl i Imām Khairābādī 252[6]
M. Faiḍ Allāh 753, 1246 [and 739 (*Khizānah i Rasūl-Khānī*)]
M. Faiḍ-Bakhsh b. Ghulām-Sarwar 706
M. Faiḍ-Bakhsh Aurangābādī 749
M. Fakhr al-Dīn Ḥusain 528
M. Farhād Qandahārī 34 (73)
M. Farīd al-Dīn Khān 759 (9)
M. Fidā-'Alī " Ṭālib " 448[26]
M. Ghauth b. M. Fā'iq 649 (4)
M. Ghauth Guwāliyārī 834 n.7
M. Ghauth Khān " A'ẓam " 897
Muḥammad Ghauth Qādirī 1056 (22)
M. Ghauthī b. Ḥasan Shaṭṭārī 984
M. Ghulām-Sarwar Lāhaurī 1043
M. Ḥabīb Allāh Akbarābādī. See Ḥabīb Allāh Akbarābādī
M. Hādī (Kāmwar Khān) 459, 517
M. Hādī b. Abī 'l-Ḥasan al-Sharīf al-Nā'īnī [= M. H. N. mentioned below ?] 235 (8)
M. Hādī b. M. Mahdī Ḥusainī Ṣafawī. See Mahdī Khān Ṣafawī
M. Hādī Nā'īnī [= M. H. b. Abī 'l-Ḥasan al-Sharīf al-N. mentioned above ?] 172 (49), 230 (26)
M. Ḥaḍrat (Pīr) 205 (11)
M. Ḥafīẓ Jāland'harī 555, 1316
M. Ḥaidar *Tārīkh i Kashmīr* 687
M. Ḥaidar Dūghlāt 273, 1273
M. Ḥakīm Amīnā " Ātashī " 743
M. Ḥakīm Khān Tūrā 388
M. Ḥasan 32 (39)
M. Ḥasan (S.) 32 (44)
M. Ḥasan b. 'Abd al-Raḥmān Mujaddidī 1051
M. Ḥasan b. Ma'ṣūm Qazwīnī (¹) 221, 1263
M. Ḥasan b. M. 'Alī ('Alī M. Khān) 729
M. Ḥasan Amrōhawī 26, 1204
M. Ḥasan Āqā Khān Ḥusainī 1266[27]
M. Ḥasan Harawī 1297
M. Ḥasan Khān " Badī' " 428 (6)
M. Ḥasan Khān Marāghī 154, 1248; *Ā'īnah i Sikandarī* 1308; *Durar al-tījān* 246; *Ḥujjat al-sa'ādah* 225; *Khairāt ḥisān* 1163; *al-Ma'āthir wa-'l-āthār* 1174; *Maṭla' al-shams* 356; *Mir'āt al-buldān i Nāṣirī* 344; *Rūz-nāmah* 344–5; *al-Tadwīn fī aḥwāl jibāl Sharwīn* 362; *Tārīkh i Farānisah* 429; *Tārīkh i inkishāf i Yangī Dunyā* 429; *Tārīkh i Īrān* 1269; *Tārīkh i muntaẓam i Nāṣirī* 154
M. Ḥasan Khān Qājār 322[24]
M. Hāshim b. 'Abd al-Ghafūr Sind'hī

(¹) He died in 1240/1824–5 according to *Ṭarā'iq al-ḥaqā'iq* III p. 153 ult. (Cf. *Rauḍāt al-jannāt* p. 180.)

(d. 1174/1760–1: see Raḥmān ʿAlī p. 253) 1259 (35)
M. Hāshim b. Ismāʿīl Shīrāzī 1201
M. Hāshim b. M. Mīrzā 320, 1282
M. Hāshim b. M. Qāsim Badakhshānī 987
M. Hāshim Khāfī (Khāfī Khān) 460, 1310
M. Ḥusain b. ʿAbd [al-Ḥusain ?] al-Iṣfahānī 1144
M. Ḥusain b. ʿAbd al-Salām 233 (65), 1267 antepenult.
M. Ḥusain b. ʿAlī Riḍā Garakānī 1178 n.5
M. Ḥusain b. Bāqī Bukhārī *Qiṣaṣ i Ḥusainī* 387 (9); *Tadhkirat al-shuhadā'* 1267 (63*b*)
M. Ḥusain b. Karam-ʿAlī Iṣfahānī 148
M. Ḥusain b. M. ʿAlī Kirmānī 222
M. Ḥusain b. M. Hādī ʿAqīlī Shīrāzī 965[19], 1344[14]
M. Ḥusain b. M. Mahdī ("Furūghī") 240, 249, 1269
M. Ḥusain b. M. Masʿūd Murādābādī 1044
M. Ḥusain b. M. Riḍā *Rauḍat al-auliyā'* 1060 (67)
M. Ḥusain b. M. Riḍā *Wasīlat al-najāt* 234 (70)
M. Ḥusain b. M. Riḍawī Ṭihrānī 171 (36)
M. Ḥusain [b. M. Sirāj al-Dīn] *al-ʿAjā'ib* 1185; *Armaghān i aḥbāb* 1180
M. Ḥusain [b.] ʿUmar [b.] . . . ʿAbd al-Salām Harawī 233 (65), 1267 antepenult.
M. Ḥusain "Āyatī" Khurāsānī 1353
M. Ḥusain "Āzād" 1180 n.2
M. Ḥusain "Giryān" Shahrābī 1184 (40)
M. Ḥusain Khān 1188 (22)
M. Ḥusain Khān b. Bāyram ʿAlī Khān 1148
M. Ḥusain Khān "Furūghī" b. M. Mahdī (not M. ʿAlī) 240, 249, 1269
M. Ḥusain Khān Niẓām al-Daulah 1338[7]
M. Ḥusain "Mahjūr" 340
M. Ḥusain Nā'īnī 233 (63)
M. Ḥusain Qarīb Garakānī 1178 n.5
M. Ḥusain al-Sharīf b. M. ʿAlī Kirmānī 222
M. Ḥusain Tafrishī 313
M. Ḥusainī Madanī Aurangābādī 1183 (23)
M. Ibrāhīm [i.e. probably M. I. Zubairī, for whom see below] 1060 (66)
M. Ibrāhīm b. M. Ḥusain Ardalānī 369
M. Ibrāhīm b. M. Taqī 232 (49)
M. Ibrāhīm b. Zain al-ʿĀbidīn Naṣīrī 319
M. Ibrāhīm "Jauharī" Harawī (not Marwī) 234 (66), 1268
M. Ibrāhīm Shīrāzī 430
M. Ibrāhīm Zubairī 745, probably also 1060 (66)
M. Iḥsān b. Ḥasan Aḥmad 1023
M. Ikrām al-Dīn b. Niẓām al-Dīn 221, 1263[17]
M. Ikrām ʿAlī Qalandar 1061 (76)
M. Irtaḍā ʿAlī Khān 1038, 1344 ult.
M. Isḥāq (Ishaque) 921
M. Islām 976[9]
M. Ismāʿīl Khān "Abjadī" 778, 1334
M. Ismāʿīl Khān Zand Tūsirkānī 246
M. Jaʿfar *Silk al-bayān* 46 (21)
M. Jaʿfar b. Mīrzā M. Khān *Majmūʿah i Jaʿfarī* 1102
M. Jaʿfar Badr i ʿĀlam 1138[4]
M. Jaʿfar Khān Khūrmūjī 343; *Āthār i Jaʿfarī* 352; *Ḥaqā'iq al-akhbār i Nāṣirī* 344
M. Jaʿfar Shāmlū 398
M. Jaʿfar Shīrāzī 50
M. Jān 1102[28]
M. Jān "Qudsī" 568, 1316
M. Jaunpūrī 1056 (21) and (28)
M. Jawād Ḥusain (S.) 1114
M. Kabīr b. Ismāʿīl Ḥaziyā (?) 516
M. Kalb-ʿAlī Khān 1156, 1184 (38)
M. Karāmat ʿAlī b. Ḥayāt ʿAlī Dihlawī 251
M. Karīm Khair al-Dīn Ḥasan Ghulām-Ḍāmin 779, 1334
M. Karīm Khān Kirmānī 1065 (116)
M. Kashmīrī (Ḥājjī) 175
M. Kāẓim, *Wazīr* of Marw, 325
M. Kāẓim b. M. Amīn 585, 1317
M. Kāẓim "Ḥādhiq" 198, 218, 1257
M. Kāẓim Kākōrawī 1036 n.4, 1047[3]
M. Khair al-Dīn Khān Ḥaidarābādī 22[2]
M. Khair al-Dīn Khān Maḥmūd-Jang [possibly identical with the preceding] 780
M. Khalīl (Khwājah) 604
M. Khalīl b. ʿAbd al-Ghafūr Qādirī Kashmīrī 1046[20]
M. Khalīl b. Dāwud Mīrzā 319, 1282
M. Khān (S.) 1093[24]
M. Khān Lawāsānī 1069

M. Khān Razzāqī 1058 (39)
M. Khiyābānī 1184 (34)
M. Laṭīf (Abū 'l-Munīf) 1183 (26)
M. Māh 134
M. Mahdī b. Abī Dharr Nirāqī 219, 1263
M. Mahdī b. Khalīl Aḥmad Jaunpūrī 1121
M. Mahdī b. M. Hādī Shīrāzī 320
M. Mahdī b. M. Ja'far Mūsawī [Tunakābunī] (1) 1266[34]
M. Mahdī [Arbāb] b. M. Riḍā Iṣfahānī 349, 1292
M. Mahdī Iṣfahānī, known as al-Muḥibb, 1285
M. Mahdī Khān b. M. Naṣīr Astarābādī 322, 1283
M. Mahdī Qazwīnī 'Abd-al-Rabbābādī 1174[1]
M. Mahdī Shīrwānī Anṣārī 422 (3)
M. Mahdī Ṭabāṭabā 762[15]
M. Ma'rūf b. M. Sharīf 'Abbāsī 966[5]
M. Mashhadī 1263
M. Mas'ūd Shāh (Raḥīm-Bakhsh) 1062 (82)
M. Ma'ṣūm 48 (4)
M. Ma'ṣūm (= Sharaf al-Dīn Ḥusain) 974 n.5
M. Ma'ṣūm b. Aḥmad Sirhindī 991[32], 1024[7]
M. Ma'ṣūm b. Bābā Samarqandī 33 (49)
M. Ma'ṣūm b. Ḥasan b. Ṣāliḥ 582, 1317
M. Ma'ṣūm b. Khwājagī Iṣfahānī 313, 1280 ult., 1281
M. Ma'ṣūm "Nāmī" 651, 1324
M. Ma'ṣūm Sharīf Iṣfahānī 1063 (99)
M. Mīrak b. Mas'ūd 237
M. Mīran-jān (2) Ilāhābādī 223
M. Mubīn Lak'hnawī 220
M. Mufīd Mustaufī Yazdī *Jāmi' i Mufīdī* 352, 1293; *Majālis al-mulūk* 237; Memoirs 1142; *Mukhtaṣar i Mufīd* 237
Muḥammad "Muḥammad" Ṣūfī Māzandarānī 806
M. Muḥsin (Ḥājī), of Hoogly 724 n.2, 1329
M. Muḥsin b. Samī' 1225[5]
M. Muḥsin Mustaufī 136, 1243

(1) For his *Khulāṣat al-akhbār*, on the Prophets and the Imāms, etc., see *Dharī'ah* vii, p. 210
(2) Mīran, with a short a in the second syllable.

M. Muḥsin Ṣiddīqī 325
M. Muḥsin al-Dīn 762[21]
M. Muḥtasham Khān 708
M. Muḥyī 'l-Dīn (Ṣafdar 'Alī Shāh) 763
M. Mu'min b. 'Abd al-Karīm Qāri' 1223[29]
M. Mumtāz al-Ḥaqq Ṣiddīqī 53 (3)
M. Mun'im Ja'farābādī 604
Muḥammad Munshī (Mīrzā). See Muḥammad (Mīrzā, fl. 1920)
M. Muqīm b. Raḥmat Allāh 677 (8)
M. Muqīm Ḥusainī Astarābādī 1136[20]
M. Murād 156 (7)
M. Murād b. Shihāb al-Dīn 610
M. Murād Kashmīrī 38[12]
M. Mushīr (or Bashīr) 648
M. Muṣṭafā al-Baghdādī 1060 (68)
M. Mustajāb Khān 696
M. Muẓaffar Khwāfī 242 (6)
M. Nabī Khān Qazwīnī 1067[10]
M. "Nadīm" b. M. Kāẓim 333, 1284
M. Nādir 218
M. Na'īm Allāh Bahrā'ichī 1032
M. Na'īm (Nu'aim ?) Badakhshī 50 (3)
M. Najaf 'Alī Khān Jhajjarī 551[13], 1314
M. Najīb b. Aḥmad 'Alī 1057 (32)
M. Najīb Qādirī Nāgaurī 1023
M. Naqī Burūjirdī 219
M. Naqī Pashāwarī 670
M. Naqshband b. M. Ma'ṣūm Sirhindī 1024[8]
Muḥammad Narshakhī 369, 1300
M. Naṣīr "Furṣat" 353, 1295
M. Naṣr Allāh Khān. See Naṣr Allāh Khān
M. Nāẓim al-Islām 347, 1287
M. Nu'aim (Na'īm ?) Badakhshī 50 (3)
M. Nu'mān 988[7]
M. Nūr Allāh 1054[1]
M. Nuṣrat 'Alī. See Nuṣrat 'Alī
M. Pārsā 7, 1193
M. Qāḍī 966, 973[21]
M. Qādir Khān "Munshī" Bīdarī. See Qādir Khān (M.)
M. Qāsim *Aḥwāl al-khawāqīn* 610
M. Qāsim (Munshī) 776[29]
M. Qāsim b. M. Sharīf 1268
M. Qāsim b. Muḥsin Tabrīzī 1217 (6*a*)
M. Qāsim Hindū-Shāh Firishtah 442
M. Qāsim "'Ibrat" Lāhaurī 607
M. Qāsim "Riḍwān" 987
M. Qiyām al-Dīn b. Abū 'l-Ḥasan Fārūqī 1022
M. Qudrat Allāh "Shauq". See Qudrat Allāh

M. Raḍī [*sic lege*] " Bandah " 147, 429[26], 1245
M. Rafī' " Bādhil " 199, 1257
M. Rafī' al-Zamān Ilāhābādī 1063 (98)
M. Rāḥat 1249[15]
M. Raḥīm Khān Kirmānī 1212[28]
M. Riḍā b. Asad Allāh Yazdī 1228
M. Riḍā b. Dildār Ḥusain Hāshimī 1158
M. Riḍā b. Ghulām-M. [Sahāranpūrī ?] 133[23]
M. Riḍā b. M. Amīn Hamadānī (d. Jumādā I 1247/Oct.–Nov. 1831 : see *Ṭarā'iq al-ḥaqā'iq* iii, p. 117) 23, 1202
M. Riḍā b. M. Mahdī Sabzawārī 1200
M. Riḍā b. M. Mu'min Khātūnābādī *Jannāt al-khulūd* 218, 1262
M. Riḍā b. M. Zamān Khān Durrānī 1181 (12)
M. Riḍā 'Alī Banārasī 46 (20)
M. Riḍā " Bandah ", apparently an error for M. Raḍī " Bandah " 147, 1245
M. Riḍā Bēg 688
M. Riḍā Hamadānī (1) 23, 1202
M. Riḍā " Najm " Ṭabāṭabā 148 ; *Akhbārāt i Hind* 488 ; *Baḥr al-zakhkhār* 148–9, 488, 523 ; *Mafātīḥ al-ri'āsat* 523 ; *Majma' al-mulūk* 148 ; *Naghmah i 'andalīb* 901 ; *Zubdat al-gharā'ib* 148, 1245
M. Riḍā " Riḍā " 608
M. Riḍā [read M. Raḍī] Tabrīzī 429[26]
M. Sa'd Allāh Murādābādī 44, 1222
M. Ṣādiq [Kashmīrī Hamadānī ?] *Manāqib i anbiyā* [?] 166
M. Ṣādiq (Ṣādiq Khān) 577
M. Ṣādiq b. 'Abd al-Bāqī Farghānī 31 (30)
M. Ṣādiq b. M. Ṣāliḥ Iṣfahānī 125, 1241–2
M. Ṣādiq " Akhtar ". See M. Ṣādiq Khān
M. Ṣādiq " Āzād " 200, 218
M. Ṣādiq Dihlawī 567
M. Ṣādiq " Humā " Marwazī 335, 1285 ; *Tārīkh i jahān-ārā* 336 ; *Zīnat al-madā'iḥ* 884
M. Ṣādiq Kāshgharī *Tadhkirah i Khwājagān* 392, 1026, 1302 ; *Tārīkh i Rashīdī* (trans.) 274
M. Ṣādiq Kashmīrī Hamadānī *Kalimāt al-ṣādiqīn* 985 ; *Ṭabaqāt i Shāhjahānī* 1171 ; probably also *Āthār i Shāh-Jahānī* 568, and possibly *Manāqib i anbiyā* [?] 166
M. Ṣādiq Khān " Akhtar " 707, 1328 ; *Guldastah i maḥabbat* 707 ; *Makhzan al-jawāhir* (by the same author?) 151
M. Ṣādiq Mūsawī Khwānsārī 29 (7)
M. Ṣādiq " Nāmī " 331, 1284
M. Ṣādiq Shihābī Sa'dī Qādirī 1013
M. Ṣādiq Yārkandī 1035
M. Ṣadr Hāshimī 1289 (17)
M. Ṣafī b. Walī Qazwīnī 19, 130, 1200
M. Sa'īd (Ḥāfiẓ) 1012
M. Sa'īd b. Aḥmad Sirhindī 991[32], 1257[30]
M. Sa'īd Aslamī 25, 1203
M. Sa'īd 'Umarī b. Aḥmad Sirhindī 991[32], 1257[30]
M. Sa'īd Ustād *al-Nā'it* 1084
M. Saif al-Dīn Kashmīrī 1326[3]
M. Saif al-Dīn Qādirī 1065 (121)
M. Ṣalāḥ 38[16]
M. Ṣalāḥ Siyāhgirdī Balkhī 378
M. Salāmat Allāh " Kashfī " 223, 1264
M. Ṣāliḥ *Baḥr al-sa'ādat* 708, 1328
M. Ṣāliḥ *Gulshan* 598 (4), 1319
M. Ṣāliḥ b. 'Abd Allāh 980, 1297[10]
M. Ṣāliḥ b. Aḥmad Māzandarānī 1132[2]
M. Ṣāliḥ b. Bāqir Khān Shīrāzī 1148
M. Ṣāliḥ b. M. Bāqir Qazwīnī 1260[26]
M. Ṣāliḥ Burghānī 223, 1264
M. Ṣāliḥ Kanbō 578, 1317
M. Ṣāliḥ [Kanbō ?] *Takmilah i Akbar-nāmah* 548[1]
M. Ṣāliḥ " Kashfī ". See " Kashfī " 214, 1262
M. Ṣāliḥ " Qudrat " 624, 1321
M. Salīm (Ḥājjī Mīr) 380
M. Sāqī (Musta'idd Khān) 592, 1318
M. Sātqīn 1035
M. Shafī' b. M. Sharīf 133[12]
M. Shafī' Gushtāsb Māzandarānī *Rūz-nāmah* 1161 (9) ; *Safar-nāmah* 1161 (14)
M. Shafī' Khān 1182
M. Shafī' " Wārid " 610, 1319
M. Sharīf *Multaqaṭ al-tawārīkh* 384
M. Sharīf *Ṣaḥīfat al-a'rās* 1028
M. Sharīf b. Dōst-M. See Mu'tamad Khān
M. Sharīf b. M. Naqī [or Taqī] 382
M. Sharīf b. Muṣṭafā 146
M. Sharīf al-Khādim 1253[7]
M. Sharīf Najafī 450
M. Sharīf " Wuqū'ī " 122, 1241
M. Shēr 1062 (81)

(1) For whom see *Ṭarā'iq al-ḥaqā'iq* iii, p. 117 sqq.

M. Shighā'ul [*sic lege*] 391, 1301
M. Ṣibghat Allāh b. M. Ghauth 222[32], 482[17], 1188 (25), 1263
M. Ṣiddīq (Ḥāfiẓ) 396
M. Ṣiddīq Ḥasan Khān. See Ṣiddīq Ḥasan Khān
M. Sikandar " Wāṣil " Khāliṣpūrī 1059 (57)
" Muḥammad " Ṣūfī Māzandarānī 806
M. Sulaimān 1064 (103) (104)
M. Sulaimān Chishtī Taunsawī 1044[22], [23], 1045[4, 14, 24]
M. Sulṭān b. Ṭīpū Sulṭān 775, 1333
M. Ṭabāṭabā'ī Iṣfahānī 400
M. Ṭāhir *Aḥwālāt i . . . Aḥmad . . . al-Aḥsā'ī* 1345[12]
M. Ṭāhir *Tajwīd i lā-yanfakk* 50 (2)
M. Ṭāhir b. M. Yūsuf Qazwīnī 316
M. Ṭāhir " Āshnā " 577
M. Ṭāhir Iṣfahānī 1219[31]
M. Ṭāhir Mālmīrī 1294
M. Ṭāhir Naṣrābādī 818
M. Ṭāhir al-Qāri' 48 (7)
M. Ṭāhir " Waḥīd "' Qazwīnī 314, 1282
M. Ṭālib (Abū 'l-'Abbās) 1004
M. Taqī b. Maqṣūd 'Alī Majlisī 1132[1]
M. Taqī b. M. Bāqir [Iṣfahānī] ([1]) *Faḍā'il al-A'immah* 229 (15), 1266 ; *Kashf al-anwār* 216 ; *Kāshif al-niqāb* 210.
M. Taqī b. M. Burghānī 1264
M. Taqī b. M. Kāẓim Kirmānī. See Muẓaffar 'Alī Shāh
M. Taqī 'Alī-ābādī 337, 1285
M. Taqī Fakhr Dā'ī Gīlānī 1186 (8), 1213[11]
M. Taqī Farāhānī 1349 n.5
M. Taqī Iṣfahānī. See M. Taqī b. M. Bāqir
M. Taqī Khān (Colonel) 1183 (32)
M. Taqī Khān " Ḥakīm " *Ganj i dānish* 242 (3) ; *Tārīkh i Mā warā' al-Nahr* 386
M. Taqī " Mīr " 849
M. Taqī " Sipihr " Kāshānī 152, 343, 1247–8
M. Ṭarāghāy (Ulugh Bēg) 271, 1273
M. Taufīq Kashmīrī 682
M. 'Ubaid al-Raḥmān ('Abd Allāh Mushtāq) 203
M. 'Umar b. Ibrāhīm Nīshāpūrī (Pashāwarī ?) 1015[4]

([1]) Called Āqā Najafī (d. 1332/1914: see Brockelmann *Sptbd.* ii, p. 838, *Dharī'ah* iii p. 304[3]).

M. 'Umar Pashāwarī 1014
M. 'Uthmān b. M. Iḥsān Bilgrāmī 1115[23]
M. 'Uthmān Damānī 1057 (36)
M. 'Uthmān Khān " Qais " 58 (7)
M. Wafā 'Aẓīmābādī 714
M. Wafā' Karmīnagī 381
M. Wajīh [al-Dīn] " 'Ishqī " 880
M. Walī Allāh. See Walī Allāh Farrukhābādī 25, 694
M. Wārith 575, 1317
M. Wārith Rasūl-numā 1040[10]
M. Wāsi' 202
M. Yaḥyā " Yaḥyā " Kāshī 569
M. Ya'qūb b. M. Dāniyāl 384
M. Ya'qūb Bukhārī 384, 1301
M. Yūsuf b. Khwājah Baqā 379, 1301
M. Yūsuf b. Khwājam-birdī 1237[17]
M. Yūsuf b. Raḥmat Allāh Aṭakī Kan'ānī 127
M. Yūsuf 'Alī Qādirī 1062 (81)
M. Yūsuf " Wālih " 130, 1243
M. Zabardast 407 (7)
M. Ẓahīr al-Dīn Bilgrāmī 56
M. Zamān b. M. Ṭāhir Tabrīzī 48 (6)
M. Zamān Khān 432 (3)
M. Zamān Khān Shāhjahānpūrī 1155
M. Zanjānī 1182 (18)
M. Zubair 1024[10]
M. Ẓuhūr b. Ẓuhūrī 1331
Muḥammad-Bakhsh " Āshōb " 616, 1321
Muḥammad-Qulī Mughūl Ḥiṣārī 533
Muḥammad-Qulī Qājār 134
Muḥammad-Qulī " Salīm " Ṭihrānī 567
" Muhandis " (Khair Allāh) 501[14]
" Muhandis " (Luṭf Allāh) 788[31]
Muḥarram " Mariḍ " Qarābāghī 429[1]
al-Muḥibb (M. Mahdī Iṣfahānī) 1285
Muḥibb 'Alī Khān " Ḥikmat " 200–1, 218
Muḥibb al-Nabī Dihlawī 1030[5], 1038[5]
Muḥibb Ḥusain Khān 1147[31]
Muḥsin 1064 (108)
Muḥsin b. al-Ḥanīf 325
Muḥsin (M.), of Hoogly 724 n.2, 1329
Muḥsin (M.) Mustaufī 136, 1243
Muḥsin (M.) Ṣiddīqī 325
Muḥsin al-Dīn (M.) 762[21]
Muḥsin 'Imād Ardabīlī 1207
Muḥtasham (Abū 'l-Qāsim) 916
Muḥtasham Khān 708
Muḥyī Ḥiṣārī 183
Muḥyī 'l-Dīn (Mīrān) 936 n.4
Muḥyī 'l-Dīn (Mirzā) 685

Muḥyī 'l-Dīn b. Ḥusain Riḍawī Ḥusainī 1066 (123)
Muḥyī 'l-Dīn b. M. Shāh Aḥmadī 1052
Muḥyī 'l-Dīn b. Rūḥ Allāh Ghaznawī 54, 1227
Muḥyī 'l-Dīn, "Dhauqī" (d. 1194/1780: see Ivanow 1st Suppt. p. 8) 694, 1326
Muḥyī ['l-Dīn] Ḥiṣārī 183
Muḥyī 'l-Dīn "Miskīn" 1052
Muḥyī 'l-Dīn Pīr-zādah 744
Muḥyī 'l-Dīn Yaḥyā Madanī 1038[3]
Mu'īn b. Maḥmūd Shīrāzī 32 (41)
Mu'īn al-Dīn b. Khairāt 'Alī Kaṛawī 56
Mu'īn al-Dīn b. Sirāj al-Dīn Maḥmūd Khāwand-Shāh 195
Mu'īn al-Dīn Chishtī 943 n.3; 987[1]; 1000, 1051[1], 1065 (113), 1066 (124), 1066 (125)
Mu'īn al-Dīn Farāhī 11, 1194; *Khulāṣah i Baḥr al-durar* 1195[19]; *Ma'ārij al-nubuwwah* 187, 1254; *Tafsīr i Sūrah i Fātiḥah* 11, 1194; *Tafsīr i Sūrah i Yūsuf* 11, 1194; *Tārīkh i Mūsawī* 162, 1250
Mu'īn al-Dīn Isfizārī 355, 1296
Mu'īn al-Dīn Minbarī (?) 977[6]
Mu'īn al-Dīn Naṭanzī 1234[5–29]
Mu'īn al-Dīn Shīrāzī 351, 1294
Mu'īn al-Dīn "Thabāt" 1064 (107)
Mu'īn [al-Dīn] Yazdī 277, 1273
Mu'īn al-Dīn Zamajī 355, 1296
Mu'īn al-fuqarā' (Aḥmad b. M.) 953
Mu'īn al-Ḥaqq b. Shihāb al-Ḥaqq 948
Mu'īn al-Miskīn. See Mu'īn al-Dīn Farāhī
Mu'īnī (M. b. Ḥusain) 1192[2]
Mu'izz al-Dīn b. Ẓahīr al-Dīn Ardistānī 1199
Mu'izzī (Najaf-Qulī) 1289 (19)
Mujaddid i alf i thānī 988 n.5, etc. (see Aḥmad Sirhindī)
Mujāhidī (S. Ismā'īl Khān) 429[19]
"Mujhar Ben Aysa Dáwud Am" 407 (2)
Mujtabā Lāharpūrī 1036[7], 1036 n.4, 1047[3]
Mujtabā Mīnuwī. See Mīnuwī
Mujtahidī (Mahdī) 1288 (8), 1350, 1352
"Mukhliṣ" (Anand Rām) 612, 1319–21
Mukhtār A'mā Iṣfahānī 1221
Mukhtārī (Ḥabīb Allāh) 1290
Muktēsar 1320[2]
"Mulhamī" (Ibrāhīm) 420
Mulk-ārā ('Abbās Mīrzā) 1287
Mullā-zādah (= Mu'īn al-fuqarā' ?) 953
"Mumaiyiz" 1339
Mūminābādī (Uwais) 180n.
"Mumtāz" (Iḥsān Allāh) 168 (7), 204 (1)
Mumtāz al-Ḥaqq Ṣiddīqī 53 (3)
Mumtāz-Maḥall 1163 (1) and (2)
Munawwar [b. ?] Maḥmūd Adīb 56 (4)
Munawwar 'Alī Khān 619[19]
Mun'im (M.) Ja'farābādī 604
Mun'im Khān Hamadānī Aurangābādī 749
"Mun'imī" (M. Aslam) 684, 1325
Munnā Lāl (Munshī) 643, 1322
Munnā Lāl (Rāy) 739 (4)
Munnī Bēgam 725[6], 1329
"Munshī" (Bud Sing'h) 767
"Munshī" (Jaswant Rāy) 777
"Munshī" (M. Qādir Khān Bīdarī). See Qādir Khān (M.)
Munshīs 1088
"Munṣif" ('Abd al-Raḥīm b. M. Bāqir) 889
"Munṣif" (Ṣafdar 'Alī Shāh) 763
Muntajab al-Dīn Badī' Juwainī 260
Muntajab al-Dīn Zarzarī [vocalisation ?] Zar-bakhsh 1025[2]
Munyarī (Sharaf al-Dīn) 1049 n.2
Muqarrab Khān (Muṣṭafā b. M. Sa'īd) 51, 1225–6
Muqtadir (Ghulām-Ḥusain) 1271[6]
Murādābād 698[12], 1044[19]
Murray (*Sir* John Macgregor) 1145 n.1
Murshid (S.) 976
Murshid b. Aṣīl 1079
Murshid-Qulī Khān (Ja'far Khān Naṣīrī) 649[13]
Murtaḍā 'Alam al-Hudā 230[4], 1266
Murtaḍā "Bīnish" '*Aẓīm al-tawārīkh* 482[25]; *Ishārāt i Bīnish* 904
Murtaḍā Ḥusain Bilgrāmī 142
Murtaḍā Khān (Sh. Farīd Bukhārī) 1241[17]
Murtaḍā-Qulī Khān Ziyād-oghlī 314[15], 1281[26]
Mūsā (Ṣadr al-Dīn) 939[17]
Mūsā 'l-Mubarqa' 228 (7)
"Musāfir" 717
Muṣaiyib b. Khuzā'ī 233 (57)
Muṣannifak 10, 1194
Mūsawī (M. b. Faḍl Allāh) 89, 1236
"Muṣḥafī" (Ghulām-Hamadānī) 875
"Mushfiqī" 373, 1301
Mushīr al-Daulah (Ḥasan Pīr-niyā) 249 (1)–(3), 1270

Mushīr al-Daulah (Ḥusain Khān) 1350[21]
Mushīr al-Daulah (Ja'far Khān) 1070
Mushkīn-qalam 1003[8]
Mushtāq ('Abd Allāh) 203
Mushtāq Aḥmad Amēt'hawī 1211[15]
Mushtāq Aḥmad Ṣābirī 1057 (29)
" Mushtāqī " (Rizq Allāh) 512
Muṣliḥ al-Dīn Lārī 116, 1240; *Mir'āt al-adwār* 117; *Shamā'il i Nabawī* 174
" Muslimī " (Abū 'l-Ma'ālī M.) 977
Muṣṭafā (S.) 52
Muṣṭafā b. 'Abd Allāh (Ḥājjī Khalīfah) 127, 1242
Muṣṭafā b. Ibrāhīm al-Qāri' 43, 1221
Muṣṭafā [Khān] b. M. Sa'īd [Kāshī] 51, 1225–6
Muṣṭafā (M.) al-Baghdādī 1060 (68)
Muṣṭafā Khān " Shēftah " 895, 1338; *Gulshan i bī-khār* 896; *Rah-āward = Targhīb al-sālik* 1152
Muṣṭafā Ṣādiq al-Rāfi'ī 1228[17]
Muṣṭafā-Qulī Mūsawī Sarāwī Sabalānī 333
Musta'idd Khān (M. Sāqī) 592, 1318
Mustajāb Khān 696
Mustaufī ('Abd Allāh) 1179, 1288 (14)
Mūsyū Farānsīsī 1161 (15)
Muta'allawī [Musta'lawī ?] Saiyids 1348[22]
Mu'tamad (Maḥmūd Farhād) 1350
Mu'tamad al-Daulah Minūchihr Khān 902[20], 1103[10]
Mu'tamad Khān (M. Sharīf) 560; *Aḥwāl i shāh-zādagī i Shāh-Jahān* 565; *Iqbāl-nāmah i Jahāngīrī* 561, 1316; *Jahāngīr-nāmah* (continuation) 557[11]
" Muṭī'ī " 727
Muṭlaq 'Alī Shāh 693[26]
" Muṭribī " al-Aṣamm al-Samarqandī 814
al-Muttaqī ('Abd al-Wahhāb) 980 n.1
al-Muttaqī ('Alī b. Ḥusām al-Dīn) 979 n.3
Muttra (Mat'hurā) 692[21]
Mūyīnah-dūz (Maḥmūd) 970 n.6
Muẓaffar al-Dīn Shāh Qājār 346, 1288 (9)
Muẓaffar 'Alī 657
Muẓaffar 'Alī Khān " Asīr " 230 (24)
Muẓaffar 'Alī Shāh Allāhī 1184 (35)
Muẓaffar 'Alī [Shāh] Ni'mat-Allāhī 1209[26]; *Baḥr al-asrār* 29 (5), 1209; *Majma' al-biḥār* 30 (18), 1211
Muẓaffar Ḥusain Mahārat Khān 139, 1244
Muẓaffar Ḥusain " Ṣabā " 915
Muẓaffar Kābulī 276 (2)
Muẓaffar (M.) Khwāfī 242 (6)
Muẓaffarids 277, 1273
Muẓaffar-Jang (Nawwāb) 522[13]
Mysore 767–77, 1333–4
Mystics, etc., 923–1066, 1342–7

Nābhājī 1055 (12)
Nabī Khān Qazwīnī (M.) 1067[10]
" Nabīl " Zarandī 1287 antepenult.
Nadhīr al-Dīn Aḥmad 699[9]
Nadhr-'Alī Jā'isī 719
Nadhr M. Nes' [?] 388 (18)
Nadhr Muḥammad Uzbak 581[5], 598 (5)
" Nadīm " ('Abd al-Karīm Bukhārī) 382
" Nadīm " (M. b. M. Kāẓim) 333, 1284
" Nādir " (Shankar Nāt'h) 1326
Nādir 'Alī " Ra'd " 1134[20]
Nādir Mīrzā b. Badī' al-Zamān Qājār 1299
Nādir Shāh 20 (33), 322–9, 1024[13], 1283–4, 1319[32]
Nafīsī (Sa'īd) 918, 1291 (1), 1340
Nāgaurī. See Ḥākim b. 'Imād, Ḥamīd al-Dīn and Najm al-Dīn
Nahrawālī (Sharaf al-Dīn) 1023[6], 1346[4] (where Shahrawānī is apparently a corruption of Nahrawālī)
Nailī Aḥmad 270[15]
Na'īm Allāh Bahrā'ichī 1032
Nā'īnī. See M. Hādī Nā'īnī
Nā'īnī (M. Ḥusain) 233 (63)
Nā'īnī (Pīr-zādah) 1157
al-Naisābūrī (Isḥāq b. Ibrāhīm) 159, 1250
al-Naisābūrī (M. b. Maḥmūd) 4, 1191–2
Nā'iṭīs 779 n.1, 1083–4, 1332[20], 1348
al-Najaf, Wahhābī rule in, 428 (7)
" Najaf " 200
Najaf 'Alī (S.) 1265
Najaf 'Alī Khān 206 (30)
Najaf 'Alī Khān b. M. 'Aẓīm al-Dīn Jhajjarī 551, 1314
Najaf Khān (Nawwāb Dhū 'l-Faqār al-Daulah) 474 n.3, 624[15], 880[21]
Najaf-Qulī Mīrzā 1153; (*Safar-nāmah*) 338 (433) (?), 1154
Najaf-Qulī Mu'izzī 1289 (19)
Najafī (Āqā) [i.e. M. Taqī b. M. Bāqir Iṣfahānī] 210[6], 216[14], 229 (15)

Najīb (M.) b. Aḥmad 'Alī 1057 (32)
Najīb al-Daulah 649[12], 694[19, 26], 1147[18], 1327
Najīb al-Dīn Mutawakkil 971 n.6, 987[2]
Najīb al-Ījī 211
Najīb (M.) Qādirī Nāgaurī 1023
"Najm." See M. Riḍā "Najm"
Najm al-Dīn (M.) 1160 (4)
Najm al-Dīn Chirīyākōtī 1181 (8)
Najm al-Dīn Ghauth al-dahr 1036 n.4, 1047[3]
Najm al-Dīn Kubrā 1032 n.2
Najm al-Dīn Nāgaurī 1045
Najm al-Dīn Qādirī (M.) 1181 (10) 1266
Najm al-Dīn Qāsim Madhmakīnī 1266[25]
Najmābādī (Maḥmūd) 1351
Nālāgaṛh (= Hindūr) 678 (13)
"Nāmī" (M. Ma'ṣūm) 651, 1324
"Nāmī" (M. Ṣādiq) 331, 1284
Namīdīhī ('Abd al-Karīm) 109, 1238[26]
Nānak (Bābā) 663–4, 677 (4)
Nand Kumār 725[8]
Napoleon 1274[8], 1288 (12)
Naqīb Khān 118, 1240
Naqsh 'Alī 855
Naqshband (Bahā' al-Dīn) 948[5], 973[5], probably also 1060 (69)
Naqshband (M.) b. M. Ma'ṣūm Sirhindī 1024[8]
Narāyan Kaul "'Ājiz" 681, 1325
Narshakhī 369, 1300
Narsing'h (Barsing'h, Bīrsing'h ?) Dēō 738[3]
Nasafī ('Umar b. M.) 371, 1300
Nasawī (M. b. Aḥmad) 1088, 1349
"Nashāṭī" (M. al-Kātib al-Shīrāzī) 940[27]
Naṣīb [al-Dīn] Kashmīrī 985
"Nāṣiḥ" (M. 'Alī Khān) 1349[5]
Nāṣiḥ b. Ẓafar Jarbādhaqānī 251
Nasīm Ḥasan 1182 (20)
Nāṣir b. Khusrau 922 (5), 1138
Nāṣir al-Dīn Kirmānī 357, 1297
Naṣīr al-Dīn Maḥmūd Chirāgh i Dihlī 942 n.1
Nāṣir al-Dīn M. Abū 'l-Manṣūr Dihlawī 31 (33), 1212
Nāṣir al-Dīn Shāh Qājār 340, 1286, 1289 (22)
Naṣīr Allāh Sulṭān (Mīrzā) 1161 (10)
Nāṣir al-Mulk (Abū 'l-Qāsim Khān) 329
Nāṣir-Jang (Amīn al-Daulah) 1152[12]
Naṣr al-Aṭibbā' 430[2]
Naṣr al-Dīn (Bābā) 985
Naṣr Allāh "Falsafī" 1249 n., 1283 n., *Tārīkh i rawābiṭ i Īrān u Urōpā* 1283; *Tārīkh i 'umūmī* 1249
Naṣr Allāh Khān "Fidā'ī" 490
Naṣr Allāh Khān Khwēshgī Khūrjawī 756, 1332; *Bayāḍ i dil-gushā* 1042; *Gulshan i hamīshah-bahār* 904; *Jāmi' i Fatḥ-Khānī* 1103; *Tārīkh i Dakan* 757
Naṣr Allāh Khān Nawwāb Shīrāzī 1298[3]
Naṣr Allāh "Surūsh" 1341
Naṣrābādī (M. Ṭāhir) 818
Naṭanzī (Mu'īn al-Dīn) 1234[5–29]
Nat'han (Mirzā) 714, 1329
Nat'han Lāl 1055 (12)
Naubakht (Ḥabīb Allāh) 1290
Naubakhtīs 1085, 1348
Naurōz Rīshī 986[1]
Naurūz 'Alī b. M. Bāqir Bisṭāmī (d. 1309/1891–2) 234 (69), 234 (71), 1268
"Nawā" (Darwīsh Ḥusain Kāshānī) 894
"Nawā'ī" ('Alī-Shīr) 789, 1334
Nawal Rāy Ilāhābādī 693
Nawanagar 731[27]
Nawāyat. See Nā'iṭīs
Nawwāb (Mīr, i.e. S. Asad Allāh) 740
Nawwāb i Daulah (M. 'Alī Khān) 233 (60)
Nawwāb Khān 598 (1)
Naẓar b. Ḥasan Jīlānī 192
"Nāẓim" (Farrukh Ḥusain Harawī) 823[24]
Nāẓim al-Islām Kirmānī 347, 1287
"Nāẓir" (Bishan La'l) 649
Naẓmī-zādah 270[5], 270[10]
Neave (Robert) 1160 (4)
Nepalese War 646[19]
Nikpay b. Mas'ūd 79, 1232
Ni'mat Allāh b. Ḥabīb Allāh Harawī 393, 1302
Ni'mat Allāh b. Raḥmat Allāh Lāhaurī 43
Ni'mat Allāh Riḍawī 1065 (116)
Ni'mat Allāh Walī Kirmānī 8 (*Sharḥ Fātiḥat al-Kitāb*), 9 (*Risālah i Ikhlāṣ*), 952[1], 1057 (34), 1061 (77) 1193
Ni'mat-Allāhī *shaikhs* 1051[32]
Ni'mat Khān "'Ālī" 589, 1318; *Bahādūr-Shāh-nāmah* 600; *Jang-nāmah* 592, 1318; *Ni'mat i 'uẓmā* 20; *Rāḥat al-qulūb* 1172; *Waqā'i' i Ḥaidarābād* 590

Nīmchah i 'Ālamgīrī 597[12]
Nirāqī (Mahdī b. Abī Dharr) 219, 1263
Nirmal 753[15]
Nīshāpūrī (Isḥāq b. Ibrāhīm) 159, 1250
Nīshāpūrī (M. b. Maḥmūd) 4, 1191–2
" Nithārī " Bukhārī 802
" Niyāz " (Sadāsuk'h Dihlawī) 481
Niyāz M. b. 'Ashūr M. Khōqandī 391
" Niẓām " (Mīr Shihāb al-Dīn entitled 'Imād al-Mulk Ghāzī al-Dīn Khān) 1028
Niẓām (Siyāqī) 308
Niẓām al-Daulah (M. Ḥusain Khān Iṣfahānī) 1338[7]
Niẓām al-Dīn *Sharḥ i Shamā'il i Tirmidhī* 1252
Niẓām al-Dīn (Munshī) 402 n.2
Niẓām al-Dīn b. M. 'Azīz Balkhī Mazārī 1039
Niẓām al-Dīn b. Saif al-Dīn. See Bhīkan (Sh.)
Niẓām al-Dīn Aḥmad b. M. Ṣāliḥ Ṣiddīqī Ḥusainī 1008
Niẓām al-Dīn Aḥmad Harawī 433, 1309; *Ṭabaqāt i Akbarī* 433; *Tārīkh i alfī* 119, 1240–1
Niẓām al-Dīn Auliyā 941 n.5, 943[6], 1014[1], 1343
Niẓām al-Dīn Aurangābādī 1038[4]
Niẓām al-Dīn Balkhī Mazārī 1039
Niẓām al-Dīn Banārasī *Ghāyat al-taḥqīq* 1228; *Ma'din al-asrār* 46
Niẓām al-Dīn " 'Ishrat " Siyālkōṭī 397, 328 (12)
Niẓām al-Dīn M. Sihālawī 1016
Niẓām al-Dīn Qārī. See Bhīkan
Niẓām [al-Dīn] Shāmī 278, 1273
Niẓām al-Dīn T'hānēsarī 18
Niẓām al-Dīn Yaḥyā b. Shams al-Dīn [Karrābī ?] 182[17], 1253–4
Niẓāmī (Ḥasan) 493, 1310
" Niẓāmī " (Maḥmūd Malik-zādah) 1306[4]
Niẓāms of Ḥaidarābād 748–59
Niẓām-Shāhs 740–2
Northbrook (1st Earl of) 648[28]
" Nudrat " ('Aṭā' Allāh) 828
Nu'mān (M.) 988[7]
Nu'mānī (M. Shiblī) 1186 (8)
Nuqrah-kār 1194 n.1
Nūr al-aṣfiyā' 232 (50)
Nūr al-Dīn b. Aḥmad Ḥusain Riḍawī 733
Nūr al-Dīn b. Burhān al-Dīn Fārūqī 602
Nūr al-Dīn b. Shams al-Dīn 271
Nūr al-Dīn [Ḥusain Khān] " Fā'iq " [Riḍawī] 904
Nūr al-Dīn Ḥusain Khān Fakhrī 694, 1326
Nūr al-Dīn Ja'far Badakhshī 946
Nūr al-Dīn M. birādar-zādah i Faiḍ 1212
Nūr al-Dīn M. b. Ḥusain Qazwīnī 975
Nūr al-Dīn M. Iṣfahānī 194
Nūr al-Dīn M. Kāzarūnī 186
Nūr al-Dīn M. Qārī' 42, 1220
Nūr al-Dīn M. Shīrāzī. See Ni'mat Khān
Nūr al-Dīn M. Wā'iẓ 17
Nūr al-Dīn Walī Rīshī 684[12], 985[20], 986[15]
Nūr al-Dīn " Zaidī " Ẓafarābādī 1121
Nūr al-Ḥaqq (Shāh) 1180[1]
Nūr al-Ḥaqq Dihlawī 441, 1309
Nūr al-Ḥasan Khān 913
Nūr al-Ḥasan Mārahrawī 57
Nūr 'Alī (S.) 1259[5]
Nūr Allāh (M.) 1054[1]
Nūr Allāh b. 'Alī M. Ḥusainī 744, 1331
Nūr Allāh Shūshtarī 1126, 1354
Nūr-Muḥammad 31 (25)
Nūr-Muḥammad (Abū 'l-Qāsim) 493 (4)
Nūr-Muḥammad Chēlā 676
Nūr-Muḥammad Khurāsānī 482
Nūr-Muḥammad Mahārawī 1038[6], 1045[23]
Nūr-Muḥammad " Naurī " Qandahārī 407 (5)
Nūrī Saiyids 1123 penult., 1124[12]
Nūr-zādah (Ismā'īl) 1307[18, 30]
Nuṣrat b. 'Umar (Sikandar) *Tuḥfat al-ḥuffāẓ* 47 (26), 1224; *Zīnat al-qāri'* 47 (28), 1224
Nuṣrat 'Alī [Khān " Qaiṣar " Dihlawī b. Nāṣir al-Dīn Abū 'l-Manṣūr (cf. p. 1212 *supra*), b. 1264/1848, owner of the Nuṣrat al-maṭābi' at Delhi and author of various Urdu works: see Raḥmān 'Alī p. 237] 1185 (4)
Nuṣrat-Jang (Nawwāb) 723

Officials 1088, 1349
Orientalists 1104
Orissa 714, 1329
Oudh 520[8], 703, 1147[8], 1328

Pādshāh Bēgam 708[9], 1328
Painters and calligraphists, 1071, 1347
Paklī (not Paglē) 685[6]

Pāk-Pattan 941[18]
Paléologue (Maurice) 429[20]
Panjāb 663–78, 1324–5
Panjū (Akhūn) 1065 (122)
Parasrūr 677 (8)
Parasrūrī (M. Aslam) 140, 1244
Parīchhatgaṛh 692
Pārsā (M. b. M. Ḥāfiẓī Bukhārī) 7, 1193
Parsees 1180 (5), 1182 (14)
Parwīz Rāhbar 1188 (24)
Pasand 'Alī Bilgrāmī 200–1
Pashāghirī 1250[5]
Patar [?] Chand (Rājah) 882[1]
Pāyandah Ḥasan Ghaznawī 533
Pazdawī [*sic*, for Maibudī] (Abū 'l-Faḍl Aḥmad b. M.) 30 (14), 1190, 1211
Persian Gulf 428 (4), 1307
Peshawar 678[1], 1115 n., 1321[13–23]
Peter the Great 430[25]
Philanthropists 1181 (9)
Philosophers, etc., 1104, 1350
P'hulwārī 1040 n.2, 1179 antepenult.
Physicians, etc., 1104, 1350
Pilgrims, etc., 1138–62
Pinnock (W.) 155 (3)
Pīr 'Abd al-Raḥmān b. 'Abd al-Qaiyūm 1051
Pīr 'Alī ('Alā' al-Daulah) 183[10]
Pīr Ibrāhīm Khān Khwēshgī 661; *Sairistān* 1103, 1155; (*Tārīkh i Bahāwalpūr*) 662
Pīr Mu'aẓẓam Shāh 396
Pīr Muḥammad (Shāh) [possibly Pīr M. Lak'hnawī, for whom see below] 1060 (71)
Pīr Muḥammad Ḥaḍrat 205 (11)
Pīr Muḥammad Lak'hnawī 1010 n.2
Pīr Muḥammad Shaṭṭārī 990
Pīrah 939[6], 939 n.2
Pīrmastī (" Afḍal ") 917
Pīr-niyā (Ḥasan) 249 (1)–(3), 1270
Pīr-zādah (Ghulām-Muḥyī 'l-Dīn) 745[1]
Pīr-zādah Nā'īnī 1157
Poets 781, 1334
Postans (T.) 659[25]
Pratāp Sing'h Kachhwāhah 690[23]
Prophets 158–207
Punnōchhī (Ḥabīb) 1156
Pūran Chand 711

Qābūs b. Washmgīr 1088[6]
Qāḍī (Shāh) Yazdī 1198
Qāḍī Khān (= M. Qiyām al-Dīn Fārūqī) 1022
Qādir 'Aẓīm Khān 1083, 1334
Qādir Khān (M.) " Munshī " Bīdarī *Sair i Hind* 1152; *Shams al-madhāhib* 1187; *Tārīkh i Āṣaf-Jāhī* 755; *Tārīkh i Qādirī* 748; *Tārīkh i Quṭb-Shāhī* 748; *Tawārīkh i farkhundah* 755
Qādir Walī 1057 (32)
Qādir-Bakhsh Sahāranpūrī 1062 (83)
Qāḍī-zādah = Kabīr b. Uwais Laṭīfī Ardabīlī 416 penult., 1168[6], 1306[15], 1355
" Qadrī " 309, 1280
Qahqahah 798 n.6
" Qā'im " Chāndpūrī 852
Qā'im-maqām (Abū 'l-Qāsim Farāhānī) 338, 1285
Qā'im-maqāmī 1288 (13)
Qā'ināt 923 (9), 1353[21]
" Qais " (M. 'Uthmān Khān) 58 (7)
Qaiyūm i awwal 1024[4]
Qājārs 332, 1179[10], 1284
Qalandarī Ṣūfīs 1032[2], 1036 n.4, 1046[32], 1047[30], 1061 (76)
Qalmāqistān 685[5]
" Qamar." See Naṣr Allāh Khān
Qamar al-Dīn (M.) 34 (67)
Qamar al-Dīn 'Alī b. Sanā' Allāh Ḥusainī Nāṣirī 833[4]
Qamar al-Dīn Aurangābādī 22, 1027[15], 1201
Qamar al-Dīn Siyālkōtī 1059 (56)
Qandahār 574[14]
" Qāni' ". See 'Alī Shēr
" Qāni'ī " 727
Qāqshāl 849 n.1
Qarā-Khitā'īs 358[3]
Qarā-quyūnlū 299
" Qarīb " Garakānī 1082 n.1
Qāshānī ('Abd Allāh b. 'Alī) *Tārīkh i Ūljāytū Sulṭān* 267, 1272; *Zubdat al-tawārīkh* (?) 79, 1232
" Qāsim " (Qudrat Allāh) 882
Qāsim b. Ibrāhīm Qazwīnī 39 (8)
Qāsim b. M. Madhmakīnī 1266[25]
Qāsim b. Nūr Allāh 1220
" Qāsim " Akbarābādī 402, 1304
Qāsim 'Alī (S.) 44
Qāsim 'Alī Khān Āfrīdī 1080, 1347
Qāsim 'Alī Khān Akbarābādī 402, 1304
Qāsim Ghanī 919, 1340, 1351
Qāsim Jaunpūrī 43
" Qāsimī " Gūnābādī 291, 1276; *Shāh-nāmah i Ismā'īl* 305, 1279; *Shāh-nāmah i Ṭahmāsp* 305, 1279; *Shāh-Rukh-nāmah* 292

Qaṣūr, The Afghāns of, 663[16], 1009 n.5, 1011[24]
" Qāṭi'ī " 813
" Qaṭrah " ('Abd al-Wahhāb) 150
Qazwīnī (Alī b. Ḥusain) 85
Qazwīnī (Faḍl Allāh) 243
Qazwīnī (M. b. 'Abd al-Wahhāb) 1176
Qazwīnī (M. b. Mubārak) 793
Qazwīnī (M. Ḥasan b. Ma'ṣūm) (1) 221, 1263.
Qazwīnī (Yaḥyā b. 'Abd al-Laṭīf) 111, 1239
al-Qifṭī ('Alī b. Yūsuf) 1106
Qilich Ṭamghāch Khān Ibrāhīm 431[12]
Qilich Ṭamghāch Khān [Mas'ūd] 1086[18]
Qilīj (Abū M. Shihāb al-Dīn) 1063 (96)
Qilīj Bēg (Mīrzā) 58 (6)
Qipchāq Khān 136, 1243
Qiwām al-Dīn Chishtī ['Abbāsī Lak'hnawī] 983[19]
Qiwām al-Dīn M. (Amīr) 210[25]
Qiwām al-Dīn M. Bukhārī 47 (32)
Qiyām al-Dīn (M.) b. Abū 'l-Ḥasan Fārūqī 1022
Qiyām al-Dīn " Ḥairat " 854
Qiyām al-Dīn " Qā'im " 852
Qubāwī (Aḥmad b. M.) 370[1], 1300
" Qudrat " (M. Ṣāliḥ) 624, 1321
" Qudrat " (Qudrat Allāh Khān Gōpāmawī) 900
Qudrat Allāh (Shāh) 1056 (23)
Qudrat Allāh Khān " Qudrat " 900
Qudrat Allāh " Qāsim " 882
Qudrat Allāh " Shauq " 143 ; *Jām i jahān-numā* 143, 1244 ; *Jām i Jamshīd* 877 ; *Ṭabaqāt al-shu'arā'* 877 ; *Takmilat al-shu'arā' Jām i Jamshīd* 877
Qudrat-Jang b. Qādir al-Daulah 1259[5]
" Qudsī " (M. Jān Mashhadī) 568, 1316
Quhistān 1353
Qum 348, 1291
Qummī (Aḥmad Ḥusainī Ibrāhīmī) 1074, 1279
Qurbān b. Ramaḍān 222, 1263
Qurbān-'Ali " Kāmyāb " Pāzawārī 224
Qurbān i Nabī 407 (7)
Quṭb al-Dīn b. S. Shāh Islāmābādī 201

(1) He died in 1240/1824–5 according to *Ṭarā'iq al-ḥaqā'iq* iii, p. 153 ult. (cf. *Rauḍāt al-jannāt* p. 180).

Quṭb al-Dīn Bakhtyār Ūshī Kākī 943 n.4, 987[1], 1014[12]
Quṭb al-Dīn Bīnā-dil Jaunpūrī 1036 n.4, 1047[3]
Quṭb al-Dīn Ḥusain [really Kamāl al-Dīn Ḥusain Khwārazmī ?] 974[21]
Quṭb al-Dīn Kaidarī 181
Quṭb al-Dīn Sihālawī 1048 n.3
Quṭb al-Madār 1006[3]. See Madār
Quṭb al-Mulk 1066
Quṭbī (Abū Bakr Q. Aharī) 1233, 1269
Quṭb-Shāhs 300[1], 746–8
Qutlugh Khāns 358[4]
Qūzānlū (Jamīl) 1271 (6)–(8), 1284[11]

" Rābiṭ." See 'Abd al-Aḥad
Raḍī (M.) Tabrīzī 147, 429[26], 1245
Raḍī (Sharīf) 1136[13]
Raḍī al-Dīn Abū 'l-Khair 'Abd al-Majīd 42
Raḍī al-Dīn M. b. M. Naṣīr Majlisī 1256
Raḍī al-Dīn Tafrishī 319
al-Raḍī al-Kātib 1260[9]
Ra'fat (Sh.) 588
Rafī' al-Dīn Dihlawī 24, 1203
Rafī' al-Dīn Ibrāhīm Shīrāzī 742
Rafī' al-Dīn M. [?] " Ghāfil " Balkhī 682
Rafī' al-Dīn Murādābādī 1146
Rafī' al-Dīn Qandahārī 880
Rafī' al-Zamān Ilāhābādī (M.) 1063 (98)
al-Rāfi'ī (Muṣṭafā Ṣādiq) 1228[17]
Rafīqī order of Ṣūfīs 1063 (96)
Rāḥat (M.) 1249[15]
Rāhbar (Parwīz) 1188 (24)
Raḥīm 'Alī Khān 675
Raḥīm Allāh Qādirī 759 (2)
Raḥīm-Bakhsh called M. Mas'ūd Shāh 1062 (82)
Raḥmān 'Alī 1120
Raḥmat Allāh " Wāḍiḥ " Bukhārī *Mālik al-mamālik* 387 (6) ; *Tuḥfat al-aḥbāb* 916
Raḥmat Khān (Ḥāfiẓ) 396, 696–7, 1303, 1327[9]
" Rā'iq " ('Alī-Riḍā Nā'iṭī, surnamed Bāqir Ḥusain Khān) 890, 1338 ; *'Aẓīm al-tawārīkh* 482 ; *Guldastah i Karnātak* 890
Ra'īs al-Umarā' (Nawwāb) 1147[27]
Rajā' M. b. 'Abd al-Raḥmān Kāzarūnī 1343[13]
Rajab al-Dīn (Bābā) 985[23]
Rajab 'Alī Khān 26, 1203

Rājan (Sh.) 1038[2]
" Rājī," author of the *Ḥaqā'iq* 1265
" Rājī " (Bamūn 'Alī Kirmānī) 221, 1263
Rājpūtānah 519, 688, 1326
Rājū Qattāl 1025[3]
Rām-Dayāl Sing'h, Rājah of Land'haurah 692
" Rāmī " 607
Rāmpūr 695[18], 697[13], 698[20], 1156[16]
Ranchhōṛ-jī b. Amar-jī 731
Rāprī 1007 n.3
" Rāqim " Dihlawī (Ghulām-Muḥammad) 1076
Rāqim Samarqandī 377, 1301
" Rasā " (Aḥmad 'Alī Lak'hnawī, d. 20 Shawwāl 1292/19 Nov. 1875 : see *Sham' i anjuman* p. 178 ult.) 1104
Rashīd b. Bahrām Harawī 45 (7)
Rashīd al-Dīn Faḍl Allāh 71, 1106[10], 1230–2
Rashīd al-Dīn Khān (M.) 1347
Rashīd al-Dīn Maibudī 1190
Rashīd al-Dīn Maudūd Lālā (?) 1059 (55)
Rashīd Khān (M. Badī') 573
Rashīd Yāsimī 919, 1340
" Rashkī " (1) b. Mannū Lāl Falsafī 1065 (115)
" Rāsikh " ('Ināyat Khān) 1183 (25)
Rāsikhī ('Abbās) 1209 antepenult.
Rasūl-numā (M. Wārith) 1040[10]
Rasūl-numā (S. Ḥasan) 1024[23]
Ratan Sing'h " Zakhmī " 709, 1328–9 ; *Anīs al-'āshiqīn* 890 ; *Sulṭān al-tawārīkh* 709
Rauḍah, or Khuldābād 858 n.2, 1024[31]
Ra'ūf Aḥmad Muṣṭafā-ābādī 1035[4]
" Raunaq " ('Abd Allāh Kurdistānī) 903
Raushan al-Daulah Bahādur-Jang 780 (2)
Raushan 'Alī Jaunpūrī 699[19]
Rāwandī (Maḥmūd b. M.) 175[22]
Rāwandī (M. b. 'Alī) 256
Rāwandī (Sa'īd b. Hibat Allāh) 1253
" Rāwī " (M. Fāḍil Khān Garrūsī) 886, 1337
Rāy Barēlī 1042[1]
Rāzī (Abū 'l-Futūḥ) 4, 1191
Rāzī (Amīn) 1169, 1355
" Rāzī " ('Āqil Khān) 584

(1) Probably a mistake or a misprint for " Ashkī " (cf. p. 1246).

Rāzī (Fakhr al-Dīn) 1106[9]
Rāzī (M. b. Zakarīyā') 1351[14]
Rēwāṛī (Rājah of) 677 (10)
Rich (Claudius James) 1150[9]
" Riḍā " (Mīr M. Riḍā) 608
Ridā 'Alī b. Sakhāwat 'Alī Banārasī 46 (20)
Riḍā 'Alī-zādah 156 (6) (7), 204 (3), 205 (5), 1079 (1), 1187 (11)
Riḍā Ṣāḥib 482[20] (see " Rā'iq")
Riḍā Shāh Pahlawī 348, 1289
Riḍā-Qulī 48 (8)
Riḍā-Qulī Khān " Hidāyat " 906 ; *Ajmal al-tawārīkh* 239 ; *Fihris al-tawārīkh* 342 ; *Majma' al-fuṣaḥā'* 911, 1338 ; *Maẓāhir al-anwār* 224 ; *Nizhād-nāmah i pādshāhān i Īrānī-nizhād* 239 ; *Rauḍat al-ṣafā-yi Nāṣirī* 342, 1246 ; *Riyāḍ al-'ārifīn* 911 ; *Sifārat-nāmah i Khwārazm* 342
Riḍā-Qulī Mīrzā *Safar-nāmah* 338[25] (cf. 1153–4)
Riḍā-zādah " Shafaq " 1183 (32), 1184 (34)
" Riḍwān " (M. Qāsim) 987
" Rif'at " (Ghulām-Jīlānī Rāmpūrī) 697, 1327
" Rif'at." See M. 'Abbās
Rīshī 985 n.3, 1052[19]
Rizq Allāh " Mushtāqī " 512
Rohillas 473 (635), 474[18], 694–8, 1147[18], 1326
Rohtās 676[1]
Rome 430[10]
Rūdakī 918[28]
Rudaulawī (Aḥmad 'Abd al-Ḥaqq) 968[14]
Rudaulī 967[24], 1005[7]
Ruhtās 676[1]
Rukn al-Dīn b. Burhān al-Dīn 1053[11]
Rukn al-Dīn Abū 'l-Fatḥ (S.), great-grandson of Makhdūm i Jahāniyān 954[5]
Rukn al-Dīn Abū 'l-Fatḥ (Sh.) b. Ṣadr al-Dīn 'Ārif 971 n.4
Rukn-zādah Ādamīyat 1288 (6)
Rūmī (Ḥājjī) 946
Rūmī. See Jalāl al-Dīn Rūmī
" Rumūz " (?) 1275[12]
Russia, 430, 1069[26], 1161 (11), 1187 (11), 1291 (3), 1308
Rustam 'Alī Shāhābādī 471
Rustam Khān 318[28]
Rūyān 361
Rūzbihān al-Baqlī 934 n.1

"Saʻādat" 681
Saʻādat-Yār Khān *Gul i Raḥmat* 697; Treatise on the Jewish origin of the Afghāns 407 (14)
"Ṣabā" (Fatḥ-ʻAlī Khān Kāshānī) 333, 1284–5
"Ṣabā" (Muẓaffar Ḥusain) 915
Ṣābir (ʻAlāʼ al-Dīn ʻAlī) 1031 n.5
Ṣābirī order of Ṣūfīs 1031[15], 1032[9]
al-Ṣābūnī 160, 1250[9]
"Ṣabūrī" 922 (1)
Sabzawārī (*Sawāniḥ*) 1027
Sabzawārī (Ḥasan b. Ḥusain) 182, 1253
Sabzawārī (M. b. M.) 54[28], 1227[15]
Sabzawārī (M. Waḥīd Allāh) 1352
Sabzawārī (Ṭāhir M.) 122, 1241
Saʻd (Khwājah) 976[12]
Saʻd (Sh.) [Chishtī] 983[19]
Saʻd al-Dīn b. Ḥasan Jān 117
Saʻd al-Dīn Jalālābādī 207 (31)
Saʻd Allāh Khān 779
Saʻd Allāh "Masīḥ" Kairānawī 196, 1256
Saʻd Allāh Murādābādī 44, 1222
Ṣadārat 960 n.6
Sadāsuk'h "Niyāz" Dihlawī 481
Sādāt i Mutaʻallawī [Mustaʻlawī ?] 1348[22]
"Saʻdī" (ʻAbd al-Bāqī) 415[31]
Saʻdī Lāhaurī 1015[9], 1344, 1346 n.1
"Saʻdī" Shīrāzī 6, 1341[31], 1342[14]
Sadīd al-Salṭanah 1307[22]
"Ṣādiq" (Mīrzā Ṣādiq) 383
Ṣadīq [Ṣiddīq ?] al-Mamālik 1249[9]
Ṣādiq Bēg "Ṣādiqī" Afshār 1335
Ṣādiq Hamadānī 985, 1171, probably also 568 and possibly 166
Ṣādiq Hidāyat 1348
Ṣādiq (M.) "Humā" Marwazī 335, 884, 1285
Ṣādiq Iṣfahānī 125, 1241–2
Ṣādiq (M.) Kāshgharī *Tadhkirah i Khwājagān* 392, 1026; *Tārīkh i Rashīdī* (trans.) 274
Ṣādiq Khān (M. Ṣādiq) 577
Ṣādiq Khān "Akhtar". See M. Ṣādiq Khān "Akhtar"
Ṣādiq "Nāmī" 331, 1284
Ṣādiq (M.) Yārkandī 1035
"Ṣādiqī" Afshār 1335
Ṣādiqī (Ḥusain Nūr) 1293
Ṣadr al-Dīn (M.) 922 (6)
Ṣadr al-Dīn b. M. Ṣādiq (Mīr) 1108 n.3
Ṣadr al-Dīn Aḥmad Būhārī 224
Ṣadr al-Dīn ʻĀrif 971 n.2
Ṣadr al-Dīn M. b. Zabardast Khān 1093
Ṣadr al-Dīn Mūsā 939[17]
Ṣadr al-Dīn Ẓahīr-al-Islām-zādah Dizfūlī 1298
Ṣadr al-Sharīʻah 171 (41)
Ṣadr al-shuʻarāʼ 225[30]
Ṣadr i Jahān (Faiḍ Allāh Banbānī) 109, 1238[31]
Ṣadrī (M. b. M.) 54 (2), 1227[15]
Sadū Mīr Afghān 407 (4)
Safarghābādī (?) 213, 1261
Ṣafawī (Ibrāhīm-zādah) 1271 (10)
Ṣafawids 301, 1278
Ṣafdar ʻAlī b. Ḥaidar ʻAlī Dihlawī *Aḥsan al-ḥadāʼiq* 25; *Tadhkirat al-aṣfiyāʼ* 1265
Ṣafdar ʻAlī Shāh "Munṣif" 763
Ṣafdar Ḥusain 233 (61)
Ṣafdar-Jang 615[27], 616[1]
Ṣafī (Shāh) 1056 (23)
Ṣafī b. Walī Qazwīnī *Anīs al-ḥujjāj* 1141; *Tuḥfat al-akhyār* 130; *Zēb i tafāsīr* 19
Ṣafī al-Dīn Balkhī 1296 penult.
Ṣafī al-Dīn Isḥāq 318[9], 939[15]
Ṣafī ʻAlī-Shāh "Ṣafī" 1205
Ṣafī Allāh, Mullā-yi Bāndah, 1346[17]
"Ṣafī" Kāshifī 962
Ṣafī-Qulī 156 (11), 1249
Ṣafīpūrī (ʻAbd al-Raḥīm) 202, 1258
Saḥāb (Abū 'l-Qāsim) 1104, 1228[35]
Ṣaḥḥāf-bāshī (Ibrāhīm Khān) 1162 (24)
Ṣāḥib Ḥaḍrat (Ghulām Murtaḍā) 745
Saʻīd b. Hibat Allāh Rāwandī 1253
Saʻīd b. Masʻūd Kāzarūnī 179, 1253
Saʻīd Nafīsī 918, 1291 (1), 1340
Saʻīdī (M.) 428 (4)
Saif b. M. Harawī 354, 1296
Saif al-Dīn (Mīrzā) 685
Saif al-Dīn Darwājakī (?) 1190
Saif al-Dīn Ḥājjī b. Niẓām al-Faḍlī 1090
Saif al-Dīn Kashmīrī 1326[3]
Saif al-Dīn Qādirī (M.) 1065 (121)
Saif al-Naẓar Ṭūsī 29 (10), 1210[18]
"Saifī" Harawī 354, 1296
Saints, mystics, etc., 923, 1342
Saiyāḥ (Jaʻfar) 1290
"Saiyid." See ʻAlī Kabīr
Sājī (Jamāl) 5
Sakkākī (Aḥmad b. M.) 1226[28]
Saksēnah 471 n.4
Ṣalāḥ b. Mubārak Bukhārī 947
Salām Allāh b. ʻAlī al-Bakrī 185, 1254
Salāmat Allāh "Kashfī" 223, 1264

Sālār-Jang (Dargāh-Qulī Khān) 1118, 1352
Sālār-Jang (Lā'iq 'Alī Khān) 1157
Ṣāliḥ b. Bāqir Khān Shīrāzī 1148
Ṣāliḥ Nāẓim b. M. 53 (2)
" Salīm " (1) ('Alī Ḥasan Khān b. Ṣiddīq Ḥasan Khān) 914, 1339
" Salīm " (Ghulām-Ḥusain Zaidpūrī) 718
" Salīm " (M.-Qulī Ṭihrānī) 567, 1316
Salīm Allāh 715
Saljūqids 254–60, 358, 409–10, 1272, 1305
Salmān Fālī 214
Salmān Qazwīnī 298
Salmān Sāwajī 919[18]
Salmānī (Tāj) 291, 1275
Sām Mīrzā 797, 1335
Samā' al-Dīn Dihlawī 969 n.1, 971[6]
Sāmānī (M. 'Alī) 949
Samarqand 371, 1060 (70), 1123, etc.
Samarqandī (M. b. 'Abd al-Jalīl) 371, 1300
Samarqandī (M. b. 'Alī) 1086
Samarqandī (M. b. Maḥmūd) 40, 1217–18, possibly also 48 (9)
Samhūdī 426, 1307
Sammākī (M. b. Ḥusain) 17, 1198
Samrū (Bēgam) 691–2
Ṣamṣām al-Daulah Khān i Daurān 614[13, 29], 618[8]
Ṣamṣām al-Daulah Shāh-nawāz Khān. See Shāh-nawāz Khān Aurangābādī
" Sanā " (Jalāl al-Dīn Humā'ī) 1187 (17), 1345[27]
Ṣan'ān (Ṣūfī) 520, 1312
Sāndawī (Aḥmad) 1180[3]
Sandīlawī (Aḥmad 'Alī Khān) 880
Sang M. Badakhshī 382, 1301
Sanglajī (M. b. Ḥasan) 1207
Sanglajī (Sharī'at b. Ḥasan) 1207
Sanglākh Khurāsānī 1077, 1347
Ṣanī' al-Daulah. See M. Ḥasan Khān Marāghī
" Sanjī " (Ghulām-Muḥyī 'l-Dīn) 1061 (79)
Sāqī (M.) 592, 1318
Sārā-bhā'ī [this is presumably the correct spelling] 732
" Sarbāz " (Ismā'īl Khān Burūjirdī) 228 (5), 1265
Sar-birahnah ('Abd al-Khāliq Pūnī) 726
Sardār i As'ad ('Alī-Qulī Khān) 1161 (17)
Sardār Khān (Khān i Jahān) 666[19]
Sard'hanah 691
Sarfarāzī (M. b. M.) 55[1], 1227
" Ṣarfī " Kashmīrī 193, 1255
Ṣārim b. M. Amāsī 36[1]
" Sarkhwush " (M. Afḍal) 821
Sarmast ('Alī) 1014[22]
al-Ṣarrāf (Mas'ūd b. 'Alī) 160 antepenult.
Sārū'ī (M. b. M. Taqī) 332
Sarūp Chand 478, 1310
" Sarwar " (M. Khān) 883
Sātqīn (M.) 1035[28]
Saund'hā Safīdūnī 1019 n.2
Sāvanūr 766[2, 24]
Sayāls 676[28]
Scott (Jonathan) 142[15], 429[12], 1244[35]
Seignobos (Charles) 430[3], 1188 (20)
Senna (Sinandij) 903[25]
Sha'bān al-Millah 946[11]
Shabānkāra'ī (M. b. 'Alī) 84
Sha'bī ('Āmir b. Sharāḥīl) 244
" Shādān " (Basāwan La'l) 690
" Shādān " (Chandū La'l) 1100
Shādī-ābād = Māndū 727[4]
" Shafaq " (Riḍā-zādah) 1183 (32), 1184 (34)
Shafī' al-Dīn Ḥasan Shūshtarī 1103
Shāfi'ī (Imām) 1227[28]
Shafī'ī 156 (11), 1249
" Shafīq." See Lachhmī Narāyan
Shaft, The Imām-zādahs of, 1086
Shāh (Khwājah) b. S. Aḥmad Khwārazmī 932[11]
Shāh (Mullā) 18, 998[8], 1001[7], 1009 n.2, 1200
Shāh 'Alī b. 'Abd al-'Alī 793[16]
Shāh Bēg Khān 1159
Shāh Gul Imām Chū [Imām-jīw ?] 1042[10]
Shāh Mīrzā. See Mahdī Khān Ṣafawī
Shāh Qāḍī Yazdī 1198
Shāh-'Ālam (Gujrātī saint) 997[11]
Shāh-'Ālam (the Gujrātī saint ?) 1346[24]
Shāh-Jahān Bēgam 734, 1329–30
Shāh-Jahān Pādshāh 564–81, 1316
Shāh-Maḥmūd Churās 392
Shāh-Mardān 1062 (89)
Shāh-Muḥammad Badakhshī 18, 998[8], 1001[7], 1009 n.2, 1200

(1) He used also the *takhalluṣ* " Ṭāhir ", but Edwards was mistaken in supposing that he was " called 'Āshiḳī ". That was the *takhalluṣ* of Ḥusain-Qulī Khān 'Aẓīmābādī, who is mentioned in the preface to the *Ṣubḥ i gulshan.*

Shāh-Muḥammad Qazwīnī 793[6]
Shāh-Muḥammad Shāhābādī 679[17], 1325[16]
Shāh-nawāz Khān Aurangābādī ('Abd al-Razzāq) 1094; *Bahāristān i sukhun* 854; *Ma'āthir al-umarā'* 1097
Shāh-nawāz Khān Dihlawī ('Abd al-Raḥmān) 146, 1100[20], 1245
Shāhābādī (Shāh-Muḥammad) 679[17]
Shahāmat 'Alī 663[2]
Shāhfūr (Ṭāhir b. M. Isfarāyinī) 3, 1190
Shahīd i Rābi' 1128 penult.
Shahīd i Thālith (M. Taqī Burghānī) 1128 n.4, 1264
Shahīd i Thālith (Nūr Allāh Shūshtarī) 1126
Shahīd i Thānī 1136[26]
Shāhjahānpūr 473[19, 22]
Shāh-Mardān (or Shāh [title] Mardān ?) 1062 (89)
Shâhnoor (= Sāvanūr) 766[2, 24]
Shāhqulīpūrī 1050[4]
Shahrābī (M. Ḥusain "Giryān") 1184 (40)
Shahrawānī [probably a corruption of Nahrawālī] 1346[5] (cf. 1023[7])
Shahrazūrī (M. b. Maḥmūd) 1107, 1350
Shāh-Rukh 87, 292
Shāh-Shujā' (Sulṭān) b. Shāh-Jahān 582[13]
Shaibānī ('Abd al-Ḥusain) 1249 (13*c*)
"Shaidā" (Ḥasan Chelebī) 1101
Shaikh al-ḥuffāẓ 231 (43)
"Shā'iq" (Khudā-Bakhsh) 1058 (40)
"Shā'ir" (M. b. 'Abd al-Jalīl Bilgrāmī) 712, 1329
Shajā'at 'Alī Khān (M.) 1180 (7)
Shajarah (S. Ḥusain) 1341
Shakar-ganj 941 n.4, 944[1], 987[2]
Shakespear (John Dowdeswell) 708[4], 1328
Shākir Khān 621, 1321
Shāmī (Niẓām al-Dīn 'Abd al-Wāsi') 278, 1273
"Sham'ī" 368
Shamkhālī 830[18] (cf. 830 n.8)
Shāmlū 868 n.
"Shams" (Asad Allāh Gulpāyagānī) 1206
Shams Bukhārī 385
Shams al-Dīn b. Sirāj al-Dīn 'Afīf 509
Shams al-Dīn b. Wārith 'Alī Banārasī 860[24]
Shams al-Dīn al-Aṣīl 155 (5)
Shams al-Dīn 'Alī Khān 210
Shams al-Dīn Kāshānī 266
Shams al-Dīn Qādirī 973
Shams al-Dīn [Tabrīzī ?] 1057 (34)
Shams al-Hudā 1037[26]
Shams i Sirāj 'Afīf 509
Shanbī (Niẓām al-Dīn) 278, 1273
Shankar Nāt'h "Nādir" 1326
Shanūzānī (?) (Abū 'l-Fatḥ b. Niẓām al-Dīn) 1056 (25)
Sharaf (Sh.) 204 (3)
Sharaf al-Dīn b. Nūr al-Dīn 376, 1301
Sharaf al-Dīn Aḥmad Manērī (Munyarī) 1049 n.2
Sharaf al-Dīn A'lam 376, 1301
Sharaf al-Dīn 'Alī Yazdī 283, 1274
Sharaf al-Dīn Ḥusain (alias M. Ma'ṣūm) 974 n.5
Sharaf al-Dīn Munyarī 1049 n.2
Sharaf al-Dīn Nahrawālī 1023[6] (cf. 1346[4])
Sharaf al-Dīn . . . Shahrawānī [*sic*, apparently for Nahrawālī] 1346[4]
Sharaf Khān Bidlīsī 366
"Sharar" (M. 'Abd al-Ḥalīm) 1186 (5)
Sharī'at b. Ḥasan Sanglajī 1207
Sharīf al-Dīn M. Chishtī 1058 (42)
Sharīf (M.) al-Khādim 1253[7]
Sharwīn 362[14]
Shash-angushtī 830 n.7
al-Shāṭibī 39, 1217
al-Shaṭṭanūfī 933
"Shauq." See Qudrat Allāh "Shauq"
"Shauqī " Farghānī, 392
Shāyān ('Abbās) 1353
"Shēftah" (Muṣṭafā Khān) 895, 1152, 1338
Shēō-Dās, Shēō-Parshād. See Shīv-Dās, Shīv-Parshād (though the former transliterations, and not the latter, are probably correct)
Shēr (M.) 1062 (81)
Shēr Aḥmad Jalālābādī 405, 1304
Shēr 'Alī "Afsōs" 456[26]
Shēr Ḥasan Khān 1185 (3)
Shēr Khān Lōdī 823
Shēr Muḥammad Khān Gandah-pūr 407 (13), 1080
Shērgaṛh 978 n.1
Sherley (Anthony) 1161 (17)
Shērmand Īrānī 1182 (14)
Shiblī Nu'mānī (M.) 1186 (8)
Shīftah (Muṣṭafā Khān) 895, 1152, 1338
Shighā'ul 1301 antepenult.

" Shihāb " ('Abd Allāh Turshīzī) 329
Shihāb al-Dīn (Qāḍī of Aḥmadnagar) 742
Shihāb al-Dīn b. Shams al-Dīn Daulatābādī 9, 1194 ; *Baḥr i mawwāj* 10, 1193 ; *Manāqib al-sādāt* 211, 1261 ; *Tārīkh i Madīnah* (?) 427
Shihāb al-Dīn (Mīr) entitled 'Imād al-Mulk Ghāzī al-Dīn Khān 623, 1028
Shihāb al-Dīn Aḥmad Ṭālish 582, 1317
Shihāb al-Dīn Qilīj 1063 (96)
Shihāb Efendī *Sharḥ al-Shifā'* 1252
Shihāb i Ḥakīm ('Alī b. Maḥmūd) 734
Shihāb-pūr ('Aṭā' Allāh) 1207
Shī'ites 1126, 1354
Shīr. See also Shēr
Shīr 'Alī " Banā'ī ". See " Banā'ī "
Shīrāz 888[23], 1123
Shīrāzī (Ḥājī Āqā) 1289 (21)
Shīrāzī. See M. b. M. Rafī'
" Shi'rī " (Ḥasan Qādirī Kashmīrī) 1046
" Shi'rī " (Ṭāhir Iṣfahānī) 904
Shīrīn-raqam (Jān i 'Ālam) 690[19]
Shirwānī (Aḥmad b. M. Yamanī) 226 n.1, 916[12], 1265[25]
Shirwānī (M. 'Abbās " Rif'at "). See M. 'Abbās
Shitāb Khān ('Alā al-Dīn Iṣfahānī) 714, 1329
Shīv[(1)]-Dās Lak'hnawī 608
Shīv[(1)]-Parshād (Munshī) 695, 1327
Shīv[(1)]-Parshād (Rāy) 738[6]
Shōlāpūr 741[11], 776[25], 1330
" Shōrish " (Ghulām-Ḥusain) 868
Shu'aib Firdausī 1058 (43)
Shujā' al-Mulk Durrānī 400
" Shujā'ī " 205 (16)
Shukr al-Dīn (Bābā) 985[23]
Shukr Allāh (Ḥājjī) 48 (10)
Shukr Allāh b. Aḥmad Rūmī 91, 1236
Shukrī (Ustād) 48 (10)
" Shūrish " (Ghulām-Ḥusain) 868
Shūshtar 365, 1123
Shūshtarī ('Abbās b. M. 'Alī) 1271[2]
Shuster (W. Morgan) 347
Shyām Parshād 723
Ṣibghat Allāh b. M. Ghauth 222 ; *'Aẓīm al-tawārīkh* 482 ; *Dāstān i gham* 223, 1263 ; *Tuḥfah i A'ẓamīyah* 1188
Ṣiddīq [Ṣadīq ?] al-Mamālik 1249[9]
Ṣiddīq Ḥasan Khān 27, 1204 ; *al-Far' al-nāmī* 1181 ; *Ifādat al-shuyūkh* 27, 1204 ; *Iksīr fī uṣūl al-tafsīr* 28 ; *Itḥāf al-nubalā' al-muttaqīn* 1137 ; *Sham' i anjuman* 913 ; *Tiqṣār juyūd al-aḥrār* 1347
Ṣiddīq Khān b. Amīr Muẓaffar 923 (13)
Sifarghābādī (Waḥīd al-Dīn M.) 213, 1261
Sihālawī (Quṭb al-Dīn) 1048 n.3
Sihālī 1016 n.2
Sihrindī. See Sirhindī
Sijāsī (Ḥusain b. 'Alī) 1206
Sijistānī (Abū Sulaimān Manṭiqī) 1104, 1350
Sikandar *Mir'āt al-madhāhib* 215
Sikandar (Nuṣrat b. 'Umar) 47 (26), (28), 1224
Sikandar b. Manjhū 728, 1329
Sikandar (M.) " Wāṣil " Khāliṣpūrī 1059 (57)
Sīl Chand 693
Sinān al-Dīn Yūsuf b. Khiḍr 932[19]
Sinandij 903[25]
Sind 650, 1125, 1323
Singers 1183 (25)
Sipahdār Khān 125[2, 10]
Sipahsālār (Farīdūn) 935
Sipahsālār i A'ẓam (Ḥusain Khān) 1350[21]
" Sipihr." See 'Abbās-Qulī Khān
" Sipihr " (M. Taqī Kāshānī) 152, 343, 1247–8
" Sirāj " Aurangābādī 853
Sirāj al-Dīn b. Kamāl al-Dīn 1038[1]
Sirāj al-Dīn 'Alī Khān " Ārzū " 834
Sirāj al-Dīn 'Uthmān 1031 n.4
Sirhatti 766[7, 13]
Sirhindī ('Abd al-Aḥad) 1257
Sirhindī. See Aḥmad Sirhindī
Sirhindī (Badr al-Dīn) 1001
Sirhindī (Ilāh-dād " Faiḍī ") 537[20], 551
Sirhindī (Walī) 560
Sirhindī (Yaḥyā) 512
Sirmūr 677 (7)
Sīstān 364
Sītā-Rām 763
Sit'hānah 674, 1325
Sīwand 353[3]
Sīwās 411[14]
Siyāhgirdī (M. Ṣalāḥ) 378
Siyālkōt 677 (8)
Siyāqī Niẓām 308
Skinner (James) 688
Sōhan La'l Sūrī 671, 1325
Sōlāpūr (Shōlāpūr) 741[11], 776[25], 1330
Sōraṭ'h 731[26]

(1) Shēō is perhaps the correct transliteration in such names as this.

Spain 431
Stanley (H. M.) *In darkest Africa* 1161 antepenult.
Ṣūbadār Khān Tālpur 658
Ṣubḥ i Azal 345[31]
Subḥān 'Alī b. Ḥasan 'Alī Khān 699[30]
Ṣubḥī (Faiḍ Allāh Muhtadī) 1182 (15)
Ṣubḥī Pāshā 1187 (18)
Sud'hārī La'l 581
" Ṣūfī " (Aḥmad Khān) *Bilqīs u Sulaimān* 169 ; *Jang-nāmah* 205 ; *Nabī-nāmah* or *Ḥamlah i Aḥmadī* 206
" Ṣūfī " (Muḥammad Ṣūfī Māzandarānī) 806
Ṣūfī Ṣan'ān 520, 1312
" Suhail " ('Abd al-Raḥīm Dunbulī) 350
" Suhailī " (Aḥmad b. Ghulām-Riḍā Khān Khwānsārī) 922 (2), 1342[8]
Suhrāb (Aḥmad) 1061 (73)
Suhrawardī (Abū Najīb 'Abd al-Qāhir) 1032 n.1
Suhrawardī (Shihāb al-Dīn) 1106[8]
Sujān Rāy Bhanḍārī 453, 1309
Sujān Sing'h D'hīr 453, 1309
Sulaimān (M.) 1064 (103), (104)
Sulaimān Taunsawī 1044[22–3], 1045[4, 14, 24]
Sulaimānī (A. b. Ḥasan) 4, 1190
Sulaimān-Shukōh 875[20], 884[29]
Sulṭān b. S. Khwājagī Ḥusainī 19
Sulṭān Aḥmad b. Khāwand-Shāh Ḥusainī 288
Sulṭān Aḥmad Qājār ('Aḍud al-Daulah) 339
Sulṭān Aḥmad Shāh Qājār 1288 (11)
Sulṭān 'Alī Ḥusainī Ṣafawī Ardabīlī 520
Sulṭān al-Shuhadā' 1006[15]
Sulṭān-Muḥammad b. Tāj al-Dīn Ḥasan 216
Sulṭān-Muḥammad Ajnālawī 1057 (37)
Sulṭān-Muḥammad " Fakhrī ". See " Fakhrī " b. " Amīrī " 792[19], 795
Sulṭān-Muḥammad Khān " Khāliṣ " 404
Sulṭān-Muḥammad Qājār 892, 1338
Sulṭān-Murād Mīrzā Qājār 1157
Sulṭān-Qulī Quṭb al-Mulk 299 antepenult.
Sulṭānum Ṣafawīyah 1197[25]
Ṣun' Allāh Ni'mat-Allāhī 1061 (77)
Sundar Lāl b. Naubat Lāl 692
Sūrābādī ('Atīq b. M.) 3, 1189
Sūrat 732[32]
Surkhakatī (M. b. 'Adnān) 431, 1308
" Surūsh " Iṣfahānī 1183 (30)
" Surūsh " (S. Naṣr Allāh) 1341
al-Suyūṭī *al-Itqān* 1228
Sykes (Percy Molesworth) 1297

Ṭabarī (Abū 'l-Ḥasan) 245
Ṭabarī (M. b. Jarīr) *Tafsīr* 2, 1189 ; *Tārīkh* 61, 1229
Ṭabaristān 359, 1298, 1353
al-Ṭabarsī (1) (al-Faḍl b. al-Ḥasan) 14 penult., 1197
al-Ṭabarsī (al-Ḥasan b. al-Faḍl) 176, 1252
Ṭabarsī (Ḥusain Nūrī) (2) 228 (7)
Ṭabrisī 1252[30]
Tabrīz 420[18], 982[22]
Tabrīzī (Aḥmad) 270
Tādifī (M. b. Yaḥyā) 972
Taftāzānī (Mas'ūd b. 'Umar) 7 (but see 1192)
Ṭā-Hā Quṭb al-Dīn Qādirī Kairānawī 29 (8), 1210[3]
" Ṭāhir " (3) ('Alī Ḥasan Khān) 914, 1339
Ṭāhir (M.) *Aḥwālāt i . . . Sh. Aḥmad . . . al-Aḥsā'ī* 1345[12]
Ṭāhir (M.) [Iṣfahānī ? See below] *Tajwīd i lā-yanfakk* 50 (2)
Ṭāhir (M.) al-Qārī' [al-Iṣfahānī ? See below] *Risālah i tajwīd* 48 (7)
Ṭāhir b. 'Arab-Shāh. See Ṭāhir Iṣfahānī
Ṭāhir b. Ḥasan Ṭūsī 1188 (19)
Ṭāhir b. M. Isfarāyinī 3, 1190
Ṭāhir (M.) b. M. Yūsuf Qazwīnī 316
Ṭāhir b. Raḍī al-Dīn Dak'hanī 740, 1330
Ṭāhir Bēg 328 (8)
Ṭāhir Iṣfahānī *Durr al-farīd* 41, 1219 ; *Manhal al-'aṭshān* 41, 1219[8, 10] ; *Nihāyat al-itqān* 1219[12,28] ; (*Risālah dar wuqūf*) 1219[30] ; (*Risālah i mufrad i Ḥamzah*) 1219[23] ; possibly also (*Risālah i tajwīd*) 48 (7) and *Tajwīd i lā-yanfakk* 50 (2)
Ṭāhir M. " Nisyānī " Tattawī 654
Ṭāhir M. Sabzawārī 122, 1241
Ṭāhir Naṣrābādī 818
Ṭāhir " Shi'rī " Iṣfahānī 904
Ṭāhir " Waḥīd " Qazwīnī 314, 1282

(1) For this word see p. 1252[22]
(2) Cf. Brockelmann *Sptbd.* ii, p. 832.
(3) But *not* " 'Āshiqī " : see the footnote to " Salīm " above.

Ṭāhirī (Aḥmad) 1294
Ṭahmās Khān 625, 1321[32–38]
Ṭahmāsb ('Abd Allāh Khān Amīr Ṭ.) 348, 1289
Ṭahmāsp I (Shāh) 305, 1279
al-Ṭā'ifī (Abū 'l-Qāsim M.) 1082[14]
Taimūr Mīrzā 1153[20]
"Ṭaiyib" (Nūr al-Ḥasan Khān) 913
Ṭaiyib Allāh 524[27]
Ṭaiyib Allāh Ruhtāsī 671
Ṭaiyib Ni'mat-Allāhī 205 (6)
Tāj b. M. Hāshimī 37[11]
Tāj Sa'īdī 1196
Tāj Salmānī 291, 1275
Tāj al-Dīn b. Zakarīyā' al-'Abshamī *Tarjamat Nafaḥāt al-uns* 956[13]; *Tarjamat Rashaḥāt 'ain al-ḥayāt* 965
Tāj al-Dīn Ṭūsī 29 (10), 1210[18]
Tajallī 'Alī 749
Tājpūr 1142[26]
Ṭālib (M.) 1004
Ṭālibōf (Talibov, Taliboff). See 'Abd al-Raḥīm b. Abī Ṭālib Tabrīzī
Tālishistān 233 (57)
al-Tamīmī (A. b. M.) 54, 1227
Tanakābunī (M. b. Sulaimān) 1133, 1354
Tanīsh Bukhārī 374, 1301
Tansar 360
Taqī (M., "Mīr") 849
Taqī al-Dīn M. b. Sharaf al-Dīn 'Alī Kāshī 803
Taqī al-Dīn M. Naqawī 946[9]
Taqī 'Alī b. Turāb 'Alī Kākōrawī 1046
Taqī 'Alī-ābādī 337
Taqī Auḥadī 808
Taqī Kāshī 803
Taqī Khān (Mīrzā) 1354[32]
Taqī Khuwaiyī 1040
Taqī Muttaqī (Qāḍī) 1161 (13), 1355
Taqī-zādah (S. Ḥasan) 241[28], 1350[16]
"Tarbiyat" (M. 'Alī Khān) 1111, 1352[2]
Ṭārumī ('Imād al-Dīn) 1196
Ṭarzī (Maḥmūd). See Maḥmūd Ṭarzī
Tattah 655[7], 1028[3], 1031[2]
Tattawī (Ibrāhīm b. Ismā'īl) 1258[32]
"Taufīq" Kashmīrī 682
Taunsah 1044 n.4
Tawakkul Bēg Kūlālī 1008
Tawakkulī b. Ismā'īl Ardabīlī 939
Tēgh-Jang Bahādur 759 (4)
Ṭēk Chand 644
"Thabāt" (Amīn Aḥmad Firdausī) 1049
"Thabāt" (Mu'īn al-Dīn) 1064 (107)
"Thamar" Nā'īnī 1338
"Thamīn" (Ghulām-Ḥasan Bilgrāmī) 620, 1115
Thanā' Allāh Pānīpatī 1034[2]
"Thanā'ī" (Abū 'l-Qāsim Farāhānī) 338, 1285
T'hānēsarī (Ghulām-Muṣṭafā) 23
T'hānēsarī (Jalāl al-Dīn) 17, 1198
T'hānēsarī (Niẓām al-Dīn) 18
"Thāqib" (Aḥsan Allāh Khān) 675
"Thuraiyā" (Ḥusain Ṭihrānī) 352
Tibet 685[5]
Tiflīs 1354[32]
Ṭihrān 1049[7]
Tikēt Rāy 874 n.3
Tīmūr 280, 1274
Tīmūrids 278, 1273; (in India) 516, 1312
Ṭīpū Sulṭān 767
al-Tirmidhī (M. b. 'Īsā) 174, 1252
Tōnk 691[9]
Torunxa = Tūrān-Shāh 359
Traditionists 1136, 1354
Travellers 1138, 1354
Tribes, families, etc., 1085, 1347
Tulasī-Rāma 1055 (12)
Tunakābunī (M. b. Sulaimān) 1133, 1354
Turāb 'Alī *Siyāḥat i Turāb* 1161 (21)
Turāb 'Alī b. M. Kāẓim Kākōrawī 1035, 1046[31]
Tūrān-Shāh b. Quṭb al-Dīn 358
Turkey 408–22, 1185 (4), 1305–6
Ṭūsī (Aḥmad b. M.) 29 (10), 1210[19]
Ṭūsī (Naṣīr al-Dīn) 1106[9]
Ṭūsī (Ṭāhir b. Ḥasan) 1188 (19)
Ṭūsī (Tāj al-Dīn) 29 (10), 1210[18]
Tustarī (M. b. As'ad) 162[29], 1250[22]
"Ṭūṭī" ('Abbās Māzandarānī) 227

'Ubaid Allāh b. 'Abd Allāh Ḥusainī 1079
'Ubaid Allāh b. Maḥmūd Shāshī. See Aḥrār
'Ubaid Allāh Abū Sa'īd Harawī 1296
'Ubaid Allāh Aḥrār. See Aḥrār
'Ubaid Allāh Khān Dihlawī 32 (48), 33 (57)
'Ubaid Allāh Khwēshgī Qaṣūrī 1009
'Ubaid Allāh Naqshband Samarqandī 981
Uchh 945[1]. 1042[11]
Ūdaipūr 519[21, 31], 592[4]
"'Udhrī" (Isḥāq Bēg) 872[25], 1337
Ujjain 737[21]
"Ulfat" (M. 'Alī) 1063 (98)
Ulugh Bēg 271, 1273

" 'Ulwī " or " 'Alawī " 598 (5)
'Umar b. al-Khaṭṭāb 233 (65)
'Umar b. M. Nasafī 371, 1300
" Umbeylah " campaign 674, 1325
Ummī (M. Barārī) 1242
Ūpādyah Kurjī Jādēv Mīr 733
" 'Urūj " (Bahā' al-Dīn Ḥasan Khān) 923 (12)
'Urwat al-wuthqā. See Ma'ṣūm (M.) b. Aḥmad Sirhindī
'Utbī (M. b. 'Abd al-Jabbār) 250
'Uthmān (Sirāj al-Dīn) 1031 n.4
'Uthmān b. 'Abd al-Raḥmān Ṭālaqānī 46 (10)
'Uthmān (M.) b. M. Iḥsān Bilgrāmī 1115
'Uthmān b. 'Umar called Kahf 1056 (26), 1345
'Uthmān Akbar 952
'Uthmān Damānī (M.) 1057 (36)
'Uthmān Khān " Qais " 58 (7)
Uwais b. Fakhr al-Dīn Mūminābādī 180 n.
Uwais al-Qaranī 1023[16], 1032[5]

Vaishnava saints 1055 (12)
Vámbéry (A.) 1161 (18)
Voltaire *Histoire de l'Empire de Russie sous Pierre le Grand* 430; *Tārīkh i Impirātōrān i Ālmān u Pāphā-yi Rum* 429[31]

" Wāḍiḥ " (Irādat Khān) 601
" Wāḍiḥ." See Raḥmat Allāh Bukhārī
Wafā (M.) 'Aẓīmābādī 714
" Wafā'ī " (Zain al-Dīn Khwāfī) 532, 1313
Wahhābī incursions 428 (5), 1307
Wahhābī rule in al-Najaf 428 (7)
" Waḥīd " (M. Ṭāhir Qazwīnī) 314, 1282
Waḥīd al-Dīn M. Jāmī SFRGHābādī 213, 1261
Waḥīd Allāh (M.) Sabzawārī 1352
Wāḥidī Balkhī 65[6]
Wais. See Uwais
Wājid 'Alī Khān 763
Wājid 'Alī Qalandar 1061 (76)
Wajīh al-Dīn (Shāh) 1059 (60)
Wajīh al-Dīn Ashraf 1031
Wajīh [al-Dīn] " 'Ishqī " 880
" Walī " (Banwālī-Dās) 450, 1309
Walī Allāh b. Ḥabīb Allāh Lak'hnawī 1047
Walī Allāh Dihlawī 20, 1201; *Anfās al-'ārifīn* 1020; *Āthār al-muḥaddithīn* 1137; *Fatḥ al-Raḥmān* 21, 1201; *al-Fauz al-kabīr* 22, 1201; *al-Intibāh* 1021; *al-Juz' al-laṭīf* 1021; *Qurrat al-'ainain* 219, 1263; *Surūr al-maḥzūn* 179, 1253
Walī Allāh Farrukhābādī 25; *Naẓm al-jawāhir* 25; *Tārīkh i Farrukhābād* 694
" Walī " Dak'hanī 213
Walī M. Qandahārī 9[22]
Walī Rām (Banwālī Dās) 450–2, 1309
Walī Sirhindī 560
" Wālih " *Asās al-īmān* 228 (3)
" Wālih " ('Alī-Qulī Khān) 830
" Wālih " (M. Yūsuf) 130, 1243
Walī-Qulī Shāmlū 317, 1282
Wallace (Donald Mackenzie) 430
al-Wāqidī 173
Warāmīnī (M. b. Abī Zaid) 211, 1261
Wardājakī [?] (Abū Naṣr) 1190
" Wārid " (M. Shafī') 610, 1319
Wārith (M.) 575–7, 1317
Wārith (M. Baqā) 232 (44)
Wārith 'Alī Saifī 403[29]
Wārith 'Alī Shāh 1058 (40)
Warnūsfādarānī (M. b. Ḥaidar 'Alī) 1215
" Waṣfī " 1003[6]
" Wāṣifī " ('Abd Allāh b. Hāshim) 215[11]
" Wāṣifī " (Zain al-Dīn Maḥmūd) 373, 1301
" Wāṣil " Khāliṣpūrī 1059 (57)
Wāsiṭī Saiyids 855 n.2
Waṣṣāf Shīrāzī 267, 1272
Wazīr 'Alī " 'Ibratī " 899
Wazīr al-Daulah Wazīr Khān 298, 1041 n.2
Wazīr al-Sulṭān. See Amīr 'Alī Khān
Wazīrōf (Wazirov, Waziroff). See Ḥaidar Wazirov, 249 (5), 426
Wazīrs, etc., 1088–1104, 1349
" Wilā " (Maẓhar 'Alī Khān) 514[23]
Wilāyat 'Alī Khān (M.) 1346[8]
Wilson (Arnold) 428 (4)
Women 1162, 1355
" Wuqū'ī " (M. Sharīf) 122, 1241

Xavier (Jerome) 163, 1251

Yādgār (Aḥmad) 515, 1312
Yādgār Akhsīkatī 391[21]
al-Yāfi'ī 53; *al-Durr al-naẓīm* 53, 1226; *Khulāṣat al-mafākhir* 936; *Rauḍ al-rayāḥīn* 935

" Yaghmā " 922[4], 923 (14)
Yaghmā'ī (Ḥabīb) 921, 1341
Yaghmā'ī (Iqbāl) 1345[18]
Yaḥyā b. 'Abd al-Laṭīf Qazwīnī 111, 1239
Yaḥyā b. Aḥmad Sīhrindī 512
Yaḥyā b. Burhān al-Dīn 1053[12]
Yaḥyā b. Hādī Daulatābādī 1175
Yaḥyā b. Ḥusain (S.) 1059 (60)
Yaḥyā b. M. (Ibn i Bībī) 408
Yaḥyā b. Shams al-Dīn [Karrābī ?] 182[17], 1253–4
" Yaḥyā " Kāshī 569
Yaḥyā Khān (Mīr Munshī) 471
Yaḥyā (Muḥyī 'l-Dīn) Madanī 1038[3]
Yaḥyā Ṣubḥ i Azal 345[31]
" Yak-dil " (Aḥmad-bakhsh Chishtī Lāhaurī) 668[24]
" Yaqīn " ('Abd Allāh) 460
Ya'qūb Charkhī 9, 1193
Ya'qūb " Ṣarfī " 193, 1255
Yār-Muḥammad b. Khudā-dād Samarqandī 41, 1219
Yār-Muḥammad b. Rājī Kamman Kōlawī 1022
Yār-Muḥammad b. Tāj-Muḥammad 1045
Yār-Muḥammad Khān Tālpur 658
Yasawī (Aḥmad) 977[2]
Yāsimī (Rashīd) 919, 1340
Yazd 352, 1125, 1293
Yazdī (A. b. M. Maibudī) 1190
Yazdī (Ghiyāth al-Dīn 'Alī) 278, 1273
Yazdī (Ḥasan b. Shihāb) 91, 1236
Yazdī (Mu'īn) 277, 1273
Yazdī (Sharaf al-Dīn 'Alī) 283, 1274
Yūsuf b. 'Abd al-Laṭīf 156 (11), 1249
Yūsuf b. Aḥmad Sijzī (or Sanjarī) 1167[32]
Yūsuf b. Āqā Bēg Dihkhwāraqānī 215
Yūsuf b. Khiḍr (Khwājah Pāshā) 932[20]
Yūsuf b. M. Ni'am Allāh Gardēzī 953
Yūsuf b. Raḥmat Allāh Aṭakī Kan'ānī 127
Yūsuf b. 'Umar Tabrīzī 171 (39)
Yūsuf 'Alī Khān 139 ; *Ḥadīqat al-ṣafā'* 140 ; *Tadhkirah i Yūsuf 'Alī Khān* 868 ; *Tārīkh i Mahābat-Jang* 717, 1329
Yūsuf Bud'h 1236[14]
Yūsuf Khān Gilīm-pōsh 1153
Yūsuf Lāhijī 1078[31]
Yūsuf Miṣrī 1199
" Yūsufī " 953
Yūsufōf [Yusufov, Yusufoff] (Mīrzā) Bukhārī 385
Ẓafar 'Alī " Ẓafar " 1066 (125)
Ẓafar Khān " Aḥsan " 815 n.6, n.11
Ẓafarābād 1126
Ẓāhidī (?) (A. b. Ḥasan Sulaimānī) 4, 1190
Zāhidī (Ḥusain b. Abdāl) 318
Ẓahīr al-Dīn Ardabīlī 416 penult., 1168[6], 1306[15], 1355
Ẓahīr al-Dīn Bilgrāmī 56
Ẓahīr al-Dīn Mar'ashī 361 ; *Tārīkh i Gīlān* 362 ; *Tārīkh i Ṭabaristān* 361
Ẓahīr al-Dīn Samarqandī 1086
Ẓahīr al-Islām-zādah (Ṣadr al-Dīn) Dizfūlī 1298
Zaidān (Jurjī) 157 (14), 1249
Zaidarī (Nūr al-Dīn M.) 1090[1]
Zaidī Saiyids of Ẓafarābād 1126[12]
Zain al-'Ābidīn (Imām) 1248[3, 8]
Zain al-'Ābidīn b. Iskandar Shīrwānī 1150
Zain al-'Ābidīn 'Alī Shīrāzī 1239
Zain al-'Ābidīn Birādar " Dīwān " 1200
Zain al-'Ābidīn Chishtī Hindālawī 987[3]
Zain al-'Ābidīn Khān Kirmānī 1206
Zain al-'Ābidīn Sabzawārī 48 (11)
Zain al-'Ābidīn Shūshtarī 773
Zain al-Dīn (Bābā) 985[22]
Zain al-Dīn al-'Āmilī 1136[26]
Zain al-Dīn Dāwud Shīrāzī 1025[4]
Zain al-Dīn M. Amīn Ṣadr Kāshgharī 382
Zain al-Dīn " Wafā'ī " Khwāfī 532, 1313
Zainab 227[12], 1265
" Zā'ir " (Kamāl al-Dīn Ḥaidar) 710
Zakarīyā' (Bahā' al-Dīn) Multānī 970 n.7
" Zakhmī " (Ratan Sing'h) 709, 1328–9 ; *Anīs al-'āshiqīn* 890 ; *Sulṭān al-tawārīkh* 709
Zamajī (Mu'īn al-Dīn) 355, 1296
Zamān (Mīrzā) 328 (9)
Zands 329, 1284
Zanjānī (Abū 'Abd Allāh) 1228 antepenult.
Zanjānī (M.) 1182 (18)
Zarāb 44[2]
Zarqānī (Maḥmūd) 1054 (9), 1345[16]
Zartusht b. Bahrām 162, 1250
Zar-bakhsh (Muntajab al-Dīn) 1025[2]
Zarzarī [vocalisation ?] (Muntajab al-Dīn) 1025[2]
Zauzanī (M. b. 'Alī) 1106[28]
Zauzanī (M. b. M.) 38
Zawārī ('Alī b. Ḥasan) *Āthār al-*

akhyār 29, 1209; *Lawāmi' al-anwār* 211; *Majma' al-hudā* 163; *Makārim al-karā'im* 177; *Tarjamah i Tafsīr i Ḥasan i 'Askarī* = *Āthār al-akhyār* 29, 1209; *Tarjamat al-khawāṣṣ* 14, 1197; *Tarjamat al-manāqib* 210, 1260
Zawārī [?] (M. b. Aḥmad) 55²
Zawārī (M. 'Alī b. M.) *Ma'āthir al-Bāqirīyah* 891
Zēb al-Nisā' Bēgam (= Bēgam Samrū) 691-2

Zēb al-Nisā' bint Aurangzēb 19²², 1017 n.4
Zhandah Pīl 950 n.3
Zindah 'Alī al-Muftī 1012
Ziyād-oghlī family 314⁵
Zōrāwar Sing'h 607
Zoroaster 162¹¹, 169 (10), 1347²⁶
Ẓuhūr (M.) b. Ẓuhūrī 1331
Ẓuhūr al-Islām 1006¹³
Zūzanī (M. b. 'Alī) 1106²⁸
Zūzanī (M. b. M.) 38